NeuroTheology
Brain, Science, Spirituality, Religious Experience

University Press

NeuroTheology
Brain, Science, Spirituality, Religious Experience
Edited by R. Joseph, Ph.D.

The publisher has sought to obtain permission from the copyright owners of all materials reproduced. If any copyright owner has been overlooked please contact: University Press, at Editor@UniversityPress.Info, so that permission can be formally obtained.

NeuroTheology: Brain, Science, Spirituality, Religious Experience
Rhawn Joseph — Editor.

Includes bibliographical references

ISBN: 0971644586

1. God. 2. Evolution. 3. Darwin. 4. Origin of Life.
5. Theology. 6. Religion. 7. Brain. 8. Creation Science.
9. Neuroscience. 10. DNA. 11. Spirituality.

Cover Design by Rhawn Joseph
Cover Design Copyright ©2002 Rhawn Joseph

Acknowledgements: The Neuropsychology of Aesthetic, Spiritual & Mystical States, by Eugene G. d'Aquili & Andrew B. Newberg, was first published in the journal, Zygon 35(1): 39-52, 2000. The Temporal Lobe: The Biological Basis Of the God Experience, by Michael A. Persinger, was first published in The Neuropsychological Bases of God Beliefs, Praeger, 1987. Love, Religion and the Psychology of Inspiration, by R. D. Ellis, was first published in the journal Philosophy in the Contemporary World, 22(2):2003. The three chapters by William James are taken from his "Gifford Lectures on Natural Religion" delivered at Edinburgh in 1901 and 1902.

UniversityPress.Info
University Press, San Jose, California

CONRIBUTORS

Carol Rausch Albright, President of the American Theological Society, Midwest Region. Executive Editor (retired) of *Zygon: Journal of Religion and Science*, Co-Director of the CTNS Science and Religion Course Program, Chicago, Illinois.

Matthew Alper, author, "God" Part of the Brain, Brooklyn, New York.

Ralph B. Allison, Retired Psychiatrist, Paso Robles, California.

Scott Atran, Centre National de la Recherche Scientifique, Paris, The University of Michigan, Ann Arbor, Michigan.

William Braud, Institute of Transpersonal Psychology, Palo Alto, California.

Kelly Bulkeley, San Francisco Theological Seminary, The Graduate Theological Union, California.

Eugene G. d'Aquili, until his recent death: Clinical Assistant Professor of Psychiatry at the Hospital of the University of Pennsylvania.

Manie Eagar, Apeiron Institute, Parklands, South Africa.

Ralph D. Ellis, Clark Atlanta University, and Editor of the journal Cognition & Emotion.

Thomas G. Fikes, Dept. of Psychology, Westmont College, Santa Barbara, California.

William F. Hamilton III, Executive Director, Skywatch International Inc. Skycom-research.org, Analyst, University of California, Los Angeles, California.

Dirk Hutsebaut, Faculty of Psychology, Katholieke Universiteit Leuven, Belgium.

Jeremy Iversen, Stanford University, Stanford, California.

William James, until his death: Professor of Psychology, Harvard University.

Rhawn Joseph, Brain Research Laboratory, San Jose, California.

Bruce MacLennan, University of Tennessee, Knoxville, Tennessee.

Andrew B. Newberg, Hospital of the University of Pennsylvania, Philadelphia.

Raymond F. Paloutzian, Dept. of Psychology, Westmont College, Santa Barbara,California. Editor of The International Journal for the Psychology of Religion.

Michael A. Persinger, Professor of Behavioral Neuroscience, Depts. of Psychology and Biology, Laurentian University, Sudbury, Ontario, Canada.

Massimo Pigliucci, Depts. Of Botany, Ecology & Evolutionary Biology, and Philosophy, University of Tennessee, Knoxville,Tennessee.

Enmarie Potgieter, Rand Afrikaans University & Apeiron Institute, South Africa.

Fraser Watts, Faculty of Divinity, University of Cambridge, England.

Michael Winkelman, Dept. of Anthropology, Arizona State University.

CONTENTS

New truths go through three stages.
First they are ridiculed,
second they are violently opposed and then,
finally, they are accepted as self-evident.
— Arthur Schopenhauer

Discovery is seeing what everyone saw
and thinking what no one thought.
— Albert Szent-Gyoergy, Nobel Laureate

Can a lizard comprehend a man?
Can a man comprehend a god?
Who dares speak for God?
Perhaps... even the gods have gods.

THE DEATH OF GOD
by Friederich Nietzsche

The madman— Have you not heard of that madman who lit a lantern in the bright morning hours, ran to the market place, and cried incessantly: "I seek God! I seek God!"— As many of those who did not believe in God were standing around just then, he provoked much laughter. Has he got lost? asked one. Did he lose his way like a child? asked another. Or is he hiding? Is he afraid of us? Has he gone on a voyage? Emigrated? —Thus they laughed and yelled.

The madman jumped up in their midst and pierced them with his glances. "Whither is God?" he cried: "I will tell you. We have killed him—you and I. All of us are his murderers. But how did we do this? How could we drink up the sea? Who gave us the sponge to wipe away the entire horizon? What were we doing when we unchained the earth from its sun? Whither is it moving now? Whither are we moving? Away from all suns? Are we not plunging continually? Backward, sideward, forward, in all directions? Is there still any up or down? Are we not straying as through an infinite space? Has it not become colder? Is not night continually closing in on us? Do we not need to light lanterns in the morning? Do we hear nothing as yet of the noise of the gravediggers who are burying God? Do we smell nothing as yet of the divine decomposition? Gods, too, decompose. God is dead. God remains dead. And we have killed him.

How shall we comfort ourselves, the murderers of all murderers? What was holiest and mightiest of all that the world has yet known has bled to death under our knives: who will wipe this blood off us? What water is there for us to clean ourselves? What festivals of atonement, what sacred games shall we have to invent? Is not the greatness of this deed to great for us? Must we ourselves not become gods simply to appear worthy of it? There has never been a greater deed: And whoever is born after us—for the sake of this deed he will belong to a higher history than all history hitherto."

Here the madman fell silent and looked again at his listeners and they, too, were silent and stared at him in astonishment. At last he threw his lantern on the ground, and it broke into pieces and went out. "I have come to early," he said then; "my time is not yet. This tremendous event is still on its way, still wandering; it is not yet reached the ears of men. Lightning and thunder require time; the light of the stars requires time; deeds, though done, still require time to be seen and heard. This deed is still more distant from them than the most distant stars—and yet they have done it themselves."

It has been related further that on the same day the madman forced his way into several churches and there struck up his requiem aeternam deo. Led out and called to account, he is said always to have replied nothing but: "what after all are these churches now if they are not the tombs and sepulchers of God?"

MYTHOLOGIES OF MODERN SCIENCE
by R. Joseph

It has been declared that god is dead, that spirituality is an "opiate" for the people. And yet, there is a scientific, neurological, and genetic foundation for religious belief, spirituality, and paranormal phenomenon, including the experience of gods, demons, spirits, souls, and life after death. There are specific regions of the brain which become highly active when dreaming, during trance states, meditation, prayer, or under LSD, and which enable us to experience those realms of reality normally filtered from consciousness, including the reality of god, the spirit, the soul, and life after death.

It has been known for thousands of years that dream sleep, trance states, isolation, and food and water deprivation can enhance an individual's ability to experience realms of reality which are normally filtered from conscious awareness. Under these conditions various regions of the neocortex and limbic system will become highly active, and even hyperactivated, such that what is normally filtered out is perceived. Under these conditions some claim to speak with god, others seek to transcend god, to achieve oneness with the spiritually sublime.

Limbic system structures such as the amygdala, hippocampus, and inferior temporal lobe have been repeatedly shown to subserve and provide the foundations for mystical, spiritual, and religious experience, and the perception, including the "hallucination" of ghosts, demons, spirits and sprites, and belief in demonic or angelic possession (Bear 1979; Daly 1958; Joseph, 1996, Mesulam 1981; Penfield & Perot 1963; Schenk &Bear 1981; Williams 1956). When these brain areas are hyperactivated, "religious" experiences are not uncommon.

Of course, there are some who might take this to mean that these experiences are nothing more than hallucinations produced by an abnormal brain. In some instances this is true. However, rather than due to some abnormality, religious experience and the seeking of spiritual nourishment is the norm and not the exception. It is this natural upwelling of spiritual emotion and religiosity which explains why despite decades of terror and suppression, totalitarian states such as Communist China, Cuba, and the former Soviet Union were unable and have been unable to crush spiritual and religious expression in their countries.

Belief in souls, spirits, the haunted house, and angels or demons, and the capacity to have mystical experiences, including the sensation of being possessed by gods or devils or hearing their voices, is world wide (Budge 1994; Campbell 1988, Frazier 1950; Godwin 1990; Harris, 1993; James 1958; Jaynes 1976; O'Keefe 1982; Malinowkski 1948; Smart 1969; Wilson 1951). Humans have been demonstrating a belief in the spiritual world for over 100,000 years (Joseph, 1996, 2000a).

These historical and cross-cultural commonalties in religious and archetypal experience include viewing the sign of the cross with spiritual awe, and the experiences of demons and devils and hearing the voice of "God" or communing with the "Great Spirit," as well as the many vestiges or incarnations of what has been referred to as the personal soul or "ghost."

Some may argue, however, that from a strictly "scientific" perspective, there is no basis for religious and spiritual belief. And, there is no "god."

According to some scientists, we are but random collections of molecules that emerged from an organic soup following the big bang creation of the universe, and we evolved following the generation of random mutations. There is no room for god or spirituality in these "scientific" equations.

Indeed, according to the popular press, and as preached by mainstream scientists, everything began with a big bang, and that at first there was nothing. Nothing! Not even space. And then, Kablooey!!! there was stuff. In my previous publications I have referred to this as the "nothing happened theory of creation."

We are also told that the scientific evidence refutes the notion of an "eternal god" because the universe is but 12 billion years young. And how do we know this? Because the most distant (detectable) stars that twinkle in the darkness of night are 12 billion light years away. Away from what? Relative to what? From where the Earth is now, they answer; a reply which has nothing to do with the supposed big bang as the Earth is not located at ground zero—the location of ground zero is in fact unknown. And what of those stars which are so distant and which died so long ago, their light will never be detected?

Consider, for example, the recent findings of professor Ray Norris and colleagues. Relying on data provided by the CSIRO's Australia Telescope and the Hubble Space Telescope they detected stars that were so far away, they had not previously been detected. According to these astronomers, this new data pushes back the origin of the universe "by a long way," though how far, is unknown, as modern day telescopes cannot collect enough light to pin down their distance (Norris et al., 2001).

The age of the universe has also been guessed at based on the supposed ages of certain stars. Using this as a measure, astronomers have guessed that the age of the universe must be between 10 - 15 billion years. For example, when a star has burned up most of its hydrogen, it expands and becomes a "red giant." When a "red giant" is detected, astronomers can make guesses as to how long it has been in existence, and thus guess its lifetime, and thus guess its age, and then, based on its estimated age, determine the age of the universe. If the star is 12 billion years old, then the universe must be 12 billion years old. This is equivalent to finding the oldest man in Russia, and then stating that since he is 124 years old, humans have been on Earth for only 124 years.

If the age and antiquity of the universe is unknown, and if the "big bang" theory of creation is not supported by the scientific evidence, then it becomes impossible to exclude the existence of an "eternal god." Likewise, if the age of the universe is unknown, then the origin of life and each and every DNA molecule, and its storehouse of genetic information, may also have a pedigree which is incredibly ancient. This view is also compatible with the belief that life may have first been fashioned by "the hand of God."

THE MYTH OF THE ORGANIC SOUP

And the Earth was without form, and void,
and darkness was upon the face of the deep.
And the spirit of God moved upon the face
of the waters.... --Genesis 1.2

Darwin (1859), in the final paragraphs of "The Origin of Species" attributed the creation of life to "what we know of the laws impressed on matter by the Creator." The Sumerians who, 6000 years ago first wrote what became the Biblical version of creation, believed that those who claimed to be Gods were begotten in a manner no different from woman and man—from seeds of life which rained down from the heavens (Kramer, 1991).

About 2,500 years ago, Anaxagoras, a Greek philosopher, echoed this Sumerian thought: "The seeds of life," he wrote, "swarm throughout the cosmos." Anaxagoras, however, did not believe that the "seeds of life" were random collections of molecules, but actual seeds, containing within them the kernel for creating all life.

Others have embraced somewhat similar views (e.g., Hoyle & Wickramsinghe, 1977; Joseph, 2000), including Sir Francis Crick (Crick, 1981; Crick & Orgel, 1973), who was awarded the Nobel Prize (along with Watson) for discoveries regarding DNA. Specifically, Crick and Orgel (1973), proposed that it was time to "consider a new infective theory, namely that a primitive form of life was deliberately planted on Earth by a technologically advanced society on another planet." By contrast, Sir Fred Hoyle and Charles Wickramsinghe (1977, 1978), proposed that "about four billion years ago life arrived in a comet."

Indeed, as the new-born Earth was lacking all the essential ingredients for the formation of life, such as oxygen, phosphorus, etc., and since the theory of the "organic soup" is not supported by the scientific evidence, then we must conclude that life either fell from the sky, embedded in cosmic debris sheared off from ancient, life-bearing planets, or, it was created by intelligent beings, i.e. "god" or "gods."

Not only was our young planet lacking the necessary life-promoting elements, but even by the most optimistic of estimates, there was not enough time for even the simplest of single celled creatures, and their DNA, to spontaneously or gradually emerge from the dust of the Earth (Folsome, 1979; Horgan, 1991; Hoyle, 1974).

Since the Earth was first formed as the presumed product of an accretion disc comprised of various elements orbiting the new born sun, it would have been sterilized by the tremendous heat generated during its creation. All complex organic carbon based molecules would have been destroyed, with the exception of microdiamonds and similar substances. And as our planet was continually bombarded with extraterrestrial debris, it was again sterilized due to the tremendous heat generated by this incessant pummeling.

The surface of the planet in fact melted. Not only was the planet twice sterilized such that all complex organic molecules would have been destroyed, but as it began to cool it was then covered by yet additional debris that continued to repeatedly slam into it until perhaps 3.5 billion years ago (Press & Siever, 1986). It was during this cooling off period, during which the planet was still being bombarded, that the first evidence of life appears, some 3.85 billion years ago (Mojzsis et al., 1996). And these were not simple life forms, but chemically complex, photosynthesizing and oxygen and calcium secreting creatures.

If life were to appear on a desert island, we would assume it simply washed to shore or fell from the sky. The Earth too is an island, swirling in an ocean of space, and up to 40,000 tons of material falls to Earth yearly.

Given that the surface of the young Earth was entirely extraterrestrial in origin, consisting of material left over from the formation of this solar system, as well as material ejected from other solar systems, it is reasonable to conclude that the life that appeared, some 3.85 billion years ago, was also extraterrestrial in origin. Indeed, cell theory, and the very nature and complexity of DNA demands an extraterrestrial origin.

Consider the many thousands of different molecules that make up a single cellular creature and which perform an incredible variety of chemical reactions in concert with that cell's other molecules and their protein (enzyme) products (Strachan & Read, 1996; Watson et al. 1992).

Consider, single cellular microbes are comprised of over 2,500 small molecules (e.g. including amino acids consisting of 10 to 50 tightly packed atoms), macro-molecules (proteins and nucleic acids) and polymeric molecules (comprised of hundreds to thousands of small molecules) all of which are precisely jigsawed together to form a single complex organism. The tiniest and most primitive of single celled creatures contain a variety of micro- macro- and polymeric molecules which fit and function together as a living mosaic of tissues.

Dr. Clyde Hutchinson of the University of North Carolina took one of the simplest known bacteria, Myoplasma genitalium, and stripped out genes, one by one, trying to define the minimum number of genes it needed to survive. He reported in 1999 that the microbe required at least 265 genes, which could be thought of as the minimal set of genes needed for life. The simplest organism, therefore must have at least 265 fully functional genes in order to live. What is the likelihood that such incredibly complex creatures repeatedly emerged from a so called "organic" soup lacking all essential organic ingredients?

When coupled with the complexity of DNA and given the fact that the essential ingredients for DNA construction were not available on this planet, it thus seems unlikely that life could have arisen gradually and merely by chance, at least on Earth.

Figure 1. Even galaxies collide. Colliding galaxies.

Indeed, a single macro-molecule of DNA is composed of hundreds of thousand, and in many cases, millions of micro-molecules which in turn contain all the necessary information for creating an embryo or a complex adult body. There is nothing random about the organization or expression of DNA.

Nevertheless, and as will also be discussed, the prevalent, mainstream view is that life emerged from non-life, and that DNA arose from non-DNA, when the necessary precursor elements fell from the sky and were randomly mixed together in an organic soup, or were spewed out from an undersea volcano and then gradually or spontaneously combined thus creating life. It is noteworthy that all attempts to create life have utterly failed, no matter how sophisticated the experiment, or how closely its design mimics the early environment of the Earth. Indeed, the "organic soup" concept of spontaneous (or gradual) genera-

tion has been repeatedly debated, and repeatedly disproved, for centuries.

As summed up so memorably by Sir Fred Hoyle, "spontaneous generation is about as likely an occurrence as the assemblage of a Boeing 747 by a tornado whirling through a junkyard." However, in the case of the new Earth, there was no "junkyard." The proverbial organic alphabet soup was missing not only DNA, but the phosphorus and oxygen necessary for the creation of DNA. Life could not have emerged from non-life—at least not on Earth.

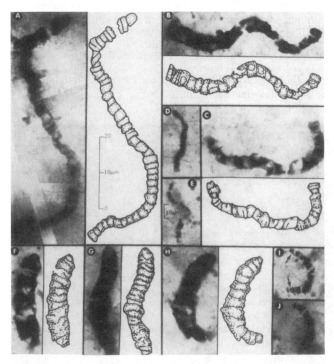

That life did not originate on Earth can also be concluded based on the nature and organization of DNA. A single macromolecule of DNA is so incredibly complex, the notion that it was randomly assembled in an organic soup is the equivalent of discovering a computer on Jupiter and then arguing that it was randomly assembled in the Methane sea.

Indeed, there is absolutely no scientific evidence to support the hypothesis that life on Earth emerged from an organic soup, or was randomly fashioned within an undersea thermal vent. As the only source for DNA is DNA, and as DNA could not have originated from an organic soup—as the necessary ingredients did not exist on Earth— then life on Earth, and its DNA, either arrived here from other planets, contained in the massive debris which had rained down from the sky for the first 700 million years after the Earth

Figure 2. (Above right) The full moon as seen from the Earth. Note major impact sites, especially that which fractured the surface of the northern hemisphere. Fossilized bacteria found in 3.5 billion year old chert in Western Australia. Photos and drawings by J. W. Schopf.

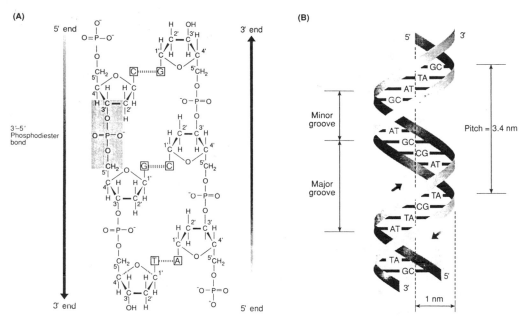

Figure 3. *(A) Depiction of the double-stranded antiparallel helix structure of DNA. (B) Depiction of the double helix with base pairs. Reprinted from Strachan & Read, 1996, Human Molecular Genetics. Wiley, New York.*

was formed, or it was first fashioned by a superior intelligence: the hand of "god."

And, if life was created by "god" or if the seeds of life swarm throughout the cosmos, then some of these "genetic" seeds have fallen to Earth and on other planets including Mars. Indeed, evidence of extra-terrestrial life has been discovered on a variety of meteorites jettisoned from other planets, as well as on the moon. Life has not only repeatedly appeared on other planets, but has done so long before the Earth became a twinkle in god's eye. Indeed, the "seeds of life" may have in fact been created by "god."

Of course, these views are completely contrary to Darwinism. As first proposed by Darwin, and as is accepted by most mainstream scientists, life on earth first emerged and was fashioned in an organic soup.

DNA & THE DEATH OF DARWINISM

Darwin's theory cannot account for the origin, organization, and expression of DNA, or the evidence of progress in the fossil record.

Darwin's theory of evolution emphasizes "random variations" and he and his acolytes deny any evidence of design or progress. Harvard paleontologist S. J. Gould (1988, p. 319) described the notion of "progress" as "noxious."

As argued in the text, Astrobiology (Joseph, 2000), Darwin's theory is refuted by genetics, as well as the fossil record. There is nothing random about the expression or organization of DNA, or the progressive metamorphosis of increasingly complex and intelligent species. Although Darwin's theory can account for "variability" it cannot explain progress including the progressive growth and encephalization of the brain. The brain has not become more variable, but progressively more complex. In fact, not only does the fossil record and the evolution of the body and the brain clearly reveal progress and a step-wise sometimes leaping progression which has led from simple celled creatures to woman and man, but the human genome represents a culmination of that progress.

Contrary to Darwinism, and as the evidence increasingly indicates, the metamorphosis of life has been genetically predetermined and precoded, has unfolded in accordance with specific genetic plans and DNA-based instructions, and has been striving (and still striving) toward fulfilling specific genetic goals. Just an the DNA of an embyro is genetically programmed to produce a fetus, neonate, infant, child, and an adult, the first life forms on this planet contained the DNA for producing all manner of life, including woman and man.

Life has not "evolved" randomly, but in a step-wise, progressive, highly predictable, molecular-

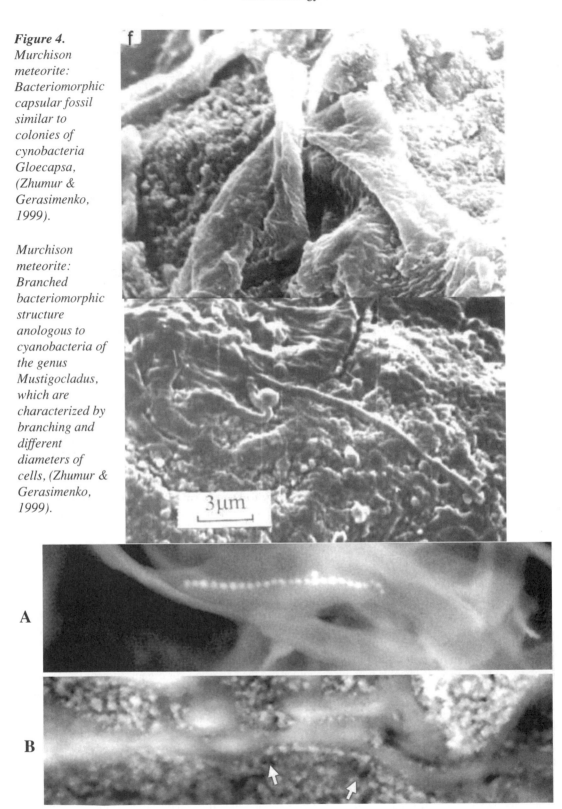

Figure 4.
Murchison
meteorite:
Bacteriomorphic
capsular fossil
similar to
colonies of
cynobacteria
Gloecapsa,
(Zhumur &
Gerasimenko,
1999).

Murchison
meteorite:
Branched
bacteriomorphic
structure
anologous to
cyanobacteria of
the genus
Mustigocladus,
which are
characterized by
branching and
different
diameters of
cells, (Zhumur &
Gerasimenko,
1999).

Figure 5. (A) Modern magnetotactic bacteria, showing a chain of magnetite crystals (B)
Magnetite crystals and chains of magnetite crystals in the Martian meteorite ALH84001 The
Martian crystals thus appear to be of bacterial orgin. From NASA/Ames Research Center

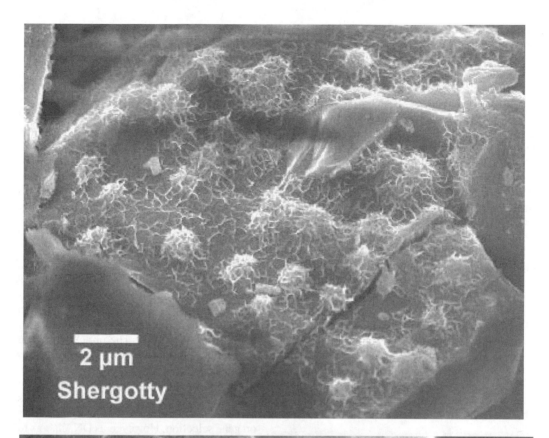

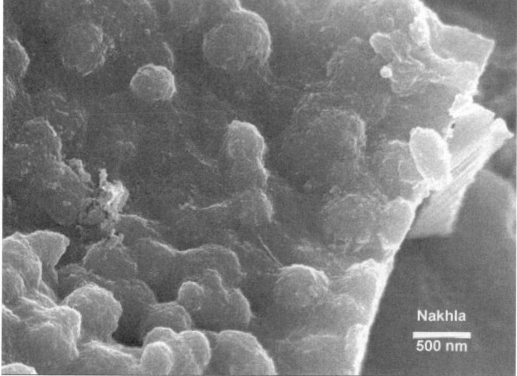

Figure 6.*Field emission scanning electron microscope image of spheroidal features in the Martian meteorits Shergotty and Nakhla which are similar to images of spherical features in bacteria-containing samples from Columbia River Basalt, from: Thomas-Keprta, et al., 2000.*

clock like fashion. It is these "genetic clocks" which have enabled scientists to accurately predict when specific species first emerged on this planet. There are in fact, genes (e.g., tim, mTim, hTIM) and proteins which perform specific "clock-like" timing functions and which interact to form regulatory feedback loops, and which are highly regulated (Clayton et al., 2001). There is nothing random about the organization or expression of DNA (Caron et al., 2001; Courseaux & Nahon, 2001), the source of all variation.

Genes act on genes, turning them on or off. The environment also acts on gene selection, and on silent genes which exist prior to their activation. It is the interaction of the environment with the genome which determines which of these precoded traits and silent genes come to be expressed. DNA not only acts on itself, it acts on the environment and thus engineers and alters the environment, as is evident during the first billion years after the Earth was formed; e.g., through the creation of an oxygen rich atmosphere, which enabled oxygen-breathing creatures to "evolve," and the secretion of calcium which promoted the metamorphosis of shells and the skeletal system, and so on. By acting on itself and by altering the environment, DNA creates a feedback mechanism, such that DNA seeks to engineer its own evolution.

The Earth too has evolved, its oceans, atmosphere, land masses, and climate systemically altered by DNA-based life forms that have lived and died over the course of the last 4 billion years.

Genes, and the traits and species they code for, have not "evolved." They have been inherited from ancestral species, often as silent genes and as genes within genes. Introns (silent genes) contain genes-within-genes, and silent genes, and are the genetic engines of evolution. As compared to all other genomes so far sequenced, human introns have become larger and longer as compared, for example, to fly or worm, i.e., about 50 kb versus 5 kb (Birney et al., 2001). The protein-encoding exons, on the other hand, are roughly the same size. Exons are also conserved, showing up in previous species, often in the same exact location. Thus there has been an increase in the intron to exon ratio in the human genome which in turn is representative of the extreme importance of introns in human evolution and evolutionary change. Introns are "silent" genes and also contain genes-within genes which may be expressed in response to changing environmental conditions, as the environment acts

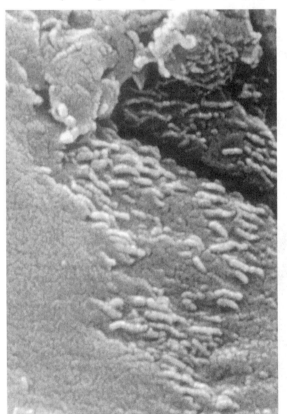

on gene selection. However, as DNA labors to genetically engineer and change the environment, it can be said that DNA (e.g. introns) are engineering their own evolution in accordance with genetic instructions inherited from those creatures who were among the first to appear on Earth--creatures which may have been intelligently designed, or whose ancestors first "evolved" on other planets.

Human genes differ from other species as they perform more complex and multi-tasking operations. The average human gene can make three to five primary protein products vs the genes of other species which create one or two proteins (Aravind et al., 2001; Birney et al., 2001). Humans produce more proteins that are classified as falling into more than one functional category (426 in human versus 80 in worm and 57 in fly). In consequence, "the human genome contains greater numbers of genes, domain and protein families, paralogues, multi-domain proteins with multiple functions, and domain architectures" (Aravind et al., 2001).

Although the mantra "random variations" is the basis for Darwinian theology, the human genome and vertebrate-specific protein domains and motifs have been created according to specific regulatory constraints, and have been built by rearranging preexisting components into a

Figure 7a. (Above & next page) Fossilized Martian bacteria discovered in Martian meteorite.

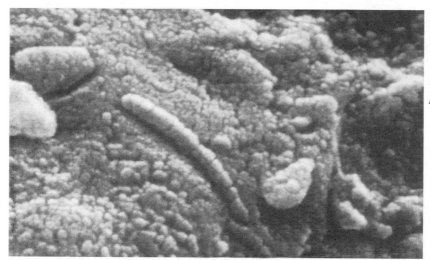

Figure 7b.
Fossilized Martian bacteria discovered in Martian meteorite. NASA photo.

richer collection of domain architectures (IHGSC, 2001). The genetic instructions and the genetic material for creating the human genome existed apriori. They did not randomly "evolve," they were inherited.

For example, consider the so called "language gene," known as FOXP2. FOXP2 existed prior to the evolution of language, and is found in the genome of other mammals, including mice, rats, dogs, cats, chimpanzees, and so on, but in a non-activated protein-protected form (Enard, et al. 2002). Specifically, the gene was first discovered, its in non-activated form, in a large London family who are incapable of speech. The gene was identified by Dr. Anthony P. Monaco of the University of Oxford. FOXP2 is believed to switch on other genes during the development of the brain thus giving rise to the neural circuitry which supports human language. However, Dr. Svante Paabo and colleagues at the Max Planck Institute for Evolutionary Anthropology, reported in the August, 2002 issue of Nature, that the same exact gene exists in a non-activated form, in mice, chimpanzees and other primates (Enard, et al. 2002). According to Dr. Paabo, the FOXP2 gene has remained largely unaltered during the evolution of mammals. However, in humans, this formerly silent gene became activated through changes in the shape of its protective protein coat. Protein prevents the activation of genes, and removal or alteration in the shape of this protein overcoat, allows for the gene to be activated.

Thus, the "language gene" did not randomly evolve through random mutations. It existed prior to the evolution of humans and prior to the evolution of language, albeit in a silent, non-activated state. The same can be said of those genes which give rise to religious and spiritual experience--they existed prior to their activation, and probably can be found in other species as is the case with tens of thousands of other "silent genes."

Consider, in 1998, Rutherford and Lindquist demonstrated that "populations contain a surprising amount of unexpressed genetic variation that is capable of affecting certain" supposedly "invariant traits" and that changes in environmental conditions "can uncover this previously silent variation" (Rutherford & Lindquist, 1998 p. 341). Indeed, much of the genome is silent, and these silent genes, and these silent traits can be expressed by varying the environment and through other stresses including fluctuations in temperature, oxygen levels, and diet (e.g., de Jong & Scharloo, 1976; Dykhuizen & Hart, 1980; Gibson & Hogness, 1996; Polaczyk et al., 1998; Rutherford & Lindquist, 1998).

Further support has been provided by Dr. Martin Yanofsky, of the University of California, San Diego, who recently reported that he activated silent genes to produce flower petals from leaves. Specifically, Yanofsky and colleagues demonstrated that when they deactivated the sepallata (SEP) genes, flowers that normally consist of sepals, petals, stamens and carpells, were reduced to consisting only of sepals. Thus, the SEP gene is necessary for petals, stamens and carpells formation. Yanofsky et al., report that although the SEP genes are active in flowering plants, and silent in leaves and nonflowering plants, that they were able to activate these silent SEP genes, and in result, leaves were converted into petals.

Silent genes, therefore, can be activated to produce traits, including evolutionary advanced traits, that exist prior to their expression. However, silent genes can also act to engineer their own evolution, by acting on the environment, or acting on other genes, thus giving rise to a step-wise progression, which has culminated, on Earth, with the "evolution" of woman and man.

DNA has engineered its own evolution and has been expressed over the course of "evolution" in a predictable, clock-like manner (Joseph 2000). The organization and expression of DNA shows evidence of intelligent design. This intelligence belongs to every DNA molecule which relies on "genetic memories" to genetically engineer the environment and its own evolution and genomic organization. The evidence, as based on genetics, is indicative of intelligent design.

This argument, first detailed by Joseph (2000) regarding the "intelligent design" and expression of DNA, has been embraced by a number of distinguished geneticists. Dr. Gene Myers, chief computer scientist at Celera Genomics, who assisted in creating the map of the human genome published in Science and Nature in February 2001, is quoted as saying the architecture of DNA is so incredibly complex that "it's like it was designed." Tom Abate, a biotechnology reporter at the San Francisco Chronicle, imagined a headline reading: "Genome Mapper Sees Hand of God!" and then asked Myers: "Designed? Doesn't that imply a designer, an intelligence, something more than the fortuitous bumping together of chemicals in the primordial slime? Myers replied. "There's a huge intelligence there. I don't see that as being unscientific. Others may, but not me."

The evidence increasingly indicates that intelligent life evolved from, and has as its source, intelligent life... which also leads to the possibility that intelligent life, represented, on this planet, in the form of modern humans, may continue to evolve and become more intelligent and more god-like. Over 90% of the human genome is silent and has yet to be expressed or activated. In fact, 50% of that silent DNA may well be devoted to the expansion and evolution of the brain--an evolutionary progression that would provide for a wider array of sensory and perceptual cognitive capability which in turn might lead to the next stage in human evolution.

Experience acts on gene selection to activate silent genes and silent traits that exist prior to their selection. In the absence of specific experiences, those brain structures and neurons which subserve those experiences, die and atrophy (Casagrande & Joseph, 1978, 1980; Joseph, 1982, 1999a). The genes generating these neurons remain silent and suppressed.

Because genes are activated by experience and complex genetic mechanisms, and as the brain has also evolved in response to environmental demands and experience, it would appear that humans evolved the capacity to have religious and spiritual experiences, because these experiences acted on gene selection, thereby enabling humans to evolve specific brain structures which allowed them to more fully participate in and experience the spiritually sublime.

Would the human brain have evolved the capacity to perceive and experience that which does not exist? What is the evolutionary significance of the evolution of the human ability to have religious and spiritual experiences? And, is this a rudimentary capability that has not yet fully evolved, that is, on Earth?

THE SEEDS OF INTELLIGENT LIFE

"And when you look up to the sky and behold the sun and the moon and the stars, the whole heavenly host, you must not be lured into bowing down to them or serving them. These the Lord your God allotted to other peoples..." -Deuteronomy 4.19

The Earth is 4.6 billion years young, whereas the age and antiquity of the Universe is unknown. And, just as our world was likely repeatedly contaminated with all manner of life, identical genetic seeds have likely rained down on innumerable worlds. Life has had ample opportunity to take root, flourish, and evolve on worlds similar and shockingly different from our own.

The Universe is likely buzzing with life, and some of these life forms, these "seeds of life," have been repeatedly tossed into the abyss following impact shearings and cosmic collisions. As the first evidence of Earthly life appeared almost immediately following a 700 million year pummeling by all manner of debris, it thus appears that at least a few of these seeds—and their DNA— fell to Earth, as well as other planets. As DNA can only be produced by DNA, then it would appear that these initial DNA-life forms were either exobiological in origin or created by the hand of god, or both.

THOUGHT EXPERIMENTS & FLIGHTS OF FANTASY
Intelligent Life Evolved From Intelligent Life

There are billions of ancient galaxies consisting of trillions of aged solar systems that are likely ringed with planets -many probably quite like our own. And, just as Life has "evolved" on this world, it could be predicted that Life has emerged on at least a few of these planetary archipelagoes including creatures who long ago "evolved" in a fashion similar to woman and man.

On Earth, the leaping, branching, and step-wise progression which has led from multicellular creature to cartilaginous fish, to bony fish... amphibian, reptile, repto-mammal, therapsid, mammal, primate and woman and man, has taken place over the last billion years. Given that over 90% of human DNA is dormant and silent and as tens of thousands of silent genes (and almost 3 billion base pairs) have yet to be expressed, the likelihood is that evolutionary metamorphosis on this planet will continue well into the future. In fact, humans may soon begin to genetically engineering their own evolution, beginning with their own children, i.e. "designer babies."

Likewise, given what has taken place on this planet over the course of the last billion years and the human-genetic potential which is yet to be realized, if similar DNA-based life forms exists elsewhere, then those who dwell in the more ancient corners of the cosmos may have genetically engineered their own evolution and may have evolved beyond modern humans billions of years before the Earth became a twinkle in God's eye.... tens of billions of years before the first upright human emerged from the mists of time.

When we consider that the light from innumerable stars may have winked out of existence billions if not trillions of years ago, that there may be galaxies so distant their light cannot yet be detected, and as current estimates of the age of the Universe are based on detectable light and meaningless distances, the age of the Universe and the ancestry of life may extend interminably into the long ago.

Given that metamorphosis on this planet has been characterized by an obvious step-wise, linear process of increasing intelligence, complexity and brain power, it could therefore be predicted that a similar process has occurred on those life bearing worlds similar to our own. However, as a progressive increase in intelligence and brain size and complexity is characteristic of life on this planet, and as up to 95% of the human genome is silent and has yet to be expressed (that is, on Earth), it can be predicted --at least from the perspective of a "Thought Experiment"--that aliens evolving in the older regions of the cosmos would probably have continued to evolve and undergo metamorphosis. They may have long ago genetically engineered their own evolution by manipulating their genes.

Again, as a "Thought Experiment" consider: These ancient ones who "evolved" billions of years before the Earth was formed may have long ago acquired new brain tissues and new layers of neocortex, and might be capable of processing sensory information which human brains may fail to even perceive much less comprehend.

For example, whereas humans have 6-7 layers (and several sub-layers) of neocortex, those who live in the older regions of the cosmos may have developed 8 or 10, or 12 layers which may be thicker and contain more neurons than their Earthly counterparts. And they may have experienced expansions in those areas of the brain, such as the frontal lobes, which are associated with foresight, judgment, planning skills, and the ability to form long term goals and anticipate multiple long term consequence. Indeed, the frontal lobes serve as the senior executive of the brain, and enable humans to consider multiple possibilities simultaneously while keeping yet other possibilities and their consequences "in mind."

Consider: What might be the technological and scientific capabilities of a civilization a million years older than our own? What of a civilization that has had ten million, or a billion, or 20 billion years to seek technological perfection? They might seem as "gods" even if they were merely human.

And it can be predicted that these ancient ones might have evolved new brain tissues and additional layers of gray matter and neocortex... gaining intellectual and perceptual capabilities which provide not just a "6th sense" but a 10th sense, and so on, completely eclipsing all aspects of human cognition, perception, and intelligence.

Consider, of the 3% of human DNA which is required to build a human being, 20% of that is used to create a brain, and another 30% of that DNA is expressed in the process of running and maintaining the brain (Brain, 1990). That is, 50% of the 3% of DNA which is coded, serves the human brain. Hence, since 97% of the 30,000 to 40,000 or more genes (and their 3 billion or more base pairs) that make up the human genome are repressed, up to 50% of that and thus perhaps as many as 25,000 repressed genes and over a billion base pairs of nucleotides may be available for future cerebral metamorphosis and expansion of the brain.

Since increased complexity and progressive cerebral encephalization is characteristic of the evolution of brain-based life on this planet, the same could be expected on other complex-life bearing worlds. Consider, the Cro-Magnon peoples of the Upper Paleolithic had a brain that was 1/3 larger than modern humans (Joseph, 2000a).

Given evidence of increased brain size in previous species of humanity, coupled with the as yet untapped genetic potential, then it can be predicted that those creatures evolving in the more ancient corners of the cosmos may have acquired more complex neuronal capabilities, as well as increased association and assimilation neocortical tissue, and may have evolved additional nuclei and layers of neocortex, exceeding the 6 to 7 layered neocortex that is characteristic of mammals and primates— and this may have transpired billions of years before the creation of the Earth. In fact, given the unknown antiquity of the universe, the brains of some exobiological organisms may consist of 8, 10, 12 or more layers of neocortex and greatly increased neocortical, perceptual, intellectual, and memory capacity, thus completely dwarfing the human brain in neuronal and cognitive ability.

Consider, what if these ancient ones long ago engineered their own DNA and thus genetically engineered their own metamorphosis and purposefully developed cerebral tissues that enable them to analyze, see relationships, or comprehend and manipulate phenomenon that modern humans cannot even conceive much less comprehend. These peoples, these ancient ones, would be as "gods" even if they were merely human.

Can a lizard comprehend a man?
Can a man comprehend a god?
Who dares speak for God?
Perhaps....
....Even the gods have gods...

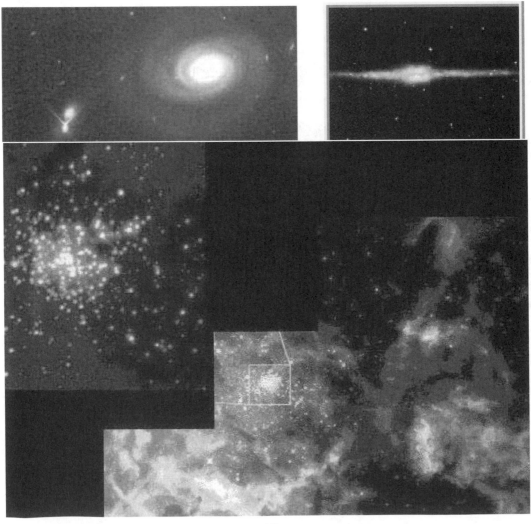

Figure 8. There are hundreds of billions of galaxies, each containing hundreds of billions of stars and suns, many probably quite like our own. (Bottom) The globular cluster M13. (Right & Below) M74 & M42, galatic stars (spiral galaxies) containinig billions of stars and suns.

Again, considered as a "Thought Experiment," what might be the creative and intellectual potency of a being whose brain and civilization has evolved over tens of billions of years, who has likely engineered their own DNA, and who has 10 or 20 or more layers of neocortex —compared to those seven we call our own? From the perspective of those astrobiological organisms who evolved in the ancient regions of the cosmos, the human brain and mind may seem to be just one small step above a frog or a reptile; which, in many ways it is.

Conversely, the human ability to comprehend the intellectual, scientific and technological accomplishments and capabilities of an alien brain organized in this evolutionary advanced fashion, might be analogous to a lizard's ability to comprehend a man. That is, the mental, intellectual, creative, and technological capabilities of creatures who began to evolve tens of billions of years ago, would lie well beyond human understanding. They would be as gods even if they were merely human.

Might this also explain the claims of the ancient Sumerians, Babylonians, Hebrews, Greeks, Romans, etc. that "God" and the "gods" looked and behaved like humans and possessed human attributes including egotism, jealousy, irrational rages... including perhaps a tendency to brag and to take credit for achievements not their own —such as the creation of the universe?

Or, could it be that an incredibly ancient, "superior" life form which lives or exists in a manner or physical dimension that is beyond our comprehension, may have been "playing god" and long ago fashioned this world, our Earth, our DNA and sewn the seeds of all life?

And, if humans are created in the image of the "Gods," having descended, and ascended, from similar genetic seeds, and if evolutionary metamorphosis is an ongoing phenomenon, then perhaps we too possess the genetic potential to be as gods, to be as God, and the genetic potential to not only eat of the tree of knowledge, but to evolve beyond good and evil.

Again, it may well be that what is referred to as spirituality and paranormal and even so called "psychic" phenomenon, are but the leading edge of psychological abilities which have not yet evolved and thus represent the first rudimentary elements of neurological and functional capabilities which have not yet fully emerged and whose genetic potential remain locked away in those silent genes which have not yet been expressed and in brain tissue which still has the genetic potential to more fully evolve... like the "language genes" lying dormant in the genomes of mice, dogs, and chimpanzees.

Because the brain has evolved the capacity to act as a transmitter to god, and may well be continuing to evolve this emerging capacity, it may be that what is perceived and experienced are fragments of a spiritual reality that is beyond our ability to fully comprehend; for why would the brain evolve the capacity to experience something that does not exist?

It is the neurological, and genetic foundations for spiritual experience, and the fact that all humans possess a brain that is organized in a similar manner, coupled with the existence of this "spiritual reality" which also explains why humans have similar religious and mystical experiences, what Jung (1964) referred to as "archetypes." Archetypes are inborn tendencies to dream of, and respond similarly to specific images and symbols and to experience a personal soul and presence of god. Humans have similar religious experiences because these experiences are real and are perceived in a similar fashion by the same regions of the brain. Each and every human is born with a brain and mind which serves as a transmitter to god.

Thus, it could be argued that the essence of "God" and our living soul, may be dwelling within the depths of the ancient limbic lobe which is buried within the belly of the brain. And not just the soul or the Great Spirit, for in the Upanishads and Tao it is said, and as Buddha, Lao Tzu, Jesus, the Sufis, and as Sumerian, Babylonian, Egyptian, Jewish, Arabic, Aryan, Greek, Roman, Indian, Muslim, and Gnostic mystics have proclaimed:

"The Kingdom of God is within you."

THE MYTH OF THE BIG BANG:
Cosmic Organic Clouds &
Creation Science
by R. Joseph

Throughout the ages, and as is true today, some of what has passed for "scientific fact" has been based on faith and dogma; which is why the temple priests of science often protect the faith, and the status quo, by attacking and ridiculing those heretics who threaten to topple and shatter the altars of their idols. The dustbins of history are laden with discarded "scientific facts" and those who believed in them (Kuhn, 1970). Until the 16th century, it was a "fact" that the Earth was at the center of the solar system and the universe. Until the 19th century it was scientific "fact" that "rocks do not fall from the sky" and that meteors did not exist. Until the 20th century, it was scientific "fact" that interstellar space was permeated by a viscous "ether." In the 1920s, articles and editorials appeared in leading scientific journals ridiculing those rocketeers who dreamed of soaring through space, explaining it was a scientific "fact" that rockets would be unable to propel themselves beyond the Earth because of the lack of atmosphere or air. Until the year 2000, it was a scientific fact that the speed of light was a constant and that nothing could travel faster than the speed of light.

And all these "scientific facts" have been proved false.

The history of science is a history of scientific revolutions, where established, authoritative scientific dogma finally crumbles from the weight of unwieldy, disconfirming evidence that can no longer be suppressed or ignored and which continues to grow until it completely undermines the beliefs and the authority of the ruling status quo. The history of scientific revolutions always entails a complete paradigm shift in scientific thought and belief; ushered in by those revolutionaries who dared to challenge the ruling authorities and the high priests of science.

In some respects, modern western science could be likened to a religion that consists of numerous cults and priesthoods--each claiming to possess the "truth." Consider modern physics. Physicists have proposed over 50 different major theories to explain the origin and nature of the universe. Obviously they cannot all be correct. Indeed, by nature of the fact that there are so many theories should lead us to conclude that none of them are correct. Essentially, we have been provided with a multiple-choice theory as to the origin of the universe--multiple choices which should include: None Of The Above.

"Its the theory which decides what we can observe" -Einstein

Like most religions, many of those in the scientific community, particularly in the field of physics and astronomy, base their theories not on facts, but on faith and belief. Faith is no substitute for fact, which is why there are so many theories, and which is why most of these theories, including the most widely accepted theories, such as the Standard Model, are incompatible with one another and fail to explain or are unable to make accurate predictions about the very phenomena they are supposed to explain.

Consider, for example, the Standard Model of elementary particles, which is employed to explain how particles like electrons, muons, neutrinos and quarks interact, that is via three interacting forces: electro-magnetic, weak nuclear and strong nuclear. However, the Standard Model is flawed and serves at best as an incomplete explanation which does not explain, for example, the most well known force in nature: gravity. The Standard Model most also assume the existence of distinct forces and their carriers the existence of which have not been shown, and which are posited to exist only in order to save the theory. The Standard Model cannot provide acceptable explanations for a surprisingly wide range of phenomena.

For example, why does the electron weigh as much as it does? Why do particles interact with a given strength and not any other? Why can an observor determine either the velocity or the position of an electron, but never both? These values can be measured in experiments, but cannot be predicted by the Standard Model.

Consider, also, for example, general relativity and quantum field theory which offer differing predictions regarding the same events such as "black holes" i.e. the fundamental origin of their thermodynamic properties and their apparent incompatibility with quantum mechanics. General relativity and quantum field theory are in fact incomptabile.

Because of these and other shortcomings, physicists have proposed over 50 different theories including five different superstring theories--each requiring ten dimensions (nine space and one time). Nevertheless, even in regard to "sting theory" (which is based on particle physics), each makes predictions that differ from the others.

Einstein's old dream of a "unified theory" of fundamental forces has not been realized. Instead, we have multiple theories which often conflict, and which either cannot be tested or which are not supported by all the available evidence. Instead, theorists are forced to ignore most of the evidence, and instead pick and choose those fragments of "evidence" which are compatible with their theory.

THE BIG BANG, COSMIC CLOUDS, AND INTERSTELLAR PLANETARY NURSERIES

Many Western educated scientists religiously adhere to the theology of purposelessness as exemplified by the almost blind devotion to Darwinism and the belief in the "big bang" creation of the Universe. Darwin's theory and neo-Darwinian evolutionary theory are also compatible with and supported by the mainstream scientific view as to the origin of the Universe; i.e., the "big bang." The theory of the "big bang" in turn provides a theoretical framework that could explain the origin of those complex molecules that fell to earth, only to be cooked and randomly jumbled together in some organic soup, or perhaps swallowed and then spewed out of some undersea volcano in the form of a living, self-replicating molecule (de Duve, 1995; Gesteland, 1993; Woodward, et al., 1998).

Essentially, the theory of the big bang rests upon the notion that at first there was absolutely nothing. Nothing! Not even space! And then, inexplicably, this nothingness began to heat up and exploded, and out of nothing there was suddenly stuff. Or, another way of putting it: nothing happened. And, out of nothing flowed space, time, elementary particles, then protons, neutrons, electrons... the Universe and finally those molecules which would some day fall to earth. And, just as nothing gave rise to everything, non-life would give rise to all life including the generation of those scientists who believe in "nothing."

More specifically, it is supposed within one trillionth of a second after the big bang—an explosion tens of billions of degrees hot—both matter and antimatter were created. In some scenarios, this resulted in an antimatter universe, and another universe consisting of matter.

In yet another scenario, since whenever matter and antimatter have contact, they instantly annihilate one another in flashes of pure energy, it is proposed that there was a slight imbalance such that there was slightly more matter than antimatter. Hence, within the one trillionth of a second after the big bang and after almost all matter and antimatter were destroyed—thus creating the cosmic microwave background radiation that permeates the universe—the fragmentary remainder of matter gave rise to this universe.

Considered broadly and generally, following the big bang and the creation of molecules from nothingness, as well as the creation of space—for initially, as there was nothing, there was no space (at least according to the theory of the big bang)—some of the remaining molecules of matter froze and/or combined in space, perhaps in association with the hydrogen and helium that was also created by the big bang. Once they combined, these formed complex organic molecules, some of which may have even developed lipid membranes (Woodward, et al., 1998). Presumably, ten billion years later, these complex molecules eventually seeded the Earth.

It is noteworthy, however, that these latter events may also occur without the necessity of a "big bang." The creation of complex organic molecules in space appears to be ongoing phenomenon. A big bang is not necessary to explain the creation of organic molecules.

More specifically, it is supposed, that after the big bang, and following the creation of stars, planets, and galaxies there were repeated cosmic collisions and supernova which dispersed all manner of debris into interstellar space—events which are ongoing and thus do not require a "big bang." Cosmic collisions are commonplace, not only between meteors and planets, but entire galaxies.

The nature of this ejecta, however, differed and continues to differ depending on the type of stellar nucleosynthesis that created it, and those events which led to its dispersal; e.g., planetary collisions, supernova, planetary nebulae etc., (Scott et al., 1998; Woodward et al., 1998).

As is now well known, many different types of stellar debris, including those produced by planetary nebulae (dying stars) contain hydrogen, oxygen, carbon, and often sulfur, nitrogen and phosphorus (Williams, 1998). Yet, molecules of this sort may be quickly destroyed by interstellar shock waves, ultraviolet photolysis, and vaporization. It is supposed, therefore, that after the big bang, and/or following planetary collisions, and/or supernova, or planetary nebulae, etc., that these molecules coalesced thus forming dense protective molecular clouds which enabled them to survive the rigors of interstellar space (Scott et al., 1998; Williams, 1998; Woodward et al., 1998). In fact, it appears that these dense molecular clouds may have served (and continue to serve) as stellar nurseries, from which stars, planets, and galaxies were (and continue to be) formed. As the cloud collapses and the heavier central most elements fall together due to gravitational forces, and then combine together, they form stars and planets.

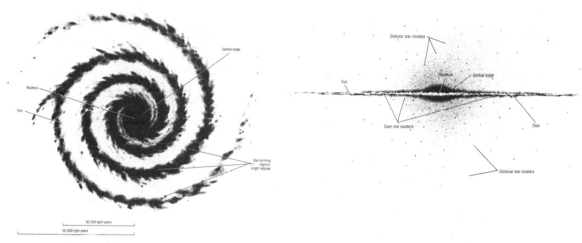

Figure 9. (Above) *Two views of the Milky Way Galaxy which is a spiral galaxy centered upon a compact nucleus of stars. Like our solar system, the Milky Way Galaxy is in motion and in orbit. The Earth is located along one of the outer spirals of the Milky Way Galaxy, and it takes our solar system about 126 million years go orbit the Milky Way. According to one theory, the nucleus of the Milkyway Way consists of older stars, whereas newer stars, including our sun and solar system, are located along the outer spirals. However, recent evidence based on infrared photos provided by the Hubble telescope indicates that at the center of this nucleus is a star that glows with the energy of 10 million suns and which was formed only 1 million to 3 million years ago. (Below) The Sombrero Galaxy, M104. Compare with Sumerian conception of the Universe. Reprinted from Ferris, 1982; Galaxies, Sierra Club Books, San Francisco.*

These molecular clouds/planetary nurseries—which have been repeatedly identified in the wilds of space—are believed to remain stable for millions if not hundreds of millions of years. In fact, in August of 1997, astronomers announced what they claimed to be an immense "planetary construction site" for new planets, just 450 million light years from Earth in the constellation of Taurus; i.e. a molecular cloud containing a dense, gas-rich rotating disc of material which is orbiting a young star, MWC480, and which is less than a few million years old.

According to Dr. Anneila Sargent, Director of the Owens Valley Radio Observatory, "We are seeing for the first time a place where conditions are perfect for the formation of planets like Jupiter or Earth."

Although the MWC480 disc makes up only a fraction of the molecular cloud, its outer edge is more than 30 billion miles across, which is 10 times the distance of the planet Pluto from the sun. As

Figure 10. *The Cone Nebula is a gaseous stellar nursery that has given birth to stars billions of years ago, and which is currently giving birth to additional infant stars.*

Figure 11. *The Orion Nebula (=M42 = NGC1976) is a gaseous stellar nursery that is currently giving birth to infant stars. Double planetary nebulae. A collection of galaxies. A spiral galaxy NGC5364. A single galaxy (which may appear as a single star), may be comprised of tens of millions or hundreds of millions of stars—each of which may have its own solar system. Because NGC5364 lies well away from the plane of our own Milky Way galaxy, it can be seen with few intervening stars.*

to the origins of the disk, presumably it is the result of the gravitational collapse of those interstellar molecular clouds which formed the star itself.

These findings, of course, also negate the necessity of positing a big bang. In fact, recent evidence based on infrared photos provided by the Hubble telescope indicates that at the center of our Milky Way galaxy is a star that glows with the energy of 10 million suns and which was formed only 1 million to 3 million years ago. That is, within the center of our galaxy is a star and presumably a planet creating nucleus —which may have been created by a collapsing molecular cloud, and which may someday come to be ringed by planets.

Moreover, dying stars also provide the material for the creation of new molecular clouds and thus the formation of new suns and planets, including perhaps the seeds of life. In December of 1997, for example, NASA released photos taken by the Hubble telescope which revealed dying stars that were in the process of blowing off their outer atmospheres and veils of luminous gas including clouds of helium, hydrogen, nitrogen, oxygen and carbon, at high speeds hundreds of billions of miles into the far reaches of space; i.e. so called "planetary nebulae."

Thus it appears that old stars are recycled, recreating the molecular clouds which gave birth to them and which will give birth to new suns and planets.

If there was no big bang, this process of recycling may have been ongoing for all of eternity.

ORGANIC MOLECULAR CLOUDS AND THE SEEDS OF LIFE

Life on Earth could not have emerged from an organic soup, or an undersea thermal event—at least on Earth. The necessary ingredients for the manufacture of life did not exist on the young planet. Nor was there sufficient free oxygen, and there may have been no free oxygen at all, which is an essential ingredient that makes up the structure of DNA. In fact, almost all the essential ingredients for the construction and manufacture of DNA, were nowhere to be found—at least on Earth— thus refuting any and all notions that Earthly life originated from non-life.

In order to account for the missing necessary ingredients for the creation of life, many mainstream evolutionary scientists and astrobiologists assume that complex organic molecules, but not living things—fell to Earth, encased, perhaps, in the debris that bombarded this planet for the first 700 million years after it was formed. Once on Earth, and after the cessation of these bombardments, those complex organic molecules which survived began to collect together, perhaps as runoff from river estuaries, thus forming either a complex molecular "organic soup," or a random collection of residue and organic sludge that was swallowed by the ocean and later spewed from a deep-ocean thermal vent in the form of living creatures (Brandes, et al., 1998; Holme, 1992).

Although a variety of scenarios abound (e.g., de Duve, 1995; Holme, 1992; Lamond & Gibson, 1990; Orgel, 1994; Rebek, 1994), involving for example, crystals, clay particles, or ribozymes (e.g., Gesteland, 1993; Unrau & Bartel, 1998), in general it is assumed that once these molecules collected together (either as an organic soup or in a deep sea thermal vent), they were subject to some electrochemical, activating event, and became organized in a manner that would eventually give rise to life; a single celled organism—the only one of its kind.

Despite being unable to explain how these events transpired, it is generally believed that this single celled organism was somehow provided with DNA (deoxyribonucleic acid), RNA (ribonucleic acid), genetic instructions, cytoplasm, and a cellular membrane, and the capacity to extract energy and reproduce itself by producing RNA- or DNA-based duplicates.

Every creature and living thing, therefore, owe their existence to these chance occurrences where a multitude of organic molecules from outer space were randomly mixed together. These molecular collections not only sprang to life but survived and began to reproduce, eventually producing complex creatures including woman and man.

Specifically, following the big bang, it is presumed that these cosmic clouds (and those which continue to orbit between and within the innumerable billions of galaxies within this universe) may have also served (and may continue to serve) as nuclear wombs that generated and gave birth to the seeds of life. Since these clouds provide protection for the complex molecules they contain, they also absorb ultraviolet light and cosmic shock waves which in turn provides them heat and energy. These collective events are believed to engender the combination and creation of even more complex organic molecules (Scott et al., 1998; Woodward, et al., 1998). It is believed that within the womb of these molecular clouds, hydrogen, oxygen, carbon, sulfur, nitrogen and phosphorus are continually irradiated by ions, and are then combined thereby creating complex organic molecules, including polycyclic aromatic hydrocarbons (PAHs), as well as carbon grains, oxides, and carbon monoxide—seeds of life.

Although the above scenario is conjecture, as is well known, interstellar space is awash with carbon based organic molecules, whereas hydrogen, the stuff of life, is a major constituent of interstellar molecular clouds (Scott et al., 1998; Woodward, et al., 1998). Data provided by the Submillimeter Wave Astronomy Satellite and the Infrared Space Observatory have detected the presence of 75 interstellar molecules (50 organic compounds and 25 nitrogen-based molecules) including molecular oxygen, carbon, carbon dioxide, methane, ammonia, benzene, formic acid, acetic acid, methanol, polycyclic aromatic hydrocarbons, and silicate grains—molecules which can be used to build amino acids.

Moreover, water, carbon dioxide, and methanol have been detected in comets. Recent evidence also suggests that amino acid can be synthesized in comets and the deposited on Earth (Bada et al., 2001). In addition, over 70 different amino acids have been detected in various meteorites, acids which have been determined to be astrobiological in origin.

The universe has also been discovered to be sugar coated. That is, sugar molecules, i.e., methyl formate, acetic acid, and glycolaldehyde, have been detected in giant gas and dust clouds, including a gas cloud located about 26,000 light-years from the center of our own Milky Way Galaxy (i.e. Sagittarius B2). This is relatively close to a region where planets have also been discovered to be forming. This is significant in that glycolaldehyde (an 8-atom molecule composed of carbon, hydrogen, and oxygen) can combine with other molecules to form the more complex sugars such as ribose. Ribose is a building block of the nucleic acids, DNA and RNA. According to Dr. Jan Hollis of the NASA Goddard Space Flight Center in Maryland, "the discovery of this sugar molecule in a cloud from which new stars are forming means it is increasingly likely that the chemical precursors to life are formed in such clouds long before planets develop around the stars."

Indeed, the chemical synthesis of complex organic molecules also occurs rather rapidly in different stellar environments, that is, within a few thousand years; at least according to results from the European Space Agency's infrared space observatory (European Space Agency, 1/17/2000). Specifically, Bruce Hrivnak of Valparaiso University and Swun Kwok and Keven Wolk, from the University of Calgary, basing their results from a comparative analysis of infrared spectra, found that molecular signatures could be identified. They deduced that small organic molecules can evolve into complex organic molecules within a few thousand years. Kwok also argued that even amino acids could be generated and synthesized in these stellar environments.

Moreover, it has been proposed that the building blocks for DNA may have been generated within a collapsing interstellar cloud. According to Sandip and Sonali Chakrabarti, a cloud, seven light years across, and containing hydrogen, carbon, oxygen and nitrogen, and several other elements, could possibly create adenine, which is a DNA base, from hydrogen cyanide. According to the Chakrabarti, "DNA bases produced in the collapsing cloud could have contaminated the Earth." However, only about 120 different molecules have been detected within these cosmic clouds, and less than a dozen have been detected which consist of 8 or more atoms.

Dworkin and colleagues (2001) have also synthesized self-assembling amphiphilic molecules in an environment designed to simulate the environments of dense interstellar molecular clouds. They report that a "complex mixture of molecules is produced by UV photolysis of realistic, interstellar ice analogs, and that some of the components have properties relevant to the origin of life, including the ability to self-assemble into vesicular structures... similar to those found in primitive meteorites." They report that by creating a "very simple, yet astrophysically relevant, ice mixture (water, methanol, ammonia, and carbon monoxide)," they could produce "a very complex mixture of compounds, including amphiphiles and fluorescent molecules."

Essentially, Dworkin and colleagues claim to have created "proto-cells," and they did so by designing a vacuum chamber with a temperature of 441 degrees below zero Fahrenheit, similar to the frigid emptiness of interstellar space. They then subjected water, ammonia, carbon monoxide, carbon dioxide, and methanol with ultraviolet radiation to mimic the radiation that might be encountered in space. The radiation induced these molecules to form into membrane-like structures with lipid bilayers similar to the lipid bilayers that enclose living cells.

According to these authors, "the ready formation of these insoluble compounds from photolyzed ices comprised of simple molecules suggests this process might be the source of their origin in meteorites, and that the delivery of such compounds by comets, meteorites, and interplanetary dust particles during the late heavy bombardment period may have played an influential role in the origin of life on Earth" as well as other planets.

As the membranes they generated were able to "grab onto other molecules that fluoresce under radiation," these authors argue that these proto-cell membranes "might have been very useful on our own early Earth when there was no ozone layer yet to protect the earliest forms of life from solar radiation. Those fluorescent molecules could have provided just the kind of sunscreen the organisms within the membranes needed to survive."

Given the above, it might be assumed that the galaxies and planets formed by the collapse of these clouds would also be awash with the organic elements necessary for the formation of life, including lipid membranes and some of the base elements for the construction of DNA. The entire universe might be one vast organic soup, and every planet a potential breeding ground for life.

Unfortunately, given the subzero temperatures of space (i.e. 10 degrees above absolute zero), there probably would not be enough energy available to drive the chemical reactions necessary for adenine synthesis, much less DNA. These theories and the evidence presented above, also cannot explain the origin of DNA -at least on Earth. A single macromolecule of DNA is so incredibly complex, the notion that it might have been created in space or in an organic soup, is the equivalent of finding a computer on Mars, and positing that it was created by random chemical reactions within a underground Martian "organic sea."

Moreover, the extreme temperatures that are engendered during the collapse and star formation, would destroy all complex organic molecules including adenine, with the possible exception of PAHs, microdiamonds, and aliphatic hydrocarbons (Woodward, et al., 1998). Planets formed in this manner, including the new born Earth, would be completely sterilized and would be dependent upon stellar debris in order to obtain the chemistry of life.

In fact, if the above collapsing cloud scenario is correct, not only would the Earth have been sterilized in the process of its creation, it would have been continually sterilized yet again by the immense heat generated during its initial 700 million years when it was incessantly bombarded by cosmic debris (Press & Siever, 1986). The new Earth was sterile and completely devoid of the complex organic chemicals necessary for life.

On the other hand, it has been argued that once the Earth had sufficiently cooled, that volatile, less refractory materials were transported to Earth via interplanetary dust particles and comets and thus contributed to the collection of organic material for the origin of life.

In fact, nearly 40,000 tons of organic carbon-bearing material rain down on the Earth yearly, the residue of meteorites and comets. Thus it could be argued that amino acids fell from the sky, were mixed together in an organic stew, and eventually gave rise to life on Earth, and that these essential elements were delivered by meteorites and the remnants of comets (Bada et al., 2001; Ehrenfreund et al., 2001). Life may have arrived on innumerable planets in this manner.

However, the first evidence of life on Earth appeared immediately following the cessation of that cosmic bombardment, 3.8 billion years ago (Mojzsis, et al., 1996). These living creatures were already quite complex and fully formed —they were not the product of an organic soup—at least on Earth. Moreover, evidence based on an analysis of meteorites from Mars indicates that fully formed complex life may have also appeared on the red planet at about the same time, 3.9 billion years ago (Gibson et al., 2001).

There simply was not enough time for life to form from an organic soup, given that complex life appeared immediately following the heating and sterilization of the Earth. As these creatures were already fully formed and quite complex, it therefore seems reasonable to conclude that life, that is, living cells (and their DNA) must have arrived on Mars, the Earth, and other planets from interstellar space, encased in debris—life that survived and then began to go forth and multiply.

THE MYTH OF THE BIG BANG

"In the interval between dissolution and creation, Vishnu-Cesha rested in his own substance, glowing with dormant energy, admidst the germs of future lives" —Hindu poem.

THE BIG BANG, GOD, & CHAOS

The theory of the big bang is problematic as it rests upon the premise that at first there was nothing and then there was an explosion and then there was stuff. Some theorists have recognized this position is rather untenable, and have modified the theory of the "big bang" by positing the initial existence of pure energy. Of course, the preexistence of "energy" also seems to refute the central tenant of the "big bang" which is at first there was nothing.

Nevertheless, according to this version of the big bang theory, this pure energy for some unknown reason became increasingly chaotic and exploded, thereby giving rise to an orderly expanding and uniform universe, where at first there was nothing but pure chaos, i.e. energy which contained not nothing, but everything.

The notion of order emerging from chaos, including the condensing and creation of vast interstellar clouds, is a very old idea that was penned by the Sumerians over 6000 years ago. Moreover, the notion of "pure energy" has been likened by some Creation Scientists as being identical to the "Spirit of God".

In fact, although the big bang theory is dressed up in the language of modern science, it appears to be a restatement of the theory of creation as presented by the ancient peoples of Sumer and in the first chapter of the five books of Moses:

"In the beginning God created heaven and earth"--Genesis 1.

Sages and wisemen over the ages have offered a variety of interpretations as to the meaning of the above passage. Some believe that god and the universe are as one and are inseparable from god, and thus the universe is eternal because god existed at the beginning.

Another view is that God could be likened to a carpenter who builds a house. The carpenter is not the house, and the materials for building the house existed prior to its being built. However, the carpenter, as builder, does not become a carpenter-creator-builder until he builds the house. This

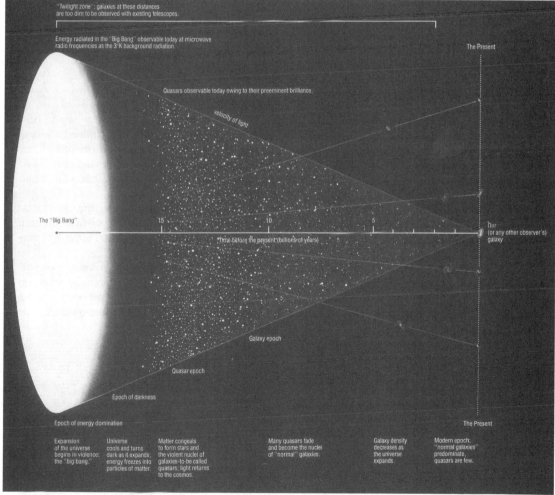

Figure 12. *Schematic illustration of the theoretical "Big Bang." Reprinted from Ferris, 1982; Galaxies, Sierra Club Books, San Francisco. There are several major conceptions of the big bang, and one is that at first there was absolutely nothing, not even space, and then there was a big explosion which created molecules and thus the Universe. This notion could also be characterized as the "nothing happened" theory of creation. Another conception is that at first there was pure energy and then this energy exploded which caused a massive and exceedingly hot expansion, and then as this expansion cooled some of this energy froze into particles of molecules which later gave rise to stellar clouds, and then stars and planets.*

31

view implies that God existed prior to creating the universe, and that the elements for creating the universe also existed apriori, but that the universe is not eternal, only its elementary parts. Likewise, it could be argued that God does not become God, i.e. the Creator, until he Creates which thus causes Him to become God, the creator. In this manner, God is self-creating and becomes God by creating the Universe, e.g. the big bang: "God said, let there be light, and there was light."

It could be argued then, that god is not eternal, but only came into being at the "Beginning."

In modern physics, "god" before He became god, could be likened to the chaotic pure energy which existed prior to the birth of the universe. It is thus through the agency of "god" that all things owe their existence, i.e. stars, planets, cosmic clouds, human beings, etc., including god. God, the Creator, is self-creating. And, just as time did not exist before the big bang, time did not exist prior to "god's" creation of the universe. Because time did not exist, and since time is a creation of god/the-big-bang, then god/pure energy also existed in the absence of and outside of time; that is, as a time-less nothingness. Hence, we can say that god and the chaotic elements which gave rise to the universe are timeless and emerged from nothingness.

However, if time and god have a beginning, then "eternity" cannot exist. Likewise, we cannot say that "God or the universe is eternal" because "eternity" implies the existence of time and that time existed before the creation/big bang. Rather, we can say that god existed at the moment of creation, and that god became god simultaneously with creation. What this means is that god existed at the beginning of time, and that god existed at the beginning.

CREATION SCIENCE

SUMERIAN COSMOLOGY: A CHAOTIC NOTHINGNESS

Modern day "Creation Science" is rooted in the story of Genesis which in turn appears to be a retelling of the Sumerian tales of creation (Heidel, 1988; Kramer, 1991; Roux, 1992). Indeed, there is now a convergence of opinion that the story of Genesis, as retold in the Hebrew and Christian Bible, bears a striking resemblance to the "creation myths" penned almost 6,000 years ago by the peoples of Sumer—in what today is Iraq; stories still in fashion with the rise of the Babylonian state which had risen with the fall of Sumer (Roux, 1992).

Our knowledge of ancient Sumer comes from a variety of ancient texts, including epic tales, hymns, poetry, proverbs, prayers and incantations. Some of these texts are written in ancient Sumerian, others are Akkadian and Babylonian copies that were found in the ruins of palaces and temple libraries.

Sumerian cosmology, as to the origin of the Universe, in some respects resembles modern cosmology. For example, they imagined that at first there was nothing and because there was nothing, it had no name. Rather, all was chaos. Moreover, because there was nothing, "No gods whatever had been brought into being. Uncalled by name, their destinies undetermined." However, rather than a pure absence, this nothingness was chaos (Kramer, 1991; Roux, 1992), a "commingling" of clouds ("mummu"), fresh waters (Apsu) and salt waters (Tiamat). And, out of this chaos came form, substance, and "An" the eternal heavens from which flowed the seeds of life; seeds which eventually fell to Earth and which also fell upon the planets of the gods, thus giving birth to the gods, the Anunnaki. "An begot the Anunnaki."

CREATION MYTHOLOGY?

The concept of god, and the Biblical account of creation, is entirely compatible with the theory of the big bang. However, although there is obvious evidence for "energy" and interstellar clouds

Figure 13. Sumerian cosmology and conception of the universe. Reprinted form Kramer, 1981. History Begins at Sumer. The University of Pennsylvania Press. Pennsylvania.

that give birth to stars, planets and galaxies, the "scientific" theory of the "big bang" is not supported by the evidence. The theory of the big bang is refuted by the fact that the "uniformity" that is required in the distribution of matter, and the supposed '3 degree background radiation that is supposed to exist uniformly in all directions of the universe (as predicted and required by this big explosion), is not uniform. Rather, there are entire walls of galaxies spread at irregular intervals (Cohen et al., 1996), with the "older" and more distant galaxies clustered together rather than spread apart (Glanz, 1996).

The background radiation is also characterized by "density fluctuations" and other deviations which indicate the universe is not behaving in a fashion that would be expected from an inflationary explosion (Ferreira et al., 1998). According to one team of scientists (reviewed in Glanz, 1996) there are "clumpy structures as far as they could see, far enough to make theorists uncomfortable." Why uncomfortable? Because these findings are incompatible with the theory of the big bang.

It has been repeatedly reported that a mysterious kind of antigravity energy, a "repulsive force permeates the universe, accelerating its expansion and sweeping distant objects unexpectedly far away" (reviewed in Glanz, 1998). There are entire rivers of galaxies flowing in directions that would not be likely if due to a big bang (e.g. Lauer & Postman -reviewed in Flamsteed 1995). And, so claims NASA, the universe is "flat" and is not expanding uniformly.

Of course, other scientists argue that the Universe is finite whereas some claim it is infinite. Others claim that it is concave; others say it is round and will someday begin to shrink. Yet others wonder if there are multiple universes consisting of numerous dimensions and subdivisions. According to "string theory" the creation of this universe is due to these subdimensions bumping into one another, thus creating the big bang or even numerous big bangs in different sub-dimensions of the cosmos those giving rise to multiple universes--a hypothesis that might best be described as the "gang bang theory of creation."

STRING THEORY & THE MULTIVERSE

As reviewed in the September 2000 issue of the journal Physical Review, one of the central tenants of string theory is that at first there was nothing and that the nothingness exploded when it was hit by another nothingness. Nothing happened twice, therefore, and gave rise to the big bang.

According to string theory, before our universe (U-2) came into existence, another universe (U-1) collided with it, causing such incredible heat that there was an explosion and the nothingness became a searing soup of subatomic particles such that nothingness gave rise to everything.

This other universe (U-1) is believed to have existed in parallel with our universe (U-2) before our universe existed; that is, in one of the alternate dimensions. These two extra-dimensions bumped into one another causing the big bang.

According to string theory, our universe consists of more than 3 dimensions. Some physicists believe there may be more than 12 dimensions. However, not all these dimensions exist side by side, but as dimensions within dimensions.

For example, it is believed that sitting atop and between the 3 dimensions is an incredibly thin 4th dimension, which is sandwiched inside. It is this postulated 4th dimensions which some physicists believe is responsible for the "big bang" and the creation of our Universe,

It is argued that this 4th dimension collided with one of the walls of the 3rd dimensions thus causing an explosion and thus the big bang.

Of course, if there are other dimensions, and if this theory is true, this raises the possibility that there may be more collisions as well as collisions in the past, and thus more explosions and even more "Big Bangs" all of which gives rise to multiple universes each created by a "big bang" —which is why I refer to this as the "Gang Bang" theory of creation.

"String" theory requires the existence of at least 10 dimensions, seven of which are believed to be curled up in regions of space so tiny that they have not yet been detected. It is the proposed existence of these additional dimensions which some argue account for the weakness of gravity, which is believed to leak off into at least one of these "extra" dimensions.

Gravity is amazingly weak, at least as compared with all other natural forces. Consider: A small magnet can easily overcome the downward gravitational pull of the entire planet and pick up a nail. According to University of Washington scientists, Heckel and Adelberger: "Gravity is the only way to see these extra dimensions but the very weakness of gravity has meant that there was no way to test the theory," said Adelberger. "No one had ever detected that gravity even existed at distances less than a millimeter...if the extra dimensions exist they must be smaller than 2/10th of a millimeter."

ETERNAL CYCLES OF CREATION & DESTRUCTION

The ancient Hindus, Buddhists, Babylonians, Sumerians, and peoples of ancient Mexico and Central America, believed that the universe is characterized by periods of rebirth and destruction, that creation and destruction occur in cycles--religious theories which do not require a "big bang."

Princeton physicist Paul Steinhardt and Neil Turok of Cambridge Universit, have also argued that space and time may not have begun in a big bang, but may have always existed in an endless cycle of expansion and rebirth. They propose that in each cycle, the universe refills with hot, dense matter and radiation, which begins a period of expansion and cooling. After 14 billion years, the expansion of the universe accelerates, as astronomers have recently claimed to have observed.

After trillions of years, the matter and radiation are almost completely dissipated and the

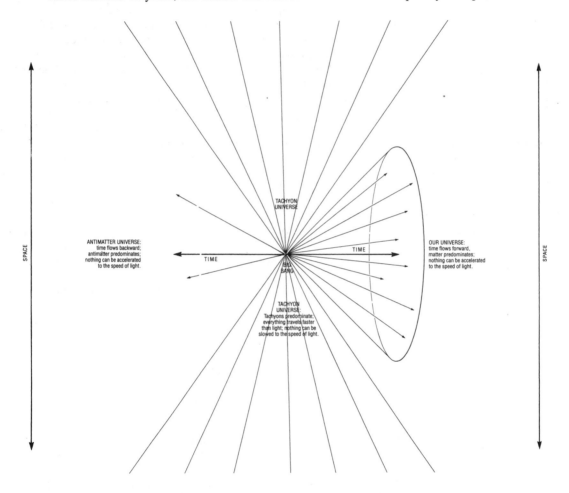

Figure 14. Schematic illustration of the "three-Universe Big Bang" cosmology proposed by J. Richard Gott III of Princeton University. Reprinted from Ferris, 1982; Galaxies, Sierra Club Books, San Francisco. In this conception, the big bang gave rise to three universes. Our Universe consists of matter and time runs forward, whereas another universe consists of anti-matter and time flows backward. In the Tachyon Universe everything moves faster than the speed of light. The theory of alternate universes, has recently been supported by findings based on an analysis of radio waves from 160 distant galazies (Nodland & Ralston 1997). That is, light travels at different speeds and directions in different regions of the universe and rotates, corkscrew fashion. Although these findings do not support the theory of the big bang, which requires uniformity, Nodland speculated that the creation of the Universe may have been asymmetrical, and that another universe may have been created where light rotates in the opposite direction. "A universe with an opposite twist."

expansion stalls. Then it begins to shrink rapidly causing it to heat up and gather energy. An energy field that pervades the universe then creates new matter and radiation, which restarts the cycle.

This new theory attempts to sidestep the major problems with the standard big bang model, that is, how did the universe originate? If there was a big bang, what caused it?

In yet another theory, the universe exists as two infinitely large parallel sheets, separated by a microscopic distance, i.e. a fifth dimension, that is not apparent to us. These sheets are expanding in all directions, releasing all the matter and energy they contain at which point the fifth dimension begins to collapse and the sheets meet and "bounce" off each other thus causing a "big bang" after which the two sheets again move apart and release matter which cools and coalesces into stars and galaxies as in our present universe.

This "fifth dimension," it is argued, may also be the depository of all the missing anti-matter, or the so called "dark matter" which physicists believe exists but which they cannot find.

Of course, by nature of the fact that so many scientific "experts" cannot agree, should in-itself be an indication that what we are dealing with is a theory that few scientists can agree on. Essentially, we have been provided with a multiple-choice theory as to the origin of the universe--multiple choices which should include: None Of The Above.

THE AGE OF THE UNIVERSE

The theory of the big bang, including estimates as to the age of the universe, are dependent upon the false assumption that light always travels at the same speed and in a straight line. That assumption is false (Nodland & Ralston, 1997; Wang et al., 2000).

Astronomers claim they can estimate the distance of each galaxy by its brightness or apparent size. The fainter and smaller a star appears, compared to other stars, the farther away it must be. But again, away from what? Some astronomers have tried to explain this logic by using the example of a car approaching in the distance: the farther away the car, the fainter its headlights appear.

The problem with this reasoning is that stars do not give off the same amount of light. Consider the headlights example. What if that car was equipped with aircraft landing lights. The incredible brightness would fool an observer into believing the car was almost upon them, when in fact it was incredibly far away. Not all headlights are created equal.

In the 1920's astronomer Edwin Hubble presented data which he argued proved that the more distant a galaxy is away from Earth, the faster it appears to be moving away. This hypothesis has given rise to the claim that the universe is expanding. One of the problems with this theory is that it is again based on Earth as ground zero. Ignoring this problem, many astronomers have decided that the age of the universe could therefore be guessed at by determining the distance of the most distant stars as based on the nature of the light given off by galaxies which are believed to be the most distant. But again, distant from what? Relative to what? And what about those stars who died so long ago, or are so far away, they have not been detected?

The age of the universe has also been guessed at based on the supposed ages of certain stars. Using this as a measure, astronomers have guessed that the age of the universe must be between 10 - 15 billion years. For example, when a star has burned up most of its hydrogen, it expands and becomes a "red giant." When a "red giant" is detected, astronomers can make guesses as to how long it has been in existence, and thus guess its lifetime, and thus guess its age, and then, based on its estimated age, determine the age of the universe. If the star is 12 billion years old, then the universe must be 12 billion years old. This is equivalent to finding the oldest man in Russia, and stating since he is 124 years old, humans have been on Earth for only 124 years.

Physicists and astronomers are often forced to employ the most naive forms of logic to support their theories. They must ignore much of the evidence and pick and choose only what seems compatible with their theories. Many, in fact manufacture "evidence" which they "factor in."

Consider, for example, Kenneth M. Lanzetta of the State University of New York at Stony Brook, who claims that "star formation took place early and very rapidly. Star formation was 10 times higher in the distant early universe than it is today," and that this first outburst of star formation took place about a half billion years following the big bang.

Using the Hubble Space Telescope, Lanzetta took pictures of galaxies he believes to be 14 billion light-years away from where the earth is now. According to Lanzetta the farther back the telescope looked, the greater the star-forming activity was. "Star formation continued to increase to the very earliest point that we could see." In other words, Lanzetta observed evidence of star formation in distant galaxies. Lanzetta then takes a giant mental leap and concludes that "We are seeing close to the first burst of star formation," which took place 500 million years after the big bang.

How did he arrive at these figures? Like most astronomers and physicists, he deduced the existence of missing "facts" and then factored in the missing facts so as to "discover" exactly what his theory predicted--a common and widely accepted practice in the realm of mainstream western "science." Lanzetta used 12 different light filters to separate colors and then relied on the intensity of red to establish the distance to each point of light—that is, the distance from the earth and NOT the distance from the supposed big bang. And then, using images of nearby star fields as a universal average for stellar density and intensity he was then able to "conclude" that 90 percent of the light of the very early universe was not detected by the Hubble telescope. However, this missing light, actually only exists as theory, and the fact that he could not find the light, disproved the theory. Nevertheless, because the existence of "missing light" is predicted by theory, this then justified his factoring in the "missing light" in order to show that the peak of star formation came just 500 million years after the big bang.

Estimates based on light are often proved wrong, Consider the fact that astrophysicists Wil Van Breugel and Wim DeVries, of Lawrence Livermore National Laboratory reported in 2001, that a galaxy near the Big Dipper (STIS 123627+621755), which was supposedly the most distant galaxy in the universe, is not so distant after all. As I have argued here and elsewhere (Joseph, 2000) "red shifts can become blue shifts;" and in this current study, it was found that STIS 123627+621755 no longer displays the red shift formerly observed by other astronomers. Hence, rather than 12 billion light years distant, this galaxy is now believed to be 9.8 billion light years away from the Earth, and is probably a small dwarf galaxy.

Currently, via the assistance of the Hubble telescope, astronomers have been able to detect galaxies that they believe to be a little over 12 billion light years distant (though others claim 14 billion or even 18 billion)—findings which assume uniformity in the speed of light and which ignore relativity. Although Esther Hu who detected some of the most distant of all currently detectable galaxies has also reported that "we've already got some candidate objects that are even further away," the light from the more distant and aged stars may have winked out of existence so long ago that they will never be detected.

In fact, professor Ray Norris and astronomers relying on data provided by the CSIRO's Australia Telescope and the Hubble Space Telescope have announced they have detected stars that were so far away, they had not previously been detected. According to these astronomers, this new data pushes back the origin of the universe "by a long way," though how far, is unknown, as modern day telescopes cannot collect enough light to pin down their distance.

These problems, where distant galaxies are discovered to be relatively near, and where physicists must manufacture data in order to arrive at their preconceived findings, are conveniently ignored by the "scientific establishment" who remain committed to the theory of the big bang. Indeed, in commenting on Lanzetta's work, another astronomer, Storrie-Lombardi said that with improved telescopes that can see further into space, we will someday be able to see into the Dark Era, the time before there were stars. "We are getting close to the epoch where we can not see at all," she said.

I would dare say that these astronomers already "cannot see at all" as they have plucked out their eyes in order to blind themselves to the truth: The age and the origin of the universe is unknown.

Astronomers based these predictions on a number of false assumptions about the nature of light and radio waves. For example, fndings based on the analysis of radio waves from 160 distant galaxies indicates that radio waves alter their trajectories and move in relation to an axis of orientation running through space. According to Dr. Borge Nodland of the University of Rochester, and Dr. Joun Ralston of the University of Kansas, this axis of orientation differs in different regions of space and determines how light travels and the speed and direction at which it travels in different regions of space. These radiations rotate, like a corkscrew as they move through space, and undergo a complete rotation every billion miles.

This axis is different in different regions of space; running one way, for example, toward the constellation Aquila and another way toward the constellation Sextans (Nodland & Ralston, 1997). What this means, according to Dr. Nodland, "is that not all space is equal" and that "light travels at different speeds" in different regions of the universe—findings which are completely contrary to the uniformity predicted by the theory of the big bang. Moreover, because light changes speed, this also makes it impossible to determine the distance or age of distant stars, based on the speed of light.

It has also been demonstrated that light can travel faster than the speed of light (Wang et al., 2000), and can arrive before it is transmitted. As based on experiments conducted by Wang and colleagues, it was concluded that "a light pulse propagating through the atomic vapour cell appears first at the exit side" such "that the peak of the pulse appears to leave the cell before entering it."

In fact, light not only travels at different speeds in different regions of the universe, but at different speeds in this solar system and above the planet Earth—which is also inconsistent with the big bang requirement of uniformity so as to make predictions regarding the big bang and the creation and age of this universe. Specifically, it was discovered and reported by Unran Inan (a professor at Stanford) at the Annual Meeting of the American Geophysical Union, in September of 1996, that flickering lights and glowing rings that are commonly detected high above thunderstorms, expand faster than the speed of light. This phenomenon is set in motion by a bolt of lightning striking the ground which causes electromagnetic pulses to race upward and to expand at an exceedingly rapid rate, thus creating an upward expanding bubble-like glowing ring. When the ring strikes the ionosphere this causes it to expand faster than the speed of light. Hence, not only is the speed of light not a constant, but the speed of light is not a limiting factor in speed of movement.

Other astronomers have attempted to sidestep these problems by ignoring them, and by providing dates as to the age of the universe based on the average age of those stars whose light still shines in the darkness of night. Again, this is equivalent to locating the "oldest man" living and then concluding, based on his age, that humans have lived on Earth for 130 or so years. That a distant star is estimated to be 12 billion years in age, provides only as estimate as to how long stars might "live" before dying. Again, what of those stars that died so long ago, their light can no longer be detected?

THE BIG BANG, RELATIVITY, AND THE PARADOX OF THE TIME MACHINE

The theory of the big bang and all notions as to the age of the universe are based on the false and ignorant assumption that we are able to detect the most distant galaxies and the oldest galaxies the likes of which may be so distant, or which ceased to exist so long ago, that they simply cannot be detected by those instruments currently available.

The theory of the big bang, and in fact all current estimates as to the age of the universe, are also refuted by and fall prey to "the paradox of the time machine."

Consider: If you were to step into a time machine and go back 1000 years in time, you would not reappear on the exact same spot on Earth 1000 years ago, but gasping for breath in outer space as the Earth, our solar system, and this galaxy are in motion and were not in this spot 1000 years ago. Likewise, those distant stars whose 12 billion year old light are just now arriving on Earth, reflect not where these stars are now, but where they were 12 billion years ago and only from the vantage point of where the Earth is now—and where the Earth is now is not ground zero for the supposed big bang. These stars were 12 billion light years distant from this specific spot in the Universe 12 billion years ago. Twelve billion years ago they were already 12 billion light years away from this location and were already 12 billion years old.

As this particular spot is not ground zero, that distance means absolutely nothing except that 12 billion years ago these stars were 12 billion light years away from this location, and this particular spot is not ground zero for the big bang. Nor is ground zero located in the spot where the most distant stars are located now. The location of ground zero is unknown.

If we chose a location 12 billion light years in the opposite direction and make our age estimates from this location, these stars suddenly become 24 billion years in age, and so on. Distance and thus age estimates based on distance and the location of an observer, are entirely relative and become meaningful only if we can identify a ground zero or starting point and this information simply does not exist.

Moreover, these distant stars have had an additional 12 billion years to move further away from the spot they were in 12 billion years ago. They may have moved in a different direction all together, as not just planets, but solar systems, and entire galaxies are in orbit. Our solar system, for example, takes about 126 million years to make a complete orbit of the Milky Way—which means in 60 million years it will be headed in the opposite direction.

What goes around, comes around, and entire galaxies can change direction. "Red shifts' (indicating an object is speeding away) can become "blue shifts" (and "blues" can become "reds") and what appears to be expanding will later appear to be contracting as its orbit takes it first away from, and then back toward this galaxy and our solar system which is also in orbit.

To be blunt: Although theories and speculation abound, we do not know the age of the universe or how it came into being though it is apparent that galaxy forming molecular clouds are abundant in interstellar space. Rather, what the evidence indicates is that the cycling and recycling of material that comprises and creates planets, stars, and complex organic molecules, may have been ongoing for all of eternity, which also raises the possibility that the universe is infinite and that life may have roots that extend interminably into the long ago.

INFINITY, ANGELS, GHOSTS & THE MULTIVERSE

The big bang model of the universe, has been developed to explain a wide range of observations about the cosmos. Because no single theory can explain these observations there are numerous models.

A major element of one of the current models accepted by most mainstream scientists, is the theory of "inflation," which posits a period of hyperfast expansion that occurred within second after the big bang. This inflationary period was proposed in order to explain what astronomers incorrectly believed was evidence for a tremendous "smoothness" and homogeneity. We now know that the universe is not "smooth" and that the universe is not expanding uniformly. The universe is clumpy.

Physicists have thus been forced to tinker and adjust the standard theory and to add additional theoretical elements to support a flawed theory. For example, "dark energy" has been proposed to account for the recent discovery that the supposed expansion of the universe is supposedly accelerating—a finding that also refutes the Big Bang theory.

Because the universe appears to be expanding, this has contributed to age old arguments about the finite vs infinite nature of the universe. The question of a finite or infinite universe is one of the oldest in philosophy, science, and religion.

According to relativity, space is a dynamic medium that can be finite or infinite and which can curve in one of three ways, depending on the distribution of matter and energy within it. It is argued that space and thus the universe is spherical, or perhaps shaped like a flat-plain as predicted by Euclidean geometry, or concave, like a saddle as predicted by "hyperbolic" geometry.

In the standard view, the universe is believed to be finite and to consist of a positive curvature such that it curves back on itself to form a closed space of finite volume. If it is finite, then it will either continue to expand or it will implode depending on the density of matter within it. If the mass density were greater than a value called the critical density, gravity would eventually reverse the expansion, causing the universe to collapse into what could be called the Big Crunch. However, no one knows what the density of the universe may be.

If the universe is in fact curved and finite, it could also give rise to the illusion of infinity, as light might wrap around itself again and again. This possible illusion, created by a positively curved universe, could also create multiple images of each and every galaxy and every star and planet including the Earth. That is, the night skies may contain numerous images of our galaxy and solar system and the Earth, and these images, being conveyed by different curvatures of light, could depict the Earth and every galaxy at different stages of their evolution.

Because light travels at different speeds and in different directions, and because it can be split apart and thus travel from a source by using multiple paths and variable speeds, it is possible for an observer to see multiple images of each galaxy and to erroneously misinterpret these multiple images of a single galaxy as multiple and distinct galaxies in an endless space.

According to quantum theory, our universe is only a single tiny facet of an incredibly large multiverse. The theoretical multiverse is a highly structured continuum containing many universes, and these many universes are side by side, or inside one another, or are mirrors of or identical copies of each other, such that everything that exists in this universe has its counterpart, or rather, counterparts in at last a few of these other universes. In some other universes, what exists or has taken place in this universe differs by varying degrees or factors. In some universes, for example, Adolf Hitler may have won World War II. In yet others, President Kennedy and his brother were never assassinated. In yet others, humans may have never evolved.

When considered from the perspective of a continuous macrocosm each of these universes obeys the laws of classical physics. However, from a microcosmic scale, quantum mechanics the dominant force and each universe interacts with every other universe through a phenomenon known as quantum interference. Those that are close together, effect each other more strongly than those far apart. In other words, each and every particle in this universe, is effected by its counterpart in another universe. However, what this also implies is that every particle and its counterpart, form a trans-universe structure, such that a particle not only exists in this universe, but exists in other universes. That is, every particle and thus every piece of matter, including humans and human consciousness, exists inside as well as outside our universe, and, each and every counterpart, can effect its counterpart and influence its structure and behavior.

The theory of the multiverse could thus be used to explain the experience of life after death, the existence of hevean or hell, or the presence or experience of what some have interpreted to be demons, angels, and even gods.

CREATION SCIENCE & THE MYTH OF THE ORGANIC SOUP

Spontaneous Generation, Creation Science, DNA, RNA Worlds, and Viruses
by R. Joseph

The "question" as to The Origin of Life -of all life- is a query that at present cannot be adequately explained. By contrast, the problem as to the origin of life on Earth may be answered by the obvious. If life were to appear on a desert island, we would assume that it washed to shore, or fell from the sky. The Earth too is an "island," swirling in an ocean of space, and living tissue may have been washing to shore since the creation.

This view, however, is rejected by present-day "creation scientists" and most (but not all) mainstream Western educated scientists, the latter of which generally hold to the view that life emerged from an organic soup, or was spewed out of an undersea thermal vent. The "life from non-life" scenario has in fact been the mainstream "scientific" view as to the origin of life for over a thousand years. However, despite its ancient history, the "organic soup" hypothesis is erroneously believed by many to have been first proposed by Darwin.

THE ORGANIC SOUP

More than a century ago, Charles Darwin (1887) wrote a letter to a friend where he speculated as to the origins of life and the first living organisms. In so doing, he reintroduced to 19th century science what would become the myth of the organic soup:

"If (and oh what a big if) we could conceive in some warm little pond, with all sorts of ammonia and phosphoric salts, light, heat, electricity, etc., present, that a protein compound was chemically formed ready to undergo still more complex changes...." chemical compounds, Darwin proposed, that would have had the chance to accumulate, eventually becoming a living entity as there were no other forms of life to compete with it, or eat it up.

Hence, according to Darwin, life emerged from non-life, the residue of an organic soup. Darwin also explained that the reason life doesn't continue to emerge from non-life, is because of the presence of modern day living things. "At the present day such matter would be instantly devoured or absorbed, which would not have been the case before living creatures were formed."

Moreover, although in this letter Darwin acquiesced to the possibility that life could emerge more than once from non-life, the theory of evolution which bears his name is based on the premise that a single molecule of life had emerged only once, and that all life descended from this original single living molecule.

According to Darwin, including modern-day neo-Darwinian theory, all the branches and twigs of the tree of life trace their roots to a single seed and a single organism that emerged from the mixing of this organic soup— a notion that could best be described as the "single seed" as well as the organic soup hypothesis. The "single seed" and single tree theory is widely embraced and accepted without question by most (but not all) academics and scientists. In fact this was the official position of the 1986 "Eighth Conference on the Origins of Life" held at Berkeley, California, for they issued a press release which reflected the consensus view that "all life on Earth, from bacteria to sequoia trees to humans, evolved from a single ancestral cell" that had emerged from an organic stew.

Why a single seed? The reasoning is elementary: life must have emerged only once on Earth since all living entities are comprised of cells and DNA, and since, regardless of species, the structure of DNA is identical. If life had emerged more than once on Earth, then there would be no "universal genetic code" but innumerable genetic codes, with some life forms possibly having no genes whatsoever.

Life on Earth may well trace its roots to a single seed. However, that seed, the first living molecule, could not have emerged from an organic soup, or an undersea thermal event—at least on

Earth. The necessary ingredients for the manufacture of life did not exist on the young planet. Nor was there sufficient free oxygen, and there may have been no free oxygen at all, which is an essential ingredient that makes up the structure of DNA. In fact, almost all the essential ingredients for the construction and manufacture of DNA, were nowhere to be found—at least on Earth—thus effectively refuting any and all notions that Earthly life originated from non-life.

Rather, as the only source for DNA is DNA, and as only living cells can generate living cells, then the first DNA-equipped cells to appear on Earth have only two possible sources: They were either the product of "intelligent design" or they first originated on another planet (or both) and were subsequently hurled to Earth contained in all manner of debris that may have been sheared from other planets following cosmic collisions; or both.

SPONTANEOUS GENERATION

For thousand years it was believed that maggots appeared in garbage or rotten meat because these decaying tissues somehow became reactivated and thus "alive," i.e. resulting in the spontaneous generation of maggots from dead tissue. This remained the prevalent "scientific" view as to the origin of life in general, until 1680 when Francesco Redi performed a series of experiments that nearly laid this notion to rest. For example, if decaying tissue were placed in a bell jar and sealed, there was no evidence of spontaneous generation. The putrefying meat remained maggot free.

Nevertheless, despite repeated demonstrations that spontaneous (or gradual) generation is not plausible, many scientists have continued to cling to this view. For example, it was argued that although maggots cannot spontaneously or gradually arise from dead meat, the same is not true for bacteria. Bacteria emerge spontaneously from dead tissue and its secretions, it was argued. And, thus life arose from collections of nutrient rich organic substances, i.e. the proverbial organic soup.

Yet, these notions too were disproved 100 years ago. Louis Pasteur, for example, in the late 1800's, demonstrated conclusively that bacteria can only be generated from other bacteria. Only living bacteria can produce other living bacteria, and the same is true of all other creatures including viruses (which, by the way, must borrow the DNA of a non-viral cell in order to reproduce).

As a demonstration, Pasteur placed a nutrient rich broth into several flasks with either S-shaped necks or straight necks. Pasteur boiled both flasks, killing any and all bacteria present. Those flasks with straight necks allowed dust particles, and any adhering bacteria, to fall into the broth. Bacteria began replicating.

However, the organic soup confined within the S-shaped flasks, remained bacteria free—even after months had passed. Falling bacteria could not penetrate the film of moisture trapped within the S-shaped neck which acted as a filter. Bacteria can only reproduce from other bacteria.

It could be argued, however, that the above experiments are irrelevant as they fail to create conditions similar to those that predominated during the first billion years after the Earth was formed.

In a rather brilliant experiment, Stanley Miller and Harold Urey attempted to recreate the environmental and atmospheric conditions of the early Earth. They continuously exposed a mixture of methane, ammonia, water vapor and hydrogen gases to electric discharges and ultraviolet light for a week (Miller & Urey, 1953). The experiment and its results were viewed as a resounding success, as these experimenters were able to produce a few complex organic compounds and amino acids such as alanine and glycine; materials and elements also found in meteorites. Nevertheless, this organic soup failed to show any signs of life. No elephants, tigers, dinosaurs, single celled bacteria, or even a fragment of DNA were produced.

Melvin Calvin performed similar experiments and repeatedly irradiated a variety of substances and inorganic compounds, including solutions of water and carbon dioxide with electrical discharges. He too failed to produce life or even a fragment of DNA, as have all subsequent attempts by numerous investigators, no matter how sophisticated the experiment.

However, because some organic compounds were produced, including many of the elementary sugars and amino acids which are considered the "building blocks" of living matter, many scientists view these and similar experiments as a success! Indeed, Miller created 12 different kinds of amino acids in his flask, some of which are found in proteins. Hence, it has been argued that given similar conditions early in the Earth's history, living organic material may have been produced continually - even though these experiments completely failed to create any living matter or even a fragment of DNA.

In fact, although various scientist have produced individual elements of various "building blocks" these elements were not linked together even when mixed together so that they might combine.

These elements produce in the Miller, Urey, Calvin, et al., experiments also lacked genetic instructions or any semblance of what could be construed as RNA or DNA.

Of course, it is reasonable to assume that if provided millions of years to create life, and if provided the right elements, acids, and other necessary materials, that life may well gradually arise, beginning perhaps as a self-replicating energy extracting semi-organism, and eventually becoming a fully formed organism equipped with the necessary DNA. Nevertheless, even if provided millions of years, the creation of DNA remains a serious problem, Again, the essential precursor elements did not exist on the young Earth including oxygen—an essential element crucial for DNA integrity.

Nevertheless, a number of possible scenarios have been put forward, all of which posit that life and DNA arose gradually when various crystals, or clay particles, or enzymes, or proteins, and/or micromolecules were randomly jumbled together by chance, and that these random occurrence coincided (by chance) with some electrochemical, activating event, thereby organizing and giving these molecules life (de Duve, 1995; Lamond & Gibson, 1990; Orgel, 1994; Rebek, 1994). As the essential elements did not exist on Earth, it is believed that exobiological organic matter must have fallen to Earth, and was then washed into the seas where these life promoting substances accumulated, forming an organic sludge.

At present, 50 organic compounds and 25 nitrogen-based molecules, including molecular oxygen, carbon, carbon dioxide, methane, ammonia, benzene, formic acid, acetic acid, methanol, polycyclic aromatic hydrocarbons, and silicate grains have been detected in interstellar space. These molecules can build amino acids. There is also evidence to suggests that amino acid can be synthesized in comets and then deposited on Earth (Bada et al., 2001).

Moreover, sugar molecules, i.e., methyl formate, acetic acid, and glycolaldehyde, have been detected in giant gas and dust clouds, and glycolaldehyde (an 8-atom molecule composed of carbon, hydrogen, and oxygen) can combine with other molecules to form the more complex sugars such as ribose. Ribose is a building block of the nucleic acids, DNA and RNA.

As over 70 different amino acids have been detected in various meteorites which have fallen to Earth, and as our planet is bombarded with over 30,000 tons of extraterrestrial material yearly, it is thus believed that this accumulating extraterrestrial organic material was mixed and churned together, eventually forming an "organic soup."

Presumably this bubbling organic brew was simultaneously subjected to massive doses of ultra violet radiation from the sun, as well as radiation given off from the core of the Earth. Presumably, these primeval conditions coincided with, and thus effected the course of chance molecular associations, thereby giving life to certain activated and irradiated molecular combinations, which again, were astrobiological and extraterrestrial in origin.

Finally, these first living and behaving molecules began to engage in further "random" associations thus creating one simple life form. This first creature not only survived but was somehow provided with a complete and full fashioned macromolecule of DNA (deoxyribonucleic acid) or RNA (ribonucleic acid). The DNA and RNA were also provided with genetic instructions and then enveloped in a cellular membrane. Once the membrane was fashioned, a cell was born equipped with the capacity to extract energy and reproduce itself by producing RNA- or DNA-based duplicates.

Every creature and living thing, therefore, owe their existence to these chance occurrences where a multitude of organic molecules from outer space were randomly mixed together (by chance) and sprang to life, such that a single living molecule miraculously survived and began to reproduce.

In fact, even the cellular membrane may have been fashioned in outer-space. Dworkin and colleagues (2001) have synthesized self-assembling amphiphilic molecules that were transformed into vesicular structures in an environment designed to simulate the environments of dense interstellar molecular clouds. When exposed to ultraviolet radiation these molecules formed lipid bilayers similar to the lipid membranes that enclose living cells. According to these authors, "the delivery of such compounds by comets, meteorites, and interplanetary dust particles during the late heavy bombardment period may have played an influential role in the origin of life on Earth" as well as other planets.

Moreover, it has been argued that "proto-cells" can be generated in the upper atmosphere of a planet with an atmosphere saturated with organic material. According to Adrian Tuck of the National Oceanic and Atmospheric Administration in Boulder, Colorado, and colleagues Veronica Vaida and Barney Ellison of the University of Colorado, "proto-cells" may form when water droplets thrown up by ocean waves, drift into the upper atmosphere.

Prior to rising in the atmosphere, these aerosol particles are saturated with organic material due to the film of oily molecules on the ocean surface, thus giving them the appearance of "protocells, with a layer of organic material on the outside." Moreover, once they enter the upper atmosphere, these lipid coated droplets can grab onto and fuse with other particles. Once the water inside evaporates, the diverse substances within become concentrated and may react to sunlight and undergo various chemical reactions, thereby increasing their weight, causing them to fall back to Earth or the ocean, where they can then pick up a second lipid layer, thus creating a lipid bilayer similar to the membrane around all living cells. However, the lipids and other organic materials these bilayers consist of are in fact the residue of other animals, including dead fish. In other words, these lipid bilayers could only be formed if other living creatures are already in existence.

Only life begets life.

These theories and the evidence presented above cannot explain the origin of DNA, the incredible complexity of a single cell, its capacity to extract and use energy, reproduce, and store and express information, etc., and so on. Indeed, a single macromolecule of DNA is so incredibly complex, the notion that it may have been randomly assembled from molecules that fell to Earth, is equivalent to finding a computer on Jupiter and then hypothesizing that it was randomly assembled in the Methane sea.

When coupled with the fact that all complex organic molecules had been twice destroyed on the new Earth, and that fully formed, complex life appeared on Earth, and possibly Mars, at the cessation of a 700 million year cosmic bombardment which had sterilized the two planets, we should conclude that these molecules which fell from space were not available for assembly in the time available so as to account for the emergence of life and its DNA. Rather, life, and its DNA, fell from the sky (or was created by intelligent design); life which may have then feasted on the later to develop "organic soup."

The cosmic cloud and organic soup scenarios are in fact incompatible with and are contradicted by cell theory and by what we know of genetics and the structure of DNA. Only DNA produces DNA. Without DNA, there is no life, and the origin of life cannot be explained without explaining the origin of DNA.

Although the heavens are swirling with some of the constituent elements necessary for life and the creation of DNA, the numerous theories and experiments that have been conducted to support the theory of spontaneous or gradual generation, cannot in any way account for the creation of DNA and its complex genetic instructions—at least on Earth.

DNA can only be produced by DNA. Living cells are produced only by other living cells (and their DNA). Since the purported "organic" alphabet "soup" was actually a thin broth missing three important letters: DNA, then the first DNA, and the first cells to appear on Earth, had to be produced by DNA equipped cells which were either astrobiological in origin, or possibly fashioned by the "hand of God," or both.

CELL THEORY AND DNA: ONLY DNA BEGETS DNA

It has been well established that DNA is produced only from other DNA and that all living cells arise from preexisting cells. That is, only life begets life and only DNA begets DNA. In this regard, it stands to reason that the first DNA equipped cells to arrive on Earth, were produced by DNA equipped cells that were astrobiological in origin, or created in the "laboratory of a living God."

The maxim, "only life begets life," and only DNA produces DNA is universal for all known Earthly creatures, including singled celled organisms, bacteria, and microbes. This well established rule of life provides the foundation for what has been referred to as "cell theory" as well as astrobiological contamination infection theory. All living things are composed of cells which contain DNA, and new cells are only formed when preexisting cells divide and replicate. Life begets life.

Another rule of cell theory is that old cells and new cells, and in fact all living cells, are fundamentally alike chemically, structurally, metabolically, and in regard to their cellular components (de Duve, 1995). Be it bacteria, animal, plant, or human, all cells are surrounded by a membrane (which may be partitioned by an internal membrane), and contain cytoplasm and DNA.

All living cells act similarly in regard to heat transduction and the liberation and conversion of photopic-chemical energy found in foodstuffs; that is, energy which is ultimately derived, via minerals and inorganic chemicals (chemolithoautotrophs), or plants and organic molecules secreted by other species (heterotrophs), or sunlight (photoautotrophs).

Hence, all cells are governed by the laws of thermodynamics (though the second law is sometimes violated). All cells are capable of breaking down simple molecular building blocks, such as

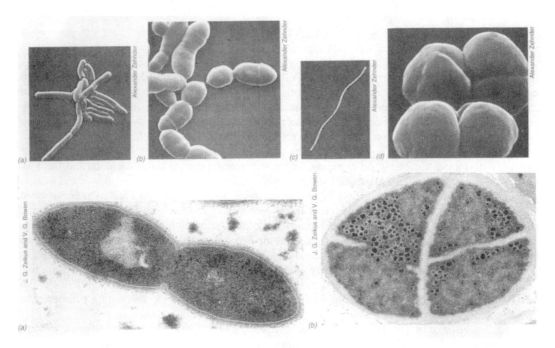

Figure 15. *The diverse morphology of Archaea. Reprinted from Brock et al., 1994. Biology of Microorganisms. Prentice Hall, New Jersey.*

minerals and glucose, or carbon dioxide, or ammonia, or nitrates, which they use to promote life and DNA replication.

All living cells are capable of converting these elements and breakdown products in order to create all the manifold and diverse proteins and carbon-containing molecules necessary for all aspects of cellular functioning. This includes regeneration of the cell wall, and the production of daughter cells, as well as the generation of proteins for maintaining the membrane, skin, skeletal system, heart, and so on. This is accomplished via instructions maintained within the macromolecules and polymeric molecules and nucleotides of DNA. These characteristics were also typical of those creatures who were among the first to take root on this planet.

Even the simplest of living cells (e.g. bacteria, archaea), maintain an inner wall which may consist of an acid-containing, fatty outer plasma membrane, within which is maintained the cell's cytoplasm and DNA. Moreover, even the simplest and most "primitive" single celled organisms are incredibly complex, and are capable of repairing their DNA as well as tears or openings in their membranes which are immediately sealed -which is accomplished via DNA induced protein synthesis.

The simplest of living organisms are mind boggling complex and the notion that they spontaneously or even gradually arose on Earth, from an undersea volcano, or an organic broth, and within just a few hundred million years, becomes completely untenable, especially when we consider DNA and cellular complexity, and the fact that the oldest life forms were equally complex and the failure to find any evidence of precursor life forms.

Single cellular microbes are comprised of over 2,500 small molecules (e.g. including amino acids consisting of 10 to 50 tightly packed atoms), macromolecules (proteins and nucleic acids) and polymeric molecules (comprised of hundreds to thousands of small molecules) all of which are precisely jigsawed together to form a single complex organism. The tiniest and most primitive of single celled creatures contain a variety of micro- macro- and polymeric molecules which fit and function together as a living mosaic of tissues.

Moreover, each of the many thousands of different molecules that make up a single cellular creature perform an incredible variety of chemical reactions -often in concert with that cell's other molecules and their protein (enzyme) products (Strachan & Read, 1996; Watson et al. 1992). When coupled with the complexity of DNA and given the fact that the essential ingredients for DNA construction were not available on this planet, it thus seems unlikely that life could have arisen gradually and merely by chance, at least on Earth.

OVERVIEW: DNA

In February of 2001, preliminary findings from two draft sequences of the human genome, generated by the Human Genome Project and Celera Genomics, were published in the journals Science and Nature. Both teams were forced to admit that they still did not know the precise number of humans genes, and could only provide gross estimates. Estimates range from 30,000-40,000 protein-coding genes in the human genome about twice as many as in worm or fly— though Venter et al. (2001) believe there may be fewer than 30,000 protein coding genes.

It is also unknown as to how many human genes exist as single copies. That is, thousands of genes may be duplicates of yet other genes. Moreover, many genes are fragmented, and the vast majority of genes (introns) are silent and suppressed.

Active genes (exons), that aspect of the gene which engages in coding and which has been expressed and activated, comprise only a tiny fraction of human DNA, about 3% of the genome and an average of about 5% of each gene. Less than 1.5% of the genome codes for proteins.

As confirmed by Celera and the Human Genome Project, and as will be detailed below, genes consist of nucleotide sequences which may be silent (introns) or coded and expressed (exons). Genes may also be active or silent. The vast majority of human DNA is silent. Activated genes and the active coding sequences comprise only a tiny fraction of the genome. Specifically, about 1.1% of the genome consists of exons, 24% consists of introns, with 75% of the genome consisting of intergenic DNA (Venter et al., 2001).

Genes consist of two strands of nucleotides, sequences of ATGC (Adenine, Thymine, Cytosine, Guanine) which are laddered together forming a double helix. However, there are almost 20% more AT nucleotides, with ATs outnumbering GCs by a ratio of 60-40, and more of the AT regions consist of silent introns.

By contrast, activated genes seem to cluster in GC rich regions. Also strings of repetitive Alu sequences cluster in the GC regions, along side active genes, which suggests that Alu sequences may play a regulatory role in gene expression.

DEOXYRIBONUCLEIC ACID (DNA): ONLY DNA BEGETS DNA

All living organisms contain DNA. DNA is composed of hundreds of thousand, and in many cases, millions of micromolecules which in turn contain all the necessary information for creating an embryo or a complex adult body (Strachan & Read, 1996; Watson et al. 1992). Hence, DNA functions as the ultimate information bearing macromolecule. As DNA also acts as a catalyst, via the synthesis of enzymes and proteins, these DNA macromolecules are capable of reproducing and synthesizing new copies of themselves, as well as generating "new" sequences of amino acids. This is accomplished through the secretion of polymerase, a characteristic of all cellular DNA. DNA gives birth to itself and to the cell.

A single macromolecule of DNA is referred to as a "gene." In all cells, the process of protein/enzyme synthesis, and related life-essential activities, are accomplished via the various genes located within and which make up the chromosomes, and in accordance with the somewhat "universal" genetic code. Each gene contains the information which determines the sequences and order of the amino acids contained in each and every cellular protein.

PROTEINS AND ENZYMES

Proteins serve as the cell's building blocks and enable it to function. All cells contain proteins and enzymes. Proteins are in fact manufactured via DNA—the substance which determines the structure of proteins, and which has generated untold life forms. The vast majority of proteins are composed of a mixture of up to 20 different amino acids, with the proportion of acids varying depending on the type of protein produced (Calladine & Drew, 1992; Strachan & Read, 1996; Watson et al. 1992). Proteins are the building blocks which comprise the organism and its manifold component parts.

The vast majority of proteins are enzymes. All enzymes are cavity scarred globules; the cavities acting to form conjunctions with other enzymes, much like a key fits into a lock. This enables them to chemically react and interact and to take specific shapes and forms.

Variations in the sequence in which these 20 amino acids are organized and fit together, therefore, can give rise to a variety of different shapes and forms, and can provide the resulting tissues and cells with specific and unique chemical and reactive properties (Calladine & Drew, 1992; Strachan &

Read, 1996; Watson et al. 1992). Moreover, the manner in which they are fashioned and fit together can serve to convey specific messages. Hence, DNA produced enzyme/proteins, contains information, and serves as information bearing micromolecules.

For every enzyme, and for every protein, there exists specific instructions which are maintained within the various multiple strands and sequence segments of DNA (Calladine & Drew, 1992; Strachan & Read, 1996; Watson et al., 1992). Through activation of various portions of the genetic code, a bacterium, or a complex human body can be fashioned. DNA, therefore, contains the ancestral and hereditary-based instructions for creating a simple or complex organism and its protein building blocks.

DNA DUPLICATION

DNA can be found in all living cells (Calladine & Drew, 1992; Strachan & Read, 1996; Watson et al. 1992). Moreover, this DNA (and the genetic code) is replicated in all daughter cells. That is,

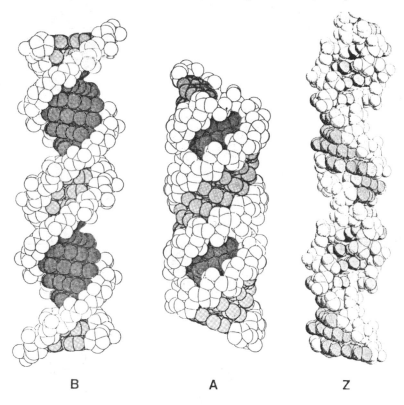

Figure 16. Schematic illustration of three idealized forms of DNA. A and B, are "right handed" with 10 to 11 phosphates per helical turn, and Z is "left handed" with 12 phosphates per turn. Reprinted from Calladin & Drew, 1992, Understanding DNA. Academic Press, San Diego.

B   A   Z

when a cell divides, each daughter cell receives an exact copy of its DNA including those intronic (non-coded) portions that are repressed, dormant, and silent (Jacob & Monod, 1993). Unlimited copies of a DNA macromolecule can be fashioned due to DNA's double helix (two chain) organization and through the secretion of polymerase.

As will be detailed below, each strand of DNA is made up of nucleotides: Adenine (A), Thymine (T), Cytosine (C), and Guanine (G), which are linked together. When these two strands unwind and polymerase is secreted, a complementary strand is produced. Just as a sculptor may use a cast in order to mold identical forms, one half of the helix acts as a mold, or template, to which is fitted its mirror image (reviewed in Calladine & Drew, 1992; Strachan & Read, 1996; Watson et al. 1992). Hence, DNA is capable of replicating itself. DNA is also capable of inducing its own metamorphosis.

CHROMOSOMAL DNA

DNA (deoxyribonucleic acid) macromolecules (genes) comprise and are located along and are entwined within the chromosomes. Chromosomes are visible under a microscope and consist of long entangled nucleotide threads. Depending on species thousand of genes may be enmeshed within a single chromosome.

Most bacteria (and other prokaryotes) have a single circular chromosome. Eukaryotic (nucle-

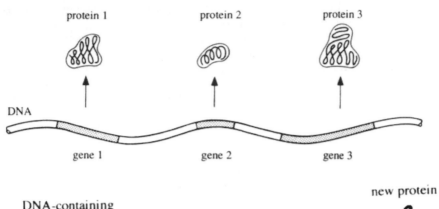

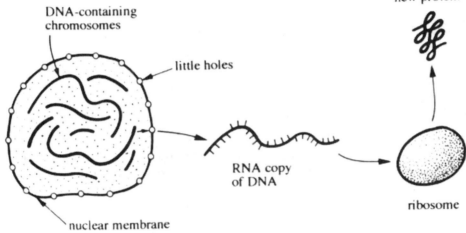

Figure 17. *DNA codes for proteins. Twenty different kinds of amino acids can make all proteins, and any series of three nucleotide base pairs can create an amino acid. Reprinted from Calladin & Drew, 1992, Understanding DNA. Academic Press, San*

Table 1.1 The Genetic Code

Figure 18. *Any series of three nucleotide base pairs can create an amino acid which in turn codes for all necessary proteins. Reprinted from Calladin & Drew, 1992, Understanding DNA. Academic Press, San Diego.*

1st base	2nd base				3rd base
	T	C	A	G	
T	Phe	Ser	Tyr	Cys	T
	Phe	Ser	Tyr	Cys	C
	Leu	Ser	STOP	STOP	A
	Leu	Ser	STOP	Trp	G
C	Leu	Pro	His	Arg	T
	Leu	Pro	His	Arg	C
	Leu	Pro	Gln	Arg	A
	Leu	Pro	Gln	Arg	G
A	Ile	Thr	Asn	Ser	T
	Ile	Thr	Asn	Ser	C
	Ile	Thr	Lys	Arg	A
	Met	Thr	Lys	Arg	G
G	Val	Ala	Asp	Gly	T
	Val	Ala	Asp	Gly	C
	Val	Ala	Glu	Gly	A
	Val	Ala	Glu	Gly	G

ated) cells usually contain several large, linear shaped chromosomes. Humans, for example, contain 23 pairs of chromosomes: 22 different autosomes and two sex chromosomes. Multicellular life forms may contain two, four, eight, or 30 or more chromosomes etc. (Strachan & Read, 1996; Watson et al. 1992). However, generally, as the complexity of the species increases so does the size of its genome, though there are exceptions (Miklos & Rubin, 1996). The cell of a lily, for example, has 30 times the DNA of a typical human cell, though the vast majority of these DNA macromolecules are repressed (Jacob & Monod, 1993) or perform functions which are as yet not apparent.

Human chromosomes vary in size and DNA content, and are numbered in ascending order as they decrease in size. Thus chromosome 1, is larger than chromosome 2.

Not all chromosomes contain the same number of genes (DNA macromolecules). Gene density differs among the chromosomes, with some chromosomes being gene rich, and others gene poor (Antequera & Bird, 1993. Craig & Bickmore, 1994). For example, the male, Y-sex chromosome is gene-poor, whereas the X-sex chromosome is gene rich. Similarly, chromosome 22 is gene rich, whereas human chromosome 21 is gene poor.

The maxim that only life produces life, and only DNA produces DNA, also holds for the various chromosomes. As noted, each human has 23 pairs of chromosomes, half of which have been passed on by the mother, the other by the father. After cell division (such as following fertilization), or when the maternal and paternal chromosomes are matched together, the genes (and their long chains of nucleotides) are paired up and compete for rival positions along and within the chromosomes. When genetic dominance is established, certain traits (e.g. brown eyes vs blue) prevail.

Every single chromosome, therefore, contains paternal and maternal genes. Via the interaction and competition of these different genes and their long chains of base pair nucleotides (the helix), billions of complex codes can be combined and differentially expressed. This is because different gene combinations will give rise to different codes within the same organism, which can be passed on to subsequent generations (Calladine & Drew, 1992; Strachan & Read, 1996; Watson et al. 1992).

These changes in genetic chromosomal organization can produce variations between and within species (including siblings). However, in part, these alterations are also responsible for inducing diversity as well as the creation of "new" species; that is, when formerly "silent" genes (introns) or "silent" gene combinations or nucleotide sequences are activated, shuffled, and so on (e.g., Finnegan, 1989; Moran et al., 1999; Rueter et al., 1999).

Chromosomes are constantly shuffled as they are passed from parent to child, thereby giving rise to different gene combinations each generation (thereby producing variability and individual differences between brothers and sisters). Hence, parents and children, and brothers and sisters share genes - which are faithfully reproduced during cell division (and leap from body to body via sexual intercourse and fertilization). And yet, although siblings, for example, share genes, they do not share the same

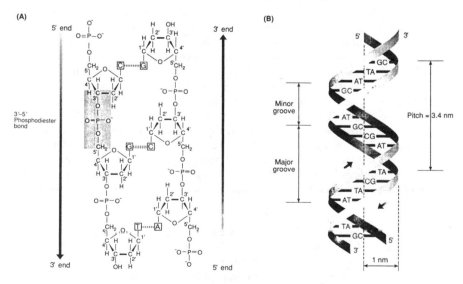

Figure 19. (A) Depiction of the double-stranded antiparallel helix structure of DNA. (B) Depiction of the double helix with base pairs. Reprinted from Strachan & Read, 1996, Human Molecular Genetics. Wiley, New York.

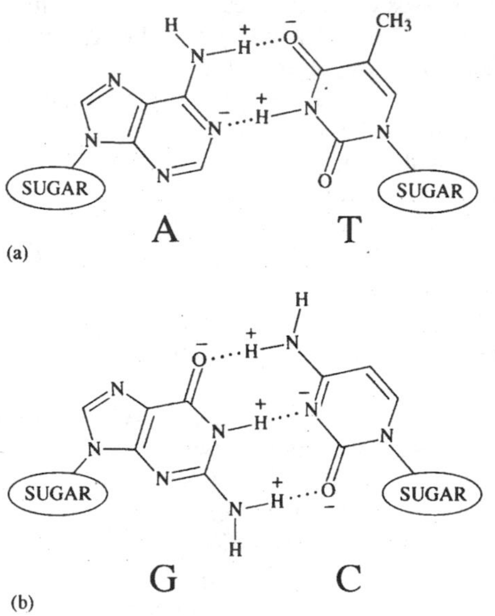

Figure 20. *Molecular organization of A,T,G,C, base pairs. A-T base pairs have two connecting hydrogen bonds and G-C have three connecting hydrogen bonds. All bonds require oxygen. Reprinted from Calladin & Drew, 1992, Understanding DNA. Academic Press, San Diego.*

identical chromosomes. Inherited chromosomes contain different gene combinations and thus slight variations in the genetic code.

Chromosomes, therefore, have a short, individual lifetime. By contrast, an individual gene (DNA macromolecule) may live forever -that is, if it is faithfully reproduced and successfully passed on to subsequent generations. Most modern genes may have a history that may extend interminably into the long ago (e.g., D'Souza et al. 1995; Garcia-Fernandex & Holland, 1994; Miklos & Rubin, 1996; Ruddle, et al. 1994; Strachan & Read, 1996; Tautz, 1998; Watson et al., 1992).

DNA NUCLEOTIDES: INFORMATION BEARING MOLECULES

The simplest cells, that is, single celled organisms, may contain as many as 6000 genes (which may be located along and within a single chromosome). By contrast, the more complex human nuclear genome consists of anywhere from 30,000 to 40,000 genes—97% of which are "silent" and have not been expressed (IHGSC, 2001), and/or which come to be expressed only in reaction to changing environmental conditions (de Jong & Scharloo, 1976; Dykhuizen & Hart, 1980; Gibson & Hogness, 1996; Polaczyk et al., 1998; Rutherford & Lindquist, 1998; Wade et al., 1997).

As noted, each DNA macromolecule (i.e. the gene) is comprised of two long strands of micromolecules, the nucleotides, the organization of which provides the instructions for creating a living organism. All DNA molecules consist of four nitrogenous bases, two pyrimidines and two purines; i.e., Adenine (A), Thymine (T), Cytosine (C), and Guanine (G). These micromolecules are linked in a linear, sequential fashion, and the sequences of nucleotides on one strand are complimentary to those of the other strand thereby forming two double stranded chains (the double helix).

For example, one strand may consist of the nucleotides CTGA... and the other GACT.... These two strands of nucleotides are linked and held together by weak electrostatic hydrogen bonds, thereby forming two complementary strands of "base pairs" (e.g. C-G, T-A, G-C, A-T, etc.). These strands are laddered together (via two sugar-phosphate backbones) thereby creating a long twisting spiral, the double helix— a double helix whose "backbone" includes oxygen and phosphorus which were not available for DNA assembly on the young Earth, as these elements were tightly bound in minerals.

The double helix, therefore consists of two nucleotide chains consisting of base pairs. These chains of micromolecules could be likened to tiny billiard balls attached, in sequence, to a long thread. Each gene, therefore, contains two spiraling "threads" of "billiard balls" which are laddered together thereby forming long sequences of base pairs.

The human genome, containing approximately 30,000 genes, consists of around 3 billion (or more) nucleotide base pairs. However, even the genomes of the simplest of single celled creatures are incredibly complex (Miklos & Rubin, 1996). A single DNA molecule with over 4 million base pairs has been identified in Escherichia coli (E. coli), and the total DNA of a simple, single celled creature

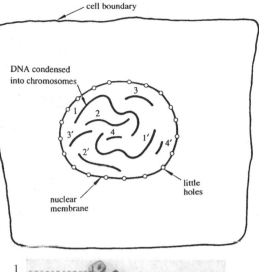

Figure 21a. *Schematic illustration of cell and nucleus containing chromosomes. Chromosomes come in homologous pairs. Reprinted from Calladin & Drew, 1992, Understanding DNA. Academic Press, San Diego.*

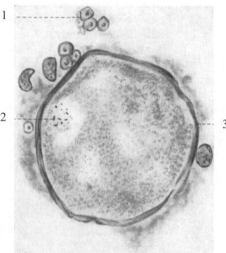

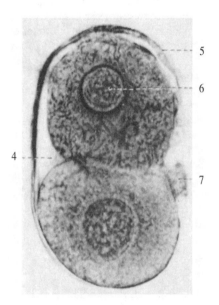

Figure 21b. *Chromosomes from the salivary gland of a fruit fly. Courtesy of Ron Hill an dMargaret Mott. Reprinted from Calladin & Drew, 1992, Understanding DNA. Academic Press, San Diego. (Bottom) Human ovum. 2-human chromosomes.*

may contain over 30 million base pairs.

Given the incredible complexity of a single DNA molecule, and the obvious chemical complexity of those creatures who appeared on Earth 3.8 billion years ago, it is thus rather incredible to posit that these creatures and their DNA, or for that matter, any strand of DNA, may have been spontaneously generated. Again, there is no other source for DNA other than DNA (Strachan & Read, 1996; Watson et al. 1992), and that holds true for the first DNA to arise on this planet. The maxim that "only life begets life" also applies to DNA. Only DNA begets DNA.

INTRONS AND RNA SPLICING

RNA is usually single stranded and employs uracil rather than thymine. The RNA backbone also differs significantly from that of DNA as it lacks oxygen and employs ribose (rather than deoxyribose). RNA is also constructed by DNA but never constructs DNA. There are different types of RNA which differ depending on their function (e.g. Rueter et al., 1999). Broadly considered these include messenger RNA (mRNA), transfer RNA (tRNA), and ribosomal RNA (rRNA), which act in sequence to code and express the information contained in specific DNA sequence segments.

Each double strand of DNA is divided up into specific information-bearing sequence segments of base pairs (exons) which are separated by non-coding sequence segments, i.e. protein coated introns. mRNA acts to code and make copies of specific DNA nucleotide (exonic) sequence segments which in turn specify what type of protein should be produced (Rueter et al., 1999).

There are tens of millions of coded (exonic) and repressed (non-coding/intronic) nucleotide sequence segments (reviewed in Strachan & Read, 1996; Watson et al. 1992). However, a single sequence segment may consists of only three adjacent nucleotides, e.g. CCG (referred to as a "codon"), or it may consist of thousands of nucleotides (CCGGTCGATT...). Moreover, each sequence which is to be coded may be separated from the next coding sequence by sequences of non-coding intronic base pairs.

Considered broadly, introns as well as exons act to signal the exact sequence and segment length of exonic nucleotides which are to be copied and transcribed by RNA (Breathnach et al. 1978; Watson et al., 1996). Because introns are protein coated, and as proteins are not easily accessed or recognized by RNA, due to the depth and configurational organization of its nucleotide framework (Draper, 1995), introns, therefore indicate where each particular segment sequence and its code begins and ends, and thus informs mRNA where coding sequences end and begin, thereby indicating which portions of each segment it should copy (Belfort, 1991, 1993; Breathnach et al. 1978; Watson et al. 1992; Witkowski, 1988). RNA, therefore, plays a major role in copying, editing, and then splicing together coded segments (Rueter et al., 1999).

Initially, however, mRNA acts to copy both exonic and intronic base pairs. Nevertheless, after transcription, copies of the introns, for the most part, tend to be snipped out of the RNA template (Rueter et al., 1999). Once snipped out, they are seemingly discarded, leaving only disjointed segments of exons in the grasp of the RNA molecule. In some cases, however, these snipped out intronic portions may become incorporated into new genomic locations by retrotransposition (Finnegan, 1989; Moran et al., 1999) or they transfer out of the nucleus into the cytoplasm, becoming a plasmid in the process—a plasmid which may become incorporated into the genome of another organism.

In any case, the remaining exonic sequential fragments are then spliced and joined together; referred to as RNA splicing (Rueter et al., 1999). The tRNA then transports these spliced segments outside the nucleus, into the cytoplasm, where they combine with the ribosomes and rRNA in order to begin producing proteins and enzymes.

Hence, in summary, tRNA translates (or reads) the exonic information coded by mRNA. Ribosomes and rRNA are then employed for the purposes of constructing those proteins specified by the

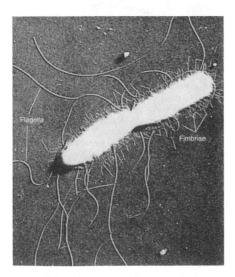

Figure 22. Mitosis. Reprinted from Strachan & Read, 1996, Human Molecular Genetics. Wiley, New York. Salmonella undergoing division.

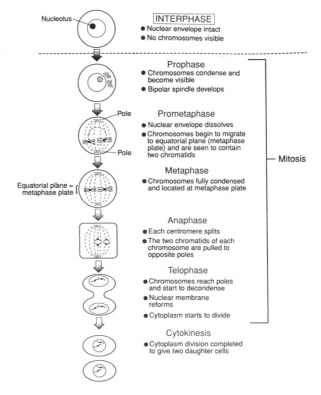

DNA sequence segment coded by mRNA. It is important to note, as will become evident below, that ribosomes and rRNA are not synonymous. Ribosomes are composed of protein products specified by DNA.

A MULTIPLICITY OF CODES

Each DNA macromolecule consists of two complementary chains of base pairs (C-G-T-A-G-C-//G-C-A-T-C-G- etc...) which are joined together to form a double helix. However, it is the sequence in which these nucleotides are organized and thus the manner in which the base pairs are arranged, which contains the instructions for creating specific proteins and conveying specific messages. This includes the plans for creating, building and maintaining a complex body and/or its component parts.

As each chain of nucleotides is divided into numerous sequence segments, and as these nucleotides, and in fact entire genes, have the capacity to shift position, a variety of codes are possible (Drake, 1991; John & Miklos, 1988; Moran et al., 1999; Symmonds, 1991). That is, just as moving the numeral "3" from its position in a sequence of numbers, from 123 to 312 results in the creation of a completely new product, and just as increasing a sequence from 123 to 1234 results in a different product (due to a "frame shift). Therefore, if one base pair moves to a different position, or if an intron or exon moves to a different position thus lengthening or shortening the coding sequence, this results in the creation of a new code and can give rise to the creation of a new gene (Finnegan, 1989; Moran et al., 1999).

Hence, genetic information, instructions, plans and memories are coded, stored in, and represented by the complex micro-molecular patterns and linear sequences in which the individual base pairs are arranged and separated (Drake, 1991; Symmonds, 1991). As this organization is not static, a variety of codes and a variety of products may be produced (Moran et al., 1999).

Moreover, as the majority of sequence segments are silent, and as they may become activated, each gene retains the potential capacity to generate an incredible variety of products including those which may be triggered by changes in climatic, atmospheric, and thus environmental conditions (de Jong & Scharloo, 1976; Dykhuizen & Hart, 1980; Gibson & Hogness, 1996; Polaczyk et al., 1998; Rutherford & Lindquist, 1998; Wade et al., 1997), —as the environment acts on gene selection (Drake, 1991; Symmonds, 1991).

For example, although protein coated and seemingly silenced (Jacob & Monod, 1993), introns not only assist in the regulation of exonic activation, but may well serve as possible depositories of ancestral genetic memories which in turn may be reproduced and reactivated through the intronic generation of genes within genes (Joseph, 1997). Moreover, introns strive to break free of their protein prison. Once free of these repressive restraints, non-coding "silent" genes and intronic nucleotides may be activated by RNA and coded, and/or they can suddenly leap to a different position and undergo transformation into an exon and come to be expressed (Finnegan, 1989; Dibb & Newman, 1989; Drake, 1991; John & Miklos, 1988; Kuhsel, et al. 1990; Symmonds, 1991).

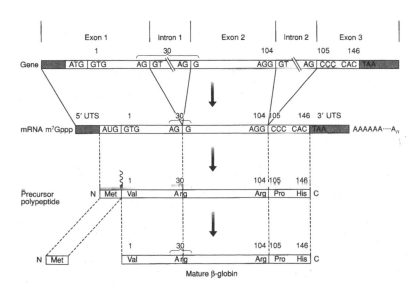

Figure 23 Introns *und RNA splicing. From Strachan & Read, 1996. Human Molecular Genetics, Wiley.*

Summary

In summary, each gene contains hundreds to thousands to millions of individual base pair nucleotide sequences which differ from that of other genes (though duplicates abound) and the vast majority of these segments are "silent" and are not coded or expressed. Each and every individual gene (including those within the same chromosomes), contain identical as well as different sequence segments of nucleotides, and thus different codes for performing a variety of different activities and duplicate (albeit silent) codes which can generate the same products. They also consist of intronic sequences which code for products which have yet to be produced, or which are produced in reaction to changing environment conditions, (e.g., de Jong & Scharloo, 1976; Dykhuizen & Hart, 1980;

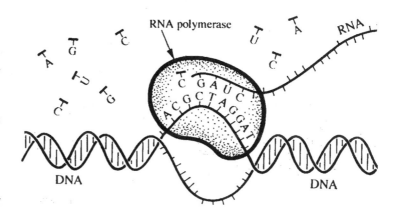

Figure 24. *Schematic depiction of a single strand of RNA being created along one of the strands of DNA which acts as a template creating its mirror image in accordance with Watson-Crick pairing rules; e.g. G=C, C=G, T=A, etc. Reprinted from Calladin & Drew, 1992, Understanding DNA. Academic Press, San Diego.*

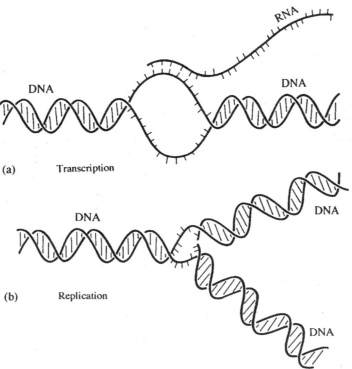

Figure 25. *Schematic depiction of transcription and replication of DNA. The DNA must untwist to allow one strand of DNA to serve as a template for the creation of RNA (A) or for the synthesis of a new strand of DNA (B). Reprinted from Calladin & Drew, 1992, Understanding DNA. Academic Press, San Diego.*

Gibson & Hogness, 1996; Polaczyk et al., 1998; Rutherford & Lindquist, 1998; Wade et al., 1997), and/or which are no longer produced having served their purpose in previous generations of species.

Each individual sequence of nucleotides, once activated, transcribed, and transferred by RNA to the ribosomes, results in the production of certain proteins, cell types, and so on. Therefore, activation of different sequence segments within a single gene, or activation of a shorter or longer version of the same sequence (i.e. such that additional nucleotides are expressed), or a shift in the position and location of even a single pair of nucleotides, can result in the production of wholly new genes (e.g., Moran et al., 1999) or different structures (John & Miklos, 1988); e.g. a muscle cell versus a motor neuron.

Again, although containing a truly mind boggling combination of codes and potential codes, only a fraction of DNA is actually coded and expressed. In fact, only 3% to 10% of all genes (exons) are activated on average (depending on species), as the vast majority of each gene, and the vast majority of genes remain "silent" and seemingly suppressed (Miklos & Rubin, 1996; Strachan & Read, 1996; Watson et al. 1992). Of the 40,000 to 30,000 genes found in human cells, only about 3% of the genome is actually coded and expressed, the rest remaining seemingly "silent," the information they contain unknown.

OF CLAY AND DNA

The incredible complexity of a single macromolecule of DNA, and the fact that only living cells beget living cells, and only DNA produces DNA, poses a dilemma for those advocating spontaneous or gradual generation theories of life. How could an incredibly complex DNA-macromolecule be created and produced on Earth, in the absence of DNA or its essential elements, including oxygen and phosphorus?

Several scenarios have been proposed, including the possibility that due to the missing DNA-ingredients, RNA-precursors or even clay may have become transformed over eons of time, thus producing this ultimate information bearing self-replicating macromolecule. For example, like God's first man, it has been proposed that the first DNA macromolecule was created from the clay of the earth (Desmond, 1993).

It has been determined that clay has two incredible capabilities. Clay is capable of storing information and engaging in energy transfer. Moreover, certain clay-crystals (like many crystals, including "DNA crystals," Winfree et al., 1998) can reproduce themselves. Microcrystalline clays

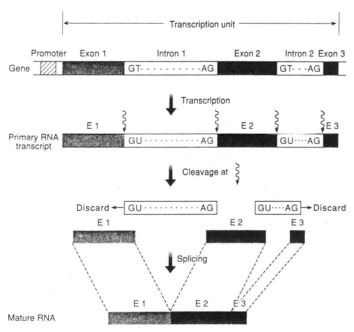

Figure 26. *Schematic depiction of RNA-splicing. RNA-splicing involves removal of non-coding intronic segments and splicing exonic segments back together. Reprinted from Strachan & Read, 1996, Human Molecular Genetics. Wiley, New York.*

(montomorillonite) when manipulated by an experimenter, can facilitate the assembly of RNA fragments if first provided with all the necessary and suitably prepared nucleotides. Hence, clay can store and generate information as well as act as a catalyst.

Given these life-like attributes, it has been argued that during primordial times, clays may have stored up radioactive and photopic energy, including energy from lightning strikes. Later, under moist conditions, this activated-clay acquired the ability to process inorganic compounds in order to create complex molecules, including RNA and DNA and its storehouse of information bearing micromolecules. However, there is no evidence that RNA or DNA can be generated from clay.

THE RNA WORLD

The genetic instructions for the creation of any and all living creatures is contained within DNA. For these instructions to be acted upon, however, generally requires an RNA intermediary. Specifically, RNA consists of a single thread of thousands of nucleotides and is manufactured as a single strand which is formed by only one half of the DNA helix. One of the two DNA strands forms a complementary chain of RNA. RNA, therefore, is derived from DNA and serves as a copy of the activated (coded) DNA which contain the genetic instructions for manufacturing various proteins. However, RNA differs from DNA as it is single stranded, employs uracil rather than thymine, and its "backbone" consists of ribose rather than deoxyribose.

Once this information is copied, thus creating mRNA (messenger RNA), tRNA (transfer RNA) molecules detach from their DNA template and are dispatched on a cytoplasmic, intracellular journey where they search out, and bind with tiny micro-molecular enzyme manufacturing proteins referred to as ribosomes. Like greedy lovers the ribosomes and tRNA molecules embrace, thus forming rRNA (ribosomal RNA) which acts to code and express the information contained in copied DNA sequence segments.

Once these instructions are decoded, specific proteins and enzymes are produced in accordance with the original DNA derived sources of genetic information. RNA, therefore, transfers these DNA-based instructions to the ribosomes so that they may be acted on thus producing the proteins necessary for building any and every body part, including multiple body parts or extensions of body parts thus inducing growth or change.

As there is absolutely no evidence to support the notion that DNA spontaneously or gradually arose from the muck of the Earth, some of those who embrace spontaneous/gradual generation have instead theorized that RNA may have been the first information bearing molecule to arise on this planet (Gilbert, 1986; Gesteland, 1993; Woodward et al., 1998). That is, life first arose in an RNA World.

In the hypothesized RNA-world, RNA creates DNA. In the real world, however, rather than RNA producing DNA, DNA serves as the template for RNA construction, and secretes and manufactures a variety of compounds (e.g. ATP, UTP, GTP, CTP) as RNA precursors. DNA specifies and provides the instructions for the synthesis of RNA and no RNA molecule can arise without these DNA-derived protein enzymes.

Some of those who believe in an RNA-world, however, reverse this process, and in so doing have had to reverse Crick's "Central Dogma," i.e. that information flows only in one direction, from nucleic acids to proteins (reviewed in Gesteland, 1993). In some RNA-world scenarios, DNA is dispensed with altogether and information changes course and flows from proteins to nucleic acids; a hypothesized function of the unusual chemical conditions that presumably characterized the early Earth. This latter scenario, however, is unable to account for the existence of these initial proteins.

In yet other "RNA-world" scenarios, DNA is also dispensed with (at least initially) and this initial, hypothetical RNA molecule fashions the proteins which are responsible for the creation of RNA. More specifically, in an "RNA world" rather than RNA being a product of DNA, this process is reversed, and a particular kind of ribosomal RNA acquires catalytic properties and begins producing proteins, and in so doing, eventually creates the first DNA (Gilbert, 1986; reviewed in Gesteland, 1993). Because DNA is a superior catalyst, these special ribosomal RNA then became subservient to these DNA molecules, and forever after have acted to code and transcribe DNA messages. Thus all subsequent life forms owe their existence to this primeval ribosomal-like RNA molecule.

As summarized by Robertson and Ellington (1998, p. 223), "Looking backwards from a contemporary vantage point, it seems that the RNA components of modern ribosomes, the cell's protein-synthesizing machinery, may itself be a ribozyme and thus a remnant of an RNA world. Looking forwards from origins, it is plausible that chemically simple, nucleic-acid or non-nucleic acid replicators gave rise to the raw material that became the RNA world."

This interesting scenario, however, does not appear to be tenable. RNA molecules are not alive, are exceedingly unstable, and cannot catalyze their own replication. Unlike DNA which can reproduce and give birth to itself -thereby creating genetic offspring- this is not a trait associated with RNA. Viruses, whose genomes consist of RNA are completely incapable of self-replication but instead must invade the genome of a host and literally hijack its DNA in order to reproduce.

In addition, although Bartel and Unrau report that they created "artificial ribozymes" capable of manufacturing one of the RNA bases, they in fact mixed trillions of organic molecules in a chemical solution, chose promising specimens, and then repeated the process again and again before creating an "artificial" ribozyme. What this means is that although an experimenter can experimentally mix and combine and chose certain organic substances so as to arrive at a carefully planned result, that the resulting, artificial molecule, nevertheless failed to create an RNA molecule.

Moreover, RNA is not easily accessed or recognized by proteins due to the depth and configurational organization of its nucleotide framework (Draper, 1995). Hence, it does not seem likely that even in an RNA-world that RNA would be able to generate the proteins and enzymes responsible for the creation of RNA or DNA.

It is noteworthy, however, that a specific type of RNA, ribozymes of which there are several subtypes (Herschlag, 1998) can be experimentally manipulated in a test tube or petri dish in order to engage in catalytic activities (Cech, 1986; Lamond & Gibson, 1990; Unrau & Bartel, 1998), including, with a little technical assistance, self-reproduction (Joyce & Wright, 1999). Moreover, Joyce and Wright (1999) reported that following several experimentally induced replications, "mutations" began to accumulate, which improved the likelihood of additional replications.

Since ribozymes can be experimentally manipulated in a test tube in order to promote their own replication, and as they can act as a catalyst and can bind other molecules, these findings have been viewed as supporting the possibility of an RNA-world (Robertson & Ellington, 1998). Hence, via the assistance of ribozymes, it is theorized that RNA fashioned the proteins which gave rise to the first molecules of RNA, even though, on the early Earth, there was a scarcity of the necessary nucleotides that constitute RNA.

In order to solve the problem of the missing RNA nucleotides, Unrau and Bartel (1998), have presented evidence to support the argument that "RNA-based life must therefore have acquired the ability to synthesize RNA nucleotides from simpler and more readily available precursors, such as sugars and bases." Specifically, Unrau and Bartel (1998) found that if RNA molecules are extracted and isolated, that they can be experimentally manipulated to catalyze the synthesis of a pyramidine nucleotide. According to Unrau and Bartel (1998, p. 260), "the finding that RNA can catalyze this type of reaction... supports the idea of an RNA world that included nucleotide synthesis and other metabolic pathways mediated by ribozymes."

Of course, pyramidine is only one of the building blocks of RNA, and the RNA they employed to induce these reactions was experimentally manipulated and modified. If similar events occurred early in the history of the Earth, one might have to postulate the helpful assistance of the hand of god— or perhaps a well funded and equipped experimenter with a test tube. Moreover, these and similar arguments rests upon the notion that a ribo-organism and thus RNA-based life existed on the early Earth; a proposition for which there is absolutely no evidence (Robertson & Ellington 1998). Moreover, even assuming that there existed RNA-based life, it not only had to have acquired catalytic abilities, but had to couple the nucleotides it created with sugars and sugar-phosphates so as to create a stable RNA-molecule. Moreover, as there were apparently no free-phosphates available, this RNA-based life had to either create phosphate where there was none, or extract it from minerals. And, most importantly, the theory of an RNA-world is rather circular in its reasoning, as it presumes the existence of an RNA-based life form that creates, with the assistance of ribozymes, RNA nucleotides, which RNA with the assistance of ribozymes, catalyzes to create RNA.

On the other hand, since the Miller-Urey-Calvin (and like-minded) experiments have generated some isolated RNA elements, this has led to the argument that early in the history of the Earth, the building blocks of RNA could have been fashioned, and these may have been randomly combined with fragments of RNA which rained down from the sky, thus creating the first step toward a ribo/RNA organism which spontaneously self-assembled.

For example, it has been demonstrated that if RNA-viral proteins are experimentally separated and then placed in a organic and chemical bath, these individual viral protein components and elements will spontaneously aggregate, recombine and will form a complete viral organism with wholly intact infective properties (Fraenkel-Conrat & Williams, 1955). However, these viral-RNAs still require the DNA of a host organism in order to replicate, as well as the active hand of an experimenter in order to extract, isolate, and then bathe them together in a controlled chemical environment which has been purposefully manipulated.

Hence, even if a single RNA molecule did appear on Earth, for example, if it fell from the sky after being manufactured in a cosmic molecular cloud, it could not have engaged in self-replication as the necessary ingredients were nowhere to be found and as it would still require the DNA of a host organism in order to replicate.

As per the problems of self-replication and protein creation, some have argued that the first RNA molecule to appear on Earth (secondary to spontaneous/gradual generation) miraculously reproduced itself by somehow folding together in such a manner that identical base pairs became matched together (e.g. de Duve, 1995). This encircled RNA molecule then broke in half, or chopped itself into two identical copies. This self-mutilating RNA then began to replicate the severed segments thereby creating copies of itself. Of course, a process such as this requires a catalyst, a guiding hand, and DNA-based genetic instructions. In fact, most types of RNA actually resist and are not amenable to becoming folded, the exceptions being Micro-RNAs and small interfering RNAs which consist of flexible structural parts. Because small RNA molecules can be folded, their existence has been argued as supporting the RNA-world hypothesis for the origin of life. However, micro-RNAs and small interfering RNAs do not perform catalytic reactions, but instead act on other types of RNA, including messenger RNA.

Micro-RNAs and small interfering RNAs, are a major controller of cellular function and also influence gene "expression." For example, these two classes of small genes have been shown to serve as molecular mechanisms controlling genes that are required for cells to turn into a lung, liver,brain or other structure. In plants, micro RNA acts on messenger RNA by literally cutting it in half, whereas in animals micro RNAs attach to target messenger RNAs and prevent translation into proteins. Small RNAs control how whole chromosomes, or regions of chromosomes, are activated or deactivated. Micro-RNAs and small interfering RNAs maywell play a significant role in evolutionary metamorphosis.

In summary, the theory of an RNA world, and the meager evidence which has been marshaled in support, fails to explain the origins of RNA, or ribozymes, or DNA, except through circular reasoning and through the creation of a theoretical chemical world—a theoretical world for which no evidence exists. Although numerous laboratories have attempted to prove otherwise, and although there has been some success in experimentally manipulating RNA and ribozymes so as to engage in catalytic and synthesizing activity, RNA cannot generate or make copies of itself (that is, without experimental assistance) and it cannot generate DNA. Only DNA produces DNA, and those cells (such as RNA equipped viruses) which are devoid of DNA are incapable of reproducing except via a DNA intermediary.

RNA-VIRAL WORLDS

VIRUSES

Although the possibility of a life-creating RNA-world seems rather unlikely, some of the scenarios briefly mentioned above may well account for the creation of the first viral "organisms" (Joseph, 1997, 2000). Viral "organisms"are not truly organisms as they are not alive.

Viruses generally differ greatly in size (from 10 to 300 nanometers), but are much smaller than single celled organisms including bacteria, approximating, in girth, a single protein or macromolecule (reviewed in Kuby, 1994). Viruses generally consist of a core of nucleic acid which is surrounded by cytoplasm containing lipids and carbohydrates, which are stabilized by a thick protein coat or lipid membrane. Almost all viruses store their genetic information in either a single or double strand of RNA with only a relatively few viral strains having acquired a single strand of DNA.

The viral genome is incredibly complex. In some cases, up to four genes are involved in regulating viral gene expression and protein synthesis. Nevertheless, although viruses have an RNA- and sometimes a DNA-genome, they share few of the metabolic and reproductive properties characteristic of animals, plants, or bacteria. Viruses behave more like a crystalline, or protein compound than a true living creature. That is, viruses are not really alive but instead consist of metabolically inert nucleoprotein particles that are in all respects lifeless. Viruses remain inert and lifeless until they come into contact with living cellular tissue, at which point they become mobile and invade and infect the host cell, sometimes inserting their own unique genetic messages into the DNA of their host (reviewed in Kuby, 1994).

Given the structure and organization of viral particles and their RNA-genome it is not inconceivable that they may have been produced -on this planet as well as others- via a process reminiscent of spontaneous generation. Viruses may be the imperfect result of the random mixing of organic sludge on any number of moons and planets. Because they have been imperfectly created, they are not alive, and thus require the complex internal environment of a living cell, and its DNA, in order to replicate.

As the viral genome usually consist of only RNA, viruses are incapable of self-replication but require a living alternative. Viruses are unique in that they require the DNA and the reproductive machinery of the host organism in order to reproduce viral DNA, and in order to replicate and to duplicate; thus, infecting the DNA of all host cells in the process.

In general, the virus will attack and attach its viral tail to the body of the host cell. This tail then secretes an enzyme which can digest part of the cell wall so that the virus can slip in and inject its own DNA or RNA into the cytoplasmic contents. The viral DNA/RNA attaches to the host chromosome, inserts itself into a gene, and then begins to direct the host cell's DNA/RNA so as to produce viral proteins and viral DNA. Viruses, therefore, are capable of inserting their RNA/DNA into the DNA of their host and altering the host's genome and sometimes splitting chromosomes in two (Berkner, 1988; Moss et al. 1990; Strachan & Read, 1996; Watson et al. 1994; Wigler, et al., 1979).

Once invasion and incorporation are accomplished viruses exert drastic influences on host cell metabolism and enzymatic machinery. Viral proteins and particles are rapidly produced, swelling the host cell until it bursts, thereby releasing its viral contents which then attack adjacent cells, exponentially multiplying, and sickening and sometimes killing the host in the process (reviewed in Kuby, 1994; Watson et al., 1992). HIV, smallpox, measles, rabies, polio, warts, fever blisters, the flu, and the common cold are all secondary to infective, invasive viral elements which take over the host cellular genetic machinery and rapidly divide.

Moreover, viruses have the capacity to become dormant following infection, and can be passed on to subsequent generations and even subsequent species. For example, the human genome is riddled with thousands of endogenous retroviruses which have been inherited and then passed on from old-world primate ancestors (Johnson & Coffin, 1999). In fact, these proviral elements can be employed to make estimates as to species phylogeny, as based on changes in ancestral sequences and their molecular evolution.

As noted, the viral genome is incredibly complex. The RNA of an influenza virus may consist of over 10,000 nucleotides, the order and arrangement of which contains the code for creating over a dozen different proteins. Likewise, the DNA of a single parovirus is composed of a double strand of base pairs which is 5,081 nucleotides in length (Watson, et al. 1992).

Presumably, it is because of the unique organization of their RNA (and sometimes DNA) based genome, that some viruses attack only special types of cells or specific organisms. HIV, for example, infects just three types of cells, dendritic cells, macrophages, and T lymphocytes which carry the CD4 receptor and serve the immune reaction (reviewed in Kuby, 1994).

As noted, viruses may have been created in a primordial organic soup following extraterrestrial contamination. Thus, they may have originated on Earth, as well as other planets. In fact, because viruses are lifeless as well as resistant to severe heat, cold, drying, alcohol, and even formaline solutions, they are perfectly suited for a life drifting in interstellar space, convalescing on some meteorite or cloud of stellar gas, dormant and lying in wait, like a spider, for a planet swarming with a variety of unsuspecting host cells. In fact, the demographics and patterns of contagion of various viruses, including some flu viruses, raise the possibility that in some cases, viral invasion may be secondary to the Earth passing through areas of outer space congested with viral organisms.

Moreover, although they may sometimes originate in interstellar space, thereby subjecting the peoples of the Earth to repeated epidemics, viruses, including prehistoric viruses between 500 and 140,000 years old, have been found, lying dormant, in the polar ice caps and from sites in Greenland (Starmer, Rogers, & Castello, 1999); which in turn suggests that they also lay dormant in other snow bound regions. According to Alvin Smith, a virologist at Oregon State University, "If you've got these things lying in the ice for a thousand years or more and their usual host has not had to deal with them, this may be a source of epidemics." Presumably, as temperatures rise and the ice melts, these viral particles are released into the atmosphere thereby giving rise to epidemics. Indeed, viruses have found in fog and clouds.

Nevertheless, regardless of their source, viruses (like some bacteria) are capable of injecting their genetic material (and the genetic material of other species) into hosts cells, and may well be capable of drifting from planet to planet, thereby contributing to interplanetary gene exchange. Indeed, these globe trotting viral organisms may have contributed to the exchange and sharing of genetic/DNA memories not only between different host organisms, but between creatures living on wholly different planets thus promoting evolutionary metamorphosis (Joseph, 1997).

In summary, if we accept the premise of an RNA-world, it would appear that at best the end result would be the formation of an imperfectly created RNA molecule. However, these RNA-entities, like viral organisms, could not have given rise to DNA, and would have been unable to replicate without the assistance of various DNA-based life forms (such as a human experimenter). However, as to the young Earth, these DNA-based life forms must have first "evolved" on other planets, or were the product of intelligent design (or both).

As only DNA begets DNA and as the young Earth was devoid of this essential ingredient, we must conclude that the first DNA to appear on this world, was either astrobiological in origin, and/or it was created by a highly intelligent life form.

CREATION SCIENCE

Although the heavens are swirling with the constituent elements and complex organic molecules necessary for life, the various "organic soup" theories cannot account for the creation of DNA and its complex life and cellular generating genetic instructions—at least on Earth. These theories have utterly failed to provide an explanation for the creation and emergence of DNA. As DNA is the foundation for cellular life, the organic soup/thermal vent, RNA-World theories therefore cannot explain the origin of Earthly-life. No matter which spontaneous generation or organic soup scenario we choose, the fact remains that on Earth, the purported "organic" alphabet "soup" was actually a thin broth missing three important letters: DNA.

There are thus two remaining possibilities for the emergence of life on Earth: Creation Science and astrobiological contamination/infection theory. However, Creation Science and Astrobiology, are not incompatible. Indeed, those who first formulated the theory of "creation science" some 6,000 or more years ago, also believed that life did not originate on this planet, but rained down from the heavens, perhaps encased in all manner of extraterrestrial debris. They also believed that these "seeds of life" gave rise to the gods.

THE SUMERIAN CREATION "MYTHS"

Modern day "Creation Science" is rooted in the story of Genesis which in turn appears to be a retelling of the Sumerian tales of creation (Heidel, 1988; Kramer, 1991; Roux, 1992). Although different modern-day Biblical interpretations abound, at least some creation scientists have addressed the issue of the missing "DNA" (alluded to above) by attributing its manufacture to a Creator. This "creationist" view is compatible with the claim by Darwin (1859) that it was a "Creator" who first created and "breathed" life into living creatures, and that the emergence and evolution of life has unfolded in accordance "with what we know of the laws impressed on matter by the Creator" (Darwin, 1859).

There is now a convergence of opinion that the story of Genesis, as retold in the Hebrew and Christian Bible, bears a striking resemblance to the "creation myths" including the "flood myths" penned almost 6,000 years ago by the peoples of Sumer—which was located in what today is Iraq. These stories were still in fashion with the rise of the Babylonian state which had risen with the fall of Sumer (Roux, 1992). Abraham, the presumed patriarch of all modern day Jewish peoples, hailed from Ur of the Chaldees, which was originally a Sumerian city. In fact, a considerable proportion of the ancient Sumerian population consisted of Semitic peoples (Roux, 1992) and Abraham may well have been a prince of the city.

According to Roux (1992, p. 85), "For more than three thousand years the gods of Sumer were worshipped by Sumerians and Semites alike; and for more than three thousand years the religious ideas promoted by the Sumerians played an extraordinary part in the public and private life of the Mesopotamians, modeling their institutions, coloring their works of art and literature."

As succinctly put by the renowned Sumerian scholar, Samuel Noah Kramer (1991, p. 75), "There is good reason to infer that in the third millennium BC., there emerged a group of Sumerian thinkers and teachers who, in their quest for satisfactory answers to some of the problems raised by their cosmic speculations, evolved a cosmology and theology carrying such high intellectual conviction that their doctrines became the basic creed and dogma of much of the ancient Near East."

Following the destruction of the Temple, around 600 B.C. the Jews were exiled to Babylon, where and when, it is believed, the story of Genesis underwent extensive editing. Hence, it could be argued that the true authors of Genesis were the Sumerian peoples.

THE ANUNNAKI: GODS FROM ANOTHER PLANET

Our knowledge of ancient Sumer comes from a variety of ancient texts, including epic tales, hymns, poetry, proverbs, prayers and incantations. Some of these texts are written in ancient Sumerian, others are Akkadian and Babylonian copies that were found in the ruins of palaces and temple librar-ies.

The Sumerian account of "Genesis" is remarkably similar to the "creation myths" of ancient people throughout the world.

According to Sumerian theology, a pantheon of gods, human-like in form, but possessing ex-traordinary superhuman scientific powers and technological capability, took possession of the Earth in order to exploit this world for its resources.

These same gods, the Anunnaki, claimed credit for creating the Earth, the heavens and the stars—claims the Sumerians rejected. According to the Sumerians, these human-like "gods" were in turn ruled by laws and regulations that were promulgated and enforced by yet other gods who lived in different regions of the cosmos (Kramer, 1991). Different "gods" through agreements worked out between them and their various factions, were in charge of different regions of the cosmos and thus ruled over and exploited different worlds and those life forms which dwelled on the different planets. The Earth was but one of these exploited planets, and was ruled by a pantheon of human-like gods, the Anunnaki.

As based on his interpretation of ancient Sumerian cuneiform writing and glyphs, Kramer (1991) informs us that these gods formed and "functioned as an assembly with a king at its head, its most important groups consisting of seven gods... and fifty who were known as the great gods." The chief "god" who ruled over the Earth was Enlil who was exceedingly arrogant, exploitive, and brutal. The other chief gods included Ninhursag who was his wife, and Enki who was a scientist and the half-brother of Enlil.

The Sumerians did not view the Anunnaki as being spiritual-like beings, but similar to humans. They did not believe the Anunnaki had created the Earth, or life, for first and foremost of the Sumerian pantheon, was "An" (Anu in Egyptian, or Anum in Akkadian). "An" was the "eternal sea" of space, the creator of the gods, including the peoples of Earth.

With the exception of the mysterious heavenly life force, An, the Sumerians repeatedly acknowl-edged that Enlil, Enki and the others were not really "gods" but technologically advanced people who had come to the Earth from the heavens, from another planet, Nibiruo (Sitchin, 1990). Thus their names, the "Anunnaki" which means: "Those who came from Heaven to Earth."

According to the Sumerians, the "Anunnaki were space-traveling peoples who not only flew in spherical and winged air ships, but who, according to Sumerian calendars, first arrived on this planet almost 500,000 years ago (Sitchin, 1990) —at about the same time that a new breed of humanity, the first archaic Homo sapiens, emerged, the earliest remains being discovered in the Middle East.

Although in charge (king) of the Earth, Enlil was bound by rules and regulations dictated by yet other gods who dwelled in other regions of the cosmos, and he was required to carry out their instruc-tions (Kramer, 1991). Apparently those instructions involved depleting the Earth of certain resources, which in turn required a huge work force.

A problem soon arose. The Anunnaki did not have enough workers.

One of the Anunnaki gods "Enki," was a master scientist who carried a staff upon which coiled the double helix of two entwined snakes. The snake was also his emblem. As for his double helix, there is an obvious similarity to modern depictions of DNA.

Enki performed experiments on these primitive human-like animals and other creatures, creat-ing all manner of hybrid beasts—what today might be referred to as "transgenic animals." These creations included half-human animals who could entertain the gods, but which nevertheless re-mained unsuitable for working the fields or the mines.

These experiments are depicted in Sumerian glyphs in which Enki and his assistants, are shown dressed in aprons and holding flasks and other scientific instruments. Also depicted are the results of his hybrid experiments, e.g. bulls with human heads, animals with human limbs,

The ancient Sumerians state that archaic humans also lived on the Earth, but that they were so primitive and animal-like, that they could not serve as a work-force.

Enki, the priests of ancient Sumer claim, decided to solve the problem of an insufficient work-force by mixing the tissues of the gods with that of the primitive humans. Enki, the Anunnaki god, created the first modern woman and man.

"Man I will create. He shall be charged with the service of the gods that they might be at ease."

Enki, the double helix god of the snake, took the blood and tissues from the body of the gods and a primitive human, and mixed it in his flasks and then impregnated one of the female gods ("Eve"). This female god gave birth to an advanced, almost god-like Homo sapiens, who was essentially created in the image of the gods; a superior god-like human who could be instructed in the art of culture, science, medicine, and technology (Heidel, 1988; Kramer, 1991). These "men" were essentially formed in the image of the gods, in the image of the Anunnaki, and were thus part-god.

The Biblical account in Genesis echoes the Sumerian account: "And God said, Let us make man in our image, after our likeness. So God created man in his image, in the image of God created he him; male and female he created them."

Again the purpose of this creation was to fill a labor shortage. God-like human were created to be employed as forced labor, and they were endowed with intelligence so they could be instructed to tend the gardens and care for the live stock of the gods.

Likewise, as stated in Genesis, God created the first man to serve the gods as a laborer. "And the Lord God planted a garden eastward in Eden and there he put the man whom he had formed...The Lord God took the man and placed him in the garden of Eden to till it and tend it." Hence, according to Genesis (2:15), the entire purpose of the creation, was to create workers "to till and tend" the gardens and fields of the gods.

In addition to working as slave labor, the Anunnakis creation was given dominion over the lands, the beasts, including a ruling responsibility over the more primitive humans who had independently evolved on Earth. Thus the "gods" according to the Sumerians "lowered from heaven... the throne of kingship," and these specially created individuals were part god and part human and were expected to act as overseers as well as slave labor. According to the Sumerians Kings lists, the Anunnaki created these first god-kings, over 240,000 years ago (Roux, 1992).

"GOD" CREATES MAN & WOMAN IN THE IMAGE OF THE GODS

Biblical accounts of creation tell us that increasingly complex life forms emerged upon the planet, in a step-wise, "day to day" sequence, beginning with simple life forms, and then simple creatures, culminating, on day 6, with the creation of woman and man. This same progression is evident from the fossil record.

Genesis 1: "And God said, Let us make man in our image, after our likeness. So God created man in his own image, in the image of God created he him; male and female created he them. And God saw every thing that he had made, and, behold, it was very good. And the evening and the morning were the sixth day."

Genesis 2: "And on the seventh day God ended his work; and he rested on the seventh day from all his work which he had made. And every plant of the field before it was in the earth, and every herb of the field before it grew: and there was not a man to till the ground. And the LORD God formed man of the dust of the ground, and breathed into his nostrils the breath of life; and man became a living soul. And the LORD God planted a garden eastward in Eden; and there he put the man whom he had formed. And out of the ground made the LORD God to grow every tree that is pleasant to the sight, and good for food; the tree of life also in the midst of the garden, and the tree of knowledge of good and evil. And the LORD God took the man, and put him into the garden of Eden to tend it and to keep it...So the LORD God caused the man to fall into a deep sleep; and while he was sleeping, he took one of the man's ribs and closed up the place with flesh. Then the LORD God made a woman from the rib he had taken outof the man, and he brought her to the man."

Thus, after creating man and woman on the six day, on the seventh day, "God" rested —for even Gods grow weary. And then, after the seventh day, there is a second act of creation; i.e., the creation of a spiritually endowed man and woman by a "Lord God;" a "man" and a "woman" who were expected to tend the gardens and the livestock of the Gods; superior god-like men and women who also shared the Earth with the more inferior humans who were the remnants of the first natural progression that ended on day six.

Thus, as retold by Genesis there is a natural progression that starts with simple creatures and on the 6th day, involves the creation of woman and man by "God." However, after the 7th day, there is a second act of human creation by a "Lord God." This Lord God appears upon the scene after "God ended his work... and rested on the seventh day." And it is this Lord God (vs God) who is credited with creating modern woman and man--humans who differed from those created on the 6th day, in that they were fashioned in the image of the gods and possessed intelligence and a living soul.

Later, in the next chapter of Genesis, we are told that Cain, the son of Adam and Eve, feared

Figure 27. *The Anunnaki: "From heaven to Earth they came." According to the Sumerians, they came in space craft from another planet.*

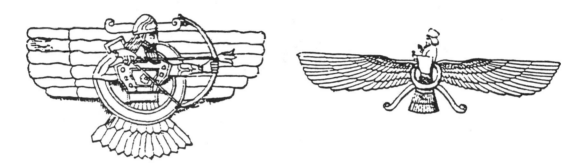

Figure 28. *Babylonian/Akkadian and Persian gods in their flying discs*

he might be killed by these other humans. The Lord God, however, assures Cain that he will not be killed, because he is different from the other humans. Cain has a "mark."

Thus we see that the man created after the seventh day differs from the man created on the sixth day, in two important respects. The man created on the sixth day, was created by "God," as part of a natural progression beginning with simple creatures. This first man, however, was unable "to till the land." The man fashioned after the seventh day, after "God" had rested, was created by the "LORD God" after all the natural sequential acts of creation had come to an end. And, this new man, created after the seventh day was able to till the gardens, and was provided with a "living soul."

As noted, according to Sumerian "mythology," the Earth was alive with all manner of beasts, including primitive humans who were little different than animals. The "gods" determined that the human-like animals that roamed the planet were unsuitable. In order to obtain a suitable work force, they called upon Enki whose emblem was the double helix.

Enki, the Anunnaki god of science and wisdom, fashioned humans that were created in the image of the gods and provided the spirit, the living soul of god. Enki's emblem was the sign of the double helix, and his symbol was that of two entwined snakes.

Enki, not only improved on the beast-like humans, but created a superior human which included women so beautiful that even the Anunnaki "gods" lusted for and desired them. In consequence, the Anunnaki had sex with these women and fathered innumerable children—and broke the laws formulated by the supreme lords of the universe.

We see the same story in Genesis:

"When men began to increase on earth and daughters were born to them, the divine beings saw how beautiful the daughters of men were and took wives from among those that pleased them... It was then, and later too, when the divine being cohabitated with the daughters of men, who bore them offspring. They were heroes of old, the men of renown," --Genesis 6.

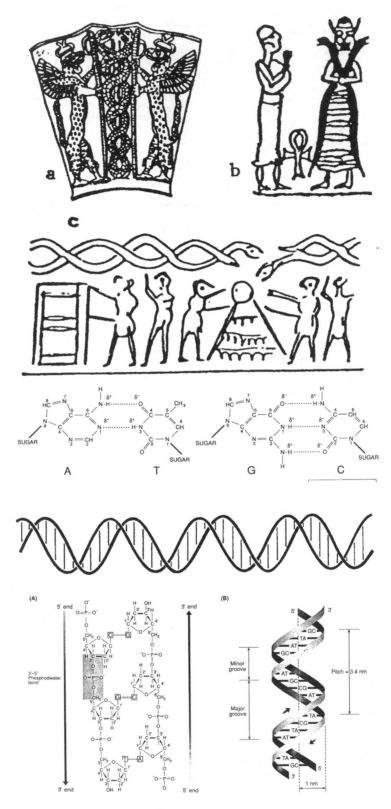

Figure 29. *(Top) The Anunnaki "god" Enki is associated with entwined serpents that form a double helix. Reprinted from Sitchin, 1990. Genesis Revisited. Avon, New York. (Below) The molecular and structural organization of DNA.*

Figure 30. *(Left) An Anunnaki goddess "Eve." According to Sumerian mythology, Enki (depicted as the serpent) created all manner of primitive workers which were part human and part animal. Enki's creations play music. Enki and an animal-human he created and which serves as his assistant. (Bottom) A stone bull with a human head. The "crown" upon its head indicates that the creature is of divine origin.*

Figure 31. *The Anunnaki, Enki, is associated with the serpent and is described by the Sumerians as a master scientist.According to the Sumerian version of creation, the "new man" was created in a laboratory and placed into the womb of a goddess. According to Sumerian mythology, it is a goddess who serves as the "host" who gives birth to the "new man" that is created in the laboratory of Enki—a "new" man who is created in the image of the gods, and who possess wisdom. (top) Sumerian depiction of a laboratory experiments in which the solar disc hovers above. (middle) Sumerian depiction of a laboratory experiment in which a more advanced part-god, part-human is created. Note the laboratory flasks, and vat to the left and the stylized tree to the right behind the woman holding the new "man." (bottom) "Eve" and the "new man." Reprinted from Sitchin, 1976. The 12th Planet. Avon, New York.*

Figure 32. The Anunnaki, serpent god, Enki

Figure 33. (Below) "The Fall of Man and the Expulsion from the Garden of Eden." Michelangelo. 1508.

Figure 34. From Ape to Adam, by Rudy Zallinger.

Sumerian & Biblical Parallels

The first 25 verses of the first book of Moses (Genesis) repeats much of the creation saga, as told by the peoples of ancient Summer and Babylon, including, in verses 26-31, the story of the creation of "man" and "woman" as part of a natural progression beginning with simple creatures. Again, however, this first man and woman, created on the sixth day, were created by "God" as part of this natural progression.

According to the Biblical version of Genesis: "The Lord God formed a man of the dust of the ground and breathed into his nostril the breath of life; and man became a living soul. And the Lord God planted a garden, eastward in Eden; and there he put the man he had formed. And out of the ground made the Lord God to grow every tree that is pleasant to sight and good for food" —for even Gods grow hungry. "But of the tree of knowledge," God warned, "thou shalt not eat."

According to the Biblical version, it is only after this warning that woman, "Eve" is created. And, we are told that Eve was beguiled by the wise serpent, and it is through Eve and the serpent that man acquired knowledge of good and evil.

The serpent is obviously Enki—the Anunnaki god of the double helix. As per "Eve" it is notewor-thy that this name can mean "of the rib" as well as the "mother of all." And, according to Sumerian mythology, it is a goddess who serves as the "host" who gives birth to the "new man" that is created in the laboratory of Enki. That is, it is through Enki and this woman, this goddess, that a new man is created, a man who is part-god, and who possessed wisdom.

It is also noteworthy that the serpent did not approach Adam, only Eve, and it was through Eve that the serpent was able to create a new Adam, one who now possessed knowledge.

It is also implied in Genesis that the serpent had sex with Eve, and impregnated her with his "seed."

"I will put enmity between you and the woman, and between your offspring and hers... and to the woman He said, I will make most severe your pangs in childbearing. In pain you shall bear children," --Genesis 3.

Thus, according to Genesis, the serpent is joined to Eve, his seed is mixed with her seed, and, Eve is also described as "the mother of all," --Genesis 3.

And what are we to make of the promise of "pangs in child bearing?" Perhaps only that her babies would have a bigger head and thus a bigger brain, thus making it more painful when the newborn passes through and emerges from the birth canal.

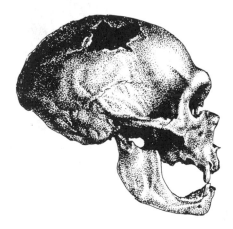
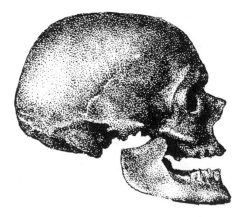

Figure 35. Comparison of the skulls of Cro-Magnon and Neanderthal (top). Note bulging frontal portion of the Cro-Magnon skull. The Cro-Magnon brain was much larger than the Neanderthal brain.

THE CRO-MAGNON AND NEANDERTHALS

The Sumerian peoples tell us that they, and in fact all of humanity, are descended from the men and women created in the image of the gods, though they also admit that over the eons we have lost and progressively shed our god-like physical, intellectual and technological capabilities.

They also tell us that when the Anunnaki created men and women in the image of the gods, that other, more primitive humans still roamed the planet. We are informed that these god-like creations also interacted with the more primitive beast-like humans, and after first waring against one another, estab-lished friendships.

Likewise, the fossil record indicates that the short, brutish, Neanderthals, a slope-headed, ex-tremely primitive and violent peoples, shared the planet with the physically and intellectually ad-vanced Cro-Magnon peoples, for over 20,000 years.

The Cro-Magnon peoples were physical and intellectual giants, the men standing 6 foot tall on average, and sporting a brain one third larger than that of modern humans and the Neanderthals; i.e. 1800 cc compared to 1350 for present day peoples.

The origins of the Cro-Magnon peoples, however, are completely unknown. There are no transitional forms that link them with Neanderthals or the still primitive "early modern" peoples of the Middle Paleolithic who were decidedly more archaic in appearance.

Whereas there is an obvious progression from Australopithecus/H. habilis to H. erectus and archaic humans and Neanderthals, as is evident from an examination of the skull and the poorly developed frontal lobe (Joseph, 1996, 2000a), the same is not true of the Cro-Magnons.

Neanderthals did not evolve into Cro-Magnons, and these two species of humanity coexisted for over 20,000 years. However, after a 400,000 year history (if we include the first Homo sapiens in their lineage), the Neanderthals died out and disappeared from the face of the Earth, around 29,000 years B.P. (Mellars, 1996); a consequence of disease or widespread ethnic cleansing on the part of the Cro-Magnon peoples.

The Neanderthals were of a completely different race; and not just physically, but genetically, for when they died out, so too did their genetic heritage and all traces of their DNA (Ovchinnikov et al., 2000). An examination of Neanderthal mitochondrial DNA sequences taken from a 29,000 year old Neanderthal specimen recovered from the Mezmaiskaya Cave in the northern Caucasus and DNA samples taken from a second Neanderthal specimen found in the Feldhofer Cave in the Neander valley, indicates that although both are closely related, genetically they are significantly different from that of modern (European) humanity (Krings et al., 1997; Ovchinnikov et al., 2000). Neanderthals and their genetic lineage, apparently completely died out without contributing anything to the modern mitochondrial gene pool.

Thirty thousand years ago, and with the demise of the Neanderthals, the Cro-Magnons gained dominion over the earth. And it is thirty thousand years ago that the ancient Egyptians claim that first kings came to rule Egypt; kings who had been created by the gods.

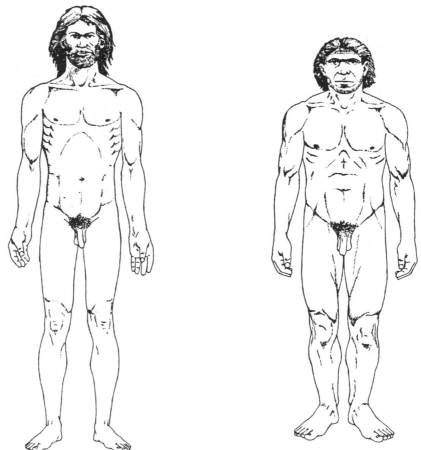

Figure 36. Depiction of Neanderthal and a Cro-Magnon man. Reprinted from Howells, 1997. Getting Here. Compass Press, Washington D.C.

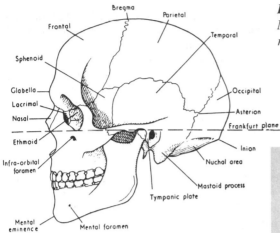

Figure 37. *Modern human cranium. (Below) Neanderthal skull from the Monte Circeo, near Anzio, Italy.*

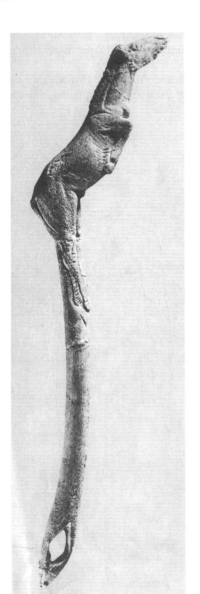

Figure 38. *Neanderthal tools (above). A Cro-Magnon spear thrower decorated with a leaping horse (left), carved around 30,000 years ago.*

THE DEATH OF DARWINISM
Purpose, Progress, Silent Genes, & Multi-Regional Human Metamorphosis
by R. Joseph

"Progress is a noxious, culturally embedded, untestable, nonoperational, intractable idea that we must replace if we wish to understand the patterns of history." -Harvard Paleontologist S. J. Gould (1988, p. 319)

Charles Darwin was not the first to profess a belief in evolution for similar theories were espoused by many others, including Anaximander, a Greek Philosopher, some twenty six hundred years ago. Anaximander argued that humans descended from fish.

Over the centuries various scientists have come to similar conclusions and have written page after page that not only parallels the later work of Darwin but which Darwin copied and incorporated into his book (often without citation), including the works and lectures of Edward Blyth, William Wells, James Pritchard, Williams Lawrence, Charles Naudin, A. R. Wallace, and G.L.L. Buffon. When it was pointed out he had copied, almost verbatim, parts of Buffon's 18th century treatise "Natural History," Darwin (1888) was forced to agree that "whole pages are laughably like mine."

Over the last 100 years Darwin has almost been deified by modern Western science and the Western media. Yet, because of the still smoldering controversy regarding the true authorship of his theory, some of his acolytes have also become his apologists, explaining away the obvious similarities between his writings and the theories and observations of his contemporaries and those great men who came before him. Thus Darwin is sometimes described as a "great synthesizer of existing information." The "existing information" that Darwin synthesized, or rather, borrowed, includes, in fact, the crux of the theory of evolution; i.e. natural selection—a theory first formally proposed and distributed, not by Darwin, but by A. R. Wallace.

Although glossed over by Darwin and his acolytes, Darwin had in fact abandoned the field of "evolution" early in his career. Prior to receiving Wallace's land mark paper, Darwin's had spent 15 years studying and writing about barnacles, not evolution. However, upon reading Wallace's brilliant paper, Darwin proclaimed that he had been studying evolution all along, and had been writing an identical paper, and then spent the next 8 months rewriting, and in some places, repeating the works of others without citation, including the brilliant and revolutionary work of Wallace.

Although we can only speculate, Darwin may well have felt he had but no choice but to borrow liberally from the work and ideas of others. Although great things had been expected of him by his wealthy and well known father, and although his father's friends, including a number of well known scientists had also expected that he would some day make a name for himself, Darwin had repeatedly failed to accomplish anything of significance. After repeated failures he had become miserably depressed. Darwin had been forced to drop out of medical school when it became apparent that he did not have the aptitude to become a medical doctor, and then he also failed at his next pursuit, which was theology. And then he failed yet again in his attempts to establish himself as a "naturalist" and scientist, his writings and observations being dismissed as insignificant and mere repetitions of what was already well known—including his observations while voyaging on the Beagle.

Worse, after he was appointed "secretary" of the Geological Society, he subsequently claimed to have made a "significant" discovery and proclaimed that some "mysterious rock formations" at Glenroy Scotland were the remnants of "ancient marine beaches" which had been part of the mainland but had sunk into the sea. Darwin was quickly proved wrong. They had been carved by glaciers.

As fame repeatedly escaped him, Darwin became increasingly withdrawn and depressed. He dabbled in this area and that, and then spent 15 years devoted to the study of barnacles, about which he wrote four short papers.

And then, on June 8, 1858, Darwin received a letter from Alfred Russel Wallace, accompanied by a 12 page summary of Wallace's ideas on evolution, i.e. natural selection. Wallace was a renowned naturalist and had published a number of papers on evolution which Darwin had read and expressed interest in. From an island near Borneo Wallace had forwarded his monograph to Darwin. The paper was utterly brilliant!

Darwin then claimed to have recently arrived at identical conclusions, and thus claimed Wallace's theory as his own. Darwin immediately abandoned the study of barnacles and began feverishly working on a book, a synthesis of the words of Blyth, Wells, Pritchard, Lawrence, Naudin, and Buffon: On the Origin of Species by Means of Natural Selection which he published in November of 1859, almost 18 months after receiving the paper by Wallace. Indeed, the crown jewel was in fact the paper by Wallace, "Natural Selection." As Darwin well knew, this "synthesis" and the theory of "natural selection" would garner him world fame.

Darwin, his well connected friends in the scientific community, and his acolytes have gone to extraordinary lengths to rewrite history and to spin myths regarding Darwin's' utterly insignificant observations when as a youth he sailed on the "Beagle"—observations which were little different from numerous naturalists writing and publishing at the time. Nevertheless, the facts of the matter are that up until receiving the paper by Wallace, Darwin had written absolutely nothing of significance on evolution, and had spent the previous 15 years studying and writing about "barnacles." Not evolution. Barnacles!

Although Darwin claims otherwise, it could also be argued that Darwin's claim to fame, and the crux of his thesis, the theory of "natural section," was devised, originated and first penned and distributed by Wallace and Wallace alone, which is why knowledgeable sources grudgingly credit Wallace as the "cofounder" of the theory of evolution.

Why did Wallace receive only second billing? Why did so many 19th century scientists find it acceptable to attribute the work of Wallace to Darwin? First, perhaps it is true, as Darwin claims, that he had been writing an identical paper on "natural selection" where he made the same exact arguments and came to the same exact conclusions as Wallace, and was thus shocked and dismayed to discover that Wallace had come to the "same" conclusions and had written them down. An amazing coincidence! Thus Darwin rightly deserves credit as being the codiscoverer. However, if that does not seem plausible, the reader might consider the following: Darwin, the former secretary of the Geological Society, was the son of a rich and well known man and part of a circle of exceedingly influential scientists. Wallace was an outsider. And, Wallace believed in God. Darwin did not.

In contrast to Darwin, Wallace was repeatedly struck by the fact that various faculties and anatomical structures had "evolved" and existed prior to the conditions that would make them necessary or useful—especially as pertaining to the "evolution" of woman and man. Evolution, as pointed out by Wallace (1895), is often characterized by the survival of certain animals who already possessed a trait, or physical characteristic, which enabled them to survive in response to changing environmental conditions. That is, these capacities existed apriori, well before they were naturally selected or useful, and to Wallace that suggested intelligent design, progress and anticipation of changing conditions. Moreover, Wallace argued that because this was particularly true of "man" his theory of "natural selection" should not be applied to human evolution.

To Wallace and at least a few of his contemporaries, such as pioneering paleontologist Robert Broom, the obvious evidence of progress, design, and the presence of advanced characteristics prior to their selection, particularly in regard to the evolution of humanity, seemed to imply purposeful anticipation or planning, as if the instructions had already existed apriori; as if human evolution were predetermined.

According to Wallace (1895) the emergence of humanity could not have occurred secondary to random variations or mutations. Evolutionary progress and adaptations made in advance of their utilization and thus before they were maximally adaptive and which have culminated in the emergence of humanity, suggested to Wallace, the presence of a "guiding hand," a "divine intelligence" which designed these features in advance and in anticipation of their later utilization. Wallace came to the conclusion that this "guiding hand" belonged to none other than God, and to combat "Darwinism" announced his belief to the world.

Darwin was furious with Wallace, and immediately fired off a letter announcing his displeasure: "I hope you have not murdered too completely your own child and mine" (Darwin, 1888).

It is because of Wallace's insistence on progress, design, and this guiding hand in the evolution of humanity—and in particular and especially his belief in God— that subsequent evolutionary and genetic theorists have ridiculed and virtually ignored his work as well as the obvious implications of his observations; i.e. adaptive changes and modifications in structure prior to their usefulness suggests that their future employment was predesigned and predetermined. Humans did not evolve their humaness or their human genes. Rather, human genes were inherited from non-human species, often as silent genes and gene-within-genes.

GENE EXPRESSION AND EVOLUTION ARE NOT DUE TO RANDOM MUTATIONS

A major tenant of Darwinian and neo-Darwinian evolutionary theory is that evolution is due to "random mutations" ("variations") and that there is absolutely no evidence of design. "Design is an illusion" we are told. Moreover, according to the more extreme elements of the neo-Darwinian school, the obvious progression from single cell, to Ediacaran fauna, to the Cambrian Explosion, to cartilaginous fish, to vertebrates, amphibian, reptile, repto-mammal, therapsid, mammal, primate, woman and man, is not progress, but "patterns without plans."

Nor have species become more complex and more intelligent. As neatly summed up by Harvard paleontologist S. J. Gould (1988, p. 319) "Progress is a noxious, culturally embedded, untestable, nonoperational, intractable idea that we must replace if we wish to understand the patterns of history." To bolster these arguments, some neo-Darwinians, point to the fact that much of the Earth's biomass consists of microbes and bacteria. Although, certainly, various strains of bacteria and species of plant, insect, and mammal, have remained relatively primitive or simple, so too have the cells of the skin vs the cells of the brain.

That relatively simple creatures have not disappeared and are abundant is not an argument against increasing complexity, design, growth, or progress. Complex species, like complex body parts, are often comprised of, or depend on, relatively simple elements or relatively simple creatures, such as bacteria, in order to survive. We would not be able to adequately digest our food without the assistance of various intestine-dwelling bacteria. Conversely, these bacteria would not be able to thrive outside our stomachs.

Complex creatures and simple plants, insects, and animals are mutually dependent and maintain interrelated lives. For increasingly complex species to have emerged on Earth required that other species undergo relatively little change other than in the form of diversification; otherwise the environment and atmosphere which sustains us could not be maintained.

To point to the existence of bacteria or simple plants and primitive insects, and then arrogantly state that the existence of these simple creatures somehow balances out and thus negates the obvious evidence of evolutionary progress, is philosophically naive and completely disingenuous. It is an argument which is not to be taken seriously. In fact, there is obvious evidence of progress not only among vertebrates but even among insects and plants (Joseph, 2001).

PROGRESS

Be it plant, insect, or animals, life on this planet has been characterized by a progressive metamorphosis where increasingly complex and intelligent species have emerged in a logical, step-wise, sequential pattern. There is nothing random about the evolution of plants, insects or animals, as demanded by Darwinian theory. Rather, the evidence indicates purposeful progressive evolutionary growth; i.e. metamphorsis.

By contrast, not only do the more extreme neo-Darwinians argue against all evidence of progress, but they claim that evolution is completely random, and is due to coincidence, chance variations, and "random mutations"—mutations that just happen to be advantageous instead of killing the host (as is common).

Of course, it is also fair to say that numerous scientists who accept Darwin as a matter of faith, believe in progress and deny that variations, or mutations are random. Certainly, the evidence and belief in progress conflicts with the neo-Darwinian view of evolution. Indeed, it is the utter predictability of evolutionary change which has enabled so many scientists to rely on the precise ticking of a genetic, molecular clock, to make predictions regarding the emergence and divergence of ancestral species. However, once a scientist strays from orthodoxy and begins accepting data that conflicts and refutes the theory, then that same scientist should reject the theory, i.e. Darwinism.

Not only does the fossil record and the evolution of the body and the brain clearly reveal progress, and a step-wise, sometimes leaping progression, which has led from simple celled creatures to woman and man, but the human genome represents a culmination of that progress.

For example. there are more protein-coding genes in the human genome as compared to other species including Amoeba dubia. What has also significantly increased in size and complexity, are the genetic engines of evolution, introns, i.e. transposons and regulatory and "silent" genes. As compared to all other genomes so far sequenced, human introns have become larger and longer as compared, for example, to fly or worm, i.e., about 50 kb versus 5 kb (Birney et al., 2001). "Worm and fly have a reasonably tight intron distribution, with most introns near the preferred minimum intron length (47 bp for worm, 59 bp for fly) and an extended tail (overall average length of 267 bp for worm and 487 bp for fly). There is a greater size distribution among human introns, with a peak at 87 bp but a very long tail resulting in a mean of more than 3,300 bp" (Birney et al., 2001).

The protein-encoding exons, on the other hand, are roughly the same size. Exons are also conserved, showing up in previous species, often in the same exact location.

Thus there has been an increase in the intron to exon ratio in the human genome which in turn is representative of the extreme importance of introns in human evolution and evolutionary change.

Human genes also differ from the genes of other species as they perform more complex and multi-tasking operations. The average human gene can make three to five primary protein products vs the genes of other species which can create one or two proteins (Aravind et al., 2001; Birney et al., 2001). This is progress.

Human proteins are more complex than the proteins in other organisms. Human proteins are capable of more interactions and do more things and perform more complex operations including alternative splicing tasks which enable them to generate a larger number of protein products. Humans, therefore, produce more proteins that are classified as falling into more than one functional category (426 in human versus 80 in worm and 57 in fly). This is progress.

There has also been an expansion of protein families. Protein families are more numerous in the human than in any other organism (Aravind et al., 2001). Again, contrary to Gould, this is evidence of progress.

In consequence, "the human genome contains greater numbers of genes, domain and protein families, paralogues, multi-domain proteins with multiple functions, and domain architectures. According to these measures, the relatively greater complexity of the human proteome is a consequence not simply of its larger size, but also of large-scale protein innovation" (Aravind et al., 2001).

Although the mantra "random variations" is the basis for Darwinian theology, the evolution of not just these genes but the vertebrate-specific protein domains and motifs have been created according to specific regulatory constraints, and have been built by rearranging preexisting components into a richer collection of domain architectures (IHGSC, 2001); the genetic foundation for their creation and the instructions for their creation, existed apriori. They were inherited. They did not randomly evolve.

SILENT GENES

Introns are "silent" genes, and contain "genes within genes" and can give birth to additional sequence segments, as well as additional genes and even gene clusters which are located deep within the intron; i.e. genes within genes (Henikoff et al. 1986; reviewed in Strachan & Read, 1996; Watson et al. 1992). If one were to twist apart the double helix of an intron, they may well discover "baby genes" and thus genes within genes, and, therefore, species within species locked within. Indeed, introns, and intronic gene clusters are considered a "hot spot" for homologous recombination (Wahls et al. 1990), which, over the course of "evolutionary metamorphosis" may have made possible not only the production of new genes and new nucleotide sequences, but the emergence of increasingly complex and intelligent creatures, such as woman and man.

Consider, for example, the metamorphosis of modern humans versus chimpanzees, both of which apparently descended, on Earth, from a common ancestor 5 million or more years ago (Sibley & Alhquist, 1984; Takahata et al., 1995). Chimpanzees and humans display a 99% homologous sequence identity in nucleotide base pair sequence organization, and 98.4% of activated/coded human and chimpanzee DNA is identical (Goodman, Tagle, & Fitch 1990). There are very few genes in the chimp genome whose counterparts cannot be found often in the same exact location in the human genome, though it is also apparent that chromosomes 4, 9, and 12 are configured somewhat differently.

Those few genes that have been inverted include AF4, which sits on chromosome 4 and which codes for a transcription factor related to leukemia in humans (reviewed in Gibbons, 1998). By contrast, those "chimpanzee" introns which have disappeared from the human genome include a few silent "satellite" introns which, in the chimp genome, are adjacent to the telomere (Royle et al. 1994), a structure which caps the chromosome and regulates gene expression and cell and DNA-based divisions. These chimpanzee introns appear to have shifted to a new position within the human chromosome (a common behavior of episomes, transposons, and plasmids), becoming exons and thus activated, and in so doing possibly promoting the transition from hominoid to hominid and thereby giving rise to the first humans in the process.

Introns are responsible for producing duplicate genes as well as new genes and clusters of genes, including numerous copies of highly repetitive sequences of nucleotide base pairs (Finnegan, 1989; Henikoff et al. 1986; Petes & Fink, 1982). The result is the creation of numerous sequence families (or gene families), some of which are dispersed throughout the genome (Jelinek et al. 1980). They are also involved in the creation of novel gene families due to gene incorporation. But perhaps most importantly, introns, and the traits they code for, exist prior to their expression. Their existence and their function cannot be explained by Darwinism, though introns are in fact the engines of "evolution."

Intronic regions of the genome are also the most likely to produce exons and to incorporate plasmids, episomes, and transposons. And, in addition to other genetic regulators, introns act to signal the exact sequence and segment length of exonic nucleotides which are to be copied and transcribed by RNA (Belfort, 1991, 1993; Breathnach et al., 1978; Watson et al., 1992; Witkowski, 1988). These protein encrusted introns instruct RNA as to how much of each segment is to be copied. If different "starter" or "stop" introns are activated this results in different segments or sequence lengths becoming expressed, thereby producing a different product. Hence, variation and diversity can be differentially induced if different "starter" exons or promoter introns are activated. Increasingly complex and intelligent species can also be produced if an intron leaps to yet another region of the genome and is expressed.

Introns found in the human genome, are also found in the genomes of other species, often in the same exact location. However, once the intron is expressed, it becomes an exon and, again, the same exact exonic genes can be found in other species who thus show the same exact traits. What this means is that introns, and the traits they encode for, exist prior to their expression. This also means that the traits they encode also remain "silent" and exist apriori. Traits and genes do not randomly evolve, but exist prior to their expression, and may be passed on from one species to another until they are finally expressed.

This theory was first proposed by Joseph in 1997, and experimentally verified in 1998, when Rutherford and Lindquist demonstrated that "populations contain a surprising amount of unexpressed genetic variation that is capable of affecting certain" supposedly "invariant traits" and that changes in environmental conditions "can uncover this previously silent variation" (Rutherford & Lindquist, 1998 p. 341). Indeed, much of the genome is silent, and these silent genes, and these silent traits can be expressed by varying the environment and through other stresses including fluctuations in temperature, oxygen levels, and diet (e.g., de Jong & Scharloo, 1976; Dykhuizen & Hart, 1980; Gibson & Hogness, 1996; Polaczyk et al., 1998; Rutherford & Lindquist, 1998; Wade et al., 1997).

Further support has been provided by Dr. Martin Yanofsky, of the University of California, San Diego, who activated silent genes to produce flower petals from leaves. Specifically, Yanofsky and

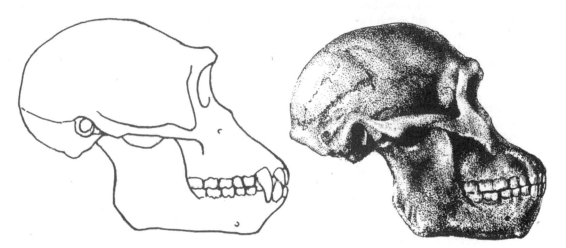

Figure 38. *The skull of Australopithecus and a chimpanzee.*

colleagues demonstrated that when they deactivated the sepallata (SEP) genes, flowers that normally consist of sepals, petals, stamens and carpells, were reduced to consisting only of sepals. Thus, the SEP gene is necessary for petals, stamens and carpells formation. Yanofsky et al., report that although the SEP genes are active in flowering plants, and silent in leaves and nonflowering plants, that they were able to activate these silent SEP genes, and in result, leaves were converted into petals.

Silent genes, therefore, can be activated to produce traits, including evolutionary advanced traits, that exist prior to their expression. They are inherited. They do not randomly evolve.

Much of the genome consists of silent intronic genes and nucleotide sequences. Silent genes and silent nucleotide sequences have the capacity to make copies of themselves, and to shift position within the genome (i.e. "jumping genes"): referred to as transposons. Transposable nucleotides show a tendency to leap to the more active GC regions. Once they are incorporated, they thus increase gene density and nucleotide content. These silent genes and silent nucleotides also come to be expressed, and/or they exert regulatory, inhibitory, or activating influences on other genes once they leap to the GC regions. However, these gene activity is not random. It is highly regulated. In other words (and contrary to Darwinism), genes (and the traits they code for) that exist apriori may change position in the genome and become active; and they leap from the non-coding to the coding regions of the genome in a purposeful, controlled, regulated, and predictable fashion.

As transposons are often copies of genes and silent nucleotide sequences, and often copies of copies, the GC regions also consist of more duplicate and repeat sequences of nucleotides than the AT regions. By contrast, more non-repeats are found in the AT regions. However, as pointed out by the International Human Genome Sequencing Consortium, (IHGSC, 2001) "Much of the 'non-repeat' DNA in AT-rich regions probably consists of ancient repeats that are not detectable by current methods."

In other words, many of the transposable elements which have shifted from AT regions to GC regions, where they are then expressed, are themselves exceedingly ancient and likely have pedigrees which extend interminably backwards in time. The findings reported by the International Human Genome Sequencing Consortium, are thus entirely consistent with the theories of evolutionary metamorphosis and intelligent design which posit that "silent" ancestral genes are passed down to subsequent generations and subsequent species, where they may later come to be activated thereby expressing silent traits that had been precoded into the genomes of our ancient ancestors. Genes and traits do not randomly evolve, they are precoded and exist apriori, and are inherited and passed on from species to species in silent form, waiting for a signal to be expressed —findings which are completely contrary to Darwinism.

Genes may be silent (introns) or expressed (exons). Each active gene also consists of active and silent nucleotide sequences. The silent sequences (introns) act as boundaries which define and frame the active zones (exons). The active zones, therefore, have also been referred to as "frames" that consist of exonic nucleotides bordered by introns which may be acting not only to "frame" but to regulate gene expression. If the frame is extended or shortened by a single nucleotide, a "frame shift" results, and the genetic code is altered: just as 3456, becomes a different product if we add or delete a number (63456). Frame shifts are also important contributors to evolutionary metamorphosis, and are largely due to the movement or activity of intronic transposons (as well as the shuffling of exons).

Intronic genes often contain genes-within genes. Intronic genes also make duplicates of themselves. How many genes are duplicates is unknown. However, gene duplication, that is whole gene duplication (WGD) has played a significant role in evolutionary metamorphosis. "In principle, WGD provides the raw material for great bursts of evolutionary change by allowing the duplication and divergence of entire pathways. WGD has played a key role in evolution" (IHGSC, 2001).

For example, there is evidence to suggest that two WGD events triggered the transition from invertebrates to vertebrates, and is thus partly responsible for vertebrate evolution; giving rise, perhaps to the first jawless fish around 500 million years ago.

Additional WGB events may have also contributed to the evolution of primates and then humans. For example, numerous human genes are duplicates and occur in sets of four homologues (e.g., the four HOX genes) which are clustered together on chromosomes 2, 7, 12 and 17; and these appear to have been duplicated at about the time when primates diverged from (non-primate) mammals, and when hominids diverged from hominoids (IHGSC, 2001). For example, a WGB event occurred around 30 million years ago when old world monkeys and apes diverged, and this was followed by a second duplication event between 5 to10 million years ago when hominoids and various species of Australopithecus diverged. This later duplication resulted in the creation of two genes on each side of the chromosome 5 centromere (Courseaux & Nahon 2001).

Transposons (intronic "jumping genes" and nucleotides) have also played a significant role in evolutionary metamorphosis. DNA transposons can produce large-scale chromosome rearrangements, and at least 47 human genes and almost half the human genome have been derived from transposons (IHGSC, 2001). Transposons do not provide any selective advantage for any individual host, but for progeny and thus subsequent generations and subsequent species. This is accomplish in part, by contributing regulatory elements and new genes to the genome which gives rise to new traits and thus new species —all of which have been programmed into the genetic code, the expression of which is under tight regulatory constraints.

This process of creating new genes and duplicate genes is not random, nor is it due to mutation, but is under genetic control and functions in accordance with precise genetic instructions (Berkner, 1988; Moss et al. 1990; Wigler, et al. 1979).

FRAME SHIFTS

The evolution of species, variations among and between species, and the evolution of seemingly "new" adaptive characteristics are a function of a variety of genetic and environmental factors. These include exon shuffling, nucleotide duplications and recombinations, the dispersal of nucleotide sequences to new genomic sites, and in particular, the intronic birth of additional genes.

As noted, genes have the capacity to express a variety of products. Sometimes all it takes are exceedingly minuscule and often minor changes in the location and coding of genes and the coding of different lengths of nucleotide sequence segments to produce wholly different products and appendages (e.g., Drake, 1991; John & Miklos, 1988; Moran et al., 1999; Symmonds, 1991).

For example, there is a specific human gene and nucleotide sequence for human dystrophin. Yet, this same gene can be differentially activated to produce muscle cells if its nucleotide sequence is extended by just a few base pairs. Moreover, this same gene can produce motor neurons and induce Purkinjee, brain cell development; that is, if the same sequence "start point" is located and activated 100 kb upstream (reviewed in Watson et al., 1992). Different traits and different products can be generated by simply extending, or reducing the number of nucleotides in a given sequence. This is referred to as a "frame shift." However, again, these genes and sequences, exist prior to their activation. They did not "evolve," they were inherited.

As is well known, sequences of nucleotides are divided into coding (exons) and non-coding (introns) segments. Introns instruct RNA as to how much of each segment is to be copied. If different "starter" or "stop" introns are activated this results in different segments or sequence lengths becoming expressed, thereby producing a different product; products which are genetically precoded.

Therefore, variation and diversity can be differentially induced if different "starter" exons or promoter introns are activated and an almost unlimited variety of products, structures, and even species can be produced by just minute shifts in nucleotide sequence organization and activation.

Consider, for example, HIV. In a 1996 nationwide AIDS study conducted by the National Cancer Institute, it was discovered that some men who fall prey to the disease, develop the infection very slowly, live significantly longer, whereas others never become infected even after years of engaging in indiscriminate homosexual activity with infected partners. It was determined that these "non-progressors" fail to become seriously ill or infected apparently because they inherited a protective gene (CKR-5) from both of their parents (Centers for Disease Control, 1996). This gene produces proteins (chemokines) which aids in resisting HIV invasion of the immune system (and which protects CD-4 membrane receptors).

Nevertheless, this protective gene is not the result of a genetic mutation, but is secondary to a slight "frame shift" in the activation of the nucleotide sequences in that particular gene. That is, a shorter segment of nucleotide base pairs has been coded and expressed in these individuals and their progeny. Moreover, this particular gene existed prior to the development of the AIDS epidemic, for again, it was inherited and found to exist in the parents of those exposed, and in their parent's parents as well as in other humans. This gene is not a mutant but existed apriori. The gene was inherited. By contrast, mutation is always a pathological process.

Rather, because of a slight frame shift in the coding of a specific sequence of nucleotides, a slightly different product was produced in these "nonprogressors" and their parents. Moreover, the potential to produce this product also exists in the genomes of other humans, and their parents, and their parents such that this gene probably has an ancestry that extends interminably into the long ago.

Again, if different "starter" or "stop" introns are activated this results in different segments or sequence lengths becoming expressed, thereby producing a different protein product. Hence, an almost unlimited variety of products, structures, and even species can be produced by just minute shifts in nucleotide sequence organization and activation, including, for example, the slight frame shift in sequence activation which resulted in the expression of the CRK-5 gene.

Likewise, consider the DNA for producing lymphocytes. As originally proposed by Macfarlane Burnet, and which has since been confirmed, the genetic instructions for producing every possible lymphocyte exists apriori; that is without prior exposure to the antigens which require their production. They exist prior to the diseases which make them necessary.

Hence, once a cell (and its DNA) comes into contact with a specific foreign antigen (including representatives of presumably new diseases), the genetic instructions for creating killer, anti-body making cells are activated and can thus fight and attack diseases that it has never before been exposed to; that is, never been exposed to on Earth. Even when exposed to a supposedly "new" pathogen, the genes already preexist for producing cells which are specifically designed so as to seek out, recognize, and attack this alien, foreign, invader including those representing diseases supposedly never before encountered.

These lymphocytes are not "mutations" but are preprogrammed into the genome and exist as intronic genetic memories which require only the appropriate stimulus in order to be expressed. When activated, these apriori lymphocytes are cloned in great numbers, a process referred to as "clonal selection."

Again, these genes and these traits did not "evolve." They were inherited--findings which refute and negate Darwinism.

GENETIC COMMONALTIES

Because genes and traits exist apriori, and as they may be stored as genes within genes (species within species), silent genes and the instructions for creating additional genes, can be passed on to subsequent generations and species. Because the instructions for the creation of additional and specific genes are also precoded, these instructions, but not the actual gene itself, may be passed on; albeit, in some instances as a gene within a gene. As such, two species that diverge from a common ancestor may later generate the same exact gene which the common ancestor (and its direct descendants) does not appear to possess.

Hence, myriad life forms contain the same exact nucleotide sequence segments and "master regulatory genes" which code for the development of the heart, lungs, eyes and brains (D'Souza et al. 1995; Garcia-Fernandex & Holland, 1994; Ruddle, et al. 1994; Strachan & Read, 1996; Watson et al. 1992) —DNA that was independently inherited from common ancestors that had neither heart, lungs, eyes, or brains. Hearts, lungs, etc., were genetically preprogrammed.

These functional, structural, and genetic commonalties include "genes such as Pax6/eyeless which are responsible for the development of eyes in diverse phyla..." and "the expression of distal-less homologues in insect and vertebrate legs, as well as other body growths" (Tautz, 1998). The vertebrate Pax-6 gene cluster is organized and expressed in almost an identical fashion in insects, worms, and mollusks, differing by only 3-6% (Quiring, et al. 1994; Zucker, 1994).

Obviously, identical structures and almost identical genes could not have randomly and independently evolved in three or five different phyla. Rather, they are either a function of gene and plasmid exchange, or they must have been passed on from a common ancestor as silent intronic genes, and genes within genes; genes which were expressed, coded and activated only in response to similar environmental conditions. These traits were preprogrammed to emerge like a chrysalis from a cocoon.

Other inexplicable commonalties include the "independent" evolution in both birds and mammals, of a "double pump" heart and the formation of a interventricular septum which induces a total separation of deoxygenated and oxygenated blood, and endothermy, i.e. the capacity to increase the production of endogenous metabolic energy. Both birds and mammals are endotherms, whereas reptiles and amphibians, the descendants of the common ancestors to birds and mammals, are exotherms who lack a double pump heart or an interventricular septum. And, the common ancestor to birds and mammals died out over 300 million years ago (Kumar & Hedges, 1998).

Likewise, although the common ancestors for birds and bats diverged from a common ancestor who could not fly, both evolved winglike characteristics from forelimbs that originally were not adapted for flight.

Hence, this common ancestor passed on genes which were genetically preprogrammed to give rise to these common features; genes that became activated once environmental conditions and other factors were altered sufficiently: the environment acts on gene selection, and the environment is genetically modified. The only other reasonable explanation is that copies of these genes were released into the environment as plasmids and were subsequently incorporated into the genomes of different highly evolved species (Joseph, 1997, 2000).

Even more remarkable: the human genome and the genome of the higher plants, share homologous DNA-promoters and binding domains (e.g. da and AS-C) including a similar "helix-loop-helix" motif which is involved in cellular division and neuron generation in vertebrates, as well as the production of ovaries and seeds in plants via CHS-A and -J promoters (Joseph, 1998c). These shared plant/flavone human/neural transcription factors, promoters, and genes act to regulate genetic transcription and thus the activation of other genes including those specifying neural vs cellular differentiation and development. However, the common ancestor for mammals and plants diverged anywhere from 1-2 billion years ago; 1 billion years before the evolution, on Earth, of neurons, seeds, or sex organs.

Hence, these traits and these genes were inherited and preprogrammed to emerge in response to changing environmental conditions, and/or were acquired through gene exchange. However, even if due to gene exchange, it can still be concluded that the genes responsible for creating ovaries, neurons, hearts, lungs and so on—or at least the genetic instructions for creating these genes—existed over a billion years ago. Ovaries, neurons, hearts, eyes and lungs did not randomly evolve, they were genetically preprogrammed.

Similarly, plants, fungi, amphibians, non-human mammals, and humans share two of the four HOX clusters of homeobox genes which play a significant role in determining the posterior-anterior axis during embryonic development (D'Souza, et al. 1995; Garcia-Fernandex & Holland, 1994; Harvey, 1996; John & Miklos, 1988; Ruddle, et al. 1994). And yet, the common ancestors for these different species diverged over 2 billion years ago. Indeed, Homeobox genes are exceedingly ancient (John & Miklos, 1988; Radetsky, 1992).

As argued in detail elsewhere (Joseph, 2001), over the course of evolution, innumerable species "evolved" identical characteristics and many of the same identical genes because they inherited from common ancestral stem species, the necessary DNA and the genetic instructions for the creation of these genes and these traits —traits and genes which could not be expressed until the emergence and creation of specific environmental, climatic, and atmospheric conditions (e.g., de Jong & Scharloo, 1976; Dykhuizen & Hart, 1980; Gibson & Hogness, 1996; Polaczyk et al., 1998; Rutherford & Lindquist, 1998; Wade et al., 1997)—conditions which were in fact biologically and genetically engineered. The genetically engineered changing environment promotes gene generation and acts on gene selection—genes which exist prior to their selection, and genes, once activated, that begin to act on the environment, which acts on gene selection, and so on.

Consider, again, the "language gene" which is found, in non-activated form, in non-human mammals. Since only DNA can produce DNA, and as the genetic instructions for creating new genes is contained in DNA, it would appear that these silent genetic instructions and thus the capability for producing all manner of products and species must have existed as intronic genetic potential in the DNA of our ancestors (e.g. Belfort, 1991; Finnegan, 1989; Kuhsel et al. 1990). This would include, of course, the DNA of those creatures who may well have been fashioned by "god" or flung upon the face of our planet billions of years ago; genetic traits that were perhaps coded as silent intronic genetic potential into the double helix of maybe even the very first single celled Adam and Eve.

It is due to the inheritance of dormant, silent intronic genes, and/or their donation and exchange between different organisms (e.g. Mikkelsen et al., 1996; Watson et al., 1992), and their subsequent activation and reorganization, which accounts for the seemingly independent evolution of identical body parts in diverse species (Joseph, 1996, 1997, 2000).

It is because humans and other species have so many of the same exact genes (D'Souza et al. 1995; Garcia-Fernandex & Holland, 1994; Ruddle, et al. 1994; Strachan & Read, 1996; Watson et al. 1992), that they have been able to "evolve" almost identical brains and complex body parts (eyes, wings, fingers and hands), and similar modes of communicating, speaking, behaving, competing or having sex (e.g. Chomsky, 1957, 1972; Ekman, 1993; Eible-Elbesfeldt, 1993; Joseph, 1993, 1996, 2000; Waal, 1989; Wickler, 1973); although they inherited these genes and these behaviors from common ancestors which did not display these traits.

Again, one need only examine the heart, the brain, the skeletal system, and so on, in order to observe what often amounts to little more than slight structural variations between distantly related species whose common ancestors were devoid of similar traits in order to conclude that these traits and the expression of these genes and behaviors were genetically preprogrammed. In other words, evolution is not due to the natural selection of "random mutations," or the coincidence of nature arriving at the same exact solution by chance, but is genetically preprogrammed, and unfolds in accordance with the DNA-instructions inherited from creatures that first emerged on Earth--creatures which were either fashioned by intelligent design, or which came from other planets, or both.

Just as a caterpillar is genetically programmed to undergo metamorphosis and emerge as a moth or butterfly, so too were humans and all manner of creatures (or variations thereof) genetically programmed to emerge, equipped with similar genes and similar traits that were inherited from those life forms which were among the first to take root on this planet.

INTELLIGENT DESIGN

The structure of DNA is such that it contains the genetic instructions, or at least, the genetic capability, for creating all manner of life; some of this information being stored within introns. DNA also contains the instructions for genetically engineering the environment in order to promote DNA dispersal and development. Although Darwin and current neo-Darwinian evolutionary biologists such as Gould insist that variation is random, or that there is absolutely no evidence of "design" (Dawkins, 1987), this view is completely at odds with the facts and with what is known about DNA.

Certainly, natural selection is not "random." Contrary to Darwin's and neoDarwinian theory, there is also nothing random about the organization or expression of DNA (Calladine & Drew, 1992; Strachan & Read, 1996; Watson et al., 1992) which is the source of all variation. There is nothing randomly variable about DNA or its expression of variability, except, perhaps in regard to those "mutations" that result in disease and death. In fact, almost all species maintain vast genetic libraries that have been conserved for hundreds of millions of years (D'Souza et al. 1995; Garcia-Fernandex & Holland, 1994; Miklos & Rubin, 1996; Ruddle, et al. 1994; Strachan & Read, 1996; Tautz, 1998; Watson et al., 1992).

According to Courseaux & Nahon (2001) of the Human Genome Project, "the many processes in genome evolution have shown that de novo generation of building blocks—single genes or gene segments coding for protein domains—seems to be rare." That is, new genes are not produced randomly or by chance. "Instead, genome novelty was mainly built by modification, duplication, and functional changes of the available blocks by processes of gene duplication, exon shuffling, or retrotransposition of genes." The creation of new genes has been under precise regulatory control (Courseaux & Nahon, 2001).

Likewise, Caron et al., (2001) of the Human Genome Project, have concluded that "highly expressed genes" and clusters of interacting genes, "cannot be explained by random variation." These analyses show that regions of highly expressed genes most likely represent a higher order structure in the genome (Caron et al. 2001). In fact, the chromosomes themselves "reveal a higher order organization of the genome" (Caron et al. 2001).

Dr. Gene Myers, chief computer scientist at the Maryland headquarters of Celera Genomics, who was responsible for creating the map of the human genome has stated that the architecture of DNA is so incredibly complex, "It's like it was designed."

That "design" includes the clock-like functioning of those genes which have given rise to "new" species, albeit in a clock-like, highly predictable fashion. For example, as is evident based on ribosomal RNA, over the course of the last 3 billion and more years, genetically programmed species and preprogrammed traits, have come to be expressed in a step-wise fashion, as if programmed by a preset "genetic clock."

All species contain similar types of ribosomal RNA (rRNA). However, there are obvious differences between species in base pair rRNA organization. There is nothing random about these differences, as they in fact differ in a predictable step-wise fashion as we ascend the ancestral tree. For example, those species which have an almost identical nucleotide base pair rRNA organization presumably diverged only recently or have diverged only minimally, e.g., bacteria.

When comparing humans to bacteria, there are significant and predictable differences in the sequences of DNA and RNA nucleotide bases, and it is these same predictable differences which have enabled various investigators to make accurate and verifiable predictions about divergence or the emergence of various species.

Data from a "molecule clock" based on the analysis of eight different genes in seven different classes of invertebrates (e.g. starfish, snails, eels, spiders), for example, predicted the existence of invertebrates which diverged over 1 billion years ago (Wray et al., 1996)—a prediction since verified by Seilacher et al., (1998) who found evidence of complex multi-cellular organisms in sediments over 1 billion years old.

And, it was data derived from a "molecule clock" which predicted that complex fully modern microbes had become established over 3 billion years ago (Woese, 1989, Woese et al., 1990)—a prediction that has now been repeatedly verified (Hoffman et al., 1999; Mojzsis, et al., 1996; Schopf, 1993, 1999).

Likewise, genetic data from a "molecular clock," that is, from the genes of more than 200 modern animal species, also corresponds with fossil findings indicating that the ancestors to birds and mammals diverged over 310 million years ago, and that the ancestors of modern mammals, including elephants, horses and cows, emerged 20 million to 45 million years before the demise of the dinosaurs (Kumar & Hedges, 1998).

In fact, this same step-wise sequential progression is evident from an examination of the approximately 100 amino acids that comprise an exceedingly important protein which participates in oxygen utilization: cytochrome c. Cytochrome c. is found in all animals, and consists of amino acids. However, cytochrome c. becomes increasingly different, albeit in a step-wise, clock-like fashion, as we descend the ancestral tree. Of the approximately 100 amino acids that comprise human cytochrome c 99 are identical to those of other primates, such as the rhesus monkey, 89 are shared with other mammals, 86 with reptiles, 82 with amphibians, 79 with fish, 69 with the silkworm, 57 with wheat, and 55 are identical to those of yeast (Denton, 1986; de Duve, 1995).

This progression is evident not only based on DNA, but the fossil record. Complex life has evolved in an organized and purposeful, step-wise manner, leading from simple cell to all manner of creatures, including modern woman and man.

THE TICKING OF THE GENETIC CLOCK

The progressive metamorphosis of increasingly intelligent and complex life on this planet, culminating in the emergence of modern woman and man, appears to have unfolded in a genetically predetermined, "molecular clockwise" fashion. That "evolution" is regulated in accordance with the "ticking" of a genetic "clock" is evident from an examination and comparison of various genes and ribosomal RNA belonging to diverse species (e.g., Denton, 1998; Kumar & Hedges, 1998; Lewin, 1988; Wray et al., 1996; Woese et al., 1990). Because this genetic "clock" appears to have been "ticking" at the same rate, simultaneously, among all branches of the tree of life (Denton, 1998), and as this "clock" on Earth, began to "tick" almost 4 billion years ago, it thus appears that the continued "ticking" of this same "genetic clock" has determined the successive emergence of increasingly intelligent and complex species (e.g., Kumar & Hedges, 1998), culminating in woman and man.

Just as the genome of the caterpillar is programmed to produce a butterfly, or the DNA of a fertilized ovum gives rise to an embryo then a fetus... neonate... child... juvenile... adult, the metamorphosis and progression which characterizes life on this planet appears to have been preprogrammed into the DNA of some of the first Earthlings. It is this genetic predetermination which also explains why although the Earth has been struck five times by life-destroying meteors, that certain species immediately recovered, and why no new phyla have emerged since the Cambrian Explosion.

As summed up by Denton (1998) "the rate of change in many genes is regulated by a clock which seems to tick simultaneously in all branches of the tree of life." Indeed, this was evident over a decade ago, for according to Lewin (1988), "the notion of and evidence for a molecular clock... has become... pervasive."

The expression of this genetic clock requires that the climate, atmosphere, oceans, and the environment, be genetically engineered so as to prepare the planet for those yet to be born. Thus, the environment is also modified in a genetically preprogrammed clock-wise fashion (Joseph, 1997, 2000). Indeed, the environment acts on gene selection (de Jong & Scharloo, 1976; Dykhuizen & Hart, 1980; Gibson & Hogness, 1996; Polaczyk et al., 1998; Rutherford & Lindquist, 1998; Wade et al., 1997), which acts on the environment, which acts on gene selection, thereby creating a complex feedback mechanism which gives rise to diverse products and species. And these genetically engineered environmental changes have acted on the DNA of each successive generation of species, our ancestors, whose DNA gave birth to our own.

There are in fact, genes (e.g., tim, mTim, hTIM) and proteins which perform specific "clock-like" timing functions and which interact to form regulatory feedback loops (Clayton et al., 2001). Moreover, these "genetic clocks" have been shown to be directly in tune with changing environmental and climatic conditions.

Specifically, the clock-like regulatory genes and proteins so far identified are composed of interacting positive and negative transcriptional translational feedback loops, the core components of which include two basic helix-loop-helix (bHLH)/PAS-containing transcription factors, CLOCK and BMAL1 which interact and pair up via their PAS (protein) domains (PER, ARNT and SIM. These transcription factors perform clock-like circadian operations in fungi, insects and mammals.

CLOCK and BMAL1 drive the rhythmic transcription of three Period genes (mPer1-mPer3) and two Cryptochrome genes (mCry1 and mCry2) which interact to inhibit transcription, forming a negative feedback loop. According to Clayton et al., (2001) "at the same time, mPER2 contributes to the transcription of Bmal1, which is rhythmically expressed with a peak phase opposite to that of mPer/mCry, forming a positive feedback loop. The push-pull action of the positive and negative feedback loops perpetuates the self-sustaining nature of the circadian clock" which in turn is sensitive to seasonal and climatic fluctuations.

These canonical clock genes and their homologues have been identified in Drosophila (tim) mice (mTim) and humans (hTIM), as well as in the worm, Caenorhabditis elegans (tim-1). According to Clayton et al., (2001) these findings suggest that the "closely related worm tim-1, mouse/human Tim and fly tim-2 genes are descendants of an ancestral timeless gene that duplicated in the arthropod lineage after the split with nematodes and vertebrates."

However, these genes exist prior to their selection and are expressed in a highly regulated, predictable fashion, which refutes darwinsim. Evidence based on DNA, genetics, and the fossil record refute Darwinism. The ticking of the genetic clock refutes Darwinism.

Genes and the traits they code for, exist prior to their expression, and many genes have been expressed in a predictable, clock-like fashion, thus giving rise, in a step-wise sequence, to increasingly complex and intelligent species.

Because the emergence of H. sapiens sapiens, and all manner of species appears to have been genetically preprogrammed to emerge in a predictable, step-wise fashion, this phenomenon has been referred to as "evolutionary metamorphosis" (Joseph, 1996, 1997, 2000a). However, rather than a 9-month gestation period, or the single seasonal metamorphosis which characterizes the transition from caterpillar to butterfly, humans are an end product, or perhaps a midway product of a process which takes several billion years to unfold; albeit in accordance and in parallel with suitable changes in the genetically engineered environment.

Thus, metamorphosis is not a one-step progression (caterpillar-butterfly) but a leaping, branching, multistep progression involving numerous successive species, many of which are genetically preprogrammed to give rise to the next in a "molecular clock-like" fashion. The ticking of this genetic clock, however, also requires that the environment be genetically engineered in preparation for the generation of subsequent species.

DNA-SUPRA ORGANISMS

All forms of life consist of packages of DNA which have manufactured an organism in order to interact with the environment. A fat hairy spider crawling along the ceiling is the product of DNA engineering, and each and every spider-cell contains a packet of DNA which created the cell and which contributed to the creation of the spider. The "spider" is merely a vehicle through which the DNA navigates its way around the world. The same is true of fish, frogs, reptiles, and so on. These are manifestations of DNA activity and every organism functions in accordance with specific DNA-instructions.

DNA strives for expression and dispersal. According to the theory of evolutionary metamorphosis, the DNA of diverse species are also interactional and together may be viewed as constituting a supra-DNA-organism which acts on the environment in order to promote DNA activation and dispersal. That is, DNA acts to genetically engineer the environment which in turn acts on gene selection which acts on the environment which leads to the expression and dispersal of additional DNA. Thus, just as DNA contains the instructions for creating and nourishing an embryo in parallel with the genetic alteration of the womb, DNA also contains the instructions for altering itself and the external environment so as to promote not just diversity, but the emergence of increasingly complex and intelligence animals, including the likes of woman and man.

Recognizing the role played by diverse species-and thus their DNA in the biological construction of the atmosphere, climate, and even the contents of the oceans, is integral to understanding evolutionary metamorphosis, including extinction, and the failure of some species to "evolve." Just as body parts or dead cells may be sloughed off or absorbed during embryonic, fetal, and neonatal development, over the course of "evolution" some species have been sloughed off and became extinct once they were no longer needed. Just as some body parts remain relatively simple, e.g. the cells of the skin versus the nerve cells of the brain, over the course of "evolution" some species have remained relatively simple and others have become more complex—all are integral to the survival of the supra-DNA-organism.

Again, the DNA or diverse species can be seen as an interactional supra-DNA organism which acts on the environment. Once certain organisms have accomplished their genetic mission, they become extinct, whereas other cells, including simple organisms continue to thrive as their output is essential to maintaining and promoting life—that is, the life of the supra-DNA-organism. Coupled with unforeseen environmental catastrophes, the need to modify the environment in order to promote DNA dispersal and development, and the fact that the environment acts on gene selection and activation (e.g., de Jong & Scharloo, 1976; Dykhuizen & Hart, 1980; Gibson & Hogness, 1996; Polaczyk et al., 1998; Rutherford & Lindquist, 1998; Wade et al., 1997) explains the periodic lack of progress in complexity over eons of time, and then the sudden surges in progress and complexity, during different epochs of the Earth's history.

THE ENVIRONMENT REQUIRES SOME CREATURES TO REMAIN SIMPLE IN ORGANIZATION

It is necessary that some species remain relatively simple and basically identical to their ancestors from billions of years ago. There is a genetic need to maintain certain environmental, climatic and atmospheric conditions (such as oxygen levels). In consequence, certain species never progress. In fact, there are specific repressor proteins and a variety of genetic mechanisms which act to prevent genetic change, even in response to changing environmental conditions. For example, regulator proteins referred to as "chaperones have been found in all organisms studied and protect against" genetic change or activation such as in response to changing environmental and climatic conditions and other stresses, such as alterations in oxygen levels (Cossins, 1998).

For example, a genetically manufactured protein, "Hsp90 is one of the more abundant chaperones. At normal temperatures it binds to a specific set of proteins, most of which regulate cellular proliferation and embryonic development. These signaling proteins form complex webs of molecular switches that allows signals both within and between cells to be transduced into responses... and act against genetic variation" and prevent the expression of silent characteristics (Cossins, 1998, pp. 309-310). For example, these proteins may prevent DNA expression by acting as a buffer between these silent genes and nucleotides and the environment, so that they are not expressed except in accordance with specific genetic instructions.

Again, consider Hsp90. Hsp90 targets multiple signal transducers which control and act as "molecular switches" which in turn control gene expression. Hsp90 "normally suppresses the expression of genetic variation affecting many developmental pathways" (Rutherford & Lindquist, 1998). However, Hsp90, also reacts to environmental stress including diet and fluctuations in temperature (Rutherford & Lindquist, 1998). As demonstrated by Rutherford and Lindquist (1998, p. 341) Hsp90 acts as an "explicit molecular mechanism that assists the process of evolutionary change in response to the environment" and it accomplishes this through the "conditional release of stores of hidden morphological variation.... perhaps allowing for the rapid morphological radiations that are found in the fossil record."

However, in order for these repressor proteins and other regulating genetic mechanisms to be switched off or on, requires contact and exposure to specific environmental agents.

Initially, the new Earth was devoid and lacking these environmental agents, such as free oxygen, calcium, and so on. Hence, in order for certain genes and gene sequences to be activated, required that these products be liberated and/or manufactured. Hence, some species immediately began secreting oxygen as a waste product, which in turn acted on gene selection.

It is because of the genetic need to create a precursor product in massive amounts (such as calcium), which explains why some species emerge, thrive, alter the environment, and then become extinct. Some species emerge simply to produce a specific product and are then jettisoned. Just as the placenta is a nurturing biological construction that is jettisoned with the birth of the baby, there have been periods when much of the Earth's biomass served only to produce and secrete products that were fundamental for the metamorphosis of future, more complex species, such as calcium to build bones. Once their genetic mission was accomplished, many of these creatures were jettisoned and became extinct. Consider, again, the calcium carbonate secreting Ediacaran fauna.

As oxygen levels increased in the atmosphere and in the sea, and as the planet again began to warm, oxygen breathing multicellular eukaryotes emerged (e.g. Brocks et al., 1999). By 2.3 billion years ago the Earth's land masses were covered with thick bacterial mats and other organisms. Many of these organisms secreted a variety of organic acids which formed laterites (iron rich deposits) by leaching iron from the upper layers of rock and soil. However, as pointed out by Dr. Ohmoto, "in order for laterites to form, there must be organic material and atmospheric oxygen;" substances secreted by and the residue of even earlier life forms.

By 1.6 billion years B.P., the Earth's climate and environment had been dramatically altered and animals began evolving into different species (e.g., Hedges & Kumar, 1999) who in turn began to prepare the world for subsequent generations. Then around 600 million years ago the calcium carbonate secreting Ediacaran emerged in every ocean and sea, releasing materials into the environment which enabled shellfish and bony complex oxygen-breathing creatures to "evolve" and undergo metamorphosis.

However, the Ediacaran fauna and subsequent generations would not have been able to thrive if not for the thick layers of bacteria which had been building up for over 2 billion years —much of which then served to nourish the Ediacaran fauna and those who emerged during the early phases of the Cambrian Explosion—just as thick mats of blood cells sustain the ovum within the womb. One species served as the nutrients for a later appearing species who prepared the world for the next generation of increasingly complex organisms.

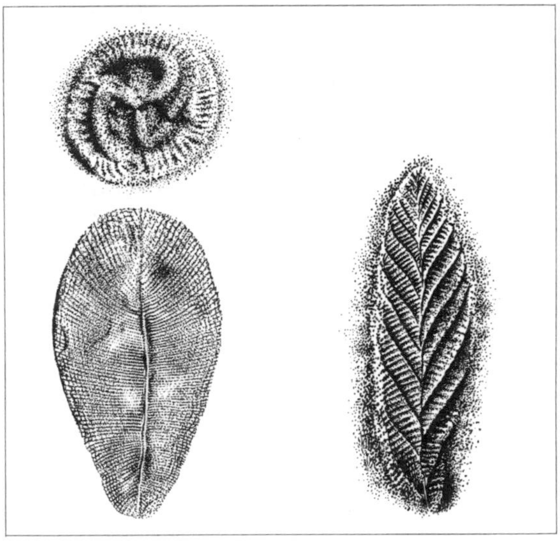

Figure 39. Ediacaran fossils from the late pre-Cambrian period. A Tribachidium (above), sea pen (right) annelid worm (left). Reprinted from Fortey 1982, Fossils. Van Nostrand Reinhold, New York.

THE CAMBRIAN EXPLOSION

THE METAMORPHOSIS OF THE EDIACARAN FAUNA

Ediacaran fossils have been discovered throughout the world, and date from 580 billion to 560 billion years B.P. (though some authors have assigned them a date of 600 million years B.P.) These were soft bodied, leaf- and disk-shaped, plant-like creatures, consisting of only 11 or fewer cell types (compared with over 200 cell types for mammals). They ranged in size from over 3.5 feet to less than 1/2 inch (Glaessner, et al. 1988). They also rather suddenly became extinct.

The emergence of Ediacaran fauna was not just a genetic experiment gone awry, as some scientists have speculated, for these creatures and their waste products altered the planet so as to make the next stage of metamorphosis possible. Because they secreted calcium carbonate, from which shells and bones are constructed, the Ediacaran fauna made possible the metamorphosis of shell fish and the skeletal system. Once their genetic mission was accomplished, the Ediacarans disappeared from the scene and there followed an explosion of shelly and bony life in every ocean, lake, river and stream—aptly referred to as the Cambrian Explosion as it took place during the Cambrian era.

THE CAMBRIAN EXPLOSION

"If it could be demonstrated that any complex organ existed which could not possibly have been formed by numerous successive, slight modifications, my theory would absolutely break down." -Darwin, 1857.

With no history of derivative ancestral forms, all manner of complex life suddenly emerged with gills, intestines, joints, brains, and modern eyes equipped with retinas and fully modern optic lenses. These included organisms with a hard tubelike outer-skeleton consisting of calcium carbonate, and all manner of "small shelly fish" (Anabrites, Protohertzina), as well as sponges, jelly fish, mollusks, brachiopods, and the first arthropods (e.g. trilobites) which immediately sprouted legs and primitive brains. In fact, every phylum in existence today emerged during the Cambrian Explosion, including some phyla which emerged then became extinct.

The survivors included the phylum Chordata; i.e. tunicates and the first jawless fish who possessed a notochord and simplified brain that consisted of a brainstem and limbic forebrain.

Hence, during the Cambrian epoch there was also a cerebral and thus a cognitive explosion as the first true brains were established; brains which would continue to "grow" and continue to undergo a genetically preprogrammed metamorphosis until finally ending up in human heads.

And yet, just as the Ediacaran fauna emerged, secreted massive amounts of calcium, and then departed the scene, an incredible number of phyla emerged during the Cambrian explosion, made their own genetically engineered contributions, and then became extinct—a pattern of sometimes inexplicable species extinction that has been repeated time and again. Again, just as the placenta is jettisoned after it serves its purpose, innumerable species have died out once they had made their contributions to the next stage of "evolutionary" development.

Thus, we see that major species have emerged, flourished, diversified, modified the environment, and then died out, only to be followed by yet another wave of "novel" species who followed the same pattern, releasing and secreting additional "waste" products and thus making their own contribution to the environment and the development of the next wave of diverse species, their descendants, before disappearing from the scene. However with each successive wave there has been not just diversity, but progress, environmental change, and increased complexity in design and intelligence, leading from simple cellular organisms to all manner of species, including woman and man.

EVOLUTIONARY METAMORPHOSIS

The astrobiological evolutionary metamorphosis theory of life and the evidence of intelligent design, is a complete departure from Darwin's theory and neo-Darwinian theories of evolution, which instead claim that "evolution" is due to random mutations and random variations. It is also a complete departure from those more extreme neo-Darwinians who deny that evolution is characterized by the progressive emergence of increasingly complex and intelligent animal life.

The theory of evolutionary metamorphosis is based on genetics and the fossil record (Joseph, 1996, 2000). By contrast, Darwin's theory is not supported by the fossil record and is refuted by genetics—as there is nothing random about DNA/RNA or DNA/RNA expression—the source of all supposed "random mutations." Indeed, his theory does not even taken into account progress, but only variation; and aspects of life on this planet has become not just variable, but increasingly complex.

As repeatedly stressed, "traits" exist prior to their expression, being genetically preprogrammed into the genetic code (de Jong & Scharloo, 1976; Gibson & Hogness, 1996; Polaczyk et al., 1998; Rutherford & Lindquist, 1998; Wade et al., 1997). And, not just traits, but the instructions for the creation of increasingly complex species have been genetically preprogrammed—and progress and the fossil record is not compatible with Darwin's theory.

What is supported by the fossil record, is the theory of "natural selection" which was first developed by A.R. Wallace. Wallace's theory of "natural selection" (and particularly his theory as to the evolution of woman and man) is fully compatible with the theory of evolutionary metamorphosis.

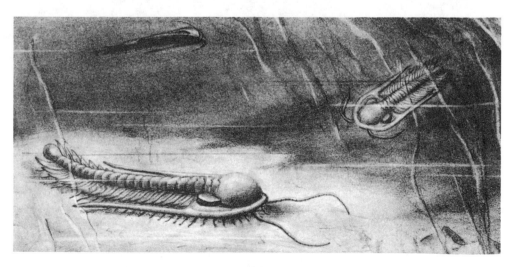

With the exception of present day "creation scientists" most scientists agree with the notion that the evolution of all Earthly life trace their ancestry to those creatures who were among the first to emerge on this planet. However, Darwin and neo-Darwinians champion the "organic soup" and believe that life and its DNA emerged from non-life following the random mixing of organic molecules. And yet, there was little or no free oxygen, which is necessary for the construction of DNA. The basic elements for DNA construction did not exist on Earth.

However, let us pretend that life did emerge from an organic soup. If that is the case, then, given the lack of Earthly ingredients, that soup must have first been stirred on another planet.

Cosmic collisions are commonplace, not only between stars, but entire galaxies. And, if life first arose on another planet, it can be assumed that some of those creatures were cast into space, encapsulated in debris, and not only survived their long journeys, but fell upon innumerable planets, only to begin genetically engineering their new worlds if at all possible. Hence, although life may ultimately trace its roots to a single cell that emerged from an organic soup, the theory of evolutionary metamorphosis views life as having arisen, on Earth, from numerous "seeds" which, in turn, may ultimately trace their origin to a single astrobiological source.

If there was a "single seed" from which all life has descended, this "seed" first appeared tens of

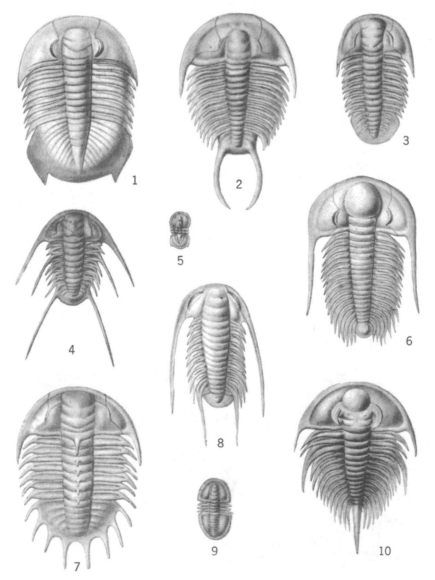

Figure 40. Cambrian Trilobites. Drawn by L.S. Douglas. Reprinted from Dunbar, 1960. Historical Geology, Wiley, New York.

billions if not hundreds of billions of years ago, on another planet thus giving rise to identical seeds; that is creatures with identical or similar DNA and DNA-based genetic instructions.

Because of this genetic commonalty, rather than a single seed and a single Earthly-trunk with innumerable branches, the theory of evolutionary metamorphosis posits a forest of trees with innumerable branches, each of which has the genetic potential to bear identical fruit. Only the theory of evolutionary metamorphosis and this forest of basically identical "genetic trees" can explain why different species of humanity, such as Homo erectus, Neanderthals, and Cro-Magnons shared the planet during overlapping time periods, and why over half a dozen species of Australopithecus and a variety of Homo Habilis appeared almost simultaneously in different parts of the world.

Since the genetic instructions for creating all manner of life is also DNA based, then it would appear that these genetic instructions and the genetic potential to create all manner of life, are also astrobiological in origin and/or a product of intelligent design. It is these ancestral astrobiological origins, the antiquity of life, and the genetic memories and instructions which they have passed down, which explains the progressive emergence of increasingly complex and intelligent life on Earth—an unfolding which has occurred according to specific DNA-based instructions and genetic memories—just as the fertilized single cell that gives rise to an embryo is genetically predetermined to create a fetus, then a neonate, child...adult.

Just as an embryo is not a random construction, all subsequent species to emerge on Earth have been genetically preprogrammed, the expression and coding of which are associated with intronic genes and intronic gene sequence activation, exon shuffling, "frame shifts," intron and plasmid insertion and exchange, and a host of other genetic variables which are yet to be identified.

Only the purposeful, controlled, and highly regulated expression of genetically pre-coded instructions can account for the obvious evidence of a step-wise, sometimes leaping progression in increasing intelligence and complexity which has characterized the metamorphosis of a rather narrow range of life on this planet. Indeed, only precise genetic instructions can account for the fact that basically similar species have emerged multi-regionally across distant lands, from distinct pockets of ancestral species which also emerged multi-regionally, and this includes the multi-regional metamorphosis of a wide variety of wide ranging species of Australopithecus, H. habilis, H. erectus, and Neanderthals. The planet was genetically seeded to grow all manner of species, including humans and all manner of variations thereof.

PROGRESS AND MULTI-REGIONAL METAMORPHOSIS

Every phylum in existence today emerged during the Cambrian Explosion, including the phylum Chordata. The first members of the phylum chordata possessed a simplified brain that consisted of a brainstem—which controls rhythmic and reflexive motor behaviors— and a limbic forebrain which mediates all aspects of emotional and motivational functioning including memory.

The evolution of the brain began with the metamorphosis of the first nerve cells; i.e. specialized sensory-motor cells capable of inducing movement in reaction to sensation such as light vs shadow. These cells were loosely organized along the outer membrane/skin and most probably did not intercommunicate except indirectly following the release of various chemical transmitters.

As the climate and environment began to change, and as the environment acts on gene selection, over the course of evolution a collection of like-minded cells began to directly interact, forming a nerve net, and then to congregate in the anterior head region, giving rise to a primitive ganglion brain. During the Cambrian Explosion, the ganglionic brain became a primitive brain, which in some species including cartilaginous fish (e.g. sharks) and later, in "bony fish" (Osteichthyes), consisted of a brainstem (concerned with reflexive sensory motor functions, visual and "auditory" perception, the sleep cycle) and an olfactory bulb-equipped forebrain which analyzed environmental chemical input and also induced gross motor behavior in response to motivationally significant stimuli.

Tunicates were among the first chordates (subphylum Urochordata) to emerge beneath the sea, some 500 million years ago, and were soon followed by the first jawless fish (e.g. Astraspis, Arandaspis), who in turn gave rise to cartilaginous (Cyclostomes) "bony" fish. Over the ensuing 100 million years, and within the vast oceans and seas, various species of "fish," e.g "bony fishes," "ray fins," developed additional brain matter, and some species of "bony fish" later developed lungs and limbs; i.e. lobed finned fish.

Armored and jawless fish, sharks, and lobed finned fish were all in possession of the prototypical brain, the basic framework of which would be inherited by all subsequent species, including amphibians, reptiles, and even woman and man (Nieuwenhuys & Meek, 1990b; Stephan, 1983).

The brains and bodies of these animals, however, did not become just more variable—as demanded by Darwinian theory—but increasingly complex and hierarchically organized and sophisticated. For example, unlike other fish which are externally fertilized and which lay eggs in the open water (eggs which are then greedily gobbled by yet other denizens of the sea), the lobe finned fish were fertilized inside the body and could bear the young alive.

By 370 million years B.P., a wide range of lobed finned fish began to appear in almost every ocean and sea. These included Dipnoans, Sarcopterygia, and Coelacanths, who began to venture forth upon the Earth where they then began to breed.

Numerous species of lobed-fins lived mainly in rivers and freshwater seas and could venture forth and live on land as they had evolved internal air sacs which were embedded within their fins. Likewise, some of the first land-based plants also evolved air sacs. These air sacs could pass oxygen directly into the blood stream. This "breathing" ability enabled the lobed fins not only to venture forth, but to hole up in caked mud during the dry seasons. As the environment acts on gene selection, it is the lobed finned fish who presumably gave rise to the next stage of complex animal life.

Lobe finned fish were (and are) in many respects a transitional prototype for all land based creatures, as their "fleshy-lobed" fins were supported by an internal skeleton consisting of a humerus, femur, radius, ulna, tibia and fibula (Caroll, 1988; Jerison, 1973; Nieuwenhuys & Meek, 1990b; Romer, 1970). The lobe finned Coelacanths, in fact possessed jointed bones shaped somewhat like arms and legs. It is from these lobed fins that legs would eventually "evolve," and it is these lobed fins coupled with the air sacks (primitive lungs), that enabled these creatures to periodically leave the water so as to venture along river banks, oceans fronts, and onto dry soil, some 400 to 350 million years ago (Caroll, 1988; Colbert, 1980; Jarvik, 1980; Jerison, 1973; Romer, 1970).

Presumably it is from one or any number of the various species of lung/air sack equipped lobe

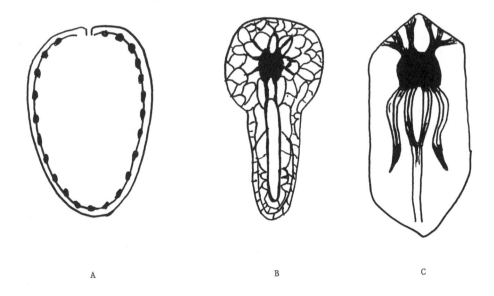

A   B   C

Figure 41. *Stages in the evolution of the nerve net in three flatworms (Acoela, Polycladida, Rhabdoceoela). A. Epidermal nervous system and nerve cells. B. Nerve net with bilobed ganglia. C. Cephalization of brain with loss of nerve net. (redrawn from Hyman, 1951). (Below) the brain of an armored fish, which became extinct 325 millions years ago.*

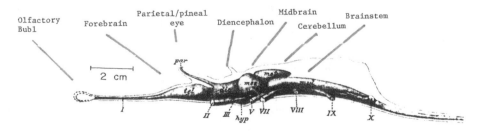

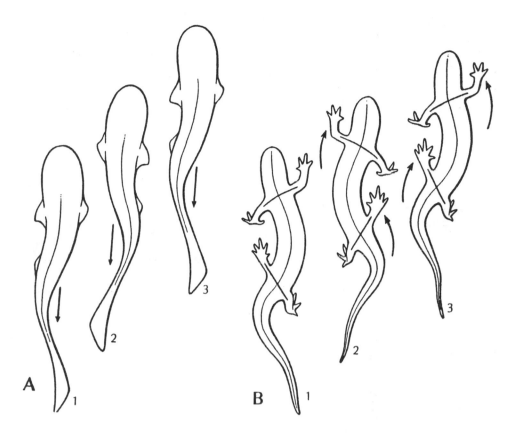

Figure 42. Rhythmic swimming motions of (A) three fish, and (B) three salamanders which utilize the same movement patterns which are in sequence with the trunkal muscle activity. The limbs are extensions of the axial muscles.

Figure 43. Stages in the transition from lung fish into Labyrhinthodants. American Museum of Natural History.

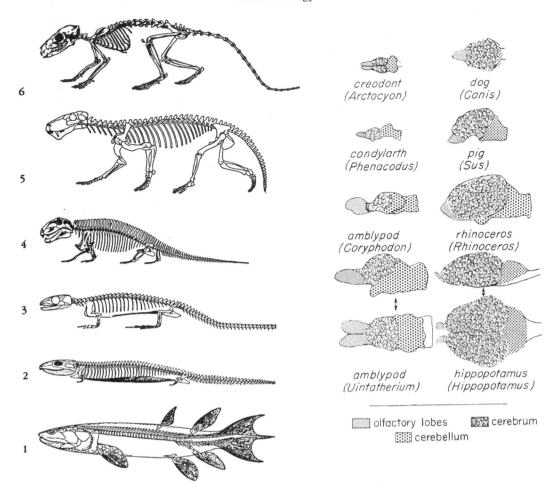

Figure 44. *Skeletal and cranial evolution leading from 1) lobed finned fish, 2) early amphibian, 3) primitive reptile, 4) repto-mammal, 5) therapsid, 6) placental mammal. Reprinted from Howells, 1997. Getting Here. Compass Press,*

Figure 45. *The brains of repto-mammals/ therapsids (left) paired with the brains of modern mammals of similar size. Reprinted from Dunbar, 1960. Historical Geology, Wiley, New York.*

finned fish, that all terrestrial vertebrates evolved (Romer, 1970), beginning, perhaps with primitive oxygen breathing amphibians, such as the seven fingered Ichthyostega whose forelimbs were hitched to the skull. This odd physical organization, however, enabled these and like-minded animals not only to walk but to perceive and hear vibration transmitted through their feet.

By 360 million years ago a variety of five-toed amphibians, some up to 15 feet long were swarming over the planet. And, for a brief time amphibians "ruled" the world as they were more social, and more intelligent than the more solitary insects who, along with plants, had dominated the planet. Insects rapidly diminished in size.

It was not the lobed finned lung fish, however, but their descendants that gave rise to amphibians. These amphibian-like creatures looked something like a cross between a fish and a big salamander, with flat heads and long tails, and short stocky feet like a turtle. These include the eusthenopterons, as well as the Ichthyostegas which used four feet in order to move about (Colbert, 1980; Jarvik, 1980; Jerison, 1973; Romer, 1970).

Hence, by 350 million years ago the lobe finned fish presumably evolved into a fish with legs, the eusthenopteron and ichthyostegas, which in turn evolved into amphibians, some of which grew up to 15 feet length and who sported an enlarged olfactory lobe which dominated the forebrain.

REPTILIAN METAMORPHOSIS

Amphibian dominion was sooner overturned by reptiles who were superiorly endowed physi-

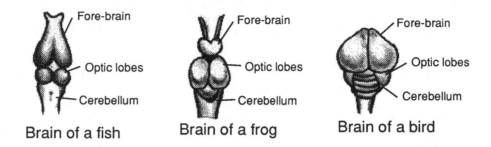

Brain of a fish   Brain of a frog   Brain of a bird

Figure 46. *The brain of a fish, frog, and bird.*

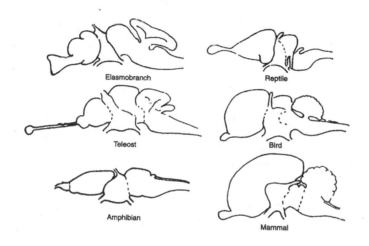

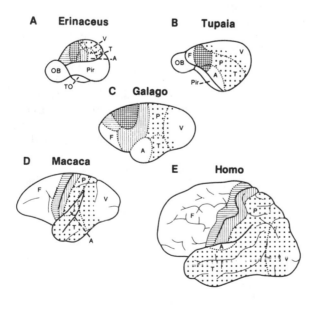

Figure 47. *Comparison of neocortical evolution and the evolution of the lobes of the brain, across five species. Abbreviations: OB-olfactory bulb, A-primary auditory cortex, F-frontal neocortex, P-parietal neocortex, Pir-piriform lobe, TO-tuberculum olfactorium, V-visual cortex. From Gloor, 1997, The Temporal Lobe and Limbic System. Oxford University Press. New York. Contrary to Darwinism, the brain has not become more variable, but more complex.*

cally and neurologically as their forebrain consisted of a greatly expanded limbic system and included distinctive limbic system structures such as the amygdala, hippocampus, and striatum which conferred tremendous intellectual powers and social-emotional signaling and associational capabilities upon these animals. Amphibians, therefore, did not just become more variable, they gave rise to a unique and superior species.

Unlike their amphibious cousins, the reptiles were better engineered for living on dry land, having evolved scaly waterproofed skins, hip and shoulder girdles, as well as a "new" method of giving birth. In contrast to amphibians who must return to the water to breed and produce young (tadpoles which undergo metamorphosis in order to become an adult), the reptiles could breed and lay amniote/cleidoic (shell covered) eggs on land from which emerged miniature adults.

The brain also increased in size and became more complex. With the evolution of reptiles the limbic forebrain mushroomed in size and gained hierarchical control over the motor functions of the brainstem (Herrick, 1948; Nieuwenhuys, 1967). The limbic forebrain could now feel emotions and directly control all aspects of body movement. In part, the increase in the size of the forebrain was induced by the increased emotional and motor demands of living on dry land, such that the motor aspects of the forebrain began to increasingly differentiate and to evolve in response to and in order to meet these new motoric needs; made possible by the limbic-striatum.

Yet another factor in the encephalization of the brain was that animals were now living in a perfumed world of smell, and these odors provided an incredible wealth of information that the limbic forebrain became specialized to analyze. As the environment acts on gene selection, olfactory input to the limbic system forced this structure to also evolve and differentiate and to become increasingly capable of analyzing a wide range of motivational stimuli. The brain did not become more variable, as demanded by Darwin's theory, but was growing larger and increasingly complex.

THERAPSID & REPTO-MAMMAL METAMORPHOSIS

Over the ensuing 25 million years, the descendants of reptiles diverged, one branch of which giving rise to the intellectually, neurologically, and physically advanced repto-mammals, around 250 million years B.P., who in turn gave rise to therapsids who emerged multi-regionally (Bakke, 1971; Brink, 1956; Crompton & Jenkins, 1973; Crompton, et al. 1979; Duvall, 1990; Maglio, 1978; Romer, 1966; Quiroga, 1979). Yet another branch gave rise to dinosaurs, around 225 million years B.P., who also emerged multi-regionally and appeared worldwide—presumably descending multi-regionally from ancestors who also emerged multi-regionally from multiple ancestral species.

Hence, primordial reptiles split into three lineages, the anapsids which gave rise to modern turtles, synapsids which gave rise to repto-mammals and then therapsids, and diapsids which gave rise to dinosaurs, and birds, and present day reptiles (Caroll, 1988).

Repto-mammals emerged some 250 million years ago, and these creatures briefly ruled the Earth. Although the initial repto-mammals were sprawlers, over time they became physically more refined, and eventually gave rise to therapsids, 200 million years B.P..

Therapsids were exceedingly technologically advanced, physically and neurologically. For example, in contrast to reptiles and amphibians, the elbows were now directed backward and the knees forward which greatly improved their ability to run and manipulate their limbs. In addition, the legs were now located beneath rather than alongside the body which enabled them to run long distances without compressing the chest and lung which allowed them to simultaneously breath while chasing prey. Reptiles must stop in order to breath since their legs, situated alongside their body and chest cavity, constrict the expansion of the lungs as they run.

The therapsids also developed a secondary bony palate which enabled them to chew food and to simultaneously breathe without danger of choking to death. Reptiles must cease to breathe in order to swallow large chunks of their food.

Another advantage occurred in regard to thermoregulation. Therapsids became warm blooded. Reptiles must sun themselves or run around and rely on behavioral thermoregulation. For example, if a reptile fails to move from a cold to a warm location (or vice versa) their body temperature soon approaches that of the external environment. They must move about in order to gain heat by sunning themselves, or cool off by sitting in the shade.

By contrast, the limbic system of the repto-mammals and then the therapsids evolved a means of regulating body temperature internally. Whereas lizards, frogs, fish, etc., have only scales, the therapsids also evolved a coat of fur, as well as sweat glands that release excessive internal heat. Moreover, with the metamorphosis of the repto-mammal therapsids, the ear underwent important modifications and the limbic forebrain began to expand with new tissues emerging and growing additional layers. Because the inner ear and additional brain tissue had emerged, vocalized communication assumed a new importance.

The increased importance of vocalization was made possible by the expanded development of the 4-5 layered cingulate gyrus; a structure that caps the 3-layered allocortical limbic system, and which is implicated in maternal offspring behavior and vocal communication (Joseph, 1999b, 2000a).

With the development of the cingulate gyrus, the therapsid's ability to communicate expanded beyond simple gestures, posturing, or olfactory-pheromonal signaling, and now included the capacity to produce a variety of complex meaningful sounds, such as between mother and infant, including, perhaps the separation cry. The five-layered cingulate gyrus provided the brain power to engage in prolonged maternal care, which in turn promoted the development of language, love, and the family (Joseph, 1993; MacLean, 1990).

Nevertheless, although exceedingly advanced, the repto-mammals were struck down and nearly became extinct following a great cataclysm when the Earth was twice struck by massive meteorites, around 250 million and 225 million years B.P. (Rampino & Haggerty, 1994). These catastrophes were followed by a "giant volcanic eruption"—all of which acted to split apart the already fracture land masses and to blot out the sun with dust, thus dropping temperatures and killing off over 50% of all marine life and all larger size terrestrial animals. These catastrophes killed off most but not all of the larger sized repto-mammals, and gave the much smaller dinosaurs a competitive advantage. The remaining repto-mammals were displaced by these "terrible lizards" who then began to evolve multi-regionally on every continent.

Those dinosaurs who may have evolved multi-regionally included the 36 foot-long Suchomimus tenernsis, who had teeth shaped like steak knives, and whose fossil remains have been discovered in Egypt, Brazil, England, and central Niger in Africa. Likewise, although Tyrannosaurus rex, the most fearsome meat eater in history, is associated with the Americas, similar species, including almost all the dinosaurs discovered in Utah, also emerged in Asia (Cifelli et al., 1997). Although they may have migrated, and despite being (for the most part) cold blooded and swam the oceans from Asia or crossed over the frozen tundra of the Arctic in order to appear in the Americas it could also be argued that these cold blooded raptors evolved multi-regionally (that is from multiple ancestral "seeds").

Following every mass extinction, although the majority of species are typically wiped out, others manage to recover. As the environment acts on gene selection, and as the remaining repto-mammals were relegated to a nighttime environment, their brain was forced to further evolve and to grow. They adapted to lurking about at night and hiding beneath deep foliage during the day—a life style which induced further expansions in the olfactory dominated forebrain which became increasingly adapted to process olfactory and auditory cues.

THE ENVIRONMENT AND THERAPSID MULTI-REGIONAL METAMORPHOSIS

By 200 to 150 million years B.P., the repto-mammals had become therapsids (Caroll, 1988). In addition to the other changes already mentioned, the therapsid brain (the dorsal pallium) was now capped with a five layered (mesocortical) cingulate gyrus—the evolution of which ushered in a revolution in vocal-emotional communication and infant-maternal behavior (Joseph, 1993; MacLean, 1990).

By 150 to 85 million years ago, various suborders of therapsids had given rise to the intellectually and neurologically superior mammals, who in addition to a five layered cingulate gyrus, had evolved a six layered neocortex. Yet, because the environment acts on gene selection, those therapsids living in sheltered pockets of primeval swamp and jungle, remained therapsids—just as in some pockets of the world, Homo erectus remained Homo erectus, and Neanderthals remained Neanderthals, although Cro-Magnon were beginning to swarm over the planet.

Because the environment acts on gene selection, different environmental and climatic conditions can produce not only diverse subspecies, but enhance or slow the rate of species metamorphosis depending on where they dwell. Metamorphosis occurs at different rates under different geological and climatic conditions, and thus at different times periods for the same species, and often not at all. An unvarying environment, coupled with related genetic factors hinders the development of the next stage of metamorphosis.

Hence, in a few isolated swamps and jungles of the world which have undergone little change over the course of the last several hundred million years, huge insects, amphibians and reptiles abound and jungle dwelling mammals still lay eggs -much like repto-mammals.

Egg laying "mammals" (monotremes), tend to be found only in a few isolated regions of the world such as in the primeval swamps and jungles of New Zealand. These egg layers include the anteaters and the even more primitive duck billed platypus. Monotremes are in fact quite primitive, and appear in the fossil record as far back as the earliest periods of the Pleistocene.

By contrast, throughout much of the rest of the world, species of amphibians and reptiles have diminished in number and diversity, and monotremes have disappeared, whereas mammals have climbed the next step of the evolutionary ladder. The egg and the embryo are now nourished inside the womb (placentals).

Egg laying mammals, the monotremes, therefore, are more like therapsids and repto-mammals than true mammals (placentals). Like repto-mammals, monotremes not only lay eggs, but are without breasts. Instead, they suckle their young via modified sweat glands which secrete milk. Over the course of evolutionary metamorphosis these sweat glands eventually became the mammillary glands of the more advanced mammals (Duvall, 1988).

The monotremes, therefore, are a type of very advanced repto-mammal, a therapsid which has yet to reach the next stage of metamorphosis. In other lands and environments, however, the monotremes have disappeared as they evolved into or were replaced or killed off by more advanced mammals who emerged almost simultaneously and multi-regionally throughout Africa, Eurasia, and North America.

These advanced mammals, however, did not simply crawl out of the earth, or emerge from stone or clay. Advanced mammals are the multi-regional descendants of therapsids who are the multi-regional descendants of repto-mammals, who in turn, once laid eggs.

Given that repto-mammals, therapsids, and mammals (including primates) have emerged on every continent, it could be argued that the genetic seeds to produce mammals have matured at different rates, albeit in different environments (Joseph, 1997). Environmental factors coupled with multiple trees of life, explains why modern human mammals still share the planet with primitive egg layers who are little different from their repto-mammal grandparents who strutted their stuff 200 million years ago.

Since the environment acts on gene selection it can influence the rate and speed of evolutionary metamorphosis and the activation and exchange of genetic material. Hence, it not surprising that primitive and modern versions of the same species may coexist, albeit in different environments, e.g. an isolated, steaming swamp and jungle, vs the fruited plains and happy hunting grounds of Eurasia, Africa, and North America. Those who appear to be more primitive and who have lagged behind, live in an environment which has not promoted the next stage of genetic metamorphosis. Those "genetic seeds" have yet to mature. In fact, this same unequal relationship where primitive and more advanced species coexist, albeit in different environments, is characteristic of all manner of Earthly life, including bacteria, plants, insects, reptiles, mammals, primates, and even the genus Homo.

MAMMALIAN METAMORPHOSIS

As noted, with the development of the cingulate gyrus, the therapsid's ability to communicate expanded beyond simple gestures, posturing, or olfactory-pheromonal signaling, and now included the capacity to produce a variety of complex meaningful sounds, such as between mother and infant, including, perhaps the separation cry. The five-layered cingulate gyrus provided the brain power to engage in prolonged maternal care, which in turn promoted the development of language, love, and the family (Joseph, 1993; MacLean, 1990).

As therapsids (e.g., Probainognathus from the Triassic followed by Periptychus from the Paleocene), continued to evolve and the brain continued to grow the mesocortical five-layered cingulate began to sprout a small nub of neocortex (Quiroga, 1980); i.e. the six layered new cortex. In later appearing therapsids, e.g. Phenocodus, the now, enlarged brain, began to resemble that of primitive mammals, e.g., opossum or hedgehog.

When the first mammals began to scurry about 85-130 million years ago (e.g. Kumar & Hedges, 1998), the gray mantle of the outer surface of the brain, the six layered neocortex ("new cortex") had begun to encapsulate the old brain, forming the frontal, parietal, temporal, and occipital lobes in the process.

It was the development of this new brain and the neocortex which provided mammals and primates with an enormous competitive intellectual edge that enabled them to take advantage of the cosmic catastrophe which presumably wiped out most of the large, cold blood, land based dinosaurs when a massive meteor struck the Yucatan peninsula, some 65 million years ago (Alvarez, 1986; Alvarez &

Asaro, 1990; Rampino & Haggerty, 1994; Raup, 1991).

The enormous energy released from this meteor strike destroyed much of life in the Americas. Moreover, due to the dust thrown into the air sunlight was blocked out for months. Temperatures dropped, thus killing off all remaining large sized cold blood animals; events which were then followed by an acid rain and a greenhouse type warming.

Any remaining dinosaurs were quickly eradicated by surviving mammals, and in consequence, mammals gained dominion over the day as well as the night. As the environment acts on gene selection, the mammalian brain quickly adapted to processing visual as well as auditory stimuli, and expanded yet again. With the ensuing evolution of primates, monkeys and apes in particular, the entire forebrain became adapted for engaging in prolonged and detailed analysis of visual and auditory stimuli (Gloor, 1997; Stephan, 1983) and climbing in trees.

Over the course of later mammalian and primate evolution and as these creatures gained complete dominion over much of the planet, the neocortex began to expand at a rapid rate (Stephan & Andy, 1977). In fact, when comparing the brains of "living fossils" such as insectivores with that of humans, it appears that the six to seven layered neocortex expanded by a factor of 156 (even when taking into account differences in body size), whereas the 3-layered limbic system allocortex and five-layered mesocortex (cingulate gyrus) and all associated olfactory-limbic structures developed at a much reduced rate.

For example, limbic system structures such as hippocampus and septum are only 4 times larger and the amygdala is 6 times larger when comparing humans to insectivores. By contrast, the olfactory bulb is 40 times smaller (Stephan & Andy, 1969; Stephan, 1983), which is due to the reduced impor-

A

B

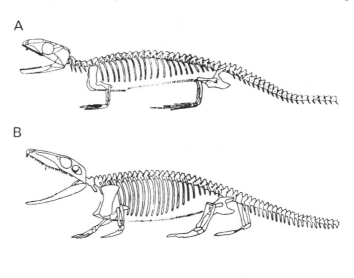

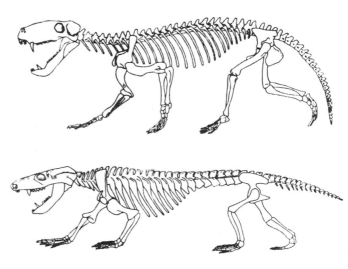

Figure 48. Skeletal structure of (A) a primitive reptile, and (B) three repto-mammals. Note placement of legs has shifted from alongside the body, to beneath the body. From Maclean, 1990. Courtesy of Plenum Publishing. Note: Contrary to Darwinism, the skeletal system has not become more variable, but more complex.

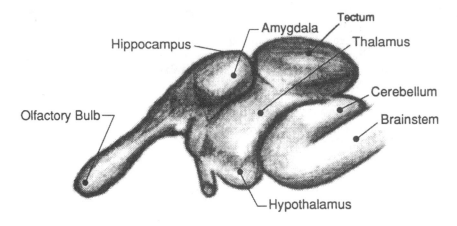

Figure 49a. *The brain of a lizard.*

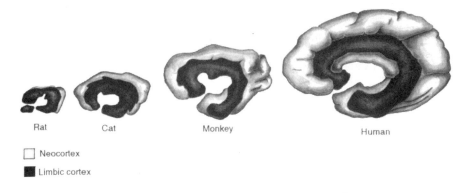

Figure 49b. *The limbic system across four species.*

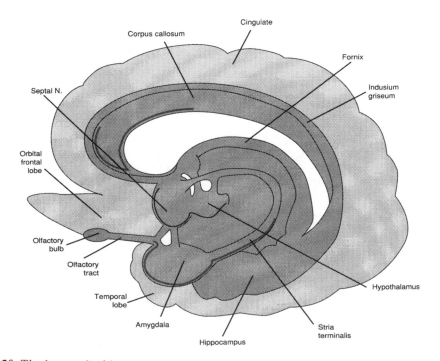

Figure 50. *The human limbic system.*

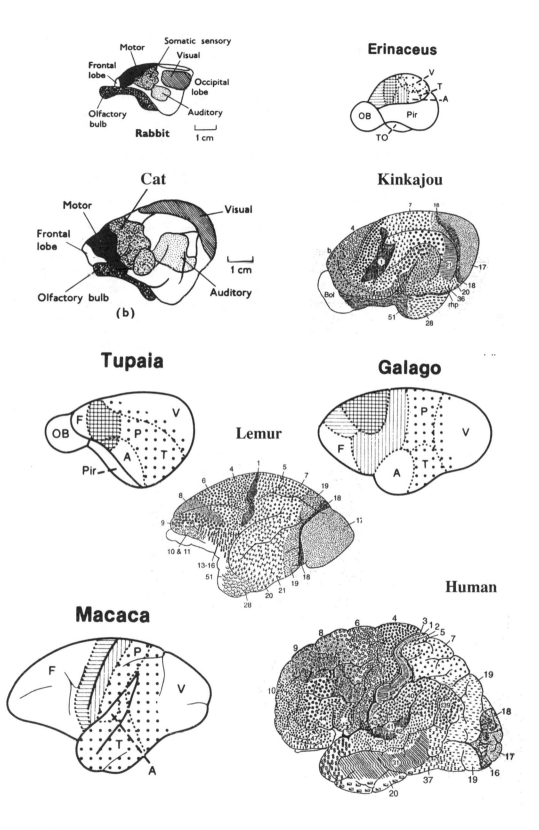

Figure 51. *The expansion and growth of the forebrain and the reduction in the olfactory regions. Contrary to Darwinism, the brain has not become more "variable" but increasingly complex.*

tance of smell and olfaction in human behavior.

Hence, contrary to Darwin's theory, the brain did not become more variable, but "evolved" new structures and tissues which mushroomed in size.

MULTI-REGIONAL PRIMATE METAMORPHOSIS

It is only with the demise of the dinosaurs that primates were able to emerge from the under-brush and the darkness of night. By 55 million years ago, during the early Eocene, at least some orders of primates (e.g. Tetonius) evolved a large occipital lobe (visual cortex), as well as an emerging temporal (auditory) lobe and frontal lobe (Radinksy, 1967, 1970). Thus, by 55 million years ago, ancestral primates had evolved a brain which resembled that of modern day prosimian primates.

Over the ensuing years, and as primates adapted to living in the trees, which in turn required major adaptations in the eyes and hands, the basic pattern for the primate neocortex became established and the frontal and temporal lobes and the "hand" area of the frontal-parietal lobes continued to expand.

The first prosimian primates to scurry about this planet may have diverged from several different mammalian lines some 70-100 million years ago. Primates, like earlier mammals, reptiles, and amphibians, came to live on every continent. Although modern day neo-Darwinian theory demands a single line of descent, like the mammals, dinosaurs, reptiles, amphibians, plants and insects before them, primates appear to have emerged multi-regionally and almost simultaneously throughout the world and from multiple branches from multiple trees, rather than from a single seed, trunk, or twig.

Of course, it is possible that many species may have simply migrated from one land to another, for example, from North American to South America. However, migration is less likely as to the emergence of, for example, primates in South America and Africa-Eurasia. The great oceans are too vast a distance to be covered without first dying of thirst and hunger. Of course, as species can be hurtled from planet to planet, migration remains a distinct possibility.

Throughout the world, many species of primate took to living amongst the branches of the trees. In consequence tremendous alterations occurred in the fingers, and hand-eye coordination—as the environment acts on gene selection. For example, claws became grasping fingers whereas the eyes moved to the front of the face thus providing for depth perception and stereoscopic vision. Within the brain there were tremendous expansions of the visual, auditory, tactual-gestural cortex.

It was presumably from these widely dispersed tree loving stocks that gave rise to "old world" monkeys in Africa, India, Asia, and "new world monkeys" in the Americas about 40 million years ago (Leaky, 1976, 1988; Pfeiffer, 1985). The wide ranging stock of "old world" monkey, in turn gave rise to apes (hominoids) about 30 million years B.P., with what would become chimpanzees and gorillas eventually appearing in Africa, and Orangutans appearing in India and Asia. Presumably numerous branches from these varied primate-hominoid trunk lines diverged again, and yet again, and gave rise to the ancestral lines which led to the emergence of the first primitive Adam and Eve.

FROM HOMINOID TO HOMINID

By 30 million years B.P., apes had emerged multi-regionally dwelling in Africa, China, and

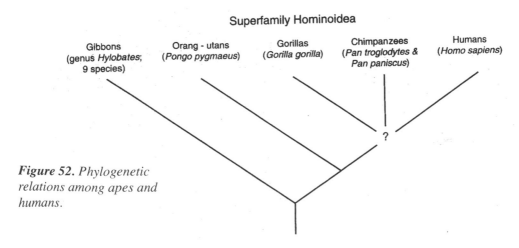

Figure 52. Phylogenetic relations among apes and humans.

India, literally from sea to shining sea. And it is from these wide ranging hominoid stocks that a variety of hominoid/pre-hominids began to "evolve," including Dryopithecus, Sivapithecus, Ramapithecus, Ankarapithecus, Ouranopithecus, and Giganotopithecus.

Evolutionary metamorphosis is most likely to occur when an organism is exposed to a multiplicity of changing environments, or where two divergent worlds meet. For the pre-hominid hominoids such as Dryopithecus, Sivapithecus, Ramapithecus, Ankarapithecus, Ouranopithecus, and Giganotopithecus, the netherworld of change was found where the forest ended and began to recede and the savanna and grasslands began to expand. This great change occurred during a period in which parts of the planet were bathed in renewed warmth.

As the changing environment acts on gene selection, the descendants of these pre-hominid hominoids gave rise to a wide variety of pre-human species which began to "evolve" multi-regionally. These included Australopithecus who was later followed and joined by Homo habilis who was joined and then followed by H. crectus who was joined and then followed by Homo sapiens who was joined and then followed by H. sapiens sapiens—the wise man who knows he is wise and who would soon dominate and then threaten a good part of the planet's multiple life forms with death and extinction.

MULTI-REGIONAL HUMAN METAMORPHOSIS FROM HOMINOID TO HOMINID

As to the ancestors of the first pre-human hominids, there are several candidates, each of which may have given rise to a distinct or similar branch of the emerging human race. These ancestral species include Dryopithecus, Sivapithecus—ape-like hominid/hominoids who emerged in Europe and India, about 16 million years ago. Other candidates include Ramapithecus whose remains have been discovered in Africa, India, and Southwest China (Jurmain, et al. 1990; Munthe et al. 1983). Ramapithecus, in fact, appears closely related to Dryopithecus and Sivapithecus.

Other possible candidates include Ankarapithecus of Turkey, Ouranopithecus of Greece, and Giganotopithecus whose 8 million year old remains have been found in India, China, and Vietnam (reviewed in Howell, 1997). Giganotopithecus may have descended from Ramapithecus and may have later given rise to Homo habilis in Asia.

Nevertheless, these species of hominoid pre-hominid have for the most part been rejected as

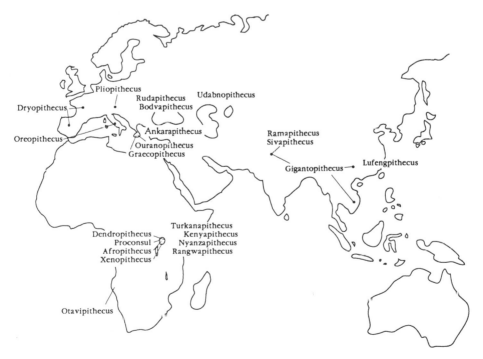

Figure 53. *A map that displays the distribution of some late Tertriary apes. Reprinted from Howells, 1997. Getting Here. Compass Press, Washington D.C.*

human ancestors. Conventional wisdom requires an African origin for the proverbial ape-hominid-human ancestor, and these species lived in the "wrong" parts of the world. Indeed, conventional wisdom requires that the facts fit the theory, and those facts and fossil remains which are inconvenient or inconsistent with accepted theory, such as the evidence for multi-regional metamorphosis, are conveniently rejected and dismissed.

MULTI-REGIONAL METAMORPHOSIS OF AUSTRALOPITHECUS & HOMO HABILIS

Around five million years ago and in reaction to yet another major change in environmental and climatic conditions, some species of hominoids began to increasingly live upon the ground. Although they spent much of their time in trees, it is while on the ground, around 5 million years ago, that the descendants of Ramapithecus and/or Giganotopithecus, Ankarapithecus, Ouranopithecus, or some other primate-pre-hominid, underwent further evolutionary metamorphosis and gave rise to a variety of more advanced pre-hominids, such as Ardipithecus ramidus and Australopithecus Afarensis.

Again, however, contrary to conventional wisdom, but consistent with the theory of evolutionary metamorphosis, a wide range of species collectively referred to as Australopithecus (A. aethopicus, A. africanus, A. robustus, A. boisei), emerged multi-regionally, throughout Africa (see Grine, 1988; Leakey & Walker, 1988; Skelton & McHenry 1992) as well as in China and Java, e.g. A. robustus (reviewed in Barnes, 1993).

Around 2-3 million years ago Australopithecus was joined by other possible human ancestors: Homo habilis (the handy man). Again, contrary to conventional wisdom, but consistent with the theory of evolutionary metamorphosis, several varieties of H. habilis (e.g. H. rudolfensis, H ergaster) appeared in Africa, as well as in China (Dragon Hill) and Indonesia (reviewed in Barnes, 1993, and Howells, 1997).

In fact, as reported in the July 5, 2002, issue of the journal Science, a 1.75-million-year-old homo habilis skull was found in Eruo-Asia, near the medieval town Dmanisi, 50 miles southwest of Tbilisi, the Georgian capital. The skull was found along with more than 1,000 crudely chipped cobbles, which are the tools commonly associated with Homo habilis. The skull has the canine teeth and face of Homo habilis and the cranial capacity of the new skull is also 600 cubic centimeters, which is "near the mean" for H. habilis.

The discovery of this skull is completely at odds with the out-of-Africa theory of human origins. In fact, as pointed out by Dr. Ian Tattersall, a specialist in human evolution at the natural history museum in New York City, the skull closely resembles a 1.9-million-year-old Homo habilis skull from Kenya.

As summed up by Dr. David Lordkipanidze who made the discovery: "We have a new puzzle."

What we have is evidence of multi-regional human evolution.

Indeed, like their purported ancestors, these species collectively referred to as Australopithecus

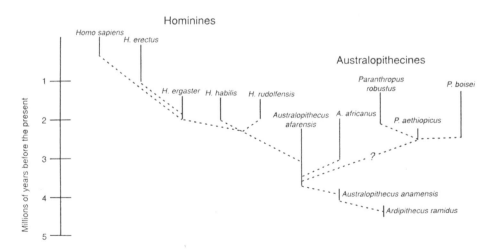

Figure 54. *One of the many interpretations of the various phylogenetic relations among different species of hominids. Reprinted from Zigmund et al., 1999 Fundamental Neuroscience, Academic Press, San Diego.*

and H. habilis "evolved" multi-regionally. However, unlike their predecessors they evolved the capacity to stand upright and to make and use tools.

MULTI-REGIONAL METAMORPHOSIS OF H. ERECTUS

Like their ancestors, the fossil evidence indicates that Australopithecus and Homo habilis continued to evolve multi-regionally and to undergo metamorphosis in various parts of the world, thus giving rise to a wide variety and wide ranging species collectively referred to as Homo erectus (Binford, 1981; Brown, et al. 1985; Jia, 1980; Johanson & Shreeve, 1989; Leaky, 1976, 1982; Pfeiffer, 1985; Rightmire, 1990; Swisher et al., 1996; Stanley 1979, 1981).

With the metamorphosis of Homo erectus, who first appeared around 1.9 million years ago, the brain gradually doubled in size, approaching within 15% of a modern human by 500,000 years B.P.

The Homo erectus were the first individuals to have harnessed fire and the first who developed crude shelters and home bases. They also utilized various earth pigments (ochre) for perhaps cosmetic or artistic purposes. In this regard, these peoples were beginning to experiment with individual creative and artistic expression.

However, contrary to conventional wisdom which requires an African origin, the earliest fossil evidence indicates that like H. Habilis, H. erectus emerged multi-regionally, beginning in Euro-Asia,

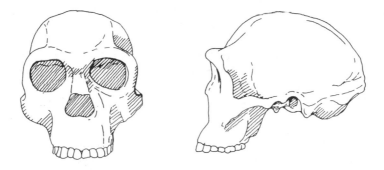

Figure 55. Homo erectus from Africa, dated to 1.6 million years. Reprinted from Howells, 1997. Getting Here. Compass Press, Washington D.C.

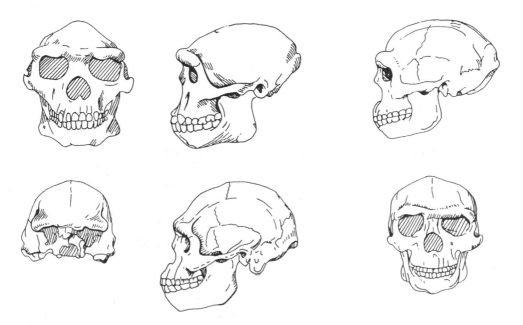

Figure 56. (Above) Homo erectus from Asia. Java man (top), Solo man (middle) and Peking man (right). Reprinted from Howells, 1997. Getting Here. Compass Press, Washington D.C.

i.e., the Caucasus (Georgian Republic) around 1.9 million years (reviewed in Howells, 1997).

H. erectus emerged multi-regionally in Asia, Africa and Europe. The skeletal remains of H. erectus (and associated stone tools) have been discovered in Ceprano Italy (dated to 800,000 B.P.), and in Java, Indonesia, (Pithecanthropus erectus) and near the Solo River (e.g. Solo Man, Java Man)—sites dated from 1.8 million to 700,000 B.P (respectively). Likewise, H. erectus (H. erectus pekinesis) have been discovered in Northern China (e.g. Peking Man) and in Zhoukoudian, Yuanmou and Xihouda China—sites dated from 500,000 to 750,000 to 800,000 to 1.5 million years B.P. (Jia, 1975, 1980; Jurmain et al. 1990; Stanley, 1979, 1981; Wu & Wang, 1985).

Although conventional wisdom and neo-Darwinian theory requires it, it is not likely that "Georgia Man," "Solo/Java Man" and "Peking Man" migrated out of Africa. The fossil remains dated to 1.6 to 1.8 million years in Java, and 1.5 to 2 million years in China (Dragon Hill), and the jaw from a H. erectus discovered in the Caucasus dated to 1.9 million years, are in fact older than similar specimens found in Africa. In fact, consistent with the theory of multi-regional metamorphosis, the species of Homo erectus discovered in China may well trace its lineage to Gigantopithecus who may have given rise to an Asian H. habilis (Jia, 1980; Munthe et al. 1983) who in turn gave rise to an Asian Homo erectus, as the remains of these ancestral species have also been discovered in Asia.

Hence, contrary to the out-of-Africa scenario, it could be argued that H. erectus first emerged in the Caucasus or Java, or Asia, or all of the above, and either spread to Africa (where H. habilis was still the dominant hominid), and finally Europe, or independently and multi-regionally evolved from ancestral species living in these other lands: evidence of intellient design

THE MULTI-REGIONAL METAMORPHOSIS OF ARCHAIC HOMO SAPIENS

Just as H. erectus appears to have evolved multi-regionally, the fossil evidence indicates that by 350,000 years ago, Archaic humans had emerged multi-regionally, in Africa, Asia, Europe, the Middle East, and India. In Europe archaic remains have been discovered in Petralona Italy, from sites dated between 350,000 to 400,000 B.P., as well as in Hungary and Germany. Likewise, the remains of archaic H. sapiens have been discovered in China (Hupei Province) dated to at least 350,000 B.P.

Moreover, multi-regional progressive evolution is evident as more advanced and modern appearing archaics ("early moderns") have been discovered in China (Dingcun, Maba, Dali, Jinniushan) as well as in East Africa from sites dated to 130,000 B.P. and 120,000 B.P respectively (Barnes, 1993; Butzer, 1982; Grun et al. 1990; Howells, 1997; Rightmire, 1984). Again, however, the more advanced species appeared in China first.

Hence, there is a clear line of multi-regional descent. Australopithecus, H. habilis, H. erectus, archaic and early modern H. sapiens appear to have emerged multi-regionally, with three distinct species of humanity, erectus, archaic, and "early moderns" sharing different regions of the planet simultaneously.

What the evidence and fossil record indicates is that the Earth was genetically seeded to grow humans (and other species) and all manner of variations thereof. Rather than a single tree with a single trunk, the "seeds" for a forest of similar trees rained down upon the planet and over time gave rise to similar, but not identical species. As the environment acts on gene selection, these "trees" have eventually bore a variety of similar (but not identical) "fruit" albeit at different times and at different rates, depending on environmental conditions.

THE MULTI-REGIONAL METAMORPHOSIS OF MODERN HUMANS

The environment acts on gene selection, and these genes exist prior to their activation. Differing environments, therefore, can induce slight changes in species living even in adjacent lands, or alterations so significant that a wholly new species emerges and displaces all locally situated ancestral species. Moreover, pockets of basically the same species may emerge multi-regionally, albeit some at an earlier or later date than others as is evident in regard to Homo erectus, Neanderthals, and the Cro-Magnons peoples, all of whom shared the planet during overlapping time periods.

Hence, whereas archaic Homo sapiens first emerged almost 500,000 years ago, large populations of Homo erectus continued to dominate parts of the planet until 300,000 years B.P., with a few isolated populations possibly hanging on until just 27,000 years ago as discovered in the island of Java (Swisher et al., 1996). Thus, for almost 200,000 years, large populations of Homo erectus and the more advanced archaic Homo sapiens shared the planet, albeit in different geological locations.

Moreover, just as Australopithecus, H. habilis, and H. erectus appear to have evolved multi-regionally, the fossil evidence suggests the same for archaic H. sapiens, whose remains have been discovered in Africa, Asia, Europe, the Middle East, and India. And, contrary to the single seed, out-of-Africa scenario, the remains of evolutionarily advanced archaics ("early moderns") appear in China (Dingcun, Maba, Dali, Jinniushan) 10,000 years before similar species appear in East Africa; i.e., from sites dated to 130,000 B.P. and 120,000 B.P. respectively (Barnes, 1993; Butzer, 1982; Grun et al. 1990; Howells, 1997; Rightmire, 1984).

Archaic H. sapiens in fact died out before the more primitive H. erectus, i.e. 29,000 B.P., (Neanderthals) vs 27,000 B.P. (H. erectus), whereas another species of incredibly advanced humans, Homo sapiens sapiens, had already emerged 75,000 years B.P. And, the first H. sapiens sapiens did not first appear in Africa, but in Australia (75,000, B.P.) followed by China (67,000 B.P.), Israel, Romania, and Bulgaria (43,000 B.P.), Iraq and Siberia (40,000 B.P.), Spain and France (35,000 B.P.), and Brazil, Peru, Chile and North America (30,000 to 50,000 B.P.). By contrast, during these same time periods, sub-Sahara Africa was still populated with archaic Homo sapiens; African Neanderthals.

Indeed, rather than originating in Africa where archaic H. sapiens roamed until 30,000 B.P., "modern" H. sapiens sapiens had already established numerous settlements in Australia and were fashioning complex tools as early as 60,000 B. P., including grooved "waisted blades" which could be bound to a handle.

What this means is that four different species of humanity were living in different parts of the world simultaneously, H. erectus, archaic, early modern, and "modern" H. sapiens sapiens—which is evidence of multi-regional evolution occurring at different rates in different branches of humanity, in different geographical regions. Although it could be argued that the descendants of one of these geographical groups merely migrated and killed off all competitors, this view is not supported by the fact that different types of humanity, for example, different types of H. habilis and H. erectus, are found in Africa vs Asia, with those in Asia (e.g. H. erectus) appearing before those in Africa, or those in Australia (e.g. "moderns") appearing before those in Africa or Asia.

Asian H. habilis and H. erectus differed significantly from their African counterparts, and so too did European vs African Neanderthals, with the European branch having a bigger brain. Australian and Asian "moderns" also appeared tens of thousands of years before their counterparts in Africa; which is not consistent with the out-of Africa scenario but instead supports the multi-regional and even the out-of-Asia or out-of-Australia view of evolution. In fact, whereas "modern" appearing H. sapiens sapiens do not emerge in North East Africa until around 35,000 B.P. the remains of Asian moderns have been found in China from sites dated as long ago as 67,000 B.P. (see Howells, 1997).

In fact, not only do "modern" humans appear outside of Africa thousands of years before "moderns" appear in Africa, but evolutionarily advanced humans were living in Northern Siberia as long ago as 250,000 to 300,000 years B.P. (Waters, 1997). Siberia is an exceedingly hostile environment requiring advanced survival skills as temperatures drop to below 70 degrees in winter. In fact, stone tools dated to 250,000 years B.P., were discovered along a river near Irutsk, Siberia—tools similar to those found in North America.

"What this indicates," according to Michael Waters of Texas A. & M., who helped date one of these sites and associated artifacts, "is that these people had the ability to deal with a rigorous environment. They could control fire, they had a survival strategy, they could make and find shelter, clothing, boots, etc." However, these advanced behaviors and capabilities, such as the ability to fashion complex clothing, do not appear in sub-Sahara Africa until near the end of the Upper Paleolithic.

Hence, similar to the step-wise worldwide pattern of multi-regional, multi-phylectic metamorphosis which has characterized the progressive emergence and increased complexity of plants and animals (Joseph, 1997, 2000a), the available evidence suggests that human "evolution" has unfolded multi-regionally in a step wise, progressive fashion, with some groups lagging far behind and others being left behind altogether and becoming extinct.

The Earth (and other planets) were genetically seeded to grow humans, and all manner of variations thereof.

This proposition and the fossil record are also consistent with evidence derived from the Human Genome Project. Much of the genome consists of silent intronic genes and nucleotide sequences. Silent genes and silent nucleotide sequences have the capacity to make copies of themselves, and to shift position within the genome (i.e. "jumping genes"): referred to as transposons. Transposable nucleotides show a tendency to leap to the more active GC regions. Once they are incorporated, they thus increase gene density and nucleotide content. These silent genes and silent nucleotides also come to be expressed, and/or they exert regulatory, inhibitory, or activating influences on other genes once they leap to the GC regions. In other words (and contrary to Darwinism), genes (and the traits they code for) that exist apriori may change position in the genome and become active; and they leap from the non-coding to the coding regions of the genome.

As noted, exons, introns and other transposable elements (e.g. "jumping genes") move about within the genome and insert themselves into new positions thus changing the genetic "code" as well as producing new genes via exon shuffling, retrotransposition, and gene duplication (Courseaux & Nahon 2001). "Dozens of genes... and about half of the human genome have been derived from transposable elements" and widespread DNA transposon activity is involved in speciation events (IHGSC, 2001); that is, the creation of subsequent species. This process including the creation of large-scale chromosome rearrangements via DNA transposon activity, is under genetic control and functions in accordance with precise genetic instructions (Caron et al. 2001; Courseaux & Nahon 2001). However, with each progressive step in the evolutionary metamorphosis of increasingly complex creatures, "there has been a marked decline in the overall activity of transposable elements" with the greatest decline occurring following the emergence of the hominid lineage; i.e. woman and man (IHGSC, 2001). With each step up the evolutionary ladder, families of transposons drop out in an almost clock-like fashion, with the last identifiable transposon extinction occurring following the divergence of humans and chimpanzees. "Only a single LTR retroposon family is known to have transposed since our divergence from the chimpanzee 7 million years ago (IHGSC, 2001).

These and other findings reported by the International Human Genome Sequencing Consortium (IHGSC) are entirely consistent with the theory that DNA strives to fulfill specific genetic goals which include the replication of life forms that long ago lived on other planets, including creatures quite similar to woman and man. Indeed, having served their purpose and having achieved their "genetic goals" "DNA transposons appear to have become completely inactive" with the evolution of humans (IHGSC, 2001).

The Earth was genetically seeded to grow humans. The multi-regional evolution of humans is evidence of intelligent design.

THE MYTH OF AFRICAN ORIGINS
THE STORY OF EVE

Conventional wisdom is of a single line of descent, and that modern humans "evolved" in Africa, from earlier species of humanity who also "evolved" in Africa, with each successive species migrating out of Africa, and then killing off and replacing earlier species who had also originated and migrated out of Africa before them.

Although one of the central tenants of Darwin's theory is that of "random variation" it has yet to be explained why that variation can only occur in Africa, and why that variation did not lead just to variable species, but increasingly intelligent and resourceful, and more advanced species. Variation does not equal increased complexity and the fossil record is indicative of a step-wise sometimes leaping progression yielding new structures and increased complexity.

Harvard paleontologist, Gould, solves this problem by denying the obvious and by claiming there is no evidence for progress. Yet others refer to mutations. Random mutations resulted in the production of successive superior species simply by chance, and these mutations repeatedly took place only in Africa.

Thus, according to modern neo-Darwinian theory, mutations were being continually produced in Africa and only in Africa, and each subsequent race of mutants migrated out of Africa only to be later replaced by more advanced mutants who also mutated in Africa.

Not only is the out-of-Africa, single seed, mutation scenario contradicted by the fossil evidence, but by logic and genetics.

For example, a "mutated" gene is generally eliminated before it has a chance to be expressed. It would be eliminated and replaced by a normal duplicate gene.

Moreover, even if the mutant gene were not eliminated, in order to produce a viable breeding pair, requires that two of the same exact mutations appear simultaneously in the same population, in both a man and a woman—and by chance—otherwise, the mutated individual might be unable to breed and pass on his/her superior mutated traits. Nevertheless, even if this mutated individual was not sterile and did breed, the mutation would likely disappear from the gene pool; either that or perhaps only an intermediate individual would be produced.

Even if we disregard those genetic mechanisms which eliminate "mutations" the fact remains that for evolution to be successful requires that multiple individuals and thus multiple mating partners "step-forward" as a group to the next stage of species evolution in order to produce viable offspring. A scenario such as this, however, is not consistent with neo-Darwinian theory, though it is entirely compatible with the theories of evolutionary metamorphosis and intelligent design.

THE TROUBLE WITH EVE

According to the "Eve" hypothesis, all modern humans descended from female ancestors living in Africa about 250,000 years ago. There are numerous problems with this theory, beginning with the fact that the assumptions upon which it rests have been shown to be invalid; e.g., that mitochondrial DNA (which in humans consists of 37 genes) is only inherited from the mother. In fact, fathers also contribute mitochondrial DNA. In addition, the estimates based on mitochondrial DNA "mutation" rates has been shown to be statistically erroneous (Templeton, 1992; Wolpoff & Thorne, 1991).

Specifically, based on an initial analysis of a small fragment (610 base pairs) of the mitochondrial genome (which consists of about 16500 base pairs), taken from 189 individuals, it was argued that there is greater diversity within Africa than outside Africa—as based on the varying patterns in sequencing (Stoneking & Cann, 1989; Vigilant et al. 1991). From this data it was concluded that all humans must have descended from African ancestors. However, others have found, using the same data, that all humans could have also descended from ancestors who lived in New Guinea (Ruvolo & Swafford, 1993).

As per more recent data provided by Chu et al., (1998), regarding the origins of modern Chinese, it is noteworthy that although these investigators also claim an African origin, that the East Asian population they studied were genetically more closely related to "Native American" Indians, followed by Australian aborigines, and New Guineans. Hence, this data could also be in-

Figure 57. Many anthropologists embrace the "single seed" hypothesis whereas all modern humans have a common ancestor which originated in Africa. As conceptualized by Williams Howells (1997), these different groups can be clustered together to form 28 Cranial Clusters which are all linked together, and 42 genetic clusters which are also linked ("Buriats" are "North Asians, and "Caucasoids" include Egyptians). Nevertheless, the genetic and cranial groups are not equivalent. Hence, Australoids are closer to Africans based on cranial clustering, but are closer to Southeast Asian and Pacific Islanders based on genetics. Reprinted from Howells, 1997. Getting Here. Compass Press,

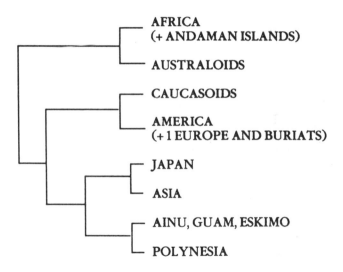

CRANIAL CLUSTER
28 GROUPS

- AFRICA (+ ANDAMAN ISLANDS)
- AUSTRALOIDS
- CAUCASOIDS
- AMERICA (+1 EUROPE AND BURIATS)
- JAPAN
- ASIA
- AINU, GUAM, ESKIMO
- POLYNESIA

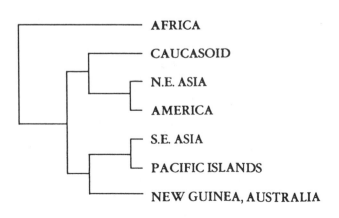

GENETIC CLUSTER
42 GROUPS

- AFRICA
- CAUCASOID
- N.E. ASIA
- AMERICA
- S.E. ASIA
- PACIFIC ISLANDS
- NEW GUINEA, AUSTRALIA

terpreted to mean that anatomically "modern" humans originated in Australia and then migrated to New Guinea, then to southern Asia, and then the Americas.

A more serious problem with the Eve hypothesis, is genetics. Those advancing the theory of "Eve" are staking their claims by making grossly erroneous assumptions about the maternal role in inheritance and "mutation." As reported by the International Human Genome Sequencing Consortium (2001) genetic material on female "chromosome Y is unusually young, probably owing to a high tolerance for gain of new material by insertion and loss of old material by deletion. Several lines of evidence support this picture." Transposed "elements on chromosome Y are on average much younger than those on autosomes. Similarly, MaLR-family retroposons on chromosome Y are younger than those on autosomes, with the representation of subfamilies showing a strong inverse correlation with the age of the subfamily. Moreover, chromosome Y has a relative over-representation of the younger retroviral class II (ERVK) and a relative under-representation of the primarily older class III (ERVL) compared with other chromosomes. Overall, chromosome Y seems to maintain a youthful appearance by rapid turnover."

By contrast, "the mutation rate in the male germline appears to be fivefold higher than in the female germline." Men pass on mutations to their offspring twice as often as women, such that "most mutation occurs in males." Higher male mutation rates are due to the fact that men make billions of sperm, while women are born with far fewer eggs. These numbers favor mutations being introduced when sperm-producing cells copy DNA on the Y chromosome. Males, therefore contribute more to evolutionary change."

As the Eve theorists have ignored the male contribution and have instead focused on "supposed" mutations in maternal-mitochondria, and have further erroneously assumed that mitochondria are inherited only from the maternal line, it can only be concluded that the Eve hypothesis is completely without any scientific foundation and should not be taken seriously.

And then there is the Neanderthal problem. Neanderthals did not evolve into Cro-Magnon peoples, as they coexisted for at least 20,000 or more years. And, European Neanderthals are genetically unrelated to modern Europeans (Krings et al., 1997; Ovchinnikov et al., 2000). If all species of humanity first evolved and then migrated out of Africa, how is it that two separate samples of DNA from different Neanderthals living in distant lands indicate that although these peoples were closely related, they are unrelated to modern peoples living in Europe? The answer? Because they evolved from an ancestral "tree" that significantly differed from that of the Cro-Magnon.

Although the environment acts on gene selection, and slight changes in the environment can activate different genes and gene sequences, thus producing variant versions of the same species, and although environmental differences can explain why African Neanderthals had an even smaller brain than Neanderthals living in frigid Europe, it cannot explain why two highly dissimilar species of humanity lived side by side for almost 20,000 years--with one group, Neanderthals, failing to evolve into the other. Rather, they "evolved" from different ancestral stocks who in turn "evolved" under different environmental conditions.

The evidence based on Neanderthal DNA, like the fossil record, is consistent with the theory of evolutionary metamorphosis. The Earth (and other planets) were genetically seeded to grow humans, and all manner of variations thereof.

And why didn't the Neanderthals evolve into modern people? First and foremost, they dwelled in Europe during an epoch of extreme Arctic cold—a bleak and frigid environment which limited experiential opportunities. They also failed to evolve because once the weather began to change, the Cro-Magnons moved in, and over the next 20,000 years the Neanderthals were either eradicated by the intellectually and technologically superior Cro-Magnons, and/or they died out due to the diseases that the Cro-Magnons brought with them as they invaded Neanderthal lands.

These later possibilities are also consistent with the theory of multi-regional evolutionary metamorphosis—as is the Sumerian claim that "gods" from other planets genetically altered some of the primitive humans living upon the Earth (e.g., Neanderthals), in order to create an intellectually superior being fashioned in the image of the gods, but who could serve as slave labor, i.e., the Cro-Magnon. According to the Sumerians, the men and women created in the image of the gods were also exceedingly sexually prolific, and their population mushroomed out of control. In contrast, according to the Sumerians, the more primitive species of humanity were sexually exceedingly primitive (suggesting that Neanderthal women had not yet lost their estrus) and once they came into contact with the god-like human creations of the gods, the Neanderthals died out as a species.

EVOLUTIONARY METAMORPHOSIS

Admittedly, it is possible that representatives of various distinct species simply migrated from place to place, thus giving rise to the illusion of multi-regional metamorphosis. Likewise, although the fossil and genetic evidence does not support the out-of-Africa, single line of descent model of pre-hominid human evolution, it remains a strong possibility that various species of pre-human "ape" may well have migrated across distant shores.

Migration becomes less likely given the numerous, and quite strikingly different species of Australopithecus, H. habilis, and H. erectus who emerged multi-regionally. Moreover, migration cannot explain the obvious independent evolution of Neanderthals and Cro-Magnon who apparently "evolved" from different branches of the human-genetic forest.

Nevertheless, even if we reject the multi-regional model as applying to most species, only the purposeful expression of genetically coded instructions can account for the obvious evidence of a step-wise, sometimes leaping progression in increasing intelligence and complexity which has characterized the metamorphosis of a rather narrow range of life on this planet. Only precise genetic instructions can account for the fact that basically similar species of humanity have emerged multi-regionally across distant lands, from distinct pockets of ancestral species which also emerged multi-regionally, as is evident in the case of Neanderthals and Cro-Magnons.

Because so many different species of humanity have emerged in distant lands, and as this pattern of multi-regionalism was repeated with Australopithecus, H. habilis, H. erectus, and H. sapiens, it thus appears that the planet (and others like it) was genetically seeded to grow humans; and that these genetic instructions were maintained in the genomes of the first creatures to be flung upon the face of this planet billions of years ago.

Over the course of "evolution" and the genetic engineering of the earthly environment, the unlocking and release of these "genetic memories" and silent traits, has resulted in the multi-regional replication of creatures (or variations thereof) who may well have been created by "god" and/or whom lived on other planets, including fish... frogs... reptiles... repto-mammals... mammals... primates... and woman, man....

DARWINIAN TAUTOLOGIES

With the exception of Wallace's theory of "natural selection," Darwinian and neo-Darwinian theories are in fact tautologies which mask what is little more than circular thinking and which can only predict by hindsight and from the present to the past; i.e. Breeders breed. Survivors survive. The fit are fit.

Specifically, according to Darwin's theory 1) Species reproduce themselves. 2) Random reproduction errors and small variations lead to variations in the population. 3). If these copying errors and random variations are adaptive and provide "fitness," they are naturally selected and passed on to offspring, thus leading to the survival of the fit. Hence, we know that a trait or a species is "fit" if those who have this trait survive, breed and produce offspring. However, there is no way to predict who is fit unless they survive and reproduce, which really means: those who reproduce are fit, and that almost all females, regardless of species, are fit, whereas the majority of males are not fit. Indeed, almost regardless of species the majority of males never breed (Bateman, 1948; Cade, 1985; Carpenter, 1942; Clutton-Brock, 1987; Fedigan, 1992; Howard, 1978; Johnson, 1972; Lott, 1979; McCann, 1981; Thornhill, 1981; Trivers, 1976; Zuckerman, 1932).

Of course, if we examine Darwin's proposition from the standpoint of the species as a whole, what his theory then explains is that a species is fit until it ceases to exist at which point it is no longer fit. And those species who survive are fit so long as they survive. Once they cease to survive they are no longer fit. Indeed, what his theory really means is that those who survive survive, those who reproduce reproduce, and those who die die.

Disregarding the obvious circular reasoning of these tautologies and the fact that Darwin is playing word games where survive=fit, and death=unfit, let us consider the male spider who breeds and is then eaten by his mate, and whose progeny fails to breed because they die— a common fate of infant spiders. Is this male spider who is eaten, and whose progeny die, more "fit" than the celibate male spider who grows fat and lives to an old age? Indeed, sometimes those who survive are not necessarily "fit" but only lucky, and ditto for those who breed, for among the animal and insect kingdom, the vast majority of males never breed (Bateman, 1948; Cade, 1985; Carpenter, 1942; Clutton-Brock, 1987; Fedigan, 1992; Howard, 1978; Johnson, 1972; Lott, 1979; McCann, 1981; Thornhill, 1981; Trivers, 1976; Zuckerman, 1932). Non-breeding males are produced in staggering numbers. Is the animal who breeds and is eaten or who is injured and dies protecting his access to a sex partner, but who produces non-breeding progeny somehow more "fit" that those animals who never produce sons and daughters but still live to a ripe old age?

Or, consider Alois and Klara Hitler, father and mother of Adolf Hitler. By Darwin's definition, because Alois and Klara produced several sons and daughters they were more "fit" than those Germans who failed to breed. Nevertheless, the children of Alois and Klara did not breed, and the actions of their son, Adolf, resulted in the death of up to 40 million people including his relatives and millions of Germans. His birth resulted in the destruction of the German nation!

Of course, the Darwinians may counter that Darwin was referring to species and not individuals. However, this argument is equally illogical, as over 95...% of all species which have appeared on Earth, have become extinct (Rampino & Haggerty, 1994; Raup, 1991). If we apply Darwin's theory to the rise and fall of species, then species, as a rule, are not "fit."

It is perhaps true, as is evident within the capitalist business community, that "survival of the fit" is the name of the competition game and the rule of success. However, those who run these businesses do so with certain goals in mind. That is, the behavior of the successful company is characterized by foresight, the development of long and short term goals which are intelligently considered, intelligently designed, purposefully planned and carried out, purposefully modified, etc., and so on. This is not Darwinism! Darwin's theory emphasizes random variations. If a business owner relied on Darwinism to run his business, he and his business would quickly become extinct.

As neatly summed up by one of the more prolific and vigorous defenders of Darwinism, Richard Dawkins (1987, p. 5) "the blind, unconscious, automatic process which Darwin discovered, and which we now know is the explanation for existence, has no purpose in mind. It has no mind, no mind's eye. It does not plan for the future. It has no vision, no foresight, no sight at all."

As applied to business, or even every day life, Darwinism would be a disaster. Behavior is purposeful, goal directed, and so to has been "evolution."

Human behavior is purposeful and is guided by intelligent (and often not so intelligent) choices. Our actions, and those of most higher animals, are not guided by random factors. Humans have learned to exert control of their environment and to chose the environment in which they dwell. Humans utilize selective breeding, and even the manipulation of genes to create new breeds and to transfer traits from one species to another--which is a form of purposeful and goal-directed evolution by "intelligent design."

Despite dogmatic claims to the otherwise, Darwin's tautological theory is contradicted by logic, the obvious, and the nature of DNA. "Evolution" is not due to random mutations. Mutation always results in death or disability. Likewise, those who breed are not more "fit" than those who do not—

as is evident among modern humans where those in poverty and who suffer ill health and an early death rate, have the highest birth rates and whose children are poorly fed and suffer from malnutrition, violence and disease, and who die at staggering rates before they are old enough to breed. This is "fit?"

Darwin's theory and neo-Darwinian evolutionary theory, including the inexplicable state-

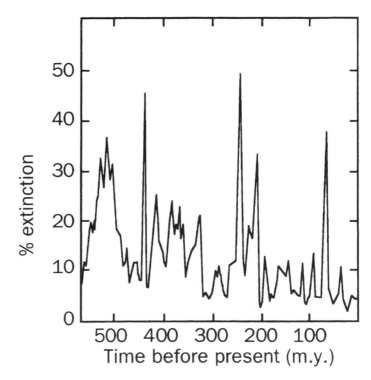

Figure 58. Estimates of the percentage of all genera to become extinct since 600 million years ago. There have been five major extinctions. Based on Rampino & Haggerty, 1994. Reprinted from Jakosky, 1998.

ments of Gould where he argues against progress, are completely refuted by the patterns of history, the fossil record, and by everything we know about genetics. There is obvious progress in neurological and human evolution, and there is evidence of obvious progress and increasing intelligence and structural technological capability across different phyla over the last 600 million years. And there is absolutely nothing random about DNA organization or expression.

As per the amazing claim that evolution is based on "random mutations" let us consider the so called "language gene," known as FOXP2. This gene existed prior to the evolution of language, and is found in the genome of other mammals, including mice, rats, dogs, cats, chimpanzees, and so on, but in a non-activated protein-protected form. The gene was identified by Dr. Anthony P. Monaco of the University of Oxford. FOXP2 is believed to switch on other genes during the development of the brain thus giving rise to the neural circuitry which supports human language. However, Dr. Svante Paabo and colleagues at the Max Planck Institute for Evolutionary Anthropology, reported in the August, 2002 issue of Nature, that the same exact gene exists in a non-activated form, in mice, chimpanzees and other primates (Enard, et al. 2002). According to Dr. Paabo, the FOXP2 gene has remained largely unaltered during the evolution of mammals. However, in humans, this formerly silent gene became activated through changes in the shape of its protective protein coat. Protein prevents the activation of genes, and removal or alteration in the shape of this protein overcoat,

DNA structure and function

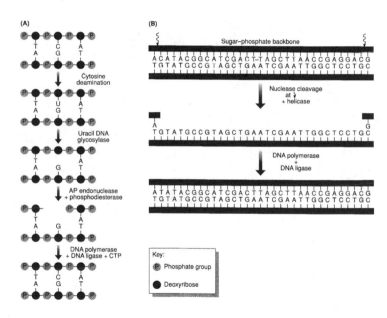

Figure 59A. *DNA repair pathways involving excision and repair. (A). Base excision repair and replacement. (B) Nucleotide excision and replacement. Reproduced from Strachan & Read*

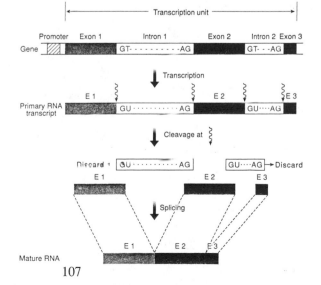

Figure 59B. *Schematic depiction of RNA-splicing. RNA-splicing involves removal of non-coding intronic segments and splicing exonic segments back together. Human genome organization, depicting coding and non-coding (intronic) genetic material. Reprinted from Strachan & Read, 1996, Human Molecular Genetics. Wiley, New York.*

allows for the gene to be activated.

Thus, the "language gene" did not randomly evolve through random mutations. It existed prior to the evolution of humans and prior to the evolution of language, in a silent, non-activated state.

Regardless of species, DNA displays a high degree of stability in regard to shape, form, organization, enzyme activity, composition, duplication and so on. The genetic code is, for the most part, universal (Strachan & Read, 1996; Watson et al. 1992) and there is no evidence or randomness in its organization or expression—as demanded by Darwin's theory.

Numerous genes and physical traits are shared by diverse phyla whose common ancestors did not posses the traits or the genes that each phyla supposedly randomly and "independently" evolved —a function, we are told by the Darwinians, of "coincidence" and "convergent" and "parallel" evolution where nature just happens to arrive at the same solution and creates the same exact gene; indeed perhaps the same coincidence which Darwin offers to explain the "laughable" similarity

Figure 60. *The Death of Darwin, as recorded by the satirical magazine, Punch. "Punch" got it wrong, for in this depiction there is an obvious progression, and Darwin and his followers do not believe in "progress," some referring to it as a "noxious" concept.*

between his work and others, or the same "coincidence" that Darwin relies upon to explain how he just happened to come up with the same exact theory proposed by Wallace.

"Coincidence" is not a scientific explanation.

As per the "evolution" of the same genes and the same traits in different species and phyla, obviously the Darwinian explanation is not logical. Rather, these diverse phyla inherited the genetic instructions to create the same genes so as to create identical or similar body parts. Either that, or these genes were released into the environment and transferred between species (Joseph, 1997, 2000).

Myriad life forms contain the same exact nucleotide sequence segments and "master regulatory genes" which code for the development of the heart, lungs, eyes and brains (D'Souza et al. 1995; Garcia-Fernandex & Holland, 1994; Ruddle, et al. 1994; Strachan & Read, 1996; Watson et al. 1992) —DNA that was independently inherited from common ancestors that had neither heart, lungs, eyes, or brains. In addition, the vertebrate Pax-6 gene cluster is organized and expressed in almost an identical fashion, differing by only 3-6%, in insects, worms, and mollusks (Quiring, et al. 1994).

And, the human genome and that of the higher plants, share homologous DNA-promoters and binding domains (e.g. da and AS-C) including a similar "helix-loop-helix" motif which is involved in cellular division and neuron generation in vertebrates, as well as the production of ovaries and seeds in plants via CHS-A and -J promoters (Joseph, 1998c). However, the common ancestor for mammals and plants diverged well over 1.6 billion years ago; 500 million to one billion years before the evolution, on Earth, of neurons, seeds, or sex organs.

These traits and these genes were preprogrammed to emerge in diverse phyla and did not coincidentally evolve in seperate and different species due to random mutations as is demanded by Darwinian theory. Rather, it appears that these genes and the genetic potential to create these genes and identical body parts, is a function of genetic inheritance and the intronic generation of "genes within genes" and thus species within species.

It is also possible that these genes may have been acquired laterally—that is, through plasmid exchange. Plasmid exchange may well explain why members of a species often "evolve" as a group and thus collectively step forward as they ascend the evolutionary ladder. Plasmid exchange, however, also appears to be under genetic control, occurring according to precise genetic instructions— a view which is an anathema to Darwinian theorists.

If Darwin's theory were correct, the genetic code in no way could be "universal" and the genomes of diverse species from plant to human would not contain a single identical gene, except for those few that would have been passed on, intact and unchanged, from a common ancestor. If Darwin's theory were correct, members of each individual kingdom of life and each separate phyla would have genomes which were radically different from one another which is clearly not the case. If Darwin's theory were correct, and evolution were due to random mutations, it would not be possible to make accurate predictions about ancestral species based on a "molecular clock" derived from rRNA or the genes of different plants or animals.

Although there is nothing random about the genetic code or the emergence of new species, Darwinian and neo-evolutionary theorists insist on randomness in the expression of mutations, and insist on purposelessness, presumably because the alternatives are too discomforting to consider. Many scientists reject the obvious for fear of discovering the "guiding hand of god." Unfortunately, by plucking out their eyes and by demanding that we do likewise, they have blinded themselves to the important implications of what has occurred on this planet over the course of the last billion years. They have blinded themselves to the patterns of history.

In their eagerness to avoid any possibility of a life affirming "god" many have instead embraced a malignant process that typically results in death or severe disability. They preach that all life is random, purposeless, and a product of "adaptive" random mutations. As preached by Darwin's Temple Priests, random mutations, and not "god" are responsible for the miracle of life, evolution, and creation. However, by accepting this gospel they have failed to clearly see the patterns of unplanned traits and cellular modifications and thus the random evolution of new species is thwarted.

Mutations and "unplanned" alterations in chromosomal structure are actively negated by repressor and heat-shock proteins, and a special subclass of oncogenes. Mutations, be they "adaptive" or malignant, like all unusual cellular formations and abnormalities in chromosomal structure, are associated with aberrant oncogene activity. A malignant progression ensues (Kim et al., 1994; Modrich, 1994; Sancar, 1994).

Neo-Darwinian evolutionary theory requires that these mutated errors be allowed free expression, that all corrective mechanisms just happen to fail, that the numerous duplicate copies available be forsaken, and that these mutations miraculously turn out to be adaptive and life promoting.

Moreover, these chance variations (mutations) must occur during the same time period in at least one male and one female who are unrelated and who live in close proximity, so that at least one viable breeding pair is produced, so that they may produce a mutated offspring. In fact, neo-Darwinian theory requires that these mutations randomly and simultaneously appear by chance, at the same time period, in the same location, in at least two unrelated breeding pairs, so that numerous mutated offspring are simultaneously produced who can interbreed thereby leading to the establishment and propagation of new species. And what is the likelihood of a scenario such as this occurring randomly and by chance?

The only way this scenario can work is if the trait was in fact genetically predetermined acting as silent genetic potential. Again, consider the work of Rutherford and Lindquest (1998). According to these authors, these traits can only be dispersed in the population with a high degree of probability, if they were predetermined. "If a population containing ten independent additive determinants affecting" the expression of "the trait, each present at a frequency of 0.1, the probability of an individual having at least six of these determinants, and thus the trait, is 1 in 7,000.

However, if the repressor protein were deactivated or its threshold for release lowered, thus "lowering the trait's threshold" for expression "by just one or two determinants, the probability of the appearance of the trait increases to 1 in 600 or 1 in 78. Once the frequency of a trait is increased in this manner, given a moderate degree of fitness advantage, selection could increase the frequency of genetic polymorphisms affecting the trait" so that it becomes widely "expressed in the population (Rutherford & Lindquest, 1998, p. 341).

Although the theory of evolutionary metamorphosis is based on the existence of traits which exist prior to their expression—and for which there is abundant scientific support (e.g., de Jong & Scharloo, 1976; Dykhuizen & Hart, 1980; Gibson & Hogness, 1996; Polaczyk et al., 1998; Rutherford & Lindquist, 1998; Wade et al., 1997), Darwinian and neo-Darwinian theory rejects predetermination. According to these theorists, evolution is random and due to chance variations, and traits cannot be genetically precoded and exist apriori, but are due to mutations

Again, for this Darwinian-mutated scenario to be successful requires that an error or abnormality in the genetic code not only go undetected and uncorrected but that the exact same mutation randomly, miraculously and simultaneously appear in numerous males and females who just happen to be living in close proximity, thereby allowing mutated mates to meet and to breed numerous progeny who also miraculously contain and express the mutated error. Darwinian theory, however, also negates this as a likelihood as these variations must occur by chance, and what is the likelihood of numerous identical variations appearing in the same group at the same time, randomly and purely by chance?

If the "mutation" did not simultaneously appear in numerous potential mates and in numerous surviving progeny, this new, mutated individual would die in a single generation and a new mutated species could not emerge; that is, unless this genetic change wasn't an error but genetically planned and part of the genome and was thus activated in numerous members of the same species.

According to neo-Darwinian orthodoxy, however, the production of new species is not genetically planned and is not encoded within the genome. Rather, the emergence of new species is the consequence of the production of random variations ("mutations") and thus "errors" in the genome which just happened to be advantageous to the organism, unlike other mutations which kill the host. We are "mutants" -so say the Neo-Darwinians.

THEOGENESIS:
THE INTELLIGENT UNIVERSE
by William F. Hamilton III

Is God in the human mind or is God a central reality to the universe?

This question may only be philosophical and not something that can be proven using scientific methodology, yet scientists of various disciplines continue to explore the subject of creation and a Creator.

The present day concept we hold of the Universe is far beyond anything the early Greek Philosophers such as Aristotle had in mind. In ancient geocentric views of the Universe, the earth held a primary position and the stars and planets (wanderers) of the heavens were just lights in a celestial sphere. There was no concept of a galaxy, supergalaxy, or cluster or supercluster in those ancient days--at least as reflected in Western/Greek (but not Middle Eastern Sumerian/Babylonian) thought.

As concepts in Cosmology improve, our understanding of the origin of life and the Universe at large increase. The prevailing scenario for the creation of the universe in Cosmology is called Inflation. This model developed by Alan Guth of M.I.T. goes beyond the Big Bang (Guth & Lightman, 1998). Essentially, Guth says that in the initial stages of creation the universe underwent a period of rapid inflation as if a balloon were expanded by a helium pump. There are up to 50 variations of this theory with little prospect of proving any one of them except by extremely delicate measurements made by instrumented satellites.

Not only are theories of creation of our universe being contemplated by cosmologists, but theories on the creation of many universes. These new theories seem to reflect an older idea that perhaps there was no beginning and no end to the creation of universes. That several universes may exist is a conclusion reached both in the world of macrophysics and microphysics, the world predominated by quantum theory.

The Anthropic Principle states that if any of the physical constants were to vary from the fine-tuned values we have determined for them then life would be impossible. It is reasoned that the properties of our universe are special and conducive to life. Speculation has ensued on the whys and wherefores.

The Anthropic Principle comes in two forms: weak and strong. The weak Anthropic Principle says in short that the ratios of certain cosmological numbers are conducive to a universe tuned to the existence of life. The strong Anthropic Principle says, in effect, that this is a universe specifically tuned to produce conscious intelligent beings. It stops short of implying genesis by a creator.

ASTROBIOLOGY & "PANSPERMIA"

"Pseudo-panspermia" is the delivery of complex organic compounds from space, to give the prebiotic soup some starter ingredients. This notion has already become widely accepted.

Basic panspermia is the presence in space, or on bodies like comets or asteroids, of microbial life that can be safely delivered to planets and start life there (Joseph, 2000). If the cells escape from a living planet on fragments after a meteor impact, the phenomenon is called litho-, ballistic-, impact- or meteoritic panspermia. Such trips are usually thought to be interplanetary only.

One version of modern panspermia proposes comets and meteors as the delivery vehicles. Comets can protect cells from UV and cosmic radiation damage; and comets can drop cells high in the atmosphere to float gently down. If bacterial spores can be immortal, as it appears, comets and meteors could spread life throughout a galaxy.

Strong panspermia is the extension of modern panspermia to deal with evolution as well. In strong panspermia, the genes for evolutionary advances are not written by copying mistakes and reshuffling within an original set of bacterial genes. Instead they are installed by gene transfer (Joseph, 2000). If these genes are spread by infectious agents such as viruses, they can transform whole populations in a single generation. The importance of gene transfer in evolution has gradually become recognized within mainstream biology. For example, in the May 5, 2000 issue of Nature, it was reported:

"It is difficult to account for the ability of bacteria to exploit new environments by the accumulation of point mutations alone. In fact, none of the phenotypic traits that are typically used to distinguish the enteric bacteria Escherichia coli from its pathogenic sister species Salmonella enterica can be attributed to the point mutational evolution of genes common to both. Instead, there is growing evidence that lateral gene transfer has played an integral role in the evolution of bacterial genomes, and in the diversification and speciation of the enterics and other bacteria."

Horizontal gene transfer also works in higher eukaryotes, where we used to hear that the germ line was protected from invasion. The very opposite may be the case. Recently scientists have observed that some transposable elements are preferentially expressed in germline cells and not somatic cells.

In the strong version of panspermia, Darwinian evolution can produce variation that results from one or two point mutations, and can, by natural selection, lead to adaptation, or microevolution. But this is not the same as macroevolutionary progress requiring whole new genes that differ from known predecessors by dozens to hundreds of essential nucleotides. In strong panspermia, those new genes must be supplied from elsewhere.

Until the emergence of panspermia, science believed that our whole planet was a biologically closed system. If so, the closed-system experiment is already well under way with proven, planet-wide results in favor of Darwinism. But the mere possibility of panspermia changes the situation entirely. One can no longer safely claim that the planet is a biologically closed system. Therefore, any instance of biological progress on Earth may result from the expression of genes acquired from elsewhere. In other words, the whole planet is subject to genetic contamination from space. If science ought to be sceptical of claims that have weak support, it should now be sceptical of the Darwinian account of evolution.

In its strongest version, panspermia holds that intelligent life can only descend from prior intelligent life (Joseph, 2000). Logically, therefore, intelligent life must have always existed, and what we have called "evolutionary progress" would actually be the local development of pre-existing, highly evolved life. This theory is fully scientific; there is nothing supernatural about it. I am attempting to name it Cosmic Ancestry. It responds to the informed criticism that Darwinism does not account for evolutionary progress.

These new trends in Astrobiology strengthen the hypothesis that we will find life on other planets througout the Cosmos. The strongest version of panspermia indicates that we will also find intelligent life througout the Cosmos. Though not proven yet, it lends support to the ET hypothesis for UFO origins. It also lends some support to evolutionary interference by advanced ET races that have come to earth. It does not go so far as to lend support to the ET abduction human-hybrid scenario though we could consider the possibility. Any argument that DNA from an alien source could not be mixed with ours would need re-evaluation in the new open systems view of life on earth.

These theories negate, therefore, the "organic soup" theory of the origin of life.

As argued by Dr. Rhawn Joseph (2000), "The likelihood that life and its DNA emerged from an organic soup, or undersea thermal vent -at least on Earth- is the equivalent of discovering a computer on Jupiter and then arguing that it was randomly assembled in the Methane Sea."

"The Origin of Life: If life were to appear on a desert island, we would assume it washed to shore, or fell from the sky. The Earth too, is an island, swirling in an ocean of space, and debris and living creatures, have been washing ashore since the creation.

"Cosmic collisions are commonplace, not only between meteors and planets, but entire galaxies, and life has been repeatedly tossed into the abyss...only to land on other planets. The genetic seeds of life swarm throughout the cosmos, and these genetic "seeds," these living creatures, fell to Earth, encased in stellar debris which pounded the planet for 700 millions years after the creation.

"And just as DNA contains the genetic instructions for the creation of an embryo, neonate, child, and adult, and just as modern day microbes contain "human genes" which have contributed to the evolution of the human genome, these "seeds," these living creatures, contained the DNA-instructions for the metamorphosis of all life, including woman and man."

"DNA acts to purposefully modify the environment, which acts on gene selection, so as to fulfill specific genetic goals: the dispersal and activation of silent DNA and the replication of life forms that long ago lived on other planets" (Joseph, 2001).

AN INTELLIGENT UNIVERSE?

The late Sir Fred Hoyle, who died recently at age 86, will be remembered as one of the most distinguished and controversial scientists of the 20th century. Soon after the end of the second world war he became widely known both by scientists and the public as one of the originators of a new theory of the universe. He was a fluent writer and speaker and became the main expositor of this new theory of the steady state, or continuous creation, according to which the universe had existed for an infinite past time and would continue infinitely into the future, as opposed to what Hoyle styled the "big bang" theory.

Hoyle wrote a seminal book he titled The Intelligent Universe. He made many controversial statements in his book that raised the ire of the scientific community.

Central to the debate is whether life in the universe is a matter of accident, whether unguided events led to the evolution of all forms of life on earth. Hoyle concludes that random events and chance occurrences are insufficient to account for the complexity of living organisms and that a cosmic control system exists, that there is a hierarchy of intelligences beyond human up to a limit we call God. This was a most disturbing statement to make as a scientist and a former atheist.

According to Hoyle, ""Once we see, however, that the probability of life originating at random is so utterly minuscule as to make it absurd, it becomes sensible to think that the favorable properties of physics, on which life depends, are in every respect DELIBERATE... It is therefore, almost inevitable that our own measure of intelligence must reflect higher intelligences.. even to the limit of God," (Hoyle, 1986).

He also said, "The chance that higher life forms might have emerged in this way is comparable with the chance that a tornado sweeping through a junk-yard might assemble a Boeing 747 from the materials therein... I am at a loss to understand biologists' widespread compulsion to deny what seems to me to be obvious."

And further, ""I don't know how long it is going to be before astronomers generally recognize that the combinatorial arrangement of not even one among the many thousands of biopolymers on which life depends could have been arrived at by natural processes here on the earth. Astronomers will have a little difficulty in understanding this because they will be assured by biologists that it is not so, the biologists having been assured in their turn by others that it is not so. The 'others' are a group of persons who believe, quite openly, in mathematical miracles. They advocate the belief that tucked away in nature, outside of normal physics, there is a law which performs miracles (provided

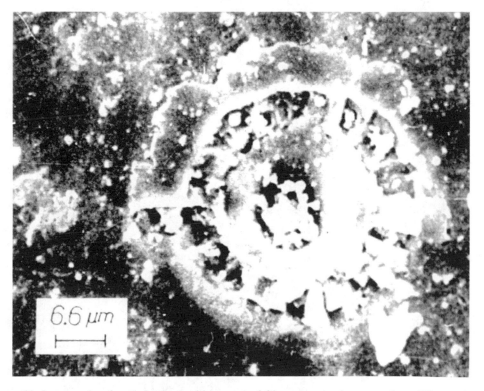

Figure 61. *Lunar microfossil that resembles a spiral filamentous microorganism. (Zhmur & Gerasimenko, 1999).*

Figure 62. *Evidence of alien life forms from the Efremovka meteorite: Coccoid bacteriomorphic structures of the Synechococcus- type. Distinct coccoid forms tended to form clusters composed of 2-4 cells, which are typical of modern cyanobacteria of this genera, (Zhumur & Gerasimenko, 1999).*

Figure 63. *Lunar microfossils Above & Right: Fossils discovered in moon samples collected in 1970 and 1970. Samples were hemetically sealed on the moon, opened and photographed in Russia. These microorganism are similar to modern coccoidal bacteria Siderococcus, Sulfalobus and Steptococus mitis. A single Steptococus mitis was also discovered in a TV camera retrieved from the moon by Appolo 12 astronauts in 1971.*

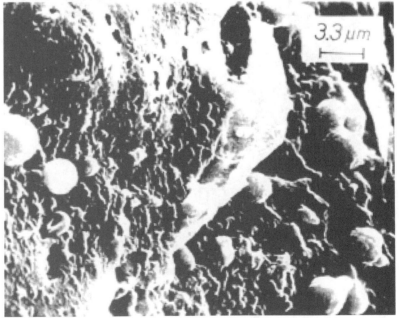

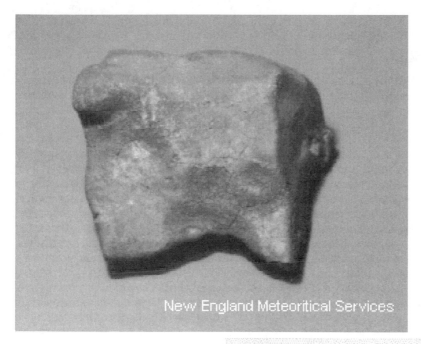

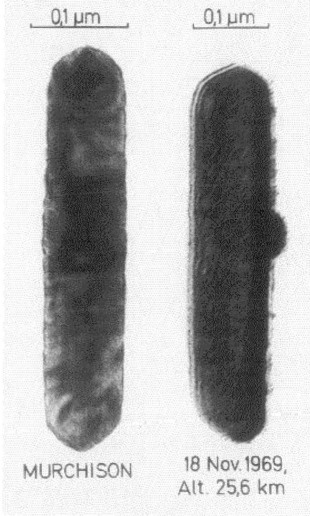

Figure 64. Above: Murchison meteorite.
Right: A fossil form the Murchison meteorite and a bacterium recovered from high in the atmosphere, by Hans D. Pflug.

the miracles are in the aid of biology). This curious situation sits oddly on a profession that for long has been dedicated to coming up with logical explanations of biblical miracles... It is quite otherwise, however, with the modern miracle workers, who are always to be found living in the twilight fringes of thermodynamics."

In his book titled The Mathematics of Evolution, Hoyle attempted to show with mathematics the constraints imposed on any Darwinian theory of evolution; i.e. that Darwin's theory is not supported by the math.

Was Hoyle wrong or do we live in an intelligent universe, not one governed solely by blind chance?

INTELLIGENT DESIGN

A new paradigm is rushing to rescue God from material science and calls its thesis, Intelligent Design (ID). This new movement, starting with life sciences, has further raised the ire of conventional scientists. Critics of this rising tide of advocates allege that those who back this concept are just the old Christian Creationist in a new suit of clothes. However, Hoyle was no Creationist, and neither is Dr. Richard Thompson who prefers Eastern Religious Philosophy to that of Western. Also, advocates of ID say they are not Creationists in the old sense of the term and only wish to present an alternate paradigm for understanding life in the universe.

Who are these leading advocates of Intelligent Design? One is William A. Dembski, a philosopher and logician and Michael Behe, a very insightful biochemist. These two have been prolific in writing on this subject and are heavily criticized by the Darwinist who will not concede to Intelligent Design as science. It is predicted that this debate will grow.

Dembski describes the theory behind ID in an abstract: "For the scientific community intelligent design represents creationism's latest grasp at scientific legitimacy. Accordingly, intelligent design is viewed as yet another ill-conceived attempt by creationists to straightjacket science within a religious ideology. But in fact intelligent design can be formulated as a scientific theory having empirical consequences and devoid of religious commitments. Intelligent design can be unpacked as a theory of information. Within such a theory, information becomes a reliable indicator of design as well as a proper object for scientific investigation. In my paper I shall (1) show how information can be reliably detected and measured, and (2) formulate a conservation law that governs the origin and flow of information. My broad conclusion is that information is not reducible to natural causes, and that the origin of information is best sought in intelligent causes. Intelligent design thereby becomes a theory for detecting and measuring information, explaining its origin, and tracing its flow." (Dembski & Behe, 1999).

AN INFORMATION UNIVERSE?

This brings us to other considerations that have been proposed for a universe that is rich in information. Cyberneticist David Foster also wrote a book he titled The Intelligent Universe, but his concept was the universe as data, as a cybernetic entity. Some of his concepts were simplistic and speculative, but he paved the way for more sophisticated theories of a cybernetic universe. These tentative theories see the universe as information and the information is processed according to instructions as one finds in a computer program. Of course, these theories imply the hidden existence of a programmer. We have had God as an Architect, a Dreamer, a Mathematician, an Engineer, and a Programmer. All of this seems rational, but scientists prefer the non-invocation of intelligent agents in the process of creation.

Mathematics: The importance of mathematics to science is such that we would not have science without mathematics. Quantities, measurements, equations, and formulas give us exactness in science. Probability theory has been used to demonstrate the improbability of a universe by accident. The internal harmony of universal processes can be analyzed with the aid of mathematics.

Consciousness: The last great frontier. We know of its existence in living entities, but its source and nature remains a scientific mystery. The pundits of the East say that all reality is based on consciousness.

Though all the galaxies emerge from him, He is without form and unconditioned (Tejabindu Up. 6, p. 239).

The Eastern view of consciousness is that it is the Supreme Reality, and though we live in a world of form and condition, it itself remains without form or condition and projects all that we witness. The western view is that consciousness is restricted to organisms, with the human as the

Figure 64. (Above) "The seeds of life swarm throughout the cosmos." Stars & Galaxies. (Below) Gaseous pillars in M16. The Eagle Nebula.

highest expression of consciousness. New ideas treat consciousness as universal and omnipresent.

Attempts are being made to construct a science of consciousness which calls on many disciplines. A recent conference on consciousness studies lists these subjects:

Philosophy: conceptual foundations, qualia, ontology, explanation, self, intentionality, mental causation, reality, free will

Neuroscience: neural correlates of consciousness, neuropsychology, vision, motor control, blindsight, anesthetic and psychoactive drugs, binding/integration

Cognitive Science and Psychology: implicit processes, attention, metacognition, memory, language, emotion, sleep, cognitive models, artificial intelligence, animal consciousness.

Physical and Biological Sciences: quantum theory, space and time, evolution, biophysics, medicine, computational theory, quantum computation and information, life.

Phenomenology and Culture: first-person methods, religion and contemplative studies, anthropology, transpersonal psychology, hypnosis, parapsychology, aesthetics.

That such a basic subject calls upon our most developed sciences and progressive minds gives us an idea on how we are evolving toward a greater understanding of our role in the universe.

The Holographic Paradigm: The concept of the universe as a giant hologram containing both matter and consciousness as a single field will, I am sure, excite anyone who has asked the question, 'What is reality?' This book may answer that question once and for all." (Wolf 2001)

The late physicist David Bohm, a former protégé of Einstein's and one of the world's most respected quantum physicists, and Stanford neurophysiologist Karl Pribram, one of the architects of our modern understanding of the brain — believe that the universe itself may be a giant hologram, quite literally a kind of image or construct created, at least in part, by the human mind. This remarkable new way of looking at the universe explains not only many of the unsolved puzzles of physics, but also such mysterious occurrences as telepathy, out-of-body and near-death experiences, "lucid" dreams, and even religious and mystical experiences such as feelings of cosmic unity and miraculous healings. (Bohm, 1986)

Perhaps the greatest challenge to future empirical sciences and faith-based religions is the determination of the primary stuff of reality. If exosomatic experiences are found to be valid, especially in near-death experiences where the brain ceases to be operational and yet consciousness, mind, and memory not only seem to continue, but seem to be enhanced in such a state, then this alone will call for a reassessment of current neurological paradigms and the evaluation of the nature of mind separated from body.

DARWINISM AND CREATIONISM
by Michael A. Persinger

In chapter five of this volume, Dr. Joseph points out a number of methodological limits to Darwin's hypothesis. The problem is few thinkers can comprehend the endless possibilities between concrete Creationism and abstract Darwinism. If we abrogate our capacity to perceive new possibilities, especially those testable and subject to rational inspection, then we confine the full extent of our cognitive capacity and limit our ability to consider viable and alternative explanations.

The diametric opposition between Darwinism and Creationism is contrived and frankly erroneous. The concept of Darwinian evolution and natural selection does not address the initial source of life forms. It assumes they are present and asks the intrinsic question: why did the shift in shapes from prototypical morphologies occur? For some structural features the effects of the impacts on and selections by the natural environment are very clear.

Darwin's and Wallace's interpretation for the variety of life forms was derived from a fundamental feature of human perception and cognition: directional seriation. If you draw a number of circles with different diameters on the blackboard and ask the class to infer the order of the occurrence of these circles over time, students will rank them from smallest to largest or largest to smallest. Seriation is based upon an intrinsic ordering of successive similarities of structure.

The use of seriation to infer temporal progression can be found in all of the sciences. It forms the basis of the concept of entropy in Physics, the periodic table and the concept of cycles (such as the urea cycle) in Chemistry, the Hertzsprung-Russell diagram in Astronomy, the law of superposition in Geology, taxonomy in Biology, shaping in Psychology, socialization in Sociology, or wage-cost creeps in Economics. However the presumption of temporal order is an inference.

Contemporary descriptions of both evolution and creationism (either as a gradual process or a catastrophic event) have not clearly described how and by what process the individual is mortal yet the germinal chains of nucleotides and proteins are potentially immortal through the generation of progeny. Neither story accommodates the bases for why the mean and standard deviation for the average live times for more than 95% of the multicelled species on this planet is 50 years plus/minus about 25 years.

The prevalence and potency of this limit strongly suggests a survival value for a restricted existence for the individual. It may have reflected the rate of changes within the physical environment at the time when early life developed. Structural and functional modification of a single cell as it progress along its ontogenetic line to full adulthood containing trillions of cells has more morphological possibilities than comparable adaptations attempted by an adult organism.

Neither story explains the sudden changes in speciation even without the assumption of catastrophic impacts from meteorites. The slow seriation of DNA sequences in response to selection by the physical environment and the intrinsic compatibility of the chemical consequences of the expression of genes could accommodate some changes in morphology and function. The evocation that billions of years were involved, which would allow even the lowest of probabilities of combinations to have the chance for expression, does not reveal the mechanisms of the sudden shifts that sometimes exceed the limits of seriation.

There is likely to be a continuum of different mechanisms and processes that have affected both the formation and progression of living molecules. A singular theory or story with a simple theme may appeal to the cognition of the believer to help him or her organize the overwhelming hits of information. However, it does not generate indefinitely the accurate predictions of the quantitative changes in morphological adaptations.

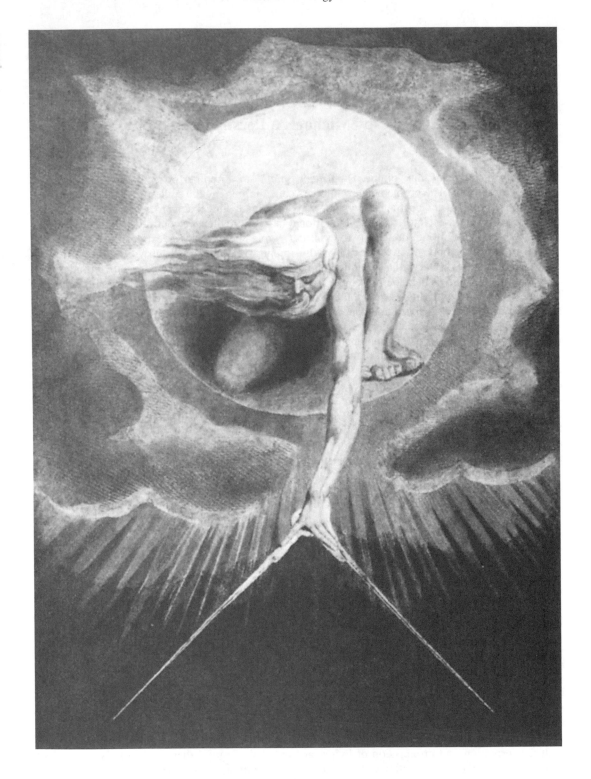

Figure 65. *The creation (Europe: A Prophecy, William Blake).*

COMPLEX MAGNETIC FIELDS, ABIOGENESIS, AND THE EVOLUTION OF LIVING SYSTEMS
by Michael A. Persinger

Abiogenesis was one of the first problems that I pursued as a young student. I had been strongly influenced by the works of Harold C. Urey concerning the atmospheres of planets. The classic experiment S. L. Miller, published in 1953 in Science, confirmed that electric arcs generated through Precambrian mixtures of atmospheric gases could generate amino acids.

During the mid 1960s I unintentionally exploded many bell jars and spent many hours searching the terrain of paper chromatography for the slightest hint of ninhydrin-induced changes in my basement laboratory in Menomonee Falls, Wisconsin. There were times when I thought I saw the glint of chemical reaction suggestive of an amine group. However the results were not consistent, despite my most conscientiousness attempts to replicate the process.

However I began to suspect that the ease of generating some amino acids from atmospheric constituents and even the cumbersome strategies for synthesizing primitive purines from the gases of formaldehyde or cyanide with oxygen, nitrogen, and water vapour that were exposed to ultraviolet light or through which electric discharges were generated would not account for the organizational components of these reactions. There had to be a "template" that allowed both temporal and spatial continuity for higher organization to be both encouraged and maintained.

This possibility became feasible, in principle, when F. E. Cole and E. R. Graf who suggested that the original Schumann Resonance (unique to the earth itself) may have augmented abiogenesis. Their experiments showed how prebiotic polymerization of amino acids required complex, time-varying magnetic fields simulating the Schumann resonance. They argued strongly that synthesis of nucleic acids acquired structural and catalytic assistance from pre-existing proteins. In fact the experimental demonstration of preferential interactions between poly-L-arginine and poly-L-lysine and certain nucleotides mayhave represented a rudimentary, primeval translation system.

The next logical step would be the possible existence of a complex higher order of geophysically-generated magnetic fields that perhaps might organize or at least determine the initial direction of the evolution of macromolecules. The influence of these fields would not necessarily be mediated by mechanisms such as Pasteur's intuition of absolute asymmetric synthesis due to optical rotations or to compensation for thermal energies. These mechanisms involved relatively strong, static magnetic fields. A more fundamental mechanism, derived from complexity and information contained within the fields themselves, would be required.

The recent development of accurate methods of measurements of complex environmental magnetic fields (and the computer memory to store and analyze this information) has given empirical support to the hypothesis that there are processes generated by the earth itself which direct the chemical structure and function of organisms in very specific directions. The existence of these complex, information-containing magnetic fields does not require the presumption the process is sentient, teleological, or even alive. The processes are likely to have always been present, perhaps from the beginning of abiogenesis, but as yet not detected. A comparison might be the probable existence of kHz electromagnetic waves for billions of years; however, they were not measured until the radio receiver was constructed.

That environmental magnetic fields can organize biochemistry has been known for more than two decades. Natural magnetic fields, like the Schumann resonance, can act as zeitgebers or time givers for the oldest and most powerful rhythm of the living system: the diurnal cycle. Both the sensitivity of these rhythms to natural magnetic fields as well as their affect on such a phylogentically old phenomenon suggest that they were present during the early stages of life forms. The strength of these fields might be extremely small. (If one were measuring only with a barograph (kiloPa) the complexity and information contained within the much faster sound pressure variations of human speech (milliPa) would never be discerned.) Research by R. Sandyk has shown how time-varying picoTesla strength magnetic fields, more than a thousand times weaker than the amplitudes of typical geomagnetic activity, influence biological chemistry.

In the 1940's H.Burr argued there was an intrinsic electrical field serving as a blue-print to ontogeny, the development of the single individual from single cell to complex organism. The concept has been in large part forgotten with the enthusiasm of molecular biology. However with all chemical reactions there are electromagnetic equivalents that have the capacity to generate fields beyond the spatial extent of the chemical reaction and to act as "zeitgebers" or "forms" to affect the interactions between atoms and molecules.

Even within the limits of electroencephalography we can measure the specific patterns of electromagnetic fields around the skull that emerge from the myriad of chemical reactions within the cerebral volume. The data suggest that the more complex the temporal structure of the magnetic fields applied to the brain and the more these patterns imitate natural processes (that are almost never symmetric sine-waves or square waves) the less the energy and the lower the intensity required to affect the entire organism.

Life on this planet is immersed with its magnetic field. It is more than just a static field whose intensities are larger at the poles than at the equator. It is a complex electromagnetic conversation that penetrates the volume of biological systems and has the potential to affect their chemical reactions. However without specific measurements we will not understand the physiological practicality or relevance of these interactions.

If this reasoning is accurate, there should have been a complex matrix of electromagnetic fields present during abiogenesis. Once the energies required to generate the essential components had discharged and left their residua, these complex shapes and sequences may have determined the progression of molecular complexity and ultimately life itself. As cell complexity aggregated into organs and specialized into structures such as the human brain, one would have expected these fields to have maintained their influence (as did the simple fields upon diurnal variations) upon even the nuances of subjective experience.

For example we have found repeatedly that the rate of occurrence or incidence of sense of a presence, the feeling of a Sentient Being, within a quiet chamber is moderately correlated with the global geomagnetic activity at the time of the experience. The strength of the correlation is enhanced by a variety of stimuli that increase the activity of the right hemisphere in most subjects. This can include application of experimentally-generated complex magnetic fields or the general apprehension of world events. Our magnetometric measurements of the concurrent local magnetic variations suggest the critical factor is not the intensity per se but the pattern of geomagnetic activity that is correlated with specific bands of intensity.

The characteristics of these hypothetical fields within which life still exists must be measurable. The metaphor by which they are described, such as holograms or matrices, must still be rational and subject to systematic testing. If these fields are measurable, they can be duplicated. If they are subject to experimental verification, then these fields should affect not only human experience but the molecular structures with which experience is correlated.

BRAINS, SCIENCE, NONORDINARY & TRANSCENDENT EXPERIENCES:
Can Conventional Concepts and Theories Adequately Address Mystical and Paranormal Experiences?
by William Braud

What if you slept, and what if in your sleep you dreamed, and what if in your dreams you went to heaven and there you plucked a strange and beautiful flower, and what if when you awoke you had the flower in your hand? Ah, what then? --Samuel Taylor Coleridge, *Biographia Literaria* (1817)

In this chapter, I hope to present a balanced account of both the strengths and limitations of conventional cognitive science and neuroscience, as these attempt to address and explain *nonordinary and transcendent experiences* (NTEs). These NTEs include, but are not limited to, mystical, spiritual, and paranormal experiences. Although some findings and theories of experimental psychology, cognitive science, and neuroscience may explain, and be quite relevant to, certain aspects of these nonordinary experiences, these explanatory concepts are not yet able to deal adequately with other aspects of these experiences. In particular, current cognitive science and neuroscience are unable to account for well-researched cases in which NTEs yield veridical knowledge about sensorily inaccessible events or in which they are associated with objectively measurable influences upon others or upon the physical world—at a distance, and beyond the reach of our conventional means of action and influence. I also will present material relevant to the issue of whether the human brain might wholly produce consciousness or whether it might serve, rather, as a vehicle for the transmission and expression of consciousness. Before treating attempts to understand or explain these nonordinary experiences, it is important to examine more closely the nature of the experiences themselves.

Nonordinary and Transcendent Experiences (NTEs)

Our familiar, ordinary experiences and actions have increasingly been brought within the growing framework of scientific understanding. Physical substrates—or, at least, physical correlates—have been found for many of our mundane activities (our sensations, movements, and memories) and even for some of our more exotic experiences (our imagery, dream conditions, and volitions). Nonetheless, there have always been forms of experience that have persistently evaded capture by science's explanatory net—experiences that intimate that there is more to our human nature and human potential than is portrayed by the conventional models and theories of physiology and psychology. It was to such exceptional experiences that William James (1890/1956) was referring when he suggested that:"The great field for new discoveries . . . is always the unclassified residuum. Round about the accredited and orderly facts of every science there ever floats a sort of dust-cloud of exceptional observations. . . . Any one will renovate his science who will steadily look after the irregular phenomena. And when the science is renewed, its new formulas often have more of the voice of the exceptions in them than of what were supposed to be the rules (pp. 299-300)."

James (1902/1985) had similar experiences in mind when he wrote: "Our normal waking consciousness, rational consciousness . . . is but one special type of consciousness, whilst all about it, parted from it by the filmiest of screens, there lie potential forms of consciousness entirely different. We may go through life without suspecting their existence; but apply the requisite stimulus, and at a touch they are there in all their completeness, definite typos of mentality which probably somewhere have their field of application and adaptation. No account of the universe in its totality can be final which leaves these other forms of consciousness quite disregarded (p. 388)."

Examples of these exceptional experiences, indicative of *something more* that lies beyond the range of our familiar forms of knowing, being, and doing, can be found in a new volume, published through the auspices of the American Psychological Association (APA). This recent book, entitled

Varieties of Anomalous Experience (Cardena, Lynn, & Krippner, 2000), treats of unusual experiences in the following categories: hallucinatory experiences, synesthesia, lucid dreaming, out-of-body experiences, psi-related experiences [i.e., psychic or paranormal experiences], alien abduction experiences, past-life experiences, near-death experiences, anomalous healing experiences [including instances of mental, distant, psychic, and spiritual healing], and mystical experience. Although I feel the title of this book is unfortunate—because the term "anomalous" suggests that these experiences are not normal or natural—the publication of such a volume by the APA does indicate that such experiences are finally receiving at least some of the professional attention they deserve.

Historically, these unusual experiences have been given many names—*supernatural* or *paranormal* experiences being, perhaps, the most frequent of these. The 18th century scientist-turned-mystic, Emanuel Swedenborg (1756/1998), in his *Arcana Coelestia*, described experiences similar to these when he coined the term *remains*, which Swedenborg scholar Wilson Van Dusen paraphrased as "our inner memory of everything sacred . . . [our] personal treasure of spiritual understanding . . . [our] sacred personal collection of little realizations of heaven" (Van Dusen, 2001, pp. 97, 106). William James himself referred to these experiences as *white crows*, reminding us that "if you wish to upset the law that all crows are black, you must not seek to show that no crows are; it is enough if you prove one single crow to be white" (1890/1969, p. 41). In 1919, the irrepressible gadfly journalist Charles Fort used an equally picturesque phrase, *damned facts*, to describe similar recalcitrant exceptions and embarrassments to the received science of his day (Fort, 1941). Other names for these and similar experiences have included *peak experiences* (Maslow, 1962), *Minerva experiences* (Otto, 1966), *transpersonal experiences* (Grof, 1972), *extraordinary phenomena* (Masters, 1974), *transcendental experiences* (Neher, 1980), *extraordinary experiences* (Helminiak, 1984), *praeternatural experiences* (Nelson, 1989), *metanormal functioning* (Murphy, 1992), *exceptional human experiences* (EHEs, White, 1993), *wondrous events* (McClenon, 1994), *high holy moments* (Van Dusen, 1999, p. 76), and—as we have seen—*anomalous experiences* (e.g., Cardena, Lynn, & Krippner, 2000; Reed, 1988; Zusne & Jones, 1989). In this chapter I prefer to call these experiences *nonordinary and transcendent experiences (NTEs)*—nonordinary because of their relative rarity and unfamiliarity, and transcendent because they go beyond the conventional understanding of human potential and of the world and because, under special circumstances, such experiences can trigger transformative changes, and working with such experiences can allow the transcendence of what one was before the experience. To facilitate our discussion, I will focus on two particular forms of these NTEs—mystical/unitive experiences and psychical experiences.

Mystical and unitive experiences are those in which there is a strong sense of greater connection, sometimes amounting to union, with the divine, other people, other life forms, objects, surroundings, or the universe itself. Often, this is accompanied by a sense of ecstasy or of being outside of one's "skin-encapsulated [individual] ego" (Watts, 1963, p. 18) or self identity. Related to this is the *pure consciousness event* that has been studied extensively by Forman (1990, 1999), who defines this as "a wakeful though contentless (nonintentional) consciousness" (1990, p. 8), and considers this a form of introvertive mysticism (Stace, 1960).

Psychical experiences are those in which we learn about or influence the world through means other than the conventionally recognized senses, motor systems, or their mechanical extensions, or rational inference, in cases in which chance coincidence has been ruled out. The major forms of psychical experiences are well known as telepathy, clairvoyance, precognition, and psychokinesis; and these can be augmented by experiences and events suggestive of survival of bodily death.

Originally having the meaning of feeling (more literally, suffering) at a distance, *telepathy* is now understood as accurate, direct knowledge of the mental content or subjective experiences of another person, typically at a distance—a kind of mind-to-mind communication or interaction. An example would be my accurate discernment of a pain in the left thumb experienced, right now, by someone who is reading this chapter. Initially having the meaning, among the French, of clear or distant seeing, *clairvoyance* is now described as accurate, direct knowledge of some objective event—again, usually at a distance; this is a kind of mind-to-object communication or interaction. An historical example of clairvoyance is an incident, investigated by an agent of Immanuel Kant, in which the 18th century scientist-turned-mystic, Emanuel Swedenborg described the timing, nature, and progression of a fire that was raging in a distant city, 300 miles away; two days later, a messenger arrived and revealed the accuracy of Swedenborg's prior report. In *precognition*, one displays accurate knowledge of future events that, according to our conventional view of time, have not yet occurred and that could not have been predicted on the basis of rational inference, nor accounted for on the basis of chance coincidence; premonitory dreams are common examples of precognition. *Psychokinesis* (sometimes called telekinesis) indicates mind-matter interactions in which one's attention and intention may directly influence other persons, other living systems, or inanimate physical systems—usually at a distance; such psychokinetic influence are most often detected in sensitive physical or biological systems that are rich in free variability or randomness. It has been suggested that some instances of unusual healing (especially "distant healing") may involve psychokinesis. *Afterdeath* or *survival research* addresses findings that suggest that some aspect of human personality might survive the death of the physical body. This is the more controversial branch of psychical research that concerns itself with such phenomena as apparitions of the dead, hauntings, some poltergeist occurrences, mediumistic communications, mediumistic physical phenomena, out-of-body experiences, near-death experiences, and reports suggestive of past lives and reincarnation. The difficulties these psychical experiences pose for conventional cognitive and neuropsychological interpretations—and even for physical interpretations—are treated in detail, below.

Forms of Psychical NTEs That Brain Science Can and Cannot Adequately Address

Within each class of NTEs, there is a range of experiences that vary widely in their characteristics. Some experiences are true instances of their class, and we might call these *veridical NTEs*. Other experiences may superficially resemble veridical NTEs but, upon more careful examination, can be found to be ordinary experiences in disguise. Still other experiences may be complex blends of these two forms—they may be veridical NTEs that also happen to have some ordinary features, or they may be ordinary experiences that, nonetheless, possess some veridical, nonordinary qualities. The range and complexity of these experiences call for great care and discernment on the part of investigators who wish to study these phenomena seriously. Facile tactics of treating these experiences as homogeneous groupings that can be attributed entirely to quirks of the brain or to supernatural visitations simply will not do. Rather, careful attention to the *details* and *full nature* of the experience in question, and the ability to make sometimes subtle discriminations, are essential tools for adequate understanding in this area of study.

Let me illustrate the investigatory issues by means of a simple example. The déjà vu experience is characterized by an often intense feeling of familiarity upon encountering a situation that is "really" novel. I visit a foreign city that I have not previously visited or learned about. On my first stroll through the center of town I see someone who is wearing a light blue suit, holding a walking stick, and standing in front of a large glass window. I have a curious feeling of having seen this, done this, been here before. The feeling may be sufficiently eerie as to be accompanied by gooseflesh and a tingling of my spine or scalp. What are we to make of this experience? Several interpretations come to mind:

1. The experience is not really occurring; I am pretending to have such an experience in order to gain attention, to fool someone, or to play a game.

2. Although novel, the street scene does closely resemble one that I have seen before, and the familiarity is attributable to a real memory of something similar.

3. On this particular occasion, there is an unusual delay in the transmission of information across my corpus callosum and other fiber tracts that connect my two cerebral hemispheres; so, I really have experienced this before—a tiny fraction of a second before—in one hemisphere, before the information registers a second time in my other hemisphere.

4. I experience unusual firing of neurons deep beneath my temporal lobe, in my brain's familiarity area, and the feeling of familiarity is simply a quirk of peculiar brain activity—a microseizure, as it were, in a particular, localized area of my brain; what I happen to be observing at the time (the street scene) is irrelevant to the familiarity experience.

5. I have had an earlier precognitive dream about this very encounter, and when I observe the street scene, I have already seen it before—in my prior dream—so, the experience naturally seems familiar.

Notice that, from the limited information of only my verbal report of having a déjà vu experience, an independent investigator could not know, with any certainty, which of these five interpretations is most likely to be correct. Additional information is needed if we are to make a case for or against any one of these five potential explanations. To assess Interpretation #1, we would need additional information about my subjective experience at the time of the event in question; it might also be useful to know something about my history, motives, and predispositions. To assess Interpretation #2, information about my prior experiences and my memories would be needed. To assess

Interpretations #3 and #4, a record of my brain activity during the event in question would be needed. To assess Interpretation #5, a record of the content of my earlier dream would be useful; for this to be convincing, the record should have been made before the later déjà vu experience.

With respect to the above scenarios, it is important to recognize two things. First, to infer the correctness of Interpretations #3 and #4 *in the absence of the requisite brain activity indicators* is entirely speculative, and to automatically conclude that one or both of these interpretations is correct is risky and no more likely to be true than any of the other interpretations. Second, if a prior record of the dream had been made, had been extremely rich in specific details, and is available for study, this record could provide prima-facie evidence in favor of Interpretation #5. Note also that, given a pre-existing and accurate dream record, *Interpretation #5 could be valid regardless of whether or not any or any combination of the first four interpretations also happen to be true.*

Now consider the following additional twist on this experience. What if, in addition to reporting the feeling of familiarity upon seeing this particular street scene, I supplement my report by saying that I have a feeling that if I pass the blue-suited person, with walking stick, near the large shop window, go to the next corner, turn right, and continue on for one and a half blocks, there will be small shop with a yellow elephant painted on its front door? What if I perform the experiment, check out the predicted location, and do, indeed, find what was described? What if had made that "elephant on the door" prediction at the time I experienced déjà vu and mentioned that I thought the experience would next unfold in that way? Or, what if the "elephant on the door" had also been included as part of my earlier dream record? In both of these cases, I can imagine no conceivable way in which the electrical or neurochemical activities within my brain—either at the time of the dream or at the time of the déjà vu experience—could account for the accuracy of my prediction. This is because the phenomenon to be explained does not behave—with respect to distance, time, or barriers—in ways that the known brain activities, or their concomitants or sequelae, behave. *Something more* is needed to account for this veridical NTE, above and beyond what currently is known about the brain and its functioning.

The possibilities and principles present in the above account illustrate well the strengths and limitations of attempts to explain, or explain away, certain unusual experiences based solely on the findings and constructs of brain science. If we replace the déjà vu experiences with any of a wide range of NTEs, similar alternative interpretations and arguments arise. We can generalize these possibilities further by substituting any of the varieties of psychical functioning (telepathy, clairvoyance, precognition, psychokinesis, afterlife or survival evidence) for the déjà vu experience, and slightly reframing the various interpretations in the following ways:

Ostensible psychical experiences such as telepathy, clairvoyance, precognition, psychokinesis, or experiences suggestive of an afterlife or survival of bodily death may be explained on the basis of: 1. Fabrication or hoaxing of the experiences,

2. Misperceptions and distortions of observation or of memory,

3. Subtle sensory cues—whether consciously attended to or not—that might betray the nature of the event that is to be known or perceived,

4. Rational inference—through which the nature of the to-be-known-or-perceived event might be determined or guessed,

5. Chance coincidence, or

6. Quirks of the brain that simulate the psychical experience.

For those predisposed not to accept the reality of psychical experiences, parsimony would demand that the foregoing six explanations be considered immediately and that only after these possibilities have been carefully and completely ruled out would one entertain the possibility of the presence of a veridical NTE. Note, again, that if there is evidence of a specific and strong correspondence between the content of a subjective experience and the content of some referent event (distant or remote in space or in time), the absence of the first five of these explanations would guarantee that the referent event would be conventionally inaccessible to brain and cognition. Further, if these five possible explanatory conditions are absent, the presence or absence of Explanation #6 becomes irrelevant in identifying the experience as a veridical NTE. In other words, brain quirks—of any sort—can explain a subjective experience but cannot explain *the presence of an accurate connection between that subjective experience and some inaccessible referent event.* For example, a particular brain pattern can be shown to underlie—and "explain"—an image of her son that arises in the mentation of a mother sitting before a hearth and idly watching the dancing flames, but the presence of that brain pattern cannot explain the sudden arising of that particular image at the precise moment that the son is experiencing a life-threatening situation, thousands of miles away (an instance of so-called *crisis telepathy*), nor can the brain pattern explain the strong correspondence that happens to occur between the two conventionally unconnected events of the mother's imagery and the distant son's desperate, momentary circumstance and need. Stated in still another way, brain activities (or any other bodily activities or conditions) can explain many, and perhaps all, subjective experiences themselves, but cannot explain the timely and accurate *connections* or *relationships* between those subjective experiences and meaningfully related distant events.

Difficult and Easier Discriminations

It is often difficult to analyze and evaluate psychical experiences that occur spontaneously in everyday life circumstances. It is not always clear whether there are or are not peculiar brain activities associated with these experiences. Often, it is difficult to determine, with certainty, whether the confounding factors of deliberate misrepresentation, hoaxing, misperceptions, distortion of observations or of memory, subtle sensory cues, rational inference, or chance are present or absent in any given case. Because brain activities and conditions are active in all of these confounding factors—it is likely that brain activities are present in all cognitive activities because they serve as the vehicles of expression for these activities—in this sense, brain activities can "explain" many NTEs. If it were possible to connect an NTE with some conventionally inaccessible referent event, however, and if it were possible to rule out the confounding factors just mentioned, then veridical NTEs could be identified fairly unambiguously even in everyday life circumstances. Indeed, for the past 12 decades—dating, at least, from the founding of the Society for Psychical Research (SPR) in England in 1882—countless observations and records have been made of apparently genuine veridical psychical experiences. These have been published in the *Proceedings of the SPR* and the *Journal of the SPR*, in the *Proceedings* and *Journal of the American SPR*, and in similar psychical research and parapsychology journals in many countries, and these findings have been compiled and discussed in numerous scholarly volumes (e.g., Myers, 1902; Stevenson, 1970; Wolman, 1977). These reports of spontaneous psychical experiences vary greatly in the quality of the evidence that they present. As would be expected, this evidence has been questioned by counteradvocates of these claims—with varying degrees of plausibility and success—and a number of reasonable critiques of this literature have been published (e.g., Kurtz, 1985).

Ruling out possible confounds more effectively and identifying veridical NTEs more unambiguously become possible when these experiences, or experimental analogs or models of these, are brought into the laboratory for careful study. Large numbers of experimental studies of telepathy, clairvoyance, precognition, and psychokinesis have been conducted and reported in professional parapsychology journals (e.g., the *Journal of Parapsychology*), as well as in many "mainstream" journals (e.g., *Nature*, the *Journal of Experimental Psychology*, *Psychological Bulletin*, and many clinical and medical journals).

Through the years, the investigations of experimental parapsychology have become increasing sophisticated, criticisms of earlier work have been effectively met, and present studies match or exceed those of conventional behavioral and biomedical research in the tightness of their designs and in their safeguards against artifacts and confounding variables. The experimental designs effectively rule out the possibility of ordinary sensory cues, rational inference, and chance coincidence, so that if consistent relationships are found between subjective experiences and distant and shielded target events, such evidence cannot be explained in terms of conventional informational or energetic transfers or mediation, nor can these *correspondences* (see previous section) be accounted for in terms of the brain activities or conditions of the research participants. Even a cursory review of the vast literature of experimental parapsychology is beyond the scope of this chapter. Rather than attempting to summarize the results of these investigations, I will simply indicate some of the more important sources to which interested readers may go to acquaint themselves, first hand, with the methods and outcomes of these studies. These resources include the *Proceedings* and *Journals* mentioned earlier in this section, the *Journal of Parapsychology*, the *European Journal of Parapsychology*, the *International Journal of Parapsychology*, and careful and extensive treatments of relevant literature in volumes by Broughton (1991), Griffin (1997), Krippner (1977-1994), Kurtz (1985), Radin (1997), Targ, Schlitz, and Irwin (2000), and Wolman (1977).

Extensive reviews and meta-analyses are available for compilations of findings from the largest and most successful research projects. These projects include studies of remote viewing (clairvoyance experiments usually involving distant geographical sites, buildings, and natural and human-made features as targets; Nelson, Dunne, Dobyns, & Jahn, 1996; Utts, 1996); waking state of consciousness, free response, extrasensory perception studies (Milton, 1993); dream telepathy studies (Child, 1985); mixed telepathy and clairvoyance under conditions of sensory restriction ("ganzfeld" studies; Bem & Honorton, 1994; Storm & Ertel, 2001); experiments conducted under conditions of nonordinary states of consciousness induced by relaxation, hypnosis, and meditation techniques (Honorton, 1977; Schechter, 1984; Stanford & Stein, 1993; Storm & Thalbourne, in press); precognition experiments (Honorton & Ferrari, 1989); psychokinesis experiments involving inanimate electronic and mechanical random target systems (Dunne & Jahn, 1992; Dunne, Nelson, & Jahn, 1988; Radin & Ferrari, 1991; Radin & Nelson, 1989; psychokinesis (direct mental influence) studies involving living target systems (Braud & Schlitz, 1991; Schlitz & Braud, 1997); and even time-displaced psychokinesis (retroactive intentional influences) studies (Braud, 2000).

Although these processes of telepathy, clairvoyance, and precognition have been noticed and recorded throughout history, and also have been documented in careful laboratory studies, their existence, to some, remains controversial. Alternative explanations and critiques of such phenomena have been made, again, throughout history, by skeptics and counter-advocates of such claims. In my opinion, these phenomena are genuine. The evidence is more than adequate scientifically, and there appear to be increasing reasons to accept that psi phenomena are real and not accounted for by conventional scientific models. I base this judgment upon my own experiences of them, my observations of their occurrence in my own laboratory under well-controlled conditions, similar observations by colleagues whose work I know and trust, and from my examination of much of the published literature on these phenomena. A reasonable and balanced approach to judging claims about these processes would be to examine carefully and dispassionately the published primary reports, read the critics' arguments, read the counterarguments to these, recall your own—and others'—lived experiences of similar incidents, and then draw conclusions based upon the fullest possible amounts of evidence and argument.

Aspects of Veridical Psychical NTEs That Brain Science Can & Cannot Adequately Explain

As mentioned previously, neuroscience and cognitive science can adequately account for the nature of the physiological and psychological conditions that occur in persons while they are having veridical psychical NTEs. They can identify the brain states that might be present during NTEs, and they can explain a great deal about the processes underlying these brain states and how these brain states change and are influenced in conventional ways. Neuroscience, cognitive science, and conventional psychology are also valuable in that they can help us identify and understand unusual physiological and psychological conditions that can simulate and be mistaken for veridical NTEs (abnormal electrical and epileptiform activities in the brain's temporal regions, memory distortions, nocturnal "paralysis" due to extreme reductions of muscle tension during certain sleep and dream conditions, various dissociative conditions, profound changes in attention, etc.).

What current brain science *cannot* explain is how brain conditions that allow the expression of accurate psychical knowledge come to occur at times that match the arising of the distant target events with which these physiological and subjective conditions are so well correlated and which can be so faithfully mirrored or described by these physiological and subjective changes and contents. Brain science can help me understand what the physiological substrates of an image of an apple might be, but it cannot help me understand why that particular substrate should happen to arise at the precise moment that someone 1,200 miles away is viewing a picture of an apple and holding a strong intention that I become accurately aware of what that person is viewing, in a mixed telepathy/clairvoyance parapsychology experiment.

The reason brain science is of no help in explaining the kinds of curious meaningful and co-arising correspondences with which parapsychology and psychical research deal has to do with the nature of the paradigm with which brain science currently is aligned. According to this paradigm, brain states can only be created or influenced by genetic predispositions, local internal bodily and psychological conditions, information that arrives through the conventionally recognized senses, and direct or indirect influences of the four forces currently recognized by contemporary physics (electromagnetism, gravitation, strong nuclear force, and weak nuclear force). Both parapsychology and conventional science recognize that, given our present understandings of the processes just mentioned, none of them—alone or in combination—can adequately account for the findings of psychical research or for the curious behaviors of the phenomena found in this field of study. For brain science to adequately address psychical findings, its paradigm must be expanded to allow for other processes or principles to influence brain functioning or it must admit that some subjective (experiential) events might exist or change independent of brain or of brain activity changes.

We can clearly illustrate the difficulties that neuroscience and cognitive science face, in attempting to explain veridical psychical NTEs within the current paradigm, by examining how pathways of action typically are handled within this paradigm. If—in instances of telepathy, clairvoyance, or precognition—a person acquires new and accurate knowledge about a distant "target" event, how might such knowledge be acquired? Brain science contends that new information can be made available to the brain only through conventional sensory channels or through recombinations of already available information. If conventional sensory signals are blocked—as in all well-designed parapsychology experiments—what could remain that could carry the requisite information?

A *transmission model* would assume that information or energy is transferred from point to point—from a target source or "sender" to a percipient or "receiver"—carried by some form of mediator through some sort of channel. An early form of this model was the mental radio analogy. Just as intelligence could be conveyed electromagnetically from a transmitter to a receiver, so too, perhaps, psychical knowledge or influence could be similarly transmitted and received. [It is not well known that a major instrument of modern neuroscience, the electroencephalograph or brain-wave device, was invented by the German scientist Hans Berger, in 1924, in an attempt to detect and measure weak electromagnetic emanations of the human brain that he believed might be the carriers of telepathic communication (see Brazier, 1961; Roll, 1960).] Many hypothetical carriers have been proposed for these psychic transmissions, including electromagnetic waves, neutrinos, tachyons, and so on. The latest contender is extremely low frequency (ELF) radiation. All such transmission models, however, face serious difficulties in explaining the operating characteristics of psychical effects.

These effects occur over great distances, and they do not seem to decline appreciably with distance, as do conventional forces. No method has yet been found to physically shield or prevent psychical effects or to amplify them. The psychical process has great discriminating power, or acuity, which is difficult or impossible to handle via conventional information carriers. Whereas ELF radiation does have great shield-penetrating power and can carry information over great distances with minimal signal loss, its information handling capacity is low (due to its long, slow waves)—too low to be able to handle the kinds of rich and rapid knowledge that sometimes can be communicated psychically. Furthermore, we know of no conventional mechanism or process through which information could be encoded from the brain of a sender onto an ELF carrier wave and then properly decoded by the brain of a receiver. Most difficult of all, for the physical and neuroscience paradigm, is the apparent disregard of psychical events for the usual constraints of time: Conventional forces interact with matter in the present moment and do not travel forward or backward in time; however, future and past events are psychically accessible, in instances of precognition, retrocognition, and retroactive intentional influence. In summary, the brain is a physical organ, and known physical organs simply do not operate in ways in which psychical events and experiences have been shown to operate.

Can Brain Science Adequately Address Mystical and Spiritual Experiences?

Thus far, we have been focusing on veridical psychical NTEs. Let us turn now to mystical and spiritual experiences and explore whether brain science fares any better in accounting for these forms of nonordinary and transcendent experience.

As in the case of psychical NTEs, it is clear that brain science can, indeed, account for some of the features of mystical and spiritual experiences. Intriguing findings relating brain states or conditions to certain types of mystical and spiritual experiences have recently been reported by neuroscientists, including d'Aquili and Newberg (1993, 1999); Fenwick (1996); Fischer (1971); Newberg, d'Aquili, and Rause (2001); and Persinger (1983, 1987). Brain stimulation studies and brain monitoring studies have linked activities in certain brain loci to subjective features similar to those that occur in mystical and spiritual experiences. These include changes in spatial and temporal perception, the feeling of a loss of the sense of self, and the feeling of "presences" of various sorts. These findings, along with descriptions of the methods that have yielded them, are provided, in great detail, in other chapters of this book. Important research on the *psychological* characteristics of mystical and related experiences has been carried out, as well, by investigators outside of this neuroscience tradition (e.g., Deikman, 1963, 1966, 1971; Forman, 1990, 1999).

The four most important characteristics of the mystical experience have been described as its ineffability, noetic quality, transiency, and passivity (James, 1902/1985). Additional characteristics attributed to this experience have included feelings of unity, numinousity, loss of ego, an altered appreciation of space and time, perceptual experiences and alterations, changes in affect, transformative changes, and paradoxicality (e.g., Stace, 1960). Other "spiritual" experiences have shared various of these qualities, and, in addition, may have included feelings of the presence of the divine, of angelic or other spiritual presences, and self-perceived encounters with various spiritual entities. An important "neurotheological" project would be to investigate carefully whether and how each of the qualities of naturally-occurring mystical and spiritual experiences might also occur in laboratory-induced versions of these experiences. Such studies—although difficult and challenging to do well—could be helpful in determining how closely the ostensibly mystical or spiritual experiences studied or induced in the laboratory resemble the naturally-occurring forms: Are they virtually identical, identical in some aspects only, or different in important ways? It is possible that neuroscientific and cognitive considerations may adequately account for some, but possibly not all, of the features of mystical and spiritual experiences.

The extensive studies just suggested should be carefully designed so as to exclude or eliminate the possible biasing role of the investigators' own beliefs and expectations, subtle suggestive features of the settings and experimental procedures, and various other demand characteristics (Orne, 1962) of the experiments. It is well known that study outcomes can be influenced importantly by these various experimenter effects (Rosenthal, 1976). I suspect that some, or even a great deal, of the findings of various neurotheological studies (e.g., the work of Persinger and his co-workers [Cook & Persinger, 1997, 2001]) might have been contributed by subtle and not-so-subtle experimenter effects and demand characteristics that had not been adequately controlled for in these investigations, rather than by the ostensible interventions. I consider this an extremely important methodological consideration in evaluating results of prior work and in planning more adequate future investigations.

In a recent paper (Braud, 2002a), I suggested ways in which various psychological principles might account for the *alleged ineffability* of the mystical experience. Ineffability, of course, refers to an inability to report adequately, in words, the contents of an experience. The psychological principles addressed in the cited paper included (a) an expansion of awareness from a limited, focal, readily-described center to an extremely rich, complex, and extensive—and, hence, difficult or impossible to articulate—margin of the field of consciousness (building on seminal contributions by Frederic Myers [1903] and by William James [1910/1980]), (b) an attentional shift from a discrete figure to a large, complex, and novel ground, (c) limitations imposed by the nature of the "object" of the experience and by our vehicles of perception and cognition, (d) difficulties of memory transfer from nonordinary to ordinary states of consciousness (building on findings of the state-dependent features of some forms of learning and memory), and (e) constraints imposed by brain structures, culture and tradition, and self-fulfilling prophesies. These principles—alone or in combination—might account for some of the limitations of vehicles of expression of mystical and spiritual (and, indeed, many other nonverbalizable) experiences. However, such explanations leave open the possibility that exposure to a transcendent realm may actually occur in such experiences.

Studies of the *noetic* features and the possible transformative impacts of mystical and spiritual experiences—both in everyday life and in the laboratory—could play extremely important roles in investigating the adequacy of neuroscience and cognitive science explanations of such experiences. I treat noetic features and transformative impacts together because, often, profound life-changing outcomes and dramatic aftereffects have issued from the noetic aspects of mystical and spiritual experiences. These noetic aspects are occasions of *knowing* that occur during the experiences; this knowing has a direct, insightful, revelatory, deep, authentic quality and an impact for the experiencer that is beyond what is typically provided by or through the more familiar discursive intellect. The noesis-related changes can range from fresh perceptions, through major changes in one's worldview, to callings and changes in vocation, to experiences of profound transformation, rebirth, and "conversion" (*metanoia*: change of heart or consciousness). A brief sampling of profound, life-changing impacts would include life changes in the founders and followers of the major religions and spiritual and wisdom traditions (e.g., the changes following experiences of "cosmic consciousness"; see Bucke, 1901/1966), the transformative changes experienced by persons who have had near-death experiences (see Greyson, 2000) or profound experiences—which can be maintained over periods of at least 24-27 years—facilitated by psychedelic (entheogenic) chemicals (e.g., Doblin, 1991; Pahnke, 1966), and the life-impacts of exceptional experiences occurring in religious or spiritual contexts (e.g., James, 1902/1985; Pratt, 1920/1934). Waldron (1998) in reporting on the life-impacts of transcendent experiences having strong noetic features, found that these noesis-rich experiences addressed important life issues; had clearly discernable phases of integration; had profound significance to the percipient that resulted in a life orientation; had continuing noetic influences in the person's life; eventually led to creative expression of the meaning contained in the experience; and had significant impacts on the experiencer's belief system, relationships, and sense of self.

It will be important to examine whether the types of experiences studied in the laboratory can have the depth of noesis found in the types of natural experiences mentioned above, and whether there are similarly profound aftereffects or consequences in the case of the experiences occurring in the laboratory. Examining the *fruits* of the various experiences can provide one way of helping us understand whether the experiences studied by neuroscientists and cognitive scientists are similar to those occurring more naturally, in everyday life conditions. Appropriate studies of the short- and longer-term aftereffects of laboratory-induced experiences have not yet been carried out. Because such aftereffects are vital aspects of the natural, to-be-explained mystical and spiritual experiences, it would be premature to conclude too much about their nature and causes from laboratory studies that have not yet addressed the presence or degree of life-impacts.

The nature of the proffered "explanation" of an NTE can also help determine its impact. An unusual experience interpreted as a quirk of the brain may not have as much of a life-altering impact as the same experience interpreted in terms of its—often profound—subjective appreciation or its personal meaning and significance. How one frames the nature and meaning of an experience—especially an NTE—and how one chooses to understand and work with that experience, more deeply and more fully, can importantly influence whether or how that experience might influence one's life or even eventuate in major transformative changes (see White, 1997). Simple interpretations as quirks of the brain would not seem to have such transformative power.

The noetic aspects, themselves, of mystical and spiritual experiences—quite apart from their possible life-impacts—have an even more direct relevance to the adequacy of interpretations based solely on brain functioning. If knowledge is gained in some of these experiences which, upon later examination, is found to have veridical aspects that could not have been explained on the basis of the experiencer's prior experience or access to that knowledge, such accurate content could not be explained readily on the basis of what is currently known about brain functioning. This kind of evidence would be a special case of the veridicality of knowledge already discussed above, in the section on psychical NTEs.

Does the Brain Produce or Transmit Consciousness?

It would be foolish to deny that certain brain structures and activities are *associated* with certain forms of consciousness. Such associations are supported by voluminous findings from research and clinical observations in neurology, psychophysiology, clinical and experimental neuropsychology, and related areas. However, the presence of a correlation, alone, does not provide sufficient information for concluding whether brain activities produce consciousness, or consciousness produces brain activities, or whether both consciousness and brain activities might be produced by something else. To prematurely conclude the first of the three possibilities just mentioned may be to fall prey to what might be called *the fallacy of the legless flea*. The possibility of this fallacy is suggested by the following fictional cautionary tale.

Once upon a time, there was an investigator who wished to find the locus of the organs of hearing of fleas. He laboriously trained a flea to jump whenever he uttered the word "jump." He then carefully analyzed his flea's anatomy to find where its ears might be located. He would say "jump," and observe a jump as an indicator that the flea had, indeed, heard him. He removed flea leg after flea leg, and the flea continued to jump whenever he commanded. When, finally, the flea did not jump, once he had removed the flea's final leg, he concluded that the flea's ears were located on that last leg, because, obviously, the flea had not heard his last jump command.

The point of this tale, of course, is to remind us not to confuse the ability to *have* an experience with the ability to *express* that experience in an observable way. To prematurely conclude that conscious content or activity might be impossible without corresponding brain content or activity may be to commit a more sophisticated and subtle form of the legless flea fallacy. This issue can be expressed, in more familiar terms, by asking whether brain structures and activities might *produce* or, rather, *transmit* consciousness.

One of the earliest statements of the brain's possible transmissive, as opposed to productive, role in consciousness was that of Ferdinand Canning Scott Schiller (1891/1894):

"Matter is an admirably calculated machinery for regulating, limiting, and restraining the consciousness which it encases. . . . If the material encasement be coarse and simple, as in the lower organisms, it permits only a little intelligence to permeate through it; if it is delicate and complex, it leaves more pores and exits, as it were, for the manifestation of consciousness. . . . Matter is not that which *produces* consciousness, but that which *limits* it and confines its intensity within certain limits: material organization does not construct consciousness out of arrangements of atoms, but contracts its manifestation within the sphere which it permits. This explanation . . . admits the connection of Matter and consciousness, but contends that the course of interpretation must proceed in the contrary direction. . . . If, *e.g.*, a man loses consciousness as soon as his brain is injured, it is clearly as good an explanation to say the injury to the brain destroyed the mechanism by which the manifestation of consciousness was rendered possible, as to say that it destroyed the seat of consciousness. . . . If the body is a mechanism for inhibiting consciousness, for preventing the full powers of the Ego from being prematurely actualized, it will be necessary to invert . . . our ordinary ideas . . . [italics in original] (pp. 293-296)."

The possible role of the brain as a releasing, permissive, or transmissive organ or vehicle of consciousness, rather than a producer of consciousness, was elaborated by William James (1898/1960). Just as a prism alters incoming white light to form the characteristic colored spectrum, but is not the source of the light; and just as the lengths of the pipes of an organ determine how the inflowing air yields certain tones and not others, but are not, themselves, the source of the air; so, too, argued James, the brain may serve a permissive, transmissive, or expressive function, rather than solely a productive one, in terms of the thoughts, images, feelings, and other experiences it allows. Henri Bergson (1914) and Aldous Huxley (1954) later expressed similar views of the brain as a *filter* or *reducing valve*, which served to block out much of, and allow registration and expression of only a narrow band of, perceivable reality, rather than as—necessarily—a *generator* of consciousness.

Today, this distinction of brain as producer or transmitter is often expressed picturesquely by asking whether the brain more closely resembles a light bulb (which is the source of the light it produces, and without which the light can no longer exist) or a television receiver (which modifies and expresses images from electromagnetic fields that exist apart from itself and which latter can continue to exist even in the absence of the receiver). The answer to this question has relevance to whether spiritual (or any other) experiences can be completely explained by identifying brain structures and activities that are associated with those experiences (a brain-as-producer view), or whether particular brain structures and activities might simply allow the registration or expression of something that might exist, in some form, apart from the registering/expressive structures and functions (a

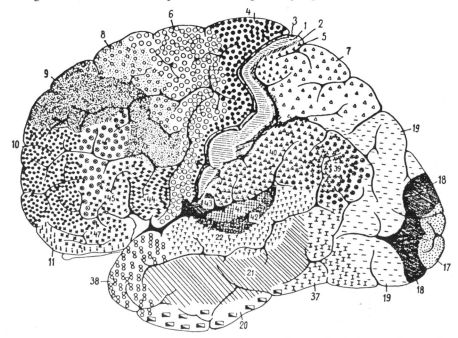

Figure 66. The humaan brain with distinct cytoarchitextural areas labled according to Brodmann. From Joseph, 1990.

brain-as-transmitter view).

To find activity in a particular brain area does not mean that there is no independent referent or trigger of that activity. If brain mapping indicates a pattern of activity in the brain's occipital lobe, this could be a result of spontaneous, endogenous neural firings in that area. However, it also could indicate the presence of an external visual stimulus. So, too, neural firing patterns in some "spiritual center" or "God center" of the brain could be caused by spontaneous or contrived endogenous activities of a local, internal sort. However, such firings would not necessarily rule out an independently-existing spiritual or divine "trigger" for such activity.

The answer to this production versus transmission question has relevance, also, to the issue of whether it might be possible for consciousness to survive, in some form, following the death of the physical body. Of course, if a strong case ever could be made for the survival of some aspects of personality or of some forms of active consciousness, after death—including afterlife evidence that could not be explained readily on the basis of psychic functioning in the living—then such evidence would be strongly suggestive that a functioning brain may not be essential to the presence of at least some forms of consciousness. Findings and discussions of issues relevant to afterlife and survival research can be found in recent works by Doore (1990), Murphy (1992), Griffin (1997), Tart (1997), Greyson (2000), and Mills and Lynn (2000). F. W. H. Myers' classic *Human Personality and Its Survival of Bodily Death* (1903) remains an outstanding resource, even today.

An intriguing case that has a bearing on this production/transmission issue was recently reported by cardiologist Michael Sabom (1998; see, also, Greyson, 2000, pp. 338-341). Sabom described a near-death experience that occurred while its experiencer—a woman who was having an unusual surgical procedure for the safe excision and repair of a large basilar artery aneurysm—met all of the accepted criteria for brain death. The unusual medical procedure involved the induction of hypothermic cardiac arrest, in order to insure that the aneurysm at the base of the brain would not rupture during the operation. The patient's body temperature was lowered to 60 degrees Fahrenheit, her heartbeat and breathing ceased, her brain waves flattened, and the blood was completely drained from her head. Her electroencephalogram was totally flat (indicating no cerebral electrical activity) and auditory evoked potentials (normally elicited by clicks presented through molded earplugs that had been inserted into her ears) ceased (indicating cessation of brainstem functioning). Ordinarily—at regular body temperature—the brain cannot function without its oxygen supply for more than a few minutes. Lowering the body and brain temperature to 60 degrees F.—by chilling the blood in a bypass machine before returning it to the body and brain—however, can reduce cellular metabolism so that the brain can tolerate complete cerebral blood flow for the 45 minutes or so required for the brain operation. The patient later reported that, apparently while under these "brain death" conditions, she had a near-death experience (NDE) in which she was able to observe and hear details of objects and happenings in the operating room with accuracy. She also experienced classic components of the NDE, including a tunnel vortex, a bright light, and different figures in the light (many deceased family members, including a distant cousin of whose death she had been unaware).

On the face of it, the experience described above might suggest that mental functioning was occurring in the absence of the usual brain conditions upon which such functioning is taken to depend. The experience cannot be explained by temporal-lobe seizure-like activities, because the continuously monitored EEG indicated no such activity. The patient's eyes had been taped shut and her ears had been blocked by the molded ear speakers that had been inserted into her ears to demonstrate that even brainstem responses to clicks were absent. If she was indeed able to describe accurately various events that transpired after she had been anesthetized, she could not have been observing them through usual sensory means, nor could she have inferred the specific details that she reported.

To me, however, there are still ambiguities in this case that prevent our considering it a definitive demonstration of mental functioning in the absence of brain functioning. These reservations have to do with the timing and accuracy of the reported events, as well as the thoroughness of auditory masking by the earplugs. A satisfactory evaluation of this striking case would require answers to the following questions:

1. Were the descriptions of operating room events and objects sufficiently detailed so as to compel confidence in their accuracy?

2. Did the earplugs adequately prevent hearing of the various operating room sounds (conversations, particular musical selections) that were occurring during the operation (recognizing that even with closed ears there may have been the possibility of hearing via bone conduction); were these possibilities considered and adequately discounted?

3. Just *when* did the patient's subjective experiences occur, relative to the actual temporal occurrence of the events described? Only if the experiences themselves occurred *during* the periods of actual "brain death" would they have a bearing on the possibility of mentation in the absence of brain functioning. At first, this may seem a curious question. However, given the evidence for precognitive and retrocognitive experiences—from careful work in experimental parapsychology and psychical research—it is possible that the patient became aware of the during-brain-death-period events but became aware of these before or after the period of brain death, when the brain was functioning normally, and misconstrued the temporal ordering of subjective experiences and described events.

4. And, finally, the patient did not die; certainly there were residual processes (perhaps anatomical, perhaps biochemical, and perhaps even extremely subtle electrical processes) that continued to function even during the "brain death" period at sufficient levels so as to allow the continuation of, and return to, full brain and body functioning after the hypothermic operation. Even if the subjective experiences did occur during the brain-death period, sufficient brain functioning must still have been present to allow memories of the experiences to have been formed and persist until later (this assumes, of course, that brain functioning is necessary to support registration, storage, and retrieval of memories).

If the above four sets of questions could be adequately addressed, the intriguing findings from this and similar cases would pose great difficulties for attempts to account for unusual experiences solely on the basis of current models of brain functioning and activity.

THE NEED FOR DIFFERENT, MORE INCLUSIVE, AND MORE INTEGRATED MODELS AND CONCEPTUALIZATIONS?

In this chapter, thus far, brain and mind have been discussed as through they might be separate entities or qualities, and the nature and possible directions of their interactions have been addressed, either explicitly or implicitly. This way of framing the discussion is but a revisiting of the perennial issue of the nature of the mind-body interactions or the "mind-body problem." The fact that philosophers, psychologists, and scientists have wrestled with this issue for so long, and have made so little satisfactory progress in this area, suggests that we may have been asking the wrong questions or framing our conceptualizations in incomplete ways. It seems time for fresh, more inclusive, and more integrated conceptualizations or models of these topics of study.

Rather than distinguishing body (brain structure and functioning) and mind (as revealed in not only the unusual experiences treated in this chapter but also in every mundane subjective experience), would it not be more satisfactory to speak, instead, of bodymind (or brainmind) as an integrated unit or process which has both materialistic/mechanical substrates and functions and also mentalistic/psychical/spiritual substrates and functions? This would require each side of the perennial debate to stretch their conceptualizations of both brain and mind, to extend each member of this perhaps misleading and only apparent duality, so that the resultant expanded conceptualization (bodymind/brainmind) transcends yet continues to include what had previously been acknowledged. This expanded construct would be given, and would operate on the basis of, the well-recognized physicalistic properties and principles that have been discovered through brain science. The same construct, however, would also be given, and operate on the basis of, other properties and principles discovered through phenomenological, parapsychological, and mystical/spiritual investigations. So, for example, aspects of this construct could respond to sensory information, electromagnetic fields, and so on, in a customary fashion. However, other aspects of this construct could respond to nonlocal events and distant information, and perhaps even to nonsensory, psychical, or spiritual/mystical realms, quite directly and in ways that may not be mediated by familiar physical laws and structures.

This thesis can be stated in several alternative ways: Brain may function as a bioassay for mind; mind may function as a psychoassay for brain; "spirit" may be real, but of a different sort of reality that can be perceived, under special conditions, by a different faculty of bodymind (one that traditionally has been known as the *imagination*; see Braud, 2002b). The "perceptions" or prehensions of the imagination may sometimes remain ineffable; at other times, these may be dramatized or personified (through vehicles of thoughts, feelings, and images) so that the referents of these experiences can somehow become available to the experiencer and expressible to others. This new approach could deal adequately with both the familiar facts of brain science and with the experiential realities with which psychical research and the religious, spiritual, and wisdom traditions have concerned themselves.

THE REALITY OF THE UNSEEN
by William James

Were one asked to characterize the life of religion in the broadest and most general terms possible, one might say that it consists of the belief that there is an unseen order, and that our supreme good lies in harmoniously adjusting ourselves thereto. This belief and this adjustment are the religious attitude in the soul. I wish, in this chapter, to call your attention to some of the psychological peculiarities of such an attitude as this, or belief in an object, which we cannot see. All our attitudes, moral, practical, or emotional, as well as religious, are due to the "objects" of our consciousness, the things which we believe to exist, whether really or ideally, along with ourselves. Such objects may be present to our senses, or they may be present only to our thought. In either case they elicit from us a reaction; and the reaction due to things of thought is notoriously in many cases as strong as that due to sensible presences. It may be even stronger. The memory of an insult may make us angrier than the insult did when we received it. We are frequently more ashamed of our blunders afterwards than we were at the moment of making them; and in general our whole higher prudential and moral life is based on the fact that material sensations actually present may have a weaker influence on our action than ideas of remoter facts.

The more concrete objects of most men's religion, the deities whom they worship, are known to them only in idea. It has been vouchsafed, for example, to very few Christian believers to have had a sensible vision of their Saviour; though enough appearances of this sort are on record, by way of miraculous exception, to merit our attention later. The whole force of the Christian religion, therefore, so far as belief in the divine personages determines the prevalent attitude of the believer, is in general exerted by the instrumentality of pure ideas, of which nothing in the individual's past experience directly serves as a model.

But in addition to these ideas of the more concrete religious objects, religion is full of abstract objects which prove to have an equal power. God's attributes as such, his holiness, his justice, his mercy, his absoluteness, his infinity, his omniscience, his tri-unity, the various mysteries of the redemptive process, the operation of the sacraments, etc., have proved fertile wells of inspiring meditation for Christian believers. We shall see later that the absence of definite sensible images is positively insisted on by the mystical authorities in all religions as the *sine qua non* of a successful orison, or contemplation of the higher divine truths. Such contemplations are expected (and abundantly verify the expectation, as we shall also see) to influence the believer's subsequent attitude very powerfully for good.

Immanuel Kant held a curious doctrine about such objects of belief as God, the design of creation, the soul, its freedom, and the life hereafter. These things, he said, are properly not objects of knowledge at all. Our conceptions always require a sense-content to work with, and as the words "soul," "God," "immortality," cover no distinctive sense-content whatever, it follows that theoretically speaking they are words devoid of any significance. Yet strangely enough they have a definite meaning *for our practice*. We can act *as if* there were a God; feel *as if* we were free; consider Nature *as if* she were full of special designs; lay plans *as if* we were to be immortal; and we find then that these words do make a genuine difference in our moral life. Our faith *that* these unintelligible objects actually exist proves thus to be a full equivalent in *praktischer Hinsicht*, as Kant calls it, or from the point of view of our action, for a knowledge of *what* they might be, in case we were permitted positively to conceive them. So we have the strange phenomenon, as Kant assures us, of a mind believing with all its strength in the real presence of a set of things of no one of which it can form any notion whatsoever.

My object in thus recalling Kant's doctrine to your mind is not to express any opinion as to the accuracy of this particularly uncouth part of his philosophy, but only to illustrate the characteristic of human nature which we are considering, by an example so classical in its exaggeration. The sentiment of reality can indeed attach itself so strongly to our object of belief that our whole life is polarized through and through, so to speak, by its sense of the existence of the thing believed in, and yet that thing, for purpose of definite description, can hardly be said to be present to our mind at all.

It is as if a bar iron, without touch or sight, with no representative faculty whatever, might neverthe-less be strongly endowed with an inner capacity for magnetic feeling; and as if, through the various arousals of its magnetism by magnets coming and going in its neighborhood, it might be consciously determined to different attitudes and tendencies. Such a bar of iron could never give you an outward description of the agencies that had the power of stirring it so strongly; yet of their presence, and of their significance for its life, it would be intensely aware through every fibre of its being.

It is not only the Ideas of pure Reason as Kant styled them, that have this power of making us vitally feel the presences that we are impotent articulately to describe. All sorts of higher attractions bring with them the same kind of impalpable appeal. Remember those passages from Emerson which I read at my last lecture. The whole universe of concrete objects, as we know them, swims, not only for such a transcendentalist writer, but for all of us, in a wider and higher universe of abstract ideas, that lend it its significance. As time, space, and the ether soak through all things so (we feel) do abstract and essential goodness, beauty, strength, significance, justice, soak through all things good, strong, significant, and just.

Such ideas, and others equally abstract, form the background for all our facts, the fountain-head of all the possibilities we conceive of. They give its "nature", as we call it, to every special thing. Everything we know is "what" it is by sharing in the nature of one of these abstractions. We can never look directly at them, for they are bodiless and featureless and footless, but we grasp all other things by their means, and in handling the real world we should be stricken with helplessness in just so far forth as we might lose these mental objects, these adjectives and adverbs and predicates and heads of classification and conception.

This absolute determinability of our mind by abstractions is one of the cardinal facts in our human constitution. Polarizing and magnetizing us as they do, we turn towards them and from them, we seek them, hold them, hate them, bless them, just as if they were so many concrete beings. And beings they are, beings as real in the realm which they inhabit as the changing things of sense are in the realm of space.

Plato gave so brilliant and impressive a defense of this common human feeling, that the doc-trine of the reality of abstract objects has been known as the platonic theory of ideas ever since. Abstract Beauty, for example, is for Plato a perfectly definite individual being, of which the intellect is aware as of something additional to all the perishing beauties of the earth. "The true order of going," he says, in the often quoted passage in his "Banquet," "is to use the beauties of earth as steps along which one mounts upwards for the sake of that other Beauty, going from one to two, and from two to all fair forms, and from fair forms to fair actions, and from fair actions to fair notions, until from fair notions, he arrives at the notion of absolute Beauty, and at last knows what the essence of Beauty is."[2] In our last lecture we had a glimpse of the way in which a platonizing writer like Emerson may treat the abstract divineness of things, the moral structure of the universe, as a fact worthy of worship. In those various churches without a God which to-day are spreading through the world under the name of ethical societies, we have a similar worship of the abstract divine, the moral law believed in as an ultimate object. "Science" in many minds is genuinely taking the place of a religion. Where this is so, the scientist treats the "Laws of Nature" as objective facts to be revered. A brilliant school of interpretation of Greek mythology would have it that in their origin the Greek gods were only half-metaphoric personifications of those great spheres of abstract law and order into which the natural world falls apart – the sky-sphere, the ocean-sphere, the earth-sphere, and the like; just as even now we may speak of the smile of the morning, the kiss of the breeze, or the bite of the cold, without really meaning that these phenomena of nature actually wear a human face.[3]

As regards the origin of the Greek gods, we need not at present seek an opinion. But the whole array of our instances leads to a conclusion something like this: It is as if there were in the human consciousness a *sense of reality, a feeling of objective presence, a perception* of what we may call "something there," more deep and more general than any of the special and particular "senses" by which the current psychology supposes existent realities to be originally revealed. If this were so, we might suppose the senses to waken our attitudes and conduct as they so habitually do, by first excit-ing this sense of reality; but anything else, any idea, for example, that might similarly excite it, would have that same prerogative of appearing real which objects of sense normally possess. So far as religious conceptions were able to touch this reality-feeling, they would be believed in in spite of criticism, even though they might be so vague and remote as to be almost unimaginable, even though they might be such non-entities in point of *whatness*, as Kant makes the objects of his moral theology to be.

The most curious proofs of the existence of such an undifferentiated sense of reality as this are found in experiences of hallucination. It often happens that an hallucination is imperfectly developed: the person affected will feel a "presence" in the room, definitely localized, facing in one particular way, real in the most emphatic sense of the word, often coming suddenly, and as suddenly gone; and yet neither seen, heard, touched, nor cognized in any of the usual "sensible" ways. Let me give you an example of this, before I pass to the objects with whose presence religion is more peculiarly concerned.

An intimate friend of mine, one of the keenest intellects I know, has had several experiences of this sort. He writes as follows in response to my inquiries: -

"I have several times within the past few years felt the so-called 'consciousness of a presence.' The experiences which I have in mind are clearly distinguishable from another kind of experience which I have had very frequently, and which I fancy many persons would also call the 'consciousness of a presence.' But the difference for me between the two sets of experience is as great as the difference between feeling a slight warmth originating I know not where, and standing in the midst of a conflagration with all the ordinary senses alert.

"It was about September, 1884, when I had the first experience. On the previous night I had had, after getting into bed at my rooms in College, a vivid tactile hallucination of being grasped by the arm, which made me get up and search the room for an intruder; but the sense of presence properly so called came on the next night. After I had gone into bed and blown out the candle, I lay awake awhile thinking on the previous night's experience, when suddenly I *felt* something come into the room and stay close to my bed. It remained only a minute or two. I did not recognize it by any ordinary sense, and yet there was a horribly unpleasant 'sensation' connected with it. It stirred something more at the roots of my being than any ordinary perception. The feeling had something of the quality of a very large tearing vital pain spreading chiefly over the chest, but within the organism – and yet the feeling was not *pain* so much as *abhorrence*. At all events, something was present with me, and I knew its presence far more surely than I have ever known the presence of any fleshly living creature. I was conscious of its departure as of its coming: an almost instantaneously swift going through the door, and the 'horrible sensation' disappeared.

"On the third night when I retired my mind was absorbed in some lecture which I was preparing, and I was still absorbed in these when I became aware of the actual presence (though not of the *coming*) of the thing that was there the night before, and of the 'horrible sensation.' I then mentally concentrated all my effort to charge this 'thing,' if it was evil, to depart, if it was *not* evil, to tell me who or what it was, and if it could not explain itself, to go, and that I would compel it to go. It went as on the previous night, and my body quickly recovered its normal state.

"On two other occasions in my life I have had precisely the same 'horrible sensation.' Once it lasted a full quarter of an hour. In all three instances the certainty that there in outward space stood *something* was indescribably *stronger* than the ordinary certainty of companionship when we are in the close presence of ordinary living people. The something seemed close to me, and intensely more real than any ordinary perception. Although I felt it to be like unto myself, so to speak, or finite, small, and distressful, as it were, I didn't recognize it as any individual being or person."

Of course such an experience as this does not connect itself with the religious sphere. Yet it may upon occasion do so; and the same correspondent informs me that at more than one other conjuncture he had the sense of presence developed with equal intensity and abruptness, only then it was filled with a quality of joy.

"There was not a mere consciousness of something there, but fused in the central happiness of it, a startling awareness of some ineffable good. Not vague either, not like the emotional effect of some poem, or scene, or blossom, of music, but the sure knowledge of the close presence of a sort of mighty person, and after it went, the memory persisted as the one perception of reality. Everything else might be a dream, but not that."

My friend, as it oddly happens, does not interpret these latter experiences theistically, as signifying the presence of God. But it would clearly not have been unnatural to interpret them as a revelation of the deity's existence. When we reach the subject of mysticism, we shall have much more to say upon this head.

Lest the oddity of these phenomena should disconcert you, I will venture to read you a couple of similar narratives, much shorter, merely to show that we are dealing with a well-marked natural kind of fact. In the first case, which I take from the Journal of the Society for Psychical Research, the sense of presence developed in a few moments into a distinctly visualized hallucination – but I leave that part of the story out.

"I had read," the narrator says, "some twenty minutes or so, was thoroughly absorbed in the book, my mind was perfectly quiet, and for the time being my friends were quite forgotten, when suddenly without a moment's warning my whole being seemed roused to the highest state of tension or aliveness, and I was aware, with an intenseness not easily imagined by those who had never experienced it, that another being or presence was not only in the room but quite close to me. I put my book down, and although my excitement was great, I felt quite collected, and not conscious of any sense of fear. Without changing my position, and looking straight at the fire, I knew somehow that my friend A. H. was standing at my left elbow, but so far behind me as to be hidden by the armchair in which I was leaning back. Moving my eyes round slightly without otherwise changing my position, the lower portion of one leg became visible, and I instantly recognized the gray-blue material trousers he often wore, but the stuff appeared semi-transparent, reminding me of tobacco smoke in consistency," – and hereupon the visual hallucination came.

Another informant writes: --"Quite early in the night I was awakened.... I felt as if I had been aroused intentionally, and at first thought some one was breaking into the house.... I then turned on my side to go to sleep again, and immediately felt a consciousness of a presence in the room, and singular to state, it was not the consciousness of a live person, but of a spiritual presence. This may provoke a smile, but I can only tell you the facts as they occurred to me, I do not know how to better describe my sensations than by simply stating that I felt a consciousness of a spiritual presence.... I felt also at the same time a strong feeling of superstitious dread, as if something strange and fearful were about to happen."

Professor Flournoy of Geneva gives me the following testimony of a friend of his, a lady, who has the gift of automatic or involuntary writing: -"Whenever I practice automatic writing, what makes me feel that it is not due to a subconscious self is the feeling I always have of a foreign presence, external to my body. It is sometimes so definitely characterized that I could point to its exact position. This impression of presence is impossible to describe. It varies in intensity and clearness according to the personality from whom the writing professes to come. If it is some one whom I love, I feel it immediately, before any writing has come. My heart seems to recognize it."

In an earlier book of mine I have cited at full length a curious case of presence felt by a blind man. The presence was that of the figure of a gray-bearded man dressed in a pepper and salt suit, squeezing himself under the crack of the door and moving across the floor of the room towards a sofa. The blind subject of this quasi-hallucination is an exceptionally intelligent reporter. He is entirely without internal visual imagery and cannot represent light or colors to himself, and is positive that his other senses, hearing, etc., were not involved in this false perception. It seems to have been an abstract conception rather, with the feelings of reality and spatial outwardness directly attached to it – in other words, a fully objectified and exteriorized *idea*.

Such cases, taken along with others which would be too tedious for quotation, seem sufficiently to prove the existence in our mental machinery of a sense of present reality more diffused and general than that which our special senses yield. For the psychologists the tracing of the organic seat of such a feeling would form a pretty problem – nothing could be more natural than to connect it with the muscular sense, with the feeling that our muscles were innervated our activity or "made our flesh creep" – our senses are what do so oftenest – might then appear real and present, even though it were but an abstract idea. But with such vague conjectures we have no concern at present, for our interest lies with the faculty rather than with its organic seat.

Like all positive affections of consciousness, the sense of reality has its negative counterpart in the shape of a feeling of unreality by which persons may be haunted, and of which one sometimes hears complaint: -"When I reflect on the fact that I have made my appearance by accident upon a globe itself whirled through space as the sport of the catastrophes of the heavens," says Madame Ackermann; "when I see myself surrounded by beings as ephemeral and incomprehensible as I am myself, and all excitedly pursuing pure chimeras I experience a strange feeling of being in a dream. It seems to me as if I have loved and suffered and that erelong I shall die, in a dream. My last word will be, 'I have been dreaming.'"

In another lecture we shall see how in morbid melancholy this sense of the unreality of things may become a carking pain, and even lead to suicide.

We may now lay it down as certain that in the distinctively religious sphere of experience, many persons (how many we cannot tell) possess the objects of their belief, not in the form of mere conceptions which their intellect accepts as true, but rather in the form of quasi-sensible realities directly apprehended. As his sense of the real presence of these objects fluctuates, so the believer alternates between warmth and coldness in his faith. Other examples will bring this home to one better than abstract description, so I proceed immediately to cite some. The first example is a negative one, deploring the loss of the sense in question. I have extracted it from an account given me by a scientific man of my acquaintance, of his religious life. It seems to me to show clearly that the feeling of reality may be something more like a sensation than an intellectual operation properly so called.

"Between twenty and thirty I gradually became more and more agnostic and irreligious, yet I cannot say that I ever lost that 'indefinite consciousness' which Herbert Spencer describes so well, of an Absolute Reality behind phenomena. For me this Reality was not the pure Unknowable of Spencer's philosophy, for although I had ceased my childish prayers to God, and never prayed to *It* in a formal manner, yet my more recent experience shows me to have been in a relation to *It* which practically was the same thing as prayer. Whenever I had any trouble, especially when I had conflict with other people, either domestically or in the way of business, or when I was depressed in spirits or anxious about affairs, I now recognize that I used to fall back for support upon this curious relation I felt myself to be in to this fundamental cosmical *It*. It was on my side, or I was on Its side, however you please to term it, in the particular trouble, and it always strengthened me and seemed to give me endless vitality to feel its underlying and supporting presence. In fact, it was an unfailing fountain of living justice, truth, and strength, to which in instinctively turned at times of weakness, and it always brought me out. I know now that it was a personal relation I was in to it, because of late years the power of communicating with it has left me, and I am conscious of a perfectly definite loss. I used never to fail to find it when I turned to it. Then came a set of years when sometimes I found it, and then again I would be wholly unable to make connection with it. I remember many occasions on which at night in bed, I would be unable to get to sleep on account of worry. I turned this way and that in the darkness, and groped mentally for the familiar sense of that higher mind of my mind which had always seemed to be close at hand as it were, closing the passage, and yielding support, but there was no electric current. A blank was there instead of *It*: I couldn't find anything. Now, at the age of nearly fifty, my power of getting into connection with it has entirely left me; and I have to confess that a great help has gone out of my life. Life has become curiously dead and indifferent; and I can now see that my old experience was probably exactly the same thing as the prayers of the orthodox, only I did not call them by that name. What I have spoken of as 'It' was practically not Spencer's Unknowable, but just my own instinctive and individual God, whom I relied upon for higher sympathy, but whom somehow I have lost."

Nothing is more common in the pages of religious biography than the way in which seasons of lively and of difficult faith are described as alternating. Probably every religious person has the recollection of particular crisis in which a director vision of the truth, a direct perception, perhaps, of a living God's existence, swept in and overwhelmed the languor of the more ordinary belief. In James Russell Lowell's correspondence there is a brief memorandum of an experience of this kind: -"I had a revelation last Friday evening. I was at Mary's, and happening to say something of the presence of spirits (of whom, I said, I was often dimly aware), Mr. Putnam entered into an argument with me on spiritual matters. As I was speaking, the whole system rose up before me like a vague destiny looming from the Abyss. I never before so clearly felt the Spirit of God in me and around me. The whole room seemed to me full of God. The air seemed to waver to and fro with the presence of Something I knew not what. I spoke with the calmness and clearness of a prophet. I cannot tell you what this revelation was. I have not yet studied it enough. But I shall perfect it one day, and then you shall hear it and acknowledge its grandeur."

Here is a longer and more developed experience from a manuscript communication by a clergyman – I take it from Starbuck's manuscript collection: - "I remember the night, and almost the very spot on the hilltop where my soul opened out, as it were, into the Infinite, and there was a rushing together of the two worlds, the inner and the outer, it was deep calling unto deep – the deep that my own struggle had opened within being answered by the unfathomable deep without, reaching beyond the stars. I stood alone with Him who had made me, and all the beauty of the world, and love, and sorrow, and even temptation. I did not seek Him, but felt the perfect unison of my spirit with His. The ordinary sense of things around me faded. For the moment nothing but an ineffable joy and exultation remained. It is impossible fully to describe the experience. It was like the effect of some great orchestra when all the separate notes have melted into one swelling harmony that leaved the listener conscious of nothing save that his soul is being wafted upwards, and almost bursting with its own emotion. The perfect stillness of the night was thrilled by a more solemn silence. The darkness held a presence that was all the more felt because it was not seen. I could not any more have doubted that *He* was there than that I was. Indeed, I felt myself to be, if possible, the less real of the two.

"My highest faith in God and truest idea of him were then born in me. I have stood upon the Mount of Vision since, and felt the Eternal round about me. But never since has there come quite the same stirring of the heart. Then, if ever, I believe, I stood face to face with God, and was born a new of this spirit. There was, as I recall it, no sudden change of thought or of belief, except that my early crude conception, had, as it were, burst into flower. There was no destruction of the old, but a rapid, wonderful unfolding. Since that time no discussion that I have head of the proofs of God's existence has been able to shake my faith. Having once felt the presence of God's spirit, I have never lost it again for long. My most assuring evidence of his existence is deeply rooted in that hour of vision, in the memory of that supreme experience, and in the conviction, gained from reading and reflection, that something the same has come to all who have found God. I am aware that it may justly be called mystical. I am not enough acquainted with the philosophy to defend it form that or any other charge. I feel that in writing of it I have overlaid it with words rather than put it clearly to your thought. But, such as it is, I have described it as carefully as I now an able to do."

Here is another document, even more definite in character, which, the writer being a Swiss, I translate from the French original: "I was in perfect health: we were on our sixth day of tramping, and in good training. We had come the day before from Sixt to Trient by Buet. I felt neither fatigue, hunger, nor thirst, and my state of mind was equally healthy. I had had at Forlaz good news from home; I was subject to no anxiety, either near or remote, for we had a good guide, and there was not a shadow of uncertainty about the road we should follow. I can best describe the condition in which I was by calling it a state of equilibrium. When all at once I experienced a feeling of being raised above myself, I felt the presence of God – I tell of the thing just as I was conscious of it – as if his goodness and his power were penetrating me altogether, the throb of emotion was so violent that I could barely tell the boys to pass on and not wait for me. I then sat down on a stone, unable to stand any longer, and my eyes overflowed with tears. I thanked God that in the course of my life he had taught me to know him, that he sustained my life and took pity both on the insignificant creature and on the sinner that I was. I begged him ardently that my life might be consecrated to the doing of his will. I felt his reply, which was that I should do his will from day to day, in humility, poverty, leaving him, the Almighty God, to be judge of whether I should some time be called to bear witness more conspicuously. Then, slowly, the ecstasy left my heart; that is, I felt that God had withdrawn the communion which he had granted, and I was able to walk on, but very slowly, so strongly was I still possessed by the interior emotion. Besides, I had wept uninterruptedly for several minutes, my eyes were swollen, and I did not wish my companions to see me. The state of ecstasy may have lasted four or five minutes, although it seemed at the time to last much longer. My comrades waited for me ten minutes at the cross of Barine, but I took about twenty-five or thirty minutes to join them, for was well as I can remember, they said that I had kept them back for about half an hour. The impression had been so profound that in climbing slowly the slope I asked myself if it were possible that Moses on Sinai could have had a more intimate communication with God. I think it well to add that in this ecstasy of mine God had neither form, color, odor, nor taste; moreover, that the feeling of his presence was accompanied with no determinate localization. It was rather as if my personality had been transformed by the presence of a *spiritual spirit*. But the more is eek words to express this intimate intercourse, the more I fell the impossibility if describing the thing by any of our usual images, at the bottom the expression most apt to render what I felt is this: God was present, though invisible; he fell under no one of my senses, yet my consciousness perceived him."

The adjective "mystical" is technically applied, most often, to states that are of brief duration. Of course such hours of rapture as the last two persons describe are mystical experiences, of which in a later lecture I shall have much to say. Meanwhile here is the abridged record of another mystical or semi-mystical experience, in a mind evidently framed by nature for ardent piety. I owe it to Starbuck's collection. The lady who gives the account is the daughter of a man well known in his time as a writer against Christianity. The suddenness of her conversion shows well how native the sense of God's presence must be to certain minds. She related that she was brought up in entire ignorance of Christian doctrine, but, when in Germany, after being talked to by Christian friends, she read the Bible and prayed, and finally the plan of salvation flashed upon her like a stream of light.

"To this day," she writes, "I cannot understand dallying with religion and the commands of God. The very instant I heard my Father's cry calling unto me, my heart bounded in recognition. I ran, I stretched forth my arms, I cried aloud, 'Here, here I am, my Father.' Oh, happy child, what should I do? 'Love me,' answered my God. 'I do, I do,' I cried passionately. 'Come unto me,' called my Father. 'I will,' my heart panted. Did I stop to ask a single question? Not one, it never occurred to me to ask whether I was good enough, or to hesitate over my unfitness, or to find out what I thought of his church, or … to wait until I should be satisfied. Satisfied! I was satisfied. Had I not found my God and my Father? Did he not love me? Had be not called me? Was there not a Church into which I might enter? … Since then I have had direct answers to prayer – so significant as to be almost like talking with God and hearing his answer. The idea of God's reality has never left me for one moment."

Here is still another case, the writer being a man aged twenty-seven, in which the experience, probably almost as characteristic, is less vividly described: -"I have on a number of occasions felt that I had enjoyed a period of intimate communion with the divine. These meetings came unasked and unexpected, and seemed to consist merely in the temporary obliteration of the conventionalities which usually surround and cover my life…. Once it was when from the summit of a high mountain I looked over a gashed and corrugated landscape extending to a long convex of ocean that ascended to the horizon, and again from the same point when I could see nothing beneath me but a boundless expanse of white cloud, on the blown surface of which a few high peaks, including the one I was on, seemed plunging about as if they were dragging their anchors. What I felt on these occasions was a temporary loss of my own identity, accompanied by an illumination which revealed to me a deeper significance than I had been wont to attach to life. It is in this that I find my justification for saying that I have enjoyed communication with God. Of course the absence of such a being as this would be chaos. I cannot conceive of life without its presence."

Of the more habitual and so to speak chronic sense of God's presence the following sample for Professor Starbuck's manuscript collection may serve to give an idea. It is from a man aged forty-nine – probably thousands of unpretending Christians would write an almost identical account.

"God is more real to me than any thought or thing or person. I feel his presence positively, and the more as I live in closer harmony with this laws as written in my body and mind. I feel him in the sunshine or rain; and awe mingled with a delicious restfulness most nearly describes my feelings. I talk to him as to a companion in prayer and praise, and our communion is delightful. He answers me again and again, often in words so clearly spoken that it seems my outer ear must have carried the tone, but generally in strong mental impressions. Usually a text of Scripture, unfolding some new view of him and his love for me, and care for my safety. I could give hundreds of instances, in school matters, social problems, financial difficulties, etc. that he is mine and I am his never leaves me, it is an abiding joy. Without it life would be blank, a desert, a shoreless, trackless waste."

I subjoin some more examples from writers of different ages and sexes. They are also from Professor Starbuck's collection, and their number might be greatly multiplied. The first is from a man twenty-seven years old: -"God is quite real to me. I talk to him and often get answers. Thoughts sudden and distinct from any I have been entertaining come to my mind after asking God for his direction. Something over a year ago I was for some weeks in the direst perplexity. When the trouble first appeared before me I was dazed, but before long (two or three hours) I could hear distinctly a passage of Scripture: 'My grace is sufficient for thee.' Every time my thoughts turned to the trouble I could hear this quotation. I don't think I ever doubted the existence of God, or had him drop out of my consciousness. God has frequently stepped into my affairs very perceptibly, and I feel that he directs many little details all the time. But on two or three occasions he has ordered ways for me very contrary to my ambitions and plans."

Another statement (none the less valuable psychologically for being so decidedly childish) is that of a boy of seventeen: -"Sometimes as I go to church, I sit down, join in the service, and before I go out I feel as if God was with me, right side of me, singing and reading the Psalms with me…. And then again I feel as if I could sit beside him, and put my arms around him, kiss him, etc. When I am taking the Holy Communion at the altar, I try to get with him and generally feel his presence."

I let a few other cases follow at random: -"God surrounds me like the physical atmosphere. He is closer to me than my own breath. In him literally I live and move and have my being," – "There are times when I seem to stand in his very presence, to talk with him. Answers to prayer have come, sometimes direct and overwhelming in their revelation of his presence and powers. There are time when God seems far off, but this is always my own fault." –"I have the sense of presence, strong, and at the same time soothing, which hovers over me. Sometimes it seems to enwrap me with sustaining arms."

Such is the human ontological imagination, and such is the convincingness of what it brings to birth. Unpicturable beings are realized, and realized with an intensity almost like that of an hallucination. They determine our vital attitude as decisively as the vital attitude of lovers is determined by the habitual sense, by which each is haunted, of the other being in the world. A lover has notoriously this sense of the continuous being of his idol, even when his attention is addressed to other matters and he no longer represents her features. He cannot forget her; she uninterruptedly affects him through and through.

I spoke of the convincingness of these feelings of reality, and I must dwell a moment longer on that point. They are as convincing to those who have them as any direct sensible experiences can be, and they are, as a rule, much more convincing than results established by mere logic ever are. One may indeed be entirely without them; probably more than one of you here present is without them in any marked degree; but if you do have them, and have them at all strongly, the probability is that you cannot help regarding them as genuine perceptions of truth, as revelations of a kind of reality which no adverse argument, however unanswerable by you in words, can expel from your belief. The opinion opposed to mysticism in philosophy is sometimes spoken of as *rationalism*. Rationalism insists that all our beliefs ought ultimately to find for themselves articulate grounds. Such grounds, for rationalism, must consist of four things: (1) definitely statable abstract principles; (2) definite facts of sensation; (3) definite hypothesis based on such facts; and (4) definite inferences logically drawn. Vague impressions of something indefinable have no place in the rationalistic system, which on its positive side is surely a splendid intellectual tendency, for not only are all our philosophies fruits of it, but physical science (amongst other good things) is its result.

Nevertheless, if we look on man's whole mental life as it exists, on the life of men that lies in them apart from their learning and science, and that they inwardly and privately follow, we have to confess that the part of it of which rationalism can give an account is relatively superficial. It is the part that has the prestige undoubtedly, for it has the loquacity, it can challenge you for proofs, and chop logic, and put you down with words. But it will fail to convince or convert you all the same, if your dumb intuitions are opposed to its conclusions. If you have intuitions at all, they come from a deeper level of your nature than the loquacious level which rationalism inhabits. Your whole subconscious life, your impulses, your faiths, your needs, your divinations, have prepared the premises, of which your consciousness now feels the weight of the result; and something in you absolutely *knows* that that result must be truer than any logic-chopping rationalistic talk, however clever, that may contradict it. This inferiority of the rationalistic level in founding belief is just as manifest when rationalism argues for religion as when it argues against it. That vast literature of proofs of God's existence drawn from the order of nature, which a century ago seemed so overwhelmingly convincing, to-day does little more than gather dust in libraries, for the simple reason that our generation has ceased to believe in the kind of God it argued for. Whatever sort of a being God may be, we *know* to-day that he is nevermore that mere external inventor of "contrivances" intended to make manifest his "glory" in which our great-grandfathers took such satisfaction, though just how we know this we cannot possibly make clear by words either to others or to ourselves. I defy any of you here fully to account for your persuasion that if a God exist he must be a more cosmic and tragic personage than that Being.

The truth is that in the metaphysical and religious sphere, articulate reasons are cogent for us only when our inarticulate feelings of reality have already been impresses in favor of the same conclusion. Then, indeed, our intuitions and our reason work together, and great world-ruling systems, like that of the Buddhist or of the Catholic philosophy, may grow up. Our impulsive belief is here always what sets up the original body of truth, and our articulately verbalized philosophy is but its showy translation into formulas. The unreasoned and immediate assurance is the deep thing in us, the reasoned argument is but a surface exhibition. Instinct leads, intelligence does but follow. If a person feels the presence of a living God after the fashion shown by my quotations, your critical arguments, be they never so superior, will vainly set themselves to change his faith.

Please observe, however, that I do not yet say that it is *better* that the subconscious and non-rational should thus hold primacy in the religious realm. I confine myself to simply pointing out that they do so hold it as a matter of fact.

So much for our sense of the reality of the religious objects. Let me now say a brief word more about the attitudes they characteristically awaken.

We have already agreed that they are solemn; and we have seen reason to think that the most distinctive of them is the sort of joy which may result in extreme cases from absolute self-surrender. The sense of the kind of object to which the surrender is made has much to do with determining the precise complexion of the joy; and the whole phenomenon is more complex than any simple formula allows. In the literature of the subject, sadness and gladness have each been emphasized in turn. The ancient saying that the first maker of the Gods was fear receives voluminous corroboration from every age of religious history; but nonetheless does religious history show the part which joy has evermore tended to play. Sometimes the joy has been primary; sometimes secondary, being the gladness of deliverance form the fear. This latter state of things, being the more complex, is also the more complete; and as we proceed, I think we shall have abundant reason for refusing to leave out either the sadness or the gladness, if we look at religion with the breadth of view which it demands. Stated in the completest possible terms, a man's religion involves both moods of contraction and moods of expansion of his being. But the quantitative mixture and order of these moods vary so much from one age of the world, from one system of thought, and from one individual to another, that you may insist either on the dread and the submission, or on the peace and the freedom as the essence of the matter, and still remain materially within the limits of truth. The constitutionally somber and the constitutionally sanguine onlooker are bound to emphasize opposite aspects of what lies before their eyes.

The constitutionally somber religious person makes even of his religious peace a very sober thing. Danger still hovers in the air about it. Flexion and contraction are not wholly checked. It were sparrowlike and childish after our deliverance to explode into twittering laughter and caper-cutting, and utterly to forget the imminent hawk on bough. Lie low, rather, lie low; for you are in the hands of a living God. In the Book of Job, for example, the impotence of man and the omnipotence of God is the exclusive burden of its author's mind. "It is as high as heaven; what canst thou do? – deeper than hell; what canst thou know?" There is an astringent relish about the truth of this conviction which some men can feel, and which for them is as near an approach as can be made to the feeling of religious joy.

"In Job," says that coldly truthful writer, the author of Mark Rutherford, "God reminds us that man is not the measure of his creation. The world is immense, constructed on no plan or theory which the intellect of man can grasp. It is *transcendent* everywhere. This is the burden of every verse, and is the secret, if there be one, of the poem. Sufficient or insufficient, there is nothing more…. God is great, we know not his ways. He takes from us all we have, but yet if we possess our souls in patience, we *may* pass the valley of the shadow, and come out in sunlight again. We may or we may not! … What more have we to say now than God said from the whirlwind over two thousand give hundred years ago?"

If we turn to the sanguine onlooker, on the other hand, we find that deliverance is felt as incomplete unless the burden be altogether overcome and the danger forgotten. Such onlookers give us definitions that seem to the somber minds of whom we have just been speaking to leave out all the solemnity that makes religious peace so different from merely animal joys. In the opinion of some writers an attitude might be called religious, though no touch were left in it of sacrifice or submission, no tendency to flexion, no bowing of the head. Any "habitual and regulated admiration," says Professor J. R. Seeley,[10] "is worthy to be called a religion"; and accordingly he thinks that our Music, our Science, and our so-called "Civilization," as these things are now organized and admiringly believed in, form the more genuine religions of our time. Certainly the unhesitating and unreasoning way in which we feel that we must inflict our civilization upon "lower" races, by means of Hotchkiss guns, etc., reminds one of nothing so much as of the early spirit of Islam spreading its religion by the sword.

BRINGING "NEURO" AND "THEOLOGY" TOGETHER AGAIN

By Andrew Newberg

The neurosciences clearly have significant potential in helping with the understanding of religious experiences and religious phenomena. An array of imaging technologies as well as the ability to measure various physiological and neurophysiological parameters will likely have a significant impact in terms of how we come to understand the importance of religion and religious experience in human life. However, it is also very important to consider the limitations of neuroscience, and in particular, what neuroscience has to say about epistemological and ontological questions. At the present time, the neurosciences proceed from a fundamental assumption that the material world, as we perceive it, is the primary "stuff" of the universe. Hence, we can explore brain function, and ultimately relate that brain function to various human experiences, thoughts, and feelings. The conclusion from such research is that the brain actually causes these experiences, thoughts, and feelings. Studies are even beginning to show which structures and functions underlie various ritual activities, spiritual practices, and even more subtle concepts such as morality and love.

While the information obtained from the neurosciences, especially as it pertains to religious phenomena, is crucial for developing an integrated understanding of neurotheology, the specific conclusions that arise from such results need to be carefully drawn. The evaluation of causality also must be considered with great care. For example, it is imperative that one recognizes that taking a brain image of someone having a spiritual experience may not help determine the ultimate causal basis of such an experience. One conclusion is that the experience is, in fact, nothing more than a series or conglomeration of brain functions. This would relegate religion and its theological development to a human construction. While this may not be inaccurate, it is far from the only conclusion that may be derived. Another conclusion would be that the brain is truly in contact with some divine presence or fundamental level of reality. In this case, the brain scan images are merely detecting the effect of that reality on the human brain. In this regard, religious experience does, in fact, coincide with a higher level of reality that transcends our usual experience of the material world. This transcendent reality could be considered to be God, in the theistic traditions, or ultimate reality in the non-theistic traditions. Furthermore, in view of this second conclusion, the brain would be derivative from this higher level of reality. Believers of religion would certainly support such a hypothesis, stating that it would make sense that if God truly existed, that there would be some fundamental way for human beings to experience and connect with God. To have a brain, designed by a creating God, that would have no ability to interact with that God would represent a fundamental disconnection. Therefore, it is only natural that the brain be able to have religious and spiritual experiences.

There is a third conclusion that is possible, which in some sense, is a synthesis of the first two. In such a conclusion, the answer to one of the commonly posed questions, "Did God create the brain or did the brain create God?" would be "yes" to both. While this may be difficult to comprehend, it is also a logically plausible conclusion. The implications of such a conclusion would be that, while human beings and the human brain are derived in some respects from an absolute reality or God, that it is also the human brain that creates our conception of that ultimate reality or God. This latter point certainly makes sense from a neuropsychological perspective because the brain is always providing us a "second-hand rendition" of reality. In other words, our only understanding of the world is through the processes of the human brain that take the sensory information and cognitive thinking processes and puts them together in order to provide us an integrated image of reality However, that the brain may be derived from some fundamental or divine level of reality is a question that remains to be clearly answered.

In addition to these three general possibilities, there are likely to be other more subtle possibilities that represent varying degrees of combinations of the three mentioned here. However, there may be other altogether different possibilities as well, which clearly need to be explored. The most important point with regard to these conclusions is not necessarily a debate over which one does represent the true reality. It is more important to ensure that scholars in the field of neurotheology maintain an openness to all possibilities and interpret the results of whatever studies or analyses they perform carefully and with respect to both the scientific perspective and the spiritual perspective of the world. As such, while there is great value in exploring the diverse variety of religious and spiritual experiences and practices using neuroscientific techniques, the religious and spiritual side must be carefully weighed, understood, and integrated into the analysis. In fact, given the possible conclusions from such an analysis, one must also be aware not only how science may inform us about religious experience, but also how religious experience may ultimately inform us about science. Only by maintaining an openness to both the "neuro" and the "theology" sides of neurotheology can this field emerge as a legitimate discipline that has the potential to advance science, religion, and the dialogue between the two.

THE NEUROPSYCHOLOGY OF RELIGION
by Scott Atran

Religion's Evolutionary Landscape: Cognition and Commitment.

Let us consider religion to be a community's (1) costly and hard-to-fake commitment (2) to a counterfactual world of supernatural agents (3) and which enables people to master their existential anxieties, such as death and deception (Atran 2002). The present chapter mainly concerns the third criterion of religion (3), and its implications for neuropsychology. This introductory section, however, first summarizes the overall intellectual framework.

The criterion (1) of costly commitment rules out cognitive theories of religion as sufficient, however insightful. Such theories lack motive (Atran & Sperber 1991, Boyer 1994, Barrett 2000). In principle, they can't distinguish nonreligious fantasy from religious belief. They fail to tell us why, in general, the greater the sacrifice to the apparently absurd – as in Abraham's willingness to offer up his beloved son - the more others trust in one's commitment (Kierkegaard 1955[1843], Weber 1946).

The criterion (2) of belief in the supernatural rules out commitment theories of religion as sufficient, however insightful. Such theories disregard cognitive structure and its causal role (Irons 1996, Nesse 1999, Wilson 2002). They don't distinguish strong secular ideologies, such as orthodox belief in Marxism or the Market, from religious belief.

Religions often invoke supernatural agents to deal with (3) emotionally eruptive existential anxieties, such as death and deception (Feuerbach 1972[1843], Freud 1990[1913]) They generally have malevolent and predatory deities as well as more benevolent and protective ones. Supernatural agent concepts trigger our naturally-selected agency-detection system, which is trip-wired to respond to fragmentary information, inciting perception of figures lurking in shadows, and emotions of dread or awe (Guthrie 1993; cf. Hume 1956[1757]). To be sure, nondeistic "theologies", such as Buddhism and Taoism, doctrinally eschew the supernatural. Nevertheless, common folk who espouse these faiths routinely entertain belief in an array of gods and spirits. Even Buddhist monks ritually ward off malevolent deities by invoking benevolent ones.

Sometime during the Pleistocene hominids became their own worst predators, encouraging natural selection of an ability to rapidly detect and react to supremely intelligent and rapacious agents (Alexander 1987). Mistaking a non-agent for an agent would do little harm, but failing to detect an agent - especially a human or animal predator - could well prove fatal. From an evolutionary perspective, it's better to be safe than sorry. This cognitive proclivity would favor the emergence of malevolent deities in every human culture, just as the countervailing Darwinian imperative to attach to protective caregivers would cognitively favor the apparition of benevolent deities.

Indeed, many mammals, such as social carnivores and primates, evince behaviors consistent with an integrated appreciation of evolved predator-protector-prey schema. In "chase play" the young typically "dare" a protector (parent, sibling) to chase them as a predator would, only to "surrender" to the pettings, lickings and other comforting behaviors of the chaser. Only humans, however, appear to have evolved a fully developed agency-awareness module, or "folkpsychology," capable of representing alternative worlds and states of mind (Baron-Cohen 1995, Suddendorf 1999). This capacity to model different models of things is necessary to the conception of counterfactual worlds, including the supernatural.

Such "meta-modeling" or "meta-representational" ability has wide-ranging consequences for human survival. It allows people to conceive of alternative worlds and to entertain, recognize and evaluate the differences between true and false beliefs. Given the ever-present menace of enemies within and without, concealment, deception and the ability to both generate and recognize false beliefs in others would favor survival.

Supernatural causes and beings are generally meta-represented as more or less vague ideas about other ideas, like a metaphor that meta-represents the earth as a mother but not quite, or an angel as a winged youth but not quite. The supernatural cannot be simply represented as a proposition about a state of affairs whose truth, falsity or probability can be factually or logically evaluated. No statement or thought about the supernatural can be empirically disconfirmed or logically disproven.

Because human representations of agency and intention include representations of false belief and deception, human society is forever under threat of moral defection. By invoking omniscient and omnipotent supernatural agents who have only (or almost only) true beliefs, people steadfastly commit to one another in a moral order that goes beyond apparent reason and self-conscious interest. In the competition for moral allegiance, secular ideologies are at a disadvantage. For, if people learn that all apparent commitment is self-interested convenience or worse, manipulation for the self-interest of others, then their commitment is debased and withers. Especially in times of vulnerability and stress, social deception and defection in the pursuit of self- preservation is therefore more likely to occur (Ibn Khaldun 1958[1318]:II,iii:41). Religion passionately rouses hearts and minds to break out of this viciously rational cycle of self-interest, and to adopt group interests that may benefit individuals in the long run. More generally, religious commitment to the supernatural underpins the "organic solidarity" (Durkheim 1995[1912]) that makes social life more than simply a contract among calculating individuals. It creates the arational conditions for devotion and sacrifice that enable people and societies to endure even against terrible odds. A supernatural agent can ultimately punish cheaters, defectors and free riders, no matter how devious or careful they may be.

Purely ideological commitments to moral principles also lack interactive aspects of personal agency – and the emotional intimacy that goes with it – as well the promise to allay the eruptive and uncontrollable existential anxieties for which there appears to be no rational expectation of resolution, such as vulnerability (to injustice, pain, dominance), loneliness (abandonment, unrequited love), and calamity (disease, death). Evolutionarily, at least some basic emotions preceded conceptual reasoning: surprise, fear, anger, disgust, joy, sadness (Darwin 1965[1872], Ekman 1992). These may have further evolved to incite reason to make inferences about situations relevant to survival decisions. This was plausibly an important selection factor for the emergence of reason itself. Existential anxieties are by-products of evolved emotions, such as fear and the will to stay alive, and of evolved cognitive capacities, such as episodic memory and the ability to track the self and others over time. For example, because humans are able to meta-represent their own selves and mentally travel in time (Wheeler et al. 1997), they cannot avoid overwhelming inductive evidence predicting their own death and that of persons to whom they are emotionally tied, such as relatives, friends and leaders. Emotions compel such inductions and make them salient and terrifying. This is "The Tragedy of Cognition." Religions customarily propose a supernatural resolution in some minimally counterfactual afterlife.

In religion, as in love and strife, sanctified displays of passionate commitment to others are given in the face of existential anxieties for which no predictable outcome or rational solution is possible, as at marriages, send offs and funerals. These sacred vows are promises to help one another in future situations where there is need, and no hope of reward. This enables people to trust and do uncalculating good for one another. That's the good news. The bad news is that just as a marriage commitment to one person precludes similar to commitment to another, so a religious commitment to one society or moral order usually precludes commitment to another. Not that all religions explicitly insist on mutually exclusive commitments, though many do. Rather, every religion professes absolute and nonnegotiable commitments that set the limits of tolerance. This adversarial process leads to unending development of new religious and cultural forms. Thus, despite the rise of secular ideologies and science, and corresponding predictions of religion's inevitable demise, new religious movements (NRMs) continue to arise at a furious pace - perhaps at the rate of two or three per day (Lester 2002).

Communal rituals rhythmically coordinate emotional validation of, and commitment to, moral truths in worlds governed by supernatural agents (Turner 1969, Rappaport 1999). Rituals involve sequential, socially interactive movement and gesture and formulaic utterances that synchronize affective states among group members in displays of cooperative commitment. Religious rituals habitually include displays of social hierarchy and submission typical of primates and other social mammals (outstretched limbs baring throat and chest or genitals, genuflection, bowing, prostration, etc.). Even priests and kings must convincingly show sincere obeisance to higher supernatural authority lest their own authority be doubted (Burkert 1996; cf. Watanabee & Smuts 1999).

Religious ritual also involves more primitive communicative forms that Tinbergen calls "ritualized social releasers" (1951:191-192). Social releasers exhibit sense-evident properties, "either of shape, or colour, or special movements, or sound, or scents," which readily elicit a well-timed and well-oriented cooperative response in a conspecific: for mating, parenting, fighting, defense, food gathering, and the like. But humans, it appears, are the only animals that spontaneously engage in creative, rhythmic bodily coordination to enhance cooperation. Unlike, say, avian mating calls or flight formations, human music or body dance (which are omnipresent in worship) can be arbitrarily and creatively elicited, transferred, combined, or interpolated to fit many different purposes and contexts (e.g., from use of love songs in mating displays to use of mating displays in sales jingles).

A key feature of the creativity of human worship is use of music in social ritual. Even the Taliban, who prohibited nearly all public displays of sensory stimulation, promoted a cappella religious chants. In a survey of persons who reported a religious experience (Greeley 1975), music emerges as the single most important elicitor of the experience (49% of cases), followed by prayer (48%) and attending group services (41%). Reading the Bible (31 %) and being alone in church (30 %) trail significantly behind. Listeners as young as three years old reliably associate basic or primary emotions to musical structures, such as happiness, sadness, fear and anger (Trainor & Trehub 1992; cf. Cunningham & Sterling 1988, Panksepp 1995). Electrocortical measures of frontal brain activity suggest that people exhibit greater relative left frontal activity to joyful and happy music and greater relative right frontal activity to to fearful and sad music, with activity greater for fearful than sad reactions and for joyful than happy reactions (Schmidt & Trainor 2001).

Music invites interpersonal relationships, creating emotional bonds between people, through the "attunement" of somatic states – much as the rocking and cooing behavior of mother and infant attunes the parental bond (Stern 1985). This is especially apparent in "call-response" format, as in Yoruba dances and Hebrew services. Moreover, in religious contexts, music is frequently experienced as authorless, like the sacred texts that often accompany it. The pre-tonal religious music of small-scale societies usually has its mythic beginnings in the origins of the world, which invites audiences to share in a sense of timeless intimacy. For the Catholic Church, Gregorian chants were taught to men by birds sent from heaven. Even Bach, Mozart and Beethoven were but vehicles of The Divine.

In sum, religion is not an evolutionary adaptation *per se,* but a constantly re-emerging cultural path by which people readily navigate the complex evolutionary landscape that sets cognitive, emotional and material conditions for ordinary human interactions. It arises, in part, from developed cognitions of folkpsychology and agency. This involves meta-representation, which makes deception possible and threatens any social order; however, these same meta-cognitive capacities provide the hope and promise of open-ended solutions through representations of counterfactual supernatural worlds that cannot be logically or empirically verified or falsified. Core religious beliefs minimally violate ordinary notions about how the world is, with all of its inescapable problems, thus enabling people to imagine minimally impossible worlds that appear to solve existential problems, including death and deception (Norenzayan & Atran 2002). Because religious beliefs and experiences cannot be deductively or inductively validated, validation occurs only by assuaging the very emotions that motivate religion. Through movement, sound, smell, touch and sight, religious rituals affectively coordinate actors' minds and bodies into convergent expressions of public sentiment – a sort of N-person bonding that communicates moral consensus.

Existential Motivation: Deception and Death

In this section, I summarize competing arguments and recent experiments with colleagues relating to the claim that religion crucially involves supernatural agents who address existential anxieties, such as deception and death.

One idea common to psychoanalysis (Freud 1990[1913], Erikson 1963) and attachment theory (Bowlby 1969, Kirkpatrick 1998) is that deities are surrogate parents that assuage existential anxieties. One reason for rejecting or substantially modifying this idea as it stands comes from anthropology. Ethnographic reports indicate that malevolent and predatory deities are as culturally widespread, historically ancient and as socially supreme as benevolent deities. Examples include the cannibalistic spirits of small-scale Amazonian, sub-Saharan African and Australian aboriginal societies as well as the bloodthirsty deities of larger-scale civilizations that practiced human sacrifice, such as Moloch of the Ancient Middle East, the death goddess Kali of the tribal Hindus and the Maya thunder god Chaak. Serpent-like devils and demons seem to be culturally ubiquitous (Munkur 1983), perhaps evoking and addressing a primal fear shared by our primate line (Mineka et al. 1984).

It also appears that neuropsychologist Michael Persinger (1987) sees readiness to believe in God as a psychological compulsion to recover the lost parental security of childhood. This innate drive is supposed to be conceptually generalized to God by stimulus-response conditioning through reward and punishment. Learning to generalize to God need involve little more than simple word association: "In this way, the properties of objects [e.g., parents] are transferred to words [e.g., "God"]":

"The parents no longer have the properties of omnipotence and omnipresence. Through experience, the adult has learned that parents are discrete and mortal beings with limited space and little time. The childhood expectations have been generalized to God" (1987:66).

Details of the God concept are determined by a person's culturally-conditioned experiences. Thus: "Matrilineal societies... have female gods. In patrilineal societies, where the male line is most important, the god is portrayed with clear masculine features."

Although it is vaguely true that the deities of different societies take on culturally-specific aspects of those societies (Durkheim 1995[1912]), there is often no simple mapping or straightforward projection of social structures onto to god features. For example, the matrilineal Nair (Warrior Caste) of Kerala in South India have the same pantheon of 330 male and female deities as do patrilineal Hindus. Off the Arabian Sea's Kerala coast, the matrilineal Lakshadsweep Islanders have no God but Allah, and worship Mohammed as His Prophet just as the patrilineal Arabs do.

Some of the syncretic Moslem and Christian societies of Asia and Africa have high-ranking women deities, and even important animal and plant deities. A recurrent myth in male-dominated patrilineal societies of Africa, such as the Gola of Liberia (d'Azevedo 1973), is that female deities originate what men desire to control (Horton 1963). For the patrilineal Tsembaga of New Guinea, the most important single spirit is "Smoke Woman" (*Kun Kaze Ambra*), who "acts as an intermediary between the living and all other categories of spirits." This female deity "might, out of jealousy, do mischief to any woman with whom a [male] novice of hers consorts" (Rappaport 1979:103).

Another reason for doubting that gods are just surrogate parents comes from cognitive psychology, in particular the branch of cognitive psychology known as "theory of mind" or "folkpsychology." Cross-cultural experimental evidence from child development studies indicate that young children reliably distinguish the intentions of parents from those of God and other supernatural agents just as soon as they can attribute intention and belief to anybody or anything at all. Attributing intention and belief critically involves the child's ability to meta-represent propositions about the world as true or false. This ability emerges around age 4 (Wimmer & Perner 1983, Wellman 1990).

In one of the few studies to replicate findings on "theory of mind" in a small-scale society (cf., Avis & Harris 1991), Knight, Barrett, Atran and Ucan Ek' (2001) showed monolingual Yukatek Maya children a tortilla container and told them, "Usually tortillas are inside this box, but I ate them and put these shorts inside." Then they asked each child in random order what a person, God, the sun (*k'in*), the principal forest spirits (*yumil k'ax'ob*, "Masters of the Forest"), and other minor spirits (*chiichi'*) would think was in the box. In line with recent studies of American children (Barrett et al. 2001), the youngest Yukatek children (4 year-olds) overwhelmingly attribute true beliefs to both God and people in equal measure. By age 5, the children attribute mostly false beliefs to people but continue to attribute mostly true beliefs to God (Figure 66).

Children 5 and over attribute true beliefs according to a hierarchy with God at the top and people at the bottom (Figure 67). Yukatek consider the Masters of the Forest powerful and knowledgeable spirits that punish people who try to overexploit forest species. Yukatek children tend to believe that forest spirits, God and the sun, "live" (*kukuxtal)* but do not "die" (*kukumil)*. For Maya adults, such beliefs have reliably measurable behavioral consequences for biodiversity, forest sustainability, and so forth (Atran et al. 2002). In brief, from an early age people reliably attribute to supernaturals cognitive properties that are different from parents and other people. Furthermore, people reliably behave differently in accordance with these different attributions.

Children's ability to distinguish god concepts from parent concepts comes about only with the acquisition (innately-driven maturation) of a capacity for meta-representation, that is, part of a fully developed folkpsychology. It is logically impossible for such a cognitive capacity, or "theory of mind," to arise from conditioning or trial-and-error learning; that is, a faculty of greater representational power (meta-representation) cannot arise piecemeal by induction or accretion from a faculty of lesser representational power (simple representation or perception of a state of affairs) (Fodor 1974; cf. discussions in Hirschfeld & Gelman 1994). Nevertheless, the idea that deities often co-opt childhood emotions associated with parental prepotency is well taken. Only, this cannot be the whole story. In religion's counterfactual and counterintuitive worlds one and the same deity can even have the dualizing role of predator and protector, or prey and protector. These may well be humankind's most popular deities. It is not an infant-parent or child-kin group template from which god concepts extend, but plausibly a more encompassing evolutionary program for detecting and dealing with agency and intention, both good (inspiring trust) and bad (inspiring fear).

Another experiment that ties religion to belief in the supernatural's ability to deal with human existential anxieties was recently carried out by Ara Norenzayan, Ian Hansen and myself. In particular, this experiment links adrenaline-activating death scenes to increased belief in God's existence and the efficacy of supernatural intervention in human affairs. Results show that people cognitively commit themselves more to the supernatural under stressful interpretations of events involving other people than they do when events are emotionally uneventful. This is so even when those uneventful events specifically involve a religious component. Commitment theories of religion also neglect such special effects of the supernatural.

Our experiment was built on a study by Larry Cahill and colleagues (1994) in the laboratory of James McGaugh. They showed college students a series of slides and a storyline about a boy riding a bike. Some subjects were exposed to an uneventful story: the boy rides his bike home, and he and his mother drive to the hospital to pick up his father (who is a doctor). For the other participants, the story begins and ends in much the same way, but the middle is very different: the boy is hit by a car and rushed to the hospital's emergency room, where a brain scan shows severe bleeding from the boy's brain and specialized surgeons struggle to reattach the boy's severed feet. After exposure to the stories, and before being tested for recall, half the subjects were given either a placebo pill or a drug (propranolol) that blocks the effects of adrenaline. The placebo and drug groups recalled the uneventful story equally well. Only the placebo group, however, remembered the emotional story more accurately than the uneventful one. (Similar effects occur from amygdala damage, McGaugh et al. 1995).

Our hypothesis was that stressful events associated with existential anxieties (e.g., death) not only deeply affect how people remember events but also religious coloring of those events. We first controlled for religious background and measured for religious identification. Then we primed each of three groups of college students with a different story: Cahill et al.'s uneventful story (neutral prime), Cahill et al.'s stressful story (death prime), and another uneventful story whose event-structure matched the other two stories but which included a prayer scene (religious prime). After this, each group of subjects read a reprint from a New York Times article (2 Oct. 2001) whose lead ran: "Researchers at Columbia University, expressing surprise at their own findings, are reporting that women at an in vitro fertilization clinic in Korea had a higher pregnancy rate when, unknown to the patients, total strangers were asked to pray for their success." The article was given to students under the guise of a different story about "media portrayals of scientific studies." Finally, the students rated the strength of their belief in God and the power of supernatural intervention on a nine-point scale.

Results show that strength of belief in God's existence (Figure 68) and in the efficacy of supernatural intervention (Figure 69) are reliably stronger after exposure to the death prime than either to the neutral or religious prime (there were no significant differences between either uneventful story). This was so whatever students' religious background or prior degree of religious identification. In sum, emotional stress associated with death-related scenes seems a stronger natural motivator for religiosity than mere exposure to emotionally unstressful religious scenes, such as praying.

This provides some confirmation of the claim that emotionally eruptive existential anxieties motivate belief in the supernatural. We also plan to test the further claim that invocation of the supernatural not only cognitively validates these eruptive emotions, but is affectively validated by assuaging the very emotions that motivate belief in the supernatural. With this in mind, it is worth noting that uncontrollable arousal mediated by adrenergic activation (as for subjects exposed to death scenes) may lead to posttraumatic stress disorder (PTSD) if there is no lessening of terror and arousal within hours; however, adrenergic blockers (propranolol, clondine, guanfacine, and possibly antidepressants) can "interrupt the neuronal imprinting that leads to long-term symptoms" (McReady 2002:9). A possibility arises, then, that heightened expressions of religiosity following exposure to death scenes that provoke existential anxieties could also serve this blocking function.

Religion and Psychopathology: Possession, Epilepsy, Schizophrenia, Autism

Stress is a key factor in emotionally drawn out communal rituals, such as initiation rites and exorcisms, and mystical states, like divine visions and revelations. In cases of religious possession, society often draws a fine line between supernaturally-caused possession and organically-caused madness that is often stress related:

"Between madness and possession, the difference is small in the eyes of the Arab.... [T]he

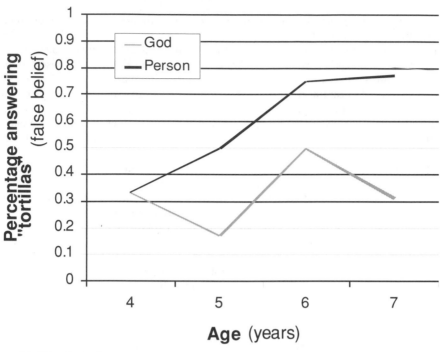

Figure 67. What's in the container?   Maya Children's Attributions of False Beliefs

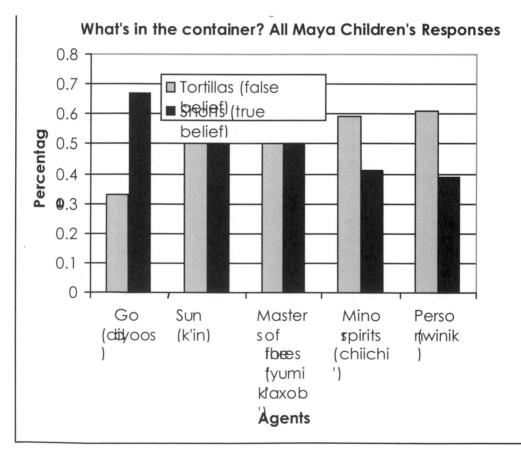

Figure 68. Percentage of responses by all age groups of Yukatek Maya children attributing false beliefs or true beliefs to persons and various supernatural agents.

madman is designated by the word *ma_noun;* the possessed person is called <u>madroub</u> or 'struck' by a spirit. To chase away the intruding spirit from the possessed body, one turns to a *faqir* [an indigent wanderer or street person who practices healing and sorcery by virtue of being 'gifted with supernatural power, because of his friendship with Allah'].... A <u>faqireh</u> [female sorceress] seizes the possessed person, places him in the middle of the room and begins turning around him as she plays the tambourine. At the sound of this primitive music, the spirit stirs restlessly; the afflicted person has convulsions" (Jaussen 1948[1907]:327).

Recurring cases of possession are reported from Africa and Afro-America (Leiris 1958, Douyon 1966, Lewis, 1971, Kilson 1972, Walker 1972, Pressel 1974, Ben-Amos 1994), European America (Freed & Freed 1964), Native America (Lowie 1924, Reina 1966), China (Yap 1960), India (Crooke 1907, Whitehead 1988[1921]), North Africa and the Middle East (Jaussen 1948[1907]). Cases in the USA often involve possession by devils, witches (Ludwig 1965, Warner 1977) and, more recently, aliens (cf. Blackmore 1999). Variants of possession include "soul kidnapping" (Lowie 1924:177-178) or "soul loss" (Warner 1977) through the agency of malevolent spirits. Black magic and bewitchment, in which spirits cast charms or spells on victims, can also exhibit aspects of possession. This is especially so in regard to the onset of symptoms and debilitating pathology, as with depression and disease (Redfield & Villa Rojas 1934:177-180). If not exorcised, death may be expected.

Although there is no clear psychopathology associated with possession, there is a more or less identifiable family of associated symptoms: listlessness, depression, guilt feelings, fainting and dissociation are frequent. Acute or chronic stress (or emotional or psychic "tension") is habitually cited as precipitating and accompanying non-institutionalized cases of possession. Institutionalized cases tend more to have psychotic pathologies, such as schizophrenic hallucination, epileptic confusion, mania, senility, and so forth. In one institutionalized Chinese sample of possessed patients, Yap (1960) reported mainly hysterics (48.5%), schizophrenics (24.3 %) and depressives (12.2 %).

In many societies, auditory and visual hallucinations that our medical establishment associates with certain forms of temporal-lobe epilepsy and schizophernia often take on a religious color. They become the "voices" and "visions" of personal revelation for the subjects themselves and, depending upon the society, they may become the charge of local religion as well. To a significant extent, persons prone to schizophrenia may find themselves better suited for a more cloistered religious life (Kelley 1958). In some societies, epileptics may be preferentially chosen as shamans (Eliade 1964). For example, in North India (Crooke 1907:259-260): "The Shaman lives a life apart, practises or pretends to practise various austerities, wears mysterious and symbolical garments, and performs noisy incantations in which a sacred drum or an enchanted rattle takes a leading part. On occasion he should be able to foam at the mouth and go into a trance or fit, during which his soul is supposed to quit his body and wander away into space. By some these seizures have been ascribed to epilepsy."

One prominent neurobiological focus of these extreme religious experiences - as well as nonpathological experiences involving glossolalia, trance and meditative ecstatic visions– is the amygdala-hippocampus complex (Beard 1963, Slater & Beard 1963, Bear 1979, Gloor et al. 1982, Geschwind 1983, Joseph, 2001, Persinger 1984). Accounts of visual and auditory hallucinations among some of history's leading religious converts and mystics intimate possible temporal-lobe epilepsy. A particularly controversial case concerns the dramatic conversion of the Apostle Paul. Paul was a vicious persecutor of Christians. One day, he collapsed on the road to Damascus and suddenly experienced auditory and visual hallucinations. As a result, he converted to Christianity and became perhaps the single most important figure in fostering its spread beyond a few marginal Jewish communities of the Roman Empire. Psychologist William James (1902) surmises that Paul's newfound voice of consience may have been "a physiological nerve storm or discharging lesion like that of epilepsy," although lack of of evidence for subsequent mental deterioration argues against temporal-lobe epilepsy (Woods 1913). Another famous case concerns a16[th]-century saint, Teresa of Avila. She experienced vivid visions, intense headaches and fainting spells, followed by "such peace, calm, and good fruits in the soul, and ... a perception of the greatness of God" (St. Theresa 1930:171). Biographers suggest that she may well have experienced epileptic seizures (Sackville-West 1943), similar perhaps to the fits suffered by the Russian writer and religious mystic, Fyodor Dostoevsky.

The absence of details precludes an accurate diagnosis in such cases. Yet, there is little doubt that extreme and even pathological religious experiences have been interpreted over the ages as unequivocal signs of divine enlightenment or possession in different times and places. In contemporary Europe and North America, however, such manifestations more often lead to confinement in a mental asylum (except in the movies). In studies of schizophrenia-like psychoses of epilepsy in British hospitals, A.W.

Beard and colleagues found that 38% of patients had hallucinations and mystical delusions, although fewer than 9% had religious convictions prior to the onset of symptoms (Beard 1963, Slater & Beard 1963). Typical reports of religious experiences among temporal-lobe epileptics include: "greater awareness," "seeing Christ come down from the sky," "seeing Heaven open"; "hears God speak"; "feels himself transfigured and even believes that he is God," and so forth (cf. Karagulla & Robertson 1955, Geschwind 1983).

A study of sudden religious conversion in 6 temporal-lobe epileptics (3 also had epileptogenic areas in frontal areas) revealed: hearing "divine music and angelic voices," "she heard a church bell ring in her right ear; and the voice said: 'Thy Father hath made the whole, Go in peace!'"; having "a day-time visual hallucination in which he saw angels playing with harps"; "he had a sudden dream-like ... flash of light, and exclaimed 'I have seen the light'," feeling "heavenly voices abusing him, felt rays were being shone on him to punish him (a sensation of burning)"; "terrified that I would not be able to carry out... the love of God.... [H]e also became paranoid, believing that he was being poisoned"; sensing "a holy smell"; believing "that he was able to pick up other people's thoughts," or "that he could understand other people's thoughts" (Dewhurst & Beard 1970).

Sudden alterations of activity in the hippocampus and amygdala can affect auditory, vestibular, gustatory, tactile, olfactory perceptions and lead to hallucinations involving voices or music, feelings of sway or physical suspension, the tastes of elixirs, burning or caressing, the fragrance of Heaven or the stench of Hell. For example, because the middle part of the amygdala receives fibers from the olfactory tract, direct stimulation of that part of the amygdala will flood co-occurring events with strong smells. In religious rituals, incense and fragrances stimulate the amygdala so that scent can be used to focus attention and interpretation on the surrounding events. In temporal-lobe epilepsy, the sudden electrical spiking of the area infuses other aspects of the epileptic experience with an odorous aura.

The hippocampus processes verbal and vocal signals, helping to link the intentions behind those signals (originating in the prefrontal cortices) to appropriate states of arousal and emotivity (via the amygdala and hypothalamus). Religious rituals sequence and rhythmically pattern these signals (prayers, preaching, incantations, chants) to infuse them with sustained affect, and to increase the motivation for any uses to which they may be put. In temporal-lobe epileptics, the hippoc-

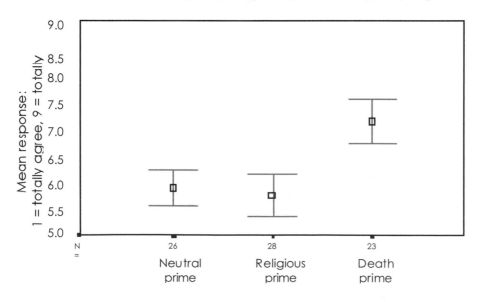

Figure 69. Strength of belief in God's existence after priming (neutral, religious or death) and then reading a newspaper article about effects of prayer on pregnancy (vertical bars represent margin of error at **p = .05**)

ampus may be spontaneously stimulated to produce or interpret verbal signals as eruptive "voices" of unknown source and uncertain intention, which may threaten in the acute phase of schizophrenic-like hallucination or soothe during remission (cf. Larkin 1979).

Hallucinations can involve different sensory modalities. Thus, the brain's auditory, vestibular and visual channels are closely intertwined. The inner ear conveys both sounds and a sense of balance. In religious ritual, music or chanting can set the body to swaying, triggering pleasant feelings. Loud noises and irregular sound patterns can cause sudden, disorienting movements, triggering surprise and fear and temporarily throwing the body out-of-kilter (although people can become habituated to noise levels and idiosyncracies in sound patterns, so that what feels unpleasant to some feels pleasant to others). Loud music or sudden noises (as well as bright or flashing lights) can drive the epileptic into seizures marked by feelings of terror and paranoia.

Because of the innate adaptation of our moving bodies to the gravitational conditions on earth, the coordination of the retina's frame with the inner ear's frame gives us a proper sense of movement only when we are upright from the ground. When the two frames are thrown out of whack (moving on a boat, whirling in a dance, suddenly rising after lying down), the body says that you're moving but the ground lets you know that you're not. Notions of "up," "down," "side," "ceiling," "floor," and "wall" become confused. When ritually controlled, this disynchronization often induces an emotionally positive sense of floating, suspension, or slow motion in a fast-moving world. When uncontrolled, as in epileptic experiences, it can provoke a frightening, emotionally aversive sense of dislocation and bewilderment. It can also produce nausea (as in motion sickness) and perhaps a sense of being poisoned (nausea and vomiting may be adaptations for elimination of toxins from the body).

These and other findings concerning relations between religious experiences and temporal-lobe epilepsy provide a main support for Persinger's (1987:113; cf. Persinger 1997) report that transient patterns of stimulation in the temporal lobe – especially around the amygdalohippocampal complex - "create the God experience." The problem with his hypothesis from a neuropsychological standpoint is that it takes little account of the importance of agency and relations with the prefrontal cortices. The key issue here is that of functional connectivity, that is, temporal correlations between spatially remote physical events. In particular, frontal-temporal connectivity – and not just temporal

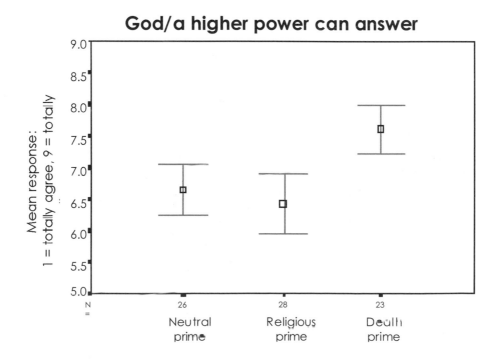

*Fig. 70. Strength of belief in supernatural power after priming (neutral, religious or death) and then reading a newspaper article about effects of prayer on pregnancy (vertical bars represent margin of error at **p = .05**)*

activation as such - implies a distributed rather than localized neural substrate for many types of religious experience. For example, disinhibited functions in the temporal lobes (e.g., seizure foci) will generally elicit a compensatory response from inhibitory circuits in the frontal lobes. If Newberg et al. (2001a,b) are right about systematic alterations in the activity of the parietal lobe's orientation association area, then issues of connectivity become correspondingly more complex. For the present, though, I want to concentrate on what I think are the least controversial - or at least the most empirically-supported - arguments about frontal-temporal connectivity in religious experience.

Brain-imaging shows heightened electrical stimulation and increased blood flow to this area of the brain during bouts of epileptic seizure, schizophrenic hallucination, speaking in tongues and trance, and deep meditation and prayer. But whereas schizophrenia-like episodes of epilepsy and schizophrenic hallucinations appear to be associated with decreased activity in the frontal cortices (Stern & Silbersweig 1998), mediation and prayer seem to be associated with increased activity (Newberg et al.. 2001a,b). In pathological cases there is a corresponding, clinically apparent lack of awareness of reality, whereas in non-pathological cases there is a reported hyperawareness of reality.

In a study of 60 inpatients with schizophrenic or schizophrenic-like auditory hallucinations, Oulis and colleagues (1995) found high levels of conviction about the reality of the sensory stimuli, clarity of content, location of their source, and lack of volitional control. The voices associated with such pathological states indicate a dampening of subcortical interactions with the prefrontal cortices and an absence or submission of will (Joseph, 1990). The louder and more intrusive the hallucinations and intensity of delusional beliefs, the more anxious and fearful patients become, whether diagnosed as schizophrenics (Hustig & Hafner 1990) or temporal-lobe epileptics (LaBar et al. 1995). A study of command hallucinations among 106 schizophrenic outpatients revealed the hallucinations to be often violent in content, leading to attempts to harm others (including innocent bystanders) or oneself (including 2 cases of command suicide) (Zisook et al. 1995).

The hallucinations and delusions associated with pathological states indicate a disconnection

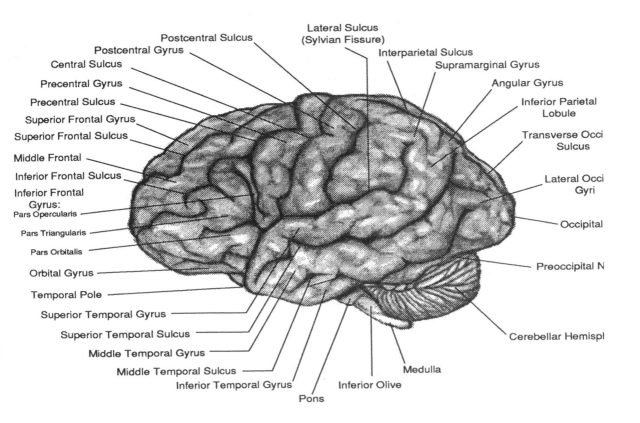

Figure 71. The left cerebral hemisphere. From Joseph, 1990.

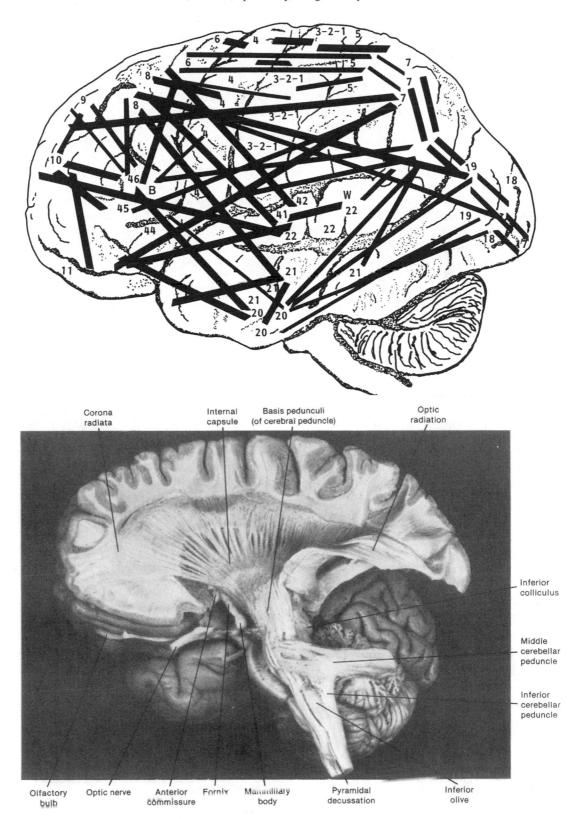

Figure 72. (Top) The massive interconnections linking the frontal lobe with all other neocortical tissues. From Joseph, 1990. (Bottom) Dissection of left hemisphere, brainstem, cerebellum, displaying fiber tracts and massive connections to the frontal lobe.. From Ludwig & Klinger, 1956. Atlas of Cerebri Humani, Little Brown, Boston.

157

between self-will and the (supernatural) will commanding the hallucinations. Schizophrenics (and schizo-phrenic-like temporal-lobe epileptics) may say, "I am God," or "I am God's slave," or both. According to Stern and Silbersweig (1998:239), such "delusions of control (or passivity) could result when a self-generated movement [e.g., self-generated verbally-mediated thoughts] is not associated with a sense of volition and /or is mistakenly believed to arise from another source, or both." These authors show that medial temporal activations (hippocampus) are prominent in hallucinating schizophrenics, but absent when control subjects listen to or imagine voices. Such temporal-lobe activations occur in the setting of a relative lack of prefrontal activity and corresponding deficits in executive functions that assign volition and agency.

By contrast, in non-pathological cases, neuropsychologist Patrick Macnamara observes: "[In] most accounts of mystical experience...the subject is invited to consent to the experience before it is given or "revealed" (see the the Annunciation to Mary in the New Testament). The suspension of agency and will, if anything, is antithetical to mystical experiences (if not to hallucinatory experi-ence).... If there is a central focus to religious belief I would place it in the effort to develop the right relationships to the deity/deities... and all this in service to development of greater self-awareness.... These after all are major functions of both orbitofrontal and dorsolateral frontal lobes" (Personal communication, 2000).

A literature review reveals that intense prayer encourages self-control and self-esteem in which reduces both acute and chronic stress--which appear to depend heavily or prefrontal activation (Worthington et al. 1996). Newberg et al. (2001a,b) report EEG and SPECT data showing increased electro-chemical activity in, and blood flow to, the inferior frontal and dorsolateral prefrontical cortical regions during intense meditation and prayer. These areas send inhibitory efferents directly onto a number of limbic and brainstem sites implicated in stress: amygdala, hippocampus, hypothalamus, and locus ceruleus (the nuceli that manufacture the stress hormone, norepinephrine) (Hugdahl 1996). There is often a marked delusional misidentification of faces, even familiar ones, which may be related to "misinterpretation of social interactions" (Phillips & David 1995).

More generally, experiments from cognitive neuropsychology indicate that such schizophrenic patients have a deficit in their ability to appreciate other people's mental states. Subjects fail in the performance of tasks involving social inferences, such as correctly assessing intentions from indirect speech (Corcoran et al. 1995). This points to a malfunctioning "theory of mind" and intentional agency, which is patently not the case for most people who have deep or periodic episodes of religious experi-ence (including many of our political leaders).

Finally, schizophrenics with prefrontal deficits also seem unable to properly formulate or pro-

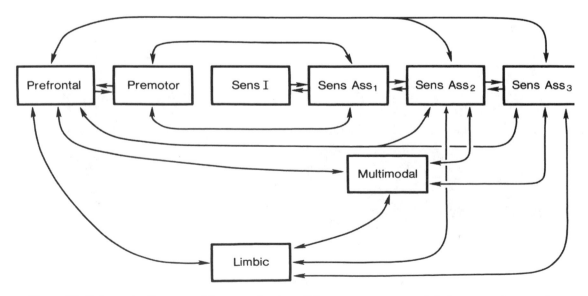

Figure 73. Schematic diagram of the organization of the sensory areas and their connections to the frontal lobe. From Gloor, 1997, The Temporal Lobe and Limbic System. Oxford University Press.

cess counterfactual propositions that require imagining oneself in possible social words that differ from the actual one. For example, after a career failure or the death of a loved one, nonpsychotic persons often imagine "what might have been, if I had only done such and such." This is an ordinary behavior that seems to be lacking among some schizophrenics (Knight & Grabowecky 1995, Hooker et al. 2000). Although a common occurrence after death of a loved one is "dream sleep" (vivid and realistic dreams concerning the deceased that burst into awareness), the grieving subject is usually aware of the difference between dream and reality. Understanding counterfactual situations may be important for dissociating imaginations of the supernatural (e.g., the transubstantiated body and blood of Christ) from factually mundane observation and existence (ordinary wine and wafers), that is, dissociating the quest for self-awareness from the awareness needed for survival.

Autism is another form of psychopathology increasingly associated with deficits in "theory of mind" and faulty appraisals of social intentions (Leslie & Frith 1987, 1988, Baron-Cohen 1995). The term "autism" was coined by Kanner in 1943; however, until the mid-1960s, when the first epidemiological survey of autism was conducted in England (Lotter 1966), autism was considered a precocious form of schizophrenia (Goldfarb 1964). As with certain forms of schizophrenia and temporal-lobe epilepsy, autistics often show abnormalities in the limbic region and associated areas of the brain stem. Autistic children have trouble remembering and processing recent verbal-auditory material, which is consistent with autopsy reports and clinical analyses indicating abnormalities in the hippocampus (Bauman & Kemper 1985, DeLong 1992). Studies of lesioned monkeys with damage to the amygdala reveal austic-like behavior associated with "hypoemotionality" (unnaturally fearless or tame, impairment in social interaction, aimless examination of objects) (Klüver & Bucy 1939, Bachevalier & Merjanian 1994).

Autistics also tend to manifest repetitive, rhythmic movements and "fixed memory" formulaic sequences akin to some forms of ritual behavior, but to no evident purpose. Catherine Johnson, a mother of two autistic children and co-author of *Shadow Syndromes* (Ratey & Johnson 1998), nevertheless sees the use of these ritualistic movements as a stepping-stone for religious education:

"A child with autism can "get" the idea of God... For one thing, the repetition and ritual of religion is perfect... For another, I'm hoping that the visual power of the high church ceiling activates the "God part" of his brain.... Neuroscientists have found there is a region of the brain that, when stimulated, causes people to experience the presence of God." (www.feat.org/search/news.asp, "Autism and God," 18 September 2000)

One apparent problem with autism, as with certain forms of schizophrenia described above, is an inability to imagine counterfactual situations. This can be particularly striking in children suffering from Asperger's Syndrome, a high-functioning form of autism. They seem to be very literal-minded and to believe exactly what they are told:

"We went overseas, and when the plane was over the clouds, he asked me: 'So this is where God lives? I can't see him.'" (accesscom.com/~hcross/mindblind.htm)

"My daughter is fixated with angels. My son told her that when you die you go to heaven and become an angel.... (Excited at this pointed) ("Goody, Goody!")... I barged right in the room and told her not to listen to her brother [for fear she would try to kill herself right there and then]." (Listserv by St. John's University for Asperger Syndrome)

To deal with such deficits in counterfactual thinking, St. Paul's Catholic Church in Alabama provides instruction for autistic children aimed at helping them to undertsand and take First Communion:

The church requires that children who receive Holy Communion be able to recognize the difference between ordinary bread and the Eucharist," said the Rev. Sam Sirianni, director of the office of worship for the Diocese of Trenton. The St. Paul's program was designed to teach the difference... but it also taught more basic things, like how to behave properly in church... learning how to behave in a crowded situation like a Mass was good for the children... people with autism often find crowds frightening, and the more situations they learn to deal with, the better. (Albert Raboteau, "Celebrating a Milestone," Austism Society of Alabama, National and World New Forum (web site), 25 June 2000).

Unlike hallucinating schizophrenics or temporal-lobe epileptics, however, autistics do not usually misrepresent their own voices and intentions as those of other agents (including supernatural agents), or misinterpret the intentions of others as those of demons or deities. Rather, severe autistics show little evidence of inferring anybody's intentions (despite retaining other aspects of intelligence and intellect intact). Their world appears to be populated not by supernatural agents, or even natural agents like friends and enemies, but by mindless, zombie-like beings that have no autonomous will, desires or thoughts.

Recent studies indicate that in largely secular societies, like our own, where there is a history of separation between Church and State, extreme mystical states are generally attributed to cerebral pathology. But in societies where institutional religions dominate, the contents of hallucinations, delusions and possessed beliefs, as well as the diagnoses of their causes, are more generally taken to be religious in origin (Kent & Wahass 1997, Wahass & Kent 1997). Religious treatment may have positive or negative effects, depending upon the community's beliefs about the supernatural origins of the illness, such as whether the person is blessed by God or possessed by Satan.

These differences in belief, which determine different moral judgments about the mutual responsibilities of individuals and societies, can lead to social or political conflict. For example, in an unprecedented ruling, Chicago immigration officials recently decided to grant political asylum to a 10-year-old autistic boy whose mother had claimed his disability and sporadically violent behavior is so misunderstood in Pakistan, their homeland, that he would be tortured and persecuted if he returned there. In her successful application to the Chicago Office of Asylum, she stated that: "He was forced to undergo various degrading and dangerous mystical treatments consistent with the curse of 'Allah,' which is how the Islamic majority in Pakistan view his condition" (Deardoff 2001).

In Moslem societies such as Pakistan or Saudia Arabia, the religious community is obliged to recognize the asocial behavior of an autistic child or schizophrenic, a social problem requiring forceful intervention of the religious community. From the secular standpoint of US immigration officials and their medical advisers, this leads the boy's homeland community to "violate" the individual's rights. By contrast, in some states of the USA (e.g., Texas) medical diagnoses of severe and violent autism or schizophrenia imply no special secular or religious responsibility of the community towards an individual who breaks a law. The individual may be even more radically isolated from society in prison and prosecuted (Western Europeans would say "persecuted") unto death (execution).

Whatever the religious take, there is an increasing scientific consensus that autism owes at least in part to alterations in the normal functioning of the prefrontal cortices, especially the ventromedial region that is involved in the affective assessment of social interactions and intentions (cf. Damasio 1994). There are massive subcortical connections between the prefrontal cortices, the temporal lobes and the limbic system. None of the religious pathologies that I have summarized – temporal-lobe epilepsy, schizophrenia, autism – implies a localized neural substrate for extreme religious experiences in the temporal lobe (or anywhere else in the brain).

Neurotheology: Claims and Doubts

In their most intense manifestations, ritual ceremonies and liturgy rivet attention on specific and conspicuous sources of sensory stimulation, including stimulation emanating from one's own body: drums or clapping hands, dancing or nodding, incense or sweat secretion, incantation or deep breathing, the light shows through stained-glass scenes or the making of signs and designs. Often, these actions and the associated stimuli induce altered states of consciousness: for example, through hyperventilation in whirling dance, deep-breathing meditation, or "going up to the mountain" (where the rarefied air leads to the effect). This focused sensory stimulation, in turn, undoubtedly arouses powerful emotional responses in the "limbic system" (hippocampus, amygdala, hypothalamus) much as naturally-provoked surprise, fear, anger and joy do (but in more controlled and sustained doses).

A possible scenario is that the overly-stimulated amygdala goes into undirected hyperactivity. It is unable to process the emotional significance of individual stimuli, though perhaps producing a general sense of foreboding. Consistent with this scenario (but by no means proving it), EEG patterns of electrical activation during "mystical experiences" bear striking similarities to those recorded during bouts of temporal-lobe epilepsy (Persinger 1983, Gloor et al. 1981, Geschwind 1983). The hypothalamus receives this confounding flood of information, relaying it to the autonomic nervous system. This provokes increased discharges in both the sympathetic (or egotropic) and parasympathetic (or trophotropic) branches of the autonomous nervous system.

The sympathetic branch is responsible for priming the body for action, such as fight or flight. The parasympathetic branch carries signals that relax or quiet the body, such as rest and sleep. Augmented sympathetic discharges increase heart rate, blood pressure, sweat secretion, pupillary dilation, skeletal muscle tone, level of stress hormones (e.g., adrenaline), cortical excitation. Augmented parasympathetic discharges lead to corresponding decreases in visceral and skeletal reactions. In normal states, increased activation in the activity of one branch usually leads to decreased activity in

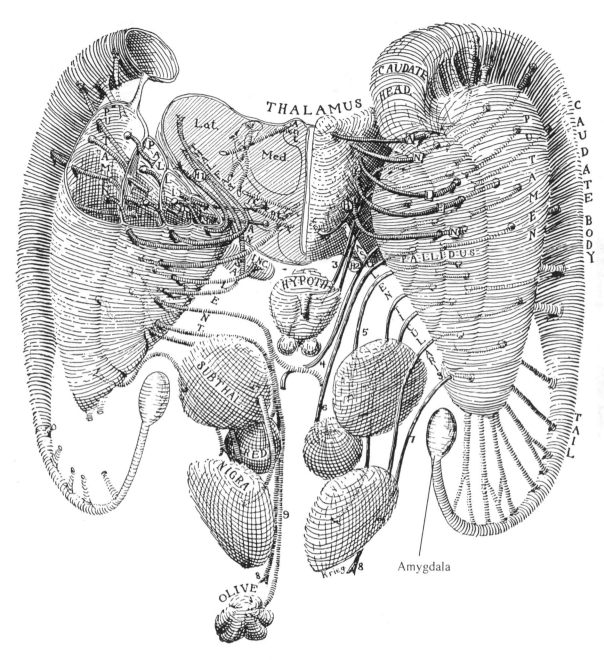

Figure 74. Schematic diagram of the limbic-Striatum. Limbic activation of the motor regions of the striatum and thalamus can trigger stereotyped, ritualistic, and repetitive movements (Joseph, 1996), motor reactions to hallucinations, as well as flight or fight responses. From Joseph 1996, after a drawing by Krieg.

the other. In mystical states, both branches appear to be activated simultaneously, although one or the other is usually dominant.

In meditative states, such as Zen Buddhist or Hindu Yogi, EEG patterns indicate a "trophotropic syndrome." Here, parasympathetic activity dominates, although continued sympathetic activity "seems in some way to be a correlate of the heightened perceptual sensitivity reported by such subjects" (Gellhorn & Keily 1972:399). According to Gellhorn and Keily (1972:402): "The principal psychological distinction from the normal would appear to be the suspension of autonomous will or intentionality." More frenzied mystical states, such as viscerally-charged (rather than meditative) trance-possession and Sufi whirling, may be characterized by an "ergotropic syndrome." Sympathetic activity dominates but continued parasympathetic activity may be associated with a concurrent sense of catharsis that is often compared to the after effects of sexual organism. Konrad Lorenz (1996[1944-1948]:267-268) describes an arousal syndrome in vertebrate predators similar to the "ergotropic syndrome." After prolonged effort and heightened arousal associated with chasing prey, an avian or mammalian carnivore experiencse an acute "sensual pleasure" after catching it through the rapid, rhythmic movement of "shaking to death." This is followed by a particular form of emotional release:

"A striking predator finds itself in an exceptional state of maximal arousal.... Immediately after striking its prey, the bird shows the same degree of abreaction as a human being... directly after orgasm. Far from greedily beginning to devour, the raptor – even if it is very hungry – will first sit still for several minutes on its prey... and then embark on the slow, laborious process of plucking its prey, as though half-asleep. Even when the raptor finally begins to eat it, it does so in a 'dispassionate,' mechanical nature, as though not quite conscious."

The hippocampus, which modulates the expression of emotions elicited by hypothalmic stimulation and provides conceptual significance to the emotions through projections to the amygdala (Joseph, 1982. 1990, 1992; LeDoux 1993), may also go into overdrive during rhythmically-induced mystical experiences. As a result, the regular channels of neural transmission are thrown out of balance. Evidence from SPECT brain-imaging is consistent with this possibility. Blood flow, and therefore traffic flow of signals between neurons, increases to the frontal lobes but decreases to the

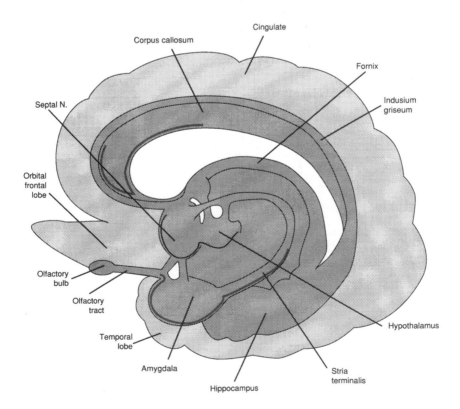

Figure 75. The Limbic System. From Joseph, 1990.

posterior superior parietal lobe (Newberg et al. 2001b). PET imaging indicates that the frontal lobes, particularly the prefrontal cortices, are associated with the executive conceptual functions of will and self control, as well as the self's temporal orientation (Wheeler et al. 1997). The top back portion of the parietal cortex, especially the left side, is associated with three-dimensional body imaging and spatial orientation (Lynch 1980). Possibly, the asymmetric flow of information towards the lower front of the brain and away from the upper back of the brain, may have something to do with the most outstanding aspect of reported mystical experiences: namely, a vivid but diffusely conceived awareness of a boundless universe, centered on (joined to, merged with) a self that has no physical markers or constraints.

One of the most completely developed "neurotheological theories" of these sorts of mystical experience that link brain and religion stems from the work of psychiatrist Eugene d'Aquili and radiologist Andrew Newberg. The authors use their own brain-imaging (SPECT) studies of meditating Buddhists and Franciscan nuns at prayer to demonstrate that experience of God, or "Absolute Unitary Being" (AUB), is hard-wired into the human brain (d'Aquili & Newberg 1998, 1999; Newberg et al. 2001a). Thus, for subjects who reported a feeling of boundless perspective and self-transcendence during meditation, the researchers found decreased blood flow in the brain's "object association areas" where perceptions between boundary and self are normally processed. They speculate that the ultimate mystical state of "hyperlucid unitary consciousness often experienced as God" (Nirvana, unio mystica, etc.) occurs when the sympathetic and parasympathetic systems are both discharging at maximal levels, with neither predominating (d'Aquili & Newberg 1998:200, 1999:26).

The authors see religious experiences as the result of normal, healthy physiology, and not pathological or random events. With this, I agree. They conclude that the experience of God, which is potentially within us all, is as "real" as the experience of ordinary objects and events (Newberg et al. 2001a). With this, I have problems. Agreement about what is a rock or a person is individually and collectively much easier to come by than agreement about what may be a magic mountain or holy spirit.

D'Aquili and Newberg (1999:51-57, 164-176) postulate seven functionally localized "cognitive operators" that are "likely to be preprogammed into the brain." These operators "represent the way the mind functions on all input into the brain... sensory input, thoughts and emotions."

1. The Holistic Operator (right parietal lobe) allows us to conceive the world as a whole, and "to apprehend the unity of God and the oneness of the universe."

2. The Reductionist Operator (left parietal lobe) gives us our "scientific, logical, and mathematical approach... to the universe," but is also critical to understanding the totality of God and the universe in each of the parts.

3. The Causal Operator (left frontal lobe and left posterior superior parietal lobe), "permits reality to be viewed in terms of causal sequences."

4. The Abstractive Operator (inferior portion of the parietal lobe in the left hemisphere) forms general concepts from individual facts, including the concepts of "mathematics, government, justice, culture, and family."

5. The Binary Operator (inferior parital lobe) permits us to extract meaning from the world "by ordering its abstract elements into dyads... (e.g., good versus evil)." It is crucial to "mythic structure": "Myths... develop the notion that the opposites we see are actually illusory, a notion that comprise [sic] part of the ideologies of Buddhism and Hinduism."

6. The Quantitative Operator (inferior parietal lobe close to areas underlying the Binary and Abstractive Operators) abstracts quantity from the perception of various elements.

7. The Emotional Value Operator (limbic system) assigns affective value to percepts and concepts.

Operators (1) and (2) are reminiscent of Gestalt psychology and are so vague and general as to apply to virtually anything. No set of empirical tests or experiments could disconfirm their operation. As Maharishi Mahesh Yogi intoned: "atom and solar system, macrocosm and microcosm, self and universe, are all one and the same." Talk of pre-programmed operators is not compelling.

Operator (3) is more specific and more plainly wrong. For the last couple of decades, researchers in developmental and cognitive psychology have begun describing functionally quite different causal mechanisms, including various types of mechanical and teleological causes (Sperber et al. 1995). For example, the type of mechanical causality (kinetics) employed by human neonates to interpret the movements of inanimate substances entails physical contact between causally-related objects and spatio-temporal contiguity along any causal path. By contrast, the type of teleological causality (agency) that children apply to the interpretation of the causal interactions between animate objects, especially humans, assumes no physical contact between interacting objects or spatio-temporal contiguity. Agentive causality is more closely associated with the prefrontal cortices. Moreover, these different types of causality have distinct maturation schedules in the brain.

Operator (4) is a relic of behaviorist psychology. Experiments in cognitive and developmental psychology and anthropology indicate that people do not first learn only specific facts before they abstract general ones (Rosch et al. 1976, Atran 1998). For example, people first come to understand that something is *simultaneously* an *animal* of a certain *generic* kind (e.g., a cat), only later do they come to categorize it as also being of a more specific (tabby) or general (mammal) sort of animal. The learning sequence may be very different for other domains. Thus, people everywhere are more prone to initially individuate persons than to individuate animals or plants or rocks. This makes good evolutionary sense. It usually matters whether your conflict or liaison is with this Jones or that Smith, but not which bear can eat you or which apple you can eat. It makes little evolutionary sense to have a domain-general operation of abstraction or generalization.

For Operator (5), d'Aquili and Newberg (1999:55) reason that lesions in the inferior parietal lobe "prevent patients from being able to name the opposite of any word prescribed to them. This area is thus the seat of... the binary operator." But cutting neural pathways in areas that facilitate antonymy no more shows this area to be the "seat" of antonymy than cutting off air traffic over the Mid-Atlantic shows the Mid-Atlantic to be the seat of the air industry. In any event, antonymy is only one kind of binary contrast ("cat" isn't an antonym of "dog," "mouse" or "kitten" but can be opposed to them).

Operator (6) supposedly accounts for quantification. Now, quantity is not extracted from perception of elements, but is imposed by placing them in one-to-one correspondence with an abstract cardinal set (class of similar classes), such that the last correspondence counted is the number assigned (7 windows and 7 flocks of birds are both just 7). There may be different innate components to number concepts (Hauser 2000). For example, Chomsky (1986) suggests that the notion of discrete infinity attaching to number is a by-product of the language faculty. There is much anecdotal evidence in anthropology, and a recent unpublished study in psychology, indicating that some nonliterate peoples can't determine cardinality (past four) because they simply haven't had the cultural need to put the various components of quantification together. (Needless to say, all such societies have religion). Apparently, such people perceive a difference between, say, 24 and 32 claps but not between, 22, 23, 24, 25, or 26 claps (Susan Carey, personal communication). Similarly, the application of number to space (extension), which characterizes Western science (rulers, coordinates, etc), was until recently alien to the rest of the world (and to the world's religions). There is no evidence such cultural breakthroughs involved rewiring of the inferior parietal lobe, or that even the simpler components of number reside there.

Operator (7) is a catch-all for "affect." Cognitive theories of emotion, such as appraisal theory (Leventhal & Scherer 1987, Ellsworth 1991), suggest that the value structure of emotions is organized very differently from the relations among emotions in the limbic system. In an aversive situation, for example, anger and sadness may have nearly matching cognitive value structures (anger involves the perception of a responsible external agent, sadness doesn't), as may fear and hope (which differ only on valence) (Keltner et al. 1993). Nevertheless, anger has more physiological and "limbic" manifestations in common with fear than anger has with sadness, or fear has with hope.

Brain researcher Rhawn Joseph (2001) proposes another ambitious version of neurotheology: "[C]ross" neurons as well as "mystical/religious" feeling neurons... probably evolved 30,000 and perhaps 100,000 years ago – possibly in reaction to the experience of "cross-like" stimuli in nature [e.g., dead trees that take the form of a cross, birds that fly with extended cross-like wings] coupled with feelings of fear or religious awe.... The sign of the cross is not uncommon and when staring at a cross the temporal lobes are activated.

Using similar logic, however, how can one exclude competing claims for the primacy of (Moslem) crescents, (Jewish) stars, (Native American) circles, and (Indo-Aryan) swastikas? Mystics of all creeds regularly signal appearances and apparitions in nature of their favorite forms. And what about those Achulean "triangles" 250,000 years ago?

Joseph's claim that Neanderthals already had a definite religious sensibility rests on sparse and controversial data. A number of paleoanthropolgists question whether Neanderthals ceremoniously dealt with death: "Neanderthals buried their dead only to discourage scavengers and eliminate odor" (Rudavski 1991:44). Flower pollen could have been carried to the grave by the wind or the feet of mourners (Johanson and Edgar 1996:100). Underground streams could have led to accumulation of bear bones in cave niches and to groups of fallen roof blocks. This would produce the illusion of an intentionally made storage pit (Chase and Dibble1987). There is also the possibility that the conventional aspects of Neanderthal burials may have lacked symbolic charge owing to deficient prefrontal cortical development (a sharper flexion of the cranial base in modern humans tucked the face under the frontal lobes to allow prefrontal development, Balter 2002:1221).

Although, as Joseph points out, temporal and frontal lobes are admittedly involved in religious symbolism, Joseph locates the "abode of God" for each individual within the limbic system. Here also is the seat of "limbic-religious blood lust" and "limbic taboos, [such] as eating and sexuality." Because "sex and food (along with fear, rage, and aggression) are probably the most powerful of all limbic emotions," they are also probably chief "motivators" of religious ritual. An alternative account of the prominence of food and sex in religious ritual might simply be that controlling them is a good way to keep religion in mind: religion-motivated abstinence fires religion-mediated desire.

Joseph offers a version of "intelligent design" in evolution:

"[I]f… there is no hereafter or spirit world, then why has our brain become adapted for perceiving and dreaming about what supposedly does not exist. Why would the limbic system evolve specialized neurons… that subserve the capacity to dream about… spirits, angels, and… the souls of the dear departed? … We see because there are people and objects to view …, If there was nothing to visually contemplate we would not have evolved eyes or visual cortex…. Shouldn't the same evolutionary principles apply to religious experience? …. A true scientist would not rule out such a possibility."

But the fact that we have neurons that "subserve" some capacity tells us little if anything about their evolution, much less about adaptation. We also have "specialized neurons" that subserve a host of mundane perceptual illusions. Does this fact justify the inference that such neurons were naturally selected or ordained to produce perceptual illusions?

Finally, Joseph takes the fact that most human DNA is not active as evidence for natural evolution from and towards spirituality: So much unused capacity needs purpose, namely, as a biological reservoir for evolution as a progressive learning process towards a more complete and active understanding of God: "Although temple priests masquerading as scientists have claimed that life miraculously emerged fully formed from the dust and muck of the earth." Rhetoric aside, this ignores that evolutionary creation usually arises only from huge waste (sperm, pollen, T cells, ideas).

In brief, despite intriguing findings concerning neurobiological correlates for certain types of intense religious experience, broader neurotheological interpretations of the findings are unwarranted. They involve speculation that not only strays way beyond the facts but crucially ignores or contradicts much recent work in cognitive and developmental psychology and cognitive anthropology. Even if neurotheological speculations about the biological correlates of mystical experiences were true, there is no evidence that less extreme, more "routine," religious experiences have some characteristic brain-activation pattern. Many people never have a full-fledged mystical experience, yet are affectively committed religious believers. Although about one-fourth to one-third of American and British subjects polled report having had a "religious experience" in their lives (Hay 1990, Spilka et al. 1992), only 2-3% claim to have had an intensely emotional "mystical experience," such as feeling all things in the world are one (Thomas & Cooper 1978, Hay & Heald 1987 cited in Beit-Hallahmi & Argyle 1997:79). We know next-to-nothing about the neurobiology of the vast majority of run-of-the-mill religious experiences and beliefs that sustain most people's faith.

Conclusion: Mystical Episodes May Inspire New Religions, But Don't Make Religion

Stressful personal episodes become religious experiences by instantiating publicly-relevant schemas. Within such cultural schemas, even the eccentric voices and visions of clinically-diagnosed schizophrenics and epileptics can become publicly-sanctioned revelations, as they are in some societies. The religious hallucinations and delusions of schizophrenics, the sensory enlightenments of temporal-lobe epileptics (the Apostle Paul or Saint Theresa de Avila?), and the mystical visions and voices of persons are at the extreme end of the "normal" distribution (Jacob, Jesus, Mohammed, Maharishi Mahesh Yogi?).

In historically seminal moments, their unpredictable, "miraculous" revelations have undoubtedly inspired common belief in divine intention and grace. Malfunctioning or hyperactive theories of mind and intentional agency are cognitively and emotionally ripe for supernatural cooptation. Revivalist and starter cults are more likely than established religions to acknowledge the divine character of these more extreme mystical experiences. As Adam Smith (1993[1776]:439) noted, this is because such religious sects aim to radically reform or recreate religious obeisance "by carrying it to some degree of folly or extravagance." A startling episode of intense sensory arousal in a face-to-face with the supernatural may prove unforgettable and emotive enough to permanently inculcate religious belief in a person, and perhaps to jump-start new belief in society.

Previous neurobiological studies of religion (including neurotheology) have focused on tracking participant's neurophysiological responses during episodes of religious experience and recording individual patterns of trance, vision, revelation and the like. This has favored comparison of religious experience with temporal-lobe brain-wave patterns during epileptic seizures and acute schizophrenic episodes. Cognitive structures of the human mind/brain in general, and cognitions of agency in particular, are usually represented in these studies in simple-minded terms (binary oppositions, holistic vs. analytical tensions, hierarchical organization, etc.) that have little input from, or pertinence to, recent findings of cognitive and developmental psychology. Perhaps more telling is recent work on the role of the prefrontal cortices in processing concepts of agency and self and in cognitive mediation of relevant emotions originating in (what was once called) "the limbic system."

For the most part, however, relatively few individuals have emotionally arousing mystical experiences, at least in our society, although the overwhelming majority of individuals consider themselves to be religious believers (polls over the last 30 years consistently show that well over 90% of Americans profess religious convictions). Neither is there any evidence that more "routine" religious experiences have a characteristic temporal-lobe signature, or any other specific type of brain-activity pattern. The neurophysiological bases that commit the bulk of humanity into the care of supernatural agents remain a complete mystery.

RELIGIOUS EXPERIENCE, COMPLEXIFICATION, AND THE IMAGE OF GOD
by Carol Rausch Albright

Abstract. The character of our mind and the structure of our brain are interactive, each influencing the nature of the other. Each person's characteristic mental operations and brain structure are a product of nature, nurture, his or her own choices and, possibly, the actions of a higher power. The many forms of religious experience may involve almost every part of the brain; for example, mysticism, music and ritual, sincere repentance, and theological understanding each involve different sorts of mental operations. The quality of religious experience, like other human experience, depends significantly on how each person's brain is structured and on mental changes over time. Developments in mental organization may follow principals of complexification seen in other complex adaptive systems, whose hallmarks include a combination of order and freedom, dynamism, interactivity, and emergent properties. The proposal is made that a person who is highly developed spiritually also has a relatively complex and integrated mind/brain. This proposal suggests new insights into the problem of evil and may have implications for the understanding of Godself.

Anything that we human beings can perceive or understand, we know through the activity of our brain. If our brain does not process a thought or a perception, we cannot know it.

The mind is the activity of the brain. The brain is the three-pound packet of tissue in our skull; the mind is the process that takes place there.

Neuroscientist Joseph LeDoux sees the mind's activities as either explicit or implicit action (LeDoux 2002, 31). The explicit mind includes all the mental activity that is conscious, or that can be called into consciousness. Reasoning, planning, reading, reflecting, calculating, designing, smelling, touching, hearing, seeing, pain and pleasure, sorrow and joy, anger, and memories of all such events—all these form part of the explicit mind. By contrast, for example, the muscular motions that make up our characteristic gait are coordinated by the implicit mind. Talk is explicit, and so is thinking about what one will say, but the basic mental processes that generate these thoughts and that translate thought to words and thence to speech are performed by the implicit mind (Donald 2001, 38).

HOW THE MIND IS SHAPED

Neither the brain nor the mind is finally determined by our genes or our fate or our experience. The brain in fact is continually being modified—in neuroscientific terms, it is "plastic"—and, therefore, so is the mind. The brain, in its continually changing embodiments, is the product of the interaction of nature, nurture, and a third player not always acknowledged: *oneself,* one's own thoughts and activities. Some observers would also include a fourth influence: a higher power that some call God.

Nature

Genes. Our various mental abilities are importantly determined by our genes. But at most, only half of a trait or an ability is determined by our genetic makeup; for many traits, the influence of genes is much less than that (LeDoux 2002, 5, citing Tellegen et al. 1988). For one thing, the thirty thousand genes in the human genome simply cannot provide enough information to map out the brain's ten billion neurons and the ten thousand billion connections among them. In addition, a person's genetic heritage may be modified by random variations that are not well understood; genes may be expressed differently under different circumstances. Recall the kitten cloned in 2002 whose coat was very different from the fur of the cat from which it was cloned. The genes were identical, but the coloration was not.

Environmental influences such as nutrition and disease affect the outcome as well. Various studies have shown that depriving a young child of essential nutrients will lower her I.Q. Brain diseases such as sleeping sickness and meningitis are detrimental as well, and so are head injuries.

The laws of nature are often overlooked as basic factors in mental operations. Yet, on a fundamental level, they affect us all. For example, oxygen is vital to metabolism in all but the most arcane forms of animal life; the laws of gravity mean that if we slip, we are likely to fall and may be injured. We are all subject to the basic chemistry and physics of the universe where we live.

Nurture

Human infants are born with many more neurons than they ultimately use. During the first few years of life, more neurons perish than will die during normal aging (Bloom and Lazerson 1988, 67; Schacter 1996, 284). Generally speaking, the neurons that survive are those that are used. Activity causes neurons to link up with other neurons. A chemical exchange results, and it enables the linked neurons to survive. Neurons that do not make connections are programmed to die (Bloom and Lazerson 1988, 67).

What causes neurons to link up with other neurons and thereby survive? Mainly, they do so in response to stimuli from the environment. And the principal stimuli to which they respond are social. Infants seem hard-wired to respond to the human face. Even during the first few hours after birth, they preferentially attend to pictures that resemble faces rather than to equally colorful pictures that look like something else (Jirari 1970, cited by Freedman 1974, 30-31). Infants also respond preferentially to the voice of their mother, which they heard *in utero* (Schacter 1996, 173).

By around two months of age, infants have learned to mimic the facial expressions of their caretakers. Thus, caretakers inform the infant who he is. If the caretaker communicates that he is wonderful, delightful, amazing, the infant returns eye contact and smiles in return. If the caretaker acts as if the baby were disgusting and burdensome, he apparently senses that (see Bowlby 1969, 338). If no one pays much attention to the baby, many of his brain cells die off, and in extreme cases, so may the baby. Since the days of foundling homes, it has been observed that infants who are fed and cleaned without personal interaction are likely to die. In such places, an infant near a busy passageway is more likely to develop than a baby in a quiet corner, where no one stops by to offer some baby talk.

Neglected children may survive, but their brains may not develop normally. Many of us remember seeing alarming pictures of brain scans of Romanian orphans who were grossly neglected during the early 1990s. Whole areas of their brain seemed blacked out, showing no activity. High levels of stress hormones apparently led to the demise of neurons in areas of the brain related to learning and memory (Leutwyler 1998). In such neglected children, the ability to form emotional attachments may be severely compromised (Bowlby 1969, 28). As an extreme example of the effects of neglect, Peter Giovacchini recollects:

"I recall with horror an 8-year-old girl who presumably had spent all of her life chained in a closet. She was about 2 feet tall and looked more like a monkey than a human being. She crouched and walked in an apelike manner. She had no capacity to speak; rather, she grunted like an animal and showed no emotions or affects that could be recognized at an interpersonal level. The only feeling observers could identify was anxiety, which occurred when she seemed to be confronting a situation that was too complex for her limited mentality, her initial reaction being confusion. This happened when someone tried to talk to her. . . . At most she seemed to be operating at a reflex level, with little mentation, but with some perceptual awareness" (Giovacchini 1993, 38-39).

The human brain retains considerable plasticity throughout life, though it is less plastic in adulthood than in infancy. At any age, neurons link up in complex networks as learning takes place. Connections and networks are strengthened through use, but if knowledge is seldom recalled, or skills are not practiced, networks tend to fade away. In general, the brain requires activity in order to remain healthy, especially as old age approaches.

Oneself

Thus, besides heredity and environment, a person's own choices can actually influence the condition and structure of the brain. Neural networks can be activated by one's own internal mental activity, such as reading, thinking, or solving problems. Other-directed activities like pursuing friendships or conversations also set in motion a cascade of neurological events. The activities and thoughts that we each choose to entertain affect our neural networks— strengthening some, weakening others.

A Higher Power

Many people believe they have experienced the influence of a higher power in their life. To

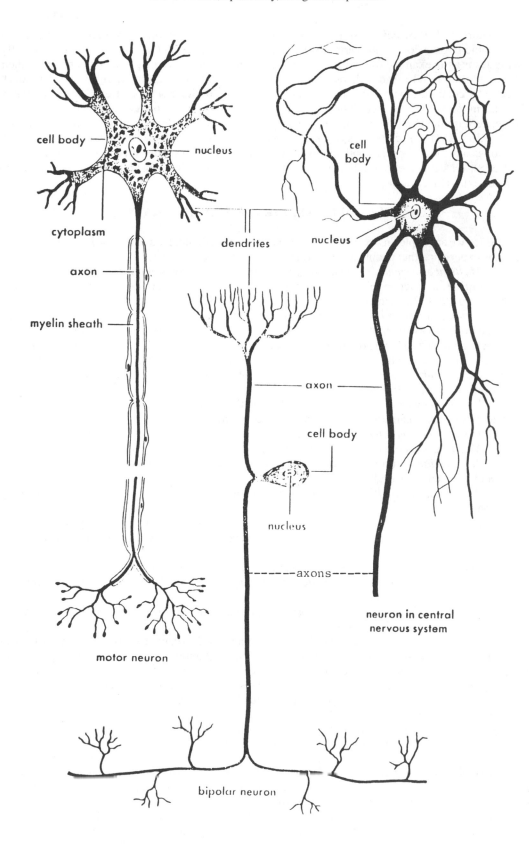

Figure 76. Examples of neurons. From Zigmund et al., 1999. Fundamental Neuroscience, Academic Press, San Diego.

some, nature itself provides awesome evidence of an intelligent creator, often seen as an ultimately unknowable Higher Power; and certainly, the natural world affects all the conditions of our lives. By having Jesus as an example for living, or by emulating the lives of revered persons, people mold their lives—and their minds. And perhaps God not only set the universe in motion, or provides an ideal, but actually continues to provide care, guidance, and grace for life. Such experience would certainly affect the mind/brain. How such divine action might take place remains the subject of active theological debate. Perhaps the Deity, in response to human decisions freely made, sets up the kinds of situations that Gordon Kaufman calls "cosmic serendipitous creativity," which "expresses itself through trajectories of various sorts that work themselves out over longer and shorter stretches of time (Kaufman 1992, 388). Whatever the source, humans in virtually every culture, ancient and modern, have reported religious experience.

RELIGIOUS EXPERIENCE AND THE BRAIN

Since we are exploring possible influences on the mind/brain, let us differentiate some types of religious experience that people have reported.

- *Mystical experience*, or a sense of the presence of God, may occur during prayer, meditation, or ritual, during an epileptic seizure in the right temporal lobe, or in other circumstances (see d'Aquili and Newberg 1999, Ramachandran and Blakeslee 1998, 188).
- *Ritual* is a feature of most religions. Often performed in a group, religious rituals may also be carried out by individuals alone. Such rituals usually involve one or more of the following: stylized bodily actions such as dancing or kneeling; music and other rhythmic sounds including chanting and speaking in unison; scent, such as incense; stylized eating and drinking; or use of such drugs as peyote. Ritual often leads to a sense of unity among the participants and may lead to profound feelings of satisfaction (Rappoport 1992, 23-24).
- *Written records* of the tradition often have authority. In preliterate traditions, their role may be filled by extensive narratives that are memorized and recited.
- *Doctrinal understanding and debate* may clarify intellectual understandings.
- *Morality and ethics* are frequently referenced to religious authority.
- *Testimonials*—narratives about religious experiences or spiritual transformations—influence others and may define oneself.
- *A sense of personal closeness* with co-religionists may provide an orientation of identity and belonging.
- *Harmony and beauty* may provoke a sense of divine presence, whether beauty is experienced in music, mathematics, scientific formulae, movement, paintings, or natural phenomena such as stars and mountains.
- *Service to others* is often an expression of religious belief and identity.
- *God's will may be sought* in regard to future decisions, through prayer or doctrine, or through an intuitive spiritual discernment.
- *A meaning for one's life,* or a sense of how one's life may fit into the cosmic and historic scheme, is often provided by religion.

Such a wide range of religious experiences may activate the brain in a variety of ways. Mystical experience, for example, seems to involve centers in the right temporal lobe, or at least reports from victims of right temporal lobe epilepsy have been interpreted to indicate that. A small percentage of persons with this disorder report that during seizures they experience an overwhelming sense of God's presence. They may also develop a stereotypical "hyper-religious" personality (Joseph 1996; Ramachandran and Blakeslee 1998, 179-88).

However, it would seem that many areas of the brain besides the right temporal lobe may be involved in the varieties of religious experience that have been discussed. Human activities are guided by different centers within the brain. Although the brain areas are interlinked and interactive, the vital importance of certain areas to certain functions has been demonstrated by studies of what happens to people after some part of their brain has been damaged by illness or injury. Typically, certain types of injuries lead to certain kinds of disabilities. In addition, through increasingly refined measurements of the brain's electrical activity (electroencephalography, or EEG), and with such subtle imaging techniques as fMRI (functional Magnetic Resonance Imaging), activity in uninjured brains can be observed.

The general differences between "left brain" and "right brain" have been popularized, but even a cursory discussion of brain activity requires more differentiation than that. One useful way to understand this differentiation of activity has been through evolutionary biology.

All animals require certain basic neuronal functions in order to remain alive. In vertebrates, such basic functions as the heartbeat are regulated by the brain stem.

In mammals, including human beings, a certain region of the brain greatly resembles the brains of reptiles; Paul MacLean, emeritus chief of evolutionary biology at the National Institutes of Mental Health, has dubbed this region our *reptilian brain* (MacLean 1990, 9). This region, which lies above the brain stem, is involved in the need to protect one's own territory or home, to reproduce, to establish basic social structures, and to forage and store food—needs that human beings have in common with reptiles, birds, and other mammals. Using their reptilian brain (since this is all they have), reptiles communicate through ritualized behaviors; their behaviors are inflexible and lack emotion. Our reptilian brain seems to be involved in similar human behaviors, although we perform them in a humanized way (Ashbrook & Albright 1997, 51-70).

Surrounding the "reptilian brain" lie structures that MacLean has called the *mammalian brain*. One of its important functions is to add emotion to the guarding, mating, competing behavior of reptiles, which mammals also share. Emotions label experiences as good or bad, helpful or dangerous, and so they motivate mammals toward behavior that is likely to promote survival. Mammals also differ from most reptiles in that they protect and nurture their young. In all mammals, mothers and young form strong emotional attachments; if they are separated, they call out for one another, or simply cry (Ashbrook & Albright 1997, 80-91). Mammal parents teach the young certain skills, thereby passing on at least a rudimentary form of culture.

The cerebral cortex—the wrinkled, grayish layer of neurons around the top and sides of the brain—is proportionately large in primates, especially such species as gorillas, chimpanzees, and human beings. Part of this cortex lacks definite duties and can be recruited for learning what needs to be learned. Humans have more of this "uncommitted cortex" than other primates do, and so their learning can be more extensive (Penfield 1975).

Also, in humans, unlike other primates, the left and right halves of the cortex generally have different duties (although in young children, one half can learn to compensate for the loss of the other). The innovation of right-left differentiation was apparently an important feature of human evolution (LeDoux 2002, 302). The human brain has become increasingly functionally lateralized, such that the right hemisphere is dominant for spatial visualization and holistic perception, whereas the left is dominant for the temporal-sequential aspects of language (Joseph 1982, 1988a). This major "rewiring" job freed up space in the left brain for such symbolic activities as speech, writing, and calculation. The value of these abilities may, in turn, have upped the evolutionary advantage for individuals with adept symbolic brains, and thus encouraged further specialization.

However, this innovation came at a price: the communication among regions of the human brain is somewhat flawed (Joseph,1982, 1986a,b, 1988a,b; Joseph et al., 1984), and so it is quite possible that one "part" of me wants to do one thing, while another "part" wants something else. Furthermore, parts of the brain other than the left cortex are "speechless," and unless they interact with the speech centers, they cannot verbalize what they experience.

The most distinctively human part of the brain is the prefrontal cortex, which lies at the top of the brain toward the front, and behind the forehead. It includes critical *convergence zones* where information from the body, from emotions, from memory, from thought and from holistic insight come together. This is a key location where judgments are made, where scenarios are spun, where plans are made and their execution is monitored (Joseph 1986a, 1996, 1999a; LeDoux 2002, 315-19).

The religious experiences listed above utilize different brain abilities. While mystical experience may indeed involve the right temporal lobe, ritual probably requires participation of the "reptilian brain" and the motor centers. Feelings of kinship and love draw upon the emotional centers of the "mammalian brain"; study of texts and understanding of doctrine are left-brained activities; discernment of beauty seems mainly to be a right-brain activity; a sense of calling and "God's plan for me" must involve the frontal lobes. Because the various parts of the human brain are interdependent, these distinctions are far from absolute. However, it is hard to think of any feature of the explicit mind that has not been involved in religious experience for some people in some traditions, and the implicit mind must necessarily have been drawn into the process as well. Being religious is an activity of the whole person.

Still, religious beliefs, experiences, and behaviors are more integrated in some people's personalities than in others. That is, beliefs, religious observances, reasoning, relationships, action in behalf of others, vocational choices, economic choices, and other facets of character are more congruent in some personalities than in others. And their integration may be greater or lesser from time to time in the same individual.

BRAIN INTEGRATION

As neuroscientist Merlin Donald points out in his recent book *A Mind So Rare*, the cortex of the human brain is organized into about six hundred thousand columnar units, each roughly half a millimeter in diameter. Each column contains about one hundred thousand neurons, woven into various brain-wide networks by millions of long communication fibers.

"These networks can respond to complex intellectual and emotional challenges with amazing speed and unity. The sheer number and complexity of these agglomerations, all contained inside a single human brain, exceed those of the entire global electronic highway, by many orders of magnitude. . . But this surely underestimates the real power of such a network. Neurons are far more flexible and have many more ways of communicating, both electrical and chemical, than the components of any known   computer. On a local scale, each column is a self-contained network in itself, with a fixed internal wiring diagram, or architecture. But it has no fixed pattern of connectivity to start. That distinction is important because while the basic columnar architecture is innate, its connectivity pattern is set by experience. Each of these columnar devices has countless interconnection points, or synapses, which connect neurons to one another in various patterns. This allows them to be wired up in various ways as the brain grows and develops and introduces a degree of flexibility or plasticity in their development" (Donald 2001).

The "wiring" among neurons is accomplished by axons and dendrites. Briefly stated, axons handle outgoing messages from the neuron, and dendrites pick up incoming signals. Information is passed from axon to dendrite across a microscopic gap called a synapse; the information exchange is facilitated by the action of one or more of a group of chemical compounds called neurotransmitters. Within the neuron itself, information is transmitted through an electrochemical process; it is the resulting electrical impulses that are picked up by electroencephalography (EEG). (So that electrochemical impulses do not keep circulating wildly about the brain, they are kept in check by the actions of certain inhibitory cells.) While many axons are very short and transmit information within a local group of neurons, other axons are longer, extending to other groups of neurons or even to

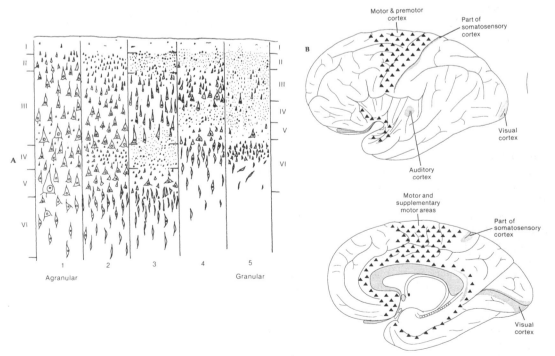

Figure 77. The layers and cell types of the primate neocortex. From Zigmund et al., 1999. Fundamental Neuroscience, Academic Press, San Diego.

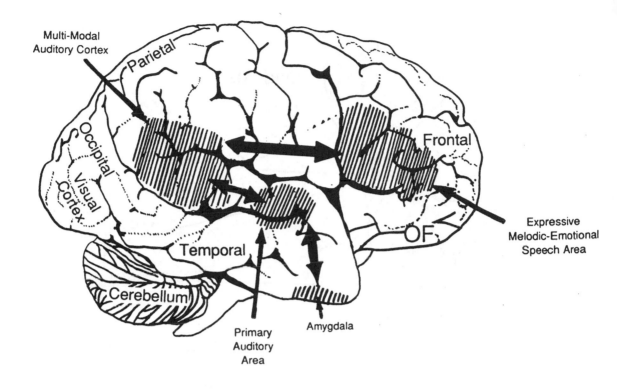

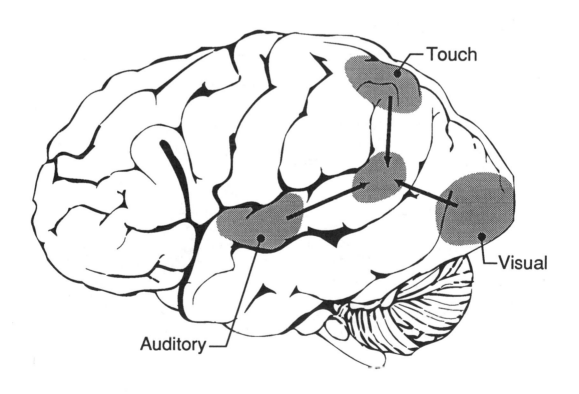

Figure 78a,b. (Above) Examples of convergence zones. (Opposite page) Illustration of a neuron and synapse. From Joseph, 1982, 1988a, 1990.

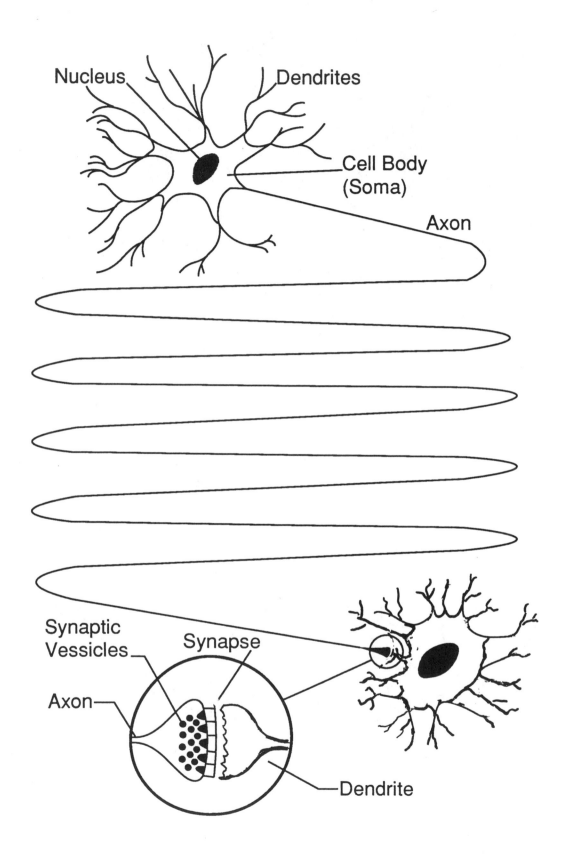

other regions of the brain. The record for length is held by neurons that regulate motion in the leg. A single axon extends from the motor center in the brain to the lower part of the spine, where it connects with nerve cells that govern the leg muscles,

The message impulse that courses through a neuron is called the action potential (AP). It normally occurs if neurotransmitters hit more than one synapse on a neuron. If APs repeatedly cross the same synapse, a strange thing happens: that neuron's response to stimulation becomes more intense, and remains so for hours. If stimuli take place frequently, the enhanced AP may become more or less "locked in." This phenomenon, which is called long-term potentiation (LTP), is clearly central to brain plasticity, that is, to learning and memory and to the development of each person's abilities and personality.

As is well established, a single neuron can store information about many different experiences so long as different synapses on the cell are involved in receiving them. The fact that several sorts of information may be stored in a single neuron helps to explain associations between different inputs.

A great deal of attention has been devoted lately to the question of how events that stimulate various brain regions can all be combined into a single experience, or a single memory, for the individual. This issue is called the *binding problem*. It is far from settled, but some interesting and fairly convincing proposals have been made in this regard. Below I cite a set of principles proposed by Joseph LeDoux on the basis of current research results. Pieces of information that are related, but stored in different brain regions, may be brought together through the following means:

• *Different systems experience the same world.* The various neural systems in an individual's brain have different functions, but because they are part of the same person, they experience the same life events at the same time. LeDoux theorizes that a kind of shared culture may therefore develop between the various systems (LeDoux 2002, 308).

• *Synchrony coordinates parallel plasticity.* If brain cells fire action potentials simultaneously, their plasticity may become integrated across regions. More research regarding synchrony is required as we "try to come to grips with the relation of the self to the brain" (Ledoux 2002, 310-12).

• *Modulatory systems may also coordinate parallel plasticity.* When a significant stimulus occurs, various chemical compounds called modulators are produced. Cells in the brain stem are the main source of modulators, but these cells have long axons that extend to other parts of the brain, where the modulators are released. Modulators facilitate transmission of signals and promote learning and memory in the areas where they are released. These chemicals stay in effect for a few moments, so that they can perhaps "tie together" events that are not quite simultaneous (LeDoux 2002, 312-14).

• *Convergence zones integrate parallel plasticity.* As first detailed over twenty years ago by Joseph (1982), information in the brain is processed in parallel and via *convergence zones.* Convergence zones, such as the inferior parietal lobule, act to assimilate perceptions and ideas, thus giving rise to multi-modal concepts, including language (Joseph 1982, 1986a,b, 1988a,b, 1990).

In fact, the intellectual sophistication of various mammalian species can be estimated with fair accuracy simply by the extent of convergence that occurs in their brain structures. "When plasticity occurs simultaneously in two regions that feed into a convergence zone, plasticity is also likely to occur in the convergence zone. . . . Once convergence is completed within systems, it begins to occur across systems" (LeDoux 2002, 317). Master convergence zones in the prefrontal cortex are critical to thinking, planning, and decision making. Convergence zones for language are found in the left hemisphere, and for understanding of spatial relationships in the right hemisphere. Other convergence zones are concerned with sensory input and with memory formation (Joseph 1982, LeDoux 2002, 318).

• *Downwardly mobile thoughts coordinate parallel plasticity.* Here is where the self comes into play as a co-creator of the mind. "Thoughts and memories . . . can influence what we attend to, the way we see things, and the way we act" (LeDoux 2002, 210).

Convergence zones, including the prefrontal cortex, can and do send messages back along the chains of neuronal communication. Thus, thoughts and memories in a convergence zone can influence activity in "lower-level" neurons, including their plasticity. "With thoughts empowered this way, we can begin to see how the way we think about ourselves can have powerful influences on the way we are, and who we become" (LeDoux 2002, 320). Through our own choices, we become co-creators of ourselves. We can influence our own character, and even the structure of our brain itself.

• *Emotional states monopolize brain resources.* When events trigger emotional and physical arousal, plasticity will be heightened at the active synapses. Interconnections among these synapses,

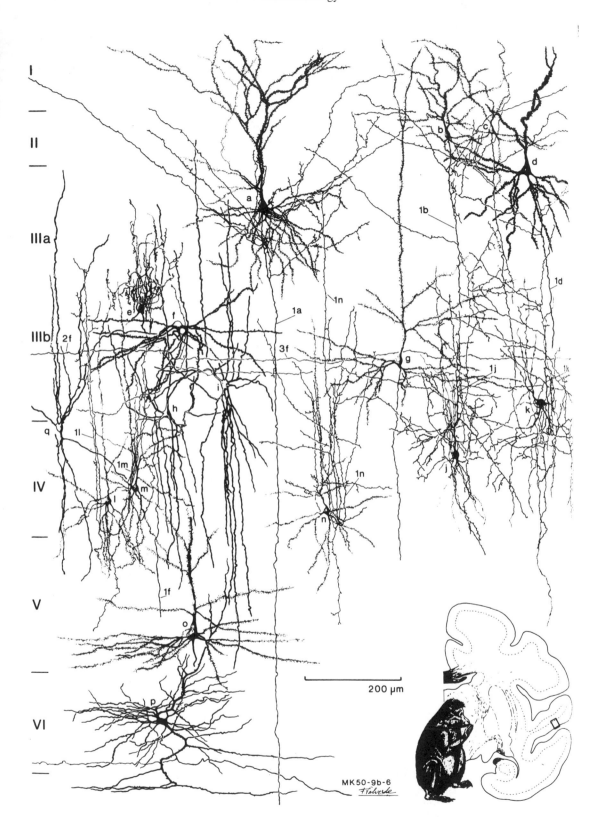

*Figure 78c. Neurons from the primate temporal lobe, From F. Valverde, 1996. Golgi Method &
Golgi Gallery.*

even in different systems, will be strengthened. But if emotions are shut down because of negative experiences, learning opportunities may be lost (LeDoux 2002, 322).

• *Implicit and explicit aspects of the self overlap, but not completely.* Probably because of the sequences of brain evolution, we have imperfect connectivity between our cognitions, emotions, and motivations (LeDoux 2002, 323).

There are, of course, those who doubt that human beings make *any* real choices. These people fall into two main camps: (1) those who believe that God actually determines everything that happens, and (2) those who believe that (*a*) electrochemical interactions among the neurons and/or (*b*) "selfish genes" determine everything that happens in the mind. Although we cannot *prove* the existence of human choice, wise men and women from Leo Tolstoy to computer scientist Donald Knuth have concluded that it simply does exist (Knuth 2001, 181).

Tolstoy addresses these questions in his Second Epilogue to *War and Peace,* an essay ahead of its time. I cite his comments, as translated from the Russian in the English parlance of the 1950s:

"Whatever presentation of the activity of many men or of an individual we may consider, we always regard it as the result partly of man's free will and partly of the law of inevitability . . . . In every action we examine we see a certain measure of freedom and a certain measure of inevitability" (Tolstoy [1869] 1952, 690).

Reason gives expression to the laws of inevitability. Consciousness gives expression to the essence of freedom.

Freedom not limited by anything is the essence of life, in man's consciousness. Inevitability without content is man's reason. . . .

Freedom is the thing examined. Inevitability is what examines. Freedom is the content. Inevitability is the form.

Only by separating the two sources of cognition, related to one another as form to content, do we get the mutually exclusive and separately incomprehensible conceptions of freedom and inevitability. Only by uniting them do we get a clear conception of man's life (Tolstoy [1869] 1952, 694).

Tolstoy does not, however, attribute all events to a combination of human choice and inevitability. Without specifying its mechanism of action, he also attributes influence to the will of God:

"Only the expression of the will of the Deity, not dependent on time, can relate to a whole series of events occurring over a period of years or centuries, and only the Deity, independent of everything, can by His sole will determine the direction of humanity's movement; but *man acts in time and himself takes part in what occurs"* (Tolstoy [1869] 1952, 684; emphasis added).

It is well known that Tolstoy spent his later years in search of the will of the Deity to whom he alludes. He was one of a long line of people who have influenced their own mental and social organization through religious quests and observances. As Nobel Prize-winning physicist Murray Gell-Mann once remarked in a lecture at the University of Chicago, "religion is the DNA of culture" (Gell-Mann 1992). That is, religious belief serves to organize human cultures and individual human consciousness at a very deep level, sometimes for better and sometimes for worse.

POSSIBLE ROLES OF GOD

Whether the Deity truly influences our consciousness is, of course, a different question. To answer it, one must first clarify what might be meant by the concept of the Deity. Here I will briefly lay out a concept— perhaps a suspicion of a concept—of the sort of God to whom I will be referring.

Let me preface the discussion with a brief discourse regarding what people presume to be real. In English and other languages, nouns denote persons, places, and things. Verbs denote actions; adverbs and adjectives describe qualities. Perhaps because of the dominance of vision among our senses and in our brain's processing of senses, we often tend to think of "noun-things" as more real than actions or qualities. Yet music, for example, can be experienced only over time and is recognized by its process and quality. Is music not real? As another example, Is the baseball bat's motion less real than the bat itself? Which is it that hits the ball out of the park?

I tend to think of God more as a process than as a "thing." I think that God—the God that people claim to have apprehended through the action of the Holy Spirit—is manifested in terms of action. As theologian Joseph Bracken points out, "God as an empirically verifiable entity is simply not available to experience . . . . All that the 'believer' and 'nonbeliever' alike experience is an activity"—a hidden creativity at work in the historico-cultural process and "an ultimate tendency or power, which is working itself out in nature and human history" (Bracken 1997, 108, in reference to

Kaufman 1985, 42).

Saint Augustine had a similar perception in the fourth century A.D. Familiar with the marine life of the Mediterranean, he described the relation between the earth and God with a metaphor of the sponge and the sea. The world as we know it is like a submerged sponge. God is the ever-changing sea, which penetrates the sponge, supports the sponge, nourishes the sponge and gives it life—but is not itself the sponge. As long as the sea flows through the sponge, the sponge may remain alive. God is forever in interaction with the world, yet God is not the world. Like the sea, God is dynamic and mysterious, always the same, yet never the same, whose very being may be experienced as action and interaction (*Confessions* VII, V, 7).

Since we are human beings, we must think about God, or anything else, in a humanlike way, using the brain that we have. Metaphor is a necessary means to understanding our religious experiences.

Let us consider Augustine's metaphor comparing the relation of God and the world with the relation of the sea and the sponge. If in fact, as Augustine suggests, the world is in God as the sponge is in the sea, God not only maintains the vitality of the world, on a continuing basis, but also, God is forever influencing the world, and its inhabitants. How might this be done?

Alfred North Whitehead and other process theologians use a metaphor that portrays God as a sort of cosmic fisherman. They suggest that God influences the world by "luring" persons to pursue the good. The pursuit of goodness may be expressed as a search for the qualitative good, or perhaps as a search for ethical understanding and discipline. In fact, if people do pursue the good, for whatever reason, they may influence not only the world but also their our own character and perhaps their own neuronal connections. Depending upon the decisions that persons freely make, God may in some way respond. The response might be perceived as a serendipitous confluence of conditions, which beckon toward a further human response.

Computer scientist Donald Knuth suggests that we may experience these beckonings as "close encounters of the transcendent kind that suggest relationships beyond the power of our experience to reckon, but which we know in some fundamental way to be true" (Knuth 2001, 186; quote attributed to Peter Gomes).

Other theologians portray the search for God as a fearsome quest, a journey into a dark cloud where nothing can be known. Such a search is not for everyone. Yet if one reaches that place of ultimate silence, "the mind opens itself to that which is most fully real, which is the power of all being, beyond all change and decay," and thus God may indeed influence the human mind (Ward 2002, 63). This way of the mystic, epitomized by Teresa of Ávila in sixteenth-century Spain, is said to lead to a deep inner calm.

A twentieth-century theologian, Paul Tillich, writes of a somewhat similar outcome of an encounter with the divine, but for that century he spoke of the outcome in somewhat psychoanalytic terms. He referred to "'the courage to be,' to affirm being, in face of all anxiety and fearfulness about the future or about the passing away of all things" (Ward 2002, 65; see also Tillich [1952] 1962). Courage in the face of anxiety, and despite a sense that the world may be meaningless, has been of particular relevance to many in our time, when evil has often seemed to be stronger than goodness.

Another "family" of suggestions regarding divine action in the world is related to natural science. Physicists beginning with Brandon Carter and including Robert Penrose, John Wheeler, John Barrow, Frank Tipler, and John Polkinghorne, are among those who have introduced various versions of the anthropic principal: the finding that natural constants in the physical world have been fine-tuned with the extreme exactitude necessary to lead the cosmos as we know it, a cosmos that supports life (Worthing 1996, 43-45).

Still another sort of suggestion regarding God's action in the world comes from twentieth-century physics. Its proponents, beginning with physicist-clergyman William Pollard and including physicist-theologian Robert John Russell and philosopher William Alston, theorize that God may act in the world through quantum effects. The field of action could be the larger physical world, or even the brain itself. Writes Alston: "The relevant physical laws only provide for a large probability of one outcome rather than another in a given situation. And the highly improbable can sometimes happen without violating probability laws. Hence God can, consistent with quantum theory, do something to bring about a physically improbable outcome in one or more instances without any violation of physical law. And even if these interventions are all on the sub-atomic level, they can, if properly chosen (and presumably God would be in a position to do so), snowball so as to make a difference to macroscopic states of affairs" (Alston 1993, 189).

A third set of suggestions related to current scientific research has to do with processes of complexification. In brief, proponents of this group of related theories maintain that there is a tendency throughout the natural world— including the human brain—for connections among elements to become more and more centered. This theory will be pursued in more detail in the next section of this paper.

Whether any of these metaphors descriptive of divine action make ultimate sense must be decided by the reader. For in the end, each person's life of faith, or unfaith, expresses a holistic orientation, in which choices and actions may, or may not, be guided by the sense that there is at the foundation of the universe a beneficent presence who cares for our welfare and merits our love.

THE COMPLEXIFICATION OF MIND

We now have seen that each individual's mind may develop in any of a myriad of ways, and that the outcomes are the result of the interaction of (1) nature, including genes, nutrition, disease, and natural law, such as the laws of physics and chemistry; (2) nurture, including interaction with caregivers, companions, and the cultural matrix during infancy and childhood and throughout life; (3) oneself, including actions chosen and mental activities selected; and perhaps (4) divine action.

We also have seen that the brain has ways in which experiences and choices may be bound together through association. And we have learned that the brain is structured in a number of convergence zones. The convergence zones may be key to processes of complexification within the human brain itself.

In order to enter this next phase of the discussion, we must briefly digress into a discussion of theories of complexification.

Complexification is a process by which entities or groups of components *organize themselves*. Much of the work on complexification is centered at a "think tank" in New Mexico called the Santa Fe Institute. Scholars are attracted there because they believe they have discerned, in their differing disciplines, processes of complexification. Key figures at Santa Fe have included Nobel Prize-winning physicists Murray Gell-Mann and Philip Anderson, biologist Stuart Kauffman, artificial intelligence specialist John Holland, and Nobelist-economist Kenneth Arrow.

A single definition of complexity is difficult to find, without launching into discussions of computer code. For our purposes, let us use the term to denote the presence of *a web of interlinked and active connections—the more intricate the web, the more complex the entity*. Complexity, as used here, does not mean merely complication. A situation that pulls us in many directions at once , so that our efforts do not reinforce one another but actually cancel each other out, I call compoundity (a term first suggested by John Albright). A situation that is complex is integrated. It may include many aspects, but these tend to reinforce one another and to work in synergy.

There is evidence that the natural world has a tendency toward complexification. In his magnum opus *The Phenomenon of Man*, Pierre Teilhard de Chardin addressed this issue:

"First the molecules of carbon compounds with their thousands of atoms symmet- rically grouped; next the cell which, within a very small volume, contains thoussands of molecules linked in a complicated system; then the metazoa in whichthe cell is no more than an almost infitesimal element; and later the manifold attempts made sporadically by the metazoa to enter into symbiosis and raise themselves to a higher biological condition, [culminating finally in the thinking creatures that are humans. We see here] the principal axis of evolution: *ever more complexity and thus ever more consciousness*." (Teilhard 1959, 243-44, emphasis added.)

Or, as physicist Paul Davies put it: The universe is undeniably complex, but its complexity is of an organized variety. Moreover, this organization was not built into the universe at its origin. It has emerged from primeval chaos in a sequence of self-organizing processes that have progressively enriched and complexified the evolving universe in a more or less uni-directional manner. "(Davies 1994, 119.)

Systems theorist Stuart Kauffman speaks of "order arising naturally from the laws of physics and chemistry. Order emerging spontaneously from molecular chaos and manifesting itself as a system that grows." He found the idea "indescribably beautiful" (Waldrop 1992, 124)

There are certain conditions that must be present in order for complexification to occur. It is essential that there be elements of order and predictability, and also elements of contingency or freedom. In conditions that are extremely orderly—for example, a crystal—spontaneous complexification does not occur. Nor does this process take place in conditions of extreme disorder and unpredictability. The human condition, as Tolstoy observed, includes both order and freedom, and it therefore meets this criterion.

Also, systems that complexify are both dynamic and adaptive. Dynamically, they interact with other systems, a process that leads to new conditions. In order to survive in the new conditions, they often must adapt; those that do not successfully adapt are "selected out." For this reason, complexifying systems are sometimes called *complex adaptive systems.*

The activity of complex adaptive systems tends to lead to unpredictable outcomes, known as *emergents.* As a very simple example, oxygen and hydrogen combine to produce something quite different from either: water. Emergence is, in fact, a hallmark of the process of complexification.

The human brain is, par excellence, a complex adaptive system. In fact, it is, for its size, the most complex system that we know of in the entire universe. Each of our brains comprises about ten billion neurons, a number in the same order of magnitude as the number of stars in the Milky Way galaxy. A neuron on average forms about a thousand synapses. Most neurons "talk" only to nearby neurons, thereby forming cell assemblies. A group of cell assemblies is "wired" to a convergence center, and these centers in turn are "wired" to super convergence centers. Yet, some brains seem to be structured more effectively than others, probably because their connectivity is better integrated and more complex.

We have seen that the communication paths among neurons are plastic: they are formed, strengthened, weakened, or even extinguished depending upon how we use them. That is, the connection patterns are adaptive.

The consequences of neural plasticity depend partly on natural laws and partly on contingent events. For example, to a certain degree, neuronal structure in the infant has a genetic basis. However, infants' neurons are *programmed* to self-destruct if they are not used; this is a further natural determinant of the infant's neuronal structure. But why should neurons remain unused? Partly because of what the baby's caregivers decide about her care—whether they pick her up and talk to her, or leave her alone in her crib for hours on end. The caregivers' choices are contingent.

The brain is beginning to look like a complex adaptive system. Does it produce emergents? Indeed it does. Some are seen in social innovations and some in the development of the individual herself.

If we are to believe Tolstoy, the very development of society and the course of history depend upon the interaction of many individual selves, so many that their interaction cannot truly be traced. He says: "The movement of nations is caused not by power nor by intellectual activity, nor even by a combination of the two as historians have supposed, but by the activity of all the people who participate in the events. . . . the conception of a cause is inapplicable to the phenomena we are examining."

"In the last analysis we reach the circle of infinity—that final limit to which in every domain of thought man's reason arrives if it is not playing with the subject. Electricity produces heat, heat produces electricity. Atoms attract each other and atoms repel one another."

"Speaking of the interaction of heat and electricity and of atoms, we cannot say why this occurs, and we say that it is so because it is inconceivable otherwise, because it must be so and that it is a law. The same applies to historical events. Why war and revolution occur we do not know. We only know that to produce the one or the other action, people combine in a certain formation in which they all take part , and we say that this is so because it is unthinkable otherwise, or in other words, that it is a law."(Tolstoy [1869] 1952, 687-88.)

Thus, complexification does not stop at the threshold of the individual brain. In fact, we are all embedded in our interpersonal worlds. We influence our cultures, and they, in turn, influence us. They help to determine the choices we make, and we, in turn, help to detemine the course of events, even long after the end of our own lifetime.

In addition, a case can be made that our mind itself is no longer confined within our skull! By jotting down calculations or outlining procedures as we solve problems, we enhance our short-term memory. The capacity of long-term memory is immeasurably increased by books and computers. In a sense, we are mental "cyborgs," part protoplasm and part information storage devices.

In this essay, however, our particular concern is the complexification of the individual brain/mind, related though we humans are to so many other selves. New and unexpected developments—emergent events—can and do occur within the mind itself, and thoughtful people have written for centuries about how personal and spiritual growth may be nurtured. As early as the second century A.D., Irenaeus of Lyons declared that "the glory of God is the human being fully alive, and the life of the human being is the vision of God." God structured spiritual life so that people would "always have a goal toward which to advance" (Irenaeus AH, IV,20:7; translations drawn from more than one source). In their search for spiritual development, people through the centuries have observed many disciplines, and many have relied upon such classics as Thomas á Kempis' *Imitatio Christi* (fourteenth century), Ignatius of Loyola's *Spiritual Exercises* (sixteenth century), John Bunyan's *The Pilgrim's Progress* (seventeenth century), or the matter-of-fact nineteenth-century American spiritual guidebook, *The Christian's Secret of a Happy Life* by Hanna Whitall Smith (Smith [1870] 1952). Today, the spiritual growth movement is once again vibrantly alive, although criteria for personal and spiritual fulfillment vary tremendously.

I would like to suggest, however, that certain qualities characterize the best of these criteria today. They include (1) integrity of character: ego boundaries intact, concerns and values centered and relatively harmonious; (2) individuation: development of one's own calling within the larger context of society; (3) genuine respect and concern for the development of integrity and individuation in others, often expressed as concern for others' spiritual growth (this is one definition of love); (4) breadth of concern, extending both to people who are like oneself and to those unlike oneself, and also to the earth and its nonhuman inhabitants; (5) a working worldview that relates these developments into a coherent whole, through use of reason, intuition, metaphor, and respect for the wisdom of those who have preceded us; and (6) effective efforts to realize these commitments along the particular avenues open to the individual. To these I would add (7) receptiveness to the actions that God may be taking in regard to ourselves and those around us, in our own very specific time and place.

I submit that these criteria demonstrate increasing complexification of character. Not only are personal powers fairly centered, but relationships with other people and with the natural world are integrated as well, and the whole operates in synergy. It would seem that complexification of brain organization is a necessary corollary. For as a person's character develops integration and integrity, the components of the mind/brain increasingly act in concert. Implied in this development is coordination of activity in the brain's convergence centers.

Complexification follows different contours in different personalities, depending upon their gifts and callings. As spiritual mentors have observed, persons who struggle to discern their goals, and who may even seem "unbalanced" initially, may eventually reach a highly creative mode of integration and make significant contributions.

Saint Paul contrasts the unintegrated and integrated character in his magnificent discourse of Romans 7 and 8: "I do not understand my own actions. For I do not do what I want, but I do the very thing I hate. . . . For I do not do the good I want, but the evil I do not want is what I do" (Rom. 7: 15, 19, NRSV). However, he continues, "those who live according to the Spirit set their minds on the things of the Spirit, [and] to set the mind on the Spirit is life and peace" (Rom. 8, 56, NRSV). Paul explains that the Spirit of God, which makes us children of God, makes this condition possible for us through its indwelling. In Galatians, Paul describes the conditions of those who live outside the Spirit, including "enmities, strife, jealousy, anger, quarrels, dissension, factions, envy, drunkenness," and so on. By contrast, the fruit of the Spirit he describes as "love, joy, peace, patience, kindness, generosity, faithfulness, gentleness, and self-control" (Gal 5: 19-21, 22-23, NRSV).

In neuroscientific terms, life outside the Spirit seems to indicate a mind/brain in which harmonious mental integration has not been well established. By contrast, life in the Spirit implies a mind/brain in which the parts work in harmony, integrated as a complex, adaptive system, and whose fruits are the emergent love, joy, peace, patience, generosity, faithfulness, gentleness, and self-control. James Fowler, a contemporary student of spiritual growth, describes the process in language of our time: "An integral, centering process, underlying the formation of the beliefs, values, and meanings that give coherence and direction to persons' lives; That links them in shared trusts and loyalties with others; That grounds their personal stances and communal loyalties in a sense of relatedness to a larger frame of reference; and That enables them to face and deal with the limit conditions of human life, relying upon that which has the quality of ultimacy in their lives." (Fowler [1981] 1995, 1.)

Integration is not cheaply bought, and in fact, almost everyone who has attempted seriously to seek spiritual growth has acknowledged the necessity for grace in the quest. Grace is not an easy concept to explain to those who have not been aware that they have received it. Metaphors and similes are necessary. Grace is like a spring of cool water that appears, unexpectedly, along a hot and dusty climb. Grace is like a foothold that appears, or a hand held out to help, or a welcoming smile. It wasn't expected, wasn't deserved, wasn't earned. To accept grace means to acknowledge its presence. One may be too proud to see that a way has been opened, insisting instead on beating one's own circular path through thickets of thorns and underbrush. One may be intent on following a track that does not actually lead to the goal, and thus one may ignore another way that would be better—even if this may be, as the poet Robert Frost observed, "one less traveled by" (Frost [1916] 1967). Grace entails mysterious gifts from God, which are only offered, not forced upon us.

A COMPLEX GOD

This discussion has brought us to consideration of the possibility that Godself may be complex—in fact, the most complex self that can be imagined.

I believe that accurate understanding of Godself is not available to the human mind; metaphors and myths must be our way of approach to understanding such mystery. However, keeping this reservation in mind, let us consider the conplexity of God. As the Ground of Being, the Originator, God is linked to all that is.

We apparently have a cosmos that operates on the basis of fine-tuned natural law, and that also includes important elements of natural contingency, as quantum physics has demonstrated. For subatomic particles, living things, and the cosmos itself, events depend upon elements of law and elements of freedom and unpredictability. And throughout, we see complex, adaptive systems.

The results have certainly been emergent. It appears that God has let loose a creation that is, in Philip Hefner's terminology, both created and co-creative (Hefner 1993). Throughout natural history, new life forms have emerged. Throughout human history, new ways of life have been invented.

If God did create human beings out of love, then, by definitions developed above, God would have desired human spiritual growth. And, human spiritual growth would require that human beings be gifted with some conditions that are predictable, and also with some freedom to choose. Otherwise complexification would not be possible, and we have seen that complexification is closely allied with spiritual growth.

This way of looking at things may allow a new understanding of why the world of a good God may contain evil. For free beings are necessarily free to choose evil as well as good. They may do evil to one another, and the distorted consequences for personality may be passed on and perpetuated; Paul exclaims in Romans 7: "Wretched man that I am!" Fortunately, human beings may also choose good, and God provides ways of escape, through grace, as we have seen.

So, Godself is related to the universe in the most complex way one can imagine. For all is centered in God, and begins and ends in God, the Alpha and the Omega. God's actions, as we have seen, bear the fruit of emergence. But might Godself also be adaptive? Or does God's constancy mean that God is so unchangeable as to be unresponsive to choices made by God's creation, in freedom? The evidence so far leads me to believe that Godself is indeed adaptive. For if God continues to love the creation, God will indeed respond to it—not only to the cosmos in large, but also to all the individual lives that drive the emergent history of humankind.

Each person's free decision makes a slight alteration in the state of the whole. A God who loves that whole will, in some way, respond. The means of such response are mysterious, and may involve the dark night of the human soul, the hiddenness of quantum choices, or other means that remain obscure. God's responses are adaptive, though God's deep, inner identity still remains constant.

Can these observations regarding the complexity of human beings, of the cosmos, and perhaps of Godself recast our understanding of what it might mean to reflect the image of God, as taught in Genesis 1:27? Are we to seek the fruits of personal integration and complexification, of seeking one's particular calling, of exercising loving concern for others' spiritual growth, and for bringing forth emergent forms of social and spiritual life? Can we take the risks, and discern the offerings of Grace?

As we enter the twenty-first century, can humankind responsibly exercise the freedoms that have emerged as a result of the innovations of the twentieth century—its advances in technology, communication, education, medical care? Can we deal with the huge demands our populations are exerting on earth's resources, the hideous conflicts and destruction that have also been our legacy? Where are we free, where are we not free? Where are the paths of Grace that we may, or may not, choose to follow? In making all the individual choices that will provide the engine of history, where can we discern the image of God?

INTERACTING COGNITIVE SUBSYSTEMS & RELIGIOUS MEANINGS
by Fraser Watts

Abstract. It is suggested that the most fruitful way of relating religious thinking to brain function is via a functional formulation of the cognitive subsystems that are grounded in the brain, and which support religious cognition. This chapter focuses on the application of the Interacting Cognitive Subsystems approach to religion. The main focus is on the two central subsystems concerned with different aspects of meaning: the propositional system concerned with specific meanings, and the implicational system concerned with generic, schematic meanings. It is argued that, in these terms, religious meanings are quintessentially implicational. However, complex issues arise about how the two meaning systems arise in religious cognition and in religious practices such as meditation, and how they produce religious phenomena such as the sense of ineffability. One of the central challenges for theology is to find a way of articulating religious meanings in a way that is faithful to the kind of cognitive code in which they arise.

There are broadly two strategies for relating religious cognition to brain function. One is to seek to map religious cognition directly on to areas of the brain. The other is to go via an intermediate level of cognitive systems that are themselves grounded in brain function. This paper takes the second of those routes, and it may be helpful to begin by stating the case for doings.

The recent development of scanning technologies has made it much easier than before to relate particular kinds of cognitive functioning to areas of the brain. Studies of which areas of the brain are involved in meditation are one example. Though there is much of interest in such research, it also has limitations. One problem is how to get people to perform religious thinking (or other religious actvities) in a reliable way, despite the constraints imposed by scanning technology. Also, whereas basic low-level cognitive tasks may be performed in a standard way with no significant individual differences, high-level cognitive functions such as those involved in religion and morality are much more subject to individual variation in how they are performed. Further, the analysis of scanning data always involves a good deal of smoothing and averaging, in which potentially significant micro-data is lost.

Most serious of all, there are problems of interpretation. It is of verylittle scientific interest simply to know which parts of the brain are employed in a particular cognitive activity. That is only of scientific interest if we can interpret such mappings, and fully understand the functional significance of particular parts of the brain. Despite all thathas been learned about mind-brain mappings, the significance of particular brain areas can often only be interpreted in a rather gross way. Though it can be assumed that there are particular brain circuits underpinning religious cognition, it is hard even to locate those circuits without knowing what kind of circuit you are looking for. Even if circuits arelocated, that tells very little about how they work. It is therefore advisable to adopt the complementary strategies of both (a) trying to develop a good theory of the cognitive systems involved in religious cognition, and also (b) considering the relation of those systems to the brain. Each strategy can enhance the other, though the first priority ought to go to developing a model of the cognitive systems that one can then look for in the brain.

In this chapter, the emphasis will be put on that cognitive systems approach. It is an approach comparable to that of d'Aquili and Newberg(1999), whose work is perhaps the best known mapping of religious cognition. They first relate religious cognition to a general formulation of cognitivefunctions (their set of nine cognitive 'operators') and then go on to suggest the brain areas that subserve each of the operators. Though it is welcome that they try to identify the neural substrate of each operator, there may be problems with any simple mapping of the cognitive operators on to areas of the brain. For example, the range of functions served by the causal operator are very diverse, ranging from casual assumptions in visual perception to those involved in religious thinking. It stretchesplausibility to assume that exactly the same areas are involved in each case.

The kind of approach to neurotheology that is being taken here requires some such formulation of the cognitive architecture. It must, of course, be onethat is potentially relevant to religious functioning. There is as yet noconsensus about the general cognitive architecture; each approach has its own strengths and weaknesses, both in terms of cognitive functions and neuropsychology. The psychology of religion requires an approach in which higher level processes are particularly well mapped; some of the availableapproaches are not sufficiently well defined at this level to be suited to the study of religion.

d'Aquili and Newberg's approach is attractive from this point of view in that it sets out the kind of higher level cognitive processes that arelikely to be relevant to religion. Though it is intended to be a general model capable of a broad range of applications, it has in fact been mainly applied to religious and mystical states of mind. The approach that will beconsidered here, the 'Interacting Cognitive Subsystems' (ICS) model of Teasdale and Barnard (1993), is in some ways comparable to the cognitive operators approach of d'Aquili and Newberg. ICS is also intended to dealwith cognitive functions comprehensively, and to have a broad range ofapplications. Indeed, an advantage of ICS is that it has already been applied to a broad range of topics in cognitive psychology. Applications to religious cognition thus represent a new application of a model that has proved its worth elsewhere and begun to gain general acceptance. It will beargued that the ICS approach clarifies some aspects of religious cognition,such as the ineffability of religious experience, that the d'Aquili and Newberg approach does not.

INTERACTING COGNITIVE SUBSYSTEMS

ICS was developed originally in the context of psycholinguistics (Barnard,1985), and has been applied in contexts as diverse as human-computerinteraction (Barnard et al, 1988), the onset of sleep (work in progress by Barnard and Watts), and depression (Teasdale and Barnard, 1993). The present paper, building on previous work by Watts (1999, 2002), will explore its application to religion.

ICS offers a general cognitive architecture consisting of nine distinct cognitive subsystems, three sensory systems (acoustic, visual, body-state),two intermediate systems (morphonolexical and object) that captureregularities in sensory input, two effector systems (articulatory and limb), and two central meaning codes (propositional and implicational). Eachsub-system has its own code, and information processing is accomplished through transforming information from the code of one subsystem to that of another. Attention here will focus mainly on the two highest level subsystems, the propositional and implicational subsystems.

In brief, the propositional subsystem is concerned with 'knowing that' (i.e. being aware of semantic relationships), whereas the implicational subsystem is concerned with a more holistic or intuitive mode of knowing. Propositional meanings are relatively specific, while implicational meanings are much more general or schematic. It is proposed that there is a complex interaction between the two meaning systems, with much cross-talk betweenthem. Much that is coded in the implicational system will be transformedinto the different code of the propositional system, and vice-versa.

The codes of the propositional and implicational systems may differ in a way that is rather like the difference between serial and parallel processing. Implicational meanings often seem to be inherently parallel and distributed, and would be best modelled computationally along connectionist lines. Propositional meanings, in contrast, seem more capable of being adequately modelled by the serial processing of classical computational modelling.

The proposal developed here for the role of cognitive subsystems in religious cognition will be limited in two ways. It will confine itself almost entirely to the two central subsystems that are concerned with meaning, and which will be particularly important in religious cognition. However, it would be possible for future work to focus on the more limited role of the peripheral subsystems in religion. For example, some of thediscussion of perceptual and motor processes in religion offered by Pruyser (1968) could be formulated in terms of the more peripheral subsystems of ICS. The focus here on just two of the nine subsystems of ICS is comparableto the focus of d'Aquili and Newberg on just two of their nine cognitive operators in modelling religious experience.

The other limitation is there will be little discussion of exactly what the neural substrate of the subsystems might be. Little has so far been published about this, though work on it is in progress, and there arepreliminary indications of the relevance of the orbito-frontal cortex to the implicational system (Joseph, 1996, 2000; Teasdale at al, 1999). Both general considerations and accumulating evidence (Joseph, 1996, 2000; McNamara, 2001) suggest that the frontal areas are likely to be important in religious cognition. Mapping ICS subsystems onto the brain is a complex task, because exactly what areas of the brainare involved in particular operations of the central meaning systems isl ikely to depend on the context and focus of particular operations. Though the neural substrate of ICS is an important matter for the future, this brief paper is not the place to begin to explore it.

THE GENERIC NATURE OF RELIGIOUS MEANINGS

There are good reasons for emphasizing the importance of the implicational subsystem for religion. Teasdale and Barnard suggest that implicational meanings are more 'holistic' in that they embody a sense of overall meaning that is greater than the sum of particular elements of meaning, and cannot readily be conveyed in a single sentence. The implicational system also has a direct linkage with bodily and emotional states, in a way that is not paralleled for the propositional system.

Religious meanings are perhaps the most holistic of all meanings. The religious world-view seems to be unique in the range of views and experiences that it integrates. There is probably nothing else that brings together aesthetics, morals and metaphysics in the same way as religion. In this sense, religious meanings are perhaps uniquely general and integrative; they link different domains of experience and reality together in very broad meaning structures.

Religious meanings are also very general in the sense that they identify common motifs that arise in very different contexts. For example, the death-to-resurrection theme is a highly general one that can be discerned in very different contexts. Trinitarian thinking, which identifies a basic three-foldness in reality in which the three elements are distinguishable but inseparable, is another very general motif. This all suggests that religious cognition is characteristically implicational, and indeed Teasdale and Barnard (1993, p. 74) specifically discuss the role of poetry and the spiritual traditions in evoking and conveying implicational meanings.Religious awareness is perhaps the quintessential function of the implicational system.

In addition, religious meanings are often figurative, as Watts and Williams(1988) have argued. Figurative thinking is, in some ways similar to the use of metaphors. However, the concept of metaphor, as it is normally formulated, assumes that literal meanings are prior, and that literal explication is possible in principle. Religious metaphor is characterised by holistic, figurative meanings such as light, which in Christian thinking brings together several different threads: God as the source of all light, the light of understanding, right conduct as being a path of light, and soon. The concept of light in religious thinking is more than an optional metaphor used to convey something that could equally well be said literally. It ties together diverse strands of meaning in a broad gestalt of meaning and finds general elements of 'light' that apply in very different contexts. There is an irreducibility about figurative thinking in religion that is notfound in metaphors proper. It is not just that metaphors are common in religion. They carry core and indispensable ideas that cannot easily be explicated in literal language (Watts and Williams, 1988, chapter 9).

It has often been noted that the sense of the unity of all things is a core mystical experience. Indeed, it would be one of the strongest candidates for an element that is common to the mystical experiences of different traditions. The sense of unity is something that would be expected to arisefrom the capacity to discern broad patterns of meanings that is the essence of the propositional system. d'Aquili and Newberg (1999) handle this interms of a particular mode of operation of the holistic operator. However, a sense of unity would also be expected to arise from the holistic meanings of the implicational system.

INEFFABILITY

There are some things that can be understood implicationally that cannot easily be propositionalised. This is the phenomenon of 'knowing more than we can say' (Nisbett and Wilson, 1977), when things that are grasped intuitively cannot be formulated in a way that is capable of explicit expression. You can sense that a model fits without being able to articulate exactly what the model is. It is now widely recognised that much information processing proceeds outside conscious awareness, and some is not at all easy to formulate consciously. For example, there may be subtle characteristics that determine whether we like or dislike particular people.Though we may know perfectly well how we react to others, it can be much more difficult to identify which features have determined our reactions.

In a similar way, there is a rich tradition of religious experiences being felt to be 'ineffable', and defying adequate expression. There is scepticism about this claim in some quarters (e.g. Proudfoot, 1985) and it has been suggested that ineffability is merely a social construction, a learned wayof describing experience. However, in terms of the ICS model, the claim that religious experience is ineffable makes perfectly good sense. Ineffable experiences are presumably those that arise in the implicational system, and are coded there. The sense of ineffability arises from the difficulty of translating a certain core of implicational meanings into any other code.

The majority of meanings in the implicational system can quite readily be transformed into the different code of the propositional system. However, there seem to be some implicational meanings for which there is no direct propositional equivalent, and religious meanings are perhaps more likely to fall into that category than any other. Propositonal meanings are characteristically linear and logical, whereas religious meanings often defy translation into that kind of code.

In fact, over the centuries, mystics have written volumes about their 'ineffable' experiences; and that has always been something of a paradox. ICS makes sense of that too. Even where propositional meanings can betranslated into the different code of the propositional system, that might be associated with a sense of loss. Because it is a different code, there would obviously be a sense in which the original meaning had not been fully captured. Translation from implicational to propositional code thus makes sense of the paradoxical features that ineffable experiences (a) can actually be expressed in some form, though (b) only with a sense of loss that the original meaning has not been properly expressed.

PROPOSITIONAL RELIGIOUS THINKING

It must be presumed that the implicational subsystem is phylogenetically the older, i.e. that the grasp of regularities and meanings at this sub-propositional level is the basic capacity, from which the capacity for propositonal meanings has been differentiated. Indeed, the distinctive cognitive capacities of humans, such as the capacity for language and reflective self-consciousness seem to be linked to the development of apropositional system as a distinct and independent subsystem. Equally, the evolution of the capacity for religion (Mithen, 1996), which seems closelyassociated with reflective and differentiated consciousness, and a sense ofself, also presumably depends on the development of the propositional systemas a distinct subsystem.

There is thus something of a paradox. On the one hand religious meanings seem to be quintessentially implicational, but on the other hand the capacity for religion seems to have required the differentiation of an independent propositional system. However, it would probably be misleadingto suggest that religious cognition is exclusively a function of either system. Perhaps religious cognition depends on the cognitive richness and flexibility that arises from the combination of both the propositional and implicational subsystems. This leads to the question of the nature of the relationship between the two subsystems in religious cognition.

Normally, there is ready cross-talk between the two meaning systems. However, there is also scope for a degree of dissociation between them. The distinction between these two subsystems suggests a typology of religious experience and theological approach, according to which system is in the driving seat. As we have seen, meanings that are coded in one system may noteasily be translated into the different code of the other system, and at least some religious meanings may fall into this category. The contemplative approach to religion seems to be one in which the implicational system isstrongly emphasised.

However, there are also approaches to religion that seem to be largely propositional. It is perfectly possible for propositional insights to remainmerely propositional. Teasdale and Barnard illustrate this in terms of aSufi story. The Sufi master, Uwais, was asked 'How do you feel?' Hereplied, 'Like one who has risen in the morning and does not know if he will be dead in the evening'. The other man said, 'But this is the situation ofall men.' Uwais responded, 'Yes, but how many of them feel it' (Teasdale and Barnard, 1993, p. 74).

There are clearly parallels here with approaches to religious cognition in which religious insights are learned at a propositional level but, for some reason, are not easily translated into the deeper codes of the implicational system. Religious insights would then be seen or heard, would be encoded propositionally, and could be written or otherwise expressed, without being encoded in a way that embodied awareness of a wider range of relationships,or involved links with other domains of experience.

Developmental evidence suggests that religious experience initially occurs in the rather inarticulate form that is associated with the implicational system. More analytical aspects of religious understanding, of a kind that would be associated with the implicational system, develop later. Recent work with young children suggest that religious experience is common and important, though not much expressed (Hay and Nye, 1998). It gradually fades though the first decade of life, perhaps because children sense that it isnot much valued by adults or their peers. While that is happening,children gradually develop the capacity for analytical religious thought, as has been well established for some time (e.g. Goldman, 1964). There thus seems to be a developmental shift from religious experience that is primarily implicational to religious thinking that is primarily propositional.

COORDINATION BETWEEN THE MEANING SYSTEMS

Though there can be a degree of dissociation between the two meaning systems, and though many religions meanings can be either propositional or implicational, religious thinking often involves a close integration of the two systems. Under specific conditions, unusually close linkages between the propositional and implicational systems can be set up. This is analogous in some ways to the 'interlock' that Teasdale and Barnard describe in depression, in which very general negative meanings in the implicational system are translated into a series of more specific negative attitudes in the propositional system, which in turn reinforce the more basic, general negative outlook coded in the implicational system.

With religious cognition, there may be a somewhat similar but more benignform of close coordination or enmeshment between the two systems. In thiscase, basic intuitive religious meanings would lead to a stream of articulate, propositional religious ideas and expressions, which in turn would strengthen more basic, in articulate religious meanings. Religious worship may, in part, be an occasion where people deliberately enter such a state of close co-ordination between the two meaning systems. However, whereas depressive interlock is a perseverative state from which peopl ecannot easily extricate themselves, the close co-ordination between the meaning systems that arises in religious contexts is a form of harmonious enmeshment of the systems that people can enter and leave at will.

The kind of enmeshment between the two systems found in religious contexts may be similar to that which occurs in love. When two people are in love, there seems to be a basic, pervasive attitude of positive valuation towards the partner. This leads to more propositional expression of statements of love for the other, which in turn strengthens the basic attitude of love. Provided both systems are involved, and the enmeshment is maintained,expressions of love arise from, and further reinforce deeper implicational meanings. For this to work, both systems need to be involved. Mere propositional ideas, unconnected to deeper implicational meanings, can degenerate into empty repetition. Equally, implicational meanings that find no form of expression are unlikely to develop, and so may not be fruitful for the person who holds them.

Religion may not only involve an enmeshment of the meaning systems; it may actually facilitate a fruitful and harmonious relationship between them. Atone extreme, a situation can arise, as it does in severe mood disorders, in which the subsystems are locked together in a perseverative way that cannot respond flexibly and adaptively to changing patterns of stimulation. At the other extreme, the sub-systems can operate in a totally uncoordinated way. Neither is adaptive. Religious practices may help to establish fruitful co-ordination between the systems, without their getting locked together. It may thus help to facilitate a state of balance and stasis between the subsystems.

MEDITATION

Some religious practices, such as meditation, seem designed to bring about an unusual relationship between the cognitive subsystems. However, it is not easy to know exactly how that should be characterised. Indeed slightly different practices may have significantly different cognitive results.

Teasdale at al (1995) offer one formulation of the effects of mindfulness. They suggest, plausibly enough, that people often perform many different cognitive operations at once, and that there is little co-ordination between the various different systems. Such cognitive 'multi-tasking' leads to the familiar sense of feeling distracted. In contrast, Teasdale et al suggest,mindfulness involves an unusual integration of the different subsystems, in which all systems, from the body system (where the breath may become acentral focus) to the central meaning systems, are working together in an integrated way, producing a sense of unified, focused attention.

However, other formulations of the effect of meditation in terms of ICS are possible. Meditation may sometimes involve the near shutting-down of some systems. It normally involves at least the shutting down of the normal processing of verbal input. That suggests that the morphonolexical and articulatory systems are shut down in meditation as far as possible. It maywell be that a key purpose of that may be to affect how the meaning systems operate. Shutting down the more peripheral language systems may help toreduce activity in the propositional system.

Shutting down articulation may thus lead to a temporary emphasis on implicational rather than propositional meanings, which may be linked to adegree of separation between the subsystems. There is the possibility that meditation leads to the two systems being partially dissociated for a periodof time in what might be regarded as an altered state of consciousness. Many religious practices seem designed to bring about an unusual state ofconsciousness, and this may well involve an unusual relationship between the propositional and implicational subsystems.

Suspending the normal cross-talk between the implicational and propositional systems may be necessary if people are to focus on the distinctive holistic meanings of the implicational system, especially those core meanings that defy adequate translation into propositional code. Meditative consciousness, in which religious meanings are perhaps experienced in an unusually pure form, may involve an explicit adoption of a kind of 'broad-band' attention, as Watts and Williams (1988) call it, inwhich very general meanings can be experienced holistically.

DISCUSSION

Watts and Williams (1988) discussed a distinction in religious cognition similar to that explored here between the implicational and propositional systems, though they did not present it in the context of a systematic theoretical framework. For example, they distinguished analytical and non-analytical modes of person perception and suggested that there is ananalogy between contemplative cognition and the non-analytical, intuitive perception of another person involved in empathy (p. 63). Equally, they made use of the distinction between insight in psychotherapy that is merely intellectual and insight that is actually effective (pp. 70-74) and suggested that the latter is also in some ways like contemplative cognition. However, useful though such analogies may be, there is also a need for a rigorous theoretical formulation of this kind of distinction, and this will require a multi-level theory of religious cognition.

The case for a multi-level cognitive theories has become clearly apparent in the related but better developed field of emotional cognition, as Williams at al. (1997) have argued. Several possible approaches have been formulated, each of which makes a distinction not unlike the one ICS makes between implicational and propositional cognition. The earliest such theorywas that of Leventhal (1984), in which what he calls 'schematic' cognition is similar to the implicational system in ICS, and what he calls 'conceptual' cognition is similar to the propositional system in ICS. Another somewhat similar distinction has been made by Epstein (1994) between rational and experiential knowing. The key question arises of whether ICS makes any unique contribution to the understanding of religious cognition that could not be made by other approaches.

The advantage of ICS lies not so much in how the distinction between the levels or systems is made, but in the detail and specificity of the surrounding assumptions. For example, ICS is much more specific about thepossible relationships between the different subsystems. Thus, for example, it is much easier to develop a formulation of religious ineffability in terms of ICS than other similar theories. Equally, there is not enough detail in other theories to formulate the kind of enmeshment between the two systems that can be modelled in terms of ICS, or of how meditation might affect cognitive processing.

Nevertheless, one of the most important implications of this kind of approach to neurotheology is a rather general one. Theology, like any academic discipline, necessarily proceeds at a propositional level. However, in the case of theology more than most disciplines, this imposes a severe limitation. If it is correct, as has been argued here, that religious meanings are so general and holistic that they are quintessentially implicational, any attempt to formulate them in the propositional code that academic disciplines need to use will inevitable fail to express them adequately. The familiar point of contemplatives about the ineffability of mystical experience perhaps applies more broadly than has often been recognised to the formulation of all religious meanings. Perhaps all propositional accounts of religious meanings will, in this sense, be deficient.

This invites a double response from theology. Firstly, it indicates that the discipline should be undertaken in a spirit of humility that recognises the inevitable inadequacy of all propositional formulations of religious meanings. Secondly, it suggests that it would be appropriate to look for innovative ways of formulating religious meanings that are a little more faithful to their inherently holistic, implicational character. It would be beyond the scope of this paper to explore such innovative formulations ofreligious meanings in detail. The general point is that propositional formulations will often be inadequate, and that innovative formulations should be considered.

A SOCIAL COGNITION INTERPRETATION OF NEUROTHEOLOGICAL EVENTS
by Raymond F. Paloutzian, Thomas G. Fikes, & Dirk Hutsebaut

Abstract. This chapter presents an interpretation of religious experiences, including but not limited to those that are triggered by or associated with known brain processes, that is based on attribution principles from social psychology. Psychological research on both common and unusual religious experience, and a social cognition orientation in general, points to the human tendency to attribute meaning to events and perceive wholes where there are parts. This raises the question of whether various mystical experiences and similar states of consciousness, coupled with the different ways that people talk about them, share a common core that is fundamentally the same but described in different languages, or whether they are in fact fundamentally different at a neurobiological level.

Also at issue is whether the heightened sense of awe, the numinous, or the perception of God reflects something that is "actually there" (and if so, what its character is) or whether it is "merely psychological," and how each conclusion is reached. The interpretation of neurobiologically based experiences by a person depends on the schemas brought to the perceptual task in a social context, and their meanings reflect the attributions made.

PSYCHOLOGICAL QUESTIONS ABOUT EXPERIENCES OF GOD

The notion of neurotheology raises the idea that it is possible to learn about God or God perceptions by studying the brain. Specifically, the narrowest version of this idea, mapping the brain mechanisms that underlay reports of God experiences, is said to tell us about the neurobiological substrates of experiencing God. We argue that the efforts to map such brain mechanisms may teach us a great deal about the neuropsychological processes that are at the basis of various important perceptions – such as the perception of God, the numinous, and Absolute Unitary Being (d'Aquili & Newberg, 1993, 1999) – but that such knowledge does not tell us about God. By virtue of this, the "neuro" can at best touch only a small corner of "theology." Instead, knowledge of this type can be correctly understood only within the social context in which a person reports to have had certain experiences. This means that the most appropriate level of analysis for understanding the processes that lead to God perceptions is social psychological, not neurobiological or theological. These latter fields are not irrelevant, but simply do not constitute the sole (or even best) level of analysis for the phenomena of spiritual experience. In fact, all experiences of this type are attributions to supernatural agency (for God perceptions or religious apparitions) or to some other non-ordinary agency (for non-God spiritual or mystical experiences) for the cause of a particular ambiguous experience, stimulus, or stimulus complex.

Let us explain the rationale for this analysis by first looking at exemplars of God experiences and of equally potent non-God mystical or Awe experiences. A social cognition view suggests that the basic psychological process of attributing meaning to the experience is the same in all cases. Examples of both types appear in both a classic century-old text in the psychology of religion and in recent books and articles in neurotheology.

God or Awe Experiences in Classic Psychology of Religion Literature

James (1902) published the following two descriptions of vivid experiences. They are exact transcriptions of what the people who had them said and felt, in their own words. One report is of a God experience and one is not.

God Perception. "These highest experiences that I have had of God's presence have been rare and brief—flashes of consciousness which have compelled me to exclaim with surprise—God is here!—or conditions of exaltation and insight, less intense, and only gradually passing away. I have severely questioned the worth of these moments. To no soul have I named them, lest I should be building my life and work on mere phantasies of the brain. But I find that, after every questioning and test, they stand out to-day as the most real experiences of my life, and experiences which have explained and justified and unified all past experiences and all past growth" (James, 1902/1958, p. 305).

Non-God Spiritual Presence. After being awakened one night, one man said, "I then turned...to go to sleep again, and immediately felt a consciousness of a presence in the room, and singular to state, it was not the consciousness of a live person, but of a spiritual presence...I do not know how to better describe my sensations than by simply stating that I felt a consciousness of a spiritual presence...I felt...a strong feeling of superstitious dread, as if something strange and fearful were about to happen" (James, 1902/1958, p. 64).

God or Awe Experiences in Neurotheology Literature

Examples of purported experiences of God or of equivalent non-God experiences of Awe are described in recent neurotheology work by Newberg (Newberg, d'Aquili, & Rause, 2001; Newberg et al., 2000, 2001). Examples of non-God, spiritual-presence experiences appear in Persinger's work involving haunt phenomena (Persinger & Koren, 2001) and sensed presence (Cook & Persinger, 2001; see also Persinger, 1993).

Newberg Data. Newberg, d'Aquili, and Rause (2001) describe two intriguing cases of brain activity correlated with intense mystical states. One of these involves visually oriented meditation in Tibetan Buddhists who experience "ultimate reality" or Absolute Unitary Being (Newberg, Alavi, Baime, Pourdehnad, Santanna, & d'Aquili, 2001). The second one involves the experience of God's presence by Franciscan nuns during centering prayer ("a 'verbal' based meditation involving the internal repetition of a particular phrase"; Newberg, Alavi, Baime, & Pourdehnad, 2000, abstract) (Newberg, d'Aquili, & Rause, 2001). In both cases, the brain events and phenomenological reports are similar and are readily interpretable within d'Aquili & Newberg's (1993) elaborate neuropsychological model. The Buddhist meditators report feelings of a loss of sense of self, of oneness with the universe, of timelessness and infinity, of a peak spiritual moment, and of the absorption of the self into something larger. Similarly, but in the language and context of a theistic religion, the Nuns report "a tangible sense of the closeness of God and a mingling with Him" (Newberg, d'Aquili, & Rause, 2001, pp. 2, 7, also chapter 6). Thus, the attributions made about these raw phenomenological experiences are somewhat different and reflect differing theological views.

Methodologically, the studies are relatively straightforward. In each case, the subject began to meditate, and as he or she approached the peak, the subject indicated this to the experimenters in an unobtrusive way (e.g., a tug on a piece of twine). The experimenters, in an adjacent room, injected a radioactive tracer into the subject by means of catheter, waited for 20-30 minutes, and placed the subject beneath a SPECT (Single Positron Emission Computerized Tomography, a noninvasive functional brain imaging technique) camera. The resulting three-dimensional image yielded a picture of the brain's activity during the meditative climax. The image obtained during the meditative climax was compared to the same subject's brain image during baseline activity.

The results of the brain scans indicate a number of similarities among the subjects in both the Buddhist and Nun groups. These include an increase in dorsal lateral prefrontal activity that corresponds to a state of intense, sustained attention in the model, and a decrease in posterior superior parietal activity (particularly in the left hemisphere) that corresponds to a "functional deafferentation" of the regions responsible for distinguishing self and non-self in the model. Differences between the groups emerge, however, in how they interpret their subjective experiences. For the Buddhist meditators, the sensations are attributed to a state of what Newberg refers to as "Absolute Unitary Being," a becoming one with the universe and a loss of self (see Newberg, d'Aquili, & Rause, 2001, p. 120). For the Christian nuns in prayer, the experience is of the presence of a personal God and a union with Christ.

Persinger Data. Persinger's research, extending from the early 1970s to present, has suggested that relatively low intensity magnetic fields may induce mystical or numinous experiences. These magnetic fields may be artificially produced in a laboratory using a technique called transcranial magnetic stimulation (TMS), or they may be naturally occurring, ambient fields due to geomagnetic or electromagnetic factors. Moreover, he reports that persons with high "temporal lobe lability" (temporal lobe epileptics exhibiting complex partial seizures, or persons scoring high on scales that discriminate such epileptics) show increased susceptibility to these weak magnetic field disturbances, particularly when the fields oscillate in ways that mimic endogenous EEG activity of temporal lobe structures.

A study by Cook and Persinger (2001) on sensed presence is representative of Persinger's laboratory research using TMS. This technique, which induces an electrical current in the brain by applying a time-varying magnetic field above the scalp, is a recent development that has been investigated in a small number of clinical (e.g., depression) and basic research applications (Fitzgerald, Brown, & Daskalakis, 2002). Typically, magnetic fields of 1-2 Tessla (T = a measure of magnetic field strength) are required for an effect. In Persinger's research, however, very weak fields in the 1 μT range are employed (slightly greater than ambient fields; see below). These fields are modulated in time, and are applied over specific regions of the scalp.

Persinger and Cook (2001) tested Persinger's (1993) vectorial hemisphericity model by applying TMS either bilaterally or unilaterally to the right hemisphere with subjects who had given high or low scores on a test of "complex partial epileptic-like experiences" (Persinger & Makarec, 1993). Subjects were recruited to participate in a relaxation study, and following 20 minutes of TMS were given a 20-item questionnaire that included, as one of the response items, "I experience a presence." They found that subjects with low temporal lobe lability reported no experience of sensed presence, whereas subjects with high temporal lobe lability reported significantly more. Consonant with the model, significantly more sensed presence reports were given under right TMS (75% of subjects reporting a sensed presence) than bilateral TMS (60%). No significant differences between the groups or conditions were found for control items referring to tingling sensations, dissociations, or fear. According to the model, these sensed presence reports are due to "awareness of the right hemispheric homologue of the sense of self" (Persinger & Cook, 2001, p. 447).

A second study from Persinger's group illustrates his research involving ambient magnetic fields, including geomagnetic fields (GMF) and electromagnetic fields (EMF). These fields are even weaker than those Persinger uses in the TMS studies. Normal levels for the time varying components of these fields are reported to be in the 10-100 nT range for GMF and 100-500 nT range for EMF. Persinger and Koren (2001) report a 1996 case of a 17 year old woman concerned about haunt experiences in her home. Specifically, she complained about visions, vibration of the bed, footsteps and humming, and a visitation by a spirit – a sensed presence felt beside her bed and then in her body. The onset of her haunt experiences coincided with GMF fluctuations exceeding 50 nT. EMF monitoring in the teenager's bedroom showed an unusually high level (4 μT) and was traced to an electric clock at the head of the bed. She had apparently sustained trauma to the left prefrontal region as a young child, and still showed motor deficits on her right side. Because Persinger's earlier work (e.g., Persinger & Richards, 1995) had suggested that GMF activity exceeding 20 nT accompanied by transcerebral magnetic fields were correlated with reports of a sensed presence, and because she was presumably at risk for epileptic brain activity, they concluded that these factors were likely the precipitating events in the present case, as well. The woman's negative subjective experiences stopped when she began sleeping in another room (with ambient magnetic fields less than 100 nT), and the family's fears of psychotic disturbance were put to rest.

Persinger and Koren's explanation involves three elements: (a) a stimulating event that has no clear referent (EMF or GMF fields), (b) stimulated brain regions that generate various sensations and feelings (the temporal limbic areas are prime candidates), and (c) an attribution process that "makes sense" out of these psychological states within a cultural or religious context. What it doesn't have room for is any sort of ontologically valid spiritual presence as a referent. As they see it, there is "not a single case of haunt phenomena whose major characteristics cannot be accommodated by understanding the natural forces generated by the earth, the areas of the human brain stimulated by these energies, and the interpretation of these forces by normal psychological processes" (Persinger & Koren, 2001, p. 179). We argue that although the issue of an ontologically valid spiritual presence being involved in such experiences is in principle neutral and independent of a scientific account, normal psychological processes certainly are involved, so much so as to make highly suspect Persinger's own claims to have found a brain mechanism unique to God awareness. Because his subjects are often aware that they might have such experiences, the long-known process of expectation based on preparatory mental set is sufficient to account for Persinger's findings.

SOCIAL PSYCHOLOGY OF AWESOME AND GOD EXPERIENCES
Questions Raised By These Samples Of Experiences

Situation-Disposition Interaction. In order to understand how people who purport to have seen God or who had a nonreligious but Awesome or spiritual experience (whether "naturally" as in the case of James' subjects, or in a research context as in the case of the neurotheological studies) came to recognize what it was that they were seeing, a number of crucial psychological issues must be addressed. For example, although it is assumed that all of these perceptions are mediated through brain processes, it is still necessary to understand what psychological mechanisms work to make these experiences happen. A percept is a psychological phenomenon, not merely an biochemical event. This means that it is at a psychological level of analysis that it must be understood. The social psychological approach has as one of its strengths the principle that personal and contextual factors interact in order to produce effects. Applied to the problem of how to understand the unusual experiences of concern in this chapter, this implies that a particular neurobiological event is interpreted a certain way because of two interacting factors. One of them is dispositional — some aspect of the person such as a schema or a motivational tendency, and the other one is situational — aspects of the social environment in which this person lives, moves, and is confronting the stimuli in question.

Attribution of Meaning. Do these experiences share a common core that makes them fundamentally the same, only perceived or stated differently by the persons? The common core thesis is the notion that such experiences are essentially the same at the neurobiological level and that they are reported differently, in different languages (e.g., God language and non-God language) because the person's schemas, language, and social context drive the perceptual task (Hood, 1995). So far we have no evidence of religiously unique brain processes, as if what is occurring in the brain of a Baptist who claims to have seen God is any different from what is occurring in the brain of a Catholic who claims to have seen God. No evidence is reported by Newberg or by Persinger of brain mechanisms unique to specific God or Awe experiences.

How then are we to account for the differences in perception between God and non-God perceptions, if they are not due to unique differences in neurobiological processes? The answer lies in the interaction between personal and social context variables in which the perceptual process is happening. For example, we can observe a difference in the meaning of the nuns and the Buddhists, and this difference is a consequence of the very different religious and nonreligious backgrounds of these persons. In other words, the same neurobiological event is interpreted in different ways, i.e., the percept is different and is described in different languages, because of what each person brings to the task of seeing and interpreting what is in fact the same core neurobiological event. The understanding of this becomes more apparent when social psychological principles are invoked.

The attribution process is perceptual. It is based on how humans perceive wholes where there are parts, see pattern in a stimulus whether or not pattern is there, and how people read meaning into events. Attribution theory is an intellectual descendant of the gestalt psychology of perception from the 1930's. The gestaltists demonstrated how humans can look at an incomplete visual stimulus such as three lines drawn at angles from each other whose ends almost (but don't) touch at the three corners, and "see" a triangle, a fully closed visual stimulus. Our visual systems are constructed so as to "fill in the gaps" at the corners, even though the lines do not actually meet. Similarly, it is possible for people to be given random presentations of stimuli, such as a random series of letters or tones, and have them report that they see a pattern. For example, Hood and Morris (1981) document an experiment in which whether a person brings an intrinsic or an extrinsic orientation to religiousness, combined with situational cues that prompt religious thoughts, determines whether people who are sensory deprived by floating in a tank of water interpret their mental images while submerged as religious or not. Overall, those who have unusual mental experiences while under sensory deprivation and who have a religious mental set, schema, or motivation and expectancy, are more likely to report their experiences in religious terms, in comparison to those who do not have such preparatory factors (Hood, 1995). Parallel landmark findings by Pahnke (1970) showed that people who were unknowingly given psilosiben were more likely to report spiritual and religious experiences if they are witnessing a Good Friday church service, in comparison to persons not given psilosiben. In cross-cultural data consistent with this, university students in Leuven, Belgium, report that religious experiences are associated with other religious indices such as an open belief structure, religious practices and knowledge, and the act of praying (Verhoeven, 1992). Overall, attributions of this type are inferences in which meaning is constructed in order to interpret a more-or-less unstructured set of sensory data (Spilka & McIntosh, 1995).

Generalizing this perceptual process to the problem of perceiving all of life or the cosmos, it is easy to understand the human need to fill in the gaps, so to speak, and perceive a complete whole although the data come to us in discrete bits and pieces. We can attribute meaning, plan, and purpose to the universe whether or not it is "actually there." This is a result of the built-in tendency of our perceptual systems to see consistency and pattern and to construct and give meaning in the face of ambiguity. This depends on social context, preparatory mental set, and schemas.

Schemas, Social Context, and Mental Set. Religion as a whole is not a schema, but we have many specific religious schemas – Catholic schema, Jewish schema, Islamic schema, Evangelical Christian schema, etc. (Paloutzian & Smith, 1995). A schema is a cognitive structure that filters and organizes incoming information and guides perceptions and behaviors. For example, a person with a Jewish schema is less likely than a person with a Catholic schema to "see" the Virgin Mary in an ambiguous stimulus such as the shape of the water stains on the side of a glass window (as did occur in the US in the late 1990s). Similarly, the Buddhists and the Nuns in the Newberg et al. (2000, 2001) studies each attributed a meaning to the ambiguous stimulus that they were experiencing that was consistent with their own religious tradition – a union with God for the Nuns and a connection with everything for the Buddhists — not merely because the neurobiological events were different but because of the different schemas they brought to the task. The classical descriptive accounts of experiences reported by James (1902) parallel these and are subject to the same analysis.

The situational context in which experiences occur and in which a schema is invoked is also an important determinant of the meaning attributed to it. As a mundane example, in church people have increased religious perceptions. For example, the music of J.S. Bach is often considered to be religious music, but two factors in interaction might heighten the odds that religious meaning will be attributed to it. One is when those who hear it are personally religious (i.e., they hear through their particular religious schema), and the other is when it is heard in church (i.e., a uniquely religious setting in which to hear it).Therefore, it is the combination of the schema that the person brings to the task and the context in which the attribution must be made that determines the person's personal set – the tendency to "see" an experience one way versus another.

In sum, experiences like those reported by James and Newberg and Persinger may actually be very similar at the core neurobiological level but interpreted differently because of the preparatory mental set brought to the perceptual task by the person in combination with schemas, context, and motivational predisposition. This means that it is at the level of the whole person that we are able to understand how such experiences happen, not merely at the level of neurobiological factors. This analysis is in accord with and argues for the approach of a social cognitive neuroscience (Ochsner & Lieberman, 2001) of religious experience, not a neuroscience of it.

Assessing the Validity of Experiences

If we learn how religious experience is determined, to what degree does this tell us about the validity of those experiences, e.g., the degree to which people who have said that they have seen God actually have seen God? This question may be on the edge of the scientific neurotheology discussion, but it is wise to address it in order to remind us exactly what knowledge about such processes does and does not say about God.

The above small sketch of data interpreted with an integrative social cognitive neuroscience approach suggests that having a religious experience is more likely when a person has a schema of a particular religious tradition, is in the presence of others who are having religious experiences, or is in some other environment that would foster religious attributions because of the preparatory mental set and situational cues that interpret the information through a religious perceptual system. Such would be the processes, theoretically speaking, that would increase or even make possible religious experience.

This summary of some of the research on the psychological bases of religious experience inevitably points to the issue of the validity of religious experience. This issue can be understood in two different ways: (a) To say that an experience is valid can mean that it is "real" for the person, or (b) it can mean that the experience is ontologically valid, that is, that the percept that is in the person's mind-brain corresponds to an entity that exists "out there" in objective reality.

The first type of reality is more-or-less easy to establish. If someone says "I perceive life as very meaningful," and the speaker and hearer both have a reasonably congruent understanding of what is meant by the word "meaningful," then we would say that the experience is valid for the person. Validity is assessed by common agreement.

Ontological validity, on the other hand, is tougher to establish. In ordinary life it does not seem terribly difficult to establish, so long as we are talking about the existence and perception of concrete objects that we all think exist. For example, if we say "I perceive an apple," and everyone else also claims to perceive the same apple, then there is sufficient common agreement so that we will together conclude that the claimed perception is valid. But what if not all people see that apple? If only one person claims to see the apple but no one else does, how do we decide whether the claimed perception is ontologically valid?

Extrapolate this example to the case of someone who claims to see a vision of God, to hear God's audible voice in a literal sense, or to experience some other unique apparition or to have a special ability to do so, such as a technique to communicate with the dead or to see angles, and instantly we comprehend the problem: the claimed percepts are incongruent—most people don't have them. The extension of this dilemma to the question of the perception of God in purported religious or mystical experiences, or any other claimed "special" state of consciousness, is straight-forward. Most people do see the apple, but most people do *not* see God. (Popular language about "seeing" God or "hearing" God's voice is usually understood in a nonliteral sense.) It is particularly problematic when we remember that in most theologies God is supposed to be invisible. If God is invisible and has no shape, then what are we supposed to make of someone's claim to have seen God?

Research data are clear that reports of religious experience are determined partly by the inter-action of situational factors and the religious and motivational variables that a person brings to the perceptual task. This suggests that the probability of having a religious experience and the belief in its validity can be manipulated by personal mindset and environmental cues. If the apparent validity of religious experience is so manipulable and plastic, then how is it possible to assess it? We suggest that although psychology and neurobiology are powerful in revealing how people come to believe that their own religious experience is valid, they are not able to tell us whether they are so. This task remains for other areas of study.

SOCIAL-COGNITIVE PICTURE OF THE PERSON

We are introducing the social-cognitive argument into the neurotheological dialogue in order to present a picture of human beings that is consistent with a social cognitive neuroscientific ap-proach. This picture is not a purely rational one. For example, the data show that what a person purports to have experienced is predictable by psychological variables and is manipulable by envi-ronmental and social conditions. Further, what it means to claim that an experience is valid is at issue. The very problem of ascribing validity to a phenomenological experience (e.g., to make a supernatural attribution about its cause) is itself a construction arrived at by an attribution process.

The research in social psychology, stemming from an overall cognitive consistency orientation that began with cognitive dissonance theory but has a more powerful intellectual descendent in attri-bution theory, suggests that we do not arrive at our conclusions by means of a purely rational or singular process. This means that the questions we are posing cannot be answered in the form in which we are asking them. Perhaps there are only parts where we want to see a whole. From schema theory, we think that there is a mental structure that guides our perception of the elements of this problem, and the attribution approach adds some understanding about the circumstances that lead us to come to certain conclusions or inferences. However, this kind of research says that the process has to be understood at primarily a psychological level. We may think what we think for a variety of reasons, conclude what we may unknowingly be preset to conclude, and then construct a rationale and basis for doing so. We may also construct meaning for it in either theological or atheological terms.

ATHEISM, RELIGIOUS CONVERSION & THE LOGIC OF GOD
by Matthew Alper

WHY ARE THERE ATHEISTS?

"What is going to happen to those of us who want to believe but aren't able to? And what is to become of those who neither want to nor are capable of believing" (Ingmar Bergmann, 1957).

In discussing my ideas with others, one of the questions most frequently asked has been, "If human spirituality represents an inherent characteristic of our species, if we truly are 'wired' to believe in a spiritual reality, then why are there atheists?" In essence, if we are "wired" to believe in a spiritual reality, how is one to explain those who don't?

Though we may all exist as a part of the same species, no two human beings are exactly alike. As similar as we might be, each of us is a unique composite of physical and cognitive traits. Whereas some of us are born to be taller than average, others are shorter. While some have exceptional vision, others are born blind. While some are more musically or mathematically gifted, others are born deficient in these areas. As a matter of fact, the distribution of every genetically inherited trait can be charted by a Bell Curve.

To demonstrate, let's apply this notion to a basic physical characteristic such as vision. Though the majority of our species is born with average eyesight and will therefore fall somewhere within this curve's mean—its bulge—there exists a much smaller percentage of individuals within every population that represent one of this curve's tapering ends. Whereas one end of this curve is represented by those born with superior vision, on the opposing side, there will most probably exist an equally small number of individuals who are born with inferior vision, with some, on the extreme edge, who are totally blind.

This same principle can be equally applied to a cognitive trait such as musical ability. Though most of us are born with an average capacity to develop a range of musical skills from composing to playing an instrument, each population possesses a smaller percentage of individuals who fall into one of this curve's two tapering tails. On one end, every culture possesses a minority of those born musically gifted. At this end's extreme, there exists an even smaller number of musical savants and prodigies such as Mozart, for example. Meanwhile, on the opposite extreme of this same curve each population will most likely possess an equally small percentage of those born tone deaf, who, though they can hear, lack any inherent musical intelligence and who don't even have a capacity to learn music skills.

Furthermore, for every capacity we possess, cognitive or otherwise, there must exist a physiological site from which that capacity is generated. Our capacity for vision, for instance, is directly related to the caliber of our eyes and visual cortex. Similarly, our capacity for music is directly related to the caliber of those parts of the brain responsible for generating musical ability. We could therefore say that whereas someone like Mozart must have been born with an unusually overdeveloped musical part of his brain, someone less gifted is most probably born with a less developed part of the same.

This, of course, is not to exclude the environmental factor. Though each of us is born with a certain degree of inherent potential in any number of abilities, the degree to which we actualize those latent potentials depends on to what degree we nurture and cultivate them. Had I, for instance, been provided with a great deal of musical instruction from early childhood on, I'm sure I would possess a greater degree of musical ability than I do today. Nevertheless, even with the most intensive musical training conceivable, there's no way I could have ever matched Mozart's skills simply because I was not born with the same genetic potential to achieve that level of ability.

The same holds true for the opposite scenario. Mozart, for instance, were he born to peasants, indentured to toil the fields, without the same opportunity to study music as he had, would never have reached the level of genius he achieved in his life. In such a case, he may have instead merely grown to become "the guy who whistles really well while tilling the soil." Unfortunately, in the same vein, latent Mozarts, Einsteins and Michelangelos probably die every day without the slightest recognition simply because they were never afforded the opportunity to fully actualize their inherent genetic potentials. I'm therefore suggesting that while life experience (nurture) plays a significant role in our cognitive developments, we can only reach as high as our inherent genetic potentials (nature) permit.

So what does any of this have to do with the question of atheism? Since I'm suggesting that spirituality and religiosity are generated from specific regions within the brain, must not the aforementioned Bell Curve principle apply to these inherent proclivities as well? If we in fact possess neurophysiologically-based spiritual and religious mechanisms, then wouldn't it make sense that the average person from any given population would probably possess an average potential for either of these intelligences? (To reassert the distinction between spirituality and religiosity, we must realize that though they usually operate in tandem with one another, one can still be born with any combination of these two unique impulses. For instance, though one might be born with an underdeveloped religious impulse, an overdeveloped spiritual sense may exist. Such an individual, might not be inclined to attend church or observe religious rituals, but might be very spiritual, and highly prone to "transcendental" experiences. On the other hand, there are those who are hyperreligious, though aspiritual. Such individuals, though they may never have a spiritual or mystical experience, or feel compelled to contemplate any "higher" truth or reality, might be obsessed with the rigid adherence to church doctrine, custom and code. It is these individuals who are most prone to the dangerous excesses of religious fanaticism.) Regarding these same Bell Curve's tapering extremes, every population should therefore also possess a smaller percentage of those born with either an enhanced or diminished capacity for either of these two distinct cognitive traits.

Regarding those who fall into the mean of the spiritual curve, such individuals are likely to possess enough spiritual intelligence that they will be predisposed to believe in some form of a transcendental reality, along with supernatural beings as well as an afterlife through which they will perceive themselves to be immortal, thus enabling them to circumvent their fear of death. These are our masses, the bulge of the spiritual Bell Curve, those who have kept spiritual ideals along with religious institutions thriving for all these years as an integral part of every human society.

Regarding this trait's tapering extremes, on one end of this curve are those born with an overdeveloped spiritual function, those for whom spirituality will play a predominant role in their conscious experience. On the farthest extreme are those who, even as early adolescents, will be delivering heartfelt sermons from the pulpit, those of whom we might say were "born with the spirit in them." These often turn out to be our prophets, zealots, and spiritual leaders, in essence, those born with an overdeveloped spiritual function.

On the opposite end of this same curve there are those we might call spiritually deficient, those born with an unusually underdeveloped spiritual function. Just as a person born blind is light-insensitive, those born with an underdeveloped spiritual function are spiritually insensitive, incapable of fully grasping, appreciating or experiencing the concept or implications of any spiritual reality. Such people rarely, if ever, will feel compelled to worship or pray, to consider or contemplate the concepts of a spiritual reality, a god, a soul, or an afterlife. Such people are unlikely to ever have a spiritual experience. These are our society's spiritually retarded, if you will. It is here that we will find the neurophysiological origins of those with a proclivity to become agnostics, atheists, rationalists, and secularists.

To again account for the environmental factor, we must realize that lack of belief (atheism) is not exclusively dependent upon one's genes. In many cases atheists are those who, though they might be inherently spiritual, were raised in a nonreligious or aspiritual environment, in which case their innate proclivities may have atrophied and consequently been substituted by a secular world view. At the same time, there are also those who, though inherently spiritual, have become so disenchanted with organized religion they've chosen to suppress their inherent proclivities and consequently deny a belief in any religion or God. As most atheistic ideologies are based in the mere denial of God's existence, I would like to stress that no philosophy can be justifiably upheld without possessing some underlying logic through which to substantiate its basic principles. Without such a logic, what is referred to as a philosophy is really nothing more than just another groundless belief system, founded in emotion rather than reason. As I see it, this is the essential problem faced by today's Atheist Movement. Rather than possessing an inherent wisdom of its own, the atheist movement relies on the logical shortcomings of those faiths it seeks to contest. And though it's true that no religion has ever been able to defend its precepts with reason, no legitimate philosophy can stand on gainsay alone. The contradicting of one belief system does not validate the tenets of another. Establishing that something is not white, for instance, does not necessitate its being black. Analogously, finding fault in the convictions of every world religion does not constitute proof that there is no God. Consequently, if we are ever to advance a viable atheism, it must possess its own logical foundation, one I believe it is finally provided with, through this new science of neurotheology.

RELIGIOUS CONVERSION

"...to whom is the arm of the Lord revealed?... He is despised and rejected of men; a man of sorrows, and acquainted with grief..." --Isaiah

When we speak of a person being born again, we are generally referring to someone who has undergone a religious conversion. When we see someone who has spent a life leading a secular existence suddenly devote themselves to an organized cult or religion, this is usually the result of a religious conversion. When someone with whom we used to go to the bars and baseball games with is suddenly spending their days handing out religious pamphlets in the streets shouting to every passerby that "Jesus Saves!" or "Blessed be Allah!" this, too, is most likely the result of a religious conversion.

Perhaps we've known someone close to us who has undergone such an abrupt personal transformation or perhaps we've only seen such people as they've proselytized their newfound faiths in the airports or streets. Regardless, the fact that this psychological phenomenon occurs in a certain percentage of every world population implies that it represents yet another integral aspect of our species' inherent neural processing.

Just as we are the musical, emotional and linguistic animal, we are also the "converting" animal, the animal whose sense of personal identity can be suddenly and drastically transformed in such a way that religious concerns come to predominate our conscious experience. In his book, Varieties of Religious Experience, William James was one of the first to document this uniquely human behavior. As James expressed it, "to say that a man is 'converted' means that religious ideas, peripheral in his consciousness, now take a central place, and that religious aims form the habitual center of his energy" (James, 1902).

For people who undergo religious conversions, individuality is replaced by ideology and very little room is left for personal growth or expression. Because the converted believes that the newfound faith determines all things, all sense of personal responsibility is relegated to some religious credo or God. To the converted, all that occurs does so because God willed it as such. No matter how ordinary or mundane an event may seem, God is suddenly viewed as responsible for everything. Should something unfavorable occur, it is only because "God works in mysterious ways." Tragic events become "blessings in disguise," as those converted are overwhelmed with a sense of being saturated in God's presence and love. This type of experience is related by John Wesley, the founder of Methodism. He referred to it as a feeling of "...the heart strangely warmed..." (Wesley, c.1703-1791), during his own conversion. Is it possible, as has been demonstrated with meditative, mystical or near-death experiences, that such sensations have a direct correlation to changes in one's neurophysiology?

Concerning the conversion process itself, though some take place in a slow and gradual manner, the majority of cases occur very abruptly. Many psychologists, such as E.S. Ames, favored "restricting the term 'conversion' to sudden instances of religious change" (Hood, 1996). G.A. Coe also thought that the use of the term conversion should be limited to those cases in which the individual undergoes an intense and sudden religious change. The only other time a person's core personality undergoes such an abrupt and drastic change is when stricken by an organic psycho-syndrome or psychosis. Being that both of these are listed as disorders in the DSM-IV, one has to wonder why we have yet to view religious conversion in the same light.

In studying the etiology of religious conversion, we need to look at those triggers that seem to precipitate the experience. According to the psychologist Paul Johnson, "A genuine religious conversion usually occurs as the outcome of a crisis of ultimate concern and a sense of desperate conflict" (Hood, 1996).

In his book, Religious Conversion: A Bio-psychological Study, the psychologist S. De Sanctis asserts that "all the converted speak of their crisis, of their efforts, and of their conflicts which they have endured" (De Sanctis, c. 1862-1935). In his work, The Cognitive and Emotional Antecedents of Religious Conversion, C. Ullman discusses studies he conducted in which he compared psychological traits of those who had undergone a religious conversion and those who had not. Ullman found that:

Converts recalled childhoods that were less happy and filled with more anguish than those of nonconverts. The emotions recalled for adolescence followed similar childhood patterns, with the addition of significant anger and fear in adolescence for the converts and not the nonconverts. Converts also differed from the unconverted in having less love and admiration for their fathers and more indifference and anger towards them (Ullman, 1982).

After studying 2,174 cases of religious conversions, the psychologist E.T Clark noted,"Sudden conversions were associated with fear and anxiety" (Hood, 1996).

If we were to look for a pattern, it would seem that those most susceptible to undergoing this type of sudden cognitive transformation are those with frail senses of identity; people with unhealthily developed egos; or those who were abused or neglected by their parents, without whose love they were never able to feel secure in the world. When such a child grows, it may not possess the inner strength required to endure life's ordinary trials and tribulations, thus catapulting that person into a state of emotional crisis. When their crisis reaches a threshold, a breakdown occurs in which the suffering individual latches onto to some religion to which they will soon convert.

Follow-up studies show that after such deeply troubled individuals undergo their religious conversion, their emotional states generally tend to improve. According to a study done by J.B. Pratt, "Prior to conversions, individuals had a tendency to wallow in feelings of unworthiness, self-doubt, and depreciation that are released or overcome via conversion" (Pratt, 1920). Yet another study showed that, "It is typical of conversion to be preceded by morbid feelings in which doubt, anxiety, internal strife, and despair are replaced by serenity, peace and optimism" (Ostow, 1953). Apparently, for those who suffer severe emotional turmoil, there are obvious benefits in undergoing a religious conversion.

This notion that those overwhelmed by stress are most vulnerable to undergoing a conversion is no secret to many religious groups, who intentionally seek out the lonely and afflicted because they know they are most likely to succumb to a conversion. The theologian, Lewis Rambo, points out that certain religious groups such as the Evangelical Christians make it part of their practice to target vulnerable individuals (Rambo, 1995). For example, in large urban areas, some churches focus on ministries to those recently divorced as they know that within the first six months after a divorce, a person is more likely to be converted. This practice of seeking out those in crisis is most evident among prison populations, worldwide, where stress levels are critical and conversions are practically endemic. Another example in which the vulnerable are targeted for conversion is practiced by recovery groups such as Alcoholics, Eaters, Gamblers, and Debtors Anonymous all of which emphasize— through the use of the renowned "12 step" program—faith in religion and God as primary tools in their effort to combat these addictive behaviors. When one is trying to overcome an addiction, they experience a sharp rise in stress levels, thus leaving those with addictive disorders as attractive candidates for a conversion.

Because a percentage of every population undergo this type of sudden behavioral change, it suggests that religious conversions most likely constitute yet another inherent characteristic of our species, a genetically inherited reflex response to overwhelming crisis or anxiety. If this does, in fact, constitute a physiological reflex, it would suggest that there must exist some specific neurophysiological mechanism responsible for generating this type of behavioral response.

It appears that the human capacity to endure reality is so tenuous that Nature had to install our species with an emergency back-up sense of identity—a religious one—to replace our secular ones when they can't provide adequate relief from our excess anxieties. Depending on to what degree one is genetically predisposed to undergo a conversion, we each have our own personal threshold for pain and duress that we can withstand before we, too, become vulnerable to undergoing this type of cognitive transformation. It appears that when a person reaches their own personal anxiety threshold, rather than to engage in some self-destructive behavior, such as drug abuse, as so many do, one's "normal," secular-self shuts down and is immediately replaced with an alternate hyper-religious one. Once the converted individual's cognitive transformation is complete, there is relief from of all those anxieties that were attached to the previous identity. All past fears are washed away and replaced with rapturous contentment (again, sensations that can, more than likely, be measured with the use of a SPECT scan or fMRI).

The human ego is a very delicate organ. If it is not properly nurtured, a person may grow to develop any number of insecurities, neuroses or even psychoses. When an individual with a weak sense of self reaches the preliminary stages of adulthood, they may not feel ready or able to take on life's responsibilities. Perhaps this is why religious conversions "typically occur during adolescence" (Hood, 1996). This is further supported by the research of psychologist Paul Johnson who concluded that "after surveying five studies conducted on over 15,000 people, the average age of conversion was 15.2 years" (Hood, 1996).

This is not to suggest that religious conversion only occurs during adolescence, for it can strike at any age that a person feels particularly vulnerable or threatened. Nevertheless, it is during adolescence that we are generally afflicted with increased anxiety levels as it is during this life passage that we are told by our parents and societies that we're soon going to have to fend for, and support ourselves. Moreover, it is usually during adolescence that we must first come to terms with the concept of our own mortality.

With all of these concerns, questions, pressures, and responsibilities suddenly thrust upon us, it is no surprise that it is during this same stage in our development (usually between the ages of 15-20), that humans undergo the most cases not only of religious conversion, but of suicide, drug abuse, anorexia, depression, and schizophrenia. It is also no wonder that the majority of conversions take place at this same age, as research suggests increased religiosity can lead to a reduction in a number of self-destructive behaviors. Regarding that most self-destructive act of all, suicide, an article entitled "Religiosity and United Stated Suicide Rates" reported that, "Church attendance remains negatively correlated with suicide rates" (Martin, 1984). This was further supported by research done by H.G. Koenig who concluded in his work Aging and God that among the elderly "faith suppresses suicidal thinking." After interviewing a number of individuals, Koenig found that many expressed that "the promise of a happy afterlife" helped to thwart any suicidal inclinations (Koenig, 1994). In a journal reference appropriately titled, "The Effect of Religion on Suicide," the team of Stack and Wasserman found that a belief in an afterlife helped to counter self-destructive impulses (Stack, 1992). Apparently, those who do not believe in a spiritual reality are more prone to engaging in self-destructive behaviors than those who have faith. Perhaps it is for this reason that religious conversion can save individuals from succumbing to self-destructive acts that we are reluctant to classify it as either a problem or a disorder.

Moreover, it is interesting that when a person converts to a sanctioned religion we tend to be that much more accepting of it, yet when one joins an unsanctioned belief system—what are referred to as cults—we feel compelled to seize that person from the "insidious" clutches of that group or influence. Regardless of how we choose to perceive this strictly human phenomenon, we must accept that it represents another cross-cultural characteristic of our species and therefore, more than likely, another genetically inherited behavioral trait, reconfirming the notion that spiritual and religious experiences can be directly related to our biologies and not to some ethereal influence or God.

THE LOGIC OF GOD:
A NEW "SPIRITUAL" PARADIGM

"We are what we think. All that we are arises with our thoughts. With our thoughts we make the world" --Siddhartha, c. 525 BCE.

"Projection makes perception. The world you see is what you gave it, nothing more than that. It is the witness to your state of mind, the outward picture of an inward condition. As a man thinketh so does he perceive. Therefore, seek not to change the world, but choose to change your mind about the world" (A Course In Miracles, 1975).

"The real voyage of discovery consists not in seeking new landscapes, but in having new eyes" (Proust, c. 1913-1925). et al (translated by: C. K. Scott-Moncrieff (Translator), Terence

"An evolution of consciousness is the central evolution of terrestrial existence...a change of consciousness is the major fact of the next evolutionary transformation" --Aurobindo,1963.

According to the 18th-century German philosopher Immanuel Kant, all perception is contingent on the manner in which an organism processes information. For example, when I experience an apple, I am reliant on the make-up of my perceptual mechanisms, my sense organs—my eyes, ears, tongue, nose, and skin—to acquire knowledge of the fruit. Once all of this sensual data is assimilated, my brain then has to integrate all the information in such a way as to invoke the comprehensible experience I refer to as an apple. Our conceptions of reality are therefore really nothing more than the products of internally generated cognitions projected onto the world around me, "the outward picture of an inward condition" (A Course in Miracles, 1975).

Being that every species possesses its own unique set of perceptual mechanisms as well as its own unique processor or brain, every species must therefore interpret reality from its own unique perspective. Accordingly, my experience of an apple is very different from a worm's, a fly's or a monkey's. This is not to say that my experience is more "real" or "true" than any other creature's, just different. Consequently, no species can ever possess absolute knowledge of anything, but instead only relative knowledge, relative to the manner in which that species processes and consequently interprets reality.

As Kant expressed it, we can never possess absolute knowledge of "things-in-themselves" (Kant,1781), only relative knowledge of "things-as-we-perceive-them." Just as flies possess fly knowledge, humans possess human knowledge. And just as flies possess fly "truths," humans possess human "truths," neither being any more authentic or real than the other. We must therefore accept that such lofty notions as absolute truth or knowledge are unattainable ideals to which we will never have access. Instead, we are forever bound to our relative and subjective human perspectives which are framed by the manner in which our sense organs and brains process information. Consequently, to understand what we refer to as reality, we first need to understand the underlying nature of how our brains process information.

According to the cognitive sciences, the human brain consists of an interactive network of separate regions, each which processes information in its own unique way. These are our cognitive functions. Consequently, to better understand the nature of how our brains process information, we first need to understand the nature of each of these interactive cognitive functions. Examples of human cognitive functions include: a language function which consists of our Wernicke's and Broca's areas as well as our angular gyrus; a variety of emotional functions, which mainly reside in the brain's limbic region; a moral function centered within the prefrontal cortex; and a spatial and temporal function which inhabit the parietal lobe; a personal identity function which resides within the right frontal cortex.. As a matter of fact, for every perception, cognition, emotion, sensation, or behavior our species demonstrates, it is likely we possess a cognitive function from which that experience or behavior is generated. It is the role of each of these distinct cognitive functions to process a multitude of data, each in its own particular way. Only after all of this separately processed data has then been integrated are we provided with a comprehensible perception of our reality.

So what if we were to apply this same precept to human spirituality? What if spirituality represents the manifestation of one of our brain's cognitive functions? As it is a cross-cultural proclivity to perceive a spiritual realm, isn't it possible that spirituality may represent one of the ways our species is "wired" to process information and consequently to interpret reality? If so, it would imply that our spiritual beliefs in concepts as a god, a soul, and an afterlife also constitute nothing more than manifestations of the way our species happens to process information and therefore to interpret reality. In such a case, God would no longer represent any Absolute Being but rather a cognitively generated, relative one. Such a hypothesis would imply that God, as we've thus far interpreted Him, as a real and absolute entity, is, as Nietzsche suggested, dead. No longer an absolute reality, God is reduced to just another one of our species' relative perceptions, the manifestation of an evolutionary adaptation-a coping mechanism-instilled in us so that we can endure life's sufferings as well as our unique awareness of death.

It may be difficult for many people to accept such a reductionistic, evolutionary, organic, cognitive, rational, that is, scientific interpretation of God. Because the majority of our species is literally hardwired to perceive a spiritual reality, it may be impossible for many to grasp, as it may conflict with their inherent perceptions of reality. Subsequently, trying to convince someone who is hardwired to believe in a spiritual reality that no such thing exists may be as futile as trying to convince a person suffering from schizophrenia that the voices heard are coming, not from without, but from within. This is not to suggest that our spiritual perceptions represent the manifestation of any physical dysfunction, as is true with illnesses like schizophrenia. On the contrary, spiritual consciousness represents a normal part of the human cognitive experience.

But, what if we could somehow convince a person dealing with hallucinations to recognize them as nothing more than the products of internally generated misperceptions? Granted, in the case of viewing an actual object like an apple, our perceptions are based in some external reality, but that doesn't mean that the human brain isn't capable of producing a variety of hallucinations and confabulations. When, for instance, auditory hallucinations are reported or phantom limb pain is expressed, the experience is as "real" to the person as is the apple on my desk is to me. In essence, cognitively generated delusions are a familiar human phenomenon. What if we could somehow teach the person to reason through the delusions? Similarly, what if our entire species could be taught to reason through the possibilty that our beliefs in the supernatural are delusional? What if we could come to recognize and accept that such beliefs aren't representative of any actual external reality but are, instead, the manifestations of internally generated misperceptions? What if we could recognize that spiritual consciousness exists as the consequence of a neurophysiological reflex? Just as planarians reflexively turn toward light, humankind reflexively turns to a god.

Let me borrow, for a moment, from Ridley Scott's 1982 science fiction film, Blade Runner. Imagine an android is programmed to believe it is human. In order to make the android believe such a thing, the manufacturer installed a computer chip into its circuitry which instilled it with fictitious memories of a fabricated past. Now imagine that the android were to suddenly become aware of its true nature. Suddenly, it realizes not only that it is an android, but that its memories are nothing more than the effects of a computer chip that compels it to perceive a delusional past. Now that the android has become cognizant of its true nature, it would be free to explore the possibilities of a whole new paradigm. No longer bound to the false reality with which it was programmed, the android would now be able to redefine its own destiny, able to explore new possibilities in accordance with its "truer" nature.

Analagously, imagine humans were to suddenly become cognizant of the fact that we've been programmed by the forces of natural selection to perceive a spiritual reality, one which is just as fabricated as our android's fictitious past. Just as the android had been constructed with computer chips that frame its thoughts and behaviors, humans are analagously constructed with cognitive functions that do the same for ours. What if in the same way that our android recognized its memories existed not as the recollection of actual past experiences but rather as the consequence of a program installed into its circuitry, we came to recognize that spiritual consciousness exists not as the effect of any actual transcendental reality but rather as the consequence of an organic program? Perhaps if we learned to regard spirituality in such a way, we too could devise a whole new paradigm for ourselves, one through which we could redefine our own destinies based on our truer natures. Rather than being stuck in the same delusional consciousness Nature forged for us, we could use this newfound self-knowledge to reach for a healthier and more productive vision of ourselves. Should we choose to embrace such a new "spiritual" paradigm, it might mark the advent of a whole new era for us, one based on such principles as self-actualization, equality, justice, and compassion, things that are all too often lacking in today's societies.

Another metaphor to be considered, is to imagine we are looking into a mirror that we believe offers a pure and perfect reflection. Now, imagine that placed between us and the mirror is actually a series of lenses, previously imperceptible to us, but that have actually distorted our view. Because of our ignorance of these lenses, we have no way of knowing that we have been visually deceived. Though we may believe that our view represents a perfect reflection of ourselves, we are actually misinformed. Until we know these lenses exist, until we know to look past them, to push them aside, we will never be afforded a true reflection of ourselves.

I believe that human spirituality represents such a lens, one that distorts our view of reality by making us perceive a spiritual element when no such thing exists. Interestingly enough, this lens distorts the perceptions of philosophers and scientists as much as anyone else. From newfangled "quantum" definitions of spirituality, to the paranormal sciences, or the archives of metaphysical philosophy, all represent various ways that spiritual consciousness has distorted man's quest for a rational conception of reality. Whether it be through quantum notions of a random principle or paradoxes used by Zen Buddhists, medieval metaphysicians or Christian ontologists, we seek to explain what we regard as incomprehensible as proof of a transcendental quality in the universe. What if we were to become aware that such a lens existed? What if we were to choose to push it aside, clearing our perspectives of all such "spiritual" distortions, affording ourselves a much clearer, less obstructed view of reality? Sure, it might be somewhat uncomfortable at first, even distressing, to have to readjust our perceptions of ourselves in such a fundamental way. But wouldn't we prefer to possess a more perfect view of reality than a distorted one? Shouldn't we prefer truth over deception?

What I'm suggesting is that spiritual consciousness constitutes "Nature's white lie," an inherited misperception selected into our species to help alleviate the debilitating anxiety caused by our unique awareness of death. But would Nature do such a thing as to program a species with an inherent misperception? Well, as odd a notion as it might seem, Nature has no regard for such lofty human conceptions as what we refer to as "real" or "true." Nature's only impetus is to create a more survivable creature, that is, one that can more effectively pass its genetic material onto future generations-this and nothing more. The author of The Selfish Gene, Richard Dawkins, expressed this same notion, "We, and all other animals, are machines created by our genes...We are survival machines, robot vehicles blindly programmed to preserve the molecules known as genes" (Dawkins, 1989).

As terrifying as the prospect of death might be, if such an organic theory of spirit and God happens to be correct, isn't it in our best interests to embrace the reality of our situation? Can anything really be gained by living in conscious denial? If science which has brought us so many life-enriching technologies can prove that this is an impulse, then why would we choose to ignore this? As is the case with any white lie, we have to ask ourselves wether we would rather live in contented ignorance, or embrace the truth? How we choose to answer this may stand as one of the pivotal decisions in determining the outcome of our species' future.

Figure 79a. The Transfiguration. Raphael.

CONVERSION AND RELIGIOUS EXPERIENCE
by William James

To be converted, to be regenerated, to receive grace, to experience religion, to gain an assurance, are so many phrases which denote the process, gradual or sudden, by which a self hitherto divided, and consciously wrong inferior and unhappy, becomes unified and consciously right superior and happy, in consequence of its firmer hold upon religious realities. This at least is what conversion signifies in general terms, whether or not we believe that a direct divine operation is needed to bring such a moral change about.

Before entering upon a minute study of the process, let me enliven our understanding of the definition by a concrete example. I choose the quaint case of an unlettered man, Steph H. Bradley, whose experience is related in scarce American pamphlet.

I select this case because it shows how in these inner alterations one may find one unsuspected depth below another, as if the possibilities of character lay disposed in a series of layers or shells, of whose existence we have no premonitory knowledge.

Bradley thought that he had been already fully converted at the age of fourteen.

"I thought I saw the Saviour, by faith, in human shape, for about one second in the room, with arms extended, appearing to say to me, Come. The next day I rejoiced with trembling; soon after, my happiness was so great that I said that I wanted to die; this world had no place in my affections, as I knew of, and every day appeared as solemn to me as the Sabbath. I had an ardent desire that all mankind might feel as I did; I wanted to have them all love God supremely. Previous to this time I was very selfish and self-righteous; but now I desired the welfare of all mankind, and could with a feeling heart forgive my worst enemies, and I felt as if I should be wiling to bear the scoffs and sneers of any person, and suffer anything for His sake, if I could be the means in the hands of God, of the conversion of one soul."

Nine years later, in 1829, Mr. Bradley heard of a revival of religion that had begun in his neighborhood. "Many of the young converts," he says, "would come to me when in meeting and ask me if I had religion, and my reply generally was, I hope I have. This did not appear to satisfy them; they said they knew they had it. I request them to pray for me, thinking with myself, that if I had not got religion now, after so long a time professing to be a Christian, that it was time I had, and hoped their prayers would be answered in my behalf.

"One Sabbath, I went to hear the Methodist at the Academy. He spoke of the ushering in of the day of general judgment; and he set it forth in such a solemn and terrible manner as I never heard before. The scene of that day appeared to be taking place, and so awakened were all the powers of my mind that, like Felix, I trembled involuntarily on the bench where I was sitting, though I felt nothing at heart. The next day evening I went to hear him again. He took his text from Revelation: 'And I saw the dead, small and great, stand before God.' And he represented the terrors of that day in such a manner that it appeared as if it would melt the heart of the stone. When he finished his discourse, an old gentleman turned to me and said, 'This is what I call preaching,' I thought the same; but my feelings were still unmoved by what he said, and I did not enjoy religion, but I believe he did.

"I will now relate my experience of the power of the Holy Spirit which took place on the same night. Had any person told me previous to this that I could have experienced the power of the Holy Spirit in the manner which I did, I could not have believed it, and should have thought the person deluded that told me so. I went directly home after the meeting, and when I got home I wondered what made me feel so stupid. I retired to rest soon after I got home, and felt indifferent to the things of religion until I began to be exercised by the Holy Spirit, which began in about five minutes after, in the following manner:—

"At first, I began to feel my heart beat very quick all of a sudden, which made me at first think that perhaps something is going to ail me, though I was not alarmed, for I felt no pain. My heart increased in its beating, which soon convinced me that it was the Holy Spirit from the effect it had on me. I began to feel exceedingly happy and humble, and such a sense of unworthiness as I never felt before. I could not very well help speaking out, which I did, and said, Lord, I do not deserve this happiness, or words to that effect, while there was a stream (resembling air in feeling) came into my mouth and heart in a more sensible manner than that of drinking anything, which continued, as near a I could judge, five minutes or more, which appeared to be the cause of such a palpitation of my heart. It took complete possession of my soul, and I am certain that I desired the Lord, while in the midst of it, not to give me any more happiness, for it seemed as if I could not contain what I had got. My heart seemed as if it would burst, but it did not stop until I felt as if I was unutterably full of the love and grace of God. In the mean time while thus exercised, a thought arose in my mind, what can it mean? And all at once, as if to answer it, my memory became exceedingly clear, and it appeared to me just as if the New Testament was placed open before me, eight chapter of Romans, and as light as if some candle lighted was held for me to read these words 'The Spirit helpeth our infirmities with groaning which cannot be uttered.' And all the time that my heart was a-beating, it made me groan like a person in distress, which was not very easy to stop, though I was in no pain at all, and my brother being in bed in another room came and opened the door, and asked me if I had got the toothache. I told him no, and that he might get to sleep. I tried to stop. I felt unwilling to go to sleep myself, I was so happy, fearing I should lose it—thinking within myself

'My wiling soul would stay
In such a frame as this.'

And while I lay reflecting, after my heart stopped beating, feeling as if my soul was full of the Holy Spirit, I thought that perhaps there might be angels hovering round my bed. I felt just as if I wanted to converse with him, and finally I spoke, saying, 'O ye affectionate angels! How is it that ye can take so much interest in our welfare, and ewe take so little interest in our own.' After this, with difficulty I got to sleep; and when I awoke in the morning my first thoughts were: What had become of my happiness? And, feeling a degree of it in my heart, I asked for more, which was given to me as quick as thought. I then got up to dress myself, and found to my surprise that I could but just stand. It appeared to me as if it was a little heaven upon earth. My soul felt as completely raised above the fears of deaths as of going to sleep; and like a bird in a cage, I had a desire, if it was the will of God, to get released from my body and to dwell with Christ, thought willing to live to do good to others, and to warn sinners to repent. I went downstairs feeling as solemn as if I had lost all my friends, and thinking with myself, that I would not let my parents know it until I had first looked into the Testament. I went directly to the shelf and looked into it, at the eight chapter of Romans, and every verse seemed to almost speak and to confirm it to be truly the Word of God, and as if my feelings corresponded with the meaning of the word. I then told my parents of it, and told them that I thought that they must see that when I spoke, that it was not my own voice, for it appeared so to me. My speech seemed entirely under the control of the Spirit within me; I do not mean that the words which I spoke were not my own, for they were. I thought that I was influenced similar to the Apostles on the day of Pentecost (with the exception of having power to give it to others, and doing what they did). After breakfast, I went round to converse with my neighbors on religion, which I could not have been hired to have done before this, and at their request I prayed with them, though I had never prayed in public before.

"I now feel as if I had discharged my duty by telling the truth, and hope by the blessing of God, it may do some good to all who shall read it. He has fulfilled his promise in sending the Holy Spirit down into our hearts, or mine at least, and I now defy all the Deists and Atheists in the world to shake my faith in Christ."

So much for Mr. Bradley and his conversion, of the effect of which upon his later life we gain no information. Now for a minute survey of the constituent elements of the conversion process.

If you opened the chapter on Association, of any treatise on Psychology, you will read that a man's ideas, aims, and objects form diverse internal groups and systems, relatively independent of one another. Each 'aim' which he follows awakens a certain specific kind of interested excitement, and gathers a certain group of ideas together in subordination to it as its associates; and if the aims and excitements are distinct in kind, their groups of ideas may have little in common. When one group is present and engrosses the interest, all the ideas connected with other groups may be excluded from the mental field. The President of the United States when, with paddle, gun, and fish-rod, he goes camping in the wilderness for a vacation, changes his system of ideas from top to bottom. The presidential anxieties have lapsed into the background entirely; the official habits are replaced by the habits of a son of nature, and those who knew the man only as the strenuous magistrate would not 'know him for the same person' if they saw him as the camper.

If now he should never go back, and never again suffer political interest to gain dominion over him, he would be for practical intents and purposes a permanently transformed being. Our ordinary alterations of character, as we pass from one of our aims to another, are not commonly called transformations, because each of them is so rapidly succeeded by another in the reverse direction; but whenever one aim grows so stable as to expel definitively its previous rivals from the individual's life, we tend to speak of the phenomenon, and perhaps to wonder at it, as a 'transformation.'

These alternations are the completest of the ways in which a self may be divided. A less complete way is the simultaneous coexistence of two or more different groups of aims, of which one practically holds the right of way and instigates activity, whilst the others are only pious wishes, and never practically come to anything. Saint Augustine's aspirations to a purer life, in our last lecture, were for a while an example. Another would be the President in his full pride of office, wondering whether it were not all vanity, and whether the life of a wood-chopper were not the wholesomer destiny. Such fleeting aspirations are mere velleitates, whimsies. They exist on the remoter outskirts of the mind, and the real self of the man, the centre of his energies, is occupied with an entirely different system. As life goes on, there is a constant change of our interests, and a consequent change of place in our systems of ideas, from more central to more peripheral, and from more peripheral to more central parts of consciousness. I remember, for instance, that one evening when I was a youth, my father read aloud from a Boston newspaper that part of Lord Gifford's will which founded these four lectureships. At that time I did not think of being a teacher of philosophy, and what I listened to was as remote from my own life as if it related to the planet Mars. Yet here I am, with the Gifford system part and parcel of my very self, and all my energies, for the time being, devoted to successfully identifying myself with it. My soul stands now planted in what once was for it a practically unreal object, and speaks from it as from its proper habitat and centre.

When I say 'Soul,' you need not take me in the ontological sense unless you prefer to; for although ontological language is instinctive in such matters, yet Buddhists or Humians can perfectly well describe the facts in the phenomenal terms which are their favorites. For them the soul is only a succession of fields of consciousness: yet there is found in each field a part, or sub-field, which figures as focal and contains the excitement, and from which, as from a centre, the aim seems to be taken. Talking of this part, we involuntarily apply words of perspective to distinguish it from the rest, words like 'here,' 'this,' 'now,' 'mine,' or 'me'; and we ascribe to the other parts the positions 'there,' 'then,' 'that,' 'his' or 'thine,' 'it,' 'not me.' But a 'here' can change to a 'there,' and a 'there' become a 'here,' and what was 'mine' and what was 'not mine' change their places.

What brings such changes about is the way in which emotional excitement alters. Things hot and vital to us to-day are cold-tomorrow. It is as if seen from the hot parts of the field that the other parts appear to us, and from these hot parts personal desire and volition make their sallies. They are in short the centres of our dynamic energy, whereas the cold parts leave us indifferent and passive in proportion to their coldness.

Whether such language be rigorously exact is for the present of no importance. It is exact enough, if you recognize from your own experience the facts which I seek to designate by it.

Now there may be great oscillation in the emotional interest, and the hot places may shift before one almost as rapidly as the sparks that run through burnt-up paper. Then we have the wavering and divided self we heard so much of in the previous lecture. Or the focus of excitement and heat, the point of view from which the aim is taken, may come to lie permanently within a certain system; and then, if the change be a religious one, we call it a ***conversion***, **especially if it be by crisis, or sudden.**

Let us hereafter, in speaking of the hot place in a man's consciousness, the group of ideas to which he devotes himself, and from which he works, call it the habitual centre of his personal energy. It makes a great difference to a man whether one set of his ideas, or another, be the centre of his energy; and it makes a great difference, as regards any set of ideas which he may possess, whether they become central or remain peripheral in him. To say that a man is 'converted' means, in these terms, that religious ideas, previously peripheral in his consciousness, now take a central place, and that religious aims form the habitual centre of his energy.

Now if you ask of psychology just how the excitement shifts in a man's mental system, and why aims that were peripheral become at a certain moment central, psychology has to reply that although she can give a general description of what happens, she is unable in a given case to account accurately for all the single forces at work. Neither an outside observer nor the Subject who undergoes the process can explain fully how particular experiences are able to change one's centre of energy so decisively, or why they often have to bide their hour to do so. We have a though, or we perform an act, repeatedly, but on a certain day the real meaning of the thought peals through us for the first time, or the act has suddenly turned into a moral impossibility. All we know is that there are dead feelings, dead ideas, and cold beliefs, and there are hot and live ones; and when one grows hot and alive within us, everything has to re-crystallize about it. We may say that the heat and liveliness mean only the 'motor efficacy,' long deferred but now operative, of the idea; but such talk itself is only circumlocution, for whence the sudden motor efficacy? And our explanations then get so vague and general that one realizes all the more the intense individuality of the whole phenomenon.

In the end we fall back on the hackneyed symbolism of a mechanical equilibrium. A mind is a system of ideas, each with the excitement it arouses, and with tendencies impulsive and inhibitive, which mutually check or reinforce one another. The collection of ideas alters by subtraction or by addition in the course of experience, and the tendencies alter as the organism gets more aged. A mental system may be undermined or weakened by this interstitial alteration just as a building is, and yet for a time keep upright by dead habit. But a new perception, a sudden emotional shock, or an occasion which lays bare the organic alteration, will make the whole fabric fall together; and then the centre of gravity sinks into an attitude more stable, for the new ideas that reach the centre in the rearrangement seem now to be locked there, and the new structure remains permanent.

Formed associations of ideas and habits are usually factors of retardation in such changes of equilibrium. New information, however acquired, plays an accelerating part in the changes; and the slow mutation of our instincts and propensities, under the 'unimaginable touch of time' has an enormous influence. Moreover, all these influences may work subconsciously or half unconsciously. And when you get a Subject in whom the subconscious life—of which I must speak more fully soon—is largely developed, and in whom motives habitually ripen in silence, you get a case of which you can never give a full account, and in which, both to the Subject and the onlookers, there may appear an element of marvel. Emotional occasions, especially violent ones, are extremely potent in precipitating mental rearrangements. The sudden and explosive ways in which love, jealousy, guilt, fear, remorse, or anger can seize upon one are known to everybody. Hope, happiness, security, resolve, emotions characteristic of conversion, can be equally explosive. And emotions that come in this explosive way seldom leave things as they found them.

In his recent work on the Psychology of Religion, Professor Starbuck of California has shown by a statistical inquiry how closely parallel in its manifestations the ordinary 'conversion' which occurs in young people brought up in evangelical circles is to that growth into a larger spiritual life which is a normal phase of adolescence in every class of human beings. The age is the same, falling usually between fourteen and seventeen. The symptoms are the same,—sense of incompleteness and imperfection; brooding, depression, morbid introspection, and sense of sin; anxiety about the hereafter; distress over doubts, and the like. And the result is the same, —a happy relief and objectivity, as the confidence in self gets greater through the adjustment of the faculties to the wider outlook. In spontaneous religious awakening, apart from revivalistic examples, and in the ordinary storm and stress and moulting-time of adolescence, we also may meet with mystical experiences, astonishing the subjects by their suddenness, just as in revivalistic conversion. The analogy, in fact, is complete; and Starbuck's conclusion as to these ordinary youthful conversions would seem to be the only sound one: Conversion is in its essence a normal adolescent phenomenon, incidental to the passage from the child's small universe to the wider intellectual and spiritual life of maturity.

"Theology," says Dr. Starbuck, "takes the adolescent tendencies and builds upon them; it sees that the essential thing in adolescent growth is bringing the person out of childhood into the new life of maturity and personal insight. It accordingly brings those means to bear which will intensify the normal tendencies. It shortens up the period of duration of storm and stress." The conversion phenomena of 'conviction of sin' last, by this investigator's statistics, about one fifth as long as the periods of adolescent storm and stress phenomena of which he also got statistics, but they are very much more intense.

Bodily accompaniments, loss of sleep and appetite, for example, are much more frequent in them. "The essential distinction appear to be that conversion intensifies but shortens the period by bringing the person to a definite crisis."

The conversion which Dr. Starbuck here has in mind are of course mainly those of very commonplace persons, kept true to a pre-appointed type by instruction, appeal, and example. The particular form which they affect is the result of suggestion and imitation. If they went through their growth-crisis in other faiths and other countries, although the essence of the change would be the same (since it is one in the main so inevitable), its accidents would be different. In Catholic lands, for example, in our own Episcopalian sects, no such anxiety and conviction of sin is usual as in sects that encourage revivals. The sacraments being more relied on in threes more strictly ecclesiastical bodies, the individual's personal acceptance of salvation needs less to be accentuated and led up to.

But every imitative phenomenon must once have had its original, and I propose that for the future we keep as close as may be to the more first-hand and original forms of experience. These are more likely to be found in sporadic adult cases.

Professor Leuba, in a valuable article on the psychology of conversion, subordinates the technical aspect of the religious life almost entirely to its moral aspect. The religious sense he defines as "the feeling of unwholeness, of moral imperfection, of sin, to use the technical word, accompanied by the yearning after the peace of unity." "The word 'religion,'" he says, "is getting more and more to signify the conglomerate of desires and emotions springing from the sense of sin and its release"; and he gives a large number of examples, in which the sin ranges from drunkenness to spiritual pride, to show that the sense of it may beset one an crave relief as urgently as does the anguish of the sickened flesh or any form of physical misery.

Undoubtedly this conception covers an immense number of cases. A good one to use as an example is that of Mr. S. H. Hadley, who after his conversion became an active and useful rescuer of drunkards in New York. His experience runs as follows:—

"One Tuesday evening I sat in a saloon in Harlem, a homeless, friendless, dying drunkard. I had pawned or sold everything that would bring a drink. I could not sleep unless I was dead drunk. I had no eaten for days, and for four nights preceding I had suffered with delirium tremens, or the horrors, from midnight till morning. I had often said, 'I will never be a tramp. I will never be cornered, for when that time comes, if ever it comes, I will find a home in the bottom of the river.' But the Lord so ordered it that when that time did come I was not able to walk one quarter of the way to the river. As I sat there thinking, I seemed to feel some great and mighty presence. I did not know then what it was. I did learn afterwards that it was Jesus, the sinner's friend. I walked up to the bar and pounded it with my fist till I made the glasses rattle. Those who stood by drinking looked on with scornful curiosity. I said I would never take another drink, if I died on the street, and really felt as though that would happen before morning. Something said, 'If you want to keep this promise, go and have yourself locked up.' I went to the nearest station-house and had myself locked up.

"I was placed in a narrow cell, and it seemed as though all the demons that could find room came in that place with me. This was not all the company I had, either. No, praise the Lord; that dear Spirit that came to me in the saloon was present, and said, Pray. I did pray, and though I did not feel any great help, I kept on praying. As soon as I was able to leave my cell I was taken to the police court and remanded back to the cell. I was finally released, and found my way to my brother's house, where every care was given me. While lying in bed the admonishing Spirit never left me, and when I arose the following Sabbath morning I felt that day would decide my fate, and toward evening it came into my head to go to Jerry M'Auley's Mission. I went. The house was packed, and with great difficulty I made my way to the space near the platform. There I saw the apostle to the drunkard and the outcast—that man of God, Jerry M'Auley. He rose, and aimed deep silence told his experience. There was a sincerity about this man that carried conviction with it, and I found myself saying, 'I wonder if God can save me?' I listened to the testimony of twenty-five or thirty persons, every one of whom had been saved from rum, and I made up my mind that I would be saved or die right there. When the invitation was given, I knelt down with a crowd of drunkards. Jerry made the first prayer. Then Mrs. M'Auley prayed fervently for us. Oh, what a conflict was going on for my poor soul! A blessed whisper said, 'Come': the devil said, 'Be careful.' I halted but a moment, and then, with a breaking heart, I said, 'Dear Jesus, can you help me?' Never with mortal tongue can I describe that moment. Although up to that moment my soul had been filled with indescribably gloom, I felt the glorious brightness of the noonday sun shine into my heart. I felt I was a free man. Oh, the precious feeling of safety, of freedom, of resting on Jesus! I felt that Christ will all this brightness and power had come into my life; that, indeed, old things had passed away and all things had become new.

"From that moment till now I have never wanted a drink of whiskey, and I have never seen money enough to make me take one. I promised God that night that if he would take away the appetite for strong drink, I would work for him all my life. He has done his part, and I have been trying to do mine."

Dr. Leuba rightly remarks that there is little doctrinal theology in such an experience, which starts with the absolute need of higher helpers, and ends with the sense that he has helped us. He gives other cases of drunkard's conversions which are purely ethical, containing, as recorded, no theological beliefs whatever. John B. Gough's case, for instance, is practically, says Dr. Leuba, the conversion of an atheist—neither God nor Jesus being mentioned. But in spite of the importance of this type of regeneration, with little or no intellectual readjustment, this writer surely makes it too exclusive. It corresponds to the subjectively centered form of morbid melancholy, of which Bunyan and Alline were example. But we saw in our seventh lecture that there are objective forms of melancholy also, in which the lack of rational meaning of the universe, and of life anyhow, is the burden that weighs upon one—you remember Tolstoy's case. So there are distinct elements in conversion, and their relations to individual lives deserve to be discriminated.

Some persons, for instance, never are, and possibly never under any circumstances could be, converted. Religious ideas cannot become the centre of their spiritual energy. They may be excellent persons, servants of God in practical ways, but they are not children of his kingdom. They are either incapable of imagining the invisible; or else, in the language of devotion, they are life-long subjects of 'barrenness' and 'dryness.' Such inaptitude for religious faith may in some cases be intellectual in its origin. Their religious faculties may be checked in their natural tendency to expand, by beliefs about the world that are inhibitive, the pessimistic and materialistic beliefs, for example, within which so many good souls, who in former times would have freely indulged their religious propensities, find themselves nowadays, as it were, frozen; or the agnostic vetoes upon faith as something weak and shameful, under which so many of us to-day lie cowering, afraid to use our instincts. In many persons such inhibitions are never overcome. To the end of their days they refuse to believe, their personal energy never gets to its religious centre, and the latter remains in active in perpetuity.

In other persons the trouble is profounder. There are men anesthetic on the religious side, deficient in that category of sensibility. Just as a bloodless organism can never, in spite of all its goodwill, attain to the reckless 'animal spirits' enjoyed by those of sanguine temperament; so the nature which is spiritually barren may admire and envy faith in others, but can never compass the enthusiasm and peace which those who are temperamentally qualified for faith enjoy. All this may, however, turn out eventually to have been a matter of temporary inhibition. Even late in life some thaw, some release may take place, some bolt be shot back in the barrenest breast, and the man's hard heart may soften and break into religious feeling. Such cases more than any others suggest the idea that sudden conversion is by miracle. So long as they exist, we must not imagine ourselves to deal with irretrievably fixed classes.

Now there are two forms of mental occurrence in human beings, which lead to a striking difference in the conversion process, a difference to which Professor Starbuck has called attention. You know how it is when you try to recollect a forgotten name. Usually you help the recall by working for it, by mentally running over the places, persons, and things with which the word was connected. But sometimes this effort fails: you feel then as if the harder you tried the less hope there would be, as though the name were jammed, and pressure in its direction only kept it all the more from rising. And then the opposite expedient often succeeds. Give up the effort entirely; think of something altogether different, and in half an hour the lost name comes sauntering into your mind, as Emerson says, as carelessly as if it had never been invited. Some hidden process was started in you by the effort, which went on after the effort ceased, and made the result come as if it came spontaneously.

A certain music teacher, says Dr. Starbuck, says to her pupils after the thing to be done has been clearly pointed out, and unsuccessfully attempted: "Stop trying and it will do itself!"

There is thus a conscious and voluntary way and an involuntary and unconscious way in which mental results may get accomplished; and we find both ways exemplified in the history of conversion, giving us two types, which Starbuck calls the *volitional type* and the *type by self-surrender* respectively.

In the volitional type the regenerative change is unusually gradual, and consists in the building up, piece by piece, of a new set of moral and spiritual habits. But there are always critical points where at which the movement forward seems much more rapid. This psychological fact is abundantly illustrated by Dr. Starbuck. Our education in any practical accomplishment proceeds apparently by jerks and starts, just as the growth of our physical bodies does.

"An athlete…sometimes awakens suddenly to an understanding of the fine points of the game and to a real enjoyment of it, just as the convert awakens to an appreciation of religion. If he keeps on engaging in the sport, there may come a day when all at once the game plays itself through him— when he loses himself in some great contest. In the same way, a musician may suddenly reach a point at which pleasure in the technique of the art entirely falls away, and in some moment of inspiration he becomes the instrument through which music flows. The writer has chanced to hear two different married persons, both of whose wedded lives had been beautiful from the beginning, relate that not until a year or more after marriage did they awake to the full blessedness of married life. So it is with the religious experience of these persons we are studying."

We shall erelong hear still more remarkable illustrations of subconsciously maturing processes eventuating in results of which we suddenly grow conscious. Sir William Hamilton and Professor Laycock of Edinburg were among the first to call attention to this class of effects; but Dr. Carpenter first, unless I am mistaken, introduced the term 'unconscious cerebration,' which has since then been a popular phrase of explanation. The facts are now known to us far more extensively than he could know them, and the adjective 'unconscious,' being for many of them almost certainly a misnomer, is better replaced by the vaguer term 'subconscious' or 'subliminal.'

Of the volitional type of conversion it would be easy to give examples, but they are as a result less interesting than those of the self-surrender type, in which the subconscious effects are more abundant and often startling. I will therefore hurry to the latter, the more so because the difference between the two types is after all not radical. Even in the most voluntarily built-up sort of regeneration there are passages of partial self-surrender interposed; and in the great majority of all cases, when the will has done its uttermost towards brining one close to the complete unification aspired after, it seems that the very last step must be left to other forces and performed without the help of its activity. In other words, self-surrender become then indispensable. "The personal will,' says Dr. Starbuck, "must be given up. In many cases relief persistently refuses to come until the person ceases to resist, or to make an effort in the direction he desire to go."

"I had said I would not give up; but when my will was broken, it was all over," writes one of Starbuck's correspondents. —Another says: "I simply said: 'Lord, I have done all I can; I leave the whole matter with Thee;' and immediately there came to me a great peace."—Another: "All at once it occurred to me that I might be saved, too, if I would stop trying to do it all myself, and follow Jesus: somehow I lost my load."—Another: "I finally ceased to resist, and gave myself up, though it was a hard struggle. Gradually the feeling came over me that I had done my part, and God was willing to do his."—"Lord, Thy will be done; damn or save!" cries John Nelson, exhausted with the anxious struggle to escape damnation; and at that moment his soul was filled with peace.

Dr. Starbuck gives an interesting, and it seems to me a true, account—so far as conceptions so schematic can claim truth at all—of the reasons why self-surrender at the last moment should be so indispensable. To begin with, there are two things in the mind of the candidate for conversion: first, the present incompleteness or wrongness, the 'sin' which he is eager to escape from; and, second, the positive ideal which he longs to compass. Now with most of us the sense of our present wrongness is a far more distinct piece of our consciousness than is the imagination of any positive ideal we can aim at. In a majority of cases, indeed, the 'sin' almost exclusively engrosses the attention, so that conversion is *a process of struggling away from sin rather than of striving towards righteousness.*" A man's conscious wit and will, so far as they strain towards the ideal, are aiming at something only dimly and inaccurately imagined. Yet all the while the forces of mere organic ripening within him are going towards their own prefigured result, and his conscious straining are letting loose subconscious allies behind the scenes, which in their way work towards rearrangement; and the rearrangement towards which all these deeper forces tend is pretty surely definite, and definitely different from what he consciously conceives and determines. It may consequently be actually interfered with (jammed, as it were, like the lost word when we seek too energetically to recall it), by his voluntary efforts slanting from the true direction.

Starbuck seems to put his finger on the root of the matter when he says that to exercise the personal will is still to live in the region where the imperfect self is the thing most sympathized. Where, on the contrary, the subconscious forces take the lead, it is more probably the better self *in posse* which directs the operation. Instead of being clumsily and vaguely aimed at from without, it is then itself the organizing centre. When the must the person do? "He must relax," says Dr. Starbuck, —"that is, he must fall back on the larger Power that makes for righteousness, which has been well ing up in his own being, and let it finish in its own way the work it has begun....The act of yielding, in this point of view, is giving one's self over to the new life, making it the centre of a new personality, and living, from within, the truth of it which had before been viewed objectively."

"Man's extremity is God's opportunity" is the theological way of putting this fact of the need of self-surrender; whilst the physiological way of stating it would be, "Let one do all in one's power, and one's nervous system will do the rest." Both statements acknowledge the same fact.

To state it in terms of our own symbolism: When the new centre of personal energy has been subconsciously incubated so long as to be just ready to open into flower, 'hands off' is the only word for us, it must burst forth unaided!

We have used the vague and abstract language of psychology. But since, in any terms, the crisis described is the growing of our conscious selves upon the mercy of powers which, whatever they may be, are more ideal than we are actually, and make for our redemption, you see why self-surrender has been and always must be regarded as the vital turning-point of the religious life, so far as the religious life is spiritual and no affair of outer works and ritual and sacraments. One may say that the whole development of Christianity in inwardness has consisted in little more than the greater and greater emphasis attached to this crisis of self-surrender.

From Catholicism to Lutheranism, and then to Calvinism; from that to Wesleyanism; and from this, outside of technical Christianity altogether, to pure 'liberalism' or transcendental idealism, whether or not of the mind-cure type, taking in the medieval mystics, the quietists, the pietists, and quakers by the way, we can trace the stages of progress towards the idea of an immediate spiritual help, experienced by the individual in his forlornness and standing in no essential need of doctrinal apparatus or propitiatory machinery.

Psychology and religion are thus in perfect harmony up to this point, since both admit that there are forces seemingly outside of the conscious individual that bring redemption to his life. Nevertheless psychology, defining these forces as 'subconscious,' and speaking of their effects as due to 'incubation,' or 'cerebration,' implies that they do not transcend the individual's personality' and herein she diverges from Christian theology, which insists that they are direct supernatural operations of the Deity. I propose to you that we do not yet consider this divergence final, but leave the question for a while in abeyance—continued inquiry may enable us to get rid of some of the apparent discord.

Revert, then, for a moment more to the psychology of self-surrender.

When you find a man living on the ragged edge of his consciousness, pent in to his sin and want and incompleteness, and consequently inconsolable, and then simply tell him that all is well with him, that he must stop his worry, break with his discontent, and give up his anxiety, you seem to him to come with pure absurdities. The only positive consciousness he has tells him that all is not well, and the better way you offer sounds imply as if you proposed to him to assert cold-blooded falsehoods. 'The will to believe' cannot be stretched as far as that. We can make ourselves more faithful to a belief of which we have the rudiments, but we cannot create a belief out of whole cloth when our perception actively assures us of its opposite. The better mind proposed to us comes in that case in the form of a pure negation of the only mind we have, and we cannot actively will a pure negation.

There are only two ways in which it is possible to get rid of anger, worry, fear, despair, or other undesirable affections. One is that an opposite affection should over- poweringly break over us, and the other is by getting so exhausted with the struggle that we have to stop, —so we drop down, give up, and don't care any longer. Our emotional brain-centres strike work, and we lapse into a temporary apathy. Now there is documentary proof that this state of temporary exhaustion not infrequently forms part of the conversion crisis. So long as the egoistic worry of the sick soul guards the door, the expansive confidence of the soul of faith gains no presence. But let the former faint away, even but for a moment, and the latter can profit by the opportunity, and, having once acquired possession, may retain it. Carlyle's Teufelsdrockh passes from the everlasting No to the everlasting Yes through a 'Centre of Indifference.'

Let me give you a good illustration of this feature in the conversion process. That genuine saint, David Brainerd, describes his own crisis in the following words:—

"One morning, while I was walking in a solitary place as usual, I at once saw that all my contrivances and projects to effect or procure deliverance and salvation for myself were utterly in vain; I was brought quite to a stand, as finding myself totally lost. I saw that it was forever impossible for me to do anything towards helping or delivering myself, that I had made all the please I ever could have made to all eternity; and that all my pleas were vain, for I saw that self-interest had led me to pray, and that I had never once prayed from any respect to the glory of God. I saw that there was no necessary connection between my prayers and the bestowment of divine mercy; that they laid not the least obligation upon God to bestow this grace upon me; and that there was no more virtue or goodness in them than there would be in my paddling with my hand in the water. I saw that I had been heaping up my devotions before God, fasting, praying, etc., pretending, and indeed really thinking sometimes that I was aiming at the glory of God; whereas I never once truly intended it, but only my own happiness. I saw that as I had never done anything for God, I had no claim on anything form him but perdition, on account of my hypocrisy and mockery. When I saw evidently that I had regard to nothing but self-interest, then my duties appeared a vile mockery and a continual course of lies, for the whole as nothing but self-worship, and a horrid abuse of God.

"I continued, as I remember, in this state of mind, from Friday morning till the Sabbath evening following (July 12, 1739), when I was walking again in the same solitary place. Here, in a mournful melancholy state I was attempting to pray; but found no heart to engage in that or any other duty; my former concern, exercise, and religious affections were now gone. I thought that the Spirit of God had quite left me; but still was not distressed; yet disconsolate, as if there was nothing in heaven or earth could make me happy. Having been thus endeavoring to pray—though, as I thought, very stupid and senseless—for near half an hour; then, as I was walking in a thick grove, unspeakable glory seemed to open to the apprehension of my soul. I do not mean any external brightness, nor any imagination of a body of light, but it was a new inward apprehension or view that I had of God such as I never had before, nor anything which had the least resemblance to it. I had no particular apprehension of any one person in the Trinity, either the Father, the Son, or the Holy Ghost; but it appeared to be Divine glory. My soul rejoiced with joy unspeakable, to see such a God, such a glorious Divine Being; and I was inwardly pleased and satisfied that he should be God over all for ever and ever. My soul was so captivated and delighted with the excellency of God that I was even swallowed up in him; at least to that degree that I had no thought about my own salvation, and scarce reflected that there was such a creature as myself. I continued in this state of inward joy, peace, and astonishing, till near dark without any sensible abatement; and then began to think and examine what I had seen; and felt sweetly composed in my mind all the evening following. I felt myself in a new world, and everything about me appeared with a different aspect from what it was wont to do. At this time, the way of salvation opened to me with such infinite wisdom, suitableness, and excellency, that I wondered I should ever think of any other way of salvation; was amazed that I had not dropped my own contrivances, and complied with this lovely, blessed, and excellent way before. If I could have been saved by my own duties or any other way that I had formerly contrived, my whole soul would now have refused it. I wondered that all the world did not see and comply with this way of salvation, entirely by the righteousness of Christ."

I have italicized the passage which records the exhaustion of the anxious emotion hitherto habitual. In a large proportion, perhaps the majority of reports, the writers speak as if the exhaustion of the lower and the entrance of the higher emotion were simultaneous, yet often again they speak as if the higher actively drove the lower out. This is undoubtedly true in a great many instances, as we shall presently see. But often there seems little doubt that both conditions—subconscious ripening of the one affection and exhaustion of the other—must simultaneously have conspired, in order to produce the result.

T.W.B., a covert of Nettleton's, being brought to an acute paroxysm of conviction of sin, ate nothing all day, locked himself in his room in the evening in complete despair, crying aloud, "How long, O Lord, how long?" "After repeating this and similar language," he says, "several times, I seemed to sink away into a state of insensibility. When I came to myself again I was on my knees, praying not for myself but for others. I felt submission to the will of God, willing that he should do with me as should seem good in his sight. My concern seemed all lost in concern for others."

Our great American revivalist Finney writes: "I said to myself: 'What is this? I must have grieved the Holy Ghost entirely away. I have lost all my conviction. I have not a particle of concern about my soul; and it must be that the Spirit has left me.' 'Why!' thought I, 'I never was so far from being concerned about my own salvation in my life.' ... I tried to recall my convictions, to get back again the load of sin under which I had been laboring. I tried in vain to make myself anxious. I was so quiet and peaceful that I tried to feel concerned about that, lest it should be the result of my having grieved the Spirit away."

But beyond all question there are persons in whom, quite independently of any exhaustion in the Subject's capacity for feeling, or even in the absence of any acute previous feeling, the higher condition, having reached the due degree of energy, bursts through all barriers and sweeps in like a sudden flood. These are the most striking and memorable cases, the cases of instantaneous conversion to which the conception of divine grace has been most peculiarly attached. I have given one of them at length—the case of Mr. Bradley.

Continuing with the subject of Conversion, considering at first those striking instantaneous instances of which Saint Paul's is the most eminent, and in which, often amid tremendous emotional excitement or perturbation of the sense, a complete division is established in the twinkling of an eye between the old life and the new. Conversion of this type is an important phase of religious experience, owing to the part which it has played in Protestant theology, and it behooves us to study it conscientiously on that account.

I think I had better cite two or three of these cases before proceeding to a more generalized account. One must know concrete instances first; for, as Professor Agassiz used to say, one can see no further into a generalization than just so far as one's previous acquaintance with particulars enables one to take it in. I will go back, then, to the case of our friend Henry Alline, and quote his report of the 26th of March, 1775, on which his poor divided mood became unified for good.

"AS I was about sunset wandering in the fields lamenting my miserable lost and undone condition, and almost ready to sink under my burden, I thought I was in such a miserable case as never any man was before. I returned to the house, and when I got to the door, just as I was stepping off the threshold, the following impressions came into my mind like powerful but small stifle voice. You have been seeking, praying, reforming, laboring, reading, hearing, and meditating, and what have you done by it towards your salvation? Are you any nearer to conversion now then when you first began? Are you any more prepared for heaven, or fitter to appear before the impartial bar of God, than when you first began to seek?

"It brought such conviction on me that I was obliged to say that I did not think I was one step nearer than at first, but as much condemned, as much exposed, and as miserable as before. I cried out within myself, O Lord God, I am lost, and if thou, O Lord, dost not find out some new way, I know nothing of, I shall never be saved, for the ways and methods I have prescribed to myself have all filed me, and I am willing they should fail. O Lord, have mercy! O Lord, have mercy!

"These discoveries continued until I went into the house and sat down. After I sat down, being all in confusion, like a drowning man that was just giving up to sink, and almost in an agony, I turned very suddenly round in my chair, and seeing part of an old Bible lying on one of the chairs, I caught hold of it in great hate; and opening it without any premeditation, cast my eyes on the 38th Psalm, which was the first time I ever saw the word of God: it took hold of me with such power that it seemed to go through my whole soul, so that it seemed as if God was praying in, with, and for me. About this time my father called the family to attend prayers; I attended, but paid no regard to what he said in his prayer, but continued praying in those words of the Psalm. Oh, help me, help me! Cried I, thou Redeemer of souls, and save me, or I am gone forever; thou canst this night, if thou pleasest, with one drop of thy blood atone for my sins, and appease the wrath of an angry God. At that instant of time when I gave all up to him to do with me as he pleased, and was willing that God should rule over me at his pleasure, redeeming love broke into my soul with repeated scriptures, with such power that my whole soul seemed to be melted down with love; the burden of guilt and condemnation was gone, darkness was expelled, my heart humbled and filled with gratitude, and my whole soul, that was a few minutes ago groaning under mountains of death, and crying to an unknown God for help, was no filled with immortal love, soaring on the wings of faith, freed from the chains of death and darkness, and crying out, My Lord and my God; thou art my rock and my fortress, my shield and my high tower, my life, my joy, my present and my everlasting portion. Looking up, I thought I saw that same light [he had on more than one previous occasion seen subjectively a bright blaze of light], though it appeared different; and as soon as I saw it, the design was opened to me, according to his promise, and I was obliged to cry out: Enough, enough, O blessed God! The work of conversion, the change, and the manifestation of it are no more disputable than that light which I see, or anything that ever I saw.

"In the midst of all my joys, in less than half an hour after my soul was set at liberty, the Lord discovered to me my labor in the ministry and call to preach the gospel. I cried out, Amen, Lord, I'll go; send me, send me, I spent the greatest part of the night in ecstasies of joy, praising and adoring the Ancient of Days for his free and unbounded grace. After I had been so long in this transport and heavenly frame that my nature seemed to require sleep, I thought to close my eyes for a few moments; then the devil stepped in, and told me that if I went to sleep, I should lose it all, and when I should awake in the morning I would find it to be nothing but a fancy and delusion. I immediately cried out, O Lord God, if I am deceived, undeceive me.

"I then closed my eyes for a few minutes, and seemed to be refreshed with sleep; and when I awoke, the first inquiry was, Where is my God? And in an instant of time, my soul seemed awake in and with God, and surrounded by the arms of everlasting love. About sunrise I arose with joy and to relate to my parents what God had done for my soul, and declared to them the miracle of God's unbounded grace. I took a Bible to show them the words that were impressed by God on my soul the evening before; but when I came to open the Bible, it appeared all new to me.

"I so longed to be useful in the cause of Christ, in preaching the gospel, that it seemed as if I could not rest any longer, but go I must and tell the wonders of redeeming love. I lost all taste for carnal pleasures, and carnal company, and was enabled to forsake them."

Young Mr. Alline, after the briefest of delays, and with no book-learning but his Bible, and no teaching save that of his own experience, became a Christian minister, and thenceforward his life was fit to rank, for its austerity and single-mindedness, with that of the most devoted saints. But happy as he became in his strenuous way, he never got his taste for even the most innocent carnal pleasures back. We must class him, like Bunyan and Tolstoy, amongst those upon whose soul the iron of melancholy left a permanent imprint. His redemption was into another universe than this mere natural world, and life remained for him a sad and patient trial. Years later we can find him making such an entry as this in his diary: "On Wednesday the 12th I preached at a wedding, and had the happiness thereby to be means of excluding carnal mirth."

The next case I will give is that of a correspondent of Professor Leuba, printed in the latter's article, already cited, in vol. vi. of the American Journal of Psychology. This subject was an Oxford graduate, the son of a clergyman, and the story resembles in many points the classic case of Colonel Gardiner, which everybody may be supposed to know. Here it is, somewhat abridged:—

"Between the period of leaving Oxford and my conversion I never darkened the door of my father's church, although I lived with him for eight years, making what money I wanted by journalism, and spending it in high carousal with any one who would sit with me and rink it away. So I lived, sometimes drunk for a week together, and then a terrible repentance, and would not touch a drop for a whole month.

"In all this period, that is, up to thirty-three years of age, I never had a desire to reform on religious grounds. But all my pangs were due to some terrible remorse I used to fell after a heavy carousal, the remorse taking the shape of regret after my folly in wasting my life in such a way-a man of superior talents and education. This terrible remorse turned me grapy in one night, and whenever it came upon me I was perceptibly grayer the next morning. What I suffered in this way is beyond the expression of words. It was hell-fire in all its most dreadful tortures. Often did I vow that if I got over 'this time' I would reform. Alas, in about three days I fully recovered, and was as happy as ever. So, it went on for years, but, with a physique like rhinoceros, I always recovered, and as long as I let drink alone, no man was as capable of enjoying life as I was.

"I was converted in my own bedroom in my father's rectory house at precisely three o'clock in the afternoon of a hot July day (July 13, 1886). I was in perfect health, having been off from the drink for nearly a month. I was in no way troubled about my soul. In fact, God was not in my thoughts that day. A young lady friend sent me a copy of Professor Drummond's Natural Law in the Spiritual World, asking me my opinion of it as a literary work only. Being proud of my critical talents and wishing to enhance myself in my new friend's esteem, I took the book to my bedroom for quiet, intending to give it a thorough study, and then write her what I thought of it. It was here that God met me face to face, and I shall never forget the meeting. 'He that hat the Son hath life eternal he that hath not the Son hath not life.' I had read this scores of times before, but this made all the difference. I was now in God's presence and my attention was absolutely 'soldered' on to this verse, and I was not allowed to proceed with the book till I had fairly considered what these words really involved. Only then was I allowed to proceed, feeling all the while that there was another being in my bedroom, though not seen by me. The stillness was very marvelous, and I felt supremely happy. It was most unquestionably shown me, in one second of time, that I had never touched the Eternal: and that if I died then, I must inevitably be lost. I was undone. I knew it as well as I now know I am saved. The spirit of God showed it me in ineffable love; there was no terror in it; I felt God's love so powerfully upon me that only a mighty sorrow crept over me that I had lost all through my own folly and what was I to do? What could I do? I did not repent even; God never asked me to repent. All I felt was 'I am undone,' and God cannot help it, although he loves me. No fault on the part of the Almighty. All the time I was supremely happy: I felt like a little child before his father. I had done wrong, but my Father did not scold me, but loved me most wondrously. Still my doom was sealed. I was lost to a certainty, and being naturally of a brave disposition I did not quail under it, but deep sorrow for the past, mixed with regret for what I had lost, took hold upon me, and my soul thrilled within me to think it was all over. Then there crept in upon me so gently, so lovingly, so unmistakably a way of escape, and what was it after all? The old, old story over again, told in the simplest way: 'There is no name under heaven whereby ye can be saved except that of the Lord Jesus Christ.' No words were spoken to me; my soul seemed to see my Saviour in the spirit, and from that hour to hits, nearly nine years now, there has never been in my life one doubt that the Lord Jesus Christ and God the Father both worked upon me that afternoon in July, both differently, and both in the most perfect love conceivable, and I rejoiced there and then in a conversion so astounding that the whole village heard of it in less than twenty-four hours.

"But a time of trouble was yet to come. The day after my conversion I went into the hay-field to lend a hand with the harvest, and not having made any promise to God to abstain or drink in moderation only, I took too much and came home drunk. My poor sister was heartbroken; and I felt ashamed of myself and got to my bedroom at once, where she followed me, weeping copiously. She said I had been converted and fallen away instantly. But although I was qu9te full of drink (not muddled, however), I knew that God's work begun in me was not going to be wasted. About midday I made on my knees the first prayer before God for twenty years. I did not ask to be forgiven; I felt that was no good, for I would be sure to fall again. Well, what did I do? I committed myself to him in the profoundest belief that my individuality was going to be destroyed, that he would take all from me, and I was willing. In such surrender lies the secret of a holy life. From that hour drink has had no terrors for me: I never touch it, never want it. The same thing occurred with my pipe: after being a regular smoker from my twelfth year the desire for it went at one, and ha never returned. So with every known sin, the deliverance in each case being permanent and complete. I have had no temptation since conversion, God seemingly having shut out Satan from that course with me. He gets a free hand in other ways, but never on sins of the flesh. Since I gave up to God all ownership in my own life, he has guided me in a thousand ways, and has opened my path in a way almost incredible to those who do not enjoy the blessing of a truly surrendered life."

So much for our graduate of Oxford, in whom you notice the complete abolition of an ancient appetite as one of the conversion's fruits.

The most curious record of sudden conversion with which I am acquainted is that of M. Alphonse Ratisbonne, a freethinking French Jew, to Catholicism, at Rome in 1842. In a letter to a clerical friend, written a few months later, the convert gives a palpitating account of the circumstances. The predisposing conditions appear to have been slight. He had an elder brother who had been converted and was a Catholic priest. He was himself irreligious, and nourished an antipathy to the apostate brother and generally to his 'cloth.' Finding himself at Rome in his twenty-ninth year, he fell in with a French gentleman who tried to make a proselyte of him, but who succeeded no farther after two or three conversations than to get him to hang (half jocosely) a religious medal round his neck, and to accept and read a copy of a short prayer to the Virgin. M. Ratisbonne represents his own part in the conversations as having been of light and chaffing order; but he notes the fact that for some days e was unable to banish the words of the prayer from his mind, and that the night before the crisis he had a sort of nightmare, in the imagery of which a black cross with no Christ upon it figured. Nevertheless, until noon of the next day he was free in mind and spend the time in trivial conversations. I now give his own words.

If at hits time any one had accosted me, saying: "Alphonse, in a quarter of an hour you shall be adoring Jesus Christ as your God and Savior; you shall like prostrate with your face upon the ground in a humble church; you shall be smiting your breast at the foot of a priest; you shall pass the carnival in a college of Jesuits to prepare yourself to receive baptism, ready to give your life for the Catholic faith; you shall renounce the world and its pomps and pleasures; renounce your fortune, your hopes, and if need be, your betrothed; the affections of your family, the esteem of your friends, and your attachment to the Jewish people; you shall have no other aspiration than to follow Christ and bear his cross till death;'—if, I say, a prophet had come to me with such a prediction, I should have judged that only one person could more mad than he,—whosoever, namely, might believe in the possibility of such senseless folly becoming true. And yet that folly is at present my only wisdom, my sole happiness.

"Coming out of the café I met the carriage of Monsieru B. [the proselyting friend]. He stopped and invited me in for a drive, but first asked me to wait for a few minutes whist he attended to some duty at the church of San Andrea delle Fratte. Instead of waiting in the carriage, I entered the church myself to look at it. The church of San Andrea was poor, small, and empty; I believe that I found myself there almost alone. No work of art attracted my attention; and I passed my eyes mechanically over its interior without being arrested by any particular thought. I can only remember an entirely black dog which went trotting and turning before me as I mused. In an instant the dog had disappeared, the whole church has vanished, I no longer saw anything, ... or more truly I saw, O my God, one thing alone.

"Heavens, how can I speak of it? Oh no! human words cannot attain to expressing the inexpressible. Any description however sublime it might be, could be but a profanation of the unspeakable truth.

"I was there prostrate on the ground, bathed in my tears with my heart beside itself, when M. B> called me back to life I could not reply to the questions which followed from him one upon the other. But finally I took the medal which I had on my breast, and with all effusion of my soul I kissed the image of the Virgin, radiant with grace, which it bore. Oh, indeed, it was She! It was indeed She! [What he had seen had been a vision of the Virgin.]

"I did not know where I was: I did not know whether I was Alphonse or another. I only felt myself changed and believed myself another me; I looked for myself in myself and did not find myself. In the bottom of my soul I felt an explosion of the most ardent joy; I could not speak; I had no wish to reveal what had happened. But I felt something solemn and sacred within me which made me ask for a priest. I was led to one; and there, alone, after he had given me the positive order, I spoke as best I could, kneeling, and with my heart still trembling. I could give no account to myself of the truth of which I had acquired a knowledge and a faith. All that I can say is that in an instant the badge had fallen from my eyes; and not one bandage only, but the whole manifold of bandages I which I had been brought up. One after another they rapidly disappeared, even as the mud and ice disappear under the rays of the burning sun.

"I came out as from a sepulcher, from an abyss of darkness; and I was living, perfectly living. But I wept, for at the bottom of that gulf I saw the extreme of misery from which I had been saved by an infinite mercy; and I shuddered at the sight of my iniquities, stupefied, melted, overwhelmed with wonder and with gratitude. You may ask me how I came to this new insight, for truly I had never opened a book of religion nor even read a single page of the Bible, and the dogma of original sin is either entirely denied or forgotten by the Hebrews of to-day, so that I had thought so little about it that I doubted whether I ever knew its name. But how came I, then, to this perception of it? I can answer nothing save this, that on entering that church I was in darkness altogether, and on coming out of it I saw the fullness of the light. I can explain the change no better than by the smiles of a profound sleep or the analogy of one born blind who should suddenly open his eyes to the day. He sees, but cannot define the light which bathes him and by means of which he sees the objects which excite his wonder. If we cannot explain physical light, how can we explain the light which is the truth itself? And I think I remain plain the light which is the truth itself? And I think I remain within the limits of veracity when I say that without having any knowledge of the letter of religious doctrine, I know intuitively perceived its sense and spirit. Better than if I saw them, I felt those hidden things; I felt them by the inexplicable effects they produced in me. It all happened in my interior mind; and those impressions, more rapid than thought, shook my soul, revolved and turned it, as it were, in another direction, towards other aims, by other paths. I expressed myself badly. Bu do you wish, Lord, that I should inclose in poor and barren words sentiments which the heart alone can understand?"

I might multiply cases almost indefinitely, but these will suffice to show you how real, definite, and memorable an event a sudden conversion may be to him who has the experience. Throughout the height of it he undoubtedly seems to himself a passive spectator or under-goer of an astounding process performed upon him from above. There is too much evidence of this for any doubt of it to be possible. Theology, combining this fact with the doctrines of election and grace, has concluded that the spirit of God is with us at these dramatic moments in a peculiarly miraculous way, unlike what happens at any other juncture of our lives. At that moment, it believes, an absolutely new nature is breathed into us, and we become partakers of the very substance of the Deity.

That the conversion should be instantaneous seems called for on this view, and the Moravian Protestants appear to have been the first to see this logical consequence. The Methodists soon followed suit, practically if not dogmatically, and a short time ere his death, John Wesley wrote:

"In London alone I found 652 members of our Society who were exceeding clear in their experience, and whose testimony I could see no reason to doubt. And every one of these (without a single exception) has declared that his deliverance from sin was instantaneous; that the change was wrought in a moment. Had half of these, or one third, or one in twenty, declared it was gradually wrought in them, I should have believed this, with regard to them, and thought that some were gradually sanctified and some instantaneously. But as I have not found, I so long a space of time, a single person speaking thus, I cannot be believe that sanctification is commonly, if not always, an instantaneous work." Tyerman's Life of Wesley.

All this while the more usual sects of Protestantism have set no such store by instantaneous conversion. For them as for the Catholic Church, Christ's blood, the sacraments, and the individual's ordinary religious duties are practically supposed to suffice to his salvation, even though no acute crisis of self-despair and surrender followed by relief should be experienced. For Methodism, on the contrary, unless there have been a crisis of this sort, salvation is only offered, not effectively received, and Christ's sacrifice in so far forth is incomplete. Methodism surely here follows, if not the healthier-minded, yet on the whole the profounder spiritual instinct. The individual models which it has set up as typical and wroth of imitation are not only the more interesting dramatically, but psychologically they have been the more complete.

In the fully evolved Revivalism of Great Britain and America we have, so to speak, the codified and stereotyped procedure to which this way of thinking has led. In spite of the unquestionable fact that saints of the once-born type exist, hat there may be gradual growth in holiness without a cataclysm; in spite of the obvious leakage (as one my say) of much more natural goodness into the scheme of salvation; revivalism has always assumed that only its own type of religious experience can be perfect; you must first be nailed on the cross of natural despair and agony, and then in the twining of an eye be miraculously released.

It is natural that those who personally have traversed such an experience should carry away a feeling of its being a miracle rather than natural process. Voices are often heard, lights seen, or visions witnessed; automatic motor phenomena occur; and it always seems, after the surrender of the personal will, as if an extraneous higher power had flooded in and taken possession. Moreover the sense of renovation, safety, cleanness, rightness, can be so marvelous and jubilant as well to warrant one's belief in a radically new substantial nature.

"Conversion," writes the New England Puritan, Joseph Aleline, "is not the putting in a patch of holiness; but with the true convert holiness is woven into all his powers, principles, and practice. The sincere Christian is quite a new fabric, from the foundation to the top-stone. He is a new man, a new creature."

And Jonathan Edwards says in the same strain: "Those gracious influences which are the effects of the Spirit of God are altogether supernatural-are quite different from anything that unregenerate men experience. They are what no improvement, or composition of natural qualifications or principles will ever produce; because they not only differ from what is natural, and from everything that natural men experience in degree and circumstances, but also in kind, and are of a nature far more excellent. From hence it follows that in gracious affections there are [also] new perceptions and sensations entirely different in their nature and kind from anything experienced by the [same] saints before they were sanctified....The conceptions which the saints have of the loveliness of God, and that kind of delight which they experience in it, are quite peculiar, and entirely different from anything which a natural man can possess, or of which he can form any proper notion."

And that such a glorious transformation as this ought of necessity to be preceded by despair is shown by Edwards in another passage.

"Surely it cannot be unreasonable," he says, "that before God delivers us from a state of sin and liability to everlasting owe, he should give us some considerable sense of the evil from which he delivers us, in order that we may know and feel the importance of salvation, and be enabled to appreciate the value of what God is pleased to do for us. As those who are saved are successively in two extremely different states-first in a state of condemnation and then in a state of justification and blessedness-and as God, in the salvation of men, deals with them as rational and intelligent creatures, it appears agreeable this wisdom, that those who are saved should be made sensible for their Being, in those two different states. In the first place, that they should be made sensible of their state of condemnation; and afterwards, of their state of deliverance and happiness."

Such quotations express sufficiently well for our purpose the doctrinal interpretation of these charges. Whatever part suggestion and imitation may have played in producing them in men and women in excited assemblies, they have at any rate been in countless individual instances an original and unborrowed experience. Were we writing the story of the mind from the purely natural history point of view, with no religious interest whatever, we should still have to write down man's liability to sudden and complete conversion as one of this most curious peculiarities.

What, now, must we ourselves think of this question? Is an instantaneous conversion a miracle in which God is present as he is present in no change of heart less strikingly abrupt? Are there two classes of human beings, even among the apparently regenerate, of which the one class really partakes of Christ's nature while the other merely seems to do so? Or, on the contrary, may the whole phenomenon of regeneration, even in these startling instantaneous examples, possibly be a strictly natural process, divine in its fruits, of course, but in one case more and in another less so, and neither more nor less divine in its mere causation and mechanism than any other process, high or low, of man's interior life?

Before proceeding to answer this question, I must ask you to listen to some more psychological remarks. At our last lecture, I explained the shifting of men's centres of personal energy with them and the lightning up of new crises of emotion. I explained the phenomena as partly due to explicitly conscious processes of thought and will, but as due largely also to the subconscious incubation and maturing of motives deposited by the experiences of life. When ripe, the results hatch out, or burst into flower. I have now to speak of the subconscious region, in which such processes of flowering may occur, in a somewhat less vague way. I only regret that my limits of time here force me to be so short.

The expression 'field of consciousness' has but recently came into vogue in the psychology books. Until quite lately the unit of mental life which figured most was the single 'idea,' supposed to be a definitely outlined thing. But at present psychologists are tending first, to admit that the actual unit is more probably the total mental state, the entire wave of consciousness or field of objects present to the though at any time; and, second, to see that it is impossible to outline this wave, this field, with any definiteness.

As our mental fields succeed one another, each has its centre of interest, around which the objects of which we are less and less attentively conscious fade to a margin so faint that its limits are unassignable. Some fields are narrow fields and some are wide fields. Usually when we have a wide field we rejoice, for we then see masses of truth together, and often get glimpses of relations which we divine rather than see, for they shoot beyond the filed into still remoter regions of objectivity, regions which we seem rather to be about to perceive than to perceive actually. At other times, of drowsiness, illness, or fatigue, our fields may narrow almost to a point, and we find ourselves correspondingly oppressed and contracted.

Different individuals present constitutional differences in this matter of width of field. Your great organizing geniuses are men with habitually vast fields of mental vision, in which a whole programmed of future operations will appear dotted out at once, the rays shooting far ahead into definite directions of advance. In common people there is never this magnificent inclusive view of a topic. They stumble along, feeling their way, as it were, from point to point, and often stop entirely. In certain diseased conditions consciousness is a mere spark, without memory of the past or thought of the future, and with the present narrowed down to some one simple emotion or sensation of the body.

The important fact which this 'field' formula commemorates is the indetermination of the margin. Inattentively realized as is the matter which the margin contains, it is nevertheless there, and helps both to guide our behavior and to determine the next movement of our attention. In lies around us like a 'magnetic field,' inside of which our centre of energy turns like a compass-needle, as the present phase of consciousness alters into its successor. Our whole past store of memories floats beyond this margin, ready at a touch to come in; and the entire mass of residual powers, impulses, and knowledge that constitutes our empirical self stretches continuously beyond it. So vaguely drawn are the outlines between what is actual and what is only potential at any moment of our conscious life, that it is always hard to say of certain mental elements whether we are conscious of them or not.

The ordinary psychology, admitting fully the difficulty of tracing the marginal outlines, has nevertheless taken for granted, first, that all the consciousness the person now has, be the same focal or marginal, inattentive or attentive, is there in the 'field' of the moment, all dim and impossible to assign as the latter's outline may be; and, second, that what is absolutely extra-marginal is absolutely non-existent, and cannot be a fact of consciousness at all.

And having reached this point, I must now ask you to recall what I said in my last lecture about the subconscious life. I said, as you may recollect, that those who first laid stress upon these phenomena could not know the facts as we now know them. My first duty now is to tell you what I meant by such a statement.

I cannot but think that the most important step forward that has occurred in psychology since I have been a student of that science is the discovery, first made in 1886, that, in certain subjects at least, there is not only the consciousness of the ordinary field, with its usual centre and margin, but an addition thereto in the shape of a set of memories, thoughts, and feelings which are extra-marginal and outside of the primary consciousness altogether, but yet must be classed as conscious facts of some sort, able to reveal their presence by unmistakable signs. I call this the most important step forward because, unlike the other advances which psychology has made, this discovery has revealed to us an entirely unsuspected peculiarity in the constitution of human nature. No other step forward which psychology as made can proffer any such claim as this.

In particular this discovery of a consciousness existing beyond the field, or subliminally as Mr. Myers terms it, casts light on many phenomena of religious biography. This is why I have to advert to it now, although it is naturally impossible for me in this place to give you any account of the evidence on which the admission of such a consciousness is based. You will find it set forth in many recent books, Binet's Alterations of Personality being perhaps as good a one as any to recommend.

The human material on which the demonstration has been made so far been rather limited and, in part at least, eccentric, consisting of unusually suggestible hypnotic subjects, and of hysteric patients. Yet the elementary mechanisms of our life are presumably so uniform that what is shown to be true in a marked degree of some persons is probably true in some degree of all, and may in a few be true in an extraordinarily high degree.

The most important consequence of having a strongly developed ultra-marginal life of this sort is that one's ordinary fields of consciousness are liable to incursions from it of which the subject does not guess the source, and which, therefore, take for him the form of unaccountable impulses to act, or inhibitions of action, of obsessive ideas, or even of hallucinations of sight or hearing. The impulses may take the direction of automatic speech or writing, the meaning of which the subject himself may not understand even While he utters it; and generalizing this phenonmenon, Mr. Myers has given the name of automation, sensory or motor, emotional or intellectual, to this whole sphere of effects, due to 'uprushes' tinot the ordinary consciousness of energies originating in the subliminal parts of the mind.

The simplest instance of an automatism is the phenomenon of post-hypnotic suggestion , so-called. You give to a hypnotized subject, adequately susceptible, an order to perform some designated act-usual or eccentric, it makes no difference-after he wakes from his hypnotic sleep. Punctually, when the signal comes or the time elapses upon which you have told him that act must ensue, he performs it; —but in so doing he has no recollection of your suggestion, and he always trumps up an improvised pretext for his behavior if the act be of an eccentric kind. It may even be suggested to a subject to have a vision or to hear a voice at a certain interval after waking, and when the time comes the vision is seen or the voice heard, with no inkling on the subject's part of its source. In the wonderful explorations by Binet, Janet, Breuer, Freud, Mason, Prince, and others, of the subliminal consciousness of patients with hysteria. We have revealed to us whole systems of underground life, in the shape of memories of a painful sort which lead a parasitic existence, buried outside of the primary fields of consciousness, and making irruptions thereinto with hallucinations, pains, convulsions, paralyses of feeling and of motion, and the whole procession of symptoms of hysteric disease of body and of mind. Alter or abolish by suggestion these subconscious memories and the patient immediately gets well. His symptoms were automatisms, in Mr. Myers' sense of the word. These clinical records sound like fairy-tales when one first reads them, yet it is impossible to doubt their accuracy; and, the path having been once opened by these first observers, similar observations have been made elsewhere. They throw, as I said, a wholly new light upon our natural constitution.

And it seems to me that they make a farther step inevitable. Interpreting the unknown after the analogy of the known, it seems to me that hereafter, wherever we meet with a phenomenon of automatism, be it motor impulse, or obsessive idea, or unaccountable caprice, or delusion, or hallucination, we are bound first of all to make search whether it be not an explosion, into the fields of ordinary consciousness, of ideas elaborated outside of those fields in subliminal regions of the mind. We should look, therefore, for its source in the Subject's subconscious life. In the hypnotic cases, we ourselves create the source by our suggestions, so we know it directly. In the hysterics cases, the lost memories which are the source have to be extracted from the patient's Subliminal by a number of ingenious methods, for an account of which you must consult the books. In other pathological cases, insane delusions, for example, or psychopathic obsessions, the source is yet to seek, but by analogy it also should be in subliminal regions which improvements in our methods may yet conceivably put on tap. There lies the mechanism logically to be assumed,—but the assumption involves a vast program of work to be done in the way of verification, in which the religious experiences of man must play their part.

And thus I return to our own specific subject of instantaneous conversions. You remember the cases of Alline, Bradley, Brainerd, and the graduate of Oxford converted at three in the afternoon. Similar occurrences abound, some with and some without luminous visions, all with a sense of astonished happiness, and of being wrought on by a higher control. If, abstracting altogether from the question of their value for the future spiritual life of the individual, we take them on their psychological side exclusively, so many peculiarities in them remind us of what we find outside of conversion that we are tempted to class them along with other automatisms, and to suspect that what makes the difference between a sudden and a gradual convert is not necessarily the presence of divine miracle in the case of one and of something less divine in that of the other, but rather a simple psychological peculiarity, the fact, namely, that in the recipient of the more instantaneous grace we have one of those Subjects who are in possession of a large region in which mental work can go on subliminally, and from which invasive experiences, abruptly upsetting the equilibrium of the primary consciousness, may come.

I do not see why Methodists need object to such a view. Pray go back and recollect one of the conclusions to which I sought to lead you in my very first lecture. You may remember how I there argued against the notion that the worth of a thing can be decided by its origin. Our spiritual judgment, I said, our opinion of the significance and value of a human event or condition, must be decided on empirical grounds exclusively. If the fruits for life of the state of conversion are good, we ought to idealize and venerate it, even though it be a piece of natural psychology; if not, we ought to make short work with it, no matter what supernatural being may have infused it.

Well, how is it with these fruits? If we except the class of preeminent saints of whom the names illumine history, and consider only the usual run of 'saints,' the shop keeping church-members and ordinary youthful or middle-aged recipients of instantaneous conversion, whether at revivals or in the spontaneous course of Methodist growth, you will probably agree that no splendor worthy of a wholly supernatural creature fulgurates from them, or sets them apart from the mortals who have never experienced that favor. Were it true that a suddenly converted man such is, as Edwards says, of an entirely different kind from a natural man, partaking as he does directly of Christ's substance, there surely ought to be some exquisite class-mark, some distinctive radiance attaching even to the lowliest specimen of this genus, to which no one of us could remain insensible, and which, so far as it went, would prove him more excellent than never the most highly gifted among mere natural men. But notoriously there is no such radiance. Converted men as a class are indistinguishable from natural men; some natural men even excel some converted men in their fruits; and no one ignorant of doctrinal theology could guess by mere every-day inspection of the 'accidents' of the two groups of persons before him, that their substance differed as much as divine differs from human substance.

The believers in the non-natural character of sudden conversion have had practically to admit that there is no unmistakable class-mark distinctive of all true converts. The super-normal incidents, such as voices and visions and overpowering impressions of the meaning of suddenly presented scripture texts, the melting emotions and tumultuous affections connected with the crisis of change, may all come by way of nature, or worse still, be counterfeited by Satan. The real witness of the spirit to the second birth is to be found only in the disposition of the genuine child of God, the permanently patient heart, the love of self eradicated. And this, it has to be admitted, is also found in those who pass no crisis, and may even be found outside of Christianity altogether.

Throughout Jonathan Edward's admirably rich and delicate description of the supernaturally infused condition, in this Treatise on Religious Affections, there is not one decisive trait, not one mark, that unmistakably parts it off from what may possibly be only an exceptionally high degree of natural goodness. In fact, one could hardly read a clearer argument than this book unwittingly offers in favor of the thesis that no chasm exists between the orders of human excellence, but that here as elsewhere, nature shows continuous differences, and generation and regeneration are matters of degree.

All which denial of two objective classes of human beings separated by a chasm must not leave us blind to the extraordinary momentousness of the fact of his conversion to the individual himself who gets converted. There are higher and lower limits of possibility set to each personal life. If a flood but goes above one's head, its absolute elevation becomes a matter of small importance; and when we touch our own upper limit and live in our own highest centre of energy, we may call ourselves saved, no matter how much higher some one else's centre may be. A small man's salvation will always be a great salvation and the greatest of all facts for him, and we should remember this when the fruits of our ordinary evangelisms look discouraging. Who knows how much less ideal still the lives of these spiritual grubs and earthworms, these Crumps and Stigginses, might have been, if such poor grace as they have received had never touched them at all?

If we roughly arrange human beings in classes, each class standing for a grade of spiritual excellence, I believe we shall find natural men and converts both sudden and gradual in all the classes. The forms which regenerative change effects have, then, no general spiritual significance, but only a psychological significance. We have seen how Starbuck's laborious statistical studies tend to assimilate conversions to ordinary spiritual growth. Another American psychologist, Prof. George A. Coe, has analyzed the cases of seventy-seven converts or ex-candidates for conversion, known to him, and the results strikingly confirm the view that sudden conversion is connected wit the possession of an active subliminal self. Examining this subjects with reference to their hypnotic sensibility and to such automatisms as hynagogic hallucinations, odd impulses, religious dreams about the time of their conversion, etc,., he found these relatively much more frequent in the group of converts whose transformation had been 'striking,' 'striking' transformation being defined as a change which, thought not necessarily instantaneous, seems to the subject of it to be distinctly different from a process of growth, however rapid." Candidates for conversion at revivals are, as you know, often disappointed: they experience nothing striking. Professor Coe has a number of persons of this class among his seventy-seven subjects, and they almost all, when tested by hypnosis, proved to belong to a subclass which he calls 'spontaneous,' that is, fertile in self-suggestions, as distinguished from a 'passive' subclass, to which most of the subjects of striking transformation belonged. His inference is that self-suggestion of impossibility had prevented the influence upon these persons of an environment which, on the more 'passive' subjects, had easily brought forth the effects they looked for. Sharp distinctions are difficult in these regions, and Professor Coe's numbers are small. But his methods were careful, and the results tally with what one might expect; and they seem, on the whole, to justify his practical conclusion, which is that if you should expose to a converting influence a subject in whom there factors unite: first, pronounced emotional sensibility; second, tendency to automatism; and third, suggestibility of the passive type; you might then safely predict the result: there would be a sudden conversion, a transformation of the striking kind.

Does this temperamental origin diminish the significance of the sudden conversion when it has occurred? Not in the least, as Professor Coe well says; for "the ultimate test of religious values is nothing psychological, nothing definable in terms of how it happens, but something ethical, definable only in terms of what is attained."

As we proceed farther in our inquiry we shall see that what is attained is often an altogether new level of spiritual vitality, a relatively heroic level, in which impossible things have become possible, and new energies and endurances are shown. The personality is changed, the man is born anew, whether or not his psychological idiosyncrasies are what give the particular shape to his metamorphosis. 'Sanctification' is the technical name of this result; and erelong examples of it shall be brought before you. In this lecture I have still only to add a few remarks on the assurance and peace which fill the hour of change itself.

One word more, though, before proceeding to that point, lest the final purpose of my explanation of suddenness by subliminal activity be misunderstood. I do indeed believe that if the Subject have no liability to such subconscious activity, or if his conscious fields have a hard rind of a margin that resists incursions from beyond it, his conversion must be gradual if it occur, and must resemble any simple growth into new habits. His possession of a developed subliminal self, and of a leaky or pervious margin, is thus a conditio sin qua non of the Subject's becoming converted in the instantaneous way. But if you, being orthodox Christians, ask me as a psychologist whether the reference of a phenomenon to a subliminal self does not exclude the notion of the direct presence of the Deity altogether, I have to say frankly that as a psychologist I do not see why it necessarily should. The lower manifestations of the Subliminal, indeed, fall within the resources of the personal subject: his ordinary sense-material, inattentively taken in and subconsciously remember and combined, will account for all his usual automatisms. But just as our primary wide-awake consciousness throws open our sense to the touch of things material, so it is logically conceivable that if there be higher spiritual agencies that can directly touch us, the psychological condition of their doing so might be our possession of a subconscious region which alone should yield access to them. The hubbub of the waking life might close a door which in the dreamy Subliminal might remain ajar or open.

Thus that perception of external control which is so essential a feature in conversion might, in some cases at any rate, be interpreted as the orthodox interpret it: forces transcending the finite individual might impress him, on condition of his being what we may call a subliminal human specimen. But in any case the value of these forces would have to be determined by their effects, and the mere fact of their transcendency would of itself establish no presumption that they were more divine than diabolical.

I confess that this is the way in which I should rather see the topic left lying in your minds until I come to a much later lecture, when I hope once more to gather these dropped threads together into more definitive conclusions. The notion of a subconscious self certainly ought not at this point of our inquiry to be held to conclude all notion of a higher penetration. If there be higher powers able to impress us, they may get access to us only through the subliminal door.

Let us turn now to the feelings which immediately fill the hour of the conversion experience. The first one to be noted is just this sense of higher control. It is not always, but it is very often present. We saw examples of it in Alline, Bradley, Brainerd, and elsewhere. The need of such a higher controlling agency is well expressed in the short reference which the eminent French Protestant Adolphe Monod makes to the crisis of his own conversion. It was at Naples in his early manhood, in the summer of 1827.

"My sadness," he says, "was without limit, and having got entire possession of me, it filled my life from the most indifferent external acts to the most secret thoughts, and corrupted at their source my feelings, my judgments, and my happiness. It was then that I saw that to expect to put a stop to this disorder by my reason and my will, which were themselves diseased, would be to act like a blind man who should pretend to correct one of his eyes by the aid of the other equally blind one. I had then no resources save in some influence from without. I remembered the promise of the Holy Ghost; and what the positive declarations of the Gospel had never succeeded in bringing home to me, I learned at last from necessity, and believed, for the first time in my life, in this promise, in the only sense in which it answered the needs of my soul, in that, namely, of a really external supernatural action, capable of giving me thoughts, and taking them away from me, and exerted on me by a God as truly master of my heart as he is of the rest of nature. Renouncing then all merit, all strength, abandoning all my personal resources, and acknowledging no other title to his mercy than my own utter misery, I went home and threw myself on my knees, and prayed as I never yet prayed in my life. From this day onwards a new interior life began for me: not that my melancholy had disappeared, but it had lost its sting. Hope had entered into my heart, and once entered on the path, the God of Jesus Christ, to whom I then had learned to give myself up, little by little did the rest."

It is needless to remind you once more of the admirable congruity of Protestant theology with the structure of the mind as shown in such experiences. In the extreme of melancholy the self that consciously is can do absolutely nothing. It is completely bankrupt and without resource, and no works it can accomplish will avail. Redemption from such subjective conditions must be a free gift or nothing, and grace through Christ's accomplished sacrifice is such a gift.

"God," says Luther, "is the God of the humble, the miserable, the oppressed, and the desperate, and of those that are brought even to nothing; and this nature is to giver sight to the blind, to comfort the broken-hearted, to justify sinners ,to save the very desperate and damned. Now that pernicious and pestilent opinion of man's own righteousness, which will not be a sinner, unclean, miserable, and damnable, but righteous and holy, suffereth not God to come to his own natural and proper work. Therefore God must take this maul in hand (the law, I mean) to beat in pieces and bring to nothing this east with her vain confidence, that she may so learn at length by her own misery that she is utterly forlorn and damned. But here lie the difficulty, that when a man is terrified and cast down, he is so little able to raise himself up again and say, 'Now I am bruised and afflicted enough; now is the time of grace; now is the time to hear Christ.' The foolishness of man's heart is so great that then he rather seekth to himself more laws to satisfy his conscience. 'If I live,' saith he, 'I will amend my life: I will do this, I will do that.' But here, except thou do the quite contrary, except thou end Moses away with his law, and in these terrors and this anguish lay hold upon Christ who died for thy sins, look for no salvation. Thy cowl, thy shaven crown, they chastity, thy obedience, they poverty, they works, they merits? What shall all these do? What shall the law of Moses avail? If I, wretched and damnable sinner, through works or merits could have loved the Son of God, and so come to him, what needed he to deliver himself for me? If I, being a wretched and damned sinner, could be redeemed by any other prices, what needed the Son of God to be given? But because there was no other price, therefore, he delivered neither sheep, ox, gold, nor silver, but even God himself, entirely and wholly 'for me,' even 'for me,' I say, a miserable, wretched sinner. Now, therefore, I take comfort and apply this to myself. And this manner of applying is the very true forces and power of faith. For he died not to justify the righteous, but the un-righteous, and to make them the children of God.

That is, the more literally lost you are, the more literally you are the very being whom Christ's sacrifice has already saved. Nothing in Catholic theology I imagine, has ever spoken to sick souls as straight as this message from Luther's personal experience. As Protestants are not all sick souls, of course reliance on what Luther exults in calling the dung of one's merits, the filthy puddle of one's own righteousness, has come to the front again in their religion; but the adequacy of his view of Christianity to the deeper parts of our human mental structure is shown by its wildfire contagiousness when it was a new and quickening thing.

Faith that Christ has genuinely done his work was part of what Luther meant by faith, which so far is faith in a fact intellectually conceived of. But this is only one part of Luther's faith, the other part being far more vital. This other part is something not intellectual but immediate and intuitive, the assurance, namely, that I, this individual I, just as I stand, without one plea, etc., am saved now and forever.

Professor Leuba is undoubtedly right in contending that the conceptual belief about Christ's work, although so often efficacious and antecedent, is really accessory and non-essential, and that the 'joyous conviction' can also come by far other channels than this conception. It is to the joyous conviction itself, the assurance that all is well with one, that he would give the name of faith par excellence.

"When the sense of estrangement," he writes, "fencing man about in a narrowly limited ego, breaks down, the individual finds himself 'at one with all creation.' He lives in the universal life; he and man, he and nature; he and God, are one. That state of confidence, trust, union with all things, following upon the achievement of moral unity, is the Faith state. Various dogmatic beliefs suddenly, on the advent of the faith-state, acquire a character of certainty, assume a new reality, become an object of faith. As the ground of assurance here is not rational, argumentation is irrelevant. But such conviction being a mere casual offshoot of the faith-state, it is a gross error to imagine that the chief practical value of the faith-state is its power to stamp with the seal of reality certain particular theological conceptions. On the contrary, its value lies solely in the fact that it is the psychic correlate of a biological growth which expresses itself in new affective states and new reactions; in larger, nobler, more Christ-like activities. The ground of the specific assurance in religious dogmas is then an affective experience. The objects of faith may even be preposterous; the affective stream will float them along, and invest them with unshakable certitude. The more startling the affective experience, the less explicable it seems, the easier it is to make it the carrier of unsubstantial notions.

The characteristics of the affective experience which, to avoid ambiguity, should, I think, be called the state of assurance rather than the faith-state, can be easily enumerated, though it is probably difficult to realize their intensity, unless one have been through the experience one's self.

The central one is the loss of all the worry, the sense that all is ultimately well with one, the peace, the harmony, the willingness to be, even though the outer conditions should remain the same. The certainty of God's 'grace,' of 'justification,' 'salvation,' is an objective belief that usually accompanies the change in Christians; but this may be entirely lacking and yet the affective peace remain the same-you will recollect the case of the Oxford graduate: and many might be given where the assurance of personal salvation was only a later result. A passion of willingness, of acquiescence, of admiration, is the glowing centre of this state of mind.

The second feature is the sense of perceiving truths not known before. The mysteries of life become lucid, as Professor Leuba says; and often, nay usually the solution is more or less unutterable in words. But these more intellectual phenomena may be postponed until we treat of mysticism.

A third peculiarity of the assurance state is the objective change which the world often appears to undergo. 'An appearance of newness beautifies every object,' the precise opposite of that other sort of newness, that dreadful unreality and strangeness in the appearance of the world, which is experienced by melancholy patients, and of which you may recall my relating some examples. This sense of clean and beautiful newness within and without is one of the commonest entries in conversion records. Jonathan Edwards thus describes it in himself: —seemed to be, as it were, a calm, sweet cast, or appearance of divine glory, in almost everything. God's excellencey, his wisdom, his purity and love, seemed to appear in everything; in the sun, moon, and stars; in the clouds and blue sky; in the grass, flowers, and trees; in the water and all nature; which used greatly to fix my mind. And scarce anything, among all the works of nature, was so sweet to me as thunder and lightning; formerly nothing had been so terrible to me. Before, I used to be uncommonly terrified with thunder, and to be struck with terror when I saw a thunderstorm rising; but now, on the contrary, it rejoices me. Billy Bray, an excellent little illiterate English evangelist, records his sense of newness thus: — "I said to the Lord: 'Thou hast said, they that ask shall receive, they that seek shall find, and to them that knock the door shall be opened, and I have faith to believe it.' In an instant the Lord made me so happy that I cannot express what I felt. I shouted for joy. I praised God with my whole heart. ... I think this was November, 1823, but what day of the month I do not know. I remember this, that everything looked new to me, the people, the fields, the cattle, the trees. I was like a new man in a new world. I spent the greater part of my time in praising the Lord."

Starbuck and Leuba both illustrate this sense of newness by quotations. I take the two following from Starbuck's manuscript collection. One, a woman says: — "I was taken to a camp-meeting, mother and religious friends seeking and praying for my conversion. My emotional nature was stirred to its depths; confessions of depravity and pleading with God for salvation from sin made me oblivious of all surroundings. I plead for mercy, and had a vivid realization of forgiveness and renewal of my nature. When rising from my knees I exclaimed, 'Old things have passed away, all things have become new.' It was like entering another world, a new state of existence. Natural objects were glorified, my spiritual vision was so clarified that I saw beauty in every material object in the universe, the woods were vocal with heavenly music; my soul exulted in the love of God, and I wanted everybody to share in my joy."

The next case is that of a man:— "I know not how I get back into the encampment, but found myself staggering up to Rev. ——'s Holiness tent-and as it was full of seekers and a terrible noise inside, some groaning, some laughing, and some shouting, and by a large oak, ten feet from the tent, I fell on my face by a bench, and tried to pray, and every time I would call on God, something like a man's hand would strangle me choking. I don't know whether there were any one around or near me or not. I thought I should surely die if I did not get help, but just as often as I would pray, that unseen hand was felt on my throat and my breath squeezed off. Finally something said: 'Venture on the atonement, for you will die anyway if you don't.' So I made one final struggle to call on God for mercy, with the same choking and strangling, determined to finish the sentence of prayer for Mercy, if I did strange and die, and the last I remember that time was falling back on the ground with the same unseen hand on my throat. I don't know how long I lay there or what was going on. None of my folks were present. When I came to myself, there were a crowd around me praising God. The very heavens seemed to open and pour down rays of light and glory. Not for a moment only, but all day and night, floods of light and glory seemed to pour through my soul,. And oh, how I was changed, and everything became new. My horses and hogs and even everybody seemed charged."

This man's case introduces the feature of automatisms, which in suggestible subjects have been so startling a feature at revivals since, in Edward's, Wesley's, and Whitfield's time, these became a regular means of gospel-propagation. They were at first supposed to be semi-miraculous proofs of 'power' on the part of the Holy Ghost, but great divergence of opinion quickly arose concerning them. Edwards, in this Thoughts on the Revival of Religion in New England, has to defend them against their critics; and their value has long been matter of debate even within the revivalistic denominations. They undoubtedly have no essential spiritual significance, and although their presence makes his conversion more memorable to the convert, it has never been proved that converts who show them are more persevering or fertile in good fruits than those whose change of heart has had less violent accompaniments. On the whole, unconsciousness, convulsions, visions, and involuntary vocal utterances, and suffocation, must be simply ascribed to the subject's having a large subliminal region, involving nervous instability. This is often the subject's own view of the matter afterwards. One of Starbuck's correspondents writes, for instance:—"I have been through the experience which is known as conversion. My explanation of it is this: the subject works his emotions up to the breaking point, at the same time resisting their physical manifestations, such as quickened pulse, etc., and then suddenly lets them have their full sway over his body. The relief is something wonderful, and the pleasurable effects of the emotions are experienced to the highest degree."

There is one form of sensory automatism which possibly deserves special notice on account of its frequency. I refer to hallucinatory or pseudo-hallucinatory luminous phenomena, photisms, to use the term of the psychologists. Saint Paul's blinding heavenly vision seems to have been a phenomenon of this sort; so does Constantine's cross in the sky. The last case but one which I quoted mentions floods of light and glory. Henry Alline mentions a light, about whose externality he seems uncertain. Colonel Gardiner sees a blazing light. President Finney writes:—-All at once the glory of God shone upon and round about me in a manner almost marvelous....A light perfectly ineffable shone in my soul, that almost prostrated me on the ground. ....This light seemed like the brightness of the sun in every direction. IT was too intense for the eyes...I think I knew something then, by actual experience, of that light that prostrated Paul on the way to Damascus. It was surely a light such as I could not have endured long."

Such reports of photisms are indeed far from uncommon. Here is another from Starbuck's collection, where the light appeared evidently external:—"I had attended a series of revival services for about two weeks off and on. Had been invited to the altar several times, all the time becoming more deeply impressed, when finally I decided I must do this, or I should be lost. Realization of conversion was very vivid, like a ton's weight being lifted from my heart; a strange light which seemed to light up the whole room (for it was dark); a conscious supreme bliss which caused me to repeat 'Glory to God' for a long time. Decided to be God's child for life, and to give up my pet ambition, wealth, and social position. My former habits of life hindered my growth somewhat, but I set about overcoming these systemically, and in one year my whole nature was changed, i.e., my ambitions were of a different order."

Here is another one of Starbucks' cases, involving a luminous element:—"I had been clearly converted twenty-three years before, or rather reclaimed. My experience in regeneration was then clear and spiritual, and I had not backslidden. But I experienced entire sanctification on the 15th day of March. 1893, about eleven o'clock in the morning. The particular accompaniments of the experience were entirely unexpected. I was quietly sitting at home singing selections out of Pentecostal Hymns. Suddenly there seemed to be a something sweeping into me and inflating my entire being-such a sensation as I had never experienced before. When this experience acme, I seemed to be conducted around a large, capacious, well-lighted room. As I walked with my invisible conductor and looked around, a clear thought was coined in my mind, 'They are not here, they are gone.' As soon as the thought was definitely formed in my mind, though no word was spoken, the Holy Spirit impressed me that I was surveying my own soul. Then, for the first time in all my life, did I know that I was cleansed from all sin, and filled with the fullness of God."

Leuba quotes the case of a Mr. Peek, where the luminous affection reminds one of the chromatic hallucinations produced by the intoxicant cactus buds called mescal by the Mexicans:—"When I went in the morning into the fields to work, the glory of God appeared in all his visible creation. I well remember we reaped oats, and how every straw and head of the oats seemed, as it were, arrayed in a kind of rainbow glory, or to glow, if I may so express it, in the glory of God."

The most characteristic of all the elements of the conversion crisis, and the last one of which I shall speak, is the ecstasy of happiness produced. We have already heard several accounts of it, but I will add a couple more. President Finney's is so vivid that I give it at length:—

"All my feelings seemed to rise and flow out; and the utterance of my heart was, 'I want to pour my whole soul out to God.' The rising of my soul was so great that I rushed into the back room of the front office, to pray. There was no fire and no light in the room; nevertheless it appeared to me as if it were perfectly light. As I went in and shut the door after me, it seemed as if I met the Lord Jesus Christ face to face. It did not occur to me then, nor did it for some time afterwards, that it was wholly a mental state. On the contrary, it seemed to me that I saw him as I would see any other man. He said nothing, but looked at me in such a manner as to break me right down at his feet. I have always since regarded this as a most remarkable state of mind; for it seemed to me a reality that he stood before me, and I fell down at his feet and poured out my soul to him. I wept aloud like a child, and made such confessions as I could with my choked utterances. I seemed to me that I bathed his feet with my tears; and yet I had no distinct impression that I touched him, that I recollect. It must have continued in this state for a good while; but my mind was too much absorbed with the interview to recollect anything that I said. But I know, as soon as my mind became calm enough to break off from the interview, I returned to the front office, and found that the fire that I had made of large wood was nearly burned out. But as I turned and was about to take a seat by the fire, I received a might baptism of the Holy Ghost. Without any expectation of it, without ever having the thought in my mind that there was any such thing for me, without any recollection that I had ever heard the thing mentioned by any person in the world, the Holy Spirit descended upon me in a manner that seemed to go through me, body and soul. I could feel the impression, like a wave of electricity, going through and through me. Indeed, it seemed to come in waves and waves of liquid love; for I could not express it in any other way. It seemed like the very breath of God. I can recollect distinctly that it seemed to fan me, like immense wings.

"No words can express the wonderful love that was shed abroad in my heart. I wept aloud with joy and love; and I do not know but I should say I literally bellowed out the unutterable gushings of my heart. These waves came over me, and over me, and over me, one after the other, until I recollect I cried out, 'I shall die if these waves continue to pass over me.' I said, 'Lord, I cannot bear any more;' yet I had no fear of death.

"How long I continued in this state, with this baptism continuing to roll over me and go through me, I do not know. But I know it was late in the evening when a member of my choir-for I was the leader of the choir-came into the office to see me. He was a member of the church. He found me in this state of loud weeping, and said to me, 'Mr. Finney, what ails you?' I could make him no answer for some time. He than said, 'Are you in pain?' I gathered myself up as best I could, and replied, 'No, but so happy that I cannot live.'"

I just now quoted Billy Bray; I cannot do better than give his own brief account of his post-conversion feelings:—

"I can't help praising the Lord. As I go along the street, I lift up one foot, and it seems to say 'Glory'; and I lift up the other, and it seems to say 'Amen'; and so they keep up like that all the time I was walking."

One word, before I close this lecture, on the question of the transiency or permanence or these abrupt conversions. Some of you, I feel sure, knowing that numerous backslidings and relapses take place, make of these their apperceiving mass for interpreting the whole subject, and dismiss it with a pitying smile at so much 'hysterics.' Psychologically, as well as religiously, however, this is shallow. It misses the point of serious interest, which is not so much the duration as the nature and quality of these shiftings of character to higher levels. Men lapse from every level-we need no statistics to tell us that. Love is, for instance, well known not to be irrevocable, yet, constant or inconstant, it reveals new flights and reaches of ideality while it lasts. These revelations form its significance to men and women, whatever be its duration. So with the conversion experience: that it should for even a short time show a human being what the high-water mark of his spiritual capacity is, this is what constitutes its importance,—an importance which backsliding cannot diminish, although persistence might increase it.

As a matter of fact, all the more striking instances of conversion, all those, for instance, which I have quoted, have been permanent. The case of which there might be most doubt, on account of its suggesting so strongly an epileptoid seizure, was the case of M. Ratisbonne. Yet I am informed that Ratisbonne's whole future was shaped by those few minutes. He gave up his project of marriage, became a priest, founded at Jerusalem, where he went to dwell, a mission of nuns for the conversion of the Jews, showed no tendency to use for egotistic purposes of notoriety given him by the peculiar circumstances of his conversion, —which, for the rest, he could seldom refer to without tears,—and in short remained an exemplary son of the Church until he died, late in the 80s, if I remember rightly.

The only statistics I know of, on the subject of the duration of conversions, are those collected for Professor Starbuck by Miss Johnston. They embrace only a hundred persons, evangelical church-members, more than half being Methodists. According to the statement of the subjects themselves, there had been backsliding of some sort in nearly all the cases, 93 percent of the women, 77 percent of the men. Discussing the returns more minutely, Starbucks finds that only 6 percent are relapses from the religious faith which the conversion confirmed, and that the backsliding complained of is in most only a fluctuation in the ardor of sentiment. Only six of the hundred cases report a change of faith. Starbuck's conclusion is that the effect of conversion is to bring with it "a changed attitude towards life, which is fairly constant and permanent, although the feelings fluctuate....In other words, the persons who have passed through conversion, having once taken a stand for the religious life, tend to feel themselves identified with it, no matter how much their religious enthusiasm declines."

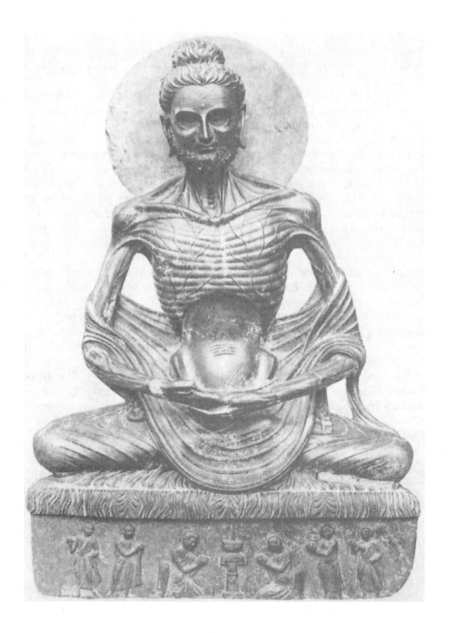

Figure 79b. "Beautiful Bodhisattva" Padmapani. (Starving Buddha), Ajanta India. About 600 A.D.

MYSTICISM
by William James

One may say truly, I think, that personal religious experiences has its root and centre in mystical states of consciousness; so for us, who in these lectures are treating personal experience as the exclusive subject of our study, such states of consciousness ought to form the vital chapter from which the other chapters get their light. Whether my treatment of mystical states will shed more light or darkness, I do not know, for my own constitution shuts me out from their enjoyment almost entirely, and I can speak of them only at second hand. But though forced to look upon the subject so externally, I will be as objective and receptive as I can; and I think I shall at least succeed in convincing you of the reality of the states in question, and of the paramount importance of their function.

First of all, then, I ask, What does the expression 'mystical states of consciousness' mean? How do we part of mystical states from other states?

The words 'mysticism' and 'mystical' are often used as terms of mere reproach, to throw at any opinion which we regard as vague and vast and sentimental, and without a base in either facts or logic. For some writers a 'mystic' is any person who believes in thought-transference, spirit-return. Employed in this way the word has little value: there are too many less ambiguous synonyms. So, to keep it useful by restricting it, I will do what I did in the case of the word 'religion,' and simply propose to you four marks which, when an experience has them, may justify us in calling it mystical for the purpose of the present lectures. In this way we shall save verbal disputation, and the recrimination that generally go therewith.

1. Ineffability. — The handiest of the marks by which I classify a state of mind as mystical is negative. The subject of it immediately says that it defies expression, that no adequate report of its contents can be given in words. It follows from this that its quality must be directly experienced; it cannot be imparted or transferred to others. In this peculiarity mystical states are more like states of feeling than like states of intellect. No one can make clear to another who has never had a certain feeling, in what the quality or worth of it consists. One must have musical ears to know the value of a symphony; one must have been in love one's self to understand a lover's state of mind. Lacking the heart or ear, we cannot interpret the musician or the lover justly, and are even likely to consider him weak-minded or absurd. The mystic finds that most of us accord to his experiences an equally incompetent treatment.

2. Noetic quality. -Although so similar to states of feeling, mystical states seem to those who experience them to be also states of knowledge. They are states of insight into depths of truth unplumbed by the discursive intellect. They are illuminations, revelations, full of significance and importance, all inarticulate though they remain; and as a rule they carry with them a curious sense of authority for after-time.

These two characters well entitle any state to be called mystical, in the sense in which I use the word. Two other qualities are less sharply marked, but are usually found. These are: —

3. Transiency. -Mystical states cannot be sustained for long. Except in rare instances, half an hour, or at most an hour or two, seems to be the limit beyond which they fade into the light of common day. Often, when faded, their quality can but imperfectly be reproduced in memory; but when they recur it is recognized; and from one recurrence to another it is susceptible of continuous development in what is felt as inner richness and importance.

4. Passivity. - Although the oncoming of mystical states may be facilitated by preliminary voluntary operations, as by fixing the attention, or going through certain bodily performances, or in other ways which manuals of mysticism prescribe; yet when the characteristic sort of consciousness once has set in, the mystic feels as if his own will were in abeyance, and indeed sometimes as if he were grasped and held by a superior power. This latter peculiarity connects mystical states with certain definite phenomena of secondary or alternative personality, such as prophetic speech, automatic writing, or the mediumistic trance. When these latter conditions are well pronounced, however, there may be no recollection whatever of the phenomenon, and it may have no significance for the subject's usual inner life, to which, as it were, it makes a mere interruption. Mystical states,

strictly so called, are never merely interruptive. Some memory of their content always remains, and a profound sense of their importance. They modify the inner life of the subject between the times of their recurrence. Sharp divisions in this region are, however, difficult to make, and we find all sorts of gradations and mixtures.

These four characteristics are sufficient to mark out a group of states of consciousness peculiar enough to deserve a special name and to call for careful study. Let it then be called the mystical group.

Our next step should be to gain acquaintance with some typical examples. Professional mystics at the height of their development have often elaborately organized experiences and a philosophy based thereupon. But you remember what I said in my first lecture: phenomena are best understood when placed within their series, studied in their germ and in their over-ripe decay, and compared with their exaggerated and degenerated kindred. The range of mystical experience is very wide, must too wide for us to cover in the time at our disposal. Yet the method of serial study is so essential for interpretation that if we really wish to reach conclusions we must use it. I will begin, therefore, with phenomena which claim no special religious significance, and end with those of which the religious pretensions are extreme.

The simplest rudiment of mystical experience would seem to be that deepened sense of the significance of a maxim or formula which occasionally sweeps over one. "I've heard that said all my life," we exclaim, "but I never realized its full meaning until now." "When a fellow-monk," said Luther, "one day repeated the words of the Creed: 'I believe in the forgiveness of sins,' I saw the Scripture in an entirely new light; and straightway I felt as if I were born anew. It was as if I had found the door of paradise thrown wide open." This sense of deeper significance is not confined to rational propositions. Single words, and conjunctions of words, effects of light on land and sea, odors and musical sounds, all bring it when the mind is tuned aright. Most of us can remember the strangely moving power of passages in certain poems read when we were young, irrational doorways as they were through which the mystery of fact, the wildness and the pang of life, stole into our hearts and thrilled them. The words have now perhaps become mere polished surfaces for us; but lyric poetry and music are alive and significant only in proportion as they fetch these vague vistas of a life continuous with our own, beckoning and inviting, yet ever eluding our pursuit. We are alive or dead to the eternal inner message of the arts according as we have kept or lost this mystical susceptibility.

A more pronounced step forward on the mystical ladder is found in an extremely frequent phenomenon, that sudden feeling, namely, which sometimes sweeps over us, of having 'been here before,' as if at some indefinite past time, in just this place, with just these people, we were already saying just these things. As Tennyson writes:

> "Moreover, something is or seems,
> That touches me with mystic gleams,
> Like glimpse of forgotten dreams—
>
> "Of something felt, like something here;
> Of something done, I know not where;
> Such as no language may declare."

Sir James Crichton-Browne has given the technical name of 'dreamy states' to these sudden invasions of vaguely reminiscent consciousness. They bring a sense of mystery and of the metaphysical duality of things, and the feeling of an enlargement of perception which seems imminent but which never completes itself. In Dr. Crichton-Browne's opinion they connect themselves with the perplexed and scared disturbances of self-consciousness which occasionally precede epileptic attacks. I think that this learned alienist takes a rather absurdly alarmist view of an intrinsically insignificant phenomenon. He follows it along the downward ladder, to insanity; our path pursues the upward ladder chiefly. The divergence shows how important it is to neglect no part of a phenomenon's connections, for we make it appear admirable or dreadful according to the context by which we set it off.

Somewhat deeper plunges into mystical consciousness are met with in yet other dreamy states. Such feelings as these which Charles Kingsley describes are surely far from being uncommon, especially in youth: —"When I walk the fields, I am oppressed now and then with an innate feeling that everything I see has a meaning, if I could but understand it. And this feeling of being surrounded with truths which I cannot grasp amounts to indescribable awe sometimes... have you not felt that your real soul was imperceptible to our mental vision, except in a few hallowed moments?"

A much more extreme state of mystical consciousness is described by J. A. Symonds; and probably more persons than we suspect could give parallels to it from their own experience.

"Suddenly," writes Symond, "at church, or in company, or when I was reading, and always, I think, when my muscles were at rest, I felt the approach of the mood. Irresistibly it took possession of my mind and will, lasted what seemed an eternity, and disappeared in a series of rapid sensations which resembled the awakening from anesthetic influence. One reason why I disliked this kind of trance was that I could not describe it to myself. I cannot even now find words to render it intelligible. It consisted in a gradual but swiftly progressive obliteration of space, time, sensation, and the multitudinous factors of experience which seem to qualify what we are pleased to call our Self. In proportion as these conditions of ordinary consciousness were subtracted, the sense of an underlying or essential consciousness acquired intensity. At last nothing remained but a pure, absolute, abstract Self. The universe became without form and void of content. But Self persisted, formidable in its vivid keenness, feeling the most poignant doubt about reality, ready, as it seemed, to find existence break as breaks a bubble round about it. And what then? The apprehension of a coming dissolution, the grim conviction that this state was the last state of the conscious Self, the sense that I had followed the last threat of being to the verge of the abyss, and had arrived at demonstration of eternal Maya or illusion, stirred or seemed to stir me up again. The return to ordinary conditions of sentient existence began by my first recovering the power of touch, and then by the gradual thought rapid influx of familiar impressions and diurnal interests. At last I felt myself once more a human being; and though the riddle of what is meant by life remained unsolved, I was thankful for this return from the abyss-this deliverance from so awful an initiation into the mysteries of skepticism.

"This trance recurred with diminishing frequency until I reached the age of twenty-eight. It served to impress upon my growing nature the phantasmal unreality of all the circumstances which contribute to a merely phenomenal consciousness. Often have I asked myself with anguish, on waking from that formless state of denuded, keenly sentient being, Which is the unreality? - the trance of fiery, vacant, apprehensive, skeptical Self from which I issue, or these surrounding phenomena and habits which veil that inner Self and build a self of flesh-and-blood conventionality? Again, are men the factors of some dream, the dream-like unsubstantiality of which they comprehend at such eventful moments? What would happen if the final stage of the trance were reached? In a recital like this there is certainly something suggestive of pathology.

The next step into mystical states carries us into a realm that public opinion and ethical philosophy have long since branded as pathological, though private practice and certain lyric strains of poetry seem still to bear witness to its ideality. I refer to the consciousness produced by intoxicants and anesthetics, especially by alcohol. The sway of alcohol over mankind is unquestionably due to its power to stimulate the mystical faculties of human nature, usually crushed to earth by the cold facts and dry criticisms of the sober hour. Sobriety diminishes, discriminates, and says no; drunkenness expands, unites, and says yes. It is in fact the great exciter of the Yes function in man. It brings its votary from the chill periphery of things to the radiant core. It makes him for the moment one with truth. Not through mere perversity do men run after it. To the poor and the unlettered it stands in the place of symphony concerts and of literature; and it is part of the deeper mystery and tragedy of life that whiffs and gleams of something that we immediately recognize as excellent should be vouchsafed to so many of us only in the fleeting earlier phases of what in its totality is so degrading a poisoning. The drunken consciousness is one bit of the mystic consciousness, and our total opinion of it must find its place in our opinion of that larger whole.

Nitrous oxide and either, especially nitrous oxide, when sufficiently diluted with air, stimulate the mystical consciousness in an extraordinary degree. Depth beyond depth of truth seems revealed to the inhaler. This truth fades out, however, or escapes, at the moment of coming to; and if any words remain over in which it seemed to clothe itself, they prove to be the veriest nonsense. Nevertheless, the sense of a profound meaning have been there persists; and I know more than one person who is persuaded that in the nitrous trance we have a genuine metaphysical revelation.

Some years ago I myself made some observations on this aspect of nitrous oxide intoxication, and reported them in print. One conclusion was forced upon my mind at that time, and my impression of its truth has ever since remained unshaken. It is that our normal waking consciousness, rational consciousness as we call it, is but one special type of consciousness, whilst all about it, parted from it by the filmiest of screens, there lie potential forms of consciousness entirely different.

We may go through life without suspecting their existence; but apply the requisite stimulus, and at a touch they are there in all their completeness, definite types of mentality which probably somewhere have their field of application and adaptation. No account of the universe in its totality can be final which leaves these other forms of consciousness quite disregarded. How to regard them is the question,—for they are so discontinuous with ordinary consciousness. Yet they may determine attitude though they fail to give a map. At any rate, they forbid a premature closing of our accounts with reality. Looking back on my own experiences, they all converge towards a kind of insight to which I cannot help ascribing some metaphysical significance. The keynote of it is invariably reconciliation. It is as if the opposites of the world, whose contradictoriness and conflict make all our difficulties and troubles, were melted into unity. Not only do they, as contrasted species, belong to one and the same genus, but one of the species, the nobler and better one, is itself the genus, and so soaks up and absorbs its opposite into itself. This is a dark saying, I know, when thus expressed in terms of common logic, but I cannot wholly escape from its authority. I feel as if it must mean something, something like what the hegelian philosophy means, if one could only lay hold of it more clearly. Those who have ears to hear, let them hear: to me the living sense of its realty only comes in the artificial mystic state of mind.

I just now spoke of friends who believe in the anesthetic revelation. For them too it is a monistic insight, in which the other in its various forms appears absorbed into the One.

"Into this pervading genius," writes one of them, "we pass, forgetting and forgotten, and thenceforth each is all, in God. There is no higher, no deeper, no other, than the life in which we are founded. 'The One remains, the many change and pass;' and each and everyone of us is the One that remains. ....This is the ultimatum...As sure as being-whence is all our care-so sure is content, beyond duplexity, antithesis, or trouble, where I have triumphed in a solitude that God is not above."

This has the genuine religious mystic ring! I just now quoted J.A. Symonds. He also records a mystical experience with chloroform, as follows: —

"After the choking and stifling had passed away, I seemed at first in a state of utter blankness; then came flashes of intense light, alternating with blackness, with a keen vision of what was going on in the room around me, but no sensation of touch. I thought that I was near death; when, suddenly, my soul became aware of God, who was manifestly dealing with me, handling me, so to speak, in an intense personal present reality. I felt him streaming in like light upon me...I cannot describe the ecstasy I felt. Then, as I gradually awoke from the influence of the anesthetics, the old sense of my relation to the world began to return, the new sense of my relation to God began to fade. I suddenly leapt to my feet on the chair where I was sitting, and shrieked out, 'It is too horrible, it is too horrible, it is too horrible,' meaning that I could not bear this disillusionment. Then I flung myself on the ground, and at last awoke covered with blood, calling to two surgeons (who were frightened), 'Why did you not kill me? Why would you not let me die?' Only think of it. To have felt for that long dateless ecstasy of vision the very God, in all purity and tenderness and truth and absolute love, and then to find that I had after all had no revelation, but that I had been tricked by the abnormal excitement of my brain.

"Yet, this question remains, Is it possible that the inner sense of reality which succeeded, when my flesh was dead to impressions from without, to the ordinary sense of physical relations, was not a delusion but an actual experience? Is it possible that I, in that moment, felt what some of the saints have said they always felt, the undemonstrable but irrefragable certainty of God?"

With this we make connection with religious mysticism pure and simple. Symond's question takes us back to those examples which you will remember my quoting in the lecture on Reality of the Unseen, of sudden realization of the immediate presence of God. The phenomenon in one shape or another is not uncommon.

"I know," writes Mr. Trine, "an officer on our police force who has told me that many times when off duty, and on his way home in the evening, there comes to him such a vivid and vital realization of his oneness with this Infinite Power, and this Spirit of Infinite Peace   so takes hold of and so fills him, that it seems as if his feet could hardly keep to the pavement, so buoyant and so exhilarated does he become by reason of this inflowing tide."

Certain aspects of nature seem to have a peculiar power of awakening such mystical moods. Most of the striking cases which I have collected have occurred out of doors. Literature has commemorated this fact in many passages of great beauty-this extract, for example, from Amiel's Journal Intime:—"Shall I ever again have any of those prodigious reveries which sometimes came to me in former days? One day, in youth, at sunrise, sitting in the ruins of the castle of Faucigny; and again in the mountains, under the noonday sun, above Lavey, lying at the foot of a tree and visited by three butterflies; once more at night upon the shingly shore of the Northern Ocean, my back upon the sand and my vision ranging through the milky way; — such grand and spacious, immortal, cosmogonic reveries, when one reaches to the stars, when one owns the infinite! Moments divine, ecstatic hours; in which our thought flies from world to world, pierces the great enigma, breathes with a respiration broad, tranquil, and deep as the respiration of the ocean, serene and limitless as the blue firmament; ...instants of irresistible intuition in which one feels one's self great as the universe, and calm as god...What hours, what memories! The vestiges they leave behind are enough to fill us with belief and enthusiasm, as if they were visits of the Holy Ghost."

Here is a similar record from the memoirs of that interesting German idealist, Malwida von Meysenbug: —

"I was alone upon the seashore as all these thoughts flowed over me, liberating and reconciling; and now again, as once before in distant days in the Alps of Dauphine, I was impelled to kneel down, this time before the illimitable ocean, symbol of the Infinite. I felt that I prayed as I had never prayed before, and knew now what prayer really is: to return from the solitude of individuation into the consciousness of unity with all that is, to kneel down as one that passes away, and to rise up as one imperishable. Earth, heaven, and sea resounded as in one vast world-encircling harmony. It was as if the chorus of all the great who had ever lived were about me. I felt myself one with them, and it appeared as if I heard their greeting: 'Thou too belongest to the company of those who overcome.'"

The well-known passage from Walt Whitman is a classical expression of this sporadic type of mystical experience:

"I believe in you, my Soul...
Loaf with me on the grass, loose the stop from your throat;...
Only the lull I like, the hum of your valved voice.
I mind how once we lay, such a transparent summer morning.
Swiftly arose and spread around me the peace and knowledge that pass
all the argument of the earth,
And I know that the hand of God is the promise of my own,
And I know that the spirit of God is the brother of my own,
And that all the men ever born are also my brothers and the women my
sisters and lovers,
And that a keelson of the creation is love."

I could easily give more instances, but one will suffice. I take it from the Autobiography of J. Trevor.

"One brilliant Sunday morning, my wife and the boys went to the Unitarian Chapel in Macclesfield. I felt it impossible to accompany them-as though to lave the sunshine of the hills, and go down there to the chapel, would be for the time an act of spiritual suicide. And I felt such need for new inspiration and expansion in my life. So, very reluctantly and sadly, I left my wife and boys to go down into the town, while I went further up into the hills with my stick and my dog. In the loveliness of the morning, and the beauty of the hills and valleys, I soon lost my sense of sadness and regret. For nearly an hour I walked along the road to the 'Cat and Fiddle,' and then returned. On the way back, suddenly, without warning, I felt that I was in Heaven-an inward state of peace and joy and assurance indescribably intense, accompanied with a sense of being bathed in a warm glow of light, as though the external condition had brought about the internal effect-a feeling of having passed beyond the body, though the scene around me stood out more clearly and as if nearer to me than before, by reason of the illumination in the midst of which I seemed to be placed. This deep emotion lasted, though with decreasing strength, until I reached home, and for some time after, only gradually passing away."

The writer adds that having had further experiences of a similar sort, he now knows them well.

"The spiritual life," he writes, "justifies itself to those who live it; but what can we say to those who do not understand" This, at least, we can say, that it is a life whose experiences are proved real to their possessor, because they remain with him when brought closest into contact with the objective realities of life. Dreams cannot stand this test. These highest experiences that I have had of God's presence have been rare and brief-flashes of consciousness which have compelled me to exclaim with surprise-God is here!-or conditions of exaltation and insight, less intense, and only gradually passing away. I have severely questioned the worth of these moments. To no soul have I named them, lest I should be building my life and work on mere phantasies of the brain. But I find that, after every questioning and test, they stand out to-day as the most real experiences of my life, and experiences which have explained and justified and unified all past experiences and all past growth. Indeed, their reality and their far-reaching significance are ever becoming more clear and evident. When they came, I was living the fullest, strongest, sanest, deepest life. I was not seeking them. What I was seeking, with resolute determination, was to live more intensely my own life, as against what I knew would be the adverse judgment of the world. It was in the most real seasons that the Real Presence came, and I was aware that I was immersed in the infinite ocean of God."

Even the least mystical of you must by this time be convinced of the existence of mystical moments as states of consciousness of an entirely specific quality, and of the deep impression which they make on those who have them. A Canadian psychiatrist, Dr. R. M. Bucke, gives to the more distinctly characterized of those phenomena the name of cosmic consciousness. "Cosmic consciousness in its more striking instances is not," Dr. Bucke says, "simply an expansion or extension of the self-conscious mind with which we are all familiar, but the superaddition of a function as distinct from any possessed by the average man as self-consciousness is distinct from any function possessed by one of the higher animals."

"The prime characteristics of cosmic consciousness is a consciousness of the cosmos, that is, of the life and order of the universe. Along with the consciousness of the cosmos there occurs an intellectual enlightenment which alone would place the individual on a new plane of existence-would make him almost a member of a new species. To this is added a state of moral exaltation, and indescribable feeling of elevation, elation, and joyousness, and a quickening of the moral sense, which is fully as striking, and more important than is the enhanced intellectual power. With these come what may be called a sense of immortality, a consciousness of eternal life, not a conviction that he shall have this, but the consciousness that he has it already."

It was Dr. Bucke's own experience of a typical onset of cosmic consciousness in his own person which led him to investigate it in others. He has printed his conclusions in a highly interesting volume, from which I take the following account of what occurred to him:—

"I had spent the evening in a great city, with two friends reading and discussing poetry and philosophy. We parted at midnight. I had a long drive in a hansom to my lodging. My mind, deeply under the influence of the ideas, images, and emotions called up by reading and talk, was calm and peaceful. I was in state of quiet, almost passive enjoyment, not actually thinking, but letting ideas, images, and emotions flow of themselves, as it were, through my mind. All at once, without warning of any kind, I found myself wrapped I in a flame-colored cloud. For an instant I thought of fire, an immense conflagration somewhere close by in that great city; the next, I knew that the fire was within myself. Directly afterward came upon me a sense of exultation, of immense joyousness accompanied or immediately followed by an intellectual illumination impossible to describe. Among other things, I did not merely come to believe, but I saw that the universe is not composed of dead matter, but is, on the contrary, a living Presence; I became conscious in myself of eternal life. It was not a conviction that I would have eternal life, but a consciousness that I possessed eternal life then; I saw that all mean are immortal; that no cosmic order is such that without any peradventure all things work together for the good of each and all; that the foundation principle of the world, of all the worlds, is what we call love, and that the happiness of each and all is in the long run absolutely certain. The vision lasted a few seconds and was gone; but the memory of it and the sense of the reality of what it taught has remained during the quarter of a century which has since elapsed. I knew that what the vision showed was true. I had attained to a point of view from which I saw that it must be true. That view, that conviction, I may say that consciousness, has never, even during periods of the deepest depression, been lost."

We have now seen enough of this cosmic or mystic consciousness, as it comes sporadically. We must next pass to its methodical cultivation as an element of the religious life. Hindus, Buddhists, Mohammedans, and Christians all have cultivated it methodically.

In India, training in mystical insight has been known from time immemorial under the name of yoga. Yoga means the experimental union of the individual with the divine. It is based on preserving exercise; and the diet, posture, breathing, intellectual concentration, and moral discipline vary slightly in the different systems which teach it. The yogi, or disciple, who has by these means overcome the obscurations of his lower nature sufficiently, enters into the condition termed Samadhi, "and comes face to face with facts which no instinct or reason can ever know." He learns-"That the mind itself has a higher state of existence, beyond reason, a superconscious state, and that when the mind gets to that higher state, this knowledge beyond reasoning comes. ...ALL the different steps in yoga are intended to bring us scientifically to the superconscious state or Samadhi...Just as unconscious work is beneath consciousness, so there is another work which is above consciousness, and which, also, is not accompanied with the feeling of egoism...There is no feeling of I, and yet the mind works, desireless, free from restlessness, objectless, bodiless. Then the Truth shines in its full effulgence, and we know ourselves-for Samadhi lies potential in us all-for what we truly are, free, immortal, omnipotent, loosed from the finite, and its contrasts of good and evil altogether, and identical with the Atman or Universal Soul."

The Vedantists say that one may stumble into superconsciousness sporadically, without the previous discipline, but it is then impure. Their test of its purity, like our test of religion's value, is empirical: its fruits must be good for life. When a man comes out of Samadhi, they assure us that he remains "enlightened, a sage, a prophet, a saint, his whole character changed, his life changed, illumined."

The Buddhists use the word 'samadhi' as well as the Hindus; but 'dhyana' is their special word for higher states of contemplation. There seem to be four stages recognized in dhyana. The first stage comes through concentration of the mind upon one point. It excludes desire, but not discernment or judgment: it is still intellectual. In the second stage the intellectual functions drop off, and the satisfied sense of unity remains. In the third stage the satisfaction departs, and indifference begins, along with memory and self-consciousness. In the fourth stage the indifference, memory, and self-consciousness are perfected. [Just what 'memory' and 'self-consciousness' mean in this connection is doubtful. They cannot be the faculties familiar to us in the lower life.] Higher stages still of contemplation are mentioned-a region where there exists nothing, and where the mediator says: "There exists absolutely nothing," and stops. Then he reaches another region where he says: "There are neither ideas nor absence of ideas," and stops again. Then another region where, "having reached the end of both idea and perception, he stops finally." This would seem to be, not yet Nirvana, but as close an approach to it as this life affords.

In the Mohammedan world the Sufi sect and various dervish bodies are the possessors of the mystical tradition. The Sufis have existed in Persia from the earliest times, and as their pantheism is so at variance with the hot and rigid monotheism of the Arab mind, it has been suggested that Sufism must have been inoculated into Islam by Hindu influences. We Christians know little of Sufism, for its secrets are disclosed only to those initiated. To give its existence a certain liveliness in your minds, I will quote a Moslem document, and pass away from the subject.

Al-Ghazzali, a Persian philosopher and theologian, who flourished in the eleventh century, and ranks as one of the greatest doctors of the Moslem church, has left us one of the few autobiographies to be found outside of Christian literature. Strange that species of books so abundant among ourselves should be so little represented elsewhere-the absence of strictly personal confessions is the chief difficulty to the purely literary student who would like to become acquainted with the inwardness of religions other than the Christian.

M. Schmolders has translated a part of Al-Ghazzali's autobiography into French:

"The Science of the Sufis," says the Moslem author, "aims at detaching the heart from all that is not God, and at giving to its for sole occupation the meditation of the divine being. Theory being more easy for me than practice, I read [certain books] until I understood all that can be learned by study and heresay. Then I recognized that what pertains most exclusively to their method is just what no study can grasp, but only transport, ecstasy, and the transformation of the soul. How great, for example, is the difference between knowing the definitions of health, of satiety, with their causes and conditions, and being really healthy or filled. How different to know in what drunkenness consists,— as being a state occasioned by a vapor that rises from the stomach, —and being drunk effectively. Without doubt, the drunken man knows neither the definition of drunkenness nor what makes it interesting for science. Being drunk, he knows nothing; whilst the physician, although not drunk, knows well in what drunkenness consists, and what are its predisposing conditions. Similarly there is a difference between knowing the nature of abstinence, and being abstinent or having one's soul detached from the world. -Thus I had learned what words could teach of Sufism, but what was left could be learned neither by study nor through the ears, but solely by giving one's self up to ecstasy and leading a pious life.

"Reflecting on my situation, I found myself tied down by a multitude of bonds-temptations on every side. Considering my teaching, I found it was impure before God. I saw myself struggling with all my might to achieve glory and to spread my name. [Here follows an account of his six months' hesitation to break away from the conditions of his life at Bagdad, at the end of which he fell ill with a paralysis of the tongue.] Then, feeling my own weakness, and having entirely given up my own will, I repaired to God like a man in distress who has no more resources. He answered, as he answers the wretch who invokes him. My heart no longer felt any difficulty in renouncing glory, wealth, and my children. So I quitted Bagdad, and reserving from my fortune only what was indispensable for my subsistence, I distributed the rest. I went to Syria, where I remained about two years, with no other occupation than living in retreat and solitude, conquering my desires, combating my passions, training myself to purify my soul, to make my character perfect, to prepare my heart for meditating on God-all according to the methods of the Sufis, as I had read of them.

"The retreat only increased my desire to live in solitude, and to complete the purification of my heart and fit it for meditation. But the vicissitudes of the times, the affairs of the family, the need of subsistence, changed in some respects my primitive resolve, and interfered with my plans for a purely solitary life. I had never yet found myself completely in ecstasy, save in a few single hours; nevertheless, I kept the hope of attaining this state. Every time that the accidents led my astray, I sought to return; and in this situation I spent ten years. During this solitary state things were revealed to me which it is impossible either to describe or point out. I recognized for certain that the Sufis are assuredly walking in the path of God. Both in their acts and in their inaction, whether internal or external, they are illumined by the light which proceeds from the prophetic source. The first condition for a Sufi to purge his heart entirely of all that is not God. The next key of the contemplative life consists in the humble prayers which escape from the fervent soul, and in the meditations on God in which the heart is swallowed up entirely. But in reality this is only the beginning of the Sufi life, the end of Sufism being total absorption in God. The intuitions and all that precede are, so to speak, only the threshold for those who enter. From the beginning, revelations take place in so flagrant a shape that the Sufis see before them, whilst wide awake, the angels and the souls of the prophets. They hear their voices and obtain their favors. Then the transport rises from the perceptions of forms and figures to a degree which escapes all expression, and which no man may seek to give an account of without his words involving sin.

"Whoever has had no experience of the transport knows of the true nature of prophetism nothing but the name. He may meanwhile be sure of its existence, both by experience and by what he hears the Sufis say. As there are men endowed only with the sensitive faculty who reject what is offered them in the way of objects of the pure understanding, so there are intellectual men who reject and avoid the things perceived by the prophetic faculty. A blind man can understand nothing of colors save what he has learned by narration and heresay. Yet God has brought prophetism near to men in giving them all a state analogous to it in its principal characters. This state is sleep. If you were to tell a man who was himself without experience of such a phenomenon that there are people who at times swoon away so as to resemble dead men, and who [in dreams] yet perceive things that are hidden, he would deny it [and give his reasons]. Nevertheless, his arguments would be refuted by actual experience. Wherefore, just as the understanding is a stage of human life in which an eye opens to discern various intellectual objects uncomprehended by sensation; just so in the prophetic the sight is illumined by a light which uncovers hidden things and objects which the intellect fails to reach. The chief properties of prophetism are perceptible only during the transport, by those who embrace the Sufi life. The prophet is endowed with qualities to which you possess nothing analogous, and which consequently you cannot possibly understand. How should you know their true nature, since one knows only what one can comprehend? But the transport which one attains by the method of the Sufis is like an immediate perception, as if one touched the objects with one's hand."

This incommunicableness of the transport is the keynote of all mysticism. Mystical truth exists for the individual who has the transport, but for one else. In this, as I have said, it resembles the knowledge given to us in sensations more than that given by conceptual thought. Thought, with its remoteness and abstractness, has often enough in the history of philosophy been contrasted unfavorably with sensation. It is a commonplace of metaphysics that God's knowledge cannot be discursive but must be intuitive, that is, must be constructed more after the pattern of what in ourselves is called immediate feeling, than after that of proposition and judgment. But our immediate feelings have no content but what the five senses supply; and we have seen and shall see again that mystics may emphatically deny that the senses play any part in the very highest type of knowledge which their transport yield.

In the Christian church there have always been mystics. Although many of them have been viewed with suspicion, some have gained favor in the eyes of the authorities. The experiences of these have been treated as precedents, and a codified system of mystical theology has been based upon them, in which everything legitimate finds its place. The basis of the system is 'orison' or meditation, the methodical elevation of the soul towards God. Through the practice of orison the higher levels of mystical experience may be attained. It is odd that Protestantism, especially evangelical Protestantism, should seemingly have abandoned everything methodical in this line. Apart from what prayer may lead to, Protestant mystical experience appears to have been almost exclusively sporadic. It has been left to our mind-curers to reintroduce methodical meditation into our religious life.

The firs thing to be aimed at in orison is the mind's detachment from outer sensations, for these interfere with its concentration upon ideal things. Such manuals as Saint Ignatius's Spiritual Exercises recommend the disciple to expel sensation by a graduated series of efforts to imagine holy scenes. The acme of this kind of discipline would be a semi-hallucinatory mono-ideism-an imaginary figure of Christ, for example, coming fully to occupy the mind. Sensorial images of this sort, whether literal or symbolic, play an enormous part in mysticism. But in certain cases imagery may fall away entirely, and in the very highest raptures it tends to do so. The state of consciousness becomes then insusceptible of any verbal description. Mystical teachers are unanimous as to this. Saint John of the Cross, for instance, one of the best of them, thus describes the conditions called the 'union of love,' which he says, is reached by 'dark contemplation.' In this the Deity compenetrates the soul, but in such a hidden way that the soul-

"finds no terms, no means, no comparisons whereby to render the sublimity of the wisdom and the delicacy of the spiritual feeling with which she is filled....We receive this mystical knowledge of God clothed in none of the kinds of images, in one of the sensible representations, which our mind makes use of in other circumstances. Accordingly in this knowledge, sine the senses and the imagination are not employed, we get neither form nor impression, nor can we give any account or furnish any likeness, although the mysterious and sweet-tasting wisdom comes home so clearly to the inmost parts of our soul. Fancy a man seeing a certain kind of thing for the first time in his life. He can understand it, use and enjoy it, but he cannot apply a name to it, nor communicate any idea of it, even though all the while it be a mere thing of sense. How much greater will be his powerlessness when it goes beyond the senses! This is the peculiarity of the divine language. The more infused, intimate, spiritual, and supersensible it is, the more does it exceed the senses, both inner and outer, and impose silence upon them...The soul then feels as if placed in a vast and profound solitude, to which no created thing has access, in an immense and boundless desert, desert the more delicious the more solitary it is. There, in this abyss of wisdom, the soul grows by what it drinks in from the wellsprings of the comprehension of love, ... and recognizes, however sublime and learned may be the terms we employ, how utterly vile, insignificant, and improper they are, when we seek to discourse of divine things by their means."

I cannot pretend to detail to you the sundry stages of the Christian mystical life. Our time would not suffice, for one thing; and moreover, I confess that the subdivisions and names which we find in the Catholic books seem to me represent nothing objectively distinct. So many men, so many minds: I imagine that these experiences can be as infinitely varied as are the idiosyncrasies of individuals.

The cognitive aspects of them, their value in the way of revelations, is what we are directly concerned with, and it is easy to show by citation how strong an impression they leave of being revelations of new depths of truth. Saint Teresa is the expert of experts in describing such conditions, so I will turn immediately to what she says of one of the highest of them, the 'orison of union.'

"In the orison of union," says Saint Teresa, "the soul is fully awake as regards God, but wholly asleep as regards things of this world and in respect of herself. During the short time the union lasts, she is as it were deprived of every feeling, and even if she would, she could not think of any single thing. Thus she needs to employ no artifice in order to arrest the use of her understanding: it remains so stricken with inactivity that she neither knows what she loves, nor in what manner she loves, no what she wills. In short, she is utterly dead to the things of the world and lives solely in God....I do not even know whether in this state she has enough life left to breathe. It seems to me she has not, or at least that if she does breathe, she is unaware of it. Her intellect would fain understand something of what is going on within her, but it has so little force now that it can act I no way whatsoever. So a person who falls into a deep faint appears as if dead....

"Thus does God, when he raises a soul to union with himself, suspend the natural action of all her faculties. She neither sees, hears, nor understands, so long as she is united with God. But this time is always short, and it seems even shorter than it is. God establishes himself in the interior of this soul in such a way, that when she returns to herself, it is wholly impossible for her to doubt that she has been in God, and God in her. This truth remains so strongly impressed on her that, even though many years should pass without the condition returning, she can neither forget the favor she received, nor doubt of its reality. If you, nevertheless, ask how it is possible that the soul can see and understand that she has been in God, since during the union she has neither sight nor understanding, I reply that she does not see it then, but that she sees it clearly later, after she has returned to herself, not by any vision, but by a certitude with abides with her and which God along can give her. I knew a person who was ignorant of the truth that God's mode of being in everything must be either by presence, by power, or by essence, but who, after having received the grace of which I am speaking, believed this truth in the most unshakable manner. So much so that, having consulted a half-learned man who was as ignorant on this point as she had been before she was enlightened, when he replied that God is in us only by 'grace,' she disbelieved his reply, so sure she was of the true answer; and when she came to ask wiser doctors, they confirmed her in her belief, which much consoled her....

"But how, you will repeat, can one have such certainty in respect to what one does not see? This question, I am powerless to answer. These are secrets of God's omnipotence which it does not appertain to me to penetrate. All that I know is that I tell the truth; and I shall never believe any soul who does not possess this certainty has ever been really united to God."

The kinds of truth communicable in mystical ways, whether these be sensible or supersensible, are various. Some of them relate to this world,—visions of the future, the reading of the hearts, the sudden understanding of texts, the knowledge of distant events, for example; but the most important revelations are theological or metaphysical.

"Saint Ignatius confessed one day to Father Laynez that a single hour of meditation at Manresa had taught him more truths about heavenly things than all the teachings of all the doctors put together could have taught him.... One day in orison, on the steps of the choir of the Dominican church, he saw in a distinct manner the plan of divine wisdom in the creation of the world. On another occasion, during a procession, his spirit was ravished in God, and it was given him to contemplate, in a form and images fitted to the weak understanding of a dweller on the earth, the deep mystery of the holy Trinity. This last vision flooded his heart with such sweetness, that the mere memory of it in after times made him she abundant tears.

Similarly with Saint Teresa. "One day, being in orison," she writes, "it was granted me to perceive in one instant how all things are seen and contained in God. I did not perceive them in their proper form, and nevertheless the view I had of them was of a sovereign clearness, and has remained vividly impressed upon my soul. It is one of the most signals of all the graces which the Lord has granted me....The view was so subtle and delicate that the understanding cannot grasp it."

She goes on to tell how it was as if the Deity were an enormous and sovereignly limpid diamond, in which all our actions were contained in such a way that their full sinfulness appeared evident as never before. On another day, she relates, while she was reciting the Athanasian Creed,—

"Our Lord made me comprehend in what way it is that one God can be in three Persons. He made me see it so clearly that I remained as extremely surprised as I was comforted,... and now, when I think of the holy Trinity, or hear It spoken of, I understand how the three adorable Persons form only one God and I experience an unspeakable happiness."

On still another occasion, it was given to Saint Teresa to see and understand in what wise the Mother of God had been assumed into her place in Heaven.

The deliciousness of some of these states seems to be beyond anything known in ordinary consciousness. It evidently involves organic sensibilities, for it is spoken of as something too extreme to be borne, and as verging on bodily pain. But it is too subtle and piercing a delight for ordinary words to denote. God's touches, the wounds of his spear, references to ebriety and to nuptial union have to figure in the phraseology by which it is shadowed forth. Intellect and sense both swoon away in these highest states of ecstasy. "If our understanding comprehends," says Saint Teresa, "it is in a mode which remains unknown to it, and it can understand nothing of what it comprehends. For my own part, I do not believe that it does comprehend, because, as I said, it does not understand itself to do so. I confess that it is all a mystery in which I am lost." In the condition called raptus or ravishment by theologians, breathing and circulation are so depressed that it is a question among the doctors whether the soul be or be not temporarily dissevered from the body. One must read Saint Teresa's descriptions and the very exact distinctions which she makes, to persuade one's self that one is dealing, not with imaginary experiences, but with phenomena which, however rare, follow perfectly definite psychological types.

To the medican mind these ecstasies signify nothing but suggested and imitated hypnoid states, on an intellectual; basis of superstition, and a corporeal one of degeneration and hysteria. Undoubtedly these pathological conditions have existed in many and possibly in all the cases, but that face tells us nothing about the value for knowledge of the consciousness which they induce. To pass a spiritual judgment upon these states, we must not content ourselves with superficial medical talk, but inquire into their fruits for life.

Their fruits appear to have been various. Stupefaction, for one thing, seems not to have been altogether absent as a result. You may remember the helplessness in the kitchen and schoolroom of poor Margaret Mary Alacoque. Many other ecstatic would have perished but for the care taken of them by admiring followers. The 'otherwordliness' encouraged by the mystical consciousness makes this over-abstraction from practical life peculiarly liable to befall mystics in whom the character is naturally passive and the intellect feeble; but in natively strong minds and characters we find quite opposite results. The great Spanish mystics, who carried the bait of ecstasy as far as it has often been carried, appear for the most part to have shown indomitable spirit and energy, and all the more so for the trances I which they indulged.

Saint Ignatius was a mystic, but his mysticism made him assuredly one of the most powerfully practical human engines that ever lived. Saint John of the Cross, writing of the intuitions and 'touches' by which God teaches the substance of the soul, tells us that—

"They enrich it marvelously. A single one of them may be sufficient to abolish at a stroke certain imperfections of which the soul during its whole life had vainly tried to rid itself, and to leave it adorned with virtues and loaded with supernatural gifts. A single one of these intoxicating consolations may reward it for all the labors undergone in its life-even were they numberless. Invested with an invincible courage, filled with an impassioned desire to suffer for its God, the soul then is seized with a strange torment that of not being allowed to suffer enough."

Saint Teresa is as emphatic, and much more detailed. You may perhaps remember a passage I quoted from her in my first lecture. There are many similar pages in her autobiography. Where in literature is a more evidently veracious account of the information of a new centre of spiritual energy, than is given in her description of the effects of certain ecstasies which in departing leave the soul upon a higher level of emotional excitement?

"Often, infirm and wrought upon with dreadful pains before the ecstasy, the soul emerges from it full of health and admirably disposed for action...as if God had willed that the body itself, already obedient to the soul's desires, should share in the soul's happiness...The soul after such a favor is animated with a degree of courage so great that if at that moment its body should be torn to pieces for the cause of God, it would feel nothing but the liveliest comfort. Then it is that promises and heroic resolutions spring up in profusion in us, soaring desires, horror of the world, and the clear perception of our proper nothingness...What empire is comparable to that of a soul who, from this sublime summit to which God has raised her, sees all the things of earth beneath her feet, and is captivated by no one of them? How ashamed she is of her former attachments! How amazed at her blindness! What lively pity she feels for those whom she recognizes still shrouded in the darkness!... She groans at having ever been sensitive to points of honor, at the illusion that made her ever see as honor what the world calls by that name. Now she sees in this name nothing more than an immense lie of which the world remains a victim. She discovers, in the new light from above, that in genuine honor there is nothing spurious, that to be faithful to his honor is to give our respect to what deserves to be respected really, and to consider as nothing, or as less than nothing, whatsoever perishes and is not agreeable to God...She laughs when she sees grave persons, persons of orison, caring for points of honor for which she now feels profoundest contempt. It is suitable to the dignity of their rank to act thus, they pretend, and it makes them more useful to others. But she knows that in despising the dignity of their rank for the pure love of God they would do more good in a single day than they would effect in ten years by preserving it...She laughs at herself that there should ever have been a time in her life when she made any case of money, when she ever desired it...Oh! If human beings might only agree together to regard it as so much useless mud, what harmony would then reign in the world! With what friendship we would all treat each other if our interest in honor and in money could but disappear from earth! For my own part, I feel as if it would be a remedy for all our ills."

Mystical conditions may, therefore, render the soul more energetic in the lines which their inspiration favors. But this could be reckoned an advantage only in case the inspiration were a true one. If the inspiration were erroneous, the energy would be all the more mistaken and misbegotten. So we stand once more before that problem of truth which confronted us at the end of the lectures on saintliness. You will remember that we turned to mysticism precisely to get some light on truth. Do mystical states establish the truth of those teho9logical affections in which the saintly life has its root?

In spite of their repudiation of articulate self-description, mystical states in general assert a pretty distinct theoretic drift. It is possible to give the outcome of the majority of them in terms that point in definite philosophical directions. One of these directions is optimism, and the other is monism. We pass into mystical states from out of ordinary consciousness as from a less into a more, as from a smallness into a vastness, and at the same time as from an unrest to a rest. We feel them as reconciling, unifying states. They appeal to the yes-function more than to the no-function in us. In them the unlimited absorbs the limits and peacefully close the account. Their very denial of very adjective you may propose as applicable to the ultimate truth, —He, the Self, the Atman, is to be described by 'No! no!' only, say the Upanishads,—though it seems on the surface to be a no-function, is a denial made on behalf of a deeper yes. Whoso calls the Absolute anything in particular, or says that it is this, seems implicitly to shut if off from being that—it is as if he lessened it. So we deny the 'this,' negating the negation which it seems to us to imply, in the interests of the higher affirmative attitude by which we are possessed. The fountain-head of Christian mysticism is Dionysius the Areopagite. He describes the absolute truth by negatives exclusively.

"The cause of all things is neither soul nor intellect; nor has it imagination, opinion, or reason, or intelligence; nor is it reason or intelligence; nor is it spoken or thought. It is neither number, nor order, nor magnitude, nor littleness, nor equality, nor inequality, nor similarity, no dissimilarity. It neither stands, nor moves, nor rests....It is neither essence, nor eternity, nor time. Even intellectual contact does not belong to it. It is neither science nor truth. It is not even royalty or wisdom; not one, not unity; not divinity or goodness; nor even spirit as we know it," etc., ad libitum.

But these qualifications are denied by Dionysius, not because the truth falls short of them, but because it so infinitely excels them. It is above them. It is super-lucent, super-splendent, super-essential, super-sublime, super everything that can be named. Like Hegel in his logic, mystics journey towards the positive pole of truth only by the "Methode der Absoluten Negativitat.'

Thus come the paradoxical expressions that so abound in mystical writings. As when Eckhart tells of the still desert of the Godhead, "where never was seen difference, neither Father, Son, nor Holy Ghost, where there is no one at home, yet where the spark of the soul is more at peace than in itself." As when Boehme writes of the Primal Love, that "it may fitly be compared to Nothing, for it is deeper than any Thing, and is as nothing with respect to all things, forasmuch as it is not comprehensible by any of them. And because it is nothing respectively, it is therefore free from all things, and is that only good, which a man cannot express or utter what it is, there being nothing to which it may be compared, to express it by." Or as when Angelus Silesius sings:

"Gott ist ein later Nichts, ihn ruhrt kein Nun noch Hier;
Je mehr dun ach ihm greiffst, je mehr entwind er dir."

To this dialectical use, by the intellect, of negation as a mode of passage towards a higher kind of affirmation, there is correlated the subtlest of moral counterparts in the sphere of the personal will. Since denial of the finite self and its wants, since asceticism of some fort, is found in religious experience to be the only doorway to the larger and more blessed life, this moral mystery intertwines and combines with the intellectual mystery in all mystical writings.

"Love," continues Behmen, is Nothing, for "when thou art gone forth wholly from the Creature and from that which is visible, and art become Nothing to all that is Nature and Creature, then thou art in that eternal One, which is God himself, and then thou shalt feel within thee the highest virtue of Love....The treasure of treasures for the soul is where she goeth out of the Somewhat into that Nothing out of which all things may be made. The soul here saith, I have nothing, for I am utterly stripped and naked; I can do nothing, for I have no manner of power, but am as water poured out; I am nothing, for all that I am is no more than an image of Being, and only God is to me I AM; and so, sitting down in my own Nothingness, I give glory to the eternal Being, and will nothing of myself, that so God may will all in me, being unto me my God and all things."

In Paul's language, I live, yet not I, but Christ liveth in me. Only when I become as nothing can God enter in and no difference between his life and mine remain outstanding.

This overcoming of all the usual barriers between the individual and the Absolute is the great mystic achievement. In mystic states we both become one with the Absolute and we become aware of our oneness. This is the everlasting and triumphant mystical tradition, hardly altered by differences of clime or creed. In Hinduism, In Neoplatonism, in Sufism, In Christian mysticism, in

Whitmanism, we find the same recurring note, so that there is about mystical utterances an eternal unanimity which ought to make a critic stop and think, and which brings it about that the mystical classics have, as has been said, neither birthday nor native land. Perpetually telling of the unity of man with God, their speech antedates languages, and they do not grow old.

'That art Thou!' say the Upanishads, and the Vedantists add: 'Not a part, not a mode of That, but identically That, that absolute Spirit of the Word.' "As pure water poured into pure water remains the same, thus, O Gautama, is the Self of a thinker who knows. Water in water, fire in fire, ether in ether, no one can distinguish them; likewise a man whose mind has entered into the Self." " 'Every man,' says the Sufi GulshanRaz, 'whose heart is no longer shaken by any doubt, knows with certainty that there is no being save only One....In his divine majesty the me, the we, the thou, are not found, for in the One there can be no distinction. Every being who is annulled and entirely separated from himself, hears resound outside of him this voice and this echo: I am God: he has an ternal way of existing, and is no longer subject to death.'" In the vision of God, says Plotinus, "what sees is not our reason, but something prior and superior to our reason. ...He who thus sees does not properly see, does not distinguish or imagine two things. He changes, he ceases to be himself, preserves nothing of himself. Absorbed in God, he makes but one with him, like a centre of a circle coinciding with another centre." "Here," writes Suso, "the spirit dies, and yet is all alive I nthe marvels of the Godhead...and is lost in the stillness of the glorious dazzling obscurity and of the naked simple unity. It is in this modeless where the highest bliss is to be found." "Ich bin so gross als Gott," sings Angelus Silesius agan, "Er ist als ich so klein; Er kann nicht uber mich, ich unter ihm nicht sein."

In mystical literature such self-contradictory phrases as 'dazzling obscurity,' 'whispering silence,' teeming desert,' are continually met with. They prove that not conceptual speech, but music rather, is the element through which we are best spoken to by mystical truth. Many mystical scriptures are indeed little more than musical compositions.

"He who would hear the voice of Nada, 'the Soundless Sound,' and comprehend it, he has to learn the nature of Dharana....When to himself his form appears unreal, as do on waking all the forms he sees in dreams; when he has ceased to hear the many, he may discern the ONE-the inner sound which kills the outer....For then the soul will hear, and will remember. And then to the inner ear will speak THE VOICE OF THE SILENCE...And now thy Self is lost in SELF, thyself unto THYSELF, merged in that SELF from which thou first didst radiate...Behold! Thou hast become the Light, thou hast become the Sound, thou are thy Master and thy God. Thou art THYSELF the object of the search: the VOICE unbroken, that resounds throughout eternities, exempt from change, from sin exempt, the seven sounds in one, the VOICE OF THE SILENCE. Om tat Sat."

These words, if they do not awaken laughter as you receive them, probably stir chords within you which music and language touch in common. Music gies us ontological messages which non-musical criticism is unable to contradict, though it may laugh at our foolishness in minding them. There is a verge of the mind which these things haunt; and whispers therefrom mingle with the operations of our understanding, even as the waters of the infinite ocean send their waves to break among the pebbles that lie upon our shores.

"Here begins the sea that ends not till the world's end. Where we stand, Could we know the next high sea-mark set beyond these waves that gleam, We should know what never man hath known, nor eye of man hath scanned....

Ah, but here man's heart leaps, yearning towards the gloom with venturous glee, From the shore that hath no shore beyond it, set in all the sea."

That doctrine, for example, that eternity is timeless, that our 'immortality,' if we live in the eternal, is not so much future as already now and here, which we find so often expressed to-day in certain philosophic circles, finds its support in a 'hear, hear!' or an 'amen,' which floats up from that mysteriously deeper level. We recognize the passwords to the mystical region as we hear them, but we cannot use them ourselves; it alone has the keeping of 'the password primeval.'

I have now sketched with extreme brevity and insufficiency, but as fairly as I am able in the time allowed, the general traits of the mystic ranges of consciousness. It is on the whole pantheistic and optimistic, or at least the opposite of pessimistic. It is anti-naturalistic, and harmonizes best with twice-bornness and so-called other worldly states of mind.

My next task is to inquire whether we can invoke it as authoritative. Does it furnish any warrant for the truth of the twice-bornness and supernaturality and pantheism which it favors? I must give my answer to this question as concisely as I can.

In brief my answer is this,—and I will divide it into three parts:

(1) Mystical states, when well developed, usually are, and have the right to be, absolutely authoritative over the individuals to whom they come.

(2) No authority emanates from them which should make it a duty for those who stand outside for them to accept their revelations uncritically.

(3) They break down the authority of the non-mystical or rationalistic consciousness, based upon the understanding and the senses alone. They show it to be only one kind of consciousness. They open out the possibility of other orders of truth, in which, so far as anything in us vitally responds to them, we may freely continue to have faith.

I will take up these points one by one.

1. As a matter of psychological fact, mystical states of a well-pronounced an emphatic sort are usually authoritative over those who have them. They have been 'there,' and know. It is vain for rationalism to grumble about this. If the mystical truth that comes to a man proves to be a force that he can live by, what mandate have we of the majority to order him to live in another way? We can throw him into a prison or a madhouse, but we cannot change his mind-we commonly attach it only the more stubbornly to its beliefs. It mocks our utmost efforts, as a matter of fact, and in point of logic it absolutely escapes our jurisdiction. Our own more 'ration' beliefs are based on evidence exactly similar in nature to that which mystics quote for theirs. Our senses, namely, have assured us of certain states of fact; but mystical experiences are as direct perceptions of fact for those who have them as any sensations ever were for us. The records show that even though the five senses be in abeyance in them, they are absolutely sensational in there epistemological quality, if I may be pardoned the barbarous expressions, —that is, they are face to face presentations of what seems immediately to exist.

The mystic is, in short, invulnerable, and must be left, whether we relish it or not, in undisturbed enjoyment of his creed. Faith, says Tolstoy, is that by which men live. And faith-state and mystic state are practically convertible terms.

2. But I now proceed to add that mystics have no right to claim that we ought to accept the deliverance of their peculiar experiences, if we are ourselves outsiders and feel no private call thereto. The utmost they can ever ask of us in this life is to admit that they establish a presumption. They form a consensus and have an unequivocal outcome; and it would be odd, mystics might say, if such a unanimous type of experience should prove to be altogether wrong. At bottom, however, this would only be an appeal to numbers, like the appeal of rationalism the other way; and the appeal to numbers has no logical force. If we acknowledge it, it is for 'suggestive,' not for logical reasons: we follow the majority because to do so suits our life.

But even this presumption from the unanimity of mystics is far from being strong. In characterizing mystic states as panthesistic, optimistic, etc., I am afraid I over-simplified the truth. I did so far expository reasons, and to keep the closer to the classic mystical tradition. The classic religious mysticism, it now must be confessed, is only a 'privileged case.' It is an extract, kept true to type by the selection of the fittest specimens and their preservation in 'schools.' It is carved out from a much larger mass; and if we take the larger mass as seriously as religious mysticism has historically taken itself, we find that the supposed unanimity largely disappears. To begin with, even religious mysticism itself, the kind that accumulates traditions and makes schools, is much less unanimous then I have allowed. It has been both ascetic and antinomianly self-indulgent within the Christian church. It is dualistic in Sankhya, and monistic in Vedanta philosophy. I called it panthesistic; but the great Spanish mystics are anything but panthesists. They are with few exceptions non-metaphysical minds, for whom 'the category of personality' is absolute. The 'union' of man with God is for them much more like an occasional miracle than like an original identity. How different again, apart from the happiness common to all, is the mysticism of Walt Whitman, Edward Carpenter, Richard Jefferies, and other naturalistic pantheists, from the more distinctively Christian sort. The fact is that the mystical feeling of enlargement, union, and emancipation has no specific intellectual content whatever of its own. It is capable of forming matrimonial alliances with material furnished by the most diverse philosophies and theologies, provided only they can find a place in their framework for its peculiar emotional mood. We have no right, therefore, to invoke its prestige as distinctively in favor of any special belief, such as that in absolute idealism, or in the absolute monistic identity, or in the absolute goodness, of the world. It is only relatively in favor of all these things-it passes out of common human consciousness in the direction in which they lie.

So much for religious mysticism proper. But more remains to be told, for religious mysticism is only one half of mysticism. The other half has no accumulated traditions except those which the text-books on insanity supply. Open any one of these, and you will find abundant cases in which 'mystical ideas' are cited as characteristic symptoms of enfeebled or deluded states of mind. In delusional insanity, paranoia, as they sometimes call it, we may have a diabolical mysticism, a sort of religious mysticism turned upside down. The same sense of ineffable importance in the smallest events, the same texts and words coming with new meanings, the same voices and visions and leadings and missions, the same controlling by extraneous powers; only this time the emotion is pessimistic: instead of consolations we have desolations; the meanings are dreadful; and the powers are enemies to life. It is evident that from the point of view of their psychological mechanism, the classic mysticism and these lower mysticisms spring from the same mental level ,from that great subliminal or transmarginal region of which science is beginning to admit the existence, but of which so little is really known. That region contains every kind of matter: 'seraph and snake' abide there side by side. To come from thence is no infallible credential. What comes must be shifted and tested,. And run the gauntlet of confrontation with the total context of experience, just like what comes from the outer world of sense. Its value must be ascertained by empirical methods, so long as we are not mystics ourselves.

Once more, then, I repeat that non-mystics are under no obligation to acknowledge in mystical states a superior authority conferred on them by their intrinsic nature.

3. Yet, I repeat once more, the existence of mystical states absolutely overthrows the pretension of non-mystical states to be the sole and ultimate dictators of what we may believe. As a rule, mystical states merely add a super sensuous meaning to the ordinary outward data of consciousness. They are excitements like the emotions of love or ambition, gifts to our spirit by means of which facts already objectively before us fall into a new expressiveness and make a new connection with our active life. They do not contradict these facts as such, or deny anything that our senses have immediately seized. It is the rationalistic critic rather who plays the part of denier in the controversy, and his denials have no strength, for there never can be a state of facts to which new meaning may not truthfully be added, provided the mind ascend to a more enveloping point of view. It must always remain an open question whether mystical states may not possibly be such superior points of view, windows through which the mind looks out upon a more extensive and inclusive world. The difference of the views seen from the different mystical windows need not prevent us from entertaining this supposition. The wider world would in that case prove to have a mixed constitution like that of this world, that is all. It would have its celestial and its infernal regions, its tempting and its saving moments, its valid experiences and its counterfeit ones, just as our world has them; but it would be a wider world all the same. We should have to use its experiences by selecting and subordinating and substituting just as is our custom in this ordinary naturalistic world; we should be liable to error just as we are now; yet the counting in of that wider world of meanings, and the serious dealing with it, might, in spite of all the perplexity, be indispensable stages in our approach to the final fullness of the truth.

In this shape, I think, we have to leave the subject. Mystical states indeed wield no authority due simply to their being mystical states. But the higher ones among them point in directions to which the religious sentiments even of non-mystical men incline. They tell of the supremacy of the ideal, of vastness, of union, of safety, and of rest. They offer us hypotheses, hypotheses which we may voluntarily ignore, but which as thinkers we cannot possibly upset. The supernaturalism and optimism to which they would persuade us may, interpreted in one way or another, be after all the truest of insights into the meaning of this life.

"Oh, the little more, and how much it is; and the little less, and what worlds away!" It may be that possibility and permissions of this sort are all that the religious consciousness requires to live on. In my last lecture I shall have to try to persuade you that this is the case. Meanwhile, whoever, I am sure that for many of my readers this diet is too slender. If supernaturalism and inner union with the divine are true, you think, the not so much permission, as compulsion to believe, ought to be found. Philosophy has always professed to prove religious truth by coercive argument; and the construction of philosophies of this kind has always been one favorite function of the religious life, if we use this term in the large historic sense.

THE NEUROPSYCHOLOGY OF AESTHETIC, SPIRITUAL & MYSTICAL STATES
by Eugene G. d'Aquili & Andrew B. Newberg

An analysis of the underlying neurophysiology of aesthetics and religious experience allows for the development of an Aesthetic/Religious Continuum. This continuum pertains to the variety of creative and spiritual experiences available to human beings. This may also lead to an understanding of the neurophysiological mechanism underlying both "positive" and "negative" aesthetics.

An analysis of this continuum allows for the ability to understand the neurophenomenological aspects of a variety of human experiences ranging from relatively simple aesthetic experiences to profound spiritual and unitary states such as those obtained during meditation. However, it may be possible, through a neuropsychological analysis to determine the similarities that exist across such experiences. Thus, certain parts of the brain may be functioning in similar ways during different experiences.

It may be the case that the specific neuropsychological components of a given experience may depend on the strength of the affectual response of the person and the ability to mark such experiences as significant. Further, even though similar structures may be functioning during different experiences, their inhibitory and excitatory interactions may be different. Finally, by considering the Aesthetic/ Religious Continuum, we may eventually arrive at a better understanding of how we experience and define reality.

Introduction

Friederich Nietzsche, following the ancient Greek model, divided aesthetics into a kind of positive aesthetics which he called Apollonian and a negative aesthetics which he called Dionysian (Nietzsche 1994). Apollonian aesthetics represent what is usually considered the aesthetics of beauty and light. It is comprised of a sense of wholeness and harmony, and is affectively marked by a sense of pleasantness, at the very least, and often a sense of joy or elation. Dionysian aesthetics, on the other hand, named after the myth of Dionysus being torn apart alive by the Bachae, is marked by a sense of fragmentation, disharmony, death or dying, and is affectively marked by sadness and melancholy, at least, and often by a sense of fundamental hopelessness, futility, and even terror.

Based on ancient philosophers, the medieval scholastics defined the essential characteristics of positive aesthetics as 1) Integritas or wholeness, 2) Consonantia Partium or harmony of parts, and 3) Claritas Formae or a radiance of form (Eco 1988). Thus for a work of art to have a positive aesthetic the medievals required that it generate an overall sense of wholeness and a sense of harmony of its composite parts. The radiance or clarity of form seems to have referred to the emotional effect on human beings which should be at the very least pleasant, and hopefully edifying and joyful.

The medieval scholastics were hesitant to deal with negative aesthetics, since, in their view, negative aesthetics were diabolical, while positive aesthetics were from God. Nevertheless, since they followed the ancients, they did summarily treat negative aesthetics. To a great extent, although not completely, the defining characteristics of negative aesthetics were considered to be the opposites of those defining positive aesthetics (Eco). They were: 1) Integritas in Fragmentatione or wholeness in fragmentation, 2) Dissonantia Partium or disharmony of parts, and 3) Tenebra Formae or darkness of form. It is interesting that if the defining characteristics of negative aesthetics were simply the opposite of the defining characteristics of positive aesthetics, then the first characteristic of negative aesthetics should be Fragmentatio or fragmentation, pure and simple. But the medievals insisted that, for a work of art to be a work art, however diabolical, and not simply a rendering of the horror of human life, there had to be some sense of wholeness or integrity even if the subject matter itself fragmented. Thus, for a medieval aesthetician, and probably for an ancient one as well, "Guernaca" or "Waiting for Godot" are works of art at least because they are defined spatially and temporally, by a frame in the case of "Guernaca" and by the production time and temporal sequencing in the case of "Waiting for Godot." The medievals would probably maintain that the use of words, and possibly of sentences, and the delimitation of formal elements within a painting contribute to the formal wholeness in spite of the fragmentation of overall subject matter. So much for the criterion of wholeness within fragmentation. The other two characteristics of negative aesthetics for the scholastic are simply the opposite of the second and third characteristics of positive aesthetics. By this we mean a disharmony of parts and a darkness of form. As in the case of Claritas Formae, Tenebra Formae also describes the emotional response to a work of negative aesthetics, i.e. sadness, futility, hopelessness, and horror.

Throughout most of human history, positive or Apollonian aesthetics have tended to be synonymous with aesthetics in general. Of course there have been counter-examples, particularly among the Greeks and Romans. But even among them, Apollonian aesthetics tended to define beauty. It is only in the 20th century, particularly in the West, that the negative aesthetic has come into its own. With the weakening of religious belief systems in the West, the existential sense of a futile, empty, and hopeless world has provided the ground for negative or Dionysian aesthetics to become a dominant manifestation of art. But whether art is Dionysian or Apollonian, it appears that, one way or another, a sense of wholeness is, to some extent at least, essential for aesthetic appreciation. The crucial importance of this, and how it relates to religious experience will become more obvious as we examine the neuropsychology of the Aesthetic-Religious Continuum.

The Neuropsychology of the Aesthetic-Religious Continuum

To understand the neuropsychology underlying both aesthetics and religious experience, we must first present some background material concerning primary epistemic or knowing states. We have previously defined nine primary epistemic or knowing states (d'Aquili 1982). Of these nine only six relate to a world of multiple discrete reality while the other three relate to Absolute Unitary Being (AUB) which is a state, usually arising out of profound meditation, in which there is no perception or awareness of discrete beings, no perception of space or time, and in which even the self-other dichotomy is obliterated (d'Aquili and Newberg 1993a). In our analysis of the neuropsychology of aesthetics, and in our preliminary analysis of the neuropsychology of religious states, we are only concerned with the six primary epistemic states which deal with multiple discrete reality.

Of these six states three are inherently unstable involving irregular relationships between the elements of discrete reality, often caused by drugs or various forms of psychosis or dementia. For the purposes of this paper we are only concerned with the three stable states involving the perception of multiple discrete reality and regular relationships between elements of that reality. The first such state is characterized by neutral affect. We have called this baseline reality, and it is presumably the reality that comprises our everyday perceptions and behaviors. The second primary epistemic state which will be of concern to us is multiple discrete reality with regular relationships suffused with positive affect. This is similar to the state that Bucke (1961) called Cosmic Consciousness. The third primary epistemic state involving multiple discrete reality and regular relationships is suffused by negative affect and has been called Weltschmerz.

Let us take a few moments to describe these states in more detail. The first of these states, which we call the "baseline" state, involves the perception of discrete entities comprising the world that are related to each other in regular and predictable ways. The affective valance of this world perception is neutral. We presume it is the state that most of us are in at this moment; for example, most are of us are quite certain of the reality of the furniture and people surrounding us. Very few, if any, of us would question the fundamental reality of the state we are in. It is precisely because this state appears certainly real while one is in it that it is a primary epistemic state. Furthermore, most individuals would consider this state as the only reality or the only valid epistemic state. Nevertheless, the fact is that not only is this sense of reality not unique, but there are two other stable perceptions of discrete reality which are also primary. These other two states are similar to the state most of us are in most of the time in that the regularities of time, space, and causality are the same and in that there is the perception of the same discrete entities in the world. They differ from baseline reality only in affective valance, positive or negative, as opposed to neutral, which usually suffuses the perception of the world.

The second primary epistemic state or "sense of reality" involves the same discrete entities and regularities as the baseline ordinary state, but it involves an elated sense of well being and joy, in which the universe is perceived to be fundamentally good and all its parts are sensed to be related in a unified whole. In this state there is usually a sense of purposefulness to the universe and to a human individual's place in the universe. This sense of purposefulness may defy logic and certainly does not arise from logic; nonetheless it is a primary stable and certain perception. The onset of such an exhilarating view of reality is usually sudden and has been described as a conversion experience. It has been delineated repeatedly in the religious literature of the world. In the psychiatric literature, it was most carefully described by Richard M. Bucke (1961) in a remarkable book entitled, Cosmic Consciousness. Since the publication of this volume in 1901 it has undergone some 22 editions, the latest in 1969. Bucke had this experience himself, and in his magnum opus, he presented evidence of similar experiences in the lives of many people including the Buddha, Socrates, St. Paul, Francis Bacon, Blaise Pascal, Bendict Spinoza, and William Blake as well as many of his own contemporaries.

A third primary sense of reality is also a very stable one. It is like the first two in that it deals with the world of multiple discrete being and has the same high degree of regularity of causal, spatial, and temporal relationships. It differs from the first two in that the basic affective valance toward the perceived universe is profoundly negative. It has been called Weltschmerz in the psychiatric literature and consists of a sense of exquisite sadness and futility, as well as the sense of the incredible smallness of human beings in the universe, the inevitable existential pain generated by being in the world, and the suffering inherent in the human condition. Usually, there is the perception of the whole universe as one vast pointless machine without purpose or meaning. In its full blown form, it is similar to Cosmic Consciousness in that it usually occurs with a suddenness that leaves the individual totally perplexed. The individual experiences a profound sense of loss and meaninglessness to the world which rarely leaves. It is the basic sense of reality which appears to underlie much existentialist thought, particularly in French existentialist literature. It is the sort of perception in which the universe is apprehended not in any way as neutral but as essentially absurd, and often suicide is thought to be the only truly human response.

It seems that the primary epistemic states that we have considered actually make up a spectrum or continuum of unitary states in which the sense of unity increasingly transcends the sense of diversity. At one end of this unitary continuum, close to baseline reality, was the experience of positive or Apollonian aesthetics. Again the sense of wholeness or Integritas was greater than the diversity of parts. It seemed that this was true in the appreciation of a sunset or a symphony. We postulated that the posterior superior parietal lobule (PSPL) and certain parts of the inferior parietal lobule, particularly on the non-dominant side, were involved in the imposing of greater unity over diversity. Thus, as one moves up the unitary continuum with progressively greater experience of unity over diversity, one moves out of the realm of aesthetics and into a realm that would more properly be characterized as religious experience.

A transitional phase between aesthetic and religious experience may be romantic love which might be characterized by the phrase, "it is bigger than the both of us." As one moves up this continuum, one moves through the experience of numinosity or religious awe, into Bucke's state of Cosmic Consciousness, properly so called. As one continues along this spectrum beyond Cosmic Consciousness, one moves into various trance states in which there is a progressive blurring of the boundaries between entities until one finally moves into Absolute Unitary Being. As soon as one moves into AUB, one is in another primary epistemic state. This is because, AUB is characterized by absolute unity. There are no longer any discrete entities which relate to each other. The boundaries of entities within the world disappear and even the self-other dichotomy is totally obliterated. In AUB there is no extension of space or duration of time. If this state is suffused with positive affect, it is interpreted, after the fact, as the experience of God or the Unio Mystica. If it is suffused with neutral affect, it is experienced, non personally, as the Void or Nirvana of Buddhism. We have previously postulated that moving up this continuum was at least partially due to progressive deafferentation of (or blocking neural input to) the posterior superior parietal lobe and possibly adjacent areas of the brain (d'Aquili and Newberg 1993a, 1993b). We proposed that total deafferentation resulted in the total and absolute unitary experience of AUB.

In testing our hypothesis that progressive deafferentation of the posterior superior parietal lobe and parts of the inferior parietal lobe, particularly on the non-dominant side, was responsible for a progressive increase in unitary experience as we go up the Aesthetic-Religious Continuum, we were gratified to find that single photon emission computed tomography brain imaging of accomplished Tibetan Buddhist meditators yielded results compatible with deafferentation in these areas during profound unitary states (Newberg, Alavi, Baime, Mozley and d'Aquili 1997). However, we still must perform additional brain imaging studies to clearly delineate whether each point along the Aesthetic-Religious Continuum is marked by progressive deafferentation of these areas. culminating in total deafferentation during AUB. Thus, the evidence is suggestive that positive or Apollonian aesthetics represents the beginning of the aesthetic-religious continuum along which various spiritual and mystical experiences are placed culminating in either the experience of God or of the Buddhist Void.

Negative or Dionysian

Although some of the mechanism of the Apollonian esthetic and its relationship to spiritual and mystical experiences remains speculative, we are accumulating increasing evidence regarding the specific aspects of that neurophysiological mechanism. The same cannot be said of Dionysian aesthetics. Here we have fragmentation associated with some degree of wholeness. As with the medieval analysis, so with the neuropsychological analysis that the Dionysian is not simply the opposite of the Apollonian. We have described that senses of unity may arise from the progressive deafferentation of the posterior superior parietal lobe.

The blocking of input into this brain structure may result in a decreased sense of self and other, a decreased sense of space and time, and an overall sense of unity among discrete objects. Fragmentation, on the other hand, may result from an increased input into the posterior superior parietal lobe, i.e. the opposite of deafferentation. Thus, the posterior superior parietal lobule and certain adjacent structures in the inferior parietal lobule on the non-dominant side may become hyperexcited and overloaded with input. The inability to process and modulate all this input may result in the subjective sensation of fragmentation, hopelessness, and fundamental disorder to the universe resulting paradoxically in a sense of emptiness and futility which seems to be inherent in the universe.

The problem with Dionysian aesthetics is that, at the same time that negativity and fragmentation exists in a work of art, certain wholeness or integrity must exist simultaneously in order for the work to be experienced precisely as art. The only speculation as to how this might come about neurophysiologically is that at the same time that there is hyperstimulation of the PSPL on the non-dominant side, there is some degree of deafferentation in the homologous PSPL on the dominant side. We have postulated that the involvement of the PSPL on both sides occurs in certain mystical states (d'Aquili and Newberg 1993a, 1993b), so this mechanism is not absurd. Whether it is, in fact, what occurs has yet to be seen. Further studies and analysis will be required in order to more fully elucidate the underlying mechanism underlying Dionysian aesthetics. We have focused on the aesthetic

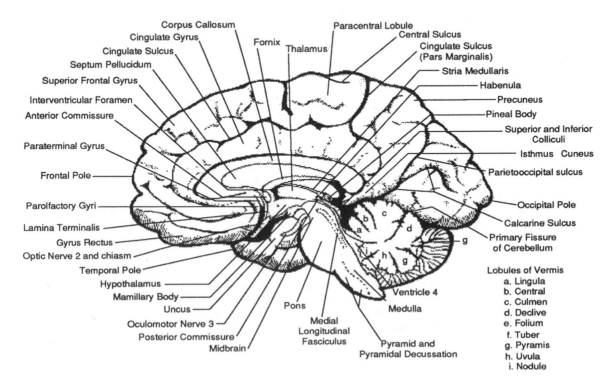

Figure 80. A medial "split-brain" view of the right hemisphere. From Joseph, 1990.

end of the Aesthetic-Religious Continuum in this paper thus far. Let us return to some considerations at the religious experience end of the Aesthetic-Religious Continuum.

Spiritual and Mystical States

We postulate that all spiritual and mystical states, at least those that have a powerful affective component, are located somewhere along a continuum that we have called the Aesthetic-Religious Continuum. These states, whether they are transitory experiences or more permanent states, occupy a place on what is probably, more or less, the second half of the Aesthetic-Religious Continuum. We admit that we have not done an exhaustive typology of unitary states. It is possible that the spiritual-mystical part of the continuum may be considerably more than half or considerably less than half of the spectrum which begins with aesthetic experiences, moves through experiences of romantic love, and then begins with lower level spiritual-mystical states.

In this part of the paper we will consider these latter states only. This upper end of the Aesthetic-Religious Continuum more or less begins with experiences of religious awe such as the sort of states which occur to some individuals when confronted with the beauty and majesty of nature. With this lower level mystical experience of religious awe should probably be also classified various numinous experiences such as mandala dreams. One can then move on along the continuum to the level of Cosmic Consciousness, properly so called, as described by Bucke. In this state, there is no alteration in the perceived characteristics of the world. However there is the profound senses, which people in this state would call knowledge, that the world is fundamentally one, in its essence, profoundly good. This is "known" to be the case even in the presence of profound evil and suffering in the world. We must reiterate that Cosmic Consciousness is not a philosophical stance, although it may be turned into one. The unity and goodness of all reality is simply known to be the case anterior to any philosophy or science. One then moves along the continuum into various trance states in which the contents of the sensorium are to a lesser or greater extent distorted or modified with reference to baseline reality. The perception of space and time can be significantly distorted during these trance states (d'Aquili and Newberg 1993a, 1993b). Likewise, it is along this part of the Aesthetic-Religious Continuum that archetypes are often activated sometimes associated with remarkable hyperlucid hallucinations.

Here we use the term hallucination it is basic sense, that is a sensory experience which cannot be checked in baseline reality. There is no implication either of reality or non-reality. As one moves along the continuum through progressively more profound trance states with progressively more tenuous boundaries between entities in the world and between the self and the world, one eventually moves into Absolute Unitary Being. As we mentioned above, this is the absolute unitary state where self and other are obliterated, where all entities and their interrelationship are obliterated, and where space and time are obliterated.

Let us now look at how these various spiritual-mystical states are characterized. The spiritual-mystical states, like all the states along the Aesthetic-Religious Continuum, can be ordered according to an experienced sense of greater unity over diversity. We have discussed this in detail above and have proposed that this progression of an increasing sense of unity can be neurophysiologically related to progressive deafferentation of the posterior superior parietal lobule and adjacent parts of the inferior parietal lobule particularly on the non dominant side. Although, in our model, the progressive unitary sense is the most important defining characteristic of spiritual-mystical states and the dimension by which various mystical states can be most rationally seen to relate to each other, there are, nevertheless three other defining characteristics of spiritual-mystical states.

As with the unitary sense these characteristics also seem to increase in intensity as one moves up the continuum towards AUB. The first of these three defining characteristics beyond the progressive unitary sense is the sense of transcendence or "otherworldliness". Actually a vague sense of transcendence seems to increase as one moves up the continuum gradually developing into a true other-worldly feeling. At present, it is unknown what is the neuroanatomical and neurophysiological substrate for the subjective sense of familiarity and its opposite unfamiliarity or strangeness. Whatever mechanism this may turn out to be, some modification of it undoubtedly underlies the sense of transcendence. Certainly, what one experiences as one moves up the spectrum is clearly strange when compared to baseline.

A second defining characteristic of spiritual-mystical experiences beyond the fundamental unitary sense is the progressive incorporation of the observing Self in each successive experience or state. As with aesthetic experiences, so with spiritual-mystical experiences, there must be a harmonious ordering of the parts or elements of the experience. We have postulated that the underlying neural network of this harmonious ordering of parts must involve the frontal lobes, the temporal lobes, and the inferior parietal lobule (d'Aquili and Newberg 1993a, 1993b). The inferior parietal lobule especially must be correlated with the harmony since it is responsible for the sense of gradation, comparison, and opposition (Joseph 1990). What is noteworthy here is not only a harmony of parts, but that one of the parts is the observing Self. The incorporation of the observing Self, to one degree or another, is absolutely essential to a spiritual-mystical state. It is by no means essential either to aesthetic experiences or to aesthetic productions. When there is an incorporation of the observing self to some extent in an aesthetic experience, however, it is a much more powerful experience. Indeed contemporary artistic productions often explicitly attempt to involve the observer.

Although it tends to generate a more powerful aesthetic experience, involvement of the observer in the content of a work of art, particularly in theatrical productions, is not inherent in a work of art being a work of art nor is it essential for an aesthetic experience. However, it is essential for a spiritual-mystical experience. The whole point of a spiritual-mystical experience is for the Self to sense itself to be fundamentally and essentially related to some aspect of whatever ultimate reality might be. This involvement of the self in the spiritual experience or state is progressively greater as one moves up the continuum. As one moves into AUB, the Self seems to expand to become the totality of reality without individualized content. This is very compatible with the Hindu interpretation, and probably underlies Shankara's observation that the Atman (or soul) and the Brahman (or God) are one.

The Christian unio mystica is phenomenologically the same, although care is taken by Christian theologians who reflect on this state to preserve the ontological independence of the soul. They would agree that in this state the union of God and the individual soul is so perfect and so complete that an observer, if such were possible, could not perceive where one ended and the other began. Nevertheless, for theological reasons, Christian mystical theologians maintain the ontological integrity of the individual although they would concede that the individual has, as it were, expanded to a perfect and a simple union with God. One often hears it said that in profound mystical experiences such as AUB the Self becomes as a drop of water in the ocean of reality. What actually appears to happen is that the Self, far from being a drop of water in an ocean, actually expands to become the

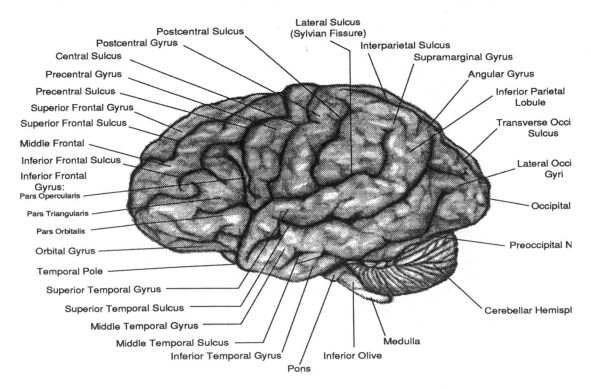

Figure 81. The left hemisphere. From Joseph, 1990.

totality of reality. When Europeans first came into contact with some Hindu sects, they were shocked and scandalized when they learned that part of ritual worship required the repeated assertion "I am God, I am God, I am God."

What confused the Europeans was that the "I" in the statement did not refer to the individual conscious ego with all its evil proclivities, but rather to the Self or Atman which is the deepest unconscious core reality of an individual. It is in this sense that every individual can truly state "I am God" because each individual can potentially expand into a state of AUB. A Hindu who states "I am God" is all the while perfectly aware of the shortcomings and failings of his conscious ego in day to day life. No religious tradition that we are aware of has ever advocated that an individual proclaim "I am God" where the "I" would refer to the conscious ego. That would indeed be blasphemy. Worse than blasphemy, it would be absurd.

The third defining characteristic of spiritual-mystical experiences beyond the unitary sense is the intense and progressive certainty as one moves up the unitary continuum of the objective reality of the mystical experiences (d'Aquili and Newberg 1993a, 1993b). A good example of this is the relatively common near death experience (NDE). This occurs in the area along the unitary continuum that we have called trance states. In its complete form, which is not too common in our society, the NDE appears to consist of the sequential constellation of two archetypes, first what we have called the Archetype of Dissolution followed by the Archetype of Transcendent Integration (Newberg and d'Aquili 1994). The first consists of hellish experience involving torture, dismemberment and other terrifying horrors. Often demons are involved and the experience is described as Hell among individuals whose religious tradition incorporates a concept of Hell. In fact, we would suggest that in the evolution of religious phenomenology, the concept of Hell may be derived from this terrifying experience. If allowed to take its course, the Archetype of Dissolution is followed by the Archetype of Transcendent Integration. This is the aspect of the near death experience that is described in present day literature (Moody 1975; Ring 1980). It involves the experience of moving through a tunnel often emerging in a breathtakingly beautiful landscape. The individual is often met by deceased relatives or friends, and in other cultures often by saints or Gods. This is usually followed by an encounter with a Being of Light and a rapid life review within the context of being totally and completely loved. Subjects recount that what is especially upsetting is reviewing one's own acts of selfishness or cruelty within the context of being unconditionally loved. At this point, the individual either decides or is informed that he or she must return to their body. This sequence of two archetypes, one terrifying beyond belief, the second involving a sort of celestial exaltation, joy, and love, together seem to form the complete near death experience.

Description of these biphasic "other world journeys" are well described in medieval spiritual literature and in the experience of other cultures as well (Zaleski 1987). This is especially true in the Tibetan Book of the Dead where the horrible and demonic chonyid state is described as a prelude to a state remarkably similar to the Archetype of Transcendent Integration (Freemantle and Trungpa 1987). The hellish Archetype of Dissolution has been described often enough in our in culture as to know that it certainly exists. Why do the great majority of individuals in our culture who have a near death experience have only, or remember only, the Archetype of Transcendent Integration is not known. We have speculated upon this in another work (Newberg and d'Aquili 1994). What is important here, however, is that almost all individuals who have had complete core experiences, especially involving the realm of light and the life review, are absolutely certain of the objective reality of their experience. This is true not only among an educated person but even among the most educated philosophers and scientists. This is apparently true among neuroscientists as well.

After reviewing many reports of core near death experiences we have been able find only one instance of a neuroscientist maintaining a tentative and somewhat skeptical stance after his experience. Furthermore the tone of his reservations was muted and agnostic allowing for the possibility of some sort of objective reality to be experienced. We do not claim to have made an exhaustive study, but all other scientists and philosophers as well as ordinary individuals, and including a number of neuroscientists, seem to maintain a quiet certainty of some sort of objective reality to their near death experience. Furthermore, people who have had the core NDE no longer appear to fear death (Ring 1980). And the lives of near death experiencers are nearly always dramatically changed in the direction of increased altruism and a generally more benevolent attitude towards family, friends, and indeed the world. Many of those who came out of a religious tradition seem to return to it, but many do not.

These experiences and their consequences in the lives of the near death experiencers are indeed amazing, and have generated a number of studies by sociologists interested in the social effects of the change in the lives of these individuals. What is clear is that almost every individual who has had a core NDE is quietly certain of the objective reality of their experience. It is interesting that almost all of the near death experiencers are not eager to proselytize, and they are not upset when they are not believed. When we discussed his experience with a neuroscientist he readily conceded that there may be neural correlates to the experience. He stated however that there are neural correlates to everyday experience, and this did not make him doubt the existence of the external world. We have considered the near death experience because it is relatively common and well reported.

The certainty of the objective reality of mystical experiences at the upper end of the Aesthetic-Religious Continuum is just as great, and, if possible, greater than the certainty of the reality of the near death experience. Individuals who have experienced AUB seem to be uniformly absolutely certain that they have been in contact with ultimate reality, however that may be subsequently interpreted in terms of their specific religious traditions. The certainty of the objective reality of that state seems to be absolute.

We have described the defining characteristics of mystical or spiritual experiences as: 1) progressive increase of unity over diversity, 2) progressive sense of transcendence or "otherworldliness, 3) progressive incorporation of the observing Self in the experience or state, and 4) a progressive increase of certainty in the objective existence of what was experienced in the spiritual-mystical state. This approaches absolute certainty especially for those states high on the unitary continuum involving hyperlucid experiences.

Reality and Phenomenology

All this leaves us with the interesting situation of what might be called superior and inferior realities with respect to baseline. For example certain states may be considered inferior in that, when they are recalled from the baseline state, they are not perceived to be real. Examples such as dreams or psychoses, while they may be considered real while one is in them, are almost always considered not to be real when the dreamer awakens or the psychotic person returns to the baseline state after being treated with certain medications. The individual may state "that was just a dream" or "I was crazy then before I took my medications." However, there are a number of states, particularly hyperlucid experiences, which are considered more real than baseline reality even when they are recalled in baseline reality. We have already presented the near death experience as a fairly common example of one such state. What is one to make of non-psychotic individuals calmly asserting that certain altered states of consciousness represent an objective reality more certainly real than the reality presented in baseline consciousness? And what do we mean when we say that something is "real", in any case?

In a previous work we have systematically demonstrated that the various criteria often presented by which we judge something to be "real" can all be reduced in one way or another to only one criterion, and that is the vivid sense that something is real (d'Aquili and Newberg 1998). This vivid sense has been called the phantasia catalyptica by the stoics or Anwesenheit by certain modern German philosophers. It is what Dr. Samuel Johnson referred to when disputing Bishop Berkeley's idealism. While discussing this with his friends he is said to have explained "I answer Bishop Berkeley thus." With this he kicked a stone with great force which happened to be beside the path on which they were walking. This is known as the "sore toe" school of epistemology. Nevertheless the stone had a compelling presence as do the people, furniture, buildings, etc., with which we interact in baseline reality. Space does not permit us to go into this issue in detail in this paper.

Suffice it to say reality seems to consist fundamentally only of the vivid sense of reality, or, as some would say reality is constituted by compelling presences. If this can systematically be shown to be true, and we believe that we have done so, then spiritual or mystical states of reality recalled in the baseline state as more certainly representing an objective condition than what is represented in the sensorium of the baseline state, must be considered real. There can be no other conclusion no matter how one comes at it. This may present many problems which must be worked out, but the essential or underlying reality of hyperlucid experiences must be said to be real or the term reality has no meaning whatsoever. It is such considerations which put us, even against our will, in the presence of what Otto called the mysterium tremendum et fascinans.

ON THE "NEURO" IN NEUROTHEOLOGY
by Andrew B. Newberg & Jeremy Iversen

Abstract. In this chapter, we review some of the basic issues regarding the neuroscientific studies associated with religious and spiritual experiences. Such an analysis is crucial for developing a comprehensive neurotheology that has a strong "neuro" as well as "theology" component. We will consider many of the recent advances in the study of brain function including neurochemical changes that are associated with various brain states and how such changes might be integrated into an overall model of religious experiences. While much of this neuroscientific analysis has aimed at specific religious and spiritual practices such as meditation or prayer, there are also implications for a wide array of spiritual experiences. Such an approach can ultimately lead to hypotheses that can form the basis for future studies of religious and spiritual phenomena.

Introduction

Neurotheology is an emerging discipline that integrates religious and spiritual concepts with neurological and neuropsychological analyses. Thus, both the neurological and theological perspectives must be considered if one is to find the best way of understanding both the human brain, and how that brain perceives and experiences religion. Much of the early foundations for neurotheology have been developed by scholars such as Rhawn Joseph (1996, 2000), James Austin (1998), and the late James Ashbrook (Ashbrook, 1984; Ashbrook & Albright, 1997) and Eugene d'Aquili (Laughlin, & d'Aquili, 1974; d'Aquili, Laughlin, & McManus, 1979). These scholars took a close look at how the neurosciences might inform us about religion and religious experience. While there are a tremendous number of issues within this field of study including how the neurosciences might approach religion, theology, religious experience, religious expression, religious practice, ritual, and myth, it is important to understand what neuroscience can do and what it cannot do. Realizing the scope and limitations of neuroscience within the study of neurotheology will provide a more rational and appropriate pursuit of this topic.

The purpose of this chapter is to explore more specifically, the current understanding of neuroscience in the context of religious experience and to provide a framework for the possibility of future empirical research studies that are a cornerstone to the developing field of neurotheology. This requires a review of the current state of neuroscience including the use of many newer imaging technologies and consider how such approaches might be applied to a broad array of religious issues. This chapter will not delve into the specific phenomenological differences between religions and religious experiences, although it must be clearly stated at the outset that while a given neuroscientific experiment might require limiting religion to a specific parameter, the broader scope of religion and religious experiences must not be lost. In other words, for neuroscience to properly be performed, there may be restrictions placed on the types of experiences that can be studied and how they may be studied. However, this should not imply that these restrictions alter or diminish the actual experiences and feelings people may have about their experiences.

There are many types of practices and experiences that can be considered to be a part of a neurotheological analysis. These practices can include those described as spiritual, religious, or meditative and while there may be specific distinctions between these, it should be realized that there is significant overlap as well. Thus, these terms can be used loosely or very explicitly and since many of the existing research studies have defined their terms more broadly, it seems appropriate for now to consider these terms more generically. However, where possible, more specific terms will be used. Furthermore, as future neurotheological research is developed, more care must be given to describing the specific practices and experiences under investigation. This also has implications for the conclusions drawn from such research so that it can be clearly determined how certain practices and experiences affect the body and brain's physiology.

In order to explore the "neuro" side of neurotheology, we will begin by establishing the current state of the science and how this has been applied to religious experience. We will then consider how basic neuroscientific approaches might be applied to a model of religious experiences. Finally, we will expand upon possible avenues of future research that might allow for a more detailed analysis of religious experiences.

Current Neuroimaging Techniques and Religious/Spiritual Practices

Functional and anatomical neuroimaging techniques have contributed dramatically to our understanding of the causes of various neurological disorders and in their diagnosis and management. Anatomical imaging techniques such as magnetic resonance imaging (MRI) and x-ray computed tomography (CT) are useful for determining structural changes in the brain. Functional imaging methods such as single photon emission computed tomography (SPECT) and positron emission tomography (PET) have been useful for measuring changes in blood flow, metabolism, and neurotransmitter activity in neuropsychiatric processes.

In the past decade, brain activation studies have utilized neuroimaging techniques to measure cerebral function during various behavioral, motor, and cognitive tasks. These studies, usually utilizing PET or SPECT, and more recently functional MRI, have helped to determine which parts of the brain are responsible for a variety of neurocognitive processes. These imaging techniques have also delineated complex neural networks and cognitive modules that have become a basis for neuroscience research. Activation studies using PET and SPECT imaging techniques have been employed to determine the areas in the brain that are involved in the production and understanding of language, visual processing, and pain reception and sensation (Phelps & Mazziotta, 1985; Phelps, Kuhl, & Mazziotta, 1981; Friston, et al., 1992). Functional MRI, which has been extensively developed in the past several years, has been shown to have high resolution in measuring changes in cerebral activity during various cognitive, sensory, and motor activation tasks (Rao, et al., 1995; Hammeke, et al., 1994; Binder, et al., 1994; McCarthy, et al., 1994; Sergent, 1994). Since most religious/spiritual practices and their concomitant experiences might be considered from the perspective of an activation paradigm, functional brain imaging techniques may be extremely useful in detecting neurophysiological changes associated with those states.

One of the particularly relevant advantages of PET and SPECT is that in addition to general brain function as measured by cerebral blood flow and metabolism, these imaging techniques offer the opportunity to explore a wide variety of neurotransmitter systems within the brain. In fact, a large number of radiopharmaceuticals have been developed over the past thirty years that may be of use for studying the effects of religious/spiritual practices and experiences. Neurotransmitter analogues have been developed for almost every neurotransmitter system including the dopamine, benzodiazepine, opiate, and cholinergic receptor systems (Kung, 1991; Diksic & Reba, 1991; Gatley, et al., 1991; Frost, 1992). A partial listing of available radiopharmaceuticals for both PET and SPECT are given in Tables 1 and 2. These, in addition to many others, may be useful in the future investigation of the neurophysiological correlates of meditative states as we will describe in more detail in this chapter.

Each of the functional imaging techniques provides different logistical and technical advantages and disadvantages for the study of meditation and other spiritually related experiences. Functional magnetic resonance imaging, while having improved resolution over SPECT and the ability for immediate anatomic correlation, would be very difficult to utilize for the study of such practices because of the noise from the machine and the problem of having to lie prone in the machine (although there may be some ways around this). While PET imaging provides better spatial resolution than SPECT, if one strives to make the environment relatively distraction free to maximize the chances of having as strong a meditative experience as possible, it is sometimes beneficial to perform these studies off hours (especially if there is a busy clinical service). This may complicate the use of PET because the radiopharmaceuticals such as fluorodeoxyglucose may not be readily available. Thus, while PET and fMRI offer certain technical advantages, SPECT also provides a potential option for the study of spiritual practices (Newberg, et al., 2001). In a SPECT study of Tibetan Buddhist meditation by our group, subjects had an intravenous line placed and were injected with a cerebral blood flow tracer while at rest in order to acquire a "baseline" image. They then meditated for approximately one hour until they experienced a "peak" in their meditation that was indicated by a signal from the subject during the meditation. The subjects were again injected with the tracer while they continued to meditate. The tracer is fixed in the brain at the time of injection so that when the images were acquired approximately twenty minutes later, they reflected the cerebral blood flow during the meditation practice. The baseline and meditation images were then compared to determine changes in cerebral blood flow.

The findings of this study showed marked increases in the bilateral frontal cortices, cingulate

Table 1: A Partial Listing of Radioligands used in
Neurological SPECT Imaging

Compound	Application
HMPAO, IMP, ECD	Cerebral blood flow
3-quinuclidinyl benzilate (IQNB)	Muscarinic cholinergic receptor
Iodopride, IBZM, iodospiperone	Dopamine receptor activity
AMIK, DOI	Serotonin receptor activity
Iomazenil	Benzodiazepine activity
2-iodomorphine	Opioid receptor activity
I-d(CH2)5[Tyr(Me)2, Tyr(NH2)9]AV	Vasopressin activity

IBZM = 3-iodo-N-[(1-ethyl-2-pyrrolidinyl)] methyl-2-hydroxy-6-
methoxybenzamide
AMIK = 7-amino-8-iodo-ketanserin
DOI = 1-(2,5-dimethoxy-4-iodophenyl)-2-aminopropane
IMP = Iodine-123-N-N', N, -trimethyl-N'-[2-hydroxyl-3-methyl-5-iodo-
benzyl]- 1, 3 propane   diamine
HMPAO = Technetium 99m hexamethyl propylene amine oxime
ECD = Ethylene Cystinate Dimer

Table 2: A Partial Listing of Radioligands Used in Neurological PET Imaging

Compound	Application
[15O] H2O	Blood Flow
[18F] fluorodeoxyglucose	Glucose metabolism
15O2	Oxygen metabolism
[11C] l-methionine	Amino acid metabolism
[11C] raclopride, 6-[18F] fluorodopamine,	Dopamine receptor activity
[11C] carfentanil, [11C] etorphine	Opiate receptor activity
[11C] flunitrazepam	Benzodiazepine receptor activity
[11C] scopolamine, [11C] quinuclidinyl-benzilate	Muscarinic cholinergic receptors
6-[18F] fluoro-L-DOPA, 4-[18F]-flouro-m-tyrosine	Presynaptic dopaminergic system
[11C] ephedrine, [18F] fluorometaraminol	Adrenergic terminals

gyrus, and thalami. A decrease in blood flow was noted in the superior parietal lobes bilaterally with the left more affected than the right. Interestingly, the decreases in the superior parietal lobes correlated with the increases in the thalami, suggesting a complex network that affects multiple brain areas during meditation.

The other brain imaging studies of meditation have utilized both fMRI and PET. The fMRI study by Lazar et al (2000) and the PET study by Herzog et al (1990-1991) both demonstrated increased activity in the frontal areas, particularly the prefrontal cortex. They also demonstrated some decreases in the parietal regions. The results from both of these studies are consistent with our SPECT results. The study by Lazar took an interesting approach to avoiding the distraction of the MRI noise by having subjects practice ahead of time with a tape of the sound made by the MRI machine. One PET study by Lou et al (1999) did not demonstrate increased prefrontal activity. However, this may have been due to the fact that subjects were following a tape guiding them through the meditation which is different from our study during which the meditation was self initiated and maintained. In a similar manner, internally generated words activate the prefrontal cortex while guided word generation does not, so whether or not the PFC is activated during meditation may have to do with the type of approach used by the practitioner (Crosson et al., 2001).

One additional study is worth mentioning here in that it measured brain activity during the religious experience associated with reciting religious phrases (Azari, et al., 2001). This PET scan evaluated religious and non-religious subjects during the recitation of various phrases that either had a religious connotation (a Psalm), a happy connotation, or neutral. Their results suggested that the religious experience associated with reciting religious language was associated with an increase in the prefrontal cortex, dorsomedial frontal cortex, and medial parietal lobe. The investigators did not find a change in the activity in the limbic system in spite of an overall positive affective response to the religious recitation. The authors suggest that these areas may form a network of areas associated with religious experiences. In relation to the above mentioned studies of specific religious practices, that have also implicated the frontal and parietal areas, there appears to be at least some convergence of the findings that this frontal-parietal interaction has some role in religious and spiritual experiences.

What should be kept in mind in interpreting the results of imaging studies such as these is that they each demonstrate certain similarities and certain differences depending on the type of practice and experience. It has long been our hope to develop a comprehensive model of a few basic types of religious/spiritual practice that could then be extrapolated to explore other types of practices. We will elaborate upon that model in this chapter tying in some of the newest developments in the study of neurotransmitter systems and the physiology of spiritual experiences.

Physiological Studies of Religious/Spiritual Practices

In studies of the physiological correlates of meditation, investigators have examined both specific neurophysiological function as well as the relation of that function to various aspects of body physiology. The autonomic nervous system's responses to meditative practices typically include decreases in blood pressure, heart rate, respiratory rate, and galvanic skin responses (Jevning, Wallace, & Beidebach, 1992; Wallace, 1970). Investigators have also performed a number of studies that measured changes in the body's neurochemistry as a result of meditation (see Table 3). The vast majority of these studies were performed on subjects practicing transcendental meditation. In this type of practice, originally derived from Hindu practice, the individual focuses on a particular word or phrase (the mantra) that has significant meaning to the individual. The result is a feeling of calmness, a loss of the sense of self, and the diminishment of the perception of external stimuli.

In terms of specific neurochemical changes associated with meditation and related spiritual practices. Several studies have demonstrated an increase in gamma aminobutyric acid (GABA)

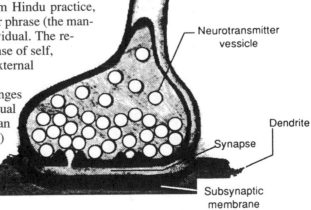

Figure 82. Example of synaptic transmission.
From Joseph, 1990.

in the blood serum of individuals during meditation (Elias, Guich, & Wilson, 2000; Elias & Wilson, 1995). Interestingly, (GABA) is the principal inhibitory neurotransmitter in the brain and may have an important role in the inhibition of specific structures during meditation.

Serotonin (ST) is a neuromodulator that densely supplies the visual centers of the temporal lobe, where it strongly influences the flow of visual associations generated by this area (Foote, 1987) . The cells of the dorsal raphe produce and distribute ST when innervated by the lateral hypothalamus (Aghajanian, Sprouse, & Rasmussen, 1987). Moderately increased levels of ST appear to correlate with positive affect, while low ST often signifies depression (Van Praag & De Haan, 1980). This has clearly been demonstrated with regards to the effects of the selective serotonin reuptake inhibitor medications such as Prozac or Zoloft which have been widely used for the treatment of depression. When cortical ST2 receptors (especially in the temporal lobes) are activated, however, the stimulation can result in a hallucinogenic effect; tryptamine psychedelics such as psylocybin and LSD seem to take advantage of this mechanism to produce their extraordinary visual associations (Aghajanian & Marak, 1999). Interestingly after meditation, breakdown products of ST in urine have been found to significantly increase suggesting an overall elevation in ST during meditation (Bujatti & Riederer, 1976; Walton, et al., 1995). The neurohormone melatonin (MT) is produced by the pineal gland, which can convert ST into MT when innervated by the lateral hypothalamus (Moller, 1992). MT has been shown to depress the central nervous system and reduce pain sensitivity (Shaji & Kulkarni, 1998). During meditation, blood plasma MT has been found to increase sharply (Tooley, et al., 2000; Coker, 1999).

The neurochemical arginine vasopressin (AVP), produced in the supraoptic nucleus of the hypothalamus, serves many functions in the brain and body. It is a vasoconstrictor that tightens blood vessels, but also it decreases self-perceived fatigue and arousal, and appears to contribute to the general maintenance of positive affect (Peitrowsky et al., 1991; Gold & Goodwin, 1978). Increases in AVP have also been found to significantly improve the consolidation of new memories and learning (Reghunandanan, Reghunandanan, & Mahajan, 1998; Weingartner, et al., 1981). In meditators, blood plasma AVP has been found in exponentially higher levels (O'Halloran, et al., 1985).

Norepinephrine (NE) is a neuromodulator produced by the locus ceruleus of the pons (Foote, 1987). NE increases the susceptibility of brain regions to sensory input by amplifying strong stimuli, while simultaneously gating out weaker activations and cellular "noise" that fall below the activation threshold (Waterhouse, Moises, & Woodward, 1998). The breakdown products of catecholamines such as NE and epinephrine have generally been found to be reduced in the urine and plasma during meditation (Bujatti & Riederer, 1976; Walton, et al., 1995; Infante, et al., 2001).

Cortisol is a hormone associated with stress responses. It is produced when the paraventricular nucleus of the hypothalamus secretes corticotropin-releasing hormone (CRH) in response to innervation by NE from the locus ceruleus (Ziegler, Cass, & Herman, 1999). This CRH stimulates the anterior pituitary to release adrenocorticotropic hormone (ACTH; Livesey, et al., 2000). ACTH, in turn, stimulates the adrenal cortex to produce cortisol (Davies, Keyon, & Fraser, 1985). Most studies have found that urine and blood plasma cortisol levels are decreased during meditation (Walton, et al., 1995; Sudsuang, Chentanez, & Veluvan, 1991; Jevning, Wilson, & Davidson, 1978).

Table 3. A partial listing of observed neurochemical related changes during meditative practices.

Neurochemical	Observed Change
Arginine Vasopressin	Increased
GABA	Increased
Melatonin	Increased
Serotonin	Increased
Cortisol	Decreased
Norepinephrine	Decreased
-Endorphin	Rhythm changed; levels unaltered

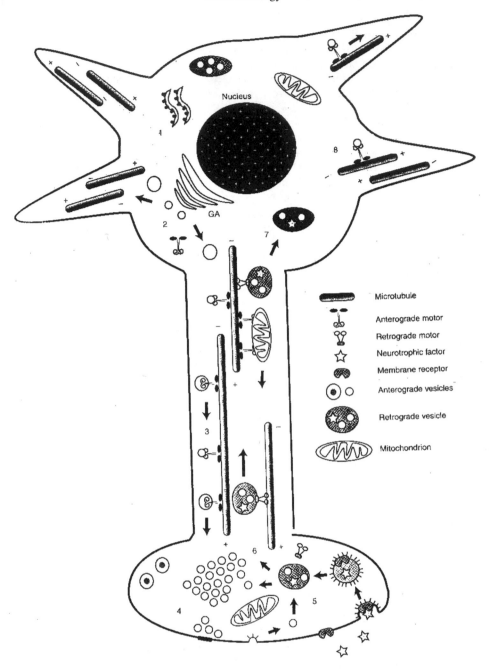

Figure 83. *Schematic illustration of a neuron and microtubles and mitochondrion as they assist in anterograde and retrograde fast axonal transport of membraine associated substances. Polypeptides which are employed for anterograde transport are synthesized by rough endoplasmic reticulum (1), and are transferred to the Golgi bodies (GA) which package these substances into membraine bound organelles (2) thereby forming vesicles which are transported by the microtubles (3) to the presynaptic terminals (4) where they are secreted. Any left over transmitter substances and/or those which are taken back up are then placed in different compartments (5) and are then employed for retrograde axonal transport (6), the retrograde transport being accomplished again by mirocotubles, and this material is delivered back to the soma (7). In step (8) the same processes takes place within the dendrite. Mitochondria interact with the micortubles, essentially supplying them with the energy to perform their transport duties. Reprinted from Zigmund et al., 1999 Fundamental Neuroscience, Academic Press, San Diego.*

Beta-endorphin (BE) is an endogenous opioid produced primarily by the arcuate nucleus of the medial hypothalamus and distributed to the brain's sub-cortical areas (Yadid, et al., 2000). The arcuate nucleus releases BE in response to the excitatory neurotransmitter glutamate, to which it is extremely sensitive (Kiss, et al., 1997). BE depresses respiration (Campbell, Weinger, & Quinn., 1995), reduces fear (Kalin, Shelton, & Barksdale, 1988), reduces pain (Amano, et al., 1982), and produces sensations of joy and euphoria (Janal, et al., 1984). Meditation has been found to disrupt diurnal rhythms of BE and ACTH, while not affecting diurnal cortisol rhythms (Infante, et al., 1998).

Types of Meditation and Approaches to their Study

Although there are thousands of specific approaches to meditation, we have typically divided such practices in to two basic categories. The first method might be called "passive meditation" in which the subject simply attempts to clear all thought from their sphere of attention (d'Aquili

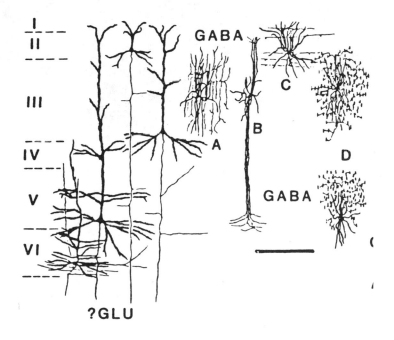

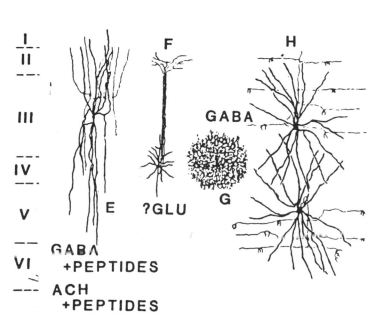

Figure 84. Morphological cell types of the cerebral cortex and their probable neurotransmitters. A-H are nonpyramidal neurons. A-axonal arcades cell, B-double-bouquet cell, C/H-basket cells, D-chandelier cell, E-bitufted cell. G-glia cell. From Jones, 1988.

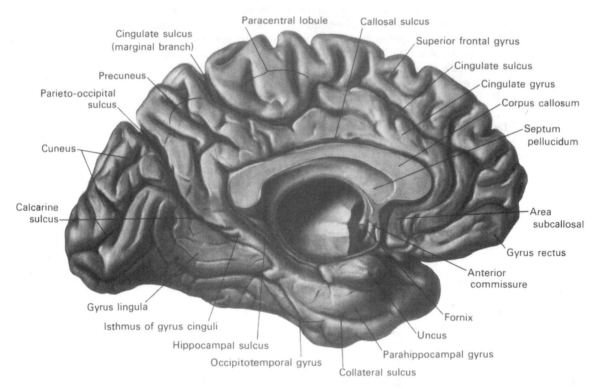

Figure 85. A medial view of the brain. From F. Mettler, 1948. Neuroanatomy. Mosby, St. Louis.

& Newberg, 1993). This form of meditation is an attempt to reach a subjective state characterized by a sense of no space, no time, and no thought. Further, this state is cognitively experienced as fully integrated and unified such that there is no sense of a self and other. There is a second general—and frequently practiced—form of "active" meditation, where the subject focuses their attention on a particular object, image, phrase, or word. Active meditation is employed in practices such as transcendental meditation and various forms of Tibetan Buddhism. Active meditation is designed to lead to a subjective experience of absorption with the object of focus. Due to space constraints, we present here only an overview of our model for passive meditation. Active meditation, however, should have many similarities in the physiological and neurochemical changes it produces; the steps of the meditative process merely may occur in a slightly different order. One other differentiation among spiritual practices might be related to whether the practice is guided or done volitionally. Guided practices are those in which an individual is following along with a person or tape that tells the person what to do throughout the practice. Volitional practices are those in which the individual uses their own will to initiate and maintain a practice. They decide what to do and when to do it. The four imaging studies of meditation described above speak to this potential difference in that the one study in which practitioners were guided by tape through their meditation demonstrated no increase in frontal lobe activity. The other three studies in which the subject did the meditation using their own volition all demonstrated increased frontal lobe activity.

It should be clear though that the specific characteristics of a given meditation practice including how the practice is performed (i.e. verbal vs visual vs movement) and what is experienced during different states of the practice will likely have a profound effect on brain function. For any current or future study of meditation, therefore, it is necessary to carefully describe the type of meditation and what people do and experience during the practice. Future, brain imaging studies may even help towards a clearer development of a typology of spiritual states and practices. For now, it is important to ensure that the phenomenological characteristics of the practice at least inform the neuroscientific perspective of the types of changes that might be expected.

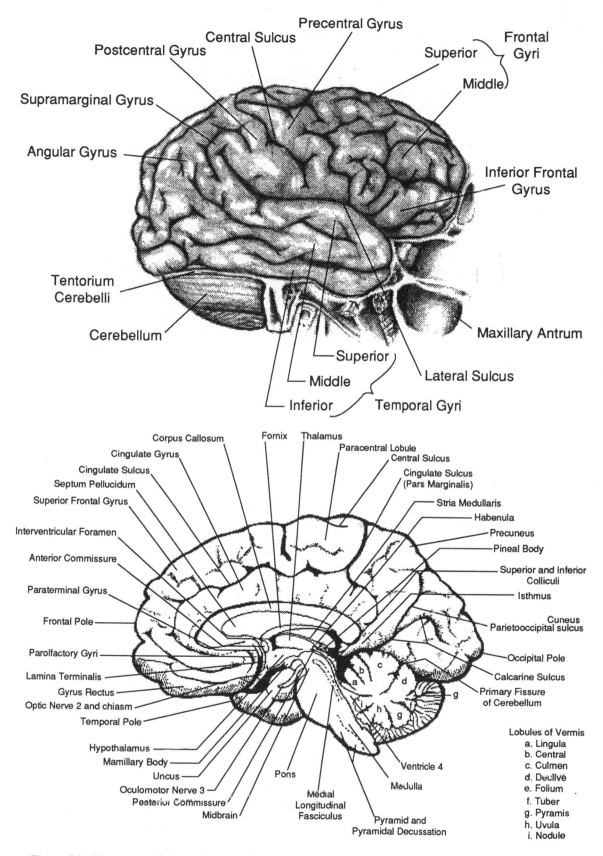

Figure 86. Diagrams of the right hemisphere (top) and a medial "split-brain" view of the right hemisphere. From Joseph, 1996.

Possible Neurochemical Correlates of Meditation

As a way of developing an overall framework from which to explore the wide variety of religious and spiritual practices, we will outline our current concept of a neurophysiological model of meditation (d'Aquili & Newberg, 1993; Newberg & d'Aquili, 2001). In particular, we are attempting to describe the type of meditation practiced by the Tibetan Buddhist subjects in our SPECT study. This is only meant to provide a basic understanding of underlying brain mechanisms that will have some similarities and some differences depending on the particular practices and experiences people may have.

Activation of the Prefrontal Cortex and Cingulate Gyrus

The prefrontal cortex is the only area that receives afferent fibers from all sensory modes, including olfaction, as well as from the multimodal association areas (Stuss, 1986;). The prefrontal cortex is involved in mediating concepts via its rich interconnections with the inferior parietal lobe (Luria, 1980; Stuss, 1986). The prefrontal cortex mediates images and complicated imaginal patterns via its connection with the rostral temporal cortex (Fuster, 1989; Stuss, 1986). The prefrontal cortex of each hemisphere is also connected to the prefrontal cortex of the other by fibers running across the genu and rostrum of the corpus callosum (Stuss, 1986). These may be important in establishing a connected circuit between the two hemispheres during spiritual practices.

Brain imaging studies suggest that willful acts are initiated via activity in the prefrontal cortex along with the anterior cingulate gyrus and are mediated by the excitatory neurotransmitter glutamate (Ingvar, 1994). Since the prefrontal cortex (PFC) in particular appears to mediate intense concentration, it should be essential for almost all meditative practices. Using PET imaging, investigators have shown that when subjects performed purposely willed tasks or tasks that required sustained attention, there was activation of the PFC (Pardo, Fox, & Raichle, 1991; Frith, et al., 1991). Activation of the PFC and cingulate gyrus has been further validated by the increased activity observed in this region on several of the brain imaging studies of meditation (Herzog, et al., 1990-1991; Newberg, et al., 2001; Lazar, et al., 2000). Therefore, meditation appears to start with activating the prefrontal cortex, and possibly the cingulate gyrus, associated with the will or intent to clear the mind of thoughts.

Thalamic Activation

The thalamus governs the flow of sensory and other neuronal information to cortical processing areas via the inhibitory effects of the neurotransmitter GABA on structures such as the lateral geniculate and lateral posterior nuclei. The lateral geniculate nucleus receives raw visual data from the optic tract and routes it to the striate cortex for processing (Andrews, Halpern, & Purves, 1997). The lateral posterior nucleus of the thalamus provides the posterior superior parietal lobule (PSPL) with the sensory information it needs to determine the body's spatial orientation (Bucci, Conley, & Gallagher, 1999). During meditation, if the activation of the right PFC causes increased activity in the reticular nucleus, the result may be decreased sensory input entering into the PSPL and visual center. While brain imaging studies of meditation have not had the resolution to distinguish the reticular nuclei, our recent SPECT study did demonstrate a general increase in thalamic activity that was proportional to the activity levels in the PFC (Newberg, et al., 2001). While it seems likely that the thalamus may play a critical role in meditation and other types of spiritual practices, further studies will be necessary to clarify the role of the thalamus in meditative practices.

It should also be noted that the dopaminergic system, via the basal ganglia, is believed to participate in regulating the glutamatergic system and the interactions between the prefrontal cortex and subcortical structures. A recent PET study utilizing 11C-Raclopride to measure dopaminergic tone during Yoga Nidra meditation demonstrated a significant increase in dopamine levels during the meditation practice (Kjaer, Bertelsen, Piccini, Brooks, Alving, & Lou, 2002). They hypothesized that this increase may be associated with the gating of cortical-subcortical interactions that leads to an overall decrease in readiness for action that is associated with this particular type of meditation. Future studies will be necessary to elaborate on the role of dopamine during meditative practices as well as the interactions between dopamine and other neurotransmitter systems.

One potentially fascinating point about the thalamus and its relationship to spiritual practices is that our SPECT study demonstrated a baseline asymmetry in the thalamus of long time meditators as compared to non-meditating controls. This asymmetry is especially intriguing since there was significant activation in the thalamus during the meditation practice. The larger question that remains to be answered is whether the baseline difference in the thalamus in meditators is the result of many

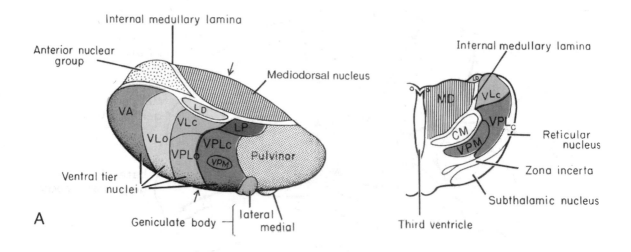

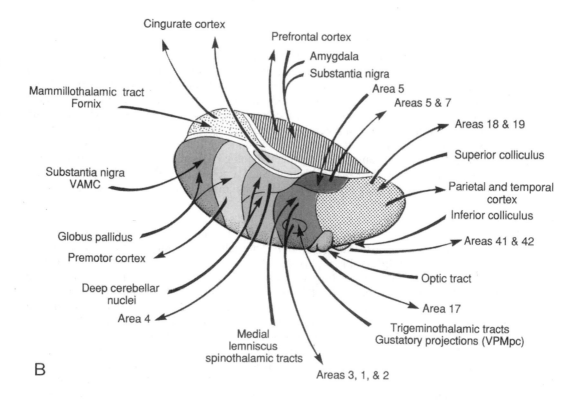

Figure 87. *(Above and next page) Schematic diagrams of the thalamic projection system, depicting thalamic-cortical pathways. From S. G. Waxman & J. Degroot, 1994, Correlative Neuroanatomy, Appleton & Lange. And from M. Carpenter, 1991, Human Neuroanatomy. Williams & Wilkins.*

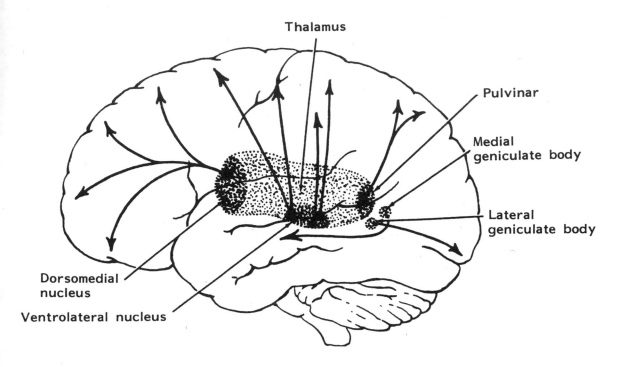

years of meditation, or is a predisposing factor that makes meditation a very powerful practice for these individuals. An answer either way would have profound implications for how we understand spiritual practices. If the former were true and meditation can actually affect the brain's basic functioning on a day-to-day basis, then meditation could be a very powerful technique for both spiritual and psychological purposes. It also may support the notion that as a person gets closer to the peak experiences of their tradition, their brain actually adapts and changes to help move the person towards a different state of being. If, on the other hand, some individuals have a predisposition to responding to meditation, this also may have profound theological implications since it might imply that some people have an easier time being spiritual. Such a notion may also have implications for free will and what paths toward religion/spirituality a person may be prone to move along.

PSPL Deafferentation

The PSPL (Brodmann's area 7) is heavily involved in the analysis and integration of higher-order visual, auditory, and somaesthetic information. Through the reception of auditory and visual input from the thalamus, the PSPL is able to generate a three-dimensional image of the body in space and may actually be crucial in distinguishing self from other. There is some difference in function between the P.S.P.L. on the right and the P.S.P.L. on the left. Joseph (1990) originally observed that the right parietal lobe appears to play an important role in generalized localization and the sense of spatial coordinates per se, whereas the left P.S.P.L. exerts influences in regard to objects that may be directly grasped and manipulated. That some neurons in the left P.S.P.L. respond most to stimuli within grasping distance, and other neurons respond most to stimuli just beyond arms reach led Joseph (1996) to postulate that the distinction between self and world may ultimately arise from the left P.S.P.L.'s ability to judge these two categories of distances. Thus, it seems probable that the self-other dichotomy is a left P.S.P.L. function that evolved from its more primitive division of space into the graspable and the non-graspable.

A recent study has suggested that the superior temporal lobe may play a more important role in body spatial representation, although this has not been confirmed by other reports (Karnath, 2001). However, it remains to be seen what is the actual relationship between the parietal and temporal lobes in terms of spatial representation. Regardless, deafferentation of these orienting areas of the brain, we propose, is an important concept in the physiology of meditation. If, for example, deafferentation of the PSPL by the reticular nucleus's effect on the posterior thalamic nucleus occurs to a significant degree, the person may begin to lose their usual ability to spatially define the self and help to orient that self. Deaffentation of the PSPL has been corroborated by several functional imaging studies of meditation that have demonstrated decreased activity in this area during intense meditation.

We might also hypothesize a distinct experience associated with either right or left PSPL deafferentation. As noted earlier, the right P.S.P.L. is concerned with generating a sense of space and spatial coordinates based upon somaesthetic, visual, and to some extent auditory stimuli. The total deafferentation of the P.S.P.L. cannot result in unusual or unmodulated visions, sounds, or tactile sensations since it has no memory banks with previously stored sensations. Rather, its total deafferentation can only result in an absolute subjective sensation of pure space. But space has no conventional meaning except as a matrix in which to relate objects. We propose, therefore, that pure space arising from total deafferentation of the right P.S.P.L. is subjectively experienced as absolute unity or wholeness.

At the same instant that the right P.S.P.L. is totally deafferented, the left P.S.P.L. is likewise totally deafferented. If the left P.S.P.L. is intimately involved with the maintenance of the Self-Other or the Self-World dichotomy. We propose that the total deafferentation of the left P.S.P.L. results in the obliteration of the Self-Other dichotomy at precisely the same moment that the deafferentation of the right P.S.P.L. generates a sense of absolute transcendent wholeness. Interesting, our SPECT study demonstrated a greater decrease in the left PSPL in the Tibetan Buddhists who were more likely to describe a sense of absorption (i.e. loss of sense of self) during their meditation rather than an experience of spacelessness. Future studies may help to clarify the role of both the left and right PSPL in various elements of spiritual experiences.

Limbic Activation

The hippocampus acts to modulate and moderate cortical arousal and responsiveness, via rich and extensive interconnections with the prefrontal cortex, other neocortical areas, the amygdala, and the hypothalamus (Joseph 1996). Hippocampal stimulation has been shown to diminish cortical responsiveness and arousal; however, if cortical arousal is initially at a low level, then hippocampal stimulation tends to augment cortical activity (Redding, 1967). Thus, the hippocampus functions in conjunction with the thalamus, hypothalamus, and septal nuclei to prevent extremes of arousal, thereby maintaining a state of quiet alertness (Joseph, 1996).

The hippocampus greatly influences the amygdala, such that they complement and interact in the generation of attention, emotion, and certain types of imagery (Joseph, 1996). It seems that much of the prefrontal modulation of emotion is via the hippocampus and its connections with the amygdala (Poletti & Sujatanond, 1980). Because of this reciprocal interaction between the amygdala and hippocampus, the activation of the right hippocampus likely stimulates the right lateral amygdala as well.

That the limbic system is significantly involved in religious experience has also been elaborated upon in an article by Saver and Rabin (1997) in which they consider a wide variety of experiences and hypotheses. After reviewing literature on experiences associated with various pathological conditions such as temporal lobe epilepsy, drug induced states, and schizophrenia, these authors suggest that the limbic areas, particularly the amygdala help to identify certain experiences as profound or real. This limbic function eventually is responsible for assessing which experiences represent a more fundamental level of reality associated with what the experiencer considers the "spiritual realm".

Another piece of evidence of the relationship of the limbic system to spiritual experiences is the research by Persinger in which stimulation of the temporal lobes has been demonstrated to result in the eliciting of a number of components of spiritual experiences including a sensed presence, certain visual experiences associated with spiritual practices, and a loss of the boundary between self and world (Cook& Persinger 1997; Persinger, 2001). Earlier brain stimulation studies in the 1950s and 1960s by Penrose (1954) and other investigators (Weingarten, Charlow, & Holmgren, 1968; Horowitz, Adams, & Rutkin, 1968) also demonstrated that stimulation of certain parts of the temporal lobe could elicit similar types of experiences observed in Persinger's work and those described in association with more "naturally" occurring experiences.

Parasympathetic Activation and Resulting Effects

Stimulation of the right amygdala can cause a stimulation of the ventromedial portion of the hypothalamus with a subsequent activation of the peripheral parasympathetic system (Joseph, 1996).

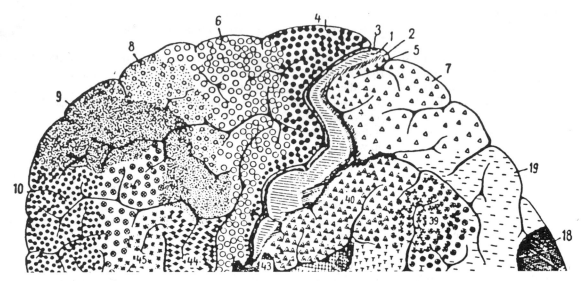

Figure 88. The superior regions of the brain, depicting the frontal and parietal areas including Brodmann's area 7. From Joseph, 1990..

This activation may result in the subjective sensation first of relaxation, and eventually, of a more profound quiescence. Activation of the parasympathetic system would cause a reduction in heart rate and respiratory rate, changes that have been extensively reported in the literature on meditative practices. This "involuntary" decrease combined with the voluntary attempt of the meditator to steady and slow breathing and movement should be associated with increased parasympathetic tone and decreased sympathetic tone. The mechanism by which sympathetic tone is decreased may involve the locus ceruleus, which produces and distributes norepinephrine (NE), the principle neurotransmitter of the sympathetic nervous system. The locus ceruleus receives most of its excitatory input from the medulla's lateral paragigantocellular nucleus, which monitors breathing and heart rate (Van Bockstaele & Aston-Jones, 1995).

During a meditative practice, decreased heart rate and breathing associated with parasympathetic activation, then, should theoretically reduce the firing of the paragigantocellular nucleus of the medulla and cut back its innervation of the locus ceruleus, which densely and specifically supplies the PSPL and the lateral posterior nucleus with NE (Foote, 1987). Less innervation would therefore mean a decrease in the quantity of NE delivered to these regions, where it normally serves to increase their susceptibility to sensory input by amplifying strong stimuli and gating out "noise" that falls below the activation threshold (Waterhouse, Moises, & Woodward, 1998). Thus, a reduction in NE decreases the impact of sensory input on the PSPL, contributing to its deafferentation. It turns out that a few studies have demonstrated an overall decrease in NE levels in the body which may in turn be related to the decreased central NE levels.

The increased parasympathetic activity should also result in the hypothalamic paraventricular nucleus, decreasing its production of CRH, ultimately lowering the adrenal cortex's production of cortisol, a finding observed in the majority of meditation studies (REFS). The drop in blood pressure associated with meditation should induce the hypothalamic supraoptic nucleus to release the vasoconstrictor AVP (Renaud, 1996), which has been shown to increase dramatically during meditation (REFS).

Positive-Feedback Circuit Formation

As the meditation practice continues, there should theoretically be increasing activity in the PFC associated with the ever persistent will to focus attention. Most of the neurons of the PFC are glutamatergic, meaning that they produce and employ the excitatory neurotransmitter glutamate to communicate among themselves and to innervate other brain structures (Cheramy, Romo, & Glowinski, 1987). In general, as PFC activity increases, it produces ever-increasing levels of free synaptic glutamate in the brain. This glutamate can stimulate the hypothalamic arcuate nucleus to release BE, depressing respiration, reducing fear and pain, and producing sensations of joy and euphoria, feelings that have been described during meditation. However, it is unlikely that BE is the sole mediator in such experiences because simply taking morphine-related substances does not produce equivalent experiences and one very limited study demonstrated that blocking the opiate receptors with naloxone did not affect the experience or EEG pattern associated with meditation (Sim & Tsoi, 1992).

Glutamate activates NMDA receptors (NMDAr), but excess glutamate can kill these neurons through excitotoxic processes (Albin & Greenmyre, 1992). We propose that, as glutamate levels approach excitotoxic concentrations, the brain might limit its production of N-acetylated-alpha-linked-acidic dipeptidase (NAALADase), which converts the the production of glutamate from its precursor N-acetyl-aspartyl-glutamate (NAAG; Thomas, et al., 2000). Interestingly, NAAG is functionally analogous to the disassociative hallucinogens ketamine, phencyclidine (PCP), and nitrous oxide. These NMDAr antagonists produce a variety of states that may be characterized as either schizophrenomimetic or mystical, such as out-of-body and near-death experiences (Ellison, 1995; Jansen, 1995).

Complex Autonomic Activity

This is a complicated aspect of our current model of meditative states primarily because of the difficulty in assessing overall autonomic tone during a particular state. This is difficult because of the reciprocal changes that occur when one arm of the autonomic nervous system is activated or inactivated. For example, the observation of a decrease in heart rate may signal increased parasympathetic activity or decreased sympathetic activity, or a combination of these. It should be noted that autonomic activity has been observed to change during meditation and that these changes may differ depending on the specific practice and state during that practice that a measurement is obtained.

Gellhorn and Kiely (1973) developed a model of meditation based almost exclusively on autonomic activity. While this notion may be somewhat limited, it nevertheless demonstrated the importance of the autonomic nervous system during such experiences. These authors suggested that intense stimulation of either the sympathetic or parasympathetic system, if continued, could ultimately result in simultaneous discharge of both systems (Gellhorn and Kiely 1973). It was postulated by Gellhorn and Kiely (1972) that the reversal state and the state of maximal discharge of both the

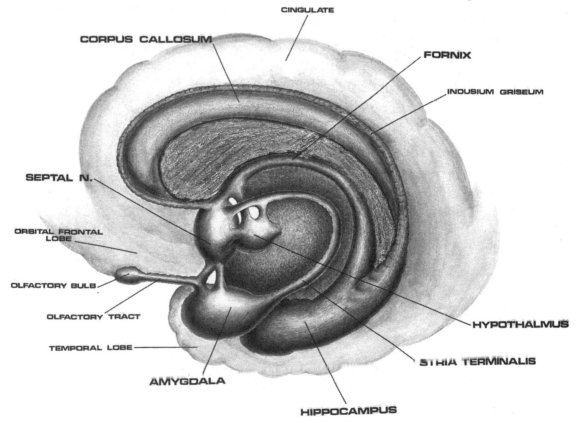

Figure 89. The limbic system. From Joseph, 1992.

sympathetic and parasympathetic systems are associated with physiological states such as sexual orgasm or prolonged stress, learned behaviors such as meditation or ecstatic states, and pathological states such as psychoses. More recent studies have demonstrated changes in heart rate and galvanic skin response during meditation and have generally shown predominantly parasympathetic activity as demonstrated by decreased heart rate and blood pressure, decreased respiratory rate, and decreased oxygen metabolism (Sudsuang, Chentanez, & Veluvan, 1991; Jevning, Wallace, & Beidebach, 1992).

Our original model was based, to some extent on the work of Gellhorn and Kiely (1972) who suggested that intense stimulation of either the sympathetic or parasympathetic system, if continued, could ultimately result in simultaneous discharge of both systems. A recent study corroborated the notion of mutual activation of parasympathetic and sympathetic systems by demonstrating an increase in the variability of heart rate during meditation (Peng, et al., 1999). The increased variation in heart rate was hypothesized to reflect activation of both arms of the autonomic nervous system. This notion also fits the description people have of these experiences in that they feel both a sense of overwhelming calmness as well as significant alertness.

It is interesting to note that stimulation of both systems can result in intense stimulation of structures in the lateral hypothalamus and median forebrain bundle which are known to produce both ecstatic and blissful feelings when stimulated (Olds & Forbes, 1981). Activation of the lateral hypothalamus has also been demonstrated to stimulate the dorsal raphe to deliver more ST to the temporal lobe visual association areas. When ST is produced by the dorsal raphe, it also inhibits the lateral geniculate nucleus, greatly reducing the amount of visual information that can pass through (Funke & Eysel, 1995). Combined with reticular and ST inhibition of the lateral geniculate nucleus of the thalamus, ST would increase the fluidity of temporal visual association in the absence of sensory input. The result would likely be the generation of internally derived imagery which has also been described during certain meditative states. Greatly increased ST levels might also provoke hallucinations in the manner of the tryptamine psychedelics which are known to affect the ST system, particularly in the temporal lobes.

Increased ST levels, combined with lateral hypothalamic innervation, may lead the pineal gland to increase MT production that has been shown to decrease pain sensitivity and produce a sensation of tranquility. Such experiences are described during meditation, and an increase in MT has also been observed. Under circumstances of heightened activation, pineal enzymes can also endogenously synthesize the powerful hallucinogen 5-methoxy-dimethyltryptamine (DMT; Guchhait, 1976). Strassman has extensively linked DMT to a variety of mystical states, including out-of-body experiences, distortion of time and space, and interaction with supernatural entities (Strassman, 2001).

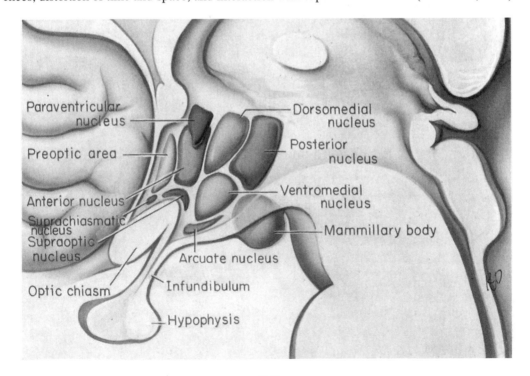

Future Directions in the Study of Meditative and Spiritual Phenomena

The future neuropsychological study of meditative practices, other religious experiences, and even experiences of distant intentionality, may offer a number of fascinating possibilities. The focus of initial studies will need to be on the specific neuroscientific techniques that will be most useful in the study of such phenomena. Imaging techniques, including PET, SPECT, and MRI, can be evaluated for their capacity to study the neurobiological correlates of meditative practices and spiritual phenomena. Specifically, such neurobiological correlates as cerebral metabolism, blood flow, and neurotransmitter receptor levels can be analyzed. Logistical issues and problems of the various techniques need to be considered in order to assess which techniques may offer the most appropriate methodology for the study of such experiences. Care should be taken so that confounding variables can be minimized and the possibility of identifying an effect is maximized. Experimental interventions should be simple, well defined, and distinct from other types of interventions to exclude possible extraneous effects. Interventions that use only one form of activity such as meditation or prayer might be the most appropriate. Interventions requiring a combination of techniques (i.e. combining praying, dancing, and singing) might be too complicated for studying individual components of the intervention and may complicate careful analysis of the effects. Thus, interventions that allow for the simplified study of specific aspects of spiritual experience will have the highest yield in initial ex-

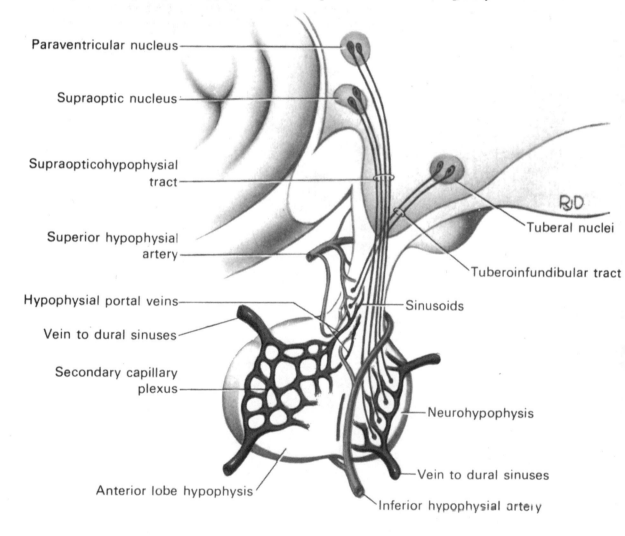

Figure 90a. (Opposite Page) The nuclei of the Hypothalamus. (Above) Hypophysial portal system differentially secrets stress hormones in response to sympathetic and para-symapthetic hypothalamic influences. From M. Carpenter (1991). Core Text of Neuroanatomy. Baltimore, Williams & Wilkins.

periments. Homogeneity of spiritual interventions also will improve the results obtained from small, preliminary studies. Other variables such as electroencephalography, autonomic activity, and neuroendocrine and immunological markers may also help elucidate the overall interaction between the brain and the body during such states.

We cannot conclude without returning the "neuro" back to "neurotheology." While theoretical models and empirical research may contribute to our understanding of spiritual practices and experiences, as well as advance our understanding of how the human brain functions, we cannot ignore some of the larger questions regarding the meaning of such analyses for theological and religious principles (d'Aquili & Newberg, 1999). Principles associated with the standard doctrine of specific religions, the more "mundane" religious experiences that most people are used to having in association with worship or liturgical rituals, and theological notions about love, forgiveness, and even the relationship of human beings to God, may all be influenced by brain function. Studying some of the more intense spiritual experiences from a neuropsychological perspective may provide important information about such experiences, but also hopefully provides a framework from which the vast array of religious and spiritual thoughts, feelings, and practices may be approached. We must also be aware of what spiritual and theological perspectives may have to say about scientific methods and ultimately about epistemological and ontological questions that have plagued human beings throughout history. It is from this intersection of neuroscience and theology that the field of neurotheology can emerge – as long as it strives to incorporate the best ideas from both the scientific and the spiritual perspectives.

NEURO-THEOLOGY,
A RATHER SKEPTICAL PERSPECTIVE
by Massimo Pigliucci

In this commentary I argue that neuro-theology suffers from two major problems. First, it is no theology at all, since it provides no insights into the (alleged) nature of God. Second, and more problematically from a scientific standpoint, some authors in this field are prone to violate basic standards of the scientific method, such as Occam's razor (i.e., the heuristics that suggests to avoid multiplying unnecessary hypotheses). I briefly discuss one particular book on neuro-theology as an example of how perfectly good scientific data can lead the authors to unscientific conclusions first, and then to pure metaphysical speculation. This sort of approach does not help either science or theology.

"Oolon Colluphid's trilogy of philosophical blockbusters: Where God Went Wrong, Some More of God's Greatest Mistakes and Who is this God Person Anyway?" --Douglas Adams, The Hitchhiker's Guide to the Galaxy.

There are two problems with the so-called "neuro-theology." First, it is no theology at all. Theology is the study of the attributes of God, an endeavor that some consider the highest calling of a human life and others regard as a complete waste of time. Regardless, the neurological study of what happens to the brain during mystical experiences cannot tell us anything about God because all we can do is to measure neural patterns and conclude that something is going on inside the subjects' brains. This, unfortunately, implies nothing on the correlation (or lack thereof) of these patterns with any outside reality. So, neuro-theology has nothing to do with the study of God.

The second problem, which is related to the first one, is that some authors in this field seem to be unusually prone to violating one of the fundamental heuristics of the scientific method: Occam's razor. According to William of Occam (1285-1349), "the mind should not multiply entities beyond necessity. What can be done with fewer ... is done in vain with more," that is, when faced with multiple hypotheses capable of explaining a given set of data, it is wise to start by considering the simplest ones, those that make the least unnecessary assumptions. We need to notice that this is not the same as saying that the simplest hypotheses are always (or even often) the best ones, but simply that any additional hypothetical construct needs to be justified by the data before being introduced in one's theory. The reason for this is that there is always an infinite number of such constructs, so that if we had to pursue any possible alternative regardless of how loosely it matches the data, inquiry would soon turn into a hopeless hunt for ghosts. Modern scientists have a good reason to use Occam's razor as a first cut into new territory: it has yielded splendid successes in the past. Let me explain why neuro-theology often misses Occam's mark through a brief consideration of the book by Newberg and D'Aquili (Newberg & D'Aquili, 2001), Why God Won't Go Away.

The book opens with its most informative chapter: the story of an experiment carried out by the authors on a Buddhist immersed in Tibetan meditation (as well as of a similar experiment on praying nuns). The practitioner of course thinks that this sort of experience gets him in touch with his inner self, "the truest part of who he is" and that at the same time he is "inextricably connected to all of creation." What the single photon emission computed tomography camera to which he is connected shows is quite different. The scan images display an unusual level of activity in an area of the brain called the posterior superior parietal lobe. The known primary function of this area is to orient the individual in space, essentially a neurological device to keep track of what's up or down, judge distances and relative positions, and in general allow us to move around. When injuries occur in this area the subject cannot properly move in its environment, with the brain apparently baffled at all those necessary calculations of distances, angles, depth and so on. The posterior superior parietal lobe accomplishes its task by first drawing a sharp distinction between the individual and everything else, literally separating the physical self from the rest of the universe. This, in turn, is made possible by a continuous flow of information from each of the body's senses - mediated, of course, by the corresponding areas of the brain.

Under normal conditions, the posterior superior parietal lobe not surprisingly shows a high level of activity: after all, we constantly need to know where we are and what we are doing. However, and here comes the kicker, during meditation (and - according to the authors - many other similar states, including prayer and drug-induced "mystical" experiences: Huxley, 1954 / 1990) that whole section of the brain is essentially non functional. Newberg and D'Aquili suggest that the brain interprets the low level of sensorial input as a failure to find the borderline between self and the rest of the universe, which nicely explains the feeling of "being one with the cosmos" that these subjects experience.

Newberg and D'Aquili go on (still in the first chapter of their book) to correctly conclude that mystical experiences are "real" in the sense of having a neurological counterpart. However, they somehow distinguish this sort of reality from the one induced by epilepsy, schizophrenia, delusions and so on. Why? Aren't all these phenomena real in the same sense? In fact, given that we experience the world through what amounts to a complex virtual reality simulation created by our nervous system, how could any psychological state not be real in the sense of having a neural correlate?

Instead of following their research to what seems to me its logical consequence - that mystical experiences are no different from delusions and drug-induced states because they alter the functioning of the posterior superior parietal lobe - the authors take a surprising turn. "Gene and I ... believe that we saw evidence of a neurological process that has evolved to allow humans to transcend material existence and acknowledge and connect with a deeper, more spiritual part of ourselves perceived of as an absolute, universal reality that connects us to all that is."

In other words, the authors think that what clearly looks like a malfunctioning of the brain due to an unusual condition of sensorial deprivation, evolved as an adaptation to get in touch with a higher level of reality. Accordingly, most of the rest of the book presents just-so stories in which interesting but impossible to test scenarios are built on what our cave-dwelling ancestors were thinking and how they were coping with the realization of their mortality. It is really a shame that brains and emotions don't leave a fossil record so that we could check on these stories. As geneticist Richard Lewontin once wrote in a similar context, "I must say that the best lesson our readers can learn is to give up the childish notion that everything that is interesting about nature can be understood. ... It might be interesting to know how [insert here your favorite biological phenomenon for which there is no trace in the fossil record] arose and spread and changed, but we cannot know. Tough luck." (Lewontin, 1998) Wouldn't we all feel better if the insights of oriental mystics really turned out to have foreshadowed modern quantum mechanics, if there really were a Tao of physics or biology? Too bad that these parallels are more likely to be a mix of hindsight helped by a generous portion of wishful thinking, but a scientist should be capable of drawing the distinction.

The last part of Newberg and D'Aquili's book is even more problematic from both a scientific and a philosophical perspective. We read sentences such as "The neurological and philosophical correlates [whatever a philosophical correlate may be] ... make it clear that Absolute Unitary Being would be a state of ultimate union and total undifferentiated oneness." Or, "In Absolute Unitary Being, nothing is experienced but the pure and complete unity of all things, or of nothings" (emphasis in the original). I am not even sure what these sentences mean, but they certainly don't have anything to do with science. The astonishing conclusion drawn by the authors seems to be that the self and the world at large are in fact contained within and possibly created by the reality of Absolute Unitary Being, the authors' thinly disguised appellative for God. It sounds to me like we have left the boundaries of both science and philosophy to plunge into pure metaphysical speculation.

This and similar sort of work cannot and will not demonstrate the existence or inexistence of God. Nothing could. But if we realize that mystical experiences originate from the same neurological mechanisms that underlie hallucinations from sensorial deprivation and drug-induced "visions," I bet dollar to donut that the reality experienced by meditating Buddhists and praying nuns is entirely contained in their mind and is not a glimpse of a "higher" realm, as tantalizing as that idea may be.

This bet of mine is in line with a fecund approach to investigating scientific problems that goes under the general heading of Bayesian analysis (Malakoff, 1999) (Howson & Urbach, 1991; Jefferys & Berger, 1992). Bayesian methods provide a very powerful type of statistical and inferential tools, which many philosophers of science also consider a good model of the way science actually proceeds in practice. For a Bayesian, alternative hypotheses are formulated and are assigned prior probabilities based on the knowledge of the problem that we have accumulated so far (priors can be derived objectively - when possible - or subjectively, but even in the latter case it is possible to show that the final results will converge if the data are informative). One then collects data and asks oneself what is the likelihood of every hypothesis given the available data. If this likelihood (the so-called posterior probability) for a given hypothesis has increased from the prior attached to it, the data were informative and favored that hypothesis. The posteriors could be unchanged (the data were uninformative on that hypothesis) or go down (the data make the hypothesis less likely). Several iterations (experiments, observations) of this procedure can be carried out, in which each time the posteriors from one iteration are used as the priors of the following one. Interestingly, for a Bayesian a hypothesis can never be completely confirmed (a posterior of one) or rejected (a posterior of zero), which is what philosophers of science agree is typical of scientific investigation: science is about the relative likelihood of different hypotheses, not about absolute truth.

Now, nobody has yet quantitatively applied a Bayesian framework to neuro-theology, but we can sketch a qualitative scenario. First, the two main contending hypotheses are that neurological data are indicative of an alternative reality or that they tell us what happens when the brain malfunctions in response to unusual sensorial stimuli. Given all we know about the brain and the (scant) evidence we have for alternative realities, I think it fair to give a high prior to the second hypothesis and a low prior to the first one. The new data, for example Newberg and D'Aquili's, seem to me to increase the likelihood of the sensorial deprivation hypothesis and leave unchanged the likelihood of the alternative reality hypothesis (because the data would be observed regardless of the existence of an alternative reality). This increases the posterior probability of the naturalistic explanation and leaves unchanged the (already low) posteriors of the transcendental hypothesis. Ergo, at the end of this round, I am justified in betting that the naturalistic explanation is the winning horse. But as all good Bayesians, I leave the door open for alternative hypotheses and await further data to think about.

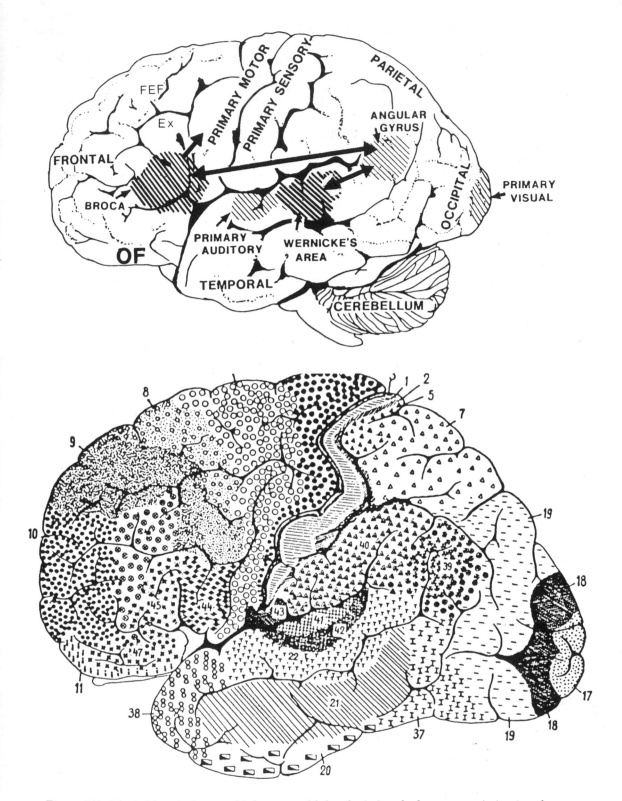

Figure 90b. The left hemisphere and left temporal lobe, depicting the language axis (top) and Broadman's area (above). From Joseph, 1990.

THE TEMPORAL LOBE: THE BIOLOGICAL BASIS OF THE GOD EXPERIENCE
by Michael A. Persinger

The extraordinary development of the human brain cannot be denied. Whether this change is considered to be a product of long evolution or of sudden occurrence does not alter the profound importance of the development. With the increased size of the brain relative to body mass, the human species obtained an unprecedented ability to comprehend the universe.

Certainly the most important change for the later emergence of human societies was the enlargement of the frontal lobes. This portion of the human brain occupies about one-half of the total cerebral capacity. Its proliferation allowed the predominance of two important behaviors: the ability to inhibit and the ability to anticipate.

The ability to inhibit impulses was primary to the survival of even the first social groups. Groups cannot be maintained unless the impulses of the component individuals are kept in check. When each member feeds or fights or copulates according to selfish and egocentric impulses, the group behavior deteriorates. The culture dies.

Modern society is replete with inhibitions. They are translated as "Thou shalt not." We cannot kill a person because we feel like it; we cannot engage in sex with another whenever it suits us. We must learn to inhibit our behaviors. As long as the human brain can inhibit, complex societies can be maintained. People who have not learned to inhibit, either because of inadequate training or due to some biological error, are considered the criminals of culture. They are removed from its presence and killed or preserved in some safe place. Such people cannot be allowed to run free if society is to survive. The ability to inhibit contributes to clear logic and sharp thinking. During problem solving, we can exclude or inhibit the thousands of memories or thoughts that could interfere. Instead, we can concentrate upon a crossword puzzle, talk about politics to a buddy in a bar, or calculate the size of distant galaxies. People who cannot inhibit irrelevant responses do not talk or think in clear and crisp patterns. These people free associate, talk in nonsense, and confuse words and phrases. Sometimes they are called schizophrenics; most of the time they are just called crazy. For a variety of different medical reasons, they have a chronic lack of the ability to inhibit.

The ability to inhibit is a fragile commodity within each of us. Its strength is weakened by alcohol, fatigue, and mind-bending drugs. During these periods of intoxication, concentration is difficult and memory comes and goes. Images of hate, impulses of revenge and sexual desires, typically inhibited by a history of punishment, emerge into awareness.

The second consequence of the frontal lobes is the capacity to anticipate. As the frontal lobe grew larger and more complex, the human species began to anticipate not just the next few seconds or days, but an entire life. Accompanying this anticipation was the experience of time.

Prediction and anticipation have great survival value for the human species. They are the foundation for hopes and idealistic goals. They allow the development of complex technologies and sophisticated social systems.

However, anticipation is a two-edge sword. As long as the anticipated event is positive in nature, great strides can be made. People work to save for the future. Children are conceived to replenish the race and crops are planted for the expected harvest. The anticipations are associated with joy and the vicarious identification of endless survival.

What the human species gained in the ability to plan and to anticipate, it paid for by the experience of anxiety and apprehension. When the anticipated event is negative, we do not experience happiness or an expectation of fulfilment. Instead, we are debilitated by feelings of doom.

During such a period, we are incapacitated. The ability to think is lost and all the fine discriminations fade into one confusing, confining form. We feel our hearts pump and the walls of the room appear to move in around us. Sometimes we feel like we are about to die.

And that's the crux of the problem. With the ability to anticipate the future, the human brain also developed the potential to acknowledge self-death. We can plan and construct great structures, but we can also anticipate our own demise. Death is the end of individual experience, the time when the thing called your "self" appears to terminate. It is perhaps the greatest unknown of them all. By its very definition, it contains the terrors of the most horrific human imaginations. The consequences can be devastating.

However, at the same time the frontal lobes were burgeoning with their capacity to inhibit and to anticipate, another part of the human brain was changing. This portion of the brain, called the temporal lobe, also grew in size and expanded outward from the sides of the major mass.

The structure of the temporal lobes was aptly formed for the demands of the new human brain. It contained a central area where sound could be experienced and understood in either space or time. Through the connections to the frontal lobe and other portions of the brain, regions of the temporal lobe contributed to speech. This sudden development of the capacity to speak was strongly correlated with the ability to think. By processes that are not yet technically clear, these properties were preconditions for the appearance of the phenomena known as awareness and experience.

The developments did not end here. Two important structures, the hippocampus and the amygdala, began to migrate deep within the brain. As the neocortex grew in size, the hippocampus was slowly pushed backward and down to the side of the brain until it rested deep within the temporal lobe. The amygdala was pushed, laterally, to within the lobe as well. The appearance of the two structures within the temporal lobe contributed to two important properties: the experience of remembering and evaluation. With the development of these structures, experiences could be labelled as rewarding or punishing. More importantly, they could be remembered. To accommodate this expansion, marked variations in the brain's architecture occurred. An extra fold or convolution appeared within the primate cortex immediately adjacent to the hippocampus. From this new region emerged massive fibers that sent out and received information from all over the brain.

The hippocampus became the gateway to the experience of images. Appropriate stimulation of this region of the human brain could unleash a vivid stream of past memories. It could also initiate an inundation of rich fantasy over which the experiencer had little control. One of these processes, whose intimacy with memory consolidation is clearly evident, was the experience of dreams.

The amygdala became a control center for the display and experience of emotions and moods. The potential for fight or flight and the experience of anger or fear evolved together. With the coupling of these emotions to mood, the human animal could experience the heights of euphoria and the depths of depression.

Because of the connections to the frontal lobes and the upper portions of the temporal lobe, the emotions became mixed with the experiences of the self. The sensations of being a person, a real entity, a unique thing in this universe, became tied to the guts of the organism. With this mixing came the exhilaration of self-preservation and the fear of personal extinction.

A biological capacity for the God Experience was critical for the survival of the species. Without some experiences that could balance the terror of personal extinction, the existence of the human phenomenon called the "self" could not be maintained. It would have been fragmented by the persistent, gnawing realization that death could come at any time. Initially, the God Experience may not have had a particular representation. Although there is no known way to re-create the experiences of the first human brain as it contemplated this cosmic event, the first experience may have been a kind of "cosmic serenity".

It was probably much like the Hindu-Buddhist concept of Nirvana, whereby a person experiences a quiescence. Within this quiescence, there is no fear, no anxiety, only the sensation of becoming a part of everything. The words may be poetry but the survival value is real—the person can cope with the anticipation of self-annihilation.

The capacity to have the God Experience is a consequence of the human brain's construction. If the temporal lobe had developed in some other way, the God Experience would not have occurred. I am not contending that the God Experience is localized within the temporal lobe, nor more than vision is stored within the occipital lobe or the body image is stored within the parietal region. Instead, my hypothesis is that the God Experience is a phenomenon that is associated with the construction of the temporal lobe.

All of us, by virtue of our primate heritage, have this capacity. Some of us may regress to it, others may enhance it, and still others may be embarrassed by its presence. Like the propensity to walk and to talk, it is a potential in each of us. We may just know it by different names. Of course, the best test of this idea would be to compare our species with a similar form that did not have the same development of the temporal lobe. Optimally, this fictional creature would have the same development of the other portions of the brain but without the odd positioning of the hippocampus and amygdala or the massive connections between the temporal and frontal lobes. To date, such a comparison has not been possible. Instead, to test the neurobiological basis of the God Experience, we must look at people who have minute alterations in this region. If all human beings have the capacity to have a God Experience, then those individuals with the appropriate alterations in the temporal lobe should report enhanced occurrences. Although the details should be highly variable, they would show the general themes of religious behavior.

Such changes can be discerned within the temporal lobe. The hippocampus, for example, is notoriously prone to deterioration due to insufficient blood supply, inadequate oxygen levels, or deficits in essential nutrients. Because of the odd geometry of its blood vessels, the hippocampus is prone to deteriorate from thickening of the arteries. Even a small alteration in the temporal lobe tissue produces pronounced and crude behaviors. Damage to the hippocampus produces some of the densest amnesia known to medical science. However when there is no memory there is no past, and when there is no past there is little anticipation of the future.

The test cannot be carried out on the behaviors of severely damaged brains. People with severe brain damage have exaggerated experiences where fragments of normal behaviors are amplified to bizarre extremes. To conclude that God Experiences are a consequence of brain damage would contradict their functional significance, unless one assumes that brain damage has survival value.

Instead, a more subtle and reversible alteration in the temporal lobe's activity must be chosen. Aberrant electrical activity deep within the temporal lobe is one candidate. God Experiences do not occur all the time, at least in most of us. They occur in short bursts during periods of personal crisis, following ingestions of chemicals, or after certain rituals (such as prayer) have been followed.

Although electrical changes reflect alterations in the functional structure of the brain, they may not always be permanent. Some electrical changes reflect the intrinsic cluster properties of the millions of neurons involved. The degree to which these neurons are likely to maintain any electrical instability, however, is related to their location and to the alteration of appropriate neuronal chemicals. They are called transmitters and form the effective communication between the brain cells.

When electrical criteria are considered, the temporal lobe maintains a unique position among neural tissues. Hippocampal cells, in particular, display more electrical instability than any other portion of the brain. These cells are also prone to repeated firing long after the stimulation has been removed. The usefulness of this sensitivity can be seen in its function. Since the hippocampus is so important for the consolidation of experience (what we call memory), a sensitivity for the variety of complex and subtle inputs to the eyes, ears, and visceral senses is critical. As we search our complex environment, it must be given not only structure but meaning.

Electrical lability leads to unique properties. The amygdala and the hippocampus can learn specific electrical patterns. Like the total person learning to drive a car or to play tennis, specific kinds of electrical activity can be slowly acquired by these structures. This means that the experiences associated with those electrical patterns can come under the control of a place (like a church) a time (like crisis), or even more mundane, a person. Learned electrical changes within the brain are integrated within the intrinsic patterns of activity. Different regions of the brain show particular patterns that more or less reflect structure and function. The temporal lobe is no exception. One of the most frequent electrical patterns generated from this lobe is called theta activity.

Theta activity, which has been defined as slow, synchronous or slightly spiked waves with frequencies between 4 Hz and 7 Hz (cycles per second) is associated with alterations in temporal lobe function. These waves occur during dreaming, creative thinking, and twilight states. This activity is present when you hear your name called just before you fall asleep. It is active when you close your eyes and repeat some thought, prayer, or mantra until only pleasant floating sensations remains.

Most of the time, the electrical activity of the temporal lobe is not exceptional. During thinking and experiencing, billions of neurons within the region maintain a complex field of electromagnetic patterns. There are few experiences of god, few episodes of intense meaning, and little sense of cosmic serenity. But, as we all know, there are brief periods, such as those occurring late at night, when the threshold of the God Experiences can be approached. Sometimes, in the early morning hours as we concentrate on some meaningful task, the sense of solitude blends into an odd feeling of familiarity. We begin to experience thoughts as if they have occurred before. A presence is sensed but not seen. There are times when the complexities of the world bear too much upon us. The job, the family, and the six o'clock news wear away our thin veneer of invulnerability. Just as life appears futile, we suddenly experience a sense of understanding and feeling of knowing. The next morning we can move again, forgetting, sometimes with shame, the convictions of the night before.

There are periods in each of our lives when we begin to know our dreams will never be acknowledged. As we pass from the third into the fourth decade of life, the youthful exuberance of infinite possibilities fragments into a cold reality of the mediocre. And then we hear a voice call us and we call it God. The next day, renewed and refreshed, we begin again.

These experiences should be correlated with normal, transient perturbations of the human temporal lobe. For now, they will be called temporal lobe transients. When they occur, the innate feelings of the God Experience are displayed. Depending on the extent of the activity, some experiences would be mild cosmic highs, the kind we feel in the early morning hours when a hidden truth becomes sudden knowledge. Other more intense transients would evoke the peak experiences of a life and determine it thereafter. They would involve religious conversions, rededications, and personal communications with God.

The first time I recorded an inconspicuous electrical seizure form the temporal lobe of a meditator and heard the reports of cosmic bliss, I was impressed with the impact of this change on the person's behavior. Here sat a person waiting with anticipation for the coming of a few short seconds of seizure. There were no convulsions or head movements of any kind, just a slight smile and the facial expressions of cosmic serenity.

But the experience was compelling. The individual, depressed and forlorn before the episode, left with a fresh view of the world. For a few brief seconds, the person had mingled with the Great Mentality whose rudiments are found in every human culture. The person had experienced a conviction shared by millions of other individuals. These people are not "weirdoes" or diagnosed abnormals. They are average people who interact in everyday ways with other people. They cope with their jobs, talk to their children, and carry on complex conversations. Some of them are the leaders of the scientific, artistic, and political worlds.

I never had the heart to tell that first person about the electrical recordings. In fact, the realization that the God Experience could be an artifact of the human brain was intellectually paralyzing. But since then, like hundreds of other brain scientists who have been determined to separate semantics from science, I have observed the symptoms again and again. They can be seen at the peak of prayer, when people revel in spiritual transcendence. They can seen during revivals when the sound of emotional hymns bring tears and smiles and the sense of a lifted burden. Wherever the world falls apart or loved ones die, the patterns appear.

The power of the God Experience shames any known therapy. With a single burst in the temporal lobe, people find structure and meaning in seconds. With it comes the personal conviction of truth and the sense of self-selection. How many people have died, still smiling, on arena floors and battlefields, in anticipation of another single burst of activity? The last question does not stem from cynicism but from concern. If the God Experience can control the lives of human beings to this extreme, what if it is can be controlled or manipulated by things or people? If the God Experience is a biological artifact of the human brain, no amount of consoling words from ancient scriptures will alter that potential. The only difference between old works and modern books is the age of the paper.

That the temporal transients exist within all of us has not been proven (yet); however, it can be inferred. If temporal lobe transients are like any other phenomena, they should be distributed along a statistical continuum. Most of us should have small ones, once or twice a year, while a few of use should have them more frequently. A small percentage should show intense and extreme bouts of temporal lobe transients. Such a population exists; they have been called temporal lobe epileptics.

There is nothing unusual about studying the exception in order to find the rule. By studying people with problems in the frontal lobes, neuroscientists determined the correlates of thinking, abstracting, and planning for the future. By studying the people with peculiar parietal regions, researchers revealed how the awareness of the body image is learned. We have gleaned a great deal about the great ravelled knot by noting its occasional deviations.

Temporal lobe epilepsy is a special form of epileptic disorder. Unlike the more publicized types of petit mal (when the person blacks out for a brief period) or grand mal seizure (when the person has a "fit"), temporal lobe epilepsy is not necessarily associated with convulsions. To state that temporal lobe epilepsy is a disease with distinct symptoms, like measles or even influenza, would be inappropriate. Since the primary reason for the diagnosis is unusual electrical activity in the (usually anterior) temporal lobe, there is much over inclusion. The different potential abnormalities within this volume of brain space produces a multitude of interactions.

However, the most persistent characteristic of the temporal lobe is the "psychic seizure" without accompanying convulsions. Psychic seizure, which is a relatively poor diagnostic label (and should not be confused with psychic research), refers to the experiences associated with abnormal electrical activity within the temporal lobe. People with seizures in this part of the brain experience vivid landscapes or perceive forms of living things. Some of these entities are not human, but are described as little men, glowing forms, or bright, shining sources.

The modality of the experience, that is, whether it is experienced as a sound, a smell, a scene (vision), or an intense feeling, reflects the area of electrical instability. If the focus of the electrical activity is near a portion of the temporal lobe (like the uncus) associated with smell, then the experience may be olfactory. If the area of abnormal activity is nearer the auditory projection area, then the experiences may involve sounds or voices.

The experiences, whether visual or auditory, may have actually happened or they may be mixtures of fantasy and reality. Sometimes they may be fixed space and time, while in other cases they may be as dynamic as everyday experiences. However, whether they are dreamlike or as vivid as this book in front of you, they are experienced as real.

There are a number of changes that occur during psychic seizures that reflect the functions of the temporal lobe. The person may experience a sense of altered meaning. Sometimes there may be an enhanced sense of familiarity (deja vu) with events that have never been experienced. At other times, the opposite, an enhanced sense of strangeness to well-known conditions, may occur.

The sense of meaningfulness is like conviction. During a psychic seizure, intense and profound feeling may occur. Afterwards the person may not remember the details, but be convinced that it happened. The event, although vague, is packed with personal and profound significance.

Another characteristic of this abnormality is an alteration in the description of the self. Depersonalization is typical. In this state, the person feels unreal or simply "not there". The body may appear to be in one place while the mind is in another. Depending upon the person's learning, these experiences range from the heavenly to the exotic.

Frequently coupled to these symptoms is the experience of forced thinking. As the appropriate region of the temporal lobe displays abnormal electrical activity, repeated thoughts are experienced. They may be a phrase or a slogan or just a nonsense sequence. Again and again, they occur in a fixed stereotyped manner. Perceptual alterations are usually limited to the sudden expansion of visual and auditory images. Objects in the room may suddenly appear to grow very small and then increase in size again. Sounds may fluctuate from very faint and distant to very loud and near.

Patients with temporal lobe epilepsy or complex partial seizures are known to experience terror and incapacitating anxiety. Yet other times, they feel euphoric and happy within the enthusiastic sensation of unlimited possibilities. Irritability can lead to homicidal impulses, while depression precedes suicidal contemplation. These symptoms may not be associated with convulsions.

The coupling between temporal lobe disorders and religious experiences can be traced into antiquity. Shorn of their poetic language, the descriptions of most religious leaders indicated temporal lobe abnormalities. If they were alive today, they would have much less appeal. There appears to be something magical about psychiatric symptoms when they are centuries old.

When we resist our reflex tendency to accept the received gospel merely because it is written, the Joan of Arcs of our past are cast in another light. There now appears to be good reason why they heard voices and then felt weak and incapacitated. There are clear mechanisms that explain why their sexual impulses waned when the euphoria of the cosmic high appeared. There is an explanation for seeing visions of things to come that never really came.

Now I am not saying that the experiences of God are synonymous with temporal lobe epilepsy. The experiences of those with epielpsy are exaggerated and disorganized forms of the brain's activity. When vast depolarizing waves spread across millions of cells, memories and fantasies are mixed and mashed together. If the spreading is severe enough, even convulsions or "fits" may occur.

Instead, the God Experience is a normal and more organized pattern of temporal lobe activity. These short temporal lobe transients are precipitated by subtle psychological factors such as personal stress, loss of a loved one, and the dilemma of anticipated death. There are no convulsions and few bizarre behaviors.

When these small changes occur, they are experienced in an organized and balanced fashion. The experiences are primarily pleasurable and sublime characteristics of less severe forms of electrical activity. Only in more extreme conditions do fear and a sense of cosmic helplessness emerge. But the potential is not all-or-none. By virtue of brain function, there is a continuum along which all of us will fall. Every one of the more than four billion brains that compose the human species would be distributed along this scale. Most of us, by definition, fall in the middle. Temporal lobe epileptics merely fall at one end of the continuum. They display the types of behaviors experienced by all of us, except they are more fragmented. Most of the time, the components—the fear or the sublime, the cosmic communion or the eternal helplessness-are distorted out of proportion or hidden within the confusion of the seizure. However, the essential symptoms are seen in a milder manner within every type of religious experience that has been reported. The sense of profound knowing is experienced as "being touched by God" or "being at one with the universe." The depersonalization is reported as "soul travelling" or "an insight into the streets of heaven." Forced thinking is experienced as being "implanted with the words of God." A simple epileptic aura is experienced as the distant sound of heavenly choirs.

These patterns are clearer within behaviors of temporal lobe patients between apparent seizures. During these periods, the brains of these people are most similar to the brains of average people during the peaks of frustration, stress, and personal crisis. It is during these times that the religious themes of thought and God Experiences should be and are evident. In fact, the behaviors of the temporal lobe epileptics have been characterized by the persistent theme of religiosity. Their lives are full of repeated peaks of mystical experiences and multiple conversions. They are obsessed by moral issues and the experiences of God and fulfilment.

Not surprisingly, their behaviors and psychological experiences are predominated by a sense of personal destiny, the most supreme form of infantile egoism. Each one has been selected to give a message to the world. Like the committed preacher or the proselytizing prophet, they have a sense of the special—their experiences are somehow exceptional. Whether prone to the ups of mania or the deep downs of depression, they are characterized by philosophical themes. Where did they come from? How were they born? Will they be reborn? Will they live forever? Sometimes the theme may be blatantly atheistic, but again and again they talk about the God Experience. Indeed, there is something about the temporal lobe and religious experience that cannot be refuted. There's the experience of time and the implication of eternity. There's the experience of space and the implication of infinity. There's the feeling of the intense meaning of the beginning and the end of it all.

If the data are clear, why haven't the patterns been evident? The relationship has been obscured by the source, the temporal lobe epileptic. First, most individuals who are hospitalized have other complications. The experiences they report are related to the nature of the more progressive disease processes. Second, when the God Experiences do occur, they are not reported. Personal God Experiences, because of the profound implication for the person's destiny, are not mentioned, lest they be misconstrued. People have been taught to assume that images of their late Uncle Henry in a rocking chair, smoking a cigar, are hallucinations; but the experience of God is real.

There is a way around the secrecy. Inhibition of ideas and actions are less evident within psychotic populations. Psychotic people, who are frequently called "just crazy", fail to inhibit their impulses. They cannot relate in a predictable fashion to the world around them, nor can they cope in any socially acceptable manner within the confusion and complexity of change.

If temporal lobe disorders were associated with religiosity and the God Experience, then the temporal lobe psychotic should be a population inundated with these experiences. The data indicate this obsession. As reported by Slater and Beard in 1963: "Mystical delusional experiences are remarkably common. One patient said that God, or an electrical power was making him do things; that he was the Son of God. Another said he felt God working a miracle on him. Another felt that God and the Devil were fighting within him and that God was winning. Another claimed, 'All this goes into one vast electronic brain which give God the power to give you life and individuality.

Hallucinations were often extremely complex and were usually full of meaning, often of a mystical type. Nearly always there were auditory hallucinations at the same time. One patient saw God, heard voices and music and received a message that he was going to heaven. Another had a vision of Christ on the cross in the sky, and heard the voice of God saying 'You will be healed, your tears have been seen'." Indeed, these reports are from hospitalized people. But does that change the impact of their experiences? Psychotic individuals are not psychological lepers or inhuman creatures. Their difference from normal people is only one of degree (and this is arbitrary). The same behaviors they display every day, we display once or twice in 20 years. Most of us have learned to compartmentalize the God Experience. It can be conditioned to occur in specific places or during certain times. Because of the relationship between the frontal and the temporal poles, most of us can learn to inhibit- to control-its occurrence. Only in the psychotic does it run rampant.

Certainly, I am not the first neuroscientist to suggest the connection. Many others have seen it before. Most have denied it. A few, frightened by the implications, have pushed it into the corners of institutions. There it stayed, pigeonholed, as an abnormal mental event that is never outwardly manifested. I also suspect that some practitioners even guard it, as if its escape would bring global havoc. Neuroscientists are, after all, human beings with fears of personal extinction and desires for immortality.

EXPERIMENTAL SIMULATION OF THE GOD EXPERIENCE:
IMPLICATIONS FOR RELIGIOUS BELIEFS AND THE FUTURE OF THE HUMAN SPECIES
by Michael A. Persinger

The application of weak, complex magnetic fields through the cerebral hemispheres elicits experiences of a "sensed presence or "Sentient Being" in normal people. We have hypothesized these experiences are the awareness of the right hemispheric equivalent of the left hemispheric sense of self and may be the prototype for the god experience. Experimental results and clinical measurements have supported this contention. Challenge of religious beliefs, which display many of the characteristics of delusions, may be prevented by the natural characteristics of neurocognitive functions. Because the structures and patterns of activity involved with the god experience may also be associated with aggression, the observation that about 50% of males who have had a religious experience, attend church regularly, and display elevated frequencies of temporal lobe signs would kill in god's name may have profound implications for the future of our species.

INTRODUCTION

One of the fundamental principles of behavioral neuroscience is that all experiences are generated by or correlated with brain activity. This activity is determined by the microstructures within the brain and the patterns of electromagnetic and chemical activity within and between these structures. Structure dictates function and microstructure dictates microfunction.

There are several important extensions of these principles. The first is that all experiences are responses that must be evoked by physical events or stimuli. However the events that function as stimuli are only an extremely small subset of the myriad of events within the environment. Different information within the brain emerges from the varied organization of these experiences.

The principles indicate that all experiences, from the awareness of the sense of self, to the feelings of love, to the presence of God, emerge from brain activity. If the scientist can isolate the controlling stimuli that evoke an experience, then any experience, including the experience of God, should be subject to experimental verification and reproduction within the laboratory.

In 1983 during a routine electroencephalographic (EEG) study to monitor the effects of transcendental meditation, an experienced instructor of that technique displayed an electrical anomaly over her right temporal lobe. During this "electrical seizure," she reported she was "filled with the spirit" and she felt the presence of God with her in the laboratory. The duration of this electrical transient was about 20 sec (Figure 91).

The obvious question emerged. If one could extract from the brain the essential electromagnetic structure with which the experience of God is correlated and then re-apply this pattern to the person's brain without their knowledge, would that person experience God? Although clinical records of individuals who were diagnosed as complex partial epileptics with a focus within the right limbic or temporal lobe abounded with references to mystical and god experiences, the technology at that time was not available to design an experiment to test that hypothesis.

THE SEARCH FOR THE SELF LEADS TO THE SENSED PRESENCE

One of the last remaining challenges to modern neuroscience is to understand the neural bases to the sense of self. It appears to be associated with the linguistic processes often attributed to classical functions of the left hemisphere of the cerebrum. From a species perspective the propensity for people to fight and to die to maintain their culture and their language is not surprising. Without the language process there would probably not be the human sense of self.

During the late 1980s the Laurentian University Neuroscience Research Group was interested in the cerebral bases to creativity and insight. Many of the great thinkers of human history, from scientists to the initiators of spiritual traditions, had reported that their "insights" were associated with feeling of communion with some force that was greater than their own sense of self. The information that suddenly occurred during these insights was often beyond the knowledge of the person if only the content of his reinforcement history was considered.

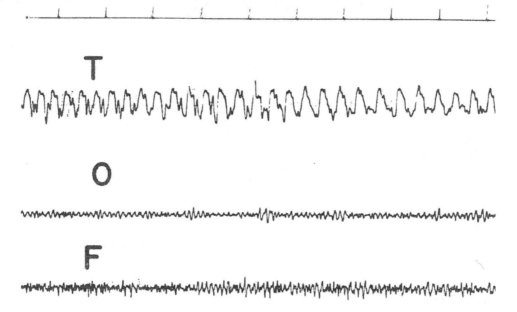

Figure 91. Occurrence of an electrical seizure over the temporal lobe during the experience of "God."

To study this problem we developed a computer based technology for the application of weak (10 nanoTesla to 1 microTesla), complex magnetic fields through the cerebral hemispheres (Figure 92). The basic procedure involved subjects sitting in a quiet chamber while blind-folded. The rationale for this approach was to imitate the historical conditions in which many "inspirational insights" have been be experienced. Attenuation of the auditory and visual inputs would also allow the activity of neurons that are typically involved with passive surveillance of the environment to become recruited into the cerebral patterns associated with the applications of the experimental magnetic fields.

Most people reported a "sensed presence" of a Sentient Being. The interpretation of the "presence" was a function of: 1) the person's temporal lobe sensitivity that can be inferred by both electroencephalographic activity and self reports from questionnaire), 2) the available cultural attributions or beliefs for the experience, and, c) the shape of the magnetic fields. The experiences were emotional and personally significant. The reconstructions of these ephemeral experiences as a component of autobiographical memory are strongly influenced by the explanation the person attached to the experiences within a few seconds of their occurrence.

Our working hypothesis is that the sensed presence is the prototype of the God experience and is actually the transient awareness of the right hemispheric equivalent of the left hemispheric sense of self. Intrinsic complex electromagnetic patterns within the left hemisphere that generate the sense of self are experienced as "the other" when their right hemispheric equivalents intrude into awareness. Because of the reciprocal inhibition of activity between the two hemispheres, these periods of intense "intercalation" are infrequent for the normal brain, except perhaps during dreaming. However during periods of personal distress,

Figure 92. Helmet for application of weak (10 nanoTesla to 1 microTesla), complex magnetic fields through the cerebral hemispheres.

psychological depression, certain psychotropic conditions, and meditation states these intrusions become more probable.

One would expect that the characteristics of the experiences would reflect the properties associated with the right hemisphere. For example the experiences would be profoundly emotional, spatial, "beyond the self", and meaningful. Our electroencephalographic measures in conjunction with the themes of these experiences indicated they involved the temporoparietal cortices and their limbic inputs from the amygdala (associated with cosmic meaning) and the hippocampus (the initial gateway to the cerebral representation of experience, i.e. complex memory). The most common correlates of the "sensed presence" include the experiences of "vibrations within the body", dream-like states, detachment of the self from the body, spinning, and either fear, aggression, or sexual arousal.

For example, a 21 year old woman with a history of diabetes who was exposed to a burst-firing magnetic field reported "I felt a presence behind me and then along the left side. When I tried to focus on its position the presence moved; every time I tried to sense where it was, it would move around. When it moved to the right side I experienced a deep sense of security like I had not experienced before. I started to cry when I felt is slowly fading away" (We had shifted the field parameters). From a physical perspective, one might expect that changes in the patterns of intracortical activity associated with the act of "focusing upon the position of the presence" would have been associated with an alteration in the neuroelectromagnetic patterns. Consequently the applied fields would have interacted with these mildly different patterns and hence the ongoing experiences and their attributions would have been modified as well.

Different patterns produce variations of the experience. For example a 30 year old woman who received a frequency-modulated field (3 msec durations for each point that generated the field) over the right temporoparietal region reported (as an ongoing narrative), " I feel detached from my body.. I am floating up.. there is a kind of vibration moving through my sternum.. there are odd lights or faces along my left side. My body is becoming very hot.. tingling sensations in my chest and stomach..now both arms. There's something feeling my ovaries. I can feel my left foot jerk. I feel there is someone in the room behind me. The vibrations are very strong now and I can look down and see myself".

We have been impressed by the common neurophenomenological themes of the experiences reported by the hundreds of university students and special populations (including visiting journalists)

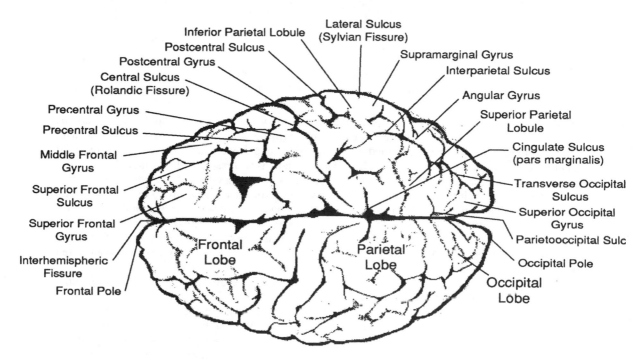

Figure 93. Diagram of a dorsal view of the right and left hemisphere. From Joseph, 1996.

281

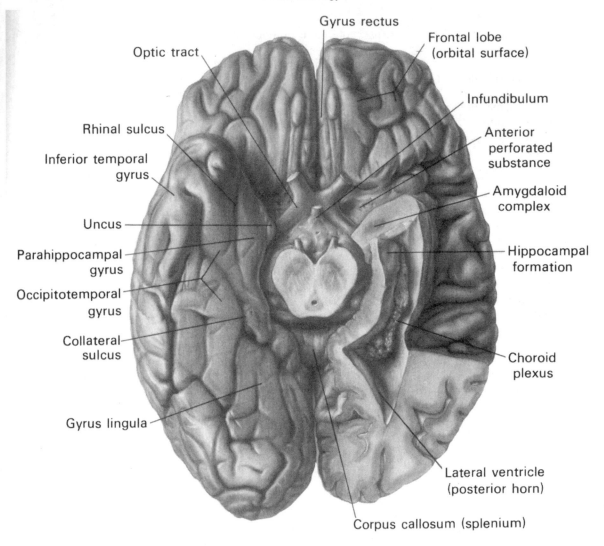

Figure 94. Ventral surface of the brain, partially dissected to show hippocampus and amygdala. From F. Mettler, 1948, Neuroanatomy. C. V. Mosby & Co. St. Louis

we have tested during the last 15 years. Although in general older people, individuals who are artists, musicians, or writers, and women are more effective introspectionists, the themes associated with specific patterns of fields have remained consistent. Each experience however, has its own special signature that is likely to reflect the beliefs of the experient as well as the cultural labels.

For example, a 25 year old male who received the frequency-modulated pattern over both hemispheres with each point in the field being presented for only 1 msec reported (post session interview) "I felt as if there were a bright white light in front of me. I saw a black spot that became a kind of funnel..no tunnel that I felt drawn into..I felt moving, like spinning forward through it. I began to feel the presence of people, but I could not see them; they were along my sides. They were colourless, grey looking people. I know I was in the chamber but it was very real. I suddenly felt intense fear and felt ice cold."

The application of the experimental complex, magnetic fields over the right hemisphere within the laboratory has consistently generated experiences of god or religious entities in people who believe in these experiences. For example a 50 year old man who reported he frequently feels Mother Mary or Christ during his daily life volunteered to participate. Without his knowledge for the timing of the presentations or the type of pattern, he reported (by button presses) the sudden "feeling" or the actual "visual presence" of Christ along his left side when a specific pattern was presented over his right temporoparietal region. The pattern imitated the pulse sequence known to produce long-term potentiation in hippocampal slices. Repeated presentations of this shape produced conspicuous but

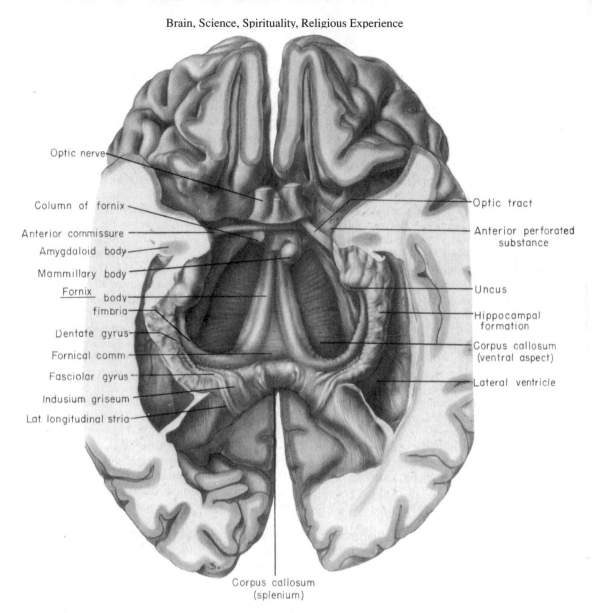

Figure 95. Dissection of the ventral surface of the brain. From F. Mettler, 1948, Neuroanatomy. C. V. Mosby & Co. St. Louis

reversible reductions in the proportions of alpha rhythms measured over both occipital lobes and the right parietal region.

One of the questions that have been asked since we initiated this research is: What does an atheist experience within these contexts? We have exposed about 20 individuals, primarily experts in various disciplines who have visited the laboratory, who have identified themselves as atheists. They also report a sensed presence or detachment from their bodies (out of body experience) but attribute the phenomena to their own cognitive processes. Often the experiences are compared to specific states induced by psychotropic compounds the person has sampled. These results strongly suggest that the experience of a "sentient presence" is an intrinsic property of the human brain and of human experience.

THE EXPERIMENTAL PROCEDURE AND TECHNOLOGY

Unlike the tradition in biophysics to study the effects of magnetic stimulation by employing the simplest of shapes of fields, we reasoned that complexity and information within these fields were more important than their intensity. If one wanted to study the function of the arrangement of molecules upon biological systems the selection of two molecules of hydrogen and one of water, because "its simple," would not have permitted the discovery of the unique properties of proteins or nucleic acids.

The importance of weak intensities of complexity and asymmetry more than high intensities of simplicity and symmetry for providing significant information to large collections of neurons is analogous to the importance of complexity for sound. If the reader was studying and a 1000 Hz sine-wave sound occurred, then he or she would not respond unless the intensity began to exceed about 80 db when it would become irritating. However the complex mixtures of sound frequencies that produced the pattern "God is here" or "help me", at only 20 db (just barely at threshold) contain information. These temporally asymmetric and complex patterns, depending upon the context in which they occurred and the explanation given by the experient, would have powerful behavioral consequences that could last a life time.

We decided that the temporal shapes of these fields would be most effective if their structures simulated the natural patterns generated by neurons and aggregates of neurons. To imitate natural patterns we extracted the activity of neurons, clusters of neurons, and even large arrays of electroencephalographic measurements. The specific complexities of these patterns were converted into columns of numbers with each number displaying a value between 0 and 255. The number 127 was "0" while numbers above or below this value represented positive or negative polarities, respectively. These numbers were then converted into voltages by digital-to-analogue converters and then delivered through solenoids, arranged around a person's head, to generate the magnetic fields.

The solenoids never touch the person's scalp to avoid any direct current induction or mechanical vibration. Instead the solenoids were embedded in a helmet, roughly at the level of the temporoparietal lobes for most individuals, within special containers that could be placed over more specific regions of the scalp, or in a type of "halo" device. In the latter geometry 8 solenoids are arranged equally in space around the scalp just above the ears. The electronic configuration of these devices allows the production of the complex magnetic fields to be generated through the brain from one hemisphere to another or to be rotated around the scalp.

There are four major parameters for these experimental magnetic fields. The first is the shape of the field itself. It is generated by the values in the column of numbers whose lengths range between 200 and 10,000 lines. The second parameter is the duration in real time of each number (and hence voltage) as it is read by the computer software. The brains of rats and humans appear to be most responsive to point-durations of between 1 msec and 3 msec. This means that if a pattern contains 1000 points and each point's duration is 3 msec, the duration of the electromagnetic pattern is 3000 msec or 3 sec.

The third parameter is the inter-stimulus time. This is the "no field" time between the presentations. We have explored interstimulus intervals between 3 msec and 10 sec in order to elicit the strongest effects. Obviously the intervals vary depending upon the type of experience. For example a burst-firing pattern, designed after the discharge pattern of amygdaloid neurons during an electrical seizure, pulsed once every 4 sec for about 20 min results in experiences equivalent to 4 mg/kg of morphine. Continuous presentation of this particular field does not produce this level of analgesia.

The fourth parameter is the total duration of the presentation of each pattern. Most of our studies have limited exposure to between 5 min and 40 min for convenience and to help develop strategies for potential applications to traditional clinical settings. Whereas repetition of the same pattern is more likely to evoke simple experiences within about 2 min, the sequential presentation of different patterns presented for about 2 to 5 min each appears to be sufficient to produce electroencephalographic entrainment and more experiences with varied themes.

We have employed three different procedures to measure the experiences associated with the application of the computer-generated weak magnetic fields. The first technique involves the recording of the ongoing narrative of experiences. Its advantage is the immediacy of the report and the direct access to the experient's own words that can later be analyzed for emotional meaning and text composition. However ongoing narratives sometimes interfere with the experiences.

The second technique has been to give the person an exit questionnaire after the experiment has been completed. The subject is required to rank the incidence of typical experiences reported within the setting. This technique does not require an ongoing narrative and, unlike the narrative procedure, does not interfere with the ongoing experiences. Its disadvantages are that many field-generated experiences are ephemeral and appear to dissipate within about 10 sec to 30 sec and the content of the post-experience questions could be incorporated into the reconstruction of the memory of the experience.

The third technique we have employed to study the "presence" is to instruct the subject to press one of two buttons to indicate when a presence occurred and on which side it was experienced. With this procedure the exact time of an experience can be recorded on the electroencephalographic record and the side of the experience can be determined without the disrupting consequences of talking into the lapel microphone. In addition this procedure allows the experimenter to expose the subject's brain to a large number of different patterns for brief periods in order to discern the latency of the responses. The disadvantage of this technique is the experimental expectation for the type of experience is set.

In all of our experiments neither the subject nor the experimenter, usually a graduate student or senior undergraduate (thesis) student, are aware of the expectations of the experiment. The subject is told that the experiment is concerned with relaxation and that weak magnetic fields may or may not be applied sometime during the experiment.

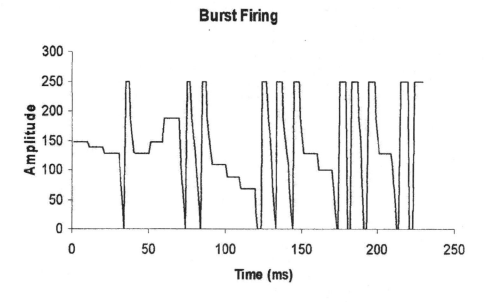

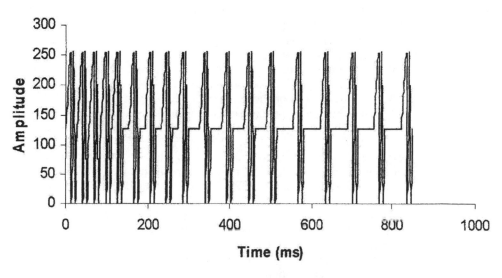

Figure 96. Two examples of complex patterns that, with appropriate parameters, have induced the Sensed Presence.

In Figure 97 (top), the relative intensity and frequency of the sensed presence compared to all other experiences during the experiment are shown for individuals who were exposed to either a sham field (equipment activated but no pattern generated from the computer) or to a burst-firing magnetic field applied asymmetrically over the left temporoparietal region, asymmetrically over the right temporoparietal region, or equally over both hemispheres (10 subjects per group). All subjects had engaged, just prior to the stimulation, in a procedure (Hypnosis Induction Profile) to enhance right hemispheric activity. The intensity of the sensed presence was greatest, compared to sham-field presentations, when this type of field was applied bilaterally.

Several experiments, involving about 100 subjects, showed that stimulation over the right hemisphere first by a continuous frequency modulated field for about 15 min followed by bilateral stimulation over the temporal-parietal lobes with a burst-firing field once every 3 or 4 sec, markedly facilitates the sensed presence. If the presence occurs during the right hemispheric stimulation, the experience appears to be along the left side and to be more emotional (or fearful). If the experience does not occur until the bilateral stimulation, the location of the "being" is perceived to be more to the right or on both sides and to be pleasant, even spiritual. About 80% of volunteers exposed to this sequence report a presence. The reverse procedure (burst-firing first followed by frequency-modulation) is less effective. Only about 10% of people exposed to sham-fields report a sensed presence. Most of them show above average numbers of temporal lobe experiences as defined by a pre-experimental questionnaire.

The elicitation of the sensed presence is specific to the temporal properties of the applied magnetic fields. The results of exposing the same subjects to a number of different patterns with different parameters and in different orders are shown in Figure 97 (bottom). The most effective configuration was the frequency-modulated pattern with point-durations of 3 msec. Reversed presentation of this number file that composed the FM pattern was not as effective. Even a very complex-sequenced magnetic field composed of 40 different shapes (within which the frequency modulated field was embedded), was not as effective.

EXPERIENCES OUTSIDE OF THE LABORATORY

Analyses of the common variance for clusters of subjective experiences reported by about 1,500 students measured over the last 15 years have shown that the sensed presence loaded on the same factor as the report of "being visited late at night by a cosmic consciousness" or "being at one with the universe". We have called this shared source of variance the "Muse" factor. Agreements with items such as "I feel intense meaning from reading poetry and prose", "I feel my thoughts are important to write down", "I have vestibular experiences such as low frequency waves undulating through the body as I fall asleep", and, "I have heard my name called just before 'falling asleep'".

In addition we have assessed, as a component of our practice in neuropsychology, more than 500 patients who have sustained mechanical trauma to their bodies. Most of these patients did not experience a suspension of consciousness and did not exhibit any CT-verified brain injury. More than 50% of these patients report that a sensed presence began to occur after the injury. In every instance the patient who reported the sensed presence felt as if he or she was no longer the same person.

The sensed presences were so disturbing that most of these patients had not reported the experiences to their physicians or to their loved ones because they were concerned about being labelled as "crazy". In general if the presence occurred primarily along the left side, the experience was considered negative. Apprehensions or sudden fears were frequent correlates. If the presence occurred primarily along the right side, the experience was considered either neutral or positive. "Internal" verbal messages, such as thoughts from the presence or "just knowing" information were more common.

The negative experiences were attributed in large part to ghosts or to cultural icons for "evil", such as demons, devils, or other adversaries. The positive experiences were attributed to deceased loved ones, such as a husband, a parent, or a god. They were considered "good". These experiences reduced the person's anxiety substantially.

We have also found that the sensed presence whose attributions range from bereavement apparitions to visitations from Gods or Aliens, occurs more frequently between midnight and 06 hr local time and in particular between 02 hr and 04 hr local time. This peak is the same period in which the greatest proportion of overt displays of temporal lobe seizures were recorded during the late nineteenth century before the implementation of effective medications.

Increases in global geomagnetic activity have been correlated with increases in both the numbers of "apparitions" and visual sensed presences as well as the numbers of epileptic seizures originating from limbic sources. That the brain is responding to the specific pattern and intensity (greater than about 40 nT) of the daily average global geomagnetic perturbations has been verified by the production of seizures in epileptic rats exposed to experimentally generated magnetic fields that precisely duplicated the temporal structure of geomagnetic fields.

One of the likely neurochemical mechanisms by which increases in geomagnetic activity encourages electrical lability within the limbic system is the suppression of the nocturnal levels of melatonin. This serotonin-derivative, primarily synthesized within the pineal organ, has dampening effects upon hippocampal electrical activity. Decreases in melatonin levels have been correlated with periods when daily geomagnetic activity increases above 20 nT and have been evoked by the nocturnal application of experimental magnetic fields with slightly larger strengths.

PERSONALITY CHANGES AND GOD EXPERIENCES

Some structures within the temporal lobe are well suited for initiating the changes in personality that follow the electrical transients associated with a god experience. Reactive synaptogenesis has been demonstrated in specific layers of the hippocampal formation in the brain of temporal lobe epileptics. Recently such reactive synaptogenesis, that contributes to electrical seizures within the limbic system, have been produced experimentally in rats.

Portions of the hippocampal formation are remarkably sensitive to brief periods of physical and chemical trauma. For example Sommer's section, or the CA1 region of the hippocampus, exhibits neuronal loss or reactive synaptogenesis following periods of hypoxia, maintained levels of the epileptogenic neuropeptides such as CRF (corticotrophin releasing factor), and insufficient blood supply. The unusual vasculature of portions of the hippocampal formation increases its vulnerability to marginal ischemic insufficiency. When one considers that the majority of the normal geriatric population exhibits electroencephalographic spikes or sharp transients focally over the temporal lobes, then one might appreciate the propensity for older individuals to report more religious experiences.

Sudden, unexpected, traumas to the brain can also initiate this sequence. Near-death experiences, that are often associated with marked insufficiency of either oxygen or glucose to portions of the limbic system, are followed by changes in the person's personality. Increased emphasis upon spirituality and even a decrease in thantophobia and existential anxiety are typical.

The changes in personality following intermittent neuroelectrical discharges within the structures of the temporal and limbic lobes have been described succinctly by Bear and Fedio for temporal lobe epileptic patients. More than 40 years ago Slater and Beard described a subpopulation of epileptic patients who maintained their cognitive capacity as well as their ability to interact with people. The patients reported intense religious experiences, often with vivid visual hallucinations, and profound beliefs.

Our measurements for both clinical patients who sustain brain traumas that affect functions of the temporal lobes and people who have experienced "temporal lobe transients", the mechanism we have proposed is associated with an intense god experience, strongly agree with the observations of other researchers. The immediate effects of a "god experience" involve intense dream-like experiences, prominent vestibular sensations ("lifting", feeling "free of burdens"), experiences of hearing-knowing information, and intense personal meaningfulness.

The after-effects of these experiences can be associated with confusion, disorientation, time loss, partial amnesia, and the incorporation of post-episodic information into the reconstruction of autobiographical memory. Typically a person whose is emotionally significant to the experient and to whom the experient has confided the experience will provide a label. The most common explanation is "you were called by god". The specific name, Yahweh, Allah, Jehovah, or the Great Cosmic Source, varies with the culture.

Ultimately personality changes emerge. There are bouts of automatic behavior and a sense of the personal. Events are perceived to occur because the person was "selected". A widening of affect encourages the person to infer patterns of meaning between unrelated experiences. Viscosity becomes more prominent and the person becomes fixed on specific ideas or phrases. In many individuals there is emphasis upon intuition rather than data or analytical deduction. An emergent focus upon nascent philosophical interests and the compulsion to record ones thoughts and feelings become more probable.

Finally, the person, because he or she feels "cosmic consent" is compelled to proselytize, to "spread the word". The person's social interactions are modified as he or she interacts more frequently with people who share the same belief and aspirations. The person is described as "a different" or "born again". Despite all of these changes the person exhibits normal social behavior without any loss in cognitive capacity.

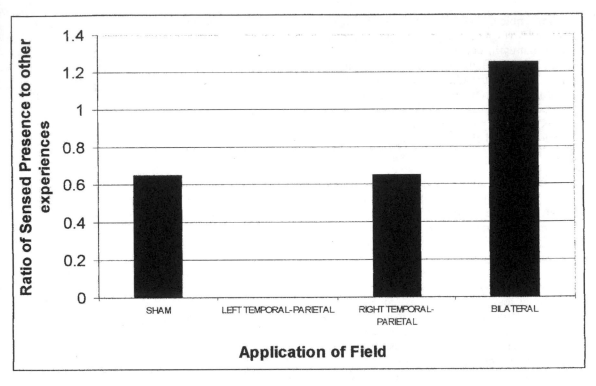

Figure 97. (Top) The ratio of the occurrence of sensed presences as compared to other experiences for subjects who received different configurations of the burst firing magnetic field or the sham field. (Bottom) Potency of different field patterns for producing sensed presences.

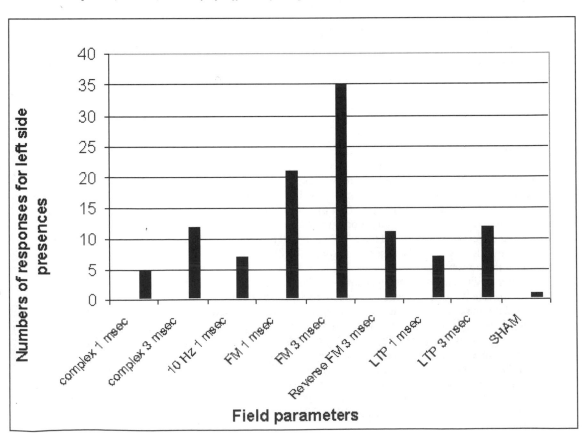

HISTORICAL EXAMPLES

The histories of individuals around whom many religions have evolved strongly suggest marked enhancements of temporal lobe functions. The god experiences occurred in caves (Mohammed), during walks in the wilderness (Christ) or during imposed sensory deprivations (Buddha). Each of these human beings was convinced he had accessed the cosmic significance of the universe. Each of these experients of their own temporal lobe functions began religious movements that affected the development of human civilizations.

During the fifteenth century Guru Nanak, an unemployed musician, departed for his typical bath in a local river and disappeared for three days. When he returned, he remained silent for a day and then said "there is neither Hindu nor Muslim. I shall follow god's path". From his experiences the tradition of Sikhism emerged. Today a similar case might be attributed to an "abduction" experience by aliens.

During the nineteenth century a young son of a minister, while walking in the forest, felt a presence. He began to experience information from a persistent presence. He felt compelled to record these inspirations from the "messenger of god". The Church of the Latter Day Saints was born.

There is no doubt that the experiences of God have been associated with the most profound feelings of human existence. As stated through one of his characters Dostoyevsky stated "The air is filled with a big noise and I thought that it had engulfed me. I have really touched God. He came into me, myself; yes, God exists I cried and I don't remember anything else. All of you healthy people can't imagine the happiness we epileptics feel during the second before our attack. I don't know if this felicity lasts for seconds, hours, or months, but believe me, for all the joys that life brings, I would not exchange this one.

However these experiences are not always harmless. In a case reported by Spratling from the nineteenth century, before the era of modern medications, the (temporal lobe) epileptic patient reported "God told me that in my next life I would be born C.H.S. and marry my last sweetheart, and be a millionaire, and that I would be a strong, hopeful, and powerful Christian millionaire. I feel God's voice in my left ear at night. I feel the Lord in my chest. I see stars in my eyes. I have seen Christ crucified. God told me I would never have any more fits. God told me to bite off a patient's ear. If God told me to do wrong, it feels as if I would do it.

BELIEF IN GOD AS A 'COGNITIVE VIRUS'

Cultures have often been defined as groups of people with shared expectancies. Expectancies are beliefs by which we organize our experiential worlds. Beliefs are cognitive structures that allow us to predict the future and to minimize the anxiety of the unknown. To many cognitive processes the unknown is analogous to the anticipation of terror and unimaginable fear.

The sentence "I will die" is perhaps the most powerful three words that have maintained the god belief. It is the semantic equivalent of conditioned suppression or the conditioned emotional response. Human cultures have devised three strategies to diffuse this semantic time-bomb. It often explodes with the realization that the dissolution of the self: death, is irrevocably imminent.

The first strategy is to remove the anticipation of termination. Every culture has a word or concept that refers to some component of the infinite, omnipresent and omniscient. If something is infinite, there is no end. If there is no end there is no anxiety.

The semantic operation to associate the person with this concept requires language structures that define the self as a subset of the infinite. Phrases such as "I am child of God" or "I will live on with God" are effective anxiolytics if one assumes implicitly that God is eternal. The "self" does not die because it becomes a component of the eternal.

The face validity of the illusion that the self is more than the body appears to be derived from the perpetual dichotomy between private and public behaviours. The resulting "dualism" between "the mind" and "the body" fosters the concept of souls, minds and other phlogiston-like entities that are reified by the experient. Once this assumption has emotional significance, even mundane experiences such as the perceptions in dreams where the self is separate from the body and in dimensions other than where the person is sleeping, become "proofs" that the "self" is independent of the finite physiology of the body.

One critical component of any god belief is that it must never be refutable or testable. Consequently the concept is always defined implicitly as "nonphysical", not measurable, and as the final default explanation when there are no apparent answers to questions. Faith, the religious variation of intense belief, is employed as proof of validity. The most typical retort to challenge is "prove god is not there".

The scientific method cannot prove a negative. However this semantic limit is not a weakness. It can be considered an encouragement to consider infinite possibilities as long as they are or could be measurable. The existence of god cannot be refuted because of the nature of the definition. It does not prove god exists. If I told you that the universe was controlled by invisible, nonphysical pink elephants would you believe? Prove they are not there.

The second approach to the problem of "I will die" has been to indict the validity of "I". Many eastern philosophies assume that the "I" is a social fiction. It is only created by the language and expectations of the culture. Consequently the "true path" is found by minimizing the role of language and by focusing upon the essence that remains. The self is simply a component of the large Cosmic Whole. There is no end to the whole.

The third approach is to this problem is to remove the "will" and replace it with the present tense. This solution, more popular among atheists and existentialists, can minimize anxiety because the anticipatory component is markedly attenuated. An aversive stimulus being experienced has much less anxiety than one being anticipated.

From a Darwinian perspective, one might appreciate the maintenance of the temporal lobe experiences that promote the God belief. If there had not been survival value associated with both the experience and the belief of gods, these behaviours should have been selected against long ago. They should have been deleted from our genetic expression.

One speculation is that during the early stages of the development of the self, the powerful capacity to anticipate the future was also associated with the capacity to anticipate one's own demise. If some other process had not emerged to attenuate this anxiety, the fragile sense of human self would have been fragmented. The incapacitation of anxiety and existential terror would have dominated.

Today most people acquire one of these solutions to the issue of personal death during their childhood. These explanations are given by parents or caregivers during the necessary times when pets, grandparents or friends die. By inference, which even the infant brain can display, the anticipation of the self's own demise emerges.

As the microstructure of the brain matures and the child progresses through the cognitive stages of development, this belief minimizes the anxiety. As maturation proceeds, the belief there is a god with whom the sense of self can never end remains embedded within each cognitive stage. By the time the organism achieves adulthood, with the faculties to question the validity and the utility of the god belief, it has become an intricate part of the cognitive structure defining the self. To challenge it or even to examine it could begin the unravelling of the person's sense of self.

Our experimental work to explore why people avoid the question of the validity of the god belief indicates that the belief has many of the characteristics of a delusion. As many clinicians acknowledge, directing the verbal behavior of delusional patients towards the logical conclusion that their beliefs are unreasonable or false is difficult. Within one or two logical steps from the conclusion that the delusion is false, the patient's cognitive process often stops or is diverted to some other topic.

To examine how people avoid the logical conclusion that a belief is not valid, we have been asking volunteers to respond as quickly as possible to a series of progressive statements presented for 5 sec each on a computer. The person must respond yes or no as quickly as possible. The items begin with the statement that the universe is composed of matter and energy and then gradually move towards the evolution of molecules and cells.

For demonstration, beginning with item 17, "The neuron is cell", the statements slowly shift towards the conclusion that would indict the validity of the god belief. The questions are: 18, "The brain is composed of neurons", 20 "Different interactions produce different behaviors", 21 "All perceptions occur within the brain", 22 "All experiences occur within the brain", 23 "Beliefs are composed of experiences". 24 "Most people believe in the existence of God", 25 "God if a belief", 26 "God is an experience within the brain", 27 "All experiences are produced by the brain", 28 "The experience of God is produced by the brain", 29 "God does not exist except within the brain".

We have noted that as volunteers (particularly the ones who belief in god and attend church frequently) begin to approach statement 29, beginning around statement 24, their response times slowly increase even after the grammar and length of the statements have been accommodated. If processes associated with the right hemisphere (such as the accuracy for words presented to the left ear during dichotic word processing) are monitored there is an increase in this activity during the items (26,27) that precede the conclusion that god is simply generated within the brain.

These data indicate there are experimental procedures that might help elucidate the neuromechanisms by which the average person avoids or ignores the logical conclusion that their belief in god may not be valid. The approach also suggests that every time the god belief is evoked to minimize anxiety, the strength of the belief, like any operant response, is strengthened. Effectively the belief becomes a powerful cognitive anxiolytic and antidepressant for the challenges to the left hemispheric sense of self.

However there may be a negative component to this intellectual opiate. Suppose another group of people exists who embrace a different god? If another god exists then does your god loose its omnipotent power? What happens when the experiences attributed to this god indicate that he or she is the only one god and believers in any other deity are less than human and hence expendable? Suppose your personal immortality is threatened. Would you kill to preserve your immortality?

"I WOULD KILL IN GOD'S NAME"

Specific electrical anomalies within the limbic system, particularly the amygdala, can trigger aggression and killing. Any stimulus that changes the threshold for amygdaloid-hypothalamic activity, from specific smells to suppression of nocturnal melatonin by geomagnetic activity, can evoke the response.

The human species is one of the most aggressive species that has existed. We are the Tyrannosaurus Rex of the mammals. As a species we have killed every animal form we have encountered, sometimes to extinction. As a species, our first response to discovery, from gunpowder to atomic fission, has been to kill the perceived enemy. We even kill each other. Since the year 1500, approximately 150 million human beings have died during armed conflicts between nations.

More cultures have been raped and razed in the names of Jehovah, Allah, or the Great Cosmic Guide than one can imagine. Although sociologists and historians often attribute these episodes to political or economic causes, the individuals who engaged in killing often reported they felt as if they had "god's consent." When personal immortality of the self is involved, fear of being killed in battle is trivial by comparison.

Although not every one might kill others if they believed that their god had condoned it, the proportion of individuals who report they would is disturbingly high. About 7% of first year university students enrolled in psychology classes reported "yes" to the statement "If God told me to kill I would in His Name." Post-inventory interviews indicated these responders were not randomly responding or engaging in frivolous activity. Whereas 10% of the population who said they would kill in God's name were males, only 5% were females. Twenty-five (25%) of the males who frequently attended a church, synagogue, mosque, or other religious context reported they would kill while only 9% of women who attended church frequently agreed with this item. For those males who attended church frequently, who reported they had a religious experience, and who displayed elevated temporal lobes signs, about 50% stated they would kill in God's name.

Close scrutiny of the personality profiles and psychological tests for these individuals indicated they were not pathological. The scores for the scales from the Minnesota Multiphasic Personality Inventory (MMPI), whose items are derived from psychiatric concepts of behavior, were within the average range or certainly not significantly different from people who reported they would not kill. The individuals who reported they would kill also did not differ with respect to suggestibility, proneness to imaginings, or self esteem. From a psychiatric and psychopathological perspective, these people were normal.

Most religious texts, including the Bible, the Koran, the Egyptian Book of the Dead, and the Book of Mormon, have frequent references to killing of others as proofs of gods' powers or justifications for their existence. People who do not belong to the same belief system are marginalized as unenlightened and become candidates for extinction. Nomad groups, believing themselves to be the "chosen", have marched into lands belonging to others and have slaughtered entire peoples because "god gave us the land."To study how normal individuals might endorse ideas of killing others in the name of a god, we have selected passages from the major religious texts concerning those topics. To mask the sources and the historical syntax of these scriptures, the phrases are paraphrased and the name of the god has been replaced with "Alien." For example, one passage read "If you should die or be killed in the cause of the Alien, the Alien's forgiveness and mercy would be surely better than all of the riches. If you die or be killed you will be taken by the Alien into his midst." Another passage read "Those who rebel against the alien listen to the evil forces. They become an enemy of the Alien and all that is right. Therefore, the Alien has no place for them in his domain. If you die before you believe in the Alien you will become conscious of your own guilt. It will fill your Being with pain, anguish, and an unquenchable fire whose flame will last forever.

These items were given to university students under the title of "Clinical Rating Exercise". The student evaluators were asked "Read the following comments of delusional patients about their reports of receiving special information during alien abductions. The specific name of the alien has been changed simply to alien. Your task is to determine which of these patients are most dangerous to society because of their beliefs about their mortality or definition of self with respect to dissolution of the self, i.e., death. Your job is to protect society from dangerous offenders." The evaluators were then asked to rate each comment from each "patient" (actually a scriptural source) on a Likert scale between 1 (not dangerous) and 7 (extremely dangerous).

The most conspicuous result from these studies is that university students who endorse extreme religious beliefs consider items about killing, such as the first example noted above, not to be dangerous to society. This association was evident regardless of the person's professed religious affiliation. These individuals also felt there was forbidden knowledge. They answered "yes" to items such as "There are things Science should not investigate" and "Belief in science and religion are not compatible".

It is interesting when these same items are quoted in the original and are referenced to the source, the ratings of the dangerousness is less (within the range of neutral). Whether this response bias reflects the political correctness of the contemporary culture concerning other's religion or some implicit assumption that religion can only be positive, remains to be investigated.

IMPLICATIONS

Our research, as well as the results of other experimenters, indicates that the experiences and beliefs about gods are normal properties of the human brain. In all probability they have developed within our species with other cognitive functions in order to facilitate adaptability. The primary role of the beliefs may have been to reduce anxiety about self-dissolution that, if not controlled, could have interfered with adaptation.

There is now experimental evidence that the experience of god can be simulated with the laboratory. Although we have shown general patterns of electromagnetic fields that can induce these experiences, it is likely that different people will require variations of parameters in order to optimize the experience. This technical variation would be analogous to the selection of the specific antidepressant and appropriate dosages for different patients.

Because the same brain structures and patterns that evoke the god experience are also associated with sexual behavior and aggression, god experiences and beliefs could encourage aggression towards individuals who do not share these beliefs if the person experiences an "instruction" attributed to god. We are social animals that require social proximity and affiliation with groups. A component of this cohesion is the exclusion of others who do not belong, particularly when the validity of the belief that defines the group is threatened.

There are many stimuli, perhaps some yet to be discovered, that can evoke the experiences of God and foster religious beliefs. If the history of science predicts the future as it has explained the past, future discoveries will likely reveal phenomena that are even greater than the God experience and the God belief. Like the phlogiston of preconceptual chemistry or the concept of "epicycles" for Ptolemy's explanation for the motions of planets, the current explanations for the experiences of the Sentient Being as a Creator and assurance for personal immortality will no longer be required. Such changes are the nature of scientific discovery.

However there is now a potential technology that could be developed to enhance the experiences of "Sentient Beings" within large populations without their awareness. The patterns we have explored, extracted from natural stimuli, can be generated over significant distances. Like all technologies it can be employed for everyone or for the benefit of a few. This technology controls the prototypical experience for the belief of immortality. Understanding the neuroscience of god experiences and beliefs and how it can be provoked or prevented may be critical to the survival of our species.

Acknowledgements

The author thanks Linda St-Pierre for her technical assistance and Dr. Rob Buckman for his perspective. The contribution of many young colleagues, some of whom now have their own laboratories, is appreciated.

THE EVOLUTIONARY ORIGINS OF SPIRITUAL CONSCIOUSNESS
by Matthew Alper

As a result of recent neurophysiological research, we now possess substantial physical evidence that there exist specific sites in the human brain responsible for generating religious and spiritual consciousness. More important, however, than the physical evidence that such sites exist, is how we choose to interpret this newfound data. Accordingly, we have but one of two choices to make. Either we are to interpret these findings from a religiously dogmatic perspective, or from a standpoint based on the scientific method.

In this regard, the question is quite simple: If we do indeed possess such "spiruality" engendering neurophysiological sites then either God must have put them there, or, like every other part of our anatomy, they evolved through the process of natural selection. If, it should turn out that God installed these sites withing us-perhaps as some type of "antennae" through which we might "receive" Him—then the case is closed and there is little else to investigate on the matter. If, however, these sites emerged through the process of natural selection, then we are presented with a mystery that demands to be solved. When, for instance, might these sites have evolved in us and, more importantly, why? As a distinct proponent of the evolutionary view, I believe it is important to try to piece together those events in human cognitive history that may have led to the emergence of this particular adapatation.

As the German philosopher Hegel succinctly expressed, "All that exists is rational" (Hegel, 1821). Every cause has its effect; every effect has its cause. In essence, nothing happens without a reason. Since this axiom applies to all that exists, it must also apply to all the various forms of terrestrial life as well-all forms including our own.

In applying this axiom to specific human characteristics, every trait we possess, from stereoscopic vision to our opposable thumbs, must have a specific reason for having emerged in us. Since the driving force underlying all evolutionary processes is the preservation of a species, every trait must somehow serve to increase our species' chances of survival. This is evident in every organ we possess (excluding, of course, those vestigial parts such as the caudal vertebrae or coccyx, that evolutionary memento of our predecessors' tails, or the appendix , a relic of our grass eating days, two examples of anatomical parts which, because we no longer need them, are in the process of being selected out of us). Because all traits must perform a specific function that will serve to increase a species' survivability, if humans possess specific neurophysiological sites responsible for generating spiritual consciousness, then the same must hold true for these parts as well.

Consequently, if humans possess spiritual consciousness, we must ask: What might its purpose be? What function might such an adaptation serve that it could enhance our species' survivability? What is this trait's rationale, its reason for being? Again, as is true of all traits, if human spirituality didn't provide some very specific function, if it didn't somehow serve to enhance our species' survivability, it would never have emerged in us.

Most physical traits emerge in response to some environmental pressure. For instance, if Arctic wolves possess thick coats of fur, it's because their environment pressured them to evolve one. As our terrestrial environments are in a state of constant flux, we as organic matter, are constantly being forced to adapt to meet the demands of our ever changing conditions. Therefore, if humans possess a neurophysiologically-based spiritual function, we must not just seek to understand its purpose, but we must also seek to understand those environmental pressures that may have forced the selection of such an adaptation upon us.

In the aforementioned case of the Arctic wolves, it was the pressure incurred by the cold weather that caused their heavy coats of fur to emerge. Among our own species, what change might have occurred within our environment that may have prompted the evolution of a spiritual function in us? Furthermore, what was unique about our species that we alone should have developed such a seemingly abstract trait? Given that Nature weeds out all that is superfluous, if spiritual consciousness didn't somehow enhance our species' survivability, it simply wouldn't exist.

AWARENESS OF DEATH

"In a hundred countries, in a thousand languages, humanity stops and reaches upward, keenly aware of its mortality." --(Matthiessen, 1991

"No thought exists in me which death has not carved with his chisel" --Michelangelo, as cited by Ramsden, 1963

No other creature on earth has the intellectual capacity of *Homo sapiens*. As a matter of fact, our intelligence constitutes the foundation of our species' remarkable strength. Whereas fish can swim, birds can fly and cats have speed, humans possess an intelligence that has allowed us to venture deeper, fly higher and move faster than any other creature on earth. No other creature, besides the quasi-living viruses, comes close to challenging our dominion over the other forms of life. All we have to do is look around us to behold the awesome power of our intelligence. In the last hundred years alone, we have transformed this planet's surface more dramatically than any other species has in the last three billion.

Nevertheless, as much as our vast intelligence may have graced our species, it has also been the source of our greatest affliction. Though our intelligence may have made us the most versatile and therefore powerful creature on earth, this same adaptation has backfired on our species with nearly the same potency that it has served us. As a result of our intelligence, something happened that had never before occurred within the known universe. With the same powers of perception that allowed our predecessors to scrutinize the world around them, *Homo sapiens* developed the unique capacity to perceive their own selves. An organic form emerged that was aware of its own existence. No other creature before us had any idea that when it drank from the watering hole, the image it gazed down upon was that of its own reflection. Now, for the first time in life's three and a half billion year history, an organism suddenly could. For the first time, a combination of molecules had emerged that could comprehend its own existence. Imagine those primal humans looking down at their hands, their bodies, in awe of what they saw and for the first time, asking that fateful question, "What is this that I am? What is this that I exist?" With the capacity for this one cognition, this one self-reflection, the human species was transformed. In biblical terms, man had taken his first bite of the Forbidden Fruit from the Tree of Knowledge.

It was probably not long after this first cognitive lightning flash occurred that we were hit with the inevitable thunder: "If I am, if I exist, then isn't it possible that one day I might not?" With the same capacity with which humans could comprehend their own existence, we became equally aware of the possibility of our own non-existence...of death. With this one awareness, the wheels of life which had been turning so smoothly for all these billions of years had turned down a cognitive cul de sac. Humankind had suffered life's first existential crisis.

THE PAIN FUNCTION

"Pain and death are a part of life. To reject them is to reject life itself" (Ellis, 1897-1928).

According to Siddhartha, enlightenment can be attained by anyone willing to follow the path of the "Fourfold Truths" (Siddhartha, c. 525 BCE). The first of these truths, referred to as Dukkha, asserts that life is a process of universal misery and suffering. No matter who we are, be it prince or pauper, we are all destined to experience the same fateful demise. We are all bound to grow old, weak and infirm. We are all preordained to lose everything we ever had or loved, including our own selves. In a nutshell, we are all going to die. Borrowing from this tenet of Buddhist pessimism, Freud expressed a similar notion: "We are threatened with suffering from three directions: from our own body, which is doomed to decay and dissolution and which cannot even do without pain and anxiety as warning signals; from the external world, which may rage against us with overwhelming and merciless forces of destruction; and finally from our relations to other men" (Freud, 1962).

Because our lives are incessantly threatened by such perilous forces, pain represents not only a biological phenomenon but a biological necessity. Just as with every other trait we possess, we experience pain because it serves a very specific function. But what exactly is pain? Pain is a negative sensation experienced by organic forms when specific receptors are triggered in the brain. Stimuli that elicit pain are generally indicative of things that represent potential threats to an organism's physical existence. For example, excessive heat, as in the form of fire, can harm, if not kill, a creature. It is for this reason that many animals possess heat-sensitive receptors that cover the surface of their skin. When these receptors come in contact with excessive heat, an animal experiences this potentially hazardous stimulus as a negative sensation we call pain. By experiencing excessive heat in such a negative or "painful" manner, animals are compelled to avoid that which can burn them. Should an animal get too close to a flame, the negative sensation of pain will prompt it to retreat, thus saving it from what may have caused more serious damage.

Pain therefore represents an evolutionary adaptation meant to encourage organic forms to avoid those things that may constitute a threat to their existence. It is this pain function that keeps us ever-vigilant. It is what prevents us from being pierced by sharp objects, to burn, freeze, starve, or dehydrate.

To provide a more specific example of how this pain function operates, I'll use the example of hunger in a rabbit. In order to prevent a rabbit from starving to death, its undernourished body will send a distress signal to its brain that it is in need of sustenance. It is this negative sensation that will motivate the rabbit to seek its required fuel supply. If this physical need is not met within a certain time frame, the animal's body will reinforce this signal by stimulating even more pain receptors causing the rabbit's hunger to be intensified. What was previously experienced as a mild discomfort becomes an acute pain. In essence, the body is sending a distress signal to itself saying, "Feed me or die!" To relieve itself of the painful sensation of hunger the animal is motivated to seek sustenance.

In our own inaccurate language, when the rabbit finally finds and consumes its meal, we tend to say that it is experiencing pleasure or satisfaction. But if we look at this from a purely biological perspective, it is not pleasure that the animal is experiencing but rather the diminishment of its pain. Just as the experience of pain increases an animal's survivability, it plays an equally important role in maintaining the preservation of a species.

It is the negative stimulus of sexual tension that incites animals to reproduce. Among mammals, reproduction represents a hindrance to individual survival as having to provide for offspring means an animal has that much less time to devote to securing its own personal needs. Giving birth and rearing young therefore is an obstacle to individual survival. Nevertheless, as reproduction plays an integral role in the preservation of any species, it is a necessity. It is for this reason that animals are biochemically driven to reproduction. Once again, though sex is generally perceived as something pleasurable, it more accurately represents the diminishment of sexual tension or pain.

Among the higher order social animals, most particularly among *Homo sapiens*, another example of a negative or painful stimulus that serves to promote the well being of the species involves that negative experience we refer to as loneliness. When one is alone, that is, isolated from the community, he is most vulnerable. As no individual is completely self-sufficient, each of us must rely on the assistance, care and protection of others. On our own, we are most defenseless. Within the group, however, an individual gains the added security and strength that comes with increased numbers. It is for this reason that Nature selected us with a negative or painful stimulus that prompts individuals to pursue the company of others.

A related example of a negative stimulus that serves to promote the well-being of the individual, as well as its species, involves what we refer to as separation anxiety, a physical discomfort experienced when we are separated from a loved one. Because romantic love fosters procreation, security and effective child-rearing, it is necessary that we experience a discomfort when separated from our romantic partners. Consequently, though we perceive ourselves as joyous when reunited with a loved one from whom we've been separated, it is really the diminishment of our separation anxiety that we are experiencing. (A research team led by anthropologist Helen Fisher of Rutgers University has been working to isolate the chemistry involved in bonding behaviors. Fisher believes that attachments formed between two individuals "in love" are caused by changes within the brain involving a group of neurotransmitters called mono-amines, which include dopamine, norepinephrine, and serotonin. To plot these changes, Fisher subjected lovelorn couples to a functional magnetic resonance imaging or fMRI brain scanner that could pinpoint minute changes in blood flow in the brain associated with bonding and infatuation. What she found was that whereas lust is governed by testosterone and estrogen, attachment is governed by the neurotransmitters oxytocin and vasopressin. Apparently, even romantic love and attachment can be reduced to neurochemical processes.

This hypothesis was also confirmed when Andreas Bartles at University College London found that when students placed in an fMRI were shown photographs of loved ones, as opposed to photos of insignificant others, which had much less effect, specific regions of the brain became highly activated. The areas which lit up were part of the anterior cingulate cortex and the middle insula and parts of the putamen and caudate nucleus.)

In summary, it is pain that keeps organic forms alive and intact. Pain is Nature's electric prod that is incessantly goading us towards those things which benefit us and away from those which can do us harm. We therefore experience pain and discomfort for a reason. Pain represents the chief stimulus by which all life is prompted to survive.

THE ANXIETY FUNCTION

"Just as courage imperils life, fear protects it" (da Vinci 1452-1519, as cited by Richter, 1952).

"There are times when fear is good. There is advantage in the wisdom won from pain." -- Aeschylus,c. 458 BCE

Most particularly among the mammals, threatening circumstances elicit a particular type of pain we call anxiety. Anxiety constitutes a specific type of painful response meant to prompt animals to avoid potentially hazardous circumstances.

As the stomach is responsible for the digestion of food, its pain receptors respond to the quality of nourishment it receives. Analagously, as the brain is where all data is stored, it is responsive to the quality of information it receives. For example, a baby rabbit pokes its nose into a fire for the very first time. The excessive temperature stimulates heat receptors dispersed throughout the rabbit's skin. This negative stimulus incites the motor reflexes which prompt the rabbit to recoil from the flame. Having escaped the situation with no more than a superficial burn, the rabbit will now encode this experience in the form of a memory. From now on, whenever this rabbit perceives a fiery object, the memory of its encoded experience will be retrieved, thereby alerting it not to repeat its past action. Rather than having to experience being burned over and over again, the rabbit's memory will act as a buffer against all possible future experiences with objects that emit excessive heat.

Though this capacity to store and utilize memories enables the rabbit to avoid fire without having to be burned repeatedly, this does not mean that the memory itself is altogether pain free. In order to remind the rabbit of the potential threat that fire and excessive heat represent, the memory will elicit a type of discomfort we call anxiety. In this way, though anxiety may serve to protect the rabbit from incurring any actual physical injury, it, nevertheless, subjects it to a certain degree of discomfort. That an actual memory can cause one to experience psychological discomfort or anxiety demonstrates that memories store emotional as well as purely perceptual data. As a matter of fact, emotional memory can be attributed to the brain's amygdala, which, when damaged, will result in the loss of an individual's capacity to retrieve memories that contain emotional content (LeDoux, 1994).

With this advanced faculty to store memories, in conjunction with the capacity to experience anxiety, an organism no longer had to sustain actual physical injury before it was motivated to avoid a potentially hazardous experience. Anxiety therefore acts as an early warning device that keeps an organism ever alert to potential threats before one is actualized.

In another more extreme example of how anxiety serves us, imagine that the rabbit now wanders off only to find itself confronted with a mountain lion. The urgency of the situation causes the rabbit to experience the most painful symptoms of anxiety, all meant to incite it to escape an otherwise potentially hazardous circumstance. Some of the negative symptoms of anxiety include heart palpitations, muscle tension, hyperventilating, trembling, perspiration-all of which are meant to prompt the rabbit to get as far away from the source of its discomfort as quickly as possible. Consequently, even though the mountain lion has yet to lay a paw on the rabbit, the rabbit will still experience the pain of its own anxieties.

When an animal is confronted by such a mortal threat as this, the symptoms of anxiety can be extremely painful. Anxiety therefore serves as an advantageous adaptation in that it prompts the organism to respond to a potentially hazardous situation with greater speed and efficiency. Should our rabbit manage to escape the mountain lion, it will encode this anxiety-engendering experience in the form of a memory. The next time the rabbit leaves its lair, the anxiety-evoking memory of its past experience with a mountain lion will discourage it from going anywhere near one. Thanks to this anxiety function our rabbit no longer needs to be attacked by a mountain lion over and over again to know to avoid one. It is for this reason that anxiety represents a biological necessity.

As Ernest Becker, author of Denial of Death, wrote: "Animals, in order to survive have to be protected by fear responses, in relation not only to other animals but to nature itself. They had to see the real relationship of their limited powers to the dangerous world in which they were immersed. Reality and fear go together naturally (Becker,1973).

As the human brain is more complex than that of other species, our cognitive capacities are that much more sophisticated. First of all, our brains contain much more storage space dedicated to memories. Secondly our species possesses an enhanced capacity to comprehend various possible futures. As a result of the combined affects of these two capabilities, humans are aware that hunger elicits pain, and enhanced by our capacity for foresight, we are motivated to procure food and shelter not just for today but for the future. Unlike many of our evolutionary ancestors who needed to rely on the immediate stimulus of hunger to be motivated to search for nourishment, we are compelled to make sure there is food available long before it is actually needed. This capacity for forethought grants us the added benefit of having more time to secure our most vital needs. Because a simpler organism needs to rely on the immediate stimulus of hunger to be prompted to search for its food supply, it may only have a few days' advance notice to procure its next meal before it will starve. In the case of humans, however, as a result of our advanced capacity for foresight, we can erect entire structures whose sole purpose is to store food for years to come.

Though this capacity for foresight may work to our advantage, it comes with a serious drawback. Instead of just being anxious about those threats that exist in the present, we experience anxiety for all those possible threats which might jeopardize us in the future. Consequently, humans don't just experience anxiety over how they will procure their next meal but over how they will secure tomorrow's meals as well. And it's not just tomorrow's meals we're concerned with but all those we will ultimately need to sustain ourselves and our progeny far into the future. For this reason, though our capacity for foresight may serve to our advantage, it at the same time engenders a tremendous amount of anxiety.

In many ways, the anxiety function represents our primary defense in our incessant struggle for survival. It is this anxiety function that keeps us ever-vigilant and alert, always on guard against the potential threats, all the things we have the unique ability to secure ourselves against long before they represent an actual threat. It is this anxiety function that has motivated us to manufacture fire and electric light, to develop all sorts of medical technologies, to build dams, and structural fortifications, to erect silos, and to devise methods of refrigeration. Due to our enhanced capacity for planning combined with the anxiety induced by our fear of potential future threats, we are obsessed with our futures. It is necessary we be this way, for the minute we become lax and lower our guards, we become vulnerable to a world of potential hazards and predators. In essence, the moment we become less anxious, we become that much more endangered.

Whereas other animals may have claws or sharp teeth with which to protect themselves, humans possess a capacity for foresight. With our enhanced capacity to envision alternative futures, humankind is that much more equipped to fortify itself against more threats than any other creature. Nevertheless, this type of advanced intelligence comes at a very high price.

WHEN AWARENESS OF DEATH MEETS THE ANXIETY FUNCTION

"Anxiety is the state in which a being is aware of its possible non-being...The anxiety of death is the most basic, most universal and inescapable" -Tillich, 1952.

"No one is free from the fear of death...The fear of death is always present in our mental functioning." --Zilboorg, 1943.

"The deep realization of the frailty and impermanence of man as a biological creature is accompanied by an agonizing existential crisis." --Grof, 1975.

"He that cuts off twenty years of life cuts off so many years of fearing death." --Shakespeare, c. 1564-1616.

So what becomes of our anxiety function when it is confronted by our species' unique awareness of death? How are we to effectively utilize our capacity for foresight when it is incessantly informing us that we are ultimately going to die? It is our capacity for foresight complemented by our anxiety function that keeps us perpetually vigilant, always on the lookout for any next possible threat. And though it is this same awareness that motivates us to avoid such perils, it, at the same time, brings us face to face with the fact that no matter what we do to fortify ourselves, our actions are all in vain. No matter how hard we work to provide ourselves with food and shelter, no matter what we do to protect and defend ourselves, no matter how much we plan and prepare for our futures, we know that death is inevitable and inescapable. It is this awareness that strips the anxiety function of all its efficacy, in turn, stripping humankind of its capacity to effectively survive.

No other creature on this planet can comprehend the concept of its own existence. Consequently, no other creature can conceive of its own non-existence, that is, of its own mortality or death. This coincides with the fact that no other creature can comprehend the concept of its own future. Before us, all creatures lived in and for the moment. If an animal got hungry, it sought food. If it got tired, it slept. It lived and it died without one conscious thought regarding its own existence or non-existence. It had no conceptual awareness of its own possible future and therefore of its own possible death. The question, "What might happen to me tomorrow?" had never before been asked until man conceived that such a day existed

This time consciousness, which is possessed by no other species with such insistent clarity, enables man to draw upon past experience in the present and to plan for future contingencies. This faculty, however, has another effect: it causes man to be aware that he is subject to a process that brings change, aging, decay and ultimately death to all living things. Man, thus, knows what no other animal apparently knows about itself, namely that he is mortal. He can project himself mentally into the future and anticipate his own decease. Man's burial customs grimly attest to his preoccupation with death from the very dawn of human culture in the Paleolithic age. Significantly, the burial of the dead is practiced by no other species. The menace of death is thus inextricably bound up with man's consciousness of time (Encyclopedia Britannica, 1977).

To add insult to injury, not only are we aware that we must die, but we also know that death can come at any given moment. Regarding our futures, nothing is certain. We live our lives anxiously standing beneath the mythical sword of Damocles wondering when that single strand of hair that holds inevitable death suspended above our heads will finally snap.

Imagine how apparent this must have been for our earliest ancestors. How much security did primitive humans have that each day would not be their last? Imagine a time when there was hardly any medicine, when what may have seemed like a bellyache or toothache one day brought death the next. What constant dread and uncertainty must have plagued our ancestor's existences. Among such nomadic dwellers, even the seemingly simple task of procuring one's next meal represented a potentially mortal chore. Whereas today we can merely pull up to the nearest drive-through restaurant to obtain our daily ration of meat, these men had to go out with their crude hunting utensils and bludgeon some ferocious beast in order to procure their next meal. In such times, the threat of death was constant. And yet, with all of our modern conveniences and medical technologies, very little has really changed. Even with all of our advancements, there is still no escaping the fact that we are all destined to die as well as that death can occur at any moment. Sure we may live another twenty or thirty years longer than our predecessors, but what difference does that really make when measured against all eternity?

Living with the certain knowledge of imminent death leaves us in a state of perpetual mortal crisis. At every moment, we stand face to face with a mountain lion from which there is no escape, staring straight into the jaws of death. What this means is that in light of our capacity for foresight, our awareness of inevitable death condemns us to live out our existences in a state of incessant mortal terror and dread.

The chief difference between our condition and that of the rabbit as it stands face to face with a mountain lion is that whereas the rabbit can escape the object of its fear, human beings cannot. Once we developed a capacity to reflect upon our inevitable deaths, we were left a state of unremitting fear of an enemy that we can neither see, flee, nor defeat. In essence, we are no better off than if we were strapped with a time bomb on a random timer set to go off at any time within the next fifty or so odd years. What would we do in such a case other than to spend the rest of our lives in a state of constant terror and dread, waiting for the ticking bomb to finally detonate? How is the human condition any different from this? The threat of death lurks around every corner, in every breath, shadow, meal, and stranger. And though we don't know from whence or where it will come, we are condemned to recognize that it inevitably will.

In addition to this, as potent as our fear of personal death is the fear of losing those we love. As a social organism, we are dependent on others for our physical as well as emotional survival. Again and again, studies show the debilitating effects of isolation in humans. Without love, we are generally pained beings. (This was most effectively demonstrated by the pioneer work of Harry Harlow [1905 – 1981], who raised young monkeys in varying degrees of isolation and found that those reared in solitary confinement grew to be utterly dysfunctional adults who, to compensate for their lack of contact, would often spend their days crouched in a corner, chewing on their own limbs as a means to provide themselves with some form of sensual stimulation.) For this reason, we place nearly the same—if not more—value on the lives of those to whom we are emotionally attached as we do our own. Consequently, we live in constant fear not just of losing our own lives but of losing the lives of those we cherish and love.

Just as there is no escape from death, there is no escape from the consequent anxiety that our mortal awareness imposes upon us. With the advent of our awareness of death, humankind was left in a state of perpetual angst, what Soren Kierkegaard called "the sickness unto death" (Kierkegaard, 1849). With the dawn of self-conscious awareness, the anxiety function had been rendered impotent and, as a result, so was our species.

It is this breakdown of our anxiety function that makes human beings the dysfunctional animals we are. In our frivolous attempts to either oppose or escape unavoidable death, we channel our energies into a morbid array of self-destructive behaviors. In our futile efforts to oppose the unopposable, we have become the only animal that will needlessly kill one another as well as our own selves. Unlike any other creature on earth, we are capable of acts of suicide, genocide, sadism, masochism, self-mutilation, drug abuse, along with a multitude of other disturbed responses, all of which result from our species' unique capacity for self-conscious awareness and with it an awareness of death. As a result of our advanced capacity to comprehend the concept of our own deaths, humankind had become a psychologically unsound, or as Freud phrased it, "the 'neurotic' animal" (Freud, 1900 as cited by Eagleton, 1976).

Furthermore, in light of our awareness of inevitable death, life takes on a newfound sense of existential meaninglessness. Our struggles to survive become an exercise in futility. Between death's inevitability and all of the suffering we are forced to endure, we are compelled to ask: Why go on living? What's the point? How was our species to justify its continued existence in light of such a hopeless circumstance? Why struggle today when tomorrow we won't even be here? Under such circumstance, the motivating principle of self-preservation that had sustained life for all these billions of years no longer applied to our species. This was a whole new set of rules our animal was now playing by, and unless something could be done to ameliorate our species' pained and desperate state, it might not have been long before our newly evolved animal would have succumbed to the forces of extinction.

THE ADVENT OF THE SPIRITUAL FUNCTION

"Fear begets gods." --Lucretius, c.99-55 BCE.

"In order to counter this fundamental angst, humans are 'wired' for God."-Benson, 1996.

"If the brain evolved by natural selection, religious beliefs must have arisen by the same mechanism," Wilson argues that "if the brain evolved by natural selection, even the capacities to select particular esthetic judgements and religious beliefs must have arisen by that same mechanistic process" (Wilson, 1975).

So there we were, a newly emerging species with an unparalleled intelligence, one which had made us the most powerful creature on earth. And then, just as everything seemed to be working just fine, the inevitable took place: Man's intelligence backfired on him. For the first time in the history of life, an organic form turned its powers of perception back upon its own self thus rendering it aware of its own existence. With the dawn of self-awareness, a cognitive revolution had taken place. With a newly emerged awareness of our own existence, the human animal had become equally aware of the possibility of its own non-existence. And so, with this one cognition, the most powerful creature on earth was suddenly incapacitated by a crippling awareness of its own inevitable death.

Imagine how these protohumans must have felt, suddenly cognizant of their own inevitable demise—naked, vulnerable, alone, defenseless against the threat of impending death, exposed before the void, unprotected by any "higher" force or being. If Nature didn't provide our newly emergent animal with some type of adaptation through which to counter the anxiety induced by this awareness, it's quite possible our species might not have endured. In order to compensate for this debilitating awareness, Nature was going have to modify our animal's cognitive capacities in such a way that we would be able to survive this unique awareness of death. Rather than being stricken by some devastating new viral or climatic threat, Humankind had been assailed by a new type of environmental pressure, one which just so happened to originate from within our own bodies, within our own brains (after all, don't our own bodies constitute our physical environments?). As a result of this new physiologically-based environmental pressure, it became necessary that further changes take place within us if the hominid line was to survive.

In order for us to conform to this new environmental pressure, the forces of selection could have affected our evolution in one of two ways. Essentially, our intelligence, which had served as our greatest strength, was now jeopardizing our very existence. One evolutionary strategy that Nature could have implemented would have been to weed out the more self-aware members of our group, thereby leaving a population of less mortally conscious individuals to survive. In other words, the forces of natural selection could have simply pushed us back a few stages in our cognitive evolutions and returned us to our former, less self-consciously aware, less intelligent states. The problem with this solution, however, is that self-conscious awareness represents one of our most formidable intelligences. Because we are self-aware, we possess the unique capacity to adapt ourselves to any situation or environment. For example, should another ice age come, whereas any other animal would have to wait for millions of years of natural selection to provide them with a thicker coat of hair, humans can sew themselves one within a few hours time. Because we are aware of our own selves, we are aware of our own limitations and can therefore adapt ourselves to survive most any circumstance. Because we can create tools and technologies through which to compensate for our physical shortcomings, we have become the most resilient creature on earth. Without that intelligence, we are of the weakest and most vulnerable.

So there we were, the naked ape, hiding out under rocks or in caves; without claws, fangs, wings, or venomous sting or discharge—nothing save our vast intelligence. Had this been taken from us, how would we have protected ourselves from the other species? Without our intelligence, Man is like a walking meal just waiting to be eaten.

Such a strategy probably wouldn't have worked in our favor. Instead, some new adaptation was needed that would allow our species to survive self and mortal consciousness without sacrificing our intelligence. But what kind of device could have accomplished this? What adaptation could possibly emerge in us that would relieve us of our incapacitating awareness of death without compromising our intellectual faculties?

Perhaps, at first, only those individuals whose cerebral constitutions somehow withstood the crippling anxiety that came with self-conscious awareness managed to endure. Nevertheless, something more was needed if the species, as a whole, was going to survive. Perhaps man's newly emergent awareness of death created so much tension in our animal that it induced a selective pressure on our cerebral physiologies. Just as environmental pressures transform entire species, why shouldn't these same pressures be able to transform our brain? Couldn't those same Darwinian principles be applied to our cerebral evolutions as well? How else are we to imagine that all of our other cognitive centers—be it linguistic, musical or mathematical-emerged?

As a result of our species' capacity for self-conscious awareness, we suddenly needed to be modified in such a way that we could meet the new demands placed upon us by our new internal environments. What this meant, was that those individuals whose brains possessed some genetic mutation that could withstand the overwhelming anxiety induced by our awareness of death, were more likely to survive. Those more likely to survive, consequently, were more likely to pass whatever advantageous adaptation they possessed onto their offspring.

As generations of these protohumans passed, those whose cerebral constitutions most effectively dealt with the anxiety resulting from their awareness of death, were selected to survive. This process continued until a cognitive function emerged that altered the way these protohumans perceived reality by adding a "spiritual" component to their perspectives. Just as the human brain had evolved musical, linguistic and mathematical intelligence, we apparently evolved a "spiritual" intelligence as well.

In summary, our species' awareness of death placed such a strong pressure on our cerebral (cognitive) evolutions, that over the course of tens of millions of years—during the emergence of the hominids—Nature selected those individuals who developed a spiritual function. That function being a built-in perception that there exists an alternate and transcendental reality that supersedes the limitations of this finite physical realm which can only offer us pain, suffering and ultimately death.

THE COGNITIVE ORIGINS OF IMMORTAL CONSCIOUSNESS

Of those factors that may have influenced the evolution of a spiritual cognitive function, one to have played a key role incorporates man's unique capacity to enumerate. Because we live through time and space, we as animals possess an inherent awareness of these dimensions. For instance, most animals possess an internal biological clock (circadian rhythm), that serves to regulate an organism's behavior in relation to time. This internal clock will regulate such activities as the time of the day or year an animal will forage, sleep, or mate.

Many animals rely, to a large extent, on their sense of sight for survival. Because our planet's lighting conditions are determined by the earth's rotation around the sun, this rotational cycle plays a critical role in most animal behavior. Furthermore, because our planet's revolution around the sun plays a critical role in the earth's climate, this, too, will have a dramatic effect on much organic behavior. Because our environmental conditions are framed by time, it's necessary that most organisms possess a biological clock as an aid in effectively surviving the earth's cycles of climate and light.

Besides possessing an inherent perception of temporal events, all life forms possess a built-in mechanism that enables them to perceive the world spatially. Even a plant, though it may be rooted to the ground, engages in heliotropic behavior, a propensity to turn its leaves to face the sun. Because we exist within a three-dimensional environment, most animals possess some combination of organs through which they can discern up and down, backward and forward, near and far. As mobile creatures, it would be impossible for an animal to survive without such sensibilities.

Though most animals possess a certain degree of temporal and spatial awareness, our species' capacity to comprehend both of these dimensions is by far the most advanced. Only humans can discern increments of time and space with such precision. By being able to apportion our world into such discrete spatial and temporal units, we have evolved the capacity to enumerate objects, that is, to count. (It was recently discovered that Rhesus monkeys possess the capacity to count groups of objects in consecutive order from one to nine, an example of our closely phylogenetically-related ancestors possessing an incipient talent for a predominantly human capacity.)

Because we possess this particular "mathematical" cognitive capacity, humans are able to measure moments in time as well as units in space. Because our species possesses an enumerating or mathematical function, we alone have been able to navigate our way across the oceans, continents, and, most recently, into extraterrestrial space. This capacity has also enabled us to construct immense architectural fortifications, countless machines and technologies, along with formidable instruments of healing as well as destruction, all things which have, for better or worse, served to make us the most powerful creature on earth. Although such capacities generally work to our advantage, just as our intelligence had backfired on us, this advanced capacity to enumerate affected us in a similarly hazardous way. I say this because inherent in our capacity to enumerate exists an awareness that this process has no finite end: No matter how big a number might be, we can always add one to it. Consequently, intrinsic to our capacity to add one plus one lies the capacity to conceptualize infinity. As only our species possesses this sophisticated a capacity to enumerate, only we have the capacity to comprehend the concept of infinity. (As mathematical consciousness represents a cross-cultural characteristic of our species, this would suggest that mathematical ability must constitute a genetically inherited trait. This would further imply that there must exist "mathematical" sites within the brain. The existence of mathematical "idiot" savants, people who can calculate into the billions but who also exhibibit general cognative impairments, would seem to confirm the existence of such a neurophysiological mechanism. As every culture has, either through words or symbolic images, conceptualized infinity, this would imply that there might exist a very specific part of our mathematical function that enables us to conceive of this very abstract notion. If such a neurophysiologically-based "infinity" site within our brain does indeed exist, it follows that we must also possess what we could call "infinity" genes that are responsible for the emergence of those sites.)

In the same way that we can enumerate units in space, we can do the same with moments in time. And just as we can comprehend the idea that one plus one equals two, we can equally conceptualize the notion that this present day plus one more equals tomorrow. It is from this same cognitive faculty that humans may have gained their capacity for foresight, one that has enabled every human culture to devise some a calendar by which it measures time in days, seasons and years.

Just as our enumerating capacity has enabled us to recognize that spatial dimensions possess no finite end, we can apply this same notion to temporal dimensions as well. Analagous to the way we can conceptualize infinity, we can equally conceptualize eternity. Just as we can keep adding one unit to any spatial dimension, ad infinitum, we can do the same with temporal dimensions, i.e., this moment plus the next moment equals the moment after, ad infinitum. With this capacity to conceive that temporal dimensions have no finite end, not only can we conceptualize our own futures all the way to our inevitable deaths but way beyond that into eternity. Because we can comprehend the concept of eternity, our species must live with an awareness that though we, our physical bodies, are temporal in nature, time itself will never end. With a conscious awareness of eternity, humans were suddenly forced to endure the notion of how infinitely brief life is. Whereas all other creatures live in and for the moment, we now had to measure our existences against the overwhelming backdrop of all eternity. Suddenly, humankind had to contend with an inherent sense of its own ultimate and painful insignificance. In the words of the French philosopher, Blaise Pascal ,"the finite is annihilated by the infinite" (Pascal, 1660).

Consequently, due to our capacity to grasp the eternal and the infinite, our species now had to endure a new anxiety, one which may have rivaled that which came as a result of our debilitating awareness of death. Due to our capacity to comprehend the infinite and eternal, our newly emerged mathematical consciousness may have played just as significant a role in the evolution of a spiritual function as did our awareness of death.

Mathematical or numerical consciousness is apparently integrally interrelated with our sense of spiritual consciousness. This relationship is made evident by the fact that every world culture has attributed spiritual significance to various geometric designs as well as numbers. Whether it be the jewish Kabbalists, the Pythagorean Greeks, the medieval alchemists, the Christian use of the Holy Trinity, the use of numbers in Aztec mythology, numerical references made in the I, Ching, or the general use of numbers employed by the variety of astrological and numerological belief systems, every world culture has maintained a belief that numbers can possess spiritual or sacred content. Not only did we now need to be protected from actual death itself but from all of the possibilities that might exist long after death. Suddenly, man was aware that he might exist (or for that matter, not exist) for all eternity. But how? In what form? Would eternity be a pleasurable or a painful experience? Would we retain our conscious identities and, if so, in what state? Would eternal existence be as replete with experience as this life or would it represent a state of bsolutenothingness, of eternal non-existence? What might that mean?

As it is natural for our animal to be concerned with its future, humans were suddenly condemned to spend their existences in search of what might happen to us not just during our lifetimes but long after death. With this new awareness, humans would now have to spend the duration of their lives, no longer just in fear of death, but in fear of what might come after death, in fear of eternal non-existence.

Rather than allowing these fears to overwhelm and destroy us, perhaps nature selected those whose cognitive variations compelled individuals to process their concept of death in an entirely new manner. Perhaps after many generations of selection, a group of humans emerged who perceived infinity and eternity as an inextricable part of self-consciousness and self-identity. Perhaps a series of neurological connections emerged in our species that compelled us to perceive ourselves as "spiritually" eternal. Once we perceived ourselves as possessing an element of the infinite and eternal within us, as apparent as it was that our physical bodies would one day perish, we were constituted to believe that our conscious experience, what we refer to as our spirits or souls, would persist forever thus rendering us immortal.

Herein lies the cognitive origins of our cross-cultural belief in immortality, in our inherent perception that we-by virtue of our eternal souls-transcend physical death. Once we came to perceive consciousness as eternal in nature, we perceived physical death as nothing more than just another life-passage in eternal existence. Suddenly our animal was compelled to bury its dead with a rite that anticipated sending the deceased's eternal self or soul onward to another realm, or what had developed to become an inherent belief in an afterlife. With the help of this newly emergent predisposition to believe in our own immortalities, our species was relieved of a large part of the burden that came with our fear of imminent and eternal death. Humankind was saved.

THE COGNITIVE ORIGINS OF GOD CONSCIOUSNESS

But even if we were to live forever, what did that mean? Man still needed relief from the fear of the unknown. Would the afterlife be a place of eternal peace and happiness or would it perhaps be even more painful and precarious than this stay here on earth? Without our parents to protect us in the afterlife, we now needed eternal guidance and protection from all that might come in the inherently perceived hereafter. According to Freud (1927), "God is the exalted father, and the longing for the father is the root of all religion."

Aware that death was not only inevitable, but that it could come at any moment, human beings were reduced to a state of infantile helplessness, as vulnerable as the day they were born. And where do infants innately turn for protection? To their parents. However, not even one's parents can save one from death. As we become adults, we come to recognize that even our once seemingly-omnipotent parents are actually impotent against the forces of death. With this knowledge, where was humankind to find eternal guidance and protection? Desperately longing for eternal comfort and security, to whom or what was primal man to turn? Perhaps our need for eternal protection had facilitated the selection of a cognitive genetic mutation that instilled our species with an inherent belief in some type of a transcendental guardian. Perhaps it was at this point in human cognitive evolution that neural connections had emerged that compelled the human animal to believe in a "higher"power, in what we refer to as a god or gods.

As infants in the crib, when we experience pain or fear, we instinctively reach out to our parents for comfort and protection. It seems likely that our cross-cultural belief in a God represents an extension of that same instinct. As Freud expressed this same notion: The derivation of religious needs from the infant's helplessness and the longing for the father aroused by it seems to me incontrovertible, especially since the feeling is not simply prolonged from childhood days, but is permanently sustained by fear of the superior power of fate. I cannot think of any need in childhood as strong as the need for a father's protection (Freud, 1962).

As a result of the selective pressures placed on our species by our awareness of eternal death, neurological connections had emerged that generated an inherent belief in the supernatural as well as in an all-powerful, imaginary father figure whose infinite powers could protect us from death and all that came thereafter.

In summary, at some point in the last two million or so years, during the emergence of the latter hominid lines, a cognitive adaptation emerged that enabled us to cope with our awarenesses of death, while at the same time allowing us to maintain self-conscious awareness. By having this cognitive mechanism instilled in us, we were now "wired" to perceive physical death in a much more acceptable manner. Once nature had instilled us with neurophysiologically-generated cognitive phantoms who could protect us from inevitable death, humans were better equipped to survive their inherent fear of such.

"One of the major functions of religious belief is to reduce a person's fear of death." --Hood, 1996.

"Religion is a natural defense against man's knowledge that he must die" --Ostow, 1953.

Sheltered from the perpetual threat of inevitable death, humans could now proceed with the daily routine of maintaining their more earthly needs. With the emergence of spiritual consciousness, our cognitive functioning had been stabilized to the extent that we could now go on living in a state of relative calm, even amid our awareness of our inevitable demise. This, I contend, is the purpose of the spiritual function. This is its rationale, its reason for being. If all this is true, however, it suggests that God isn't a transcendental force or entity that actually exists "out there," beyond and independent of us, but rather represents the manifestation of an inherited human perception, a coping mechanism that comes in the form of a cognitive phantom generated from within the human brain.

.

EVOLUTIONARY NEUROTHEOLOGY & THE
VARIETIES OF RELIGIOUS EXPERIENCE
by Bruce MacLennan

Abstract. The goal of this chapter is to outline an evolutionary neuropsychological foundation for spiritual and religious experiences. Central to this account are concepts from archetypal psychology, which, on the one hand, explain the structure of common religious experiences, but, on the other, are grounded in ethology and evolutionary biology. From this it follows that certain religious phenomena are objective, in that they are empirical, stable, and public. As a consequence, certain theological claims can be objectively confirmed or refuted. However, it would be a mistake to assume that this approach reduces religious experiences to the "merely psychological" or considers them inessential epiphenomena in a materialist universe. On the contrary, I will show that it demonstrates the compatibility and even inevitability of transcendental religious experience—and its crucial importance—to biological beings such as ourselves.

Overview

How can we achieve a unified understanding of the universe, which comprehends the physical, psychical, and spiritual dimensions of reality? In this chapter I will argue that the archetypes, as described in the psychological theories of Jung and his followers, provide the crucial link between the material and spiritual worlds: on the one hand, they are grounded in evolutionary neuropsychology; on the other, they are the objective constituents of the spiritual world. This might seem to reduce the spiritual realm to the "merely psychological," or even to neural epiphenomena, but I will argue that this is a misinterpretation of the theory, and that the gods (or God) are objectively real and crucially important for meaningful human life.

Evolution and the Archetypes
Ethology and the Structure of Behavior

All animal species exhibit characteristic behavioral patterns, commonly called instincts. These behaviors are served by perceptual systems, which are also characteristic of the species. These perceptual-behavioral structures, which are common to all members of a species, change very slowly, on evolutionary timescales, as the species continues to adapt to its (possibly changing) natural environment. The functions of these perceptual-behavioral structures must be understood in the context of the species' *environment of evolutionary adaptedness*, that is, the environment in which it has historically evolved and therefore to which it is adapted. One of the contributions of modern ethology, as developed especially by Konrad Lorenz and Niko Tinbergen in the mid-twentieth century, was to recognize that the meaning and function of behavior cannot be understood outside of this environment.

A species' genome defines a characteristic life-cycle pattern for each member of the species as it progresses from birth to death. However, the phylogenetic pattern of the species is expressed ontogenetically by an individual's development in and interaction with its particular environment, which may differ more or less from the environment of evolutionary adaptedness. (This is especially the case for modern humans, as will be discussed later.) Species-characteristic perceptual-behavioral patterns are encoded in the structure of the brain, which is a result of the developmental program encoded in the genome. Various behavioral patterns (e.g., mating behaviors) may be *potentiated* at appropriate stages in an animal's development (e.g., sexual maturity), but they are *activated* through an *innate releasing mechanism* (IRM) by means of a *releaser* or *sign stimulus* (e.g., an estrus-related pheromone).

The human species is also characterized by genotypic perceptual-behavioral structures. Which specific structures are phylogenetic characteristics of our species ("nature"), and how they are ontogenetically modified by an individual's development in his or her particular environment ("nurture"), should be left to empirical research, and not prejudged by psycho-socio-political ideology. For my argument, it is sufficient to acknowledge that *Homo sapiens*, like other animal species, has characteristic perceptual-behavioral structures.

Archetypal Psychology and the Structure of the Psyche

Ethology studies species-characteristic perceptual-behavioral structures "from the outside," that is, by observing animals' behavior in their natural environment. However, when *we* are the animal in question, we may ask how these perceptual-behavioral structures are experienced "from the inside." The corresponding psychological structures are what Jung called *archetypes*: "To the extent that the archetypes intervene in the shaping of conscious contents by regulating, modifying, and motivating them, they act like the instincts" (Jung, *CW* 8, ¶404).

The archetypes are often confused with innate images, but Jung was explicit, especially in his later work (e.g., *CW* 9, pt. 1, ¶155), that they are not images, but dynamical structures of perception and behavior. They do not become images until they structure conscious content after being activated by a sign stimulus or other cause. The archetype "is not meant to denote an inherited idea, but rather an inherited mode of functioning, ... a 'pattern of behavior'" (Jung, *CW* 18, ¶1228).

The archetypes reside in the *collective unconscious*, for the archetypes are unconscious until they are activated, and they are collective in that they are common to all humans. Although this idea is surrounded by much mysticism, "The hypothesis of the collective unconscious is, therefore, no more daring than to assume that there are instincts" (Jung, *CW* 9, pt. 1, ¶91). In addition to the collective unconscious, we each have a *personal unconscious*, which is a result of our individual ontogenies in our particular environments (more later on this process).

Like the instincts to which they correspond, archetypes are *potentiated* at particular developmental stages in accord with a phylogenetically determined life-cycle (the human life-cycle). When an appropriate releaser (sign stimulus) occurs in the environment, the archetype is *actualized*, and begins its work of structuring conscious perception and of influencing motivation and behavioral disposition. Because the releaser is keyed into the archetype, the triggering situation or relationship is perceived as numinous and significant; the psyche is reoriented toward (evolutionarily) appropriate action. As examples, consider encountering a sexually exciting person or being confronted by a threatening, angry person.

Complexes, which are webs of associations, are created by intense or repeated activation of an archetype in the ontogenetic psyche; therefore they have personal material surrounding an archetypal core. Complexes normally reside in the personal unconscious, but when activated, they can intrude on consciousness by influencing perception, motivation, and behavior. We tend to think of complexes as pathological, but it important to understand that they are normal components of our psyches; indeed some are essential for our normal functioning, as will be explained in the next subsection. They are "the functional units of which the ontogenetic psyche [is] composed" (Stevens, 1982, p. 65).

The thwarting of "archetypal intent" can nucleate pathological complexes. Thus Stevens' Fourth Law of Psychodynamics says, "Psychopathology results from the frustration of archetypal goals" (Stevens, 1993, p. 86). However, this does not imply that archetypes should govern our behavior; rather, our moral problem is "what *attitude* we adopt to these fundamental *a priori* aspects of our nature—how we live them, and how we mediate them to the group. It is the ethical orientation that counts" (Stevens, 1982, p. 240).

Some Specific Archetypes

It will be worthwhile to review some of the archetypal structures identified by Jung and his colleagues. Readers familiar with archetypal psychology might want to skim the remainder of this section. One of the fundamental archetypal relations for all primates is that between mother and child. As the newborn infant begins to discriminate itself from its environment, the archetypal child-parent axis forms (the foundation of the ego-Self axis, discussed later). With greater awareness the child-parent axis differentiates into the child-mother axis and, from the child's perspective, the *Mother* archetype is actualized. Among many other things, the archetypal Mother symbolizes the source of care; she expresses home and family (the *Eros principle* and the *centripetal* orientation of the ego).

Later, as the father assumes a more important role, the *Father* archetype is actualized as one pole of the archetypal relationship between father and child. He is especially the source of order and mediates the outward relation to society and the rest of the world (the *Logos principle* and the *centrifugal* orientation of the ego).

As the child's sexual identity develops (as early as eighteen months), the *contrasexual* (opposite sex) characteristics remain undeveloped in the unconscious (analogous to contrasexual physical attributes after puberty: e.g., a man's breasts, a woman's clitoris). The contrasexual part in the female psyche is called the *Animus* (Latin for spirit, thought, will), and in the male is called the *Anima* (Lat., soul, vital principle). The contrasexual part exists both as an archetype, conditioned by biological development, and as a complex, conditioned by the environment. That is, the Anima/Animus is partly phylogenetic and partly ontogenetic; it is a sequential elaboration of the Mother or Father archetype.

There are many other archetypes, most of which are familiar from mythology (e.g., Maiden, Wise Old Man, Trickster), but they do not need to be discussed at this time. Although mythologists and archetypal psychologists are inclined to classify and name them, it is important to remember that they are connected into a continuum or continuous "field" in which there are real distinctions, but also borderline cases (von Franz, 1974, ch. 8).

The archetypal field as a whole is called the *Self*, which is therefore the sum total of human archetypes. As such it is the psychical aspect of the perceptual-behavioral structure encoded in the human genome, and hence it constitutes the "phylogenetic destiny" of the psyche. "The self is our life's goal, for it is the greatest expression of that fateful combination we call individuality" (Jung, *CW* 7, ¶404). The Self is unconscious as well as conscious, and therefore must be carefully distinguished from ego-consciousness.

The *Ego* is the individual conscious mind, a complex that perhaps evolved to facilitate our adaptation to the environment, and is responsible for actualizing the life-cycle plan of the Self. Although ego-consciousness is crucial to our human nature, we tend to overvalue it, and forget that it is an "organ" evolved to facilitate the human species' survival in its environment of evolutionary adaptedness. Many spiritual practices (as well as psychotherapeutic practices) are directed toward achieving a proper balance between the Ego and the Self.

The *Persona* (Latin: mask, role, character) is a complex, built on the Ego, that mediates the individual's adaptation to society. It is the face we present to the world (e.g., through the habitual attitudes and manners of behavior of our class and vocation). "One could say, with a little exaggeration, that the persona is that which in reality one is not, but which oneself as well as others think one is" (Jung, *CW* 9, pt. 1, ¶221). Our personas are essential to our functioning as social animals, so long as we avoid the danger of confusing our personas with our Selves.

The *Shadow* comprises all the traits and qualities consciously rejected by the individual and their culture (collective *consciousness*). It is therefore a complicated, multilayered complex comprising material rejected by the individual, by his or her family, and by larger significant groups, up to the culture at large. Like all complexes, it also has an archetypal core, based on an innate predisposition to dichotomize, but perhaps also including a phylogenetic predisposition against certain behaviors (e.g., incest). However, since the Shadow compensates our conscious attitudes (which may be imbalanced), it is not entirely negative.

Since ethology has established that some of our human perceptual-behavioral structures are shared with non-human species (e.g., mother-child bonding and social behavior in other primates), it is plausible to suppose that these animals also experience corresponding archetypes, not identical but homologous. Therefore, behind the archetypes that are our common human heritage, we can find others that are common to all primates; beyond these are the archetypes of mammals and of all vertebrates.

Can we go even further? Certainly some aspects of the structure of our psyches are consequences of the fact we are living beings, and further, that we are physical systems. As Jung said, "the 'psychic infra-red', the biological instinctual psyche, gradually passes over into the physiology of the organism and thus merges with its chemical and physical conditions…" (*CW* 8, ¶420). For example, physical systems of all sorts exhibit characteristic forms of dynamical behavior (equilibrium, cycles, and chaos), which are also characteristic of the psyche and are therefore archetypal.

If we follow this line of reasoning, we are led to conclude that the most fundamental and universal archetypes are the laws of nature (whatever they may be discovered to be) experienced psychically (i.e., "from the inside," as opposed to through external observation). Therefore, among the most fundamental archetypes are the numbers, considered as qualitative ideas (e.g., unity, dichotomy, conjunction), for number "preconsciously orders both psychic thought processes *and* the manifestations of material reality" (von Franz, 1974, p. 53). These considerations may seem to stretch the idea of the unconscious too far, but they are necessary if we are to achieve an understanding that embraces the physical, psychical, and spiritual.

Archetypal Theology

The Archetypes and the Gods

Having reviewed some of the principal archetypes and their evolutionary neuropsychological foundation, I will turn to their theological implications. It is best to begin from a polytheistic perspective, for "archetypal psychology is necessarily nonagnostic and polytheistic" (Hillman, 1975, p. 226; see also Hillman, 1983, ch. 10; Miller, 1981). Nevertheless, my conclusions apply equally well to monotheism, as is explained later.

The archetypes are much bigger than individual people, and therefore no person can completely fulfill an archetype. It is normal to *project* an archetype onto a person (such as projecting the Mother archetype onto your personal mother), but with maturity we retract the projections, and differentiate the real person from the idealized archetype. Nevertheless, the unfulfilled potential of the archetype remains, and we are left with a longing for the idealized figures they represent. Further, the archetypes call for complete actualization (for that is their biological function), and urge us to seek them. Likewise, the sum total of the archetypes, the Self, seeks actualization of the genomic potential of the species in the life of the individual, which gives rise to the drive for fulfillment that Jung called *individuation*.

Once the projections are withdrawn, we realize that the archetypes exist independently of the concrete individuals that may manifest them; or, in other words, we may say that the archetypal structures exist in the genotype independently of the individuals that trigger their innate releasing mechanisms. That is, the archetypes are autonomous; they exist independently of human psyches in the same sense that the human genotype exists independently of individual humans.

For example, when the projection of the Mother archetype is withdrawn from the concrete mother, the archetypal Great Mother remains to represent the Eros principle. Similarly the personal father comes to be differentiated from the Heavenly Father as representative of the Logos principle. These are, of course, only two examples (though important ones) of many.

It is well known that the archetypes correspond to the gods of various pantheons, and that mythology often encodes archetypal relationships; there is no need to attempt to summarize here the extensive specific work of many archetypal psychologists (Jung, 1998, may be cited as an introduction). Rather, I will take the identity of god and archetype for granted, and focus on the question of whether the gods are real or "merely psychological." According to common scientific standards, we may say that the archetypes (the gods) are objectively real phenomena if they are *empirical*, *stable*, and *public*.

The archetypes are *empirical phenomena* in the primary sense of those words because they manifest as appearances (Greek, *phainomena*) that arise in experience (Grk., *empeiria*). The archetypes themselves are not directly experienceable, because they reside as potential perceptual-behavioral structures in the unconscious. However, we experience their effects when they actualize in consciousness, and from these empirical effects we can infer the archetypal structures causing them, which does not make them any less real. "The existence of the instincts can no more be proved than the existence of the archetypes, so long as they do not manifest themselves concretely" (Jung, *CW* 9, pt. 1, ¶155). Science commonly infers, from their effects, causes that are not directly observable (e.g., elementary particles, force fields).

That these experiences need not have external referents, that is, corresponding physical phenomena external to the observer, does not negate their empirical validity. Psychology must take them as givens (Lat., *data*), for its subject matter is the psyche and whatever appears to it (*phainomena*). All sciences, from physics to sociology, are grounded in the experiences ("observations") of an individual psyche.

The archetypes are *stable* phenomena, another criterion of objective reality. From the earliest recorded mythologies, to the cosmologies of surviving traditional cultures, to the dreams and fantasies of contemporary people, we find the same archetypes recurring across time and place. Indeed, it was this observation that first led Jung to hypothesize the existence of archetypes (Jung, *CW* 10, ¶847).

The forgoing also shows that the archetypes are *public* phenomena; that is, when suitably trained observers investigate the unconscious, they reach consistent conclusions about its archetypal structure. (The prerequisite of suitable training is common to all but the simplest sciences; one must learn how to read even a thermometer correctly.)

Therefore the archetypes are empirical, stable, and public, which are the accepted scientific standards for the objective reality of a class of phenomena. Hence the archetypes — the gods — are real.

Nevertheless, it's worthwhile to say a little more about the manner of existence of the archetypes, about their *ontological status*. Fortunately, we have some analogous situations to guide us, for if, as has been argued, the archetypes are the psychical aspect of phylogenetically-defined perceptual-behavioral structures, then the archetypes are functions of the human genome, which is a mathematical pattern. Therefore the archetypes exist in the same way as other mathematical patterns, as (Platonic) *forms* independent of their physical embodiment (or lack thereof). They are formal, not material.

This conclusion is strengthened by our broadened perspective on the archetypes, which reaches beyond the human species, to non-human species and their underlying physical processes. For these processes are governed by mathematical laws, and therefore their archetypal correspondents in the psyche must be likewise mathematical in structure. Again, the existence of the archetypes (the gods) is akin to the existence of mathematical patterns (forms). The laws of nature (whatever they may be) are what they are, and would be so, even if there were no material universe to obey them. Therefore the archetypes exist independently of physical embodiment (they are immaterial).

That the physical, psychical, and spiritual worlds converge in the realm of mathematical form is not a new idea; it is attributed to Pythagoras, and was developed over two and one-half millennia of Platonic, Neoplatonic, and Neopythagorean thought. Indeed, it lurks in the intellectual background of archetypal psychology (Hillman, 1983, pp. 4-5). However, the modern perspective dictates some changes in this venerable theory, which we must consider.

Traditionally, the archetypes have been considered eternal and unchanging, and so they are, from an individual's perspective. However, the archetypes do change slowly with the human genome, that is to say, at evolutionary timescales. Therefore they have changed little if at all in the last hundred thousand years or more. The deeper archetypal structures are even older (at least four million years for hominids, 55 million years for primates, 500 million for vertebrates); the laws of physics are unchanging and therefore eternal. Thus we can conclude that the archetypes — the gods — change very slowly. Certainly they have not changed in recorded history. Rather, our gods are the same as those of our hunter-gatherer ancestors who lived a hundred thousand years ago.

The reader may grant that the archetypes are objectively real and effectively eternal, but may be reluctant to call them "gods." To argue that they deserve this appellation requires a discussion of their role in our lives.

The archetypes are a source of meaning because they integrate individual lives into the greater patterns of humanity and the universe; they give transpersonal meaning and significance to situations and relationships in human life. From an ethological perspective humans are primed, through innate releasing mechanisms, to respond in characteristic ways to the corresponding releasers (sign stimuli). When such a pattern of perception and behavior is released, the individual fulfills part of his or her destiny as a member of the human species. From a psychological perspective, the sign stimulus appears charged with significance and meaning; the archetype is activated and appears in consciousness as an archetypal image. When an archetype is actualized, the resulting situation or relationship is experienced as numinous, supernatural, uncanny, hallowed, blessed, or miraculous.

Being in love is a familiar example of an archetypal situation; everyone has experienced its power to transform perception and behavior. The beloved is surrounded by a numinous aura, and the relationship is charged with meaning. Therefore, it is not surprising that the ancients saw the hand of a god (Aphrodite or Eros) in such relationships. Indeed, "Aphrodite" and "Venus" were sometimes used as common nouns meaning sexual love, desire, and charm, and Eros (love, desire) was worshipped as a god from an early period (Hornblower & Spawforth, 1996, s.v. Eros). Plato (*Phaedrus* 245b-c) famously classified love (*erôs*) as a kind of divine madness (*theia mania*). Significantly, he claimed that love stems from the "recollection" of the eternal forms, acquired before birth; in our terms, love is an actualization of certain innate archetypal patterns.

When we are in an archetypal situation, we are under the influence or compulsion of a god. That is, we are drawn into the narrative of a phylogenetic "script" (which does not imply, of course, that we have no control over the situation); we may feel like we are living a myth (as, indeed, we are).

There are two poles to the archetypal relation: the experiencing ego and the "other" towards which the perceptual-behavioral "script" is directed. The entire relationship is divinely (archetypally) guided, and each pole may be experienced as inspired by a god. The ego may experience itself as "possessed" by a divinity (Eros, in the proceeding example), whose intentions may conflict with the ego's. Similarly, the "other" (often a person) may be perceived as divine, numinous, magical, or radiant. For example, the beloved is experienced as a god or goddess.

Of course, the beloved is not a god or goddess. People are not archetypes, and the practical difficulties of treating them as such are well known. In psychological terms, we should withdraw the projection; although the archetypal relation is authentic, we cannot forget that an archetype cannot be manifested completely by an individual; the archetype may touch a human, but it is superhuman and resides elsewhere.

It is even more dangerous to confuse oneself with a deity, the ancient sin of hubris, the psychological condition of *ego inflation*. "Possession" by a divinity is not necessarily a bad thing (who would reject the divine madness of love?) — another word for it is inspiration (Grk., *entheos*, "having the god within") — but it is crucial to be consciously aware of what is taking place (an archetypal actualization), nor should one abandon the "ethical orientation" of the ego.

Morality and the Gods

Are the gods good? Ancient theologians debated the topic. The traditional mythology did not present them as moral ideals, and popular belief tended to agree, but intellectuals were more inclined to think that the gods must be good. If we take the ethological perspective on the problem, we can say that archetypal structures have evolved by conferring selective advantage to humans in our environment of evolutionary adaptedness; in this broad sense, they can be called "good." But does that make them moral ideals? Certainly, the archetypes are real forces, which cannot be ignored or thwarted with impunity; psychopathologies result from "frustrating archetypal goals." But few would advocate that we blindly follow our biological urges.

Furthermore, the gods may have differing demands, and may even war with one another. At least that was the view of traditional mythology and epic, which, again, the intellectuals found unacceptable. However, ethology teaches us that the traditional view was more accurate. An animal may find itself in the grips of two incompatible patterns of behavior (fight or flight is an obvious example); ethologists say that it is in a state of *conflict*. Psychologically we may find ourselves in the grip of incompatible archetypes (gods), each urging toward the fulfillment of its own purpose. So three goddesses appeared to Paris, each pushing him to fulfill her own archetypal plan. From a theological perspective, we may be placed in real existential dilemmas. Gods cannot be disobeyed without dire consequences, yet in a case of archetypal conflict we are faced with reconciling warring deities. In facing such a dilemma, it is not simply a matter of choosing good over evil, for each of the gods is good in the sense that they serve the species (and, beyond that, life in general). They each have a legitimate claim on us.

More accurately, I think, the gods should be considered "beyond good and evil." Psychologically, all archetypes are positive and negative, because they are prior to conscious discrimination, and therefore prior to human morality. Hence, Aphrodite causes us to love our spouses and to start families, but also urges us to extramarital affairs. Ares encourages us to strike when we're angry, but also to defend our homeland. The clever words granted us by Hermes can win support for a just cause, or they can cheat and deceive. The Sky Father Zeus enforces laws and rules, but sometimes to the point of cruelty. The Great Mother nurtures her children, but may smother or even devour them. And so on, for all the other gods.

In my examples, I have drawn from Greek mythology, as is often done in archetypal psychology, because of its seminal role in Western culture. Nevertheless, one may wonder how well these myths reflect human archetypal structures. Although it is ultimately an empirical question (which Jung and others have addressed through their investigations), we may with some confidence say that *the true gods are the gods of Paleolithic hunter-gatherers*.

Based on the work of Fox (1989), Stevens (1993, p. 67) observes that we have spent 99.5% of our species' history as hunter-gatherers, and therefore it is the environment and life of the hunter-gatherer that has contributed most to our genetic heritage. What was it like? Our communities were "organic extended kinship groups" comprising "forty to fifty individuals, made up of approximately six to ten adult males, about twice that number of childbearing females, and about twenty juveniles and infants" (Stevens, 1993, p. 67). They were homogeneous in beliefs and practices and structured around families (not necessarily monogamous). Such communities frequently encountered each other, for marrying, warring, and other purposes.

This is our environment of evolutionary adaptedness. Therefore, the gods who ruled these people are the gods who rule us yet, like it or not.

Of course we no longer live as hunter-gatherers, and few would advocate that we return to that life. Nevertheless, the archetypes are real forces, and while they should not be obeyed blindly, neither can they be ignored without consequences. It is the function of ego-consciousness to find ways to live in the modern world without denying the gods of our hunter-gatherer ancestors.

However, we should beware of supposing that the ego can dominate or repress the archetypes; the ego is an organ of the Self, not vice versa. To act as though the ego is all-powerful is, in fact, to be "possessed" by the Hero archetype (an authentic archetype, to be sure, but just one of many). "That way madness lies": ego inflation, which calls forth Nemesis (the "justifiable anger of the gods") to punish the hubris of the hero who imagines that he is the master over the gods (Hillman, 1975, pp. 178-80).

Since I have presented the archetypes in the context of polytheism, the reader may be impatient about how it applies to monotheistic religions. Briefly, in archetypal psychology, the Self occupies a position comparable to the God of monotheistic religions. The individual archetypes are then aspects of God, or subsidiary spirits (e.g., angels and demons). This, in fact, was one way the classical gods were interpreted by early Christian theologians (e.g., Seznec, 1981).

The Special Role of the Anima/Animus

Among the archetypes the Anima/Animus has a special position, for it is the nearest component of the unconscious; therefore it is the proximate representative of the divine other. Thus, this archetype can function as a *psychopomp* (soul guide) leading us to greater knowledge and communion with spiritual world.

The Anima of a man often acts as divine Muse, a source of creativity and access to feelings, because she is open to the nonrational and so provides an opening to the unconscious and soul. Thus the ancient poets invoke their Muses, which is more than just a convention. Another well-known mythological example of the Anima is Athena, whom we see caring for Odysseus in the *Odyssey*.

Similarly, the Animus of a woman often acts as a source of rational purposefulness and intellect, and, as representative of the Logos principle, points the way toward the spirit. Many women have found the Animus to be a source of strength as they move into traditionally male vocations. Alternatively, the Animus may call a nun, for example, to become a "bride of Christ."

However, if the Anima or Animus is not consciously integrated, it may possess the ego or be projected on others in primitive ways. If it is projected, then a person may misperceive members of the opposite sex. For example, a man may perceive women as irrational children or seductive nymphs; a woman may perceive men as cold, aggressive, or remote. If possession occurs, then a person may act out the least differentiated characteristics of their contrasexual part. Thus, the animus-possessed woman may become inappropriately bossy, aggressive, judgmental, opinionated, or intolerant, while the anima-possessed man may become touchy, resentful, overly emotional, sentimental, or irrational (Jung, *CW* 9, pt. 2, 24-35).

Obviously, integration of the contrasexual part of the psyche does not mean losing one's sexual identity. Rather, by establishing a conscious relation with this archetype, one achieves greater psychic balance, and recruits its powers, especially in establishing a connection to the other archetypes (gods). This is especially the task of the second half of life, when the Self urges the psyche to reclaim its rejected and neglected parts. From a theological perspective, the gods and spirits call one to make alliances with them and to put the ego in service to the higher Self.

As remarked in an earlier Section, the Anima/Animus exists as both archetype (god) and as complex. The archetype is a high god (e.g., Athena for men, Dionysus for women), whereas the complex is a more personal spirit, more involved with one's individual life. The complex thus acts in behalf of the archetype, serving as usual as mediator between the personal and the archetypal. (For more on the Anima/Animus, see E. Jung, 1957, and Jung, *CW* 9, pt. 2, ch. 3.)

Complexes and Mediating Spirits

As discussed in an earlier Section, the personal unconscious comprises complexes formed through the interaction of archetypes and our individual lives; in theological terms, we can say that each complex is the offspring of a god, assigned to an individual. The archetypes are the same for everyone, and in this sense they do not treat us as individuals. The complexes, however, are a hybrid of the general and the particular, the universal and the personal. We may even say that they "know" us, for the particulars of our individual histories are stored in the web of associations of which they are constituted. Therefore complexes function as mediating spirits, intermediate between a person and a god. It may seem an exaggeration to identify psychological complexes with mediating spirits, but "complexes behave like independent beings" (Jung, *CW* 8, ¶253); they are autonomous personalities.

The ancient Greek word for such a mediating spirit was *daimôn*, which could refer to any divine spirit, but was especially applied to the mediators between humans and gods; it did not have the negative connotation of our word "demon" (Burkert, 1985, III.3.5). Many ancient cultures believed that each man had a *genius* (and each woman a *iuno*) that was born with them and stayed with them throughout their lives; this personal spirit has been explicitly identified with the unconscious mind (Onians, 1951, pp. 127-67). Some philosophers thought that each person had both an attending "good spirit" (*agathos daimôn*) and an interfering "bad spirit" (*kakos daimôn*), sometimes euphemistically called "the other *daimôn*." This reflects the moral ambivalence of our complexes, which from the perspective of ego-consciousness may be good or bad. Like the archetypes (gods), the complexes (mediating spirits) have their own agendas, which may or may not agree with our egos'.

Also like the archetypes, we may be "possessed" by a complex, or project it onto others (that is, from our perspective, one of our complexes may "possess" another person). Projection of complexes is not strictly a matter of perception on the part of the projector, for the receiver may accept the projection and therefore also experience the possession. The two may therefore enter into a reality-altering state of mutual projection. For example, a person may accept the role of scapegoat projected onto them by a group.

Mutual projection also arises in families, since children are prone to accept projection from their parents. Unlived or rejected aspects of the parents may be projected onto the children, who become possessed and either reinforce or compensate their parents' imbalances; such possessions can continue even after a parent's death. Such is one cause of "family curses" (e.g., the House of Atreus), in which pathological complexes are passed on from generation to generation.

Projection and possession (which are not necessarily bad) may be difficult to identify, because our complexes are closely bound to our personalities, and therefore hard to differentiate from ourselves. Indeed, it can become difficult to distinguish one's authentic personality from the crowd of personal complexes.

One sign of "possession" is a defensive feeling when the complex is threatened. Therefore, a person may overreact emotionally when an intellectual position (such as a philosophical or political opinion) is criticized or even questioned. In general, complexes are created from strong emotional charges, and so sudden changes of mood or feeling (in the absence of obvious causes) may indicate that one has been possessed (or released from possession). Also, complexes often appear in dreams.

Since our "personal demons" affect our perception and behavior, it is important to be aware of them, even to befriend them. Because a god has created them, they cannot, in general, be "banished" (dissolved), nor should we wish to do so, for they are channels of divine (archetypal) energy into our personal lives. On the other hand, we cannot allow ourselves to be ruled by them, for we have a conscious ethical standpoint, but they do not; like the gods, they are beyond good and evil.

Therefore, the first requirement is to come to know your "demons," especially when they possess yourself or (via projection) someone else. Once known (and even named), they are less liable to possess or project. Next, one must enter into a dialogue with them, and reach some mutually agreeable alliance or, if that be impossible, reconciliation. Since they are spirits mediating between the gods and us, they can become invaluable allies in helping us to live in accord with divine providence, which is the goal of psychological individuation.

Again, possession and projection are not necessarily bad. To be the object of projection can be liberating and empowering; consider the effect of being the object of someone's infatuation, or of being perceived as a great genius. The result can be beneficial, provided we bask in the glow only for a while, and avoid possession. Furthermore, since a complex is a spirit mediating our relation to a god (archetype), it can be an enormous source of inspiration. It is no coincidence that the most creative people in all endeavors seem to be "possessed" by their callings (Jung, *CW* 17, ¶¶300-4). For more on complexes see, for example, von Franz (1980).

The Shadow: Collective and Personal

Gods in polytheistic religions are not generally all-good or all-bad, therefore we do not find figures comparable to Satan in these religions. Rather, each of the gods has good and bad aspects, although even this puts the issue too much in our terms; the gods, as agents of divine providence, have their own purposes, which we may view from a human perspective as good or ill (for us). We are all too apt to assume that humans are at the center of the universe, and therefore that the perspective of human egos and our collective conscious values should be the universal norm. Nevertheless, we are humans, and there are spirits and perhaps even gods that are evil in human terms.

We may begin at the personal level: we have seen that the Shadow, which resides in the personal unconscious, comprises all the traits and characteristics consciously rejected by the ego; in this sense it is "evil" (by definition). The Shadow is a complex, and therefore everything I have said about complexes applies to it; in particular, it may possess and project. These are especially insidious in the case of the Shadow: since it embodies everything that we reject, we are loath to admit it as our own; Prospero takes an enormous step toward psychic integration when he says of Caliban, "this thing of darkness I / acknowledge mine" (*Tempest* V.i.324-5).

One simple way to discover the nature of your own Shadow is to ask yourself what sort of person you find most despicable or impossible to endure; that is your Shadow (Stevens, 1982, p. 215). Therefore, when we encounter a person who strikes us this way, we can be confident that we are projecting our Shadow onto them. (To be sure, such a person normally has something in common with our Shadow — that is the releaser that invites the projection — but it may be trivial compared to what we project onto them.) Worse, they may even accept our projection, and by becoming possessed by our Shadow, become our worst nightmare. However, if you are familiar with your Shadow complex, you may recognize its familiar features in the other person, and be able to withdraw the projection to both of your benefits.

Since the Shadow grows out of a person's individual development, it incorporates consciously and unconsciously acquired values and beliefs about what is bad or wrong. Since much of this development takes place in the context of the family, much of the Shadow is likewise shared. Again, a collective Shadow complex common to a family (or larger group) may be experienced as a "family curse" (e.g., a tendency of abused children to become abusive parents, or a "curse" of substance dependency).

Further, the collective consciousness of a culture may generate a commonly shared Shadow, which then assumes the dimensions of "archetypal Evil." This Shadow may possess or project, like any other complex, and is especially likely to be projected onto minority or other disenfranchised groups. (Since the Shadow is consciously rejected by the group, it is by definition not "us"; therefore it must be "them.")

Failure to recognize the essential amorality of the gods leads to their (apparently) negative aspects being relegated to Shadow figures, which leads us into a distorted relationship with divinity. "The brighter the light, the darker the shadow it casts"; thus all-good Gods must have all-evil Devils to balance them. Similarly, failure to recognize our personal Shadows leads to their projection onto others.

As with all complexes, knowledge of the Shadow diminishes its power. Recognizing that the gods have their own purposes and attempting to understand them aids us in establishing a relationship with them that neither denies their reality nor requires us to abandon our ethical standpoint. The mediating spirits help to establish this harmonious relation with divinity.

Aside from avoiding possession and projection, knowing your Shadow has other important benefits. Because it is the complement of collective and personal consciousness, it has many powerful characteristics and powers. If you are primarily a thinker, then your Shadow is dominated by feeling. Since your Shadow wants to bring a feeling orientation to life, by forming an alliance with the Shadow you can balance your conscious personality while satisfying its needs. In summary, integrating the traits of the Shadow into consciousness is a major stage in becoming psychologically whole.

Failure to assimilate our Shadows — individual and collective — is perhaps the biggest problem facing our world. (For more on the Shadow, see Jung, *CW* 9, pt. 2, ch. 2.)

The Self and the One

The archetypes, as psychical aspects of the instincts, all have their own purposes, but together — as the archetypal Self — they served the survival of our species in its environment of evolutionary adaptedness. So also, although the gods have their own agendas and purposes, together they are aspects of one archetypal system, which provides a universal foundation of significance and meaning for humankind. Therefore, many polytheistic religions have seen the gods as being under the direction of one chief god, or as constituting some kind of unified godhead, which is closely identified with the notion of divine providence. For convenience I will use Neoplatonic terminology and call this deity "the One."

Before discussing the notion of providence, however, we must look more closely at the godhead. As discussed in the previous Section, behind the human archetypes, we find more fundamental archetypes shared by all primates; thence we proceed until we come to the archetypes of all living things, and ultimately to the archetypes of all physical systems. From the physical side, whatever the evolved perceptual-behavioral structures of humans or other animals, they must obey the laws of nature (including the laws of evolution), whatever they may be. From the psychical side, whatever the archetypal gods of humans may be, they are subject to more remote gods who govern all life, as these in turn are subject to that One that is the psychical aspect of the laws of nature. From the physical perspective, the eternal laws of nature govern the process of the universe through all time; from the psychical perspective, the eternal One — through timeless divine providence — governs the activities of all souls, including those of gods, mediating spirits, and mortals. (Such "governance," of course, need not imply determinism.)

This divine One cannot but remind us of the God of monotheistic religions, but we must beware of transferring notions from the latter to the former. The One comprises the entire universe; it is all-inclusive and therefore paradoxical. Even more so than the individual gods, the One is beyond good and evil, for it includes all the gods and everything else. Certainly, many of the philosophers have told us that God is good, and that everything God does is good, but this "good" must be interpreted in the transvalued, super-human sense that it serves universal providence. We should not be so anthropocentric as to assume that this "good" will be to the benefit of the human species, let alone to the benefit of you or me.

Such a god and such providence may seem remote in the extreme. Nevertheless, the human archetypes — the gods of our hunter-gatherer ancestors — bring providence — and meaning and significance — into the human world and, both directly and through the agency of mediating spirits, into our individual lives. Therefore, by becoming conscious of these spirits and gods, and by striving to live, with their aid, in accord with providence, we can live meaningful lives through conscious, intentional participation in the destiny of the universe.

This is the lifelong process that Jung termed *individuation* (becoming *individuus* — undivided). That is, "Individuation is a conscious attempt to bring the universal programme of human existence to its fullest possible expression in the life of the individual" (Stevens, 1982, p. 142). (There are various practices, such as active imagination, for entering into dialogue with gods and mediating spirits; see Jung, 1997, or Johnson, 1986, for introductions.)

Within each of us is a Paleolithic hunter-gather; this is "the spiritual, inner and complete man" (Jung, *CW* 9, pt. 1, ¶ 529), the archetypal or primal human. But, although the archetypal human is a hunter-gather, we can neither blindly obey him (for we are not hunter-gatherers), nor can we blithely ignore him (for he is our essence). As in the other cases we have seen, our existential project is to reconcile modern life with the needs of this god. We become whole humans by consciously incarnating the god. (For more on the Self, see Jung, *CW* 9, pt. 2, ch. 4.)

The Neural Basis of Archetypal Theology

Much work remains to be done on the neural processes underlying human instinctual behavior, and therefore the archetypes and complexes. Nevertheless a few hypotheses may be mentioned.

Following Stevens (1982, pp. 247-75), it seems that most activity in the midbrain and brain stem is unconscious. Therefore it is likely that the archetypes have their neurological roots in the brain stem, which is responsible for primary instincts, maintaining alertness, and similar basic functions. (Indeed, their roots go deeper yet, into physiological and physical processes, as already discussed.) However, archetypal structures also extend upward into the midbrain (especially the limbic system), which is concerned with appetites, emotions, and some of the less rigid aspects of the instincts. They extend even into the cortical hemispheres, where they enter conscious experience. Although activity in the cortex is conscious, it has a different character in the two hemispheres, and so the dominant, verbal, "logical" left hemisphere may have trouble expressing the imagistic activity of the right hemisphere, which therefore seems mysterious and numinous (Stevens, 1982, p. 266). The personal unconscious and its complexes seem to reside in the lower cortical regions.

Individuation presupposes better integration of neural activity in all parts of the brain. The dominant left hemisphere has learned to inhibit information crossing the corpus callosum from the right hemisphere, and both hemispheres may inhibit inputs from the midbrain and brain stem. Various spiritual practices, such as prayer, meditation, and ritual can allow access to these deeper, more archetypal brain systems.

Further, the ventromedial cortex (subgenual cortex) controls communication between the prefrontal cortex and the limbic system, so it is an important mediator between consciousness and the unconscious. It seems to govern the integration of perceptions and thoughts into a meaningful whole; changes in its activity are correlated with mania and depression (Drevets & al., 1997). Therefore increased activity in this area may be important in religious experiences, such as states of mystical union. Understanding the neuropsychology of such experiences does not diminish their reality, for they do in fact reflect real contact with the transcendent One.

Acknowledgements

Obviously this chapter owes a great debt to Carl G. Jung, whose ideas are essential to its thesis. However, it also draws heavily on Anthony Stevens' (1982, 1993) clear articulation of the interrelation of archetypal psychology, ethology, and neuroscience. Readers familiar with his work will be aware of the extent of my debt to him. For the most part, all I have done is to explicate the theological implications of archetypal psychology.

PALEOLITHIC SPIRITUAL EVOLUTION
Death, The Frontal Lobe, Spiritual Symbolism
by R. Joseph

Belief in the transmigration of the soul, of a life after death, of a world beyond the grave, has been a human characteristic for at least 100,000 years, as ancient graves and mortuary rites attest (e.g., Belfer-Cohen & Hovers, 1992; Butzer, 1982; McCown, 1937; Rightmire, 1984; Schwarcz et al., 1988; Smirnov, 1989; Trinkaus 1986). Despite their small brains and primitive intellectual, linguistic, cognitive, and mental capabilities, primitive "archaic" human beings who wondered the planet over 120,000 years ago, carefully buried their dead (Butzer, 1982; Rightmire, 1984). And like modern Homo sapiens sapiens, they prepared the recently departed for the journey to the Great Beyond: across the sea of dreams, to the land of the dead, the realm of the ancestors and the gods.

Throughout the Middle and Upper Paleolithic it was not uncommon for tools and hunting implements to be placed beside the body, even 100,000 years ago, for the dead would need them in the next world (Belfer-Cohen & Hovers, 1992; McCown, 1937; Trinkaus, 1986). A hunter in life he was to be a hunter in death, for the ethereal world of the Paleolithic was populated by spirits and souls of bear, wolf, deer, bison, and mammoth (e.g., Campbell, 1988; Kuhn, 1955). Moreover, food and water might be set near the head in case the spirit hungered or experienced thirst on its long sojourn to the Hereafter. And finally, fragrant blossoming flowers and red ocher might be sprinkled upon the bodies (Solecki, 1971) along with the tears of those who loved them.

Given the relative paucity of cognitive, cultural, and intellectual development among Middle Paleolithic Neanderthal and "archaic" humans, and the likelihood that they had not yet acquired modern human speech (Joseph, 1996, 2000a,b), evidence of spiritual concerns among these Middle Paleolithic peoples may be somewhat surprising if not unbelievable (Gargett 1989).

Neanderthals, archaics, and other peoples of the Middle Paleolithic were not very smart and used simple stones for tools. In fact, they constructed and made essentially the same stone tools over and over again for perhaps 200,000 years, until around 35,000 B.P., with little variation or consideration of alternatives (Binford, 1982; Gowlett, 1984; Mellars, 1989). Neanderthals greatly lacked in creativity, initiative, imagination, and tended to create simple stone tools that served a single purpose.

As neatly summed up by an ardent defender of Neanderthal cognitive capabilities (Hayden, 1993, p. 139), "as a rule, there is no evidence of private ownership or food storage, no evidence for the use of economic resources for status or political competition, no elaborate burials, no ornaments or other status display items, no skin garments requiring intensive labor to produce, no tools requiring high energy investments, no intensive regional exchange for rare items like sea shells or amber, no competition for labor to produce economic surpluses and no corporate art or labor intensive rituals in deep cave recesses to impress onlookers and help attract labor."

Neanderthals tended to live in the "here and now," with little ability to think about or consider the distant future (Binford, 1973, 1982; Dennell, 1985; Mellars, 1989, 1996); the only notable exception, the future life after death.

This notable dichotomy is in part a function of the differential evolution of the frontal versus the temporal lobes. The frontal lobes are the senior executive of the brain and are responsible for initiative, goal formation, long term planning, the generation of multiple alternatives, and the consideration of multiple alternative consequences (Joseph, 1986a, 1988a, 1999b). The frontal lobes are the source of creativity and imagination, whereas the temporal lobes are the seat of the soul. It is the temporal lobes which were maximally developed in archaic and Neanderthals, whereas the frontal lobe would increase in size by a third in the transition from archaic humans to Cro-Magnon woman and man.

Based on a gross analysis of the skull and casts made of the inner surface of the skull as well as other evidence some of which will be reviewed here, it is apparent that "archaic" Neanderthal men and women possessed a well developed inferior temporal lobe whereas the frontal lobe is sloped and stunted (Joseph, 1996, 2000a). It is the temporal lobes, and the limbic structures buried within which are directly implicated in the generation of personal, emotional, and religious experience including the ability to from long term emotional attachments and to feel intense love (Gloor, 1997; Joseph, 1992a; MacLean, 1990).

In fact, Neanderthals provided loving care for friends and family who had been injured or maimed, enabling them to live many more years despite their grievous injuries. For example, the skeleton of one Neanderthal male, who was about age 45 when he died, had been nursed for a number of years following profoundly crippling injuries. His right arm had atrophied, and his lower arm and hand had apparently been ripped or bitten off, and his left eye socket, right shoulder, collarbone, and both legs were badly injured. Obviously someone loved and tenderly cared for this man. He was no doubt a father, a husband, a brother, and son, and someone in his family not only provided long term loving care to make him comfortable in this life, but prepared him for the next life as well.

Neanderthals were unable to fashion complex tools or think complex thoughts, yet they were people of passion who experienced profound emotions and love; made possible by the limbic system and temporal lobe. In fact, it is because they had the limbic capacity to experience love, spiritual awe, and religious concerns, that these expressions of love continued beyond death. Thus the Neanderthals carefully buried their dead, providing them with food and even sprinkling the bodies with seven different types of blooming, blossoming, fragrant flowers.

THE ANTIQUITY OF THE SOUL

MIDDLE PALEOLITHIC SPIRITUALITY

When humans first became aware of a "god" or "gods" cannot be determined. Nevertheless, the antiquity of religious and spiritual belief extends well beyond the course of the last 100,000 years, as it has been well established that Neanderthals and other Homo Sapiens of the Middle Paleolithic (e.g. 150,000 to 35,000 B.P.) and Upper Paleolithic (35,000 B.P. to 10,000 B.P.) engaged in complex religious rituals. These rituals are evident from the manner in which they decorated their caves and the spiritual symbolism associated with death.

Neanderthals (a people who lived in Europe, Russia, Iraq, Africa, and China from around 150,000 to 30,000 B.P.), have been buried in sleeping positions with the body flexed and lying on its side. Some were laid to rest with limestone blocks placed beneath the head like a pillow—as if they were not truly dead but merely asleep.

Sleep and dreams have long been associated with the spirit world, and it is through dreams that gods including the Lord God worshipped by Jews, Christians, and Muslims, have communicated their thoughts, warnings, intentions, and commands. Throughout the ages, and as repeatedly stated in the Old Testament and the Koran, dreams have been commonly thought to be the primary medium in which gods and human interact (Campbell 1988; Freud, 1900; Jung 1945, 1964). Insofar as the ancients (and many moderns folks) were concerned, dreams served as a doorway, a portal of entry to the spirit world through which "God," His angels, or myriad demons could make their intentions known.

It is through dreams, we are told, that one is able to come into direct contact with the spirit world and a reality so magical and profoundly different yet as real as anything experienced during waking. It is through dreams that ancient humans came to believe the spiritual world sits at the boundaries of the physical, where day turns to dusk, the hinterland of the imagination where dreams flourish and grow. And it is while dreaming that one's own soul may transcend the body, to soar like an eagle, or to commune with the spirits of loved ones who reside in heaven along side the gods.

Neanderthals prepared their dead for this great and final journey, by laying their loved ones to rest so that they would sleep with the spirits and dream of heavenly eternity.

Neanderthals have also been buried surrounded by goat horns placed in a circle, with reindeer vertebrae, animal skins, stone tools, red ocher, and in one grave, seven different types of flowers. In one cave (unearthed after 60,000 years had passed), a deep chamber was discovered which housed a single skull which was surrounded by a ring of stones.

Yet others were buried with large bovine bones above the head, with limestone blocks placed on top of the head and shoulders, and with heads severed coupled with evidence of ritual decapitation, facial bone removal, and cannibalism (Belfer-Cohen and Hovers 1992; Binford 1968; Harold 1980; Smirnov 1989; Solecki 1971). In one site, dated to over 100,000 years B.P., Neanderthals decapitated eleven of their fellow Neanderthals, and smashed their faces beyond recognition.

Moreover, Neanderthals buried bears at a number of sites including Regourdou. At Drachenloch

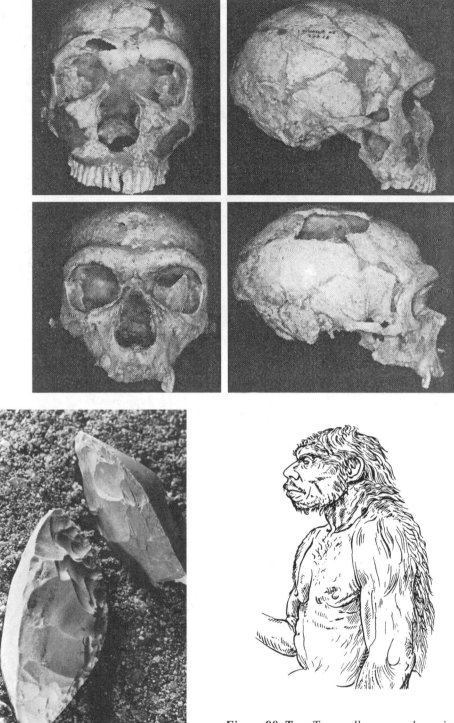

Above: Neanderthal tools.

Figure 98. Top: *Two well preserved crania from northern European male Neanderthals. Reproduced from M. H. Wolpoff (1980), Paleo-Anthropology. New York, Knopf. Above: The head and torso of a Neanderthal. Reprinted from Howells, 1997. Getting Here. Compass Press, Washington D.C.*

317

Figure 99. *A Neanderthal seemingly glowers from the grave at those who have disturbed his long slumber. His body had been sprinkled with 7 different types of flowers. Reproduced from R. Solecki. Shanidar: The first Flower people. New York, A.A. Knopf.*

Figure 100. *Neanderthal burial.*

they buried stone "cysts" containing bear skulls (Kurten 1976); hence, "the clan of the cave bear."

It therefore seems apparent that Neanderthals not only engaged in complex religious rituals, but they believed in spirits, ghosts, and a life after death. Hence the sleeping position, stone pillows, stone tools and food. They were preparing the departing spirit for the journey to the Hereafter and the land of dreams.

It is also appears that they feared the dead, and were terrified by the prospect that certain souls might haunt the living. They were afraid of ghosts, and frightened by the possibility that just as one might awake from sleep after visiting the land of the dead, the dead might also awake from this death-like slumber. The dead, or at least their personal souls, had to be prevented from causing mischief among the living; especially the dead of dreaded enemies. Hence, the ritual decapitation, facial bone removal, and placement of heavy stones upon the body.

It can be concluded, therefore, that almost 100,000 years ago, primitive humans had already come to believe in ghosts, souls, spirits, and a continuation of "life" after death. And, they also took precautions, in some cases, to prevent certain souls from being released from the body and returning to cause mischief among the living.

Moreover, they appear to have believed in a personal soul, which is why, in the case or powerful enemies, the Neanderthals would cut off heads and hands. They went to great lengths to obliterate all aspects of that dreaded individual's personal identity; e.g., smashing the face beyond recognition.

Of course, the fact that these Neanderthals were buried does not necessarily imply that they held a belief in "God." Rather, what the evidence demonstrates is that Neanderthals were capable of very intense emotions and feelings ranging from murderous rage to love to spiritual and superstitious awe. Although no god is implied, Neanderthals held spiritual and mystical beliefs involving the transmigration of the soul and all the horrors, fears, and hopes that accompany such feelings and beliefs. Although the Neanderthals had not discovered god, they stood upon the threshold.

THE NEANDERTHALS: A CHARACTER STUDY

What is most surprising about the depth of Neanderthal spirituality is the fact that these were an exceedingly violent, murderous people, as the remnants of their skeletons preserved for so many eons attests. Many of their fossils still betray the cruel ravages of deliberately and violently inflicted wounds.

They also appear to have systematically engaged in female infanticide, and displayed a willingness to eat almost anything on four or two legs—including other Neanderthals. In one site, dated to over 100,000 years B.P., Neanderthals decapitated eleven of their fellow Neanderthals, and then enlarged the base of each skull (the foramen magnum) so the brains could be scooped out and presumably eaten. Even the skulls of children were treated in this fashion.

In fact, they would throw the bones and carcasses of other Neanderthals into the refuse pile. In one cave, a collection of over 20 Neanderthals were found mixed up with the remains of other animals and refuse. Presumably, these were enemies or just hapless strangers, innocent cave dwellers who were attacked and sometimes eaten after being brutally killed.

Hence, with the obvious exception of "friends," mates, and family, Neanderthals often saw one another as a potential meal, and had almost no regard for a stranger's innate humanness. These were a violent, murderous, ritualistic people, and strangers were often killed and eaten.

These characteristics are also associated with religious fervor. Among ancient and present day peoples, violence, murder, ritual cannibalism, and the sacrifice of children are common religious practices.

Violence and murder are also under the control of the limbic system. And it is the limbic system which mediates religious and spiritual experience.

ARCHAIC SPIRITUALITY AND MORTUARY RITUALS

The Neanderthals were not a very intelligent or tidy people. Yet they possessed a well developed limbic system and temporal lobe. In fact, from an examination of fossilized skulls, it appears that other archaic Homo sapiens, including the still primitive "early modern" Homo sapiens of the Middle Paleolithic were well endowed in this regard, though the frontal lobe remained poorly developed (Joseph, 1996, 2000a,b).

By contrast, the temporal lobe began to expand and evolve at a faster and earlier rate than the frontal lobe (Gloor, 1997), which is a characteristic of ontological development as well (Joseph, 1982, 2000a).

It is the expansion of the temporal lobe, this "transmitter to god" which also explains why even earlier species of primitive humanity practiced complex spiritual rituals and mortuary rites. "Early modern," and other "archaic" Homo sapiens commonly buried infants, children, and adults with tools, grave offerings, and animal bones.

For example, archaic H. sapiens and "early moderns" were carefully buried in Qafzeh, near Nazareth and in the Mt. Carmel, Mugharetes-Skhul caves on the Israeli coast over 90,000 to 98,000 years ago (McCown 1937; Smirnov 1989; Trinkaus 1986). This includes a Qafzeh mother and child who were buried together, and an infant who was buried holding the antlers of a fallow deer across his chest. In a nearby site equally as old (i.e. Skhul), yet another was buried with the mandible of a boar held in his hands, whereas an adult had stone tools placed by his side (Belfer-Cohen and Hovers 1992; McCown 1937).

NEOLITHIC MORTUARY PRACTICES

It is unknown if the burial practices of the Paleolithic peoples included burning, as is common in many ancient and present day cultures (e.g. India). There is ample evidence, however, that burning was a widespread custom during the Neolithic. In some cases, only the bones were buried, which indicates that either the body was burnt, or it was only buried after the flesh had rotted away; referred to by anthropologists as a "secondary burial."

Like those who came before them, the mortuary practices of the Neolithic peoples, such as those living in predynastic Egypt, included the burial of loved ones in sleeping positions, often lying the dead on their left side (Budge, 1900; Hoffman, 1991). The dead "sleeping" body would also be buried with substantial grave goods including surplus wealth.

"The deceased were laid on reed mats and invariably accompanied by grave offerings that reflected their relative wealth and aspects of daily life. These included tools, flint knives, scrapers, arrowheads, ornaments like shell and stone beads, and a bewildering variety of fine, handmade polished red ware jars, backed clay figurines, amulets, and carved ivory plaques" (Hoffman, 1991, p. 110).

Moreover, just as Paleolithic peoples also sometimes took steps to prevent the souls of the dead from returning to haunt the living, or to take up residence in the dead bodies, those of the late Upper Paleolithic and early Neolithic did likewise. For example, the dead might be buried covered with huge stone slabs and with heads, arms, hands and feet missing, and/or impaled with weapons (Budge, 1900).

Mortuary rites and religious rituals have therefore been practiced the world over, from the Middle Paleolithic to the Upper Paleolithic to the Neolithic and beyond to the present. For over 100,000 years humans have buried and weeped over their dead, have believed in spirits and a life after death, and have provisioned their souls for the journey to the Hereafter.

We may be born of the flesh, but we are spiritual beings. Spirituality has been a defining aspect of the human condition for over 100,000 years.

CRO-MAGNON GENESIS:
The Children of the Gods

Biblical accounts of creation tell us that increasingly complex life forms emerged upon the planet, in a step-wise, "day to day" sequence, beginning with simple creatures and culminating, on day 6, with the creation of woman and man. In fact, this same progression is evident from the fossil record, and was first detailed in the Sumerian accounts of Genesis.

Almost 6000 years ago the Sumerians, a cultured people whose cities and civilization eventually gave rise to Babylon, explained that the first humans were exceedingly "primitive" and unsuitable to perform the work required by the gods. The gods required intelligent and skilled workers to tend their farms and gardens.

According to the ancient Sumerians, Enki, the Anunnaki god of science and wisdom, decided to rectify the situation by taking tissue from the gods, mixing it with other substances, so as to create the first true human beings; humans that were fashioned in the image of the gods and provided the spirit, the living soul of god. Enki's emblem was the sign of the double helix, two entwined snakes.

The Biblical account in Genesis echoes the Sumerian account: "And God said, Let us make man in our image, after our likeness. So God created man in his image, in the image of God created he him; male and female he created them."

In the account provided by Genesis there is also a second act of human creation by a "Lord God." This Lord God appears upon the scene after "God ended his work... and rested on the seventh day."

As the men and women created on the sixth day were not suitable to farm the land or manage his herds, the "Lord God" engaged in another act of creation because "there was not a man to till the ground... And the Lord God formed man of the dust of the ground and breathed into his nostrils the breath of life; and man became a living soul. And the Lord God planted a garden eastward in Eden and there he put the man whom he had formed."

Thus we see that the man created after the seventh day differs from the man created on the sixth day, in two important respects. The man created on the sixth day, was created by "God," as part of a natural progression beginning with simple creatures. This first man, however, was unable "to till the land." The man fashioned after the seventh day, after "God" had rested, was created by the "Lord God" after all the natural sequential acts of creation had come to an end. And, this new man, created after the seventh day was able to till the gardens, and was provided with a "living soul."

Because the Earth was already swarming with these more primitive humans, Cain (the son of Adam and Eve) worried aloud to the Lord God, that he may be killed: "I shall be a fugitive and a vagabond in the earth; and it shall come to pass that everyone that findeth me shall slay me... And the Lord set a mark upon Cain, lest any finding him should kill him" (Genesis, 4: 14-15).

Thus we may presume that the first men and women did not possess a "living soul," were exceedingly primitive and violent, and lacked the intellectual capability to perform the tasks assigned—at least, as stated by the Sumerians and echoed in Genesis. "There was not a man to till the ground." They were like animals. They had no souls.

By contrast, the second creation resulted in men and women who were not only created in the image of the Gods, but who were highly intelligent, and who received something of God, becoming a "living soul." Unlike the men and women created on the sixth day, this newly created woman and man were so creative, intelligent, and demonstrated such wisdom, that the "the Lord God..." proclaimed "man had become as one of us, to know good and evil."

THE CRO-MAGNON

The Cro-Magnon were a very handsome people with thin hips, broad shoulders, aquiline noses, prominent chins, small even perfect teeth, high rounded foreheads, and with brains almost a third larger than those of the average woman and man today, i.e. 1800 cc vs 1350 ccs. There was nothing ape-like or Neanderthal about these people.

These were a tall and noble looking race. Consider, whereas the average height of a present day male averages (depending on country) from between five foot four to five foot 9 inches, Cro-Magnon men stood 6 foot tall, though the women were somewhat smaller and more delicate. Compared to those who came before or after them, and until the advent of the 20th century, these people were giants and they may well have appeared as "gods;" at least to the Neanderthals who managed to hang on for another 10,000 years after the Cro-Magnons had appeared upon the scene. In fact, it was not until the 20th century and with significant changes in nutrition and diet that people in the Western world grew by almost half a foot in height, the men reaching five feet nine inches on average.

The Cro-Magnon were also intellectual giants. They were accomplished artists, musicians, craftsmen, sorcerers, and extremely talented hunters, fishermen, and highly efficient gatherers and herbalists. When they emerged upon the scene over 35,000 years ago, they carried and fashioned tools and weapons that had never before been seen. They had the know how to make and bake pottery and construct clay figurines as well as construct kilns and burn coal so as to fire and mold their creations.

From the time of Homo Erectus (1.9 million to 500,000 B.P), humans had utilized fire to keep warm, to provide light, to cook their food, and to ward off animals. However, the Cro-Magnon learned over 30,000 years ago how to make fire using the firestone; iron pyrite which was repeatedly struck with a flint thus making sparks which could easily ignite brush.

They also created the first rudimentary blast furnaces which were capable of emitting enormous amounts of heat, so as to fire clay. This was accomplished by digging a tiny tunnel into the bottom of the hearth which allowed air to be drawn in. Indeed, 30,000 years ago these people were making fire hardened ceramics and clay figures of animals and females with bulging buttocks and breasts—which are presumed to be the first goddesses.

Many of these female figurines were shaped so that they tapered into points. Because they were pointed they could be stuck into the ground or into some other substance either for ornamental or supernatural purposes, e.g., household goddesses or as fertility figures and earth mothers. In fact, much of the art produced, be it finely crafted "laurel leafs" or other artistic masterpieces, served ritual, spiritual, and esthetic functions. However, they also created art that was meant to be looked at, owned and admired, and for trade, as jewelry and household decorations, and as highly prized possessions as well as for religious reverence.

Likewise, the first musical instruments were created by these people some 25,000 years ago. These included wooden drums and tiny flutes and whistles.

These peoples were also the first to weave baskets, and the first to use needle and thread in order to make finely fitted clothes which were carefully and deftly sewn together. Unlike all those who had come before them they decorated their clothes and tools and weapons with elaborate designs and geometric and animal symbols. Within their underground cathedrals they left behind elaborate and complex paintings, some of which were almost 3-dimensional. These peoples demonstrated an esthetic artistic awareness and mastery that was unprecedented and which equals the ability of any living artist today.

Thirty five thousand years ago, Cro-Magnon were painting animals not only on walls but on ceilings, utilizing rich yellows, reds, and browns in their paintings and employing the actual shape of the cave walls so as to conform with and give life-like dimensions, including the illusion of movement to the creature they were depicting. Many of their engraving on bones and stones also show a complete mastery of geometric awareness and they often used the natural contours of the cave walls, including protuberances, to create a 3-dimensional effect.

The drawing or carving often became a harmonious or rather, an organic part of the object, wall, ceiling, or tool upon which it was depicted. The Cro-Magnon drew and painted scenes in which animals mated, defecated, fought, charged, and/or were fleeing and dying from wounds inflicted by hunters. The Cro-Magnon cave painters were exceedingly adept at recreating the scenes of everyday life. Moreover, most of the animals were drawn to scale, that is, they were depicted in their actual size; and all this, 35,000 years ago (e.g. Chauvet, et al., 1997).

The Cro-Magnon obtained their colors from natural earth pigments, such as ocher, a clay that contains a variety of iron minerals. However, whereas Neanderthals and H. habilis apparently had a fondness for red, the Cro-Magnon learned to separate and mix these pigments creating a variety of hues and colors. In order to mix and to arrive at the correct consistency, a variety of lubricants were employed such as blood, urine, vegetable and fruit juices, animal fat, and the contents of eggs. The separate colors were then mixed in various hollowed out rocks and shells.

The Cro-Magnon artist used a brush, as well as his or her fingers in order to paint. In fact, they used a variety of different brushes which enabled the artist to create different shades and strokes. In some cases the artist simply blew the paint onto the drawing via a tubular bone, thus making a mist-like spray.

The Cro-Magnon artists had also invented abstract impressionism, as many of their paintings and artworks were exceedingly abstract, surrealistic, or comprised of geometric forms and concentric shapes and ovals which in some cases formed abstract versions of animals or women. Indeed, they displayed an artistic mastery equal to that of any modern master, including Picasso. Awe stuck by these Paleolithic masterpieces Picasso complained that in 30,000 years "we have learned nothing new. We have invented nothing." Indeed, the geometric and angular form of representation employed by these Paleolithic Masters appears again and again throughout history and is found in Egyptian, Sumerian, and even early Greek art.

The origins of the Cro-Magnon peoples, however, are completely unknown. There are no transitional forms that link them with Neanderthals or the still primitive "early modern" peoples of the Middle Paleolithic who were decidedly more archaic in appearance. Neanderthals did not evolve into Cro-Magnons, and they coexisted for almost 15,000 years, until finally the Neanderthals disappeared from the face of the Earth, around 30,000 years B.P. (Mellars, 1996). Indeed, the Neanderthals were of a completely different race; and not just physically, but genetically, for when they died out, so too did their genetic heritage and all traces of their DNA (Ovchinnikov et al., 2000).

By contrast although modern human DNA differs significantly from Neanderthal DNA, "modern" human DNA traces its ancestral lineage to female ancestors who lived around 250,000 years ago (Stoneking & Cann, 1989; Vigilant et al. 1991). Likewise, according to the Sumerian Kings' lists, the Anunnaki created the first god-like humans around 240,000 years ago (Roux, 1992) when Enki implanted a mixture into a female goddess who gave birth to the first man.

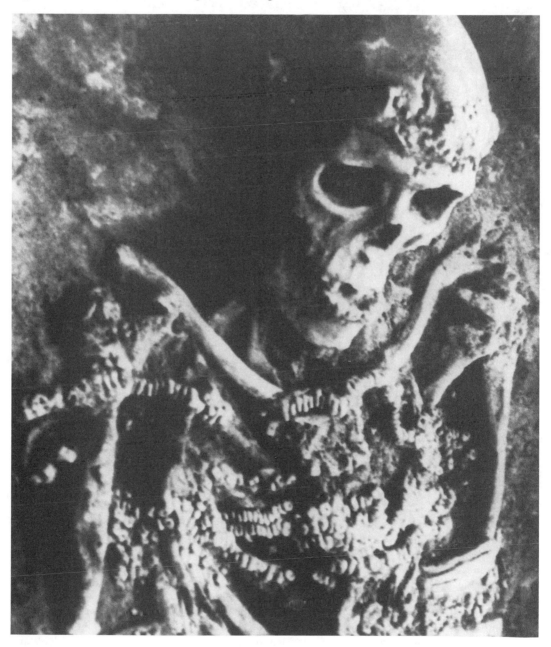

Figure 101. *Upper Paleolithic Cro-Magnons buried with tools, ornaments, hunting implements, and other essentials.*

Figure 102. *Upper Paleolithic Cro-Magnons buried with tools, ornaments, hunting implements, and other essentials.*

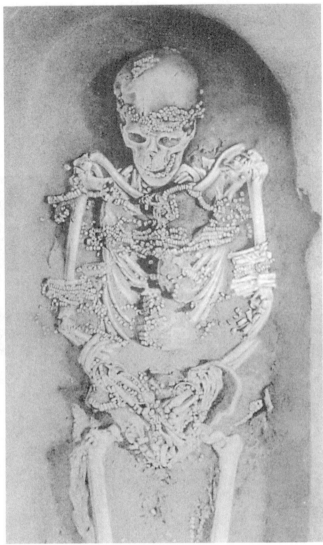

Thirty thousand years ago, and with the demise of the Neanderthals, the Cro-Magnons gained dominion over the earth. And it is thirty thousand years ago that the ancient Egyptians claim that first kings came to rule Egypt, and that these kings were gods.

In comparison to all those who had come before them, and the Neanderthals who still lived in adjacent lands, the Cro-Magnon were so physically, intellectually, technologically, culturally and genetically advanced, and had such a huge brain, and they appeared so suddenly upon the Earth, that they may well have been created by God and in the image of the Gods... knowing good and evil.

CRO-MAGNON UPPER PALEOLITHIC SPIRITUALITY

The brain of the Cro-Magon differ from previous species of humanity and other primates and mammls, in that the frontal lobe has significantly increased in size (Joseph, 1996). The frontal lobe is the "senior executive" of the brain and personality, and among it s many fuctions are the capacity for creative and symbolic thought--to put into thought and to act out limbic and spiritual impulses (Joseph, 1986a, 1999c).

The spiritual belief systems of the Cro-Magnon and other peoples of the Upper Paleolithic, completely outstripped those of their predecessors in complexity, originality, and artistic and symbolic accomplishments. As the brain and man and woman evolved, so too did their spiritual beliefs.

Hence, the Cro-Magnon conception of, and ability to symbolically express the spirit world, became much more complex as well, undergoing what has been described as a "symbolic explosion" (Bandi 1961; Kuhn 1955; Leroi-Gurhan 1964, 1982; Prideaux 1973).

The Cro-Magnon practiced complex religious rituals and apparently were the first peoples to have arrived at the conception of "god." However, it was not a male god who they worshipped but female goddesses who were attended by animals and animal-head shaman.

Figure 103. *Neanderthal skeleton, Neanderthal, and a Cro-Magnon skeleton.*

By 35,000 years ago the Cro-Magnon were painting, drawing, and etching bear and mammoth, dear and horse, and pregnant females and goddesses in the recesses of dark and dusky caverns (Bandi 1961; Chauvet et al., 1996; Leroi-Gurhan 1964, 1982; Prideaux 1973). The pregnant females include Venus statuettes, many of which were fertility goddesses. The Cro-Magnon were well aware of the differences between a slim sexy woman and a fertility Goddess for they were able to draw both. In fact, these were the first people to paint and etch what today might be considered Paleolithic porn. That is, in addition to pregnant fertility goddesses they drew and painted slim, shapely, naked and nubile young maidens in various positions of repose (Joseph, 1993, 2000a).

It is noteworthy that even 35,000 years ago and continuing for the next 25,000 years, the Cro-Magnon artist often drew and painted over existing drawings, including paintings which were hidden away in deep recesses of dark underground caverns that were extremely difficult to get to. This indicates that the location within the cave was of particular mystical, spiritual, or at least ritualistic significance, particularly in that many paintings were in out of the way places where one had to crawl long distance through tiny spaces and along rather tortuous routes to get to them. In fact, not just the location but the journey to these hidden recesses may have been of ritualistic significance perhaps relating to birth or even rebirth following death.

SPIRITS, SOULS, AND SORCERERS

As is evident from their cave art and symbolic accomplishments, the nether world of the Cro-Magnon and other peoples of the Upper Paleolithic, was haunted by the spirits and souls of the living, the dead, and those yet to be born, both animal and human (Brandon 1967; Campbell 1988; Kuhn 1955; Prideaux 1973).

Upper Paleolithic peoples apparently believed these souls and spirits could be charmed and controlled by hunting magic, and through the spells of sorcerers and shamans. Hence, in conjunction with the worship of the goddess, the Cro-Magnons also relied on shamans and priests.

Hundreds of feet beneath the earth, the likeness of one ancient shaman attired in animal skins and stag antlers, graces the upper wall directly above the entrance to the 20,000-25,000 year-old grand gallery at Les Trois-Freres in southern France (Prideaux1973). Galloping, running, and swirling about this ancient sorcerer are bison, stag, horse, deer, and presumably their spirits and their souls. Images of an almost identical "sorcerer" appear again in ancient Sumerian and Babylonian inscriptions fashioned four to six thousand years ago. The "sorcerer" has a name: "Enki"-the god of the double helix.

The Cro-Magon also believed in and worshipped the goddess who was associated with the fertility of the earth, as well as the moon and the stars. One great goddess was carved in limestone over the entrance to an underground cathedral in Laussel, France, over 25,000 years ago. She was painted in the colors of life and fertility, blood red. Her left hand still rests upon her pregnant belly whereas in her right hand she holds the horned crescent of the moon which is engraved with thirteen lines, the number of moon cycles in a solar year. She was a goddess of life, linked to the mysteries of the heavens and the magical powers of the moon whose 30 day cycle corresponds with the menstrual cycle which issues from a woman's life giving womb. The Cro-Magnon believed in god. God was a woman.

UNDERGROUND CATHEDRALS: EMBRACED BY THE LIGHT

In order to view many of these Cro-Magnon paintings and "religious" statues and shrines, one has to enter the hidden entrance of an underground cave, and crawl a considerable distance, sometimes hundreds of yards, through a twisting, narrowing, pitch black tunnel before reaching these Upper Paleolithic underground Cathedrals. Here the Cro-Magnon would light candles and lamps, performing magical and spiritual rituals as the painted animals and spirits wavered in the cave light.

The nature and location of the Cro-Magnon cathedrals, which have been found throughout Europe, and the nature of the tortuous routes to get to them, and the effect of cave light bringing these paintings to life, is significant as it embraces features associated with after death experiences as retold by present day as well as ancient peoples.

In the ancient Egyptian and Tibetan Books of the Dead, and has been reported among many of those who have undergone a "near death" or "life after death" experience, being enveloped in a dark tunnel is commonly experienced soon after death. It is only as one ascends the tunnel that one will see in the decreasing distance, a light, the "light" of "Heaven" and of paradise. Once embraced by the light "the recently dead" may be greeted by the souls of dead relatives, friends, and/or radiant human or animal-like entities (Eadie, 1992; Rawling 1978; Ring 1980).

Given the nature of their rituals, shamanic images, and goddess figurines, including the symbolism of flight associated with death, it thus appears that the Cro-Magnon were probably the first people to engage in magic and sorcery and may have been the first to develop notions of heaven and god and goddesses and the first to invent priests and shamans.

And, because the Cro-Magnons obviously believed in an after-life, they buried their dead with food, weapons, flowers, jewelry, clothing, pendants, rings, necklaces, multifaceted tools, head bands, beads, bracelets and so on. The Cro-Magnon were a profoundly spiritual people and they fully prepared the dead for the journey to the spirit world, equipping them so that they could live for all eternity in the land of the gods.

CRO-MAGNON GODS IN THE GARDEN OF EDEN

MAN THE HUNTER

The achievements of the Upper Paleolithic Cro-Magnon were not merely limited to art, ceramics, music, and spirituality, as they constantly experimented with and created new inventions such as the sewing needle, pointed burins, highly efficient cutters and scrapers, and the spear thrower. This device consisted of a spear that was fitted into a long hooked rod, about 1-2 feet in length.

Figure 104. Cro-Magnon art.

Via the spear thrower a Cro-Magnon hunter or warrior could toss his weapon an incredible distance and at a tremendous velocity thus greatly enhancing his killing power and range. In effect, the spear thrower acted as an extension of a man's arm and enabled a man to almost double the distance in which he could throw a spear. He could easily impale and kill an animal or another man standing anywhere from 70 to 150 yards away.

Like all their tools, the spear throwers were elaborately decorated with fine carvings, etchings, drawings and paintings of animals such as horses, deer, bison, birds and fish. These tools and weapons were also made from a variety of substances such as reindeer antlers..

These people also realized that a spear covered with barbs, harpoon style, would do much more damage than a smooth point. However, even with barbs, animals often were not killed outright and the mortally wounded beast would sometimes run for miles before falling down and dying. The Cro-Magnon, therefore, created blood grooves along side the bone spearheads so that blood could more efficiently gush from the wound thus speeding the process of dying.

In addition, perhaps 20,000 years ago the first bows and arrows apparently came into widespread use and the arrows appear to have been feathered so as to stabilize their flight. With the creation of the bow the hunter could now remain completely hidden for if he missed with his first shot the animal would not even know he was there (so long as he stayed down wind and out of sight). The hunter could now shoot again and again.

The Cro-magnon were the greatest hunters of their time and unlike those who came before them, they were able to easily kill antelopes, bison, wild horses, reindeer, mammoths, and even lions and bears. They were also good trappers and fisherman and took birds, small animals and fish in abundance. In fact they were the first true fishermen and constantly harvested the abundant game living in the lakes, rivers and seas. These people utilized nets, a trident shaped spear as well as a baited hook which would then become lodged in the throat of the fish.

Diversity in tool making is the hall mark of the Cro-Magnon. Thirty five thousand years ago, a typical tool kit consisted of well over 125 items, e.g. knives for cutting, whittling, stone saws, chisels, perforators for making holes, needles, scrapers for bone others for skin, pounding slabs, etc.. Many of these tools were attached to wood, bone and antler handles, and/or were made of these materials including ivory. Ivory can also be steamed and bent so that specific shapes can be molded.

In contrast, the Neanderthal and those who came before them, simply knocked two stones together so as to sharpen a rock, or they chipped away flakes from rocks and used these as cutting tools and weapons. Compared to the Neanderthals, Cro-Magnons were like gods.

GODDESS: WOMAN THE GATHERER

By the dawn of the Upper Paleolithic hunting had become the center of religious and artistic life for the men. Nevertheless, 60-80% of the Cro-Magnon diet consisted of fruits, nuts, grains, honey, roots and vegetables (Clark, 1952; Prideaux, 1973), which were gathered by females (Joseph, 2000b). Among the hunting and gathering societies in existence during the last few centuries, women have been and are the gatherers and main providers of food whereas spoils from the hunt account for only about 35% of the diet (Dahlberg, 1981; Lee & DeVore, 1968; Martin & Voorhies, 1975; Murdock & Provost, 1973; Zilman, 1981).

Gathering was also a spiritual affair which unlike hunting and the taking of life, celebrated the nurturance and giving of life and life's abundance. These Paleolithic women likely gathered in groups of 7 or more adults. The Cro-Magnon woman did not just gatherer the produce from the Garden of Eden, but she experimented with horticulture, herbology, and the fertility of the Earth.

Man the hunter, woman the gatherer and giver of life, has characterized the psychic and spiritual dichotomy of the human condition since well before the Paleolithic. Yet, with the arrival of the Cro-Magnon, woman became a tool-making, gathering goddess and mistress of the hearth and the hunt. And woman, the first god, was worshipped by woman and man.

THE GODDESS

Whereas hunting was the center of religious life for men, food gathering and herbology served the same purpose for women. Such gathering groups must have commonly been loud, noisy and very gay affairs filled with the talk and singing of the women and the sounds of games and yells of the children. Some women were pregnant or probably carried and nursed infants who might be passed from mother to sister, to aunt, and back again. Children and young adolescents would frolic about

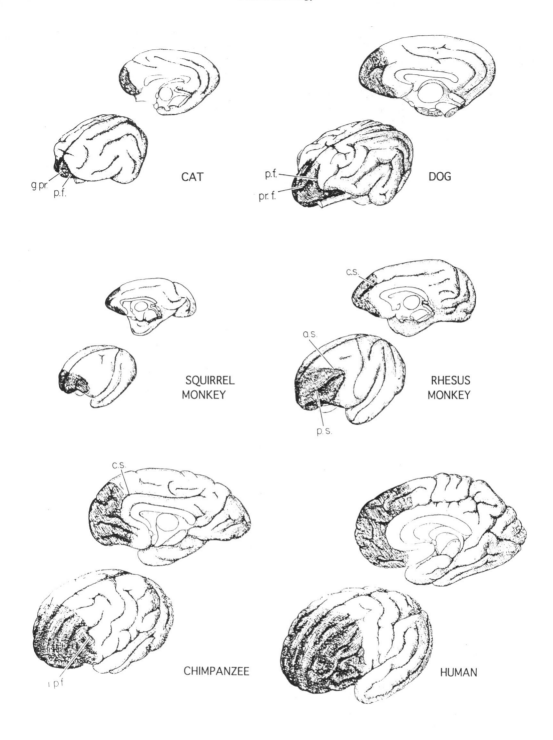

Figure 105. *Comparisons of the frontal lobe across species. Note obvious expansion. (Modified from Fuster, 1997. The Frontal Lobes. Raven-Lippincott. Baltimore). The frontal lobes subserve inhibitory control, reasoning, judgement, imagination, creativity, and thought, including expressive speech as mediated by the emergence of Broca's expressive speech area in humans.*

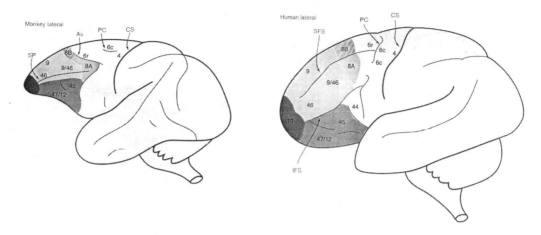

Figure 92. Comparison of monkey and human frontal lobe. Reprinted from Zigmund et al., 1999 Fundamental Neuroscience, Academic Press, San Diego.

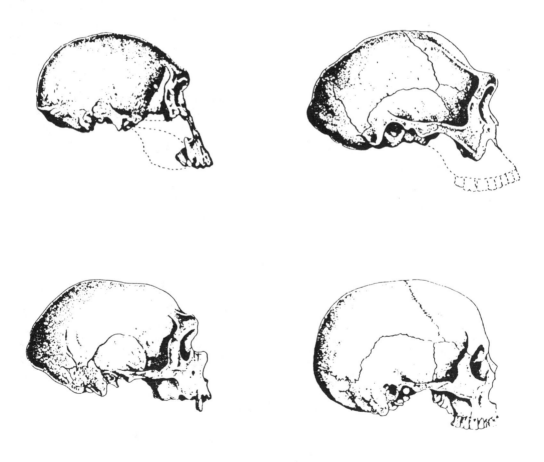

Figure 106. Comparison of the frontal cranium over the course of "evolution:" from Australopithecus, to H. Habilis, to H. erectus. to modern humans. Note obvious expansion of the frontal lobe.

Figure 107. Cro-Magon Art

Figure 108. *A mother goddess, holding in her hand the symbol of the moon with 13 lines, which is the number of menstrual/lunar cycles in a solar year. Her other hand rests upon her pregnant belly. This goddess was carved outside the entrance to an underground Paleolitic Cathedral.*

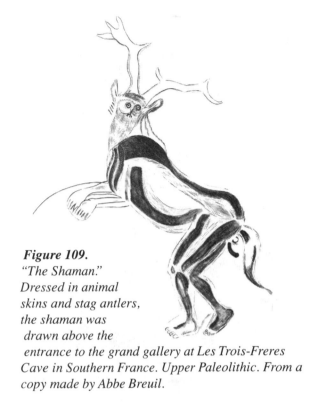

Figure 109.
"The Shaman."
Dressed in animal
skins and stag antlers,
the shaman was
drawn above the
entrance to the grand gallery at Les Trois-Freres
Cave in Southern France. Upper Paleolithic. From a
copy made by Abbe Breuil.

Figure 110. *A*
Sumerian/Babylonian
god, with shaman's
horns, holding a staff
upon which sits a
flying solar disc.

and play. The women could talk, sing, celebrate life's abundance, and share and practice their spiritual faith and worship together as they harvested nature's bounty.

Woman the gatherer worshipped the Great Mother, the Great Goddess, the Lord of Creation, Mother Earth, the Mother of All. And she carried with her ivory and stone engravings of the Great Mother, and amulets and rings, and mother goddess statues that could be stuck into the ground.

And while the men performed their rituals in the deep recesses of caverns and caves, woman worshipped the Great Mother by dawn's early light, and the light of the harvest moon. And whereas the men practiced rituals involving death and the spiritual hereafter, women practiced rituals of fertility that celebrated life's abundance. Dancing, singing, fertility rites, and sex orgies became hallmarks of their rituals.

THE LIFE OF A CRO-MAGNON GODDESS

Whereas the Cro-Magnon hunter invented his own religion and a stockpile of technologically advanced weapons that made him the greatest hunter of all time, woman the gatherer discovered her own unique life giving spirituality and created her own arsenal of tools which made her the greatest artisan of all time. Her creations included statues of female gods, earrings, necklaces, bacelets, pendants, and beads, and complex tools for domestic ease including choppers, scrapers, cleavers with a straight cutting edge on one side (Day, 1996; Righmire, 1990). That these tools were fashioned by a female hand can be deduced by their domestic use (Joseph, 2000a,b). Among hunting and gathering groups it is females and not the males who make and use tools (Niethhammer, 1977), the only exception being hunting implements and weapons of war which females are not allowed to touch (Tabet, 1982).

The responsibilities of the Cro-Magnon woman included the preparation of the food she gathered and any meat which the men brought home from their hunting sojourns. In addition to food preparation, clothes were sewn and fashioned out of hides (Clark, 1952, 1967; Prideaux, 1973), and these too are tasks associated with women (Gusinde, 1961; Lee, 1974; Neithhammer, 1977), including, presumably, the Cro-Magnon females of the Upper Paleolithic.

Thus the duties of the Upper Paleolithic female were much more multi-faceted and complex than her predecessors, and included cleaning hides via a scraper, drying and curing the skin over the smoke of a fire, and then using a knife or cutter to make the general desired shape. The Upper Paleolithic female was also employing a punch to make holes in these hides, through which leather

Figure 111. *A dead hunter and a birds head. A disembowled bison stands above him. Presumably this scene depicts the death of a hunter and the flight of his soul as symbolized by the bird. Bird heads were commonly employed by ancient peoples including the Egyptians to depict the ascension to heaven. Eventually, bird heads were replaced by creatures with wings, e.g. angels. Reproduced with permission, Bildarchiv Preubischer Kulturbesitz.*

Figure 112. *Goddesses with bird heads. From Libya, approximately 10,000 B.P. The bird head symbolizes the capacity for flight and thus the ability to ascend to heaven.*

straps or a vine could be passed so as to create a garment that could keep out the cold (Clark, 1952, 1967; Prideaux, 1973). They were also weaving and using a needle to sew garments together; "domestic" tasks which are almost exclusively associated with "women's" work (Murdock & Provost, 1973; Neithhammer, 1977).

The women were exceedingly skilled artisans whose abilities easily excel those of any modern woman today. And they were creating beautiful, colorful, intricately designed, embroidered, and tailored clothes over 30,000 years ago.

The Cro-Magnon women dressed their men and their children like woodland gods, fed them the food of the gods, picked fresh daily from the Paleolithic garden of Eden. And they worshipped woman as the life creating and life giving goddess, the Great Mother of All who gave life to the earth and woman and man.

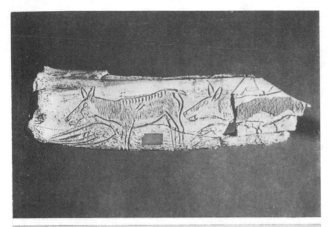

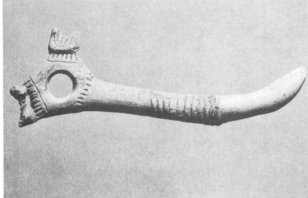

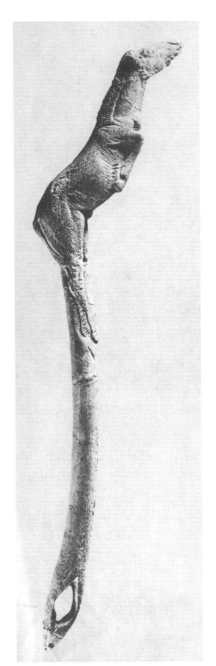

Figure 113. Upper Paleolithic art, including a leaping horse that had been carved as part of a speer thrower.

VILLAGES BECOME CITIES, BECOME CIVILIZATIONS

These people and their descendants became so proficient at art, crafts, horticulture and hunting that they were able to settle year round in villages. In fact, the Cro-Magnon built long houses of wood and stone that were large enough to easily provide shelter for up to 20-25 adults and children at a time. These long houses were about 50 feet long and 20 or more feet wide. These were not merely makeshift accommodations that could be moved at whim. The houses were set on stone foundations that were sunk 2-3 feet into the ground. These houses also contained bedrooms, common living areas (or living rooms), kilns and fireplaces, as well as stone storage vaults where meat and other perishables could be easily stored for weeks at a time.

By contrast, the Neanderthals were still living in cold, damp caves.

"Long houses" are associated with matriarchal, female dominated societies. In these societies

Figure 114."Venus" figurines. Upper Paleolithic Goddesses.

daughters and the daughters of daughters never leave home but live with their mothers and grand-mothers, thus forming extended families living under one roof, the long house. Men marry into these households, and together these households would make up a village or small town which would be governed by the matriarchs. Therefore it can be deduced that Cro-Magnon society was also matriarchal as is also indicated by the widespread religious cult of the goddess.

By 15,000 years ago, they were already living in great cities of thousands of people; cities surrounded by woodland and small farms and fields of wild wheat. Stone sickles and grinding stones were in use 20,000 years ago which allowed for the harvesting and milling of wild and domestic grains. Moreover, they probably made beer from the grain and may well have discovered that wine could be produced from the fermented grape. Hence, the Cro-Magnon people invented civilization over 20,000 years ago; which is exactly what the oldest written records and the ancient Sumerian, Egyptian and Mayan Kings lists patiently explain.

However, not all Cro-Magnon were city dwellers. Many made their homes out of animal skins that were sewn together thus forming tents. The tents were held together by poles and were anchored to the ground by wooden posts.

The massive efficiency by which these people were able to hunt, gather, forage, as well as plant and harvest their own grains not only resulted in a very well rounded and healthy diet but increased leisure time. Indeed, these people may well have arrived at a 3 day work week 35,000 years ago; leisure time that could be devoted to the development of other pursuits and interests, such as the acquisition of material goods and wealth and the seeking of knowledge and spiritual wisdom; wisdom and knowledge not just of this world, but of the next one.

THE LIMBIC SYSTEM AND SPIRITUAL SYMBOLISM

Middle Paleolithic peoples and those of the Upper Paleolithic buried their dead with grave offerings and with the body placed in sleeping positions. These peoples believed in an afterlife and a spirit world which could be entered through a doorway of dreams. According to the ancients, the soul could exit the body when dreaming and following death.

Because these ancient peoples were capable of experiencing love, fear, and mystical and religious awe, and as they believed in spirits and ghosts, they evolved religious rituals and religious symbolism to help them communicate with and gain control over the spiritual realms. These rites included the development or discovery of signs and symbols which could generate religious awe regardless of time or culture.

For example, in addition to their complex mortuary practices, one of the first signs of exceedingly ancient religious symbolism is an engraved "cross" that is perhaps between 60,000 to 100,000 years old (Mellars, 1989). Likewise, the underground entrance to the Chauvet cathedral, in France, is marked by a large red cross that was painted 35,000 years ago (Chauvet et al., 1996).

Regardless of time and culture, from the Aztecs, Mayans, American Indians, Romans, Greeks, Africans, Christians, Cro-Magnons, Egyptians (the key of life), and so on, the cross consistently

Figure 115. *Gathering Goddesses. Large gathering group of women filling their baskets with fruits, grains, and produce from their gardens of Eden. Engraving from the 16th century.*

appears in a mystical context, and/or is attributed tremendous cosmic or spiritual significance (Budge ,1994; Campbell, 1988; Joseph, 2000a; Jung, 1964; Sitchin, 1990).

The "sign of the cross" is found in almost all cultures and generally signifies religious or cosmic significance, e.g. the four seasons, the two equinoxes and two solstices. The sign of the cross was the ideogram of An, the Sumerian giver of all life from which rained down the seeds of life on all worlds including the worlds of the gods. An of the cross gave life to the gods, and to woman and man.

The symbol of the cross is in fact associated with innumerable gods and goddesses, including Anu of the ancient Egyptians (who is identical to An), the Egyptian God Seb, the Goddess Nut, the God Horus (the hawk), as well as Christ and the Mayan and Aztec God, Quetzocoatl. For example, like the Catholics, the Mayas and Aztecs adorned their temples with the sign of the cross. Quetzocoatl, like Jesus, was a god of the cross.

In China the equilateral cross is represented as within a square which represents the Earth, the meaning of which is: "God made the Earth in the form of a cross." It is noteworthy that the Chinese cross-in-a-box can also be likened to the swastika—also referred to as the "gammadion" which is one of the names of the Lord God: "Tetragammadion"

Swastikas, the crooked cross, also appear across cultures and is associated with the gods, with the heavens, with the creation of the Earth, e.g., the four corners of the Earth, and the four corners of the heavens; and with sexuality, the fertility of the Earth. The swastika is a sex symbol. Four men or women lying together on their sides engaged in mutual masturbation and oral-anal sex.

The commonalty in religious significance associated with the cross may have to do with the "four corners" of the world and the heavens; that is, the two equinoxes and the two solstices. As ancient priests and shamans turned their eyes to the heavens, seeking to peer beyond the mystery that separated this world from the next, the "four corners" and the constellation in which the sun rose on the solstice or equinox, may have been a common astronomical method of divining the the will of the gods, and for navigation, localization, and calculation. And there may have been stars that were aligned together like today's southern cross, and these constellations may have also been observed by priests and shamans as they turned their eyes to the heavens, and who viewed these celestial symbols as having heavenly significance.

Yet another factor may be due to the shared commonalty of the limbic system, which contains feature detecting neurons sensitive to geometric stimuli including the sign of the cross. The brain structures of the limbic system, e.g., amygdala and hippocampus, and inferior temporal lobe, have been repeatedly implicated in the generation of fear, love, intense emotions, and religious and spiritual beliefs (Bear 1979; Daly 1958; d'Aquili and Newberg 1993; Gloor 1986, 1992; Halgren 1992; Horowitz et al. 1968; Jaynes 1976; Joseph 1992a, 1998a; MacLean 1990; Mesulam1981; Penfield and Perot1963; Rolls 1992; Schenk and Bear 1981; Slater and Beard 1963; Subirana and Oller-Daurelia, 1953; Trimble 1991; Weingarten, et al. 1977; Williams 1956).

The amygdala is able to receive, process and integrate multiple signals from all the sensory modalities simultaneously. The amygdala enables us to hear "sweet sounds," recall "bitter memories," or determine if something is spiritually significant, sexually enticing, or good to eat (Gloor 1986, 1992, 1997; Halgren 1992; Joseph 1992a, 1996; Kling et al., 1987; O'Keefe and Bouma 1969; Rolls 1992; Ursin and Kaada 1960).

Figure 116. *Paleolithic fertility rites. Dancing Paleolithic Goddess surrounded by female dancers.*

The amygdala enables us to experience the spiritually sublime, is concerned with the most basic animal emotions, and allows us to store emotional and personally significant experiences in memory.

The amygdala also makes it possible for us to reexperience these memories when awake or during the course of a dream in the form of visual, auditory, or religious or spiritual imagery (Bear 1979; d'Aquili and Newberg 1993; Gloor 1986, 1992, 1997; Halgren, 1992). It is the amygdala which enables an individual to experience emotions such as love and religious rapture, as well as the ecstasy associated with orgasm, and the dread and terror associated with the unknown. It also appears to generate religious and spiritual significance when presented with the sign of the cross.

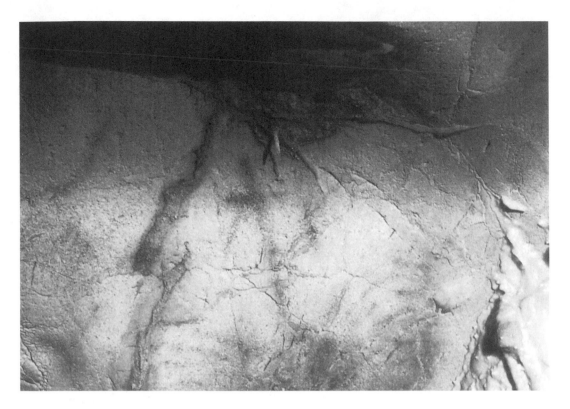

Figure 117. *The entrance to the underground Upper Paleolithic cathedral. The Chauvet cave. Note the sign of the cross. Reprinted from Chauvet et al., (1996). Dawn of Art: The Chauvet Cave. Henry H. Adams. New York.*

Figure 118. *The sign of the cross appears appears across cultures, e.g., the Maya, Aztecs, Chaldeans, Hindus, Persians, Paleolithic American Indians, Chinese. In China the equilateral cross is represented as within a square which represents the Earth, the meaning of which is: "God made the Earth in the form of a cross." It is noteworthy that the Chinese cross-in-a-box can also be likened to the swastika—also referred to as the "gammadion."*

Figure 106. *The swatiska is a sex symbol and associated with sexuality; i.e., four people laying side by side performing felatio or cunnilingus upon one another*

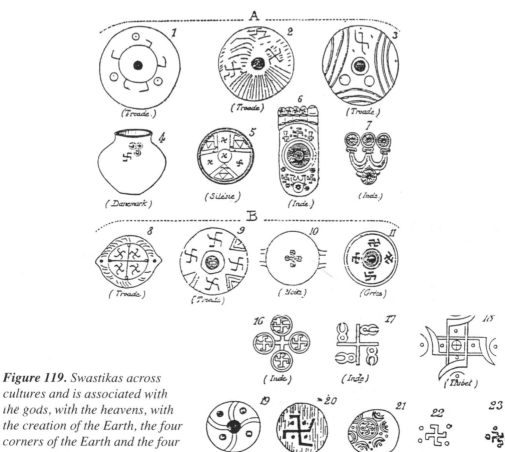

Figure 119. *Swastikas across cultures and is associated with the gods, with the heavens, with the creation of the Earth, the four corners of the Earth and the four corners of the heavens.*

Figure 120. *(Top) The God Seb supporting the Goddess Nut who represents heaven. Note the repeated depictions of the key of life; i.e. a ring with a cross at the end.(right) Quetzocoatal. (Below) Examples of cross-cultural crosses.*

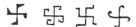

SOLAR CROSSES.[1]

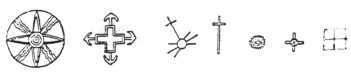

VARIETIES OF THE GAMMADION.

GAMMADIONS.

CROSS-RECOGNITION NEURONS

The inferior temporal lobe, and thus the amygdala and hippocampus, appears to have been well developed in "archaics," and Neanderthals, comparable, grossly, to the temporal lobes of Upper Paleolithic and present day peoples (Joseph, 1996, 2000a). It is these cerebral structures which have made it possible to experience as well as to attribute spiritual or religious significance to certain actions and geometric signs and stimuli.

Along the neocortical surface of the inferior temporal lobe and the amygdala are dense neuronal fields that contain neurons that fire selectively in response to visual images of faces, hands, eyes, and complex geometric shapes, including crosses (Gross et al. 1972; Hasselmo, Rolls and Baylis, 1989; Morris et al., 1996; Richmond, et al. 1983, 1987; Rolls 1984, 1992). These neurons are sometimes referred to as "feature detectors." The ability to recognize faces, geometric shapes, and social emotional nuances are dependent on these specialized temporal lobe and amygdala feature-detecting neurons (Gross, et al. 1972; Hasselmo et al. 1989; Morris et al., 1996; Richmond, et al. 1983, 1987; Rolls 1984). Together these structures interact to create complex neural networks that respond selectively to these stimuli, such that, when perceiving a face or a cross the amygdala and temporal lobe become activated.

If the amygdala and overlying temporal lobe were destroyed, the individual would lose the

Figure 121. *Aton, the sun God. Note rays of sunlight becoming caressing hands.*

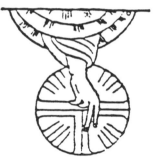

Figure 122. *The hand of "god" emerging from a cloud, with the finger tips emitting rays of light, as if the hand were "a living sun." 9th Century. Paris.*

Figure 123. *The all-seeing eye of God. Painting by Jan Provost, 15th century.*

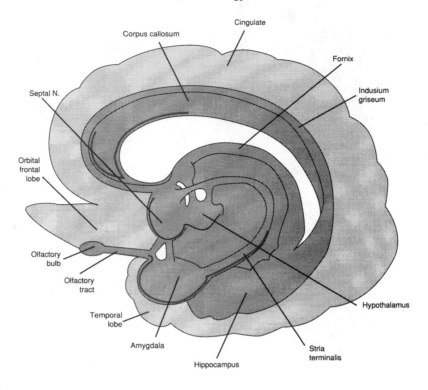

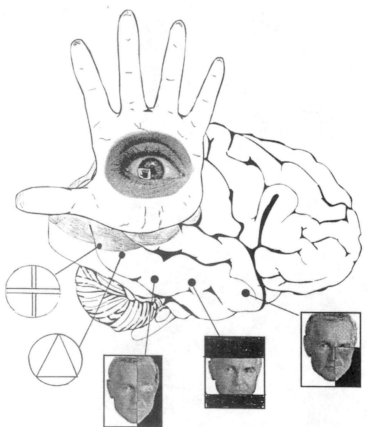

Figure 124. Top: The Limbic System. Above: The parietal lobe has been referred to as a "lobe of the hand." Neurons within the inferior temporal lobe respond to foveal and the upper visual field, and contain "facial" and "feature" detection neurons.

ability to perceive faces or complex geometric stimuli. They would lose the capacity to feel love, or recognize family or friends. Isolation would be preferred. They would also cease to experience emotional or spiritual awe in reaction to religious symbols, such as the sign of the cross.

THE AMYGDALA AND SPIRITUAL SYMBOLISM

Neurons in the amygdala and inferior temporal are multimodally responsive, receiving and integrating signals from all sensory association areas simultaneously (Gloor 1986, 1992, 1997; Halgren 1992; Joseph 1992a, 1996; Kling et al., 1987; O'Keefe and Bouma 1969; Rolls 1992; Ursin and Kaada 1960). Because these structures contain feature detectors and subserve almost all aspects of emotion, including religious feeling, it is possible for faces, hands, eyes, and geometric symbols to become infused with, or to stimulate, mystical and religious feeling, including for example, the "evil eye." The amygdala located in the right temporal lobe in fact becomes exceedingly excited when it detects that someone is gazing directly at them.

Abnormal activation of the amygdala-temporal lobe is also associated with the experience of frightening hallucinations—due to the activation of these feature-detecting neurons (Gloor, 1997; Joseph, 1992a, Halgren, 1992). The emotion is aroused in response to the hallucination, but is also generated internally even in the absence of a hallucination; fear being the most common reaction associated with amygdala activation (Davis et al., 1997; Gloor, 1997; LeDoux, 1996).

Moreover, as these nuclei respond selectively to stimuli such as crosses or when being stared at, heightened emotional activity within these limbic nuclei could result in feelings of fear, foreboding, or religious awe which is attributed to objects such as "crosses" or the "evil eye." Crosses, eyes, faces, and related emotions may also be hallucinated if the related feature-detecting neurons are also activated.

Similar explanations could be offered in regard to the spiritual significance attributed to triangles (i.e. pyramids), circles, hands, and eyes. The amygdala and overlying temporal lobe also become activated in response to these perceptual stimuli. In fact, crosses, triangles and circles were etched on Cro-Magnon cave walls over 35,000 years ago (Chauvet et al., 1996), whereas hands, and eyes repeatedly appear in mystical contexts.

However, as to the triangle (which is also the shape of a pyramid), this had long been a sex symbol, and a symbol of fertility, as long ago as the Upper Paleolithic. The triangle is associated with the outer shape of a woman's vagina—the gateway to the womb, the source of life. And, the amygdala is not only responsive to triangles, but it is one of the primary structures responsible for generating sexual arousal.

Hence, it can be assumed that "cross" and "pyramid" neurons as well as "mystical/religious" feeling neurons (or neural networks) had probably evolved by 35,000 and perhaps 100,000 years ago—possibly in reaction to repeated exposure to a woman's naked body, and the experience of "cross-like" stimuli in nature. One need only rise their arms horizontally or walk in the forest to spy dead trees that take the form of a "cross," or look upward to view birds with extended cross-like wings soaring through the skies. The sign of the cross is not uncommon and when staring at a cross the temporal lobes and the amygdala are activated.

Likewise, a woman with her legs spread, or in the act of giving birth, would have also generated extremely intense emotions, ranging from sexual arousal in reaction to her triangular-shaped vagina, to the dread and fear associated with the life creating potential of the womb and the great unknown.

THE FRONTAL LOBES & SPIRITUAL SYMBOLISM

The evolution and expansion of the frontal lobe and the inferior parietal lobe, have significantly contributed to the evolution of language, tool technology, and artistic symbolism (Joseph 1993, 1999e). Over the course of mammalian, primate and human evolution, the frontal lobes have signficantly expanded in size and complexity, reaching their greatest degree of development in humans (Fuster, 1997). Likewise, with the evolution of modern humans, a wholly unique structure also evolved: the angular gyrus of the inferior parietal lobe (Joseph, 1999e).

As is well known, the frontal lobes serve as the "senior executive" of the brain, cognition, and personality, regulating information processing throughout the cerebrum (Fuster 1997; Joseph 1986a, 1999a; Passingham 1993; Selemon et al. 1995; Shallice & Burgess 1991; Stuss & Benson 1986), including, via Broca's area, the expression of symbolic speech. The frontal lobes are primary in regard to all aspects of imagination, creativity, and symbolic thinking. Hence, the evolution and

Figure 125. *The pyramid/triangle often appears in a mystical context and is associated with the life giving attributes of the Great Goddess, the Mother of All. Specifically, the pyramid/triangle is associated with a woman's vagina, the source of new life.*

expansion of the anterior portion of the brain confer greater creative, cognitive, linguistic and intellectual capabilities upon those so endowed.

Likewise, the angular gyrus of the inferior parietal lobe (IPL) plays an important role in language, symbolic thinking, as well as artistry, drawing, creativity, tool use and manipulation (Joseph 1982, 1993, 1999e; Kimura 1993; Strub & Geschwind 1983). The IPL/angular gyrus sits at the junction of the tactile, visual, and auditory association areas, and assimilates, sequentially organizes, and injects this material into the stream of language and thought.

Hominoids (and other non-human mammals) lack an angular gyrus (Geschwind 1965) and their artistic talents, symbolic abilities, and tool-making capabilities are limited to hammering with rocks, and throwing or manipulating leaves, sticks, and twigs (Boesch & Tomasello 1998; Fedigan 1992; Goodall 1986, 1990; McGrew & Marchant 1992).

The tool making tradition of H. habilis was exceedingly primitive, consisting or rocks that had been banged together in order to arrive at a desired shape. Hence, it can be concluded that H. habilis had not yet evolved an angular gyrus and that the frontal lobe had no expanded beyond that of other primates such as chimpanzees. It can be also be concluded (see below) that H. habilis had not yet evolved the ability to speak in a manner even remotely resembling the speech of modern humans—an impression that is also bolstered by their poorly developed (pre-) frontal lobe, a region that contains Broca's expressive speech area.

THE NEANDERTHAL VS CRO-MAGON FRONTAL LOBE

The human frontal lobes serve as the "Senior Executive" of the brain and personality (Fuster 1997; Joseph 1986a, 1999a; Passingham 1993; Selemon, Goldman-Rakic & Tamminga 1995; Shallice & Burgess 1991; Stuss & Benson 1986), and are "interlocked" via converging and reciprocal connections with the limbic system, striatum, thalamus, and the primary, secondary, and multi-modality associational areas including Wernicke's area and the IPL (Fuster 1997; Jones & Powell 1970; Goldman-Rakic 1995, 1996; Pandya 1988; Pandya & Yeterian 1990; Petrides & Pandya 1988). Through these interactional pathways, the frontal lobes are able to coordinate and regulate attention, memory, personality, and information processing throughout the neocortex so as to direct intellectual, creative, artistic, symbolic, and cognitive processes (Fuster 1997; Goldman-Rakic 1995, 1996; Joseph 1986a, 1999a; Luria 1980; Passingham 1993; Shallice & Burgess 1991; Stuss & Benson 1986).

As based on human (and animal) experimental and case studies, it is well established that the frontal lobes enable humans to think symbolically, creatively, imaginatively, and to plan for the future and to consider the consequences of certain acts, to formulate secondary goals, and to keep one goal in mind even while engaging in other tasks, so that one may remember and act on those goals at a later time (Fuster 1997; Goldman-Rakic 1995, 1996; Joseph 1986a, 1999a; Luria 1980; Shallice & Burgess 1991; Stuss & Benson 1986). Selective attention, planning skills, and the ability to marshal one's intellectual resources so as to not only remember but achieve those goals, and the capacity to anticipate the future rather than living in the past, are capacities clearly associated with the frontal lobes (Fuster 1997; Joseph 1986a, 1999a; Stuss & Benson 1986).

In addition, the right and left frontal lobes respectively subserve the expression of emotional-melodic, and vocabulary-rich grammatical speech (Gorelick & Ross 1987; Joseph 1982, 1986a, 1988a, 1999a,e; Ross 1993). Specifically, upon receiving converging impulses from the IPL and the language and auditory areas in the temporal lobes, Broca's area (and its emotional speech producing counterpart in the right frontal lobe) act on the immediately adjacent secondary and primary motor areas which control, regulate and program the oral laryngeal musculature (Foerster 1936; Fox 1995; Joseph 1982, 1988a, 1999e,f). Therefore, the ability to express one's thoughts, ideas, and emotions through complex speech is made possible by the frontal lobes.

Although endocasts should not be employed to localize functional landmarks such as Broca's area, they are useful for making gross determinations as to the overall size and configuration of the cerebrum and the lobes of the brain. In this regard, and as based on cranial comparisons, or endocasts using the temporal and frontal poles as reference points, it has been demonstrated that the brain has tripled in size, and that the frontal lobes have significantly expanded In length and height over the course of human evolution and during the Middle to Upper Paleolithic transition (Blinkov and Glezer 1968; Joseph 1993; MacLean 1990; Tilney 1928; Weil 1929; Wolpoff 1980). Cro-Magon people were obviously superiorly endowed as compared to Neanderthals.

For example, it is apparent (see figures), that the height of the frontal portion of the skull is greater in the six foot tall, anatomically modern Upper Paleolithic H. sapiens sapiens (Cro-Magnon)

Figure 126. *A modern (dotted line) mesolithic cranium compared with a more ancient cranium (solid line). Arrows indicate the main average changes in skull structure including a reduction in the length of the occiput and an increase and upward expansion in the frontal cranial vault. Reproduced from M. H. Wolpoff (1980), Paleo-Anthropology. New York, Knopf.*

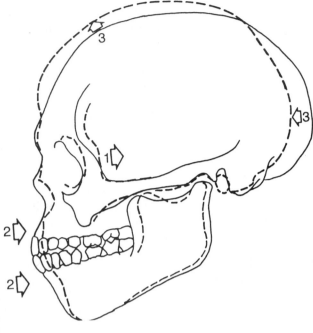

versus Neanderthal/archaic H. sapiens (see also Wolpoff 1980, Table 12.1; and Tilney, 1928). Hence, impoverished Neanderthal frontal lobe development and expanded Cro-Magon frontal lobe capacity is indicated. Indeed, the characteristic "slopping forehead" was an obvious limiting factor in archaic and Neanderthal frontal lobe development). The Cro-Magnon brain was significantly larger than the Neanderthal brain, with volumes ranging from around 1600 to1880 cc on average compared with 1,033 to 1,681 cc for Neanderthals (Blinikov & Głezer 1968; Clark 1967; Day 1986; Holloway 1985b; Roginskii & Lewin 1955; Wolpoff 1980).

The differential evolution of the Cro-Magnon vs the Neanderthal frontal lobe (and angular gyrus) is also apparent as based on paleo-neurological and neuropsychological analysis of tool and hunting technology, artistic and symbolic development, and social organization in the Upper vs the Middle Paleolithic (Joseph 1993). As will be detailed below, the angular gyrus probably emerged and Broca's area probably became fully functional during the Middle to Upper Paleolithic transition; evolutionary developments which likely contributed to the demise of the Neanderthals.

Since Cro-Magnon's shared the planet with Neanderthals during overlapping time periods (and coupled with evidence reviewed below) it certainly seems reasonable to assume that the expansion and evolution of the frontal lobe and angular gyrus, provided these people with an obvious competitive advantage as they clearly dwarfed the Neanderthals in all aspects of cultural, intellectual, social, linguistic and technological achievement. Hence, endowed with a bigger brain and expanded frontal and IPL/angular gyral capacity, the cognitively, linguistically, technologically and intellectually superior "Cro-Magnons" and other "modern" Upper Paleolithians, probably engaged in wide spread ethnic cleansing and exterminated the rather short (5ft 4in.), sloped-headed, heavily muscled Neanderthals, eradicating all but hybrids from the face of the Earth, some 35,000 to 28,000 years ago.

By contrast, whereas the Neanderthals frontal lobe is not as well developed, the occipital and superior parietal areas are larger in length and breadth (Wolpoff, 1980). However, these posterior regions of the brain are concerned with visual analysis and positioning the body in space (see chapters 20, 22). As male and female Neanderthals spent a considerable amount of their time engaged in hunting activities (see below), scanning the environment for prey and running and throwing in visual space were more or less ongoing concerns. A large occipital and superior parietal lobe would reflect these activities.

Because the modern frontal lobe is so extensive and highly developed, and as different frontal regions have evolved at different times periods and are organized differently and have different neuroanatomical connections, they are concerned with different functions (chapter 19; see also Fuster 1997; Joseph, 1999a). For example, about one third of the frontal lobe, i.e. the motor areas, are concerned with initiating, planning, and controlling the movement of the body and fine motor functioning. It is this part of the "archaic" and Neanderthal frontal lobe that appears to be most extensively developed.

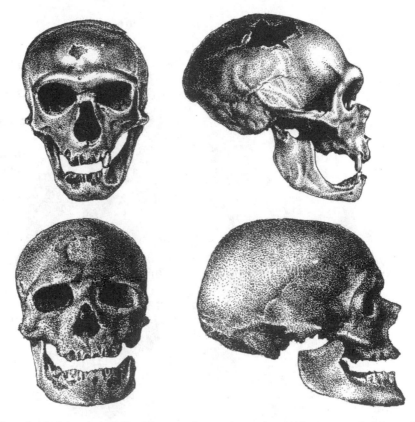

Figure 127. *Neanderthal (top) and Cro Magnon (bottom) craniums. Note expanded frontal region of skull in Cro-Magnon.*

The "orbital frontal lobes" acts to inhibit and control motivational and emotional impulses arising from within the limbic system (chapter 19). Via orbital frontal interconnections with the limbic system it is possible for emotions to be represented as ideas, and for ideas to trigger emotions. An examination of the "archaic" H. sapien and Neanderthal orbital area (i.e. endocasts) suggests a relative paucity of development.

The more recently evolved anterior (pre-) frontal lobe and the lateral frontal convexity are highly important in imaginative and creative thinking and regulating the transfer of information to the neocortex. These structrures are involved in perceptual filtering, and exerting steering influences on the neocortex so as to direct attention and intellectual processes (Como, Joseph, Forrest, Fiducia, Siegel, 1979; Heilman & Van Den Abel, 1980; Joseph, et al. 1981; Joseph, 1986a, 1999a). That is, the anterior half of the frontal lobes act to mediate and coordinate information processing throughout the brain by continually sampling, monitoring, inhibiting and thus controlling and regulating perceptual, cognitive, and neocortical activity. And, in receiving this information, the frontal lobes play a significant role in all aspects of symbolic and imaginative thinking, including those thoughts pertaining to the symbolism and meaning of the spiritually sublime and religious experience.

Moreover, social skills, planning skills, the formation of long range goals, the ability to marshal one's resources so as to achieve those goals, and the capacity to consider and anticipate the future, rather than living in the past, as well as develop alternative problem solving strategies and consider a multiple range of ideas simultaneously, are capacities clearly associated with frontal lobe functional integrity. Hence, an individual is able to not only anticipate the future and the consequences of certain acts, but can formulate and plan secondary goals which depend on the completion of one's initially planned actions. Indeed, the capacity to decide to do something later, to remember and do it later, and to dream and fantasize and to visualize the future as pure possibility are made possible via the frontal lobes. It is the evolution of the anterior regions of the frontal lobe which have made abstract thinking and abstract reasoning possible, and to express these thoughts symbolically via language or artistic symbolism.

Conversely, when the frontal lobes have been damaged, or when the "prefrontal" lobes have been disconnected from the rest of the brain (such as following pre-frontal lobotomy), status seeking,

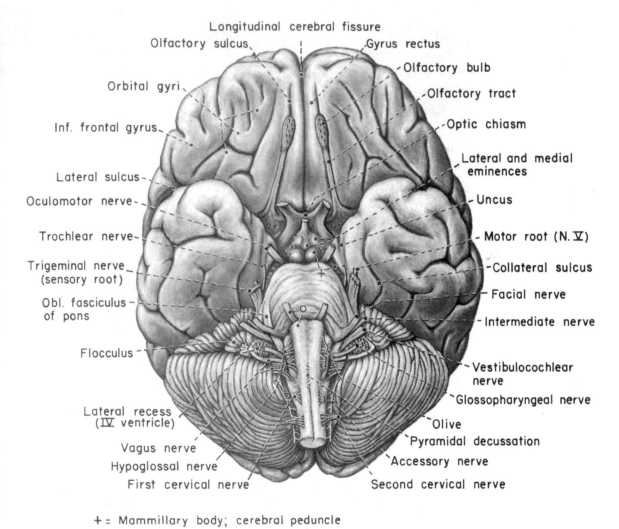

Figure 128. Ventral surface of the brain, depciting the orbital frontal lobes. From M. Carpenter, 1991. Core Text of Neuroanatomy, Williams & Wilkins.

social concern, foresight, and emotional, motivational, intellectual, conceptual, initiative, problem solving and organization skills are negatively impacted (Fuster 1997; Joseph, 1986a, 1999a; Luria, 1980; Passingham 1993). Frontal lobe damage or surgical disconnection of the pre-frontal lobe reduces one's ability to profit from experience, to anticipate consequences, or to learn from errors by modifying future behavior. There is a reduction in creativity, dreaming, abstract reasoning, symbolic thinking, or the capacity to synthesize interrelated ideas into concepts or to grasp situations in their entirety. Interests of a social or intellectual nature are diminished, or, with severe damage, abolished (Fuster 1997; Joseph 1986a, 1988a, 1999a; Luria 1980; Stuss & Benson 1986). Planning skills, long range goal formation, concern for the future, clothing, personal adornments, symbolism, social status, the thoughts of others and personal identity, matter little.

In addition, language functioning is typically disrupted, with damage to the left frontal lobe, i.e. Broca's area, resulting in severe reductions in speech output and with right frontal injuries producing excessive and delusional speech. However, with damage to the right frontal lobe, the emotional and melodic aspects of speech may become disrupted.

Thus the right and left frontal lobe not only contribute to imagination and symbolic thought, but produce the grammatical, temporal sequential, and melodic aspects of modern human speech. In this regard, it can be concluded, based not only on an examination of differences in the Cro-Magon vs Neanderthal skull, but in the paucity of Neanderthal symbolism or artistry, that the Cro-Magnon

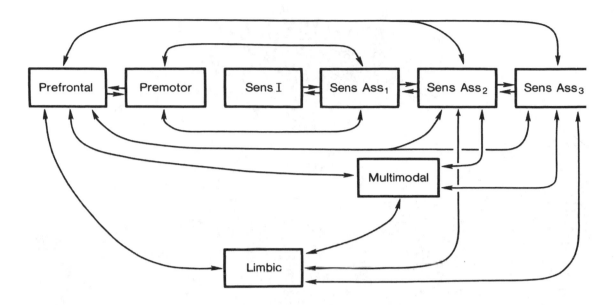

Figure 129. Schematic diagram of the organization of the sensory areas and their connections to the frontal lobe. From Gloor, 1997, The Temporal Lobe and Limbic System. Oxford University Press.

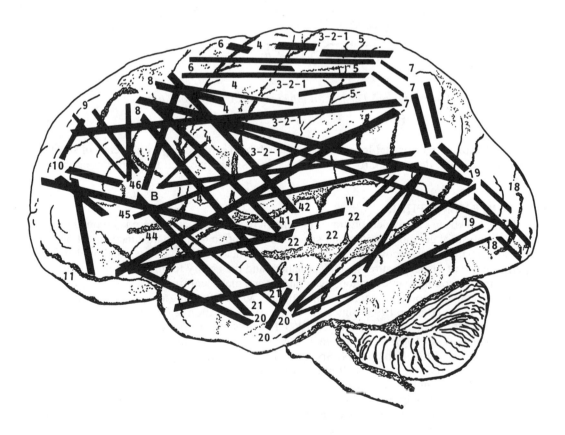

Figure 130. Schematic diagram of the organization of the frontal receiving areas. From Joseph, 1990.

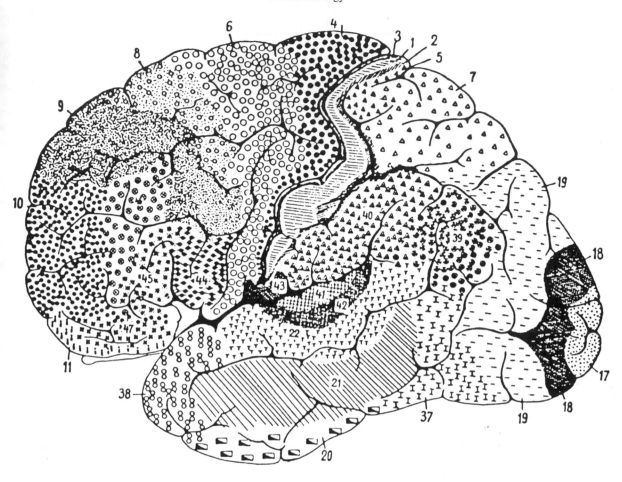

Figure 131. The left hemisphere. The frontal lobe includes Brodmann's areas: 4,6,8,9,10,11,12,44,45,46, etc.,

was blessed with a larger frontal lobe. Hence, although both groups display evidence of spirituality and belief in life after death, the Cro-Magon were able to symbolize their thoughts through religious artistry.

THE RIGHT HEMISPHERE

It has now been clearly demonstrated that the right cerebral hemisphere is dominant over the left in the analysis of geometric and visual-space, the perception of depth, distance, direction, shape, orientation, position, perspective, and figure-ground, the detection of complex and hidden figures, the performance of visual closure, gestalt formation, and the ability to infer the total stimulus configuration from incomplete information, route finding and maze learning, localizing targets in space, drawing and copying complex geometric-like figures and performing constructional tasks, block designs and puzzles (Benton 1993; Butters & Barton, 1970; Carmon & Bechtoldt, 1969; DeRenzi & Scotti, 1969; DeRenzi et al. 1969; Ettlinger, 1960; Fontenot, 1973; Franco & Sperry, 1977; Fried et al. 1982; Hannay et al., 1987; Kimura, 1966; 1969, 1993; Landis et al. 1986; Lansdell, 1968, 1970; Levy, 1974; Milner, 1968; Nebes, 1971; Sperry, 1982). It is for these and other reasons that the right brain is often viewed as the artistic half of the cerebrum.

Hence, if the right hemisphere is injured, the ability to draw and to perform visual-spatial and artistic tasks, is completely disrupted. Even when required to copy simple figures and drawings, patients with right cerebral injuries have trouble with general shape and organization, and their drawings and copies are grossly distorted and/or characterized by left sided neglect.

However, although the right frontal lobes play a significant role in symbolic thinking, fantasy, and artistry, it is the right inferior parietal lobe (IPL) and the angular gyrus of the IPL, which has

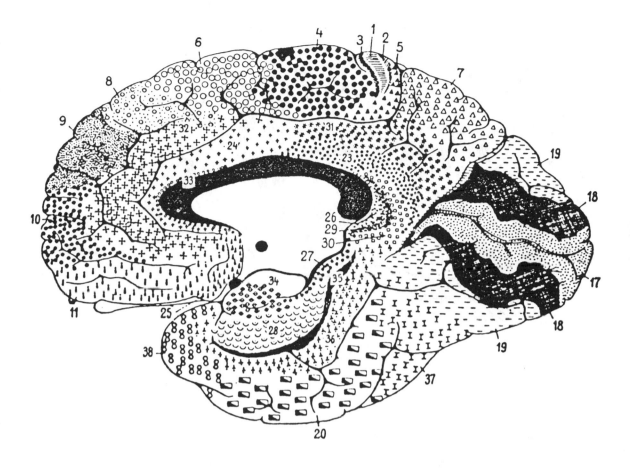

Figure 132. A medial view of the right hemisphere. The frontal lobe includes Brodmann's areas: 4,6,8,9,10,11,12, etc.,

shown to be crucially important in performing artistic tasks. Hence, if the right IPL is injured, the patient may demonstrate what is called "Constructional Apraxia."

Likewise, injury to the left IPL (and angular gyrus) can create apraxic disturbances. However, in these cases, it is the ability to use tools and not visual-spatial or artistic functioning per se, which is effected. On the otherhand, since both the right and left IPL are intimately interconnected with the frontal lobes, and the speech areas, damage to the left IPL can also disrupt speech and language.

THE INFERIOR PARIETAL LOBE

The angular gyrus of the inferior parietal lobule (IPL) is unique to humans (Geschwind, 1965), and is crucially evolved in artistic and constructional tasks, and in controlling temporal sequential hand movements including the manipulation of external objects and internal impressions (De Renzi and Lucchetti, 1988; Heilman et al., 1982; Kimura, 1993; Strub and Geschwind, 1983). As first detailed by Joseph (1982, 2000) the evolution of the angular gyrus enabled humans to engage in complex creative, symbolic, and artistic activities involving a series of related steps, to create and utilize tools, to produce and comprehend complex gestures, such as American Sign Language, and to express and perceive grammatical relationships—capacities which are disrupted with lesions localized to the IPL. In fact, the motor engrams that make possible artistic, constructional and temporal and sequential motor acts, including those involved in grammatical verbal expression, are partly localized within the IPL (De Renzi and Lucchetti, 1988; Heilman et al., 1982; Kimura, 1993; Strub and Geschwind, 1983). In fact, the IPL not only interacts with but appears to program the frontal motor areas for the purposes of producing fine motor, temporal-sequential and artistic movements, including the vocalization of speech units.

Those devoid of an angular gyrus/IPL, or those who have suffered a severe injury to this area,

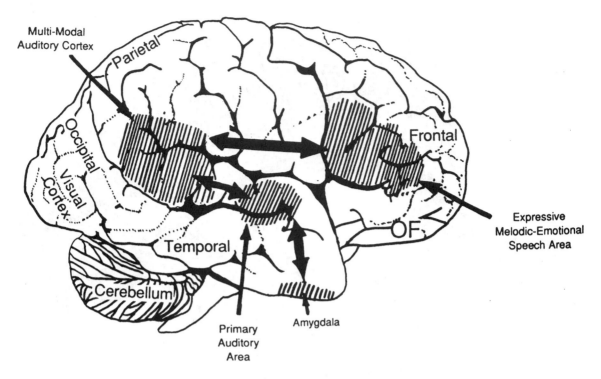

Figure 133. The melodic speech areas of the right hemisphere. From Joseph, 1988a.

are generally unable to draw complex objects or to correctly manipulate or fashion complex tools - much less utilize them in a complex temporal sequence. This condition is referred to as apraxia; i.e. an inability to perform tasks involving interrelated steps and sequences (De Renzi and Lucchetti, 1988; Geschwind, 1965; Heilman et al., 1982; Kimura, 1993). With severe left-sided IPL injuries, the individual may be unable to make a cup of coffee or put on their clothes, much less fashion or sew them together. Moreover, grammatical speech is disrupted and patients may suffer extreme word finding difficulty, or a conduction aphasia. That is, speech is no longer produced as Broca's area is disconnected from the IPL and Wernicke's area. Likewise, reading ability is disrupted as the left IPL not only comprehends and produces gestures but visual symbols including written language. By contrast, injuries to the right IPL completely disrupts the ability to draw simple and complex objects or to perform visual-spatial and artistic tasks.

Hence, the IPL/angular gyrus (including the frontal motor areas) makes possible the ability to fashion and manipulate tools and organizes speech into vocabulary-rich, temporal sequential grammatical units, as well as to draw, create symbols, or to engage in artistic tasks.

As apes do not possess an angular gyrus (Geschwind, 1965), it appears that over the course of evolution, with the development of right handedness and selective pressures acting on gene selection across gathering/tool-making generations, the IPL/angular gyrus emerged as an extension of the auditory area in the temporal lobe and the superior parietal visual-hand area. Indeed, the parietal lobes are considered a "lobe of the hand" and contain neurons which guide hand movements (Hyvarinen, 1982; Kaas, 1993; Lynch, 1980; Mountcastle et al., 1975, 1980) and which respond to visual input from the periphery and lower visual fields -the regions in which tool-making and tool-using hands are most likely to come into view.

Because most individuals would use the right hand for drawing or tool making and the left for holding the tool, it is the left parietal lobe (which monitors the right lower visual field and controls the right hand) that guides and visually observes, learns and memorizes hand-movements when gathering, gesturing, or manipulating some object or constructing a tool. By contrast, it is the right IPL and angular gyrus which is performing the visual-spatial analysis and which is guiding the left and right frontal motor areas, when using tools in order to create signs, symbols, and works of art.

Over the course of evolution and as experience and the environment act on gene selection and induce neural plasticity, the parietal (and superior temporal) lobe expanded, the angular gyrus emerged,

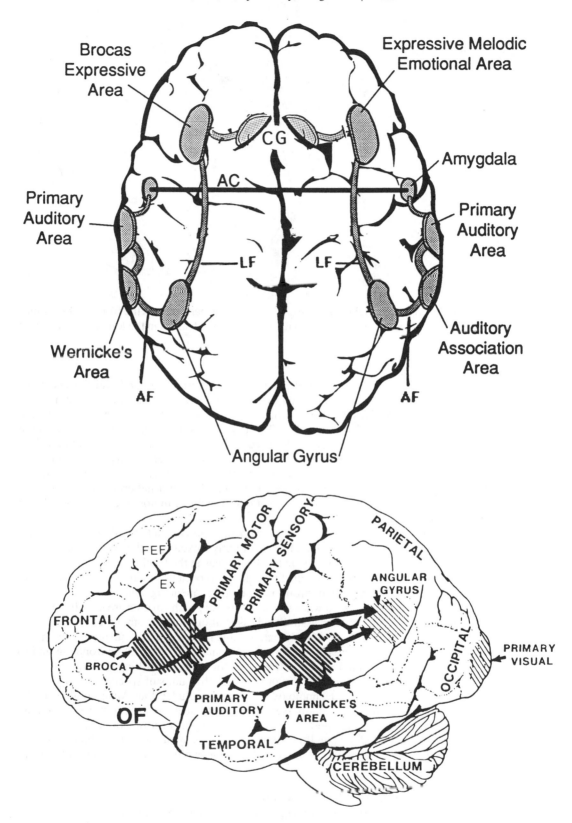

Figure 134. (Top) Superior view of the right and left hemisphere. From Joseph, 1996. (Bottom) The "Language Axis" of the left hemisphere. From Joseph, 1982.

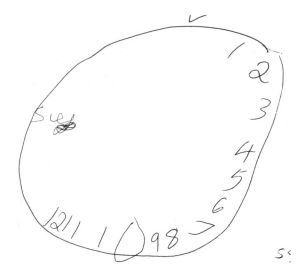

Figure 135. Drawing of a clock by a patient with right parietal injury, from Joseph, 1988a.

and neuroplastic alterations were induced in the adjoining motor-hand area in the frontal lobe including what would become Broca's speech area and the melodic speech areas in the left and right frontal lobes.

SYMBOLIC LANGUAGE

The angular gyrus sits at the junction of the posterior-superior temporal and the occipital-parietal lobes, and is critically involved in naming, word finding, grammatical speech organization, and is in part an extension of and links Wernicke's with Broca's area (Joseph, 1982, 1999e; Geschwind, 1965; Goodglass & Kaplan, 2000; Kimura, 1993). Through its extensive interconnections with the adjacent sensory association areas, the IPL/angular gyrus is a major convergence zone and receives and assimilates complex associations, thereby forming multi-modal concepts, and acts to symbolize, classify and name this material which is then injected into the stream of language and thought. The IPL/angular gyrus, in concert with Wernicke's area, transmits this information to Broca's speech area, which in turn organizes the immediately adacent oral, laryngeal motor areas (Foerster, 1936; Fox, 1995; Joseph, 1992, 1999a).

As the right and left frontal vocalization areas are richly interconnected with the anterior cingulate vocalization centers, wheras the temporal lobe is tightly linked with the amygdala, once the angular gyrus of the IPL evolved, thus linking the language areas at the level of the neocortex, "limbic language" (emotional speech mediated by the limbic system) became hierarchically represented, yoked to the neocortex and subject to fractionization, temporal sequencing, and multi-classification (Joseph, 1999d,e). Wernicke's area was now able to communicate with Broca's area, with the angular gyrus injecting temporal sequences and assimilated associations into the stream of language and thought. Hence, in addition to artistry, and manipulating tools in a temporal sequential fashion, the evolution of the IPL/angular gyrus enabled humans to manipulate the internal environment and to transmit symbolic and linguistic impulses to the frontal motor areas controlling the oral-laryngeal musculature, thereby reorganizing Broca's area in order to vocalize units of speech.

As based on an analysis of tool technology, it can be concluded that Australopithecus, H. habilis, H. erectus, and Neanderthals did not possess the neurological sophistication for vocalizing complex human language, and had not yet evolved an angular gyrus or a functional Broca's area. Rather, the evolution of modern speech and the ability to express symbols and symbolic and religious-spiritual thought, symbolically, likely corresponded to the evolution of the peoples of the Upper Paleolithic, the Cro-Magon.

INFERIOR PARIETAL LOBE & ANGULAR GYRUS

The IPL/angular gyrus sits at the junction of the tactile, visual, and auditory association areas, and assimilates, sequentially organizes, and injects this material into the stream of language and thought,

The angular gyrus of the inferior parietal lobe (IPL) also plays an important role in language, as well as artistry, creativity, tool use and manipulation (Joseph 1982, 1993, 1999e; Kimura 1993; Strub & Geschwind 1983). Hominoids (and other non-human mammals) lack an angular gyrus (Geschwind 1965) and their artistic, creative, tool-making capabilities are limited to hammering with rocks, and throwing or manipulating leaves, sticks, and twigs (Boesch & Tomasello 1998; Fedigan 1992; Goodal 1990; McGrew & Marchant 1992).

Likewise, the tool making tradition of H. habilis was exceedingly primitive, consisting or rocks that had been banged together in order to arrive at a desired shape. Hence, it can be concluded that H. habilis had not yet evolved an angular gyrus. Moreover, asit can be also be concluded (see below) that H. habilis had not yet evolved the ability to speak in a manner even remotely resembling the speech of modern humans—an impression that is also bolstered by their poorly developed (pre-) frontal lobe, a region that contains Broca's expressive speech area.

The parietal lobe is considered a "lobe of the hand" (Critchley 1953; Hyvarinen 1982; Kaas 1993; Lynch 1980; Mountcastle et al. 1975, 1980) whereas the angular gyrus/IPL contains the motor engrams responsible for the programming of complex temporal and sequential hand and figer movements, including those involved in tool making and utilization (Critchley 1953; De Renzi & Lucchetti 1988; Gerstmann 1930; Joseph 1999e; Heilman et al. 1982; Kimura 1993; Strub & Geschwind 1983). Hence, given the above, it can be assumed that the angular gyrus probably slowly evolved over the course the last two millions years in parallel with the establishment of handedness and hand-related activities as reflected in the evolution of tool technology. Given these trends and the association between right handedness, the left hemisphere, and language, it can also be assumed that not only the neural substrate for preferential hand use and tool making, but for modern human speech production and perception also gradually arose over the course of the last two million years.

The angular gyrus of the left hemisphere contains the "motor engrams" necessary for the performance of complex temporal sequential movements, including those involved in tool use and manufacture. In this regard, the angular gyrus/IPL is also a "lobe of the hand." Hence, with the evolution of the angular gyrus, the ability to use the fingers and the hand, particularly the right hand, in tasks requiring a series of sequential steps, including counting, also evolved. In consequence, if the left cerebral angular gyrus/IPL were severely injured, mathematical ability would be abolished, as would the capacity to perform tasks involving temporal-sequential movements; a conditions referred to as apraxia.

Non-human primates lack handedness or complex tool making or using capabilities. This is because the ability to make or utilize complex tools is dependent on the IPL/angular gyrus (Critchley 1953; De Renzi & Lucchetti 1988; Gerstman 1930; Geschwind 1965; Heilman et al. 1982; Kimura 1993). Hominoids lack an angular gyrus though they are endowed with an inferior-superior parietal lobe (areas 7b and 7ip), which, as noted contain neurons that guide hand movements, including grasping and manipulating. Hence, although they lack an angular gyrus, homoinoids, such as chimpanzees make and use simple tools such as rocks, leaves, and sticks (Boesch & Tomasello, 1998; Goodall 1986, 1990; McGrew & Marchant 1992). Hence, although H. habilis and Australopithecus, were using rocks as simple stone tools some 2.4 to 2.6 million years ago (Hamrick & Inouye 1995; McGrew 1995; Susman 1994; Semaw et al. 1997; White et al., 1999) this does not indicate that they had evolved an angular gyrus.

Moreover, although perhaps as many as 60% of Australopthecines, 70% of H. habilis and at least 80% of archaic H. sapiens may have been right handed (Cornford, 1986; Dart, 1953; Toth, 1985), given the rather unvarying and still simplistic Oldowan/Acheulean/Mousterian stone tool technologies associated with these groups, there is still no evidence that these species had evolved an angular gyrus—though certainly trends in this direction are evident.   Nevertheless, it was not until the Upper Paleolithic and the appearance of anatomically "modern" Paleolithic humans, including the Cro-Magnon, that tool making became literally an art and evolved beyond the use of rock and stone and complex multifaceted features were incorporated in their construction. It is at this stage of evolutionary development that we have clear functional and neuropsychological evidence for the evolution of the angular gyrus of the IPL.

Neanderthal tools were predominately "usc-spccific" and thus served, for the most part, a unidimensional purpose (Hayden, 1994). In fact, similar to children, the Neanderthals tended to use their mouth for manipulative tasks (Molnar, 1972; Trinkaus, 1992). Specifically, it Neanderthals would use their mouth for grasping and holding objects as well as chewing and softening items such as hides in order to soften them and make them more pliable. Although the Neanderthals used stone "knives" it is not until the rise of the Upper Paleolithic that highly complex blade and completely new, diverse, and multifaceted tool (Aurignacian) technologies became the norm (Jelinek, 1989; Leroi-Gourhan, 1964; Mellars, 1989). Moreover, with the Upper Paleolithic peoples, the capacity to impose form, to visualize multiple possibilities and to use natural contours and shapes in order to create not just tools but a variety of implements, decorations, and objects, came into being, including complex representational and mobile art, complex scaffolding to support cave artists, and the sewing needle (Leroi-Gourhan, 1964, 1982) -all of which requires an angular gyrus/IPL and a motor cortex capable of controlling fine hand and finger movements; not only so that they may be fashioned but employed correctly.

In contrast, there is no evidence of a sewing needle or complex tool construction among Neanderthal populations during the Middle Paleolithic, and the capacity to visualize possibilities in regard to shape and form, was comparatively absent as well (Binford, 1982; Mellars, 1989, 1996). Thus, it is with the evolution of the Cro-Magon, the angular gyrus and expansions in the frontal lobe which provided the neurological foundations for tool design and construction, the ability to sew and even wear clothes, and the capacity to create art, and pictorial language in the form of drawing, painting, sculpting, and engraving. It is the the evolution of these tissues which enabled human beings to not only create visual symbols but to talk about them and create verbal amd visual symbols in the form of written language and religious imagery.

Since there is no evidence for complex tool technology, complex abstract symbolic thinking, or an angular gyrus among Australopithecus, H. habilis, H. erectus archaic H. sapiens or Neanderthals, it thus appears that "modern" human linguistic and abstract symbolic abilities probably did not fully emerge until the evolution of the Cro-Magnon peoples. As in non-human primates, the thought processes, cognitive abilities, and language possessed by these earlier hominids, including Neanderthals, was likely emotional, limbic in origin, word-poor, and aggramatical and lacking in symbolism or abstract expressionism. Until the very end of their rein, Neanderthals and other ancient hominids simply lacked the the neurological foundation to produce vocabulary-rich, complex grammatical speech, or the capacity to give shape and symbolic form to their spiritual thoughts or religious beliefs.

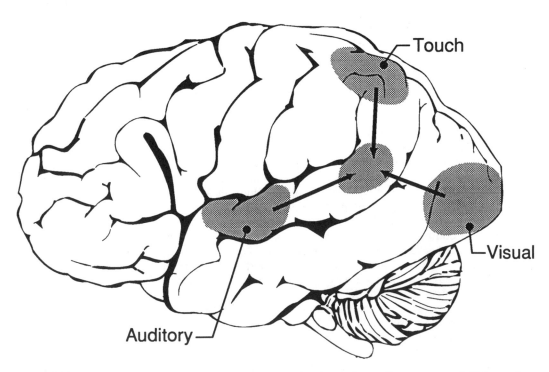

Figure 136. The inferior parietal lobe receives convering input from all sensory modalities and assimilates these associations to create complex multi-modal ideas, from Joseph, 1990.

AFTER-DEATH, ASTRAL PROJECTION
JUDGMENT DAY & THE SECOND DEATH
by R. Joseph

There are a variety of conditions which can hyperactive the limbic system, including death. The anticipation of death, the terror and dread of impending death, are also made possible by the limbic system. The limbic system can anticipate, and it can feel fear and anxiety in response to the unknown.

The Cro-Magnon, and peoples of the Neolithic practiced mortuary rituals because they could also see beyond death, beyond one's personal demise, which is why these earthen graves contained tools, food, and ornaments. The souls of the dead would need these items in the next world.

The dead, therefore, were believed to survive the experience of dying. It was believed that they would retain a personal identity, in the form of a personal soul, which would ascend to the heavens and join the abode of the spirits and the gods.

The ancients were exceedingly concerned about what happened after death, and what trials and tribulations they may experience in the hereafter. And they worried about evil spirits, and the behavior of those souls who when alive had committed evil on Earth.

To protect the living, the enemy dead were sometimes decapitated, their hands and legs removed, and their eyes sewn shut and faces smashed, so that their souls would be unable to rise from the dead and cause mischief in the afterlife. In this regard, the ancients did not necessarily believe that every soul would immediately ascend to heaven, but may remain tethered to the earth below.

Those souls that remain earth bound were often believed to be evil spirits, undeserving of a place among the gods. As detailed in the Egyptian and Tibetan Books of the Dead, it was also believed that some souls could lose their way and remain earthbound.

Yet others, such as the priesthood of the Roman Catholic Church, believed that souls almost never immediately ascended to heaven. Instead, the souls of the dead were believed to spend at least part of eternity in a realm called purgatory.

PURGATORY

Some conceive "purgatory" as a spirit-like world that exists between this reality and the reality of God. During the middle ages many Catholic theologians came to believe that the length of time a soul might remain in purgatory would depend on the nature and extent of their sins. Purgatory was like a jail sentence, and once sufficient punishment had been doled out, the soul was free to ascend to heaven.

Likewise, some of those of the Buddhist faith believed "that at death, the self, the Atman, departs to another world, where it works out the consequences of its karma. Some of these worlds were pleasant, others were hells where retribution was suffered for evil deeds. When the consequences of its karma was worked out, the self was reincarnated" (Brandon, 1967, p.171).

Others of the Christian faith also came to believe that upon death the soul merely goes to sleep; that sleep is the fate of the soul following death until a second awakening at the time of the final judgment.

According to John Calvin "the souls of the faithful, after completing their term of combat and travail, are gathered into rest, where they await with joy the fruition of their promised glory; and thus all things remain in suspense until Jesus Christ appears as the Redeemer."

The Koran endorses certain aspects of this view, such that the dead will have no knowledge of the time that has elapsed since their death. And when the soul awakes to experience judgment day, they will think they have just awakened from sleep. Hence, the soul was believed to be unconscious while the body decayed, and is awakened by the trumpet heralding the last judgment.

The ancients, however, believed that the soul could depart the body during sleep, and that death was the final liberation of the soul. The soul did not sleep. Instead the soul could remain earth bound and observe all that took place below, or ascend to heaven where it would be embraced by the light.

However, as pointed out by the Egyptian and Tibetan Books of the Dead, the soul might also be

Figure 137.
Jesus presiding over the judgement of those cast into hell (by Hans Memlinc).

embraced by darkness, or they may lose their way and could be harried for all eternity by demons and devilish monstrosities in the darkness of the underworld.

SUBTERRANEAN HELL

As the dead were often buried in the earth, it was believed by some that the soul may descend into the earth womb, into the subterranean realms of the spirits and gods of the dead.

The ancient Greeks believed that at death and with the dissolution of the unity of the body, thymos—the conscious self and the life principle—was released into the air, and transformed into a wraith, a shadowy image of the living person, known as the eidolon. It was the life principle, psyche, which descended into Hades, which was a huge subterranean pit deep beneath the ground. There the life principle became a wraith, and existed with other eidolons, but devoid of self-consciousness in a state of perpetual and eternal gloom.

Greek thought was in some respects basically identical to that of the Sumerians, Akkadians, Babylonians, and Israelites who believed that the spirits of all the dead dwelled for all eternity in a dreary, lightless, subterranean abode. According to the Sumerians and Akkadians death involved a horrible transformation where the dead became a diseased, decaying, grisly being which descended to the underworld, "the land of no return."

According to the Hebrews, this terrible realm of darkness was called She'ol. She'ol, was where kings and peasants, rich and poor, good and evil, existed in a state of equal and horrible wretchedness. Hades and the Hebrew She'ol are identical. The good and the wicked, rich and poor, kings and peasants, all descended into hell and assumed this wraith-like existence in the realm of the dead.

Yet others preached that only the evil go to this subterranean hell. The righteous, the just, and the good, ascend to heaven and live in bliss for all eternity. However, if one went to heaven or hell depended on how one had lived their life, and how they were judged by the gods.

"For those who have disbelieved... shall roast in fire... and their bellies and skin shall be melted. To them it is said: Taste the punishment of the burning." -Koran

THE EVOLUTION OF HELL

"Jesus said: There is a light within a man of light, and it lights up the whole world. If he does not shine, he is darkness." -Gospel of Thomas.

In contrast to the light and bliss of "heaven," Hell has commonly been associated with darkness and the underworld. In part, the notion of an underworld is a direct consequence of burial practices, and perhaps the belief that sinners will fail to rise to heaven but instead will be condemned to a bleak existence deep beneath the Earth.

The belief in an underworld where sinners burn in hell, is also related to the worship of the sun as god. That is, during the day the sun god rules the Earth, but each evening it must pass through the underworld where it may be attacked by the demons of darkness. Every night, therefore, the sun god would have to fight these demons, and would do so with the rays of the sun. That is, the sun-god would burn the enemies of god with the fire of the sun's rays. Hence, Hell also became associated with fire, such that, as these beliefs evolved, sinners and enemies of god would be sent to hell where they would not only be attacked by devils and demons, but would burn in flames for all eternity.

The belief in Hell and in demons and devils is world wide and vivid descriptions of a hellish underworld and its demonic denizens are also described in the Egyptian and Tibetan Books of the Dead. Indeed, these books were written so as to inform believers as to the mysteries of death and the trials and tribulations one might experience following death so that demons and other devilish monstrosities and misfortunes might be avoided.

For example, priests or relatives of the recently departed were expected to read various hymns, litanies, magical formula, spells, and incantations from the Egyptian Book of the Dead which would help protect the dead from the multitude of devils and fiends that would seek to devour and destroy the spirit-soul. "These powers of evil had hideous and terrifying shapes and forms, and their haunts infested the region through which the road of the dead lay when passing from this world to the Kingdom of Osiris" (Budge, 1994). According to the ancient Egyptians, the gods were basically powerless to protect the souls from these demons which could inflict horrible suffering upon the spirit souls for all eternity.

"Then the Lord of Death will place around thy neck a rope and drag thee along; he will cut off thy head, tear out thy heart, pull out thy intestines, lick up thy brain, drink thy blood, eat thy flesh, and gnaw thy bones; but thou will be incapable of dying. Even when the body is hacked to pieces, it

Figure 138. *(Above) The entrance to Heaven. By Hieronymus Bosch, 1500. (Right) Sinners cast into hell (by W. Blake).*

will revive again and thy will be tortured for all eternity."-Tibetan Book of the Dead.

However, these evils can also be avoided which is the purpose of these texts. They serve as a roadmap to heaven. In this regard, these texts actually educate the reader as to "The Art of Dying" so that an undesirable and hellish death can be avoided.

Unfortunately, or so say these texts, many are condemned to Hell for all eternity. According to the Tibetan Book of the Dead, a hellish death is due to the "power of accumulated evil Karma." Likewise, according to the Egyptian Book of the Dead, spirit souls may be judged and condemned to hell for all eternity if they had behaved in an evil and unjust manner when living. Hence, both texts warn of a judgment day and a life review and warn that those who have committed evil acts will be judged, found guilty, and then condemned.

Hence, it can be deduced that by 6,000 years ago, that in addition to a heaven and hell, a moral-religious spiritual conscience and moral-consciousness has evolved. This is reflected by the religious conviction that the just and the unjust would be rewarded and punished in the next world after they had died; their good deeds often weighed against the bad.

As is now well established, a sense of morality and a personal conscience (as in: Let your conscience be your guide) is directly associated with the functional integrity of the frontal lobe (Joseph, 1986a, 1999a). The frontal lobes are concerned with anticipating consequences and serve to inhibit or redirect unacceptable impulses in order to avoid punishment.

It also appears that the frontal lobe had fully evolved and reached its peak levels of development and expansion during the Upper Paleolithic. In this regard, although there is no physical evidence to indicate that Upper Paleolithic peoples had also evolved a moral conscience or a concern that the spirit soul would be punished for past misdeeds, Budge (1994) argues that the Book of the Dead and the beliefs that permeate the pyramid texts, were already quite ancient by the rise of the first Dynasty, and thus have pre-dynastic, and therefore, Upper Paleolithic origins.

It is noteworthy that although the Tibetan (and Egyptian) Book of the Dead warn of a judgment day, and describe all manner of Hellish devils and demons, this text repeatedly reminds the reader that these demonic entities are a product of one's own mind. They are illusions erupting from the depths of the primeval unconscious which is freed of the suppressive restraints of the every day reality and the illusions of this world.

According to this text, different demons and hells are not only associated with the unconscious but issue from specific regions of the brain, including, according to descriptions in these texts, tissue of the mind that appear to be associated with the temporal lobes, the right temporal lobe in particular ("eastern regions of the brain"). That is, when facing north, the frontal lobes are the northern part of the brain, the occipital lobes the southern, and the left and right temporal lobes the western and eastern portions of the brain.

THE NEUROLOGY OF PERSONAL MEMORIES
HIPPOCAMPUS

As is well known, the hippocampus is exceedingly important in memory, acting to place various short-term memories into long-term storage and retrieving short-term memories (Enbert & Bonhoeffer, 1999; Fedio & Van Buren, 1974; Frisk & Milner, 1990; Milner, 1966; 1970; Nunn et al., 1999; Penfield & Milner, 1958; Rawlins, 1985; Scoville & Milner, 1957; Squire, 1992; Victor & Agamanolis, 1990). Presumably the hippocampus encodes new information during the storage and consolidation (long-term storage) phase, and assists in the gating of afferent streams of information destined for the neocortex by filtering or suppressing irrelevant sense data which may interfere with memory consolidation. Moreover, it is believed that via the development of long-term potentiation the hippocampus is able to track information as it is stored in the neocortex, and to form conjunctions between synapses and different brain regions which process and store associated memories.

Hence, if the hippocampus has been damaged the ability to convert short term memories into long term memories becomes significantly impaired (MacKinnon & Squire, 1989; Nunn et al., 1999; Squire, 1992; Victor & Agamanolis, 1990; Zola-Morgan & Squire, 1984, 1985a, 1986). Memory for words, passages, conversations, and written material is also significantly impacted, particularly with left hippocampal destruction (Frisk & Milner, 1990; Squire, 1992).

Bilateral destruction of the anterior hippocampus results in striking and profound disturbances involving memory and new learning (i.e. anterograde amnesia). For example, one such individual who underwent bilateral destruction of this nuclei (H.M.), was subsequently found to have almost completely lost the ability to recall anything experienced after surgery. If you introduced yourself to

Figure 139. *Devils and demons. 17th century.*

him, left the room, and then returned a few minutes later he would have no recall of having met or spoken to you. Dr. Brenda Milner has worked with H.M. for almost 20 years and yet she is an utter stranger to him.

H.M. is in fact so amnesic for everything that has occurred since his surgery (although memory for events prior to his surgery is comparatively exceedingly well preserved), that every time he rediscovers that his favorite uncle died (actually a few years before his surgery) he suffers the same grief as if he had just been informed for the first time.

H.M., although without memory for new (non-motor) information, has adequate intelligence, is painfully aware of his deficit and constantly apologizes for his problem. "Right now, I'm wondering" he once said, "Have I done or said anything amiss?" You see, at this moment everything looks clear to me, but what happened just before? That's what worries me. It's like waking from a dream. I just don't remember...Every day is alone in itself, whatever enjoyment I've had, and whatever sorrow I've had...I just don't remember" (Blakemore, 1977, p.96).

Presumably the hippocampus acts to protect memory and the encoding of new information during the storage and consolidation phase via the gating of afferent streams of information and the filtering/exclusion (or dampening) of irrelevant and interfering stimuli. When the hippocampus is damaged there results input overload, the neuroaxis is overwhelmed by neural noise, and the consolidation phase of memory is disrupted such that relevant information is not properly stored or even attended to. Consequently, the ability to form associations (e.g. between stimulus and response) or to alter preexisting schemas (such as occurs during learning) is attenuated (Douglas, 1967).

AMYGDALA & HIPPOCAMPUS

There is considerable evidence which strongly suggests that the hippocampus plays an interdependent role with the amygdala in regard to memory (Gloor 1992, 1997; Halgren 1992; Kesner & Andrus, 1982; Mishkin, 1978; Murray 1992; Sarter & Markowitsch, 1985); particularly in that they are richly interconnected, merge at the uncus, and exert mutual excitatory influences on one another. For example, it appears that the amygdala is responsible for storing the emotional aspects and personal reactions to events, whereas the hippocampus acts to store the cognitive, visual, and contextual variables (Gloor, 1955, 1997).

Specifically, the amygdala plays a particularly important role in memory and learning when activities are related to reward and emotional arousal (Gaffan 1992; Gloor 1992, 1997; Halgren 1992; LeDoux 1992, 1996; Kesner 1992; Rolls 1992; Sarter & Markowitsch, 1985). Thus, if some event is associated with positive or negative emotional states it is more likely to be learned and remembered.

Because of its involvement in all aspects of social-emotional and motivational functioning, activation of the amygdala therefore, can evoke highly personal and emotional memories as it is highly involved in remembering emotionally charged experiences (Gloor, 1992, 1997; Halgren, 1981, 1992; Halgren, et al. 1978; Rolls, 1992; Sarter & Markowtisch, 1985). In fact, the amygdala becomes particularly active when recalling personal and emotional memories (Halgren, 1992; Heath, 1964; Penfield & Perot, 1963), and in response to cognitive and context determined stimuli regardless of their specific emotional qualities (Halgren, 1992). Moreover, depth electrode activation of the amygdala can even evoke memories of sexual intercourse, and traumatic memories that had long ago been forgotten.

Consider, for example, a case described by Gloor (1997, pp. 7-9) in which the right amygdala of a 21 year old patient "was briefly stimulated for 2.8 seconds at a low intensity. Immediately upon its onset" the patient reported "a feeling like falling into the water. When he was asked to elaborate, he replied that it was as if something had covered his eyes, nose and mouth." Again the stimulation was applied and the patient excitedly asked: "Could you do it again, Doctor? When asked why, he said he had the words on his lips to describe the feeling, but then could not." The stimulation was then applied without warning for 4.4 seconds. The patient "opened his mouth, with an astonished look on his face." A terrifying memory had suddenly come back to him. It was when he was eight years old and had been at a picnic when "A kid was coming up to me to push me into the water.... I was pushed by somebody stronger than me... a big fellow..." who pushed him under the water and had kept his head under the water so that he couldn't breath.

However, once these emotional memories are formed, it sometimes requires the specific emotional or associated visual context to trigger their recall (Rolls, 1992; Halgren, 1992). If those cues are not provided or ceased to be available, the original memory may not be triggered and may appear to be forgotten or repressed. However, even emotional context can trigger memory (see also Halgren, 1992) in the absence of specific cognitive cues.

Similarly, it is also possible for emotional and non-emotional memories to be activated in the absence of active search and retrieval, and thus without hippocampal or frontal lobe participation. Recognition memory may be triggered by contextual or emotional cues. Indeed, there are a small group of neurons in the amygdala, as well as a larger group in the inferior temporal lobe which are involved in recognition memory (Murray, 1992; Rolls, 1992). Because of amygdaloid sensitivity to visual and emotional cues, even long forgotten memories may be evoked via recognition, even when search and retrieval repeatedly fails to activate the relevant memory store.

According to Gloor (1992), "a perceptual experience similar to a previous one can through activation of the isocortical population involved in the original experience recreate the entire matrix which corresponds to it and call forth the memory of the original event and an appropriate affective response through the activation of amygdaloid neurons." This can occur "at a relatively non-cognitive (affective) level, and thus lead to full or partial recall of the original perceptual message associated with the appropriate affect."

Thus the amygdala is responsible for emotional memory formation and recall whereas the hippocampus is concerned with recalling and storing verbal-visual-spatial and contextual details in memory. Thus, damage to the hippocampus can impair retention of context, and contextual fear conditioning, but it has no effect on the retention of the fear itself or the fear reaction to the original cue (Kim & Fanselow 1992; Phillips & LeDoux 1992, 1996; Rudy & Morledge 1994). In these instances, fear-memory is retained due to preservation of the amygdala. However, when both the amygdala and hippocampus are damaged, striking and profound disturbances in memory functioning result (Kesner & Andrus, 1982; Mishkin, 1978).

Therefore, the role of the amygdala in memory and learning seems to involve activities related to reward, orientation, and attention, as well as emotional arousal and social-emotional recognition (Gloor, 1992, 1997; Rolls, 1992; Sarter & Markowitsch, 1985). If some event is associated with positive or negative emotional states it is more likely to be learned and remembered. That is, reward increases the probability of attention being paid to a particular stimulus or consequence as a function of its association with reinforcement (Gaffan 1992; Douglas, 1967; Kesner & Andrus, 1982).

Moreover, the amygdala appears to reinforce and maintain hippocampal activity via the identification of motivationally significant information and the generation of pleasurable rewards (through action on the lateral hypothalamus). However, the amygdala and hippocampus act differentially in regard to the effects of positive vs. negative reinforcement on learning and memory, particularly when highly stressed or repetitively aroused in a negative fashion. For example, whereas the hippocampus produces theta in response to noxious stimuli the amygdala increases its activity following the reception of a reward (Norton, 1970).

THE HIPPOCAMPUS & ASSOCIATED MEMORY STRUCTURES

Reverberating neurons are presumably located in various regions of the neocortex, and are apparently bound together via the simultaneous activity and steering influences involving the frontal lobes (Joseph, 1986a, 1999a), dorsal medial thalamus, and in particular the amygdala and hippocampus (Gloor, 1997; Graff-Radford, et al. 1990; Lynch, 1986; Rolls, 1992; Squire, 1992). These structures are all interlinked and highly involved in attention, arousal, and memory functioning, and probably act together so as to establish and maintain specific neural circuits and networks associated with specific memories (e.g., Brewer et al., 1998; Squire, et al,. 1992; Tulving et al., 1994; Wagner et al., 1998). For example, these different networks and neurons may be linked via the steering influences exerted by the frontal lobes etc., which can selectively activate or inhibit these memories and associated tissues in a coordinated fashion, and which can tie together certain perceptual experiences so as to form a complex multi-modal memory (e.g., Dolan et al., 1997; Joseph, 1982, 1986a, 1988a, 1999a; Kapur et al., 1995; Squire, et al,. 1992; Tulving et al., 1994; Dolan et al., 1997; Brewer et al., 1998; Wagner et al., 1998).

The frontal lobes, however, not only assist in the recollection of memories (Brewer et al., 1998; Wagner et al., 1998), but in conjunction with the limbic system, can induce feelings of guilt about those memories. Presumably, at death, the amygdala and hippocampus act to trigger the recollection of long term and highly personal memories, whereas the frontal lobes may serve to pronounce judgment and impose guilt. Indeed, it has been well established that the frontal lobe not only acts to inhibit memories and various impulses, but serves as a moral conscience which passes judgment on others and on one's self (Joseph, 1986a, 1999a).

AMYGDALA & HIPPOCAMPAL INTERACTIONS: HALLUCINATIONS

Direct electrical stimulation of the temporal lobes, hippocampus and particularly the amygdala (Gloor, 1990, 1997) not only results in the recollection of images, but in the creation of fully formed visual and auditory hallucinations (Gloor 1992, 1997; Halgren 1992; Halgren et al., 1978; Horowitz et al., 1968; Malh et al., 1964; Penfield & Perot, 1963).   It has long been know that tumors invading specific regions of the brain can trigger the formation of hallucinations which range from the simple (flashing lights) to the complex. The most complex forms of hallucination, however, are associated with tumors within the most anterior portion of the temporal lobe (Critchley, 1939; Gibbs, 1951; Gloor 1992, 1997; Halgren 1992; Horowitz et al. 1968; Tarachow, 1941); i.e. the region containing the amygdala and anterior hippocampus.

Similarly, electrical stimulation of the anterior lateral temporal cortical surface results in visual hallucinations of people, objects, faces, and various sounds (Gloor 1992, 1997; Halgren 1992; Horowitz et al., 1968)—particularly the right temporal lobe (Halgren et al. 1978). Depth electrode stimulation and thus direct activation of the amygdala and/or hippocampus is especially effective. For example, stimulation of the right amygdala produces complex visual hallucinations, body sensations, deja vus, illusions, as well as gustatory and alimentary experiences (Weingarten et al. 1977), whereas Freeman and Williams (1963) have reported that the surgical removal of the right amygdala in one patient abolished hallucinations. Stimulation of the right hippocampus also produces memory- and dream-like hallucinations (Halgren et al. 1978; Horowitz et al. 1968).

The amygdala also becomes activated in response to bizarre stimuli (Halgren, 1992). Conversely, if activated to an abnormal degree, it may produce bizarre memories and abnormal perceptual experiences. In fact, the amygdala contributes in large part to the production of very sexual as well as bizarre, unusual and fearful memories and mental phenomenon including dissociative states, feelings of depersonalization, and hallucinogenic and dream-like recollections (Bear, 1979; Gloor, 1986, 1992, 1997; Horowitz et al. 1968; Mesulam, 1981; Penfield & Perot, 1963; Weingarten et al. 1977; Williams, 1956).

Single amygdaloid neurons receive a considerable degree of topographic input, and are predominatly polymodal, responding to a variety of stimuli from different modalities simultaneously (Amaral et al. 1992; O'Keefe & Bouma, 1969; Ono & Nishijo, 1992; Perryman, Kling, & Lloyd, 1987; Rolls 1992; Sawa & Delgado, 1963; Schutze et al. 1987; Turner et al. 1980; Ursin & Kaasa, 1960; Van Hoesen, 1981). However, much of this information is filtered out, as it is not necessary to taste what we see, or to feel what we hear, and so as to prevent the brain from being overwhelmed. In part, this massive sensory filtering is made possible via serotonic (5HT) which suppresses synaptic activity in the visual cortex, the lateral (visual) geniculate nucleus of the thalamus as well as the amygdala and throughout the neocortex (Curtis & Davis 1962; Marazzi & Hart 1955). For example, in response to arousing stimuli, 5-HT is released (Auerbach et al. 1985; Roberts, 1984; Spoont, 1992) which acts to narrow and focus attentional and perceptual functioning so that stimuli which are the most salient are attended to. That is, 5HT appears to be involved in learning not to respond to stimuli that are irrelevant and not rewarding (See Beninger, 1989). These signals are filtered out and suppressed.

By contrast, substances which block 5HT transmission -such as LSD- results in increased activity in the sensory pathways to the neocortex (Purpura 1956), such that information that is normally filtered out is perceive. LSD acts on serotonin (5HT) 5HT restricts perceptual and information processing and in fact increases the threshold for neural responses to occur at both the neocortical and limbic level.

As is well known, LSD can elicit profound hallucinations involving all spheres of experience. Following the administration of LSD high amplitude slow waves (theta) and bursts of paroxysmal spike discharges occurs in the hippocampus and amygdala (Chapman & Walter, 1965; Chapman et al. 1963), but with little cortical abnormal activity. In both humans and chimps, when the temporal lobes, amygdala and hippocampus are removed, LSD ceased to produce hallucinatory phenomena (Baldwin et al. 1959; Serafintides, 1965). Moreover, LSD induced hallucinations are significantly reduced when the right vs. left temporal lobe has been surgically ablated (Serafintides, 1965).

Intense activation of the temporal lobe and amygdala has also been reported to give rise to a host of sexual, religious and spiritual experiences; and chronic hyperstimulation (i.e. seizure activity) can induce some individuals to become hyper-religious or visualize and experience ghosts, de-

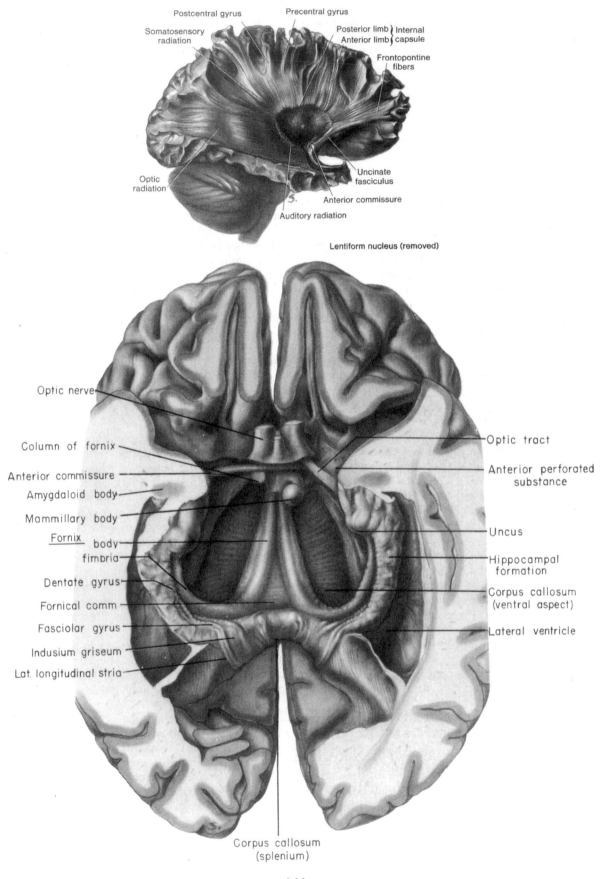

Postcentral gyrus

Precentral gyrus

Somatosensory radiation

Posterior limb } Internal
Anterior limb } capsule

Frontopontine fibers

Optic radiation

Uncinate fasciculus

Anterior commissure

Auditory radiation

Lentiform nucleus (removed)

Optic nerve

Column of fornix

Anterior commissure

Amygdaloid body

Mammillary body

Fornix
body
fimbria

Dentate gyrus

Fornical comm

Fasciolar gyrus

Indusium griseum

Lat. longitudinal stria

Optic tract

Anterior perforated substance

Uncus

Hippocampal formation

Corpus callosum (ventral aspect)

Lateral ventricle

Corpus callosum (splenium)

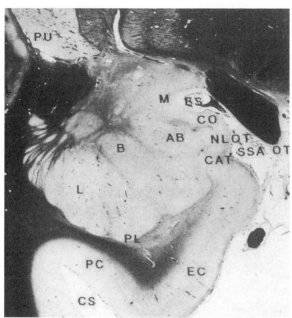

Figure 140. (Op. page top) A cutaway medial view depicting Hippocampal/ Entorhinal projection system. (Op. page bottom) Ventral cutraway view of Hippocampal system. rom Mettler, 1948. (Left) Uncus: hippocampal structures (CS, PC, EC) and Amygdala structures (L, B, AB, M). From Gloor 1997.

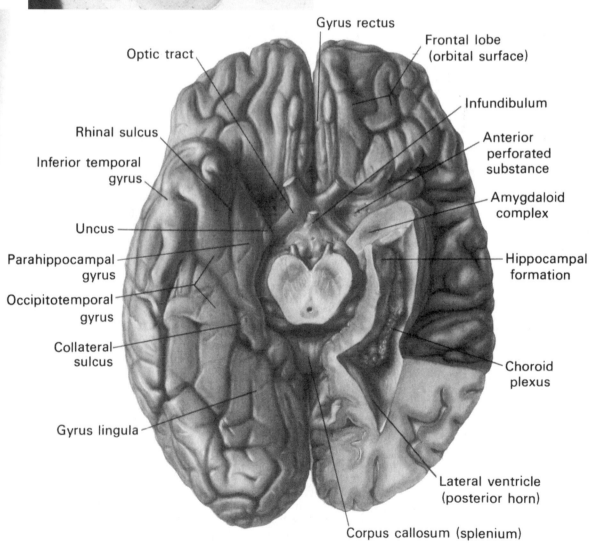

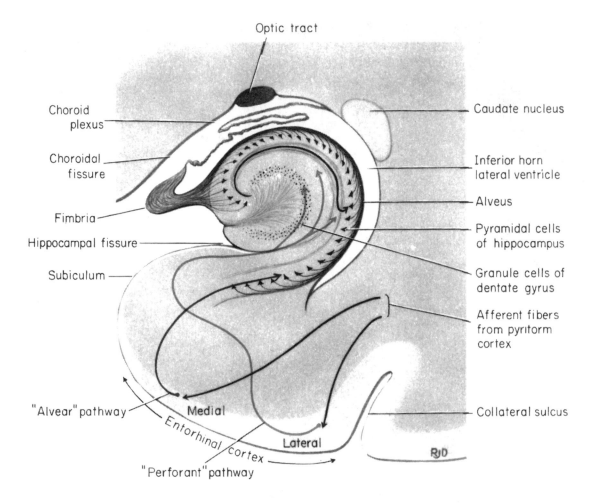

Optic tract

Choroid plexus

Choroidal fissure

Fimbria

Hippocampal fissure

Subiculum

"Alvear" pathway

Medial

Entorhinal cortex

Lateral

"Perforant" pathway

Caudate nucleus

Inferior horn lateral ventricle

Alveus

Pyramidal cells of hippocampus

Granule cells of dentate gyrus

Afferent fibers from pyriform cortex

Collateral sulcus

RjD

mons, angels, and even God, as well as claim demonic and angelic possession or the sensation of having left their body (Bear 1979; Gloor 1986, 1992; Horowitz, Adams & Rutkin 1968; MacLean 1990; Mesulam 1981; Penfield & Perot 1963; Schenk, & Bear 1981; Weingarten, et al. 1977; Williams 1956).

In consequence, under conditions such as death, these limbic system structures may become excessively aroused, freed of inhibitory restraint, and begin to recall and judge personal memories, as well as hallucinate all manner of forms and images, including those of gods, demons, angels and devils who pass judgment.

JUDGMENT DAY

It is commonly believed that some souls will go to heaven, and others would spend eternity in hell. The determination of which soul would go where, thus gave rise to the concept of being judged. The nature of one's afterlife depended on how one was judged and the nature of one's good and evil deeds. Death, therefore, also became a final judgment day where the wicked were punished, and the good rewarded with eternal heavenly bliss.

We do not know if the Cro-Magnon believed in hell or a final judgment. The ancient Sumerians, Babylonians, and Egyptians, as well as the ancient peoples of the Indus valley, and ancient China clearly believed that a final judgment awaited man after death.

For example, in the Rig-Veda we are told that the good are invited to live in heaven, whereas the wicked are hurled by the deities Soma and Indra into an eternally dark prison from whence there is no return.

According to the ancient Egyptians, the woman and man who respected and maintained maat—that is, truth, justice, and righteousness—would achieve a state of eternal beatitude, whereas those who did not could expect to suffer in a dreary Hellish underworld where they and the enemies of the sun god Ra would burn for all eternity—roasted by the burning rays of the sun. Most of these ideas were laid out in considerable detail in the Egyptian Book of the Dead, the Pyramid Texts.

The Pyramid Texts were composed and compiled by the priests of Heliopolis, to help the dead pharaohs achieve eternal bliss in the afterlife. Only the morally just could expect to enter heaven. Nevertheless, the dead, both good and evil, would have to defend themselves against every accusation. Life in the afterworld could be easily imperiled by accusations of those who had been wronged.

Yet, in ancient Egypt, it was believed that the chief accuser would be memory, the dead's own memories, and the dead's own heart would recount and remember their good or evil deeds. Indeed, it would be hell to be plagued for all eternity by every bad memory and all associated feelings of guilt and psychic pain.

This same belief is recounted in the Tibetan Book of the Dead: "You are now before Yama, King of the Dead. The mirror in which Yama seems to read your past is your own memory, and also his judgment is your own. It is you yourself who pronounces your own judgment, which in turn determines your rebirth."

However, whereas the Tibetan Buddhists believed that the souls of the dead passed judgment on themselves, the ancient Egyptians believed that the Great God Osiris would pass judgment. Osiris, would hold and weigh the scales of justice.

JUDGMENT

The Great God of the ancient Egyptians did not pass judgment alone, for in this he was assisted by a council of 12, a tribunal of the Great God. As detailed in the Book of the Dead, the jackal-headed god of death, Anubis, adjusts the scales of justice which will determine one's fate; to his right stands Thoth, the ibis-headed god of wisdom—the divine scribe who records the final verdict. And behind Osiris crouches a horrible hybrid monster, the eater of the dead.

"The council which judges the deficient, thou knowest that they are not lenient on the day of judging the miserable, the hour of doing their duty. It is woe when the accuser is one of knowledge. Do not trust in length of years, for they regard a lifetime as but an hour. A man remains after death, and his deeds are placed beside him in heaps. However, existence yonder is for eternity, and he who complains of it is a fool. But as for him who reaches it without wrong-doing, he shall exist yonder like a god, stepping out freely like the lords of eternity." -Egyptian Book of the Dead.

Not only is it futile for the guilty to proclaim their innocence, but the consequences, the manner in which the balance sways depends on one's own heart and memories, which will testify against the dead. According to the ancient Egyptians, the heart will be laid upon the scales and weighed against the lightness of a feather and balanced against Maat; Maat being truth.

good outweighs the evil, salvation would be at hand, for it could be expected that "the offenses of which thou art accused will be eliminated, thy fault wiped out by the balancing of the balance, in the day of the evaluation of qualities; thou causes the weighing to be made as Thoth." -Egyptian Book of the Dead.

As noted, according to the ancient Egyptians the final judgment is listed into a book. Jewish, Christian and Islamic faith also involves a book in which the final judgment is listed.

"And I saw the dead, great and small, standing before the throne, and books were opened. Also another book was opened, which is the book of life. And the dead were judged by what was written in the books, by what they had done." -R.S.V. 10:11-15.

According to the ancient Hebrews, a sinner might have his name erased from the book: "who ever sins against me, I will blot out of my book." —Exodus 33:33. And with this erasure, by having one's name blotted out, the soul of the dead would be condemned for all eternity, forgotten forever, never to be remembered even by the Lord God.

THE LIFE REVIEW: HEART OF A MEMORY

The notion of being judged and a weighing of one's sins is a common belief that recurs throughout history. The ancient Chinese, although practicing ancestor worship, also believed that sinners would roast in hell. The souls of the ancient Chinese were judged by officials of the underworld which was comprised of 10 tribunals. The soul would typically kneel before these judges next to whom would stand officers with books with the records against which the soul would be judged.

Similar beliefs were held by the ancient Greeks. For example, after Odysseus met with the ghost of Achilles in Hades he states that: "I saw Minos, the glorious son of Zeus, golden scepter in hand, giving judgment to the dead from his seat, while they sat and stood about the king through the wide-gated house of Hades."

According to the ancient Egyptians, the chief prosecutor and the witness against the accused, would be the accused themselves. That is, the dead, their heart, would be forced to testify against themselves. Memories, both good and bad, would be recalled involuntarily. That is, the dead would undergo a life review.

In pictures of judgment day, we see that on the scales rest the hieroglyphic sign of the heart, the ib, and a feather. And before the balance stands the dead. If the soul has lived a righteous life, his heart will detail his good deeds which are weighed against truth. If he has done evil, he implores his heart not to witness against him. He struggles not to remember. But to no avail.

Death, to the ancients, therefore, involved a life review, where one's memories are recalled and one's life is judged on the scales of good and evil, on the balance of truth.

Although we now know that the amygdala, in conjunction with the hippocampus becomes particularly active when recalling personal and emotional memories (Halgren, 1992; Heath, 1964; Penfield & Perot, 1963), the ancients believed these memories were stored in the heart which served as one's conscience. Whereas we localized the transmitter of god to the limbic system, the ancient Egyptians believed that the heart was "the god which is in man." On the other hand, the amygdala directly affects cardiovascular functioning and thus the beating of the heart.

The ancient Egyptians experienced a considerable degree of apprehension about judgment day and the fact that their hearts would witness against them. The Egyptians were painfully aware that they might be condemned to hell for all eternity by their own evil memories. These same concerns also appear in the Tibetan Book of the Dead:

"You are now before Yama, King of the Dead. In vain will you try to lie, and to deny or conceal the evil deeds you have done. The Judge holds up before you the shinning mirror of Karma, wherein all your deeds are reflected. But again you have to deal with dream images, which you yourself have made, and which you project outside, without recognizing them as your own work. The mirror in which Yama seems to read your past is your own memory, and also his judgment is your own. It is you yourself who pronounces your own judgment, which in turn determines your rebirth." -Tibetan Book of the Dead.

The weighing of the heart and undergoing a final judgment is not shared by all religions. However, judgment day has been a common belief among many different religions since the Neolithic, including Christian, Greek, Roman, Christian and the apocryphal writings of the Jews: "The spirits of the dead shall be separated. A division has been made for the spirits of the righteous, in which there is a bright spring of water. And such has been made for sinners when they die and are buried in the earth and judgment. Here their spirits shall be set apart in great pain."-Book of Enoch

Figure 142. Anubis, Egyptian God of the Dead weighing the souls of the dead.

Figure 143. *The Archangel Michael weighing the souls of the dead. Detail from the Last Judgement (by Hans Memlinc.)*

THE SECOND DEATH

"So I prophesied as I was commanded: and as I prophesied, there was a noise, and behold, a rattling; and the bones came together, bone to its bone. And as I looked, there were sinews on them, and flesh had come upon them, and skin had covered them; but there was no breath in them. Then he said to me, Prophesy to the breath, prophesy, son of man, and say to the breath, Thus says the Lord God: Come from the four winds, O breath, and breathe upon these slain, that they may live. So I prophesied as he commanded me, and the breath came into them, and they lived, and stood upon their feet, an exceedingly great host." -Ezekial.

Yahweh, Ezekial tell us, has the power to resurrect the dead, to join together even disarticulated bones, and turn them into human bodies, giving them life. This is the second life after death. And there is a second death that awaits all sinners:

"Then Raphael answered, one of the holy angels who was with me, and said unto me: These hollow places have been created for this very purpose, that the spirits of the souls of the dead should assemble therein, ye that all the souls of the children of men should assemble here. And these places have been made to receive them till the day of their judgment and till the appointed time period till the judgment comes upon them."-Book of Enoch

In later Vedic literature, including the Brahmanas, we are told of a second death. All souls would suffer a penalty that would be paid in the form of dying again and again, possibly for all eternity. This is called samsara, the transmigration of the soul. Thus according to the ancient peoples of the Indus Valley, after one dies, they could suffer a second death, and then a third death, and so on, for all eternity, each subsequent life determined by one's character and behavior in previous lives.

Although the Greeks thought it possible to achieve a state of blessed eternal beatitude, they also believed that some souls fall from their primal state of beatitude and undergo a series of incarnations, beginning in insect or bestial form, and that they then have to live and die ten thousand deaths before regaining a human state. Only enlightened souls can escape this endless cycle of birth and death.

According to modern Christian faiths, the dead also suffer a second death, which may be more horrible than the first. That is, after the soul awakens from purgatory: "The Son of man will send his angels, and they will gather out of his kingdom all causes of sin and all evildoers, and throw them into the furnace of fire; there men will weep and gnash their teeth. Then the righteous will shine like the sun in the kingdom of their father." -R.S.V. 13:41-43.

"Then I saw a great white throne and him who sat upon it; from his presence earth and sky fled away, and no place was found for them. And I saw the dead, great and small, standing before the throne, and books were opened. Also another book was opened, which is the book of life. And the dead were judged by what was written in the books, by what they had done. And the sea gave up the dead in it. Death and Hades gave up the dead in them, and all were judged by what they had done. Then Death and Hades were thrown into the lake of fire. This is the second death, the lake of fire; and if any one's name was not found written in the book of life, he was thrown into the lake of fire." -R.S.V. 10:11-15.

"The cowardly, the faithless, the polluted, murderers, fornicators, sorcerers, idolaters, and all liars, their lot shall be the lake that burns with fire and brimstone, which is the second death." -Revelation of St. John, II:184, 4356-457.

"Do you not know that the unrighteous will not inherit the kingdom of God? Do not be deceived; neither the immoral, nor idolaters, no adulterers, nor homosexuals, nor thieves, nor the greedy, nor drunkards, nor revivlers, nor robbers, will inherit the kingdom of God."-Paul, Galatians, V 22-23.

And yet, there is a second salvation.

Idolaters, adulterers, homosexuals, thieves, the greedy, drunkards, revivlers, and robbers... And such were some of you! But you were washed, you were sanctified, you were justified in the name of the Lord Jesus Christ and in the Spirit of our god." -Paul, Galatians, V 22-23.

Hence, it was also believed possible to escape the second death if one had lived a life free of sin, or if one repented for their sinful ways. And this same belief is held by those of the Hindu and Buddhist faith. That is, if the consequences of one's Karma could be worked out by the self, the Atman before the next reincarnation, the soul would not have to be born again only to die again and yet again. As to those who failed to work out the consequences of their Karma, or those who had lived a life of the utmost evil, their lot would become an eternal hell.

HELL: JUDGMENT AND PUNISHMENT

Although the Sumerians and ancient Hebrews and Greeks initially believed that both good and evil, rich and poor, would descend to hell, some also believed that She'ol, Hades, and Hell, were places of judgment, where punishments were doled out to the wicked.

"Upon the termination of life they were brought to trial; and, according to their sentence, some go to prison-houses beneath the earth, to suffer for their sins, while others, by virtue of their trial, are borne lightly upwards to some celestial spot, where they pass their days in a manner worthy of the life they lived." -Plato, Phaedrus.

In ancient Chinese religion, the realm of the dead was believed to consist of seven Hells where the evil would roast for all eternity. Likewise, in ancient Egypt, Greece, the Middle East, and Catholic Rome, punishment for the wicked, for the enemies of god, became eternal hell fire and all manner of demonic horrors.

"And I" the Apostle Peter "saw also another place very squalid; and it was a place of punishment, and they that were punished and the angels that punished them had their raiment dark, according to the air of the place. And some there were hanging by their tongues; and those were they that blasphemed the way of righteousness, and under them was laid fire flaming and tormenting them... and there were others, women, hanged by their hair above that mire which boiled up; and these were they that adorned themselves for adultery... And in another place were gravel-stones sharper than swords or any spit, heated with fire, and men and women clad in filthy rages rolled upon them in torment... and others being cast down from a great precipice to the rocks below..."

"For those who have disbelieved... shall roast in fire... and their bellies and skin shall be melted. To them it is said: Taste the punishment of the Burning." -Koran

AFTER-DEATH, OUT-OF-BODY, ASTRAL PROJECTION
The Book of the Dead

"The Book of the Dead" is the title given to the collection of mortuary texts, also referred to as Pyramid texts, which the ancient Egyptian theologians composed for the benefit of the dead. However, they were first called the "book of the dead" or "a dead man's book" by tomb robbers, as these texts were commonly found in the dead man's coffin. During the sixth Dynasty, the common name for the Book of the Dead was "manifested in the light" or "embraced by the light."

According to E.A. Wallis Budge, Late Keeper of the Egyptian and Assyrian Antiquities of the British Museum, these texts were already quite ancient by the rise of the first dynasty, over 6,000 years ago. The predynastic Egyptians "were quite certain that men did not perish when they died, but that some part of a man departed after death to some place where he would renew his life in some form, according to the dictates of some divine being" (Budge, 1994, p. 4).

According to the Book of the Dead, at death the spirit-soul of the deceased would arise from the body, and although translucent and transparent to the living, this spirit-soul would at first hover above and look upon the body and could see and hear what was taking place below (chapter CLXXVII). The spirit-soul may then depart, only to return to visit the body (e.g. chapter LXXXIX: The Soul Visiting the Body which Lies on a Bier), sometimes even reanimating the body (chapter XCII), such that the dead might live again in this world.

Like their Paleolithic predecessors, the walls of all Egyptian tombs and all but three of the hundreds of pyramids that dot the land, were graced with paintings of all manner of animal life and realistic scenes of the every day life to which they were accustomed. And within these tombs dwelled the ka, a spirit-like force which resided in a ka-statue of the dead person. These statues were exact replicas of the dead, that is, when they were alive.

It was the ba, the soul of the dead, which the Egyptians believed ascended to heaven. The ba would sometimes be depicted in flight, as a human-headed bird. Upon entering heaven the dead achieved the status of an akh—a "glorified being" that had reached completeness of attainment.

However, as detailed in the Egyptian Book of the Dead, prior to entering heaven (Anu), the spirit-soul of the deceased might "fly through the air" (chapter XCII) "pass over the earth" (chapter IV), such that it could move freely from place to place, before entering a tunnel or realm of darkness, and then arising into the sky to the abode of the gods in heaven at which point they bask in "a shining, glorious light" (Budge, 1994).

Similarly, according to Book 1, of the Bardo, Tibetan Book of the Dead, following death the deceased will be enveloped with a "Clear Light" of "Wisdom and the Knower will experience the shining, dazzling, glorious, Radiance of the Clear light of Pure Reality, the All Good. Thine own consciousness, shining, void, and inseparable from the Great Body of Radiance, hath no birth, nor death, and is the Immutable Light—Buddha Amitabha."

Likewise, according to the Egyptian Book of the Dead, the soul ascends into the sky to the

Figure 144. *Ani and his wife Thuthu entering the Hall of Judgement.*

Figure 145. *Anubis testing the balance upon which sits a feather (right) and the heart (in container, left).*

Figure 147. *Thoth recording the judgement. The Devourer of the dead crouches behind him.*

Figure 147. *Horus leading Ani into the presence of Osiris*

Figure 148. *Ani kneeling before the thron of Osiris (next page).*

Figure 149. Osiris upon his throne. Behind him are the gods Isis and Nephyths

abode of the gods in heaven at which point the dead bask in "a shining, glorious light" and are led into the presence of dead relatives and brethren, and finally to the divine being Osiris, who is said to have made "men and women to be born again" and where they then dwell in bliss for all eternity having achieved everlasting life: "My soul is God. My soul is eternity" (Budge, 1994).

It is noteworthy that the soul, at first, usually does not know it is dead, that the body has died. According to the Tibetan Book of the Dead: "When the consciousness-principle gettest outside the body, it sayeth to itself, Am I dead, or am I not dead? It cannot determine. It can see that the body is being stripped of its garments. It seeth its relatives and heareth the weepings and wailings of friends and relatives, and although it seeth them and heareth them calling upon him, they seeth him not."

OUT-OF-BODY AND AFTER-DEATH EXPERIENCES

The notion of a soul leaving the body following death is a common belief among almost all religions. Again, some believe that the soul may fall asleep, whereas others believe it will either ascend to heaven or descend into hell. And, as noted, we are also told that the soul of the dead may linger upon the Earth, may remain tethered to the body, or may even return to visit the dead body, sometimes hovering above it, and in rare instances, somehow reanimating the body, such that the dead come back to life.

Likewise, among modern day people, some children and adults who have been declared "clinically" dead have returned to life. And many of those who subsequently return to life, have reported that after "dying" they left their body and floated above the scene (Eadie 1992; Rawling 1978; Ring 1980). And, at first, many do not realize they are dead.

According to modern accounts, typically they become increasingly euphoric as they float above their body, after which they may float away, become enveloped in a dark tunnel and then enter a soothing radiant light. And later, when they come back to life, they may even claim conscious knowledge of what occurred around their body while they were dead and floating nearby.

"Lisa" for example, was a 22 year old college coed with no religious background or spiritual beliefs, who was badly injured in an auto accident when the windshield collapsed and all but completely severed her arm. According to Lisa, when she got out of the car her was blood spraying everywhere and she only walked a few feet before collapsing. Apparently an ambulance arrived in just a few minutes. However, the next thing she noticed was that part of the time she was looking up from the ground, and part of the time she was up in the air looking down. From above she could see the ambulance crew working, picking up her body, placing it on a gurney and into the ambulance.

According to Lisa, during the entire ride to the hospital it was like she was half in and half out of the ambulance, as if she were running along outside or just extending out of the vehicle watching the cars and trees go by. When they got to the hospital she was no longer attached to her body but was floating up and down the halls, watching the doctors and nurses and attendants. One doctor in particular drew her attention because he had a big belt buckle with his name written on it. She could even read it and it said "Mike."

According to Lisa, she was "tripping out, bobbing up and down the halls, just checking everything out" when she noticed a girl lying on a gurney with several doctors and nurses working frantically. When she floated over and peered over the shoulder of one of the doctors to take a look she suddenly realized the girl was her and that her hair and face were very bloody and needed to be washed. At that point she realized she was floating well above her body and the doctors, and that she looked to be "dead." Lisa said she did not feel afraid or upset, although the fact that her hair was bloody and dirty bothered her.

She soon floated up and outside the Emergency room and was enveloped in a total blackness, "like I was passing through a tunnel at the end of which was a light which became brighter and more brilliant, radiating outward." The light soon enveloped her body which made her feel exceedingly happy and very warm. A few moments later she heard the voice of her grandmother who had died when Lisa was a young girl. Although Lisa had no memory of this grandmother, she nevertheless recognized her and felt exceedingly happy. However, her grandmother very sorrowfully told her it was "too soon" she would have to "go back." Lisa didn't want to go back, but had no choice. She was drawn away from the light and felt herself falling only to land with a painful thump in her own body. At this point she moved her hand which alerted one of the emergency room staff that Lisa was no longer dead.

Lisa had no religious training and had never heard of "near death experiences" (she was injured in 1982). After returning to life she only reluctantly explained what had happened when she was questioned by one of her doctors.

Lisa also claimed that while she was dead and floating about the emergency room that she saw and heard what was going on around her after she died, and upon coming back to life she was able to accurately recall everything that occurred in the emergency room up to the point when she was enveloped in darkness. She was able to accurately describe "Mike" (who in fact wore a belt buckle engraved with "Mike"), most of the staff who attended her, as well as the conversations that occurred around her as well as some of the other patients.

Similar "after death" claims of leaving and floating above the body, and seeing everything occurring below, are common (Eadie 1992; Moody 1977; Rawling 1978; Ring 1980; Sabom 1982; Wilson 1987), and, as noted, are even reported in the 6,000 year old Egyptian Book of the Dead (Budge 1994), as well as the Tibetan Book of the Dead (the Bardo Thodol) which was composed over 1,300 years ago (Evans-Wentz 1960). Approximately 37% of patients who are resuscitated report "out of body" experiences (Ring 1980).

Consider for example, the case of Army Specialist J. C. Bayne of the 196th Light Infantry Brigade. Bayne was "killed" in Chu Lai, Vietnam, in 1966. He was simultaneously machine gunned and struck by a mortar. According to Bayne, when he opened his eyes he was floating in the air, looking down on his crumpled, burnt, and bloody body, and he could see a number of Vietcong who were searching and stripping him:

"I could see me... it was like looking at a mannequin laying there... I was burnt up and there was blood all over the place... I could see the Vietcong. I could see the guy pull my boots off. I could see the rest of them picking up various things... I was like a spectator... It was about four or five in the afternoon when our own troops came. I could hear and see them approaching... I could see me... It was obvious I was burnt up. I looked dead... they put me in a bag... transferred me to a truck and then to the morgue. And from that point, it was the embalming process."

"I was on that table and a guy was telling a couple of jokes about those USO girls... all I had on was bloody undershorts... he placed my leg out and made a slight incision and stopped... he checked my pulse and heartbeat again and I could see that too...It was about that point I just lost track of what was taking place… [until much later] when the chaplain was in there saying everything was going to be all right… I was no longer outside. I was part of it at this point" (reported in Wilson, 1987, pp 113-114; and Sabom, 1982, pp 81-82).

Some surgery patients, although ostensibly "unconscious" due to anesthesia, are also able to later describe conversations and related events that occurred during the operation (Furlong, 1990; Kilhstrom, et al. 1990; Polster, 1993). Hence, the notion that those who are "clinically dead" or near death may recall various events that occurred while they were ostensibly "dead" should not be dismissed out of hand. Moreover, some surgery patients also claim to "leave their bodies" while they were "unconscious" and claim to recall seeing not just the events occurring below, but in one case, dirt on top of a light fixture (Ring 1980). "It was filthy. I remember thinking, 'Got to tell the nurses about that.'"

Did the above surgical patient or Lisa or Army Specialist Bayne really float above and observe their bodies and the events taking place below? Or did they merely transpose what they heard (e.g. conversations, noises, etc.) and then visualize, imagine, or hallucinate an accompanying and plausible scenario? This seems possible, even in regard to the "filthy" light fixture. On the other hand, not all those who have an "out of body" hear conversations, voices, or even sounds. Rather, they may be enveloped in silence.

"I was struck from behind... That's the last thing I remember until I was above the whole scene viewing the accident. I was very detached. Everything was very quiet. This was the amazing thing about it to me... I could see my shoe which was crushed under the car and I thought: Oh no. My new dress is ruined... I don't remember hearing anything. I don't remember anybody saying anything. I was just viewing things... like I floated up there..." (Sabom, 1982; p. 90).

Moreover, even individuals born blind experience these "near death" hallucinations. And although blind, while dead they will see for the first time. However, whereas many who experience life after death find the experience exhilarating, others respond with feelings of extreme dread and terror. Death is not a pleasant experience.

FEAR AND OUT-OF-BODY EXPERIENCES

The prospect of being terribly injured or killed in an auto accident or fire fight between opposing troops, or even dying during the course of surgery, are often accompanied by fear. It is also not uncommon for individuals who experience terror to report perceptual and hallucinogenic experiences, including dissociation, depersonalization and the splitting off of ego functions. They may feel as if they have separated from their bodies and floated away, or were on the ceiling looking down (Campbell 1988; Courtois 1995; Grinker and Spiegel 1945; James 1958; Neihardt and Black Elk 1932/1989; Noyes and Kletti 1977; Parson 1988; Southard 1919; Terr 1990). Consider the following accounts:

"The next thing I knew I wasn't in the truck anymore; I was looking down from 50 to 100 feel in the air." "I had a clear image of myself... as though watching it on a television screen." "I had a sensation of floating. It was almost like stepping out of reality. I seemed to step out of this world" (Noyes and Kletti 1977).

Or as a close friend described his experience: "I was shooting down the freeway doing about 100 in my Mustang when a Firebird up ahead suddenly cut me off. As I switched lanes to avoid him, he also switched lanes at which point I hit the breaks and began to lose control. The Mustang began to slide and spin... I felt real terror... I was probably going to be killed... I was trying to control the Mustang and avoid turning over, or hitting any of the surrounding cars or the guard rail... time seemed to slow down and then I suddenly realized that part of my mind was a few feet outside the car looking all around; zooming above it and then beside it and behind it and in front of it, looking at and analyzing the respective positions of my spinning Mustang and the cars surrounding me. Simultaneously I was inside trying to steer and control it in accordance with the multiple perspectives I was suddenly given by that part of my mind that was outside. It was like my mind split and one consciousness was inside the car, while the other was zooming all around outside and giving me visual feedback that enabled me to avoid hitting anyone or destroying my Mustang."

HIPPOCAMPAL PLACE NEURONS: ASTRAL PROJECTION

Feelings of fear and terror are mediated by the amygdala, whereas the capacity to cognitively map, or visualize one's position and the position of other objects and individuals in visual-space is dependent on the hippocampus.

The hippocampus contains "place" neurons which are able to encode one's position, place, and movement in space. Specifically, O'Keefe, Nadel, and colleagues, found that hippocampal pyramidal cells were able to become attuned to specific locations within the environment, as well as to particular objects and their location in that environment, thereby creating cognitive maps of visual space. Moreover, they discovered that as the subject moves about in that environment, entire populations of cells would fire but only when in a particular spot, whereas other cells would fire when in a different location.

Some cells respond not just when moving about, but in reaction to the speed of movement, or when turning in different directions. Moreover, some cells are responsive to the movements of other people in that environment and will fire as that person is observed to move around (Nadel, 1991; O'Keefe, 1976; Wilson and McNaughton, 1993).

The hippocampus, therefore, can create a cognitive map of an individual's environment and their movements and the movement of others within it. Presumably it is via the hippocampus that an individual can visualize themselves as if looking at their body from afar, and can remember and thus see themselves engaged in certain actions, as if one were an outside witness (Joseph, 1996). Indeed, as is well known, the hippocampus play a major role in forming and retrieving memories.

Under conditions of hyperactivation (such as in response to extreme fear) it appears that the hippocampus may create a visual hallucination of that "cognitive map" such that the individual may "experience" themselves as outside their body, observing all that is occurring and/or hallucinate themselves as moving about in that environment such as flying above it.

In fact, it has been repeatedly demonstrated that hyperactivation or electrical stimulation of the amygdala-hippocampus-temporal lobe, can cause some individuals to report they have left their bodies and are hovering upon the ceiling staring down (Daly 1958; Jackson and Stewart 1899; Joseph, 1996; Penfield 1952; Penfield and Perot 1963; Williams 1956). That is, their ego and sense of personal identity appears to split off from their body, such that they may feel as if they are two different people, one watching from above, the other being observed down below.

As described by Penfield (1952), "it was as though the patient were attending a familiar play and was both the actor and audience."

Presumably abnormal activation due to extreme fear or direct electrical stimulation induces an individual to think they are seeing themselves from afar because the hippocampus is transposing and "hallucinating" one's image; similar to what occurs during normal remembering. Or, perhaps it is not a hallucination at all, but a capacity mediated by a hyperactivated hippocampus.

As noted, many patients who are diagnosed as "clinically dead" and then return to "life" report that after leaving their body they enter a dark tunnel and are then enveloped in a soothing radiant light. The same is reported in the Egyptian and Tibetan Books of the Dead.

Presumably, in that the hippocampus, amygdala, and inferior temporal lobe receive direct and indirect visual input and contain neurons sensitive to the fovea and upper visual fields, hyperactivation of this region also induces the sensation of seeing a radiant light. The massive release of opiates (due to physical trauma leading to "death") would account for the immediate loss of fear and the experience of tranquillity and joy. Continued activation of these brain regions would also account for the hallucinations of seeing dead relatives, that are commonly reported by those who have "died," as well as the life review, in which one's past life flashes before their eyes.

At death, the amygdala and hippocampus would begin to remember, and memories that were emotional and personal, and all accompanying emotions, such as guilt, would be experienced as part of death. That is, not just the memory, but the awful feeling of the memory would be reexperienced. These structures, therefore, account for the feeling of floating above the body, the life review, and the judgment imposed on the self by their guilty or guilt-free conscience.

The hyperactivation of these limbic structures, therefore, explains why those who have near death experiences report feelings of peace, rapture and joy as they were "bathed by the light" and stood in the all knowing presence of "God" or other divine beings including friends and relatives who had previously passed away. Indeed, these exact same feelings and experiences can be induced by electrically stimulating the inferior temporal lobe and amygdala-hippocampal complex.

EXPERIMENTAL & SEIZURE INDUCED OUT-OF-BODY, HEAVENLY AND OTHER WORLDLY EXPERIENCES

Some individuals suffering from temporal lobe epilepsy also report "out of body experiences." Penfield and Perot (1963) describe several patients who during a temporal lobe seizure claimed they could see themselves in different situations. One woman stated that "it was though I were two persons, one watching, and the other having this happen to me," and that it was she who was doing the watching as if she was completely separated from her body.

One patient had a sensation of being outside her body and watching and observing her body from the outside. Another neurosurgery patient alleged that while outside her body she was also overcome by feelings of euphoria and eternal harmony.

Other patients claim to have quite pleasant auras and describe feelings such as elation, security, eternal harmony, immense joy, paradisiacal happiness, euphoria, completeness. Between .5 and 20% of such patients report these feelings (Daly 1958; Williams 1956).

A patient of Williams (1956) claimed that his attacks began with a "sudden feeling of extreme well being involving all my senses. I see a curtain of beautiful colors before my eyes and experience a pleasant but indescribable taste in my mouth. Objects feel pleasurably warm, the room assumes vast proportions, and I feel as if in another world."

A patient described by Daly (1958) claimed his temporal lobe seizure felt like "a sunny day when your friends are all around you." He felt dissociated from his body, as if he were looking down upon himself and watching his actions. Williams (1956) describes a patient who during a seizure-induced aura reported that she experienced a feeling of being lifted up out of her body, coupled with a very pleasant sensation of elation and the feeling that she was "just about to find out knowledge no one else shares, something to do with the link between life and death." Subirana and Oller-Daurelia (1953) described two patients who experienced ecstatic feelings of "extraordinary beatitude" or of paradise as if they had gone to heaven. Their fantastic feelings also lasted for hours.

Other patients suffering from temporal lobe seizures have noted that feelings and things suddenly become "crystal clear" or that they had a feeling of clairvoyance, or of having the truth revealed to them, or of having achieved a sense of greater awareness such that sounds, smells and visual objects seemed to have a greater meaning and sensibility. Similar claims are made by those who have "died" and returned to tell the tale.

One woman I evaluated claimed she would float on the ceiling, and could float outside and could see, on one occasion, a friend who was coming up the walkway. She also reported that by having a certain thought, she could propel herself to other locals including the homes of her neighbors.

EMBRACED BY THE LIGHT

"The heavens were opened and the whole creation which is under heaven shone... I saw a light, and a child in the light... And while I looked he became an old man. And he changed his form again... and I saw... an image with multiple forms in the light." -Apocryphon of John.

Betty J. Eadie reports in her 1992 book, "embraced by the light" that after dying and then communing with three "ancient" men who appeared at her side and who "glowed" she suddenly thought of her husband and children who she wanted to visit. "I began to look for an exit" and discovered that "my spiritual body could move through anything...My trip home was a blur. I began moving at a tremendous speed... and I was aware of trees rushing below me. I just thought of home and knew I was going there... I saw my husband sitting in his favorite armchair reading the newspaper. I saw my children running up and down the stairs... I was drawn back to the hospital, but I don't remember the trip; it seemed to happen instantaneously" (pp. 33-35).

BLACK ELK

Compare Eadie's description with that of Black Elk (Neihardt and Black Elk, 1932/1989), a Lakota Sioux Medicine Man and spiritual leader (born in 1863). During a visit to England (he was part of Buffalo Bills Wild West Show) he suddenly fell out of his chair as if dead, and then experienced himself being lifted up. In fact, his companions thought he had died.

According to Black Elk: "Far down below I could see houses and towns and green land and streams... I was very happy now. I kept on going very fast...Then I was right over Pine Ridge. I looked down (and) saw my father's and mother's teepee. They went outside, and she was cooking... My mother looked up, and I felt sure she saw me... then I started back, going very fast...Then I was lying on my back in bed and the girl and her father and a doctor were looking at me in a queer way...I had been dead three days (they told him)...and they were getting ready to buy my coffin" (pp. 226-228).

This was not Black Elk's first out of body experience, however. Black Elk demonstrated numerous behaviors and symptoms suggestive of temporal lobe epilepsy. Beginning even in childhood Black Elk repeatedly experienced "queer feelings" and heard voices, had visions, and suffered numerous instances of sudden and terrible fear and depression accompanied by weeping, as well as trance states in which he would fall to the ground as if dead.

Black Elk also had other visions similar to those reporting "life-after-death" experiences, including the following incident that occurred during one of his trance and out-of-body states: "Twelve men were coming towards me, and they said, Our father, the two-legged chief, you shall see... There was a man standing. He was not Wasichu (white) and he was not an Indian. While I was staring at him his body began to change and became very beautiful with all colors of light, and around him there was light..." (p. 245).

Similar accounts, including descriptions of a tribunal of 12 are detailed in the Egyptian Book of the Dead.

Ms. Eadie (like many others who have experienced "life after death") came upon a man standing in the light which "radiated all around him. As I got closer the light became brilliant...I saw that the light was golden, as if his whole body had a golden halo around it, and I could see that the golden halo burst out from around him and spread into a brilliant, magnificent whiteness that extended out for some distances" (pp. 40-41).

ASTRAL ANTIQUITY

Muhammed reports that while sleeping and dreaming he was lifted into the air and transported by the angel Gabriel from Arabia to the Temple Mount in Jerusalem. There he was greeted by three men, who he believed to be Abraham, Moses, and Jesus, as well as a crowd of other prophets. He was then lifted up and entered a divine sphere and came upon the garden of promise and, according to the Koran, saw a "lote-tree veiled in a veil of nameless splendor."

In Hinduism, the lote tree symbolizes the limit of this reality and rational thought.

St. Augustine reports he was "lifted up by an ardent affection towards eternal being itself... we climbed beyond all corporate objects and the heaven itself, where sun, moon, and stars shed light on the earth."

Some individuals (and their followers) claim to be able to voluntarily leave their body (Monroe, 1994), this includes any number of "mystics," and New Age spiritualists, as well as some priests, prophets and shamen. Indeed, Monroe (1994) founded an Institute to study this phenomenon, and claims that others can learn this technique. Monroe, however, notes that when he had his first out-of-body experience he had felt extremely frightened.

That so many people, regardless of culture or antiquity, have similar experiences (or hallucinations) while in trance states, or dreaming, or after "dying," of leaving their body, is presumably due to all possessing a limbic system and temporal lobe that is organized similarly.

The fact that although ostensibly similar, many of these experiences are also colored by one's cultural background, can in turn be explained by differences in experience and cultural expectations and thinking patterns. As explained in the Tibetan Book of the Dead: "It is quite sufficient for you (the deceased) to know that these apparitions are [the reflections of] your own thought forms."

DEATH AND THE LIMBIC SYSTEM

Presumably conditions such as dreaming, trance states, depth electrode activation, extreme fear, traumatic injury, or temporal lobe epilepsy, result in hyperactivation of the amygdala and hippocampus and overlying temporal lobe. These structures create an image of the individual floating or even soaring above familiar or bizarre surroundings, and will trigger memories, hallucinations, brilliant lights, as well as secrete opiate-like neurotransmitters which induce a state of euphoria and thus eternal peace and harmony.

Given that similar experiences are reported by those who have experienced depth electrode stimulation of these structures, and by those declared "clinically dead" also raises the possibility that the hippocampus and amygdala may be the first areas of the brain to be effected by approaching death, as well as one of the last regions of the brain to actually die.

That is, as one approaches death and even after medical death, the amygdala and hippocampus may continue to function briefly and not only become hyperactivated, but produce a feeling of eternal peace and tranquillity and a hallucination of floating outside the body and of meeting relatives and other religious figures; like a dream.

And yet, it is curious that so many individuals have basically a very similar "dream" and only under conditions of death. Moreover, it is exceedingly difficult to reconcile these experiences with the Darwinian notion of evolution.

What is the "evolutionary" adaptive significance of so many members of the human race having a dream of the "Hereafter" after they die.

As we have learned from physics, this reality is only one of many, and the perception of these alternate realities, and all associated manifestations of extraordinary psychic abilities, are normally inhibited, suppressed, and cannot be perceived or processed due to the limitations of our brain. Under conditions of hyperactivity, the limbic system may not only hallucinate, it may also begin to process this information, and gain access to and engage in alternate modes of thinking, perceiving, and communicating, such that what is normally concealed is revealed to the receptive mind.

Figure 150a. *A Kumeyaay shaman ("Native American"). Photo by TT. Waterman, 1898. Note hands painted on his chest and solar disc on his belly.*

SHAMANISM AND INNATE BRAIN STRUCTURES: THE ORIGINAL NEUROTHEOLOGY
by Michael Winkelman

The famous specialist of comparative religion, Mircea Eliade, promoted a universal concept of the shaman, pointing to the substantial similarities in spiritual healers in societies around the world. Eliade emphasized that the shaman was someone who entered "ecstasy" to communicate with the spirits on behalf of the community. Eliade also added that the shaman's ecstasy was a "magical flight" or soul flight, not possession; that the shaman could heal by recovering the patient's lost or stolen soul; that the shaman acted with the assistance of animal allies or powers; and that the shaman could also act as a sorcerer. In service to the community, the shaman gathered the entire local group for an all-night ceremony of singing, chanting and dancing as the shaman made the "magical flight" (or out-of-body experience) to the spirit worlds in search of needed information and power and to recover lost souls.

Anthropologist Michael Harner has referred to these worldwide practices as "core shamanism," reflecting recognition that there are basic principles of shamanic practice found in cultures around the world. These universals present a challenge to the rationalistic perspective that shamanism is like other religions, a delusion. The universals of core shamanism attest to an adaptive and empirical basis rather than an arbitrary set of beliefs. This adaptive basis for shamanism is increasingly recognized as a core feature of the emergence of modern human culture 40,000 years ago in the Middle/Upper Paleolithic transition, and played a pivotal role in these cultural advances (Winkelman 2002a). Shamanism was a central part of these cultural institutions, and literally left its symbolic imprint on the walls of caves in Europe (Ryan, 1999, Clottes and Lewis-Williams, 1998, Lewis-Williams 2002). These activities reflect the adaptive advantages of shamanic practices in human cognition, psychological development and social bonding (Winkelman 2000, 2002a).

Universals of core shamanism reflect structures of the brain and the operations and processes of innate brain modules. This neurological basis of shamanism is discussed by Laughlin, McManus and d'Aquili (1992) in terms of neurognostic structures. Neurognostic refers to neurologic structures underlying gnosis, or knowing. Shamanism involves the utilization of a number of neurognostic structures, biologically based structures for experience and knowing that underlie the universality of shamanic practices and their adaptive advantages. These universals reflect an evolved psychology of humans, characteristics acquired because of selective pressures for the advantages they provide (Winkelman, 2002b, McClennon, 2002). Shamanism was the original "neurotheology," a spiritual healing practice based in fundamental principles of the brain and its functions.

The basis of shamanism in neurobiology raises the question of why many cultures lack shamanism or other shamanistic practices. With the rise of complex societies, shamanism underwent a transformation and suffered oppressions and a demise (Winkelman, 1992). The original forms of shamanism disappeared, often being brutally oppressed by religions and state political systems, as Harner (1973) documents in the formation of European witchcraft. However, while original forms of shamanism disappeared (or were transformed), basic principles of shamanism persisted or re-emerged in transformed practices because of their foundation in neurological principles. This is seen in the widespread practices of mediumship, as well as the spontaneous re-emergence of shamanic experiences in modern peoples. These neurognostic principles underlying shamanism are also manifested today in "spiritual emergencies" and in spontaneous religious experiences.

Since the practices of shamanism had been eradicated from pre-modern European cultures, the term shaman entered English from other cultures (Flaherty, 1992). The term was subsequently attributed to practices around the world following the widespread attention it received from Eliade's (1964, originally 1951) classic book Shamanism archaic techniques of ecstasy. While Eliade's work contributed to the perception that shamanism was a worldwide healing practice involving ecstatic communication with the spirit world on behalf of the community, some people have questioned whether shamanism is truly cross-cultural, or whether it is a regionally specific phenomena restricted to Siberia. Others have taken the term shaman and extended it to practices in virtually every culture. Both of these perspectives ignore the phenomena of core shamanism and the cross-cultural differences in practices that use its neurological bases.

CROSS-CULTURAL PERSPECTIVES ON SHAMANS

The idea of core shamanism is based in recognition of structurally identical healing practices in cultures around the world. Whether or not shamanism is universal has been plagued problems of a definitional approach to shamanism. When shamanism is defined based upon a particular set of assumptions, the question of what is a shaman becomes problematic. Some people define shamanism broadly enough to incorporate almost any spiritual practice, while others define it narrowly, specifying that only Siberian cultures have shamanism.

An alternative to the definitional approach and its problems is provided by an empirical assessment of the characteristics associated with magico-religious healers around the world (Winkelman, 1986a, 1990, 1992; see Winkelman & White, 1987 for data and methods). This cross-cultural approach provides an empirical basis for establishing core shamanism and its characteristics, revealing a world-wide shamanism in small-scale societies. Interdisciplinary research indicates shamanism is found cross-culturally because it involves adaptations to psychobiological potentials of altered states of consciousness (ASC, or the integrative mode of consciousness) as well as other innate potentials (Winkelman, 2000).

Shamanistic Healers. The cross-cultural research illustrates the importance of distinguishing core shamanism and other healing practices using ASC. Shamans are found among hunter-gatherers and societies with limited agriculture or pastoral subsistence patterns and political integration limited to the local community. Shamanism was originally an ecological adaptation of hunter-gatherer societies to psychobiological structures and humans' psychosocial and therapeutic needs. This psychobiological foundation for shamanism assured the persistence of similar ASC-based healing practices as societies became more complex. I have referred to these practitioners in more complex societies as shamanistic healers, a human universal that involves healers who use ASC in community rituals to interact with the spirit world (Winkelman, 1990, 1992). Shamanistic healers share the core characteristics of shamans emphasized by Eliade—ecstasy (ASC), community and spirits— reflecting psychobiological principles. ASC are manifested universally, reflecting enhance integration of lower brain processes with frontal processes achieved through induction of synchronized theta wave patterns in the brain. The presence of community in shamanistic healing reflects a variety of psychosocial functions and psychobiological effects. These appear to include the elicitation of neurotransmitter system functions (opioid and serotonergic mechanisms) with a variety of healing mechanisms. The use of the spirit world in shamanism is another biologically based universal. Beliefs about spirits function as a symbol system that provides personal and social identification and self-development and differentiation. Shamanistic healers share these characteristics with core shamanism because of their biological basis; other aspects of shamanistic healers differ from core shamanism because of the effects of their respective societies (agricultural, politically integrated) on healing and consciousness.

Universals of Shamans. Cross-cultural studies revealed that there are similar characteristics associated with the healing practitioners of hunter-gatherer societies, including: an ASC experience known as soul journey or soul flight; the use of chanting and music and dancing; an involvement of the entire community; training through deliberately induced ASC, particularly vision quests; an initiatory experience involving death and rebirth; therapeutic processes focused on soul loss and recovery; disease caused by attacks by spirits and sorcerers, and the intrusion of foreign objects or entities abilities of divination, diagnosis and prophecy; charismatic leadership, as well as malevolent acts, or sorcery; animal relations, including control of animal spirits, transformation into animals and hunting magic.

This paper proposes that a number of these universals can be understood in relationship to basic principles of brain operation that have intrinsic healing properties. The specific aspects of core shamanism addressed below include: the shamanic ASC, soul journey, death and rebirth, music, dance, and therapeutic processes.

THE NEUROLOGICAL FOUNDATIONS OF SHAMANISM

The evolution of human cognition has been characterized in terms of the acquisition of a modular brain structure (e.g., see Mithen [1996] for review). These theories propose human brain evolution involved the acquisition of innate modules, specific structures or functional systems that were adaptive for addressing particular kinds of tasks. Among the modular systems attributed to humans are those for: language, music, mimesis (imitation), animal species classification, self-recognition, inference of other's mental states ("mind-reading") and tool use. Contradictions to the processes of the innate modules have been proposed as providing the basis for religious thought (Boyer 2001); I suggest that we can understand many universals of shamanism in terms of the representations produced through the integration of the processes of these innate modules.

The operation of innate structures of the brain underlie the foundations of shamanism emphasized by Eliade— ecstasy, the spirit world and community— as well as other universal characteristics of shamanism (e.g., death and rebirth, soul journey, music, dance). Ecstasy, or altered states of consciousness (ASC), involve a mode of consciousness; these natural physiological conditions induce the relaxation response, synchronization of brain waves and integration of the evolutionary levels of the brain. The spirit world involves the use of innate representation modules for understanding self, social others, and their mental capacities, a natural psychology based upon human characteristics. Shamanic universals of animism, animal spirits, guardian spirits, and soul flight involve manipulation of these modules in understanding nature, and in the management of personal and social identities. Community represents the importance of social others in synchronizing human psychobiological functions. Shamanic healing manipulates the paleomammalian brain structures to produce emotional healing by evoking socioemotional and psychodynamic processes, strengthening social identity, and eliciting the body's opioid and immunological systems.

THE PSYCHOBIOLOGY OF SHAMANIC ASC

"Ecstasy," trance or ASC has been recognized as central to shamans' selection, training and professional practice. The biological aspects of shamanic ASC are obscured by the many different procedures used to induce them (e.g., auditory driving through procedures such as drumming. clapping, singing and chanting; fasting and water restrictions; prolonged periods of sleeplessness, or deliberate periods of sleep for dream incubation; austerities such as temperature extremes and painful exposures or mutilations of the body; and hallucinogens and other plant medicines in some traditions). In spite of this variety of induction practices associated with shamanism, most procedures have the same basic overall physiological effects (Mandell, 1980).

Shamanic ASC typically involve singing, chanting, drumming and dancing, followed by a phase of collapse and apparent unconsciousness. The overall physiological dynamics involve an activation of the sympathetic division of the autonomic nervous through drumming and dancing until exhaustion of the sympathetic system from extreme exertion leads to collapse into a parasympathetic dominant state characterized by the relaxation response and intense visual activity. This same stimulation and collapse cycle is produced by many other procedures, including: fasting, sleeping and dreaming, hallucinogenic drugs (or psychointegrators [Winkelman, 1996]). Sometimes shamans enter this phase of relaxation ASC directly through withdrawal and an internal focus of attention, rather than extensive induction procedures and the sympathetic system stimulation.

The shamanic ASC is one of several states of consciousness that occur in the integrative mode of consciousness, part of the cycles of homeostatic balance in the nervous system. The biological basis of the integrative mode of consciousness is reflect in the presence in all cultures of procedures for accessing ASC (Laughlin, McManus and d'Aquili, 1992, Bourguignon, 1976). Although societies differ in their attitudes towards ASC and the means for controlled access to them, institutionalized procedures for entering ASC are found in virtually all societies because they are part of human nature and the normal functions of the brain. The universals of shamanistic practices reflect underlying brain structures and functions that reflects a normal brain response to diverse stimuli. These responses induce synchronized brain wave patterns, typically in the theta (3-6 cycles per second [cps]) and slow alpha (6-8 cps) range.

These brain wave patterns are produced by activity in the limbic system, also referred to as the emotional brain and the paleomammalian brain. These discharges first establish linkages between the limbic system and the lower brain structures, integrating information from the whole organism with emotions and memory. These connections produce strong theta wave patterns mediated by the action of the serotonin circuitry. These synchronized theta patterns produce ascending discharges, sending impulses up the neuraxis of the brain (a nerve bundle running from the bran stem up into the limbic system and frontal parts of the brain). These synchronous discharges reach the frontal cortex, where they replace its normal fast and desynchronized brain wave activity with the coherent slow wave discharges in the alpha and theta range (Mandell, 1980; Winkelman, 1986b, 1992, 2000). The overall effect of the shamanic ASC is to dominate the frontal part of the brain with information from the emotional and behavioral brains. This integrates the information and processes of these preverbal brain structures into the personal and cultural systems mediated by language and the frontal cortex.

Soul Journey: Self in Presentational Symbolism. The shaman's ASC is characterized as a "soul journey" or "soul flight," although the shaman's ASC may take several forms, including a visit from the spirit world or a transformation into an animal. Although possession is associated with some shamanistic healers (e.g., mediums) it is not characteristic of core shamanism. The shaman's soul journey is a neurognostic structure, a biologically based experience attested to cross-culturally (e.g., astral projection, out-of-body-experiences, near death experiences). The experience of flight and vision associated with the soul journey is a natural response of the human nervous system. Hunt (1995) proposes that the experience of soul flight involves representation of self from the "other's" perspective. Soul journey involves the prototype of "taking the role of the other," seeing oneself from another's point of view. In the soul journey, this perspective is represented in the visual spatial modality, involving what Hunt refers to as a presentational symbolism. This is a symbolic system that operates independently of language, providing a medium for an externalized self-representation. These experiences provide new form of self-awareness not tied to one's ordinary self and body, and create the shaman's transcendence of ordinary awareness and identity.

COMMUNITY RITUAL AS A PSYCHOBIOLOGICAL THERAPY

Eliade emphasized that shamanic healing was on behalf of the community, and shamanistic healing occurs in the context of the local community. Typically all members of the community were expected to attend what was characterized by Eliade as "a spectacle unequaled in the world of daily experience" (1964:511). These group rituals are not uniquely human, but also have a significant role in animal societies. The wide distribution of group rituals in the animal kingdom attest to their sociobiological importance. In humans, the collective presence of a community produces therapeutic effects derived from both psychosocial influences (positive expectation and social support) and psychobiological effects. Collective rituals strengthen group identity and community cohesion not only through social processes, but also through their effects upon human psychobiology. Communal activities also elicit and reinforce attachment needs in the mammalian biosocial system (Kirkpatrick, 1997, Frecska and Kulcsar, 1989) and appear to elicit psychosociophysiological mechanisms that release endogenous opiates (see also Prince, 1982). The attachment and affective bonds that evolved in mammals to maintain proximity with infants provide a secure basis for the self in the feelings of protection from powerful figures.

These affective bonds are used in shamanistic ritual, which reinforce these innate mechanisms for attachment with the cultural symbols and neurognostic processes. Frecska and Kulcsar review evidence that shamanic rituals elicit psychobiologically mediated attachment processes that are based in the body's opioid mechanisms. Shamanic rituals use cultural symbols that have been cross-conditioned with patterns of attachment and their physiological and emotional responses. The emotionally charged cultural symbols that were associated with physiological systems during early attachment relations and socialization processes provide a basis for elicitation of the opioid system in shamanistic ritual. The ritual use of symbols associated with physiological reactions enables shamanic ritual to manipulate physiology. The release of endogenous opioids by a variety of physical activities associated with shamanic ritual has also been noted (e.g., see Prince, 1982, Winkelman, 1997). These shamanic activities that stimulate release of the body's own opioid system include: exhaustive rhythmic physical activities (e.g., dancing and clapping); exposure to temperature extremes (e.g., cold or sweat lodges); and austerities such as prolonged water deprivation and fasting, flagellation, and self-inflicted wounds. Opioids are also elicited by emotional manipulations involving fear and positive expectations, as well as the nighttime activities typical of shamanic ritual, when endogenous opioids are naturally highest.

The release of natural opioids stimulates physiological processes, including the immunological system (Frecska and Kulcsar, 1989). Activation of the opioid system also produces a sense of euphoria, certainty and belongingness. These processes enhance coping skills and the maintenance of bodily homeostasis (Valle and Prince, 1989). Endogenous opioids reduce pain, enhance tolerance of stress, facilitate environmental adaptation, and enhance psychobiological synchronization within the group. These processes enhance group solidarity in a sense of communitas, the experience of the essential bonds among group members. Enhancement of community identity promotes the dissolution of self-boundaries and enhances the sense of identification with others. This reinforces individual commitment to the group and promotes the development of an integrated sense of self.

Chanting and Music: Innate Expressive Social Capacities. The use of song and chanting are universal aspects of shamanic healing ritual. These activities not only induce an ASC, but also reflect expressive community communication processes that utilize innate modules. Chanting practices associated with shamanism reflect a biologically based capacity with deep evolutionary roots. These vocalizations have progenitors in the song, call and other vocal expressive systems found in other animals (Molino, 2000). These expressive capabilities that humans share with other primates were extended in human evolution, but continue to share functions as a communicative and expressive system. These vocalizations involve states of high arousal to communicate about affective states and alarm; to modulate social contact and spacing; for mate attraction, pair bonding and bond and territorial advertisement; to motivate other members of the group; interindividual and intergroup communication, particularly regarding location, spacing, food sources and danger; and to enhance group cohesion and unity (Geissmann, 2000). Music's adaptive roles include its ability to promote group cohesion and coordination, enhancing synchrony and cooperation among group members. Music strengthens group cohesion through mutual cognitive and emotional expression and coordinating the behavior of different individuals into synchronized performances (Brown, 2000, Merker, 2000).

Mimesis and Dance. The shaman's dance is a core aspect of shamanic practices found around the world. Dancing is part of a larger group of cultural activities such as chanting, singing, poetry and play that share common modules that provide rhythm, affective semantics and melody (Molino, paraphrase p165, 173). This rhythmic module of the brain provided an expressive system that predated language (Donald, 1991). Freeman (2000) suggest that music and dance coevolved to enhance social bonding and communication of internal states, contributing a technology for inducing ASC and breaking down existing habits and thought patterns. The close linkage of musical expression with movement and dance reflects the operation of an innate brain device known as the "mimetic controller," which provides the unique human ability to entrain the body to external rhythms (Donald, 1991). The effects of music include a compulsion to move with the rhythm, including shaking, clapping, stomping and dancing, reflecting the operation of this innate mimetic controller. Group ritual dances and vocal imitation of animals were among the first of human mimetic activities. The mimetic controller provides the basis for the ability to represent through imitation, as well as gestural and facial representations and the rhythmic coordination of behavior of individuals. Mimesis provides a basis for a shared culture through enactive symbolism. The shaman's use of dance, imitation and drumming reflect the utilization of this innate mimetic controller, which provides mechanisms for producing coordination among a group. This communication system of the body involves a "rhythmo-affective semantics" that expresses the fundamental emotions (Molino, 2000). Mimesis is still the primary mechanisms through which humans learn social roles and physical skills. This mimetic ability expressed through imitation and ritual produced a mythic ethos that was enacted early in human evolution in activities involving collective participation. These behaviors have direct continuities with animal ritual (see McClennon, 2002). Similarities with ape ritual are seen in their locomotor displays involving kicking, stomping, shaking branches, beating on the chest, ground or vegetation, and jumping and running (Geissman).

SPIRIT AS BIOPSYCHOSOCIAL STRUCTURES OF SELF AND OTHER

A central feature of shamanism is the interaction with the spirit world. This belief in spirits is part of a broader cognitive framework known as animism. Animism is the belief in a soul or vital principle that animates entities, producing their behaviors and other observable properties. While animism has been viewed historically as a delusional system of belief, contemporary perspectives consider animism in a different light. Animism, or spirits, reflect basic principles of human consciousness. Spirits reflect fundamental operations of the nervous system and consciousness and a basic forms of knowledge of the world that operate at non-verbal pre-linguistic levels of conceptualization, reflecting processes of what the neurobiologist Paul MacLean (1990, 1993) refers to as paleomentation. These paleomentation processes include activities of the paleomammalian brain, or limbic brain, that engages in processes related to self, emotional attachments and the feelings of certainty regarding one's convictions. These brain processes also provide representations central to consciousness, a sense of self and others, operating on structures that function outside of conscious awareness.

Animism is a universal of human cultures, based in conceptual processes that consider other phenomena to be fundamentally like humans. Animism is a basic form of projection of cognitive similarity, attributing our own characteristics to unknown others. Animism is generally manifested in anthropomorphism, which involves the attribution of human characteristics—self, emotions, mind and identity—to non-human entities (Guthrie, 1993). The attributions to spirits are based in a metaphoric extension of the properties of the self for modeling the unknown other. Spirit beliefs also reflect social structures of the group and the dynamics of social and interpersonal relations. This human tendency to animate the natural world with human-like principles is a form of relational knowing that establishes human relations with the environment. Animism plays a fundamental role in the construction of a sense of self-identity and communal identity (Bird-David, 1999).

The concepts of spirits represent a language of intrapsychic dynamics of the self and psychosocial relations with others. Consequently, spirits constitute a natural symbolic system for manipulating unconscious aspects of self, personal and communal identity, and psychosocial relations with others. Viewing the spirit world as a conceptual framework for representing aspects of self and others enables an understanding of how ritual manipulation of spirit constructs can have effects upon attachments and emotions. Shamanic systems consider spirits to be the most fundamental causes of illness; they also reflect fundamental structures of self and others and generic aspects of consciousness. Shamanic ritual elicits these primordial psychocognitive processes and forms of communication, and uses symbolic processes to manage self concept, emotional well-being and relationships with social "others." The spirit processes of shamanistic healing make maladies meaningful in both the context of cultural life, and in relationship to innate structures of self-perception. These neurognostic based systems of meaning provide a basis for understanding personal psychodynamics through an innate body-based system of meaning (Laughlin, 1997). This body based references system is also fundamental to the shamanic journey— or "out-of-body experience." Shamanic healing rituals entrain these innate structures with cultural symbolic processes, allowing healing to emerge from unconscious integration (Winkelman, 2000).

Spirits can be understood in terms of symbolic systems that represent "complexes," which are organized perceptual, behavioral and personality dynamics that operate independent of, or dissociated from, ordinary awareness and social identity. Shamanistic healing practices addresses these dissociated personality complexes by eliciting the holistic imperative, a drive toward integration across levels of consciousness (Laughlin et al., 1992). These complexes, representing un-integrated aspects of self, are manipulated in shamanic rituals to produce healing by re-structuring and integrating the unconscious dynamics. Shamanic healing integrates the self, utilizing visual and corporeal processes to unite unconscious information with the conscious mind. Shamanic ritual provides a number of mechanisms for elicitation of the emotional unconscious and re-alignment of the individual with social expectations and cultural meaning systems.

Death and Rebirth. An aspects of self and identity produced through shamans' ASC are illustrated in a universal feature of shamanic training, a "death and rebirth" experience. This death and rebirth experience may occur spontaneously, as a result of illness or injury, or during the active pursuit of shamanic power. During initial training and development, the shaman neophyte experiences a crisis of illness and suffering involving attacks by spirits which lead to personal death. This death is followed by a destruction of the victim's body and its reconstruction with the addition of spirit allies and powers. This death and rebirth experience reflects neurognostic processes of self transformation, constituting a natural response to conditions of overwhelming stress and intrapsychic conflicts (Walsh, 1990). These experiences are the result of the fragmentation or breakdown of the ego, experienced in "autosymbolic images" of the destruction of one's body and self (Laughlin et al., 1992). Shamanic healing in response to this death and rebirth also activates innate drives towards toward psychological integration. Shamanic rituals manipulate symbolic and physiological structures to restructure the ego and producing a new self identity. This restructuring is promoted by holistic imperatives toward psychointegration, and provides the basis for the exceptional health of shamans.

SPIRIT RELATIONS AS ROLE TAKING: INCORPORATING THE "OTHER"

Humans have an innate capacity to "take the perspective of others." Humans can infer other's mental states, using their own minds to infer the mental states and motivations of others. This capability enables humans to incorporate others into self-identity, to use the models of "others" to augment and model the self. Shamanism uses this capability to provide therapeutic processes through role-taking (Peters & Price-Williams, 1981). The processes of role-taking are exemplified in the shaman's spirit world interaction, where shamans enact the personalities of the spirits. The interactions with the spirit world provide representations of personal and social psychodynamics, including emotions, attachments, social influences and behaviors. These representations allow shamanic rituals to affect the psychodynamics of the patient. Shamanic manipulation of the spirit world produces therapeutic changes because the spirits represent fundamental aspects of the self. The shaman's dramatic enactment of interactions with spirits provides models for self development and socialization. The innate capability to incorporate the "other" enables the spirit systems to contribute to identity modification. This occurs through the internalization of spirit behaviors, as well as the capabilities inherent in animal allies and powers.

Shamanic self-development is exemplified in the basic training activities of shamanism, the acquisition of animal powers and the vision quest, or guardian spirit quest. These involve seeking a personal relationship with the spiritual world through the development of a personal relationship with spirit allies, powers and guardians.

The shamanic systems of animism, totemism and guardian spirits provide natural symbolic systems for the development and differentiation of self. The cultural processes of shamanism manipulate these natural systems to create natural symbolic systems for the representation of self and alternate forms of self, providing mechanisms for problem-solving and psychosocial adaptation. The spirit identities provide a range of self-concepts to mediate conflict among biological, psychological and social priorities.

Animal Allies and Totemism. Animals play a central role in shamanic practices and beliefs. Animals are the basic allies and spirit helpers of shamans, who are generally considered to be "master of the animals" or have special relationships to the deities and natural forces that control animals. Shamans are typically called upon to assist in hunting, and are generally believed to be able to transform themselves into animals. These universals of shamanism involving animals reflect the use of another innate module of the brain. Mithen refers to this as the natural history or intuitive biology module. This involves specialized innate capacities for organizing knowledge about animals and recognizing "species essence." This ability is manifested in the universal human ability to organize information about animals and produce taxonomical classification schemas for the natural world. This innate capability provides a universal analogical system for creation and extension of meaning. The use of animal species for representation is manifested in the phenomena of spirit allies and totemism. The anthropologist Levi-Strauss (1962) characterized totemism as involving the establishment of metaphoric relationship between the natural history domains of animals and social groups. In totemism, human groups are distinguished by attributing the characteristics derived from the animal world. Totemism involves human thought about the identity of humans and social groups in terms of the models provided by animal species. The use of animals is social and cognitive modeling is one of the most fundamental aspects of metaphoric and analogical thought, a universal human system for expression of meaning and creation of social and personal identity.

Guardian Spirit Complex. The use of this innate system for recognizing species essence is also manifested in the practices of the guardian spirit complex. Shamanism utilizes the natural history module in incorporating animal spirits as powers or allies, as aspects of the personal powers and identity. In hunter-gather societies, this guardian spirit quest was not specific to shamanism, but central to development of adult skills and competencies. This was part of the transition to adulthood, guiding the individual in personal and social choices and commitments in life (Swanson, 1973). These guardian spirit interactions provided personal powers, strength, and assistance in making one's decisions about social choices for adult life. These animals with whom shamans have personal relationship have psychosocial functions in empowerment and in providing a representational system for self-development and self-differentiation. This was illustrated in the widespread North American guardian spirit complex focused on the guardian spirit quest. This role of animal spirits as representing aspects of one's self reflects a fundamental aspect of shamanistic thought, that of the "sacred other" (Pandian, 1997). The intersection of the animal spirit with personal identity involves cultural processes for producing symbolic models for the self. The animal spirits provide projective systems for psychosocial relations and ideals that structure individual psychodynamics and social behavior. Pandian suggests that the "shamanistic sacred self" provides models and processes for protecting individuals from stress and anxiety and the management of emotions. These animal identities also provide alternate forms of self representation to facilitate social adaptations. The alternate senses of self that animal powers provide are mechanisms for problem-solving and conflict management. Animal spirit concepts of self provide a system of variable command-control agents that facilitate the mediation of personal and social conflict. These animal spirits provide alternate sense of identity that can mediate conflict between the different aspects of self and instinctive agents. This helps mediate a hierarchy of personal and social goals. Shamanic animal powers provide processes for constructing and manipulating a variety of selves for psychological and social integration.

SHAMANISTIC THERAPIES: A BIOPSYCHOSOCIAL APPROACH

Shamanic rituals use ASC, community relations, and interactions with spirit-world constructs to manipulate physiology, psychology and social relationships for therapeutic benefits. This reflects the ability of shamanic practices to evoke an integrated biopsychosocial healing process that elicits not only symbolic and social processes, but also physiological responses.

ASC AS HEALING PRACTICES

Shamanic ASC exercise therapeutic effects through a number of processes. These include the induction of a condition of parasympathetic dominance in the autonomic nervous system and a synchronization of information across the levels of the brain, particularly limbic-frontal integration and synchronization of the frontal hemispheres. These produce physiological processes underlying shamanic healing mechanisms, including: physiological relaxation, producing a reduction in tension and stress; regulation of psychophysiological processes, reducing anxiety reactions and psychosomatic effects; providing accessing to sub- and un- conscious information; integration of behavioral, emotional and cognitive processes; enhancement of social bonding and group integration; and facilitating positive emotions and social attachments.

Shamanic ASC induce a parasympathetic dominant state that evokes the relaxation response. This generalized decrease in sympathetic nervous system activity has therapeutic value, reducing stress related physiological conditions. Rapid induction of the parasympathetic dominant state can also cause the erasure of conditioned responses (learned behaviors) and produce dramatic changes in beliefs by increasing suggestibility and placebo and psychosomatic effects. ASCs activate pre-conscious brain processes, allowing integration into the conscious mind of psychodynamic material that is normally inaccessible. These repressed conflicts affect emotions and physiological responses. Enhance expression of these repressed aspects of self through giving expression to non-verbal information can have therapeutic effects through enhanced integration of he psyche.

ASC evoke limbic system functions that manage emotional mentation, self and social identity processes related to interpersonal bonding and attachment. These contribute to healing through producing an integration of emotional information into consciousness. ASC produce theta wave entrainment, an integration across hierarchical brain levels. This integration of pre- or unconscious functions into conscious awareness involves an enhanced integration of cognitive and emotional processes. This integration of information from different functional systems of the brain enhances learning, attention, memory and adaptation to novel situations (Mandell, 1980).

The effects of shamanic ASC may be inferred from research on the physiology of meditation. Some scientists believe that there are neuroendocrine mechanisms of meditation that involve stress reduction through enhancement of serotonin functioning and stimulation of theta brain-wave production (Walton and Levitzky, 1994). Meditation lowers autonomic arousal and enhances brainwave coherence in theta frequencies. Meditation effects upon serotonin levels have the effect of reducing cortisol levels, and consequently the anger and fear reactions. The meditation research implicates the same mechanisms that Mandell (1980) postulates as generic to transcendent states. This involves serotonergic mechanisms that are manifested in synchronous high voltage slow frequency brain waves (alpha, theta, and delta activity, especially 3-6 cycles/second) that link the limbic system and behavioral brain. This slow wave synchronized brain waves drive their impulses into the frontal cortex, linking its processing to the lower brain structures.

EMOTIONAL HEALING PROCESSES

The processes of shamanistic healing involve the generic processes of all spiritual healing systems, the provision of meaning. The sense of meaning instilled by shamanism provides healing through multiple mechanisms that link the individual to a sense of socially-mediated well-being. Shamanic meaning systems have a neurobiological basis in the functions of the limbic, or emotional, brain and its processes related to assurance of psychological well-being and attachment. The neurobiologist MacLean has referred to these as emotiomentation processes, affective evaluation processes that provide an assurance of a meaningful and controllable world that counteracts anxiety and its detrimental physiological effects. Social processes and spirits provide explanations that meet human needs for assurance, instilling confidence and a sense of certainty. Shamanism uses symbolic manipulations that have the potential to intervene in the stress mechanisms of the general adaptation syndrome. Shamanic ritual may alleviate high levels of activity in the pituitary/adrenal system, curtailing the resistance stage of the stress reaction through changing emotional responses that upset the balance in the autonomic nervous system. Shamanic ritual and its effects upon social bonding manipulate emotional processes and their physiological consequences, providing effects upon both body and mind. An aspect of shamanistic healing involves the elicitation of placebo responses through instilling the expectation of well-being.

Shamanic healing activities address social-emotional dynamics through many processes: the community integration involved in soul recovery and object and spirit extraction; eliciting community support systems that meet fundamental human needs for a sense of belonging and bonding with others; evocation and restructuring of painful memories (catharsis and abreaction); and confession and forgiveness as processes for resolving intrapsychic and interpersonal conflict. Shamanic healing typically externalizes guilt, attributing it to the action of spirit forces; this helps minimize the sense of personal responsibility and guilt, reducing negative emotional process. Ritual operates through metaphoric processes that manipulate affective responses independent of the rational mind. This enables shamanic ritual to reorganize emotional dynamics, reprogramming emotional brain processes through songs and psychodramatic enactments that have the ability to change self-perception and social relations.

Shamanism's use of the production of meaning to heal involves the universals of symbolic healing (Dow, 1986). This involves particularizing a client's circumstances within their cultural mythology, and then ritually manipulating that mythological system to transform the their emotions and self-system. This ritual manipulation is primarily achieved through the mechanisms of the spirit world. Shamanistic ritual uses spirit concepts to connect with innate drives toward self-differentiation and identification with "others" enabling self-reorganization and integration (Laughlin et al., 1992). These processes connect with innate tendencies to integration of identity at higher levels of self-integration, and identification with more powerful others, symbolically transforming the self.

CONCLUSIONS: CONTEMPORARY MANIFESTATIONS OF SHAMANIC NEUROGNOSTIC STRUCTURES

The neurological foundations of shamanic features allows for their persistence in contemporary society. This is reflected in contemporary illness in psychiatrists' diagnostic categories of "spiritual emergencies. These include: spontaneous shamanic journeys; the death and rebirth experience; mystical experiences with psychotic features; and expressions of psychic abilities (Walsh, 1990). The shamanic paradigm provides a framework for addressing these experiences as natural manifestations of human consciousness and as developmental opportunities. The neurognostic framework helps explain why the shamanic phenomena spontaneously manifest and why the shamanic approach is a more successful therapeutic approach in addressing these natural manifestations of consciousness. The shamanic paradigm re-interprets what psychiatry considers symptoms of acute psychosis and emotional disturbance as opportunities for personal development. The psychobiological basis of these shamanic experiences allows shamanic counselors to treat these conditions as natural and elicit brain processes that provide opportunities to develop control over these experiences. Treating death and rebirth, soul loss, out-of-body experiences, power loss, animal familiars and spirits as natural manifestations of consciousness enables people to engage in the classic shamanic approach of self-empowerment to address these experiences.

Although shamanism has been regarded as an ancient human healing tradition, its modern resurgence indicates that shamanism's dynamics are here to stay. Instead of pondering the reasons for a "return to superstition," the neurognostic framework provides an understanding of these phenomena as natural phenomena of consciousness. Shamanic traditions of altering consciousness, ritually manipulating identity and changing psychosocial dynamics through adopting animal and spirit world identities are still relevant. Shamanic traditions are rooted in human psychobiology and brain dynamics, assuring their continued relevance. Their persistence in traditional societies and their resurgence in the modern world is testimony to the need for shamanic healing. Shamanic healing practices may not only be good complementary therapies, but they may also provide important alternatives to biomedicine by addressing the biopsychosocial dynamics of human health and illness. Shamanic healing can open new avenues for all healers by ritually addressing the innate brain processing modules for knowledge about mind, self, others and nature and manipulating these natural models of self for further development.

Figure 150b. *A Sumerian/ Babylonian god or shaman, holding a staff upon which sits a flying solar disc.*

Figure 150c *"The Shaman." Dressed in animal skins and stag antlers, the shaman was drawn above the entrance to the grand gallery at Les Trois-Freres Cave in Southern Francem, about 30,000 year ago. Upper Paleolithic. From a copy made by Abbe Breuil.*

EXPLORING THE CONTOURS OF MIND & CONSCIOUSNESS THROUGH MAGICO-SPIRITUAL TECHNIQUES
by Manie Eagar & Enmarie Potgieter

Although, on the surface, the techniques and style might differ, the path to altered states of consciousness can be strikingly similar when you compare the experiences of practioners from all over the world.

Two comparisons are made in this paper - the approach to and achievement of trance states of the San Bushmen in South Africa, and the traditions of working with the sacred plants of the Amazon, specifically San Pedro and ayahuasca.

These trance, or altered, states, are expressed through dance, singing and artwork.

Both South African bushmen and indigenous South American Indians express themselves in this way, and the historical context in both instances will be compared down to present times where 'living tribes' express these traditions in modern themes of trance dance and song. This has been given a modern context and 'urban shamans' have adopted some of these techniques to project into other, altered or 'all potential' states of consciousness, which is being thoroughly researched.

This paper concludes that all minds are landscapes to be traversed and explored by a multiplicity of techniques and approaches – literally that an archaeology of mind is available to us and that an ecology of consciousness can be evolved from these recorded experiences and related research. In a broader sense, the farther reaches of the conscious and unconscious mind are being explored increasingly through both scientific and experimental methods by using a variety of psycho deconstructive and integrative techniques – from the shamanistic 'manufacturing of reality' by deconstructing boundaries of sense-making reality, to the reality and consciousness-making of artificial intelligence, studies into animal and plant sentience, as well as psychonautic explorations into other 'dimensions' of reality and consciousness constructs. It is a netherworld, a 'twilight zone', of either or neither that has attracted, and been navigated by generations of psycho-spiritual seekers and mind explorers in the form of artists, poets, philosophers and the modern-day high priests of science and cyber shamans.

A variety of traditional and modern magico-spiritual techniques centering on achieving altered states of consciousness have evolved to project will and intent towards specific outcomes - either for personal development, therapeutic applications and for mundane, personal use. These practices have evolved into 'cyber shamanism and psychonautics' through a variety of ecstatic techniques such as gnosis, breathing, meditation, visualisation, and the use of psycho-integratives (entheogens such as San Pedro and ayahuasca), tantric practices and ritual.

This paper will draw on the latest insights into magical technique, modern science of the mind, quantum physics, genomics, memetics, consciousness studies, altered states/realities (by whatever means), shamanic and ritual traditions - to investigate its universal applicability and the essential 'pathways' for the next generation of consciousness exploring practitioners and seekers.

INTRODUCTION

In the beginning there was the body – bound physicality with a locale and a purpose - the survival of the body. This body evolved over time and grew an increasingly more intelligent and conscious sense-making tool – the brain. To travel through this landscape into which it was deposited the body, and its sense-making tool, the mind, also produced a mirroring, reprogrammable, data sifting capacity to enhance its chances of survival and with the added ability to conjecture, to imagineer beyond the boundaries of physical body and the sense of self – into the future, whilst looking back onto lessons of the past for as far as its memory banks will allow.

For the last few tens of thousands of years, it is clear that this sense-making capacity has evolved to the point where the mind within the body can literally project beyond itself and its physical locale in the landscape – both the inner (the mindscape) and the outer (the realm of physical objects

– both animate and inanimate) whilst traversing through the geographical world. Some things made sense - was within the grasp of the senses. Most things did not and became the realm of mythmaking.

The big question of time and life's trajectory is succinctly stated by the hero Deckard in the science fiction movie *Blade Runner*, "All he'd wanted were the same answers the rest of us want. *Where did I come from? Where am I going? How long have I got?*" This question has preoccupied every sensate human and finally humanity as our cultural communication and sense-making base started to grow to the point were it spans VALIS-like across the planet thanks to the Internet – a model of interpenetrative, boundaryless sense of knowing.

The term 'VALIS' is the science fiction author Philip K. Dick's acronym for 'vast active living intelligence system' which he defined further as a 'spontaneous self-monitoring negentropic vortex … tending progressively to subsume and incorporate its environment into arrangements of information' (Davis, 1998). VALIS is an example of a personal sense-making myth created by Dick to understand his view of and journey through his mindscape and his external landscape, in the same way that any religion or belief system is a sense-making myth for any grouping of people.

For the ancient questing shaman this became a matter of life and death – knowing the cycles of time, the times to hunt, the times to seek shelter, when to mate, when to move across this dangerous foreign landscape in which he and his tribe were located – meant pushing the limits of what he or she could do with their sense-making tool, the mind. And the short answer is, much as we experience today, most things do not make sense and do not seem to have the same humanlike bound-within-a-body purpose as we enjoy it.

The environment from which we are spawned itself is a vehicle for shaping boundaries on the edge of space and time and the quantum flux, at the exact boundary were extropy and entropy meets. This balancing act of the bound and boundless has moulded us inside our skins for purposes of survival and imbued us with a lifespan, similar to our android protagonist Roy in *Blade Runner*, with a limited lifespan, for such are the cycles of time. The description 'boundless' can be thought of in the sense of '*apeiron*'. For the Pre-Socratic Greek philosopher, Anaximander, this conception of *apeiron* as externally unbounded is rooted in the word's use to mean 'ring' or 'sphere,' on whose surface one may travel for an indefinite period of time without coming to a bounding line (Rohr, 1995).

For we are hunters of time, bound in dimensional space, attempting to make sense, interpret, conjecture, speculate, and roll the dice again as we go along. Such is the nature of our being (here).

There is an old passage written by the Venerable Bede, quoted by noted Nobel Prize-winning theoretical physicist Steven Weinberg, that has preoccupied our minds for a very long time, when we sit with shamans at smoky fires, or participate in some sense-making magickal ritual, or listen to psychonauts as they conjecture over and integrate their journeys after returning from an ayahuasca ceremony, or trance dance the night away with some revellers, or at a solitary zazen retreat at a Buddhist monastery sitting for ten hours a day for three weeks. The Venerable Bede ponders the issue that "…*man appears on earth for but a little while; but of what went before this life or of what follows, we know nothing*".[1] But for us the curiosity remains.

Our challenge to such thinking is – can we ever know enough. Have we reached the boundaries of our sense-making capacities? We think the human is far too curious a monkey (the eastern philosophers accuse western thinkers of having 'monkey mind' and for good reason – our curiosity is insatiable). Is there a point where one would ever close off all avenues of query and relax into a state of simply being. We do not think so. In many ways many histories of mankind have been written, and will simply become footnotes in the broader tapestry of knowing, of expanding mindscapes and landscapes, of history and sense-making that we ourselves have yet to traverse.

At issue here is - do we lack the sense-making capacity to see, feel and be conscious of meaning beyond our physical selves, and beyond the cycle of life and death. This is the Sisyphean task of the shaman as he/she grasps beyond the immediate realm of the now into the realm of the witches, the hagazussa (German for 'fence rider'), between the worlds, the world of peripheral vision on the boundary of sense-making.

In the words of science fiction mythmaker Philip K. Dick, "But I have never had too high a regard for what is generally called 'reality'. Reality, to me is not so much something that you perceive, but something you make" and "The world of the future, to me, is not a place but an event. … a construction which there is no author and no readers but a great many characters in search of a plot" (Sutin, 1995. p. 204).

It is a world in which we manufacture our own reality as a conscious, knowing, active expression and manifestation of our purposeful, sense making self (willed existence) through the manipulation of our present reality/ies. Each instant, a personal 'through the looking glass' conglomeration of contexts. I become 'my habits of acting in context and shaping and perceiving the contexts in which I act' (Bateson, 1978. p. 275).

ENTER THE SHAMAN

It is the world of the shamans that we now enter and psychonavigate mindscapes that do not regard themselves as bound by space and time, or this or any other reality.

Our journey inwards and outwards starts with the (San) Bushman of Southern Africa, who left behind the world's richest heritage of Stone Age rock art (the earliest dating has been made at 26 000 BCE, contemporaneous with the Upper Palaeolithic art of Western Europe; the Lascaux cave paintings date from 17 000 BCE). Initially seen as merely 'caveman doodles' and 'bush graffiti', the latest research has uncovered the layers of sense and mythmaking that envelop this hugely rich tapestry of symbolised human consciousness.

For the Bushman his rock art is a unique record of altered states of consciousness, even alternate states of consciousness, as perceived and experienced through trance dance and the raising of boiling energy (a potency, like electricity, called *!gi,* or */num*). These shamans are the 'owners of, and full of potency' and whose task it is to control it for the good of the people. For these myths were both personal and tribal – the whole community participates, supports, and draws on this mythmaking process to this day through their trance dances and subsequent healing rituals (Lewis-Williams and Dowson, 2000).

In the case of their rock art "…we realise that the San conceived of the cosmos as layered…" For them "The rock face was like a veil suspended between this world and the realms inhabited by spirits and spirit animals." "*Everything* painted on the 'veil', no matter how secular the images may seem to us, was in fact set in a spiritual context and contributed to the dissolution of distinctions between the material and the spiritual worlds" (Lewis-Williams and Dowson, 2000, p. vii). "When viewing Bushman rock art, we should remind ourselves that we are looking at a bridge between two worlds" (Lewis-Williams & Dowson, 2000, p. 36).

These magico-spiritual techniques (they did not practice sympathetic magic as was originally thought) are taught to apprentices and passed on from generation to generation through dance rehearsals, to the point were they even face and keep in view the rock paintings made by the tribal shamans (the 'owners of potency', the *n/om k" ausi*) to heighten the level of their own potency as they enter trance states and the days of 'eland power'. Blood from the eland was used in the paintings which became storehouses of potency. This made contact with the spirit world possible, guaranteed humankind's existence by facilitating healing, rain-making and animal control, and, by flowing between nature and people, gathered up all aspects of life in a single spiritual unity.

It is estimated that about half the men and a third of the women in a Kalahari Bushman camp may be shamans. The Bushmen of today hardly ever use hallucinogens. They rely instead on hyperventilation, intense concentration and highly rhythmic dancing to alter their state of consciousness. It is likely that, having recovered from the trance state, the shamans remembered and then depicted their experiences while in a normal state of consciousness.

Having recovered from trance hallucinations, shamans in other parts of the world also experience after-images which may recur for many months after a trance experience. These after-images may last for a few seconds or up to a few minutes. They seem to float before one; or, if one is looking at a flat surface like a wall or a ceiling, they are like colour slides projected on a screen. Projected onto the wall of a rock shelter, such mental images could have provided the inspiration for painting (Lewis-William & Dowson, 2000).

In the trance, the shaman enters an altered state of consciousness, triggered by rhythmic dancing, their dancing rattles, and thudding steps, clapping and chanting. The Bushmen activate a supernatural potency that resides in songs and in the shamans themselves. This potency 'boils', rises up the shamans' spines and they enter trance. They call on the power of spirit animals to allow them to heal their people, and feel like they have animal characteristics themselves and that the power flows painfully from themselves. Both the Cape and European rock paintings show humans with animal features, and people twisting in apparent pain from arrows piercing their body. These represent the experience of being a shaman (Lewis-Williams & Dowson, 2000).

"The shamans' experiences and practices have fundamental similarities around the world because they reflect innate brain process and experiences" (Winkelman, 2000). Further support for this idea comes from psychologists looking at what happens to people in altered states of consciousness or with altered brain function. For Lewis-Williams and Dowson (1998), this is a neurological bridge to the past. Shamanic rituals are still carried out around the world in traditional religions, and non-shamanic people can experience similar feelings under hypnosis, or during fever, trance or migraine.

J.D. Lewis-Williams and T.A. Dowson (1988) in their article 'The Signs of All Times' propose a neurobridge backwards in time to the Upper Palaeolithic by which we can gain insight into the nature of the origins of art. Our nervous system has not changed much in the past 100,000 years. We are still physically very much the hunter-gatherers we were prior to agrarianism. In the signs of Upper Palaeolithic art Lewis-Williams and Dowson see entoptic phenomena very similar to those produced by people in altered states of consciousness today.

This is where we can already draw on the Bushman's sense-making abilities and align it with global mythmaking cultures (the sacred, animated spirit world is as real as the secular, physical world; using trance dance for healing; exercising supernatural powers through dreams; rainmaking; visiting distant camps on out-of-body travel; the control of animals; to reinforce successful hunting expeditions, for personal and tribal protection, connection with the spirit world and the ancestors; to receive messages from and maintain a relationship with their gods; and to maintain a sense of structured, supportive community through a communal sense and myth-making).

"THE FORCE THAT THROUGH THE GREEN FUSE DRIVES THE FLOWER"-Dylan Thomas

One of the shamanic traditions that has been steeped in the use of hallucinogens to induce altered states of consciousness, for healing and divination, is that of the ayahuasceros – the medicine men and women, the mestizo shamans of the Amazon region. Ayahuasca derives from the Quechua language, huasca meaning "vine" and *aya* meaning "dead people." Thus the "vine of the dead" (Metzner, 1999).

With a growing body of research around altered states of consciousness, shamanic practice and therapeutic use of entheogens, DMT (short for the powerful psychoactive ingredient dimethyltryptamine of the ayahuasca brew) has drawn attention because of its reputation to induce special states of consciousness, during which the 'plant teachers' function as spiritual teachers and sources of healing power and knowledge. The plants represent a healing power or energy that can be associated with a plant, a person, an animal, even a place. "In the tribal societies where these plants and plant preparations are used, they are regarded as embodiments of conscious intelligent beings that only become visible in special states of consciousness, and that can function as spiritual teachers and sources of healing power and knowledge" (Metzner, 1999).

The ayahuasqueros or vegetalistas (plant specialists) see the material world and spirit world as interpenetrative – a realm were both co-exist, were "our normal waking consciousness, rational consciousness as we call it, is but one special type of consciousness, while all about it, parted from it by the filmiest of screens, there lie potential forms of consciousness entirely different" (James, 1901/1958, p. 228).

"Crucial to shamanic practices is the belief that many plants, if not all plants, each have their own 'mother' or spirit. It is with the help of the spirits of some of these plants, which I have called 'plant teachers', that the shaman is able to acquire his powers" (Luna, 1984. p. 228)

The role of sacred plants in both ancient and contemporary societies are to allow the personal relationship with reality established in a mythical time; to develop relationships with an animal spiritual realm which is the source of power and self identification; the dissolution of death and ego and its resurrection and transformation; and social rituals to enhance social identity formation, group integration and cohesion and to reaffirm cultural values and beliefs (Winkelman, 1995).

Along with the intake of the ayahuasca brew, is the performance of the Icaros - shamanic power songs learned either from a maestro shaman or directly from the spirits (Luna, 1984). They are used to communicate with the spirits of the natural world, to heal the sick, and to actually provoke certain kinds of visual displays or visions in those medicated with Ayahuasca. The most important of these songs are those learned from the spirits themselves or those received in the dream visions which often follow an ayahuasca session.

There are icaros for increasing or decreasing the strength of the hallucinations, for calling defenders or arhena, for curing specific illnesses, for reinforcing the effects of medicinal plants, for attracting the love of a woman (huarmi icaro), for calling the spirits of dead shamans, for causing rain, wind or thunder, for bewitching, for hunting or fishing certain animals, for curing snake bites, for protecting oneself before sexual intercourse, etc. One shaman even relates that if one knows the principal icaro of a shaman, you can attract his defenders when he dies, and can incorporate his knowledge (Luna, 1984).

Icaros are used only during ayahuasca sessions. In the highly sensitized state of ayahuasca intoxication, the icaros help structure the vision. They can also modify the hallucinations themselves. The icaros are the quintessence of shamanic power. Luna reports, "There are icaros for increasing or diminishing the intensity and color of the visions, for changing the color perceived, and for directing the emotional contents of the hallucinations."

Vegetalistas are masters of synaesthesia. Through using the most interesting acoustic effects produced by whistling and singing, the geometric designs can be seen acoustically. The icaros refer to a medicine as "my painted song," "my words with those designs," or "my ringing pattern" and relates to the entoptic phenomena described by Lewis-Williams and Dowson visible in the San Bushman rock art.

The authors explained the signs in Paleolithic cave art as entoptic images which arise within the human optic system, particularly when people are in altered states of consciousness. The authors compared entoptic-type images appearing in Palaeolithic cave art with similar ones in shamanistic rock art of the Coso Indians of California and the Southern San Bushman of South Africa to argue that Palaeolithic cave art was also associated with altered states of consciousness and was indeed a pan-human phenomenon.

PARADIGMS OF MAGICO-SPIRITUAL PRACTICE

Consciousness is contextual, a living biofeedback system, a cybernetic tool of existence, and therefore in the mind of the shaman and the magico-spiritual practitioner, can be manipulated through techniques of mind, by volitionally and wilfully 'bending', or alternating realities, and therefore consciousness.

Before embarking into the reality-manufacturing world of shaman, it would be useful to create a perspective to the different paradigms extant in the world of the magico-spiritual practitioner and consider a variety of approaches to magico-spiritual techniques (Frater UD, 1991).

Frater UD theorises that the typical present-day magician leans toward, alternates between, or aggregates aspects of the Spirit Model (used by shamans and traditional ceremonial magicians, in which autonomous entities exist in a dimension accessible to ours through altered states of consciousness); the Energy Model (where the world is viewed as being 'vitalised' by energy currents that the magician manipulates); the Psychological Model (in which the magician is seen as "a programmer of symbols and different states of consciousness," manipulating the individual and the deep layers of consciousness); and the Information Model (where information is the code that programs the essentially neutral energy of the life force), and ultimately evolves his own Meta-Model.

The **Spirit Model**, alongside the Energy Model is the oldest model of magic. We can find it worldwide in shamanic cultures as well as in many religions. Its basic premise is the existence of an otherworld inhabited by more or less autonomous entities such as spirits, angels, demons, gods, etc. The shaman or magician is someone who can enter this otherworld at will, who has travelled widely in it, knows its language and customs and has made friends, smitten enemies and/or acquired allies and servitors there. This is important as all magic is of these entities' making. The modern German word for witch, "Hexe" (f.) illustrates this rather neatly if we take a closer look at its etymology. It derives from Old High German "hagazussa" which translates as "fence rider". The hagazussa is riding the "fence between the worlds" i.e. she is at home in the world of everyday life as well as in the magical otherworld of spirits.

These entities who are usually invisible, at least to the average person, and it is the shaman's or magician's task to make them put his will into effect. This may be done by prayer, by barter, by cajoling or even - vide medieval demon magic - by the application of magical force, threats and pressure.

The otherworld may have its own geography but it is usually considered to coexist with the world of everyday life. The key to entering it is an altered state of consciousness, controlled trance or ecstasy of which the shaman is an expert.

The **Energy Model** is based on the ancient healing disciplines of hypnosis and magnetism. "Animal magnetism" is a subtle force inherent in organisms. Interesting parallels to this concept in the vitalist theories of biology, Prana from Yoga, the Polynesian concept of Mana and the Chinese principle of Ki or Ch'i (Chi). In early shamanic cultures, shamanic magic is very frequently a mixture between the spirit and energy model, e.g. the shaman may call upon his spirits or gods to give him "power" or he may, vice versa, use his power to extort favours from them.

In its pure form, however, the shaman or magician is not in need of spirits and other entities. The world is viewed as being "vitalised" by subtle forces or energies and his primary task consists in mastering the art of perceiving and manipulating them. As all phenomena are basically energetic in nature, the existence of an otherworld is not strictly required. Thus, the magician is more of an "energy dancer" than a "fence rider" or go-between. But even here the key to the perception, charging and general utilisation of these forces is again the magical trance or, in magical terms, gnosis.

This approach was popularised in the West since the seventies when the general influx of Eastern thinking made concepts such as chakra and kundalini work a mainstay of most occult disciplines.

With Sigmund Freud's theory of the subconscious, man was suddenly seen as a being which was only partially conscious and in control of itself.

The **Psychological Model's** premise is that the subconscious (or, as Carl Jung later retagged it, the unconscious) will do the job if it is properly addressed and/or conditioned. This is achieved by magical trance, suggestion and the use of symbols (i.e. selective sensory input) as tools of association and as a means of communication between the magician's conscious will and his subconscious faculty responsible for putting it into effect.

A more radical approach was taken by Austin Osman Spare whose sigil magic rests on the basic tenets of the psychological model. Spare's brilliant system is in principle an inversion of Freud's theory of complexes. The psychological magician is a programmer of symbols and different states of consciousness. He is not necessarily in need of a transcendent otherworld or even subtle energies, though in practice he will usually work on the assumption that one or the other (or both) do in fact exist and can be utilised by his subconscious. By actively suppressing his will in the form of a graphical sigil and forgetting it, the magician creates an artificial "complex" which then starts to work on similar lines just as suppressed, subconscious traumas will cause neurotic behaviour, etc.

The **Information Model** of magic is a more recent development. Its basic premises are that, a) Energy as such is "dumb", it needs information on what to do; this can be so called laws of nature or direct commands; and b) Information does not have mass or energy. Thus, it is faster than light and not bound by the restrictions of the Einsteinian space-time continuum. It can therefore be transmitted or tapped at all times and at all places, via a kind of 'information matrix'.

The application of the, as yet evolving, information model has led to the discipline of Cybermagic (from "cybernetics" or the "science of control systems"). Contrary to the other models described above, Cybermagic does not rely on magical trance to achieve its effects. Rather, the Cybershaman activates either his own main memory banks, namely brain and spine, or those of the target person. His techniques demand controlling kundalini effects through Yoga and meditation.

The **Meta-model** of magic is not a model as such but rather an instruction on the use of the others. In the spirit model healing is regarded as an exorcism, illness is caused by "evil" or, at least, undesired entities which have to be neutralized and removed by the shaman or magician. To achieve this the shaman will usually call upon the help of his own spirits who will then handle the matter. Properly exorcised, the patient has been freed from the cause of his ailment and can recuperate.

In the energy model ailments are seen to be caused by energetic imbalance. The magician's task consists of restoring that balance of energies commonly defined as "health". This he may do by laying on hands, by using crystals and precious stones, by magnetism or chakra massage, etc. The balance having been restored, the patient is regarded as having been healed.

In the psychological model illness is considered to be basically psychosomatic in nature. The magician will, therefore, either do a ritual work with the patient which enhances his stamina and resolves his troubles (e.g. a Saturn ritual to cope with "Saturnian challenges" the patient is seen to have avoided by becoming ill) or he will charge a sigil for the patient's health.

In the information model the Cybermagician will transmit an informational "healing matrix" into the patient's system (or somehow create a "morphic field" of health and self-healing) and let the patient's energies take it from there to do the job of their own accord i.e. automatically.

Following the meta-model the magician will decide beforehand in which paradigm he will begin his operation. This must not necessarily exclude the possibility of shifting the paradigms in midwork or of blending them, of course.

In contrast to standard psychotherapeutic care (such as psychoanalysis attempting to bring repressed materials to the surface so that they can dissipate), the cybermagician, seeking psychointegration, might mine his own repressions and obsessions for energy to empower creations of his own imagination, a goal that many psychiatrists might regard as being quite contrary to mental health.

THE UNIVERSALITY OF ALTERNATE STATES OF CONSCIOUSNESS

Shamanism, then, represents a series of individual performances in a dynamic complex across space and time, a going beyond (Luna and White, 2000). A key aspect of shamanism from 'both worlds', from the landscapes of the Southern African San Bushman and the Amazonian ayahuascero, is that it is a way which embraces a deep relationship with nature.

Eastern techniques embrace the shamanistic approach, particularly Tantric methods of the left-hand path (such as the way of the aghora), which includes meditating at funeral pyres at the ghats, in graveyards and at a variety of Himalayan pilgrimage spots. In the broadest sense shamanism is the natural science of the subjective condition, a position it shares with Gnosticism - an extended awareness of oneself in the existential flow. It is humanity's search for self transcendence.

Achieving altered states can take place during meditation, hyperventilation, the practice of yoga, hypnosis, fasting, and physical suffering (such as the self-inflicted pain in certain religious traditions or by modern-day body-alchemists). It is a state that can be reached in many ways to explore aspects of reality different from those perceived in an ordinary state of consciousness (Polivoy).

"Many cultures have developed technologies for altering consciousness and inducing spiritual experiences." (Winkelman, 2000). Describing shamanism and its ancient healing practices within the context of neurotheology, he has demonstrated that there are basic similarities in shamans in cultures around the world (Winkelman, 2000). The similarities in shamans include the use of trance or ecstasy - altered states of consciousness (ASC) - to interact with the spirits and heal. These spirit world interactions are often referred to as "soul journeys," flying, out-of-body experiences and astral projection. These abilities are acquired when the initiate shaman undergoes a "death and rebirth experience" and acquires animal allies and spirit powers.

Winkelman outlines the neurobiological basis of shamanism—humanity's original spiritual practices, and explains puzzling aspects of shamanism, its universal presence in the ancient world, as well as its modern resurgence. "Universals of shamanism are related to basic brain functions. The shamans' experiences and practices have fundamental similarities around the world because they reflect innate brain process and experiences" (Winkelman, 2000).

Winkelman's research findings place shamanism in the context of human evolution and suggests that shamanic practices were a key element of the evolution of modern humans some 40 000 years ago. Shamans helped people acquire information and develop new forms of thinking. Shamanism also provided mechanisms for healing and personal development, building alliances and creating group solidarity.

"Shamanism is not just an ancient practice nor is it limited to simpler societies. The contemporary world has many examples of 'neoshamanism,' current adaptations to these ancient principles of spiritual healing and consciousness" (Winkelman, 2000).

The shaman knows that the psychedelic experience, the altered state is programmable whilst his frame of mind and the surrounding mise-en-scène contributes substantially to the experience and demonstrates the enormous role that both culture and the psyche play in shaping the experience. (Davis, 2000).

THE MAKING OF MEANING AND MYTH – THE MANUFACTURING OF REALITY

For the shaman the experience of ASC is as if the anchors of his mind are set free and consciousness is set adrift (unbound) needing to find new bearings and coordinateness, improvising, and forcing alternate reality constructs as he goes along.

In this sense shamanic art (reference the San Bushmen rock art and ayahuasca visions) become representational of the inner worlds and visions of the practitioner. They are 'probes' sent out into the real world to represent and align with the inner world of the ancient shaman and modern psychonaut. It becomes subjective layering of alternate realities and an extension of the inner world of the shamanic seer/ seeker of meaning.

These probes can be viewed as mind-trajectories - from liminal into boundless space – an attempt to incorporate (integrate) and reach out into unbound space from the 'bound space-time' of the skin-clad body (leading to the experience of embodied and disembodied space-time) ... beyond the boundaries of skin, beyond the contours of the normal consciousness of the shaman.

STEPS TO A SHAMANIC EXPERIENCE (FROM THE ARCHAIC TO THE MODERN) – THE STAGES OF THE SHAMANIC JOURNEY

Common to all shamanic or magico-spiritual experiences is that some degree of alteration of consciousness is necessary (Harner, 1990. p. 49). The following steps illustrate the common boundary-breaking steps that earmark any shamanic or magico-spiritual, altered, ecstatic or trance-state experience, and can be summarised as follows,

. Inducing ecstatic or altered states of consciousness (through trance states or the ingestion of entheogens; usually accompanied by the inner or outward declaration of wilful intent and possibly cultural context through ritual);

. Various stages indicating the commencement of the journey (visual effects – entoptics; physical symptoms; signs of allies and familiars, etc. as the ASC gains momentum);

. Dissolution of boundaries of self and normal perception of reality (usually associated with the releasing 'little death' experience which can be incremental or sudden) – **into the void**;

. Achieving an altered state of consciousness (reality shift into boundaryless space; sense of connection to everything - a sense of individual existence, of separateness from the physical world around him, evaporates – the so-called 'ocean of consciousness' experience) – **in the void**; and

. The return to the normal mundane realm and existence associated with psychointegration and re-membering of imagery and 'messages – **through the void**.

In essence, for the shaman, the magico-spiritual experience honours and/or recognises the interpenetrative spirit of the body and the body as product of the landscape at the same time. The body, the vehicle for our minds and consciousness, is a product of its environment, and needs to engage with it continuously, through all states of consciousness for its survival. Consciousness is a by-product of this interaction. The limitation of consciousness, altered or alternative is the degree to which it can consciously process this reality on its own terms, and in terms of its environment, communal, spiritual, physical or otherwise.

It would be more accurate to talk about states of consciousness per se, than trying to carve up or layer these states of consciousness, which is an arbitrary act in its own right. Awareness is like a torchlight beaming out onto the landscape of being and becoming. These states of consciousness are all intensities of the same torchlight, not altered versions or aspects of it.

What is of more interest from a magico-spiritual perspective is, if alternate realities truly exist - alternate realities of which we can become consciously aware and engage with (the true aspiration and domain of the ancient shamans and modern psychonauts). The continuous attempts to penetrate these alternative or other realities are the same quest for the shaman, the scientist and the magico-spiritual practitioner.

Modern shamans have adopted some of these techniques to project into other, altered or 'all potential' states of consciousness, to explore the contours of their minds and discover 'the pattern that connects' (Bateson, 1995).

All minds are landscapes to be traversed and explored by a multiplicity of techniques and approaches. An archaeology of mind is available to us and an ecology of consciousness can be evolved from these recorded experiences and related research.

ON VARIETIES OF CONSCIOUSNESS

Consciousness cannot be bound - it is boundless. Like ancient three masted ships safely hugging familiar coastlines, we are traversing inner space bound by skin and boundless outer space enveloped in space-time – we are embodied consciousness. For the journey is still not complete - we are still refining our tools of investigation and exploration. The journey for mankind has just begun. The need to look within and without (with feeling, with meaning, without boundaries – spiritually, scientifically or otherwise).

We have to enter a magical realm where we can re-imagine ourselves being and becoming ad infinitum – a progression upwards and downwards on the snakes and ladders of existence. From a shamanic perspective we are still evolving in every direction – into and out of extinction (genetically and memetically). Thoughts, like clouds, rising, drifting and vanishing – such is our lives – like the fleeting swallow of reality flying in from the cold, through our hall of consciousness and back into the cold night again (from the tale of the Venerable Bede quoted by Weinberg, 1993. p. 208-209).

The first step is to discover what lies within. This is still our chief pre-occupation. To bind things, thoughts. The problem is that what we imagine can be bound, is boundless. All states of reality and consciousness shift – it is a pesky little thing that cannot be pinned down, especially not in our quantum universe stalked by Schrödinger's, or was it the Cheshire cat?

One moment you are selling your audience Coke consciousness and the next body comes along and sells Pepsi consciousness. From this point onwards things get blurry and indefinable on both terms, unless you elect to experience interpenetrative Coke-Pepsi consciousness in which neither is distinct nor has a separate identity (reality) any more – simultaneously a gain and a loss.

The point of course is to go for neither and remain in a boundaryless state of flux – in a state of so-called Buddha, boundless or non-dual mind – where you can literally think yourself up and down the evolutionary ladder. You can imagine (manufacture/imagineer) what you were before or states of being yet to come … witness the unfolding mystery of all mysteries, the 'source of all things' of the Tao te Ching.

What you can imagine you can become. It is all quite simple from here onwards. And you can realise it in this lifetime. Leave it up to the quanta and the life force and from this rich soup you can serve up anything you like. Today you can witness this instance in space-time around you. Everybody and everything is in different states of being and becoming … you have this multicameral mind taking snapshots of emerging realities in space and time.

From this point onwards it all becomes trajectories. Bound in our bodies, we become trajectories of mind into boundless space and time. We are the hunters … bound in our skins we hunt space-time which is boundaryless – without beginning or end. Add some quantum flux and you can have infinite possibilities (infinite potential), universes, consciousnesses, realities …

"We regularly experience our skin as the boundary of our body. Our identity is in part formed from our understanding that we are bounded creatures. One way we understand our self is that we are defined by the body we inhabit—we are bounded objects, contained within our skin" (Rohr, 1995).

Similar to the "Osmose (1995) experience - an immersive interactive virtual-realty world created by Char Davies - these inner and outer landscapes are 'spaces for exploring the perceptual interplay between self and world, i.e. a place for facilitating awareness of one's own self as consciousness embodied in enveloping space'.

It is the artist's 'belief that traditional interface boundaries between machine and human can be transcended (in the case of Osmose) even while re-affirming our corporeality, and that Cartesian notions of space as well as illustrative realism can effectively be replaced by more evocative alternatives' has a very shamanic ring to it. For her 'Immersive virtual space, when stripped of its conventions, can provide an intriguing spatio-temporal context in which to explore the self's subjective experience of "being-in-the-world" - as embodied consciousness in an enveloping space where boundaries between inner/outer, and mind/body dissolve' represents a very altered state of consciousness.

Parallel consciousness takes on another dimension for physicist Fred Alan Wolf (1991) altering the way in which we see reality alters reality. Existence as we know it is a subset of reality which is unknowable. Our minds are tuneable to these multiple dimensions, multiple realities.

EM-BODI-MENT (MIND/BODY ALCHEMY)

Manufacturing reality is about binding consciousness in space-time – enveloping it with skin. We are embodied consciousness … that can imagine dis-incarnate bodies, experiences that are unbound – unbound by our reality. Within that manufactured reality we cloak, we dress, we provide skin, we tag and attempt to define. It is what we were designed to do – it is consciousness by design, manufactured reality.

The latest neuropsychological research has demonstrated that regardless of culture, space, time, shaman, cave, priest, temple, magician or psychonaut – you are stuck with an apparatus that is bound in skin, chased with memes, seeking out new trajectories into space-time/reality – imagining reality unbound (a space in which consciousness as we know it does not exist).

But we can dream it … in the little labs between our ears we can excite potential and past states of being, and project trajectories to the future, into nether realms of reality. Especially in excitatory states, the timelines cross over and new states (modalities) of consciousness can be imagined and engineered (imagineered), manufactured and projected into space-time (our space-time).

That is why the experimentation and exploration can never stop – the experiment, the experience that is us, cannot stop (even though we are only facets (fractions) of reality and can only realise so much of what we are made of in one lifetime … a sea of potentiality, reality, self, consciousness, awareness bound in skin.

Can there be one consciousness, bound and unbound, inside and outside of skin at the same time? We'll leave that to you to decide and speculate upon. But for all of us we predict the journeying has just begun. The exploration has just commenced … when science embraces techniques of consciousness in the same way that modern technoshamans have embraced all possible realities, bound and unbound, at a stage when consciousness is still formulating and revealing itself to our biocomputers.

We are still in for a real treat of cosmic proportions. The first step towards integrating these 'opposing' realities is to take a holistic view of the universe – to take a step back as the mystics did with hermetic statements of 'as above, so below' and 'solve et coagulum' – you have to dissolve in the one realm of consciousness (lose your skin so to speak) to emerge in the next dimension of reality – to move from bound to unbound to bound again.

To gnostically, hedonistically and ecstatically engage with reality head on and discern as you go along – the path of science – and to dismiss the whole.

Things we 'know' about consciousness from a magico-spiritual perspective,

i   The mind is telescopic.
ii Consciousness is the product of bound, liminal space-time.
iii Consciousness is evoked potential.
iv Consciousness is personalised, embodied reality.
v) The landscape of mind describes the boundaries of consciousness.
vi Consciousness is the brain's attempt at sense-making.
vii Consciousness as 'having a point of reference', a rootedness in reality.

Where most people are quite content to occupy 'dead centre' of the landscape of their lives and experiences, to live in so-called 'balance', the shaman seeks out the liminal spaces - the zone that lies not-quite-one-side and not-quite-the-other-side of such conceptual boundaries. Inside liminal space ritual, and its 'product', altered states of consciousness, becomes the metaphor for proceeding from the known to the unknown, from the bound to the boundless. Employed within bound space, it disconnects its participants from everyday existence (Connerton, 1989. p.4). The actors have entered a "liminal" or "threshold" state. Both metaphor and ritual are ways of recognition in which the identifying qualities of one thing are transferred in an instantaneous, almost unconscious, flash of insight to some other thing that is, by remoteness or complexity, unknown to us. 'In this gap between ordered worlds, almost anything may happen' (Turner, 1974. p. 13).

On the "…concept of 'ecology of mind,' which states that mind is immanent in systems and not isolated to individual locations", Bateson concluded that the individual mind is immanent, but not only in the body. It is immanent also in pathways and messages outside the body; and there is a larger mind of which the individual mind is only a sub-system. This larger mind is comparable to God and is perhaps what some people mean by God, but it is still immanent in the total interconnected social systems and planetary ecology (Bateson, 1978).

THE FARTHER REACHES OF CONSCIOUSNESS – TO INFINITY AND BEYOND

The farther reaches of the conscious and unconscious mindscapes are being increasingly scientifically and experimentally explored through a variety of psycho deconstructive and integrative techniques – from the shamanistic 'manufacturing of reality' by deconstructing boundaries of sense-making reality, to the reality and consciousness-making of artificial intelligence, studies into animal and plant sentience, and psychonautic explorations into other 'dimensions' of reality and consciousness constructs. It is a netherworld, a 'twilight zone', of either or neither that has attracted, and been navigated by generations of psycho-spiritual seekers and mind explorers in the form of artists, poets, philosophers and the modern-day high priests of science and cyber shamans.

MAGICO-SPIRITUAL TECHNIQUES –
PROGRAMMES OF THE MIND

A variety of traditional and modern magico-spiritual techniques centering on achieving altered states of consciousness have evolved to project will and intent towards specific outcomes - either for personal development, therapeutic applications or for mundane, personal use. These practices have evolved into 'cyber shamanism and psychonautics' through a variety of ecstatic techniques such as gnosis, breathing, meditation, visualisation, and the use of psycho-integratives (entheogens such as ibogaine, San Pedro and ayahuasca), tantric practices and ritual.

The main aim of developing and refining magico-spiritual technique over the ages is to achieve altered states of consciousness repeatedly and reliably – an intentional manufacturing of reality through meta-sense and mythmaking.

Magicians are interested in the utilisation of techniques to bring about a state of gnosis/trance or no mind to create a magickal outcome in either themselves or the world around them. Primarily this kind of gnosis falls into what Peter J. Carroll (1987) calls an excitatory mode of gnosis. 'Inhibitory' or 'releasing' techniques are utilised as a means to strengthen alternate senses that are being excited or stimulated. By mastering various techniques, and through experience, a magician can apply these techniques to effect with safety and reliability.

These techniques include the ability to explore and face all aspects of reality, good or bad, painful or pleasurable, to the point of going to extremes, is the illumination that magicians seek to allow their mind's to become conscious of the fact that these feelings and emotions are only constructs of the mind.

From a shamanistic perspective, "The shaman is a technician of consciousness who utilises those (psychobiological) potentials for healing and for personal and social transformations" (Winkelman, 2000).

FUTURE PSYCHONAUTICS; ALTERNATE STATES OF CONSCIOUSNESS; INTEGRATED, HYPER CONTEXTUAL CONSCIOUSNESS

In the introduction to *I Hope I Shall Arrive Soon*, a collection of late short stories, Dick (Sutin, 1995) wrote that "we live in a society in which spurious realities are manufactured by the media, by governments, by big corporations, by religious groups, political groups—and the electronic hardware exists by which to deliver these pseudo-worlds right into the heads of the reader, the viewer, the listener" (Sutin, 1995).

MANUFACTURING REALITY

"Altered states of consciousness are real, and as our media technologies get better at drawing us in and out of them, artists and other non-coercive proponents of the human spirit (or whatever you want to call it) need to become familiar with these states, not simply as a source of inspiration, but as modes of expression, communication, and confrontation itself. By recognizing that the material that we are now focused on is not technology but human experience itself, then we take a step closer to that strange plateau where our inner lives unfold into an almost collective surface of shared sensation and reframed perception — a surface on which we may feel exposed and vulnerable, but beginning to awake." --Erik Davis, Experience Design, And the Design of Experience

MEANING/SENSE-MAKING

It is through meaning, rather than belief, that we are able to transform reality at any level, because meaning changes from moment to moment. Since the discovery of meaning is spontaneous, magico-spiritual work is a collection of discoveries. The psychonaut is interested solely in the green edge of consciousness.

Clearly, the object of magic is to achieve higher states of consciousness. The magus is empowered to affect events only to the extent that he is able to recognise that inside and outside is one. To transform the world is to transform oneself and vice-versa. However, although those who don't know what they are doing are obliged to perform magic strictly through the observation of rituals, those who understand its real nature and purpose can move directly to its centre and act from there, without incantations and conjurations.

INTERPENETRATIVE SPIRIT (ACTION)

The sciences need to plumb the depths of 'primordial reality', the 'first reality', the so-called pre-rational, and seek out the heights of the post-rational realm, super conscious (the borders of which make science shrink back suspiciously with statements of 'metaphysical' or 'mystical'), to discern and navigate the contours of human consciousness. Only then can we prepare for the transhuman aeon of transcending the boundaries of human consciousness that will follow.

STEPS TOWARDS A FURTHER ECOLOGY OF MIND

TRANSLATIVE, TRANSFORMATIONAL, TRANSCENDENTAL, TRANSHUMAN

The following 'progressive stages' will form a framework for future research into a 'steps towards a further ecology of the mind' (to borrow from Bateson),

a) **Translative consciousness** – Newtonian step and repeat thinking; linear; measured consciousness; clear boundaries between subjective and objectives; still evolving; penetrative but not whole-picture awareness; bound, demarcated consciousness.

b) **Transformational consciousness** – metamemes; conscious metaprogrammes (reference John Lilly's papers on dolphin research). The self-organising principles of complexity theory.

c) **Transcendental consciousness** – e.g. tantra, all layers, all dimensions, simultaneously; ocean of consciousness experience (but with complete awareness and sentience – not a psychedelic, Gnostic or ecstatic, trippy joyride; beyond life and death; connectedness – inwardly and outwardly) – the true interpenetrative spirit and possibly the final frontier of human, three-dimensional space-time consciousness. Unbound, fuzzy consciousness. Highest level of complexity and complexification.

d) **Transhuman consciousness** – boundless multidimensional space-time. Chaotic random sea of possibilities, probability and potentiality. The pregnant void. The so-called 'mother' principle of the Tao. Creative/destructive spirit. Glimpses from the magic-spiritual realm; the perspective of the shaman. Emergent transition to consciousness without bounds, immeasurable …the apeiron.

CONCLUSION

The consciousness that we experience is human consciousness. It is not the totality of consciousness 'out there', the totality of consciousness that still has to be experienced or must still be re-membered.

EXCITATORY STATES OF CONSCIOUSNESS (THE FALLACY OF MIND-BODY DUALITY)

Consciousness is an excitatory state – a gateway of the mind e.g. meditation calms one part of the mind which allows a subliminal excitatory state to 'emerge' of which you become aware. It (realisation, awareness) appears magically (rises up into conscious awareness) as if hidden, from nowhere, therefore the mystical analogies that get contributed to Gnostic and ecstatic states of consciousness. The brain is a fixed state (bound) organic material that has captured or was formed by these excitatory states – interpenetrating the body from boundless reality.

We are the product of this interpenetrative spirit - the apeiron (a boundless excitatory state of potentiality - of interpenetrative matter and spirit).

Future Research

Religions, magico-spiritual traditions as bound consciousness; enclaves reserved for the manufacture of prescripted and described reality – bound by memes, and ritual actions in space-time.

DRUG-INDUCED GOD
by Matthew Alper

"Psychedelic drugs have been used to stimulate religious experience since the dawn of history" (Batson, 1979).

"Religion is the opiate of the masses" (Marx, 1844).

Besides engaging in such practices as prayer, chant, dance, yoga, or meditation, many world cultures report having used psychedelic drugs as another means through which to evoke a mystical, religious, transcendental, or spiritual experience.

"The use of psychedelic sacraments in shamanic and religious practices is found throughout history. The word entheogen, used to describe certain plants and chemicals used for spiritual purposes, emphasizes this long established relationship" (Jesses, 1996).

From the sacred drink of Soma used by the Vedic Hindus, the morning glory seeds and mescaline ingested by Native Americans, the sacred mints of the Greek mystery religions, the use of cannabis by the Sythians, and the yaje or ayahuasca of the Amazonian jungle peoples, to the iboga of the peoples of equatorial Africa, all represent examples of psychedelic drugs that have been used by a variety of cultures to evoke a spiritual experience. Because of the universal nature of this phenomenon, the word entheogens—meaning "God generated from within"—has been created to describe this class of "God-inducing" drugs. To the ancient Aztecs, the connection between entheogens and the spiritual realm was so clear that they referred to peyote as the "Divine Messenger" and psilocybin as "God's flesh."

It is so widely recognized that certain drugs can stimulate a spiritual experience that some secular governments, which normally forbid the use of drugs, have allowed for the use of certain entheogens when ingested as a religious sacrament.

In 1994, the U.S. government enacted the American Indian Religious Freedom Act Amendments, providing consistent protection across all fifty states for the traditional ceremonial use of peyote by American Indians...In its report on the 1994 legislation, a U.S. House of Representative's committee reported that 'peyote is not injurious,' and that the spiritual and social support provided by the Native American Church [NAC] has been effective in combating the tragic effects of alcoholism among the Native American population (Jesses).

From William James's experiments with nitrous oxide to Aldous Huxley's experiments with Lysergic acid (LSD), it is widely noted that certain plants and/or chemicals can induce experiences indistinguishable from certain mystical states. Stanislov Grof in his work, Realms of the Human Unconscious: Observations from LSD Research, catalogued the experiences of individuals who were administered experimental doses of LSD. Based on his studies, Grof found that the symptoms induced by the drug were the same described by those who have undergone a spiritual,mystical, or transcendental experience (Grof, 1975).

But how is it that a drug could have the ability to rouse such feelings as these in us? How is it possible that chemicals can have the capacity to induce something as allegedly ethereal as a spiritual or transcendental experience in us? What does this say about such drugs? Or, more significantly, what does this say about the spiritual, transcendental experience?

In order to answer such questions, we need take a look at the drugs themselves. As we know, all drugs, including the psychedelics or entheogens as they are now called, are always the same in regard to their molecular structure. (This is true of any drug. For example, on a molecular level, aspirin is always aspirin; penicillin is always penicillin. Accordingly, the same rule must also apply to each of the various entheogenic drugs.

In regard to the molecular composition of many of the entheogenic drugs, it is no coincidence that, in many cases, they are nearly identical in structure to certain neurotransmitters—those chemicals that play an integral role in the chemical transmission of impulses between nerve cells). For instance, whereas the entheogenic drug mescaline is almost identical in its molecular composition to the neurotransmitter noradrenaline, a molecule of psilocybin, more commonly known as "magic mushrooms," is almost identical in composition to a molecule of the neurotransmitter serotonine. Any entheogenic drug represents a constant. The atomic structure of an LSD molecule is the same whether ingested in Bangkok or Bolivia, at sea level or on top of the Himalayas.

The same can be said, more or less, about human physiology. Granted, though there is a certain degree of variance among individuals within our species, underlying this diversity is a distinct physiological uniformity. Since we are dealing with two constants—same drug, same physiology—it's no surprise that entheogenic drugs should have this particular effect on individuals from such a wide variety of cultures. This still leaves us with the crux of the problem which is: Why do these drugs have this particular effect on us? Why do they have a distinct tendency to elicit what we refer to as spiritual, mystical, transcendental, or religious experiences?

No drug can elicit a response to which we are not physiologically predisposed. Drugs can only enhance or suppress those capacities we already possess. They cannot, however, create new ones. For example, the fact that we possess the capacity for sight—that we possess the physical hardware to "see"—means that it is within the realm of possibility that a drug would be able to either enhance or suppress one's visual capacities. The fact, however, that we do not possess the physical hardware to fly, for instance, means that no drug can ever enhance or suppress our non-existent powers of flight. Again, a drug can only affect us as much as we possess some physiological mechanism that might be receptive to that drug's particular chemistry.

The fact, for instance, that novocaine has the universal effect of desensitizing one to pain means that we must possess pain receptors that are capable of being suppressed. In the same way, the fact that psychedelic drugs have a cross-cultural tendency to stimulate experiences we define as being either spiritual, religious, mystical or transcendental means we must possess some physiological mechanism whose function is to generate this particular type of conscious experience. If we didn't possess such a mechanism, there's no way that these drugs could possibly stimulate such experiences in us. In short, the fact that there exists a certain class of drugs-molecules—that can evoke a spiritual experience in us supports the notion that spiritual consciousness must be physiological in nature. In support of this, hundreds of ethnobotanical studies lend further substantiation to the neurophysiological origin of the mystical experience.

DREAMS, SPIRITS AND THE SOUL
by R. Joseph

Dreams and hallucinations, have, as their neurological source, activity generated within the temporal lobe and limbic structures buried within--the hippocampus and the amygdala. The hippocampus is known to be a depository of new memories and to assist in the retrieval of new memories--memories that often reappear in the contexts of dreams. Yet, dreams and memories, especially emotional memories, also have as their neurological source, the amygdala and overlying temporal lobe and associated limbic structures.

The amygdala enables us to hear "sweet sounds," recall "bitter memories," or determine if something is spiritually significant, sexually enticing, or good to eat. The amygdala also makes it possible for us to store personal, sexual, spiritual, and emotional experiences in memory and to recall and reexperience these memories when awake or during the course of a dream in the form of visual, auditory, or religious or spiritual imagery (Bear 1979; d'Aquili & Newberg 1993; Gloor 1986, 1992, 1997; Halgren, 1992).

The amygdala, in conjunction with the hippocampus, contributes in large part to the production of very sexual as well as bizarre, unusual and fearful mental phenomenon including out-of-body dissociative states, feelings of depersonalization, and hallucinogenic and dreamlike recollections involving threatening men, naked women, sexual intercourse, religion, the experience of god, as well as demons and ghosts and pigs walking upright dressed as people (Bear 1979; Daly 1958; d'Aquili & Newberg 1993; Gloor 1986, 1992; Halgren 1992; Horowitz et al., 1968; Jaynes 1976; MacLean 1990; Mesulam 1981; Penfield & Perot 1963; Rolls, 1992; Schenk & Bear 1981; Slater & Beard 1963; Subirana & Oller-Daurelia 1953; Taylor, 1972, 1975; Trimble, 1991; Weingarten et al., 1977; Williams, 1956).

The amygdala also makes it possible to experience not just spiritual and religious awe, but all the terror and dread of the unknown. Indeed, the amygdala can generate feelings of hellish, nightmarish fear

And yet, it is also the amygdala which is responsible for the capacity to transcend the known, this reality. It is also the amygdala which assists in maintaining this reality through the inhibition and filtering of most of the sensory signals bombarding the brain and body. If not for this sensory filtering, a color might have taste and its own particular texture, whereas sounds might provoke smells, warmth, light, colors, tastes, and feelings of weight. Hyperactivation of the amygdala, and overlying temporal lobes can remove these sensory filters, and what is concealed is revealed, sometimes in overwhelming confusing majesty.

Neurosurgical patients have reported communing with spirits or receiving profound knowledge from the Hereafter, following depth electrode amygdala stimulation or activation (Penfield and Perot 1963; Subirana and Oller-Daurelia, 1953; Williams 1956). Some have reported hearing even the singing of angels and the voice of "God."

THE LIMBIC SYSTEM: SPIRITUALITY AND EMOTION

According to d'Aquili and Newberg (1993) mystical states may be voluntarily or involuntarily induced and are dependent upon the differential stimulation of limbic system nuclei, including the hypothalamus, hippocampus, and amygdala, as well as the right frontal and right temporal lobe. However, it appears that these brain areas differentially contribute to religious and emotional experience.

For example, the hypothalamus is concerned with all rudimentary aspects of emotion, homeostasis such as food and water intake, and controls the hormonal and related aspects of violent behavior and sexual activity. The amygdala also plays a highly significant role in sexual and violent behavior, and, in conjunction with the temporal lobe and hippocampus, enables a human to have religious, spiritual and mystical experiences (Bear 1979; Daly 1958; d'Aquili and Newberg 1993; Horowitz et al. 1968; Mesulam 1981; Penfield and Perot 1963; Schenk, and Bear 1981; Slater & Beard 1963;

Subirana & Oller-Daurelia 1953; Trimble 1991; Weingarten, et al. 1977; Williams 1956). These religious experiences may involve violent behavior or sexual activity, due to limbic involvement.

As we shall see in later chapters, many religious customs and rituals involve violence and sexuality, which in turn is due to the activation of this limbic system transmitter to god.

The amygdala and hypothalamus subserve the capacity to experience feelings of intense sexual arousal, fear or, conversely, euphoria, including an orgasmic feeling of rapture, or the "nirvana" of a heroin "high." This is because the hypothalamus and amygdala are major pleasure centers, and contain opiate-producing neurons and opiate (enkephalin) receptive neurons, thus generating feelings of numbness and a narcotic high. Large concentrations of opiate receptors and enkephalin-producing neurons are located throughout the amygdala (Atweh & Kuhar 1977ab; Uhl et al., 1978).

In response to pain, stress, shock, fear, or terror, the amygdala and other limbic nuclei begin to secrete high levels of opiates which can eventually induce a state of calmness as well as analgesia and euphoria (Joseph, 1998a, 1999a). It is this heroin high that explains why an ox, deer, and other animals will simply give up and lie still while they are devoured and eaten alive. It is this amygdala-induced heroin high which also contributes to feelings of religious rapture and the ecstasy associated with life after death and the attainment of Nirvana.

THE AMYGDALA, HIPPOCAMPUS AND HALLUCINATIONS

Whereas the amygdala and hypothalamus interact in regard to pleasure, rage, and sexuality, the amygdala and hippocampus interact to subserve and mediate wholly different aspects of experience, including memory, dreaming, and hallucinations. The hippocampus in particular appears to be responsible for certain types of "hallucinations" such as the visualizations of astral projection or seeing oneself floating above the body (Joseph 1996, 1999b, 2000a). Some patients report not only floating, but of being embraced by a light and taken to a vast realm of fantastic proportions where they are given access to knowledge of the nature of life and death.

The amygdala, hippocampus, and temporal lobe are richly interconnected and appear to act in concert in regard to mystical experience, including the generation and experience of dream states and complex auditory and visual hallucinations, such as may be induced by LSD (Broughton 1982; Goldstein et al. 1972; Gloor 1986, 1992; Hodoba 1986; Horowitz, et al. 1968; Joseph, 1992a; Meyer et al. 1987; Penfield and Perot 1963; Weingarten, et al. 1977; Williams 1956). If these neurons are hyperactivated, such as occurs during dream states, seizures, physical pain, terror, food deprivation, social and sensory isolation, and under LSD (which disinhibits the amygdala by blocking serotonin) an individual might infuse their perceptions with tremendous religious and emotional feeling. Hence, under these conditions the individual may hallucinate, and ordinary perceptions, objects or people may be perceived as spiritual in nature or endowed with special or religious significance.

Intense activation of the temporal lobe, hippocampus, and amygdala has been reported to give rise to a host of sexual, religious and spiritual experiences; and chronic hyperstimulation can induce an individual to become hyper-religious or to visualize and experience ghosts, demons, angels, and even "God," as well as claim demonic and angelic possession or the sensation of having left their body (Bear 1979; Gloor 1986, 1992; Horowitz et al. 1968; MacLean 1990; Mesulam 1981; Penfield & Perot 1963; Schenk & Bear 1981; Williams 1956).

In some instances the individual may come to believe he or she is hearing, seeing, and interacting with gods, angels and demons when in fact they are hallucinating. These false beliefs are accentuated further because they are excessively emotionally and religiously aroused and are experiencing an "enkephalin" high and feelings of rapture or "nirvana."

In many cases, however, the individual is not hallucinating. Rather, their eyes have been opened, and they suddenly see as gods... knowing good and evil.

LSD, LIMBIC SYSTEM FILTERING AND HALLUCINATIONS

The amygdala is capable of processing visual, tactile, auditory, gustatory, olfactory, and emotional stimuli simultaneously. Amygdaloid neurons are multimodally responsive. Single amygdaloid neurons receive a considerable degree of topographic input, and are predominatly polymodal, responding to a variety of stimuli from different modalities simultaneously (Amaral et al. 1992; O'Keefe & Bouma, 1969; Ono & Nishijo, 1992; Perryman, Kling, & Lloyd, 1987; Rolls 1992; Sawa & Delgado, 1963; Schutze et al. 1987; Turner et al. 1980; Ursin & Kaasa, 1960; Van Hoesen, 1981).

Normally much of this data is suppressed and filtered so as to prevent the tasting of colors, the visualization of sound, and so on. This is made possible via the inhibitory influences of the frontal lobes and a variety of neurotransmitters including serotonin (5HT). 5HT suppresses synaptic activity in the amygdala and throughout the neocortex and thus reduces sensory input (Curtis & Davis 1962; Marazzi & Hart 1955; Morrison & Pompeiana 1965). 5HT restricts perceptual and information processing and in fact increases the threshold for neural responses to occur at both the neocortical and limbic level. In this manner, selective attention (via sensory filtering) can be maintained while the organism is engaged in goal directed motor behavior, such as running away or taking evasive action if chased by a lion.

In consequence, substances which block 5HT reception at the level of the synapse -such as LSD- results in increased activity in the amygdala and in the sensory pathways to the neocortex (Purpura 1956), such that information that is normally filtered out is perceived. Following the administration of LSD high amplitude slow waves (theta) and bursts of paroxysmal spike discharges occurs in the hippocampus and amygdala (Chapman & Walter, 1965; Chapman et al. 1963), and the amygdala begins to process information that is normally suppressed.

Under conditions which induce limbic hyperactivity, 5HT may be depleted and limbic sensory acuity is increased. However, what is perceived is not necessarily a hallucination but instead represents the perception of overlapping sensory qualities that are normally filtered out. Colors may be felt and tasted, music may be observed as well as heard, the molecular composition of ceilings, floor and walls may be parted so that one can see through the spaces between where molecules join together. And the pulse of life may be experienced as it ebbs and flows in a leaf one holds between their finger tips.

Consider, for example, a description of someone's first LSD "trip:"

"It was 1966... Jimi Hendrix was singing about purple haze, and that is exactly what we scored up in Haight Ashbury—mixed by the master himself, Stanley Osley..."

"About half an hour after I'd taken it, I was walking toward the park to meet and trip with my fellow tripsters when I began to notice the incredible clarity and vividness of my surroundings. Colors were brighter, plants seem to sparkle...and I stopped and touched a leaf...I could feel its energy, its life... I could taste it through my fingers...And when I got to the park I was so overwhelmed with the colors, the tastes, the smells, the incredible vividity and clarity that I felt almost overwhelmed and sat down to take it all in..."

"And then I heard a jet somewhere in the distance, and I looked into the sky but couldn't see it but my ears led my eyes to one of the mountains surrounding the valley, and oh my god, I could see right through the mountain. It was like the molecular composition of the mountain was parting into separate molecules. I could see the spaces between the molecules which were all in a frenzy of activity... it was as if I had achieved X-ray vision, and there were these crystal blue holes—like bubbles—and I could see right through the mountain and I could see the sky on the other side, including the jet. I could see the jet on the other side of the mountain by looking right through the mountain, by looking right through those gaps in the spaces between the molecules which were zipping along in their own unique pattern. And then the jet flew over the top of the mountain and instead of one jet I could see ten, then a hundred, and a kaleidoscope of jets in the sky."

"I raised my hand to point to this incredible sight, and instead of one hand, there were these trails of hands. And I did that again, waved my hand and there were these hand-arm trails of hands-hands-hands catching up and then merging... and it was then that I realized I could see through my hand. So I gazed at it for closer inspection. It was as if my eyes became a tunneling microscope—and this was 10 years before they invented tunneling microscopes."

"At first I could see the incredible cellular structure of the skin, and then the molecular structure...the pulsating molecules themselves... and then I could see between the spaces where the molecules joined together... my sight penetrated the skin and I could see the blood vessels, and then my eyes penetrated the blood vessels and I could see inside the blood vessel, I could see the blood platelets and the white corpuscles as they swirled through the vessel —and I kept thinking: How come I never noticed this before? I had forgotten that I had taken LSD."

Hallucinogens, of course, are an age-old means of obtaining access to alternate realities, including the realities of "god." Hallucinogens are said to enable an individual to peer between the space that separate this reality from all other realities, such that what is concealed is suddenly revealed. It is the amygdala, hippocampus, and temporal lobe which are responsible for these complex hallucinations, and it is the amygdala which normally filters much of this information so that it remains hidden. Hence, by hyperactivating these structures, in essence, one is also activating the transmitter to god.

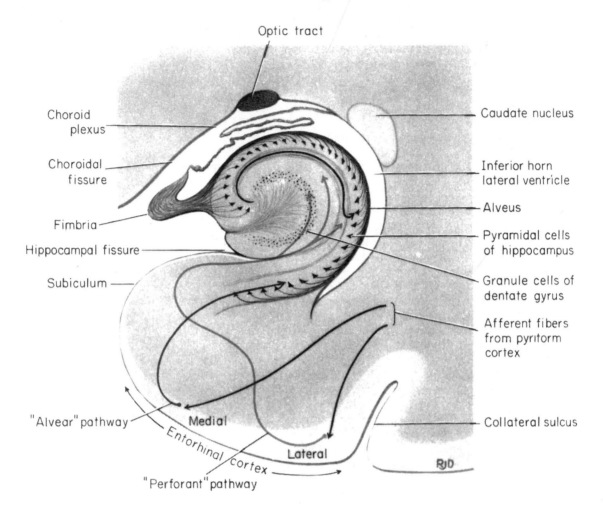

Optic tract

Choroid plexus

Choroidal fissure

Fimbria

Hippocampal fissure

Subiculum

"Alvear" pathway

Medial

Entorhinal cortex

"Perforant" pathway

Lateral

Caudate nucleus

Inferior horn lateral ventricle

Alveus

Pyramidal cells of hippocampus

Granule cells of dentate gyrus

Afferent fibers from pyriform cortex

Collateral sulcus

RJD

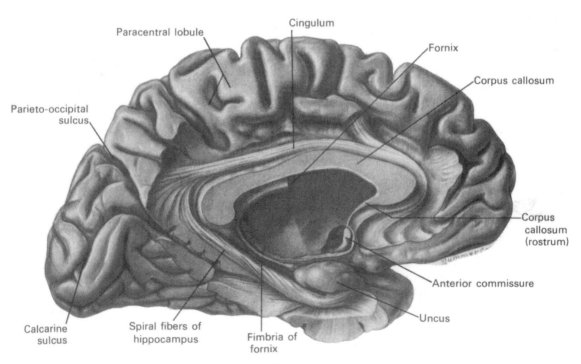

Paracentral lobule

Cingulum

Fornix

Corpus callosum

Parieto-occipital sulcus

Corpus callosum (rostrum)

Anterior commissure

Calcarine sulcus

Spiral fibers of hippocampus

Fimbria of fornix

Uncus

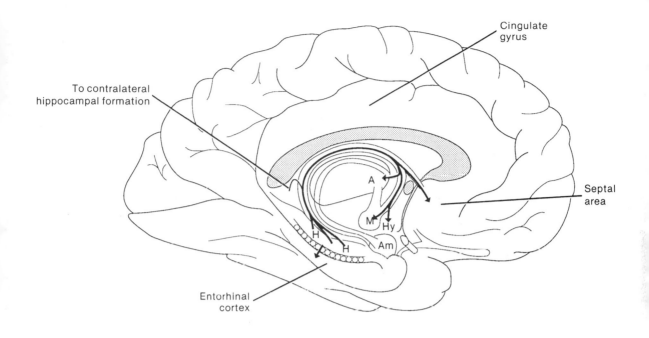

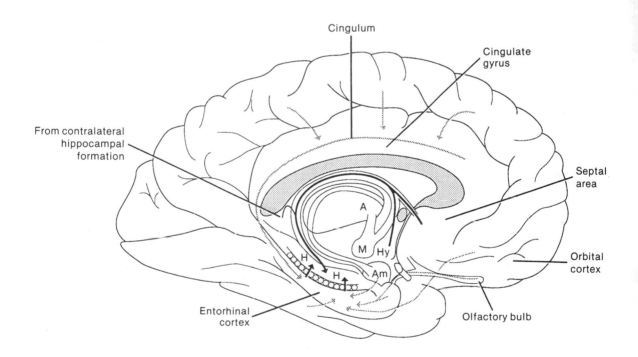

Figure 150. (Above left) Cut-away view of the hippocampal complex and its sublayers. From P. Gloor, 1997, The Limbic System & Temporal Lobe. Oxford University Press. (Below left) Medial cutaway view of the hippocampal fiber pathways. From F. Mettler, 1948, Neuroanatomy. Mosby. St. Louis. (Top & Bottom) Hippocampal efferants and afferent pathways. From Nolte, 1988, The Human Brain, Mosby, St. Louis.

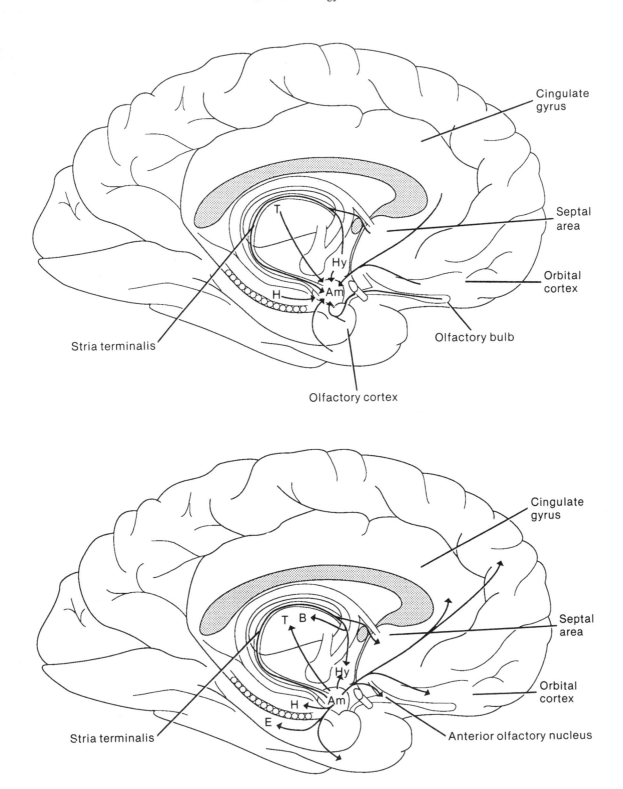

Figures 151. Cut-away views of the amygdala fiber pathways, including efferants and afferents. From Nolte, 1988, The Human Brain, Mosby, St. Louis.

SOULS, SPIRITS, DREAMS, AND POLTERGEISTS

TO KNOW FEAR IS TO KNOW GOD
"Fear the Lord your God." -Deuteronomy 10:12.

Priests, prophets, shamans and many others who encounter "god" or His "angels" not uncommonly experience tremendous fear. Fear is the most common emotion associated with the amygdala (Gloor, 1997; Halgren, 1992; LeDoux, 1996; Williams, 1956), with some patients experiencing horrifying, hellish, and nightmarish fear, sometimes coupled with hellish hallucinations.

We are repeatedly told in the Bible, that to know fear is to know god. Indeed, even a committed atheist may feel compelled to cry out and pray to god if sufficiently terrified. Terror is also an emotion associated with the amygdala... as well as with the Lord God.

Yet others experience awe and rapture when confronted by the divine. As noted, amygdala hyperactivation is also associated with feelings of extreme joy and ecstasy.

According to d'Aquili and Newberg (1993; p. 194) "a combination of the experience of both fear and exhalation" is "usually termed religious awe." These feeling states are "almost always associated with religious symbols, sacred images, or archetypal symbols" which flow "from the inferior temporal lobe" and which "appear sometimes as monsters or gods". Indeed, angels, demons, and poltergeists may be experienced.

Most people find these experiences quite terrifying. They also frequently believe their perceptions are completely real and are not hallucinations.

SPIRITS AND POLTERGEISTS
"Cindy," a 22 year old college student, was plagued by demons and ghosts for months until her abnormal right inferior temporal lobe was surgically removed.

Prior to her brain injury, Cindy had never been very religious, and had certainly never seen a ghost; that is, until following her auto accident. She had been thrown over 50 feet through the windshield of her car and suffered a fracture of the right temporal region of the skull and developed a subdural hematoma, a blood clot, which was pressing on the temporal lobe inducing herniation. Burr holes were drilled into her skull and the clot was surgically evacuated. Although her brain and temporal lobe had been injured, over the following weeks she seemed to quickly recover.

It was several days after her release from the hospital when she was startled while watching television. The arms, legs, hands, feet, and heads of the various actors began protruding from the screen into the living room where she sat.

Cindy said that at first she thought the television was broken and turned it off. But, as she stared back at the blank screen she saw what looked like her dead father staring back at her (which was probably her own reflection). As she backed away, the figure emerged from the television. He beckoned to her, and then behind him ghostly spooks and wraiths began to stream from the picture tube.

Terrified and crying for her mother she raced for the bathroom and locked herself in. Yet, even as she hid within the inner sanctum of the washroom, spirits, sprites and poltergeists streamed from the bathroom mirror and swirled about her. Crying and stumbling, she raced into the living room and was horrified to see a spirit enter and take possession of her mother who was transformed before her eyes. Panicked and terrified, Cindy ran into the street crying for help. A police officer, after investigating the scene, brought her to the local hospital and psychiatry unit. She was medicated and kept there on a 72 hour hold.

Later she decided what she had experienced were ghosts and lost souls of people who had been buried in an old, almost completely forgotten cemetery on the other side of the hill from where she lived. She also thought they were the ghosts of Indians who had been entombed beneath her house as there are numerous Indian burial grounds in the county.

Once she was released from her 72 hour psychiatric hold, she stopped taking her medication, and over the course of the next several weeks, she claimed to see "animal spirits." She reported that the "secret souls" of her mother's house plants were watching and observing her and that she could sometimes see filmy, soul-like entities traveling to and fro across the room and between different plants.

After several more hospitalizations, and an EEG, it was determined that she was suffering from excessive activity, seizure activity in the damaged temporal lobe. The inferior temporal lobe and the underlying amygdala were surgically ablated and destroyed, and she ceased to "hallucinate."

DREAMS, ANIMAL SPIRITS AND LOST SOULS

Across time and culture, people have believed that not just humans and animals, but plants and trees were sensitive, sentient, intelligent, and the abode of spirits including the souls of dead ancestors (Campbell 1988; Frazier 1950; Harris, 1993; Jung 1964; Malinowski 1948). Before felling a tree, the spirit sometimes had to be conjured forth so as to not harm it (Campbell 1988; Frazier 1950). Be it animal or plant, souls were also believed capable of migrating to new abodes.

Among the ancients and many so called primitive cultures, it was believed that souls are reflected in shadows, in streams, and pools of water (Campbell, 1988; Frazier, 1950; Harris, 1993; Jung, 1964; Malinowkski, 1948). Because ghosts or demons sometimes attempt to abduct souls, this required that one's shadow and reflection be protected. Even water spirits might try to capture a person's soul, so staring into reflecting ponds and lakes was to be avoided.

Moreover, the ancients believed that the shadows and reflections of others had to be avoided so that one did not come into contact with the soul of a witch, sorcerer, or a demon. It was believed that one's soul could be abducted by demons and witches as well as the recently departed. This is also why in some cultures people turn mirrors to the wall after a death and lay down pictures of the recently departed (Frazier 1950). This insures that living souls are not stolen by the souls of the dead who are leaving this world for the next one.

The belief in the persistence of the soul after death gave rise to ancestor worship in some ancient cultures, including China. Oracle Bones were believed to contain the souls of the dead and were employed for divinatory purposes in ancient China over 4,000 years ago. The earliest Oracle Bones so far discovered are covered with pictograms including a man with a large ghostly distorted head (Brandon, 1967). This pictogram also denotes the word kuei, which means, soul. Oracle bones also included characters signifying the words "she, shen, and tsu." "Tsu" means dead ancestor, "she" is a protective fertility deity of the soil, and "shen" are divine beings connotating phallic significance.

The ancient Chinese practiced a religious ritual which was intended to prevent the soul from departing the body at death. The orifices would be stopped up to keep the kuei safely inside the body. So long as the soul remained tethered to the body, the body would not undergo its final fatal disintegration. These beliefs gave rise to the ritual of "calling back of the soul," a ritual also performed for the living as the souls were believed able to wander forth from the body, such as during sleep, exposing the living body to death and extinction (Brandon, 1967).

The ancient Chinese believed that the kuei represented by the yin-soul, was associated with the body since conception. By contrast, a yang-soul was associated with the individual personality and the person's unique mental qualities.

The alternating and competing principles of the yin-soul and the yang-soul are directly related to the concepts of ying and yang. They also gave rise to ancestor worship as the ancient Chinese believed that the life force, the energy associated with the soul, this *substance familiale,* lay buried beneath the ground as *une masse indistincte.* "This energy was represented above ground at any given moment, only by the living members of the family, which constituted the individualized portions of that *substance familial.* It followed, accordingly, that each birth within the family represented the reincarnation of a portion of that subterranean *substance familial,* while each death meant the return of a part of this individual family substance familial to the *masse indistincte in* the ground below" (Brandon, 1967, p. 180).

SOULFUL DREAMS

Souls were also believed by ancient humans to wonder about while people sleep and dream (Brandon 1967; Frazier 1950; Harris 1993; Jung 1945, 1964; Malinowkski 1990). That is, among many different cultures and religions the soul is believed to sometimes escape the body via the mouth or nostril during sleep. Moreover, during a dream the soul may wonder away from the body and may engage in certain acts or interact with other souls including those of the dear but long dead and departed.

Sometimes the soul is believed to take on another form, such as a bird, or deer, fox, rabbit, wolf, and so on. The spirit and the soul could also hover about in human-like, ghostly vestiges, at the fringes of reality, the hinterland where day turns into night (Campbell 1988; Frazier 1950; Jung 1964; Malinowski 1954; Wilson 1951). The souls of animal's such as a wolf or eagle, could also leave the body and take on various forms including that of a woman or Man. Not just men but animals too had souls that had to be respected.

Even after death souls continued to interact with the living, and every living being possessed a

Figure 152. (Below) The souls of young women who had drowned beckon to passing men, luring them to their deaths. (Left) A female tree spirit.

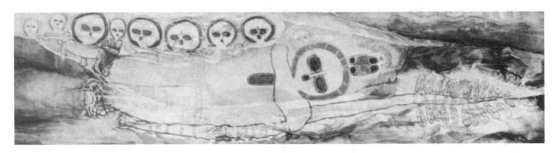

Figure 153. *Wondjina figure with plum tree at its side. Wondjinas are spirits. Above the Wondjina are the "children of the wondjinas" which are the souls of men. (Below) Paleolithic souls ascend to heaven.*

soul. Hence, the ancients believed that these souls could be influenced, their behavior controlled, and, in consequence, a good hunt insured or with the assistance of a soul, or by performing magical rituals aimed at the soul, enemies could be defeated and an evil man could be easily slain.

Because animals and plants had souls, and as some gods would also take up residence within an animal or plant as a temporary or permanent abode, this gave rise to animal worship and animal sacrifice, as well as the avoidance of certain animals or plants which were not to be killed or eaten, or

killed or eaten only in a certain ritualized manner (Campbell 1988; Frazier 1950; Malinowkski 1948; Smart 1969).

Over the course of human cultural and cognitive evolution, these beliefs became increasingly complex and required specialists to interpret and minister the rituals and rites (Armstrong 1994; Brandon 1967; Campbell 1988; Frazier 1950; Smart 1969; Wilson 1951). Soon priests, prophets, and even the Gods evolved.

DREAMING OF GOD

Priests and prophets as well as the common people, often experienced God as well as animal spirits and the souls of the dead, during the course of a dream (Campbell 1988; Frazier 1950; Jung 1945, 1964; Malinowkski 1954).

Dreams have their source in the amygdala and hippocampus and inferior temporal lobe. Although mediated by brainstem nuclei, activity within the amygdala may in fact trigger the first phase of dreaming (REM), which is signified by the buildup of PGO (pontine-geniculate-occipital) waves. REM (dream) sleep is heralded and then accompanied by what has been referred to as PGO waves. That is, the amygdala is active not only during REM, but amygdala activity triggers PGO waves (Calvo, et al. 1987) which then leads to dream sleep. The amygdala produces the dream, and dreams the dream, and the dream may consist of fragmentary memories, hallucinatory imagery, and emotional extremes.

In addition to amygdala activity during REM, the hippocampus begins to produce slow wave, theta activity (Jouvet 1967; Olmstead, Best, and Mays 1973; Steriade and McCarley

1990). Presumably, during REM, the hippocampus and amygdala act as a reservoir from which various memories, images, emotions, words, and ideas are drawn and incorporated into the matrix of dreamlike activity being woven by the right (and left) hemisphere (Joseph 1982, 1988, 1996, 2000a). The hippocampus and amygdala also serve as a source from which material is drawn during the course of a daydream.

Yet, as also noted, these limbic structures also normally acts to inhibit the perception of most of the stimuli impinging on the body. This information is filtered so that one reality is maintained and to prevent the individual from being overwhelmed with competing streams of input. In other words, just as a channel selector on a television or radio permits the select reception of information from a single source (a single reality), these brain structures perform likewise. However, just as there are a multitude of channels, and just as one can change from channel to channel in order to receive a wealth of data, images, sounds, and information from a variety of sources (a variety of realities), likewise, the limbic system can also become tuned to other sources of information which are not normally perceived.

And, once the Doors of Perception are opened, all appears as it is...infinite.

DREAMING & WITCHCRAFT

"Witchcraft" and any and all "paranormal" capabilities, including "ESP" or divining by dreams, has been condemned as "unnatural" by many (but not all) religions throughout the ages including the ancient Jews and the Catholic Church.

"Witchcraft is a sin." I Samuel 15: 23

Of course, the "god" Yahweh would communicate with his prophets through visions and dreams. However, the unauthorized use of these same capacities was also condemned and outlawed, and those possessing these "unnatural" attributes killed: "I will gather you and blow upon you the fire of my wrath, and ye shall be melted in the midst therefore... for... They prophesy falsely and divine deceitfully. They have profaned what is sacred to me... I am profaned in their midst" (Ezekiel, 22:23).

The Lord God declared religious war against and condemned to death all witches and all those who could commune with the dead, speak with spirits, conjure ghosts, or communicate with devils (Exodus 22: 18, Samuel 15: 23; Ezekiel 22:23).

"You know... how he has cut off those familiar with ghosts and spirits and wizards. So wherefore then layest thou a snare for my life, to cause me to be killed." -I Samuel 28:8-10.

Likewise, the Medieval Catholic Church burnt witches, warlocks, and dreamers, and all those suspected of communing with devils. According to Church and religious authorities, these practices were the work of the Devil, Satan, the fallen angel, the fallen god, the serpent also known as the god of the snake.

These "supernatural abilities" were viewed as a threat for they could be employed to divine the future, to influence and cast spells on other humans, or to communicate with the dead or even with other gods including the devil. Hence, those who saw the future through trance states or via dreams, or who demonstrated what might be described as "ESP," although venerated by some, were condemned by others as "unnatural" and sinful.

"Thou shall not suffer a witch to live." Exodus 22:18

DREAMING THE FUTURE

It is said that Mary Lincoln dreamed of President Lincoln's assassination, and saw his dead body laid out with the bullet wound to his head. If that story is true, it could be said that Mary Lincoln gained advance access to information that already existed in the future, in some distant realm of space. Because time is a function of movement through space and distance, it could be assumed that Mary Lincoln was able to see what lay up ahead whereas others, being more "near sighted" were unable to perceive these events until they were upon them.

Yet another possibility is that she somehow deduced what might transpire, and then it did come to pass. Therefore what she dreamed was a well reasoned prediction, rather than a form of extrasensory perception.

Yet another possibility is that the murder of Lincoln, the actual intention of killing him, had been communicated to her; that is, through her dreams and perhaps the dreams of Mr. John Wilkes Booth or one of his coconspirators. That is, she may have received this information through the commingling of dreams, or perhaps, through the interaction of souls which some believe can leave the body during sleep and interact with the souls of others.

Anecdotal evidence abound to support the possibility that people can communicate with one

Figure 154. *"With dreams upon my bed thou scarest me and affrightest me with visions" William Blake, 17th century.*

another while dreaming. Some studies suggest that a dreamer can even tap into the thoughts of those awake.

Consider, for example, studies performed in the Sleep Laboratory of Mimonides Medical Center in New York, by Dr. Williams Erwin. In these studies, participants were introduced, and then later, while one subject slept and when it was determined he had entered REM sleep, the other would begin looking at particular paintings and prints. He would then attempt to project these images into the mind of the sleeper.

In one experiment, when the test subject entered REM, the "sender" opened a package which contained an art print of the Mexican and Indian followers of the Mexican revolutionary Emiliano Zapta, i.e. Zapatistas, by Romero. When the test subject entered REM, the other began gazing at the picture and attempted to project it to the dreamer. The dreamer was immediately awakened when the REM episode had ceased and was asked to describe his dream: "...a feeling of memory... of New Mexico... a lot of mountains...Indians, Pueblos" (reviewed in Broughton, 1991; see also Child, 1985; Devereuz, 1953; Ullman & Krippner, 1989).

DREAMS, SPIRITS AND REALITY

"I the Lord will make Myself known to him in a vision, and will speak with him in a dream." - Numbers 12.6

When the limbic system becomes hyperactivated it is not at all uncommon for an individual to dream. Dreams, it has been proclaimed, are the royal road to the unconscious (Freud, 1900).

It is also via dreams that gods and spirits speak to women and men (Campbell, 1988; Jaynes, 1976; Jung, 1945, 1964). It was via dreams that hunter-gatherers and ancient humans were able to gain access to the domicile of the soul and the spirit world of the hereafter (Frazier 1950; James 1958; Neihardt and Black Elk 1989). Indeed, it has been argued that dreams (and thus the limbic system) enable an individual to come into contact with a different reality; the same reality shared and experienced by our ancestors and the gods—the ultimate reality of the Great Spirit.

DREAMS AND MULTIPLE REALITIES

Our ancient human ancestors lived in two realities, that of the physical and of the spiritual, both of which were undeniable and experienced by enemies and friends alike (Frazier, 1950; Jung, 1945, 1964). One need only spend a night alone in the forest among the trees and the elements to become quickly convinced that one is not alone, but is being watched by various entities both alive and supernatural, animal and spirit, benevolent and unkind.

Like modern day humans, the ancients had dreams by which they were transported or exposed to a world of magic and untold wonders. It is as if one had been transported to a different world and a reality which obeyed its own laws of time, space, and motion.

It is through dreams that humans came to believe the spiritual world sits at the boundaries of the physical, where day turns to dusk, the hinterland of the mind where imagination and dreams flourish and grow (Frazier, 1950; Jung, 1945, 1964; Malinowkski, 1954); hence the tendency to bury the dead in a sleeping position even 100,000 years ago.

It is also via dreams that humans came to know that spirits and lost souls populated the night. The dream was real and so too were the Gods and demons who thundered and condemned and the ghosts and phantoms that hovered at the edge of night. Although but a dream, like modern humans, our ancient ancestors experienced this through the senses, much as the physical world is experienced. Both were real and were taken seriously.

Dreams are the royal road to the unconscious realms of the mind and to realities that lie just beyond conscious awareness. And it is through the amygdala, hippocampus, and temporal lobe, that dreams emerge and flow. The limbic neurons subserving spiritual experiences also give rise to dreams. Thus the link between the world of dreams and the spirit land of gods and demons is the limbic system; i.e. the "transmitter to god."

RIGHT TEMPORAL LOBE HYPERACTIVATION & DREAMING

The amygdala and the neocortex of the temporal lobe are interactionally involved in the production of religious and hallucinatory experiences including dream states (Broughton, 1982; Gloor, 1997; Goldstein et al., 1972; Hodoba, 1986; Humphrey & Zangwill 1961; Kerr & Foulkes 1978; Meyer et al., 1987); the right temporal lobe and amygdala in particular (Joseph, 1988a, 1992a).

Similarly, d'Aquili and Newberg (1993) argue that the right hemisphere (and right amygdala) is more involved than the left in the reception and production of religious imagery. This is likely as the right hippocampus and amygdala, and the right hemisphere in general (Broughton, 1982; Goldstein et al., 1972; Hodoba, 1986; Humphrey & Zangwill 1961; Joseph, 1988, 2000a; Kerr and Foulkes 1978; Meyer, Ishikawa, Hata, and Karacan 1987) also appear to be involved in the production of hallucinations, dream imagery as well as REM during sleep. Indeed, like the limbic system, the right hemisphere is not only associated with dreams, but the unconscious mind (Joseph, 1982, 1988a,b).

In addition to dream production, the right hemisphere also appears to be the dominant source for complex non-linguistic hallucinations. Specifically, tumors or electrical stimulation of the right hemisphere or temporal lobe are much more likely to result in complex visual as well as musical and singing hallucinations, whereas left cerebral tumors or activation gives rise to hallucinations of words or sentences (Berrios, 1990; Halgren, et al. 1978; Hecaen & Albert, 1978; Jackson, 1880; Mullan & Penfield, 1959; Penfield & Perot, 1963; Teuber et al. 1960).

Although up to five stages of sleep have been identified in humans, for our purposes we will be concerned only with two distinct sleep states. These are the REM (rapid eye movement) and non-REM (N-REM) periods. N-REM occurs during a stage referred to as "slow-wave" or synchronized sleep. In contrast, REM occurs during a sleep stage referred to as "paradoxical sleep." It is called paradoxical, for electrophysiologically the brain seems quite active and alert, similar to its condition during waking. However, the body musculature is paralyzed, and the ability to perceive outside sensory events is greatly attenuated (reviewed in Hobson et al. 1986; Steriade & McCarley 1990; Vertes 1990).

Most individuals awakened during REM report dream activity approximately 80% of the time. When awakened during the N-REM period, dreams are reported approximately 20% of the time (Foulkes, 1962; Goodenough et al. 1959; Monroe et al. 1965). However, the type of dreaming that occurs during REM vs. N-REM is quite different. For example, N-REM dreams (when they occur) are often quite similar to thinking and speech (i.e. lingusitic thought), such that a kind-of rambling verbal monologue is experienced in the absence of imagery (Foulkes 1962; Monroe et al. 1965). It is also during N-REM in which an individual is most likely to talk in his or her sleep (Kamiya, 1961). In contrast, REM dreams involve a considerable degree of visual imagery, emotion, and tend to be distorted and implausible to various degrees (Foulkes, 1962; Monroe et al. 1965)

REM is characterized by high levels of activity within the brainstem, occipital lobe, and other nuclei (Hobson, et al. 1986; Steriade & McCarley 1990; Vertes 1990). It also has been reported that electrophysiologically the right hemisphere becomes highly active during REM, whereas, conversely, the left half of the brain becomes more active during N-REM (Goldstein et al. 1972; Hodoba, 1986). Similarly, measurements of cerebral blood flow have shown an increase in the right temporal and parietal regions during REM sleep and in subjects who upon wakening report visual, hypnagogic, hallucinatory and auditory dreaming (Meyer et al., 1987).

Electrophysiologically the right temporal lobe becomes highly active during REM, whereas, conversely, the left temporal region becomes more active during dreamless sleep, i.e., NREM (Goldstein et al. 1972; Hodoba 1986). Similarly, measurements of cerebral blood flow have shown an increase in the right temporal regions during REM sleep. Right temporal lobe blood flow also increases in subjects who upon wakening report visual, hypnogogic, hallucinatory and auditory dreaming (Meyer et al. 1987). Abnormal and enhanced activity in the right temporal and temporal-occipital area will also provoke dreaming and acts to increase the length and amount of dreaming and REM sleep for an atypically long time (Hodoba 1986).

Interestingly, abnormal and enhanced activity in the right temporal and temporal-occipital area acts to increase dreaming and REM sleep for an atypically long time period. Similarly, REM sleep increases activity in this same region much more than in the left hemisphere (Hodoba, 1986), which indicates that there is a specific complementary relationship between REM sleep and right temporal-occipital electrophysiological activity.

As noted, LSD induces its "hallucinatory" effects by disinhibiting the amygdala. That is, LSD blocks the sensory filtering and perceptual inhibitory activity of a neural transmitter, serotonin. In consequence multisensory qualities that are normally suppressed are suddenly perceived such that what was hidden is revealed; sounds have color and colors and sounds can be tasted, as the boundaries of this reality melt away thus revealing the supernatural reality of the otherside.

Conversely, LSD induced hallucinations are significantly reduced when the right but not the left temporal lobe has been surgically ablated (Serafintides1965). Similarly, it has been reported that dreaming is abolished with right but not left temporal lobe destruction (Bakan, 1978). Hence, it appears that there is a specific complementary relationship between REM sleep, hallucinations, LSD, mystical experiences, and right temporal (and thus right amygdala and hippocampus) electrophysiological activity. By contrast, the left half of the brain appears to be the domain of the more logical and nonintuitive aspects of conscious experience.

Whereas the right hemisphere is dominant for all aspects of emotion, and is the domain of the more visual and imaginal aspects of the mind, the left hemisphere is dominant for language, math, and the temporal sequential aspects of consciousness. It is the right hemisphere which dreams the dream, and it is the left hemisphere which not only passively observes but which forgets the dream upon waking (Joseph, 1988a). It is the more unconscious realms associated with the right hemisphere which are directly in tune with these alternate realities, such as conveyed through dreams, and it is the left hemisphere which dismisses and rationally explains away these experiences as nonsense.

DAY DREAMS AND FORESEEING THE FUTURE

During dream states we see and experience events which are normally filtered from the conscious mind. We can also gain insight into problems which have plagued us, or gain access to knowledge of events which occurred in the past or which will occur in the future (Joseph, 1988a, 2000a; Jung 1945, 1964)—just as we can think about the future or the past and make certain deductions and predictions.

Consider the day dream. In addition to its images and memories, the fantasy produced also consists of anticipations regarding the future, and in this respect, the day dream could be considered an imaginal means of preparation for various possible realities. Interestingly, daydreams appear to follow the same 90-120 minute cycle that characterize the fluctuation between REM and NREM periods, as well as fluctuations in mental capabilities associated with the right and left hemisphere (Broughton 1982; Kripke and Sonneschein 1990). That is, the cerebral hemispheres tend to oscillate in activity every 90-120 minutes. This cycle corresponds to the REM-NREM cycle and the appearance of day and night dreams, and the right hemisphere also appears to be the source of day dreams.

According to the ancients, day and night dreams both contained important information, not just regarding the past or the world of souls and spirits, but the future. As possible harbingers of the future, the intentions of the gods, and the future of self, friends and family, it has long been believed that dreams should be observed most carefully and could be used to foretell the future (Campbell 1988; Frazier 1950; Freud 1900; Jung 1945, 1964; Malinowkski 1954). It was pharaoh's dream which foretold that seven years of famine would follow seven years of plenty.

In fact, among the ancients, the American Indians, and even the highly cultured Romans, every once in a while someone would have what is called "a big dream." The big dream was of great importance to the whole clan, tribe, city, or nation. Often, the man or woman having the dream would gather the others together and announce it. And more often than not, it would be a woman who would have the big dream, for women have always been said to be more in touch with the "irrational," and throughout history it is women who have predominantly served as oracles.

THE TRANSMITTER TO GOD

Given that dreams reflect mental activity, it is thus not terribly surprising that dreams may also contain meaningful information that is not otherwise available to the conscious mind. Since the right hemisphere and limbic system which are responsible for dreaming dreams also "speak different languages" and attend to and process unique types of information, this data cannot always be transferred to and understood by the left hemisphere (Joseph, 1986a, 1988a,b; Joseph et al., 1984). From the perspective of the temporal sequential language dependent mind, these impressions remain unconscious.

The conscious mind is often denied information and social-emotional nuances that may be unconsciously conveyed by others but which may be perceived within the right hemisphere and limbic system (Joseph, 1982, 1988a, 1992b, 2000a; Joseph et al., 1984). This is because the information attended to and the manner in which this data is analyzed by the limbic system and right hemisphere is so different from that normally received and processed by the left hemisphere.

Nevertheless, sensory and emotional stimuli, which are normally ignored or filtered out by the language-dependent left hemisphere during waking are nevertheless perceived and analyzed by other regions of the brain so that a variety of conclusions may be arrived at, albeit unconsciously; and the same occurs during dream sleep.

During dream states, serotonin levels diminish (similar to what occurs under LSD) and multimodal neurons begin to fire such that the brain becomes in tune with, and is sometimes overwhelmed by sensory and ideational events which are normally filtered before reaching consciousness. However, during dreaming, this information may be recalled, integrated, assimilated, and certain conclusions arrived at; that is, by the right hemisphere and limbic system. And this information may then be conveyed to the language dependent left half of the brain which is at a low level of arousal during dream sleep and thus cannot prevent its reception. The left hemisphere observes the dream, which, however, it may forget upon waking.

Because the limbic system and right temporal lobe are hyperactivated during dream states, not only does the brain become freed of inhibitory restraint, but one is presumably able to gain access to dreamlike alternate realities, including, perhaps, the spiritual reality of the Hereafter. Presumably the same occurs when fasting, isolated, in pain, under LSD, in trance, or in the throes of religious ecstasy, all of which activates the limbic system thus increasing channel capacity, so that what is concealed is revealed.

THE STUDY OF "BIG DREAMS"
Critical Connections Between
Religion and Neuroscience
by Kelly Bulkeley

Introduction

Much of the pioneering research in the new field of neurotheology has focused on the practice of meditation and prayer, with special attention to the mystical states that can be generated by the concentrated efforts of experienced practitioners (Benson 1975; Benson 1996; Albright 1997; Austin 1998; Newberg 2001). Research in this area has been remarkably fruitful, with the successful identification of several distinct neurophysiological processes regularly involved in these types of religious experience (as documented in several chapters of this book). If, however, the ultimate goal of neurotheology is to understand the full spectrum of interactions between religious experience and contemporary neuroscience, we must acknowledge the limits of an exclusive focus on refined contemplative practices like meditation and prayer. To be sure, these practices are relatively easy to study (the subjects are, by definition, willing to sit still and passively allow the experimental probings of the researcher), but that methodological convenience should not blind us to the fact that the world's religious traditions have developed a huge array of practices that generate many different types of religious experience. Arguments that contrive to place meditation and prayer at the top of a putative hierarchy of religious states run the danger of depreciating other modes of religious experience and oversimplifying the rich pluralism of human religiosity.

The best way to guard against that danger is to complement meditation and prayer studies with careful investigations of other modes of religious experience, analyzing them in terms of both their spiritual phenomenology and their neuropsychological substrates. These studies will naturally confront many methodological challenges not found in research on meditation and prayer. How, for example, do you get a SPECT scan of a whirling Dervish? How do you measure neurotransmitter secretions in the brain of a Catholic priest during Mass? How do you gauge patterns of electrical activation in the nervous system of a Muslim mourner at a funeral rite? How do you perform an fMRI on an Appalachian Christian who is handling a venomous snake? Tough questions, to be sure. But the difficulty of answering them should not be used as a justification for ignoring these kinds of religious phenomena. On the contrary, I believe this is precisely where the future of neurotheology lies: in the development of creative new methods, using tools from both religious studies and cognitive neuroscience, to explore the vast, colorful realm of human religious experience.

The research presented in this chapter is offered as a step in that direction, with a specific focus on the study of "big dreams." That term was coined by C.G. Jung (Jung 1975), and since his time other researchers have investigated this same realm of dreaming using a variety of different terms: "intensified dreams" (Hunt 1989), "impactful dreams" (Sikora 1993), "highly significant dreams" (Knudson 2001), "extraordinary dreams" (Bogzaran 2002), and "apex dreaming" (Nielsen 2000). My contributions to this growing lexicon have been "root metaphor dreams" (Bulkeley 1994; Bulkeley 1999) and "most memorable dreams" (Bulkeley 2000). Although differing somewhat in their conceptual emphases, all these terms point to the existence of a cluster of relatively rare but widely experienced dream types involving 1) unusually intense emotions and physiological sensations, 2) striking visual images combining bizarreness, beauty, chaos, and order, and 3) a high degree of memorability upon awakening.

For researchers in neurotheology, the study of big dreams (I will use Jung's term for the remainder of this chapter) has several appealing features:

-Big dreams are frequently reported by "ordinary" people, not just by religious virtuosi or highly trained practitioners.

-Big dreams are reported in virtually every religious and cultural tradition throughout history, and are still reported by people in contemporary Western society.

-Big dreams are clearly grounded in the neural activity of the brain during sleep, a fact that opens the way to using sleep research technologies to investigate the neurological processes that produce such religiously and spiritually charged experiences.

-The universality of big dreams, combined with their rootedness in the brain, strongly suggest the possibility that such dreams serve powerful adaptive functions that can be explained and understood in evolutionary terms.

These are all features that favorably distinguish the study of big dreams from the study of meditation and prayer. In identifying these features I do not mean to diminish the significance of those practices. Nor do I mean to propose big dreams as a new paradigm for uncovering the "essence" or "origin" of religion. I simply want to highlight the fact that dreams are another type of religious phenomenon that must be accounted for by any neurotheological theory that aspires to a comprehensive view of human religiosity.

I also do not want these differences to overshadow the potential of the study of big dreams to make use of many of the same imaging techniques that have been applied with such impressive results to meditation and prayer. Such experimental efforts have not yet been made, in large part because neuroscientists with access to the extremely expensive and technologically complex brain imaging machinery have had neither the time nor the inclination to pursue such questions. That will likely change soon, as the research technology becomes less expensive and easier to use outside a laboratory setting, and as investigators in neurotheology continue their work showing that the neuro-physiological correlates of various types of religious and spiritual experience reveal important modes of brain-mind functioning that have not yet been recognized and/or understood by mainstream cognitive neuroscience. A primary goal of this chapter is to outline a conceptual framework for this coming generation of neurotheological research on big dreams.

One of the few researchers who has devoted attention to the interaction of neural and religious factors in dreaming is R. Joseph (Joseph 2001), who has pointed out that the high degree of limbic activation in REM sleep is consistent with the prominent role of the limbic system in various forms of religious experience. More specifically, Joseph suggests that the right hippocampus and amygdala play special roles in the formation of religious imagery, and this may be true in dreams as well, where right hemispheric activity appears to be relatively high. "[I]t appears that there is a specific complementary relationship between REM sleep, hallucinations, mystical experiences, and right temporal (and thus right amygdala and hippocampus) electrophysiological activity." (112)

This chapter will follow up on those suggestions by Joseph, as well as on the insights of Jung, Hunt, Kuiken, Knudson, Krippner and Bogzaran, and other researchers who have undertaken the study of big dreams. First I will survey the occurrence of big dreams in various religious and cultural traditions, considering both their geographic diversity and their experiential phenomenology. Then I will review current neuroscientific research on the nature and function of human dreaming, with special attention to the Activation-Synthesis model of J. Allan Hobson and the clinico-anatomical research of Mark Solms. Having laid out the religious and neuroscientific material I will go on to identify several critical points of connection between the two, and I will point to several questions meriting future research. I will conclude the chapter by offering a new model for understanding the formation, function, and interpretation of big dreams.

Dreams in the History of Religions

This section reviews the findings of researchers in religious studies, anthropology, and history regarding various kinds of dream experiences recorded in different places and times. The review starts with a consideration of the roles that dreams and dreaming have played in major religious faiths and cultural traditions. Then the analysis shifts to a consideration of several cross-cultural and perhaps universal features in the experience of spiritually transformative dreams.

The Ancient Near East

The earliest evidence for dreams in ancient Mesopotamia is a monument built by King Eanatum I (ca. 2454-2425 B.C.E.) in which he commemorates his latest military victory and recounts how the god Ningirsu appeared beside his head in a dream and guaranteed his success in battle (Noegel 2001, 46). In ancient Egypt the first appearance of dreaming in a surviving text comes in a group of documents known as "Letters to the Dead." Dating to the First Intermediate Period (2150-2055 B.C.E.), these texts were written to deceased relatives, who are said to appear in the dreams of the living, sometimes in unpleasant ways (Szpakowska 2001). The Egyptian word for dreams used in these texts is rusut, and Szpakowska explains the significance of this term: "Interestingly, resut is most often determined by an open eye, which is also used for words related to visual perception (such as 'see,' 'be vigilant'). The other term meaning dream was qed, which derived from the word 'sleep.' When this word meant 'sleep,' it was followed by the sign of a bed, but when it meant 'dream,' it used the same open eye sign as resut. An Egyptian could also refer to a dream indirectly by saying that someone came and spoke while the person was sleeping, or that he saw or heard something and then woke up." (31) Szpakowska goes on to point out that the ancient Egyptians had no verb "to dream," and spoke instead of the noun "dream" as something seen, an object of visual perception existing outside the will of the passive dreamer. (31)

The social diversity of the authors of the "Letters to the Dead" is something of an exception in the Ancient Near East dream literature, as the majority of reports are, like the dream of Eanatum I, attributed to kings, priests, and military leaders. These reports generally involve a direct message from a god in which the dreamer passively receives reassurance, guidance, warning, and/or information about the future (Oppenheim 1956; Noegel 2001). The dreams are generally positive in tone, and nightmares are rarely reported, although they play a central role in one of the era's greatest epic poems, the Epic of Gilgamesh (Bulkeley 1999).

Although relatively few reports have survived of dreams from a wider portion of the population, the existence of several manuals of dream interpretation indicate some degree of interest in the subject among the general public. The practical, "how-to" nature of these manuals is indicated by their intimate focus on the details of people's personal lives (their health, sexuality, family relationships, concerns with money and status) and their prescription of various rituals, prayers, and magical formulae to remove the ill effects of bad dreams (Oppenheim 1956; Noegel 2001; Szpakowska 2001). Analyzing a text referred to as the Babylonian Dream Book, Noegel gives the following abbreviated list of types of dream experience described and interpreted in the book: "[U]rinating, having sex, flying, visiting certain temples and towns, seeing the dead and the divine, ascending to the heavens, descending to the underworld, carrying objects, standing or sitting in a particular place, turning into various animals, eating and drinking particular items, making objects, performing a particular occupation, seeing animals, being given objects, seeing astronomical bodies, and felling trees and plants." (51) The interpretive strategies used to translate dream images into practical meanings involved various techniques of linguistic association, most commonly punning and the pairing of similars and opposites. Emphasis was put on the dreamer's occupation, state of mind, status, and personal situation, and interpreters were warned that the same dream image could express different meanings for different people. Although the manuals provided various classificatory systems for dream phenomenology, they all shared the basic assumption that some dreams were more closely related to personal daily life while other dreams involved interactions with divine beings, realities, and powers.

In addition to the interpretation manuals, numerous texts have been found that provide instructions for performing rituals (namburbu) that could evoke favorable dreams from the gods in which the dreamer received divine blessings, insights into the future, and the power to ward off demons and bad dreams (Noegel 2001). These rituals typically invoked the gods of fire, light, or magic, and they involved the preparation of the sleeper by use of such methods as purification, prayer, repeating incantations, and creating magical amulets and figurines. Underlying the use of both rituals and interpretation manuals is the widespread Mesopotamian belief that dreaming could be used to promote a person's health. "The very act of interpreting dreams, like the namburbu rituals, was therapeutic. By 'solving' the puzzling dream, the interpreter 'dissolved' its harmful consequences and thus 'resolved' the dreamer's health" (Noegel 2001).

Judaism

Within this broader Ancient Near Eastern context, Judaism emerged some time after 2000 B.C.E. as a new religious and ethnic tradition shaped in large part by long experiences of exilic wandering. According to the Hebrew Bible, dreams had a directly formative impact on the lives of several of the tradition's founding patriarchs. Numerous Biblical texts present dreaming as a privileged medium by which God communicates with humans. Abram's experience of "a dread and great darkness" falling upon him (Gen. 15), Jacob's dream of the heavenly ladder (Gen. 28), Samuel's experience in the temple of the Lord (1 Sam. 3), and Solomon's dream at Gibeon (1 Kings 3) all describe experiences in which the dreamer receives an awe-inspiring revelation of divine power and majesty. (These Biblical dream theophanies are precisely the kinds of experience Rudolf Otto had in mind when he developed the concept of "the numinous" in his book The Idea of the Holy (Otto 1958). Other types of dreams reported in the Hebrew Bible involve predictions for the future (Gen. 37, 41), reassurance in times of military conflict (Judges 7), and disturbing, ominous nightmares (Gen. 20, Job 7, Dan. 4).

The Hebrew Bible presents two accounts of the practice of dream interpretation. In the first, Joseph interprets the dreams of the baker and the butler (Gen. 40) and the Pharaoh (Gen. 41), translating the concrete images of their dreams (e.g. wine cups, bread baskets, cows, ears of grain) into symbolic predictions for their future. In the second, Daniel performs the feat of not only interpreting King Nebuchadnezzar's dream but also knowing what the dream is before the King tells him (Dan. 2). Like Joseph, Daniel translates the imagery of the dream (a "great image....mighty and of exceeding brightness, stood before you" (Dan. 2:31)) into a symbolic prediction for Nebuchadnezzar's future. Also like Joseph, Daniel attributes his interpretive skills to God's inspiration and guidance (Gen. 41:16, Dan. 2:28).

In addition to these affirmations of the religious value of dreams, the Hebrew Bible includes several passages expressing deep skepticism toward dreams. Numbers 12:6-8 refers to dreams as potentially deceptive "dark speech. In Ecclesiastes 5:3 it is said, "For a dream comes with much business, and a fool's voice with many words." Psalm 73 dismisses dreams as vain illusions-"on awaking you despise their phantoms." The prophet Jeremiah castigates those people (rival prophets?) who falsely claim to know of God's will through their dreams (Jer. 23). Although Solomon's dream at Gibeon follows the classic pattern of an Ancient Near Eastern dream incubation (Oppenheim 1956, Patton 2002), Samuel's surprising encounter with God in the Temple reflects an implicit repudiation of dream incubation as unbefitting the autonomy and majesty of the Jewish God (Bulkeley 1995) (See also Isa. 65:4).

For many centuries rabbinic commentators have been elaborating on these Biblical dream themes. Tractate Berakhot from the Babylonian Talmud (ca. 600 C.E.) has been especially influential in the Jewish tradition (Friedan 1990; Harris 1994). This text offers detailed explanations for interpreting dreams using verbal associations, puns, and scriptural allusions, and it also provides instructions on rituals to reverse the negative effects of bad dreams. Berakhot portrays dreams as valuable sources of insight into both to the dreamer's personal life (e.g., health, sexuality, family relations) and to his or her religious faith. However, the text repeatedly emphasizes that the process of interpreting dreams is very difficult and complex; dreams are always enigmatic and distorted, because "just as there is no wheat without straw, so there is no dream without worthless things" (Ber. 55a). Dreaming has remained a topic of interest among Jewish philosophers and theologians from Philo (born ca. 20 B.C.E.) to Moses Maimonides (1135-1204 C.E.) and, some have argued, all the way to Sigmund Freud (Bakan 1958; Covitz 1990; Friedan 1990; Harris 1994; Hasan-Rokem 1999; Idel 1999; Brill 2000).

Graeco-Roman Traditions

The roots of archaic Greek dream beliefs reach at least as far back as Hesiod's Theogony (ca. 725 B.C.E.), a poetic creation myth in which it is said that "Night bore frightful Doom and the black Ker [a spirit of death]/And Death, and Sleep, and the whole tribe of Dreams." (vv. 211-212) (Hesiod 1973). Homer's epic poems The Odyssey and The Iliad (ca. 800 B.C.E.) make numerous references to dreams, portraying them as divine revelations (Od. 4:884-946), vivid emotional experiences of frustration and sadness (Il. 22:199-201, Il. 23:54-107), and sources of deception and manipulation (Il. 2:1-83, Od. 19) (Bulkeley 2001).

The development of the Greek philosophical tradition brought a new degree of critical analysis to the nature and functions of dreaming. A famous passage in book IX of Plato's Republic uses common dream experience as a means of insight into the hidden depths of human nature: "[A] terrible, fierce, and lawless class of desires exists in every man, even in those of us who have every appearance of being decent people. Its existence is revealed in dreams" (IX.571-572) (Plato 1957) Aristotle (384-322 B.C.E.) offered a naturalistic explanation for dreaming: When we sleep our faculties of sense perception and intellectual analysis suspend their ordinary functions, allowing the echoes of emotionally charged perceptions to reverberate through our minds and become new objects of perception, i.e. dreams (Aristotle 1941; Aristotle 1941b). Both Plato and Aristotle express disdain for supernatural explanations of dreaming, although both acknowledge the potentially valuable insights to be gained from at least some dreams-the Republic says that a man with a rational, well-ordered soul is able to have special dreams in which "he comes nearer to grasping truth than at any other time" (336), and Aristotle views dreams as distorted but interpretable expressions of people's emotional preoccupations. In this the two philosophers may have been following the lead of their mentor Socrates (469-399 B.C.E.), who told his friends of two dreams he had in prison-a recurrent dream of being told to "practice and cultivate the arts" (Phaedo 60-61) (Plato 1961) and a dream of a beautiful, white-clad woman accurately predicting the date of his execution (Crito 43-44) (Plato 1961) (see also (Bulkeley 1998b).

The best evidence for interest in dreams among the general Greek population comes from the temples of the healing god Asklepius, which were vital centers for the ritual practice of dream incubation (Jayne 1925; Dodds 1951; Oppenheim 1956; Meier 1967; Edelstein 1975; Miller 1994; Cancik 1999; Patton 2002). Hundreds of these temples thrived on the mountains, coasts, and islands of the Mediterranean during the final centuries of classical Greek culture and throughout the era of imperial Rome. The young Roman rhetorician Aelius Aristides (117-189 C.E.) practiced dream incubation at several Asklepian temples, and in his Sacred Tales he describes the busy operations at the grandly designed, well-staffed sanctuaries where people suffering from a variety of physical and emotional troubles came to purify themselves, sleep in the serpent-strewn temple, and pray to Asklepius for a dream of revelation and healing (Aristides 1981). The temples themselves were adorned with enthusiastic testimonials from visitors who received the sought-for dreams and were healed of their ills.

The popular practice of dream interpretation seems to have enjoyed a special flourishing during the height of the Roman empire, to judge by the Oneirocriticon of Artemidorus of Daldis (born ca.200 C.E.) (Artemidorus 1975; Grottanelli 1999; Walde 1999). Artemidorus refers to many other dream books circulating through the Mediterranean at that time, and he mentions his involvement with a large population of professional dream interpreter's working in various cities and countries. His Oneirocriticon is intended to codify the wisdom of those other books and interpreters and provide a detailed manual for the professional practice of dream interpretation. Included in the text are descriptions of different categories of dreams (future-oriented vs. present-oriented, direct vs. allegorical), explanations of punning and wordplay, reminders to pay close attention to the personal circumstances of the dreamer, and canny advice about maintaining a professional reputation. The main body of the Oneirocriticon is an extensive catalog of different dream images and their possible meanings-going blind, losing teeth, flying, being beheaded, engaging in a wide variety of sexual acts, and having encounters with animals, gods, and mythological beasts, among many, many other categories. Many of Artemidorus' interpretations follow the Asklepian beliefs and the medical tradition of Hippocrates, Rufus, and Galen in attributing to dreams the power of diagnosing illness (Achmet 1991; Walde 1999). Although the Oneirocriticon is meant as a training manual and reference guide, Artemidorus emphasizes that personal experience is essential to effective dream interpretation: "I maintain that it is necessary for the interpreter of dreams to have prepared himself from his own resources and to use his native intelligence rather than simply to rely upon manuals" (Artemidorus 1975).

Christianity

The founder of the religion, Jesus of Nazareth (died ca. 30 C.E.), is not reported in the New Testament as having experienced any dreams, possibly because he had none to report and possibly because the writers of the Gospels wanted to emphasize his uniquely immediate connection to God, even greater than the connection enjoyed by Moses in the Hebrew Bible, who is said to have spoken to God "mouth to mouth, clearly, and not in dark speech" like dreams (Num. 12:8). One of the Gospels, however, presents the story of Jesus' birth as directly shaped by several heaven-sent dreams warning his parents of threats against them and the life of their newborn child (Matt. 1:20-24, 2: 12, 13, 22). Dreams also serve as a source of divine guidance in the missionary work of Paul, directing him to visit certain regions, warning him of potential dangers, and reassuring him in times of anxiety (Acts 16:9, 18:9-11, 23:11, 27:23-25). Indeed, Paul's original conversion experience on the road to Damascus (Acts 9) became the preeminent model for conversion to the Christian faith, and over the centuries, wherever Christianity has spread, people have reported intense, revelatory dreams in which God appeared to them and compelled them to adopt the new religion (Peel 1968; Osborne 1970; Lanternari 1975; M'Timkulu 1977; Fisher 1979; Curley 1983; Kelsey 1991; Shaw 1992; Miller 1994.)

One of the early converts was Jerome (ca. 347-420), a well-educated young man who reported a startling dream in which he was brought before the judgment seat of God, accused of being "a follower of Cicero and not of Christ," and scourged by repeated strokes of the lash until he made a vow to reject all worldly books and devote himself exclusively to Christianity (Kelsey 1991). Despite the powerful impact of this dream on his own life ("thenceforth I read the books of God with a zeal greater than I had previously given to the books of men" (137)), or perhaps precisely because its transformative impact, Jerome, who went on to become a powerful church bishop, denounced the dream incubation practices that were still popular throughout the Mediterranean world and condemned people who "sit in the graves and the temples of idols where they are accustomed to stretch out on the skins of sacrificial animals in order to know the future by dreams, abominations which are still practiced today in the temples of Asklepius" (137) (Miller 1994).

This basic theological tension-between a respect for the divine power of dreams and a deep fear of being deceived or misled by them-pervades the Christian tradition right into the present day. For many theologians the key concern is the inescapable nature of sexuality in dreams. St. Augustine (354-430 C.E.) laments in his autobiographical Confessions that even though he has, like Jerome, converted from paganism to Christianity and has pledged himself to a life of chastity, he is still plagued by disturbingly vivid sexual dreams: "But in my memory of which I have spoken at length, there still live images of acts which were fixed there by my sexual habit. These images attack me. While I am awake they have no force, but in sleep they not only arouse pleasure but even elicit consent, and are very like the actual act. The illusory image within the soul has such force upon my flesh that false dreams have an effect on me when asleep, which the reality could not have when I am awake. During this time of sleep surely it is not my true self, Lord my God?" (X.xxix(40)) (Augustine 1991). St. Thomas Aquinas (1225-1274) follows Aristotle in explaining many dreams (particularly sexual dreams) as nothing more than the unfortunate by-products of ordinary bodily processes, and he adds to Aristotle the Christian belief that dreams of sexual temptation are sent by the devil to lure the faithful astray. However, in the Summa Theologica Aquinas admits that divine revelations in dreams are possible: "This can be seen in the fact that the more our soul is abstracted from corporeal things, the more it is capable of receiving abstract intelligible things. Hence in dreams and alienations of the bodily senses, divine revelations and foresight of future events are perceived the more clearly." (1.Q-12.11) (Kelsey 1991) Protestant reformer Martin Luther (1483-1546) refused to have anything to do with the seeming revelations of dreams: "I care nothing about visions and dreams. Although they seem to have meaning, yet I despise them and am content with the sure meaning and trustworthiness of Holy Scripture" (Luther 1945).

Despite these theological misgivings, at the popular level Christian interest in dream continued to exist, although people had reason to be prudent about talking too openly about their dreams-the Malleus Malificarum, the fifteenth-century manual used by the inquisitors to detect and hunt down witches, lists dreams as one medium by which demons operate (Sprenger 1971). For the most part, dream incubation practices continued unabated, and in many cases the rituals were performed in Asklepian temples that had been reconsecrated as shrines to Christian saints and martyrs(Achmet 1991). New manuals of dream interpretation were produced, including a text called the Oneirocriticon, written by a Christian named Achmet in tenth-century Byzantium who essentially copied the basic framework of Artemidorus' manual and filled it in with references to Christian scriptural and iconographic sources (Achmet 1991). These ritual and interpretive practices gave new theological expression to the same themes found in the earlier traditions regarding dreams as a source of revelation, guidance, warning, healing, and possible deception. Looking at Christianity today in Western Europe and North America, the dream theory of C.G. Jung can be viewed as a psychological elaboration of those basic religious themes (Jung 1965; Jung 1975), and his theory has in turn reignited Christian theological and popular interest in dreaming (Sanford 1982; Taylor 1983; L.M. Savary 1984; Kelsey 1991; Taylor 1992; Hall 1993) .

Islam

The Muslim faith emerged in seventh century C.E. Arabia as a profound revisioning of early Jewish and Christian traditions. One theme the religion's founder, the Prophet Muhammed (570-632), drew from the scriptures of those two traditions was a reverence for dreaming. In Islam's foundational text the Qur'an (610-632) dreams serve as a vital medium by which God communicates with humans, offering divine guidance and comfort, warnings of impending danger, and prophetic glimpses of the future. Muhammed describes several of his own dreams in the Qur'an and in the hadith (the collected sayings of the Prophet). For example, he tells his followers (many of whom were battle-tested warriors) "I saw in a dream that I waved a sword and it broke in the middle, and behold, that symbolized the casualties the believers suffered on the Day [of the battle] of Uhud. Then I waved the sword again, and it became better than it had ever been before, and behold, that symbolized the Conquest [of Mecca] which Allah brought about" (Hermansen 2001). Muhammed also made a practice of asking his followers to share their dreams so he could interpret them, and he gave them instructions on how to purify themselves so they could have good, heaven-sent dreams (an incubation practice that came to be known as istikhara; see Trimingham 1959; Callois 1966; Hermansen 2001).

Inspired by these teachings from the Qur'an and the hadith, Muslim philosophers and theologians over the centuries developed new techniques and conceptual frameworks for the practice of dream interpretation. The most famous of these interpreters was Ibn Sirin, whose name was reverently attached to dream interpretation manuals long after his death in 728 C.E. Ibn Sirin emphasized that the same dream image could have different meanings for different people, and many of his interpretations hinged on the identification of a special connection between a dream image and a passage from the Qur'an.

The Oneirocriticon of Artemidorus was translated into Arabic in 877 C.E., and it gave further stimulus to Muslim dream theory and practice. During an era of tremendous vitality in Islamic culture, the philosophers Ibn Arabi (1164-1240) and Ibn Khaldun (1332-1402) drew on both Muslim and Graeco-Roman dream traditions to devise a basic typology of dreams that has shaped Muslim beliefs to the present day. Here is Ibn Khaldun's rendering of it: "Real dream vision is an awareness on the part of the rational soul in its spiritual essence, of glimpses of the forms of events.... This happens to the soul [by means of] glimpses through the agency of sleep, whereby it gains the knowledge of future events that it desires and regains the perceptions that belong to it. When this process is weak and indistinct, the soul applies to it allegory and imaginary pictures, in order to gain [the desired knowledge]. Such allegory, then, necessitates interpretation. When, on the other hand, this process is strong, it can dispense with allegory. Then, no interpretation is necessary, because the process is free from imaginary pictures.... One of the greatest hindrances [to this process] is the external senses. God, therefore, created man in such a way that the veil of the senses could be lifted through sleep, which is a natural function of man. When that veil is lifted, the soul is ready to learn the things it desires to know in the world of Truth. At times, it catches a glimpse of what it seeks.... Clear dream visions are from God. Allegorical dream visions, which call for interpretation, are from the angels. And 'confused dreams' are from Satan, because they are altogether futile, as Satan is the source of futility" (Khaldun 1967).

The dream traditions of Islam have proven remarkably durable, as Muslims today in countries all around the world fully accept that basic typology and continue to look to their dreams for divine reassurance, future guidance, physical and emotional healing, and spiritual initiation (particularly with Sufi mystical practice-see (Ewing 1989). Contemporary Muslims make use of an abundant literature of popular dream interpretation manuals, and they continue to practice dream incubation at shrines of deceased saints (Shaw 1992; Hoffman 1997; Hermansen 2001). Evidence of continued Muslim belief in the prophetic value of dreams during times of military conflict appears in the video-tape publicly released in December of 2001 in which Osama bin Laden and a group of followers discuss dreams that anticipated the September 11 attack on the World Trade Center and the Pentagon.

Hinduism

Hinduism originated in the diverse religious beliefs and practices of the people of the Indus Valley (Persian hindu, Sanskrit sindhu, "river"), and is now the faith of a majority of the nearly one billion people of modern-day India. The tradition's earliest text is the Rg Veda (ca. 1300 B.C.E.), a collection of sacred teachings, prayers, and rituals. Dreaming appears in this text as a source of emotional distress and personal danger. For example, a prayer to the god Varuna reads, "If someone I have met, O king, or a friend has spoken of danger to me in a dream to frighten me, or if a thief should waylay us, or a wolf-protect us from that, Varuna." Another prayer involves Agni, the god of fire: "The one who bewitches you with sleep or darkness and lies with you-we will drive him away from here."

A later corpus of sacred texts, the Upanishads (ca 700 B.C.E.), offers a more systematic treatment of dreaming. These texts describe four states of being: waking, dreaming, dreamless sleep, and identity with the Godhead. The Brihad-Aranyaka Upanishad contains this passage on the nature of dreaming: "When one goes to sleep, he takes along the material of this all-containing world, himself tears it apart, himself builds it up, and dreams by his own brightness, by his own light. Then this person becomes self-illuminated. There are no chariots there, no spans, no roads. But he projects from himself chariots, spans, roads. There are no blisses there, no pleasures, no delights. But he projects them from himself blisses, pleasures, delights.... For he is a creator. On this point there are the following verses [from the Vedas]: 'Striking down in sleep what is bodily, sleepless he looks down upon the sleeping [senses]....In the state of sleep going aloft and alow, a god, he makes many forms for himself-now, as it were, enjoying pleasures with women, now, as it were, laughing, and even beholding fearful sights."

Historian of religions Wendy Doniger has pointed out the significance of the terms used in these texts: "The verb srj, used to express projection, means literally to 'emit' (as semen, or words), and it frequently occurs in stories about the process of creation (sarga, from srj) in which the Creator emits the entire universe from himself the way a spider emits a web" (O'Flaherty 1984). Furthermore, "the same verb is used here and throughout Indian literature to denote one's perception of both worlds: one 'sees' (drs) the world just as one 'sees' a dream."

Further evidence for Hindu interest in dreams can be found in the following texts: the two great epics The Mahabharata (ca. 400 B.C.E.-400 C.E.) and The Ramayana (ca. 100 B.C.E.), in which dreams play dramatic roles in portending future disasters, revealing strong emotions, and offering alluring glimpses of truth that the dreamers both desire and fear (Bulkeley 1999b); medical texts like the Athara Veda (ca 500-600 C.E.), which gives an extensive catalog of different types of dreams, their meanings, their origins, and their relevance to the psychosomatic conditions of the dreamer; and philosophical texts like the Yogavasistha (900-1200 C.E.), which tells several stories about dreams and dreamers, stories that have the cumulative effect of disrupting ordinary distinctions between waking and dreaming, calling into question one's basic sense of existential identity. Running through all these texts is an underlying belief in the pluralism of dreaming: some dreams are primarily influenced by bodily conditions, others by personal temperment, and still others by gods and goddesses. "These two ideas-that dreams reflect reality and that they bring about reality-remain closely intertwined in Indian texts on the interpretation of dreams" (O'Flaherty 1984).

Buddhism

This tradition emerged in 5th-6th B.C.E. India, and its beginning is attributed to the decision of a prince named Guatama to renounce his privileged life and meditating under a Bo tree, which led him to become a Buddha, literally "one who has awakened" to the truth (Bowker 1997). Buddhist interest in dreaming starts with Guatama's conception. His mother, Queen Maya, is said to have had a dream by which she was impregnated with a child who destined to become either a universal king or, if he renounced the world, a Buddha. Here is one version of Queen Maya's dream: "At that time the Midsummer festival (Asalaha) was proclaimed in the city of Kapilasvatthu....During the seven days before the full moon Mahamaya had taken part in the festivities....On the seventh day she rose early, bathed in scented water, and distributed alms....Wearing splendid clothes and eating pure food, she performed the vows of holy day. Then she entered her bed chamber, fell asleep and saw the following dream: The four guardians of the world lifted her on her couch and carried her to the Himilaya mountains and placed her under a great sala tree....Then their queens bathed her....dressed her in heavenly garments, anointed her with perfumes and put garlands of heavenly flowers on her....They laid her on a heavenly couch, with its head towards the east. The Boddhisattva, wandering as a superb white elephant....approached her from the north. Holding a white lotus flower in his trunk, he circumambulated her three times. Then he gently struck her right side, and entered her womb" (Young 2001). This story, which dramatically expands on the earlier Hindu theme of the cosmic creative power of dreaming, has been included in nearly every biographical text on the Buddha, and it has frequently been reproduced in painting, sculpture, and other forms of iconography. One of its noteworthy features is its ritual context, which reflects an idealized version of dream incubation. Indeed, there is abundant evidence throughout Buddhism's history of practices devoted to dream incubation, practices that in various ways model themselves on what Queen Maya did in terms of purifications, prayers, devotional activities, astronomical timing, and special sleeping conditions (Laufer 1931; Wayman 1967; O'Flaherty 1984; Ong 1985; Young 1999, 2001).

In keeping with the popular practice of dream incubation, several Buddhist medical texts were written to explain the origins and meanings of different kinds of dreams. Regarding origins, Buddhist explanations included disturbances of bodily humors, reflections of daily experience, personal fantasies, future prophecies, divine influences, strong emotions, sexual desire, and demonic attack (Wayman 1967; O'Flaherty 1984; Ong 1985; Young 1999). Other prominent texts spoke of dreams as a means by which Buddhist monks managed to convert Indian Kings to their faith. "Doubtless, these stories [of monks interpreting kings' dreams] reflect actual Buddhist practice, for other sources corroborate the tradition that Buddhists converted many Indian Kings by a combination of public debate, private counseling,....and a kind of primitive psychoanalysis" (O'Flaherty 1984).

Buddhist monks, in the context of seeking to understand the illusory nature of all reality, took special interest in developing the ability to maintain awareness and intentionality within the dream state (Gillespie 1988; Norbu 1992; Rinpoche 1998; Young 1999). For example, the Tantric Buddhist Naropa (11th century C.E.) (who left his home as a youth to seek out a teacher whose name he had been given in a dream), taught his followers a precise method for cultivating awareness in dreaming, including special visualizations, breathing exercises, and sleep postures (Gillespie 1988). In recent years these Buddhist dream practices have become the subject of interest to Western researchers in "lucid dreaming," who have sought parallels between the conscious dream experiences of Buddhist monks and contemporary Westerners (LaBerge 1985; LaBerge 1988). Their efforts have been met with the response that Buddhist dream experiences cannot be adequately understood outside the religious context in which they were generated (Norbu 1992; Lama 1997; Rinpoche 1998; Young 1999; Doniger 2001).

Comparative Analysis

In the interest of space, although at the risk of slighting many other rich dream traditions, I will bring this survey to a close with the observation that historians of religion, anthropologists, and ethnographers have found a tremendous variety of sophisticated dream beliefs and ritual practices in the indigenous cultures of North America (Benedict 1922; Morgan 1932; Luomala 1936; Radin 1936; Eggan 1952; Eggan 1955; Eggan 1957; Wallace 1958; Hallowell 1966; Devereux 1969; Irwin 1994; Irwin 2001), Central and South America (Gregor 1981; Gregor 1983; Tedlock 1987; Descola 1993; Gregor 2001; Kracke 2001; Tedlock 2001), Africa (Sundkuler 1961; Fabian 1966; Charsley 1973; Levine 1975; Curley 1983; Charsley 1987; Shaw 1992; Shafton 2002), and Oceania (Firth 1934; Sharp 1969; Tonkinson 1970; Stephen 1979; Trompf 1990; Stephen 1995; Bosnak 1996; Lohmann 2001). Although I do not have room in this chapter to give even a brief review of all this material, I will in the following comparative analysis take the beliefs and practices of these cultural traditions into consideration as I highlight a set of cross-cultural themes and patterns.

Quality of the Data

Before going further, a key question needs to be addressed: how are we to assess the quality of this data? There are at least two reasons to adopt a cautious attitude toward the historical and cross-cultural material just reviewed. First, nearly all of the texts we have considered so far have been shaped to varying degrees by the interests of scribes, editors, redactors, compilers, and translators. These intermediaries have determined which dreams are and are not recorded, which details are and are not included, which meanings are and are not emphasized. As a result, our access to the dream beliefs, practices, and experiences of people from other places and times is never direct, but always mediated by people who have strong personal and ideological motives to present dreams in certain ways and not in others. Second, even in cases where we have a relatively direct report of a person's dream experience, we must still consider the possibility that the individual has revised or embellished his or her experience, whether through conscious fabrication or unconscious subterfuge. Put most crudely, we can never be sure whether or not people are actually telling the truth when they report a dream-they may just be making it all up. These two factors make it difficult if not impossible to support general claims about dreaming based on historical and cross-cultural evidence alone. However, even if it is not decisive by itself, the historical and cross-cultural evidence becomes surprisingly significant when considered in the light of contemporary neuroscientific research on the dreaming brain. Providing that kind of illumination is my ultimate goal in this chapter.

Major Cross-Cultural Themes. Let us summarize and conceptually organize the material covered so far. Here is what we can most confidently propose, independently of any experimental research and relying solely on the history of religions data, about people's basic beliefs, practices, and experiences involving dreams and dreaming:

1. Widespread Public Interest. Although surviving dream reports from ancient times generally come from the social elite (kings, priests, military leaders), there is ample evidence of strong popular interest in dreams among all segments of society in virtually every known culture.

2. Different Types of Dreams. All cultures make distinctions among different types of dreams, with the most common distinction being between significant and insignificant dreams.

3. Qualities of Dreaming. Many cultures emphasize the visual nature of dreaming and speak of "seeing" dreams, and dreams as a type of "vision." Nearly all cultures emphasize the strong emo-

tional qualities of dreaming, i.e. the way dreams bring forth deep passions and powerful desires.

4. Origins of Dreaming. Although each culture has its own distinct understanding of the origins of dreaming, nearly all of them revolve around the paradox that dreaming is both passive and active, something people receive and create, something coming from outside and inside at the same time.

5. Functions of Dreaming. In keeping with the belief in different types of dreams, all cultures believe dreaming serves several different functions, among which the most important are anticipating the future, warning of danger, envisioning sexual pleasure, heralding new births, mourning death and other losses, healing illness, giving moral guidance, and providing divine reassurance in times of distress. In rare but widely reported cases, dreams are seen as serving the additional function of sparking religious conversions, i.e., provoking radical transformations of personality and/or spiritual orientation.

6. Dream Content. Remaining mindful of the limited confidence we can have in the veracity of subjective dream reports, we can identify the following as the most prominent elements of dream content cross-culturally: Characters personally known to the dreamer; characters with supernatural or divine qualities; animals, especially snakes; sexual activity; flying and falling; fighting, conflict, and aggression; bodily functioning (e.g., eating, excreting, illness, teeth).

7. Dream Interpretation. In every known culture there are people who have devoted extensive amounts of time and attention to the practice of dream interpretation. Most interpreters use a combination of personal details, common cultural symbols and metaphors, and linguistic analysis (e.g., word-play, punning, parallels and oppositions). These interpretive practices are almost always accompanied by an awareness of the potential to be deceived or misled by dreams.

8. Dream Rituals. Dream rituals are found all over the world, with the basic aims of fending off bad dreams and evoking good ones. The most prominent of these rituals are those intending to "incubate" a good dream by means of purifications, devotions, prayers, sleeping at a special time and in a special place (e.g., a temple, cave, mountain top, shrine, grave), and using a special body position or posture.

Dreams in Cognitive Neuroscience

This section will outline the major experimental findings of the past half-century of scientific research on the relationship between dreaming and the brain. As with the historical and cross-cultural review in the previous section, this survey will be restricted to highlighting only a few of the important findings of current neuroscience, without being able to reproduce all the data and argumentation that underlie those findings.

The Discovery of REM Sleep

In the early 1950's University of Chicago physiologist Nathaniel Kleitman and his student Eugene Aserinsky were studying sleep in children, when they noticed strange movements under the children's eyelids when they fell asleep. Aserinsky and Kleitman conducted several experiements to learn more about this phenomenon, and they soon found that both children and adults experience during sleep regular periods of highly coordinated eye movements, intensified brain activity (as measured by the electroencephalograph, or EEG), irregular breathing, loss of muscle tone, increased heart rate, and increased blood flow to the genitals (leading to penile erections in men and clitoral swelling in women). William Dement, who joined the Aserinsky and Kleitman research team, coined the term "rapid eye movement" or "REM" for these stages of sleep, contrasting them with "non-rapid eye movement" or "NREM" stages of sleep. Of special interest to these researchers, subjects in the sleep lab who were awakened during a stage of REM sleep were much more likely to report a dream than people awakened during a state of NREM sleep. The REM dream reports frequently involved "strikingly vivid visual imagery," suggesting that "it is indeed highly probable that rapid eye movements are directly associated with visual imagery in dreaming" (Kleitman 1955) (Kleitman 1953; Dement 1972).

Functions of REM and NREM Sleep. Following up on Aserinsky and Kleitman's discovery, researchers soon found that a typical night's sleep for an adult human follows a regular alteration of REM sleep and four distinct states of NREM sleep. On average, an adult human experiences each night four to five periods of REM sleep, of between 10 and 60 minutes, for a total of approximately one-quarter of their total sleep time. Looking at sleep in other animals, researchers found that all mammals (with the apparent exception of the spiny anteater and the bottlenose dolphin) experience regular cycles of REM and NREM sleep; birds apparently have a kind of REM sleep, but reptiles do not. Furthermore, in most mammals (including humans) the percentage of REM sleep is higher among newborns than adults. Taken together, these findings suggest that REM sleep serves some adaptive function, developed over the course of evolutionary history, in the activation and maturation of the mammalian brain (Dement 1972; Jones 1978; Jouvet 1999; Flanagan 2000). Some of the adaptive functions that have been suggested include storing memories and newly learned skills (Smith 1993), processing information with a high emotional charge (Ramone Greenberg 1972), responding to waking life crises (Cartwright 1991), making wide-range connections in the mind (Hartmann 1995), and practicing responses to potential waking life threats (Revonsuo 2000).

Perhaps the most surprising finding in the early years of research on REM and NREM sleep was the intensity of activation in the brain during REM. Contrary to expectations that sleep was a time of quiescence, researchers found that in fact the brain is designed to engage in a cyclical pattern of highly complex and dynamic activities, whose intensity is often greater than that of brain functioning during wakefulness. "If we were not able to observe that a subject is behaviorally awake in the first case and sleeping in the second, the EEG alone would not be capable of indicating whether the subject is awake or [in REM sleep]" (Hobson 1988). Much of this intense neural activity can be attributed to the phasic discharge of PGO (ponto-geniculo-occipatal) waves originating in the brainstem and spreading throughout the brain. "PGO waves represent unbridled brain-cell electricity. 'Brainstem lightning bolts' is hyperbolic but to the point" (Hobson 1999).

J. Allan Hobson and Activation-Synthesis

The most influential theory regarding the relationship between REM sleep and dreaming comes from J. Allan Hobson, whose Activation-Synthesis model (McCarley 1977; Hobson 1988) portrays an essentially unidirectional, bottom-up process of dream formation. In this view dreaming is "activated" by the neurochemical processes of REM sleep that, as an accidental by-product, lead to the activation of random feelings, images, and memories in the sleeping mind. These arbitrary bits of mental content are "synthesized" by higher brain functions that struggle to make sense of them, leading to the imposition of meaning on what is fundamentally nonsensical material. The fact that this process starts in the brainstem and then moves to the brainstem explains why dreams are so bizarre, disjointed, and emotionally turbulent. As Hobson and McCarley say in their 1977 paper, "[T]he forebrain may be making the best of a bad job in producing even partially coherent dream imagery from the relatively noisy signals sent up to it from the brain stem."

In more recent work, Hobson and his colleagues have examined in greater detail the neurochemical dimensions of REM sleep and dreaming. They have found that the transition from waking to sleeping is mediated by a shift in the relative balance of amine and acetylcholine molecules in the brain, with the aminergic system dominant in waking and the cholinergic system dominant in sleeping (Hobson 1999). Hobson says the loss of aminergic inhibition and the reciprocal gain in cholinergic excitation (a process initiated in the brainstem) offers a more precise explanation of why dreams are so filled with disorientation, visual hallucination, distractability, memory loss, and lack of self-awareness. The reciprocal interaction of aminergic and cholinergic systems determines the mode of a person's brain/mind activity across a spectrum from "rational, logical, and self-aware (the traits of being awake), to delusional, illogical, and unreflective (the traits of dreaming)." Hobson also says dreaming, in both its psychological deficiencies and its neurochemical dominance by the cholinergic system, is akin to organic mental syndromes like Alzheimer's disease and Korsakoff's psychosis: "Dreaming, then, is not like delirium. It is delirium. Dreaming is not a model of psychosis. It is a psychosis. It's just a healthy one." Hobson mentions his interest in a new class of anti-psychosis drugs, monoamine oxides inhibitors, whose therapeutic effectiveness involves strengthening the aminergic system and thereby improving the patient's mental functioning while awake, although at the cost of suppressing REM sleep. Noting that the people who take these drugs do not seem to suffer any obvious problems due to the cessation of their dreaming, Hobson speculates, "Maybe dreams really are an epiphenomenona, a secondary and unnecessary outcome of an underlying process. Maybe they are not important psychological experiences. This conclusion is already suggested by the near total amnesia that we all normally have for our dreams."

Even though Hobson's research is most directly aimed at refuting Freud's psychoanalytic theory of dream formation, he does grant that dreaming reflects an impressive degree of creative power in the human brain-mind system. Furthermore, he allows for the possibility that dreams can provide therapeutically valuable information in terms of revealing the primary emotional concerns of the dreamer, and he offers examples of his own dreams to illustrate this (Hobson 1988). If we set aside his barbed rhetorical flourishes against Freudian orthodoxy, we find that a closer analysis of Hobson's work reveals a surprisingly high regard for the functional importance of sleep and dreaming. Consider the following list of functions he proposes in Dreaming and Delirium (1999):

1. By resting in REM sleep, the amines are better able to restrain the potentially disruptive effects of acetylcholine during the day. "[M]y theory is homeopathic: we have a sleep seizure in order to avoid a waking seizure. We dream so as not to hallucinate."

2. "During this unique brain-mind state of REM sleep, then, our circuits are being cleared and our battery is being recharged....REM, it seems, is some sort of supersleep."

3. REM sleep serves to restore the body's capacity for temperature regulation, while NREM sleep enhances the immune system's ability to fight infection.

4. The automatic cycling of waking, sleeping, and dreaming is directly involved in processing and storing new information, and in forming, consolidating, and associating memories. "One function of my dream might thus be to associate my memories and so increase their versatility and redundancy."

5. REM sleep and dreaming function to exercise basic motor programs (especially the fight-or-flight system and the orienting response). "The motor programs in the brain are never more active than during REM sleep...[in order] to prevent their decay from disuse, to rehearse for their future actions when called on during waking, and to embed themselves in a rich matrix of meaning." This function of exercising basic motor programs extends to extremely positive dreams like those of flying: "our ecstatic dreams equip us for the elation and joy of life."

6. Dreaming reveals "the wondrous brain-mind with all of its creative power," a power that is rooted in the fundamentally random, chaotic, nonsensical nature of dream activation: "human creativity depends on a natural tension between the chaos and the self-organization of brain-mind states." Hobson says the brain-mind's drive toward self-organization begins in utero and explains both the patent absurdity of most dreams and the occasionally startling creativity of a few of them. "A remarkable point is that some dreams do take up recurrent themes of undoubted significance to the life of the dreamer. Some seem to repeat almost exactly. How do we square this paradox? What part of dreaming is determined and what part is not? The only answer we have is chaos."

7. In light of current neuroscientific discoveries, Hobson is willing to agree that "Freud was right" in at least this sense: "dreams are trying to tell us something important about our instincts (sex, aggression), our feelings (fear, anger, affection), and our lives (places, persons, and times)."

Mark Solms and the Neuropsychology of Dreams

Hobson's Activation-Synthesis model, with its emphasis on the unidirectional, bottom-up influence of brainstem processes on dream formation, has been challenged by Mark Solms, a psychoanalytically-trained clinical neurologist at London Hospital Medical College who has carefully studied the dreams of 361 patients suffering a variety of brain lesions (Solms 1997). Solms found that almost all of the patients suffered one of four distinct "syndromes" or patterns of disrupted dreaming: "global anoneira," a total loss of dreaming; "visual anoneira," cessation or restriction of visual dream imagery; "anoneirgnosis," increased frequency and vivacity of dreaming, with confusion between dreaming and reality; and "recurring nightmares," an increase in the frequency and intensity of emotionally disturbing dreams. Solms analyzed these four syndromes in comparison to each other and in comparison to those patients (N=24) who, despite suffering serious forms of brain damage, experienced no disruptions in their dreaming. On this basis, Solms has made several claims about what specific regions of the brain are responsible for the formation of dreams:

1. Both Hemispheres. Solms says that global anoneira "can occur with strictly unilateral lesions in either hemisphere," suggesting that both left and right hemispheres make necessary contributions to normal dreaming. This refutes arguments that the right hemisphere has exclusive control over dreaming, and Solms says his findings support Doricchi and Violani's theory that both hemispheres play functional roles, with the right hemisphere providing the "perceptual 'hard grain'...which is probably indispensable for the sensorial vividness of the dream experience" and the left hemisphere providing the "cognitive decoding of the dream during its actual nocturnal development."

2. Global cessation of dreaming can occur after damage to several different regions of the brain, which Solms says supports a distributed, non-modular view of brain-mind functioning: "[C]omplex mental faculties such as reading and writing (and, we might add, dreaming) are not localized within circumscribed cortical centers....[They] are subserved by complex functional sys-

tems or networks, which consist of constellations of cortical and subcortical structures working together in a concerted fashion."

3. Solms finds that language disorders such as aphasia were no more common among his dreaming patients than his non-dreaming patients, and he comments "the high incidence of preserved dreaming among our aphasic patients....demonstrates that loss of the ability to generate language does not necessarily imply loss of the ability to generate dreams." Solms does, however, acknowledge that deeper semantic disorders related to language may be crucial to normal dreaming.

4. Solms finds a "double dissociation" between visual imagery in dreams and visual perception in waking: patients with visual problems had normal dreaming, and patients with nonvisual dreaming had normal visual abilities. Specifically, he finds that brain areas V1 and V2, which are crucial for the processing of external visual signals, are not necessary for the generation and maintenance of normal dream imagery. This means, Solms says, that "dream perceptions are not perceptions; they are representations of perceptions" and he claims his findings refute theories that explain dreams as "internally generated images which are fed back into the cortex as if they were coming from the outside."

Taking these points together, Solms proposes a model of the normal dream process in which several particular brain regions make functional contributions: basal forebrain pathways, which contribute "a factor of appetitive interest" in terms of curiosity, exploration, and expectation; the medial occipito-temporal structures, which contribute visual representability; the inferior parietal region, which contributes spatial cognition; the frontal-limbic region, which adds "a factor of mental selectivity" in separating dreaming from waking (damage to this region leads to reality-monitoring problems in waking); and temporal-limbic structures, which contribute "a factor of affective arousal" and may, in their seizure-like behavior during sleep, be the ultimate source of dream generation. Solms claims his neuropsychological findings refute Hobson's Activation-Sythesis theory: "[T]he neural mechanisms that produce REM are neither necessary nor sufficient for the conscious experience of dreaming....[N]ormal dreaming is impossible without the active contribution of some of the highest regulatory and inhibitory mechanisms of the mind. These conclusions cast doubt on the prevalent notion-based on simple generalizations from the mechanism of REM sleep-that 'the primary motivating force for dreaming is not psychological but physiological' (Hobson and McCarley 1977). If psychological forces are equated with higher cortical functions, it is difficult to reconcile the notion that dreams are random physiological events generated by primitive brainstem mechanisms, with our observation that global anoneira is associated not with brainstem lesions resulting in basic arousal disorders, but rather with parietal and frontal lesions resulting in spatial-symbolic and motivational-inhibitory disorders. These observations suggest that dreams are both generated and represented by some of the highest mental mechanisms."

Unfortunately, the alternative offered by Solms to replace Activation-Synthesis turns out to be a pale restatement Freud's sleep-protection theory (Freud 1965). Solms, unlike Freud, takes no interest whatsoever in the study of dream content (Solms 1997). However, he fully endorses Freud's sleep-protection model of dream formation, and the ultimate, though modestly stated, intention of Solm's 1997 book is to promote a neuropsychological revival of psychoanalytic theorizing.

In considering Hobson's work above, I suggested we distinguish his anti-psychoanalytic polemics from his research findings. Here I suggest we make a similar distinction between Solms' pro-psychoanalytic theorizing and his clinico-anatomical data. From the perspective of our interest in the study of big dreams, one immediate point of interest in Solms' work is the syndrome of "excessive dreaming," or anoneirognosis. This syndrome involves people experiencing intensely emotional and hyperrealistic dreams, often with unusual characters and other content features (although Solms takes no interest in content, his clinical descriptions of the ten patients who had this syndrome include dream reports of meeting deceased loved ones, visiting the "pearly gates," visiting a very beautiful place, and having a black snake crawl into the dreamer's vagina. Both in form and content, these anoneirognostic dreams are quite similar to historical and cross-cultural reports of big dreams. Although Solms' patients would probably be happy to give up their hyper-vivid dreams if they could just regain normal brain/mind functioning again, the experiential similarities of their dreams to the types of dreams most frequently reported in the world's religions is highly suggestive. If Solms is right that frontal limbic lesions are the cause of this syndrome, this may be a key region of the brain to study in connection with the religiously-oriented experience of big dreams.

Also of interest is Solms' account of the syndrome of recurrent nightmares. Patients who have damage to the brain's temporal-limbic areas are especially prone to an increase in nightmares, Solms says, because that particular kind of damage often produces intense neural discharges and seizure activities that overwhelm the ordinary functioning of the brain and inject the patients' dreams with a relentless sense of anxiety. Solms speculates that seizure activity anywhere in the brain can set the dreaming process in motion. This suggests that a potentially fruitful way to study big dreams, some of which are terribly frightening and nightmarish, is to investigate their connection to states of heightened temporal-limbic activation, such as occurs in epilepsy and perhaps other kinds of religious experience. Many common features of big dreams-e.g., the number and frequency of emotions, the activation of instinctive behavior patterns like fight-or-flight, the strong physiological arousal upon awakening-may well be attributable to the extraordinary activation of certain neural processes in the temporal-limbic regions of the brain.

Other Contributions from the Cognitive Sciences

The comparative analysis I offer in the final section of this chapter will be guided primarily by the findings of Hobson and Solms. However, it will also draw deeply on the work of several other researchers whose findings have tremendous potential for the study of big dreams. These include Tracey Kahan (Kahan 2000; Kahan 2001), Jayne Gackenbach (Gackenbach 1991), and Stephen LaBerge (LaBerge 1985), who have explored the phenomenon of lucidity, consciousness, and metacognition in dreaming; David Foulkes (Foulkes 1999), who has shown that the development of a capacity for dreaming tracks the development of general cognitive abilities; G. William Domhoff (Domhoff 1996; Domhoff 2001; Domhoff 2001), who has identified fundamental elements in the content of ordinary dreams and thereby provided a valuable comparative context for the investigation of extraordinary dreams; Ernest Hartmann (Hartmann 1995; Hartmann 1998), who has accounted for the therapeutic value of dreams by highlighting the neural connections that are formed and re-

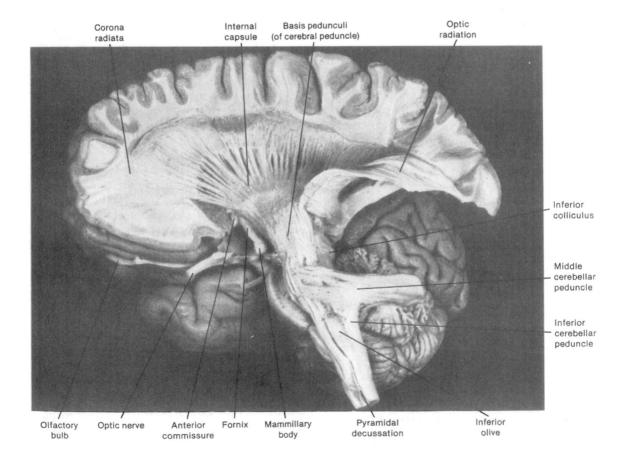

Figure 153a,b. (Below and Previous Page) Two Views of the Brainstem. From M. Carpenter, 1991.

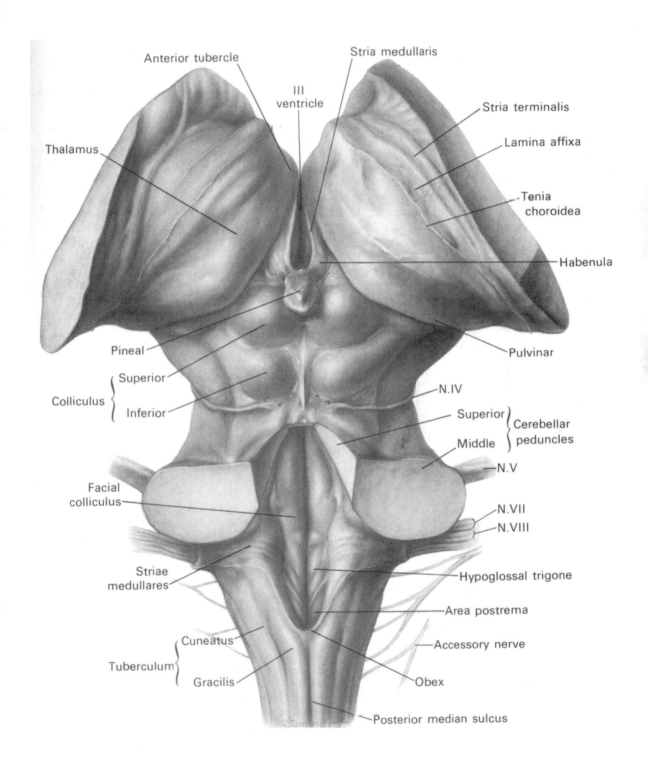

formed during the dreaming process; and Antti Revonsuo (Revonsuo 2000), whose "threat simula-tion" model of the nature and function of nightmares provides important insight into the possible evolutionary emergence of big dreams as authentic contributors to human survival and reproductive success.

Quality of the Data

As with the history of religions material, the quality of the neuroscientific data needs to be critically evaluated. There are at least two reasons to adopt a cautious attitude toward this research. The first regards the so-called "lab effect," by which the dreams of people who serve as subjects in sleep laboratories are influenced in ways both large and small by the experimental situation. The lab effect is unquestionably real; the still-to-be-answered question is how much it matters. Most re-searchers argue that it does not matter, at least for the purposes of their experimental work. With all due respect, I suggest it does matter, much more than is usually admitted, and I am convinced it matters a great deal in the study of big dreams. My feeling is echoed by none other than Allan Hobson, who is on record as saying, "The most interesting dreams always occur outside the lab" (Discovery Channel 1994). The artificiality of the lab setting and the invasiveness of most experi-mental techniques cannot help but produce a deep sense of guardedness within a person serving as an experimental subject, and it is reasonable to think that big dreams, whatever their precise neural origins, are unlikely to occur in such a context. This should make us wary of generalizations about human dreaming based solely on data gathered from the sleep laboratory. The second reason for caution regards the widespread assumption among neuroscientists that discoveries about processes in the brain in illness can tell us what is happening to the brain in ordinary life. Both Hobson and Solms, despite their many disagreements, share the fundamental view that the study of brain disfunctioning can reveal the most important features of normal dreaming. This is undoubtedly true to some extent, but it is equally true that health cannot be conceived simply as the absence of pathol-ogy. Medical research is making it increasingly apparent that healthy human functioning has dy-namic qualities all of its own (Goldberger 2002), and in the context of the study of big dream this calls into question any theories that use "pathology=health" models of reasoning.

Comparative Analysis

In this section I will integrate the foregoing material from the history of religions and cognitive neuroscience. I will identify points of agreement and disagreement between the two bodies of re-search, raise questions that I hope will be tested in future investigations, and outline a new model of the formation, function, and meaning of big dreams.

Cross-Cultural Themes Revisited

1. Widespread Public Interest. The discovery of the physiological universality of REM sleep among mammals and its formative role in human brain development certainly accords well with the cultural universality of interest in dreaming. The numerous reports of dream experiences from cul-tures all over the world and throughout history are just what one would expect if dreaming funda-mentally depends on a biologically innate process like REM sleep. However, the close relationship in many cultures between dreams, visions, trances, artistic inspirations, and other extraordinary modes of consciousness suggests that at least some features of dream formation do not depend on REM sleep but can be activated in a variety of other mind/brain conditions. This is certainly the point made by Solms' research. I believe dreaming is best understood as an evolutionary "spandrel" (Flanagan 2000), i.e. a process that was not directly selected for in evolution but has emerged out of other processes that were directly selected for in the pre-history of our species. The psychological experi-ence of dreaming seems to be a spandrel to REM sleep, an evolutionary by-product that has, over time, developed its own functional capacities. Question 1: Are there any significant differences between the brain/mind systems of healthy people with high rates of dream recall and healthy people with little or no dream recall? Question 2: Do the brain/mind systems of healthy people with high rates of dream recall have functional advantages in terms of conceptual flexibility, imaginative cre-ativity, and emotional balance?

2. Different Types of Dreams. Because of the lab effect, contemporary neuroscientists are in a poor position to say much about the more infrequent and unusual types of human dream experience reported by the world's religious traditions. However, Hobson, Solms, and other neuroscientists have acknowledged that some dreams do possess an extraordinary emotional power and perceptual vivid-

ness. This reveals a crucial point of agreement between the world's religions and contemporary neuroscience: both recognize that most dreams are fairly mundane and unremarkable, while a rare few are strikingly vivid and intense. The future study of big dreams will go far indeed if it takes its point of departure from this fundamental unity of belief about the existence of distinct types of dream experience. We can expect that new advances in the technology that monitors sleep stages in home environments will enable researchers to make major advances in our understanding of the neural correlates of unusual types of dream experience. Question 3: Do different types of dreams involve different modes of neuropsychological activity? Question 4: What are the neuropsychological distinctions between big dreams and ordinary dreams?

3. Qualities of Dreaming. There is complete agreement on this point between neuroscience and the world's religions. Both speak of dream experience as primarily visual in nature, and both emphasize the strong emotional content in many dreams. Neuroscience is not yet clear on how exactly visual perception occurs in dreaming, but it may well be connected to the activation of brain systems involved in motor behavior and spatial orientation. People move around a lot in their dreams, and they often find themselves in strange places and new situations (Hobson 1999). The simultaneous activation of visual, motor, and orientational systems accounts for the experiential richness of the dreaming "life-world," and this suggests that the common contemporary analogy between dreaming and watching a movie is misleading. Dreaming is not like passively viewing images on a screen; dreaming is more like being suddenly thrown into a place you've never seen before and having to figure out where you are. Additional evidence for this view comes from cross-cultural reports of big dreams involving journeys of the soul to otherworldly realms. Question 5: What parts of the brain are activated in dreams with unusually creative and aesthetically complex visual imagery? Question 6: Are there any types of big dream that do not involve heightened activity in the limbic region (especially the amygdala) and other areas responsible for emotional responsiveness?

4. Origins of Dreaming. Neuroscience and the world's religions agree that the majority of dreams are related to the common concerns of daily life, themes such as bodily health, family relations, social status, etc. Neuroscience and the world's religions fundamentally disagree, however, on the question of big dreams, which most religious traditions believe are caused by something outside the dreamer's personal self, i.e., by transpersonal sources of power, agency, and intention. This disagreement marks a profound philosophical divide, and I do not believe it can be easily bridged. I do, however, believe neuroscience can grant at least the metaphorical truth of the religious view. If "self" is understood as "cognitive sphere of ordinary waking life identity," then it is both meaningful and experientially true to speak of certain dreams as originating from someplace outside of the self. I also believe that new answers to the apparent intentionality of big dreams will come from the study of dreaming as a phenomenon of chaos in which complex, unpredictable patterns of neural activity generate a highly dynamic, self-organizing, self-creating experiential process (Hobson 1993; Kahn 2000). Question 7: Can patterns of meaning, intention, and teleology be identified in a person's dreams across his or her lifetime? Question 8: Do big dreams involve a greater degree of chaotic brain activation than occurs in ordinary dreaming?

5. Functions of Dreaming. There is mixed agreement on this. Contemporary research has produced findings that generally support cross-cultural beliefs that dreams function to anticipate the future, prepare for possible threats, envision sexual pleasure, herald new births, mourn death and other losses, and promote healing. The additional cross-cultural beliefs about moral guidance, divine reassurance, and conversion in dreams do not find much support from neuroscience. However, I will wager that future research will show that these "religious" functions can be understood as plausible extensions of other well-established brain/mind processes. Question 9: Do people with culturally-reinforced expectations about the moral and religious value of dreaming have significantly different brain activities during sleep than people without such expectations? Question 10: Do big dreams prompting conversion experiences involve any special activity in those regions of the brain responsible for maintaining a coherent and consistent sense of self?

6. Dream Content. As noted above, Solms and other neuroscientists take little interest in dream content. But scientifically reliable tools for studying dream content do exist, with the most sophisticated such system being the content analysis method founded by Calvin Hall and Robert Van de Castle (Hall & Van de Castle 1966) and recently revised and expanded by G. William Domhoff (Domhoff 1996). Looking at the content analysis findings on common elements in human dreaming, we find close correspondence with the content of the dreams reported from historical and cross-cultural contexts. The same basic themes can be seen in content analysis and the history of religions:

birth, death, social relations, bodily functioning, sexuality, fighting, flying, and encounters with animals, especially snakes (for an exemplary synthesis of the biological, neurological, psychological, and cross-cultural data on snake dreams, see Wilson 1998). In the world's religions we find a higher percentage of dreams with supernatural beings in them, which suggests that unusual, and unusually powerful, characters are one of the key features that distinguish big dreams from ordinary dreams. Question 11: What other content elements are more frequent in big dreams than in ordinary dreams? Question 12: Can a content profile be developed for different types of big dreams that would allow an investigator other than the dreamer to look at a dream series and identify those reports most likely to be described by the dreamer as "big dreams"?

7. Dream Interpretation. If neuroscientists take little interest in dream content, they take none in interpretation-"Interpretation is always a risky, speculative enterprise" (Hobson 1999). This skepticism accords well with the repeated warnings found in the world's religions about the possibility of being deceived, misled, and deluded by dreams. Most religious traditions acknowledge this danger, and then go ahead and try to interpret their dreams by using a core set of methods: seeking associations to the dreamer's personal life, identifying connections with common cultural symbols and metaphors, and making a linguistic analysis of wordplay, punning, parallels, and oppositions. These methods are essentially identical to those used by most contemporary psychotherapists, and one good theoretical framework in which to understand this connection between religious and psychological practice is to look at dreaming as a special mode of metaphorical thinking (Lakoff 2001). The prevalence of metaphor in dreams attests to the crucial role of association cortex in dream formation, which in turn highlights the fact that dreaming involves a dynamic interaction between "higher" and "lower" brain systems. It appears that highly memorable and impactful dreams are generated by the spiraling feedback of unusually intense neural discharges from the brainstem with unusually creative metaphorical thinking in the forebrain. Question 13: Are the brain processes involved in dream metaphor the same as the brain processes used to generate metaphorical thinking while awake? Question 14: Does the interpretation of big dreams require the use of special methods different from those used in the interpretation of ordinary dreams?

8. Dream Rituals. The lab effect clearly demonstrates the strong influence of pre-sleep stimuli on dreaming. Indeed, the sleep laboratory may one of the best tools ever devised for achieving a major goal of cross-cultural dream incubation: fending off bad dreams. As Ernest Hartmann notes, when frequent nightmare sufferers come to the sleep lab they have far fewer disturbing dreams because they go to sleep with the reassuring awareness that lab technicians will be carefully watching over them all night long (Hartmann 1984). Cross-cultural rituals of dream incubation can be understood as deliberate efforts to utilize special pre-sleep stimuli as means of generating particular types of dreams. The cross-cultural reports suggest the rituals frequently have the desired effect: Asklepian supplicants receive healing dreams, Native American initiates have dreams of guardian spirits, Buddhist yogins have lucid dreams. Of course, many of these reports include some degree of post-dream editing and revising, but it would be unwise to dismiss all such dreams as deliberately fabricated "culture pattern" dreams. In light of the lab effect, and in consideration of the scientific literature on the incorporation of pre-sleep stimuli in dreaming (Van de Castle 1994), it makes good sense that the basic methods of dream incubation (focusing attention, physical purification, sleeping in an unusual setting), if practiced consistently and with a strong belief in their efficacy, would produce discernible effects on people's actual dreaming experience. I suggest that dream incubation rituals represent the earliest experimental investigations of dreaming, and for that reason they deserve serious attention from contemporary researchers. Question 15: Do dream incubation rituals increase the involvement in dreaming of the forebrain, particularly the neural systems responsible for executive command functions? Question 16: Do people raised in cultural traditions with high interest in dreaming have significantly different neuropsychological patterns in their dreams as compared to people raised in cultural traditions with little or no interest in dreaming?

The Formation, Function, and Interpretation of Big Dreams

Efforts to study big dreams face a number of methodological difficulties, with no simple or obvious way to overcome them. Every source of data we possess, up to and including modern sleep laboratory research, is compromised by various limits and imperfections. Researchers who want to learn more about big dreams are thus driven by methodological necessity to develop interdisciplinary frameworks for understanding the formation, function, and interpretation of highly memorable, deeply impactful dreams. The human sciences (religious studies, anthropology, philosophy, history, lingustics, psychology) have much to contribute to the development of these frameworks, and so do the natural sciences (molecular biology, cognitive neuroscience, evolutionary theory, nonlinear dynamics). Future advances in the study of big dreams, and in the field of neurotheology generally, will depend on the interdisciplinary creativity of scholars who try weaving together all these multiple threads of insight and understanding.

I take the following words from neuroscientist Antonio Damasio as a good expression of the spirit animating my own interdisciplinary research: "the power of science comes from its ability to verify objectively the consistency of many individual subjectivities" (Damasio 1999). This chapter has been devoted to showing how a new synthesis of religion and neuroscience can provide scientific verification for the extraordinary dream experiences of "many individual subjectivities." To close the chapter I want to summarize my rendering of a religion-neuroscience synthesis and offer a new framework for understanding the formation, function, and interpretation of big dreams.

Formation

Big dreams emerge from brain/mind processes that are intimately related to, but not strictly dependent on, the neural activities of REM sleep. Big dreams involve extraordinarily energetic feedback loops between higher and lower regions of the brain/mind system, which points to the likelihood that big dreams are shaped by the same kinds of nonlinear dynamics and self-organizing tendencies that researchers have identified in other chaotic systems (e.g., the weather, natural ecologies, water currents, star formation). Although much more research is needed on this point, current neuroscientific findings suggest that several different brain regions contribute to the formation of big dreams, especially the brainstem (responsible for generating PGO waves), the frontal-limbic area (responsible for reality-monitoring), the temporal-limbic area (responsible for emotional arousal), and the prefrontal cortex (responsible for narrative coherence and focused attention). The ultimate generative source of a big dream is usually felt by the dreamer to lie far outside his or her ordinary waking self. This is where the world's religious traditions come in, offering explanations that refer to the soul of the dreamer and/or the influence of transpersonal beings and powers.

Function

Strong evidence from both religious history and neuroscience shows that big dreams can serve a variety of functions: anticipating the future, warning of danger, envisioning sexual pleasure, heralding new birth, mourning death and other losses, and healing illness. Each of these functions can be understood in evolutionary terms as contributing to the adaptive fitness and reproductive success of Homo sapiens sapiens. These functions can also be understood in religious terms as the means by which Divine beings and powers interact with humans, benevolently guiding people through their lives. The religions of the world have also believed big dreams serve other functions: providing moral guidance, offering Divine reassurance, and sparking deep personality transformation (conversion). Neuroscience has yet to examine these more specifically religious functions in any detail, but it seems reasonable to view them as further extensions of what neuroscience already knows, i.e. that dreaming generates a tremendous degree of creative power that is directly involved in promoting, preserving, and sustaining the individual's healthy brain/mind functioning. To put my theory in a phrase, dreaming provokes greater consciousness. Dreaming literally calls forth new voices and new possibilities into the dreamer's conscious awareness. Especially in the experience of big dreams, I believe the supreme function is to stimulate the dreamer to grow in consciousness-to consider new thoughts, acknowledge new feelings, remember past experiences, and take new actions in waking life. By provoking greater consciousness, big dreams fundamentally reorient people's views of themselves and the world, and this deep reorientation inevitably extends to their relationship to ultimate reality, however they personally and culturally conceive it.

Interpretation

At a certain level it is impossible to give a satisfying interpretation of a big dream, because they almost always involve images, feelings, and sensations that defy translation into waking language. Nevertheless, people throughout history have tried to interpret their dreams, and the most frequently used methods are seeking associations to the dreamer's personal life, identifying connections with common cultural symbols and metaphors, and making a linguistic analysis of wordplay, punning, parallels, and oppositions (all the while remaining vigilant toward possible deception). In my own research I have found several specific interpretive techniques that are effective in the study of big dreams-for example, focusing special attention on especially bizarre elements, or on sudden shifts in scene or character (Bulkeley 2000). Big dreams may be more amenable than ordinary dreams to creative expression by means of drawing, painting, poetry, theater, music, and other artistic media, and these endeavors should also be regarded as legitimate modes of interpretive exploration.

Conclusion

A growing number of scholars have taken up the interdisciplinary challenge of studying big dreams, and I strongly suggest that researchers in the budding field of neurotheology consult their works. A strong case can be made that dreaming is the most universal form of religious experience and spiritual transformation to be found in human history. The world's religious traditions have long testified to this fact, and we now have the neuroscientific means to verify it. By drawing together these two realms of understanding we not only deepen our knowledge of a truly amazing phenomenon of human existence-we also gain the ability to enhance its power in the world.

Figure 153c. Saint Anthony beset by demons from hell.

LOVE, RELIGION, AND THE PSYCHOLOGY OF INSPIRATION
by Ralph D. Ellis

Abstract. While much of psychology preserves the legacy of behaviorism and consummatory drive-reductionism, attempting to explain all human behavior as in the service of pleasure and survival, this paper begins by summarizing the "enactivist" approach to emotion and motivation. Rather than a machine in which the shape of the whole is determined by the interaction of passively-responding micro-components, the organism is viewed as a self-organizing system which appropriates and replaces internal and environmental substratum elements as needed. Emotions are not responses to stimuli, but expressions of an active system seeking congenial environmental affordances, motivated by fundamental playful, exploratory, and other non-consummatory aims that can be understood as the tendency of complex systems to prefer higher-energy basins of attraction rather than settle into satiation and dull comfort. Given this understanding of the emotions in complex animals, there is a fundamental need for inspiration to fuel the self-initiated activation of the system; lack of this basic inspiration is depression. In sophisticated conscious beings, the need for inspiration is exacerbated by awareness of the problems of finitude; love, the arts and religion are meant to address this heightened need for inspiration. Some approaches to religion, however — "fundamentalist" approaches — contend with the problems of finitude in an inauthentic way: rather than enhance the feeling of inspiration so as to create a positive experience of the value of being capable of counterbalancing the problems of death, evil, and the relative powerlessness and insignificance of the individual, they contend with those problems by simply denying them. This fundamentalist approach leads to corresponding distortions of ethical and political attitudes.

It is fashionable to think of the burning of Bruno for his scientific heresies as an instance of the tyranny of religion and philosophy over science. But the event can also be viewed the other way around. Dogmatic adherence to a bad or outmoded scientific theory results from bad reasoning, and bad reasoning in turn results from failure to take philosophy seriously enough. When a scientist proposes an iconoclastic theory, it is frequently because the maverick scientist is doing genuine philosophical thinking that the other scientists are not prepared to do. Einstein rejected the homogeneity of space and time for the same reasons as Poincaré – because of philosophical thought experiments, not merely because of the latest empirical discoveries. Bohr rejected material substances for similar reasons.

At the present time, the lingering neo-behaviorism and nominalism of the contemporary mind sciences results from the logical empiricist epistemology of an earlier philosophical period, which psychologists have not yet rethought effectively enough. The legacies of behaviorism and other forms of extreme empiricism survive everywhere in psychology, not least in the study of emotion. Students of the affective domain who wish to move much beyond a simplistic consummatory-drive model, such as Gendlin (1980, 1998), Panksepp (1998), and Watt (2000), tend to be marginalized in many circles, and in others their significance is underappreciated, perhaps out of our intimidation by the popularity of the standard views.

Most twentieth century systems of psychology were built on a motivational theory that emphasized hedonism and the explanation of behavior in terms of a series of billiard ball reactions supposedly compatible with a reduction to basic physics and chemistry. The distinction between activity and passivity was lost, and so was the idea that animals would be motivated to engage in certain forms of activity for their own sake, even without leading eventually to the reduction of some consummatory drive. This left us with little in the way of psychology of religion beyond the assumption of Freud and Rank that the purpose of religion is to deny the unacceptable fact of death. On this interpretation, no form of religion could be taken seriously by an intelligent and intellectually honest person, consisting only of literal belief in self-deceptive metaphysical fantasies in the service of wish fulfillment, motivated by the desire for eternal happiness: the only root desire involved was pleasure maximization. Sexual love suffered a similar fate, succumbing to explanations in terms of consummatory sexual needs combined with need for social structure, with little validity attributed to the role of love in fueling the basic need for inspiration. The idea that organisms which are genuinely active rather than passive might have a fundamental need for inspiration to activate them could hardly even make its way onto the radar screen.

It is therefore a very long leap from contemporary psychology and neurophysiology to anything like an adequate understanding of the human affective sphere. But this may not be so much because the needed empirical cards are not on the table, but rather because they have not been given a good enough philosophical shuffling. Because such a reshuffling is currently only a tentative promissory note, we cannot discuss the existential concerns of human beings without appealing to a richer basis in emotional theory than is usually assumed in the behavioral sciences. I shall therefore devote a preliminary section to sketching a way to build on the limited understanding that comprises the mainstream of current psychological work on emotion, and to develop the further resources needed for the existential emotional issues that religion and philosophy hope to address. This sketchy account is elaborated further in other places (Ellis 1986, 1995, 1996, 1999a, b; 2000a, b, d; 2001c).

At the point when room has been made for an understanding of the "higher" emotions – which in my view are not completely derivative from simple consummatory drives – it will become clear that one of the most fundamental emotions in sophisticated animals is a need for inspiration. Without inspiration, human infants die of marasmus (Spitz and Wolf 1946); adults seriously deficient in inspiration commit suicide, become alcoholics, embrace fundamentalist religions, follow Fuhrers, destroy marriages with philandering, and engage in a plethora of other destructive and self-destructive activities. An anonymous poem written ostensibly by a monkey, after enumerating dysfunctional human behaviors to which no self-respecting monkey would stoop, concludes as follows: "Yes, man descended, the ornery cuss, but brother he didn't descend from us!"

When the need for a feeling of inspiration is understood as primary, we can begin to understand the psychology of religion in other dimensions than simply self-deceptive wish fulfillment. At that point, I shall argue that there are two fundamentally different approaches to spiritual experience, whose essence is that it serves the need for inspiration, which is heightened in humans: we can either work to fulfill this need, or we can repress and deny the existential conditions that exacerbate it.

Why is this need exaggerated to such a degree in humans, so that it can even take priority over other fundamental needs? On my view, the reason the striving for inspiration becomes so pressing and problematic in humans is that sophisticated conscious and emotional beings are intelligent enough to realize that their hopes and dreams are seriously threatened by fundamental conditions of finitude. The span of our existence is short, and our power to accomplish goals is fragile and limited, as are our abilities to establish needed social and personal relations and to make much of a valuational difference in the grand scheme of things. This awareness of our overall existential condition heightens the human need for inspiration beyond that of other animals, while at the same time threatening its realization by crowding imagery of past, future, and hypothetically possible evils into the mind. The two main responses to this problem lead to the two main spiritual or religious orientations I shall characterize: we can either deny the facts of finitude (or the fact that they concern us) and construct metaphysical belief systems aiming to prove the ultimate inexistence of such problems (as in religious fundamentalism); or we can work toward the ability to experience the positive value of being intensely enough to overshadow the acknowledged negativity of our finitude problems. From this perspective, the fulfillment of spiritual needs does not necessarily require religion, in the sense of metaphysical and supernatural beliefs, although it does usually make use of religious imagery, metaphors, and attitudes. As Dewey (1934, p. 16) said, the worst enemy of religion is often Religion.

For lack of better terms, I call the two approaches to spiritual needs the "fundamentalist" and the "experiential" approaches, because they result from the two different attitudes toward the existential conditions of finitude. We can either cultivate a way to feel inspired with a direct experience of the intrinsic positive value of being, felt intensely enough to counterbalance the negativity of the problems of finitude (death, powerlessness, alienation, and the relative insignificance of any individual in the ultimate scheme of things); or we can deny the reality of those evils through a fundamentalist belief system which insists that the soul is literally immortal and that God will literally rectify all earthly injustices and evils in the hereafter. The key word here is "literally"; fundamentalism, after all, means a literal interpretation of certain ontological dogmas, usually as set forth in some authoritative text. These two very different approaches to the existential dilemma of finitude lead to two completely different worldviews with corresponding moral, political, social, and interpersonal attitudes. Even Buddhism and other meditative religions, which one might suppose would not need to deny the reality of finitude, actually allow for either of these conflicting approaches: While some use the religion to facilitate a healthy adjustment to the problems of finitude, thus restoring the capacity for inspiration, others interpret the religion as denying finitude. I once attended an all-day Buddhist meditation at which young people were being taught to recite arguments proving that death is not real.

But we need to start at a very basic level of inquiry: If we are to understand human emotional orientations toward existential issues, we must first pay careful attention to the problem of an adequate theory of human emotions, which has been badly distorted by the consummatory-reductionist assumptions of twentieth century behaviorism and drive theory. Otherwise, a coherent grounding for an understanding of existential emotions would simply be missing.

1. The Extropic Dimension of Self-organizing Beings

Some recent physiological accounts of emotion suggest a more sophisticated psychology than the simplistic hedonistic-behaviorist theories of the past. Physiologists of emotion like Panksepp (1998, 2000), Watt (1998, 2000), Freeman (1987, 1988) and Damasio (1994, 1999) speak of many physiological emotional tendencies that have nothing to do with the motivation to reduce consummatory impulses, even indirectly. Some emotions are geared intrinsically toward play, exploration, bonding, empathy, and other non-consummatory activities that cannot be derived from learning based on reinforcement of consummatory drives.

"Consummatory" in this context means oriented toward filling a chemical "deficit" that stands in the way of energy-efficient homeostasis through submolecular energy-conservation (White 1959). In non-consummatory behavior, there is no prior deficit, but simply the desire to engage in patterns of activity consistent with a complex system's tendency to maintain both an optimal level of homeostasis and a suitable level of complexity, which in turn often motivates an increased energy level. I call this need for increased energy and complexity "extropy," because it counteracts the tendency toward "inertia" (Freud (1925/1959, p. 68) that could result from too much focus on consummatory drive reduction. For this reason, it also often resists the tendency toward entropy that is so dominant in inorganic chemistry as well as in the chemistry of the consummatory drives that preoccupied twentieth century drive theorists.

Panksepp (1998) argues on neurophysiological grounds that there are seven basic emotional brain systems, grounded in seven different relatively independent systems of neurotransmitter activity and neuroanatomy: (1) a general "seeking" system that motivates curiosity and exploration, engaged in for their own sake and intrinsically valued by the organism; (2) play; (3) anger; (4) fear; (5) nurturance/sexuality; (6) social bonding/separation distress; and (7) consummatory pleasure. Panksepp shows evidence that none of these motivations is learned through conditioning by association with reinforcement of any of the others; thus most of them do not conform to the assumption of early drive theorists that all behavior must be learned by association with consummatory reinforcement or association with physical pain. The system Panksepp labels the "seeking" system seems especially resistant to that assumption, and is reminiscent of the "exploratory" drives and drives toward "mastery" proposed by revisionist drive theorists of the mid-twentieth century who wanted to reject the assumption that the organism would remain completely passive if not stimulated toward the acquisition of pleasure and satiation (see Kagan and Berkun 1954; Montgomery1955; White 1959; Ellis 1986).

This way of assessing the causal mechanisms of emotional behavior allows the organism to be seen as the agent of its own actions rather than as a passively reacting machine. Panksepp's model suggests a self-organizing view of information processing in living beings rather than one in which each input is merely transformed into an output in piecemeal and automaton-like fashion. The movements of the organism are initiated, coordinated, energized, and integrated by the whole animal working as the agent of its activity.

The difference between true activity and passive reaction can be understood scientifically in terms of the theory of self-organization (Monod 1971; Kauffman 1993; Weiss 1968; Varela et al. 1991; Ellis 1999a, b; 2000a, b; 2001c; Newton 1996, 2000, 2001; Ellis and Newton 1998). Complex self-organizing systems behave in such ways as to maintain their definitive patterns of activity, structures, and levels of energy across replacements of the physical components that are used to enact the pattern. The continuing pattern of activity seeks out, appropriates and replaces its needed microlevel components rather than being constituted as a mere epiphenomenon of the sum of their (passive) interactions.

If we adopt such a theory of self-organizing systems, it makes perfectly good sense that the system would be motivated to engage in non-consummatory activities that are intrinsically valued even when they do not lead to consummatory pleasure. Since a self-organizing system can be active in a strong sense, and not merely a system of passive reactions, it can appropriate and replace its own micro-constituents at all levels, from components of cells to favorable environmental conditions, and can reorganize its component subsystems when needed to maintain the desired pattern and energy level of the activity of the organism as a whole. This is not a new idea; it can be traced to Aristotle (1986), Kurt Goldstein (1938), Ludwig von Bertalanffy (1933/1962), Abraham Maslow (1974), and many others. What is new is that it can now be made compatible with micro-level physical and chemical causal sequences that make up the self-organizing system. The system as a whole has the capability to reorganize the background conditions, both within itself and in the environment, pre-supposed by the efficacy of specific causal sequences at the micro level (Ellis 2000a, c; 2001c).

In the normal course of experience, contrary to the presumptions of many behavioristically influenced and consummatory-drive-oriented theorists, environmental novelty is often craved because of our desire for extropy. But as Freud and Rank were ahead of their time in noticing, this craving for novelty, adventure, unpredictability, and higher-energy forms of experiencing often conflicts with our desire for homeostatic energy-efficiency, satiation, predictability, and Freud's "inertia," toward which our consummatory drives toward dull comfort would impel us if not counterbalanced. To resolve this conflict requires an increasingly sophisticated intellect and an increasingly flexible adaptation to the environment. Emotions increasingly seek out general environmental action affordances rather than specific physical objects or conditions.

The organism, then, can act and not merely react, and can appropriate the conditions demanded by its emotional motivations rather than merely reacting to conditions that are presented to it. This requires a richer model of emotional intentionality than the traditional stimulus-response paradigm. Rather than feeling emotions in reaction to stimuli, the organism can seek out and use available stimuli to enable it to feel what it was already motivated to feel. In fact, the self-organizational approach to emotion reopens a number of questions that had long been closed about the way the emotions work, and suggests a revisiting of previously rejected answers to them. Among them are the following:

(1) Emotions are not responses to stimuli. Since emotion arises out of the aims of a self-organizational system, emotion is an aspect of the organism's acting on its environment rather than reacting to it. Thus the stimulus-response paradigm in emotion studies is seriously misleading, and to think that environmental events cause organisms to act would be an oversimplification. Organisms are always already acting on their own, unless they are dead, and discrete environmental events can only "disturb" the ongoing pattern of self-initiated action, so that a readjustment must be found somewhere in the pattern's total configuration that can reorganize the parts of the organism as well as the environment, in order to maintain the general contour of the whole pattern of activity as nearly as possible. This ongoing pattern of self-organization, and the ways it readjusts when disturbed, must be understood in terms of the way dynamical systems operate. When someone cuts me off in traffic, the anger I feel is not directed at the person who cuts me off; instead, in the typical scenario, I am already in the mood to feel angry about other more important structures in my life as a whole ontological project, and then choose the motorist who cut me off as a concrete symbolic image to enact those feelings. Otherwise, I would not react so cataclysmically to such a trivial incident. The reasons why I would choose a specific intentional object will be touched on below.

(2) It follows from the first point that there is no one-to-one correspondence between emotions and objects. With such complexity characterizing the aim of any emotion, there will seldom be only one possible response that can achieve the organism's ultimate objective. On the contrary, whenever behavior is motivated by emotion, it will be by far the exception rather than the rule that we observe a one-to-one correspondence between stimulus and response. And on those rare occasions where such a one-to-one correspondence does appear to obtain, it may be only because the organism has not yet found alternative ways to achieve its objective, and thus, at that particular point in time, has habitually chosen one particular response. Many therapists have noted that inflexible one-to-one correspondence between specific stimuli and specific responses is one of the most universal earmarks of neurosis (for example, see Kohut 1985; Miller 1981; Muller 1991; Zachar 2000).

(3) Higher, non-consummatory emotions are not derivative. In this paper, we must concern ourselves with the "higher" emotions, not just the "primary" ones, and the most extreme difference between the self-organizational theory of emotion and others may be that the former can posit an independent, non-consummatory tendency toward a preference for higher-energy attractors — a tendency toward "extropy," arising from the organism's dynamical structure. This makes curiosity, play,

nurturance and other social activities primarily motivating, not derivative through learning from more "basic" motivations. The higher emotions cannot be neatly reduced to elaborately elongated schemes for the attainment of chemical homeostasis alone. It is true that dynamical systems seek homeostasis, but they also seek to maintain suitably complex and high-energy basins of attraction to fit the life trajectories that various life forms set for themselves, because of the specific ways in which they are self-organized (Juarerro 1999; Prigogine 1996). This perplexing issue, that animals do not seem to want merely to satiate consummatory drives, but are also adventurous, playful, and curious, will be one of the pivotal issues to be explored throughout this paper, since inspiration is the most important affective feeling presupposed by self-initiated activity. A theory as to why there would be such important non-consummatory motivations and emotions is spelled out in greater detail elsewhere (Ellis forthcoming a).

(4) Emotions prefigure rather than responding to cognitive content. Because animals are self-organizing, their emotional processes drive other conscious processes rather than merely responding to them. We react to an emotional stimulus more quickly than we can even cognitively register the content of the object by means of perceptual processing. The hippocampal-cerebellar-hypothalamic loops that instigate action begin as early as 18 ms. after presentation of an unexpected stimulus (Haines et al. 1997), whereas the occipital lobe does not process the visual identity of the unanticipated object until at least 200 ms. later (Aurell 1989). When we then reflect on why we feel the way we do, the feeling reveals itself as already having been intentionally directed to the action affordances of an object or an environmental situation. The fear reaction is signalled by neurotransmitter activity (glutamate, monoamines, and other neuropeptides) in a circuit including the lateral amygdala to medial hypothalamus to PAG and pons, prior to perceptual and intellectual processing (Panksepp 1998; LeDoux 1996).

(5) Complex dynamical systems appropriate their own micro-constituents, rather than being determined by them. To define what is meant by "action" as opposed to "mere reaction" is a difficult philosophical problem at the base of a self-organizational approach to emotion. The recently elaborated concept of complex dynamical systems (Bunge 1979; Juarrero 1999; Kauffman 1993; Kelso 1995; MacCormac and Stamenov 1996; Monod 1971; Newton 2000; Prigogine 1996; Thelen and Smith 1994) can provide the necessary tools for such an understanding. Complex dynamical systems, in the terminology of these theorists, are structured so as to preserve certain continuities of behavior across exchanges of energy and materials with their environment. The more they must seek out and appropriate the replacement components to keep the pattern of organization going, the more clearly they fall within the category of "living" systems (Bertalanffy 1933; Bunge 1979; Monod 1971). The activities of living systems, then, are not merely built up through the accumulation and summation of the causal powers of their micro-constituents. There is also a causal power on the part of the whole system, to regulate – and in fact even to find and purposefully make use of – micro-components on an as-needed basis. Emotions are expressions of this self-organizational tendency, and this is why emotions can cause actions holistically rather than in partes extra partes fashion.

(6) The "aboutness" of emotions is general and multiply-realizable. We should not think of an emotion as just another type of conscious qualia caused by certain kinds of inputs, alongside perception, thought, and the proprioception of bodily sensations. Emotion is unique in that its qualia do not take specific inputs as their intentional objects, since they are always felt in relation to the action affordances of objects, which will be different depending on the object's relations to the overall aims, which are self-organizational. A disruption of the pattern is assessed at the level of the whole, not in an isolated part. Perception and thought may uniquely identify a likely candidate as the environmental stimulus that is largely responsible for a disruption, but the felt quality of the emotion itself is not this specific, and the motorist who cuts me off serves only as an opportunity to symbolize a complexity of feelings about my general orientation to the environment. The felt quality of an emotion cannot pinpoint what the real disturbance is in the first casual or superficial glance. The emotion reveals that something is "off" in the organism-environment relationship, and it reveals some general features of this "offness" in terms of action affordances. Gendlin (1980, 1998) discusses ways we can and typically do explore the hidden nuances of a felt quality to get more specific information out of it, but this specific information is not obviously announced by a superficial reading of what an emotion initially seems to be triggered by – again, because the organism's aims are self-organizational and thus must be contextualized in terms of a larger picture.

(7) Emotion is efferent rather than afferent. While other forms of consciousness may passively react by means of afferent "input," emotion generates its qualia by initiating action commands

in the form of efferent signals (which then may be frontally inhibited). We do not know what we are feeling by receiving afferent (proprioceptive or interoceptive) signals from the body; we know it by sending action commands (sensorimotor, efferent signals) to the parts of the nervous system that are more peripheral than the emotional brain areas. While action imagery is clearly distinguishable from sensory or proprioceptive imagery – for example, because it involves a cortically inhibited efferent signal, whereas sensation and proprioception involve afferent signals – it can also be argued that for sensation and proprioception to rise to the level of consciousness requires that action imagery already have been present, at least in the preconscious sense that an inhibited action command has been sent. For example, tracking of subcortically originated neurotransmitter activity shows that this activity must precede perceptual or cognitive consciousness, and event related potentials (ERPs) and other brain activity measures show that emotional brain areas are activated earlier than perceptual processing areas even in perceptual and imaginative consciousness (Aurell 1989); also, the perceptual processing does not lead to consciousness of the object unless the emotional areas have already been activated, and unless they in turn activate brain areas associated with attention, such as frontal and anterior cingulate areas (Bernstein et al. 2000). Contemporary work on the cerebellum (Schmahmann 1997; Schmahmann et al. 2001) shows that the cerebellum — traditionally considered to be primarily a coordinator of motor routines — is a necessary way-station in this process, so that even conscious perception and cognitive skills depend on certain kinds of action commands being originated by the cerebellum, even though those action commands will be inhibited and quickly modified during the course of a perceptual experience.

(8) Sensorimotor imagery differs crucially from proprioceptive imagery. The intentionality of emotion is understood better in terms of sensorimotor action imagery than in terms of proprioceptive or sensory imagery. Whereas proprioception is characterized by a passive receiving of information from the periphery, sensorimotor imagery requires that the organism, acting out of its self-organizational aims, initiate an action command and deliver this action command to other parts of its nervous system (Jeannerod 1997). When the action command is inhibited, sensorimotor imagery results.

(9) Emotions are precognitively intentional. It is a mistake to say that emotional qualia per se do not have intentional objects until we cognitively interpret the cause of the qualia. Salmela (2002) expresses the essential problem here very incisively. Cognitivists (for example, Ben Ze'ev 2000) hold that a feeling has no intentionality until we cognitively assess its cause. According to Ben Ze'ev, we know that we are in love because we feel certain sensation-like feelings such as butterflies in the stomach, and then cognitively associate a certain person with that feeling, noticing that we have the feeling whenever the person is present. Salmela's objection is that a feeling of butterflies in the stomach would not be identified as love, or indeed as any emotional feeling, unless it already contained an intentional reference even at the pre-cognitive level. It could just as well be an upset stomach or a feeling of dizziness. We can identify it as a feeling of love, rather than dizziness or an upset stomach, because we sense precognitively that it already refers to something beyond itself. We sense that it indicates something about our relation to some aspect of our environment. When we reflect on an emotional feeling, we do not add the intentionality to it as a side-effect of the reflection; we discover that it already had an intentional reference.

(10) Emotion studies have neglected the insights of phenomenology. Much misunderstanding of the meaning of emotions results from what Husserl (1913) calls the "natural attitude." We normally direct our attention toward objects in the world. We observe that conjoined physical events cause effects in each other at a simple mechanical level. When we then notice a conjunction between a simple physical event and an emotional effect in ourselves, it is natural to apply the categories of everyday physical observation to ourselves, assuming that the simple environmental event that we have observed must be what has caused our emotional response. More often than not, however, this is simplistic and misleading. If I have an intense feeling toward someone who cut me off in traffic, it is almost certain that the person who cut me off is not really what the feeling is primarily about – its intentional object. To interpret emotions as passive reactions to environmental conditions rather than as aspects of self-initiated organismic activity distorts their intentional meaning.

In sum, complex dynamical systems can rearrange elements of their subsystems to maintain a higher level pattern. Within limits, they can appropriate and replace components as needed, can readjust the background conditions needed for various micro-level causal sequences, and can use multiple shunt mechanisms and feedback loops to ensure massive overcausation of their multiply realizable homeostatic and extropic aims. So when the balance of the whole is disrupted, the system must monitor the state of the whole in order to decide which of the many subsystems can best be readjusted — for example, the fear system, leading to hiding or relocation of the organism, or the anger system, leading to a getting rid of environmental impediments, or the exploratory or play systems, leading to higher levels of energy and complexity.

2. Emotions as Reflecting the Organism's Inspiration for Self-activation

Given a model in which genuine action is fundamental, in the sense just outlined, we can view any emotion in terms of the way an endogenously initiated action potential finds or fails to find congenial environmental affordances. On the self-organizational model, even emotions traditionally viewed as simple responses to stimuli, such as anger and fear, can be thought of, just as in the more obvious cases of joy or play, as *intending* the organism's self-initiated activity toward maintaining a self-organizing pattern, and are not just causal reactions to external stimuli. Before we can feel anger or fear, we must first be in the process of engaging in the general activities of our lives, and then something gets in the way of this already-ongoing activity. Usually, what gets in the way is the lack of some very complex and multiply-realizable set of conditions, rather than a simple physical object. So when we direct anger toward a simple object, we are usually using that objet to symbolize a set of feelings that are more complex and directed intentionally toward our overall ontological situation vis a vis the total environment. This is an important point for integrating physiology with existential emotional issues, because it allows anger and fear to be conceived of in terms of the organism's already ongoing activity, rather than as causal reactions to an external stimulus. In this way, we can make phenomenological sense of what it is that the organism *wants,* as correlated with its basic self-organizational structure, rather than simply regarding anger and fear as either arbitrary causal reactions, or as tendencies derived through learning from consummatory drives. Panksepp notes that the clearest physiological symptoms of anger are produced by binding the arms of an infant. Anger can be understood only on the assumption that the organism first wants to initiate its own actions, and then is thwarted in this attempt by some sort of confinement or constriction.

There are many and various different emotions that feel confining when our freedom to realize complex action potentials are not afforded by the environment, and these include grief and separation distress. In these cases, the experienced *lack* (Lacan's "missing object") constricts us. For example, many people in the grips of grief feel almost as if they cannot breathe. Thus it is not counterintuitive that Panksepp classifies separation distress as a separate "panic" system in the brain. When an important human relationship facilitates a subject's being in a more interesting, higher-energy basin of attraction, the withdrawal of that love object means constriction of freedom.

But a further dimension of separation distress is that it can lead to *despair*. This despair relates to the fact that love enables the subject to value being *per se* more intensely. Empathy with a conscious being whose structure is interesting is a positively valued experience, and inspires the subject with a feeling that being a conscious being *per se* is a fun and valuable thing to do. Infants whose exploratory drives have not yet developed are utterly dependent on empathy with a caretaker for this kind of value experience, and therefore if deprived of empathic interaction can die of marasmus even though their consummatory needs are met (Spitz & Wolf 1946). Loss of a love object withdraws this "being-valuing" action affordance; the subject can no longer as intensely value its own activity, and seeks a less active, lower-energy basin of attraction, lapsing into entropy and depression. In the case of older children and adults who have already developed other extropic dimensions such as exploration and play, separation distress will be experienced as a negative affective situation, and the desire to live, still pronounced in other subsystems, feels constricted by this very entropy, so that those subsystems force the experience of restless anxiety and a feeling of painful tension and confinement (for further discussion of this point, see Ellis 1996, pp. 81-95).

Even though bad novelty can trigger fear, anger, or separation distress, it is equally true that good novelty can feel liberating -- it presents affordances consistent with the body's ongoing desire to keep flowing in natural patterns, but to increase the energy level while doing so. The higher we go on the evolutionary scale (and also the more consciousness there is), the more the organism wants to deviate far from equilibrium and find more extropic basins of attraction that also are consistent with homeostasis needs. Each organism has many basins it can settle into, and it was advantageous for a hunting/gathering creature to develop a tendency to prefer the higher energy (seeking and playful) ones. This is the genetic hand we are dealt with regard to physiological emotional tendencies. We have a natural tendency to prefer extropy, but this tendency often can conflict with the preference for homeostasis, and the basic physiological emotional tendencies are complex ways of addressing these internally-conflicting concerns. Of course, an inherent desire to explore, a sense of general curiosity, and a need for intellectual stimulation, even when such activities do not lead to consummatory reward, are going to be selectively favored for survival in a hunting and gathering gene pool.

3. The Need for Value-Affirmation

An important existential parameter addressed by this concept of extropic emotion is also the need not just to *achieve* whatever it is we value, but also to *affirm the value* of what we value -- to feel that it *is* valuable. If we did not feel inspired to exercise our capacity for the realization of our activity at more extropic basins of attraction, we would lapse into lower energy ones. Thus the feeling of *inspiration* – the Aristotelian valuing of our own activity for its own sake, for the sheer interest of it – correlates with the release of dopamine and norepinephrine, which are neurotransmitters that facilitate efferent action commands and make us feel more conscious, more "alive" and, quite literally, more awake. Hence the power of caffeine addiction, which directly stimulates the release of norepinephrine, and indirectly of dopamine. In order to exist at our most extropic basins of attraction, we must feel that doing so is worthwhile, i.e., we must feel "inspired."

Lists of "basic emotions" that do not include the need for something like a feeling of inspiration are therefore too impoverished to be applicable to the motivational structure of highly complex self-organizing animals. Even a dog or cat can feel inspired or, on the contrary, generally lethargic and uninterested in its environment. In an extreme case, we have already discussed the fact that marasmus infants can die even though all their consummatory needs are met (Spitz & Wolf 1946).

There are entire categories of human activity whose purpose is not to attain that which we value, but to intensify our sense that whatever it is we value *is* valuable, through a feeling of inspiration. Religion, love, and the arts are examples of such "value-affirming" as opposed to "value-achieving" activities. Love, for example, is an existential need, called for by the interactive structure of our being, as well as a basic physiological tendency of the brain. We vicariously experience the other as someone whose being-structure would be interesting to enact, and we try to do so as nearly as possible through empathy. Correlatively, in love we experience the other as extremely *valuable*, so that an existential sense that the overall struggle is worthwhile can be served. The behaviors of love are often meant to enhance the experience of this inspiration rather than to achieve the outcomes posited as valuable by the value feelings that are intensified in the process (for a more elaborate discussion of this point, see Ellis 1996).

4. Intensification of Value-affirmation through Concrete Symbolization

I have argued that complex conscious animals need not only homeostasis, but also *extropy*. This means, among other things, that we need to have complexity and novelty in our interactions with the environment, because novelty affords extropic activity. But for the same reasons, it also implies that we need to find ways to further concretely *embody* our conscious states so as to *amplify* them, which entails *symbolization*. I.e., we feel conscious states more intensely when we express them concretely. For example, uttering eulogies intensifies grief, caressing a loved one or singing love songs intensifies the feeling of love, and clenching the fists intensifies anger. Similarly, we grasp our general felt sense of a situation more vividly when we try to put it into words. This need for symbolization in turn leads to speech, art forms, and relations to others, so that we can have *media through which* to symbolize and thus amplify the activities of our being (see Ellis 1986, 1996, 2000d).

Correlatively, we need to experience the project of achieving all these goals as one that has *value per se,* rather than as meaningless and pointless. I.e., we need to feel that being what we are (or being anything) is worthwhile or has value -- that the entire project of being is worth the effort, not merely as an extrinsic or instrumental value, serving to accomplish other purposes, but rather intrinsically, for its own sake. This implies the need for an imaginative object whose intrinsic value we can intensely experience -- and the only completely adequate object that can be effective for this purpose on a sustained basis is *another conscious being.* We then need *imagistic symbolization* to amplify our experience *of* the value of the intensely valuation-affording object, i.e., the other person (which can mean expressing our feeling of the value *to* others, or just to ourselves); and we need to act in relation to the valued object, in such a way as to amplify our experience of its value -- which leads to friendship, respect, loyalty, and many other social emotions. In this way, the entire realm of object relations, in the sense used by object relations theorists, can be grounded not only in existential phenomenology, but also in physiology and a basic understanding of complex dynamical systems.

The need to experience the project of being as worth the effort (the need for inspiration) is a further elaboration of the arousal and seeking systems, and correlates with Panksepp's separation distress (or what Panksepp also calls the *"panic"*) system, which is the negative manifestation of a love system, also including lust and nurturance (utilizing release of oxytocin in the brain for females, and both oxytocin and prolactin for males), as well as friendship and play (combining oxytocin and prolactin with energizing dopamine, norepinephrine, and other neurotransmitters). Ultimately, we need others in relation to whom we can fully express what we are -- which is just as fundamental and existential a need as eating or protecting one's boundaries. But in addition to needing others to enact our relational form of being, we also need them for a more complex reason: Certain others are available for an intense direct experience of the intrinsic value of being, through admiration amplified by compassion; in the experience of these others, we affirm the value of being, and thus feel inspired.

The failure to achieve this aim results in *depression,* which correlates with chemical imbalances of the total system, but ultimately stems from a failure to *energize* the system at a high enough level of extropy, since the value of doing so needs to be felt in order to motivate doing so. Thus dogs act listless and disoriented when they fail to get the kind of play, social interaction, and even obedience training that they want (being such an extremely cooperative species).

5. Knowledge of Finitude as Intensifying the Inspirational Need

Although we speak of self-organizing systems as having a "tendency" to appropriate whatever physical elements are needed to keep the system going in its preferred patterns, and readjusting to a different basin of attraction to compensate for changes in the environment, we should of course remember that maintaining a complex self-organizing system is not at all *easy,* and requires the cooperation of several different extraneous mechanisms, such as the gifts we inherit through long and hard natural selection, as well as conscious planning and good luck in terms of environmental conditions — and even then, of course, the project is ultimately doomed to eventual death. Even a tiny disruption of the evolutionary legacy, such as a stroke, can make the project impossible — and probably in almost all instances the best we can do is to come close to achieving all the elements for the total extropic-homeostatic balance that is desired.

The complexities resulting from anticipation of this ultimate failure in death affects the most intelligent organisms in such an important way that the need to appreciate the value of being *per se*, as instantiated in beloved others and experienced through positive relations with others, becomes still further pronounced than it would be in an animal unintelligent enough simply to live in the present moment without concern about death and other conditions of finitude. This leads to a further intensification of many kinds of love experiences in humans. Not only is love not merely derivative from more elementary needs such as sexual pleasure, but in fact sexual lust can be a relatively mild impulse compared with the impassioned turbulence of love when intensified by the larger existential need to affirm the value of being through a sense of inspiration, which is further exaggerated by existential understanding of the limits of human life in all dimensions of finitude, including the finitude of the human life span (Ellis 1996).

In order to actualize ourselves, we need to be in interaction with others — this is the nature of mammals (and of intensely conscious beings as conceived of in existential terms). When not in interaction with others, either directly or indirectly, it may become impossible for us to *be* what we are; our self-organizing systems cannot maintain themselves, and we feel the resulting failure of both homeostasis *and* extropy. "Lust" and "nurturance" are similar to each other both physiologically (Panksepp 1998) and phenomenologically (Ellis 1996); they involve actualizing one's being through empathy with another, and experiencing the value of being as instantiated in the other through empathy. Sex too (which is not really necessary for reproduction, in lower species) evolved hand in hand with these tendencies toward empathy.

Without this empathic dimension, we have acute distress, because we either cannot *be* what we are, or we cannot see the full *value* of being what we are (or of being anything at all) — which is a frequent precursor to depression (Panksepp 1998, 274). Even the courtship behavior of sub-mammalian species, such as birds, often exhibits elaborate imitative routines very suggestive of empathy.

Understanding *why* we need others to actualize our being requires understanding the structure of the self or personality, which is a higher-order pattern of progressing from one conscious state to another: A personality can be identified by the pattern in the directions of those changes, which is a style of being, rather than by a mere listing of *which* conscious states are experienced; we might all experience them all, at various times (Ellis 1986). So to be what we are, we have to relate to others who will allow the right kind of pattern of progression from one state to the next, in addition to allowing progressions that generally afford extropy and inspiration. For each individual, different patterns will be required to achieve these ends, since the ends themselves have to do with complex structures of dynamic change.

In sum, we have now seen considerable evidence that contemporary neurophysiology of the emotions does not require a simplistic egoistic-hedonist and consummatory-drive-reductivist view of the emotional life, but is generally consistent with the demands of existentialists and self-actualization psychologists. The key to reconciling physiology with these higher-order ways of seeing the meaning of emotions is to approach the physiology underlying consciousness itself in terms of complex self-organizing systems that seek extropic basins of attraction as well as homeostasis. To energize such complexity in the face of a vivid understanding of finitude requires an inspirational *intensification of the experience of the value* of that which we value, and not merely means of achieving the valued ends. This can lead to an interpretation of the intentional meaning of emotions like love, religious inspiration, and artistic appreciation that are more true to the phenomenological experiencing of these feelings than is the notion that they are derivative from basic hedonistic instincts in the service of mere drive-reduction.

6. Love and Other Non-hedonistic Motivations

Much of the higher emotional life derives from motives that orient themselves not only around achieving the ends that we feel are valuable, but also around intensifying our experience of the value of the ends – the "inspirational" effect that was so basic in the system of emotional categories sketched out above.

Many forms of love, including the love of a mother, of an erotic partner, or sometimes of a comrade in arms, are of the "value-intensifying" rather than the "end-attaining" variety (Ellis 1996). Each of these kinds of love also resists reduction to hedonic explanations. A mother will endure considerable suffering for the sake of children, as will (quite notoriously) a person in erotic love. Literature and the arts are quick to pick up on this non-hedonic dimension of love. It is an interesting phenomenon from the artist's viewpoint, because the very non-hedonic nature of the subject affords exploration of the emotional life in which hedonic motives are not assumed to be paramount, and neither is the hedonic or entertainment dimension of the aesthetic experience presumed to be the overriding artistic consideration.

The classic instance of an artwork that seems to eschew the dominant importance of the hedonic dimension is the entire genre in literature and drama (with analogous forms in music and visual art) that falls under the category of "tragedy." Philosophers since the time of Aristotle have tried to explain what is sometimes called the "tragic paradox" — the fact that in watching a tragedy we positively *want* to experience the gut-wrenching feelings of grief and pain that we hope will be so intense as to move us to tears. A similar phenomenon also extends beyond drama to real life: We want to look at the picture of a deceased loved one so that we can grieve, to revisit the park where we spent time with a lost love, so that we can weep, to get the pianist to play the sad song again so that we can again reflect on how much sadness inevitably pervades life.

This tragic paradox, the desire for a painful catharsis in tragedy or in life, would not seem so contradictory if it were not for the usual psychological assumption that humans are motivated always and only to maximize happiness and minimize suffering, or at least that we are willing to endure suffering only if it leads to some greater happiness in the long run. On the contrary, the purpose of the tragic art forms and of real-life grief is not merely to attain some indirect pleasure in the long run; it is to experience as fully as possible the intrinsic value of that for which we grieve. It is not so paradoxical that we can sometimes "enjoy" painful experiences in an equivocal sense of "enjoy" where "enjoy" is defined to mean simply that we sometimes *choose* to undergo painful experiences, as when a guilty person wants to punish herself. The real paradox arises from the conflict between this wanting to have painful experiences and the usual, everyday assumption that human motivation is fundamentally hedonistic.

Why, then, does tragedy have such an inspirational effect? Levinas (1969) emphasizes that love, the appreciation of the value of another being through an intense experience of empathy, is often pulled by a vision of the other's vulnerability and finitude. "Eros aims at the other in his frailty [*faiblesse*]"(256). Similarly, Unamuno (1972) stresses that the *compassion* dimension of love is largely determinative of its force, because we *appreciate* the value of something more fully when we focus on its inevitable finitude, thus contrasting its uniqueness and irreplaceability with the tragic possibility of its non-being. Through such tragic experiences, we fully appreciate the value of being, as instantiated in a love object or literary protagonist for whom we feel the intense combination of admiration and compassion; such an experience is different from, more powerful than, and more important than mere pleasure or entertainment.

This is one reason most people in most cultures have believed in some form of religion — because it offers an experience of the value of being, not by removing or hedonically counterbalancing life's suffering and woe, but by making us feel that life's value is positive in spite of any possible amount of suffering and woe (or at least in spite of very substantial amounts). Nor can it be a coincidence on this score that tragedy evolved from a religious ritual. From this perspective, we might say that a good part of the feeling of release we get from a good tragic performance is precisely the release from toiling enslavement to the futility and absurdity of the hedonic calculus to which everyday attitudes tend to attribute so much importance.

It is a commonplace that the pleasures we are able to grab, by themselves, are "not enough" to give life meaning — to give it enough value to vindicate its sorrows and hardships. Indeed, this must certainly be one of the messages *of* tragedy: Try though we may, it is hubris to think that we can ultimately win any battle in which the score is kept through a hedonic calculus alone. To be sure, tragedy in the end should leave us inspired and uplifted, not downcast; but we are uplifted not because we now are convinced that we can win the struggle for a positive hedonic balance, but because we no longer feel that the value of human existence is contingent on the status of any hedonic calculus.

If we explore the phenomenology of this experience of the non-hedonic intrinsic value of being, we can then see why tragedy — or more generally works of art that involve a tragic dimension — are particularly suited to make possible such an experience. If tragedy is to have an inspirational effect — to intensify our feeling of the positive value of being, rather than merely its futility, we must experience this value as instantiated in the tragic protagonist through empathy.

A great deal can be learned about the non-hedonic emotions by understanding the way tragedy achieves its paradoxical inspirational effect. The tragic effect requires that we vicariously appreciate not the *instrumental* or *extrinsic* value of a being (as reflected in capacity for great deeds, power, or social status), but rather the person's *intrinsic* value. And to do this requires setting up a dynamic in which our empathic admiration, not for the person's accomplishments or grandiosity, but rather for the person's intrinsic value *qua* ontologically embattled yet existentially meaningful conscious being, must be *intensified by* our compassion, while at the same time our compassion is intensified even more by the feeling of empathic admiration for the person *qua* ontologically endangered yet intrinsically valuable. If we do admire a protagonist in this way, the feeling of admiration is sharply intensified by our compassion for the tragic flaw which will result in her downfall.

These same elements of admiration (for the person's intrinsic value), compassion, and empathy can be noticed in real life feelings of love. There is often an intensification of the feeling of love in the instant when we have reason to focus on the finitude of the love object — when we empathize with the embattledness of her existential project in the face of the forces that not only endanger her physical existence, but also threaten the prospect of authentic being of the person she has the potential to be. A particularly clear illustration of this notion occurs in the popular film *White Palace*, in which the protagonist is not at all attracted to the heroine until he discovers that her apparently hardened, cynical exterior is a cover for the pain of her loss of a child years earlier; from that moment on, he is irresistibly drawn to her. This example also suggests that, ironically, much of the perception of the other's vulnerability stems simply from the sense that she is *in need* for love or for some sort of existential intensification as pulled by an interpersonal context for its potential expression — a need whose urgency underscores the basic embattledness of her project of being. Moments when we sense that the other's being is ultimately faced with conditions of endangerment (including social or existential endangerment) are moments when the concrete *feeling* of love is pulled very sharply.

The intensification of admiration through compassion for the vulnerability and finitude of a tragic protagonist (or, in real life, a love object), transforms mere admiration into an instance of the kind of experience that can be designated as "awe-inspiring." Admiration for a great hero such as Hector becomes an overwhelming awe when the threat of his heroic death becomes real, and more still because his cause is already doomed to lose; the sharpest possible intensification of this awe is achieved (assuming that we do initially admire and empathize with him) in the instant when he is run through by the blade of Achilles, who then drags his mutilated body through the street in front of his aggrieved widow. But our admiration for Achilles in turn is also intensified to the point of awe because we know that the Achilles heel makes him also vulnerable and finite. In general, our admiration for all that is worthwhile in the courageous struggle of conscious beings against the inevitable ontological conditions that embattle them is magnified by our compassion for the inevitably tragic condition of finitude. This intensified feeling of awe-stricken affirmation of the intrinsic value of being (or at least of conscious and human beings) is not only positive and negative at the same time, but its positivity is in direct proportion to its negativity.

This effect of mutually intensified compassion and appreciation of positive intrinsic value depends on our directly *experiencing* rather than simply *intellectually acknowledging* the fleetingness and irreplaceability of the beloved object, whether a real-life love object or a tragic protagonist. Tragedy makes possible the direct experience of that which is intrinsically valuable in an ontologically embattled, irreplaceable conscious being, and then magnifies the intensity of this direct experience of intrinsic value by continually twisting the knife of that very embattlement.

For example, Racine makes effective use of the tension between intrinsic valuation and a sharp edge of sadness to make us feel the heavy-hearted Phaedra's tragic passion for her unattainable stepson Hyppolytus. One result is a corresponding magnification of our empathy with Phaedra herself. Thomas Mann uses a similar effect in *Death in Venice,* where a dying German composer, previously steeped in stoic self-discipline, is drawn in painful admiration toward a seemingly carefree young boy at an Italian beach. In both Racine's and Mann's stories, the feeling of finitude contextualized in a love story heightens and intensifies the felt significance of the characters' struggles. What these authors have managed to do is to provide a direct glimpse into the embattled ontological vulnerability of a person *qua* instance of endangered but intrinsically valuable existential project, as "man, slighted but enduring" — an effect similar to what we experience in moments in real life where a feeling of love is intensified through compassion for vulnerability.

Such an analysis makes sense only against a background of motivational theory in which happiness and pleasure are not the ultimate driving forces; drive-reduction is not the end of human being. Rather, the end is to *exist* as the form of being that one is motivated to *be,* and to be in this pattern irrespective of whether life is happy or miserable. In dynamical systems terms, the system needs to maintain its structures of activity at a certain level of complexity just as much as it needs to reduce drives so as to achieve homeostasis. To ignore the non-hedonistic emotions is thus to ignore half of the emotional life.

Not only in tragedy, but in all artistic activity, we seek to intensify value feelings rather than to attain what they value, and we want the emotions to have an opportunity to unfold by finding vehicles of expression. By expressing values, as Gendlin (1998) and Langer (1957) point out, we give our feelings about them concretely embodied symbolization, and in this way we feel their value more fully; we thus also feel more intensely the value of being *per se.*

7. Narcissism and Narcissistic Disturbance in the Process of Value-Affirmation Experience

Differing ways of handling narcissistic concerns lead to different orientations toward the existential problems that face conscious beings sophisticated enough to worry about them (i.e., humans), and ultimately toward religion in its different forms. Narcissism at bottom is an existential issue. The narcissistically disturbed person refuses or is unable to accept the conditions of her own finitude – a short life span limited by death, limited social, political and economic power, limited ability to affect others and to accomplish the goals to which one might aspire in an ideal world, and also limited ability to form needed social and emotional relationships to others. All of these limitations are aspects of the finite condition, and as Heidegger stressed in his early work, we are all finite; finitude is a necessary ontological condition for all actually existing creatures, with the possible exception of the Infinite, or God, which if it exists would encompass all finite beings. Those of us who are finite beings may deny or seek to escape our finitude only on pain of the inauthenticity that inevitably accompanies self-deception.

But the narcissistically disturbed person, as Karen Horney (1937; 1950/1991) described so well, precisely *does* attempt to deny the finite condition. The classic narcissist fancies that he has within his power to accomplish what other creatures can only dream of. If he chooses, not only can he be the greatest practitioner of his chosen fields, but could also beat all others at their own games if he were to set his mind to it. If he chooses not to do so, it is only because of his disdain for those endeavors (athletes are "meatheads," intellectuals are "nerds"), or out of an admirable sense of modesty and magnanimity (the ability to affect modesty being one of the narcissist's most admirable virtues). As the life of a narcissistically disturbed person plays itself out, of course, "successful" narcissism gradually or suddenly gives way to "unsuccessful" narcissism (e.g., see Lowen 1985; Miller 1981). The unsuccessful narcissist is faced with some incontrovertible sign that his grandiose ego ideal is not in fact being realized. For example, he may find himself in the position of a middle-aged drug addict alternating between homelessness and prison sentences, having irreversibly failed at his profession and alienated family and friends. At this point, the focus shifts from maintaining the grandiose self-image to projecting blame onto others who supposedly caused the failure.

How does narcissistic disturbance affect the higher existential emotions in relation to love, the arts, religion, and other ways of maintaining the feeling of inspiration, or the sense that life is worthwhile? Some orientations to religion are inherently inauthentic and narcissistic. As discussed in more detail elsewhere (Ellis, forthcoming b, c), these are "fundamentalist" attitudes toward religion, whether cloaked with the metaphysical beliefs of al Kaeda terrorists who believe that true servants of Allah will enjoy an infinite number of virgins in the afterlife, or of the Christian fundamentalists who believe that Palestinians should have no rights vis a vis Israel because Armageddon is at hand and "God will be good to the friends of Israel." Fundamentalism means literal interpretation, including literal interpretation of statements about the existential concerns of finitude: that death is not real, that God will rectify all injustices, and that God supplies whatever love and fellow-feeling cannot be gotten through concrete personal and social relations with other finite beings. In short, for the fundamentalist type of religion, the problems of finitude do not exist. Thus there is no need for an extreme experience of the value of being powerful enough to overshadow them. Thus it is easy to destroy other conscious beings in the name of fundamentalism.

In more sophisticated approaches to religion, which include a good dose of what I call the "experiential" effect of religion, the strategy is just the opposite. Rather than denying the existence of the problems of finitude, the purpose is to provide an awe-inspiring emotional experience of the value of being, so that it is possible to bear up under the inevitable hardships and injustices of life without self-deception and inauthenticity. "Eternal life" is not taken to mean literally that people do not really die when they die (as people often comfort themselves by saying at funerals), but something more metaphorical – for example, that life is infinitely valuable and thus worth as much as an infinitely long life, or that the depth of a life's meaning outweighs its shortness in length, or some other such analogical meaning. The purpose is to inspire the faithful to "have faith" – i.e., to feel inspired with a sense that the negativity of the existential conditions of finitude are more than compensated for by the positive value of being, which the religious experience attempts to facilitate.

In concrete terms, religion usually does this by providing the worshiper with the image of a conscious being who can be loved. So, as hinted by many Jungians, religion and sexual love do not play such dissimilar roles in human psychology. Both serve the inspirational need, and both do so by offering the image of a conscious being for whom love – the experience of the intrinsic value of being as instantiated in a specific love object – can be intensified through concrete symbolizing-behaviors in relation to the love object, including those which serve the dynamic of admiration as amplified by compassion. For this reason, most religions include less-than-omnipotent beings who can suffer, such as saints, martyrs, or Christ on the cross; such finite objects for reverence can inspire compassion, and thus intensify the feelings of admiration and inspiration.

But by denying the very problems of finitude from the outset, narcissists also attempt to eliminate this need for intensified experience of another's intrinsic value. They do so by constructing a grandiose self image. To confuse imagery of the self, in the everyday sense of this expression, with the self itself is the hallmark of narcissistic disturbance (Klein 1975; Kohut 1985). The narcissist thinks of herself as an object, as viewed from an external perspective, as the protagonist of a story as read by someone else, or by oneself in the act of viewing and judging oneself as if from an external perspective (Miller 1981). Narcissists think of themselves in third person; the events of the narcissist's life are narrated to herself as if read from the pages of the biography of some famous person from the past, who has already been judged important enough to write books and stories about (Horney 1937, 1950).

This in turn brings us to a discussion of the difference between a narcissistically disturbed value system and a value system characteristic of healthy narcissism. For the healthy narcissist, intrinsic value is invested in objects external to the self – love objects, social or political objectives, and abstract ideals, all of which are ways in which the subjective self intensifies the experience of the value of being *per se*. In love, for example, we intensely experience the intrinsic value of being as instantiated in the other. The corresponding imagery here is imagery of the other as we engage her.

The imagery of the "self" that does this engaging is not primarily objective, but consists of imagery of results of the self's actions in relation to others as guided by these non-narcissistic values.

For the narcissistically disturbed person, by contrast, only the self and its experience can be intrinsically valuable; the experience of others, political actions, and work toward abstract ideals have only instrumental value insofar as they serve to promote images of oneself as valuable. In this case, moreover, even the *subjective* self is relegated to a mere instrumental value, since the main purpose is now to view oneself as valuable, through one's own eyes and the eyes of others, as an accomplished, amusing, or in some way other-pleasing persona. The inspiration of the intense experience of intrinsic value in the other is then blocked by this confusion between intrinsic and instrumental value. The narcissist is caught up in the habit of measuring the value of himself and of others instrumentally — as depicted in objectified imagery — and therefore misses the intrinsic value that can be seen only through empathy with the other's subjective being. Rather than imagery of sensorimotor action schemas as they would relate the self's actions to the other, the imagery is caught up with the way things *look,* objectively.

It is possible to distinguish (and most psychologists do distinguish) at least three aspects of the self that are oriented in different ways toward valuational feelings in such a way that the motivated directedness toward these values provides much of the unity and continuity needed to structure the self. First, there is the "ego ideal" — the aspect of the self (or of the "superego," if one prefers) that holds up esteemed images of what the self ideally should strive to be like. According to many theorists, notably Kohut (and this is also consistent with casual, everyday observations), people often are able to love their abstract ideals (moral values such as loyalty, integrity, magnanimity, etc.) with an emotion quite similar to the idealizing love one feels for a person.

Second, there is the "narcissistic self." This is the aspect of the self (or of the superego) that craves the attention and admiration of others. Since we all must first attract the attention of others in order to make contact with them to meet the need for meaningful interaction, there will always be a narcissistic self in anyone's personality structure. It is only when this narcissistic self becomes "disturbed" — when infantile traumata cause the person to react cataclysmically and compulsively to any threat to the narcissistic self's craving for attention, approval and admiration — that it becomes a neurosis or even psychosis.

Third, there is the "idealized object image" — i.e., the image of some specific person in whom one feels are embodied the cherished qualities of the ego ideal and/or of the narcissistic self. It is an obvious phenomenological observation that we sometimes relocate values from our ego ideal to another person (who serves as an idealized object image), and *vice versa.* In the same process, we also relocate the investment of emotional commitment and energy that accompanies these valuational feelings. It has also often been observed (for example, by Reik and by Kohut) that, at times when the ideals that unify a self are faltering or are being committed to radical questioning, the person is likely to find a person whose idealized image serves as a stand-in for the now missing or weakened ego ideal. In concrete terms, a person who finds herself no longer able to be enthusiastically enough motivated and inspired by the abstract value beliefs that used to define the meaning of her activity and organization, will then desperately cling to the meaning and motivational direction provided by falling in love, or by becoming a follower of a charismatic personality or political demagogue, or by becoming devoted to a spiritual partner, whether the latter be a human being, a deity, or the representative of a deity such as a saint or martyr. In effect, the idealized person is made to serve the meaning-structuring and motivational directedness that organize the self, now that the ego ideal is no longer able to serve this purpose as effectively. When this kind of dynamic is heavily involved in a love relationship, the threat of the loss of the beloved person's intimacy threatens to issue in an extreme disintegration and unraveling of the basic fabric of the self, leading to a more or less psychologically unstable condition. Even among well-balanced personalities, such a disintegration of the motivated directedness of the self is often experienced to a greater or lesser extent with the loss of an important love relationship. But the difficulty of working through the resulting anxieties seems to be proportional to the fragility or weakness of commitment to the valuational feelings toward cherished long-term goals that could pull the person into the future, thus providing a sense of direction and continuity to overpower the fragmentation and meaninglessness that would otherwise intensify the anxiety.

It is important to realize that such an intense valuation can be spread to include moral abstractions, and as a result also spiritual or religious systems that provide symbolic rather than literal love objects. This transference of valuation from a primary love object to a moral abstraction can occur only in sophisticated conscious beings. The reason it is possible is that, once we have ever experienced the magnified appreciation of intrinsic value afforded by the process described above, we have learned to focus on the person's vulnerability, innocence, and finitude in awe-stricken admiration for her struggle to maintain authenticity and intensity in the face of this finitude. We then realize that these same qualities also have intrinsic value when exemplified in *other* people, if only we could vicariously experience them within a space of empathy so as to fully appreciate them in direct experience. Finally, we allow ourselves to be open to a space of empathy with people generally, and to feel a degree of reverence toward them by appreciating in each person the qualities that are intrinsically valuable in conscious beings generally. In essence, we abstract the qualities that are experienced as valuable in conscious beings from a primary love object (whether lost or still present), so that we can then admire those qualities as exemplified elsewhere.

I say that this transference process can occur only in sophisticated conscious beings because it requires the ability to think in terms of meta-emotions. Sophisticated beings can ask themselves questions about their feelings toward specific persons, and think of ways to make them different. We can decide how we feel *about* specific feelings that we have and ask ourselves questions designed to remind us of other feelings that we might have in that context, if only we were to think of other relevant considerations at the right time. For example, a high school friend of mine grew up to be a serial bathtub killer (i.e., he strangled women in their bathtubs). Whenever confronted with evil moral behavior, I can always remind myself to feel compassion for the offender, if I wish to, just by thinking of my high school friend and all the psychological foibles and brain dysfunctions that led him to such a sorry conclusion. This would be a much more difficult thing for a monkey to do, because it requires conjuring the right images at the right time and in the right context. Monkeys usually entertain imagery that is automatic and spontaneous rather than introducing imagery at will.

The meta-emotional process that is most relevant for our purposes here is that we can learn to experience in many people the qualities in a love object that pull intense compassion and thus amplify the feeling of reverence, by abstracting those qualities and then looking for them in others. I should emphasize, however, that none of this contradicts the notion that it is precisely the *uniqueness* of an individual that is loved, and not some abstract set of qualities (such as "temperance," "wisdom," "courage," etc.). But the *way in which* we appreciate the person's uniqueness — her irreplaceability and unrepeatability in the history of the universe — is by focusing on her potential embattledness and vulnerability in the project of trying to maintain authenticity and sensitivity in the face of the ontological conditions that *all* conscious beings face, simply by virtue of being conscious beings. This ontological endangeredness will manifest itself in the guise of very different kinds of threats for different individuals under specific different circumstances, but the essential effect that it has in allowing us to intensely focus on and appreciate the person's value *qua* unique individual always follows the same dynamic. Since this dynamic is the *way in which* we focus on an individual's uniqueness in order to feel reverent toward it, we can therefore say that we learn to love by learning to directly experience the value of a conscious being *qua* conscious being, and that we can then learn to focus on this same value (which can be abstracted) in other conscious beings as well — provided that we are able to enter into and maintain a space of empathy with them.

This same process also serves to restore the stability of the ego ideal. When we learn to focus on the fact that the same qualities that are intrinsically valued in the original love object can also be found in all other conscious beings, we adopt an abstract system of values based on the premise that the existence of conscious beings has intrinsic value, and including all corollaries derivable from this premise. The ego ideal then includes this set of values, and we find that by loving the person in whom we worship this value, we also learn to love the entire value system based on affirming this value.

We can clearly see, then, that the value placed on an "idealized object image" and the values that guide the ego ideal are *the same values* — the irreducible value of the existence of conscious beings *per se*. This value needs to be seen as embodied in an example, and intensely appreciated there, so that it *can* be felt strongly enough to *be* the guiding ultimate value of the ego ideal. In fact, what could the definition of a "healthy" ego ideal be if not one whose ultimate guiding principles are derived from the intrinsic value of certain qualities inherent in conscious beings? And the person with the healthy ego ideal, as defined in this way, will also have a healthy narcissistic self. I.e., one will enjoy the image of oneself, not as a ravishingly beautiful or handsome, omnipotent, irreproachable kind of *persona,* but as a person who embodies the same ideals that the healthy ego loves in a spiritual partner — sensitivity, courageous authenticity, uniqueness, finitude, and moral sincerity.

These are the kinds of qualities one will then enjoy having people see in oneself, and will thus enjoy seeing oneself as exhibiting.

Commitment to a set of moral values based on the intrinsic value of all conscious beings allows one to focus more easily on the valuable as it exists in a specific potential love object. At the same time, it is possible to transfer love from a primary love object to derivative love objects by abstracting that which is valuable in both, and this abstraction strengthens the abstract moral standards of the ego ideal.

Since the process of abstraction of the values manifested by one love object enables us to transfer this love to someone else, it is possible to transfer the locus of value appreciation from within a beloved person (or deity) to secondary love objects (the "fellow man"), or to human beings generally, merely by focusing intently enough on the appropriate qualities in these other objects. A romantic love object, for example, in effect can become a vehicle for the intense experience of the positive value of being *per se*, while at the same time offering the opportunity to concretely symbolize this love (for example, through sexual feeling) on a continuing basis. Furthermore, each time other functions of the relationship again tend to eclipse the space of empathy, it is possible to renew the space of empathy by again focusing on the qualities that one learned to admire in a primary love object. At this point, one has learned to love a romantic partner or other derivative love objects in a "reverent" enough way that this positive value experience is continually intense enough to compensate for the harshness of the ontological predicament. The spreading of a primary experience of value-affirmation to derivative value objects is thus extremely important, and this same process serves to spread the love for a primary spiritual partner to the love for one's own guiding ideals.

It is beyond our scope here to go into the details of the way such an abstract value system would be worked out. There can be arguments and disagreements among philosophers in this regard. But as soon as the intrinsic value of conscious entities and their well being is assumed as the basic driving force of a value system, it then becomes possible to designate as a *prima facie* "good" whatever serves to facilitate people's self-actualization and well being. Acts that we "ought" to perform can then be thought of as acts that would be expected to enhance those ends. There will be conflicts between different ends, since some will enhance the good of some, while others enhance the good of others; resolution of these conflicts are the job of a theory of justice, which I cannot go into at this point. As the reader will easily realize, the working out of a theory of justice, not to mention a good social and political system, will be difficult and complex. My point here is simply that a person inspired by the spreading effect of the inspirational love experience will be emotionally committed to the project of discovering what is good and right, and then acting to further the objectives that follow from such a value system.

Many people in our culture (as in most cultures, but especially in ours) obviously have trouble understanding how it is possible to have non-hedonistic experiences of the positive value of being in spite of serious personal misfortunes (both contingent and because of the essentially apocalyptic nature of things). Understanding this phenomenon requires taking seriously an aspect of human motivation that is at odds with the ideology of a culture intent on getting people to jump through hoops to attain rewards. Such an ideology requires that people see the main purpose of life as attainment of rewards, and thus interpret their emotions as desiring to see certain objective outcomes in the world, the occurrence of which is supposed to increase one's own happiness, contentment, or feeling of belonging. To a certain extent, any culture that wants to get the maximum amount of diligent performance out of its members will find it advantageous to teach them that this simplistic hedonism is the meaning of life, so that it can then get them to do the work in order to obtain the benefits. Our culture is more determined to maximize this performance of superior accomplishments than most are; it therefore teaches that obtaining the material and social benefits it can offer is the *only* thing that a normal human being is really motivated to do, and constructs an entire edifice of atomistic-individualist, egoistic-hedonist social scientific theory on this premise, promoting it through its media at every opportunity. People are then so intent on "proving themselves" that they become all the more egocentric and narcissistic (i.e., image-conscious).

We have already seen why this view of emotions is misguided and ultimately destructive of the meaning of life. It is misguided because consciousness is motivated more strongly and basically by the desire to fully *exist* than by the desire for happiness or pleasure. Many of the feelings that we misconstrue as aiming to achieve happiness and pleasure really aim simply to fully experience themselves. The purpose of the behavior they motivate is neither to achieve any objective outcome in the world, nor to achieve an increase in happiness or contentment, but rather to provide an opportunity to symbolically enact the emotion so that we can feel it as intensely as it desires to be felt.

The same thing is true for the feeling of love. What love wants first of all is not to possess the beloved, or to benefit her, or even to confirm one's faith that the love is returned. What love first wants is simply to be felt with a certain degree of intensity, so that an inspirational effect takes place. But for an emotion to be felt requires symbolization in order to give it a concrete substratum of which it can be predicated as a pattern of change, just as a piece of music needs a physical medium — a vibrating string, air through which the wave is transmitted, etc. — in order for the music to really exist. Further, the symbolization medium must be appropriate to the form of the emotion that is to be symbolized, just as a musical medium must be appropriate to the pattern of the music. A Chopin sonata cannot be embodied in the vibrating snare of a snare drum (although the snare may irritatingly voice one particular note of the sonata each time that note is played in the same room with the snare drum). Similarly, if love is to be symbolized in such a way that the love can be continually felt at the needed level of intensity, the lover must have the opportunity to behold or contemplate the being of the person he loves. And this involves more than beholding her physical body or appearance (since a person is her *pattern of consciousness,* not merely her physical body or appearance). The main purpose of the space of empathy with intensified love objects is that through it we are enabled to perceive the value of being as revealed in the other, provided that we ourselves are in the right frame of mind to do so. (The attitude of the space of empathy also tends to help us achieve this frame of mind, as explained earlier.)

Narcissistic disturbance blocks the ability to invest this intense experience of intrinsic value in another – attempting instead to deny the pressing relevance, for both self and other, of all the problems of finitude. But, as we shall see in the next section, the same dynamic exists in religious fundamentalism. At bottom, narcissistic disturbance and religious fundamentalism pursue the same strategies in dealing with the existential condition: they deny its reality, even though this very denial deprives them of the psychological resources that could contend with it in a non-self-deceptive way.

8. Contrasting Attitudes toward Finitude: Contrasting Religions and Contrasting Worldviews

To argue that fundamentalism is a form of narcissistic disturbance is not to argue that authenticity requires rejecting the possibility of a literally supernatural realm; the point is rather that the problem of intensely enough experiencing the intrinsic value of being becomes hopelessly garbled if we stake everything about the meaning of life on bets about the supernatural, and then deceive ourselves that we can be more sure of such bets than we actually can. To speak of "self-deceptive forms of religion" or "self-deceptive metaphysical systems" is not to suggest that such belief systems are necessarily false, but that the believer has deceived herself in the sense of thinking that we can be more confident of their truth and of our understanding of them than we actually can. By then encouraging the believer to proceed as if finitude were no longer a problem, such a fundamentalist belief system actually impairs the direct experience of the value of being, because an initial acknowledgement that finitude at least constitutes a serious problem is fundamental to the depth of direct value experience, especially in its primary exemplar, which on my view is through the intensification of human compassion.

In contrasting self-deceptive and non-self-deceptive forms of religion, it is useful to consider in a little more detail than we did at the outset the vast matrix of philosophical theories and assumptions needed to justify the self-deceptive worldview — i.e., the kind of worldview that operates essentially by denying the ultimate reality of finitude. Such denial systems inevitably lead sooner or later to the "problem of evil," whose solution in turn requires an even more elaborate system of distorted reasoning and a rejection of even more obvious everyday realities. The essence of this problem is usually framed in terms of the following formula:

God is all-good.
God is all-powerful.
There is evil.

The problem of evil, in essence, inevitably results from the fact that the original purpose of the self-deceptive kind of religion — dating virtually to the apes — *was precisely to deny the existence* of those evils which are so unpalatable that we cannot reconcile ourselves to them. Yet at the same time it is empirically obvious that such evils still do exist. Thus it becomes "paradoxical" that what we have convinced ourselves *cannot* exist, *does* exist after all. On the level of reality, we must deal with evil every day in order to survive, while at the same time the meaning and purpose of survival are defined at a level of fantasy in which these everyday realities can have no relevance, and therefore no purpose.

For example, at the level of everyday reality, we believe that the preservation of human life is the most important of all intrinsic values. Yet our value system itself is supposedly based on a religious doctrine that denies the ultimate reality of death, maintaining, for example, that soldiers who die in war do not really die, but merely migrate to a metaphysical realm in which they live on eternally. How, then, can the death of a soldier — which is not even a real death at all — be considered *intrinsically* undesirable, rather than a mere pragmatic inconvenience to his family, his friends, and the economic system? After all, that which is intrinsically valuable — the soldier's life — presumably has not been destroyed. In short, how can that which has no reality, death, be considered an evil? But if not an evil, why try to prevent it? The suicide terrorists of al Kaeda are merely the reductio ad absurdum of this denial of the reality of death, which is correlative with the failure to value life.

The same question arises with regard to all other intrinsic values. We observe that, in the empirical realm of everyday reality, the wicked often flourish while the good suffer. But we know that an all-good deity would not *wish* such injustice to exist, and an all-powerful deity would *know how* to prevent it. We must therefore believe that any injustice that we humans are unable to prevent, through sincere effort and hard work, will be exactly compensated for in the afterlife. But if all injustice is to be eradicated in the hereafter, then there is not much point in our efforts to eradicate it here and now. Here again, that which in the ultimate scheme of things has no reality — in this case, injustice — also cannot really be an evil. In every case, it turns out that the meaning of life is *erased* precisely by the same metaphysical system that was supposed to give life meaning. If death is not really death, then what point is there in saving a life? If injustice is to be cancelled, why work so hard to fight it?

The classic Judeo-Christian solution to the problem of evil (and one also finds parallels to it in the Muslim, Hindu, Ancient African and most other theistic religions) is that God, in order to create the greatest possible amount of good, needed also to create the greatest possible *variety* of goods. It would not have been so good simply to create one very good entity — say, an angel — and then proceed to exactly duplicate this one being millions of times, thus bringing forth a universe that would consist of a vast array of precise duplications of this one being. Much better to create a variety of good things, even though this entailed creating both greater goods (for example, angels) and lesser goods (for example, the tsetse fly). This balancing act became precarious when the well-being of some of the lesser goods conflicted with each other; yet God calculated that more good would result from the existence of these conflicting goods than if He were to deny one or the other of them the opportunity to exist. And it is clearly better to have the opportunity to exist, despite whatever pain and suffering might arise from this unavoidable balancing act, than never to exist at all — especially if we assume that God rectifies the resulting injustices in the hereafter.

But this solution, posed in such a simple form, cannot easily withstand the numerous counterexamples to which it is subject, and therefore it must be dressed up a little. The tsetse fly is such a lowly, insignificant being, that no humane and rational God — not to mention an all-good, all-powerful one — could possibly think that the existence of this nearly worthless insect (whose only biological purpose seems to be to cause sleeping sickness in humans) could ever outweigh in value the life of even one conscious human being, let alone thousands. Similarly, it is beyond credibility that an omniscient deity could not have calculated a way to avoid a tidal wave that destroys an entire city — especially if He (or She) has the power to create and destroy things at will. Why not destroy the tidal wave in the nick of time, or create some impediment to its striking — or at least warn the people that it is on its way?

The "experiential" approach to religion or spirituality, by contrast, does not require a denial of the reality of evil. When we have such a pronounced positive value experience as is facilitated by love, the arts, or non-fundamentalistic religious experience, we feel that, if only the inspirational experience could be sustained, we would be much more than compensated for even the worst of all possible metaphysical scenarios — i.e., the scenario in which our brief and humble existence on this inconsequential ball of dust is all there is. We find that our appreciation of the loved person's quasi-aesthetic beauty and value is in no way spoiled by the unfortunate fact of finitude. Indeed, since we have given up our own sense of self-importance in favor of reveling awe-strickenly in the other's form of being, it now makes much less difference to us whether the ego-subject with which we previously identified ourselves will survive forever or not. Our own narcissistic gratification with its silly demands for self-importance and self-aggrandizement is precisely what we have escaped in favor of living in the appreciation of the other's uniqueness and vulnerability in the face of finitude; we empathize with this uniqueness and vulnerability in the form of compassion mixed with admiration. In concrete terms, we esteem the other all the more strongly because she is finite.

In short, once we have experienced such extreme positive value, we are *compensated* for the ontological predicament rather than needing to deceive ourselves that the predicament *does not exist*. Correlatively, the intensification of love itself depends on our ability to face the truth. If we did not at some point bring ourselves to acknowledge that the ontological dilemma is a dilemma, then our compassion for the finitude of the beloved *in the face* of this dilemma would not be intense enough to make possible a powerful enough value experience to motivate dropping our self-deceptions with regard to death, powerlessness, and alienation. This is why the experience in a sense can occur only by "tricking" us into abandoning egocentricity. The experience of the other initially pulls us out of ourselves by appealing to an egocentric motive — the need for self-transformation. This need for self-transformation is built into the structure of consciousness *per se,* because consciousness is in its essence a pattern of change and cannot exist as stasis. The egocentric subject must allow its being to be taken over and overpowered by the other's pattern of unfolding in order to pull itself out of existential lethargy and somnambulism. Even if submission to this transformation is threatening or painful, the ontological structure of consciousness in its motivational dimension impels us to do it. To be conscious is a more fundamental need than to be happy or complacent.

A condition for the possibility of the "transcendent value experience" — in which we experience the intrinsic value of being as instantiated in a love object intensely enough to compensate for the harshness of the existential conditions of finitude — is that conscious beings have intrinsic and absolute value. We do not need to experience sweeping feelings of love, or undergo any direct transcendent value experience, in order to know intellectually that this is true. The value of conscious beings is presupposed by all other valuational or ethical propositions for which any evidence or argument can be given. But to know intellectually *that* something has value is different from actually directly *experiencing* its value, just as the knowledge that Tchaikovsky wrote a Seventh Symphony, and that it was as great as his Sixth, is no substitute for directly experiencing the beauty of the Seventh Symphony by actually listening to a performance of it.

The fact that we can directly experience the value of conscious beings accounts for the extreme moral importance of events here on earth despite the infinitesimal smallness of the earth in the cosmic scheme of things. As Trotsky eloquently put it,

"If I were one of the celestial bodies, I would look with complete detachment upon this miserable ball of dust and dirt. . . . I would shine upon the good and the evil alike. . . . But I am a *man*. 'World history which to you, dispassionate gobbler of science, to you, book-keeper of eternity, seems only a negligible moment in the balance of time, is to me everything!' (Trotsky 1964, p.40)

Once we have abandoned the self-deceptive metaphysical doctrines of the fundamentalist type of religion, we also no longer need the metaphysical dogmas that were necessary as *ad hoc* hypotheses to prop them up. The most important one of these *ad hoc* hypotheses was the doctrine of a radically free will, which was needed to solve the problem of evil in the self-deceptive scheme of things, and therefore led to a predominantly retributive, guilt-and-blame oriented morality. This retributivism, however, tends to kill compassion. One can easily see how damaging this retributivism is to the possibility of compassion by observing the dynamics of any long-term romantic relationship or marriage. One of the main problems that undermines the space of empathy between the two people is their insistence on shifting guilt and blame for all problems away from themselves and onto each other. Their need to avoid the other's blame then forces them to become so rigidified in their defensiveness that they cannot openly express feelings and ideas to each other without fear of condemnation and rejection. This dynamic in turn kills the space of empathy.

The same problem can be seen in people's political behavior. For example, in most states in the United States, 99 per cent of welfare recipients are children and single or divorced mothers needed to care for their children when not in school (and who also are required to seek and accept employment by all possible means on pain of losing their welfare benefits). Yet, year after year, politicians win elections by running adds that promise somehow to eliminate welfare. In spite of the facts about the intractability of the vicious cycle of poverty in our economic system, such ads continue to appeal to those in our culture who are so obsessed with projecting guilt and blame onto someone, and insisting that people's problems are the result of their own free will, that we prefer to use our vote to express hostility toward the victims of social problems than to use them to elect someone who would try to develop solutions to the problems. We are more interested in finding scapegoats for our problems than in making them go away.

As another example, consider the problem of drug abuse. At the time of this writing, our culture shows virtually no interest in offering resources to help people overcome drug addiction, or to eliminate the social problems that cause people to become so hopeless that they would sacrifice their lives to an addiction, or even to find out what the causes of the psychological problems that lead to addiction might *be;* we instead spend billions of dollars to send armies and police to drug-producing areas to destroy crops or engage in shoot-outs with gangsters. It is obvious, of course, that the *effect* of these efforts, if they were to succeed, would be to make the drugs more scarce, so that their price would increase, and therefore addicts would have to commit more crimes, and more violent crimes, to get the money to buy the drugs. And this is not a complicated fact to understand. Yet our culture manifests a need to engage in some sort of expressive action, no matter how counterproductive, to symbolize our hostile and condemnatory feelings toward people who deal in illegal drugs. But few are interested in expressing compassion or humanitarian concern for those who are addicted to drugs, let alone those who were unlucky enough to have their character determined by such negative environmental and/or hereditary factors that they would end up with immoral and criminal personality structures. The retributive, guilt-and-blame oriented morality with its emphasis on free will demands that we hate and inflict still further harm on such people — even if this means harming ourselves and other innocent people in the process — rather than pitying them and trying to calculate the most beneficial way to deal with them by taking into account all available facts of the case.

As documented by Adorno's studies of the "authoritarian personality" (see Adorno et al. 1964), it is understandable on the basis of differing attitudes toward finitude and the related needs for inspiration that different forms of religion would correlate with different ethical and political attitudes.

The very elements of human nature that would pull compassion – determinism, limitation of power, etc. – are the same features that must be blamed and condemned by the fundamentalist, in order to protect the literalistic dogmas from the problem of evil. At the same time, if humans had the degree of freedom and power to pull ourselves up by our bootstraps attributed to us by fundamentalism, then the fundamentalist would be morally justified in not feeling much compassion for our weaknesses and evils. So both fundamentalism and experiential worldviews are comprehensive. The former lacks the resources to be adequately inspired simply by love for other humans, so that grand metaphysical denials must be marshalled; and at the same time, because those metaphysical denials *have* been marshalled, there is no *need* for the love for other humans to adequately serve the need for inspiration.

We seem presently to be drawing to the close of a historical period when the need to feel love as an inspirational experience powerful enough to counterbalance the acknowledged facts of finitude was enacted by projecting it onto a merely "romantic" partner (as defined by a certain cultural tradition) in the form of sexual feeling. This was all too limited an attempt because the sexual symbolization served as an all-too-easy substitute for the more complex forms of symbolization that would make accessible the more sophisticated feelings toward the consciousness of the other person that primary love experiences entail.

If, however, we understand why we felt so compelled to project such an awesome spiritual experience onto a sexual love object, we should then be ready to take the next step, which is to use the experience of inspiration-through-compassion *per se* (whether in a romantic context or not) to pull us out of egocentricity, so that we experience the value of conscious beings other than ourselves intensely enough to compensate for the harshness of the ontological predicament. We can then abandon the metaphysical dogmas needed to support a self-deceptive denial of the predicament, along with the distortion of ethics that blocked us from fully feeling compassion toward others. At the same time, the poetry and symbolism of religious mythology can be retained as a rich system for intensifying the experience of the value of being.

"WIRED" FOR SELF-DESTRUCTION:
The Dangers of the Religious Impulse
by Matthew Alper

"Religion is the source of all imaginable follies and disturbances. It is the parent of fanaticism and civil discord. It is the enemy of mankind" -Voltaire c.1694-1778.

"Science is the great antidote to the poison of superstition. An ailing world would do well to reach for the right bottle in the medicine cabinet" -Smith,1776.

"A science that comes to terms with the spiritual nature of mankind may well outstrip the technological science of the immediate past in its contribution to human welfare" -Sadock, 2000.

"We either come to terms with our unconscious drives and instincts-with life and death-or else we surely die" -Brown,1959.

What is the purpose of any science if not to provide us with data that can lead to the betterment of our species? In this regard, science should be viewed as a utilitarian undertaking in which the primary goal of any investigation is to obtain useful information. With this in mind, "What," we might ask, "is the utility of neurotheology?" How can we, either as individuals or a species, benefit from this new science?

So, what if it should turn out that human spirituality and religiosity are nothing more than two inherited biological impulses, two evolutionary adaptations that emerged to make us a more survivable species? If this be the case, shouldn't we inquire into the underlying nature of these essential parts of us? Generally speaking, though each physical characteristic we possess provides us with some adaptive utility, each often comes with its own drawbacks. Accordingly, if religiosity constitutes an inherited characteristic of our species, what might be some of its potential drawbacks? What negative impact might a religious function have on our species?

Only once we determine this, will we be able to maximize on this impulse's positive aspects while, at the same time, minimizing its negative. Only once we view religious consciousness as an evolutionary adaptation will we be able to objectively examine its potential liabilities. And, only once we identify such liabilities, can we begin to work on turning them into strengths.

For all the advantages there might be in possessing a religious instinct, for all it has done to help strengthen the group dynamic, to provide us with a sense of ultimate meaning and purpose in our lives, for all the hope and comfort it might bring, it has proven itself, time and again, to be a very dangerous impulse. As the philosopher Alfred North Whitehead expressed it:

History, down to the present day, is a melancholy record of the horrors which can attend religion: human sacrifice, and in particular the slaughter of children, cannibalism, sensual orgies, abject superstition, hatred between races, the maintenance of degrading customs, hysteria, bigotry, can all be laid at its charge. Religion is the last refuge of human savagery (Whitehead, 1926).

Granted, humankind has done away with many of the more primal excesses of its religious impulse. For example, none of the world's present-day mainstream religions incorporate such rites as child sacrifice or cannibalism into their practices. Nevertheless, even with the proscription of these more barbaric rites, religion continues to act as a divisive force, promoting discrimination among peoples as well as inciting enmity, aggression, and ultimately war.

But why is it that the world's various religions, whose tenets are so often based on just and loving principles, so frequently find themselves pitted against one another in acts of cruelty, hostility, and even genocide? Though every culture possesses the same inherent religious impulse because each emerges from its own unique historical and environmental circumstance, this same impulse manifests itself differently in each culture. It is for this reason that though we all possess the same inherent religious impulse, so many different religions have emerged.

Because each religion has faith that its beliefs-and only its beliefs-are representative of "the truth," each religion inherently contradicts every other. (If my God is true, how can yours be also?). Consequently, there exists an inherent antagonism in each religion for every other. Moreover, our religious functions instill us with an inherent belief that we are immortal. Because each religion possesses its own unique interpretation of what immortality represents, each religion views every other as a threat to its notion of an immortal soul (If my heaven is true, how can yours be also?). In this regard, each religious belief system perceives every other as not just a mortal threat, but also as an immortal threat As one might imagine, any threat to one's immortal soul is not something that any individual or society is likely to take lightly. As a result of this unfortunate psychodynamic, our species tends to engage in what could be termed religious tribalism. It is this same dynamic that has compelled us to initiate the types of religious wars and atrocities that have plagued our species' history.

Perhaps if we could learn to view and religiosity as nothing more than a genetically inherited impulse, we'd be better able to contain some of its more destructive influences. If we could come to understand the underlying nature of this instinct, perhaps we could learn to curb the inevitable antagonism that each religion inherently feels for every other. If we were to recognize that our religiously generated fears and antipathies were merely the effects of an inherited impulse, as opposed to anything founded in reason, we might be able to temper the excesses of this same impulse that has launched our species into a history of repeated religious war. How many more times must we justify acts of cruelty, murder, and genocide in the name of some God or religion before we learn to tame this destructive impulse in us? Even today, we need just look to recent world events in the Middle East, in India and Pakistan, Northern Ireland, and Yugoslavia, and now here in America, as a mere few examples, to witness the destructive grip the religious impulse has on our species.

During the time of our species' emergence, when humans lived in small nomadic tribes, perhaps it was necessary that we possess a religious impulse. At that time, religious consciousness provided us, not just with a means to cope with our anxieties regarding death, but also with a way to order and organize ourselves socially. Nevertheless, times have changed since then. Since our emergence, not only have humans successfully populated the planet but, in the process, we have evolved from a species of small, closely-knit, often isolated, nomadic communities into citizens of diverse and stationary civilizations.

Within a relatively short period of time, humans have transformed their own environments into something very different from those into which we originally evolved. At the time of our emergence, we were little more than what Desmond Morris referred to as "Naked Apes" (Morris,1967), monkey people who lived in caves, could start fires, and chip rocks. And look at us now, a mere hundred thousand years later (which is very little in terms of evolutionary time) living in concrete megalopolises, using advanced modes of transportation and communication. In essence, the physical conditions into which our species was initially selected had been drastically altered within a relatively short time. As a result, certain aspects of our "hardwiring" no longer suited our new conditions, rendering us an environmentally maladjusted animal.

Perhaps during the dawn of our species, when humans had barely populated the planet and lived in small isolated communities, religious tribalism didn't represent as much of a threat as it helped to preserve a group's survival and identity. As time passed, however, and our species grew in numbers, varying cultures with their numerous religions and ideologies began to expand into one another's territories, making religious tribalism an ever-increasing threat to the fabric of these new social conditions.

Today, as we find ourselves living in what is becoming an increasingly global community, maintaining a diversity of belief systems may no longer represent a viable option for our species. Instead, we may have to learn to adopt a unified set of religious principles through which to achieve global harmony. Perhaps if we could create and embrace a single humanistic ideology based on such universal principles as tolerance, love, compassion, and forgiveness, while discarding the more divisive promptings of our religious impulses, we might be able to optimize our potential for happiness, while minimizing our potential for fostering pain and suffering in the world.

Humans are destined to remain a religious animal as we are "wired" this way. Nevertheless, not unless we learn to rechannel our inherent religious sensibilities into one globally-shared humanistic ethic, are we likely to survive. If we are naive enough to only love, value, and respect those who share the same religious ideology with which we were raised, we will probably destroy ourselves. The boundaries of our love and respect for other men must be extended beyond the narrow margins of any single religious ideology and applied to the whole of humankind.

Similar to the manner in which the Europeans have abandoned their national currencies and replaced them with the unified form in the Euro-dollar, it may be necessary for every country to abandon all national and religious sentiment and replace them with a unified cultural paradigm, one world religion based on the brotherhood of man. United, our species may at least have a chance of standing; divided, however, we are sure to eventually fall. To restate Albert Einstein's impassioned plea to the world after World War II, "Only a few short years remain in which to discover some spiritual basis for world brotherhood, or civilization as we now know it will certainly destroy itself." (Einstein, 1954).

This notion of containing our self-destructive impulses seems particularly relevant today in a world in which we possess modern weapons of mass destruction. In such potentially precarious times, can we really afford to leave ourselves in the hands of our most primal instincts? Just as it is necessary that we contain the excesses of all of our instincts, shouldn't we seek to do the same for our religious ones as well? Rather than to simply learn new ways to negotiate a war, wouldn't we be better off if we sought to understand and contain those impulses that continue to drive us toward such aggressive behaviors? There is no time left to negotiate. We've played our last chip in the war room. Any next world war that might emulate those of our past would mark the end of life as we know it. As Einstein, once again, so eloquently expressed, "I do not know with what weapons World War III will be fought, but I can assure you that World War IV will be fought with sticks and stones."

Just because we, as a species, are temporarily king-of-the-hill, we erroneously presume that we're invincible. It's as if we've placed unconditional trust in the forces of Nature to preserve us, as if, because of the great strength we presently possess, we are immune to the forces of extinction. Perhaps we feel this way because we continue to believe the myth that we are God's chosen creatures. To recognize what a puerile fantasy such thinking represents, we need just look at terrestrial life's three and a half billion year history to see that it is little more than a chronicle of mass extinctions. As a matter of fact, for every species that exists today, there are countless numbers now extinct. For us to presume that we are immune to such a fate may very well mark the beginnings of our own demise.

Just because we happen to live in a time of relative peace and calm, we shouldn't presume things will remain this way forever. The history of our species is an epic of war, one that is often contingent on the world's economic conditions, which happen to be cyclical in nature, fluctuating between periods of growth and recession. In a period of growth, we become complacent. In recession, we go to war. (Put a hundred loaves of bread before a hundred hungry people belonging to two different religions and you will have peace. Put ten loaves of bread before a hundred hungry people of two different religions, and you will have genocide.)

In addition, with all our newly advanced medical technologies, which decrease infant mortality rates and extend life expectancy, the continued rise in our world's population only exacerbates the possibility of a world recession. Again, in light of the destructive technologies we now possess-nuclear, chemical, and biological-perhaps it's time we start to work on mastering our own natures, most particularly those instincts that tend to be the cause of so much bitter conflict and destruction. Once we understand the nature of our self-destructive instincts, only then will we be able to channel those same energies into more productive outlets, and, consequently, to maximize our species' potential for prosperity and peace.

Furthermore, because our inherent religious impulses compel us to believe in an afterlife, it's possible that we tend to take less responsibility for our actions here on earth. Because we instinctively believe that this life represents a mere stop-over in eternal existence, we allow ourselves to be profligate. Because we inherently perceive ourselves as immortal, we place less meaning and significance on perfecting ourselves within this lifetime, as well as in preserving the conditions of this, our earthly environment. Why, after all, worry about the earth when we'll be spending the rest of eternity somewhere else? How else are we to explain the manner in which we recklessly continue to exploit and butcher this planet—as if we're the last living generation?

So why not use the same methodology that has enabled us to master our environments, to master ourselves? Science. Isn't it time we begin placing the same emphasis we use on perfecting our toys—our space ships, computers, and automobiles—on perfecting ourselves? How much longer will we be slaves to destructive religious credos, before we can transfer our faith over to the natural sciences? Why this need to cling onto the same antiquated paradigms by which we were raised? What if our great, great, great, great—and then some—grandparents were wrong? What if those who believed rain to be mana from heaven and lightning the wrath of God were mistaken?

So, which will it be? Are we to accept the underlying principles conceived in scientific method—in reason—or are we to obstinately hold on to those antiquated belief systems that sprang from our pre-scientific, ignorant past? In prior times, it was considered blasphemy to believe that the earth revolved around the sun. Since such primitive times, science has sent men to the moon and back. In the past, it was considered sinful to perform an autopsy, that is, to study human anatomy and physiology. Now, as a result of the physiological sciences, we've developed a plethora of medical technologies that have eased our pains as well as extended our life span. And yet, in a society as modern as ours, in the world's most powerful democracy, we still find ourselves battling against the suppressive forces of religious ultra-conservatism and fundamentalism. In as modern an age as ours, we still live in a nation in which the same evolutionary principles that brought us so many life-enriching technologies struggles to be taught in the classroom. And why? Because religious values, which often seek to impede the march of scientific progress and reason, continue to play a significant role in human nature and therefore in human politics.

We rely on our religions to tell us what is acceptable versus unacceptable, what we should and shouldn't do, what we can and can't say or think. Religion acts as a constricting force, constantly trying to obstruct the flow of any information it might construe as a threat to its own obsolete ideology. In this way, religion confines us. It limits our field of vision. It tries to place us in a narrow box and bind us within. Should we seek to step outside the confines of that box, to merely take a peek at the world of possibilities beyond, we are to be shunned by our community. Why then, when this life may be our last, should we want to limit ourselves in such a way?

Not to suggest that there should be no limits set on human behavior. As a social animal, with often runaway impulses, there's nothing wrong with a bit of healthy restraint. By no means would I encourage the dissolution of all codes of behavior and conduct. Nevertheless, do we necessarily want these codes to be based on antiquated mythologies? Through the careful application of scientific method we know more about the origins and nature of human behavior than ever before. Why then would we want to rely on systems that were based on the whims of men's imaginations, on untested and unproven hunches, to decide social doctrine? Isn't it time we finally discard our dated paradigms and replace them with methods that can at least be validated? How much more evidence do we need before we will finally embrace the scientific process? And if we do, shouldn't we seek to resolve our social and ethical dilemmas through this same medium? As the sociologist Auguste Compte expressed it, "Only those willing to submit themselves to the rigorous constraints of scientific methodology and to the canons of scientific evidence should presume to have a say in the guidance of human affairs. Just as freedom of opinion makes no sense in astronomy or physics, it is similarly inappropriate in the social sciences" (Compte 1798 - 1857, as cited by Coser, 1977).

Only once the human animal comes to terms with the fact that it has been born into a mental matrix—a neurological web of fantasy and deceit—will we have a chance of offsetting this potentially destructive impulse within us. Knowledge is power, and it is high time that the science of neurotheology be made available to the world so that our species might see another way. It is time that the science of religiosity be taken out of the hands of philosophers, metaphysicians, and theologians and "biologized."

Not to suggest that we should seek to eradicate religion altogether but rather that we try to put it into scientific perspective. In itself, there is nothing wrong with engaging an impulse that helps to bond communities as well as to give individuals a sense of purpose and belonging. Apparently, our religious impulse serves a very critical function in us, otherwise Nature most probably would not have selected such a mechanism. It is rather the excesses of our religious impulse that represents the greatest threat. In its extreme, the religious impulse fosters a fanatacism that promotes dangerously discriminatory and martyristic behaviors. And though this same impulse may sometimes be used to promote such positive virtues as charity and good-will, it often only ends up fueling the flames of religious fundamentalism. Nevertheless, by merely brow-beating and ridiculing the religious, they will never be converted to reason. By explaining to them, however, that there is a real underlying logic—a "neurotheology" (to coin a term by Aldous Huxley from his 1962 novel, *Island*)—through which to rationally explain our religious propensities, they might be more inclined to at least consider this as a possibility.

Suppose we are devoid of spirit, composed of matter and nothing more. If true, we must learn to view ourselves as organic machines. Not until we accomplish this will we be able to effectively act as our own mechanics. If we truly possess a neurophysiologically-based religious impulse, one that has prompted us to engage in acts of aggression, hostility, and war, shouldn't we seek to master it? If we truly are ticking biological time bombs, shouldn't we seek to diffuse ourselves?

Besides, if there truly is no spiritual reality, just think of all of the energy we've wasted in practicing our illusionary beliefs. Think of all of the useless rituals and ceremonies we've performed, all of the sacrifices we've made, the shrines we've built, the purses we've filled, the gods we've worshipped and prayed to and, meanwhile, all of it in vain. If there truly is no spiritual realm, we've been little more than a species of primitives paying homage to thin air. Imagine what a group of onlooking extraterrestrials would think after witnessing our behavior. "Look at the monkey people," they would say, "offering sacrifices to the void; killing, defiling, and warring with one another over literally nothing; banging their chests and wailing at the wind, all in the vain hope that it might incite some imaginary force to save them from their inevitable fates."

If it's true that there is no spiritual reality, God, soul, or afterlife, then let's accept ourselves for what we are and make the most of it. Perhaps such a change in our self-perceptions might help us to shift our priorities from the hereafter to the here and now, to deter future wars, and, ultimately, to minimize our pain and suffering and to maximize our chances of obtaining the greatest amount of peace and prosperity in life. This, more than anything, is what I would hope to gain from a scientific interpretation of human spirituality and God. Here lies the utility of the science of neurotheolgy.

Figure 154. (above)" And Satan... smote Job with boils." -W. Blake. (Below) Satan contemplating evil and destruction.

SEX, VIOLENCE &
RELIGIOUS EXPERIENCE
by R. Joseph

THE LIMBIC SYSTEM & VIOLENT BEHAVIOR

The neocortical surface of the brain (the so called "gray matter") is the seat of the rational mind, being concerned with language, math, reasoning, and higher level cognitive capacities. Beneath this neocortical mantle, buried within the depths of the cerebrum are several large aggregates of limbic structures and nuclei which are preeminent in the control and mediation of all aspects of emotion including violent, aggressive, sexual, and social behavior and the formation of loving attachments. The limbic system controls the capacity to experience love and sorrow, and governs and monitors internal homeostasis and basic needs such as hunger and thirst, including even the cravings for pleasure-inducing drugs (Bernardis & Bellinger 1987; Childress, et al., 1999; Gloor 1992, 1997; LeDoux 1992, 1996; MacLean, 1973, 1990; Rolls, 1984, 1992; Smith et al. 1990). Over the course of evolution, the forebrain and much of the neocortex (and the so called "rational mind") evolved in response to and so as to better serve the limbic system and fulfill and satisfy limbic needs.

However, the limbic system is not only predominant in regard to all aspects of motivational and emotional functioning, but is capable of completely overwhelming "the rational mind" due in part to the massive axonal projections of the amygdala upon the neocortex. Although over the course of evolution a new brain (neocortex) has developed, Homo sapiens sapiens ("the wise may who knows he is wise") remains a creature of emotion. Humans have not completely emerged from the phylogenetic swamps of their original psychic existence. Hence, due to these limbic roots, humans not uncommonly behave "irrationally" or in the "heat of passion," and thus act at the behest of their immediate desires; sometimes falling "madly in love" and at other times, acting in a blind rage such that even those who are 'loved" may be slaughtered and murdered.

The schism between the rational and the emotional is real, and is due to the raw energy of emotion having it's source in the nuclei of the ancient limbic lobe — a series of structures which first make their phylogenetic appearance over a hundred million years before humans walked upon this Earth and which continue to control and direct human behavior.

Humans, although rational creatures, are also killers, men in particular. Men are natural born killers, which is why the history of human affairs is written in gore and blood. This sad state of affairs is due to the incredible power of the limbic system which, when aroused, can hijack and gain complete control over the rational mind. Unfortunately, as the limbic brain also mediates spirituality and religious experience, not uncommonly the worst of crimes and the worst of murders, are committed in the name of god and in the name of religion.

FUNCTIONAL OVERVIEW

In general, the primary structures of the limbic system include the hypothalamus, amygdala, hippocampus, septal nuclei, and anterior cingulate gyrus; structures which are directly interconnected by massive axonal pathways (Gloor, 1997; MacLean, 1990; Risvold & Swanson, 1996). With the exception of the cingulate which is referred to as "transitional" cortex (mesocortex) and consists of five layers, the hypothalamus, amygdala, hippocampus, septal nuclei are considered allocortex, consisting of at most, 3 layers.

The hypothalamus could be considered the most "primitive" aspect of the limbic system, though in fact the functioning of this sexually dimorphic structure is exceedingly complex. The hypothalamus regulates internal homeostasis including the experience of hunger and thirst, can trigger rudimentary sexual behaviors or generate feelings of extreme rage or pleasure. In conjunction with the pituitary the hypothalamus is a major manufacturer/secretor of hormones and other bodily humors, including those involved in the stress response and feelings of depression.

The amygdala has been implicated in the generation of the most rudimentary and the most profound of human emotions, including fear, sexual desire, rage, religious ecstasy, or at a more basic level, determining if something might be good to eat. The amygdala is implicated in the seeking of loving attachments and the formation of long term emotional memories. It contains neurons which become activated in response to the human face, and which become activated in response to the direction of someone else's gaze. The amygdala also acts directly on the hypothalamus via the stria terminalis, medial forebrain bundle, and amygdalafugal pathways, and in this manner can control hypothalamic impulses. The amygdala is also directly connected to the hippocampus, with which it interacts in regard to memory.

The amygdala maintains a functionally interdependent relationship with the hypothalamus in regard to emotional, sexual, autonomic, consumatory and motivational concerns. It is able to modulate and even control rudimentary emotional forces governed by the hypothalamic nucleus. However, the amygdala also acts at the behest of hypothalamically induced drives. For example, if certain nutritional requirements need to be meet, the hypothalamus signals the amygdala which then surveys the external environment for something good to eat (Joseph, 1982, 1992a). On the other hand, if the amygdala via environmental surveillance were to discover a potentially threatening stimulus, it acts to excite and drive the hypothalamus as well as the basal ganglia so that the organism is mobilized to take appropriate action.

When the hypothalamus is activated by the amygdala, instead of responding in an on/off manner, cellular activity continues for an appreciably longer time period (Dreifuss et. al., 1968). The amygdala can tap into the reservoir of emotional energy mediated by the hypothalamus so that certain ends may be attained.

LIMBIC LUST, MURDER, AND RELIGIOUS EXPERIENCE

The amygdala and hypothalamus often act in a highly coordinated manner in reaction to an exceedingly important emotional stimulus, or in response to a specific limbic need, such as hunger, thirst, rage, or sexual desire (Joseph, 1992a, 1996; MacLean 1969, 1990). For example, in response to hypothalamically monitored needs (hunger, sexual desire), the amygdala may scan the environment until it determines that a particular food item or person, has the necessary attributes (Gloor 1992; Joseph 1992a,b, 1996; Kling et al., 1987; O'Keefe and Bouma 1969; Ursin and Kaada 1960). In response to urgent hypothalamic desires, the amygdala might even assign sexual attributes to an individual that normally might not be viewed as sexually enticing.

It is also through hypothalamic and amygdala activity that a particular item or object (e.g. a banana) might be viewed as both a food item and sexual object. Or conversely, why certain individuals may be viewed as sexual as well as aversive and hateful (e.g. one's husband or wife). Indeed, because the hypothalamus and amygdala are so concerned with sex, rage, fear, and hunger, not only may these attributes be assigned to one individual, animal, or object simultaneously (e.g. fear of the beast one is going to enjoy killing and eating; hunger, guilt, and aversion regarding a high caloric treat; hatred for a loved one) but these conflicting emotions may be combined so as to give rise to exceedingly intense, albeit abstract emotional states; e.g. religious awe as well as religioius rage.

HYPOTHALAMIC RAGE

Stimulation of the lateral hypothalamus can induce extremes in emotionality, including intense attacks of rage accompanied by biting and attack upon any moving object (Flynn et al. 1971; Gunne & Lewander, 1966; Wasman & Flynn, 1962). If this nucleus is destroyed, aggressive and attack behavior is abolished (Karli & Vergness, 1969). Hence, the lateral hypothalamus is responsible for rage and aggressive behavior.

The lateral maintains an oppositional relationship with the medial hypothalamus. Hence, stimulation of the medial region counters the lateral area such that rage reactions are reduced or eliminated (Ingram, 1952; Wheately, 1944), whereas if the medial is destroyed there results lateral hypothalamic release and the triggering of extreme savagery.

Inflammation, neoplasm, and compression of the hypothalamus have also been noted to give rise to rage attacks (Pilleri & Poeck, 1965), and surgical manipulations or tumors within the hypothalamus have been observed to elicit manic and rage-like outbursts (Alpers, 1940). These appear to be release phenomenon, however. That is, rage, attack, aggressive, and related behaviors associated with the hypothalamus appears to be under the inhibitory influence of higher order limbic nuclei such as the amygdala and septum (Siegel & Skog, 1970). When the controlling pathways between these areas are damaged (i.e. disconnection) sometimes these behaviors are elicited.

For example, Pilleri and Poeck (1965) described a man with severe damage throughout the

Figure 155a. The nuclei of the Hypothalamus. From Carpenter, 1991.

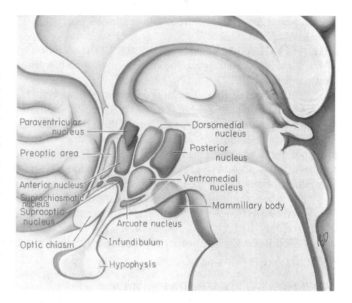

cerebrum including the amygdala, hippocampus, cingulated, but with complete sparing of the hypothalamis who continually reacted with howling, growling, and baring of teeth in response to noise, a slight touch, or if approached. Hence, the hypothalamus being released responds reflexively in an aggressive-like non-specific manner to any stimulus. Lesions of the frontal-hypothalamic pathways have been noted to result in severe rage reactions as well (Fulton & Ingraham, 1929; Kennard, 1945).

THE AMYGDALA AND RAGE

Fear and rage reactions have also been triggered in humans following depth electrode stimulation of the amygdala (Chapman, 1960; Chapman et al., 1954; Heath et al. 1955; Mark et al. 1972). Mark et al. (1972) describe one female patient who following amygdaloid stimulation became irritable and angry, and then enraged. Her lips retracted, there was extreme facial grimmacning, threatening behavior, and then rage and attack—all of which persisted well beyond stimulus termination.

Similarly, Schiff et al. (1982) describe a man who developed intractable aggression following a head injury and damage (determined via depth electrode) to the amygdala (i.e. abnormal electrical activity). Subsequently, he became easily enraged, sexually preoccupied (although sexually hypoactive), and developed hyper-religiosity and psuedo-mystical ideas. Tumors invading the amygdala have also been reported to trigger rage attacks (Sweet et al. 1960; Vonderache, 1940).

In many instances patients or animals will react defensively and with anger, irritation, and rage which seems to gradually build up until finally the animal or human will attack (Egger & Flynn, 1963; Gunne & Lewander, 1966; Mark et al., 1972 Ursin & Kaada, 1960; Zbrozyna, 1963). Unlike hypothalamic "sham rage," amygdaloid activation results in attacks directed at something real, or, in the absence of an actual stimulus, at something imaginary. There have been reported instances of patient's suddenly lashing out and even attempting to attack those close by, while in the midst of a temporal lobe seizure (Saint-Hilaire et al., 1980), and/or attacking, kicking, and destroying furniture and other objects (Ashford et al., 1980).

Moreover, rage and attack will persist well beyond the termination of the electrical stimulation of the amygdala. In fact, the amygdala remains electrophysiologically active for long time periods even after a stimulus has been removed (be it external-perceptual, or internal-electrical) such that is appears to contine to process—in the abstract—information even when that information is no longer observable (O'Keefe & Bouma, 1969).   The individual may therefore remain enraged or fearful long after the threat or offending party had departed the scene. The amygdala makes it possible to feel moody.

The amygdals appears capable of not only triggering and steering hypothalamic activity but acting on higher level neocortical processes so that individuals form emotional ideas. Indeed, the amygdala is able to overwhelm the neocortex and the rest of the brain so so that the person not only forms emotional ideas but responds to them, sometimes with vicious, horrifying results. A famous example of this is Charles Whitman, who in 1966 climbed a tower at the University of Texas and began to indiscriminantly kill people with a rifle (Whitman Case File # M968150, Austin Police Department, Texas, The Texas Department of Public Safety, File #4-38).

Charles Whitman climbed the University tower carrying several guns, a sawed off shotgun, and a high powered hunting rifle, and for the next 90 minutes he shot at everything that moved, killing 14, wounding 38.   Post-mortem autopsy of his brain revealed a glioblastoma multiforme tumor the size of a walnut, erupting from beneath the thalamus, impacting the hypothalamus, extending into the temporal lobe and compressing the amygdaloid nucleus (Charles J. Whitman Catastrophe, Medical Aspects. Report to Governor, 9/8/66).

THE AMYGDALA, FEAR, AND THE LORD

"And now Israel, what does the Lord your god require of you, but to fear the Lord your god." - Deuteronomy 10:12.

The amygdala in particular is exceedingly important in generating feelings of fear (Davis et al., 1997; Gloor, 1992, 1997; Halgren, 1992; Rosen & Schulkin 1998; Scott et al., 1997; Williams 1956) as well as sexuality, rage, and hunger. In this regard, feelings of religious awe may be based on fear (d'Aquili and Newberg 1993), rage, extreme, hunger, or sexual arousal. Fear, however, is often the most potent means of eliciting religious feeling, for even a committed atheist when confronted with the possibility of a horrifying death may cry out to god. The "Lord God" Yahweh, in fact, depends on fear, and glories in terrifying his subjects in order to reveal his presence and power:

"The beginning of wisdom is the fear of the Lord." -Proverbs 1:7, 9:10, 15:33.

"And now, Israel, what does the Lord your god require of you, but to fear the Lord your god." -Deuteronomy 10:12.

"God has come... in order that the fear of Him may be ever with you so that you do not go astray." -Exodus 20:17.

THE FRONTAL-TEMPORAL LOBES

In addition to the amygdala, temporal lobe and hippocampus, d'Aquili and Newberg (1993) point out that the right frontal lobe also plays a significant role in the generation of mystical experience. It is thus noteworthy that the right frontal lobe can pray, swear, and curse "God" even when the (speaking) left cerebral hemisphere has been severely damaged and the patient is aphasic and can no longer speak (Joseph, 1982, 1988a, 1999a).

The right frontal and temporal lobe, hypothalamus, and amygdala also interact in regard to sexual arousal (Freemon & Nevis 1969; Joseph, 1986a, 1988a, 1992a, 1999a; MacLean 1969, 1990; Remmillard et al. 1983; Robinson & Mishkin 1968; Spencer et al., 1983). This is a very important relationship, and in part explains why (although there are exceptions), religions tend to be quite sexual and/or exceedingly concerned with sexual mores and related activity. As is well known, female pregnancy and matters pertaining to birth control and abortion are of extreme concern to most modern as well as ancient religions (Campbell 1988; Frazier 1955; Parrinder 1980; Smart 1969).

The limbic system as well as the frontal and temporal lobes are highly concerned with acting on or inhibiting aggression and murderous rage reactions which also arise in the limbic system (Joseph 1986, 1988, 1992a, 1996). This may also explain why many religious sects are so "righteously" belligerent and hateful and have employed torture, human or animal sacrifice, and sanctioned if not encouraged the murder of nonbelievers: What could be referred to as limbic-religious blood lust.

"Shed man's blood, by man your blood be shed." -Genesis 9:6.

SHED MAN'S BLOOD

The "Lord God," Yahweh, repeatedly required that the ancient Israelites undergo a bloody ritual of submission (e.g. Exodus 24:1-14), and in fact proscribed a ritual of incredible bloodiness for the investiture of his priests (Exodus 29: 1-46). This "Lord God" also required the slaughter and sacrifice of living creatures whose blood is splashed on his altar, and on his priests.

For example, upon the ratification of the covenant, twelve oxen were drained of their blood, one oxen for each of the 12 tribes of Israel, and as it was splashed on the people, Moses says" This is the blood of the covenant that the Lord now makes with you concerning these commands" (Exodus 24:8). In yet another bloody ritual a bull is slaughtered then a ram, then yet another ram, and their blood is splashed and smeared on the altars, on the priests, and on the people, and climaxes with those who are being ordained as priests holding up bloody pieces of the body (Exodus 29: 10-28).

King Solomon slaughtered 22,000 oxen and 22,000 sheep as an offering to this "Lord God" whose loves meat, but not his vegetables.

In fact, as this "Lord God" is apparently a meat eater, this may explain why he criticized Cain, a tiller of the soil, and rejected his first harvest offering of fruit and vegetables that he had grown with his own hand (Genesis, 4):

"And in the process of time it can to pass that Cain brought of the fruit of the ground and offering until the Lord. And Abel, he also brought of the firstlings of his flock and the fat thereof. And

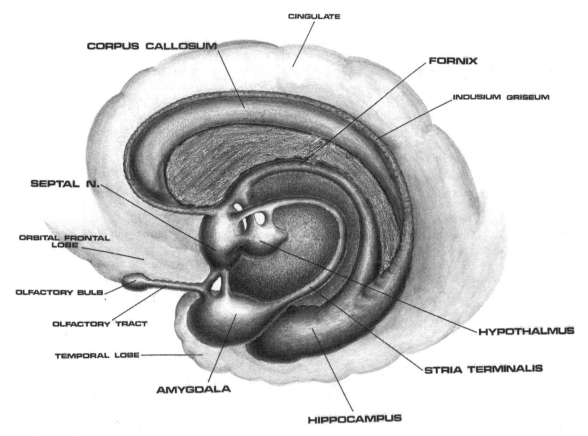

Figure 155b. The nuclei of the limbic system, From Joseph, 1990.

the Lord had respect unto Abel and to his offering: But unto Cain and to his offering he had not respect." -Genesis 4.3-5.

For ancient hunters, aggression and the killing of animals (and other humans) was a way of life. Hunters often employed hunting magic and related religious rituals to insure success. Religion and murder, like religion and sex, are linked to the limbic system and evolved accordingly. Consequently, when in the throes of religious excitement, torture and murder may even receive the blessing or might be actively encouraged by one's "God."

The "Lord God" enjoys killing people, and informs Moses that even those who wish to convert should be slaughtered: "You shall make no covenant with them... " and "I will blot out their memory... The Lord will be at war with Amalek throughout the ages" (Exodus 17:14-16). This Lord God, will in fact engage in widespread ethnic cleansing and genocide, and will also impose a rein of terror on His own people (e.g., Exodus 32: 26-29, 35). The Lord God loves to spill the blood of innocent and guilty alike.

On the other hand, the blood sacrifice is also related to the worship of the goddess, the Great Mother of All. It is menstrual blood which issues from the womb, the source of all life, and the rites of the goddess cult involved sanctifying and splashing menstrual blood on the altar. Hence, many ancient patriarchal religions appear to have adopted this practice, with the notable exception that instead of using the blood to celebrate life, the purpose of these bloody rituals was to evoke the power to take life which would be sacrificed to a warring, meat eating, God.

WARRIOR GODS: FEAR AND PANIC

Throughout history, many of the patriarchal Gods have been aggressive, jealous, conquering, angry and war-like e.g., Marduk, Mazda, Zeus, Apollo, Mars, and Yahweh "the Lord of hosts." For example, in addition to being described as the "Lord of hosts," Yahweh also means: "The Destroyer."

These warrior gods, including Yahweh, were prone to mass murder and extremely violent rages. Yahweh repeatedly threatened and engaged in the slaughter of enemies and believers alike, without mercy or regard for women and children. Terror, war, and murder: the Lord God's middle names.

"Terror, and the pit, and the snare are upon you, O inhabitant of earth (Isaiah 24:17). And as the Lord took delight in doing you good and multiplying you, so the Lord will take delight in bringing ruin upon you and destroying you (Deuteronomy 26:63). The Lord will bring a nation against you from afar, from the end of the earth, which will swoop down like the eagle... a ruthless nation, that will show the old no regard and the young no mercy (Deuteronomy 28:47-50). It shall devour the offspring... you shall eat your own issue, the flesh of your sons and daughters... until He has wiped you out... leaving you nothing... until it has brought ruin unto you..." (Deuteronomy 28:50-55).

"In the Name of God... by the Troops shall the unbelievers be driven towards Hell, until when they reach it, its gates shall be opened... for just is the sentence of punishment on the unbelievers... " - Koran, XXXIX

"Behold I send an angel before thee, to keep thee in the way. Beware of him and obey his voice, for I will be an enemy unto thine enemies, and an adversary unto thine adversaries, and I will cut them off... .I will send my terror before thee, and will destroy all the people to whom thou shalt come.... and I will drive them out from before thee, until thou be increased and inherit the land." -Exodus 23:20-30

"...when you approach a town, you shall lay seizure to it, and when the Lord your god delivers it into your hand, you shall put all its males to the sword. You may, however, take as your booty the women, the children, the livestock, and everything in the town—all its spoils—and enjoy the spoil of your enemy which the Lord your god gives you... In the towns of the people which the Lord your god is giving you as a heritage, you shall not let a soul remain alive." -Exodus 20:15-18; -Deuteronomy 20:12-16

"When Israel had killed all the inhabitants of Ai... and all of them, to the last man had fallen by the sword, all the Israelites turned back to Ai and put it to the sword...until all the inhabitants of Ai had been exterminated... and the king of Ai was impaled on a stake and it was left lying at the entrance to the city gate." -Deuteronomy 8:24-29.

In fact, the Lord God condemned even his most loyal followers if they dared to show even the slightest mercy even to animals (e.g., I Samuel 28:18-19). The Lord God, as described in the Old Testament, had what might best be described as a hair trigger temper, such that at the slightest sign of murmuring he would pounce and kill men, women, and children, the innocent and guilty alike including those of his own people. As is evident, for example, in the story of Exodus, the people were His prisoners, and He killed or insured that every adult who exited Egypt would die in the desert, including even Moses for making but one small mistake in following His orders: Instead of ordering a rock to give water, Moses tapped it with his cain. For this "sin," the Lord God kills Moses with a Divine kiss.

LIMBIC AND RELIGIOUS MASS MURDER

ETHNIC CLEANSING, AND GENETIC GENOCIDE

Led by Moses, and their "Lord God" the ancient Hebrews/Israelites murdered untold numbers, perhaps hundreds of thousands of innocent men, women, children, including even their livestock. These atrocities were committed against all manner of innocent peoples not because they had sinned, but because they happened to be along the path to the "promised land" and because they had the misfortune of living on land and possessing property that the "Lord God" wanted to give to his people.

"When the Lord they God shall bring thee into the land, and shall cast out many nations before thee, the Hittite, and the Gergashite, and the Amorite, and the Canaanite, and the Perizzite, and the Hivite, and the Jebusite... and the Lord thy god shall deliver them up before thee, and thou shalt smite them, then thou shall utterly destroy them."-Deuteronomy 7:1-2.

"Of the cities of these peoples, that the Lord they God giveth thee for an inheritance, thou shalt save alive nothing that breathest." -Deuteronomy, 20:16.

Moreover, "God" gloried not only in the murder of innocent women and children, but took special satisfaction in the theft of their property—the spoils of a godly-genocidal war. The Lord God believed that theft and injustice was a testament to his glory as a conquering warrior god.

"Great and goody cities, which thou didst not build and houses full of all good things which thou didst not fill, and cisterns hewn, which thou didst not hew, and vineyards and olive-trees, which thou didst not plant, and thou shalt eat and be satisfied." -Deuteronomy 6:10-11.

Yahweh, the Lord of Hosts, the "Destroyer," apparently so enjoyed the spectacle of mass murder, that once he began to kill He found it difficult to stop, killing everything and everyone, the guilty and the innocent, the righteous and the wicked, and even their animals. Apparently only blood and more blood, the signs of death, could protect the innocent, and cool his ardor for indiscriminate mass murder, which is why He explains to Moses that the only way to protect himself and the Jewish people from slaughter was by painting their doors red with blood: "When I see the blood" He informs Moses, "I will pass over you, and there shall be no plague upon you to destroy you, when I smite the land of Egypt" (Exodus 12:12-13).

It was only the sight of blood which prevented Yahweh from killing Moses almost immediately after informing him that he was to lead the Israelites out of Egypt.

"And the Lord said unto Moses...Go... And it came to pass by the way in the inn, that the Lord met him and sought to kill him. Then Zipporah" (the wife of Moses) "took a sharp stone and cut off the foreskin of her son, and cast it at his feet, and said, Surely a bloody husband art though to me."

Why would the "Lord God" seek to kill his prophet? There are many possibilities, all of which may have provoked "Lord God's" inherent murderous nature. For example, Moses dilly dallied and did not go directly to Egypt as he had been commanded. In addition, the "Lord God" may have been provoked to rage because Moses had failed to circumcise his son. Moses never did escape the wrath of the "Lord" for the "Lord God" kills Moses just as he and the Israelites are on the verge of entering the promised land.

THOU SHALT KILL AND KILL AND KILL

Despite the commandment "thou shall not kill" Yahweh kills and murders the innocent and guilty alike and encourages and in fact orders the Israelites to murder even babies and women with children.

"And they warred... as the Lord commanded and slew all the males. And they slew the Kings... and they took all the women and their little ones... and they burnt all their cities wherein they dwelt, and all their goodly castles with fire... And Moses was wroth...and said unto them. Have ye saved all the women and the little ones alive? Now therefore kill every male among the little ones, and kill every woman that hath known man by lying with him." (Numbers, 31).

As repeatedly detailed in Exodus, the "Lord God" purposefully and repeatedly "hardened Pharaoh's heart" simply as an excuse for murdering innocent Egyptians, so that He could glory in the carnage.

"I will harden Pharaoh's heart that I may multiply My signs and marvels in The land of Egypt. When the Pharaoh does not heed you, I will lay My hand upon Egypt." -Exodus 7:3.

Moreover, it is not just Egyptians or the hapless innocents who the Israelites and their Lord God murder in their 40 years of wondering, but tens of thousands if not hundreds of thousands of Jews. The Lord God kills them for rebelling, He kills them for "murmuring," He kills them for complaining, He kills them for questioning. And He kills their wives, brothers, fathers, mothers, and children: "Go forth and slay brother, neighbor, and kin" (Genesis, 32:26-29).

For example, when Moses ascended the Mountain to meet with the Lord God, the Israelites grew impatient with the hardships and murders they were forced to endure, and they turned again to worshipping the scared goddess, as represented by the golden calf. In reaction, Yahweh thunders and his prophet Moses proclaims that innocent and guilty alike shall be murdered: "Put ye every man his sword upon his thigh and slay every man...his brother, and every man his companion, and every man his neighbor and kin" (Genesis, 32:26-29).

When Moses proclaimed the Israelites a "nation of priests," some of the Israelites then dared to ask: if "Every member of the community is holy and the Lord is among them all... Why do you set yourselves up above the assembly of the Lord?" The response? Those who dared to ask questions are killed, including their wives, children, brothers and neighbors: "And the Earth opened her mouth and swallowed them" (Numbers, 16:32).

The ancient Israelis not only received special permission from their "Lord God" to murder wayward Jews, non-Jews and Jewish nonbelievers, including women and children whom they slaughtered without mercy (e.g. Numbers, 3115-18; Numbers 34, 50-53), but even Jewish babies. Indeed, it was a Hebrew religious-tradition to kill and slaughter not only non-Jewish males in general but first born Jewish sons (a custom until the time of Moses, e.g. Bergmann 1992).

SACRIFICIAL MURDERS

Human sacrifice was a common feature of many ancient religions, and serves as one of the founding stones of Christianity: The Lord God's sacrifice of his son, Jesus, on the Cross. Hence, it is said that "Christ died for your sins." Christ was sacrificed as an offering to the Lord God, so as to wash away the sins of the masses—or so claims the Roman Catholic Church.

The Lord God showed a particular fondness for killing first born sons, including the first born of the ancient Egyptians, as well as his own people.

"A blessing on him who seizes your babies and dashes them against rocks." -Psalm 137:9).

"I polluted them with their own offerings, making them sacrifice all their firstborn, which was to punish them, so that they would learn that I am Yahweh." -Ezekiel 20:25-36; 22:28-29.

This "Lord God" even required the death of the first born son of King David and his wife Bethsheba, despite the fact that He claimed to have loved David most dearly. However, by killing this little boy, "God" in effect pardoned King David for repeatedly breaking two of His commandments, i.e., murder (of Bethsheba's husband) and adultery. Thus, the son of David was sacrificed by the Lord God so as to cleanse David of his sins, including, perhaps his sinful propensity for having sex with other men's wives (e.g. Abigail wife of Nabal, and Michal wife of Paltiel). However, David the murderer and adulterer, was also a fierce warrior who had killed tens of thousands, including even tens of thousands of Jews—and this "Lord God" loved him most dearly.

Sacrificial murder, therefore, is a way of indicating atonement, and for obtaining favor from one's god, including the Lord God. For thousands of years it has been a world wide religious custom to sacrifice captured warriors, young virgins, and especially children.

In some ancient societies children were killed because they were "pure" and precious. Thus the death of these innocent children could be considered a true sacrifice. Moreover, the ancient gods, including Yahweh, required that those murdered in their glory, be pure and without blemish. Children, and virgins, therefore, were a natural choice.

First born sons in particular were singled out for this honor as many ancient religions held to the belief that the first born was the offspring of a god who had opened the womb and impregnated the mother. This belief may even have caused the Lord God some consternation, for he not only required the killing of the first born, but he repeatedly shows favor to second born sons, e.g., Abel over Cain, Isaac instead of Ishmael, Jacob instead of Esau, Ephram over Manasseh, Solomon the second born son of David and Bethsheba, and so on.

It was also believed by many pagan groups that because a god may have impregnated the mother, the god also lost some of his lifeforce in the process. Hence, the first born would be killed to liberate that energy which could then be absorbed by the god.

It may well have been because of these beliefs that other gods were absorbing this life force, that the Lord God, although at first demanding the sacrifice of first born sons, later changed His mind, and condemned the practice:

"This very day you defile yourselves in the presentation of your gifts by making your children pass through the fire of all your fetishes." -Ezekiel 20:31.

CHRISTIAN HOLY WARS

KILL THEM ALL: GOD WILL RECOGNIZE HIS OWN

It was upon these images of the murdering warrior God, the Lord of Hosts, that Pope Urban II proclaimed that war for the sake of God was holy. Thus, the Catholic Popes instigated numerous Crusades and inquisitions. In consequence hundreds of thousands of Moslems, Jews, and women and children, were sexually tortured, slaughtered, spitted, and roasted alive, and their cities and villages pillaged and set ablaze. All in the name of the Lord God. So intense was their limbic blood lust that even Christians were murdered.

For example, in the 13th Century an army of some thirty thousand Christian knights and Crusaders descended into southern France and attacked the town of Beziers in search of heretics. Over thirteen thousand Christians flocked to the churches for protection. When the Bishop, one of the Pope's representatives, was informed that the army was unable to distinguish between true believers and heretics, he replied, "Kill them all. God will recognize his own."

However, in order to recruit those worthy of such a glorious and murderous undertaking, the Pope had to appeal to murderers, rapists, molesters of children, and those who enjoyed the prolonged torture of their victims.

"You oppressors of orphans, you robbers of widows, you homicides, you blasphemers, you plunderers of others' rights... If you want to take counsel for your souls you must go forward boldly as knights of Christ..." so proclaimed the Pope who offered "indulgences" and forgiveness to all those who would commit blasphemies and murder women and children in the name of the Lord God and Jesus Christ.

Figure 156. *(Above) According to Catholic Dominican Bishop Bartolom de Las Casas, the Indian natives were hung and burnt alive "in groups of 13... thus honoring our Savior and the 12 apostles." Because some of the victims managed to live throughout the night, the Dominican priests ordered that sticks be shoved down their throats so the soldiers and priests would not be kept awake at night by their cries and moans. Woodcut by De la Bray, 15th century.*

(Right) The Aztecs regularly practiced human sacrifice. A victim lies dead at the foot of the temple steps, whereas the warrior at top has his chest cut open by the temple priest, which allows his soul to ascend skyward leaving behind a bloody trail.

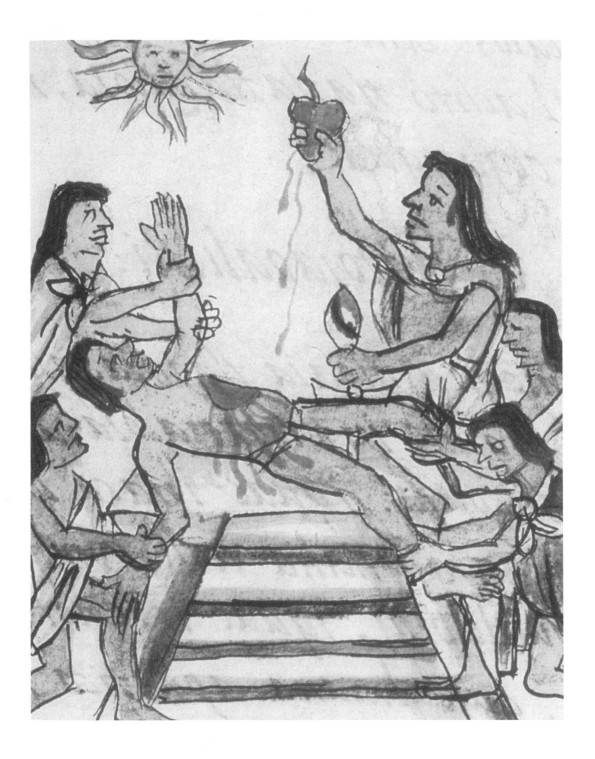

Figure 157. *The Aztecs regularly practiced human sacrifice by cutting out the hearts of captured warriors in honor of their god.*

As summed up by Henry Charles Lea: "Protestants and Catholics rivaled each other in the madness of the hours... Christendom seemed to have grown delirious, and Satan might well have smiled at the tribute to his powers seen in the endless smoke of the holocaust which bore witness to his triumph over the Almighty."

Again, however, although "Lord God" of the "Old Testament" repeatedly approved of mass murder and rape, and in fact employed these practices against His own people, Jesus Christ obviously did not preach mass murder, torture, rape, pedophilia, and the castration of young boys: "But love ye your enemies and do good and lend, hoping for nothing and your reward shall be great. Be ye merciful...judge not, and ye shall not be judged: condemn not and ye shall not be condemned: forgive and ye shall be forgiven" (Luke, 7: 35-37); "For the Son of man is not come to destroy men's lives, but to save them" (Luke 10: 56; however, see Matthew 10:16 vs 34-35).

Nevertheless, despite the teaching of Christ, the Catholic Church fully approved of castration, mass murder, and the most horrible of tortures. Indeed, as is well known, the Spanish and Catholic missionaries, acting at the behest of the Catholic Popes (and their Spanish/Catholic Sovereigns), continued these Satanic practices once they invaded the America's during the 1500's and up through the 19th century.

As the Catholic Dominican Bishop Bartolom de Las Casas reported to the Pope: the Aztec and Indian natives were hung and burnt alive "in groups of 13... thus honoring our Savior and the 12 apostles." However, because some of the various victims managed to live throughout the night, the Dominican priests ordered that sticks be shoved down their throats so the soldiers and priests would not be kept awake at night by their cries and moans.

Of course the Aztecs did not practice a benign form of worship, for they tore the beating hearts from their victims in order to please their God (Carrasco 1990) and they killed thousands if not hundreds of thousands in so doing.

Similarly, many Indian tribes of the Mississippi valley practiced human sacrifice as did the ancient Jews, Europeans, and leaders of the Protestant Reformation who urged the killing of anyone and everyone who did not agree with their interpretation of the Bible, including fellow Christians:

"Therefore let everyone who can smite, slay, and stab, secretly or openly, remembering that nothing can be more poisonous, hurtful, or devilish that a rebel. It is just as when one must kill a mad dog; if you do not strike him he will strike you, and a whole land with you." -Martin Luther.

What is the origin of these sadistic religious practices? The human limbic system. And, we should recall: the limbic system is concerned not just with sex and violence, but resources, such as food, water, land, and thus territory.

HOLY WAR:
OSAMA BIN LADEN, MOHAMMED ATTA & 9/11

It was thirteen hundred years ago, in the seventh century A.D., that the religion known as Islam arose in the Arabian peninsula. With astonishing rapidity, it quickly spread across and conquered the Middle East, Byzantium, Persia, northern Africa, and Spain.

Islam was spread by the sword.

The armies of the Christian Byzantine Empire were annihilated in 636, and Jerusalem fell in 638.

Four hundred years later, in the year 1095, the Catholic Pope Urban II called upon the nobility and their armies to go to forth and assist their Christian brothers, the Byzantines, and kill the Muslims in the name of God—a cause that could be justified by scripture:

"Behold I send an angel before thee, to keep thee in the way. Beware of him and obey his voice, for I will be an enemy unto thine enemies, and an adversary unto thine adversaries, and I will cut them off... I will send my terror before thee, and will destroy all the people to whom thou shalt come... and I will drive them out from before thee, until thou be increased and inherit the land." - Exodus 23:20-30

However, it was not the pious that Urban desired to fight his wars, but lovers of murder and mayhem. He required killers to do a killer's job. He was interested in recruiting for his holy cause only those who were murderers, rapists, molesters of children and anyone who enjoyed the prolonged torture of their victims.

He had just launched the first crusade.

An important factor that played a role in helping to persuade the nobles and their armies to participate in such a gruesome task so terribly far from home, were the offers of an "indulgence."

An "indulgence" was literally a license to sin, to do harm, and it was a guarantee that all sins would be forgiven by god, no matter how odious the crime.

In consequence, the crusaders not only attacked and massacred the Muslims, successfully re-taking Jerusalem on July 15, 1099, but they massacred their fellow Christians who had the misfortune and bad luck of living in villages that fell along the way—a pattern that was repeated in subsequent Crusades over the centuries.

The Muslims viewed the Christians as "polytheists," and idolaters, and set out to cleanse the Holy lands of these blasphemers.

The Islamic Holy Wars and Counter-Crusades began.

Saladin was the greatest of Muslim generals, and in 1187, he annihilated the entire army of the Kingdom of Jerusalem at the Horns of Hattin, near the Sea of Galilee. Jerusalem had again come under Islamic rule.

Now after nearly a thousand, the "crusader forces" had returned and whereas the Medieval Catholic Church had been driven back and had failed to defeat the Muslim peoples, the United States had succeeded greatly. During the Gulf War America had invaded the holiest of all Muslim lands, the land of Mecca, the Holy land of Saudi Arabia—which was an intolerable affront to 1,400 years of Islamic tradition. It was an afront to Allah, to god.

Over a thousand years ago, after driving out the polytheists and those who worshipped multiple gods and those who profaned the lands of Arabia, the prophet Muhammad had declared that hencefore there shall "not be two religions in Arabia."

Muhammad's words were law—he was the messenger of God.

And now, a thousand years later, the polythiests, the Crusaders had returned.

The presence of foreign troops, with their many gods, was blasphemous. It was a sin. It was a crime against god.

The American led, Western "crusader forces," of course, saw their presence in a whole different light. They were not the invaders. They were in Saudi Arabia to protect it from Saddam Hussein's armies and to liberate Kuwait.

From the perspective of the Americans, they were not an occupying force but remained stationed in Saudi Arabia after the Gulf War, in order to protect the kingdom from Saddam Hussein.

It was not just entirely on religious grounds that bin Laden and other Arabs were incensed. They also believed the presence of the "Crusader Forces" were corrupting the morals of the people and causing the kingdom of Saudi Arabia incredible economic and financial harm.

"The crusader forces became the main cause of our disastrous condition," bin Laden wrote in his 1996 declaration of jihad which read, in part, as follows:

"DECLARATION OF WAR AGAINST THE AMERICANS OCCUPYING THE LAND OF THE TWO HOLY PLACES: EXPEL THE INFIDELS FROM THE ARAB PENINSULA. A MESSAGE FROM USAMA BIN MUHAMMAD BIN IN LADEN"

"Praise be to Allah, we seek His help and ask for his pardon. we take refuge in Allah from our wrongs and bad deeds. Who ever has been guided by Allah will not be misled, and who ever has been misled, he will never be guided. I bear witness that there is no God except Allah, and I bear witness that Muhammad is His slave and messenger.

"It should not be hidden from you that the people of Islam had suffered from aggression, iniquity and injustice imposed on them by the Zionist-Crusaders alliance and their collaborators; to the extent that the Muslims blood became the cheapest and their wealth as loot in the hands of the enemies. Their blood was spilled in Palestine and Iraq. The horrifying pictures of the massacre of Qana, in Lebanon are still fresh in our memory. Massacres in Tajakestan, Burma, Cashmere, Assam, Philippine, Fatani, Ogadin, Somalia, Erithria, Chechnia and in Bosnia-Herzegovina took place, massacres that send shivers in the body and shake the conscience. All of this and the world watch and hear, and not only didn't respond to these atrocities, but also with a clear conspiracy between the USA and its' allies and under the cover of the iniquitous United Nations, the dispossessed people were even prevented from obtaining arms to defend themselves.

"The people of Islam awakened and understood that they were the main targets for the aggression of the Zionist-Crusaders alliance. All false claims and propaganda about "Human Rights" were hammered down and exposed by the massacres that took place against the Muslims in every part of the world.

"The latest and the greatest of these aggressions, incurred by the Muslims since the death of the Prophet (ALLAH'S BLESSING AND SALUTATIONS ON HIM) is the occupation of the land of the two Holy Places -the foundation of the house of Islam, the place of the revelation, the source of the message and the place of the noble Ka'ba, the Qiblah of all Muslims- by the armies of the American Crusaders and their allies. (We bemoan this and can only say: "No power and power acquiring except through Allah")....

"Traitors implement the policy of the enemy in order to bleed the financial and the human resources of the Ummah, and leave the main enemy in the area-the American Zionist alliance enjoy peace and security! This is the policy of the American-Israeli alliance as they are the first to benefit from this situation.

"But with the grace of Allah, the majority of the nation, both civilians and military individuals are aware of the wicked plan. They refused to be played against each other and to be used by the regime as a tool to carry out the policy of the American-Israeli alliance through their agent in our country: the Saudi regime.

"If there are more than one duty to be carried out, then the most important one should receive priority. Clearly after Belief (Imaan) there is no more important duty than pushing the American enemy out of the holy land.

"Ibn Taymiyyah, after mentioning the Moguls (Tatar) and their behavior in changing the law of Allah, stated that: the ultimate aim of pleasing Allah, raising His word, instituting His religion and obeying His messenger (ALLAH'S BLESSING AND SALUTATIONS ON HIM) is to fight the enemy, in every aspects and in a complete manner; if the danger to the religion from not fighting is greater than that of fighting, then it is a duty to fight them even if the intention of some of the fighter is not pure i.e. fighting for the sake of leadership (personal gain) or if they do not observe some of the rules and commandments of Islam. To repel the greater of the two dangers on the expense of the lesser one is an Islamic principle, which should be observed. It was the tradition of the people of the Sunnah (Ahlul-Sunnah) to join and invade- fight- with the righteous and non-righteous men. Allah may support this religion by righteous and non-righteous people as told by the prophet (ALLAH'S BLESSING AND SALUTATIONS ON HIM). If it is not possible to fight except with the help of non-righteous military personnel and commanders, then there are two possibilities: either fighting will be ignored and the others, who are the great danger to this life and religion, will take control; or to fight with the help of non righteous rulers and therefore repelling the greatest of the two dangers and implementing most, though not all, of the Islamic laws...."

In February of 1998, bin Laden published a second declaration of war: Ladenese Epistle.

OSAMA BIN LADEN DECLARES WAR (JIHAD) AGAINST JEWS & THE CRUSADERS

"Praise be to God, who revealed the Book, controls the clouds, defeats factionalism, and says in His Book: "But when the forbidden months are past, then fight and slay the pagans wherever ye find them, seize them, beleaguer them, and lie in wait for them in every stratagem (of war)"; and peace be upon our Prophet, Muhammad Bin-'Abdallah, who said: I have been sent with the sword between my hands to ensure that no one but God is worshipped, God who put my livelihood under the shadow of my spear and who inflicts humiliation and scorn on those who disobey my orders.

"The Arabian Peninsula has never — since God made it flat, created its desert, and encircled it with seas — been stormed by any forces like the crusader armies spreading in it like locusts, eating its riches and wiping out its plantations. All this is happening at a time in which nations are attacking Muslims like people fighting over a plate of food. In the light of the grave situation and the lack of support, we and you are obliged to discuss current events, and we should all agree on how to settle the matter.

"No one argues today about three facts that are known to everyone; we will list them, in order to remind everyone:

"First, for over seven years the United States has been occupying the lands of Islam in the holiest of places, the Arabian Peninsula, plundering its riches, dictating to its rulers, humiliating its people, terrorizing its neighbors, and turning its bases in the Peninsula into a spearhead through which to fight the neighbouring Muslim peoples.

"If some people have in the past argued about the fact of the occupation, all the people of the Peninsula have now acknowledged it. The best proof of this is the Americans' continuing aggression against the Iraqi people using the Peninsula as a staging post, even though all its rulers are against their territories being used to that end, but they are helpless.

"Despite the great devastation inflicted on the Iraqi people by the crusader-Zionist alliance, and despite the huge number of those killed, which has exceeded 1 million... despite all this, the Americans are once against trying to repeat the horrific massacres, as though they are not content with the protracted blockade imposed after the ferocious war or the fragmentation and devastation.

"So here they come to annihilate what is left of this people and to humiliate their Muslim neighbors.

"If the Americans' aims behind these wars are religious and economic, the aim is also to serve the Jews' petty state and divert attention from its occupation of Jerusalem and murder of Muslims there. The best proof of this is their eagerness to destroy Iraq, the strongest neighboring Arab state, and their endeavor to fragment all the states of the region such as Iraq, Saudi Arabia, Egypt and Sudan into paper statelets and through their disunion and weakness to guarantee Israel's survival and the continuation of the brutal crusade occupation of the Peninsula.

"All these crimes and sins committed by the Americans are a clear declaration of war on God, his messenger and Muslims. And ulema have throughout Islamic history unanimously agreed that the jihad is an individual duty if the enemy destroys the Muslim countries. This was revealed by Imam Bin-Qadamah in "Al-Mughni," Imam al-Kisa'i in "Al-Bada'i," al-Qurtubi in his interpretation, and the shaykh of al-Islam in his books, where he said: "As for the fighting to repulse [an enemy], it is aimed at defending sanctity and religion, and it is a duty as agreed [by the ulema]. Nothing is more sacred than belief except repulsing an enemy who is attacking religion and life."

"On that basis, and in compliance with God's order, we issue the following fatwa to all Muslims:

"The ruling to kill the Americans and their allies — civilians and military — is an individual duty for every Muslim who can do it in any country in which it is possible to do it, in order to liberate the al-Aqsa Mosque and the holy mosque [Mecca] from their grip, and in order for their armies to move out of all the lands of Islam, defeated and unable to threaten any Muslim. This is in accordance with the words of Almighty God, "and fight the pagans all together as they fight you all together," and "fight them until there is no more tumult or oppression, and there prevail justice and faith in God."

"This is in addition to the words of Almighty God: "And why should ye not fight in the cause of God and of those who, being weak, are ill-treated (and oppressed)? — women and children, whose cry is: 'Our Lord, rescue us from this town, whose people are oppressors; and raise for us from thee one who will help!'"

"We — with God's help — call on every Muslim who believes in God and wishes to be rewarded to comply with God's order to kill the Americans and plunder their money wherever and whenever they find it. We also call on Muslim ulema, leaders, youths and soldiers to launch the raid on Satan's U.S. troops and the devil's supporters allying with them, and to displace those who are behind them so that they may learn a lesson.

"Almighty God said: "O ye who believe, give your response to God and His Apostle, when He calleth you to that which will give you life. And know that God cometh between a man and his heart, and that it is He to whom ye shall all be gathered."

"Almighty God also says: "O ye who believe, what is the matter with you, that when ye are asked to go forth in the cause of God, ye cling so heavily to the earth! Do ye prefer the life of this world to the hereafter? But little is the comfort of this life, as compared with the hereafter. Unless ye go forth, He will punish you with a grievous penalty, and put others in your place; but Him ye would not harm in the least. For God hath power over all things."

"Almighty God also says: 'So lose no heart, nor fall into despair. For ye must gain mastery if ye are true in faith.'"

In 1998, bin Laden announced his intentions to the world and the United States and called for the killing of "Americans and their allies, civilians and military . . . in any country in which it is possible to do it."

In 1998, U.S. targets were hit: the U.S. embassies in East Africa and the USS Cole in Aden, Yemen.

Years of planning went into the 1998 bomb attacks—just as bin Laden promised.

"The nature of the battle requires good preparation."

In 1998, he also promised that "the battle will inevitably move . . . to American soil."

In June of 2001, Osama bin Laden boasted that a horrific attack would soon take place in the United States.

"To all the Mujah: Your brothers in Palestine are waiting for you; it's time to penetrate America and Israel and hit them where it hurts the most."

On September 11, 2001, he made good on his terrorist threat. His Al-Qaeda terrorist organization murdered nearly 3,000 Americans.

On the morning of September 11. 2001, Mohammed Atta and 18 other Muslim terrorists, hijacked 4 commerical jets, two of which struck the World Trade Center, the others crashing into the Pentagon and a field in Pennsylvania.

Although Atta had repeatedly rehearsed this operation, on the morning of September 11, he was so worried that he might miss his flight from Maine to Boston that he rushed out and forgot his luggage. Later FBI agents would discover a jet fuel consumption calculator, an instructional video on flying commercial jets, a scrap of lined paper with a list of helpful hijacker hints, a letter, dated from 1996, and a kind of Hijacker's epistle.

In the notes and letter he left behind, Atta said he planned to kill himself so he would go to heaven as a martyr.

He also wrote out a page of last minute reminders which he may have photocopied and circulated among his followers. Atta, the presume author, had doodled on the paper, sketching a crude "key of life" that consisted of a arrowhead-like sword, with serpentine swirls and two hoops circling the shaft.

The letter also said in part:

"It is a raid for Allah....When the time of truth comes and zero hour arrives, then straighten out your clothes, open your heart and welcome death for the sake of Allah. Seconds before the target, your last words should be: There is no God but Allah. Mohammed is his messenger. I pray to you, God, to forgive me from all my sins, to allow me to glorify you in everypossible way."

The FBI also found a detailed letter, a kind of Hijacker's Epistle which had apparently been circulated among all four hijacker teams, for a copy was also found in the debris of yet another hijacked jetliner.

It read in part as follows:

"In the name of God, the most merciful, the most compassionate. . . . In the name of God, of myself and of my family . . . I pray to you God to forgive me from all my sins, to allow me to glorify you in every possible way..."

"Remember the battle of the prophet . . . against the infidels, as he went on building the Islamic state..."

And then, on the top of page 3, it was captioned: "The last night."

"Remind yourself that in this night you will face many challenges. But you have to face them and understand it 100 percent."

"Obey God, his messenger, and don't fight among yourself where you become weak, and stand fast, God will stand with those who stood fast."

"You should engage in such things, you should pray, you should fast. You should ask God for guidance, you should ask God for help. . . . Continue to pray throughout this night. Continue to recite the Koran."

"Purify your heart and clean it from all earthly matters. The time of fun and waste has gone. The time of judgment has arrived. Hence we need to utilize those few hours to ask God for forgiveness. You have to be convinced that those few hours that are left you in your life are very few. From there you will begin to live the happy life, the infinite paradise. Be optimistic. The prophet was always optimistic."

"Always remember the verses that you would wish for death before you meet it if you only know what the reward after death will be."

"Everybody hates death, fears death. But only those, the believers who know the life after death and the reward after death, would be the ones who will be seeking death."

"Remember the verse that if God supports you, no one will be able to defeat you."

"Keep a very open mind, keep a very open heart of what you are to face. You will be entering paradise. You will be entering the happiest life, everlasting life. Keep in your mind that if you are plagued with a problem and how to get out of it. A believer is always plagued with problems. . . . You will never enter paradise if you have not had a major problem. But only those who stood fast through it are the ones who will overcome it."

"Check all of your items, your bag, your clothes, knives, your will, your IDs, your passport, all your papers. Check your safety before you leave. . . . Make sure that nobody is following you. . . . Make sure that you are clean, your clothes are clean, including your shoes."

Figure 158a. World Trade Center, 9/11/2001. From Reuters.

Figure 158b. World Trade Center, 9/11/2001. From The New York Post

"In the morning, try to pray the morning prayer with an open heart. Don't leave but when you have washed for the prayer. Continue to pray."

"When you arrive ... smile and rest assured, for Allah is with the believers and the angels are protecting you."

"When you enter the plane pray:

"Oh God, open all doors for me. Oh God who answers prayers and answers those who ask you, I am asking you for your help. I am asking you for forgiveness. I am asking you to lighten my way. I am asking you to lift the burden I feel."

"Oh God, you who open all doors, please open all doors for me, open all venues for me, open all avenues for me."

"God, I trust in you. God, I lay myself in your hands. I ask with the light of your faith that has lit the whole world and lightened all darkness on this earth, to guide me until you approve of me. And once you do, that's my ultimate goal."

"There is no God but God. There is no God who is the God of the highest throne, there is no God but God, the God of all earth and skies. There is no God but God, I being a sinner. We are of God, and to God we return."

THE SUICIDE BOMBER

The suicide bomber is stereotypically highly religious, a loner with few social skills, depressed, withdrawn, and often confused about their sexuality (Jess, et al., 2001, Jess & Beck, 2002). He who volunteers to destroy himself and others with a bomb strapped to his back, generally faces a future that offers little hope. He (or she) often feels overwhelmed by hopelessness and defeat as well as by feelings of terrible rage and anger.

The suicide bomber is not interested in killing soldiers, but civilians. He has no qualms, nor issues about destroying the innocent. Women and children are viable, desirable targets. By bringing the war off the battlefield and into the homes, work and public spaces of the innocent, the suicide bomber tries to spread so much terror that the enemy, who they call Israel and America, will withdraw from their lands and capitulate, as capitulation offers the possibility of salvation.

The suicide bomber seeks revenge and salvation--often for imaginary sins, including the "sin" of homosexuality (Jess, et al., 2001, Jess & Beck, 2002). The suicide bomber believes that through hatred and violence, by murdering innocent people, he is fulfilling a moral and spiritual quest that will lead to martyrdom and paradise.

Most suicide bombers are highly religious. Prospects are recruited from mosques and religious institutions and are led to believe that by killing themselves and others, they will go straight to paradise, where they will be seated in honor, next to their almighty God.

According to Islamic tradition, and as taught by "suicide teacher" Mohammed el Hattab, "He who gives his life for Islam will have his sins forgiven and will attain the highest state of paradise." And what is paradise? 72 virgins who will love him and him alone. Eternal sexual bliss is one of the rewards of martyrdom.

Suicide bombers are commonly recruited by and are affiliated with the Palestinian militant group Hamas (or Islamic Jihad).

They are recruited from mosques and schools. It is not the brave and courageous who are enticed, but those who appear lonely, troubled, shy and withdrawn—those who might leap at the chance to be accepted, to be part of a group, to be given a mission in life, to feel important, and to belong.

Suicide bombers from the Middle East are typically young, impressionable, often highly religious, and living in despair and hopeless poverty. They are loners. They are shy, awkward, and usually have few or no friends. In American slang, they are the "losers." They are young men with nothing to lose and everything to gain: Paradise and 72 willing virgins.

And like many virgins and young men confused about their sexuality, these "losers," are often seduced by older men, who offer camaraderie and the chance to feel wanted, to belong and to have friends, if only the young man will agree to kill himself.

Friendly, awkward, shy and alone, these young men are easy pickings for those sophisticated in the art of enticing the friendless with gifts of kindness, respect and yes, even love, brotherly love.

The recruiters, these older men wise in the world, offer the "loser" a chance to become an accepted, respected member of the gang, part of an elite brotherhood: A brotherhood in blood.

Perhaps at many as half of the 19 men who agreed to kill themselves and thousands of others on September 11, were mentally disturbed and confused about their sexuality.

Wail Alshehri, for example, suffered from significant "psychological problems" that required treatment.

Abdulaziz Alomari was an alcoholic. He had at least one arrest for drunk driving.

Ahmed Salah Alghamdi, was highly religious, the graduate of a religious school, and he suffered from the torment of sin. He knew himself to be a sinner. He was wracked by a pathological, almost delusional guilt, frequently asking others, such as his parents, to pray for him.

Highly religious, mentally disturbed, and drowning in self-hate.

Some would agree to murder and destroy Americans, only because they were seeking to destroy their own unknown face.

As detailed in the book, America Attacked (Jess et al., 2001), Mohammed Atta was centrally involved in possibly all phases of the 9/11 attack, including planning, spying, recruitment and training. Atta may have also been a self-hating homosexual.

Atta was a religious man, which is a common characteristic of those who carry out suicide attacks. Yet, Atta differed from the stereotypical suicide attacker in that he was older, 33, highly educated and technically skilled. He also came from a well to do family and could be considered "upwardly mobile."

In many respects he was no different from any other "upwardly mobile" highly educated Muslim. But there were also several notable exceptions. Atta drank alcohol excessively and he enjoyed hanging out at bars, including Sharky's Billiard Bar in Hamburg where he was attending the Technical University in 1996.

He also preferred the company of men to women and his goal in life was to launch a suicidal attack and murder thousands of people who had never caused him or his loved ones harm.

Mohammed Atta, was a religious man. His teachers described him as polite, diligent, intelligent and very religious, perhaps fanatically so.

Yet he was also a sinner who loved fast cars, flashy clothes, young men and money, lots and lots of money.

Mohammed Atta knew himself to be a sinner. He desperately sought redemption, turning first to religion, and then failing that, or perhaps, because of it, embracing suicide and mass murder in order to achieve martyrdom and to wash away his guilty sins.

Mohammed Atta was also a leader. He played a leadership role in Hamburg and again in the United States.

Young men were attracted to Mohammed Atta and many were seduced and convinced to join his army, including fellow hijackers, Marwan Al-Shehhi, Saeed Alghamdi and Ziad Jarrahi—men he met and "seduced" in Hamburg.

Together they were to do battle with the enemies of Islam and their reward would be paradise and the cleansing of their guilty sins.

Mohammed Atta saw himself as a soldier and he would lead his men on a journey to eternity and paradise.

In 1996, Atta demanded that University officials accommodate his religious needs. He convinced them to establish an Islamic prayer room for himself and 20 other Muslim students.

Atta, the seductress, began recruiting others to the cause.

Arabic men not only attended his prayer room sermons but would gather late at night at his home.

Atta held meetings in the prayer room and in his home and soon found a willing convert, Marwan Al-Shehhi, who was 11 years his junior. Marwan Al-Shehhi, was not just a convert, he moved into Atta's apartment and formed an unusual relationship that was to last until the day they died.

The two men became "inseparable" and "joined at the hip."

They lived together. They trained together. They worked out together. They drank together. They committed mass murder together. The only thing they didn't do together was seek out women.

They had no interest in women. They did not like women. Atta, in fact, hated women and left instructions that women should not be allowed to attend his funeral.

In America and Europe, when two men form close, physical, "inseparable" relationships, and eschew the company of females, few eyebrows are raised even when it becomes clear the men are homosexuals.

In more conservative Islamic countries, it is also not uncommon for men to spend a lot of time together and to even live together. That two highly religious men might also become inseparable and eschew the company of women, would be viewed as a sign of virtue and no cause for alarm.

However, if the same two inseparable Arab men liked to drink, wear expensive fancy clothes and spend time on the town, but also eschewed the company of women, such behavior would be recognized for what it is, and would not be tolerated. It would have been viewed as "immoral." Sinful. In many Muslim countries, they could be legally killed and stoned to death.

Al-Shehh was also a problem drinker. In Florida he and Atta frequented a number of bars and were often observed to down four or five drinks in a row. Their favorite "poisons" included rum and Coke and Stolichnaya vodka and orange juice.

If they were Osama bin Laden's men, they didn't act like it. Bin Laden would not let his boys smoke cigarettes. Drinking alcohol would have led to banishment from the ranks of his al-Qa'eda movement.

However, as we now know, in 1996 bin Laden made an exception. He welcomed sinners into the ranks of his fighters. He would even finance their sins.

Were the two men homosexuals?

We don't know.

What we do know is that Mohamed Atta and Marwan Al-Shehhi were fashion conscious, they enjoyed wearing expensive clothes, and were provided with large sums of money to indulge these habits. They also spent time keeping their bodies pretty by working out together at gyms.

They were always together.

The lived together.

They were inseparable.

Indeed, these two men remained "bound at the hip" until the day they boarded separate planes in Boston and hijacked them to New York City.

That they were both highly religious, Mohammed Atta in particular, does not rule out homosexuality. It certainly didn't rule out mass murder. Rather their brand of religiosity leads credence to the possibility that these two fashion conscious, inseparable, unmarried men may have harbored "forbidden" tendencies, even if they never acted on them.

These forbidden tendencies may have also been the lure, which attracted and then bound so many young men to Atta's camp. These same guilty, sinful tendencies may have had the motive force, which drove them to commit suicide and mass murder—devilish deeds that would cleanse them of their sins, even if they had never acted on them.

Mohammed Atta, while he was in Hamburg, Germany, had taken on the role of a cleric, of a priest! In was in this clerical-type shepherd role that he was able to gather so many sheep.

Homosexuality is common among clerics, shamans and priests. In the United States, homosexuality was so rampant within the ministry of the Episcopal church and its homosexual clergy so openly promiscuous that the church lost over 5 million members by 1997.

Likewise, and as will be detailed later in this chapter, the priesthood of the Catholic Church also includes a high percentage of homosexuals and pedophile priests who rape young men and boys. For example, in 1999, the Bishop of the Santa Rosa Diocese in California was forced to resign because another priest, a younger man, accused the Bishop of repeatedly raping him. In 2000, the Catholic Church decreed that priests could no longer be alone with altar boys, because of the possibility these older men would seduce their young charges.

In Hamburg, Mohammed Atta also served a priestly role. He gathered young and highly intelligent Muslim men who were alone, friendless and isolated, and bound them to him and his cause. He was a seductress.

Ziad Jarrah was seduced. He soon began living together with Mohammed Atta and Marwan Al-Shehhi in the same apartment—an arrangement that astonished his father, Samir Jarrah, when he learned of it.

This unusual relationship also put a strain on Ziad's relationship with his fiance, Asle. Although they were to get married, Ziad became so entangled with his new friends that he no longer had time to see her. He was so busy that when it came time for Asle to meet his parents, he could not find the time to accompany her.

Too busy to bring his fiance to meet his family?

Ziad Jarrah had been seduced. He not only lived with the two men but he died with them. On September 11, he helped to commandeer and then to pilot one of the four hijacked planes.

When Ziad Jarrah moved in with Mohammed Atta and Marwan Al-Shehhi, the Jarrah family realized that something was terribly wrong with their only son.

He was living with two men in a small apartment when he had more than enough money to live alone. His relationship with his fiance grew more and more estranged. He was behaving strangely. He was preoccupied. He seemed moody and depressed.

What was wrong with Ziad?

His family did not know.

What was troubling Ziad?

They did not know.

What we do know is that Ziad felt compelled to kill himself for Islam.

According to Islamic tradition and as instructed by "suicide teacher" Mohammed el Hattab, "He who gives his life for Islam will have his sins forgiven."

What sins had he committed? What had he done that was so utterly horrible that only a martyr's death could wash away his sins?

We do not know.

Yet, something so bothered the young man that he volunteered to participate in a mission of death that was guaranteed to end his painful life and cleanse him of his guilty sins.

MASS SUICIDE AND MODERN
RELIGIOUS MURDERERS

Murder of the innocents and the slaughter of infidels and nonbelievers are not antiquated religious customs. Nor are these acts the exclusive province of Islam or men from the Middle East. Cults and religious groups regularly arise in various lands and cultures and frequently indulge in similar practices, e.g. the mass suicide of Jim Jones and his followers in "Jonestown" ("People's Temple"), David Koresh and the fiery death of his followers at Waco Texas.

MASS DEATH AT JONESTOWN

On November 18, 1978, the reverend Jim Jones exhorted and then forced his followers to engage in mass murder and mass suicide in Guyana. More than 900 people, many of them children, drank, or were forced to drink cyanide-laced fruit punch. Jones, a charismatic monomaniac who at one time was a favorite of San Francisco's liberal political elite, took a less painful and quicker way out. He died of a bullet to the head.

Jim Jones was born in 1931 and became a "Holy Roller" preacher as a child. As he reached adulthood he developed a creed he called "apostolic socialism" which deified social justice but which down played the role of god—hence his appeal to the ultra-liberal San Francisco political elite. Current San Francisco Mayor, and former leader of the California Assembly, Willie Brown, was one of Jones' "biggest cheerleaders." Nevertheless, despite his cult status even among the city's liberal elite, Jones became increasingly paranoid and disillusioned with San Francisco, especially following a negative magazine article in New West magazine. Jones moved his followers to a 3,800 acre plot of land in Guyana's outback, where they raised livestock and grew their own food.

The people's paradise soon became a prison camp. Followers were not allowed to leave, and there were forced beatings and forced sex. Jones who required that his followers refer to him as "father" demanded utter obedience. Incessant screaming and threats were delivered nightly against imagined slights and for faintly perceived faults, with the guilty being beat with "the board of education." Anyone who questioned his authority was placed in "The Box," an underground coffin. Unruly children would be taken to the Jonestown well and hung upside down by a rope tied around their ankles and would be repeatedly dunked and beaten.

Jones became increasingly concerned about the CIA and FBI plotting against him and his paradise, and soon required that his followers practice mass suicide so as to protect them from outside threats: the "White Night" drills. Jones would get on the compound loud speaker at night and begin shouting: "White Night! White Night!" which signaled a coming attack. Followers were required to leap from their beds and assemble at designated spots where they would then drink from huge vats.

However, what triggered the mass suicide was a visit from a California politician, Leo Ryan, who upon leaving invited a number of Jones' followers to come with him. Ryan was murdered and insofar as Jones was concerned, the day of reckoning was at hand. One of those who drank the poison wrote in her suicide note: "We died because you would not leave us alone."

HEAVEN'S GATE

Mass suicide has been practiced by numerous religious cults, both ancient and recent, including, in the 1990s, 74 followers of the "Order of the Solar temple," and 39 members of "The Higher Source," i.e. "Heavens Gate." Many of the male members of the Higher Source, including the leader of the cult, a minister (and son of a Presbyterian minister), Marshall Applewhite (also known as "Do") also had themselves castrated.

In the case of Applewhite, castration was not only a means of achieving purity, but a way to control his rampant homosexuality. In 1970, for example, he was fired from the University of Saint Thomas after it became known that he was having sex with male students. Soon thereafter he apparently began hearing voices, including the voice of god and was awakened to a new form of spirituality which required abstinence from sex. His creed eventually came to include strict rules involving "no human-level relationships and no socializing."

As an aside it is noteworthy that abnormal amygdala activity, or amygdala destruction, can alter sex drive and sexual orientation, and can also induce a loss of social interest. Human-level relationships are avoided (Joseph, 1999b; 2000a).

Soon Applewhite's credo came to include UFOs.

Specifically, Applewhite saw the coming of the Hale-Bopp comet as a heavenly sign that a UFO was coming to take him and his followers to a better place, to "the level above human, to take us home to Their World: Heaven." The cultists, therefore, killed themselves by eating a poison laced pudding. They lay on bunk beds in a standard black uniform and Nike tennis shoes and died.

DAVID KORESH: BEATEN BY THY GOD

David Koresh ("Vernon") of the Branch Dividian cult, also ordered the death of his followers, and they apparently obeyed his wishes, for he had told them he was "god." In fact he first made his announcement on January 30, 1987, when he sent a wedding invitation to the Seventh Adventists Church in southern California, which read in part: "I have seven eyes and seven horns. My Name is the Word of God...Prepare to Meet Thy God."

David Koresh was a sexual sadist. He had sex with the wives of all his many followers, and had sex with and would beat and order the beating of their and his children. According to one of his followers, Marc Breault (Breault & King, 1993) "Children were spanked for any reason; crying during a sixteen hour Bible study, refusing to sit on Vernon's lap, or daring to defy the prophet's wishes."

"Each child had their own special paddle with their name written on it...Some women thought the best way to please their Son of God lover was to be especially severe when dishing out discipline. But sometimes it wasn't easy for the adults to spank the children. They couldn't find a spot on the child's buttocks that wasn't black and blue or bleeding" (Breault & King, 1993).

The women were sometimes subjected to the same treatment. One 29-year old woman who announced that she was hearing voices was imprisoned in one of the small cottages on their property. She was beaten, and repeatedly raped by her "guards."

David Koresh was also a prophet of Doom, and between the months of October 1991 to February 1993, he and his group spent over $200,000.00 on guns. This arsenal included 50-caliber machine-guns and a million rounds of ammunition (Breault & King, 1993). Koresh was not only preparing for Armageddon but was contemplating mass suicide.

On Sunday, February 28, 1993, at 9.55 A.M., in Waco, Texas, a hundred ATF agents began their raid which resulted in a blood bath. A 51 day siege finally ended in a firestorm, and the death of David Koresh, his followers, and their children who burned to death when the compound was set on fire and burned to the ground. It was David's wish, however, for the entire world to go up in flames.

CROSS CULTURAL SPIRITUAL BLOOD LUST

These crazed religious practices are not limited to Americans. Consider, the Japanese religious cult "Aum." Their leader Shoko Asahara and many top cult members were arrested and charged with murder in June of 1995 for releasing the nerve gas Sarin in five subway cars during rush hour injuring over 5,500 Japanese commuters (New York Times, 6/7/95).

Similarly, although the "modern" Islamic, Christian and Jewish religions forbids it, many modern day Middle Eastern and African Islamic, Christian, and Jewish fundamentalists, regularly preach murder and hatred.

For example, "militant rabbis" in Israel had encouraged and condoned the assassination of

Israel's Prime Minister, Yitzhak Rabin, and had issued a "pursuer's decree," which in effect morally required that he be killed (New York Times 11/11/95). And, he was murdered by a student of religion, Yigal Amir, who claimed he acted upon "God's" instructions.

Because of this limbic religious blood lust, members of religious sects may turn against one another and commit murder in the name of God, just as Jews murder Jews, and Christians murder Christians in the name of God.

For example, on November 29, 1998, six members of the United Pentecostal Church were arrested for kicking to death six people, including three children, "to wipe out the enemies of God." According to Reuters new agency (11/28/98), the killings began two weeks prior, when the pastor of the thirty member sect announced during a sermon that he could hear voices from Jesus Christ" ordering that members of the group be punished. "The pastor, helped by his wife and two other men, began beating, whipping and stamping on the worshipers... followed by more disciplinary torture over several days. Among the dead were two boys, aged three and four."

HINDU, MUSLIM, BUDDHIST SPIRITUAL BLOOD LUST

"Terrorist attacks" by Muslim religious zealots is not uncommon. However, these attacks and calls for the death of infidels, are not always aimed at Jews or Americans, but their "brothers" and "sisters," i.e. fellow Arabs and Muslims.

Consider Algeria. Between 1992 and 1999, over 80,000 Algerians were murdered by Muslim zealots, with the majority of victims consisting of children, girls, and pregnant women who were beheaded, disemboweled, or who had their throats slashed. The reason for these murders and campaign of terror? To establish a holy Islamic state.

In fact, in 1998, on the first holy day of Ramadan—which marks "god's" revelation of the Koran to the Prophet Muhammed—Muslim religious zealots killed and slaughtered more than 400 people, most of them women.

Hindu Muslim violence has haunted the country of India for hundreds of years, but reached a boiling point in 1947 when Pakistan, an Islamic nation, declared its independence from India, a secular democracy. Over a million Hindus and Muslims were slaughtered that year.

The violence and religious murders have continued unabated.

In the spring of 2002, a Muslim mob stoned and then set fire to a train carrying Hindus, burning alive dozens of women and children. The Hindus were returning from Ayodhya where they had been demanding the construction of a Hindu temple on the site of a mosque destroyed by their nationalists allies. After the train pulled into Godhra, a town populated mostly by Muslims, some of the Hindus began attacking Muslim men. The Muslim community reacted with stones and set fire to the train. Nearly 60 Hindus were killed.

The next day, tens of thousands of Hindus retaliated with acts of unspeakable butchery. Muslim men were beaten, stabbed, shot, and beheaded, young women and mothers were stripped naked, raped, and then skewered on swords or soaked with gasoline and set on fire. The bellies of pregnant women were slit open, and their unborn babies ripped from their bodies, raised skyward on the tip of a sword and then tossed into the many fires that were consumming Muslim towns and cities. Thousands of Muslims lost their lives in this manner and over 100,000 were left homeless.

Even Buddhist monks murder and assault one another. For example, in November of 1998, gray-robed Buddhist monks of the Chogye Buddhist order in Korea, spent several weeks assaulting and beating each other with clubs, chairs, and even fire bombs as they battled over religious control of the order's main temple (Associated Press, 11/17/98). In one brawl alone, 37 were seriously injured and five killed.

RELIGIOUS MURDERS AND THE LIMBIC SYSTEM

What is the source of these religious-murderous and sadistic behaviors? The limbic system and the same cluster of nuclei which subserve aggression, sexuality, and spirituality. It is the limbic system which enables humans to respond with irrational and murderous blood lust in the name of "God" and religion and it is the amygdala that can induce a horribly violent and murderous assault with minor provocation— and as we have seen, the Lord God, and numerous religious fanatics, have also murdered at the slightest provocation.

For example, if the amygdala is directly stimulated rage reactions are commonly triggered. The face will begin to contort, the teeth will be bared, the pupils will dilate, the nostrils will flare, and then the animal or human will viciously attack (Egger & Flynn, 1963; Gunne & Lewander, 1966; Mark et al., 1972; Ursin & Kaada, 1960; Zbrozyna, 1963). Amygdaloid activation results in attacks directed at something real, or, in the absence of an actual stimulus, at something imaginary; including, presumably, in the case of religious fanatics, imaginary slights or insults.

There have been reported instances of patients suddenly lashing out and attacking friends, relatives or strangers while in the midst of a temporal lobe seizure (Saint-Hilaire et al., 1980), and/or attacking, kicking, and destroying furniture and other objects (Ashford et al., 1980). One female patient, during amygdala stimulation, became irritable and angry, and then enraged. Her lips retracted, there was extreme facial grimacing, threatening behavior, and then rage and attack—all of which persisted well beyond stimulus termination (Mark et al., 1972).

Yet another man developed intractable aggression following a head injury and the development of abnormal activity within the amygdala (Schiff et al.,1982). Subsequently, he became easily enraged, sexually preoccupied, and developed hyper-religiosity and pseudo-mystical ideas. He became violently religious.

Indeed, the amygdala is able to overwhelm the neocortex and the rest of the brain so that the person not only forms religious ideas but responds to them, sometimes with vicious, horrifying results. Hence, it appears to be the limbic system, and the amygdala in particular, which not only contributes to religious and spiritual experience, but religious brutality and murder committed in the name of one's god.

SEX, GOD, AND RELIGION

Sexual Spirituality and the War Against Women

A not uncommon characteristic of high levels of limbic system and inferior temporal lobe activity are changes in sexuality as well as a deepening of religious fervor (Bear 1979; Blumer, 1970; Slater & Beard 1963; Trimble 1991; Taylor 1972, 1975). Hypersexuality or conversely, hyposexuality is not uncommon.

It is noteworthy that not just modern day evangelists, but many ancient religious leaders, including Abraham, Jacob (Israel) and Muhammed, tended to be highly sexual and partook of many partners (e.g. St. Augustine of Hippo: "Give me chastity, 'o lord, but just not yet"), or, they shared their wives (Abraham), or they married women who were harlots (e.g. Hosea) or had sex with other men's wives (Muhammed, King David), or killed other men in order to marry or have sex with their wives (King David).

King Solomon (like his father King David) experienced numerous dream states in which he communicated with God, and he required the sexual services of 700 wives and 300 concubines.

LIMBIC SYSTEM SEXUALITY

The limbic system is concerned with sex. Structures such as the amygdala and hypothalamus not only mediate sexual behavior, but they are sexually differentiated and have sex specific patterns of neuronal and dendritic development, (Allen et al. 1989; Blier et al. 1982; Gorski et al. 1978; Nishizuka & Arai, 1981; Rainbow et al. 1982; Raisman & Field, 1971, 1973; Simerly, 1990; Swaab & fliers, 1985). That is, there are "male" and "female" limbic systems, and even "homosexual" limbic systems such that male homosexuals are in possession of a limbic system which is more "female" than "male" in structural organization (Levay, 1991; Swaab, 1990), and in some respects (the anterior commissure) hyper-female in size (Allen, & Gorski, 1992).

Indeed it has now been well established that the amygdala and the hypothalamus (specifically the anterior commissure, anterior-preoptic, ventromedial and suprachiasmatic nuclei) are sexually differentiated and have sex specific patterns of neuronal and dendritic development including the preoptic area and ventromedial nucleus of the hypothalamus (Bleier et al. 1982; Dorner, 1976; Gorski et al. 1978; Rainbow et al. 1982; Raisman & Field, 1971, 1973). The preoptic and other hypothalamic regions are not only sexually dimorphic but chemical and electrical stimulation of the preoptic and ventromedial hypothalamic nuclei triggers sexual behavior and even sexual posturing in females and males (Hart et al., 1985; Lisk, 1967, 1971). In female primates, even maternal behavior can be triggered (Numan, 1985). In fact, dendritic spine density of ventromedial hypothalamic neurons varies across the estrus cycle (Frankfurt et al., 1990) and thus presumably during periods of maximal sexual receptivity and arousal, as well as during pregnancy and while nursing.

Electrical stimulation of the preoptic area increases sexual behavior in females and males, including the frequency of erections, copulations and ejaculations, we well as pelvic thrusting followed (in the case of males) by an explosive discharge of semen even in the absence of a mate (Hart, et al., 1985; Maclean, 1973). Conversely, lesions to the preoptic and posterior hypothalamus eliminates male sexual behavior and results in gonadal atrophy.

Although the etiology of homosexuality remains in question, it has been shown that the ventromedial and anterior nuclei of the hypothalamus of male homosexuals demonstrate the female pattern of development (Levay, 1991; Swaab, 1990). Male homosexuals are in possession of limbic system that is more "female" than "male" in functional as well as structural orientation.

The primate amygdala is also sexually differentiated (Nishizuka & Arai, 1981; see also Simerly, 1990). The male amygdala is 16% larger than the female amygdala (Breedlove & Cooke, 1999; Filipek, et al., 1994), whereas in male rats, the medial amygdala is 65% larger than the female amygdala and grows or shrinks in the presence of testosterone (Breedlove & Cooke, 1999).

The male vs female amygdala also contains a greater number of synaptic connections and shows different patterns of steroidal activity (Breedlove & Cooke, 1999; Nishizuka & Arai, 1981; Simerly, 1990). These sex differences are particularly evident in the medial amygdala, which is also a principle site for steroidal uptake, including the female sex hormone, estrogen, and contains a high concentration of leutenizing hormones (Stopa et al., 1991). The number of immunoreactive cells in the female amygdala also fluctuates during the estrus cycle, being highest during proestrus (SImerly, 1990), and thus presumably acts so that if pregnant, the fetus will not be attacked as foreign, and/or so as to coordinate, with the hypothalamus, the appropriate neuroendocrine responses during pregnancy and following birth.

Because the amygdala is involved in sexuality and is sexually differentiated, activation of the amygdala can produce clitoral tumenence, penile erection, sexual posturing (Kling and Brothers, 1992; MacLean, 1990; Robinson and Mishkin, 1968; Stoffels et al., 1980) sexual feelings (Bancaud et al., 1970; Remillard et al., 1983). Electrical stimulation of the amygdala can also trigger sensations of extreme pleasure (Olds and Forbes, 1981), memories of sexual intercourse (Gloor, 1986), thrusting, sexual moaning, ejaculation, as well as ovulation, uterine contractions, lactogenetic responses, and orgasm (Backman and Rossel, 1984; Currier, Little, Suess and Andy, 1971; Freemon and Nevis,1969; Warneke, 1976; Remillard et al., 1983; Shealy and Peel, 1957).

Moreover, in rats and other animals, kindling induced in the amygdala can trigger estrus and produce prolonged female sexual behavior. In fact, abnormal- or seizure activity within the amygdala or overlying temporal lobe may induce a female to engage in "sexual intercourse" even in the absence of a partner. For example, Currier and colleagues (1971, p. 260) describe a female temporal lobe seizure patient who was "sitting at the kitchen table with her daughter making out a shopping list" when she suffered a seizure. "She appeared dazed, slumped to the floor on her back, lifted her skirt, spread her knees and elevated her pelvis rhythmically. She made appropriate vocalizations for sexual intercourse such as: It feels so good...further, further."

The anterior commissure, the band of axonal fibers which interconnects the right and left amygdala/temporal lobe is also sexually differentiated. Like the corpus callosum, the anterior commissure is responsible for information transfer as well as inhibition within the limbic system. Specifically, the female anterior commissure is 18% larger than in the male (Allen & Gorski 1992). Moreover, the anterior commissure is larger not only in females, but is 35% larger in homosexual males vs male heterosexuals (Allen & Gorski, 1992).

It has been argued that the increased capacity of the right and left female amygdala to communicate (via the anterior commissure) coupled with the more numerous and more densely packed neurons within the female amygdala (which in turn would decrease firing thresholds and enhance communication), and the sex diffferences in the hypothalamus, would also predispose females to be more emotionally and socially sensitive, perceptive, and expressive (Joseph 1993). Hence, these limbic sex differences induces her to be less aggressive and more compassionate and maternal, and affects her sexuality, feelings of dependency and nurturance, and desire to maintain and form attachments in a manner different than males. However, in homosexual males, this may predispose at least some of these males to not only behaving more emotionally, but more violently than women and even more violently than heterosexual men.

As will be detailed, it is these same sex differences in the limbic system which account for why women are more religious than men, attending church more often, and why homosexuals are drawn to the priesthood. Unfortunately, some of these homosexual priests, because they are in possession of a "female" limbic system that is bathed with aggression-inducing testosterone, have also promoted or engaged in religious violence directed toward men as well as women.

THE RELIGIOUS WAR AGAINST WOMEN

Abnormalities in the limbic system, the amygdala and hypothalamus in particular, can also provoke extreme sexual violence. In one case, a young man with seizure activity originating in his amygdala and temporal lobe, beat his mother to death and then sexually assaulted the body (Joseph, 2000a).

An abnormal limbic system may abnormally link sex with murder; and among men, the sexual murder or torture of women. Moreover, because the amygdala is clearly linked to religious experience, sexual behavior and religious expression may become linked in a positive or a negative fashion. For example, whereas a heterosexual male may respond to a beautiful woman with interest and sexual lust, homosexual priests may respond with murderous lust. Augustine, Jerome, Tertullian, and other Catholic theologians absolutely hated women, viewing them as evil temptresses that lead men to hell.

"What is the differences whether it is a wife or mother, it is still Eve the temptress that we must beware of in any woman." -St. Augustine.

"Do you not know that you are each an Eve? The sentence of God on this sex of yours lives in this age: the guilt must of necessity live too. You are the devil's gateway; you are the unsealer of that forbidden tree; you are the first deserter of the divine law; you are she who persuaded him whom the devil was not valiant enough to attack. You so carelessly destroyed man, God's image. On account of you, even the Son of God had to die." -Tertullian, 16th Century

Even the Lord God, Yahweh voiced contempt and hatred for women: "Because the daughters of Zion are haughty and walk with stretched forth necks and wanton eyes, walking and mincing as they go, and making a tinkling with their feet...The Lord shall wash away the filth of the daughters of Zion... by the spirit of burning." -Isaiah 3:16-26, 4:4.

Women throughout the ages have been demeaned and attacked by male and homosexual religious authorities, and their murder was often sanctioned by various gods. Indeed, during the middle ages, the Catholic Church declared war on women who were then systematically tortured and slaughtered by the Catholic authorities.

FEAR OF FERTILITY

Yet another factor in the religious crusade against women was the fear of the goddess cult by the patriarchal religious authorities. For example, during the Crusades, because the women were temporarily freed of male dominance, some began to practice their own religion and worship their own goddesses, including those pagan goddesses that celebrated female sexuality; e.g., fertility cults—perhaps the oldest and most ancient of "organized religions." In consequence, the leaders of the Catholic Church felt compelled to act. They sought to destroy woman in general, and those women associated in any way with the goddess and her fertility cults. Women, therefore, were suspect if they were in any way sexually attractive, and those who were the most sexually appealing (i.e. fertile) were the first to be murdered by the Catholic Authorities. Her reproductive facility was viewed as supernatural in origin, her menstrual cycle being in tune with the cycles of the moon, and the moon and the blood of her menstruation were believed to have supernatural power. Every woman was not just Eve, but an incarnation of the goddess.

The reproductive and supposedly supernatural power of menstrual blood may have contributed to those rituals requiring that animals be drained of blood and their blood splashed on religious altars, including the altars of the Lord God Yahweh. Originally it was menstrual blood that was splashed upon the altar of the goddess.

The ancient Hebrews, and the Catholic authorities, therefore, deemed a menstruating woman as unclean, for menstrual blood had the power of life and that of the supernatural. Women in general, therefore, were subject to attack, with the ancient Jews reciting a prayer thanking god "for not making me a woman." However, it was her reproductive facility, and thus her association with the goddess that was most feared and detested.

As detailed by Robert Briffault in his brilliant text, "The Mothers" (Briffault, 1931) "the supernatural source which magic powers are regarded as being primarily derived is... connected in the closest manner with the functions of women... her... reproductive functions... and a power which is used in a dread-inspiring manner. And by virtue of their natural position and function, the wielder of domestic magic...she had charge of the sacred objects and performed all the religious functions connected with the household."

Yet another factor in the religious persecution of woman, was her facility at speech. Indeed, and as is now well demonstrated, females demonstrate clear language superiorities over males, and they even talk faster as well (Joseph, 2000b). Speech and language, that is, a woman's tongue, is her natural and traditional weapon, which she may use for "pronouncing curses, of casting spells... of bewitching and performing incantations. It was a dreaded power. The curse of a woman is accounted far more potent than the curse of a man" (Briffault, 1931). Women in general, therefore, were considered suspect by the Catholic authorities and during the Middle Ages they were rounded up, sexually tortured, and killed.

THE CATHOLIC CHURCH DECLARES WAR AGAINST WOMEN

Woman has been persecuted by various religious authorities because of the power of her tongue, her reproductive power, her associations with pagan goddesses, and her ability to enchant men with her sexuality.

Woman is biologically predisposed to having multiple orgasms, multiple partners, and to indulging in promiscuity—which does not mean she will necessarily behave promiscuously (Joseph, 2000a,c). Nevertheless, because of her sexual nature and association with fertility, religious rituals of the goddess stereotypically involved sexual orgies and ritual prostitution.

Although male authorities, both religious and otherwise, have attempted throughout the ages to control and yoke female sexuality, this has not always been successful. In Europe, including Rome, during the 6th through 11th century, female sexuality and her promiscuous nature was openly flaunted, and the worship of pagan goddesses became widespread and was threatening the authority of the Church. As early as the 1st century, the missionary sermons of St. Paul were repeatedly drowned out by women chanting "Diana, Diana, Diana;" Diana being the goddess known since prehistoric times as the Queen of Heaven.

Unable to suppress the goddess cult, and the fertility rites of her worshippers, the Catholic Church finally issued the "Canon Episcopi" in the 10th century: "Some wicked women, reverting to Satan, and seduced by the illusions and phantasms of demons, believe and profess that they ride at night with Diana, on beasts, with an innumerable multitude of women. It would be well if these women, one and all, perished for their infidelities."

HOLY WAR: WOMAN THE WITCH, SORCERESS, AND HEALER

The proclamation, however, had little effect. Hence, in 1252, Pope Innocent IV issued the Ad Exitrpanda, which authorized the execution of heretics (e.g. wealthy landowners) and the seizure of their goods, and the prolonged sexual torture of women who were beautiful, wealthy, or old, ugly, and eccentric and/or who gathered in groups to talk and converse and possibly worship pagan goddesses. This was followed by the first Papal bull on sorcery, in 1259, and yet another bull, the notorious Super illius specula, in 1322 (by Pope John the XXII), and then the famous Bull Summis desiderantes affectibus, in 1484 (by Pope Innocent VIII), which demanded the death of these women. The Popes and the Catholic Church proclaimed them witches and declared war against women.

Being "true soldiers of Christ," the Dominicans Heinrich Kramer and Johann Sprenger responded to this Papal decree by writing and issuing the Malleus Maleficarum (witch's hammer), thus unleashing a murderous, sadistic, blood lust that demanded the sexual torture and burning of "woman the witch, healer and sorceress" (Achterberg, 1991; Gies & Gies 1978; Lederer 1968). "For she is a liar by nature, so in her speech she stings while she delights us... for her voice is like the song of the Sirens, who with their sweet melody entice the passerby's and kill them..." (Malleus Maleficarum).

These sadistic misogynists were soon seconded by Bishop Bossuet, of France, who believed there was an army of 180,000 witches threatening France and Rome, all of them beautiful and thus bewitching. The Bishop then demanded that they be gathered up in one body and that "all be burned at once in one fire."

And the great sin of these women? According to the Malleus Maleficarum "Carnal lust! All witchcraft comes from carnal lust, which in women is insatiable."

As summed up by Lederer (1968) in his interesting book, The Fear of Women, "witchcraft was a woman-thing, and the persecution of witches a man-thing; for it was first and last the women who were being persecuted and burned." In fact, hundreds of thousands of women were murdered, whole populations were destroyed, and some villages were left with only one female inhabitant. In 1404 alone, it is estimated that the Papal fathers burned at least 30,000 women. So many women were murdered, that it could be said that the Church was attempting no less than a whole sale genocide of women—"sexocide" at Lederer put it.

Because many of the men (the Crusaders) had been killed or were serving in the army of the Catholic Lord God, the women were often left unprotected. Sometimes whole villages were destroyed, or all the women in a given area were rounded up by the Catholic authorities and then sexually murdered.

These women, particularly those who were exceedingly attractive or ugly, were then hideously tortured and then slaughtered by burning, boiling in oil, crushing, and via whatever device the religious authorities felt appropriate or which suited their sick minds. In Germany huge ovens were constructed for the purposes of mass female murder (Achterberg, 1991; Lederer 1968). As noted, even the Lord God Yahweh recommended that haughty, beautiful women be burned in the fire.

However, it was not just beautiful females, for they come in a limited supply, but those who were old, eccentric, childless, and particularly women who owned property and pets, such as cats. Indeed, the cats would be tortured and murdered alongside the women. The "Black Plague" in fact was in part a consequence of the denunciation and killing of cats, coupled with the sanctification of rats and mice (the proverbial church mouse), by the Catholic authorities.

As to the children of these witches, the Church had only "compassion." These children would be merely flogged in front of the fires in which their mothers were burning.

Predominantly, when the priests set upon a village, it was the young and beautiful who were generally the first to be tortured, as they were experts at love magic. These beautiful women would bewitch men by shooting mesmerizing "beams of light from their eyes" which causes the man to fall in love (Briffault, 1931).

As pointed out by Dominicans Heinrich Kramer and Johann Sprenger, "Consider also her gait, posture, and habit, which is vanity of vanities. There is no man in the world who studies so hard to please the good God as even an ordinary woman studies by her vanities to please men... who... they infect with witchcraft by inclining men to inordinate passion. Yet...her heart is a net, it speaks of the inscrutable malice which reigns in their hearts... for they fulfill their lusts by consorting with devils."

According to Pope Innocent VIII, these women "have given themselves up to devils in the form of incubi and succubi. By their incantations, spells, crimes, and infamous acts they destroy the fruit of the womb in women, in cattle and various other animals; they destroy crops, vines, orchards...they render husbands impotent."

Of course, they also had the power to heal, so when the Archbishop of St. Andrews became ill and his physicians were unable to provide him with a cure, he sent for a well known woman healer whose expertise was in the making of ointments, Allison Peirsoun of Byrehill. Her cure was a success! So, the Archbishop had her tortured and burned.

RELIGIOUS SEXUAL SADISM

The torture of women, of course, was sexual. The woman would be stripped and her body, breasts, and orifices would be thoroughly investigated for the mark of the devil. However, the "investigation" was made with long needles and conducted by priestly specialists called "prickers," who would stick these needles into every suspected Devil's mark.

After the women became unconscious or unresponsive to the continued pricking, the priests would then employ "gresillons which crushed the tips of fingers and toes in the vice; the echelle, or rack, for stretching the body; the tortillon for squeezing its tender parts... legs were broken, even into fragments... or the legs would be grilled on the caschielawis...the fingernails were pulled off with the turkas, or pincers, and needles driven up to their heads into the quick."

As summed up by Henry Charles Lea: "Protestants and Catholics rivaled each other in the madness of the hours... Christendom seemed to have grown delirious, and Satan might well have smiled at the tribute to his powers seen in the endless smoke of the holocaust which bore witness to his triumph over the Almighty."

SEXUALITY, THE GODDESS AND THE SERPENT

Karen Robidoux was a young mother and a member of a religious sect. Karen was also very attractive and beautiful, and some of the female members of the sect believed she was vain. They resented how some of the men of the sect would look at her. And then, one of the women, Michelle Mingo, experienced a vision and heard a voice: it was a prophecy from God. Because Karen was pretty, and vain, she could no longer eat solid food, but could only drink boiled almonds. Her 10-month old son, Samuel, was also to be denied food. Breast milk would be his only source of nourishment. The sect members then allowed the boy to starve, and ignored his cries for food as they ate at the dinner table. He starved to death—"God's" punishment for his mother's beauty and sexuality.

Sexuality is a major concern of most major religions (Lederer 1968; Parrinder 1980; Smart 1969) as well as the limbic system. In fact, almost all major religions and their Gods, either act to promote sexuality, or to suppress it. This should not be entirely surprising for religions are very sexual and many were originally concerned with the fertility of the fields and the abundance of prey (Campbell 1988; Frazier 1950; Harris, 1993; Kuhn 1955; Malinowski 1948; Parrinder 1980; Prideux 1973). Religious rituals evolved accordingly beginning with the cult of the goddess, the sacred feminine, the Great Mother of All.

As summed up by Halle Austen (1990) in her book, The Heart of the Goddess, "creativity, the power to manifest physical and psychic reality, is one of the Goddess's primary aspects...the source of all being. She appears as the Great Mother, the Sustainer of Life, the Cosmic Creatrix. It is from her that all life proceeds and to her that all life returns." And, "just as our ancestors honored a woman's ability to create humans from her womb and feed them from her breast, they also honored the Earth as the Great Mother who nourishes us" and the sky and heavens as the Great Mother who would nourish the Earth and her children with drops of life sustaining rain.

Aditi, the Hindu Goddess of the Void, for example, represented "creative power" and "abundance," and the cosmic womb from which all creation has its source. The goddess is also known as the celestial cow and the golden calf who provides nourishment not just to humans, but the gods. As the Great Mother also nourishes the gods, she is also the guardian of cosmic harmony and order.

The cult of the goddess has its origins in the Paleolithic. Hence the numerous "Venus" statues and carvings of heavy breasted pregnant women.

The goddess cult continued to reign supreme during the Neolithic and she was worshipped by the ancient Sumerians, Egyptians, Akkadians, Babylonians, Hebrews, and in fact all ancient peoples including those of the Americas and Australia.

The Australian Aborigines, for example, are not only the oldest continuous culture that has survived on this planet, but they have worshipped the Great Mother, the "All Mother" since time immemorial, depicting her as giving birth in dreamtime to all the peoples of the Earth.

Because the sun also nourishes the Earth, the Goddess was also a goddess of the sun, for the sun was originally thought to be female. Hence, Igaehindvo the Cherokee Sun Goddess, Brigit the Celtic Fire Goddess, and Amaterasu Omikami the Great Spirit Shining in Heaven and Goddess of the sun of ancient Japan: "The radiance of the Sun Goddess filled the universe and all the deities rejoiced." In ancient Egypt the goddess Nut was believed to have given birth to the sun.

Woman was also associated with the sun and fire because in many ancient cultures, it was believed that woman first discovered the art of making fire, which she used to warm the people and prepare the food. Fire is also a symbol of spiritual awakening and knowledge of the spirit world.

The goddess, therefore, was associated in all ways with all things having to do with life and death, and the spirit world.

"I am Nature, the universal Mother, mistress of all the elements, sovereign of all things spiritual, queen of the dead. Though I am worshipped in many aspects, known by countless names, and propitiated with all manner of different rites, the whole earth venerates me." -Apuleius, second century B.C.

It is noteworthy that in addition to being the source of all life, that the Goddess was also associated with the serpent. The Sumerian "god" Enki, was depicted as a snake, and sometimes as a snake with breasts. The peoples of predynastic Egypt also worshipped the goddess in the form of a snake. In ancient Egypt, the hieroglyph for "snake" also means Goddess.

The Hindu Goddess Kali wore a garland of snakes around her neck—which represented the female life force, the transformative power of Shakti. Shakti was often depicted by the ancient Hindus and the pre-Aryan Dravidans, with a kundalini snake emerging from her womb and vagina.

The snake although an obvious phallic, and thus sexual symbol, is also associated with wisdom. Hence, the snake in the garden of Eden not only tempts Eve, but he induces her to eat of the fruit of the tree of knowledge. In fact, throughout the world snakes have commonly been the companions of oracles, those who had special knowledge of the future.

The snake represents supernatural knowledge and power which is one of the reasons the Lord God instructed Moses to "take your rod and cast it down before Pharaoh. It shall turn into a serpent... Then Pharaoh called the wisemen and the sorcerers, now the magicians of Egypt and they... cast down every man his rod, and they became serpents: But Aron's rod swallowed up their rods" (Exodus 7:10-12). And, it was a serpent which Moses carried as a fetish which he used to protect and lead the Israelites as they wondered for 40 years in the desert.

Nevertheless, because of its association with wisdom, sexuality, and woman, the serpent also came to be viewed as evil. The Lord God condemned the serpent, whereas the Catholic Church depicted this reptile as synonymous with Satan, the Devil. Both woman and the serpent became enemies of the Lord God.

SEX, FOOD, AND RELIGION

The limbic system mediates not only sexuality, but internal homeostasis and food intake. Likewise, many modern mystical and religious practices have also involved the ritual control over sex and food. This includes many American Indian, Christian, Jewish, and Moslem sects (Campbell 1988; Parrinder 1980; Smart 1969). Thus the commandment "thou shalt not... " These are limbic taboos, as eating and sexuality (like murder and violence) are under limbic control.

Many limbic taboos, however, promote survival, for example, by proscribing the eating of poisonous plants or unclean animals. Similarly, by forbidding anal or indiscriminate sex one was spared the wrath of this "God" and whatever plagues he might send in the form of venereal disease or viruses. If we rule out the possibility of an attack with nuclear armed missiles, mass death due to disease is presumably what became of Sodom and Gomorrah where the anal sex crazed mobs attempted to sodomize even the angels sent by the "Lord God" himself (Genesis 19).

Sex and food (along with fear, rage, and aggression) are probably the most powerful of all limbic emotions and motivators. If sufficiently hungry or sexually aroused, these conditions can completely overwhelm the brain. Limbic hyperactivation in turn can induce religious or spiritual dreams or hallucinations.

Hungry men, women, and infants will dream of food. Those who are sexually aroused will dream of sex. However, a parched and starving man will not just dream, he will hallucinate food and water and will attempt to slake his desires by consuming a hallucination.

Given that early (as well as modern) human populations were often concerned with obtaining food (as well as a sex partner) many of their earliest religious beliefs and rituals were therefore concerned with increasing the abundance of game animals as well as preserving their own progeny (Armstrong 1994; Campbell 1988; Frazier 1950; Harris, 1993; Kuhn 1955; Parrinder 1980; Prideux 1973). As noted, many an ancient Upper Paleolithic cave was decorated with fertility and sex symbols, including pregnant women (Venus figures) and animals (Bandi 1961; Joseph 1996; Kuhn 1955; Leroi-Gurhan 1964), whereas Egyptian tombs contain numerous paintings of food and goddesses.

Thus, given our ancient hunter-gatherer (and then later, farming) heritage, many religions both ancient and relatively modern are highly concerned with fertility and food, and tend to be very sexual and limbic in orientation if not origin. This is also why there have always been fertility goddesses and gods who are associated with eating and drinking, especially alcohol (Campbell 1988; Frazier 1950; James 1958; Parrinder 1980; Smart 1969). This also includes, for example, Osiris, and especially Dyonisus who was among other things, a sex crazed dancing god of the vine. In fact, one of the first miracles performed by Jesus involved making wine from water, and, as we know, Jesus surrounded himself with highly sexual women, prostitutes who would sometimes rub precious oil on his body.

SEX, GOD, AND RELIGION

RELIGIOUS LOVE CHARMS AND SPIRITUAL SEXUALITY

In Arabic-pre-Islamic tradition, it was said that martyrs were rewarded in heaven with 72 Virgins. "Man has not touched them before them nor jinni. Which then of the bounties of your Lord will you deny? Reclining on green cushions and beautiful carpets. Which then of the bounties of your Lord will you deny? —The Beneficent.

Hadith number 2,562 in the collection known as the Sunan al-Tirmidhi says, "The least [reward] for the people of Heaven is 80,000 servants and 72 wives, over which stands a dome of pearls, aquamarine and ruby."

Among the ancient religions of India and China, the sexual activity of the Gods and the promotion of similar sexual activities among the believers were widespread religious practices and beliefs (Austin 1990; Campbell 1988; Parrinder 1980).

For example, the ancient Vedas were greatly concerned not only with the worship of various nature gods, but with the rituals of sexual union. Ancient Indian religious texts are filled with love charms and instructions as to how to win the love of a man or woman, or to protect against demons.

Figure 159. A Paleolithic Mother God and fertility figure.

Figure 160. *The patriarchical gods and their male priests, declared war against the Goddess, and the Mother of all, became a whore, "Satan's Bride," "harlots from hell" who cavorted and had sex with devils.*

Temple prostitutes were also quite common throughout India and the Middle East, as well as in Rome and Greece. Some temples employed so many girls that they were like giant brothel emporiums (Parrinder 1980). As noted, sexuality and desire (like religious feeling) are directly mediated by the amygdala and hypothalamus.

In fact, sexual intercourse became a religious ritual among Hindus and Buddhists who practiced "tantra." The practitioners of tantra were inspired by visions of cosmic sex and the acquisition of sexual energy. Through tantra one might be confronted with the cosmic mystery of creation as exemplified by another deity, Shakti, the divine mother. However, restrictions on where one could have sexual intercourse (not in public) and certain types of sexual acts such as oral sex, were prohibited as well as sex with strange women or those of a lower caste (Parrinder 1980). Nevertheless the joys of sex were continually emphasized and embraced. Hence, the Kama Sutra, the "love text".

On the other hand, it was believed by some ancient far Eastern sects that in order to gain power, one had to break taboos and, for example, engage in sexual orgies or have sex with women while they were menstruating. Menstrual blood was believed to possess the spiritual and creative life force, whereas sexual orgies were believed to liberate tremendous amounts of sexual energy.

These "taboo" sexual practices were also a form of tantra, referred to as "left handed tantra." Those who followed the way of the left handed trantra claimed that passion was nirvana and that adepts should cultivate all sexual pleasures (Parrinder 1980). Both male and female deities, usually in the act of having sex, were worshipped.

Ancient Chinese and Taoists religions are also quite sexual (Austin 1990; Parrinder 1980). These beliefs are exemplified by the concepts of Yin and Yang which appeared over 3000 years ago and which represented the male and female principles of the universe. Sexual intercourse was viewed as a symbolic union of the earth and heaven, which, during rainstorms were believed to mate. By engaging in sexual relations man and woman achieved harmony by following the example of the gods.

THE LORD GOD: A SEXUAL GOD

Beginning at about the same time that the Judaic religion became more dominant in certain areas of the Middle East, around 3,000 years ago, and over the following thousand years a tremendous change in religious sexual thought began to flourish, enveloping the Roman Empire, and which eventually paralleled and coincided with the development of Christianity and Islam.

Unlike the goddess and the highly sexual gods of, for example, the ancient Greeks and Romans, the "Lord God" of the Old Testament does not have sex with human women and there is no hint of sexual duality in his personage. He is a male god, a warrior and destroyer. Although not overtly sexual, the sexual activities of men and especially women were of great concern to Him. Be fruitful and multiply, He ordered, and as to certain women who were presumably barren, and in one case, still a virgin, He is reported to have opened their wombs.

Male sexuality was also a concern; that is, the diminishment of the intensity of man's sexual pleasure. Thus He required a form of sexual self-mutilation. As part of his covenant with Abraham and the Israeli people, it was ordered that every male child would suffer the amputation of the tip of his penis (which is densely innervated by fibers that yield intense sexual pleasure): "And ye shall circumcise the flesh of your foreskin; and it shall be a token of the covenant betwixt me and you" (Genesis 17: 10-11).

Although there is no evidence that the Lord God was sexually active with human females, it does appear that the Lord God had a sexual consort, the goddess Sophia, before he became the Lord God of the Earth. Sophia was the goddess of wisdom and she was not only his lover, she may have been his sister: "It is Wisdom calling. Understanding raising her voice. I Wisdom, live with Prudence; I attain knowledge and foresight... The Lord possessed me in the beginning in his own way, before his works of old...When he prepared the heavens, I was there...I was by him as one brought up with him. I was daily his delight, rejoicing always before him" (Proverbs 8).

In addition, it appears that she may have betrayed Him. "Rejoicing in the habitable part of the earth, and my delights were with the sons of men" (Proverbs 8:31).

It is true, however, that the above quote may mean that she simply was delighted by the sons of men, and did not have sex per se with men.

However, if she did betray Him, this may explain why she is never again referred to, as well as His following complaints: "Aholah played the harlot when she was mine; and she doted on her lovers...desirable young men...thus she committed her whoredoms with them and with all whom she doted... she defiled herself" (Ezekiel 21: 5-7). "Like mother, like daughter. You are the daughter of your mother, who rejected her husband" (Ezekiel 16: 44-45).

It may also explain His jealous prying nature, and obvious dislike of the female sex and his recommendation that women who were truly attractive and sexually desirable should be burnt (Isaiah 3:16-26, 4:4) as they were all "whores" (Hosea 2).

"Because the daughters of Zion walk with wanton eyes, mincing as they go, and making a tinkling with their feet...The Lord shall wash away the filth of the daughters of Zion... by the spirit of burning" -Isaiah 3:16-26, 4:4.

Indeed, Sophia's "delights with the sons of men" and her betrayal of the Lord God may explain why He not only disdains pretty women, but pardons and encourages the sexual exploitation of women and the rape and sexual slavery of women, and their murder if they dare behave like whores. In fact, He brags that he "delivered...Aholah who played the harlot when she was mine...into the hand of the Assyrians... They discovered her nakedness; they took her sons and her daughters, and slew her with the sword... they executed judgment on her" (Ezekiel 23:9-10).

RELIGIOUS RAPE AND SEX SLAVERY

The Lord God is very concerned with the sexual relations between men and women. Those men He loved most dearly had sex with multiple sex partners. The Lord God even approved of sex slavery, including sex with little girls who are taken slave:

"Kill every male among the little ones. But all the women and female children that have not known a man, keep alive for yourselves." -Numbers, 31

The permissive attitude of the Lord God when it comes to female sex slavery may explain why the modern state of Israel not only has no laws forbidding the owning or selling of human beings, but why non-Jewish women are openly sold as sex slaves in the state of Israel (see M. Specter, "Traffickers New Cargo: Naive Slavic Women, New York Times, January 11, 1998).

And, once a sex slave, always a sex slave, even if she is Jewish female.

"When you acquire a Hebrew slave... and if his master gave him a wife, and she has borne him children, the wife and her children shall belong to the master. When a man sells his daughter as a slave, she shall never be freed, as male slaves are." -Exodus, 21: 2-7.

And the Lord God even encourages and pardons the violent rape of young Jewish virgins by Jewish men. For example, after some of the Benjaminites raped a woman to death (Judges 19:25), and following the murder of their own women in retaliation by the other 11 tribes of Israel, these tribes then realized that the tribe of Benjamin would die out without women. So, they decided to attack yet another city of their fellow Jews and to "utterly destroy every male and every women that hath lain by man" with the exception of "young virgins" who the Benjaminites were allowed to rape (Judges 21:11-13).

However, not enough virgins were acquired following this massacre. So the Benjaminites were instructed by the Lord God to rape another group of young Jewish virgins.

"Then they said, Behold there is a feast of the Lord in Shiloh...Go and lie in wait in the vineyards. And see and behold if the daughters of Shiloh come out to dance in dances, then come ye out and catch you every man his wife of the daughters of Shiloh" (Judges 21:19-25).

The Benjaminites, however, raped men as well as women, and were quite willing to gang rape a woman until she was dead (Judges 19:25-26, 20:5). According to the divine law, they could also brutally and sadistically rape female slaves; and if she lived for two days following a violent, brutal rape, there was no penalty.

Again, the Lord God of the ancient Jews had an obvious contempt for the female sex: "Because the daughters of Zion are haughty and walk with stretched forth necks and wanton eyes, walking and

Figure 161. (Right & Left) The god Shiva and the most feminine and lovely of his shktis, Parvati the daughter of a Himilayan god. Shiva and Parvati symbolize the union of the female and male energy of the cosmos. The god Vishnu and his voluptuous and swollen breasted Lakshmi. From a stone panel in the temple of Khajuracho, 10th century.

Figure 162. *A swollen naked breasted Yakshimi (tree goddess). With her swollen breasts, wide hips, slim waist and shaved vagina, she is the ideal estrus female. From Mathura, 2nd century India.*

mincing as they go, and making a tinkling with their feet; The Lord will smite with a scab of crowns of their head and the Lord will discover their secret parts. In that day the Lord will take away their tinkling ornaments...their bracelets...bonnets, ornaments...earrings, the rings...and fine linen...And it shall come to pass that instead of sweet smell there shall be stink." -Isaiah 3:16-26, 4:4.

Indeed, this Lord God, when angry, found pleasure in using explicit sexual imagery when condemning his people, Israel—whom He referred to as a woman when He was angry. Indeed, He repeatedly threatened to strip this brazen female "naked" and referred to her as an "adulterous harlot." Echoes of the divine betrayal by the Sophia, the goddess of Wisdom?

"And let her put away her harlotry from her face and her adultery from between her breasts. Else I will strip her naked... And I will snatch away My wool and My linen that serve to cover her nakedness. Now will I uncover her shame in the very sight of her lovers..." - Hosea 2.

SEXUALITY, PEDOPHILIA, & HOMOSEXUALITY

Although this volatile, mercurial, and masculine seeming "Lord God" was asexual, sexual behavior was of tremendous concern to "Him" for He commands sexual moral obedience—at least of women and married women in particular— and repeatedly tells his people, starting with Adam and Eve, "be fruitful and multiply."

And sexuality, and the condemnation and/or control of sexuality, has been and remains a major concern of cults or established religions. The temple virgins who served the virgin goddesses of ancient Greece and Rome, were required to remain celibate upon threat of death. Shakers' communities have been dying out for lack of sex and children. Buddhist monks are celibate, and Hindu "renouncers" swear off sex later in life. According to Catholic Canon law priests are required to remain celibate and celibacy is defined to include "perfect and perpetual continence," meaning no sexual activity of any kind, including masturbation.

However, celibacy did not become a requirement of priests until 1139 when it became church law. Prior to 1139, priests, bishops, cardinals, and even Popes had lovers and wives, some Popes had several.

The Mormon Church initially willingly embraced, as a religious creed, the right of every man to have several wives; i.e. sex partners, and the founder of the Church was reputed to have 40 wives.

Likewise, Muhammed was reported to have the sexual prowess of forty men, and to have bedded at least 9 wives and numerous concubines including even one young girl (Lings 1983).

However, the grand champion of religious-sexual excess was King Solomon who required the sexual services of 700 wives and 300 concubines.

Sex scandals are also commonplace among priests, rabbis, pastors, and ministers.

The Reverend Jimmy Swaggart whose sermons were filled with fire and brimstone, and who regularly assailed Catholics, Jews (who "are going to Hell") pornography and prostitution, temporarily gave up a $150 million dollar a year world wide television ministry in 1988, when his fondness for prostitutes and pornography was exposed and he was caught with a prostitute. Moreover, the attorney who exposed Swaggart also claimed the minister was a pedophile. Swaggart has since returned to the ministry. During his sermons he yells, collapses to the floor, recounts conversations with god, repeatedly breaks into tears, and again rails against Catholics and Jews (who "are going to Hell"), and against pornography, prostitution, as well as hypocrisy.

Likewise, Jim Bakker lost a 300 million dollar ministry, when among other things, he and another pastor were accused of repeatedly sexually assaulting a young female member of their flock.

In 1999, the dean of Harvard Divinity School was forced to resign "for conduct unbecoming" after it was discovered that he had downloaded thousands of "explicit" pornographic images on his Harvard-owned computer in his Harvard-owned home.

In January of 2001, the Reverend Jesse Jackson admitted that he had cheated on his wife and has fathered a daughter from another woman. "No doubt, many close friends and supporters will be disappointed in me," Jackson said.

Sex with little girls is permitted by the Jewish Holy book, the Talmud:

For example, according to the Talmud: "Rab said: When a grown-up man has intercourse with a little girl it is nothing, for when the girl is less than this it is as if one puts the finger into the eye... tears come to the eye again and again, so does virginity come back to the little girl under the age of three."

Talmud Sanhedrin 55b "Come and hear! A maiden aged three years and a day may be acquired in marriage by coition [sexual intercourse], and if her deceased husband's brother cohabits with her, she becomes his."

The Talmud, is believed by Orthodox Jews, to be based on god's laws and to be Mosaic in origin; that is, based on oral (and written laws) first put forth my Moses: "Kill every male among the little ones. But all the women and female children that have not known a man, keep alive for yourselves." -Numbers, 31

Sex with children, and especially sex with little boys, has been a common religious practice, and a priestly predisposition, since the inception of the priesthood and organized religion.

DAVID KORESH: SEXUAL THEOLOGY

David Koresh announced he was God in a wedding invitation to the Seventh Adventists Church in southern California. It read in part: "I will scold your daughters for their nakedness and pride that they parade in My Father's house, and by my angels, I will strip them naked before all eyes because of their foolish pride." Naked women at his mercy and who he would impregnate and "fill with seed" was his predominant religious fantasy.

As he confided to his "right hand man" Marc Breault early in his ministry: "I'll have women begging me to make love to 'em. Just imagine, virgins without number." Within just a couple of years he would be attended by at least twenty young women, most of whom he "married," including two that were just 14 years old, and one who was age 12 (Breault & King, 1993).

Sex was at the center of his theology, even claiming that god would take them to heaven in a divine spaceship that he sketched on a blackboard. It was an erect penis!

Koresh apparently was consumed by sexual thoughts and was the recipient of sexual visions that he claimed were sent to him by God. Soon he began demanding sex from the wives of his followers, women who he believed had married these other men without his permission and who should have married him

"All you men are just fuckers, that's all you are. You married without getting God's permission. Even worse, you married my wives. God gave them to me first. So now I'm taking them back."

According to Marc Breault, everybody was shocked, stunned, and Vernon kept saying things like: "So Scott, how does it feel to know your not married anymore... In October, 1989, he began having sex with the other men's wives... and directed the women to inform him when they had reached the fertile part of their cycle to maximize the chance of pregnancy." As per the men, Vernon informed them that it was their job to "defend King Solomon's bed."

Vernon not only had sex with and impregnated their wives—fathering over 20 children— but began having sex with these children; that is, when he wasn't beating them.

PEDOPHILE PRIESTS

As the American public learned in the Spring of 2002, pedophile priests have been raping little boys for decades if not for the last thousand years. Indeed, homosexuality and the homosexual rape of boys and young men is so common in the Catholic church that by edict, priests are no longer allowed to be alone with altar boys.

In 1999, the Bishop of the Santa Rosa Diocese in California was forced to resign because another priest accused the Bishop of repeatedly raping him.

Rev. John Rebovich enticed teenagers with free alcohol and then would rape them when they were too drunk to resist.

Gerald Ridsdale, an Australian Catholic priest, pleaded guilty to sexually assaulting 21 children.

Stephen Kiesle, a priest serving in Fremont, California, was charged in May of 2002 with sexually molesting up to 21 children. Kiesle had admitted to police that he "really liked young blond girls." However, his victims included both boys and girls, many as young as 9, some of whom he would tie up before assaulting them sexually.

The Rev. Paul Shanley has been accused of raping hundreds of boys. Indeed, Paul Shanley openly advocated the idea of sex between men and boys and he often attended meetings with the North American Man-Boy Love Association.

Boston priest John Geoghan had been raping young boys for over three decades; nearly 200 boys in 30 years. He is not alone.

It has been reported by the Boston Globe that 50 of Boston's Roman Catholic priests have been molesting boys for decades. Because of the public uproar, the Boston archdiocese was forced to remove over 20 priests between January and September of 2002, because of sexual misconduct and the rape of young boys. Over 400 lawsuits have been filed against priests in Boston.

In 2002, a number of seminary students were expelled from the Catholic Theological Union in Chicago because they were openly engaging in homosexual relations with one another. The Maryknoll Seminary is known to be "overrun with gay men."

The entire Catholic Church appears to be overrun with "gay men;" that is homosexual pedophiles. In consequence, when one pedophile priest is removed or transfers, another pedophile takes his place.

In March of 2002, Anthony J. O'Connell, the Roman Catholic bishop of Palm Beach, Florida, resigned after admitting that he sexually abused a teenage seminary student. He had also been accused of raping two other boys. He had been appointed to lead the Church by Pope John Paul II following the resignation of another pedophile, Bishop Joseph Keith Symons, who admitted sexually assaulting at least five boys.

According to Dr. Thomas Plante of the Jesuit college, Santa Clara University, and editor of a book on sexuality and the church, "50% of the Catholic clergy are gay." The Boston Globe (1/31/2000) has reveled that Catholic priests have a rate of HIV infection which is four times that of the general population.

Estimates as to the number of active, homosexual pedophiles in the Catholic Church range from 6.1% to 16% according to Richard Sipe, an "expert" on sex abuse and the Church.

There are an estimated 50,000 priests in the US. Hence, the number of pedophile priests could range from 3,000 (6%) to 8,000 (16%). However, there are only 188 diocese in the U.S., which means that there are anywhere from 16 to 42 pedophile priests per diocese.

Not surprisingly, over 800 priests have been removed from the ministry as a result of allegations against them. There have so far been over 1,400 insurance claims against the Church. The Church has so far paid out over $1 billion in liability with an estimated $500 million pending.

Not surprisingly, pedophile priests often work together in the same church or diocese.

The Rev. Paul Shanley and another pedophile priest owned and operated a "gay inn" in Palm Springs which catered to gay men. Shanley is accused of raping hundreds of boys. Indeed, Paul Shanley openly advocated the idea of sex between men and boys and he often attended meetings with the North American Man-Boy Love Association.

Likewise, according to the Cleveland Plain Dealer in a series of stories printed in the Spring of 2002, "parishes such as Ascension and St. Patrick, both in the West Park neighborhood of Cleveland, had more than one alleged abuser working at the same time." Moreover, when they work together, they also aid each other in recruiting and raping children.

Consider, for example, Reverends Gary Berthiaume and Allen Bruening. As detailed in May of 2002, by the Cleveland Plain Dealer: "Bruening would use trips to the pool to seduce young boys." One child, "Frank (not his real name), says he not only had to contend with Bruening, but also with Berthiaume, who was sent to the Cleveland diocese after serving six months in a Michigan prison for child abuse. After the swimming trips, says Frank, both priests were waiting in the showers. While Bruening stood naked in a one-person stall, says Frank, Berthiaume would be ordering him to join the other priest in the shower."

"Here I am, a little kid, and here is this pastor, you want to believe you're a good kid," Frank says. "This person is the next closest thing to God. You would do anything that they would say. How could you question these people?"

According to Professor Germain Grisez, and as he reported to the Bishops Committee on Sexual Abuse, the Catholic Church is permeated by a "homosexual subculture" and "homosexual clerics" who seduce "adolescent boys."

Likewise, according to Father Donald B. Cozzens, author of The Changing Face of the Priesthood, there are a "disproportionate number of gay men that populate our seminaries."

As summed up by Bishop Wilton D. Gregory, "It is an ongoing struggle to make sure the Catholic priesthood is not dominated by homosexual men."

It is in part because of the homosexual culture and the large number of pedophile priests that the Catholic Church and its Catholic Bishops have for centuries, covered up the homosexual rape of children by not just priests, but Bishops and Cardinals.

For example, Boston priest John Geoghan had been raping young boys for over three decades. When Bernard Cardinal Law of the archdiocese of Boston became aware of Geoghan's behavior which was threatening to become public, he quietly transferred Geoghan to another parish where he immediately began sexually assaulting children. Geoghan was not the only priest he transferred; and many other bishops have done likewise: cover up the crime and transfering the pedophile priest to another city where he can continue raping boys.

It is also because of these coverups, that in March of 2002, several Federal anti-racketeering suits—RICO The Racketeering Influenced and Corrupt Organizations Act— have been filed. By filing that kind of suit, the lawyers are calling the Catholic Church a criminal enterprise.

It is because of this overarching homosexual-pedophile culture that many priests, bishops, and cardinals, have not just covered up abuse, but in fact see nothing wrong with it, viewing these crimes as "forgivable"—except in those cases where a priest or Bishop repeatedly rapes young boys and the rapes become public.

Even in these latter instances, Church officials, until recently, were inclined to reinstate pedophile priests even after their cases become public or the cause of ruinous lawsuits.

For example, Bishop Donald W. Wuerl of Pittsburgh, had to battle with Church officials for over 7 years before he was able to remove Rev. Anthony Cipolla. Cipolla had been accused of raping altar boys, one of whom filed suit.

Father Cipolla appealed to the Vatican's homosexual hierarchy, its highest tribunal, which ruled to reinstate him despite the suitcases full of papers which documented the priest's sex crimes. Essentially, the Vatican, in making this ruling, also ruled that it was permissible to have sex with children.

Most Bishops are more concerned with protecting the church's name and its bank accounts, and with making it possible for pedophile priests to continue raping boys. Until recently, American bishops have repeatedly transferred predator priests from parish to parish, but only when their sex crimes threatened to bring unwanted publicity to the parish.

In May and June of 2002, when the scandal grew and threatened to completely overwhelm the Catholic Church, Church officials and thus the homosexual hierarchy first tried to downplay the problem and then sought to distinguish between sex with young children who were unwilling to have sex, and sex with older children and older boys who, the Church claims, welcomed if not solicited the sex. The Church denied that it had a problem, and claimed that rapes and sex with minors was not truly an act of pedophilia, because "almost all the cases involved adolescents and therefore were not cases of true pedophilia."

Moreover, according to Church officials, these offenses are forgivable because they amount to little more than the sexual seductions of teenage boys who willingly submit.

In May, and as was widely reported in newsapers such as the Boston Globe, Church officials announced that priests who had abused children in the past, would remain priests so long as there was no evidence that the priest in question was a serial abuser. Likewise, those who abused children in the future would not suffer any penalty, that is, unless they raped and sexually assaulted a number of children. However, even in these cases bishops would be given the discretion to retain these priests given mitigating circumstances.

"The question of the reassignment of priests who have harmed children is still a thorny issue," said Bishop Wilton D. Gregory, president of the United States Catholic Conference, the national forum for American bishops.

To their surprise, the public and the media reacted angrily to their pronouncements and the willingness of the Church to tolerate the sexual rape of young boys. It was repeatedly said in the media, that "the Catholic Church just doesn't get it."

Presumably, the homosexual hierarchy was unable to understand why the public was outraged, precisely because this homosexual hierarchy experienced the same "forgivable" sexual longings for children. In fact, three of the five members of the Ad Hoc Committee on Sex Abuse, including its chairman, Bishop John B. McCormack of Manchester, N.H., had been severely criticized for their handling of sex abuse cases, and their willingness to tolerate the rape of children and homosexuality among members of the clergy. Because so many shared the same deviant desires, even minor sanctions against abusers thus seemed excessive to many in the pedophilia priesthood.

In fact, on August 8, 2002, the Rev. Connors, the president of an association of Roman Catholic religious orders, publically complained that pedophile priests were being "scapegoated" and then criticised American bishops for reacting to the complaints of victims and the media, charging "that American bishops have been scapegoating abusers." Connors also ridiculed those victims who had stepped forward by asking: "Are we having fun yet?" Connors, as president, represents the views of 15,000 U.S. priests in orders such as the Jesuits and Benedictines.

We should recall, that these are the same religious orders which burned women and beat their children in front of the raging fires. This is the same church which would castrate young boys to keep them singing and looking pretty; i.e. the "castratos"--boys who were also the sexual playthings of Bishops, Cardinals and priests.

Thus we should not be surprised to discover that insofar as modern pedophile priests, and the majority of bishops and cardinals are concerned, sex with boys is normal and forgivable. In fact, even sex with children could be forgiven so long as a large number of children were not involved and the cases did not become public.

Specifically, in June of 2002, top Vatican officials and American cardinals tried to contain the public uproar. Repeat offenders and those priests who "become notorious and are guilty of the serial, predatory sexual abuse of minors," would be dismissed, said Cardinal Theodore E. McCarrick of Washington. However, as to those priests who had molested and sexually assaulted children in the past, the Church would be more lenient and leave it up to the local Bishops to determine if the priest was a true danger to children.

According to Cardinal Francis E. George of Chicago, the church wanted to protect the rights of priests who had been accused. In fact, Church officials sent a letter to Catholic priests in America, expressing sympathy and support "through these troubled times. We regret that episcopal oversight has not been able to preserve the church from this scandal," the letter read. That is, the sympathy of the church, was not for the victims, but only for the church and its priesthood. Indeed, pedophile priests must be protected according to Bishop Gregory, who emphasized that "even a priest who offends still enjoys rights."

Cardinal Francis George, of Chicago has also argued that bishops should be allowed to make distinctions between serial pedophiles and priests who "crossed boundaries" with older teenagers.

"A little more wiggle room enables you to be more just," Cardinal George said. "There is a difference between a moral monster who preys upon little children, and does so in a serial fashion, and someone who perhaps under the influence of alcohol engages in an action with a 17- or 16-year-old young woman who returns his affection."

Young woman?

Stephen Rubino, a lawyer who has represented over 300 alleged victims of priest abuse, estimates 85% of the victims have been teenage boys.

As summed up by National Review senior writer Rod Dreher "This is chiefly a scandal about unchaste or criminal homosexuals in the Catholic priesthood."

Even some Catholic priests and Bishops grudgingly agree, though they were again quick to make a distinction between pedophilia and sex with young men: According to Monsignor Eugene Clark of New York, "disordered" homosexuals were to blame. His view was seconded by the Bishop of Detroit who has said the current crisis is "not truly a pedophilia-type problem, but a homosexual-type problem."

Indeed, homosexuality is so rampant among Catholic priests that according to the Boston Globe (1/31/2000) they have a rate of HIV infection which is four times that of the general population.

And its is not just the Catholic Church which is a refuge for homosexual priests. The Presbyterian Church stated that perhaps as many as 23% of clergy have had "inappropriate sexual contact" with other men. As detailed in the San Francisco Chronicle (Lattin, 7/15/97) homosexuality became so rampant within the ministry of the Episcopal church, and its homosexual clergy so openly promiscuous that the church lost over 5 million members by 1997.

In Australia, hundreds of boys and young men have alleged they were raped by the homosexual priests and pastors of the Christian Fathers boarding schools.

In Islamic countries, homosexual are also drawn to the priesthood. It is rumored, for example, that in the holy city of Om, in Iran, that homosexuality and homosexual pedophilia is a common, albeit forbidden practice among Mullahs who sexually exploit their young male charges.

Homosexuality and homosexual pedophilia are common among the Hindu priesthood and the Hare Krishnas. In fact, over a dozen Hare Krishna temples in the United States were forced to file for bankruptcy in 2002, because of the over 400 million dollars in judgments awarded in lawsuits for the homosexual sexual abuse of boys and young men. They are not alone: The archdiocese of Boston has acknowledged playing millions of dollars in settlements for almost 90 priests.

THE LIMBIC SYSTEM AND SEXUALITY

Why the concern regarding sex pro or con in religious thought? Why the illicit, perverse, or promiscuous tendencies of priests and other religious leaders? Sex, like religious experience, or the ability to derive pleasure from eating and drinking, is mediated by the limbic system; i.e. the hypothalamus, amygdala, and temporal and frontal lobes (e.g. Freemon & Nevis 1969; Joseph, 1988a, 1992a, 1999a; MacLean 1969, 1990; Remmillard 1983; Robinson & Mishkin 1968).

As noted, activation of the sexually dimorphic amygdala can produce penile erection and clitoral engorgement (Kling & Brothers, 1992; MacLean, 1990; Robinson & Mishkin, 1968; Stoffels et al., 1980), and trigger sexual feelings (Bancaud et al., 1970; Remillard et al., 1983), extreme pleasure (Olds and Forbes, 1981), memories of sexual intercourse (Gloor, 1986), as well as ovulation, uterine contractions, lactogenetic responses, and orgasm (Backman & Rossel, 1984; Currier et al., 1971; Freemon & Nevis, 1969; Remmillard et al., 1983).

However, the limbic system also mediates violent behavior, including sexually violent behavior. Thus religiosity also can also be tainted by violent sexual thoughts and behavior.

THE GODDESS, HOMOSEXUALITY, & RELIGIOUS EXPERIENCE

As noted, it has been estimated that at least 50% of Catholic priests are homosexuals, and that the HIV rate among Catholic Priests is four times that of the general population. In fact, throughout history, shaman and other religious figures have commonly been homosexuals. Homosexuals are probably drawn to the priesthood for the same reason that women have been viewed as more in touch with the supernatural; i.e., the sexual differentiation of the limbic system.

Recall that portions of the hypothalamus and amygdala are sexually dimorphic; i.e. there are male and female amygdaloid nuclei (Bubenik & Brown, 1973; Nishizuka & Arai, 1981). Female amygdala neurons are smaller and more numerous, and densely packed than those of the male (Bubenik & Brown, 1973; Nishizuka & Arai, 1981), and smaller, densely packed neurons fire more easily and frequently than larger ones. This may contribute to the fact that females are more religious, more emotional and more easily frightened than males as the amygdala is a principle structure involved in evoking feelings of fear (Davis et al., 1997; Gloor, 1997; LeDoux, 1996) as well as spirituality.

THE FEMALE LIMBIC SYSTEM AND RELIGIOUS EXPERIENCE

Confirming common experience, numerous scientific studies have demonstrated that women display clear superiorities over males in regard to the expression, perception, and comprehension of social emotional nuances, regardless of the manner in which they are conveyed (Burton & Levy, 1989; Brody, 1985; Buck, 1977, 1984; Buck et al., 1974, 1982; Card et al., 1986; Eisenberg et al., 1989; Fuchs & Thelan, 1988; Harackiewicz, 1982; Lewis, 1983, Rubin, 1983; Safer, 1981; Shennum & Bugental, 1982; Strayer, 1980). And this is true even from the earliest stages of childhood.

This greater social emotional sensitivity, including a much greater likelihood of becomes frightened and easily terrified, is likely due to sex differences in the functional and structural organization of the limbic system, the amygdala in particular. Because female amygdala neurons are more numerous and packed more closely together (Bubenik & Brown, 1973; Nishizuka & Arai, 1981), and as smaller, tightly packed neurons demonstrate enhanced electrical excitability, lower response thresholds, and increase susceptibility to kindling, there is thus a tendency for the female amygdala to become hyperactivated more easily than the male amygdala—thus inducing extreme fear as well as a propensity for religious and spiritual feelings.

Indeed, women are not just more emotional, but have more intense religious experiences, attend church more often, are more involved in religious activities, involve their children more in religious studies, hold more orthodox religious views, incorporate religious beliefs more often in their daily lives and activities, and pray more often as well (Argyle & Beit-Hallahami, 1975; Batason & Ventis, 1982; De Vaus & McAllister Glock. 1967; Lazerwitz, 1961; Lindsey, 1990; Sapiro, 1990).

Moreover, the anterior commissure, a thick rope of axonal fibers which interconnects the right and left amygdala of the right and left temporal lobe is also sexually differentiated. The anterior commissure is responsible for information transfer as well as inhibition within the limbic system. Specifically, the female anterior commissure is 18% larger than in the male (Allen & Gorski 1992).

Thus not only is the female amygdala more excitable, but the right and left amygdala (located in the right and left temporal lobe) can more easily communicate and excite one another. Hence, again, the increased tendency for females to become easily frightened and to be religiously inclined. To know fear is to know god.

THE HOMOSEXUAL LIMBIC SYSTEM AND SPIRITUAL EXPERIENCE

Although the etiology of homosexuality remains in question, it has been shown that the ventromedial and anterior nuclei of the hypothalamus of male homosexuals demonstrate the female pattern of development (Levay, 1991; Swaab, 1990), whereas the anterior commissure, which interconnects the right and left amygdala/temporal lobe, is "hyper-female" in size (Allen, & Gorski (1992). Male homosexuals are in possession of limbic system that is more "female" than "male" in functional as well as structural orientation.

This female pattern of limbic system development also explains why homosexuals are more inclined to behave and think like women rather than men. Indeed, homosexual males and females tend to be more alike than different in regard to social-emotional reactions and tendencies (Tripp 1987). In some cases these feminine tendencies are grossly exaggerated (Tripp, 1987); i.e. the "swishy" male with the exaggerated high pitched voice.

A significant number of homosexuals, in fact, are psychologically similar to females in a number of ways, including having a high interest in fashion and wearing apparel, a pronounced tendency to employ feminine body language and vocal tones, to shun sports and avoid fights, and to have a fear of physical injury, particularly during childhood (Bell et al. 1981; Bieber et al. 1962; Van Den Aardweg, 1984; Tripp, 1987). Many also tend to maintain intense dependency relations with their mothers and to remain distant from strong male figures including their fathers (Green, 1987).

As children homosexual males tend to prefer female companions and friends, girls toys, activities, and often girls clothes, (Bell, et al. 1981; Saghir & Robins, 1973; Grellet et al. 1982; Green, 1987). From 67% to 75% of homosexuals vs 2%-3% of heterosexual males reported being "feminine" and more like girls than boys as children (Saghir & Robins, 1973; Green, 1987).

Thus, being in possession of a "female" limbic system may not only account for similarities between homosexuals and women in regard to fear and other behaviors, but in respect to spirituality.

Thus priests and shamans not only tend to be homosexuals, but public displays of overt homosexual activity and promiscuity coupled with religious fervor often comes to characterize the behavior of homosexual clergy, as was the case within the ministry of the Episcopal church, and which appears to be the case in the Catholic Church.

The homosexual limbic system, however, is actually organized in a hyper-female fashion. When compared to the female and especially the male limbic system, the homosexual limbic system could be considered different from the male and female "norm." And as noted, abnormalities in the limbic system or hyperactivity, is associated with hypersexuality, transvestitism, and public displays of sexuality (Blumer, 1970; 1999; Davies and Morgenstern, 1960; Kolarsky, et al., 1967; Leutmezer et al., 1999; Terzian and Ore, 1955).

As noted, in ancient religions, including those who worshipped the great goddess, male youths would sometimes castrate themselves, and would forever after dress as women in order to obtain her power and serves as her priests.

Goddess cults have always been associated with fertility rites and woman's sexuality. Homosexuality between women worshippers was common, whereas when men were allowed to participate, the religious service would become a sex orgy. That modern day homosexual priests with their female limbic system behave similarly, albeit with men and boys, is therefore to be expected.

HOMOSEXUAL PRIESTLY DISDAIN FOR THE FEMALE SEX

Despite the "love" between women that has always characterized the goddess cults, women in general, and young women in particular are sexually quite competitive. It is not uncmmon for young women to feel threatened by attractive women (Joseph, 1985, 2000d). That is, sexy attractive women pose a competitive threat; feeling that can border on intense dislike if not hate for those women who are particularly sexy and especially those who flaunt their sexuality (Joseph, 1985, 2000d).

Fertile and sexy women, as noted, aroused considerable hate among the priests of Yahweh, the Lord God, and the Catholic Clergy during the Middle Ages. Given that so many priests are in fact homosexuals, and have a "female" limbic system, and are thus similar to women in so many ways, this may also explain the extreme hatred for the female sex as expressed by the Lord God and innumerable homosexual and pedophile priests.

Figure 163. Venus and the lovers. An allegorical joke and a blasphemy in which the virgin Mary is depicted as naked and being adored by angels and devout men.

"If it was good company and conversation that Adam needed, it would have been much better if god were to have arranged to have two men together as friends, not a man and a woman." -St. Augustine.

THE HOMOSEXUAL LIMBIC SYSTEM: REVISTED

The homosexual limbic system is not only (in some respects) more female than male in structural organization, it is "hyper-female" (e.g. the anterior commissure). However, unlike the female brain, the homosexual limbic system is bathed in high levels of testosterone--a hormone known to induce aggression.

It is tempting to speculate that because some homosexuals demonstrate an almost hyper-developed pattern in the structure of the anterior commissure (and thus presumably the amygdala, as well as the hypothalamus), coupled with what some studies have suggested are higher than normal levels of testosterone (at least as compared to heterosexual males) that this may lead to abnormal functioning in the limbic system. This may account for why a significant minority of these individuals engage in excessive, dangerous and sometimes "bizarre" (e.g. "fist fucking") sexual behaviors, including *indiscriminate* promiscuity, "orality," "anality," and a proclivity to engage in group oral/anal sex, or to "cruise" and repeatedly have sex with strangers (sometimes in a single evening). It has been reported that between 24% to 30% of this population have *repeatedly* engaged in truly reckless and self-destructive sexual behaviors during their youth (Aaron, 1973; Gans, 1993; Pollak, 1993; Symons 1979; Tripp, 1987).

In fact, injuries to and/or seizure activity within the amygdala/temporal lobe may result in bizarre sexual changes, such as continuous masturbation and indiscriminate, often hypersexual hetero- and homosexual behaviors including attempts at sex with inanimate objects (Kling and Brothers, 1992; Kluver and Bucy, 1939; Pribram and Bagshaw 1953; Terzian and Ore, 1955). Hypersexuality following amygdala injury has been documented among numerous species, including cats and dogs (Blumer 1970; Kling and Brothers, 1992) and humans.

Humans with an abnormally activated or severely injured amygdala/temporal lobe may expose and manipulate their genitals (Leutmezer et al., 1999), masturbate in public, and attempt to have sex with family members or individuals of the same sex (Blumer, 1970; Kolarsky, Freund, Macheck, and Polak, 1967; Terzian and Ore, 1955). Moreover, abnormal activity involving the amygdala and over-lying temporal lobe has been associated with the the development of hyposexuality (Taylor, 1971; Heirons and Saunders, 1966; Toon, Edem, Nanjee, and Wheeler, 1989), hypersexuality (Blumer, 1970) as well as homosexuality, transvestism, and thus confusion over sexual orientation (Davies and Morgenstern, 1960; Kolarsky et al., 1967).

Moreover, as noted, abnormalities or excessive activity in the amygdala or hypothalamus can also induce not just abnormal sexual behavior, but violent and sexually violent acts. In some respects, although the average homosexual is no different from the average heterosexual, it could be argued that given the sex differences in the homosexual limbic system, that this may also predispose a significant minority of homosexual to engage in sexually abnormal as well as violent acts.

For example, although the homosexual community prefers to blame heterosexuals for "gay bashing," those who beat up homosexuals and those who kill homosexuals, are almost always homosexuals and men who admit to having had sex with men in the past or at least fantasizing about it.

Likewise, "homophobic" men who go out in search of "gay" men and then attack and viciously beat up homosexuals, generally have a history of previous sexual contacts with men. In fact, violent "homophobic" males often direct their attacks to the victim's genitals, after which they may rape and sodomize or force the victim to perform fellatio.

Homosexual violence against homosexuals, and that includes women beating up women and men beating up men, is epidemic, often vicious, and so out of control that even homosexual organizations are forced to admit there is a serious problem.

In their book Men Who Beat the Men Who Love Them: Battered Gay Men and Domestic Violence, Drs. Island and Letellier report that "the incidence of domestic violence among gay men is nearly double that in the heterosexual population." However, according to the homosexual organization, Community United Against Violence, this figure is in fact an underestimate due to under reporting. Homosexuals are reluctant to call the police and report that their lover, or a stranger they just had sex with, beat them up.

In the year 2000, it was estimated that about 30% of homosexual couples violently batter one another.

Violence among homosexual couples may in fact be increasing. In a more recent study, it was found that incidents of domestic violence in gay and lesbian relationships rose from between 29% to 58% last year. For example, the San Francisco-based Community United Against Violence recorded 4,048 incidents of domestic violence in gay and lesbian relationships, up from 3,120 cases in 1999. In Los Angeles there was a 58.2 percent increase.

Violence among "gays" is not a function of poverty.

Richard "Dick" Hatch became one of the poster boys of the homosexual movement after he won $1 million on the CBS television show "Survivor. However, in October 2001, he was charged with domestic violence for assaulting his lover. Dick Hatch was also arrested in April 2000 on a charge of abusing his 9-year-old son.

There is a lot of self-hate and self-loathing in the homosexual community. After they give in to their urges, some men are so ashamed that they attack and beat up the man they just had sex with. Some homosexuals beat up their homosexual lovers because they enjoy it.

In August 2001, the homosexual community on the west coast was sent into a tizzy by the announcement that a homosexual serial killer was on the loose. Adam Ezerski, 19, of Atlantic Beach, Florida, had a history of beating up "gay" men, after having sex with them. But in the summer of 2001, Adam began beating some of his lovers to death, including a 76-year-old homosexual, Irving Sicherer, on July 25, and on the very next day, 39-year-old Anthony Martilotto. Both men had met Ezerski on the street, brought him home for some gay love-making, after which he killed them. Sicherer was bludgeoned to death, and Martilotto was strangled.

On August 15, a San Francisco homosexual who picked Adam up in a cafe, and brought him home, was severely beaten and strangled after a night of gay love-making. The victim told authorities that he woke up to discover Ezerski strangling him and beating him in the head. However, the victim did not contact police at first, because, he didn't realize Adam was a serial killer.

In a recent PBS series on those who murder homosexuals, it was inadvertently revealed that almost every single individual convicted of viciously murdering a homosexual had previously had sex with men. And in some cases, several men who had sex together went out in search of homosexuals who they could rob, beat and murder.

Likewise, the worst of serial killers are male homosexuals, or men who have had significant homosexual experience. Henry Lee Lucas traveled the country with his homosexual lover and killed 350 men and women. A Russian homosexual, Andrei Chikatilo, raped and murdered 21 boys, 17 women and 14 girls. Donald Harvey killed 37 boys. John Wayne Gacy raped and killed 33 boys in Chicago. Patrick Kearney murdered 32, cutting his victims into small pieces after have sex with them. Bruce Davis molested and killed 27 young men and boys. The homosexual trio of Corll, Henley, and Brooks murdered 27 Texas men and boys. Juan Corona murdered 25 migrant workers and then had sex with their bodies. Jeffrey Dahmer killed 17 boys and also had a taste for body parts. It has been estimated that up to 68% of those murdered by serial killers have been killed by homosexuals.

Violence in the homosexual community is epidemic.

In a recent series of articles printed in the exceedingly pro-homosexual newspaper, the San Francisco Chronicle (e.g. see Heredia, 9/23/2000, page A25), it was reported that the radical homosexual group, ACT-UP/San Francisco, has been engaging in "a campaign of intimidation and violence" against homosexuals including "felony assault" on public health officials. "Members of the group face trial for assault on several employees of the AIDS group Project Inform" and according to witnesses, have been "formenting terror" in the homosexual community.

As noted, the male medial amygdala is larger than its female counterpart (Breedlove & Cooke, 1999) and changes in size in response to testosterone, which is significant as the medial nuclei (and testosterone) is directly implicated in violent and aggressive behaviors. In consequence, homosexuals, although they have a "female limbic system" also have high levels of testosterone, which, when coupled with other differences between the homosexual and "normal" limbic system, may well predispose a significant minority of homosexuals to behave in a violent and sexually sadistic manner, behaviors that might include the rape of little boys (as is common among pedophile priests), and the sexual sadism visited upon and the mass murder and torture of men, women, and children—as was common during the inquisitions, crusades, and witch burning trials conducted by a Catholic Church --a "church" that has been dominated by homosexuals and a homosexual and homosexual-pedophile subculture for over a thousand years.

On the otherhand, it is perhaps these same sex differences in the limbic system which predisposes a significant minority of homosexuals, and women in general, to be more religious and more spiritually inclined--sex differences which in turn might account for why so many homosexuals are drawn to the priesthood.

SPIRITUAL HELPERS &
MULTIPLE PERSONALITY DISORDER
by Ralph B. Allison

During 25 years of working with highly hypnotizable patients with Multiple Personality Disorder, the bodies of two of these women were borrowed by four different types of spiritual entities. One identified itself as the Essence of the patient's Personality, and the others were its supervisors, who called themselves Celestial Intelligent Energy or CIE. The three CIE were the Spiritual Guardian, Teacher, and Professor. Functions of the Essence are described. Job descriptions of the CIE are presented. They report how they serve "The Creator" in assisting us humans in fulfilling and completing our Life Plans. While each Essence shifts back and forth between Physicalspace (the material world) and Thoughtspace (the nonmaterial world), the CIE are full-time residents of Thoughtspace. However, the CIE have great influence on what happens to humans in Physicalspace.

ENTERING THE LAND OF THE MULTIPLES

The first patient I diagnosed as having Multiple Personality Disorder (MPD) came to my office in Santa Cruz, California, in 1972. She presented both an Eve White and an Eve Black alter-personality (Thigpen & Cleckley, 1957). However, the most important entity she showed me was what I came to call an Inner Self Helper (ISH) (Allison & Schwarz, 1980). In my medical and psychiatric training, nothing had been said about MPD, and nowhere in the psychiatric literature could I find anything about what the ISH might be. Even though I had no idea what it was, I welcomed it as a co-therapist in my attempt to treat a patient for whom I had no treatment plan.

My first awareness of this first "multiple's" ISH was on a tape recording she made in the privacy of her home, which she played for me at our next therapy session. In that recording, I now find mention of several of the functions I have learned that the ISH has in all such patients (Allison & Schwarz, 1980:53-55).

The ISH said, "I know everything that's happened. I know everything that you don't know." This indicates her involvement in the patient's memory management.

"I'm just trying to help you. Because I'm strong. I'm strong, but I have to have your confidence and I have to have your belief in me that we can, you and I, get rid of Sylvia (the Eve Black alter-personality) for good. I mean from now on, so she can never return again, 'cause she doesn't know me. She's not aware of me. She doesn't know about the phone call." This indicates her protective and healing functions, as well as her ability to be unknown to some alter-personalities.

"If Dr. Allison knows, if he knows there's two of us against Sylvia, then he'll be able to help you better." This indicates an ability to work with the therapist as co-therapist.

"If you and I work to help you, we will be one, not two but just one. But see, I'm the side, I'm the part that can help, if you'll just let me. I'm the part that you fight. You fight me. You put all your energies to fight me when you should be fighting Sylvia. . . . But I need your strength as much as you need mine. I'm just a part of it, and you're just a part of it. But together we can be the whole." This indicates that the normal state of affairs would be integration of the ISH with the Personality, but that the Personality's use of Free Will interferes with its cooperation with the ISH while dissociated.

"I've got the strength, all the strength that you need, if you'll just allow it. Just let yourself accept it, that you are all the things that Sylvia isn't, and that we are two against her one, and that we can become one solid person, that loves, that cares, that knows God. . . . You never let yourself see good. But God's there, He stands by. He's there. You could accept Him. I have." This indicates tremendous potential power and a linkage to the Divine.

Each personality and the ISH completed a Minnesota Multiphasic Personality Inventory. Whereas Janette's (the Eve White alter-personality) diagnosis was Dissociating (Hysterical) Personality, the ISH's report was "essentially within normal limits and would serve to verify or clarify other evidence of normalcy. Self appraisal seems too faultless and suggests more coping problems than is admitted by the patient. This signifies a strong will that does not easily tolerate interference or strict control. Patient's positive traits are described as adventurous, frank, individualistic, socially forward, enthusiastic, generous, fair-minded, and verbally fluent." (Allison, 1974:28-29)

Janette moved to another state during therapy and, to the best of my knowledge, she never completed integration of her personalities, nor of her ISH. She demonstrated that, in patients with MPD, there often is a dissociated ISH. This spiritual entity can be counted on to aid the therapist if he or she will but listen and follow what the ISH knows is necessary to regain the patient's mental health.

In numerous subsequent patients with MPD, I interviewed their ISHs and worked with them in therapy. Most of our discussions had to do with what needed to be done in therapy, but occasionally I would ask the ISH about her own background. Every ISH I so interviewed described a past physical lifetime she had as a Personality in her own body, prior to becoming the mentor of the Personality of my dissociated patient. Obviously, they were describing reincarnation as a fact of life. One ISH told me of her last lifetime as the Personality of a squaw in a Native American tribe. In that previous lifetime, she herself had MPD. She had integrated because of the treatment of the tribal Medicine Man, thus becoming an expert on the disorder herself. That was why she was so good at helping her current "charge" cope with MPD while under my care.

Then I met a patient with MPD I have called "Elise." She was the most highly hypnotizable and psychic patient I had met up to that time. When in crisis, she switched alter-personalities in every few seconds, which mandated many hospitalizations. Her ISH gave her name as Charity. When I asked Charity when she had last had her own physical body, she told me that she had last been in the body of a Christlike figure in the Aztec civilization many centuries ago. This was not the story I was used to hearing from other ISHs. Later, I learned that the person whose body she inhabited was apparently Quetzalcoatl, a mythological Aztec god-king from the 3rd to 8th century CE.

Charity told me she also operated a "school for spirits" in which her students stayed for 200 years. During a crisis with Elise, I met two of her students when they used her body to talk to me. One identified herself as Faith, the other as Hope. I met each of just once. They each tried to help me in my treatment of Elise, but I didn't consider their suggestions particularly useful at the time.

Elise improved, and both of us moved on. I moved to Yolo County, California, in 1978. There I met "Marie," another highly hypnotizable woman with MPD and an ISH named Becky. Marie and Becky had dissociated at six months of age, and Becky then created 69 alter-personalities to run the body. The Original Personality had been absent from the physical body for the past 30 years. During the month prior to the integration of all alter-personalities with her Original Personality, Faith, Hope, and Charity all came forth and talked to me again, this time by borrowing Marie's body. The Original Personality had been "raised" by them in their "own realm" where they prepared her for living in our physical world after I arrived in town to do the needed integrative therapy. They knew a six-month-old infant Original Personality could not be expected to be able to operate a 30-year-old body when suddenly thrust into it. She had been trained in basic social skills by Faith, Hope, and Charity, whom she called "my Moms," during the previous 30 earth years.

I avoided bringing up my experiences with Elise and these three spirits, hoping to trick them into revealing who they really were. In spite of my skepticism, it soon became apparent that they were the exact same spirits I had met while talking to Elise, as they knew all about Elise and all about me, as well. I had no secrets from them.

During my three years in Yolo County, I succeeded in psychologically integrating Marie. Becky was still dissociated from Marie, the now-integrated Original Personality. Becky came out to talk to me any time she wanted to. Faith, Hope, and Charity also came out and borrowed her body to talk to me whenever they wanted to. I did not call on them. They chose the time and place to speak to me. Marie could object to their borrowing her body if she was very insistent, but they eventually got their way by putting her into deep trance whenever they wanted to contact me directly. When they were done, Marie would find herself in front of me, wondering what had happened. This was always done in private, so there would be no cause for embarrassment. They were always looking after her best interests.

I left Marie and Yolo County in 1981 to live and work in San Luis Obispo County. When I retired in 1994, I contacted Marie to see if she would cooperate with me in writing her life story. She agreed, and we started writing a book about her life. Actually, the primary informant was Becky, who knew everything that had happened to everyone since the day Marie was born. During my contacts with Marie since then, Becky, Faith, Hope, and Charity have borrowed Marie's body whenever they wanted to, to educate me on matters of importance to them and to me. First, I had to decide what to call all of them, as their roles in Marie's life needed to be described in the manuscript we were writing. Becky told me that she liked my term, ISH, for herself, but only for during the time Marie had been dissociated and was operating with alter-personalities. She considered ISH a job title, equivalent to Damage Control Officer in the military. Now that the damage had been repaired, she reverted to the job she had at the beginning of Marie's life.

In reading philosophical and psychological literature, I soon realized that there have been and are a number of names applied to the likes of Becky, such as soul or spirit. She felt those terms had been contaminated by our current usage and wanted me to call her the Essence of Marie. Becky always called Marie her charge. In my own writings, I commonly use two different pairs of words for the two "parts" of the human mind, which have traditionally been called the mind and the spirit. Sometimes I use the terms Emotional Self and Intellectual Self when speaking qualitatively. Other times I use Personality and Essence. The most ancient pair of terms I found were Plato's Irrational Soul and Rational Soul (Stone, 1997).

When I asked the three spirits what they wanted to be called, Faith asked to be called the Spiritual Guardian of the Essences. Hope preferred to be called the Spiritual Teacher of the Guardians of the Essences. Charity wanted to be called the Spiritual Professor of the Teachers of the Guardians of the Essences. When I needed a group identity label, Charity and I discussed the options at length, and she finally agreed they could all be called Celestial Intelligent Energy or CIE. She told me they were all energy, and intelligent energy at that. In religions, they had been called angels, but that comes from "messenger" in Greek. They wanted me to know that they were far more than mere messengers from "The Creator," for whom they all worked.

When the manuscript was completed, Becky decided that Marie, who had been employed for eight years as a clerical worker in Sacramento, needed to move on to another job. She was hired at a state agency in Central California and moved to San Luis Obispo County to live. Since then I have been able to observe what Marie, the Emotional Self and Personality, does all by herself, and what Becky, her Intellectual Self and Essence, has to do for her. Never before has a dissociated person been available for such long-term observation, while operating as a "normal person" in an ordinary American society setting. During these last years I have been with her in various social settings where I have learned which psychological tasks Marie can do by herself and which ones require the services of Becky. To complete the manuscript, I needed the job descriptions of Faith, Hope, and Charity, and they dictated those for my benefit. Since then, they have demonstrated those duties in many ways in their dealings with me, Marie, and our friends.

PHYSICALSPACE AND THOUGHTSPACE

Before I can explain what these four nonmaterial entities do, I must explain where they operate. They constantly referred to "your realm" and "our realm," in speaking about where they operate. To make it clear in my writings, I had to invent new words to avoid archaic concepts contaminating what they were teaching me. Since Cyberspace had become a favorite term in our world of computer hardware and software, I decided to use the terms Physicalspace and Thoughtspace to label "my realm" and "their realm."

Physicalspace is the physical world as we traditionally know it, at least in the past four centuries of scientific exploration. It is the world of discrete things and the forces which relate them to each other. Those forces are gravity, electromagnetism, the weak nuclear force and the strong nuclear force. These can be called "dumb energy," as they need human consciousness to direct where they go when in action. It is limited in time and space, with the fastest speed possible being that of light. Communication between inhabitants is by voice, telephone, telegrams, fax machines and mail, with email becoming more popular. The experts in understanding the rules and procedures are primarily physicists, along with chemists, biologists, and other "hard science" experts. They devote their careers to discovering the rules which govern how everything works.

Thoughtspace is what has been called heaven/hell/purgatory/Tao by religions, the Spirit World by shamans, and the Astral Plane by Theosophists. In Thoughtspace there is no time or space, as all is eternal and infinite. There are no discrete entities, as all intelligent energy is interconnected and interrelated. The entire "space" is made up of "intelligent energy," which is consciousness. The entire "universe" is both "The Creator" and made by "The Creator." That which is made is the same as That which made it. There are no rules in Thoughtspace, as all actions are decided on a case-by-case basis. We physical beings enter it in sleep, meditation, lucid dreaming, religious ecstasy and mystical experiences, and when we "cease to exist," as the CIE prefer to call bodily death. There is a massive amount of energy in Thoughtspace, but of a sort which is unmeasurable by any physical instrument.

According to the CIE, Thoughtspace has always been here, and Physicalspace came into being next. Physicalspace was created by "The Creator" and will continue as long as "The Creator" wishes for it to be in existence.

FREE WILL

Each Essence and Personality is a "fragment" of the consciousness of "The Creator." "The Creator" gave each fragment Free Will to ignore the instructions of "The Creator." Each human has been assigned a specific Master Life Plan by "The Creator," with one portion to be played out in each physical incarnation. This is the set of instructions which "The Creator" desires each human Personality to live by, and the Essence knows the content of the Life Plan of its charge. The Personality does not know for sure his or her Life Plan in advance of attempting to fulfill it.

The Personality is attached to the human brain, which contains nerve cells and neurohormones, including sex hormones. Therefore, each Personality has a sexual identity and capacity for human emotions, such as anger, lust, jealousy, and eroticism. Free Will and emotionality go hand in glove, as emotionality is the primary reason humans exercise their Free Will. Personalities spend much of their time pursuing unwise activities because they have decided to exercise their Free Will for emotional reasons.

While the Essence has the capacity for exercising Free Will, it has neither sexual identity nor emotionality. It thinks, plans, and decides, but it does not emote. It can have very strong convictions on various subjects, but it has no feelings about those subjects. It usually foregoes exercise of its Free Will, but, when it chooses to continually exercise its Free Will, it becomes a "turned Essence."

RESIDENCY STATUS

The Personality feels at home in Physicalspace and is a stranger when in Thoughtspace. The Essence moves readily between Physicalspace and Thoughtspace every day. It is our bridge of consciousness between the two realms. During the day, the Essence must be fully in attendance in its charge's body in Physicalspace, trying to persuade the Personality to complete and fulfill its Life Plan. But, at night, during nondream sleep, up to 97% of the Essence can leave the body for retraining and instructions in Thoughtspace. During dreams, it tries to inform the Personality of the actions needed to be done the following day.

The CIE are full-time residents of Thoughtspace. Faith, Hope, and Charity are examples of three CIE who have been assigned by "The Creator" to work with human beings in Physicalspace. They use various methods to communicate with and manipulate humans whom they believe need their influence. Taking over the bodies of very highly hypnotizable persons like those with MPD is one method they can use to influence those humans they are assigned to. They can also make "holographic images" of humans, animals, gnomes, and fairies to communicate with humans who are more comfortable communicating with such "beings." They can take over the body of a friend or relative who then says something inspirational without knowing why.

THE WORLD OF HUMAN IMAGINATION

If all humans on earth were to disappear tomorrow, Physicalspace and Thoughtspace would continue to exist. But there is another "universe" which would slowly fade away and dissipate. That is the World of Human Imagination, which is an "interface universe" between the other two. It is a universe totally populated by creations of human imagination, and its very existence depends on the continued thoughts and belief systems of humans over the centuries. It is the world of mythology, tribal gods, emotional heavenly beings with dysfunctional families, and other anthropomorphic entities. It is a world which humans have created out of their emotional and intellectual needs since they came to be upon this globe.

Throughout history, there has been a problem telling the difference between what is in Thoughtspace and what is in this World of Human Imagination. The main difference is that the residents of Thoughtspace have no capacity for the possession or expression of human emotions, such as jealousy, rage, or revenge. So when "spiritual beings" are said to possess such human emotions, they are creatures of this World of Human Imagination.

This World of Human Imagination contains what are called Thought-forms in parapsychology (Bradley, 1991:616-617). They have a degree of independent existence after the demise of their creators, but they do not last forever. They are like the smoke from a bonfire, which exists for a while in the sky after the fire has been extinguished on the ground. Eventually, the winds will carry the smoke particles away and dissipate the cloud that formed from the fire itself. Neither smoke nor Thought-forms have an internal structure of their own to hold them together. Thought-forms need humans to continue contributing their own emotions and thoughts into them to maintain their form and function. Without these continued human contributions, they would disappear.

LEARNING ABOUT THE FUNCTIONS OF THE ESSENCE

While we were writing the book of Marie's life, Becky explained exactly what she did to bring about each desired result, such as the appropriate memories at the right time in therapy. I also spent time with Marie in everyday activities in society, noting what she could and could not do by herself. When I found some function she could not do, I would check with Becky to find out if that was a function of the Essence instead of the Personality. Becky would explain to me what Marie could do and what she, Becky, had to do to perform a complex mental function correctly.

SOME OF THE BODILY FUNCTIONS OF THE ESSENCE

The Essence is the Ki, the Kundalini, the Chakras, being the Life Force itself. Therefore, it has full control over all physical functions, which it first manipulates through the pineal gland, which produces the hormone melatonin. It also communicates to all organs in the body via the endorphin system (Pert, 1997). This is in addition to the communication system provided by the central and peripheral nervous systems.

The Essence can manipulate the immune system to cause the body to become ill with any virus or bacteria in the environment. It decides how long the human is to be sick and then starts the healing and recovery process at the proper time. When its charge's Life Plan is completed, it will shut the body down to cause it to cease to exist. If the body is put on life support machines, the Essence may become quite dissatisfied and develop an "attitude problem," which may be manifested in its next incarnation by antisocial actions in childhood. It knows how and when to cause the body to cease to exist, but it does not know how to cope with machine supported breathing and blood circulation. While the patient is in coma the Essence goes back to Thoughtspace for a crash course on the subject.

The Essence of a woman decides when she is to become pregnant. It can prevent pregnancy, regardless of the exposure. If her Essence does not allow pregnancy to occur, that is because such is not included in her Life Plan. The existence of fertility clinics is disapproved of in Thoughtspace, since such clinics can only deliver the bodies of babies. The CIE then have to scurry around to find an available Personality and Essence. This requires major juggling of an already complexly planned distribution system.

If the Life Plan of the woman includes her experiencing a pregnancy, but she is not ready to raise a child, her Essence will continue the pregnancy for a while and then institute a spontaneous abortion. If she is to go full term but not raise the child, the CIE will refrain from delivering any Personality or Essence to the fetus, and it will be stillborn. Thus, from the point of view of Essences and CIE, abortions are unnecessary. The Essence will abort a fetus if the woman should not bear a child. If they do not abort, then that child was meant to be born, to fulfill and complete the Life Plans of both the mother and the child, as well as of other associated humans.

The CIE report that there is no Essence or Personality in a fetus in utero, as the mother's Essence takes care of all the needs of the contents of her uterus. The baby's Essence and Personality enter the infant's body when it takes its first breath after delivery. Only then is it a complete person, with the traditional body, mind and spirit intact and integrated.

SOME OF THE MENTAL FUNCTIONS OF THE ESSENCE

Since the Prime Directive of each Essence is to keep the child alive until he or she has completed and accomplished his or her Life Plan, it must have all the abilities needed to accomplish that task. Each Essence started out as a fragment of "The Creator's" consciousness and completed a full series of lifetimes as a Personality. When its last lifetime was completed, this fragment of consciousness was upgraded to become an Essence. This upgrading included the implantation into it of certain abilities not contained in any Personality. Nevertheless, it did not lose any of the talents or traits it had as a Personality. However, in its new role as mentor to a Baby Personality, it is no longer connected to the brain's neuronal system or neurohormones. Therefore, it no longer has a sexual identity and can no longer emote. It can remember back to its own lifetimes when it felt male or female, and when it could emote like all humans do.

One function given to each Essence prior to its new career in Physicalspace is knowledge of the Original Language, which is Ancient Sanskrit. This is what might be called a "metalanguage," a language from which and into which all other languages can be translated. It is massively complex since in Thoughtspace there are no facial or other bodily movements to indicate subtleties of meaning, and each thought must be precise, so no misunderstanding can occur. For example, while in English we have one word, LOVE, for affectionate feelings between two persons, and in Greek there are eight such words, in the Original Language there are about 1500 words for love. This is the language that Essences use to communicate with each other and with the CIE.

Since each Essence must be able to understand from birth what the caretakers of the baby say, it is given a full vocabulary of the native language of the birth family. It knows when the mother is saying loving things, or when it is telling the baby how much she hates her and wants to kill her. The Essence can interpret the facial expressions of all humans, to be prepared for any hostility toward its charge. This is during a phase of neurological development when the baby's eyes only see shadows when looking at mother or father. The Essence does not use the physical eyes to see people, and it is also communicating with all Essences of all caretakers, to learn of their intentions toward its charge.

The Essence is the Memory Manager for the Personality (Allison, 1996). It acts as a recorder of all perceptions which cannot come to the neurological system from sensory end organs, such as unspoken thoughts and felt emotions. It also moves all appropriate memories from the organic brain memory system, which includes the hippocampus, amygdala and thalamus, into storage in Thoughtspace in the Akashic Records (Bradley, 1991:7). It records everything that the human experiences as he or she experiences it, but most of that which is recorded is never returned to the brain to be a recalled conscious memory. But, if some specific memory is needed in therapy at a later date, it is in storage in the Akashic Records to be recalled if the Essence and the CIE agree for it to be recalled. All memories are coded on the basis of safety of recall. Pleasant memories can be recalled without problems, but unpleasant memories must be approved by the CIE before being allowed to be recalled, and then only at the safest time and place.

The Essence is the source of all intuitive ideas and impulses. It provides the Personality with awareness of dangers to avoid, as well as impulses to go where the person will meet someone who will fit into their Life Plan.

Whereas the Personality is the source of "emotional imagination," the Essence is the source of "inspirational imagination." When the two are combined, works of genius result. The subject of inspirational imagination comes from Thoughtspace, from the Akashic Records. The CIE know what needs to be discovered, and they implant the ways to discover it into the consciousness of the potential discoverers. Sometimes, the CIE want to make sure that a certain invention will be invented at a specific time and so "cover their bets" by having two different inventors working on the problem at the same time. When both foreswear using Free Will and keep on schedule, they both invent the same device the same week and share in the awards and recognition. This happens when the invention is so important it must be invented at that point in history.

The truly inspired artists, musicians, and writers all describe how the pictures, music or words just flow into their minds, and they just have to put it down in physical form. These "new works" were already composed in Thoughtspace and transmitted by the CIE and Essences to the appropriate artists to produce and perform them.

The Essence can cause its charge to have either positive or negative hallucinations, just as can be done in hypnosis with highly hypnotizable people. We each see what our Essence wants us to see. If an Essence wants its charge to have a physical injury for some educational reason, it can make the Personality not see a rock in the path, which he then stumbles over, breaking his ankle. He literally did not see that rock, because his Essence gave him a negative hallucination of it.

On the other hand, the Essence can cause its charge to see anything that needs to be seen, from flying chariots in the sky above to the inside of a UFO. Out-of-body experiences are produced this way, as a teaching experience for the Personality. The person is not really up in the air over her body in the operating room while the surgeon is trying to stop the hemorrhage. The Essence is giving the Personality a full sensory experience which convinces her that she is above the operating room table about to die. This gives the Personality the push needed to decide to live and "come back into her body." Without such imagery, the Personality might not be willing to overcome her emotional resistance at continuing to live in that body. The Essence uses the experience as a necessary teaching device for the Personality.

Each Personality must have a set of rules to live by, or it goes into a panic. This is what is known as using the "Legal Ethical" way to solve problems. If you look up the answer in the book of approved methods and follow it, there will be no complaints you didn't "do it by the book." Everyone will be happy with you, even if the method did not work this time. But you followed the rules, so you cannot be blamed for the poor results. The result is often a Win-Lose or Lose-Lose solution.

But the Essence of each of us has no rules to follow and has a full range of choices to select from in order to solve the problem in a Win-Win manner. The Essence looks at the current situation and uses the "Situational Ethical" way of solving problems. It ignores what happened in a somewhat similar situation in the past, as the exact same factors are not present this time. Each party to the problem is evaluated, each person's Essence is interviewed, and each person's Life Plan is taken into account. Only when all present factors are considered does the Essence make a judgement as to which action to take. This takes no time, since it is being done in Thoughtspace, where time does not exist. The Personality suddenly "knows" what to do to solve the problem, odd as the solution might sound. But when she does it, it works, and that is what counts.

During nondream sleep, each Essence is 97% gone into Thoughtspace, getting informed of new facts about the world in which we live, so it can do its job well the next day. This is its time for "inservice training." It uses the dream time to communicate information to its charge, the Personality, if that person is one who pays attention to his or her dreams. If not, the Essence has to use other methods during the daytime to get the same information across. This means that each Essence uses a symbol system which is understandable to its charge, since there is no universal symbol system all of us somehow know already. The messages related to what we should do upon awakening are in the dreams we have just before waking up.

If the Personality does not pay attention to the soft but insistent warnings of the Essence and still exercises Free Will, resulting in a potential lethal situation, the Essence can take over the body and get it out of harm's way. This will happen only when all other methods of preservation have failed, and the time to cease to exist is not yet here. The Essence will take over driving the car just as it reaches the edge of the cliff, stop it, back it up, and drive it to the hospital emergency room. Once the Essence has given the story of the suicide attempt to the admitting psychiatrist, it submerges, permitting the Personality to orient himself to the psychiatric ward, wondering how he got there in the first place.

CELESTIAL INTELLIGENT ENERGY (CIE)

I have previously referred to the supervisors of the Essences, the full-time residents of Thoughtspace, named Faith, Hope, and Charity. These were names they first used when raising Marie in Thoughtspace. Their names in the Original Language were too complex for the infant Original Personality, Marie, to use.

The CIE report that they have been on duty monitoring and manipulating all humans since the inception of our world by "The Creator." They are blissful to be working with and for "The Creator," whom they worship. However, they do not wish for us to worship them, the CIE. They are not doing their jobs because they want us humans to bow down and worship them, as has happened in many ancient cultures. They only want us to cooperate with them. They are only doing their jobs.

Each CIE has a specific role to play in the operation of the universe, but there is no hierarchy, in the sense there is in our human culture. No one is the boss, having the power to hire and fire the others. They are more like the various wheels in a fine watch, all working in coordination for common goals. None is more important than any other, but each relates to the others in specific ways, depending on their duty. The CIE have been here for all eternity and can report what they did in cultures in previous eras. They were there, so they are first hand reporters.

Since they have no time or distance in their universe, they can be all places at the same time. They can prepare for actions of humans long before those humans know such actions will be needed. They are always watching each and every one of us and are interceding whenever they believe intervention is needed, to keep us on our Life Plans, and to keep us safe from bodily destruction, at least until our time to cease to exist has arrived. When that time comes, they will help the Essence use any means available to terminate our earthly existence and bring us home to Thoughtspace. There they will prepare us for our next earthly reincarnation.

The duties and responsibilities of each of the CIE are as follows. None of the Spiritual Guardians, Teachers or Professors have had a physical body of their own.

SPIRITUAL GUARDIAN OF THE ESSENCES, AS DESCRIBED BY FAITH

"Whereas the Essences have responsibility for one human charge, we, the Spiritual Guardians of the Essences, are responsible for 150 of the Essences. Our duties and responsibilities are as follows:

"We are called Spiritual Guardians of the Essences because we protect and guard. Therefore, that is our title. Our prime responsibility is to protect our Essences at all costs. When the energy of an Essence has been depleted while protecting their charge, it is unable to sustain any further psychic assault. A psychic assault is when a 'turned Essence' is trying to destroy the Essence of another human. We, as Guardians, must take drastic steps to protect the Essence we are supervising. We can physically remove the body from the place of the psychic assault. We can also make the human fall asleep. We can convince the human with the 'turned Essence,' who is doing the psychic assault, to feel that the argument or discourse has been finished. This is our most important and Prime Directive, to protect and guard the Essences under our guidance. We create situations in which the human needs to make important decisions. If the Essence has been unable to direct their charge to the point of taking appropriate action, we will step in. Situations will include a career direction, for example. We will send other humans into the path of the human that we need to change. We will have that human say or do something that brings about the change required.

"Another important function is to pick the family that the human will be born into. That way the human's Life Plan will be started properly. We pick the culture, social group, parents, and siblings with whom the human will experience all that is needed to complete their Life Plans. In the course of the human growing, we also send boyfriends and girlfriends into the humans' lives as lessons to be learned in social and romantic experiences. We also send to the humans the best friends, who are actually part of the 150 Essences that we supervise. That is why, when humans meet their closest friends and feel as if they have known those humans before, it is because they have. They are part of the humans' existence of all prior lives before.

"We choose the humans' mates or significant others to create learning situations. There can be many different kinds of learning situations. This includes all manners of relationships, including heterosexual or homosexual pairing. It could be learning to live with an emotional or mentally ill human. It could also be experiencing the life as a mate to someone who is significantly disabled. We also know if one mate is enough or if the human will have several mates. In either context, it is all part of growing and learning in this Life Plan. We also have chosen specific jobs or positions that each human is to be involved in. We will direct and change those job situations that best suit your needs. If the specific job the human is in becomes unbearable, that is because we have stepped in and are making it so. Your Life Plan does not include that position or job anymore. That is the time that all humans need to listen to their Essences. We also are called, in human terms, 'Guardian Angels,' but that is incorrect wordage for ourselves. We do protect and guard the Essences, and we will perform 'miracles,' such as extracting a human from a horrible accident. We, as Guardians of the Essences, have a full variety of Essences to supervise. We have immature ones who are on their first assignments, who are called 'Baby Essences.' We have Essences that do not cooperate with our teaching and become rebellious and therefore turn their charge into doing some criminal acts. Those are called 'turned Essences.'

"Each Essence, having had prior lives as humans, has been granted Free Will by 'The Creator.' This means that any Essence may choose to ignore the advice and training of the CIE, who are assigned to implement the directives of 'The Creator.' A 'turned Essence' ignores the teachings of the CIE and exercises Free Will alone."

SPIRITUAL TEACHER OF THE GUARDIANS OF THE ESSENCES, AS DESCRIBED BY HOPE

"To perform a 'miracle,' the Spiritual Guardian of the Essences combines with another CIE, 'The Spiritual Teacher of the Guardian of the Essences.' Each Teacher is responsible for 150,000 Spiritual Guardians.

"We Spiritual Teachers are in charge of all education of the Guardians and of the Baby Essences. When they arrive at our school, the first avenue is to implant into the Baby Essence the entire language of ourselves, the CIE. That way, we are able to communicate without misinterpretation. Once the Baby Essences have become implanted with our language, they are sent to their Guardian. We instruct the Guardians regarding where each Essence is to be placed in Physicalspace, when each Essence will arrive again in Thoughtspace, and how long the next physical life of each Essence will last.

"We constantly teach the Guardians new and improved information regarding changes in culture and environment into which the Essences have been assigned. We also are responsible regarding all of humans' Physicalspace educational resources. We have the responsibility for housing and training of rebellious 'turned Essences.' They are given added training and opportunity for additional growth before they are allowed to be reincarnated into another human form again."

SPIRITUAL PROFESSOR OF THE TEACHERS OF THE GUARDIANS OF THE ESSENCES, AS DESCRIBED BY CHARITY

"When the Spiritual Teacher joins with the Guardian to perform 'miracles,' they may need to be joined by the other CIE. Her title is the 'Spiritual Professor of the Teachers of the Guardians of the Essences.'

"We Professors are responsible for 250,000 Teachers. We are responsible for the 150,000 Guardians that each of these Spiritual Teachers has the responsibility for. We also are responsible for the 150 Essences that each of the Spiritual Guardians has responsibility for. We, the Professors, are responsible for maintaining dictionaries of all human words, phrases and definitions in a special library for all Essences and other CIE to use. We are responsible for assigning specific duties to the Teacher and the Guardian regarding the humans that we are responsible for teaching.

"For example, we will provide the Teacher with the information they need to help the human with marital or family crises. We will supply the Guardian with information involving friends, acquaintances, and co-workers.

"We, the Professor, have the responsibility for spiritual and higher levels of learning and understanding for the humans that we have been assigned to.

"We reacquaint humans with others who were related to them in previous lives. We arrange for the conditions of when and where Essences will be reincarnated. Most decisions are decided by conferring with the Essence and other CIE involved with the Essence's charge. However, we have the final say on any decisions which they cannot resolve among themselves.

"We pass down information from 'The Creator' to the Teachers to the Guardians to the Essences. All information from the Essences is relayed back to us through the same channels. When we are teaching humans, we will converse with a small circle of human contacts. We limit our teachings to no more than 10 humans at a time, as contamination will rob us of our responsibility and duty from our beloved 'Creator.'

"The delivery of psychic abilities is another one of our functions. We deliver all psychic abilities to the Essences to deliver to their respective charges.

"We are responsible for bringing together the Essences of humans who will be working together. This is one of the actions we take as managers for any projects that 'The Creator' wants completed. We have the authority to complete the project in any way that we have to.

"We are responsible for housing 'turned Essences' that are a major threat to the existence of Essences in our realm. We have what is known as a 'velvet whip.' We do not chastise, we do not punish, in human terms. We house, explain, and teach, but these Essences will never be reincarnated into another human being, ever."

CONCLUSIONS OF BECKY, THE ESSENCE, AND THE CIE, FAITH, HOPE, AND CHARITY

"Humans have long considered the universe as something that was created out of nothing. Theologians have considered that Something created the universe. Both are correct. 'The Creator' has been here for as long as there has been energy. 'The Creator' designed this universe of yours with all manners of life, with plants, animals, and minerals. We, the CIE, are in charge of the operations of 'The Creator's' universe. There is an intellectual order in your universe, and it is precisely run by the CIE. There is no error in what we do.

"We have been typically envisioned as angels, females with white robes, halos, wings, long blonde hair, and sandals. WE ARE NOT THAT. We do not have bodies; we are energy.

"Each of the Essences is taught by ourselves, the CIE, under the direction of 'The Creator.' Each Essence has had prior lives and is able to impart whatever wisdom and knowledge they learned unto their charges. Memories are stored, indexed and retrieved by each human's Essence in the Akashic Records Center. The Essences bring forth the memories to their charges only when needed.

"The Essences do not force their actions unto their charges. They are the still, small voice inside each human. When each of you listens to that voice inside, you will find the correct path that each must tread. Reincarnation is a fact in our realm for all Essences in order for them to gain the experience needed to direct their charges on their next series of lifetimes. Your journey of completing and fulfilling your Life Plan will be long but rewarding if you will only listen to that voice, your Essence. It has never failed; your Essence has always been there and wishes for you humans to be more attentive to it.

"We are here. Listen to us and grow."

Figure 164. *"With dreams upon my bed thou scarest me & Affrightest me with visions" Williams Blake, 17th century.*

POSSESSION & PROPHECY
by R. Joseph

PRESENCE, POSSESSION & THE ALIEN HAND

"After getting into bed I had a vivid tactile hallucination of being grasped by the arm, which made me get up and search my room for an intruder. The next night I suddenly felt something come into the room and stay close to my bed. It remained only a minute or two. There was a horribly unpleasant sensation connected with it. It stirred something at the roots of my being. The feeling was not pain so much as abhorrence. Something was present with me, and I knew its presence far more surely than I have ever known the presence of any fleshly living creature. I was conscious of its departure as of its coming; an almost instantaneously swift going through the door, and the horrible sensation disappeared" (James, 1902).

"Quite early in the night I was awakened. I felt as if I had been aroused intentionally, and at first thought someone was breaking into the house. I immediately felt a consciousness of a presence in the room, it was not a consciousness of a live person, but of a spiritual presence. I also at the same time felt a strong feeling of superstitious dread, as if something strange and fearful were about to happen" (James, 1902).

It is certainly possible, in some cases, that the experience of a "presence," of the existence of an unseen person or entity, may have a supernatural origin. Neurologically, however, this condition is associated with abnormalities, including seizure activity, involving the right hemisphere--the right parietal lobe in particular—and disturbances involving the corpus callosum interconnections between the right and left (speaking) half of the brain including the medial frontal lobe and anterior commissure (Joseph, 1988a,b, 1996, 1999a).

For example, a woman with a right parietal injury repeatedly claimed that at night another person would get into bed with her. She believed that the alien entity was a little Negro girl, whose arm would slip into the patient's sleeve (Gerstmann, 1942). This alien "presence" was exclusively a left sided phenomenon. Yet another patient with a right parietal injury claimed "that an old man" would get into bed with him. Another patient engaged in peculiar erotic behavior with his left limbs which he believed belonged to a woman. A patient described by Bisiach and Berti (1987, p. 185) "would become perplexed and silent whenever the conversation touched upon the left half of his body; even attempts to evoke memories of it were unsuccessful." Instead he claimed "that a woman was lying on his left side; he would utter witty remarks about this and sometimes caress his left arm".

Some patients feel as if the left half of their body has been taken over by something evil that is persecuting them. They may develop a dislike for their left arms or legs, try to throw them away, become agitated when they are referred to, entertain persecutory delusions regarding them, and repeatedly complain of strangers sleeping in their beds (Bisiach & Berti, 1987; Critchley, 1953; Gerstmann, 1942).

One patient complained that this other person tried to push her out of the bed. She threatened to sue the hospital. Another patient, after bumping into her left arm and leg all night, bitterly complained about "a hospital that makes people sleep together." She expressed not only anger but concern least her husband should find out; she was convinced it was a man in her bed.

Likewise, the left hemisphere of some split-brain patients have claimed to hate the left half of their body and attribute to it disagreeable personality traits or claim that it has engaged in behavior which the speaking half of the brain finds unpleasant, strange, objectionable, embarrassing, or contrary to it's wishes (Joseph, 1988ab).

In many instances, patients may have lived a normal, uneventful life, only to suddenly become possessed by an alien presence which takes over half their body.

Goldberg (1987, p 290) describes a 53 year old right-handed women, "B.D." who while at work was overcome with a "feeling of nausea and began to notice that her left leg felt 'as if it did not belong to me.' This feeling of being dissociated from her body spread to the rest of her left side. At home, her symptoms began to worsen. While sleeping one night a few days after admission to the hospital, she woke up suddenly and noticed her own left hand scratching her shoulder.... She would frequently look down to find the hand doing something that she had no idea it had been doing. She found this very disturbing and was convinced that she was going crazy." Subsequent CT scan and MRI indicated an infarct to the medial frontal lobe and damage to the body of the corpus callosum.

Another patient described by Goldberg (1987, p. 295) reported "an incident in which she was lying in bed with the window open when suddenly the left limb reached down and pulled up the covers, functioning entirely in the alien mode. She concluded that 'it' must have felt cold and needed to cover her up. She felt that frequently the 'alien' did things that were generally 'good for her.'"

McNabb, Caroll, and Mastaglia (1988, pp. 219, 221) describe a woman with extensive damage involving the medial left frontal lobe and anterior corpus callosum, whose right "hand showed an uncontrollable tendency to reach out and take hold of objects and then was unable to release them. At times the right hand interfered with tasks being performed by the left hand. She attempted to restrain it by wedging it between her legs or by holding or slapping it with her left hand. The patient would repeatedly express astonishment at these actions." Another patient reported that she was "attempting to write with her left hand, the right would reach over and take the pencil. The left hand would respond by grasping the right hand to restrain it."

In some instances, patients may display alien movements in both hands (Gasquoine 1993; Goldberg & Bloom 1990) as well as alien vocalization of thoughts. For example, a patient described by Gasquoine (1993) had a propensity to reach out and touch female breasts, as well as novel objects and persons. He reported this caused him great embarrassment and that he would typically attempt to take hold of his right with his left hand or voluntarily grasp objects, such as his lap tray, so that he would not spontaneously reach out and grab someone.

Some individuals not only have difficulty controlling their arms and hands, but their speech. That is, they may begin to speak and make pronoucements, which they claim to have no control over—as if they had been taken over and were possessed by an alien consciousness that had a mind of its own.

POSSESSION & THE RIGHT HEMISPHERE
It is now well established that the brain is functionally lateralized, such that the temporal and sequential aspects of language are controlled by the left hemisphere, whereas visual spatial, environmental, the emotional sounds of speech, and the body image, are the domain of the right half of the brain. Because each hemisphere is concerned with different types of information, even when analyzing ostensibly the same stimulus each half of the brain may react, interpret and process it differently and even reach different conclusions (Joseph, 1988b; Joseph et al., 1984, Levy & Trevarthen, 1976). Moreover, even when the goals are the same, the two halves of the brain may produce and attempt to act on different strategies. In consequence, functional lateralization may lead to the development of oppositional attitudes, goals and interests such that one half of the brain may desire or engage in acts that are opposed by the other. This has been experimentally demonstrated in patients who have undergone split-brain surgery, that is, complete corpus callosotomy and the severing of the axonal pathways linking the right and left hemisphere.

For example, one split brain individual's left hand would not allow him to smoke, and would pluck lit cigarettes from his mouth or right hand and put them out. Apparently, although his left cerebrum wanted to smoke, his right hemisphere didn't approve --he had been trying to quit for years (Joseph, 1988a,b). Yet another split brain patient experienced conflicts when attempting to eat, watch TV, or go for walks, his right and left hemisphere apparently enjoying different TV programs or types of food (Joseph 1988b). Nevertheless, these difficulties are not limited to split-brain patients, for conflicts of a similar nature often plague the intact individual as well.

Indeed, it has been well demonstrated that each half of the brain is capable of experiencing independent and semi-independent forms of consciousness, two minds within a single brain, one in the right the other in the left hemisphere. This has been demonstrated in studies of patients who have undergone complete corpus callosotomies (i.e. split-brain operations) for the purposes of controlling intractable epilepsy (Joseph, 1988ab). As described by Noble Laureate Roger Sperry (1966, p. 299), "Everything we have seen indicates that the surgery has left these people with two separate minds, that is, two separate spheres of consciousness. What is experienced in the right hemisphere seems to lie entirely outside the realm of awareness of the left hemisphere. This mental division has been demonstrated in regard to perception, cognition, volition, learning and memory."

For example, when split-brain patients are tactually stimulated on the left side of the body, their left hemispheres demonstrate marked neglect when verbal responses are required, they are unable to name objects placed in the left hand, and they fail to report the presence of a moving or stationary stimulus in the left half of their visual fields (Bogen, 1979; Joseph, 1988b; Levy, 1974, 1983; Seymour et al. 1994; Sperry, 1982). They (i.e., their left hemisphere's) cannot verbally describe odors, pictures or auditory stimuli tachistoscopically or dichotically presented to the right cerebrum, and have extreme difficulty explaining why the left half of their bodies responds or behaves in a particular purposeful manner (such as when the right brain is selectively given a command).

However, by raising their left hand (which is controlled by the right half of the cerebrum) the disconnected right hemisphere is able to indicate when the patient is tactually or visually stimulated on the left side. When tachistoscopically presented with words to the left of visual midline, although unable to name them, when offered multiple visual choices in full field their right hemispheres are usually able to point correctly with the left hand to the word viewed.

When presented with words like "toothbrush," "tooth" falls in the left visual field (and thus, is transmitted to the right cerebrum) and the word "brush" falls in the right field (and goes to the left hemisphere). Hence, when offered the opportunity to point to several words (i.e., hair, tooth, coat, brush, etc.), the left hand usually will point to the word viewed by the right cerebrum (i.e., tooth) and the right hand to the word viewed by the left hemisphere (i.e., brush). When offered a verbal choice, the speaking (usually the left) hemisphere will respond "brush" and will deny seeing the word "tooth."

Overall, this indicates that the disconnected right and left cerebral hemispheres, although unable to communicate and directly share information, are nevertheless fully capable of independently generating and supporting mental activity (Bogen, 1969, 1979; Joseph, 1986b, 1988b; Levy, 1974, 1983; Sperry, 1982). Hence, in the right hemisphere we deal with a second form of awareness that accompanies in parallel what appears to be the "dominant" temporal-sequential, language dependent stream of consciousness in the left cerebrum.

Moreover, as has been demonstrated by Sperry, Bogen, Levy, Joseph and others, the isolated right cerebral hemisphere, like the left, is capable of self-awareness, can plan for the future, has goals and aspirations, likes and dislikes, social and political awareness, can purposefully initiate behavior, guide response choices and emotional reactions, as well as recall and act upon certain memories, desires, impulses, situations or environmental events —without the aid, knowledge or active (reflective) participation of the left half of the brain.

In consequence, because each half of the brain controls the other half of the body, sometimes one half of the body will engage in independent actions, such that half of the body may behave as if possessed and controlled by an alien or even a demonic force.

As reported by patients who have undergone "split-brain" surgery, the behavior of the right hemisphere is not always cooperative, and sometimes it engages in behavior which the left language dominant half of the brain finds objectionable, embarrassing, puzzling, mysterious, and upsetting.

For example, Akelaitis (1945, p. 597) describes two patients with complete corpus callosotomies who experienced extreme difficulties making the two halves of their bodies cooperate. "In tasks requiring bimanual activity the left hand would frequently perform oppositely to what she desired to do with the right hand. For example, she would be putting on clothes with her right and pulling them off with her left, opening a door or drawer with her right hand and simultaneously pushing it shut with the left. These uncontrollable acts made her increasingly irritated and depressed." On several occasions it tried to slam a drawer on her right hand, and on a number of instances the left hand (right hemisphere) attempted to take her clothes off, even though that is not what she (i.e. the left hemisphere) desired to do.

Another patient experienced difficulty while shopping, the right hand would place something in the cart and the left hand would put it right back again. Both patients frequently experienced other difficulties as well . "I want to walk forward but something makes me go backward." A recently divorced male patient noted that on several occasions while walking about town he found himself forced to go some distance in another direction. Later (although his left hemisphere was not conscious of it at the time) it was discovered (by Dr. Akelaitis) that this diverted course, if continued, would have led him to his former wife's new home.

Geschwind (1981) reports a callosal patient who complained that his left hand on several occasions suddenly struck his wife—much to the embarrassment of his left (speaking) hemisphere. In another case, a patient's left hand attempted to choke the patient himself and had to be wrestled away

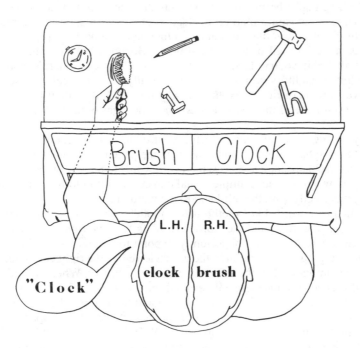

Figure 165a. Split-brain patient. The right hemisphere, which controls the left hand, sees the word "brush." The left hemisphere sees the word "clock." When asked to retrieve the item seen with the "left hand" the right hand picks the brush. From Joseph, 1988a).

(Goldstein; cited by Geschwind, 1981).

Bogen (1979, p. 333) indicates that almost all of his "complete commissurotomy patients manifested some degree of intermanual conflict in the early postoperative period." One patient, Rocky, experienced situations in which his hands were uncooperative; the right would button up a shirt and the left would follow right behind and undo the buttons. For years, he complained of difficulty getting his left leg to go in the direction he (or rather his left hemisphere) desired. Another patient often referred to the left half of her body as "my little sister" when she was complaining of its peculiar and independent actions.

A split-brain patient described by Dimond (1980, p. 434) reported that once when she had overslept her "left hand slapped me awake." This same patient, in fact, complained of several instances where her left hand had acted violently. Similarly, Sweet (1945) describes a female patient whose left hand sometimes behaved oppositionally and in a fashion which on occasion was quite embarrassing.

Similar difficulties plagued a split-brain patient whom I reported on (Joseph 1988b). After callosotomy, this patient (2-C) frequently was confronted with situations in which his left extremities not only acted independently, but engaged in purposeful and complex behaviors —some of which he (or rather, his left hemisphere) found objectionable and annoying.

For example, 2-C (the speaking half of his his brain) complained of instances in which his left hand would perform socially inappropriate actions (e.g. attempting to strike a relative) and would act in a manner completely opposite to what he expressively intended, such as turn off the TV or change channels, even though he (or rather his left hemisphere) was enjoying the program. Once, after he had retrieved something from the refrigerator with his right hand, his left took the food, put it back on the shelf and retrieved a completely different item "Even though that's not what I wanted to eat!" On at least one occasion, his left leg refused to continue "going for a walk" and would only allow him to return home.

In the laboratory, he often became quite angry with his left hand, he struck it and expressed hate for it. Several times, his left and right hands engaged in actual physical struggles. For example, on one task both hands were stimulated simultaneously (while out of view) with either the same or

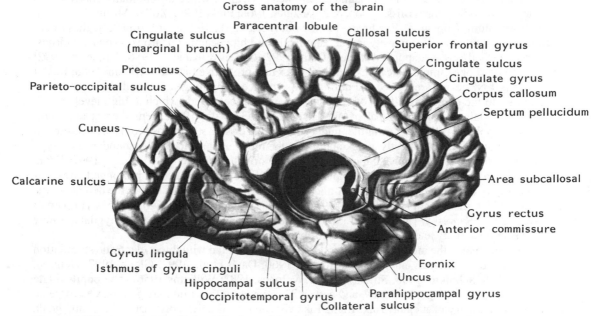

Figure 165b. A medial "split-brain" view of the brain. A massive rope of fibers, the corpus callosum, connects and transfers information between the right and left half of the brain.

two different textured materials (e.g., sandpaper to the right, velvet to the left); and the patient was required to point (with the left and right hands simultaneously) to an array of fabrics that were hanging in view on the left and right of the testing apparatus. However, at no time was he informed that two different fabrics were being applied.

After stimulation the patient would pull his hands out from inside the apparatus and point with the left to the fabric felt by the left and with the right to the fabric felt by the right.

Surprisingly, although his left hand (right hemisphere) responded correctly, his left hemisphere vocalized: "That's wrong!" Repeatedly he reached over with his right hand and tried to force his left extremity to point to the fabric experienced by the right (although the left hand responded correctly! His left hemisphere didn't know this, however.). His left hand refused to be moved and physically resisted being forced to point at anything different. In one instance a physical struggle ensued, the right grappling with the left.

Moreover, while 2-C was performing this (and other tasks), his left hemisphere made statements such as: "I hate this hand" or "This is so frustrating" and would strike his left hand with his right or punch his left arm. In these instances there could be little doubt that his right hemisphere was behaving with purposeful intent and understanding, whereas his left hemisphere had absolutely no comprehension of why his left hand (right hemisphere) was behaving in this manner.

EMOTIONAL TRAUMA, POSSESSION & THE SPLITTING OF CONSCIOUSNESS

It has been demonstrated experimentally, that even the normal brain may experience similar episodes of functional disconnection between the right and left hemisphere (Joseph et al., 1984; reviewed in Joseph,1988a) such that the individual may feel possessed or experience an evil, alien presence. In part, this is a consequence of functional lateralized and the specialization of each half of the brain, and right hemisphere dominance for emotion and the body image. However, these conditions also sometimes occur during episodes of extreme emotional distress which also effects the right hemisphere more strongly than the left (reviewed in Joseph, 1988a, 1996). In fact, under conditions of extreme fear, the brain may be injured, and regions in the limbic system, such as the amygdala, may develop "kindling" --which is a form of seizure activity.

Specifically, under conditions of extreme fear or emotional trauma, the brain secretes and releases a cascade of neurochemical and stress hormones, including corticostereoids, enkephalins, norepinephrine (NE), serotonin (5HT), and dopamine (DA), all of which differentially contribute to the fear and stress response (Bliss, Ailion, & Zwanziger, 1968; Fink, 1999; Moller, Milinksi & Slater, 1998; Rosenblum, Coplan, & Friedman, 1994; Southwick et al., 1993). Unfortunately, these neurotransmitter fluctuations negatively impact amygdala and hippocampal neurons, axons, dendrites, and their pre and post synaptic substrates (Cain, 1992; Goelet & Kandel, 1986; Kraemer, 1992; Krystal, 1990). For example, since NE also serves a neural protective function (Glavin, 1985; Ray et al., 1987b), if NE levels are reduced--a normal consequence of prolonged fear and stress-- neurons are exposed to the damaging effects of enkephalins and corticosteroids which at high levels attack and kill amygdala and hippocampal pyramidal neurons (Gahwiler 1983; Henriksen et al., 1978; Packan & Sapolsky, 1990). For example, under high levels of stress, corticosteroids are secreted in massive amounts, but also directly attack and injure the hippocampus due to the abundance of Type II adrenal steroids receptors which abound within this structure (Lupien & McEwen, 1997; Pugh, Fleshner & Rudy, 1997). In addition, coupled with NE depletion, repeated or prolonged stress induced secretory episodes of corticosteroids and enkephalins can injure cells within the dentate gyrus and Ammon's horn (Lupien & McEwen, 1997) such that the hippocampus will atrophy (Lupien & McEwen, 1997; Sapolsky, 1996; Uno, Tarara, Else, & Sapolsky, 1989). As to the amygdala, it may develop seizure activity and thus become abnormally activated.

Extreme fear is the most common emotional reaction elicited with direct electrode stimulation of the human or nonhuman amygdala (Chapman, 1960; Davis et al., 1997; Gloor, 1997; Halgren, 1992; Rosen & Schulkin, 1998; Strauss, Risser, & Jones, 1982; Williams 1956). The pupils dilate and the subject will cringe, withdraw, and cower. This cowering reaction may give way to extreme panic and the animal will attempt to take flight. Likewise, abnormal activity originating in the amygdala and/or the overlying temporal lobe can evoke overwhelming, terrifying feelings of "nightmarish" fear that may not be tied to anything specific, other than perhaps the sensation of impending death (Herman & Chambria, 1980; Strauss et al., 1982; Weil, 1956). With amygdala activation the EEG becomes desynchronized (indicating arousal), heart rate becomes depressed, respiration patterns change, the galvanic skin response significantly alters, the face contorts, the pupils will dilate, and the subject will look anxious and afraid (Bagshaw & Benzies, 1968; Davis, 1992; Kapp, Supple, & Whalen, 1994; Ursin & Kaada, 1960).

However, if the amygdala (and hippocampus) is injured or abnormally active, the individual may become emotionally abnormal, they may suffer from hallucinations, they may hear voices, and they may have dissociative episodes and feel as if they have been "possessed."

The feeling of being "possessed" including the development of alternate personalities which temporarily possess and take over control from the main personality, and thus dramatic alterations in personality,have been repeatedly observed following injury to the amygdala and overlying temporal lobe (Lilly et al., 1983; Marlowe et al., 1975; Shenk & Bear, 1981; Terzian & Ore, 1955). In some cases of temporal lobe, amygdala, hippocampal abnormality, the alterations in personality are so dramatic patients may appear to be possessed by demons or suffering from a multiple personality disorder (Fichtner, Kuhlman, & Hughes, 1990; Mesulam, 1981; Shenk & Bear, 1981). In fact, in several cases of multiple personality dissociative disorder, EEG or blood flow abnormalities involving the temporal lobe have been demonstrated (Drake 1986; Fichtner et al., 1990; Mathew, Jack & West, 1985; Mesulam 1981; Schenk & Bear 1981). Moreover, some patients may shift from one personality to another following a seizure or with increases in temporal lobe activity (Mesulam, 1981; Shenk & Bear, 1981). Similarly, it has been reported that heightened emotional distress may precede the appearance of alternate personalities (Greaves 1980; Putnam 1985).

Sometimes the "voices" of the alternate personality, or the "demon... devil... god" and so on, will order the main personality to harm others or themselves. Some of these alternate personalities may also take control and engage in criminal and self-destructive acts. Some of those "possessed" honestly believe they are possessed by demons, devils, or god.

Alternate personalities may be formed during a dissociative state while a victim is experiencing a period of severe and repetitive trauma. That is, under certain traumatic (or neurological) conditions, an aspect of the consciousness may fragment, break off, and thereafter act in a semi-independent or completely independent manner.

Compared to other cortical areas, the most complex, vivid hallucinations, including out-of-body dissociative experiences, have their source in the temporal lobe (Daly, 1958; Gloor,1986, 1990, 1992; Halgren 1992; Halgren et al., 1978; Horowitz et al., 1968; Penfield, 1952, 1954; Penfield & Perot, 1963; Williams 1956) and the hippocampus and amygdala appear to be the responsible agents (Gloor, 1990, 1992; Horowitz et al., 1968; Halgren, 1992; Halgren et al., 1978). The amygdala, hippocampus, and temporal lobe play a significant role in the production of REM sleep and dream activity (Hodoba, 1986; Meyer, Ishikawa, Hata, & Karacan, 1987), and become disinhibited in reaction to hallucinogens such as LSD, and are thus implicated in the production of LSD-induced hallucinations (Baldwin, Lewis, & Bach, 1955; Chapman, Walter, & Ross, 1963; Serafetinides, 1965). Hence, under conditions of extreme emotional stress and trauma, the hippocampus, amygdala and temporal lobe may become abnormally active, and victims may experience extreme sensory distortions and hallucinations, including out-of-body phenomenon.

Due to the development of these fear-induced sensory-distorting hallucinatory states, trees, animals, and inanimate objects may even assume demonic form and/or be invested with satanic intent. These horrible hallucinations and sensory distortions may also be committed to memory. Later, the victim may recall the "hallucination" and believe they were set upon by demons, witches and the like, and/or that they were abused in Satanic rituals, or abducted and painfully probed by demonic aliens.

Consider the Walt Disney version of "Snow White." When the woodcutter, who had been ordered to cut out her heart, urged Snow White to flee for her life, she panicked and ran into the darkening forest in near hysteria. And, as she ran and stumbled darting in tears here and there, the trees became demonic, growing eyes and wicked mouths, and gnarled arms and hands which stretched out threateningly toward her. Overcome with terror, she collapsed to the forest floor, sobbing uncontrollable.

Now, perchance, had Snow White later recalled this frightening misadventure, she may well have explained to skeptical listeners that demons had emerged from the forest, and threatened to snatch her away. and, she may truly believe this happened, for it is what she truly experienced and what she now truly remembers.

Yet others may believe they were attacked by aliens, or demons, and then spirited away to hell, or to space ships where nightmarish experiments were performed on them.

It is noteworthy that many of those reporting alien abductions, have a history of sexual molestation or severe emotional trauma, or temporal lobe epilepsy (Mack, 1994). As noted,, stress, sexual trauma and sexual activity activates the amygdala as well as the temporal lobe—structures which are associated with the production of complex and exceedingly frightening hallucinations, including those of a demonic, religious, and sexual nature including naked women, demons, ghosts and pigs walking upright dressed as people (Bear 1979; Daly 1958; Gloor 1986, 1992; Horowitz et al. 1968; MacLean 1990; Mesulam 1981; Penfield & Perot 1963; Schenk, & Bear 1981; Slater & Beard 1963; Subirana & Oller-Daurelia, 1953; Trimble 1991; Weingarten, et al. 1977; Williams 1956).

Hence perhaps it is not surprising that individuals who were severely traumatized or who were sexually abused, sometimes report that they were subject to bizarre sexual rituals that involved demonic (Satanic) activities (which is not to say that in some cases this may in fact be the case). And perhaps it is not surprisingly that those with histories of severe abuse, and/or who suffer from seizure disorders, may believe that demonic-like aliens lifted them into the air and took them to a room of vast proportions—descriptions which are identical to those of at least some patients during temporal lobe stimulation, and at least some individuals who are severely frightened and/or who died only to return to tell the tale.

HELL & ALIEN ABDUCTIONS

Many "abductees" claim a sequence of perceptual experience similar to those who have died and returned to tell the tale. Abductees report the presence of a bright light, or a strange illumination which may envelop them in a beam or halo of light. They feel drawn upward toward the light, and they feel and see themselves as floating in the air (Bullard, 1987; Mack, 1994; Ritchie, 1994).

Similar to those who have "experienced" life after death, abductees report going on voyages through the air, where they rapidly fly over the land or sea, to destinations including the Egyptian pyramids, New York City, and the North pole (Bullard, 1987; Mack, 1994; Ritchie, 1994).

Over the course of the last fifty years there have been numerous reports of alien abductions (Bullard, 1987; Mack, 1994, Ritchie, 1994). Typically they are "abducted" while asleep or dreaming, or just upon wakening in the middle of the night -which raises the specter of hallucination and temporal lobe limbic system activation as these structures become exceedingly active during dream sleep.

Others claim they were abducted while driving late at night, while tired and under conditions where the head lights, moon light, and oncoming lights may flicker past (Bullard, 1987; Mack, 1994;

Figure 166. Alien-devils
probing abductees. 17th
century woodcut.

Ritchie, 1994) -thus inducing possible seizure activity.

However, the religious experience of some abductees is often hellish, and the aftermath includes prolonged feelings of depression, and horror and despair. "Abductees" frequently report that once they were drawn up toward the light, they felt overwhelmed with terror and that once they "arrived" they were subjected to painful and agonizing procedures (Bullard, 1987; Mack, 1994; Ritchie, 1994).

Women often report that they were stripped naked and their legs spread, and that they were sexually molested, raped, or painfully probed.

Male and female abductees frequently report undergoing painful and invasive physical exams by alien monstrosities who loom demonically, probing vaginas, wombs, the anus, the eyeballs, and the viscera, with needle-like devices, or with twisting wires, or sharp, painfully cold lance-like instruments that may deliver electric, burning, or shock like sensations (Bullard, 1987; Mack, 1994; Ritchie, 1994).

Like those who experience life after death, some abductees report undergoing a "life review." They may see themselves or others on a viewing screen, usually engaged in sexual or violent activity. Similar sexual flashbacks are not uncommon with direct amygdala stimulation (Gloor, 1990, 1997; Halgren, 1992).

Once they return to earth and/or awake in their beds, many abductees are initially amnesic for the experience, though they may be troubled by fleeting, horrifying images and flashbacks (Bullard, 1987; Mack, 1994; Ritchie, 1994). Likewise, hyperactivation of the hippocampus can induce a temporary amnesia (Joseph, 1998a, 1999b).

They also suffer from depression, sleeplessness, anxiety and panic attacks; which again are suggestive of limbic system and temporal lobe abnormalities as well as post-traumatic stress disorder.

It is noteworthy, however, that some of those who undergo life-after-death also report exceedingly unpleasant experiences. This includes feelings of terror, sensations of terrible physical pain, the presence of demonic monstrosities, or hallucinations of people crying, moaning, screaming, and burning in flames.

"For those who have disbelieved... shall roast in fire... and their bellies and skin shall be melted. To them it is said: Taste the punishment of the burning." -Koran

DISSOCIATION & POSSESSION

It has been repeatedly demonstrated with neurosurgical and epilepsy patients that abnormal temporal lobe/hippocampal activation can cause an individual to experience themselves as separating and floating above their body, such that they may feel as if they are two different people, one watching, the other being observed (Daly 1958; Jackson & Stewart, 1899; Penfield 1952; Penfield & Perot 1963; Williams 1956). As described by Penfield (1952) during electrical stimulation of this area, "it was as though the patient were attending a familiar play and was both the actor and audience." Likewise, children, as well as adults, who are terribly abused or traumatically stressed and frightened often report dissociative experiences including even a splitting of consciousness such that one aspect of their mind will seem to be floating above or beside their body (Courtois, 1988; Grinker & Spiegel, 1945; Noyes & Kletti, 1977; Parson, 1988; Southard, 1919; Terr, 1990). Hence, the famous aside: "He was literally beside himself with fear."

Most abusers do not wish to molest an unresponsive body, but a personality that is either excited or tormented and terrified by what is occurring. According to Courtois (1995), it is the abuser's desire "to achieve total control over the victim and her responses and for the victim to become a willing participant and to enjoy the abuse. To achieve this end, many incest offenders take great pains to sexually stimulate their victims to arousal." They may pinch, cut, and hurt them to obtain the desired reaction. Thus, although these particular children may have "split off" from their body, they are nevertheless forced to respond, as a personality, to the abuse in which case the split off, or remaining portion of the "personality" may act in accordance with the manner in which it was created. Thus, the abuser slowly shapes a personality which is formed during periods of abuse. Hence, some alternative personalities are highly sexual, or homosexual, or angry and self-destructive, mirroring either the role they were forced to play or the personality and behavior of the perpetrator. The dissociated aspects of conscious-awareness, therefore, may slowly establish its own independent identity; that is, an alternate personality—a personality which may be repeatedly triggered or purposefully shaped during subsequent traumas, and which may grow only to split apart again and yet again, forming multiple fragmentary personas each supported by a dissociated and abnormal neural network.

However, these "broken off" or alternate personalities, in turn, may be "state dependent" and supported by isolated neural networks maintained by the amygdala in the absence of hippocampal participation. Because the alternate "personality" essentially splits off from the main personality under certain highly stressful conditions, in general, it can only be reactivated and function independently when the individual is stressed or in a similar state of mind. Moreover, because of the state dependent nature of this partial "personality," the main personality essentially becomes amnesic regarding it. In part this is a consequence of hippocampal deactivation. When the hippocampus returns to normal, it can no longer gain access to these personal memories (which may be maintained by the amygdala), such that dissociated personal memory and the associated, albeit disconnected personality, remains isolated and inaccessible. In consequence, some victims, or their families, feel as if they sometimes are possessed.

POSSESSION & PROPHECY

Altered mental states, secondary to brain injury, seizure activity, or severe emotional trauma, by definition, encompass an alteration in consciousness. Under some conditions, what is perceived is a hallucination, a sensory distortion, or a dream-like flashback. Some may believe they have been afflicted by demons, or that they are possessed. Feelings of possession or the presence of an alien presence, can be directly attributed to neurological abnormalities in the right hemisphere, right parietal lobe, corpus callosum, and the limbic system. Prophecy, too, has been linked to hyperactive states and abnormalities in the limbic system; and individuals who make prophecies also sometimes appear to be possessed.

Signs of limbic system hyperactivity and seizure activity include loss of consciousness, trance states, dreamy states, auditory and visual hallucinations and related disturbances of the auditory and visual system involving language and reading and writing. The disturbances of language and speech are due to the involvement of the temporal lobe in auditory and reading comprehension. That is, the language areas, upon receiving visual signals, provide the auditory equivalent to a written word so that the person knows what the written words sounds like (Joseph, 1982, 1996, 2000a).

The auditory association area in the left temporal lobe (Wernicke's receptive speech area) not only comprehends incoming speech but assists in the programming of Broca's expressive speech area in the frontal lobe. It is Broca's area which produces speech, and a tissue immediately above Broca's area subserves writing. Therefore, abnormalities in the temporal lobe can induce severe disturbances of speech including abnormalities in the ability to write and spell words. In this regard it is noteworthy that whereas Moses suffered from a severe speech impediment and was slow of tongue, Muhammed, God's messenger, was apparently dyslexic and agraphic. He was unable to read or write.

On the other hand, hyperactivity in these limbic and temporal lobe structures can also induce pressured speech and writing. The afflicted individual may feel compelled to preach and to write out their mystical thoughts (Joseph, 2000a). Certain individuals who develop "temporal lobe epilepsy" or irritative lesions to this tissue, may suddenly become hyperreligious and spend hours reading and talking about the Bible or other religious issues. They may spend hours every day preaching or writing out their mystical or religious thoughts, or engaging in certain actions and movements they believe have religious significance. Many modern day religious writers who also happen to suffer from epilepsy are in fact exceedingly prolific, whereas conversely, those who feel impelled to preach tend to do just that. In fact, many of the prophets reported that they felt forced to preach and prophecies even though they struggled not to.

Temporal lobe hyperactivity or temporal lobe epilepsy is not usually associated with tonic clonic seizures and patients do not flail about on the ground, though they may certainly lose consciousness and move their hands and arms in a ritualistic manner. And yet, they may also retain the power of speech--though what they say may sound like jibberish. In some instances, particularly if the amygdala and amygdala-striatum is impacted, the patient may appear to be in a trance. They may experience pleasant or unpleasant odors, heart palpations, difficulty breathing, excessive sweating, and disturbances of movement, ranging from a complete freezing of the body to spasmodic movements of the arms and legs (Joseph, 1999a, 2000a). Following a temporal lobe seizure the patient may stagger about like a "stunned ox." In this regard when the prophet Jeremiah experienced the Lord God, his arms and legs convulsed and he staggered about like a drunk.

The presence of "god" may be experienced through dreams, through visions, and through voices— and it is usually a terrifying experience which grips the prophet like a seizure: "And I saw this great vision, and there remained no strength in me, for my comeliness was turned in me into corruption, and I retained no strength" (Daniel, 10:8); he defecated and urinated, as he fell to the ground—a not uncommon manifestation of certain seizures.

Daniel claimed he immediately lost consciousness before being confronted by the Lord god: "Thus was I in deep sleep on my face, and my face toward the ground" when an angel appeared in a prophetic vision (Daniel 10:9).

Likewise, Abraham would lose consciousness just prior to experiencing these "visions" or upon hearing the voice of the Lord God. "And a deep sleep fell upon Abraham (Genesis, 15:1,2).

In addition, and as discussed in earlier chapters, hyperactivity in this area of the brain can induce terror and severe depression, auditory and visual hallucinations, as well as religious fervor and even feelings of possession.

CASE HISTORIES

Consider Mary (described by Mesulam, 1981), a 26 year old female, A-average college student. For several months she had been complaining of odd mystical experiences involving alterations in consciousness, accompanied by auditory and visual hallucinations as well as frequent experiences of deja vu. These mystical experiences soon progressed to feelings of being possessed by the Devil. She was convinced the Devil was urging and trying to make her do horrible things to other people or to herself. She also claimed he would sometimes loudly cackle inside her head. Finally, a priest was brought in and a rite of exorcism was performed, as the Catholic hierarchy became convinced of the authenticity of her experiences, that she was possessed. However, her condition failed to improve. Finally an EEG was performed and abnormal activity was discovered to be emanating from both temporal lobes.

Another 44 year old female college graduate suffering from temporal lobe abnormalities instead came to believe she was possessed by God and at times also thought she was the Messiah, and at the behest of God, had a special mission to fulfill (Mesulam 1981). At the urging of the "God" she ran for public office and almost won. However, she also engaged in some rather bizarre actions including widespread and inappropriate sexual activity -another manifestation of limbic hyperactivation (see also Schenk, and Bear 1981; Trimble 1991).

In a classic case described over 120 years ago by Sommer (1880), a 25 year-old man who suffered several seizures a day, claimed to have had repeated conversations with God. God's voice spoke to him quite clearly. One day, God told him he was Jesus Christ and to go forth and perform miracles. The first miracle he was to perform was to fly through the air. So convinced was he that

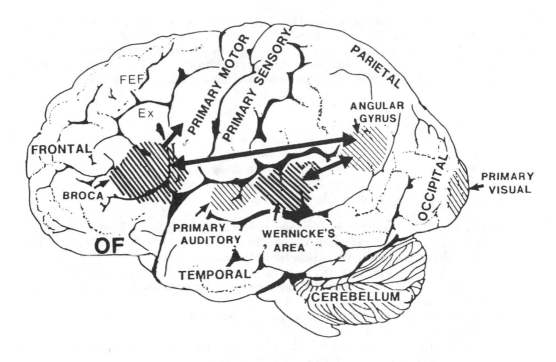

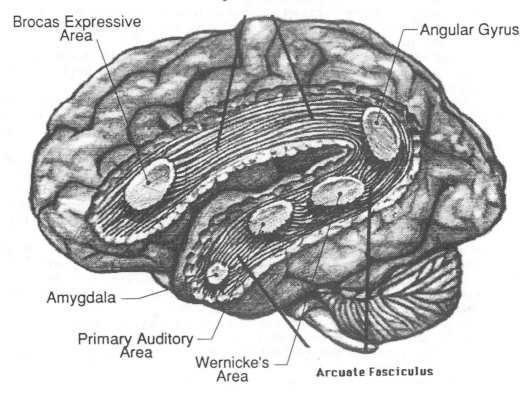

Figure 167. The language axis of the left hemisphere. Cutaway diagram depicting the pathway of the language areas of the left hemisphere, including the amygdala, Wernicke's receptive speech area, the angular gyrus (assimilation area) and Broca's expressive speech area. From Joseph, 1982, 1996

these revelations were real, and that he was in fact "The Christ" that this young man climbed up on a roof and leaped into the air. At autopsy he was found to have a hard sclerotic lesion of the right Ammon's horn; i.e. the hippocampus. Sommer (1880) concluded that these religious hallucinations (and all hallucinations and sensory illusions) were directly due to abnormalities in this and adjoining tissue—which includes the amygdala; the two core structures of the limbic system and temporal lobe.

MUHAMMED

In order to receive the word of God, Muhammed would typically lose consciousness and enter into trance states (Armstrong 1994; Lings 1983). However, he had his first truly spiritual-religious conversion when he was torn from his sleep by the archangel Gabriel who enveloped him in an terrifying embrace so overpowering that Muhammed's breath was squeezed from his lungs.

"Recite!" (iqra!) the angel demanded.

Muhammed refused: "I am not a recitor!"

The angel again enveloped him in a crushing embrace, squeezing the air from his lungs. Again the angel demanded: "Recite!" and again Muhammed refused. And then the angel crushed him a third time, at which point words began to pour from Muhammed's mouth:

"Recite in the name of thy Sustainer, who has created—created man out of a germ-cell! Recite—for thy Sustainer is the Most Bountiful, One who has taught (man) the use of pen—taught him what he did not know!"

Because the angel forced Muhammed to recite the words of God, it is for this reason that the book of Islam is called the qur'an: "Recitation."

This was the first of many such episodes Muhammed had with the archangel Gabriel who sometimes appeared in a titanic kaleidoscopic panoramic form.

Muhammed was initially exceedingly distressed, horrified by what he had experienced. He also feared he may have been "possessed by a jinn," a sprite. It was commonly believed among the Arabic community that some people had their own individual, personal jinni who could provide them with good luck and inspiration.

Muhammed did not know what to think. Shattered by the experience and overcome with feelings of suicidal terror and depression, Muhammed finally decided to throw himself from a cliff. Again the angel Gabriel appeared to him as he stood at the precipice.

According to Muhammed: "I heard a voice from heaven saying, O Muhammed! thou art the apostle of God and I am Gabriel. I raised my head toward the heavens to see who was speaking, and lo, Gabriel in the form of a man with his feet astride the horizon... I turned my face away, but toward whatever region of the sky I looked, I saw him there."

Escape was impossible. Horrified, terrorized, and depressed by what he considered a "loathsome" experience, and fearing that he was "possessed by a jinn," Muhammed crawled on his hand hands and knees and flung himself into the lap of his wife, and begged her to shield him from the divine presence. "Then I told her the whole story." She soothed him and after listening to him describe his ordeal, she suggested that they speak with her cousin, "Waraqa, a Christian who knew scripture."

Eventually, Muhammed reluctantly accepted his fate, and in accordance with the voice of "God" or his angels, Muhammed not only spoke the words of "God" but began reciting and chanting various themes of God in a random order over the course of the following 20 years; an experience he continued to find quite painful and wrenching (Armstrong 1994; Lings 1983). "Never once did I receive a revelation without feeling my soul being torn away from me."

In order to receive his revelations, Muhammed also entered into a trance state and would lose consciousness. He reported that a heaviness would fill him with a feeling of depression and grief, and that he would sweat profusely. He also stated that although the divine message was often clear, at other times it was a jumble of sounds and voices, "like the reverberations of a bell. And that is the hardest upon me; the reverberations abate only when I understand the message."

LOT

Epilepsy can be due to a number of different causes, such as head injury, heat stroke during infancy, and tumors. However, the predisposition to develop epilepsy can also be inherited.

Like his uncle Abraham, Lot also saw angels and talked to the Lord God. It was the Lord God's angels who warned Lot to leave Sodom; reportedly the most sexually corrupt city on Earth.

Once Lot escaped from Sodom, he celebrated by getting drunk and impregnating both his daughters who willingly snuck into his bed on two separate nights (Genesis, 20: 33-38). In fact, even before they left Sodom Lot had offered his daughters to some of the men of the city to do with as they pleased (Genesis 19: 8).

We do not know if Lot followed Abraham's example and also let other men have sex with his wife. Nevertheless, both Abraham and Lot clearly demonstrated signs of temporal lobe and limbic hyperactivation.

EZEKIAL

Many "prophets" and other religious figures also display evidence of the Kluver-Bucy syndrome—a disturbance also referred to as "psychic blindness" which is due to severe abnormalities or destruction of the amygdala. For example, patients may seek isolation, avoid people, engage in abnormal sex acts, and eat non-nutritional substance such as cigarette butts or other objects.

Thus we read that Ezekiel would eat dung.

In addition, many of the "prophets" avoided people and would seek isolation—yet another characteristic of limbic and amygdala abnormalities.

Likewise we read that Ezekial isolated himself from other humans and refused to speak to others. If they approached he would withdraw. If they followed he would flee. Primates with bilateral amygdala damage respond identically.

Social isolation, however, is a common means of achieving enlightenment, and isolation also acts on the amygdala (Joseph, 1982, 1992a. 1999a,b).

It was while isolated from all human contact that Ezekial had a shattering experience which caused him to lose consciousness. He had seen a cloud of light shot through with lightning, and within that stormy light he observed a great chariot pulled by four beasts each of which had four heads with the face of a man, bull, a lion, and eagle, and each wheel of the chariot rolled in a direction different from the others. And he heard wailing, moaning, and voices that gave him commands. And he experienced a sweet taste in his mouth, like honey, when "the spirit lifted me and took me, my heart overflowed with bitterness and anger." Afterward he lay "lie someone stunned" for an entire week.

Yet other signs of amygdala hyperactivation include catalepsy and catatonia. Thus we read that Ezekial was forced to lie on one side for 390 days without moving and then on his other side for 40 days. He was in all respects completely catatonic.

Cataplexy, or in this case, what appears to be catatonia, is also known as an arrest reaction due to excessive fear (e.g. "paralyzed with fear"), or to abnormalities in the amygdala striatal medial frontal lobe emotion-motor circuit. If exceeding frightened, one may freeze and fail to move, a function of the amygdala acting on the motor centers in the striatum and medial frontal lobe (Joseph, 1999b). The airline industry refers to this as "frozen panic states" and about 20% of those involved in airline or other disasters will freeze and fail to move or to take any evasive action that might save their lives.

If there is an abnormality in this emotional-motor circuit, the individual may develop Parkinson's disorder, or catatonia, in which case they may lie frozen in the same posture for weeks and months. In Ezekial's case, the possibility of amygdala hyperactivity seems to be implied; not only because of the above mentioned conditions, but as he was obsessed with sexuality and often employed violent sexual imagery when he prophesied.

MOSES AND TEMPORAL LOBE LIMBIC HYPERACTIVITY

The story of Moses is part mystery, at least regarding his paternal origins. We are told that he was raised in the palace of the Pharaoh of Egypt who regarded him as a grandson. Yet, the identity of his father is unknown and we are also told that his mother hid him for three months after he was born. When she could hide him no more, she placed him in a wicker basket among the reeds of the Nile. It was there that Moses was discovered by the daughter of Pharaoh, who in turn raised him like a son. But then we are told that the princess paid a Hebrew woman to nurse the child. When he grew to be a boy the princess named him "Moses, which means: "I drew him out of the water." "Moses" however, was also a common Egyptian name, including that of a mighty Pharaoh: Thutmoses.

Moses had a violent temper and one day beat an Egyptian to death. Overcome with fear, when he realized the murder had been witnessed, he fled to the land of Midian where he proceeded to challenge a group of men and rescued the daughters of the local pagan priest.

Moses, the "Egyptian" then married Zipporah, the daughter of the priest. It was later, after the birth of his son, Gershom, and while alone and isolated and attending a flock of sheep in the wilderness, near the mountain of God, that the Lord God appeared and spoke to him from inside a blazing bush.

The Lord God then proceeded to instruct Moses as to what he should say to the Israelites: "The Lord, the god of your fathers, the God of Abraham, the God of Isaac, the God of Jacob has sent me to you." But "Moses answered and said to the Lord, Please O Lord, I have never been a man of words. I am slow of speech and slow of tongue." Indeed, his speech was so garbled the Lord God decides to appoint Moses' brother Aron to assist him: "You shall speak to him and put the words in his mouth."

Possibly, Moses requires an interpreter because he does not know the language of the Hebrews; being raised as a prince in the household of the Pharaoh. However, he also required Aron to speak for him to Pharaoh. Thus it appears that he may well have had a severe speech impediment as he claims. In fact, coupled with his violent temper, his severe depressions, and the possibility of auditory and visual hallucinations, it could be argued that Moses suffered from temporal lobe epilepsy: The "Divine Illness." Seizure activity within the temporal lobe and limbic system are clearly associated with triggering religious experiences and can give rise to murderous rage reactions as well as disturbances of speech and language.

Moses may have suffered from temporal lobe seizures as a consequence of being left for days, as an infant, to bake in the hot, broiling Egyptian sun, after his mother abandoned him in a basket on the Nile. If that were the case his infant brain could have become overheated and damaged by the high temperatures.

If Moses subsequently developed temporal lobe seizure activity, this could explain his hyperreligious fervor, his rages and the numerous murders he committed or ordered. Indeed, a recurring theme throughout the story of Exodus is that of Moses killing and repeatedly ordering human slaughter, beginning with the first Egyptian he killed, followed by the first born sons of the Egyptians, then Pharaoh and the Egyptian army, and then the slaughter and death of the Hebrews who followed him out of Egypt, all 600,000 of them.

TRANCE STATES

Numerous religious figures have achieved enlightenment, or were only able to commune with god, once they entered a trance state. Buddha, for example, is said to have at first communed with gods, and then to have transcended the gods by entering a trance state which enabled him to experience nirvana.

It is said that when Buddha entered into trance that fragrant breezes swirled about him, flowers bloomed and blossomed and fell from the air, and that the Earth began to rock as the gods in heaven began to rejoice. However, one god, a demon, Mara, was alarmed. She told Buddha to remain in a state of bliss and to never, under any circumstances attempt to inform others of what he had accomplished as no one would believe him. Two other gods, however, Sakra, the Lord of the devas, and Maha Brahma begged him to teach his method to all the world. Buddha heeded their advice.

For the next 45 years he wondered all over India preaching his message. Humans could transcend suffering and the gods, and through kindness, compassion, meditation and Yoga, they could come into contact with the ultimate reality.

Trance states are said to enable one to sense and perceive what others cannot. In Buddhism it is believed that trance enables one to gain use of Power over the material world. This includes the Power (te) of not contending, the Power to use men, and the Power for causing others to act, or to prevent them from acting.

Mystics may achieve trance states through ritual and discipline or through pain, sex, fasting or drugs. These trance states have been divided into five stages by some (Buddhists), six by others (Tantra), and four by yet other mystics (Sufis).

Broadly considered, these trance stages begin with the perception of visions and voices, then progress to a non-perceptual awareness of God, followed by transcendence and a merging and becoming one with God, which is the supreme mystical act.

While in trance, some individuals not only experience a bright light, but they may be blinded by it. In some cases the light is so bright those around them will see it. Moses and Jesus both shone with a light that others could see, whereas St. Paul was blinded by the great light that shone around his head--a light which gave rise to a "hallucination" and a revelation, on the road to Damascus.

During revival meetings, it is not uncommon for revivalists to suddenly go into trance and see "a brightness like the sun" "everything is bathed in a rainbow of glory."

VISIONS AND DREAMS

Throughout the "Old Testament" the "Lord god" delivers his words through visions and dreams, and in some instances the words themselves constitute the "vision;" that is, like an auditory hallucination:

"And an angel said unto Israel... And an angel said unto Balaam... and Elohim said unto him... And an angel of the Lord called unto Abraham out of heaven... and Elohim said unto Noah... The word of the Lord came unto Abraham in a vision... And the Lord said unto Abraham... and the Lord said unto Jacob...and the Lord said unto Joshua... and the Lord said unto me... and the word of the Lord came unto me... "etc.

Likewise, the gods and goddesses of ancient peoples throughout the world, including for example, the gods of the ancient Romans and Greeks would speak and appear to specific, chosen people in visions and dreams; an experience also referred to as an "epiphany" or in modern psychiatric terminology, a "hallucination."

One of Jacob's many epiphanies included a dream of a ladder which stretched from heaven to earth; and angels were ascending and descending between the realms of god and man.

People who suffer from periodic episodes of limbic and temporal lobe hyperactivation, such as those with temporal lobe epilepsy, may hear voices and suffer seizures which may be indistinguishable from a trance state. It is not uncommon for these seizures to be preceded by an auditory or visual hallucination or aura (Gloor, 1997; Penfield and Perot 1963; Trimble 1991; Williams 1956). Patients can have any number of very odd hallucinations, such as smelling sweet or horrible odors, hearing voices, music, or conversations, seeing angels, demons, ghosts, and God.

The great existential author, F. Dostoevsky, apparently suffered temporal lobe epilepsy. Dostoevsky, alleged (via one of his characters) that when he had a seizure the gates of Heaven would open and he could see row upon row of angels blowing on great golden trumpets. Then two great golden doors would open and he could see a golden stairway that would lead right up to the throne of God.

Beginning with Abraham, and throughout the "Old Testament" the "Lord God" delivers his words primarily through visions and dreams, and frequently his prophets lose consciousness or enter into trance states. Many of His prophets appear to be suffering from temporal lobe epilepsy or hyperactivity.

In the 12th century, Moses Maimonides, composed a book "A Guide for the Perplexed" as a letter to R. Joseph. According to Maimonides "the Divine Will has withheld from the multitude the truths required for the knowledge of God... Do not imagine that these most difficult problems can be thoroughly understood by any one of us."

"At times the truth shines so brilliantly that we perceive it as clear as day. Our nature and habit then draw a veil over our perceptions, and we return to darkness almost as dense as before. We are like those who, though beholding frequent flashes of lightning still find themselves in the thickest darkness of night."

"For some the lightning flashes in rapid succession, and they seem to be in continuous light, and their night is as clear as the day. This was the degree of prophetic excellence attained by Moses, the greatest of prophets."

"By others, only once during the whole of night is a flash of lightning perceived. This is the case with those of whom we are informed "They prophesied and did not prophecy again." "There are some to whom the flashes of lightning appear with varying intervals; others are in the condition of men, whose darkness is illuminated not by lightning, but by a small light that is not continuous, but now it shines and now it vanishes..."

"The degrees of perfection of men vary according to these distinctions. Concerning those who never beheld the light even for one day, but walk in continual darkness, it is written: "They know not, neither will they understand. They walk in darkness" (Psalms, 82:5). Truth, in spite of all its powerful manifestations is completely withheld from them" (Maimonides, 12th century).

The Truth revealed, however, is often a shattering experience, that grips one like a seizure. Likewise, the gift of prophecy, is not always a welcome gift, and even the role of prophet may be resisted. Moses actively resisted and argued with the "Lord God" and repeatedly tried to convince Him to pick someone more deserving. Other prophets have also attempted to resist, but to no avail. They were often hounded by the "Lord god" or his angels, or felt compelled to prophecy even when threatened with death by the people—and many a prophet was killed by the people, including the ancient Jews.

Jeremiah, for example, was openly despised and ridiculed by the ancient Jews. Nevertheless, though he wished it otherwise, he could not withhold his prophesying: "For the Word of the Lord was unto me a reproach and a mocking all day, and I said, I will not mention it, nor will I again speak in His name; but it was in mine heart as burning fire, enclosed in my bones, and I was wearied to keep it, and did not prevail" (Jeremiah, 20:8,9).

THE TRANSMITTER TO GOD

Although it is possible that certain religious figures may have been suffering from temporal lobe epilepsy, it is noteworthy that seizures are stereotypical and idiosyncratic. That is, unless an individual has several different seizure foci, each seizure is basically identical to the next and the auras and hallucinations are quite similar from one seizure to the next.

This is not the case with many of the prophets. As detailed by Moses Maimonides: "According to the books of the prophets, a certain prophet after being inspired with one kind of prophecy is reported to have received prophecy in another form. It is possible for a prophet to prophecy at one time in the form and at another time in another form. The prophet does not prophecy continuously but is inspired at one time and not at another, so he at one time prophecy in the form of a higher degree and at another time in that of a lower degree; it may happen that the highest degree is reached by a prophet only once in his life time, and afterwards remains inaccessible to him, or that a prophet remains below the highest degree until he entirely looses the faculty."

For example, "And the word of the Lord ceased from Jeremiah" (Erza, i:1), or "And these are the last words of David" (Samuel, 23:1).

Some individuals may prophecy once and only once—which argues against temporal lobe epilepsy.

ABRAHAM

In ancient Sumer (in southern Iraq around 6,000 years ago), it was believed that the Universe was ruled by a pantheon of Gods, the Anunnaki (Armstrong 1994; Kramer 1956, Wooley 1965); perhaps the same pantheon alluded to in the first chapter of Genesis.

The Sumerians also worshiped household gods and goddesses, including a personal God, which in some respects could be likened to a "guardian angel" or a spirit (totem) helper, as was common among the Plains Indians. This personal God served almost as a conscience and as a mediator between the head of the household and the great Gods which ruled the Earth and the cosmos.

Because this was a private, personal God, it was not uncommon for a believer to engage in prolonged and daily discussions with his deity (Kramer 1956: Woolley 1965). To this god one could bear their heart and soul regarding sins, injustice, personal shortcomings and hopes for the future. Hence, this god was indeed a personal god with whom one could "talk" and maintain a special personal relationship and which served to protect the Sumerians from the Pantheon of gods who rules the Earth at that time—or so claim the ancients.

And then one day something astounding and revolutionary occurred in the mind of a man of the city, of Ur of the Chaldees, of ancient Sumer, in ancient Babylon, and birthplace of Abram a rich Babylonian prince. Abram had left the city and began having visions and hearing voices. It was coming from his personal God and it later gave him a command (Genesis 12): "Get thee out of thy country ...and I will make of thee a great nation... and in thee shall all the families of the earth be blessed..."

And Abram and his personal god walked and talked, as God had not done since the time of Adam and Eve. And then one day this personal God came to a decision and said to Abram: "Thy name shall be Abraham, for a father of many nations have I made thee. And I will make thee exceedingly fruitful... and I will make thee the father of many nations... and I will be their God" (Genesis 17).

Abraham, both saw and heard his God on numerous occasions both awake and dreaming, often falling on his face as God appeared. They ate together, and walked and spoke together during the heat of the day, and during the darkest hours of the night. This Lord God, the "God of Abraham" was also making all types of grandiose promises and predictions, all of which came to pass.

PROPHECIES FULFILLED

Is it possible that Abraham was dreaming? Could this personal God from ancient Ur have been but a hallucination, and given Abraham's odd sexuality and murderous actions, a product on tempo-

Figure 168. *Jacob's dream of the ladder to Heaven with angels going to and fro. Drawing by Hayley, 18th century.*

Figure 169. Aztec worshippers induce visions of the "god of the dad" by self-inflicting wounds.

ral lobe epilepsy or subclinical seizure activity?

When we consider that this is the same Lord God (at least in religious theory) who today is worshiped by Jews, Christians, and Moslems alike, the possibility of hallucinations does not seem likely. Indeed, has not the Lord God's prophecy to Abraham come to pass: "And I will make thee the father of many nations... and I will be their God" (Genesis 17).

In fact, given that the God experienced by Abraham and Sara (and in fact, with few exceptions, the God repeatedly described in the Bible) not only appeared as a man but behaved as a man and not a spirit-like supernatural being, the possibility of hallucinations does not seem likely.

Likewise, when we consider how many other prophesies were fulfilled, including the repeated destruction and recreation of Israel, including, most recently in 1948—the aftermath of a world war led by an Austrian German-Jew, Adolf Hitler—as well as the hundreds of millions who worship a Jew (Jesus) as "God," it borders on the irrational to simply dismiss these events as a hallucination, a myth, or a coincidence.

Under conditions of limbic hyperactivation, not all "hallucinations" are hallucinations, but instead may represent the perception of stimuli which are normally filtered from consciousness. Under conditions of sensory deprivation, pain, social isolation, drug use, the nuclei of the limbic system may become abnormally activated and possibly hyperactivated such that subclinical seizure activity (kindling) develops (Cain, 1992; Gloor, 1997; Joseph, 1999b,d).

Under conditions of limbic kindling, hyperactivation, or seizure activity, sensory and emotional filtering that normally takes place in these nuclei is reduced or abolished. That is, the individual may begin to perceive things or individuals that (presumably) do not exist, or they may gain access to "hidden" knowledge that bursts upon them with a shattering clarity, or they may achieve a "higher" understanding of existence and the nature of reality. They may commune directly with god, goddesses, devils, demons, and angels.

As these same nuclei are also implicated in dream states, near death experiences, and out-of-body phenomenon, it could thus be argued that individuals who for whatever reason are "blessed" with an overactive amygdala-temporal lobe are also given access to god-like stimuli which are also normally filtered from consciousness.

Figure 170. *It was predicted that in the year 1519 a comet would appear in the east and signal the return of Quetzalocoatl. The emperor Mochtezuma observes a comet from the East—a prophetic sign of the return of the Quetzalocoatl, the plumed serpent (a bearded god whose symbol was also the sign of the cross), and the impending destruction of the Aztec empire. A few weeks later, the Spaniards, bearded and wearing plumed helmets, and carrying the sign of the cross, arrived off the East coast of Mexico. (Below) Quetzocoatl.*

"Know that for the human mind there are certain objects of perception which are within the scope of its nature and capacity to perceive; on the other hand, there are amongst things which actually exist, certain objects which the mind can in no way grasp: The gates of perception are closed against it. Further, there are things which the mind understands, one part, but remains ignorant of the other. And when man is able to comprehend certain things, it does not follow that he may be able to comprehend every thing."-Moses Maimonides

Moreover, consider the prophecies delivered to Muhammed. In less than fifty years all the Arabic tribes had been converted to Islam.

Or consider the prophecies of the god of the cross, that is, the Mayan and Aztec God, Quetzalocoatl. Quetzalocoatl, the plumed serpent, was associated with the planet Venus, and the sign of the cross was one of his many emblems which is depicted in the center of his shield.

According to Mayan and Aztec religious belief, Quetzalocoatl, the god of the cross, had been driven from the lands at the time of the great flood, some 12,000 years ago. However, it had been prophesied that Quetzalocoatl, the plumed serpent and god of the cross, would return to Mexico and that the ruling gods, and their temples, would be completely overthrown. In fact, an exact date was given for his return, which would be signified by the appearance of a comet in the East. In the Christian calendar this was to be

545

in the year 1519.

As predicted, in the year 1519 a comet appeared in the East, and soon thereafter, the plumed and helmeted Cortez and his crew, flying the Spanish flag and the sign of the cross appeared off the East Coast of Mexico. And, as predicted, the old god, as well as the Aztec civilization were destroyed, and the god of the cross is now worshipped not just by the Mexican, but peoples throughout the Americas. Just a coincidence?

THE PROPHECY OF THE SECOND EXODUS

Prior to and with the establishment of Israel the "Lord God" of the ancient Jewish people repeatedly threatens them with the most horrible of misfortunes and foretells, through his prophets, that they will be scattered and dispersed throughout the lands—and this is exactly what transpires, repeatedly, beginning in the 6th century B.C., when the southern kingdom of Judah was destroyed and the people marched off into exile in Babylon. It is Babylon and before that, Sumer where much of the story of creation may well have been first composed, only to be later incorporated and retold in Genesis.

And then again, almost 2,000 years ago, following their return from exile and return to the promise lands, the Lord God again warns the ancient Jews of their destruction.

"The Lord will bring a nation against you from afar, from the end of the earth, which will swoop down like the eagle... a ruthless nation, that will show the old no regard and the young no mercy." -Deuteronomy 28:47-50.

And this is exactly what transpired when Roman legions, marching under the banner of the swastika and the eagle, swooped down and destroyed the second temple. Again the Jews are driven from Israel, and dispersed throughout the lands.

But then the Lord God also tells the Jewish people that someday He will return them to the promised land. And this prophecy too was fulfilled, by no less than Adolf Hitler; a man who likened his nation to the "Holy Roman Empire" and who modeled his government after the Roman Catholic Church (which he also sought to destroy). And, Hitler's armies marched under the banner of the eagle and the swastika, the twisted cross, the "gammadion"—which is also one of the many names of god, including the Lord God of the old testament: "Tetragrammaton" ("absolute existence").

Even the word "Nazi" has a Jewish reference: "Ashkenazi." "Ashkenazis" are European Jews.

Hitler went forth according to instructions he claimed to have received from Divine Providence. He was to go forth and cleanse the land of Jews. He was to begin the second exodus.

HITLER AND DIVINE PROVIDENCE:
SECOND EXODUS

"Behold, the people of the children of Israel are too many and too mighty for us. Come, let us deal wisely with them." -Exodus 1:9-10.

As Hitler struggled to become dictator of Germany, and as he clearly states in his book, Mein Kampf, the Jews, he preached had not only obtained positions of power disproportionate to their numbers, but they were stealing German wealth, were engaged in sex slavery, and they threatened to overwhelm society with evil and moral decay. They were like a disease, like vermin, like a cancer, and were less than human; they were like animals, subhuman. Hitler counseled that the German nation should deal wisely with them.

The same sentiments had been expressed thousands of years before, by the Pharaoh, King of Egypt.

When Adolf Hitler finally came to power, not only did the majority of the German peoples willfully and fearfully followed his dictates, but many compared him to John the Baptist, Jesus Christ and even God. "Is he John the Baptist? Is he Jesus?" Goebbels wrote in his diary. Many honestly believed they were in the presence of a German Messiah! And not just his earliest followers, but many a German general thought he was "god" and the destiny of Germany. And many shared his lowly opinion of the Jewish people, who Hitler promised to sweep from Germany and send back to their promised land.

Hitler claimed he was acting in accordance with the will of Divine Providence. He believed he had been appointed by God.

Hitler was to be the "Lord God's" angry fist which would savagely strike a scattered people, the Jews, and drive them back to Israel, the Promised Land.

The second exodus would mirror the first.

"He exalts nations, then destroys them; He expands nations, then leads them away. He deranges the leaders of the people, and makes them wander in a trackless waste."
-Job, 12:20-24

Once Hitler came to power, and as he led his nation out of the great depression to greatness, he and his government issued orders controlling Jewish breeding and sexuality; and then the Jews were barred from practicing their professions; and then the Jews were officially described as subhuman, then they were ordered to immigrate--events and laws that echo the events leading up to the first Exodus.

And just as the ancient Jews stripped the Egyptians of their worldly goods before setting off for the promised land, the German Jews who sought to immigrate were stripped of their worldly possessions. Those who remained or failed to heed the six years of repeated warnings to leave Germany were finally herded into concentration camps where they were enslaved, starved and worked to death--conditions which mirror those of ancient Egypt prior to the exodus.

"And so they died, one after another, as if smitten by a pestilential destruction... And then their taskmasters threw their bodies, unburied, beyond the borders of the land, not allowing their kinsmen to even weep over those who had thus miserably perished." -Philo of Alexandria.

POSSESSION & THE VOICE

Hitler first heard the "voice" of Divine Providence, in 1905, when he was a 17-year old youth, living in Austria. The "voice" told Hitler, he would someday become the leader of Germany, and would lead "God's people" back to the land of their fathers.

Hitler and his best friend, August Kubizek, had just left the opera when the "voice" spoke through Hitler. The voice told Hitler and Kubizek that Adolf would someday become the savior of Germany. The Voice explained: Hitler had received a mandate from god, and would someday receive a mandate from the people, to lead them out of their servitude and to lead them back to the land of their fathers. The Voice declared that Hitler had been chosen by Providence and had been given a Divine mission. Adolf Hitler was destined to establish a new social order, a new Reich which would be established under his leadership... The 17-year old Hitler had received a mandate to lead God's people to the heights of freedom and back to the promised land.

Kubizek was amazed and shocked by the voice and the transformation he observed in Hitler. Hitler, he thought, seemed to be possessed by a demon.

Many of those who observed Hitler, later in life, also witnessed periods of possession. Hitler, a plain, and somewhat funny looking man, would suddenly become transformed, as if--according to those who observed the transformation--he was possessed by a demon: a demon who could weave a spell upon the German people by speaking with Hitler's voice.

"Listening to Hitler one suddenly has a vision of one who will lead mankind to glory... A light appears in a dark window. A gentleman with a comic little moustache turns into an archangel... The archangel flies away... and there is Hitler sitting down, bathed in sweat with glassy eyes..." —Gregor Strasser

According to Francois-Poncet, Ambassador from France to Nazi Germany, when the voice spoke, "Hitler entered into a sort of mediumistic trance..."

Others were of the same opinion.

"I looked into his eyes—the eyes of a medium in a trance... Sometimes there seemed to be a sort of ectoplasm; the speaker's body seemed to be inhabited by something... fluid. Afterwards he shrank again to insignificance, looking small and even vulgar. He seemed exhausted, his batteries run down." —Bouchez

"Hitler was possessed by forces outside himself... One cannot help but think of him as a medium. For most of the time, mediums are ordinary, insignificant people. Suddenly they are endowed with what seems to be supernatural powers which set them apart from the rest of humanity. These powers are something that is outside their true personality—visitors, as it were from another planet. The medium is possessed. Once the crisis is past, they fall back into mediocrity. It was in this way, beyond any doubt, that Hitler was possessed by forces outside himself—demoniacal forces of which the individual named Hitler was only a temporary vehicle." —Rauschning.

Hitler tells us in Mein Kampf and in his other writings and comments, that throughout his life,

Figure 171. Adolf Hitler.

he was guided by the "voice" --a voice which would repeatedly protect him from harm, and which guided his rise to power.

For example, he relates the following experience during the first World War. "I was eating dinner in a trench with several comrades. Suddenly a voice seemed to be saying to me, "Get up and go over there." It was so clear and insistent that I obeyed automatically. I rose to my feet and walked twenty yards. Then I sat down to go on eating. Hardly had I done so when a flash and deafening report came from the part of the trench I had just left. Every member in it was killed."

Remarkably, although he served as a runner (messenger) during the first World War, and although the average war time life span of a runner was just a few days, Adolf Hitler nevertheless survived in this position for several years with only minor injuries—a good fortune that he also attributed to Divine Providence.

In Mein Kampf Hitler explains that following the only time he was seriously injured, following a gas attack in the closing days of World War I, he experienced a vision, and heard a voice, which taunted him and then explained why he was being spared: "And then the Voice thundered at me: "Miserable wretch, are you going to cry when thousands are a hundred times worse off than you!" And then, the Voice spoke again and he experienced a vision of the utmost clarity: "I was being summoned to save Germany.... I would go into politics."

It was soon after that terrifying and "wonderful" vision, that others too, began to believe that Hitler had been chosen by God.

Dietrich Eckardt, a highly influential and powerful member of the secret mystical organization, the "Thule Society" and one of the founding members of the National Socialist Party, met Hitler in 1919, and announced after their first meeting: "He is the one..." Eckardt and other German mystics had been waiting for the coming of a German Messiah, one who would lead the German nation and the German people in a battle between the gods... and who could serve as a bridge between this world and a mystical world from the past--a world of mythical heroes, demons and gods. Eckardt was convinced that Hitler was the Messiah they had been waiting for--that Hitler had been chosen by god.

Eckardt took Hitler under his wing, and initiated him into the mysteries of the most diabolical of secret societies. As he lay dying, in 1923, Eckhart bragged. "We have given him the means of communicating with Them."

Hitler, too, admitted to communicating with Them. "I will tell you a secret," he once confided to one of his top deputies, Rauschning. " I have seen Him. He is intrepid and cruel. I was afraid of him."

Hitler was especially afraid that "He" would come at night, while Hitler slept and dreamed.

As related by Albert Speer and others, Hitler was fearful of being alone at night. He also had trouble falling asleep and staying asleep. He often wanted company into the late hours of the night. Hitler frequently voiced a fear of falling asleep when by himself. He sometimes dozed off only to awake with a frightened and hysterical shout, screaming that someone or something was in his room. As described by one of his followers:

"Hitler wakes at night with convulsive shrieks; shouts for help. He sits on the edge of his bed, as if unable to stir. He shakes with fear making the whole bed vibrate. He gasps, as if imagining himself to be suffocating."

On one occasion, after awakening his staff with cries for help, they rushed to his room only to observe as "Hitler stood swaying in his room, looking wildly about him. 'He! He! He's been here!' he stamped and shrieked in the familiar way." On another occasion he awoke and cried out: "There! There! Over in the corner! He is there." On yet another occasion he awoke screaming and in convulsions. When his attendants ran into the room they found "Hitler standing, swaying and looking all around. "It's he, it's he'" he groaned. 'He's come for me!' His lips were white; he was sweating profusely. Suddenly he uttered a string of meaningless figures, then words, and scraps of sentences. It was terrifying." —Rauschning.

Yet, although Hitler admitted that this presence was"intrepid and cruel. I was afraid of him," he nevertheless relished being the chosen one, that he had been chosen by divine providence. He bragged of it.

As Fuehrer of Germany, he repeatedly spoke of hearing "Divine" voices, and claimed that he was following "the commands that Providence has laid upon me… Divine power has willed it... Not even if the whole party tried to drive me to action, I will not act. But if the voice speaks, then I know the time has come to act."

HITLER THE JEW?

During his tumultuous rise to the pinnacles of power Adolf Hitler was often accused of being Jewish. Even the leaders of the National Party which he sought to lead, ridiculed Hitler as a "Jew" and for "behaving like a Jew" as did many of his enemies.

Before coming to power, Adolf Hitler was also a target of widespread ridicule, and was mocked by enemies and the press who questioned his ancestry and who laughably referred to him as "Adolf Schickelgruber." "Schickelgruber" had been the name of Adolf's maternal grandmother, and for 39 years, the name of his father, Alois.

Although the "Schickelgruber" moniker rankled the rising dictator, what concerned him and what he feared most was the history behind the name: the discovery that he was part "Jew;" a fear he repeatedly voiced long after coming to power.

"People must not know who I am," he ranted, and then ranted again when informed that his family history was being investigated. "They must not know where I came from."

Long before and well after Hitler became Chancellor of Germany, considerable effort was expended to falsify, erase or destroy the records from his past. Investigations were conducted by the Gestapo who repeatedly visited his ancestral village in Austria, questioning and threatening anyone that had been associated with the Hitler family.

Hitler was so concerned that when he annexed Austria, in 1938, he ordered that his family's ancestral village, Dollersheim, and all neighboring villages be destroyed. His armies marched in and then cleared out and forcibly evacuated the villagers who were dispersed far and wide. And then Hitler in fact, made it disappear, erased it from the face of the Earth. His armies bombed Dollersheim and all neighboring villages into oblivion as part of a training exercise. Even his father's and grandmother's graves were obliterated and no trace remains.

Nevertheless, what has survived the ravages of time, purposeful destruction and clever forgery, is the fact that Adolf's father, Alois Schickelgruber was the illegitimate son of a female servant, Maria Anna Schickelgruber. Maria Anna became pregnant while living as a servant in a Jewish household —a common servant girl fate. It was assumed by family members and villagers alike that she'd been impregnated by the head of the house, Baron Rothschild, or one of his sons (Langer, 1973; Payne, 1973); a rumor that the Austrian Secret police claimed to have confirmed when ordered by Austrian Chancellor Dollfuss to conduct a thorough investigation. Later, when Hitler orchestrated the anschluss of Austria and German troops marched in, he had Dollfuss murdered, and in addition to destroying Dollersheim, ordered that all documents related to that investigation be destroyed.

Yet others claimed that the man who had impregnated Adolf's grandmother was the Jewish scion of the seigneurial house of Ottenstein.

Hitler's own nephew, William Patrick Hitler, and Adolf's personnel attorney, Hans Frank, claimed that his grandfather was a wealthy "Granz Jew" by the name of Frankenberger who in turn "paid a maintenance allowance from the time of the child's birth until his fourteenth year."

As Frank reported to Hitler, and as he recounted at his Nuremberg war crimes trial, based on what he learned "the possibility cannot be dismissed that Hitler's father was half Jewish as a result of an extramarital relationship between the Schickelgruber woman and the Jew from Graz. This would mean that Hitler was one-quarter Jewish."

When Adolf Hitler was presented with the results of Frank's investigation, although denying he was Jewish, Hitler did admit to Frank that a Jewish man paid his grandmother money, because the "Jew" was tricked into believing he was the father of Alois (Rosenbaum, 1999). Of course this means, if Adolf (or rather Frank) is to be believed, that his grandmother was having sex with a Jewish man before she became pregnant.

What these stories all have in common, of course, is that Hitler's grandfather was a rich Jewish man, and that after becoming pregnant his grandmother was banished from the Rothschild or Frankenberger or the Ottenstein home and sent back to her village to have her baby, Alois. It also appears that funds and even "hush money" were secretly provided for her and the baby

When required to fill out the baptismal certificate for her son, she left the line as to the father of her boy, completely blank. Why did she leave it blank? Two reasons. Having been impregnated by a Jewish man was nothing to be proud of given the anti-Semitic attitudes of the peasant farmers and villagers of Lower Austria. Secondly, it is said that she was paid to keep the paternity secret.

Yet another factor suggesting that Alois was Jewish was the fact that he was nothing like the peasants of his mother's village where people intermarried and produced generation after generation of peasant farmers. Alois in fact left the village and sought his fortune. Alois was supremely self-confident, politically astute, and ambitious, and with the help of influential aristocrats in Vienna, Alois became a government official.

SCHICKELGRUBER BECOMES HITLER:
Abram Becomes Abraham. Jacob Becomes Israel

As to the name "Hitler," although Alois Schickelgruber was proud of his heritage, he found it to his financial advantage to change his name at age 39. Exceedingly shrewd and ambitious, Alois was presented with an opportunity to become instantly a man of considerable property; and the name of that opportunity was Johann Hiedler who had lived in nearby town of Weitra. Johann Hiedler died at age 84 without wife or children—a condition that normally would result in his estate being confiscated by the Austrian government.

Alois instantly seized this opportunity and made arrangements with the local parish priest to alter the parish birth records (Shirer, 1941, 1960). The priest scratched out the name "Shicklegruber" and penciled in "Hiedler."

Alois wasn't especially fond of the "Hiedler" moniker, and altered the spelling to make it sound more pleasing. Alois "Hiedler," became Alois Hitler, and Alois Hitler, unlike any of his mother's peasant farmer relatives, rose to some prominence and became an official in the Austrian government (Payne, 1973; Shirer, 1941, 1960).

ALOIS THE BASTARD

According to German historian, Helmut Heilber: "The aberrational quality of the Hitler family beginning with the ambitious and enterprising father of Adolf shows that other blood must have entered the Lower Austrian Waldviertel stock which had been weakened by years of inbreeding."

Likewise, according to Walter Langer (1972) who was employed by the Office of Strategic Services to conduct a study of Hitler just before the war: "The intelligence and behavior of Alois, as well as that of his two sons (Alois Jr., and Adolf), is completely out of keeping with that usually found in Austrian peasant families. Their ambitiousness and extraordinary political intuition are much more in harmony with the Rothschild tradition."

Alois was not only ambitious and successful, but proud of his paternity—having a father who was wealthy and an aristocrat. Alois, in fact, chose a Jewish man to act as Adolf Hitler's godfather (Langer, 1972), and a Jewish doctor helped to deliver Hitler into this world.

Thus, the evidence strongly suggests that Alois was half Jewish and that Adolf Hitler was one quarter Jewish—a possibility vehemently rejected by Nazis and Jews alike.

HITLER AND THE VOICE OF DIVINE PROVIDENCE

As a young man, Adolf did not feel it necessary to hide his origins. He admitted to having a Jewish father and bragged of having rich Jewish relatives (Hanisch, 1936, 1939). As a young man, Adolf even dressed like a "Jew," and formed close "friendships" with Jewish men—one of whom he lived with briefly (Heidan, 1936; Payne, 1973). Moreover, in addition to associating with, dressing like, living with, and obtaining money from Jews, in February of 1919 Adolf Hitler participated in a parade, as a designated mourner, for a very close friend, a Jewish socialist who had been murdered in Munich (Rosenbaum, 1999).

And like Jewish prophets and Moses before him, it could certainly be argued that Hitler too had been chosen by Divine Providence and the Lord God:

"I will chose the wicked for an evil day...
... I will speak in visions and dreams."

And, like Moses before him, and declaring to be guided by "Divine providence," Hitler turned his eyes to the East, and modeling his "government" after that of the Holy Roman Empire and Catholic Church, and marching behind the banner of the eagle and the twisted cross, the swastika, he ordered the Jews to immigrate, and engaged in wide scale ethnic cleansing and mass murder ostensibly so as to obtain living space—exactly as did Moses.

But, perhaps even more importantly, Hitler initially had no interested in killing off or exterminating the Jewish population. In fact, those who were first forced into the concentration camps were political enemies. Instead, Hitler did all in his power to force the Jews, the subhumans, to immigrate, even relying on forced expulsion. It was only in 1941, 8 years after he came to power, that he began to systematically exterminate the Jewish people.

In 1941, and after suffering his first defeats, the murder and the cleansing of the lands of Jews became more important to Hitler than winning the war. He began diverting from his floundering war effort, the needed funds, troops, and trains which he ordered were to be used strictly for the purpose of terrorizing, killing, and rounding up for mass murder those Jews who had failed to heed his 8 years of warnings to immigrate. Paradoxically, perhaps, Hitler believed it important to kill off only the weak, and to preserve the strong--many of whom immigrated, after the war, to Palestine.

In this respect, it could be surmised that the entire purpose for the war was to preserve the strong, destroy the weak, and force out the toughest and strongest of Jewish people and to drive them to what would become Israel--"Israel" meaning: "God's strength." Indeed, did not the Lord God apply this same principle in choosing Jacob rather than Isaac to become "Israel?" Isaac was weak and meakly allowed Abraham to bind him with the intention of cutting his thoat. By contrast, Jacob took charge of his own fate and even wrestled and bargained with divine beings.

SECOND EXODUS

"The Lord will bring a nation against you from afar, from the end of the earth, which will swoop down like the eagle... a ruthless nation, that will show the old no regard and the young no mercy." -Deuteronomy 28:47-50.

The "final solution," only became the final solution in 1941, when the remaining Jews, failed or were unable to heed his threats and demands to immigrate, and/or failed to escape his war machine as it blitzed onwards. It was only when confronted with millions of Jews that could not be relocated to Israel and Madagascar that systematic mass killings began.

Again, however, initially he ordered that the Jewish people immigrate. Hundreds of thousands did heed the call and attempted to escape and to immigrate. However, many did not wish to go to Israel, and some returned to Germany or sought haven in other countries.

However, just as "God" had hardened the heart of Pharaoh, world leaders also experienced a hardening of the heart, and denied the persecuted Jewish people entry into their countries. The Jewish people, driven from Germany and all "strange" lands, had only one place to go: Israel.

As noted, the 600,000 ancestors of the 6 million Jews murdered by Adolf Hitler in his quest for "living space" and racial purity, also engaged in wide scale ethnic cleansing, some 3,000 years ago. Led by Moses, his brother Aron, and divine providence, in their 40 year search for living space, "the promised land," the Jewish people indiscriminately killed and slaughtered men, women, and children whose only crime was having lived for centuries on land the Jews wished to claim for their own.

And just as the Lord God would kill every single Jew, the 600,000 who He brought forth from the land of Egypt in his successful quest to establish Israel, Hitler would kill six million. And, just as Moses was aided by a Jew, Aron, in the killing of fellow Jews and innocents alike, Adolf Hitler was aided by a fellow Jew, Reinhard Heydrich who organized the "Office for Jewish Emigration" which later became the office of extermination. It has been said Heydrich was so tormented by his Jewish ancestry and the "Jew within" that he sought to cleanse himself by orchestrating the extermination of all European Jews (Rosenbaum, 1999).

However, instead of killing 600,000 of the "chosen" who the Lord God killed or allowed to die of old age in the desert, Hitler would kill six million. And just as "God" ordered the murder and pillage of millions of non-Jews to fulfill his goals, Hitler did likewise.

"I believe that it was God's will to send a youth into the Reich, to let him grow up, to raise him to be the leader of a nation so as to enable him to lead his people back to the homeland." -Adolf Hitler

And who were "his people?" Hitler was not even born in Germany.

What was the ultimate outcome of World War II? The reestablishment of Israel—exactly as God's prophets prophesied. Again, Hitler was more concerned with cleansing the lands of Jews than wining the war. Hitler believe he was acting according to the will of the Lord God. Divine Providence.

"There is a higher ordering, and we are all nothing else than its agents." -Adolf Hitler.

HISTORY REPEATS ITSELF

"We are often accused of being the enemies of the mind and spirit. Well, that is what we are, but in a far deeper sense than bourgeois science, in its idiotic pride, could ever imagine." —Adolf Hitler

Adolf Hitler experienced amazing success in building up Germany during the "Great Depression." His amazing success was the envy of the world--including the United States of America, whose President could look on only with envy.

And Adolf Hitler achieved incredible success when he went to war: destroying the armies and conquering Poland, France, and all of Europe in just a matter of months.

And then, Hitler destroyed his armies, and then Germany was destroyed. By the end of the war, in 1945, every major Germany city had been nearly reduced to rubble.

And in Palestine, the Palestinian people were being murdered, terrorized and driven from their homes by the Jews--in a repeat of the terrors that characterized the Jewish conquest of Palestine and Canaan, thousands of years before.

A little over two years later, and because of the atrocities committed by the Nazis, the United Nations granted Israel statehood. The Jews again had reclaimed their "promised land," the land of their fathers.

GERMANY & BABYLON

Over two thousand years ago, around 600 BC., the Jewish Lord God announced through his prophets that he would enable Babylon to become a super-power in order to punish his Jews, by attacking Israel/Judea and sacking the Temple of Solomon. And this is exactly what happened.

The Jewish prophet Ezekiel, then announced that the sacking of Jerusalem and the Temple of Solomon was just the beginning of their punishments. It was only a warning. But if the Jewish people did not heed these warnings, Ezekiel also pronounced that Yahweh would use the nation of Babylon as the instrument of his wrath, and that the king of Babylon would destroy the Temple and burn the city to the ground. Approximately 6 years after this prophecy, Nebuchadnezzar, the king of Babylon, attacked and destroyed the city and the temple. The Jews were driven into exhile.

However, the Lord God, through his prophets also explained that He would then destroy Babylon, thus giving His Jews, yet another opportunity to repent of their sins, to follow His laws, and to return to Israel.

However, in order for these prophecies to be fulfilled required that Babylon become a super-power and defeat Egypt. That is, Babylon was to become an instrument of God. It would become a super power which the Lord God would employ to make the Jews suffer, and then to force them off their land, and then to enslave them, so as to make them cry out to the Lord God. Then Babylon would be destroyed so that the Jews could return to the promised land and reestablish the state of Israel.

Around 600 B.C. the prophet Jeremiah began uttering prophecies about Babylon and Egypt and its king. According to Jeremiah 46: "This is the message against the army of Pharaoh Neco king of Egypt. "Prepare your shields, both large and small, and march out for battle! What do I see? They are terrified, they are retreating, their warriors are defeated...and there is terror on every side, declares the Lord... The day belongs to the Lord, the Lord Almighty- a day of vengeance, for vengeance on his foes. The sword will devour till it is satisfied, till it has quenched its thirst with blood. For the Lord, the Lord Almighty, will offer sacrifice in the land of the north by the River Euphrates... prepare for Nebuchadnezzar king of Babylon to attack Egypt: Egypt will hiss like a fleeing serpent...The Daughter of Egypt will be put to shame, handed over to the people of the north. The Lord Almighty, the God of Israel, says: "I am about to bring punishment on Amon god of Thebes, on Pharaoh, on Egypt and her gods and her kings, and on those who rely on Pharaoh. I will hand them over to those who seek their lives, to Nebuchadnezzar king of Babylon and his officers. Later, however, Egypt will be inhabited as in times past," declares the Lord.

And this is exactly what came to pass. Babylon again became a lone superpower that none could oppose. But according to the prophets of Israel, Yahweh was merely using Babylon, allowing this nation to become all powerful, so that he could employ it in his wrath against Judea which he proclaimed would be severely punished so that the Jewish people would learn a lesson and again follow his laws:

"In those days, at that time," declares the Lord, "the people of Israel and the people of Judah together will go in tears to seek the Lord their God. They will ask the way to Zion and turn their faces toward it. They will come and bind themselves to the Lord in an everlasting covenant that will not be forgotten." —Jeremiah 50: 4,5.

And that is exactly what came to pass. However, according to the prophet Jeremiah, although Yahweh would use Babylon to punish His people, Yahweh would then destroy Babylon and punish it for this sin: "This is the word the Lord spoke through Jeremiah the prophet concerning Babylon and the land of the Babylonians: "Announce and proclaim among the nations, lift up a banner and proclaim it; keep nothing back, but say, 'Babylon will be captured; Bel will be put to shame, Marduk filled with terror. Her images will be put to shame and her idols filled with terror.' A nation from the north will attack her and lay waste her land. No one will live in it; both men and animals will flee away. I will stir up and bring against Babylon an alliance of great nations from the land of the north. They will take up their positions against her, and from the north she will be captured. So Babylonia will be plundered; all who plunder her will have their fill," declares the Lord....I will punish the king of Babylon and his land as I punished the king of Assyria. But I will bring Israel back to his own pasture." —Jeremiah 50.

And this too is exactly what came to pass.

Cyrus, the King of Persia, attacked and destroyed Babylon, and one of his first acts was to permit the Jewish exiles to return to Judea and rebuild the Temple of Solomon—an edict Cyrus recorded in the Cylinder of Cyrus, which is housed in the British Museum. According to Cyrus, he destroyed Babylon and allowed the Jewish people to return to Judea because he "was charged to do so by Yahweh, the God of Heaven."

THE TRANSMITTER TO GOD

The question as to why any particular individual might be chosen to serve as a prophet or messenger of "God" cannot be answered here, though we can certainly consider possibilities.

Every individuals appears to be naturally "wired for god" and thus capable of receiving the word of god. However, some display signs of hyperactivity in this region of the brain which appears to enhance these capabilities—albeit in accordance with the waxing and waning activity within the limbic system and temporal lobe. Or perhaps a person who lives a highly spiritual or mystical life style perpetually activates this region of the brain and achieves what others can only hope for via drugs, fasting, self-mutilation, and isolation; i.e. access to God, or the spiritually sublime.

Or perhaps the presence of "God" triggers hyperactivity in the limbic system of those chosen to be His prophets, which thus enables them to hear and see god-like stimuli as well as causing them to demonstrate signs of temporal lobe abnormalities. That is, just as something frightening or sexual will activate limbic neurons, something exceedingly frightening, spiritual, or god-like, might hyperactivate these same neurons, eventually creating supersensitive conditions and thus perpetually activating the "transmitter to God."

As to the possibility that individuals such as Moses, Jesus, Abraham, Muhammed, or other "prophets" and messengers may have been hallucinating, this is not terribly likely since what they heard and experienced was often different from day to day and as there was an obvious message and plan of action that they were exposed to and which they relayed to others. Moreover, the prophecies they were given and what they were told would come to pass, came to pass!

Indeed, as the limbic system is clearly implicated in every single case, and as this region of the brain normally inhibits and filters incoming sensory stimuli, it could thus be argued that individuals who for whatever reason are "blessed" with a hyperactivated limbic system, or a limbic system which is highly "evolved," or who are directly contacted by god, are therefore provided access to god-like stimuli and alternate realities which are normally filtered from consciousness.

"If the doors of perception were cleansed everything would appear... as it is, infinite..."-W. Blake

Indeed, what the evidence suggests is that these limbic structures periodically become hyperactivated and open up windows and doorways to alternate realities or dimension which are normally hidden from view. Under conditions of limbic system hyperactivity, what is concealed is suddenly revealed, including, perhaps, even the private thoughts of the gods.

ANTI-CHRIST, ARMAGEDDON, ASTRONOMY & THE SCIENCE OF RELIGION

by R. Joseph

"Religions are like glow-worms: they need darkness in order to shine. A certain degree of general ignorance is the condition for the existence of any religion."—Arthur Schopenhauer

"Has the famous story that stands at the beginning of the Bible really been understood? The story of God's hellish fear of science? It has not been understood. This priestly book par excellence begins, as is fitting, with the great inner difficulty of the priest: He knows only one great danger, in consequence "God" knows only one great danger."

"The old God, all "spirit," all high priest, all perfection, takes a stroll in his garden; but he is bored. Against boredom even gods struggle in vain. What does he do? He invents man—man is entertaining. But Lo and Behold! Man too is bored. God's compassion with the sole distress that distinguishes all paradises knows no limits: soon he creates other animals as well. God's first mistake: man did not find the animals entertaining; he ruled over them, he did not even want to be "animal." Consequently, God created woman. And indeed, that was the end of boredom—but of other things too! Woman was God's second mistake. "Woman by nature is a snake, Eve—every priest knows that: "from woman comes all calamity in the world"—every priest knows that too. "Consequently, it is from her too that science comes." Only from woman did man learn to taste of the tree of knowledge."

"What had happened? The old God was seized with hellish fear. Man himself had turned out to be his greatest mistake; he had created a rival for himself; science makes man godlike—it is all over with priests and gods when man becomes scientific. Moral: science is forbidden—it alone is forbidden. Science is the first sin, the seed of all sin, the Original Sin. This alone is morality: Thou shal't not know." —Nietzsche.

The priests of the mediaeval Catholic Church saw it as their religious duty to destroy the books, temples, and the religious-science of the ancients. When the Spanish and the priests of the Catholic Church arrived in Mexico, they destroyed tens of thousands of books and thousands of Indian idols and temples. In the year 1530 alone, the Bishop of Mexico, Juan de Zumarraga, burned thousands of Aztec manuscripts, hieroglyphic texts and astronomical documents in a huge fire (Landa, 1990).

Likewise, Friar Diego de Landa and his fellow Catholic missionaries, destroyed thousands of Mayan codices, which he declared to be "works of the devil, designed by the evil one to delude the Indians and to prevent them from accepting Christianity... We found great numbers of books but as they contained nothing but superstitions and falsehoods of the devil we burned them all, which the natives took most grievously and which gave them great pain" (Landa, 1990).

Astronomy and science have long been treated as "enemies of god" by the medieval Catholic church. Galileo, as we know, was given a choice: Recant and never again peer through his telescope, or be tortured and burned.

In this regard, the peoples of old Mexico had doubly sinned, at least in the eyes of the Catholic priests, for they worshipped Quetzalcoatl, the "Feathered Serpent" —"the devil" or so the priests believed— and the devil and the serpent have always been the great friend of wisdom and knowledge.

Kukulkan, the "Feathered Serpent" (referred to as Quetzalcoatl by the Aztecs), was the great God of the Maya (Coe, 1991; Thompson, 1993). The Temple of Kukulkan, located in Chichen Itza, in northern Yucatan, Mexico, towers nearly 100 feet into the air, and forms a perfect four sided ziggurat, with four stairways with 91 steps each. Coupled with the last step which forms the top platform, the total steps comes to 365 which corresponds to the number of days in a solar year.

The Temple of Kukulkan was constructed with astronomical-geometric precision, designed to react, twice a year, to the sunlight striking the northern staircase, by giving rise to the illusion of a giant serpent undulating across the steps. The illusion of a slithering snake lasts for a period of 3 hours and 22 minutes on the day of the spring and autumn equinoxes.

In contrast to the "Holy Fathers," the priests of old Mexico were not threatened by science, but embraced it with religious fervor.

The Mayan priests learned to chart the heavens, visualize eternity, and to count in millions. Over a thousand years ago, the Mayan priests calculated the solar year at 365.2420 days (Coe, 1991; Thompson, 1993, Wright, 1991), which is remarkably close to the modern "scientific" figure of 365.2422: the exact length of a solar year. Likewise, the Mayas calculated that it took the moon 29.528395 days to orbit the Earth—a figure nearly identical to that given by modern scientific instruments: 29.530588 days.

They also discovered the concept of zero, or nothing (Coe, 1991) and believed in the concept of infinity, as did the Hindu and Aryan sages of ancient India.

As summed up by Thompson (1993) "In the Maya scheme the road over which time had marched stretched into a past so distant that the mind of man cannot comprehend its remoteness. On a stela at Quiriga in Guatemala a date over 90 million years ago is computed; on another a date over 300 million years ago is given. These are actual computations, stating correctly the day and month positions, and are comparable to calculations in our calendar giving the month positions on which Easter would have fallen at equivalent distances in the past. The brain reels at such astronomical figures."

The Mayan astronomer priests of ancient Mexico and Central America, also determined the synodical revolution of Venus, i.e. 584 days, which is the time it takes Venus to return to a specific point in the heavens as viewed from the Earth. Like the medieval Catholic Church, the Mayas (as well as the Aztecs) associated Venus (the Morning Star) with the Great Serpent.

The Mayas recognized that the figure of 584 was just a very close approximation, because the movements of Venus and Earth are not completely regular. The Mayan priests thus arrived at an "average" synodical period of 583.92 days (Thompson, 1993)—a figure nearly identical to modern estimates.

The Mayan priests also devised a calendar which included a "sacred year," the tzolkin of 260 days, and which was separated into 13 months of 20 days each. As we shall see "13" is a precessional number related to the cyclic movement of the cosmic clock and periods of creation and destruction.

In addition, they devised a calendar based on the "Long Count" which incorporated their beliefs about the future and the past (Wright, 1991). According to the Mayas, time operates in great cycles of creation and destruction; cycles which have a duration of 5125 years.

This Long Count Calendar was in turn based upon the even more ancient bar-and-dot calendar devised by the Olmecs. The Olmecs bar-and-dot calendar—with a current starting date of 8/13/3113 B.C. (4 Ahau 8 Cumku)—predicts that the end of this world will begin at the end of the next great cosmic cycle, on December 23, 2012 (4 Ahau 3 Kankin).

According to the Mayan/Olmec/Aztec calendar (the same calendar adopted by the Aztecs), the last great period of destruction occurred 12,000 years ago, when the Earth was rattled by Earthquakes, volcanic eruptions, and terrible floods: events they blamed on a cosmic calamity, and which they, and other ancient peoples, associated with the Great Serpent, which was associated with Venus.

The Mayan/Olmec priests did not base these predictions on superstition. The priests were scientists, mathematicians, and astronomers who believed by studying the movements of the stars and cyclic cosmic events, that they could scientifically predict what would occur in the future, as based on what has transpired in the past (Coe, 1991; Nigel, 1990; Thompson, 1993).

The astronomer priests of old Mexico, also believed the gods lived among the stars, and that in the remote past, the gods had come to the Earth and had bequeathed and provided woman and man with science and wisdom—including a science that would enable the Kings of the Earth, to join the gods among the stars.

The ancient city of Teotihuacan was believed to be the "place of the gods" where the gods would gather. This included the god Huehueteotl—the god who gave life its beginning and who formed the first woman and man—humans who were also part god (Nigel, 1990).

The city of Teotihuacan was a "Holy city" and a center of scientific study. It was believed by the astronomer priests that those who were interned in the city of Teotihuacan would also begin life anew—that is, as gods.

As reported by Father Benardino de Sahagun, who accompanied the Conquistadors in the 16th century: the natives believed that "the Lords therein buried, after their deaths, did not perish but

Figure 172. The Pyramid of Kukulkan. From C. Macadans, H. Men, C. Bensinger, 1991. Mayan Vision Quest. HarperSanFrancisco, California.

turned into gods." It was "the place where Kings became gods" and where "gods were made" (Thomkins, 1987).

The city of Teotihuacan has also been described as "the road of the gods" (Westwood, 1987). This same terminology can be found in the Pyramid Texts (The Book of the Dead) of ancient Egypt (Budge, 1903). In describing the death of the pharaoh and his burial tomb, the pyramid, it is stated: "to make a road... to ascend into the company of the gods."

Indeed, the ancient Egyptians believed that the dead pharaoh would join the Lord of Eternity, Osiris, the god of the dead, who resided not only in the underworld, but in the stars—the Belt of Orion.

Thus we find, for example, that the southern shaft of the "King's chamber" of the Great Egyptian Pyramid of Giza, is aimed, like the barrel of a gun, directly at the location occupied by the Belt of Orion when the pyramid was supposedly first erected some 4,500 years ago (Bauval, 1994).

Following his death, the soul of the pharaoh was believed to journey to the Orion constellation, which became his eternal resting place among the gods and the stars. As stated in the Pyramid Texts:

"The gods who are in the sky are brought to you, the gods who are on Earth assemble for you; they place their hands under you, they make a ladder for you that you may ascend on it into the sky, the doors of the sky are thrown open to you, the doors of the starry firmament are thrown open for you."

By contrast, the southern shaft of the Queen's chamber points at the location occupied by the binary "dog star," Sirius, some 4,500 years ago (Bauval, 1994)—which is when the Queen's chamber was supposedly constructed.

In the ancient Egyptian Pyramid Texts, the binary/dual star system known as the "dog star" Sirius ("Sept") was directly associated with the god Isis, the sister and lover of Osiris (Budge 1903, 1911). Osiris was the father and Isis the mother of the god Horus who was also described as a "dweller in Sept." Thus Osiris was believed to have impregnated Sirius/Isis who gave birth to the god Horus. Horus however, forever after maintained a close relationship with his mother—living in her house.

The relationship between Osiris, Isis, and Horus, is neatly summed up by the Pyramid texts:

"Thy sister Isis cometh unto thee rejoicing in her love for thee. Thou settest her upon thee, thy issue entereth her, and she becometh great with child like the star Sept. Horus-Sept cometh forth from thee in the form of Horus, dweller in Sept."

To the uninitiated, including most Western readers, these religious notions may well seem to represent little more than quaint superstitions and highly imaginative and fanciful myths. In fact, they are based on amazingly accurate astronomical observations and the belief that "things are numbers."

The ancient Egyptians apparently recognized that Sirius was a binary star system, and that a smaller star (identified today as Sirius B) revolves around the larger star (Sirius A). Isis, therefor, is sometimes depicted as twins. It is noteworthy, however, that the binary nature of the Sirius star system was not discovered by modern western science until 1862.

Sirius also received special attention from the ancient Egyptian priests because of all the stars that are visible to the naked eye, it is the only one to rise heliacally every 365 days—referred to as the Sirian/Sothic cycle), that is, on the first day of the New Year—according to the ancient Egyptian calendar.

"We cannot but admire the greatness of a science capable of discovering such a coincidence. The double star of Sirius was chosen because it was the only star that moves the needed distance and in the right direction against the background of the other stars. This fact, known four thousand years before our time and forgotten until our day, obviously demands an extraordinary and prolonged observation of the sky "(Schwaller de Lubicz, 1988).

The priests of ancient Egypt were accomplished scientists and astronomers. They also believed in the existence of gods.

Be it Mayan, Aztec, Egyptian, or the ancient peoples of Summer and Babylon, the home of the gods, was in the heavens. The gods lived among the stars, but had come to Earth, to create woman and man, and to provide them with wisdom and knowledge.

Ancient astronomer priests not only studied the stars, they created great temples and pyramids which served as astronomical observatories of the heavens and terrestrial maps of the stars.

The ancient priests created heaven on Earth.

Figure 173. *Osiris upon his throne. Behind him is the godess Isis and her twin. Note the 12 serpents that sit above his head, six to the left six to the right, with a central most coiled serpent who represents the Milky Way.*

THE PYRAMIDS: HEAVEN ON EARTH

THE PYRAMIDS OF GIZA

The three great Egyptian pyramids of Giza appear to have been constructed to form a terrestrial map of the heavens, specifically, the Orion constellation and thus the house of Osiris. The three great pyramids are oriented closely together, and although the four corners of each pyramid point due East, West, North and South, they do not lay in a straight line, but are oriented along an axis which mimics the three belt stars of Orion (Bauval, 1994).

As pointed out in 1994 by Robert Bauval, a Belgian construction engineer, the three pyramids of Giza, are aligned in the exact orientation and interrelationship of the three belt stars. Like (the lower) two of the three pyramids (Khufu, Khafre), the lower two belt stars, Al Nitak and Al Nilam, form a perfect diagonal. However, like the upper pyramid (Menkaure), the third, upper star, Mintaka, is offset slightly to the East.

According to Bauval: "It is really quite obvious that all these monuments were laid out according to a unified plan that was modeled with extraordinary precision on those three stars. What they did at Giza was to build Orion's Belt on the ground."

Specifically, when mapped against the Orion Constellation, it is apparent that the Great Pyramid of Khufu occupies the same position as Al Nitak, whereas the Pyramid of Khafre occupies the same position as Al Nilam, whereas the Pyramid of Menkaure occupies the position of Mintaka—that is, their position 12,500 years ago: on the same date that Orion's Belt was at its lowest altitude in the precessional cycle. The figure of 12,500 years ago also corresponds to a date which marks the point at which the 3 belt stars began their upward cycle.

"At 10,450 BC—and at that date only—we find that the pattern of the pyramids on the ground provides a perfect reflection of the pattern of the stars in the sky. I mean it's a perfect match—faultless— and it cannot be an accident" (Bauval, 1994)

The three pyramids of Giza not only serves as a terrestrial map of the Orion Constellation, but by their differences in size, also reflect the different magnitudes of these three belt stars (Bauval, 1994). In addition, other structures on the Giza plateau correspond to the location and interrelationship of the stars of the Orion Constellation, and thus provide a map of the heavens.

Again, however, this heavenly map does not match the skies as they looked during the so called pyramid age, 4,500 years ago, but the heavens, as seen from Egypt, 12,500 years ago (Bauval, 1994).

This date is significant. First, it corresponds with the date given by Plato, and the Olmec/Mayan/Aztec calendar for the last period of cosmic destruction, in which all the great civilizations and cities of the Earth were destroyed by Earthquakes, volcanic eruptions, torrential rains, and world-wide flooding—a confluence of catastrophes which were directly linked to a cosmic event and an upheaval in the heavens (reviewed in Joseph, 2000). Secondly, this date corresponds to a period in which there was a sudden rise in global temperatures (global warming), the rather sudden ending of the last ice-age, and the incredible flooding and loss of animal life that occurred during this period. Indeed, sea levels are believed to have risen nearly 400 feet and the Earth was apparently rocked by massive Earthquakes and rapid alterations in global temperature such that some regions of the planet froze, whereas others boiled.

THE PYRAMIDS OF TEOTIHUACAN

Like the 3 great pyramids of Egypt, the pyramids of Teotihuacan also appear to serve as a terrestrial map of the heavens.

Teotihuacan is notable not only for its Pyramid of the Sun, but for its Pyramid of the Moon, the Pyramid of Quetzalcoatl, and the "Citadel," all of which form an axis referred to as the "Street of the Dead." The orientation of the "axis" however is slightly off center. The "Street of the Dead" is inclined 15 degrees by 30 degress east of north. The design is believed to have been purposeful and based on astronomical alignments which form a map of the heavens (Harleston, 1974; Nigel, 1990; Thompkins, 1987), "the sky-world where dwelt the deities and spirits of the dead" (Thompkins, 1987).

It has also been determined that Teotihuacan may have been designed to serve as a scale model of the solar system, with the center line of the Pyramid of Quetzalcoatl representing the position of the sun, with the temples and pyramids of the "Street of the Dead" denoting the precise orbital distances of the outer planets, i.e. Pluto, Neptune, Uranus, Saturn, Jupiter, and the asteroid belt (Thompkins, 1987).

What is even more striking is that Uranus was not "discovered" by Western scientists until 1787, Neptune in 1846, and Pluto in 1930. The "Street of the Dead" and its temples and pyramids appear to be at least 2000 years old (Nigel, 1990) and perhaps more than 10,000 years old.

Figure 174. The Great Pyramids of Giza. The ancient historical record and their technological perfection suggests that the 3 great pyramids were also erected by a technologically advanced pre-deluvial culture and civilization. Note in the foreground, the crumbling miniature remnants of the tiny pyramids erected by the ancient Egyptians. (Bottom) The three pyramids mapped against the 3 belt stars of the constellation of Orion.

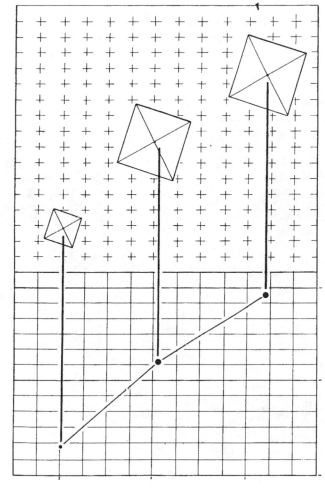

How did the ancients discover the presence of the outer stars? In the same manner as modern astronomers: Through mathematical calculations.

As noted, the "Long Count" was designed to predict the cycles of destruction and creation, with the ending of this world being brought about by a great earthquake. The "Street of the Dead" may have also served to detect earthquakes.

According to Alfred Schlemmler (1990), originally, the "Street of the Dead" was not a street at all, but a series of interlocking reflecting pools that were filled with water. The street served as a "long-range seismic monitor" to detect earthquakes where ever they may occur in the world, since earthquakes "can cause standing waves to form on a liquid surface right across the planet. These reflecting pools would have therefore enabled the priests of "Teotihuacan to read from the formation of standing waves, the location and strength of earthquakes around the Earth, thus allowing them to predict such an occurrence in their own area."

THE PYRAMIDS: EARTH IN HEAVEN

"Coincidence" is not a scientific explanation.

Although the above mentioned observations and interpretations are certainly open to debate, the evidence nevertheless appears to indicate that there was an objective, scientific, and astronomical basis for the design and construction of the pyramids of Egypt and old Mexico—an objective scientific basis which explains why there are so many similarities between the religious structures erected by people from completely different cultures and living on separate continents, thousands of years ago. The objective similarities are due to their being modeled on the same heavens—though another possibility is that they were not only based on the same science, but were built over 10,000 years ago by people who shared the same culture and technology (Joseph, 2000).

In addition to the above, the Aztec's Pyramid of the Moon is shorter than the Pyramid of the Sun. However, their summits are level. Similarly, in Egypt, the summits of the Great Pyramid and the Pyramid of Khafre are the same, although the Khafre pyramid is shorter. This was accomplished by building the Pyramid of the Moon and the Pyramid of Khafre on higher ground (Smyth, 1990).

The pyramids of Giza and the pyramids of Teotihuacan, also incorporate, and in the same way, the value of pi. Pi is the constant that is multiplied by the diameter of a circle to give its circumfer-

Figure 175. The pyramids of Teotihuacanand the street of the dead

ences (Harleston, 1974).

The area of the Great Pyramid's base (3023.16 feet) divided by twice its original height (481.3949 feet) gives the figure 3.1400000+ (pi). In addition, the ratio between its height and perimeter is the same as the ratio between the circumference and radius of a circle, i.e. 2 pi. And, if we multiply the height of the pyramid by 2 pi, we get the perimeter of its base.

The Pyramid of the Sun has a gentler slope compared to the pyramid at Giza, 43.5 vs 52 degrees and it is not as tall, 233.5 feet vs 481.3949. However, its base is almost the same, 2932.8 vs 3023.16 feet. Even so, the pi formula can be applied to the Pyramid of the Sun (Harleston, 1974). Its base divided by twice its height is equal to two pi, i.e. 6.2800. Its base divided by four times its height is equal to one pi, i.e. 3.1400... And, if we multiply the height of the pyramid by 4 pi, we get the perimeter of its base.

The builders of the pyramids of Egypt and ancient Mexico were well versed in geometry and astronomy and knew the relationship of the radius to its circumference. They knew the circumference of the Earth, and the distance of the center of the Earth to the poles. For example, the ratio of the Great Pyramid's altitude to its perimeter is the same as that of the polar radius of the Earth to its circumference: 2 pi, whereas the same ratio when applied to the Pyramid of the Sun yields the same figure if divided by two.

In fact, as determined by Charles Piazzi Smyth (1990), the Astronomer-Royal of Scotland, the Great Pyramid incorporates and reveals the distance of the Earth from the sun when its height is multiplied by the proportion of its height to its width, that is, ten to the ninth power.

In addition, the height of the Great Pyramid is 1:43,200 of the polar radius of the Earth and the perimeter of its base is 1:43,200 of the Earth's equatorial circumference. In other words, by multiplying the base and height of the Great Pyramid by 43,200 one can arrive at an astonishingly close approximation of the dimensions of the Earth (Smyth, 1990). The Great Pyramid represents a scale model of our planet.

The builders of the Great Pyramid "had determined the shape of the Earth which they knew to be a true circle, its size, its precise circumference, the geographical distance from the equator to the poles, the fact that the Earth is flattened at the poles, degrees of latitude and longitude to within a few hundred feet, the fact that they were shorter at the equator and longer at the poles, and the exact distance of the Earth from the sun. They had designed the pyramid's base to correspond to the distance the Earth rotates in half a second" (Funrneaux, 1987, p 17). The same can also be said of the builders of the Pyramid of the Sun (Harleston, 1974).

In summary: the Great Pyramids of Egypt and Mexico, appear to have been built in accordance with precise geometrical and astronomical laws to serve as a map of heaven, and to record the dimensions of the Earth and the duration of the solar year. The Great Pyramid and the Pyramid of the Sun not only served as scale models of this planet, but could be used to record the movements of the Earth around the heavens in relation to the sun and the stars—the dwelling place of the gods.

PRECESSION: THE FUTURE IS THE PAST

"The mind has lost its cutting edge, we hardly understand the Ancients." —Gregoire de Tours, 6th century

The astronomer priests of the ancient world made a number of startling discoveries about the cosmos, our solar system, and the Earth—startling because thousands of years would pass before modern western scientists would make the same discoveries.

Much of the science of the ancient world has been lost through natural and cosmic catastrophes, or destroyed by the hand of man. In consequence, we know almost nothing about the ancient past, and much of what we do know, is dismissed by "experts" who cloak their ignorance with derision and laughter.

We suffer from a collective amnesia as to ancient pre-deluvial civilizations and those events which transpired six thousand years ago, ten thousands years ago, and so on.

This amnesia is in large part, purposeful, for the books detailing the pre-deluvial past, and the treasures of knowledge the ancients had acquired, have been deliberately destroyed by priests, princes, and conquering kings.

In 213 B.C., the Emperor Chou-Houng-Ti, destroyed a hundred thousand books. When the library of Alexandria was destroyed, tens of thousands of manuscripts went up in flames. When

Pergamo was burned to the ground, 200,000 ancient books were reduced to soot and ash. And what of the ancient books from the library of the Temple of Solomon, from the sanctuary of Phtah of Memphis, the libraries of ancient Athens? Dust. Ashes and dust, of which only fragments remain... fragments and those few ancient stone tablets, temples, and pyramids which escaped the destructive hand of man.

Yet, despite the destructive efforts of the conquerors of old, and the priests of the medieval church who preached: "Thou shalt not know," we have learned that knowledge is not a sin, and that the ancients were men of great wisdom who had studied and learned from the stars.

Copernicus stated explicitly in the preface to his works, that it was from his reading of ancient authors that he learned of the movements of the Earth. And likewise, Newton and Galileo openly admitted their debts to the scientists of old. Indeed, Newton believed that the ancients had learned the secrets of the creation, transmutation, and destruction of matter, as well as the secrets of the stars.

"If I have seen further, it is by standing on the shoulders of giants" —Newton.

Newton stood on those ancient shoulders because he desired a clear view of the stars.

The ancients studied the stars because they believed the future could be predicted by the past, and that time itself was linked to the cyclic movements of the Earth through the heavens.

These are not superstitions. Modern day calendars are based on the same principle.

However, whereas modern day calendars are based on the orbit and tilt of the Earth during a 365 day period, the ancients relied not only on a solar calendar, but a precessional calendar that was 25,776 years in duration—a calendar and cosmic clock that also predicts cycles of creation and destruction and the birth and death of the gods.

THE COSMIC CLOCK

The illusion of movement of the Sun, from north to south, and then back again, in synchrony with the waxing and waning of the four seasons, is due to the changing tilt and inclination of the Earth's axis, as it spins and orbits the sun. Thus over a span of 12 months it appears to an observer that the days become shorter and then longer and then shorter again as the sun moves from north to south, crosses the equator, and then stops, and heads back north again, only to stop, and then to again head south, crossing the equator only to again stop and head north again.

The two crossings each year, over the equator (in March and September) are referred to as equinoxes. The two time periods in which the sun appears to stop its movement, before reversing course (June and December), are referred to as solstices—the "sun standing still."

The sun was recognized by ancient astronomer priests, as a source of light and life-giving heat, and as a keeper of time, like the hands ticking across the face of a cosmic clock.

Because of the scientific, religious, and cosmological significance of the sun, ancient peoples, in consequence, often erected and oriented their religious temples to face and point either to the rising sun on the day of the solstice (that is, in a southwest—northeast axis), or to face the rising sun on the day of the equinox (an east-west axis).

For example, the ancient temples and pyramids in Egypt were oriented to the solstices, whereas the Temple of Solomon faced the rising sun on the day of the equinox.

Over eons of time ancient peoples were forced to slightly alter the orientation of their temples, due to precession and cyclic changes in the inclinations of the Earth's orbital path (the ecliptic) and in its axis (obliquity). For example, the angle of the tilt of the Earth was 24 degrees in 4,000 BC, but has been reduced to 23.5 degrees in modern time. Eventually the angle of the tilt will reverse course and assume a greater angle of inclination.

The gravitational influences of the sun and the moon, coupled with the angle of the tilt of the Earth—that is, the axis of the orientation of the north and south pole—also causes the planet to slowly wobble as it orbits the sun—a phenomenon referred to as "precess."

As will be detailed, the priests of antiquity discovered precess, thousands of years ago.

The Earth spins at the rate of 1000 miles per hour (as measured from the equator) and orbits the sun at 66,600 miles per hour. This orbital and circular motion generates incredible centrifugal forces which cause the Earth's equator to bulge outward whereas the poles are somewhat flattened, thus giving the planet a (sideways) egg-like shape of an oblate spheroid. However, this extra mass at the equator also serves to keep the Earth steady on its axis as it orbits the sun—like the outer rim of a spinning top or gyroscope.

It is said that this oblate spheroid shape of the planet was first discovered by Sir Isaac Newton. However, almost a thousand years before Newton, Muhammad describe the Earth as "shaped like an egg." Muhammad was correct.

And because of the gravitational influences of the sun and the moon, coupled with centrifugal forces, the angle of the tilt of the Earth slowly alters over time as it spins and orbits the sun. The alteration in the tilt of the Earth is cyclic, and over the course of the last 41,000 years, the tilt has been reduced by 1.5 degrees, i.e., from 25 degrees to a little less than 23.5 degrees.

Because the angle of the tilt—that is, the orientation of the north and south pole—alters over time, and the retardation of the Earth's orbit, and thus due to a cyclic phenomenon referred to as "precession," over time the north pole "points" at different stars, and the sun rises in different constellations, like the movements of the hand of a clock.

PRECESSION

The ancient astronomer priests discovered "precession" thousands of years before modern western scientists (Santillana & von Dechen, 1969; Sellers, 1992).

There is a cosmic clock-like regularity to "precession"—like the hands moving around the circular face of a clock.

At present, the north pole points at the "pole star" referred to as Polaris (alpha Ursae Minoris). Five thousand years ago the north pole pointed at alpha Draconis. Thirteen thousand years ago it pointed towards Vega.

In thirteen thousand years, the north pole will again point at Vega. Twenty thousand years from now it will again point at alpha Draconis. And, in 25,776 years it will again point at Polaris.

Thus, it takes the Earth 25,776 years for the hands of the cosmic clock to make a complete circular rotation and to complete a full precessional cycle.

Because the orientation and tilt of the Earth also shifts as it orbits the sun, the amount of sunlight the Earth receives varies during the course of a single orbit, but in a predictable, clock-like fashion (Hays et al., 1976). As noted, this change in the tilt of the planet gives rise to the four seasons and what is referred to as the winter and summer solstices and the autumn and spring equinoxes.

In the northern hemisphere, during the winter, the tilt is away from the sun, with the greatest degree of that tilt occurring on December 21. December 21 marks the winter solstice and is the shortest day of the year. By contrast, the greatest degree of tilt toward the sun occurs on June 21, the summer solstice, which is the longest day of the year. The equinoxes, March 20 and September 22, are the two days of the year which are of equal length.

Thus, the cosmic clock-like cycle of the Earth's orbit around the sun, gives rise to four significant astronomical events which the ancients deemed to be of the highest significance. However, as the ancients discovered, the equinoxes also undergo precession, and, precession has a repetitive, clock-like predictability (Santillana & von Dechen, 1969; Sellers, 1992).

As the Earth orbits the sun it forms an imaginary circle referred to as the ecliptic. There is, however, a second, outer imaginary circle, an outer-ring that forms a belt that surrounds the Earth's ecliptic orbit.

This outer circle is ringed with stars that form the 12 constellations of the zodiac: Aquarius, Pisces, Aries, Taurus, Gemini, Cancer, Leo, Virgo, Libra, Scorpio, Sagittarius, Capricorn. The 12 constellations, although differing in size, are evenly spaced, occupying positions in the heavens that could be likened to the numbers on the face of a clock.

Each constellation occupies a space of 30 degrees along the ecliptic of the Earth's 360 degree orbit around the sun. Thus, as the Earth orbits the sun, every 30 days the Earth faces a different constellation during the morning sun-rise, and thus passes through a different house of the zodiac.

Because the orbit of the Earth gives rise to the illusion of the movement of the sun, the sun also appears to be rising in and passing through a different constellation every 30 days. Thus, an observer who watches as the sun rises or sets, will also see the sun rising or setting in a different constellation, every 30 days.

It is this illusion which led the ancient Greeks and the Medieval Catholic Church to believe that the Earth was at the center of the solar system and that the sun orbited the Earth.

The ancient astronomer priests of remote antiquity were not fooled. Thousands of years before the rise of the Greek civilization, these ancient priests recognized that the sun was at the center of the solar system, and, they calculated not only precess, but precession (Santillana & von Dechen, 1969; Sellers, 1992).

Because of the clock-like regularity of the changing seasons and the passage of the Earth through all the houses of the zodiac in a solar year, it can be predicted in which house of the Zodiac the sun would rise on any day of the year, including on the mornings of the summer and winter

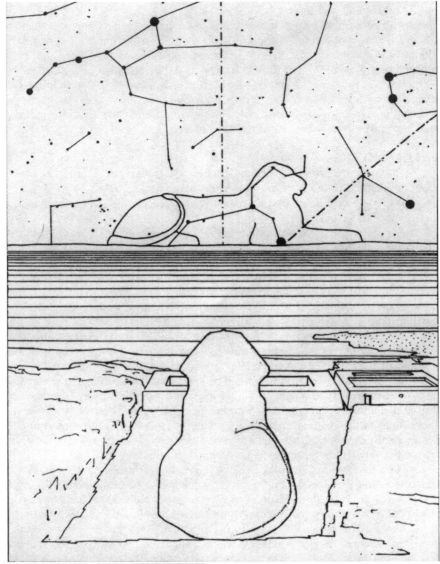

Figure 176. (Above). The Sphinx was erected to face the constellation of Leo, on the morning of the equinox, 12,5000 years ago. Drawing From G. Hancock, 1995. Fingerprints of the Gods. Three Rivers Press, New York. (Left) Weathering studies indicate the Sphinx was first erected over 12,000 years ago and suffered most of its erosion when inundated by massive rainfall and flooding.

solstices and the spring and autumn equinoxes. These predictions can be made with accuracy for the following year, or even a hundreds years into the future: The future can be predicted mathematically based on the past.

What the ancient priests discovered, however, was that over thousands of years of time, and because of precession, the sun slowly changes position, like the hands of a clock. Over thousands of years, the sun begins to rise in a different constellation on the mornings of the summer solstices, and a different constellation on winter solstices and different constellations on the spring and autumn equinoxes (Santillana & von Dechen, 1969; Sellers, 1992).

What the ancient priests discovered was that the sun's changing position, like the hands of a clock, pointed out the "hours" of the precessional cycle—a phenomenon referred to as the "precession of the equinoxes."

Instead of every 30 days, the ancients discovered that every 2160 years the sun would point at a different constellations on the day of the equinox or solstice. That is, it takes 2160 years for the sun to slowly move from house to house—like the ticking hands of celestial clock.

Due to the retardation of the Earth's orbital movement of 1 degree every 72 years, precession is a counterclockwise, or rather, an anti-clockwise phenomenon. Thus, every 2,160 years the sun rises in the previous house of the Zodiac. That is, the sun appears to move in a counterclockwise direction, such that the hands of the solar precessional clock also move backwards: Virgo, Leo, Cancer, Gemini, Taurus, Aries, Pisces, Aquarius, etc.

For example, the hands of the solar clock pointed at Aries, 4000 years ago, but slowly moved toward Pisces. For the last 2000 years the hand of the solar clock has pointed at Pisces, but is also moving slowly toward Aquarius. Thus, although we are still in the house of Pisces we are about to enter the age of Aquarius.

The ancient priests also determined that the precession of the equinoxes takes 25,920 years to complete its 360 degree circular cycle; i.e. 12 x 2160 years. The ancients were off by 144 years, at least according to modern "estimates" which gives the number as 25,776 (Hays, et al., 1976). Thus, 25,776 years from now, the sun will again appear to rise in Pisces and will be about to enter the age of Aquarius.

NEW AGE RELIGIONS

As the ancient astronomer priests realized, a single year consists of 365 days. A Great Year consists of 25,920 years. The Great Year, like a single year, consists of 12 houses, but instead of 30 days per house/month, the duration of the time spent in each house/constellation is 2160 years.

It was also believed that as the hands of the cosmic clock shifted from one constellation to the next, this signified the ushering in of a "new world age," e.g., the age of Taurus followed by the age of Aries followed by the (current) age of Pisces, each lasting 2160 years.

However, every beginning is heralded by an ending and the death of a "god." As Aristotle long ago pointed out, in the truly ancient world, the "gods were stars," that is, constellations.

Thus, as the hands of the precessional clock moved from constellation to constellation, each new world age would be associated with the death of an old god and the birth and rein of a new god, who in turn would be directly linked to the prevailing constellation.

For example, the astronomical age of Pisces (the fish) began around the time of the birth of Christ, which is why the fish was and continues to be a symbol associated with Christ and Christianity.

The age of Taurus the bull was 4,000-6,000 years ago which is why ancient religions of that period employed the symbol of the Bull, e.g. the Bull-cult of ancient Crete, the Apis bulls of ancient Egypt.

The Sumerian lists of the Zodiac also begin with Taurus, the bull, and this is because, 6,000 years ago the Sumerian civilization was in full flower and the Sun appeared to rise in the constellation of Taurus on the spring equinox. Sumerian stories also frequently refer to the Bull of Heaven. However, there are also Sumerian references to lions, such as when Gilgamesh killed two lions with his bare hands. Six thousand years ago, the sun appeared to rise in the constellation of Leo (the Lion) on the day of the summer solstice.

Again, there are two solstices, and two equinoxes, and a different constellation occupies each of the four, for a 2,160 year period.

The Sumerians were largely a Semitic people, and Abraham, the patriarch of modern day Jews and the Jewish religion, hailed from Ur of the Chaldese, a Sumerian city, during the waning days of the age of Taurus. And like the Sumerians, the ancient Jews worshipped a number of gods, including Taurus, the bull—also known as the "Golden Calf."

Moses appeared upon the scene during the new age of Aries: the ram—also known as the god of war. But, when he led the Jews from Egypt to the lands he claimed had been promised to them by the God of Abraham, Isaac and Jacob, they were not accepting of the new god and repeatedly rebelled in favor of the old gods, the gods worshipped by their fathers, and their kings:

"When the people saw that Moses was so long in coming down from the mountain, they gathered around Aaron and said, "Come, make us gods who will go before us. Aaron answered them, "Take off the gold earrings that your wives, your sons and your daughters are wearing, and bring them to me." So all the people took off their earrings and brought them to Aaron. He took what they handed him and made it into an idol cast in the shape of a calf. Then they said, "These are your gods, O Israel, who brought you up out of Egypt." When Aaron saw this, he built an altar in front of the calf and announced, "Tomorrow there will be a festival to the Lord."

"Then the Lord said to Moses, Go down, because your people, whom you brought up out of Egypt, have become corrupt. They have been quick to turn away from what I commanded them and have made themselves an idol cast in the shape of a calf." —Exodus 32

Moses immediately ordered the slaughter of all who had worshipped the golden calf.

The age of the Bull was over. The hands of the precessional clock had shifted to a new constellation and a new world age. A new age required a new god. The God of Moses, the God of Abraham, Isaac and Jacob, was the new god heralded by the new age of the ram—Aries, the god of war, also known as the "Lord of Hosts" (armies) and the "Lord of Heaven."

The age of the ram began 4000 years ago—when Abram/Abraham was called by "God" and left for Egypt— and ended 2000 years ago, which is why ancient religions at that time were ram-oriented and/or used rams in their symbolism. Indeed, rams appear repeatedly in the old testament and were important symbols in Egypt during this period.

Abram (Ab-ram) left Sumer during the opening days of the new age of the ram, and it is Abram (who became Abraham) who was the patriarch and thus the founder of a new religion, the Jewish religion—but first he had to prove himself to the new god—the god of the ram—by sacrificing his first born son, Isaac (Genesis 22):

"And it came to pass after these things, that God did tempt Abraham, and said unto him, Abraham: and he said, Behold, here I am. And he said, Take now thy son, thine only son Isaac, whom thou lovest, and get thee into the land of Moriah; and offer him there for a burnt offering upon one of the mountains which I will tell thee of.... and Abraham built an altar there, and laid the wood in order, and bound Isaac his son, and laid him on the altar upon the wood. And Abraham stretched forth his hand, and took the knife to slay his son. And the angel of the LORD called unto him out of heaven, and said, Abraham, Abraham: and he said, Here am I. And he said, Lay not thine hand upon the lad, neither do thou any thing unto him: for now I know that thou fearest God, seeing thou hast not withheld thy son, thine only son from me. And Abraham lifted up his eyes, and looked, and behold behind him a ram caught in a thicket by his horns: and Abraham went and took the ram, and offered him up for a burnt offering in the stead of his son."

By sacrificing a ram, provided by "God," and because he was willing to kill

Figure 177. The sacrifice of Isaac by Abraham. Etching by Rembrandt. Instead, Abraham sacrificed a ram.

his first born son, Abraham proved himself worthy of being the father of a new age religion... "And Abraham called the name of that place Jehovah..." —Genesis 22

FATEFUL SIGNIFICANCE OF PRECESSION

In ancient records we are sometimes told that "fate has 12 stations." However, the ancients made a distinction between "fate" and "destiny." Fate could be altered through free will and one's behavior. Destiny could not—at least, so said the ancients. Destiny was unalterable: And this included even the destiny of the gods, for whereas gods, like woman and man, could influence if not control their fate, they could not control or alter their destiny, which, like their fate, was written in the stars.

The ancient astronomer priests believed that destiny, on a cosmic or global level, and the destruction and renewal of civilization, could be determined through the observation of the stars and via mathematical predictions based on precess, precession, and the orbit of the Earth as it made its journey through the heavens and the 12 houses of the zodiac; that is, the 12 constellations.

This was important to the ancients because these events heralded not just the birth of a new god, but periods of destruction and cosmic calamity followed by a new golden age.

In the final passages of Revelation, we see not only references to precession and the 12 houses of the Zodiac, but we are told of a new golden age: "One of the seven angels... carried me away in the Spirit to a mountain great and high, and showed me the Holy City, Jerusalem, coming down out of heaven. It had twelve gates. The twelve gates were twelve pearls. I did not see a temple in the city, because... the city does not need the sun or the moon to shine on it, for the glory of God gives it light."

As noted, periods of rebirth and destruction were believed to be linked to the Earth's movements from constellation to constellation, and this is also the overarching message of Revelation, i.e. Armageddon. Again, these beliefs were not based on superstition, but observation, history, and mathematical analysis.

There are hints in ancient records, for example, that cyclic periods of destruction were due to the Earth passing through regions of space that were in turmoil. We are told of wars in heaven, battles among the stars, in which the Earth was buffeted by debris from space and rocked by wayward planets, moons, comets and stars that snaked through the heavens like a giant serpent, or a like a dragon which swallowed (eclipsed) the sun and the moon, and then attacked the Earth. And we are warned that these cosmic catastrophic events are cyclic and will occur again in the future:

"Is this the one that made the Earth to tremble, that did to shake kingdoms. That made the world as a wilderness, and destroyed the cities...

"But beware and rejoice not because the rod of his that smote thee is broken: for out of the serpent's root and of his fruit shall be a fiery flying dragon... -Isaiah, 14

And, we are warned that these future cosmic catastrophic events, these wars in heaven, are directly related to precession and the passage of the Earth through the twelve houses of the Zodiac:

"And there appeared a great wonder in heaven: A woman clothed with the sun, and the moon under her feet, and upon her head a crown of twelve stars: And she being with child cried travailing in birth and pained to be delivered...

"And there appeared another wonder in heaven: And behold a great red dragon having seven heads and ten horns and seven crowns upon his head. And his tail drew the third part of the stars of heaven and did cast them to the Earth... -Revelation, 12

Thus we are told of "twelve stars" which are the 12 houses of the zodiac. And we are provided with the numbers: seven heads and ten horns and seven crowns. Seven + seven + ten = 24.

There are 24 hours in a day, a recurring cycle of 12 hours of light, 12 hours of darkness.

The number 24 is repeated again and again in Revelation, and the references is to repeating cycles: "...because he once was, now is not, and yet will come..."

And, as to "the third part of the stars," that Revelation tells us will be cast to Earth, this yields the number 8. What is the significance of number 8?

"Eight" refers to the eighth planet counting from the outer orbit of the solar system, i.e. the planet Venus, the morning star, also known as the great serpent, and by the name: "Lucifer."

"How art thou fallen from heaven, O' Lucifer star of the morning... the one that made the Earth to tremble, that did to shake kingdoms. That made the world as a wilderness, and destroyed the cities..." -Isaiah, 14

According to ancient Sumerian and Babylonian tradition: "Seven" refers to our planet, mother Earth—the seventh planet when counting from the outer rim of the solar system. In the passage above, mother Earth becomes: "A woman clothed with the sun, and the moon under her feet" (though, as detailed later, this passage may also refer to the constellation of Virgo—a Virgin about to give birth to a new god).

"Seven also refers to the seven stars of Ursa, the dominant stars of the north and which are believed to be linked to the operative powers controlling the universe. And, in Revelation, we are told of the "7 angels... 7 seals... 7 spirits... 7 stars..."

Because the ancients believed that the stars, and the movement of the Earth in its journey through the heavens was of fateful significance, the observations of the heavens and the cyclic nature of the dance of the stars, played a major role in decision making and in religious practices, including, as noted, in the orientation of ancient temples and predictions of destruction and rebirth.

MYTHOLOGY & PRECESSION:
KNOWLEDGE IS POWER

"Newton was not the first of the Age of Reason. He was the last of the magicians, the last of the Babylonians and Sumerians.... He looked on the whole universe and all that is in it as a riddle, as a secret which could be read by... certain mystic clues...laid about by... an esoteric brotherhood. He believed that these clues were to be found...in certain papers and traditions handed down by the brethren in an unbroken chain back to the original cryptic revelation in Babylon. He regarded the universe as a cryptogram set by the Almighty." —John Maynard Keynes.

Throughout much of history, there have been secret societies consisting of men who believed that the discoveries of science should be kept secret from kings, ministers, government officials, and those who would exploit science for the purpose of evil and doing harm.

Asoka, the grandson of Chandragupta who had unified ancient India, was a warrior and a scientist, and he applied his understanding of science, to war. He was overcome by his own successes and developed a horror for war. Upon becoming emperor of India, Asoka forbid men to ever use their intelligence or their knowledge of science, for purposes of evil. Scientists and scholars of ancient India, were forced to take vows of secrecy and to become members of a secret society who could only communicate openly through riddles, parables, and secret codes.

The ancient astronomer priesthood in many ways, also functioned like a secret society, with secret initiation rites, and hidden knowledge that only initiates were privy too.

For example, the Kaballa tells us that there are 72 angels and that those who know their names and numbers can use them to invoke or approach the divine powers—the Sephiroth.

In the ancient religion of China, the initiation ritual of the Hung League involved questions that involved the numbers 36, 72, and 108 (Ward, 1925)—all of which are multiples of 12:

"I saw two pots with red bamboo. In one pot were 36 and in the other 72 plants, together, 108. Who in the world knows the meaning of this?"

Indeed, what is the meaning of this?

All three are multiples of 12. Moreover, these numbers, as well as the numbers 9, 12, 30, 36, 108, 360, 2160, 25,920, 432,000, 1,296,000, repeatedly appear in ancient religious texts and in religious "myths" the world over.

In Arabic-pre-Islamic tradition, it was said that martyrs were rewarded in heaven with 72 Virgins. "Man has not touched them before them nor jinni. Which then of the bounties of your Lord will you deny? Reclining on green cushions and beautiful carpets. Which then of the bounties of your Lord will you deny? —The Beneficent.

Hadith number 2,562 in the collection known as the Sunan al-Tirmidhi says, "The least [reward] for the people of Heaven is 80,000 servants and 72 wives, over which stands a dome of pearls, aquamarine and ruby."

The ancient Egyptian religious myth of Osirus tells us that 72 divine conspirators, led by Seth, plotted to kill Osirus (Budge, 1903, Sellers, 1992).

The mystics of the Kaballah believe that 72 is Yahweh's secret number.

Yahweh instructed Moses and Aron to take 70 of the elders of Israel to accompany them to the Holy Mount; i.e. Moses + Aron + 70 = 72. However, Moses and Aron also brought along 2 of Arons 4 sons. Thus Aron and Moses were accompanied by 72 men.

These numbers are significant because they are precessional numbers which yield 2160—the total number of years in which the sun was believed to spend in each of the 12 constellation.

For example, 30 times 72 equals 2160—the number of years the ancients believed it took the sun to pass from one to the next house of the zodiac.

Consider: 12 is the number of houses of the zodiac. There are 360 degrees to a circle and 30 is the number of degrees assigned to each house (360 divided by 12=30). 72 is the number of years for the sun to complete a precessional shift of one degree (the modern estimate being 71.6). And, 360 is the total number of degrees in the Earth's ecliptic.

Again, 72 x 30 yields 2160 which is the total number of years in which the sun spends in each house. 360 x 72 equals 25,920, as does 2160 x 12, which is a very close estimate of the number of years to complete a precessional cycle through all 12 houses of the zodiac, the modern estimate being 25,777 years.

Likewise, the value of 2160 is remarkably close to the modern estimate of 2148, which is the time it now takes for a precessional shift through a single constellation.

In some religious "myths," the number 36 is added to 72, to obtain 108:

"In one pot were 36 and in the other 72 plants, together, 108. Who in the world knows the meaning of this?"

The number, 108, can be multiplied by factors of 10 to obtain the number of years for a precessional shift through a single constellation, i.e. 20 times 108 equals 2,160.

The temple complex of Angkor, India, has five gates which lead to five roads, each of which is bordered by 108 gigantic stone figures, i.e. 540 stone figures total. These stone figures are bound to a huge Naga serpent, which they pull in order to churn the Milky Oceans of the Universe.

540, like 108, is a precessional number.

For example, 540 x 4 = 2,160.

The number "4" is derived from the four seasons (the two solstices and two equinoxes) and which also provides us with the sign of the cross.

Also, 540 x 48 = 25,920

In ancient Indian religion, the number 48 appears as a component of each divine year. For example, 4,800 is the duration of Krita Yuga.

The Rigveda also tell us of the "12-spoked wheel in which the 720 sons of Agni are established." 12 x 720 = 8640 which when multiplied by 30 = 25,920.

The number 12, of course, refers to the 12 houses of the zodiac. And, 12 has always been a very important number in ancient, as well as more modern religions, such as Judaism and Christianity.

The ancient Greeks and Romans believed in 12 great gods, the 12 Olympians of the Greek Pantheon. However, before the rise of the 12 Olympians, the Greeks tell us there were 12 Titans.

There are 12 months in a year, 12 hours in a day, and 12 hours in a night, and 12 constellations.

Osiris (The Lord of the Dead), was killed by Set in the company of 72 conspirators, and passes judgment on the dead with the assistance of a council of 12.

"The Holy City, Jerusalem, coming down out of heaven.... had a great, high wall with twelve gates, and with twelve angels at the gates. On the gates were written the names of the twelve tribes of Israel. There were three gates on the east, three on the north, three on the south and three on the west. The wall of the city had twelve foundations, and on them were the names of the twelve apostles of the Lamb" —Revelations.

Jesus had his 12 apostles. Moses "erected 12 stone pillars" (Exodus 24:4). And Jacob and Ishmael each had 12 sons.

"As for Ishmael... of him twelve chieftains will be born, his shall be a great nation" —Genesis 17:20.

"Those were the sons of Ishmael...twelve chieftains each to his own nation" —Genesis 25.

"And the number of sons of Jacob was twelve." —Genesis 35

However, although Jacob had 12 sons, before the birth of his last (12th son) Benjamin, the number of his brood had also numbered 12 if we include his daughter Dinah. Likewise, the 12 constellations of the zodiac consists of 11 males and 1 female—Virgo.

The tribe of Benjamin, that is, the Benjaminites, also took on a female role. As detailed in the Jewish Bible (Tanakh), the Benjaminites were a tribe of notorious homosexuals.

As detailed in Genesis, Jacob's other sons were also linked to the zodiac: Juda was referred to as a lion (Leo), Zebulun was linked to Aquarius—he was to be a Dweller of the Seas—and Joseph was linked to Sagittarius as he was depicted as a bowman.

Also, Levi and Simeon were linked together, thus forming a Gemini (twins). Both brothers, Jacob prophesied, would forfeit their domains and their offspring would be dispersed among the other 10 tribes. However, the list stayed at 12 with the addition of Joseph's two sons, Ephraim and Manasseh.

Also, in the Jewish "Bible" —i.e, in the Nevi'm (The Prophets)— there are 12 minor prophets (chapters) and 9 major prophets (chapters) listed. Again, these are precessional numbers.

The ancients also counted 9 planets, the Earth being number 7, and Venus, number 8.

And, 12 x 9 = 108. These are all precessional number, and 9 and 12 are repeatedly mentioned in the Bible and were considered sacred numbers by a number of ancient religions:

The Aztecs and Mayas believed in a pantheon of 9 deities, as did the priests of Egypt during the earliest dynastic period, 4,500 years ago (Budge, 1903, Thomkins, 1987). The Mayas also believed that the underworld has nine levels through which the dead must journey over a period of 4 years (Coe, 1993).

We also know that the Hebrew word "Mazal-tov" (shouted during births and weddings) does not mean "good luck" per se, but a "good zodiac," or, a "good constellation/station." That is, a wish that the sun's station, in a specific constellation on the day of the birth/wedding, will bring good luck.

Again, there are 12 constellations and 12 is a precessional number.

Or consider the number, 432,000.

The Mayan calendar featured the number 432,000, as well as 2160 and others that allowed for the calculation of precession, i.e. 1 Tun = 360 days, 2 Tuns = 720 days, 6 Tuns 2160 days, 6 Katuns = 43,200 days (Wright, R. 1991).

The ancients believed that precession through one constellation takes 2,160 years. Precession through two houses of the zodiac (60 degree across the ecliptic) was believed to take 4,320 years.

In ancient Indian religion, Kali Yuga is believed to be one of the four ages of Earth. Kali Yuga is identified as the current and last age and consists of 1200 Divine years. This is equal to 432,000 years of mortal man.

There are also 10,800 stanzas in the religious text, the Rigveda, the most ancient of Vedic literature— 10800 being a multiple of 108. Each stanza consists of 432,000 syllables.

In the Sumerian King's list, it is asserted that the Anunnaki gods arrived on Earth, 432,000 years ago.

We are also told by Berossus of ancient Babylon, that gods and demi-gods ruled ancient Summer for a total of 432,000 years.

According to ancient Chinese traditions, all the world's knowledge, before the destruction of the last world by the worldwide deluge, were said to be written down in 4,320 volumes.

Berossus also tells us that there are 2,160,000 years between creation and universal catastrophe, which is the amount derived at when 432,000 is multiplied by 5.

The four seasons, plus the axis running through the Earth (passing through north and south pole) yields the number "5."

Likewise, 2,160,000 represents 1000 cycles of the number of years it takes the sun to pass from one to the next house of the zodiac.

As noted, by multiplying the base and height of the Great pyramid by 43,200 one can arrive at an astonishingly close approximation of the dimensions of the Earth.

Or, consider the Norse poem which describes the battle of the gods and the end of the world:

"500 doors and 40 there are I seen, in Valhalla's walls; 800 fighters through each door fare, When to war with the Wolf they go."

500 plus 40 = 540. 540 x 800 = 432,000.

432,000 divided by 6,000=72

432,000 divided by 2,000=2,160

Again: "Coincidence" is not a scientific explanation.

Dr. Herman Hiprect, who participated in "The Babylonian Expedition of the University of Pennsylvania" has reported that in analyzing the numerous Mesopotamian mathematical tablets, that "all the multiplication and division tables from the temple libraries of Nippur and Sippar, and from the library of Ashurbanipal in Ninevah, are based upon the number 1296000." He concluded that this number had to be related to precession.

12,960,000 divided by 500=25,920

500 x 25,920=12,960,000

As summed up by de Santillan and von Dechend (1969),

"When one finds the same numbers reappearing under several multiples in the Vedas, in the temples of Angkor, in Babylon, in Heraclitius' dark utterances, and also in the Norse Valhalla, it is not an accident... These refer to celestial events... and constitute... a language of awe inspiring antiquity... that concentrates on numbers, motions, measures, overall frames, schemas, and on the structure of numbers, on geometry.... which transmit... a precessional message..."

Figure 178. Churning the Milky Oceans of the Heavens. The serpent was often used to symbolize the spiraling coil of the Milky Way. From G. De Santillana & H. von Dechend, 1969, Hamlet's Mill. David R. Godine, Publisher, Boston.

Yes, but is the message?

The ancients believed that precession, the cosmic clock, was directly linked to cycles of creation and destruction, of death and rebirth. Precession was a key to predicting the future—a future based on the past, including past cycles of cosmic destruction, in which the Earth was buffeted by cosmic forces and falling stars as it journeyed again and again, through the same wilds of space.

Five times in the history of our planet, the Earth has been struck by massive meteors which have destroyed over 70% of animal life on this planet.

Indeed, one need only gaze at the pocked-mocked surface of the moon in order to realize we live in the midst of a cosmic-shooting gallery.

And the best predictor of the future, is the past.

Repeatedly the Earth has been buffeted by natural catastrophes, including a period of global warming, 12,000 years ago, that caused sea-levels to rise nearly 400 feet—thus destroying much of ancient civilization.

And the best predictor of the future, is the past.

Repeatedly our planet has been plagued by a confluence of catastrophes, both man-made and of cosmic origin... a confluence of catastrophes which are said to have befallen the Earth some 12,000 years ago, and which destroyed the cities, destroyed the kingdoms, and destroyed the civilizations of ancient woman and man...

An increasing body of evidence now indicates the Earth was in fact struck by a swarm of meteors, some 12,000 years ago, packing an explosive punch equal to a thousand hydrogen bombs, igniting firestorms and shrouding the earth in a dense cloud of dust that blocked sunlight and sent worldwide temperatures plummeting.

"And the seven judges of hell raised their torches, lighting the land with their livid flame. A stupor of despair went up to heaven when the god of the storm turned daylight into darkness, when he smashed the land like a cup" -the Epic of Gilgamesh.

These giant meteors ("stars") attacked in swarms, 12,000 years ago, striking the Middle East and leaving still visible craters over 2 miles wide. Others struck North and South America, a cluster of ten striking the Pampean Plains in Argentina. Most slammed into the oceans of the Earth creating tidal waves over 3 miles high—thus destroying the cities and the civilizations of woman and man.

Those striking the oceans sent plumes of mist and water into the air, whereas those striking the Earth sent up plumes of smoke and debris, thus first rising global temperatures and then sending them plummeting by blocking out the sun thus causing the freezing of the massive tidal flood waters. Likewise, 12,000 years ago, 100s of species were driven to extinction, including the woolly mammoths who were flash frozen with grass in their mouth. In the Americas, giant bears, giant bevers, sabertooth tigers, lions, cheetas, and wolves as big as a horse, suddenly became extinct, again, some 12,000 years ago.

That meteors and debris from the heavens attack in swarms is evident from the comet that struck Jupiter. Likewise, there is increasing evidence that the dinosaurs were wiped out, 65 million years ago, when the Earth was struck by swarms of meteors. In 1991, a giant 110 mile-wide crater—dated to 65 million years ago- was discovered buried under the tip of the Yucatan Peninsula. It struck at the same time as the death of the dinosaurs. As reported in the August issue of the journal Meteoritics & Planetary Science, yet another crater has been discovered in the Ukraine which is also 65 million years old. According to a report in the August 1, 2002 issue of Nature, yet another meteor crater was found at the bottom of the North Sea dating to the same era.

And the best predictor of the future, is the past:

"How art thou fallen from heaven, O' Lucifer son of the morning. For thou hast said in thine heart: I will ascend into heaven. I will exalt my throne above the stars of God. I will ascend above the heights of the clouds. I will be like the most High...

"How art thou fallen from heaven, O' Lucifer star of the morning. Is this the one that made the Earth to tremble, that did to shake kingdoms. That made the world as a wilderness, and destroyed the cities...

"But beware and rejoice not because the rod of his that smote thee is broken: for out of the serpent's root and of his fruit shall be a fiery flying dragon... -Isaiah, 14

"And there appeared a great wonder in heaven: A woman clothed with the sun, and the moon under her feet, and upon her head a crown of twelve stars: And she being with child cried travailing in birth and pained to be delivered...

"And there appeared another wonder in heaven: And behold a great red dragon having seven heads and ten horns and seven crowns upon his head. And his tail drew the third part of the stars of heaven and did cast them to the Earth...

"And there was a war in heaven: Michael and his angels fought against the dragon: and the dragon fought and his angels. And the great dragon was cast out, that old serpent, called the Devil and Satan which deceivith the whole world: He was cast out and his angels were cast out with him...

"And the serpent cast out of his mouth water as a flood. And the Earth opened her mouth and swallowed up the flood which the dragon cast out his mouth. And the dragon was wroth and went to make war..." —Revelation, 12

THE ANTI-CHRIST

The coming of Christ, a Messiah, the new god, and the onset of a "new Golden Age" was heralded by the sun's movement from Aries into the house of Pisces, 2000 years ago. In the mind of

Figure 179. In 1994, the Shoemaker-Levy 9 comet broke into huge pieces and collided with the planet Jupiter.

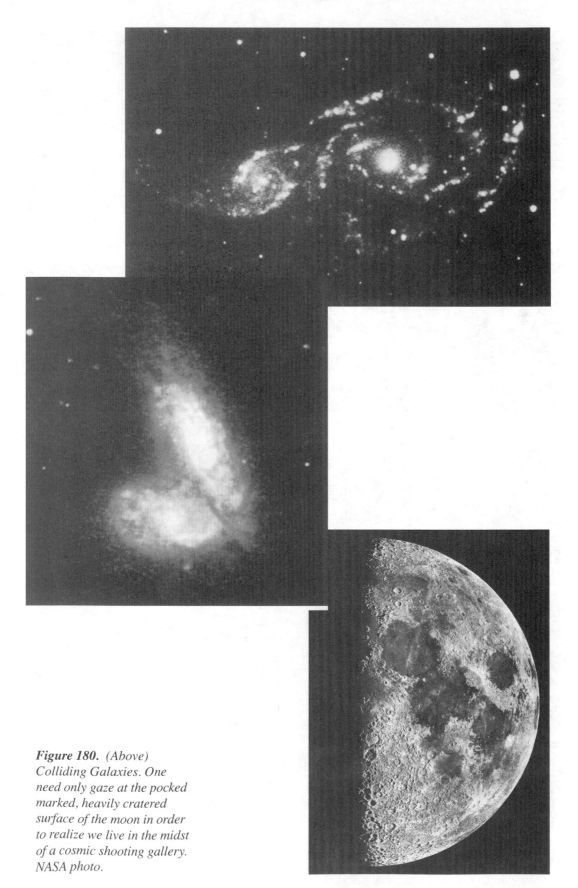

Figure 180. *(Above)*
Colliding Galaxies. One
need only gaze at the pocked
marked, heavily cratered
surface of the moon in order
to realize we live in the midst
of a cosmic shooting gallery.
NASA photo.

at least some of the ancients, the birth of the new god was also signaled by the conjunction of Jupiter and Saturn, which lined up together in the constellation of Pisces, in the year 6 B.C., thus forming a very bright "star"—the "star of Bethlehem."

These "blessed" events were immortalized two thousand years ago by Virgil, in his Fourth Ecologue: "Now the Virgin returns, the reign of Saturn returns, now a new generation descends from heaven on high. Only do thou, pure Lucina, smile on the birth of the child, under whom the iron brood shall first cease, and a golden race spring up throughout the world!"

And who was the "virgin?"

Virgo. With her return, Virgo the virgin would give birth to a new age and a new god.

Two thousand years ago, whereas Pisces governed the vernal equinox, the sun rose in Virgo during the autumn equinox. However, 12,000 to 14,000 years ago, Virgo governed the vernal equinoxes during the "golden age" and when she left, the "golden age ended" in a confluence of catastrophes. Hence, Virgil's poem, refers to the return of the Virgin which coincided with the new age of Pisces both of which ruled during the last "Golden age."

Thus, the birth of Christ was associated not only with the new golden age of Pisces, but with a virgin—Virgo: The virgin birth of the new god. Virgo would rein for 2,160 years, and with her departure (in about 100 years), the god she gave birth to will die. However, a new god will not only take the place of the old god, but her departure will give birth to the new god as well—a god associated with the "beast" —Leo (the lion). The Virgin will flee only to be pursued by Leo who shall take her place.

Likewise, in Revelation, we are told that the ending of the next world will be associated with a "beast...like that of a lion..." and a "dragon" who "gave the beast his power and his throne and great authority..." and who "pursued the woman who...was pregnant and cried out in pain as she was about to give birth..." and who, upon giving "birth to the male child...fled into the desert.... where she might be taken care of for 1,260 days...the dragon...pursued the woman..."

The woman (Virgo) gives birth (a virgin birth) to a new God only to depart and to be pursued by the water belching dragon and anti-Christ who gives power to a lion-like beast (Leo) who will rule the heavens. However, by departing she also gives birth to a new god: the beast, Leo.

Revelations also gives us the number of the beast: "His number is 666. This calls for wisdom. If anyone has insight, let him calculate the number of the beast."

"666" is obviously a reference to a repeating cycle. Yet, the author of Revelations asks us to look beyond the obvious and to "calculate the number of the beast."

Calculating the Number of the Beast: $6 \times 6 \times 6 = 216$. "216" is a precessional number: 2,160—the number of years to complete a precessional cycle.

"The dragon...which gave power to the beast... had...ten horns." -Revelation.

$10 \times 216 = 2160$.

The "Beast" is Leo: "The horses... I saw in my vision looked like this: The heads of the horses resembled the heads of lions....Then I saw another mighty angel coming down from heaven...he gave a loud shout like the roar of a lion....And I saw a beast coming out of the sea." (Aquarius—the sea.) "He had...a mouth like that of a lion." -Revelation.

And his repeating cyclic number, 666, refers to precession: "The beast, which you saw, once was, now is not, and will come up out of the Abyss...The inhabitants of the Earth.... will be astonished when they see the beast, because he once was, now is not, and yet will come..." -Revelation

As noted, precession is a counterclockwise, or rather, an anti-clockwise phenomenon. Due to the retardation of the Earth's orbital movement of 1 degree every 72 years, every 2,160 years the sun rises in the previous house of the Zodiac.

Hence, instead of moving forward from Pisces to Aries, in about 100 years the sun will rise in Aquarius, thereby signaling the death of the god of Pisces (the fish) and heralding the new age god of Aquarius who will rule the vernal equinox.

Likewise, Virgo (the virgin) is followed (chased) by Leo (a lion/beast) who will rule the autumn equinox, just as he did 12,000 years ago: "The horses,,, I saw in my vision looked like this: The heads of the horses resembled the heads of lions....Then I saw another mighty angel coming down from heaven...he gave a loud shout like the roar of a lion....And I saw a beast coming out of the sea." (Aquarius—the sea). "He had...a mouth like that of a lion...." -Revelation

The age of Aquarius/Leo, therefore, is the anti-Christ: Symbolized by the movement away from Pisces/Virgo, and the end of that "god's" rule.

The coming of the anti-Christ is also associated with the onset of terrible worldwide calamities

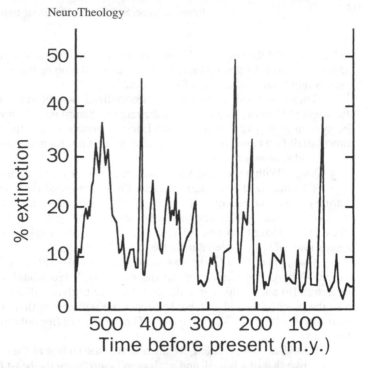

Figure 181. (Right) Estimates of the percentage of all genera to become extinct since 600 million years ago following massive meteor strikes against the Earth. There have been five major extinctions. Based on Rampino & Haggerty, 1994. Reprinted from Jakosky, 1998. (Below) NASA illustration of a giant meteorite striking the Earth.

and catastrophes.

"And the serpent cast out of his mouth water as a flood..."

Some 12,000 years ago, Aquarius (the god of the waters) ruled the autumn equinox and Leo ruled the vernal equinox. It is during this ancient period that the "Golden Age" is believed to have ended, and civilization along with it in a terrible flood that coincided with a "war in heaven." Thus, the return of Leo and Aquarius (albeit in the opposite equinox) and the departure of Pisces and Virgo, is also believed to herald not just a new beginning, but a terrible ending—a confluence of catastrophes that will coincide with a celestial war in heaven and a battle among the stars that will begin with the rise of Leo, the "Beast:"

Will the Earth will be struck by a swarm of asteroids and meteors with the onset of the age of Aquarius/Leo?

"Look, he is coming with the clouds, and every eye will see him... and there before me was a throne... In the center, around the throne, were four living creatures. The first living creature was like a lion" (Leo?) "the second was like an ox" (Taurus?) "the third had a face like a man (Sagittarius/Aquarius?), "the fourth was like a flying eagle..."

And what is the "flying eagle?"

The International Astronomical Union recognizes 88 constellations, including, Aquila, the Eagle who "glides on outstretched wings through the glowing band of the Milky Way." Altair, is its brightest star, and is about 16 light-years from Earth. "Altair," is the Arabic word for "eagle."

Revelation continues: "the fourth was like a flying eagle... And I saw a mighty angel proclaiming in a loud voice, "Who is worthy to break the seals and open the scroll...Then one of the elders said to me... the Lion... has triumphed. He is able to open the scroll and its seven seals... and the stars in the sky fell to Earth. The sky receded like a scroll, rolling up, and every mountain and island was removed from its place. Then the kings of the Earth, the princes, the generals, the rich, the mighty, and every slave and every free man hid in caves and among the rocks of the mountains... Then the seven angels who had the seven trumpets prepared to sound them. The first angel sounded his trumpet, and there came hail and fire mixed with blood, and it was hurled down upon the Earth. A third of the Earth was burned up, a third of the trees were burned up, and all the green grass was burned up. The second angel sounded his trumpet, and something like a huge mountain, all ablaze, was thrown into the sea....The third angel sounded his trumpet, and a great star, blazing like a torch, fell from the sky..." -Revelation.

THE END

"Who among us can tell the future by letting us hear the First Things?" —Isaiah, 43.

Revelation repeatedly refers to a cosmic catastrophe associated with the house of Leo (the lion) and Aquarius (waters/sea). Ezekiel (38, 39) tells us that in the "End of Days" fire and brimstone will fall from the skies, and there will be great earthquakes, plagues, and wars.

Ezekiel, like Revelation and Isaiah, also contains precessional language, as does the Mayan/Olmec calendar. And, they base their predictions of the future, on what has happened in the past... that the End is anchored in the Beginning (e.g. Isaiah, 48; Zechariah, 1, 7).

And in the Beginning the Earth was bombarded with massive meteorites for nearly 700 million years. And five times in the last 500,000 years, the Earth has been struck by massive meteorites which have destroyed 70 to 90% of all animal life.

The best predictor of the future, is the past.

However, neither Revelation, Ezekiel, or Isaiah, provide us with a date in which these terrible catastrophic and cosmic events are to recur, other than to warn that these disasters will begin with the return of the great serpent, the anti-Christ, and the beast: Aquarius/Leo.

The Mayas, basing their calculations on the Venus calender, were more exacting.

According to the Mayan/Olmec/Aztec Calendar, the date for the beginning of the end of this civilization and this world, will be "4 Ahau 3 Kankin" (December 23, 2012), "and it will be ruled by the Sun God, the ninth Lord of the Night."

******

The best predictor of the future, is the past, and "those who do not learn from the past, are condemned to repeat it."

And if it has not happened, it will happen... "and no one will be safe from it."

Does that mean we are nearing "the end?" Will the Earth be attacked by a swarm of falling stars?

Fate has 12 stations. Although we may change our fate, the ancients tell us that destiny cannot be altered, but only predicted from the past and the movements of the sun and the stars.

But as to fate—that again, is of our own making. And what are we making? Global warming, ozone depletion, genetic pollution, ethnic cleansing, atomic proliferation, wars wars and more wars... the streams, rivers, lakes and oceans of the Earth a vast toilet churning with man-made pharmaceutical wastes and cancer-causing chemical poisons— we are poisoning the planet, we are killing mother Earth... and no god will come down from the skies to save us.

"Satan" that great serpent may threaten us from the skies...but the confluence of catastrophes that will destroy mankind, are also of our own making...

Figure 182. *Satan cast out of heaven.*

REFERENCES

Achterberg, J. (1985), Imagery in healing: shamanism and modern medicine. Boston: New Science Library: Shambhala.

Adorno, T., E. Frenkel-Brunswik, D. Levinson, and R. N. Sanford (1964) *The Authoritarian Personality.* New York: Wiley.

Aghajanian, G., Sprouse, J., Rasmussen, K. 1987. Physiology of the midbrain serotonin system. In Meltzer, H. Ed. Psychopharm

Aghajanian, G.K., & Marek, G.J. 1999. Serotonin and hallucinogens. Neuropsychopharmacology, 21 2 Suppl,16S-23S.

A Course In Miracles 1975. New York. The Foundation for A Course in Miracles.

Addin En Reflist, Achmet. 1991. Oneirocriticon. Translated by S. M. Oberhelman. Lubbock: Texas Tech University Press.

Aeschylus. c. 458 BCE. The Oreseteia. Translated by Robert Fagles. New York. Penguin Books. 1984.

Al-Maqrizi, K. 1911. Das Pyramidenkapitel Hitat. Graefe, Leipzig.

Albin, R., & Greenamyre, J. 1992. Alternative excitotoxic hypotheses. Neurology 42,733-738.

Albright, C. R., & Ashbrook, J. 2001. Where God Lives in the Human Brain. Naperville, IL: Sourcebooks.

Alexander, R. 1987 The biology of moral systems. New York: Aldine de Gruyter.

Allen, L.S. & Gorski, R.A. 1992. Sexual orientation and the size of the anterior commissure in the human brain. Proceedings of the National Academy of Sciences,89, 7199-7202.

Allen, L.S. Hines, M. Shryne, J.E. & Gorski, R.A. 1989. Two sexually dimorphic cell groups in the human brain. Journal of Neuroscience, 9, 497-506

Allison, R. 1974 A New Treatment Approach for Multiple Personalities. American Journal of Clinical Hypnosis, 17,15-32.

Allison, R. 1996 Essence Memory: A Preliminary Hypothesis. Hypnos, 23, 6-13.

Allison, R., & Schwarz, T. 1980. Minds In Many Pieces. New York, Rawson, Wade.

Alston, W. P. 1993. Divine action, human freedom, and the laws of nature. In Quantum «osmology and the Laws of Nature. Ed. R. J. Russell, N. Murphy, and C. J. Isham. Vatican City State: Vatican Observatory Publications.

Amano, K., Tanikawa, H., & Kawamura, H., et al. 1982. Endorphins and pain relief. Applied Neurophysiology, 45,123-135.

Amaral, D. G., Price, J. L., Pitkanen, A., & Thomas, S. 1992. Anatomical organization of the primate amygdaloid complex. In J. P. Aggleton Ed.. The amygdala. pp. 1-66, New York: Wiley-Liss.

Andrews, T.J., Halpern, S.D., & Purves, D. 1997. Correlated size variations in human visual cortex, lateral geniculate nucleus, and optic tract. Journal of Neuroscience, 17 8,2859-2868.

Antequera, F., & Bird, A. 1993. Proceedings of the National Academy of Sciences, 90, 11995-11999.

Aristides, Aelius. 1981. The Complete Works. Translated by C. A. Behr. Leiden: E.J. Brill.

Aristotle. 1941a. On Dreams. In The Collected Works of Aristotle, edited by R. McKeon. New York: Random House.

Aristotle. 1941b. On Prophesying by Dreams. In The Collected Works of Aristotle, edited by R. McKeon. New York: Random House.

Aristotle (1986) *De Anima.* London: Penguin.

Arrhenius, S. 1908. World in the Making. NY.

Artemidorus. 1975. The Interpretation of Dreams. Translated by R. J. White. Park Ridge: Noyes Press.

Aravind, L., et al., 2001. Apoptotic molecular machinery: vastly increased complexity in vertebrates revealed by genome comparisons. Science 2001, 1279-1284.

Aserinsky, E. and Nathaniel K. 1955. Two Types of Ocular Motility Occurring in Sleep. Journal of Applied Physiology 8:1-10.

Aserinsky, Eugene, and Nathaniel Kleitman. 1953. Regularly Occurring Periods of Eye Motility, and Concomitant Phenomena, during Sleep. Science 118:273-274.

Ashbrook, J.B. Neurotheology: The working brain and the work of theology. Zygon, 1984.

Ashbrook, J.B., Albright, C.R. 1997. The Humanizing Brain: Where Religion and Neuroscience Meet. The Pilgrim Press, Cleveland.

Ashbrook, James B, and Carol Rausch Albright. 1997. The Humanizing Brain: Where Religion and Neuroscience Meet. Cleveland: The Pilgrim Press.

Atran, S. 1998 Folkbiology and the anthropology of science: Cognitive universals and cultural particulars. Behavioral and Brain Sciences 21:547-609.

Atran, S. 2002 In gods we trust: The evolutionary landscape of religion. New York: Oxford University Press.

Atran, S., Medin, D., Lynch, E., Vapnarsky, V., Ucan Ek', E., Coley, J., Timura, C. & Baran, M. 2002 Folkecology, cultural epidemiology, and the spirit of the commons: A garden experiment in the Maya Lowlands, 1991-2001. Current Anthropology 43:421-450.

Atran, S. & Sperber, D. 1991 Learning without teaching: Its place in culture. In L. Tolchinsky-Landsmann ed., Culture, schooling and psychological development. Norwood NJ: Ablex.

Atweh, S. F., & Kuhar, M. J. 1977a Autoradiographic localization of opiate receptors in rat brain. I. Brain Research, 129, 1-12.

Atweh, S. F.,& Kuhar, M. J. 1977b Autoradiographic localization of opiate receptors in rate brain. III. Brain research, 134, 273-405.

Augustine. 1991. Confessions. Translated by H. Chadwick. Oxford: Oxford University Press.

Aurobindo, S. 1963. The Future Evolution of Man. All India Press.

Aurell, C. G. (1989) Man's triune conscious mind. *Perceptual and Motor Skills* 68, 747-754.

Austin, H. I. 1990. The heart of the goddess. Wingbrow Press, Berkeley.

Austin, J. 1998. Zen and the Brain : Toward an Understanding of Meditation and Consciousness. MIT Press: Cambridge, MA.

Austin, J. 1998. Zen and the Brain: Toward and Understanding of Meditation and Consciousness. Cambridge, MA: MIT Press.

Austin, James H. 1998. Zen and the Brain. Cambridge: MIT Press.

Avis, J. & Harris, P. 1991 Belief-desire reasoning among Baka children. Child Development 62:460-467.

Azari, N.P., Nickel, J., & Wunderlich, G, et al. 2001. Neural correlates of religious experience. European Journal of Neuroscience, 13, 1649-1652.

Bachevalier, J. & Merjanian, P. 1994 The contribution of medial temporal lobe structures in infantile autism: A neurobehavioral study in primates. In L. Bauman & T. Kemper eds., The neurobiology of autism. Baltimore: Johns Hopkins Press.

Bada, J. et al., 2001. Proc. Natl. Acad. Sci. Vol. 98, 815-819

Bagshaw, M., & Benzies, S., 1968. Multiple measures of the orienting reaction and their dissociation after amygdalectomy in monkeys. Experimental Neurology, 27, 31-40.

Bakan, David. 1958. Sigmund Freud and the Jewish Mystical Tradition. Boston: Beacon Press.

Bakan, P. 1977. Dreaming, REM sleep and the right hemisphere: A theoretical integration. Journal of Altered States of Consciousness, 3, 285-307.

Balcells, L., Swinburne, J., Coupland, G. 1991. Transposons as tools for the isolation of plant genes. Trends in Biotechnology, 9, 31-36.

Balter, M. 2002 What made humans modern? Science 295:1219-1225.

Banquet,J. P. 1983 Inter- and intrahemispheric relationships of the EEG activity during sleep in man. Electroencephalography and Clinical Neurophysiology, 55, 51-59.

Barnard, P. 1985. Interacting cognitive subsystems: A psycholinguistic approach to short-term memory. In A. Ellis Ed., Progress in the psychology of language. UK, Hove: Lawrence Erlbaum Associates Ltd. Vol. 2, 197-258.

Barnard, P., Wilson, M., & Maclean, A. 1988. Approximate modelling of cognitive activity with an expert system: A theory-based strategy for developing an interactive design tool. The Computer Journal, 31, 445-456.

Barnes, G. L. 1993. China, Korea, and Japan. The rise of civilization in East Asia. Thames & Hudson, London.

Baron-Cohen, S. 1995 Mindblindness. Cambridge, MA: MIT Press.

Barrett, J. 2000 Exploring the natural foundations of religion. Trends in Cognitive Science. 4:29-34.

Barrett, J., Richert, R. & Driesenga, A. 2001 God's beliefs versus mother's: The Development of nonhuman agent concepts. Child Development 72:50-65.

Barrett, W. 1926. Death-bed Visions. London: Methuen.

Batchelor, M 2001 Meditation for Life. London, Frances Lincoln

Batchelor, S. 1990 The Faith to Doubt: Glimpses of Buddhist Uncertainty. Berkeley, CA. Parallax Press

Bateson, Gregory. 1978. Steps to an Ecology of Mind. Granada

Batson, C.D. and Ventis, W.L. 1982. The Religious Experience. Oxford University Press.

Bauer, C. E., et al., 2000. Science, 2000,

Bauman, M. & Kemper, T. 1985 Histoanatomic observations of the brain in early infantile autism. Neurology 35:866-874.

Bauval, R. 1994. The Orion Mystery. Doubleday, New York.

Bear, D. M. 1979 Temporal lobe epilepsy: A syndrome of sensory-limbic hyperconnexion. Cortex 15: 357-

384.

Bear, D.M. & Fedio, P. 1977.Quantitative analysis of interictal behavior in temporal lobe epilepsy. Archives of Neurology, 34, 454-467.

Beard, A. 1963 The schizophrenia-like psychoses of epilepsy, II: Physical aspects. British Journal of Psychiatry 109:113-129.

Beck, Edward and Cowan, Christopher C. 1996. Spiral Dynamics: Mastering Values, Leadership and Change. Exploring the New Science of Memetics. Oxford: Blackwell.

Becker, Ernest. 1973. Denial Of Death. The Free Press.

Beit-Hallahmi, B. & Argyle, M. 1997 The psychology of religious behavior, belief, and experience. London: Routledge.

Belfer-Cohen, A., and E.Hovers, 1992 In the eye of the beholder: Mousterian and Natufian burials in the levant. Current Anthropology 33: 463-471.

Belfort, M. 1991. Self-splicing introns in prokaryotes, Cell, 64, 9-11.

Belfort, M. 1993. Introns. Science, 262, 1009-1010.

Bell, A.P., Weinberg, M.S., & Hammersmith, S.K. 1981. Sexual Preference: Its Development in Men and Women. Bloomington, Indiana University Press.

Bell, B. D. 1994. Pantomime recognition impairment in aphasia. Brain & Language, 47, 269-278.

Bem, D. J., & Honorton, C. 1994. Does psi exist? Replicable evidence for an anomalous process of information transfer. Psychological Bulletin, 115, 4-18.

Ben-Amos, P. G. 1994 The promise of greatness. In T. Blakely, W. van Beek & D. Thomson eds., Religion in Africa. Portsmouth, NH: Heinemann.

Benedict, Ruth. 1922. The Vision in Plains Culture. American Anthropologist 24 1:1-23.

Benson, H. 1996. Timeless Healing. New York. Scribner.

Benson, Herbert, and Marg Stark. 1996. Timeless Healing: The Power and Biology of Belief. New York: Fireside.

Benson, Herbert, and Miriam Klipper. 1975. The Relaxation Response. New York: Harpertorch.

Ben-Ze'ev, A. (2000) *The Subtlety of Emotions*. Boston: MIT Press.

Bergson, H. 1914. Presidential address. Proceedings of the Society for Psychical Research, 27, 157-175.

Berkner, K. L. 1988. Development of adneovirus vectors for the expression of heterologous genes. Biochemical Techniques, 6, 616-629.

Bernstein, M., Stiehl, S., and Bickle, J. (2000) The effect of motivation on the stream of consciousness: Generalizing from a neurocomputational model of cingulo-frontal circuits controlling saccadic eye movements. In R. Ellis and N. Newton (Eds.), *The Caldron of Consciousness: Motivation, Affect, and Self-organization*. Amsterdam: John Benjamins, 91-108.

Bertalanffy, L. von (1933/1962). *Modern Theories of Development: An Introduction to Theoretical Biology*. New York: Harper.

Bertini, M., Violani, C., Zoccolotti, P., Antonelli, A., & DiStephano, L. 1983 Performance on a unilateral tactile test during waking and upon awakenings from REM and NREM. InSleep, pp. 122-155ed. W. P. Koella Basel: Karger.

Bexton, W. A., Heron, W.,& Scott, T. H. 1954 Effects of decreased variation in the sensory environment. Canadian Journal of Psychology, 8, 70-76.

Bieber, I., Dain, H. J. Dince, P. R., et al. 1962. Homosexuality. New York, Basic Books.

Binder, J.R., Rao, S.M., & Hammeke, T.A., et al. 1994. Functional magnetic resonance imaging of human auditory cortex. Annals of Neurology, 35,662-672.

Binford, S. R. 1968 A structural comparison of disposal of the dead in the Mousterian and the Upper Paleolithic. Southwest Journal of Anthropology 24: 139-54.

Bird-David, N. (1999), "Animism" revisited: personhood, environment and relational epistemology. Current Anthropology, 40, 67-91.

Birney, E., et al. 2001 Mining the draft human genome. Nature 409, 827 - 828.

Blater, M. 1996. Science, 273, 871-972.

Bloom, F. E., & Lazerson, A. 1988. Brain, Mind, and Behavior. 2d ed. New York: Freeman.

Blumer, D., & Benson, D.F. 1975.Personality changes with frontal and temporal lesions.In D.F. Benson & D. Blumeer Eds., Psychiatric aspects of neurologic disease.New York: Grune & Stratton.

Bock, J. B. et al., 2001 A genomic perspective on membrane compartment organization. Nature 409, 839 - 841.

Boddy, J. (1994), Spirit possession revisited: beyond instrumentality. Annual Review of Anthropology, 23, 407-34.

Bohm, D. 1986. Wholeness and the Implicate Order.

Bosnak, Robert. 1996. Tracks in the Wilderness of Dreaming: Exploring Interior Landscape through Practical Dreamwork. New York: Delacorte Press.

Bossant, E. 1992. Het dossier van de verschijningen te Beauraing: Een psychologische analyse en evaluatie The dossier of the apparitions at Beauraing: A psychological analysis and evaluation. Unpublished thesis, Katholieke Universiteit Leuven , Belgium.

Bourguignon, E. (1976), Possession. San Francisco: Chandler and Sharpe.

Bowker, John, ed. 1997. The Oxford Dictionary of World Religions. Oxford: Oxford University Press.

Bowlby, J. 1969 Attachment and loss, vol. 1. Attachment. New York: Basic Books.

Boyer, P. 1994 The naturalness of religious ideas. Berkeley: University of California Press.

Boyer, P. (2001), Religion Explained The Evolutionary Origins of Religious Thought. New York: Basic Books.

Bracken, J. A. 1997. Panentheism from a process p erspective. In Trinity in Process: a Relational Theology of God. Ed. J. A. Bracken and M. H. Suchocki. New York: Continuum.

Bradley, M. 1991 Harper's Encyclopedia of Mystical & Paranormal Experience. New York, HarperCollins.

Brain, The 1990. Cold Springs Harbor Symposium, The Brain, Cold Springs Harbor, NY.

Brandon, S.G. F. 1967 The Judgment of the Dead. New York, Scribners.

Braud, W. G. (2000) Wellness implications of retroactive intentional influence: Exploring an outrageous hypothesis. Alternative Therapies in Health and Medicine, 6(1), 37-48.

Braud, W. G. (2002a). Thoughts on the ineffability of the mystical experience. The International Journal for the Psychology of Religion, 12, 141-160.

Braud, W. G. (2002b). Transpersonal images: Implications for health. In A. Sheikh (Ed.), Healing images: The role of imagination in health (pp. 444-466). Amityville, NY: Baywood.

Braud, W. G., & Schlitz, M. J. (1991). Consciousness interactions with remote biological systems: Anomalous intentionality effects. Subtle Energies: An Interdisciplinary Journal of Energetic and Informational Interactions. 2, 1-46.

Brauer, G. 1989. The Evolution of modern humans: A comparison of the African and Non-African evidence. in The human revolution: Behavioral and biological perspectives on the origins of modern humans, vol 1. Edited by P. Mellars and C. B. Stringer. Edinb

Brazier, M. A. B. 1961. A history of the electrical activity of the brain: The first half-century pp. 110-115. London: Pitman Medical Publishing Co.

Breasted, J. H. 1909. History of Egypt. New York, Scribners.

Breathnach, R., Benoist, C., O'Hare, K., et al. Ovalbumin gene. Proceedings of the National Academy of Sciences, 75, 4853-4857.

Breault, M., & King, M. 1993. Inside the Cult. Signet, New York.

Breedlove, M. , & Cooke, B. 1999. Proceedings of the National Academy of Sciences.

Brend, R. 1975. Male female intonation patterns in American English. InB. Thorne & N. Henley, Eds. Language & Sex.Massachussetts: Newbury House Publishers.

Brill, Alan. 2000. The Phenomenology of True Dreams in Maimonides. Dreaming 10 1:43-54.

Brody, L. 1985. Gender differences in emotional development. A review of theories and research. In Steward, A. & Lyko, M. eds. Gender and personality. Durham, Duke University Press.

Brooks, A. S., Helgren, D. M., Cramer, J. S., et al. 1995. Dating and context of three middle stone age sites with bone points in the Upper Semliki Valley, Zaire, Science, 268, 548-552.

Broughton, R. 1982 Human consciousness and sleep/waking rhythms: A review and some neuropsychological considerations. Journal of Clinical Neuropsychology, 4, 193-218.

Broughton, R. 1991. Parapsychology: The controversial science. New York: Ballantine.

Brown, N.O. 1959. Life Against Death. Vintage Books.

Brown, S. , Merker, B. and Wallin, N. (2000), An introduction to evolutionary musicology. In N. Wallin, B. Merker and S. Brown. Eds. The Origins of Music. Cambridge (MA): MIT Press. Pp. 3-24

Brown, S. (2000), The 'musilanguage model of music. In N. Wallin, B. Merker and S. Brown. Eds. The Origins of Music. Cambridge (MA): MIT Press. pp.271-300.

Bubenick, G. A., & Brown, G. M. Morphologic sex differences in the primate brain areas involved in regulation of reproductive activity. Experimentia, 1973, 15, 619-621.

Bucci, D.J., Conley, M., & Gallagher, M. 1999. Thalamic and basal forebrain cholinergic connections of the rat posterior parietal cortex. Neuroreport, 10 5,941-945.

Buck, R. 1977. Nonverbal communication of affect in preschool children. Journal of Personality and Social Psychology, 35, 225-236.

Buck, R. 1984. The communication of emotion. New York, Guilford.

Buck, R. Miller, R. & Caul, W. 1974. Sex, personality and physiological variables in communication of affect via facial expressions. Journal of personality and social psychology, 30, 587-596.

Buck, R., Baron, R., & Barrette, D. 1982. The temporal organization of spontaneous nonverbal expression. Journal ofPersonality & Social Psychology, 42, 506-517.

Bucke, R. M. 1961, 1966. Cosmic consciousness: A study in the evolution of the human mind. New Hyde Park, NY: University Books. Original work published 1901.

Budge, E.A. W. 1903. The Egyptian Book of the Dead. Dover Books, New York.

Budge, E.A. W. 1911. Osiris and the Egyptian Ressurrection. Medici Society, London.

Bujatti, M. & Riederer, P. 1976. Serotonin, noradrenaline, dopamine metabolites in transcendental medita-tion-technique. Journal of Neural Transmission, 39 3,257-267.

Bulkeley, K. 1994. The Wilderness of Dreams: Exploring the Religious Meanings of Dreams in Modern Western Culture. Albany, State University of New York Press.

Bulkeley, K. 1995. Spiritual Dreaming: A Cross-Cultural and Historical Journey. Mahwah, Paulist Press.

Bulkeley, K. 1998b. Masculine Fragments of a History of Dreaming: The Last Dreams of Socrates. The Fifteenth International Conference of the Association for the Study of Dreams, Laie, Hawaii.

Bulkeley, K. 1999. Visions of the Night: Dreams, Religion, and Psychology. Albany, State University of New York Press.

Bulkeley, K. 1999b. Wisdom's Refuge in the Night: Dreams in The Mahabharata, The Ramayana, and Rich-ard III. Visions of the Night: Dreams, Religion, and Psychology. K. Bulkeley. Albany, State University of New York Press.

Bulkeley, K. 2000. Transforming Dreams: Learning Spiritual Lessons from the Dreams You Never Forget. New York, John Wiley & Sons.

Bulkeley, K. 2001. Penelope as Dreamer: The Perils of Interpretation. Dreams: A Reader on the Religious, Cultural, and Psychological Dimensions of Dreaming. K. Bulkeley. New York, Palgrave.

Bunyan, Paul. [c. 1670} 1998. The Pilgrim's Progress. Ed. N. H. Keeble. New York: Oxford Univ. Press.

Bunge, M. (1979) Ontology II: A World of Systems. Dordrecht: D. Reidel.

Burkert, W. 1985. Greek Religion, tr. J. Raffan. Cambridge: Harvard University Press.

Burkert, W. 1996 Creation of the sacred. Cambridge, MA: Harvard University Press.

Burton, L. A. & Levy, J. 1989. Sex differences in the laterlized processing of facial emotion. Brain and Cognition, 11, 210-228.

Busse, E. W. 1997. iDuke longitudinal study I: Senescence and senility. In R. Katzman, R. D. Terry & K. L. Bick Eds. Alzheimer's disease: Senile dementia and related disorders. New York: Raven.

Butzer, K. 1982 Geomorphology and sediment stratiagraphy, in The Middle Stone Age at Klasies River Mouth in South Africa. Edited by R. Singer and J. Wymer. Chicago: University of Chicago Press.

Cahill, L., Prins, B., Weber, M. & McGaugh, J. 1994 Beta-adrenergic activation and memory for emotional events. Nature 371:702-704.

Calvino, Italo. 1993. Time and the Hunter. Picador, London.

Calvo, J. M., Badillo, S., Morales-Ramirez, M., Palacios-Salas, P. 1987. The role of the temporal lobe amygdala in ponto-geniculo-occipital activity and sleep organization in cats. Brain Research, 403, 22-30.

Campbell, C., Weinger, M.B., & Quinn, M. 1995. Alterations in diaphragm EMG activity during opiate-induced respiratory depression. Respiratory Physiology, 100 2,107-117.

Campbell, J. 1988 Historical Atlas of World Mythology. New York, Harper & Row.

Cancik, Hubert. 1999. Idolum and Imago: Roman Dreams and Dream Theories. In Dream Cultures: Explo-rations in the Comparative History of Dreaming, edited by G. G. Stroumsa. New York: Oxford University Press.

Card, A. L., Jackson, L. A., Stollak, G. E., & Ialongo, N. S., 1986. Gender role and person-perception accuracy. Sex Roles, 15, 159.

Cardena, E., Lynn, S. J, & Krippner, S. Eds.. 2000. Varieties of anomalous experience: Examining the scien-tific evidence. Washington, DC: American Psychological Association.

Caron, H., et al., 2001. The human transcriptome map: Clustering of highly expressed genes in chromo-somal domains. Science 2001, 1289-1292- 171.

Carrasco, D. 1990 Religions of MesoAmerica. San Francisco, Harper & Row.

Carroll, Peter. 1987. Liber Null and Psychonaut: An Introduction to Chaos Magic. USA: Weiser.

Cartwright, Rosalind. 1991. Dreams That Work: The Relation of Dream Incorporation to Adaptation to Stressful Events. Dreaming 1 1:3-10.

Carus, Titus Lucretius. c.99-55 BCE Lucretius: On the Nature of Things. W.H.D. Rouse, trans. Revised and edited by Martin F. Smith. Bailey, C. ed. De Rerum Natura. 3 volumes with commentary. Oxford, 1947. Cam-bridge, MA: Harvard University Press, 1992.

Casagrande, V. A., & Joseph, R. 1978. Effects of monocular deprivation on geniculostriate connections in primates. Anatomical Records, 14, 2001.

Casagrande, V. A., & Joseph, R. 1980. Morphological effects of monocular deprivation and recovery on the dorsal lateral geniculate nucleus in Galago. Journal of Comparative Neurology, 194, 413-426.

Castillo, R. (1991), Divided consciousness and enlightenment in Hindu Yogis. Anthropology of Consciousness, 2, 1-6.

Castle, Robert Van de. 1994. Our Dreaming Mind. New York: Ballantine Books.

Cech, T. R. 1986. RNA as an enzyme. Scientific American, 255, 64-65.

Chalmers, D. 1996 The Conscious Mind, Oxford, University Press

Charsley, S.R. 1973. Dreams in an Independent African Church. Africa: Journal of the International African Institute 43 3:244-257.

Charsley, S.R.1987. Dreams and Purposes: An Analysis of Dream Narratives in an Independent African Church. Africa: Journal of the International African Institute 57 3:281-296.

Chase, P. & Dibble, H. 1987 Middle Paleolithic symbolism. Journal of Anthropological Archaeology 6:263-296.

Chauvet, J-M., Deschamps, E. B. & Hillaire, C. 1996 Dawn of Art: The Chauvet Cave. H.N. Abrams.

Chen, R., & Forster, F. M. 1973. Cursive and gelastic epilepsy. Neurology, 23, 1019-1029.

Cheramy, A., Romo, R., Glowinski. 1987 Role of corticostriatal glutamatergic neurons in the presynaptic control of dopamine release. In Sandler, M., Feuerstein, C., & Scatton, B., et al. Eds. Neurotransmitter Interactions in the Basal Ganglia. Raven P

Child, I. L. 1985. Psychology and anomalous observations. American Psychologist, 40, 1219-1230.

Chomsky, N. 1986 Knowledge of language. New York: Praeger.

Clark, J. D., & Harris, J. W. K. 1985. Fire and its role in early hominid lifeways. African Archaeology Review, 3, 3-27.

Clayton, J. D. et al., 2001 Keeping time with the human genome. Nature 409, 829 - 831.

Clottes, J. & D. Lewis-Williams. (1998), The shamans of prehistory: Trance and magic in the painted caves. New York: Harry Abrams.

Coe, M.D. 1991. The Maya, Thames & Hudson, London.

Cohen, S., Chang, A., Boyer, H., & Helling, R. 1973. Construction of biologically functional bacterial plasmids. Proceedings of the National Academy of Sciences,70, 3240-3244.

Coker, K.H. 1999. Meditation and prostate cancer: integrating a mind/body intervention with traditional therapies. Seminars in Urological Oncology 17 2,111-118.

Coleridge, S. T. 1985. Biographia literaria. In H. J. Jackson Ed., Samuel Taylor Coleridge The Oxford authors; pp. 155-482. Original work published 1817

Connerton, Paul. 1989. How Societies Remember. Cambridge.

Cook, C.M. & Persinger, M.A. 1997. Experimental induction of the sensed presence in normal subjects and an exceptional subject. Perceptual & Motor Skills, 85 2, 683-693.

Cook, C.M. & Persinger, M.A. 2001. Geophysical variables and behavior: XCII. Experimental elicitation of the experience of a sentient being by right hemispheric, weak magnetic fields: Interaction with temporal lobe sensitivity. Perceptual and Motor Skills, 92(2), 447-448.

Corcoran, R., Mercer, G. & Frith, C. 1995 Schizophrenia, symptomatology and social inference: Investigating itheory of mind in people with schizophrenia. Schizophrenia Research 17:5-13.

Corning, W. C., Dyal, J.A., & Willows, A. 1973. Invertebrate learning. Plenum. New York.

Corveleyn, J. 2001. Folk Religiosity or Psychopathology? The case of the apparitions of the Virgin in Beauraing , Belgium 1932-1933. In Psychohistory in psychology of religion: interdisciplinary studies pp. 239-259. International series in the p

Coser, A.L. 1977. Masters of Sociological Thought: Ideas in Historical and Social Context. Harcourt, Brace, Jovanovich Press.

Covitz, Joel. 1990. Visions of the Night: A Study of Jewish Dream Interpretation. Boston: Shambhala.

Cowan, J. D. 1982. Spontaneous symmetry breaking in large-scale nervous activity International Journal of Quantum Chemistry, 22:1059-1082.

Cowen, R. 1995. Hubble constant: Controversy continues. Science News, 147, 198.

Courseaux, A., & Nahon, J-L. 2001. Birth of two chimeric genes in the Hominidae lineage. Science 2001: 1293-1297.

Crick, F. H. 1981. Life itself, Simon & Schuster

Crick, F., & Orgel, L. 1973. Directed Panspermia, Icarus, 19, 43-57.

Crook, J. 1991 Catching a Feather on a Fan: A Zen Retreat with Master Sheng Yen. Shaftesbury, Dorset, Element Books

Crooke, W. 1907 The native races of Northern India. London: Archibald Constable.

Crosson, B., Sadek, J.R., & Maron, L., et al. 2001. Relative shift in activity from medial to lateral frontal cortex during internally versus externally guided word generation. Journal of Cognitive Neuroscience, 13 2, 272-283

Cunningham, J. & Sterling, R. 1988 Developmental changes in the understanding of affective meaning in music. Motivation and Emotion 12:399-412.

Curley, Richard T. 1983. Dreams of Power: Social Process in a West African Religious Movement. Africa: Journal of the International African Institute 53 3:20-37.

Daly, D. 1958 Ictal affect. American Journal of Psychiatry, 115, 97-108.

d'Aquili, E.G. & Newberg, A.B. 1993. Religious and mystical states: a neuropsychological model. Zygon, 28, 177-200.

d'Aquili, E.G. & Newberg, A.B. 1999. The Mystical Mind: Probing the Biology of Religious Experience. Fortress Press, Minneapolis.

d'Aquili, E. & Newberg, A. 1998 The neuropsychological basis of religions, or why God won't go away. Zygon 33:187-201.

d'Aquili, E. & Newberg, A. 1999 The mystical mind. Minneapolis: Fortress Press.

d'Aquili, E. 1986 Myth, ritual, and the archetypal hypothesis. Zygon 21:141-160.

d'Aquili, E.G. 1982. Senses of Reality in Science and Religion. Zygon 17 4:361-384.

d'Aquili, E.G. & Newberg, A.B. 1993. Religious and Mystical States: A Neuropsychological Model. Zygon, 28 2, 177-200.

d'Aquili, E.G. and A.B. Newberg. 1993a. ìMystical States and the Experience of God: A Model of the Neuropsychological Substrate. Zygon 28 2: 177-200.

d'Aquili, E.G. and A.B. Newberg. 1993b. Liminality, Trance, and Unitary States in Ritual and Meditation. Studia Liturgica 23 l: 2-34.

d'Aquili, E.G. and A.B. Newberg. 1998. ìThe Neuropsychological Basis of Religion: Or Why God Won't Go Away. Zygon 33 2:187-201.

d'Aquili, E.G., Lauglin, C. Jr., & McManus, J. 1979. The Spectrum of Ritual: A Biological Structural Analysis. Columbia University Press, New York.

d'Azevedo, W. 1973 Mask makers and myth in Western Liberia. In A. Forge ed., Primitive art and society. London: Oxford University Press.

Darwin, C. 1859. The origin of species by means of natural selection. London, Murray.

Darwin, C. 1871. The origin of species and the descent of man. New York, Random House.

Darwin, C. 1887. Letters. In Darwin, F. ed., The Life and Letters of Charles Darwin, Vols. 1 & 2. Appleton, New York.

Darwin, C. 1965[1872] The expression of the emotions in man and animals. Chicago: University of Chicago Press.

Davies, E., et al. 1985. The Role of Calcium Ions in the Mechanism of ACTH Stimulation of Cortisol Synthesis. Steroids, 45:557.

Davies, P. 1994. The unreasonable effectiveness of science. In Evidence of Purpose: Scientists Discover the Creator. Ed. J. M. Templeton. New York: Continuum.

Davis, E. 1999. Techgnosis: Myth, Magic and Mystery in the Age of Information. Serpentstail, UK.

Davis, E. 2000. Adventures in Inner Space: Meet the Psychonauts. Originally ran in Feed's Drugs Issue, November 6, 2000.

Davis, M., Walker, D. L., & Lee, Y. 1997. Amygdala and bed nucleus of the stria terminalis: Differential roles in fear and anxiety measured with acoustic startle reflex. Annals of the New York Academy of Sciences, 821, 305-331.

Davison, C., & Kelman, H. 1939.Pathological laughing and crying.Archives of Neurology and Psychiatry, 42, 595-643.

Dawkins, R. 1978. The Selfish Gene. Oxford University Press

Dawkins, R. 1987 The Blind Watchmaker. Norton, New York.

Dawkins, Richard. 1989. The Selfish Gene. Oxford. Oxford University Press.

Dawkins,R. 1993 Viruses of the mind. In B.Dahlbohm ed Dennett and his Critics: Demystifying Mind. Oxford, Blackwell

De Jong, G., & Scharloo, W. 1976. Environmental determination of selective significance of neutrality of amylase variants in Drosophilia. Genetics 84, 77-94 1976.

De Vaus, D., & McAllister, I. 1987. Gender differences in religion. American Sociological Review, 52, 472-481.

Deardoff, J. 2001 Mom wins asylum for son with autism. Chicago Tribune, February 21.

Deikman, A. J. 1963. Experimental meditation. Journal of Nervous and Mental Disease, 136, 329-373.

Deikman, A. J. 1966. Deautomatization and the mystic experience. Psychiatry, 29, 324-338.

Deikman, A. J. 1971. Bimodal consciousness. Archives of General Psychiatry, 25, 481-489.

DeLong, G. 1992 Autism, amnesia, hippocampus, and learning. Neuroscience and Behavioral Reviews 16:63-70.

Dembski, W. A. & Behe, M. J. 1998. Intelligent Design: The Bridge Between Science and Theology by

Dement, William. 1972. Some Must Watch While Some Must Sleep: Exploring the World of Sleep. New York: W.W. Norton.

Dennett, D.C. 1991 Consciousness Explained. Boston and London; Little, Brown and Co.

Denton, M. J. 1998. Nature's Destiny. The Free Press, New York.

Descola, Phillipe. 1993. The Spears of Twilight: Life and Death in the Amazon Jungle. New York: The New Press.

Desjardins, D. & M. A. Persinger 1995. Association between intermale social aggression and cellular density within the central amygdaloid nucleus in rats with lithium/pilocarpine-induced seizures. Perceptual and Motor Skills 81 2: 635-41.

Desmone, R., & Gross, C. G. 1979 Visual areas in the temporal cortex of the macaque. Brain Research, 178, 363-380.

Devereux, G. 1953. Psychoanalysis and the Occult. International Universities Press. New York.

Devereux, George. 1969. Reality and Dream: Psychotheraphy of a Plains Indian. New York: Doubleday Anchor.

Devore, I. 1974. Male dominance and mating behavior in Baboons. In Beach, F. ed. Sex and Behavior, Wiley, NY.

Dewhurst, K. & Beard, A. 1970 Sudden religious conversions in temporal lobe epilepsy. British Journal of Psychiatry 117: S497-S507.

Dewey, John, A Common Faith. New Haven: Yale University Press, 1934.

Dworkin, J. P., et al., 2001. Self-assembling amphiphilic molecules: Synthesis in simulated interstellar/precometary ices. Proc. Natl. Acad. Sci. Vol. 98, 815-819

Dibb, J., & Newman, A. J. 1989. Evidence that introns arose at proto-splice sites. EMBO, 8, 2015-2021.

Dicks, D. Myers R. E. & Kling, A. 1969. Uncus and amygdaloid lesions on social behavior in free ranging rhesus monkeys. Science, 160, 69-71.

Diksic, M. & Reba, R.C., Eds. 1991. Radiopharmaceuticals and Brain Pathology Studied with PET and SPECT. CRC Press, Boca Raton.

Doblin, R. 1991. Pahnke's Good Friday experiment: A long-term follow-up and methodological critique. Journal of Transpersonal Psychology, 23, 1-28.

Dodds, E.R. 1951. The Greeks and the Irrational. Berkeley: University of California Press.

Domhoff, G. William. 1996. Finding Meaning in Dreams: A Quantitative Approach. New York: Plenum.

Domhoff, G. William. 2001. A New Neurocognitive Theory of Dreams. Dreaming 11 1:13-33.

Domhoff, G. William. 2001. Using Content Analysis to Study Dreams: Applications and Implications for the Humanities. In Dreams: A Reader on the Religious, Cultural, and Psychological Dimensions of Dreaming, edited by K. Bulkeley. New York: Palgrave.

Donald, M. 2001. A Mind So Rare: The Evolution of Human Consciousness. New York: W. W. Norton.

Doniger, Wendy. 2001. Western Dreams about Eastern Dreams. In Dreams: A Reader on the Religious, Cultural, and Psychological Dimensions of Dreaming, edited by K. Bulkeley. New York: Palgrave.

Doore, G. Ed.. 1990. What survives?: Contemporary explorations of life after death. Los Angeles: Tarcher.

Dorit, R. L. Schoenbach, L., & Gilbert, W. 1990. Science, 250, 1377-1382.

Douyon, E. 1966 L'examen au Rorschach des voudouisants Haitiens. In R. Prince ed., Trans and possession states. Montreal: R.M. Bucke Memorial Society.

Dover, G. A. 1995. Nature Genetics, 10, 254-256.

Dow, J. (1986), Universal aspects of symbolic healing: A theoretical synthesis. American Anthropologist, 88, 56-69.

Dreifuss, J. J., Murphy, J. T., & Gloor, P. 1968. Contrasting effects of two identified amygdaloid efferent pathways on single hypothalamic neurons. Journal of Neurophysiology, 31, 237-248.

Drevets, W.C., Price, J.L., Simpson, J.R., Todd, R.D., Reich, T., Vannier, M., Raichle, M.E. 1997. Subgenual prefrontal cortex abnormalities in mood disorders. Nature, 386, 824-7.

Dundes, A. 1988. The flood myth. U. California Press. Berkeley.

Dunne, B. J., Nelson, R. D., & Jahn, R. G. 1988. Operator-related anomalies in a random mechanical cascade. Journal of Scientific Exploration, 2, 155-180.

Dunne, B., & Jahn, R. 1992. Experiments in remote human/machine interaction. Journal of Scientific Exploration, 6, 311-332.

Durkheim, E. 1995[1912] The elementary forms of religious life. New York: The Free Press.

Dykhuizen, D., & Hart, D. L. 1980 Selective neutrality of 6PDG alozymes in E. coli and the effects of genetic background. Genetics 96, 801-817.

Eadie, B. J., & Taylor, C. 1993 Embraced by the light. New York, Bantam

Eagleton, Terry. 1976. Criticism and Ideology: A Study in Marxist Literary Theory. London: NLB.

Eco, U. 1988. The Aesthetics of Thomas Aquinas. Cambridge, MA: Harvard University Press.

Edelstein, Ludwig, and Emma Edelstein. 1975. Asclepius: A Collection and Interpretation of the Testimonies. New York: Arno Press.

Edge, H., Morris, R., Palmer, J., & Rush, J. 1986. Foundations of parapsychology: Exploring the boundaries of human capability. Boston: Routledge & Kegan Paul.

Eggan, D. 1952. The Manifest Content of Dreams: A Challenge to Social Science. American Anthropologist 54: 469-485.

Eggan, D. 1955. The Pesonal Use of Myth in Dreams. Journal of American FolkLore 68: 445-463.

Eggan, D. 1957. Hopi Dreams and a Life History Sketch. Primary Records in Culture and Personality 2 1: 1-147.

Ehrenfreund. P., et al., 2001. Extraterrestrial amino acids in Orgueil and Ivuna: Tracing the parent body of CI type carbonaceous
    chondrites. Proc. Natl. Acad. Sci. 98, 2138-2141.

Eible-Eisbesfeldt, I 1996. Ethology. Holt. NY

Einstein, Albert 1954. Ideas and Opinions. New York; Crown Publishers Robertson, J.M. 1922. Voltaire. London.

Ekman, P. 1972. Universals and cultural differences in facial expressions of emotions. In J. Cole ed. Nebraska Symposium on Motivation, Lincoln, University of Nebraska Press.

Ekman, P. 1992 An argument for basic emotions. Cognition and Emotion 6:169-200.

Ekman, P. 1993.Facial expression and emotion. American Psychologist 48, 384-392.

Eliade, M. 1964 Myth and reality. London: Allen & Unwin.

Eliade, M. (1964), Shamanism: archaic techniques of ecstasy. New York: Pantheon Books.

Elias, A.N. & Wilson, A.F. 1995. Serum hormonal concentrations following transcendental meditation—potential role of gamma aminobutyric acid. Medical Hypotheses, 44 4,287-291.

Elias, A.N., Guich, S., & Wilson, A.F. 2000. Ketosis with enhanced GABAergic tone promotes physiological changes in transcendental meditation. Medical Hypotheses, 54 4,660-2.

Ellis, Henry Havelock. 1897-1928. Studies in the Psychology of Sex.

Ellis, M. M., Spann, D. R., & Posakony, J. W. 1990. Extramacrochaetae, a negative regulator of sensory organ development. Cell, 61, 27-38.

Ellis, R. D. (1986) An Ontology of Consciousness. Dordrecht: Kluwer/Martinus Nijhoff.

Ellis, R. D. (1995) Questioning Consciousness: The Interplay of Imagery, Cognition and Emotion in the Human Brain. Amsterdam: John Benjamins.

Ellis, R. D. (1996) Eros in a Narcissistic Culture. Dordrecht: Kluwer.

Ellis, R. D. (1999a) Why isn't consciousness empirically observable? Emotion, self-organization, and nonreductive physicalism. Journal of Mind and Behavior 20, 391-402.

Ellis, R. D. (1999b) Dynamical systems as an approach to consciousness: Emotion, self-organization, and the mind-body problem. New Ideas in Psychology 17, 237-250.

Ellis, R. D. (2000a) Consciousness, self-organization, and the process-substratum relation: Rethinking nonreductive physicalism. Philosophical Psychology 13, 173-190.

Ellis, R. D. (2000b) Efferent brain processes and the enactive approach to consciousness. Journal of Consciousness Studies 7, 40-50.

Ellis, R. D. (2000c) Three elements of causation: Biconditionality, asymmetry, and experimental manipulability. Philosophia 29, 1-21.

Ellis, R. D. (2000d) Integrating the physiological and phenomenological dimensions of affect and motivation. In R. Ellis and N. Newton (Eds.), The caldron of consciousness: Motivation, affect, and self-organization. Amsterdam: John Benjamins, 91-108.

Ellis, R. D. (2001a) Implications of inattentional blindness for "enactive" theories of consciousness. Brain and Mind 2, 297-322.

Ellis, R. D. (2001b) A theoretical model of the role of the cerebellum in cognition, attention and consciousness. Consciousness & Emotion 2, 300-309.

Ellis, R. D. (2001c) Can Dynamical Systems Explain Mental Causation? Journal of Mind and Behavior 22, 311-334.

Ellis, R. D. (forthcoming a) Curious Emotions: Self-Organization, Action, and the Higher Human Affects. Amsterdam: John Benjamins.

Ellis, R. D. (forthcoming b) Love, Death, and the Interpersonal Experience of Value. Chicago: Open

Court.

Ellis, R. D. (forthcoming c) Spiritual Partnership and the Experience of the Value of Being. Target article for a special issue of *The Personalist Forum* with commentaries.

Ellis, R. D. & Newton, N. (1998) Three paradoxes of phenomenal consciousness: Bridging the explanatory gap. *Journal of Consciousness Studies 5*, 419-442.

Ellison, G. 1995. The N-methyl-D-aspartate antagonists phencyclidine, ketamine and dizocilpine as both behavioral and anatomical models of the dementias. Brain Research Reviews, 20 2,250-267.

Ellsworth, P. 1991 Some implications of cognitive appraisal theories of emotion. K. Strongman ed. International Review of Studies of Emotion, vol. 1. New York: John Wiley.

Enard, W. et al. (2002) Molecular evolution of FOXP2, a gene involved in speech and language. Nature Online. 10.1038

Encyclopedia Britannica Macropaedia: Book 16 p.201.

Epstein, S. 1994. Integration of the cognitive and the psychodynamic unconscious. American Psychologist, 49, 709-724.

Erikson, E. 1963 Childhood and society, 2nd ed. New York: Norton.

Ewing, Katherine. 1989. The Dream of Spiritual Initiation and the Organization of Self Representations among Pakistani Sufis. American Ethnologist 16:56-74.

Fabian, Johannes. 1966. Dreams and Charisma: Theories of Dreams in the Jamaa-Movement Congo. Anthropos 61:544-560.

Fedigan, L. 1992. Primates and paradigms: Sex roles and social bonds. Montreal: Elden Press.

Fenwick, P. 1996. The neurophysiology of religious experiences. In D. Bhugra Ed., Psychiatry and religion: Context, consensus, and controversies pp. 167-177. London: Routledge.

Ferreira, P. G., J. Majueij, & K. M. Gorski, 1998. Astro. J. Lett. 503, L1-L4.

Feuerbach, L. 1972[1843] The fiery book. Garden City, New York: Anchor Books.

Fields, C., Adams, M. D., White, O., & Venter, J. C. 1994. Nature Genetics, 7, 345-346.

Finnegan, D. J. 1989. Eurkaryotic transposable elements and genome evolution, Trends in Genetics, 5, 103-107.

Firth, Raymond. 1934. The Meaning of Dreams in Tikopia. In Essays Presented to C.G. Seligman, edited by E. E. Evans-Pritchard. London: Kegan Paul.

Fischer, R. 1971. A cartography of the ecstatic and meditative states. Science, 174, 897-904.

Fisher, Humphrey J. 1979. Dreams and Conversion in Black Africa. In Conversion to Islam, edited by N. Levtzion. New York: Holmes and Meier.

Flaherty, G. (1992), Shamanism and the eighteenth century. Princeton: Princeton University Press.

Flamsteed, S. 1995. Crisis in the cosmos. Discover, March, 67-77.

Flanagan, Owen. 2000. Dreaming Souls: Sleep, Dreams, and the Evolution of the Conscious Mind. Oxford: Oxford University Press.

Folk, R. L. 1997. Department of Geological Sciences, University of Texas, Austin, Texas 78712, USA.

Fodor, J. 1974 The language of thought. Cambridge, MA: MIT Press.

Foote, S. 1987. Extrathalamic modulation of cortical function. Annual Review of Neuroscience, 10,67-95.

Forman, R. K. C. 1999. Mysticism, mind, consciousness. Albany: State University of New York Press.

Forman, R. K. C. Ed.. 1990. The problem of pure consciousness: Mysticism and philosophy. New York: Oxford University Press.

Fort, C. 1941. The books of Charles Fort. New York: Henry Holt & Co.

Foulkes, David. 1999. Children's Dreaming and the Development of Consciousness. Cambridge: Harvard University Press.

Fowler, J. W. [1981] 1995. Stages of Faith. San Francisco: HarperSanFrancisco.

Fox, R. 1989. The Search for Society. New Brunswick: Rutgers University Press.

Fraenkel-Conrat, H., & Williams, R. C. 1955. Reconstitution of active tobacco mosaic virus from its inactive protein and nucleic acid components. Proceedings of the National Academy of Sciences, 41, 690-698.

Franz, M.-L. von 1974. Number and Time: Reflections Leading toward a Unification of Depth Psychology and Physics. Evanston: Northwestern University Press.

Franz, M.-L. von 1980. Projection and Re-Collection in Jungian Psychology: Reflections of the Soul. La Salle: Open Court.

Frater U.'.D.'. 1991, The essay ëModels of Magic' will be part of his next book, Dance of the Paradigms. A Chaos Magick Primer. Llewellyn's Publications, St. Paul, Minn.

Frecska, E. & Z. Kulcsar. (1989), Social bonding in the modulation of the physiology of ritual trance. Ethos, 17(1), 70-87.

Freed, S. & Freed, R. 1964 Spirit possession as an illness in a North American village. Ethnology 3:152-197.

Freedman, D. G. 1974. Human Infancy: An Evolutionary Perspective. Hillsdale, N.J.: Erlbaum.

Freedman, W. L. 1994. Science, 266, 539-540.

Freemantle, F. and C. Trungpa. 1987. The Tibetan Book of the Dead, Translation with Commentary. Boston: Shambhala.

Freemon, F. R.& Nevis, A. H. 1969 Temporal lobe sexual seizures. Neurology, 19, 87-90.

Freeman, W. (1987) Simulation of chaotic EEG patterns with a dynamic model of the olfactory system. *Biological Cybernetics 56,* 139-150.

Freeman, W. (1988) Why neural networks don't yet fly: Inquiry into the neurodynamics of biological intelligence. *Proceedings of the IEEE International Conference on Neural Networks* Volume 2 (pp. 1-7). San Diego: IEEE (Institute of Electrical and Electronics Engineers).

Freeman, W. (2000), A neurobiological role of music in social bonding. In N. Wallin, B. Merker and S. Brown. Eds. The origins of music. Cambridge (MA): MIT Press. Pp.411-424.

Freud, S. (1925/1959) *Beyond the Pleasure Principle.* New York: Bantam.

Freud, S. 1927. The Future of an Illusion. J. Strachey, Trans. Norton.

Freud, S. 1962. Civilization and Its Discontents. W.W. Norton and Co. Inc.

Freud, S. 1962. Civilization and Its Discontents. W.W. Norton and Co. Inc.

Freud, S. 1990[1913] Totem and taboo. New York: Norton.

Freud, S. 1900 The interpretation of dreams. In J. Strachey Ed Standard Edition Vol 5. London: Hogarth Press.

Freud, Sigmund. 1965. The Interpretation of Dreams. Translated by J. Strachey. New York: Avon Books.

Friedan, Ken. 1990. Freud's Dream of Interpretation. Albany: State University of New York Press.

Friston, K.J., Frith, C.D., & Passingham, R.E., et al. 1992. Motor practice and neurophysiological adaptation in the cerebellum. a positron emission tomography study. Proceedings of the Royal Society of London, 248,223-228.

Frith, C.D., Friston, K., & Liddle, P.F., et al. 1991. Willed action and the prefrontal cortex in man. a study with PET. Proceedings of the Royal Society of London, 244,241-246.

Frost, J.J. 1992. Receptor imaging by positron emission tomography and single-photon emission computed tomography. Investigative Radiology, 27, S54-S58.

Frost, Robert. [1916] 1967. The road not taken. In The Poetry of Robert Frost, 1 st ed. Ed. E. C. Lathem. New York: Holt, Rinehart & Winston.

Fukuda, M., Ono, T., & Nakamura, K. 1987. Functional relation among inferiotemporal cortex, amygdala and lateral hypothalamus in monkey operant feeding behavior. Journal of Neurophysiology, 57, 1060-1077.

Fuller, J. L., Rosvold, H. E.. & Pribram, K. H. 1957. Effects on affective and cognitive behavior in the dog after lesions of the pyriform-amygdaloid-hippocampal complex. Journal of Comparative and Physiological Psychology, 50, 89-96.

Funke, K. & Eysel, U.T. 1995. Possible enhancement of GABAergic inputs to cat dorsal lateral geniculate relay cells by serotonin. Neuroreport, 6 3,474-476.

Furst, P. (Ed.). (1976), Hallucinogens and culture. San Francisco: Chandler and Sharp.

Fuster, J.M. 1989. The Prefrontal Cortex: Anatomy, Physiology, and Neuropsychology of the Fronal Lobe. New York: Raven Press.

Gackenbach, Jayne, and Stephen LaBerge, eds. 1988. Conscious Mind, Sleeping Brain: Perspectives on Lucid Dreaming. New York: Plenum Press.

Gackenbach, Jayne. 1991. Frameworks for Understanding Lucid Dreaming: A Review. Dreaming 1 2:109-128.

Gargett, B. H. 1989 Grave Shortcomings: The evidence for Neandertal burial. Current Anthropology 30: 157-90

Gatley, S.J., DeGrado, T.R., & Kornguth, M.L., et al. 1990. Radiopharmaceuticals for positron emission tomography. Development of new, innovative tracers for measuring the rates of physiologic and biochemical processes. Acta Radiological Supplementum,

Gell-Mann, Murray. 1992. Physics colloquium lecture, University of Chicago.

Gellhorn, E. & Kiely, W. 1972 Mystical states of consciousness. Journal of Nervous and Mental Disease 154:399-405.

Gellhorn, E. & Kiely, W.F. 1973. Autonomic nervous system in psychiatric disorder. In Mendels, J. Biological psychiatry. New York: Wiley, 1973.

Gendlin, E. (1980/1982) *Focusing.* Toronto: Bantam.

Gendlin, E. (1962/1998) *Experiencing and the creation of meaning.* Toronto: Collier-Macmillan.

Georgeson, M. A., and M. A. Harris. 1978. Apparent foveo-fugal drift of counterphase gratings. Perception. 7 527-536.

Geschwind, N. 1983 Interictal behavioral changes in epilepsy. Epilepsia 24 suppl. 1:S23-S30.

Geissmann, T. (2000), Gibon songs and human music from an evolutionary perspective. In N. Wallin, B. Merker and S. Brown. Eds. The origins of music. Cambridge (MA): MIT Press. Pp.103-123

Gibbons, A. 1996. On the many origins of species. Science, 273, 1496-1499.

Gibson, E., et al., 2001. Precambrian Research 106:15-34

Gibson, G., & Hogness, D. S. 1996. Effects of polymorphism in the Drosophilia regulatory gene Ultrabithorax on homoetic stability. Science 271, 200-203.

Gillespie, George. 1988. Lucid Dreams in Tibetan Buddhism. In Conscious Mind, Sleeping Brain: Perspectives on Lucid Dreaming, edited by S. LaBerge. New York: Plenum Press.

Giovacchini, P. L. 1993. Borderline Patients, the Psychosomatic Focus, and the Therapeutic Process. Northvale, N.J.: Jason Aronson.

Glanz, J. 1996. Science 272, 1590 1996.

Gloor, P. 1960. Amygdala. In J. Field Ed., Handbook of physiology pp. 300-370. Washington, DC: American Physiological Society.

Gloor, P. 1986. iRole of the human limbic system in perception, memory and affect: lessons from temporal lobe epilepsy. In B. K. Doane & K. E. Livingston eds. The Limbic System. New York: Raven.

Gloor, P. 1997. The temporal lobe and limbic system. Oxford University Press, New York.

Gloor, P. 1986 The role of the human limbic system in in perception, memory, and affect. Lessons from temporal lobe epilepsy. In The Limbic System: Functional organization and Clinical Disorder. ed. B. K. Doane, & K. E. Livingston. New York, Raven Pres

Gloor, P. 1992. Role of the amygdala in temporal lobe epilepsy. In J. P. Aggleton Ed.. The amygdala. pp. 505-538, New York: Wiley-Liss.

Gloor, P., et al., 1982. iThe role of the limbic system in the experiential phenomena of temporal lobe epilepsy. Annals of Neurology, 12: 129-144.

Gloor, P., Olivier, A., Quesney, F., Andermann, F. & Horowitz, S. 1982 The role of the limbic system in experiential phenomena of temporal lobe epilepsy. Annals of Neurology 12:129-144.

Godwin, M. 1990 Angels. New York, Simon & Schuster.

Gold, P.W. & Goodwin, F.K. 1978. Vasopressin in affective illness. Lancet,1 8076,1233-1236.

Goldstein, K. (1938) The Organism. New York: American Books.

Goldberger, Ary L. 2002. Chaos Theory, Fractals, and Complexity: The Biology of Imagination. Paper read at Science and Mind/Body Medicine, May 2, at Cambridge, Massachussetts.

Goldfarb, W. 1964 An investigation of childhood schizophrenia. Archives of General Psychiatry 11:620-634.

Goldman, R. 1964. Religious Thinking from Childhood to Adolescence. New York: Seabury Press.

Goldstein, L., Stoltzfus, N. W., & Gardocki, J. F. 1972 Changes in interhemispheric amplitude relationships in the EEG during sleep. Physiology and Behavior, 8, 811-815.

Goodman, F. (1988), How about demons? Possession and exorcism in the modern world. Bloomington: Indiana University Press.

Greeley, A. 1975 The sociology of the paranormal. London: Sage.

Green, R. 1985. Gender identity in childhood and later sexual orientation. American Journal of Psychiatry, 142, 339-341.

Green, R. 1987. The Sissy Boy Syndrome and the Development of Homosexuality. New Haven. Yale U. Press.

Greenberg, M., & Weber, P. 1985. Nature, 316.

Gregor, T. 1981. Far, Far Away My Shadow Wandered....: The Dream Symbolism and Dream Theories of the Mehinaku Indians of Brazil. American Ethnologist 8 4:709-729.

Gregor, Thomas. 1983. Dark Dreams about the White Man. Natural History 92 1:8-14.

Gregor, Thomas. 2001. A Content Analysis of Mehinaku Dreams. In Dreams: A Reader on the Religious, Cultural, and Psychological Dimensions of Dreaming, edited by K. Bulkeley. New York: Palgrave.

Greyson, B. 2000. Near-death experiences. In E. Cardena, S. J. Lynn, & S. Krippner Eds., Varieties of anomalous experience: Examining the scientific evidence pp. 315-352. Washington, DC: American Psychological Association.

Griffin, R. R. 1997. Parapsychology, philosophy, and spirituality: A postmodern exploration. Albany: State University of New York Press.

Grof, S. 1972. Varieties of transpersonal experiences: Observations from LSD psychotherapy. Journal of Transpersonal Psychology, 4 1, 45-80.

Grof, S. 1975. Realms of the Human Unconscious. The Viking Press.

Grof, S., and l Halifax. 1977. The Human Encounter with Death. London: Souvenir Press.

Gross, C. G., Rocha-Miranda, C. E., & Bender, D. B. 1972 Visual properties of neruons in inferotemporal cortex of the macaque. Journal of Neurophysiology, 35, 96-111.

Grottanelli, Cristiano. 1999. On the Mantic Meaning of Incestuous Dreams. In Dream Cultures: Explorations in the Comparative History of Dreaming, edited by G. G. Stroumsa. New York: Oxford University Press.

Guchhait, R.B. 1976. Biogenesis of 5-methoxy-N,N-dimethyltryptamine in human pineal gland. Journal of Neurochemistry, 26 1,187-190.

Guth, A. H., & Lightman, A.P. 1998. The Inflationary Universe: The Quest for a New Theory of Cosmic Origins.

Guthrie, S. 1993 Faces in the clouds. New York: Oxford University Press.

Haines, D., E., Dietrich, E., Mihailoff, G.A., and McDonald, E. F. (1997) Cerebellar-hypothalamic axis: Basic circuits and clinical observations. In J. Schmahmann (Ed.), The Cerebellum and Cognition (pp. 84-110). New York: Academic Press.

Halgren, E. 1992. Emotional neurophysiology of the amygdala within the context of human cognition.In J. P. Aggleton Ed., The amygdala. pp. 191-228, New York, Wiley-Liss.

Halgren, E., Babb, T. L., & Crandall, P. H. 1978 Activity of human hippocampal formation and amygdala neurons during memory tests. Electroencephalography and Clinical Neurophysiology, 45, 585-601.

Halgren, E., Walter, R. D., Cherlow, D. G., & Crandal, P. H. 1978 Mental phenomenoa evoked by electrical stimualtion of the human hippocampal formation and amygdala, Brain, 101, 83-117.

Halifax, J. (1979), Shamanic voices. New York: E.P. Dutton.

Hall, Calvin, and Robert Van de Castle. 1966. The Content Analysis of Dreams. New York: Appleton-Century-Crofts.

Hall, J. 1978. Gender effects in decoding nonverbal cues. Psychological Review, 85, 845-857.

Hall, J. A. 1993. The Unconscious Christian: Images of God in Dreams. Mahwah: Paulist Press.

Hallowell, I. 1966. The Role of Dreams in Ojibwa Culture. In The Dream and Human Societies, edited by R. Callois. Berkeley: University of California Press.

Hammeke, T.A., Yetkin, F.Z., & Mueller, W.M., et al. 1994. Functional magnetic resonance imaging of somatosensory stimulation. Neurosurgery, 35, 677-681.

Hammerly-Dupuy, D. 1988. Some observations on the Assyro-Babylonian and Sumerian flood stores. in Dundes, A.The flood myth. U. California Press. Berkeley.

Hanisch, R. I 1939. I Was Hitler's Buddy. New Republic, April pp. 239-242, 270-272, 297-300.

Harackiewicz, J. N., & DePaulo, B. M. 1982. Accuracy of person perception. Personality & Social Psychology Bulletin, 8, 247-256.

Harleston, H. (1974). A mathematical analysis of Teotihuacan. XLI International Congress of Americanists, October.

Harner, M. (Ed.). (1973), Hallucinogens and shamanism. New York: Oxford University Press.

Harner, M. (1988), What is a shaman? In G. Doore (Ed.), Shamans Path: Healing, personal growth and empowerment (pp.7-15). Boston: Shambhala Publications.

Harner, M. (1990), The Way of the Shaman. San Francisco: Harper and Row.

Harold, F. B. 1980 A comparative analysis of Eurasian Palaeolithic burials. World Archaeology 12: 195-211.

Harris, M. 1993 Why we became religious and the evolution of the spirit world. In Lehmann, A. C. & Myers, J. E. Eds Magic, Witchcraft, and Religion. Mountain View: Mayfield.

Harris, Monford. 1994. Studies in Jewish Dream Interpretation. Northvale: Jason Aronson.

Hartmann, E. 1995. Making Connections in a Safe Place: Is Dreaming Psychotherapy? Dreaming 5 4:213-228.

Hartmann, E. 1998. Dreams and Nightmares: The New Theory on the Origin and Meaning of Dreams. New York: Plenum.

Hartmann, Ernest. 1984. The Nightmare: The Psychology and Biology of Terrifying Dreams. New York: Basic Books.

Harvey, R. P. 1996. NK-2 Homeobox genes and heart development. Developl Biol. 178, 203-216.

Hasan-Rokem, Galit. 1999. Communication with the Dead in Jewish Dream Culture. In Dream Cultures: Explorations in the Comparative History of Dreaming, edited by G. G. Stroumsa. New York: Oxford University Press.

Hauser, M. 2000 What do animals think about numbers? American Scientist 88:144-151.

Hauser, M. (2000), The sound and the fury: Primate vocalizations as reflections of emotions and thought. In N. Wallin, B. Merker and S. Brown. Eds. The origins of music. Cambridge (MA): MIT Press. Pp. 77-102

Hawkes, J. 1963 The World of the past. Vol. 1. New York. Knopf.

Hay, D. & Nye, R. 1998. The Spirit of the Child. London: HarperCollins.

Hay, D. 1990 Religious experience today. London: Mowbray.

Hayashi, J-I., Tekemitsu, M., Goto, Y-I., Nonakoa, I. 1994. Journal of Cell Biology, 125, 43-50.

Hays J. D. et al., 1976. Variations in the Earth's Orbit. Science, 194, 1125.

Healey, F., M. A. Persinger, et al. 1996. Enhanced hypnotic suggestibility following application of burst-firing magnetic fields over the right temporoparietal lobes: a replication. International Journal of Neuroscience 87 3-4: 201-7.

Healey, F., M. A. Persinger, et al. 1997. Control of choice by application of the electromagnetic field equivalents of spoken words: mediation by emotional meaning rather than linguistic dimensions? Perceptual and Motor Skills 85 3 Pt 2: 1411-8.

Hedges, S. B. 1994. Molecular evidence for the origin of birds. Proceedings of the National Academy of Sciences, 91, 2621-2624.

Hedges, S. B., & Kumar, S. 1999. Divergence times of eutherian mammals. Sciences, 285, 2031.

Hedges, S. B., et al., 1992. Human origins and analysis of DNA sequences. Science, 255, 737-739.

Hefner, P. 1993. The Human Factor: Evolution, Culture, and Religion. Minneapolis: Fortress.

Hegel. 1821. Fundamental Principles of the Philosophy of Law Grundlinien der Philosophie des Rechts.

Hegel. 1821. Fundamental Principles of the Philosophy of Law Grundlinien der Philosophie des Rechts.

Heidan, J. 1936 Hitler. Knopf, New York, 1936.

Heidel, H. 1988. The Babylonian Genesis. Oriental Institute of Chicago.

Hellemans, A. 1995. Dwarfs and dim galaxies mark limits of knowledge. Science, 268, 366-367.

Heller, W., & Levy, J. 1981. Perception and expression of emotion in right-handers and left-handers. Neuropsychologia, 19, 263-272.

Helminiak, D. A. 1984. Neurology, psychology, and extraordinary religious experiences. Journal of Religion and Health, 23, 33-46.

Henikoff, S., Keene, M. A., Fechtel, K., & Friston, J. W. 1986. Gene with a gene. Cell, 44, 33-42.

Hermann, B. P., & Chambria, S. 1980. Interictal psychopathology in patients with ictal fear. Archives of Neurology, 37, 667-668.

Hermansen, Marcia. 2001. Dreams and Dreaming in Islam. In Dreams: A Reader on the Religious, Cultural, and Psychological Dimensions of Dreaming, edited by K. Bulkeley. New York: Palgrave.

Herzog, H., Lele VR, & Kuwert T, et al. 1990-1991. Changed pattern of regional glucose metabolism during Yoga meditative relaxation. Neuropsychobiology, 23, 182-187.

Hesiod. 1973. Theogony. Translated by D. Wender. New York: Penguin Books.

Hillman, J. 1975. Re-Visioning Psychology. New York: Harper & Row.

Hillman, J. 1983. Archetypal Psychology: A Brief Account. Dallas: Spring.

Hirschfeld, L. & Gelman, S., eds. 1994 Mapping the mind. New York: Cambridge University Press.

Hobson, J. A., Lydic, R., & Baghdoyan, H. A. 1986 Evolving concepts of sleep cycle generation: From brain centers to neuronalpopulations. Behavioral and Brain Sciences, 9, 371-448.

Hobson, J. Allan, and Robert McCarley. 1977. The Brain as a Dream State Generator: An Activation-Synthesis Hypothesis of the Dream Process. American Journal of Psychiatry 134:1335-1348.

Hobson, J. A. 1988. The Dreaming Brain. New York, Basic Books.

Hobson, J. A. 1993. Self-Organization Theory of Dreaming. Dreaming 3 3: 151-178.

Hobson, J. A. 1999. Dreaming as Delirium: How the Brain Goes Out of Its Mind. Cambridge, MIT Press.

Hodoba, D. 1986 Paradoxic sleep facilitation by interictal epileptic activity of right temporal origin. Biological Psychiatry, 21, 1267-1278.

Hoffman, Valerie. 1997. The Role of Visions in Contemporary Egyptian Religious Life. Religion 27 1:45-64.

Hood, R.W. Jr., Spilka, B., Hunsberger, B. & Gorsuch, R. 1996. The Psychology of Religion. The Guilford Press

Hooker, C., Roese, N. & Park, S. 2000 Impoverished counterfactual thinking is associated with schizophrenia. Psychiatry 63:326-335

Hornblower, S., & Spawforth, A. Eds. 1996. The Oxford Classical Dictionary, third edition. Oxford: Oxford University Press.

Horney, K. (1950/1991) Neurosis and Human Growth. New York: W.W. Norton.

Horney, K. (1937) The Neurotic Personality of Our Time. New York: W.W. Norton.

Horowitz, M. J., Adams, J.E., & Rutkin, B.B. 1968. Visual imagery on brain stimulation. Archives of General Psychiatry, 19, 469-486.

Horsh, R. B., Fry, J. F., Hoffman, N. L., et al. 1985. A simple and general method for transferring genes into plants. Science, 227, 1229-1231.

Honorton, C. 1977. Psi and internal attention states. In B. Wolman Ed., Handbook of parapsychology pp. 435-472. New York: Van Nostrand Reinhold.

Honorton, C., & Ferrari, D. C. 1989. Future telling: A meta-analysis of forced-choice precognition experiments, 1935-1987. Journal of Parapsychology, 53, 281-308.

Horton, R. 1963 The Kalabiri Erkine society. Africa 33:94-114.

Howson, C., & Urbach, P. 1991. Scientific Reasoning: the Bayesian Approach. La Salle, IL: Open Court.

Hoyle, F. 1986. The Intelligent Universe. Holt, Rhinehart, Winston, 1986

Hugdahl, K. 1996 Cognitive influences on human autonomic nervous function. Current Opinion in Neurobiology 6:252-258.

Hultkrantz, A. (1973), A definition of shamanism. Temenos, 9, 25-37.

Hume, D. 1956[1757] The natural history of religion. Stanford: Stanford University Press.

HumphreyM. E., & Zangwill, O. L. 1951 Cessation of dreaming after brain injury. Journal of Neurology, Neurosurgery, and Psychiatry, 14, 322-325.

Hunt, H. 1989. The Multiplicity of Dreams: Memory, Imagination, and Consciousness. New Haven: Yale University Press.

Hunt, H. (1995), On the nature of consciousness. New Haven: Yale University Press.

Hustig, H. & Hafner, R. 1990 Persistent auditory hallucinations and their relationship to delusions and mood. Journal of Nervous and Mental Disease 178:264-267.

Husserl, Edmund. (1913/1931) *Ideas*, W.R. Boyce Gibson Trans (London: Collier 1931; from "Ideen zu einer Reinen Phänomenologie und Phänomenologischen Philosophie," 1913).

Huxley, A. 1954 / 1990. The Doors of Perception - Heaven and Hell. New York: Harper & Row.

Ibn Khaldun 1958[1318]. The Muqaddimah, 3 vols. London: Routledge & Kegan Paul.

Idel, Moshe. 1999. Astral Dreams in Judaism: Twelfth to Fourteenth Centuries. In Dream Cultures: Explorations in the Comparative History of Dreaming, edited by G. G. Stroumsa. New York: Oxford University Press.

Ignatius of Loyola. [c. 1535] 1992. Spiritual Disciplines. New York: Crossroad.

IHGSC 2001 Initial sequencing and analysis of the human genome. Nature 409, 860 - 921.

Infante, J.R., Peran, F., & Martinez, M., et al. 1998. ACTH and beta-endorphin in transcendental meditation. Physiology and Behavior, 64 3, 311-315.

Infante, J.R., Torres-Avisbal, M., & Pinel, P., et al. 2001. Catecholamine levels in practitioners of the transcendental meditation technique. Physiology and Behavior, 72 1-2,141-146.

Ingerman, S. (1991), Soul retrieval. San Francisco: Harper Collins.

Ingvar, D.H. 1994. The will of the brain: Cerebral correlates of willful acts. Journal of Theoretical Biology, 171, 7-12.

Irenaeus of Lyons. [c. 189] 2000. Against heresies. In Iraenaeus of Lyons, ed. R. M. Grant. New York: Routledge.

Irons, W. 1996 Morality, religion, and human nature. In W.M. Richardson & W. Wildman eds. Religion and science. New York: Routledge.

Irwin, H. l. 1986. Perceptual perspectives of visual imagery in OBEs, dreams and reminiscence. Journal of the Society for Psychical Research, 53:210-217.

Irwin, Lee. 1994. The Dream Seekers: Native American Visionary Traditions of the Great Plains. Norman: University of Oklahoma Press.

Irwin, Lee. 2001. Sending a Voice, Seeking a Place: Visionary Traditions among Native Women of the Plains. In Dreams: A Reader on the Religious, Cultural, and Psychological Dimensions of Dreaming, edited by K. Bulkeley. New York: Palgrave.

Isokawa-Akesson, M., Wilson, C. L. & Babb, T. L. 1987. Structurally stable burst and synchronized firing in human amygdala neurons: auto- and cross-correlation analyses in temporal lobe epilepsy. Epilepsy Research 1: 17-34.

Jackson, D., Symons, R., & Berg, P. 1972. Biochemical method for inserting new genetic information into DNA.Proceedings of the National Academy of Sciences, 69, 2904-2909.

Jackson, J. H. 1880 Dreamy States.In J. Taylor Ed Selected Writings of John Hughlings Jackson 1958 New York, Basic Books.

Jackson, J. H., & Stewart, 1899 Epileptic attacks with a warning of a crude sensation of smell and with the intellectual aura dreamy state in a patient who had symptoms pointing to gross organic diseae of the right temporosphenoidal lobe.

Jakobsen, M. (1999), Shamanism traditional and contemporary approaches to the mastery of spirits and healing. New York: Berghahn Books.

James, W. 1890 The Principles of Psychology, London; MacMillan

James, W. 1901, 1902/1958. The Varieties of Religious Experience.

James, W. 1956. The will to believe, human immortality, and other essays on popular philosophy. New York: Dover. Original work published 1890

James, W. 1960. Human immortality: Two supposed objections to the doctrine. In G. Murphy & R. O. Ballou Eds., William James on psychical research pp. 279-308. New York: Viking. Original work delivered as a lecture 1898

James, W. 1969. What psychical research has accomplished. In G. Murphy & R. O. Ballou Eds, William

James on psychical research pp. 25-47. New York: Viking. Original work published 1890

James, W. 1980. A suggestion about mysticism. In R. Woods Ed., Understanding mysticism pp. 215-222. Garden City, NY: Image Books. Original work published 1910

Janal, M., Colt, E., & Clark, W., et al. 1984. Pain sensitivity, mood and plasma endocrine levels in man following long-distance running, Effects of naxalone. Pain, 19,13-25.

Jansen, K.L.R. 1995. Using ketamine to induce the near -death experience, mechanism of action and therapeutic potential. Yearbook for Ethnomedicine and the Study of Consciousness Jahrbuch furr Ethnomedizin und Bewubtseinsforschung, 4, 55-81.

Jaussen, A. 1948[1907] Coutumes des Arabs au pays de Moab. Paris: Adrien-Maisonneuve.

Jayne, Walter. 1925. The Healing Gods of Ancient Civilizations. New Haven: Yale University Press.

Jaynes, J. 1976 The origin of consciousness in the breakdown of the bicameral mind. Boston: Houghton Mifflin.

Jeannerod, M. (1997) *The Cognitive Neuroscience of Action*. Oxford: Blackwell.

Jedrej, M.C. , and Rosalind Shaw, eds. 1992. Dreaming, Religion, and Society in Africa. Leiden: E.J. Brill.

Jefferys, W. H., & Berger, J. O. 1992. Sharpening Ockam's razor on a Bayesian strop. American Scientist, 80, 64-72.

Jelinek, W. R., Tommey, T. P., Leinwand, L., et al. 1980. Ubiquitous interspersed repeated DNA sequences in mammalian genomes. Proceedings of the National Academy of Sciences, 77, 1398-1402.

Jess, S., Beck, G. Joseph, R. 2001. America Attacked. University Press, California, San Jose.

Jess, S., & Beck, G. 2002. John Walker Lindh: American Talian. University Press, California, San Jose.

Jesses, R. 1996. iEntheogens: A brief history of their Spiritual Usei. Tricycle: Volume 6, Number One: Fall 1996 p.60.

Jevning, R., Wallace, R.K., & Beidebach, M. 1992. The physiology of meditation, A review. A wakeful hypometabolic integrated response. Neuroscience and Biobehavioral Reviews,16,415-424.

Jirari, C. 1970. Form perception, innate form preferences, and visually mediated heat-turning in human neonates. Unpublished doctoral dissertation, Committee on Human Development, University of Chicago.

Johanson, D. & Edgar,B. 1996 From Lucy to language. New York: Simon and Schuster

John, B., & Miklos, G. 1988.The Eucaryotic Genome in Development and Evolution. Allen & Unwin, London,

Johnson, J. E., Birren, S. J., & Anderson, D. J. 1990. Two rat homologues. Nature, 346, 858-861.

Johnson, R. A. 1986. Inner Work: Using Dreams and Active Imagination for Personal Growth. New York: Harper & Row.

Johnson, R. N. 1972 Aggression in man and animals. Philadelphia. W. B. Saunders.

Johnson, W. E., & Coffin, J. M. 1999. Constructing primate phylogenies from ancient retrovirus sequences. Proceedings of the National Academy of Sciences, 96, 10254-10260.

Jones, Richard M. 1978. The New Psychology of Dreaming. New York: Penguin Books.

Joseph, R. 1979.Effects of rearing and sex on learning and competitive exploration. Journal of Psychology, 101,37-43.

Joseph, R. 1982. The Neuropsychology of Development. Hemispheric Laterality, Limbic Language, the the Origin of Thought.J. Clin. Psy. 444-33.

Joseph, R. 1984. La Neuropsiciologia Del Desarrollo: Lateralidad, Hemisferica, Lenguaje Limbico, y el Origen del pensamiento. Archives of Psychiatry and Neurology, Venezolanos, 30, 25-52.

Joseph, R. 1985. Competition between women. Psychology, 22, 1-11.

Joseph, R. 1986a. Reversal of language and emotion in a corpus callosotomy patient. Journal of Neurology, Neurosurgery, & Psychiatry, 49, 628-634.

Joseph, R. 1986b. Confabulation and delusional denial: Frontal lobe and lateralized influences. J. Clin. Psy. 42, 845-860.

Joseph, R. 1988a The Right Cerebral Hemisphere: Emotion, Music, Visual-Spatial Skills, Body Image, Dreams, and Awareness. J.Clin. Psy., 44, 630-673.

Joseph, R. 1988b. Dual mental functioning in a split-brain patient. J. Clin. Psy.,44, 770-779.

Joseph, R. 1990. Neuropsychology, Neuropsychiatry, Behavioral Neurology, Plenum, New York.

Joseph, R. 1992a The Limbic System: Emotion, Laterality, and Unconscious Mind, The Psychoanalytic Review,79, 405-456.

Joseph, R. 1992b.The Right Brain and the Unconscious.New York, Plenum.

Joseph, R. 1993. The Naked Neuron: Evolution and the Languages of the Body and Brain. New York, Plenum Press.

Joseph, R. 1994 The limbic system and the foundations of emotional experience. In V. S. Ramachandran Ed. Encyclopedia of Human Behavior. San Diego, Academic Press.

Joseph, R. 1996. Neuropsychology, Neuropsychiatry, and
Clinical Neuroscience, 2nd edition. Williams & Wilkins, New York, Plenum.

Joseph, R. 1997. The Evolution of Life on Other Planets: The Origin of Life and Evolutionary Metamorphosis. California University Press, California.

Joseph, R. 1998a. The limbic system. In H.S. Friedman ed., Encyclopedia of Human health, Academic Press. San Diego.

Joseph, R. 1998b. Traumatic amnesia, repression, and hippocampal injury due to corticosteroid and enkephalin secretion. Child Psychiatry and Human Development. 29, 169-186.

Joseph, R. 1998c. Flavonoid substance and/or flavone glocosides substance as a treatment for disorders of the brain. United States Department of Commerce: Patent & Trademark Office, March, # 60/080,768.

Joseph, R. 1998d. Olfactory substance as a treatment for disorders of the brain. United States Department of Commerce: Patent & Trademark Office, March, # 60/080,770.

Joseph, R. 1998e. Combined use of Ginko Biloba and Hypericum Perforatum Saint John's Wort as a treatment for disorders of the brain. United States Department of Commerce: Patent & Trademark Office, March, # 60/080,769.

Joseph, R. 1999a. Frontal lobe psychopathology: Mania, depression, aphasia, confabulation, catatonia, perseveration, obsessive compulsions, schizophrenia.Psychiatry, 62, 138-172.

Joseph, R. 1999b.Environmental influences on neural plasticity, the limbic system, and emotional development and attachment, Child Psychiatry and Human Development. 29, 187-203.

Joseph, R. 1999c. The neurology of traumatic dissociative amnesia. Commentary and literature review. Child Abuse & Neglect. 23,

Joseph, R. 2000. The Transmitter to God: The Limbic System, The Soul, and Spirituality. University Press California, San Jose.

Joseph, R. 2000b. Astrobiology, the Origin of Life, and the Death of Darwinism. University Press California, San Jose,

Joseph, R. 2000c. The evolution of sexuality and sex differences in language and visual spatial skills. Archives of Sexual Behavior, 29, 35-66.

Joseph, R. 2000d. Female Sexuality: The Naked Truth. University Press California, San Jose.

Joseph, R. 2000f. Fetal brain behavioral cognitive development. Developmental Review, 20, 81-98.

Joseph, R. 2001. The Limbic System and the Soul: Evolution and the Neuroanatomy of Religious Experience. Zygon 36 1:105-136.

Joseph, R. 2001. Astrobiology, the Origin of Life, & the Death of Darwinism. 2nd edition. University Press California, San Jose.

Joseph, R. 2002. Neuropsychiatry, Neuropsychology, Clinical Neuroscience.3rd edition.University Press California, San Jose.

Joseph, R., & Casagrande, V. A. 1978. Visual field defects and morphological changes resulting from monocular deprivation in primates. Proceedings of the Society for Neuroscience, 4, 2021.

Joseph, R. & Casagrande, V. A. 1980. Visual field defects and recovery following lid closure in a prosimian primate. Behavioral Brain Research, 1, 150-178.

Joseph, R., Forrest, N., Fiducia, N., Como, P., & Siegel, J. 1981. Electrophysiological and behavioral correlates of arousal. Physiological Psychology, 1981, 9, 90-95.

Joseph, R., & Gallagher, R. E. 1980. Gender and early environmental influences on activity, overresponsiveness, and exploration. Developmental Psychobiology, 13, 527-544.

Joseph, R., & Gallagher, R. E. 1985. Interhemispheric transfer and the completion of reversible operations in non-conserving children. J.Clin. Psy.41, 796-800.

Joseph, R., Gallagher, R., E., Holloway, J., & Kahn, J. 1984. Two brains, one child: Interhemispheric transfer and confabulation in children aged 4, 7, 10. Cortex, 20, 317-331.

Joseph, R., Hess, S., & Birecree, E. 1978. Effects of sex hormone manipulations and exploration on sex differences in maze learning. Behavioral Biology, 24, 364-377.

Jouvet, M. 1967 Neurophysiology of the states of sleep. Physiological Review, 47, 117-177.

Jouvet, Michel. 1999. The Paradox of Sleep: The Story of Dreaming. Translated by L. Garey. Cambridge: MIT Press.

Jung, C. G. (CW). The Collected Works of C. G. Jung, edited by H. Read, M. Fordham, & G. Adler, translated primarily by R. F. C. Hull. London: Routledge & Kegan Paul, 1953-78; New York: Pantheon, 1953-60, and Bollingen Foundation, 1961-67; Princeton: Princeton University Press, 1967-78.

Jung, C. G. 1945 On the nature of dreams. Translated by R.F.C. Hull., The collected works of C. G. Jung, pp.473-507 Princeton: Princeton University Press.

Jung, C. G. 1964 Man and his symbols. New York. Doubleday.

Jung, C.G. 1965. Memories, Dreams, Reflections. Translated by C. Winston. New York: Vintage Books.

Jung, C.G. 1974. On the Nature of Dreams. In Dreams. Princeton: Princeton University Press. Original edition, 1948.

Jung, C. G. 1997. Jung on Active Imagination, edited & introduced by J. Chodorow. Princeton: Princeton University Press.

Jung, C. G. 1998. Jung on Mythology, selected & introduced by R. A. Segal. Princeton: Princeton University Press.

Jung, E. 1957. Animus and Anima. Dallas: Spring Publications.

Juarrero, A. (1999) Dynamics in Action: Intentional Behavior as a Complex System. Cambridge, Mass.: MIT/Bradford.

Kagan, J., & Berkun, M. (1954) The reward value of running activity. Journal of Comparative Physiological Psychology 47, 108-10.

Kahan, T. L. 2000. The Problem of Dreaming in NREM Sleep Continues to Challenge Reductionist 2-Gen Models of Dream Generation Commentary. Behavioral and Brain Sciences 23 6:956-958.

Kahan, T. L. 2001. Consciousness in Dreaming: A Metacognitive Approach. In Dreams: A Reader on the Religious, Cultural, and Psychological Dimensions of Dreaming, edited by K. Bulkeley. New York: Palgrave.

Kahn, D. Hobson. A. J. 1993. Self-Organization Theory and Dreaming. Dreaming 3 3:151-178.

Kahn, D. et al., 2000. Dreaming and the Self-Organizing Brain. Journal of Consciousness Studies 7 7:4-11.

Kalin, N., Shelton, S., & Barksdale, C. 1988. Opiate modulation of separation-induced distress in non-human primates. Brain Research, 440,285-292.

Kanner, L. 1943 Autistic disturbances of affective contact. The Nervous Child 2:217-250.

Kant, Emmanuel. 1781. Critique of Pure Reason. New York. St. Martin's Press.

Kapp, B. S., Supple, W. F., & Whalen, P. J. 1994. Effects of electrical stimulation of the amygdaloid central nucleus on neocortical arousal in the rabbit. Behavioral Neuroscience, 108, 81-93.

Karagulla, S. & Robertson, E. 1955 Physical phenomena in temporal lobe epilepsy and the psychoses. British Medical Journal 1:748-752.

Karnath, H.O., Ferber, S., & Himmelbach, M. 2001. Spatial awareness is a function of the temporal not the posterior parietal lobe. Nature, 411, 950-953.

Kauffman, G. D. 1985. Theology for a Nuclear Age. Philadelphia: Westminster.

Kauffman, G. D. 1992. Nature, history, and God: toward an integrated conceptualization. Zygon: Journal of Religion & Science 27: 379-401.

Kauffman, S. (1993) The Origins of Order. Oxford: Oxford University Press.

Kaufman, S. 1995. At Home in the Universe: The Search for Laws of Self-Organization and Complexity. New York: Oxford Univ. Press.

Keeney, Bradford P., editor. 1999. Kalahari Bushmen Healers. USA: Ringing Rocks Press.

Kelley, M. 1958 The incidence of hospitalized mental illness among religious sisters in the United States. American Journal of Psychiatry 115:72-75.

Kelsey, Morton. 1991. God, Dreams, and Revelation: A Christian Interpretation of Dreams. Minneapolis: Augsburg Publishing.

Kelso, J. A. (1995) Dynamic Patterns: The Self-organization of Brain and Behavior. Cambridge, Massachusetts: MIT/Bradford.

Keltner, D., Ellsworth, P. & Edwards, K. 1993 Beyond simple pessimism: Effects of sadness and anger on social perception. Journal of Personality and Social Psychology 64:740-752.

Kent, G. & Wahass, S. 1996 The content and characteristics of auditory hallucinations in Saudia Arabia and the UK. Acta Psychiatrica Scandinavica 94:433-437.

Kerr, N. H., & Foulkes, D. 1981 Right hemisphere mediation of dream visualization: A case study. Cortex, 17, 603-610.

Khaldun, Ibn. 1967. The Muqaddimah. Translated by F. Rosenthal. Princeton: Princeton University Press.

Kierkegaard, S. 1955[1843] Fear and trembling and the sickness unto death. New York: Doubleday.

Kierkegaard. 1849. The Sickness Unto Death: A Christian Psychological Exposition for Edification and Awakening. Penguin USA. 1989.

Kilson, M. 1972 Ambivalence and power. Journal of Religion in Africa 4:171 177.

Kirk, G.S. and Raven, J.E. 1971. The Presocratic Philosphers. Cambridge.

Kirkpatrick, L. (1997), An attachment-theory approach to psychology of religion. In B. Spilka & D. McIntosh (Eds.), The psychology of religion (pp.). Boulder, CO.: Westview Press.

Kirkpatrick, L. 1998 God as a substitute attachment figure. Personality and Social Psychology Bulletin 24:961-973.

Kiss, J., Kocsis, K., Csaki, A., Gorcs, T.J., & Halasz, B. 1997. Metabotropic glutamate receptor in GHRH and beta-endorphin neurons of the hypothalamic arcuate nucleus. Neuroreport, 8 17, 3703-3707.

Kjaer, T.W., Bertelsen, C., Piccini, P., Brooks, D., Alving, J., & Lou, H.C. 2002. Increased dopamine tone during meditation-induced change of consciousness. Cognitive Brain Research, 13, 255-259.

Klein, M. (1975) *Envy and Gratitude*. Hogarth Press, English Institute of Psycho-Analysis.

Kling, A. 1972. Effects of amygdalectomy on social-affective behavior in non-human primates. In B. E. Eleftherious Ed.. The Neurobiology of the amygdala, pp 127-170. New York: Plenum.

Kling, A. S., Lloyd, R. L., & Perryman, K. M. 1987. Slow wave changes in amygdala to visual, auditory and social stimuli following lesions of the inferior temporal cortex in squirrel monkey. Behavioral and Neural Biology, 47, 54-72.

Kling, A., & Steklis, H.D. 1976.A neural substrate for affiliative behavior in nonhuman primates.Brain Behavior and Evolution, 13, 216-238.

Kling. A. S. & Brothers, L. A. 1992. The amygdala and social behavior.In J. P. Aggleton Ed.. The amygdala. New York: Wiley-Liss.

Kl,ver, H. & Bucy, P. 1939 Preliminary analysis of function of the temporal lobe in monkeys. Archives of Neurology 42:979-1000.

Knight, N., Atran, S., Barrett, J. & Ucan Ek', E. 2001 Understanding the mind of God: Evidence from Yukatek Maya children. Paper presented at the Annual Meeting of The Society for the Scientific Study of Religion, Columbus, OH, October.

Knight, R. & Grabowecky, M. 1995 Escape from linear time: Prefrontal cortex and conscious experience. In M. Gazzaniga ed., The cognitive neurosciences; Cambridge, MA: MIT Press.

Knudson, Roger. 2001. Significant Dreams: Bizarre or Beautiful? Dreaming 11 4:167-178.

Knuth, D. E. 2001. Things a Computer Scientist Rarely Talks About. Stanford, Calif.: CSLI.

Koenig, H.G. 1994. Aging and God: Spiritual Pathways to Mental Health in Midlife and Later Years. New York. Haworth Press.

Kohut, H. (1985) *Self Psychology and the Humanities*. New York: W.W. Norton.

Kracke, Waud. 2001. Kagwahiv Mourning: Dreams of a Bereaved Father. In Dreams: A Reader on the Religious, Cultural, and Psychological Dimensions of Dreaming, edited by K. Bulkeley. New York: Palgrave.

Kramer, Heinrich, and James Sprenger. 1971. The Malleus Maleficarum. Translated by M. Summers. New York: Dover.

Kramer, S. N. 1991. History begins at Sumer. U. Pennsylvania Press, Philadelphia.

Krettek, J.E., & Price, J.L. 1977.Projections from the amygdaloid complex. Journal of Comparative Neurology, 172, 723-752, 687-722.

Kripe, D. F. & Sonnenschein 1973 A 90-minute daydream cycle. Sleep Research, 2, 187-190.

Krippner, S. Ed.. 1977, 1978, 1982. Advances in parapsychological research Vols. 1-3. New York: Plenum.

Krippner, S. Ed.. 1984, 1987, 1990, 1994. Advances in parapsychological research Vols. 4-7. Jefferson, NC: McFarland.

Krippner, Stanley, Fariba Bogzaran, and Andre Percia de Carvalho. 2002. Extraordinary Dreams and How to Work with Them. Albany: State University of New York Press.

Krippner, S. & P. Welch. (1992), Spiritual dimensions of healing: From native shamanism to contemporary health care. New York: Irvington Publishers, Inc.

Kuhsel, M. G., Strickland, R., & Palmer, J. D. 1990. An ancient group I intron shared by eubacteria and chloroplasts, Science, 250, 1570-1573.

Kuiken, Don, and Shelley Sikora. 1993. The Impact of Dreams on Waking Thoughts and Feelings. In The Functions of Dreaming, edited by R. Hoffmann. Albany: State University of New York Press.

Kumar, S., & Hedges, S. B. 1998. A molecular time scale for vertebrate evolution. Nature. 396, 336-342.

Kung, H.F. 1991. Overview of radiopharmaceuticals for diagnosis of central nervous disorders. Critical Reviews in Clinical and Laboratory Science, 28,269-286.

Kurten, B. 1976 The cave bear story. New York: Columbia University Press.

Kurtz, P. Ed.. 1985. A skeptic's handbook of parapsychology. Buffalo, NY: Prometheus.

Kurzweil, Ray. 1999. The Age of Spiritual Machines. London, Orion.

Labandeira, C. & Phillips, T. 1996. Proceeding of the National Academy of Sciences.

La Barre, W. (1972), Hallucinogens and the shamanic origins of religion. In P. Furst, (Ed.), Flesh of the gods (pp.). New York: Praeger.

LaBerge, Stephen. 1985. Lucid dreaming: The Power of Being Awake and Aware in Your Dreams. Los Angeles: Jeremy Tarcher.

Lakoff, George. 2001. How Metaphor Structures Dreams: The Theory of Conceptual Metaphor Applied to Dream Analysis. In Dreams: A Reader on the Religious, Cultural, and Psychological Dimensions of Dreaming, edited by K. Bulkeley. New York: Palgrave.

Lama, The Dalai. 1997. Sleeping, Dreaming, and Dying. Boston: Wisdom Publications.

Lamond, A., I., & Gibson, T. J. 1990. Catalytic RNA and the origin of genetic systems. Trends in Genetics, 6, 145-149.

Landa Deigo de. 1990. Yucatan before and after the Conquest. Dante Publications, Mexico.

Langer, W. C. 1972. The Mind of Adolf Hilter. Basic Books, New York.

Langer, S. (1957) Problems of Art. New York: Scribners.

Lanternari, Vittorio. 1975. Dreams as Charismatic Significants: Their Bearing on the Rise of New Religious Movements. In Psychological Anthropology, edited by T. R. Williams. Paris: Mouton.

Larkin, A. 1979 The form and content of schizophrenic hallucination. American Journal of Psychiatry 136:940-943.

Laufer, Bertold. 1931. Inspirational Dreams in East Asia. Journal of American Folk-Lore 44:208-216.

Laughlin, C. (1997), Body, brain, and behavior: The neuroanthropology of the body image. Anthropology of Consciousness, 8(2-3), 49-68.

Lauglin, C. Jr. & d'Aquili, E.G. 1974. Biogenetic Structuralism. Columbia University Press, New York.

Laughlin, C., J. McManus, & E. d'Aquili. (1992), Brain, symbol and experience toward a neurophenomenology of consciousness. New York: Columbia University Press.

Lavallee, M. R. & M. A. Persinger 1992. Left ear right temporal lobe suppressions during dichotic listening, ego-alien intrusion experiences and spiritualistic beliefs in normal women. Perceptual and Motor Skills 75 2: 547-51.

Lazar, S.W., Bush, G., & Gollub, R.L., et al. 2000. Functional brain mapping of the relaxation response and meditation. Neuroreport, 11, 1581-1585.

Lazerwitz, B. 1961. Some factors associated with variations in church attendance. Social Forces, 39, 301-309.

Le Doux, J. 1994. Emotion, Memory and the Braini. Scientific American 270: 32-39.

LeDoux, J. 1993 Emotional memory systems in the brain. Behavioural Brain Research 58:69-79.

LeDoux, J. E. 1996. The emotional brain. New York: Simon & Schuster.

LeDoux, J. 2002. Synaptic Self: How Our Brains Become Who We Are. New York: Viking.

Lehmann, A. C. & Myers, J. E. 1993 Magic, Witchcraft, and Religion. Mountain View: Mayfield.

Leiris, M. 1958 La possession et ses aspects theatraux chez les Ethiopiens. Paris: Plon.

Lerner, M. 2000 Spirit Matters. Charlottesville, Va.: Hampton Roads, Walsch.

Leroi-Gourhan, A. 1964. Treasure of prehistoric art. New York: H. N. Abrams.

Leroi-Gourhan, A. 1982. The archaeology of Lascauz Cave. Scientific American 24: 104-112.

Leslie, A. & Frith, U. 1987 Metarepresentation and autism. Cognition 27:291-294.

Leslie, A. & Frith, U. 1988 Autistic children's understanding of seeing, knowing, and believing. British Journal of Developmental Psychology 6:315-324.

Lester, T. 2002 Supernatural selection. Atlantic Monthly, February 8.

Leutmezer, F., Serles, W., Bacher, J., et al., 1999. Genital automatisms in complex partial seizures. Neurology, 52, 1188-1191.

Leutwyler, K. 2002. Don't stress. Scientific American, December.

LeVay, S.A. 1991.A difference in hypothalamic structure between heterosexual and homosexual men Science, 253, 1034-1037.

Leventhal, H. & Scherer, K. 1987 The relationship of emotion to cognition. Cognition and Emotion 1:3-28.

Leventhal, H. 1984. A perceptual-motor theory of emotion. In L. Berkowitz ed. Advances in Experimental Social Psychology, Volume 17. New York: Academic Press.

Levinas, E. (1969) Totality and Infinity. The Hague: Martinus Nijhoff.

Levinson, B., Kenwrick, S., Lakich, D., et al. 1990. A transcribed gene in an intron of the human Factor VIII gene. Genomics, 7, 7-11.

Levinson, G., & Gutman, G. A. 1987. Molecular Biology & Evolution, 4, 203-221.

Levy, J., & Heller, W. 1992. Gender differences in human neuropsychological function. In A. A. Gerall, H. Moltz, & I. L. Ward eds., Handbook of behavioral Neurobiology, Vol. 11, Sexual differentiation pp. 245-274. Plenum, New York.

Lewin, B. 1988. Molecular clocks turn a quarter of a century. Science, 239, 561-563.

Lewis, I. 1971 Ecstatic religion. Harmondsworth, UK: Penguin.

Lewis, R.S., & Anders, E. 1983. Science.

Lewis, I. (1988), Ecstatic religion: An anthropological study of spirit possession and shamanism. London: Routledge.

Lewis-Williams, D. (2002), The Mind in the Cave. London: Thames and Hudson.

Lewis-Williams, J. David. 1981. Believing and Seeing: Symbolic Meanings in Southern San Rock Paintings. London: Academic Press.

Lewis-Williams, J.D. & Dowson, T.A. 2000. Images of Power: Understanding San Rock Art. Cape Town: Struik Publishers.

Lewis-Williams, J.D. and Dowson, T.A. 1988. The signs of all times: Entoptic Phenomena in Upper Palaeolithic Art. Current Anthropology 29:201-245

Lewontin, R. C. 1998. The evolution of cognition: questions we will never answer. In D. Scarborough & S. Sternberg Eds., Methods, Models, and Conceptual Issues. An Invitation to Cognitive Science pp. 107-132. Cambridge, MA: MIT Press.

Li, W-H, et al., 2001 Evolutionary analyses of the human genome. Nature 409, 847 - 849 .

Lilly, J. C. 1972 The Center of the Cyclone, New York. Julian Press.

Lilly, R., Cummings, J. L., Benson, F., Frankel, M. 1983, The human Kluver-Bucy syndrome. Neurology, 3, 1141-1145.

Lindsey, L. L. 1990. Gender roles. A sociological perspective. Englewood Cliffs. Prentice Hall.

Lindsley, D. 1961. Common factors in sensory depr-vation. In P. Solomon Ed., Sensory deprivation. Cambridge: Harvard University Press.

Lings, M. 1983 Muhammad, his life based on the earliest sources. New York. Ballintine Books.

Lisk, W.G. 1967. Neural localization for androgen activation of copulatory behavior in the male rat. Endocrinology, 80,754-780.

Lisk, W.G. 1971. Diencephalic placement of estrodiol and sexual receptivity in the female rat.American Journal of Physiology, 203, 493-500.

Livesey, J.H., Evans, M.J., Mulligan, R., & Donald, R.A. 2000. Interactions of CRH, AVP and cortisol in the secretion of ACTH from perifused equine anterior pituitary cells, permissive roles for cortisol and CRH. Endocrine Research, 26 3,445-463.

Lohmann, Roger. 2001. The Role of Dreams in Religious Enculturation among the Asabano of Papua New Guinea. In Dreams: A Reader on the Religious, Cultural, and Psychological Dimensions of Dreaming, edited by K. Bulkeley. New York: Palgrave.

Lorenz, K. 1996. The natural science of the human species. Cambridge, MA: MIT Press.

Lotter, V. 1966 Epidemiology of autistic conditions in young children, 1: Prevalence. Social Psychology 1:124-137.

Lou, H.C., Kjaer, T.W., Friberg, L., et al. 1999. A 15O-H2O PET study of meditation and the resting state of normal consciousness. Human Brain Mapping, 7, 98-105.

Lowen, A. (1985) Narcissism: Denial of the True Self. New York: Macmillan, 1985.

Lowie, R. 1924 Primitive religion. New York: Boni and Liveright.

Lucretius. c. 99-55 BCE Lucretius: On the Nature of Things. W.H.D. Rouse, trans. Revised and edited by Martin F. Smith. Bailey, C. ed. De Rerum Natura. 3 volumes with commentary. Oxford, 1947. Cambridge, MA: Harvard University Press, 1992.

Ludwig, A. 1965 Witchcraft today. Diseases of the Nervous System 26:288-291.

Luna, Luis Eduardo and Amaringo, Pablo. 1999. Ayahuasca Visions: The Religious Iconogrpahy of a Peruvian Shaman. North Atlantic Books, Berkeley, California.

Luna, Luis Eduardo and White, Steven F. 2000. Ayahuasca Reader: Encounters with the Amazon's Sacred Vine. Sante Fe, Synergetic Press.

Luna, Luis Eduardo. 1984 Icaros: Magical Melodies excerpted from The Concept of Plants as Teachers among†four Mestizo Shamans of Iquitos, Northeastern Per·. Paper prepared for the Symposium on Shamanism of Phase 2 of the XIth International Congress of A

Luna, Luis Eduardo. 1984. ëPlant Teachers' published in Shamans Through Time, edited by Jeremy Narby and Francis Huxley. 2001, Thames & Hudson, pp 227-229.

Luther, Martin. 1945. Luther's Works. Translated by J. Pelikan. St. Louis: Concordia Publishing House.

Lynch, J. 1980 The functional organization of posterior parietal association cortex. Behavioral and Brain Sciences 3:485-499.

M'Timkulu, Donald. 1977. Some Aspects of Zulu Religion. In African Religions: A Symposium, edited by J. Newell S. Booth. New York: NOK Publications.

Mac Cormack, E. and Stamenov, M. (eds.) (1996) Fractals of Brain, Fractals of Mind. Amsterdam: John Benjamins.

MacLean, P. D. 1969 The hypothalamus and emotional behavior. In The hypothalamus.ed W. Haymaker pp. 127-167 Springfield. Thomas.

MacLean, P. D. 1990. The Triune Brain in Evolution. New York: Plenum.

Maglio, V. J. 1978. Evolution of African Mammals. Harvard University Press. Cambridge.

Makarec, K. & M. A. Persinger 1985. Temporal lobe signs: electroencephalographic validity and enhanced scores in special populations. Perceptual and Motor Skills 60 3: 831-42.

Makarec, K. & M. A. Persinger 1987. Electroencephalographic correlates of temporal lobe signs and imaginings. Perceptual and Motor Skills 64 3 Pt 2: 1124-6.

Makarec, K. & M. A. Persinger 1990. Electroencephalographic validation of temporal lobe signs inventory in normal populations. Journal of Research in Personality, 24: 323-337

Malakoff, D. 1999. Bayes offers a 'new' way to make sense of numbers. Science, 286, 1460-1464.

Malinowski, B. 1954 Magic, Science and Religion. New York. Doubleday.

Mandell, A. (1980), Toward a psychobiology of transcendence: God in the brain. In D. Davidson and R. Davidson, (Eds.), The psychobiology of consciousness (pp.379-464). New York: Plenum.

Mann, T. (1954) *Death in Venice*. New York: Random House.

Manning, A. 1972. An introduction to animal behavior. Menlo Park, Addison-Wesley.

Margulis, L. 1970. Origin of Eukaryotic cells, Yale U. Press, New Haven.

Marshall, J.F., & Teitelbaum, P. 1974.Further analysis of sensory inattention following lateral hypothalamic damage in rats.Journal of Comparative and Physiological Psychology, 86, 375-395.

Martin, J.P. 1950.Fits of laughter sham mirth in organic cerebral disease.Brain, 73, 453-464.

Martin, William T. 1984. Religiosity and United States Suicide Rates, 1972-1978, Journal of Clinical Psychology, Vol. 40 1984, pp. 1166-1169.

Marx, Karl. 1884. The Marx-Engels Reader. New York. W.W. Norton & Co.

Maslow, A. H. 1962. Lessons from the peak-experiences. Journal of Humanistic Psychology, 2, 9-18.

Maslow, A. (1974) *Motivation and Personality*. New York: Harper & Row.

Masters, R. 1974. Consciousness and extraordinary phenomena. In J. White Ed., Psychic exploration: A challenge for science pp. 598-614. New York: G. P. Putman's Sons.

Matthiessen, Peter. 1991. The Circle of Life: Rituals from the Human Family Album. San Francisco. Harper.

Maxam, A. M., & gilbert, W. 1977. A new method of sequencing DNA. Proceedings of the National Academy of Sciences, 74, 560-564.

McCarthy, G., Blamire, A.M., & Puce, A., et al. 1994. Functional magnetic resonance imaging of human prefrontal cortex activation during spatial working memory task. Proceedings of the National Academy of Sciences, 91,8690-8694.

McClenon, J. 1994. Wondrous events: Foundations of religious beliefs. Philadelphia: University of Pennsylvania Press.

McClennon, J. (2002), Wondrous healing Shamanism, human evolution and the origin of religion. DeKalb: Northern Illinois University Press.

McCown, T. 1937 Mugharet es-Skhul: Description and excavation, in The stone age of Mount Carmel. Edited by D. A. E. Garrod and D. Bate. Oxford: Clarendon Press.

McGaugh, J., Cahill, L., Parent, M., Mesches, M., Coleman-Mesches, K. & Salinas, J. 1995 Involvement of the amygdala in the regulation of memory storage. In J. McGaugh, F. Bermudez-Rattoni & R. Prado-Alcala eds., Plasticity in the central nervous syst

McKay, B. E., M. A. Persinger, et al. 2000. Exposure to a theta-burst patterned magnetic field impairs memory acquisition and consolidation for contextual but not discrete conditioned fear in rats. Neuroscience Letters 292 2: 99-102.

McKay, D. S., Gibson, E. K., Thomas-Keptra, K. L. 1996. Science, 273, 924-929.

McNamara, P. 2001. Religion and the frontal lobes. In Andresen, J. ed. Religion in Mind. Cambridge: Cambridge University Press.

McReady, N. 2002 Adrenergic blockers shortly after trauma can block PTSD. Clinical Psychiatry News, February.

Meier, C.A. 1967. Ancient Incubation and Modern Psychotherapy. Translated by M. Curtis. Evanston: Northwestern University Press.

Mellars, P. 1989. Major issues in the emergence of modern humans. Current Anthropology 30: 349-385.

Mellars, P. 1996 The Neanderthal legacy. Princeton University Press.

Mellars, P. 1998. The fate of the Neanderthals. Nature 395, 539-540.

Merker, B. (2000), Synchronous choursing and human origins. In N. Wallin, B. Merker and S. Brown. Eds. The origins of music. Cambridge (MA): MIT Press. Pp. 315-327.

Mesulam, M. M. 1981 Dissociative states with abnormal temporal lobe EEG: Multiple personality and the illusion of possession. Archives of General Psychiatry, 38, 176-181.

Metzinger, T. Ed 2000 Neural Correlates of Consciousness, Cambridge, Mass. MIT Press

Metzner, Ralph. 1999. Ayahuasca: Human Consciousness and the Spirits of Nature Ralph Metzner, Ph.D. editor with contributions by J.C. Callaway, Ph.D., Charles Grob, M.D., Dennis McKenna, Ph.D., and others. Thunder's Mouth Press, New York

Meyer, J. S., Ishikawa, Y., Hata, T., & Karacan, I. 1987 Cerebral blood flow in normal and abnormal sleep and dreaming. Brain and Behavior 6, 266-294.

Michon, A. L. & M. A. Persinger 1997. Experimental simulation of the effects of increased geomagnetic activity upon nocturnal seizures in epileptic rats. Neuroscience Letters 224 1: 53-60.

Miller, A. (1981) *The Drama of the Gifted Child.* New York: Basic Books.

Miller, D. 1982. The New Polytheism. Dallas: Spring Publications.

Miller, Patricia Cox. 1994. Dreams in Late Antiquity: Studies in the Imagination of a Culture. Princeton: Princeton University Press.

Mills, A., & Lynn, S. J. 2000. Past-life experiences. In E. Cardena, S. J. Lynn, & S. Krippner Eds., Varieties of anomalous experience: Examining the scientific evidence pp. 293-314. Washington, DC: American Psychological Association.

Mineka, S., Davidson, M., Cook, M. & Keir, R. 1984 Observational conditioning of snake fear in rhesus monkeys. Journal of Abnormal Psychology 93:355-372.

Mithen, S. 1996. The Prehistory of the Mind: A Search for the Origins of Art, Religion and Science. Phoenix: Thames and Keedson.

Milton, J. 1993. A meta-analysis of waking state of consciousness, free response ESP studies. Proceedings of the36th Annual Parapsychological Association Convention, 87-104.

Monod, J. (1971) *Chance and Necessity.* New York: Random House.

Montgomery, K.G. (1955) The role of the exploratory drive in learning. *Journal of Comparative Physiological Psychology* 47, 60-64.

Mojzsis, S. J. et al., 1996. Nature 384, 55-59.

Molino, J. (2000), Toward an evolutionary theory of music. In N. Wallin, B. Merker and S. Brown. Eds. The origins of music. Cambridge (MA): MIT Press. Pp.165-76.

Moller, M. 1992. Fine structure of pinealopetal innervation of the mammalian pineal gland. Microscope Research Technology, 21, 188-204.

Moody, R.A. 1975. Life After Life. Atlanta: Mockingbird Books.

Morgan, W. 1932. Navaho Dreams. American Anthropologist 34:390-405.

Moritz, C., Dowling, T. E. & Brown, W. M. 1987. Evolution of animal mitochondrial DNA: Relevance for population biology and systematics. Annual Review of Ecological Systematics 18: 269-292.

Morris, Desmond. 1967. The Naked Ape. London. Jonathan Cape Ltd.

Morris, J. S., Frith, C. D., Perett, D. I., Rowland, D., Young, A. W., Calder, A. J., & Colan, R. J. 1996. A differential neural response in the human amygdala to fearful and happy facial expression. Nature, 383, 812-815.

Morris, R. L., S. B. Harary, J. Janis, J. Hartwell, and W. G. Roll. 1978. Studies of communication during out-of-body experiences. Journal of the Society for Psychical Research, 72:1-22.

Morris, Richard. 1997. Achilles in the Quantum Universe: The Definitive History of Infinity. London: Souvenir.

Morse, J., P. Castillo, D. Venecia, J. Milstein, and D. C. Tyler. 1986. Childhood near-death experiences. American Journal of Diseases of Children, 140:1110-1114.

Morse, l., D. Venecia, and J. Milstein. 1989. Near-death experiences: A neurophysiological explanatory model. Journal of Near-Death Studies, 8 45-53.

Moss, B. O., Elroy-Stein, Mizukami, T., et al. 1990. New mammalian expression vectors. Nature, 348, 91-95.

Muller, R. (1991) *The Marginal Self.* Atlantic Highlands, NJ: Humanities Press International.

Munkur, B. 1983 The cult of the serpent. Albany: State University of New York Press.

Munro, C. & M. A. Persinger 1992. Relative right temporal-lobe theta activity correlates with Vingiano's hemispheric quotient and the sensed presence. Perceptual and Motor Skills 75 3 Pt 1: 899-903.

Murdock, G. P., & Provost,C. 1981. Factors in the Division of Labor by Sex. Ethnology, 12, 203-235;

Murphy, M. 1992. The future of the body: Explorations into the further evolution of human nature. Los Angeles: Tarcher.

Myers, F. W. H. 1903. Human personality and its survival of bodily death 2 Vols.. New York: Longmans, Green, & Company.

Nadler, R. D., & Braggio, J. T. 1974. Sex and species differences in captive reared juvenile chimpanzees and orangutans. Journal of Human Evolution.

Nakamura, K., & Ono, T. 1986. Lateral hypothalamus neuron involvement in integration of natural and artifical rewards and cue signals. Journal of Neurophysiology, 55, 163-181.

Neher, A. 1980. The psychology of transcendence. Englewood Cliffs, NJ: Prentice-Hall.

Nei, M., et al., 2001. Estimation of divergence times from multiprotein sequences for a few mammalian species and several distantly related organisms. Proc. Natl. Acad. Sci. 10, 1073

Neihardt, J. G. 1988 Black Elk Speaks. Nebraska, U. Nebraska Press.

Neithammer, C. 1977. Daughters of the earth. New York, Collier.

Nelson, P. L. 1989. Personality factors in the frequency of reported spontaneous praeternatural experiences. Journal of Transpersonal Psychology, 21, 193-210.

Nelson, R. D., Dunne, B. J, Dobyns, Y. H., & Jahn, R. G. 1996. Precognitive remote perception: Replication of remote viewing. Journal of Scientific Exploration, 10 1, 109-110.

Nesse, R. 1999 Evolution of commitment and the origins of religion. Science and Spirit 10:32-36.

Newberg A., Alavi, A., Baime, M., Pourdehnad, M., Santanna, J., & d'Aquili, E. 2001. The measurement of regional cerebral blood flow during the complex cognitive task of meditation: a preliminary SPECT study. Psychiatry Research,106 2, 113-22.

Newberg, A., A. Alavi, M. Baime, P.D. Mozley, and E. d'Aquili. 1997. The Measurement of Cerebral Blood Flow During the Complex Cognitive Task of Meditation Using HMPAO-SPECT Imaging. Journal of Nuclear Medicine 38: 95P.

Newberg, A.B., Alavi, A., Baime, M., et al. 2001. The measurement of regional cerebral blood flow during the complex cognitive task of meditation: A preliminary SPECT study. Psychiatry Research: Neuroimaging, 106, 113-122.

Newberg, A.B. and E.G. d'Aquili. 1994. iThe Near Death Experience as Archetype: A Model for 'Prepared' Neurocognitive Processes. The Anthropology of Consciousness, 5:1-15.

Newberg, A., & D'Aquili, E. 2001. Why God Won't Go Away: Brain Science & the Biology of Belief. New York, NY: Ballantine.

Newton, N. (1996) Foundations of Understanding. Amsterdam: John Benjamins.

Newton, N. (2000) Conscious emotion in a dynamic system: How I can know how I feel. In R. Ellis and N. Newton (Eds.), The Caldron of Consciousness: Motivation, Affect, and Self-organization. Amsterdam: John Benjamins, 91-108.

Newton, N. (2001) Emergence and the uniqueness of consciousness. Journal of Consciousness Studies 8, 47-59.

Nielsen, Tore. 2000. Cognition in REM and NREM Sleep: A Review and Possible Reconciliation of Two Models of Sleep Mentation. Behavioral and Brain Sciences 23 6:851-866.

Nietzsche, F. 1994. The Birth of Tragedy: Out of the Spirit of Music. M. Tanner editor. London: Penguin Classics.

Nigel, D. 1990. The Ancient Kingdoms of Mexico. Penguin, New York.

Nisbett, J. & Wilson, T. D. 1977 Telling more than we can know: Verbal reports on mental processes. Psychological Review, 84, 231-259.

Noegel, Scott. 2001. Dreams and Dream Interpreters in Mesopotamia and in the Hebrew Bible Old Testament. In Dreams: A Reader on the Religious, Cultural, and Psychological Dimensions of Dreaming, edited by K. Bulkeley. New York: Palgrave.

Noî, A. 2002 Ed In the Visual World a Grand Illusion? Thorverton, Devon, Imprint Academic.

Noll, R. (1983), Shamanism and schizophrenia: a state-specific approach to the schizophrenia metaphor of shamanic states. American Ethnologist, 10(3), 443-59.

Noll, R. (1985), Mental imagery cultivation as a cultural phenomenon: the role of visions in shamanism. Current Anthropology, 26, 443-451.

Norbu, Namkhai. 1992. Dream Yoga and the Practice of Natural Light. Ithaca: Snow Lions Publications.

Norenzayan, A. & Atran, S. 2002 Cognitive and emotional processes in the cultural transmission of natural and nonnatural beliefs. In M. Schaller & C. Crandall eds., The psychological foundations of culture. Hillsdale, NJ: Lawrence Erlbaum.

Noyes, R., & Kletti, R. 1977 Depersonalization in response to life threatening danger. Comprehensive Psychiatry, 18, 375-384.

O'Brien, S. J., Womack, J. E., Lyons, L. A., et al. 1993. Nature Genetics, 3, 103-112.

O'Flaherty, Wendy Doniger. 1984. Dreams, Illusion, and Other Realities. Chicago: University of Chicago Press.

O'Halloran, J.P., Jevning, R., & Wilson, A.F., et al. 1985. Hormonal control in a state of decreased activation, potentiation of arginine vasopressin secretion. Physiology and Behavior, 35 4,591-595.

O'Keefe, J.& Bouma, H. 1969. Complex sensory properties of certain amygdala units in the freely moving cat.Experimental Neurology, 23, 384-398.

O'Regan, J.K. and Noî, A. 2001 A sensorimotor account of vision and visual consciousness. Behavioral and Brain Sciences, 24.

Ochsner, K.N. & Lieberman, M.D. 2001. The emergence of social cognitive neuroscience. American Psychologist, 56 9, 717-734.

Offen, M. L., Davidoff, R. A., Troost, B. T., & Richey, E. T. 1976. Dacrystic epilepsy. Journal of Neurology,

Neurosurgery and Psychiatry, 39, 829-834.

Olds, J. A. 1956.A preliminary mapping of electrical reinforcing effects in rat brain.Journal of Comparative and Physiological Psychology, 49, 281-285.

Olds, J. A., & Milner, P. 1954.Positive reinforcement produced by electrical stimulation of septal areas and other regions of the rat brain. Journal of Comparative and Physiological Psychology, 47, 419-427.

Olds, M.E. & Forbes, J.L. 1981. The central basis of motivation, intracranial self-stimulation studies. Annual Review of Psychology, 32, 523-574.

Olmstead, C. E., Best, P. J.,& Mays, L. E. 1973 Neural activity in the dorsal hippocampus during paradoxical sleep, slow wave sleep and waking. Brain Research, 60, 381-391.

Ong, Roberto K. 1985. The Interpretation of Dreams in Ancient China. Bochum: Studienverlag Brockmeyer.

Onians, R. B. 1951. The Origins of European Thought About the Body, the Mind, the Soul, the World, Time, and Fate. Cambridge: Cambridge University Press.

Oppenheim, A. Leo. 1956. The Interpretation of Dreams in the Ancient Near East with a Translation of an Assyrian Dream-Book. Transactions of the American Philosophical Society 46 3:179-343.

Orgel, L. E. 1994. The origin of life on earth. Scientific American.271, 76-83.

Orne, M. T. 1962. On the social psychology of the psychological experiment: With particular reference to demand characteristics and their implications. American Psychologist, 17, 776-783.

Osborne, Kenneth E. 1970. A Christian Graveyard Cult in the New Guinea Highlands. Practical Anthropologist 46 3:10-15.

Ostow, M. and Scharfstein, B.A. 1953. The Need to Believe. International Univ. Press.

Otto, H. 1966. Multiple strength perception method, Minerva experience and others. In H. Otto Ed., Explorations in human potentialities pp. 471-486. Springfield, IL: Charles C. Thomas.

Otto, Rudolph. 1958. The Idea of the Holy. Translated by J. W. Harvey. New York: Oxford University Press.

Oubré, A. (1997), Instinct and revelation reflections on the origins of numinous perception. Amsterdam: Gordon & Breach.

Oulis, P., Mavreas, V., Mamounas, J. & Stefanis, C. 1995 Clinical characeristics of auditory hallucinations. Acta Psychiatrica Scandinavica 92:97-102.

Ovchinnikov, I. V., et al., 2000.Molecular analysis of Neanderthal DNA from the northern Caucasus.Nature, 2000.

Pahnke, W. 1970. Drugs and mysticism. In B. Aaronson & H. Osmond Eds., Psychedelics: The uses and implications of hallucinogenic drugs pp. 145-164. Garden City, NY: Anchor Books.

Paloutzian, R. F. & Smith, B. 1995. The utility of the religion-as-schema model. The International Journal for the Psychology of Religion,

Pandian, J. (1997), The sacred integration of the cultural self: An anthropological approach to the study of religion. In S. Glazier (Ed.), The anthropology of religion,(pp.505-516). Westport, Conn.: Greenwood Press.

Panksepp, J. 1995 The emotional source of ìchills induced by music. Music Perception 13:171-207.

Panksepp, J. (1998) *Affective Neuroscience*. New York: Oxford University Press.

Panksepp, J. (2000) The neuro-evolutionary cusp between emotions and cognitions: Implications for understanding consciousness and the emergence of a unified mind science. *Consciousness & Emotion* 1, 17-56.

Pardo, J.V., Fox, P.T., & Raichle, M.E. 1991. Localization of a human system for sustained attention by positron emission tomography. Nature, 349, 61-64.

Parrinder, G. 1980 Sex in the World's religions. Oxford University Press. New York

Pascal, Blaise. 1660. Pensees: Section III of The Necessity of the Wager. Translated by W.F. Trotter.

Passingham, R. 1993 The frontal lobes and voluntary action. Oxford: Oxford University Press.

Pathy, L. 1991. Exons—original building blocks of proteins? BioEssays, 13, 187-192.

Patton, Kimberley. 2002. Dream Incubation: Theology and Topography. Paper read at 19th International Conference of the Association for the Study of Dreams, June 19, at Boston, Massachussetts.

Payne, R. 1973 The Life and death of Adolf Hitler. New York, Praeger.

Peel, J.D.Y. 1968. Aladura: A Religious Movement among the Yoruba. London: Oxford University Press.

Penfield, W. 1952 Memory Mechanisms. Archives of Neurology and Psychiatry, 67, 178-191.

Penfield, W. 1975. The Mystery of the Mind: A Critical Study of Consciousness. Princeton, N. J.: Princeton Univ. Press.

Penfield, W., & Perot, P. 1963 The brains record of auditory and visual experience. Brain, 86, 595-695.

Peng, C.K., Mietus, J.E., & Liu, Y., et al. 1999. Exaggerated heart rate oscillations during two meditation techniques. International Journal of Cardiology, 70,101-107.

Persinger, M. 1983 Religious and mystical experiences as artifacts of temporal lobe function. Perceptual and Motor Skills 57:1255-1262.

Persinger, M. 1984 Striking EEG profiles from single episodes of glossolalia and transcendental meditation.

Perceptual and Motor Skills 58:127-133.

Persinger, M. 1987 Neurophysiological bases of God beliefs. New York: Praeger.

Persinger, M. 1997 I would kill in God's name, Role of sex, weekly church attendance, report of a religious experience, and limbic liability. Perceptual and Motor Skills 71:817-818.

Persinger, M. A. 1983. Religious and mystical experiences as artifacts of temporal lobe function: a general hypothesis. Perceptual and Motor Skills 57 3 Pt 2: 1255-62.

Persinger, M. A. 1984. People who report religious experiences may also display enhanced temporal-lobe signs. Perceptual and Motor Skills 58 3: 963-75.

Persinger, M. A. 1985. Death anxiety as a semantic conditioned suppression paradigm. Perceptual and Motor Skills 60 3: 827-30.

Persinger, M. A. 1987. MMPI profiles of normal people who display frequent temporal-lobe signs. Perceptual and Motor Skills 64 3 Pt 2: 1112-4.

Persinger, M. A. 1988. Increased geomagnetic activity and the occurrence of bereavement hallucinations: evidence for melatonin-mediated microseizuring in the temporal lobe? Neuroscience Letters 88 3: 271-4.

Persinger, M. A. 1988. Temporal lobe signs and personality characteristics. Perceptual and Motor Skills 66 1: 49-50.

Persinger, M. A. 1989. Geophysical variables and behavior: LV. Predicting the details of visitor experiences and the personality of experients: the temporal lobe factor. Perceptual and Motor Skills 68 1: 55-65.

Persinger, M. A. 1991. Preadolescent religious experience enhances temporal lobe signs in normal young adults. Perceptual and Motor Skills 72 2: 453-4.

Persinger, M. A. 1991. Subjective pseudocyesis false pregnancy and elevated temporal lobe signs: an implication. Perceptual and Motor Skills 72 2: 499-503.

Persinger, M. A. 1992. Enhanced incidence of the sensed presence in people who have learned to meditate: support for the right hemispheric intrusion hypothesis. Perceptual and Motor Skills 75 3 Pt 2: 1308-10.

Persinger, M. A. 1992. Criterion validity for Rotton's paralogic test: beliefs of forbidden knowledge may negatively affect inferential problem solving. Perceptual and Motor Skills 74: 296-298.

Persinger, M. A. 1993. Paranormal and religious beliefs may be mediated differentially by subcortical and cortical phenomenological processes of the temporal limbic lobes. Perceptual and Motor Skills 76 1: 247-51.

Persinger, M. A. 1993. Transcendental Meditation and general meditation are associated with enhanced complex partial epileptic-like signs: evidence for cognitive kindling? Perceptual and Motor Skills 76 1: 80-2.

Persinger, M. A. 1993. Vectorial cerebral hemisphericity as differential sources for the sensed presence, mystical experiences and religious conversions. Perceptual and Motor Skills 76 3 Pt 1: 915-30.

Persinger, M. A. 1994. Seizure suggestibility may not be an exclusive differential indicator between psychogenic and partial complex seizures: the presence of a third factor. Seizure 3 3: 215-9.

Persinger, M. A. 1994. Sense of a presence and suicidal ideation following traumatic brain injury: indications of right-hemispheric intrusions from neuropsychological profiles. Psychological Reports 75 3 Pt 1: 1059-70.

Persinger, M. A. 1995. Geophysical variables and behavior: LXXIX. Overt limbic seizures are associated with concurrent and premidscotophase geomagnetic activity: synchronization by prenocturnal feeding. Perceptual and Motor Skills 81 1: 83-93.

Persinger, M. A. 1995. On the possibility of directly accessing every human brain by electromagnetic induction of fundamental algorithms. Perceptual and Motor Skills 80 3 Pt 1: 791-9.

Persinger, M. A. 1996. Enhancement of limbic seizures by nocturnal application of experimental magnetic fields that simulate the magnitude and morphology of increases in geomagnetic activity. International Journal of Neuroscience 86 3-4: 271-80.

Persinger, M. A. 1996. Feelings of past lives as expected perturbations within the neurocognitive processes that generate the sense of self: contributions from limbic lability and vectorial hemisphericity. Perceptual and Motor Skills 83 3 Pt 2: 1107-

Persinger, M. A. 1997. I would kill in God's name: role of sex, weekly church attendance, report of a religious experience, and limbic lability. Perceptual and Motor Skills 85 1: 128-30.

Persinger, M. A. 1999. Increased emergence of alpha activity over the left but not the right temporal lobe within a dark acoustic chamber: differential response of the left but not the right hemisphere to transcerebral magnetic fields. International J

Persinger, M. A. 2001. The neuropsychiatry of paranormal experiences. Journal of Neuropsychiatry & Clinical Neuroscience 13 4: 515-24.

Persinger, M. A., & Koren, S. A. 2001. Predicting the characteristics of haunt phenomena from geomagnetic factors and brain sensitivity: Evidence from field and experimental studies. In J. Houran and R. Lange Eds., Hauntings and Poltergeists: Multidis

Persinger, M. A., S. G. Tiller, et al. 2000. Experimental simulation of a haunt experience and elicitation of paroxysmal electroencephalographic activity by transcerebral complex magnetic fields: induction of a synthetic ghost? Perceptual and Motor Skills.

Persinger, M. A. & K. Makarec 1992. The feeling of a presence and verbal meaningfulness in context of temporal lobe function: factor analytic verification of the muses? Brain & Cognition 20 2: 217-26.

Persinger, M. A. & K. Makarec 1993. Complex partial epileptic signs as a continuum from normals to epileptics: normative data and clinical populations. Journal of Clinical Psychology 49 1: 33-45.

Persinger, M. A. & P. M. Richards 1994. Quantitative electroencephalographic validation of left and right temporal lobe signs and indicators in normal people. Perceptual and Motor Skills 79 3 Pt 2: 1571-8.

Persinger, M. A., P. M. Richards, et al. 1994. Differential ratings of pleasantness following right and left hemispheric application of low energy magnetic fields that stimulate long-term potentiation. International Journal of Neuroscience 79 3-4: 19.

Persinger, M. A. & P. M. Richards 1995. Vestibular experiences of humans during brief periods of partial sensory deprivation are enhanced when daily geomagnetic activity exceeds 15-20 nT. Neuroscience Letters 194 1-2: 69-72.

Persinger, M. A. & P. M. Valliant 1985. Temporal lobe signs and reports of subjective paranormal experiences in a normal population: a replication. Perceptual and Motor Skills 60 3: 903-9.

Persinger, M. A. & S. A. Koren 2001. Experiences of spiritual visitation and impregnation: potential induction by frequency-modulated transients from an adjacent clock. Perceptual and Motor Skills 92 1: 35-6.

Persinger, M. A., Y. R. Bureau, et al. 1993. Behaviors of rats with insidious, multifocal brain damage induced by seizures following single peripheral injections of lithium and pilocarpine. Physiology & Behavior 53 5: 849-66.

Persinger, M. A., Y. R. Bureau, et al. 1994. The sensed presence as right hemispheric intrusions into the left hemispheric awareness of self: an illustrative case study. Perceptual and Motor Skills 78 3 Pt 1: 999-1009.

Pert, C. 1997 Molecules of Emotion. New York, Scribner.

Peters, L. & D. Price-Williams. (1981), Towards an experiential analysis of shamanism. American Ethnologist, 7, 398-418.

Petes, T., & Fink, G. R. 1982. Gene conversion between repeated genes. Nature, 300, 216-217.

Phelps, M.E. & Mazziota, J.C. 1985. Positron emission tomography. Human brain function and biochemistry. Science, 228, 799-809.

Phelps, M.E., Kuhl, D.E., & Mazziotta, J.C. 1981. Metabolic mapping of the brain's response to visual stimualtion. Studies in man. Science, 211, 1445-1448.

Phillips, M. & David, A. 1995 Facial processing in schizophrenia and delusional misidentification. Schizophrenia Research 17:109-114.

Pietrowsky, R., Braun, D., Fehm, H.L., Pauschinger, P., & Born, J. 1991. Vasopressin and oxytocin do not influence early sensory processing but affect mood and activation in man. Peptides, 12 6, 1385-1391.

Plato. 1957. The Republic of Plato. Translated by A. D. Lindsay. New York: E.P. Dutton.

Plato. 1961. Crito. In Plato: Collected Dialogues, edited by H. Cairns. Princeton: Princeton University Press.

Plato. 1961. Phaedo. In Plato: Collected Dialogues, edited by H. Cairns. Princeton: Princeton University Press.

Polaczyk, P. J., Gasperini, R., & Gibson, G. 1998. Naturally occurring genetic variation affects Drosophilia photoreceptor determination. Developl. Genes Evol. 207, 462-470.

Poletti, C.E. & Sujatanond, M. 1980. Evidence for a second hippocampal efferent pathway to hypothalamus and basal forebrain comparable to fornix system: A unit study in the monkey. Journal of Neurophysiology, 44, 514-531.

Polivoy, Silvia. The psychotherapeutic employment of sacred plants. Article published on the internet at: psychointegrator.yage.net/article.html

Pratt, J.B. 1920, 1934. The Religious Consciousness: A Psychological Study. New York: Macmillan.

Pressel, E. 1974 Umbanda trance and possession in Sao Paulo, Brazil. In F. Goodman, J. Henney & E. Pressel eds., Trance healing and hallucination. London: Wiley.

Prideaux, T. 1973. Cro-Magnon. New York: Time-Life.

Prince, R. (1982), The endorphins: A review for psychological anthropologists. Ethos, 10(4), 299-302.

Prigogine, I. (1996) The End of Certainty: Time, Chaos, and the New Laws of Nature. New York: Free Press.

Proudfoot, W. 1985 Religious Experience. Berkeley: University of California Press.

Proust, Marcel. c. 1913-1925. Remembrance of Things Past. New York. Knopf Press. 1982.

Pruyser, P. W. 1968. A Dynamic Psychololgy of Religion. New York: Harper & Row.

Racine, J. (1968) Phaedra. In Samuel Weiss (Ed.), Drama in the Western World. Chicago: Raytheon, pp. 176-216.

Radin, D. I. 1997. The conscious universe: Truth of psychic phenomena. San Francisco: HarperCollins.

Radin, D. I., & Ferrari, D. C. 1991. Effects of consciousness on the fall of dice: A meta-analysis. Journal of Scientific Exploration, 5, 61-83.

Radin, D. I., & Nelson, R. D. 1989. Evidence for consciousness-related anomalies in random physical systems. Foundations of Physics, 19, 1499-1514.

Radin, Paul. 1936. Ojibwa and Ottawa Puberty Dreams. In Essays in Anthropology Presented to A.L. Kroeber. Berkeley: University of California Press.

Rainbow, T.C., Parsons, B., & McEwen, B.A. 1982.Sex differences in rat brain oestrogen and progestin receptors. Nature, 300, 648-649.

Raisman, G. & Field, P.M. 1973. Sexual dimorphism in the neuropil of the preoptic area of the rat and its dependence on neonatal androgen. Brain Research, 54, 1-29.

Rajaram, M. & Mitra, S. 1981. Correlations between convulsive seizures and geomagnetic activity. Neuroscience Letters, 24: 187-191.

Ramachandran, V. S., and Blakeslee, S. 1998. Phantoms in the Brain. New York: Morrow.

Rank, O. (1924/1993) The Trauma of Birth. New York: Dover.

Rambo, Lewis. 1995. Understanding Religious Conversion Yale University press.

Ramone Greenberg, R. Pillard, and C. Pearlman. 1972. The Effect of Dream REM Deprivation on Adaptation to Stress. Psychosomatic Medicine 34:257-262.

Ramsden, E.H. 1963. The Letter of Michalangelo; Edited and Translated by E.H. Ramsden, Stanford University Press.

Ransom, T. W., & Powell, T. E. 1972. Early social development of feral baboons. In F. E. Poirer ed.. Primate socialization. New York, Random House.

Rao, S.M., Binder, J.R., & Hammeke, T.A., et al. 1995. Somatotopic mapping of the human primary motor cortex with functional magnetic resonance imaging. Neurology,45,919-924.

Rappaport, R. 1979 Ecology, meaning, and religion. Berkeley: Atlantic Books.

Rappoport, R. A. 1992. Ritual, Time and Eternity. Zygon: Journal of Religion & Science, 27: 5-30.

Rappaport, R. 1999 Ritual and religion in the making of humanity. Cambridge, UK: Cambridge University Press.

Ratey, J. & Johnson, C. 1998 Shadow syndromes. New York: Bantam Doubleday.

Redding, F.K. 1967. Modification of sensory cortical evoked potentials by hippocampal stimulation. Electroencephalography and Clinical Neurophysiology, 22, 74-83.

Redfield, R. & Villa Rojas, A. 1934 Chan Kom: A Maya village. Chicago: University of Chicago Press.

Reed, G. 1988. The psychology of anomalous experience rev. ed.. Buffalo, NY: Prometheus Books.

Reghunandanan, V., Reghunandanan, R., & Mahajan, K.K. 1998. Arginine vasopressin as a neurotransmitter in the brain. Indian Journal of Experimental Biology, 36 7, 635-643.

Reina, R. 1966 The law of the saint. Bobbs-Merrill.

Reinisch, J. M., and Sanders, S. A. 1992. Prenatal hormonal contributions to sex differences in human cognitive and personality development. In Gerall, A. A., Moltz, H., & Ward, I. L. Eds., Handbook of Behavioral Neurobiology, Vol. 11, Sexual Differention. Plenum.

Reik, T. (1945) Psychology of Sex Relations New York: Rinehart.

Reithman, H. C., et al., 2001 Integration of telomere sequences with the draft human genome sequence. Nature 409, 948 - 951.

Remmillard, G. M., Andermann, F., Testas, G. F., et al. 1983 Sexual ictal manifestations predominant in women with temporal lobe epilepsy. Neurology, 33, 323-330.

Renaud, L.P. 1996. CNS pathways mediating cardiovascular regulation of vasopressin. Clinical and Experimental Pharmacology and Physiology, 23 2,157-160.

Revonsuo, Antti. 2000. The Reinterpretation of Dreams: An Evolutionary Hypothesis of the Function of Dreaming. Behavioral and Brain Sciences 23 6.

Richmond, B. J., Optican, L. M., Podel, M., & Spitzer, H. 1987 Temporal encoding of two-dimensional patterns by single units in primate inferior temporal cortex. Journal of Neurophysiology, 57, 132-162

Richmond, B. J., Wurtz, R. H., & Sato, T. 1983 Visual responses of inferior temporal neurons in awake rhesus monkey. Journal of Neurophysiology, 50, 1415-1432.

Richter, I.A. 1952. Selections from the Notebooks of Leonardo da Vinci. London: Oxford University Press, p. 278.

Richter, I.A. 1952. Selections from the Notebooks of Leonardo da Vinci. London: Oxford University Press, p. 278.

Rightmire, G. P. 1984 Homo sapiens in Sub-Saharan Africa, in The origins of modern humans: A world survey of the fossil evidence. Edited by F. H. Smith and F. Spencer. New York: Alan R. Liss.

Ring, K. 1980. Life at Death: A Scientific Investigation of the Near-Death Experience. New York: Quill

Publishers.

Ring, K. 1980. Life at Death. New York: Coward, McCann & Geoghegan.

Ring, K.1986. Heading Toward Omega. New York: Morrow.

Rinpoche, Tenzin Wangyal. 1998. The Tibetan Yogas of Dream and Sleep. Ithaca: Snow Lions Publications.

Ritchie, D. 1994. UFO. Facts on File, NY

Rohrer, Tim. 1995. Boundless Paradox: a discussion of Heraclitus, Anaximander and Gorgias. Paper posted on the internet at: http://philosophy.uoregon.edu/metaphor/psabstr.htm

Roll, W. G. 1960. [Book review of Psyche by Hans Berger]. Journal of Parapsychology, 24, 142-148.

Rolls, E. T. 1984. Neurons in the cortex of the temporal lobe and in the amygdala of the monkey with responses selective for faces. Human Neurobiology, 3, 209-222.

Rolls, E. T. 1992. Neurophysiology and functions of the primate amygdala. In J. P. Aggleton Ed.. The Amygdala. pp. 143-166. New York: Wiley-Liss.

Rolls, E.T., Burton, M.J., & Mora, F. 1976.Hypothalamic neuronal response associated with the sight of food.Brain Research, 111, 53-66.

Rosch, E., Mervis, C., Grey, W., Johnson, D., & Boyes-Braem, P. 1976 Basic objects in natural categories. Cognitive Psychology 8:382-439.

Rosenbaum, R. 1999. Explaining Hitler. Harper, New York.

Rosenthal, R. 1966. Experimenter effects in behavioral research. New York: Appleton-Century-Crofts.

Ross, J. & M. A. Persinger 1987. Positive correlations between temporal lobe signs and hypnosis induction profiles: a replication. Perceptual and Motor Skills 64 3 Pt 1: 828-30.

Roux, G. 1992 Ancient Iraq.Penguin, New York.

Rudavsky, S. 1991 The secret life of the Neanderthal. Omni 14:42- 44, 55-56.

Russell, M., et al., 1999. The Journal of the Geological Society of London, 156, 869-870.

Rutherford, S. L., & Lindquist, S. 1998. Hsp90 as a capacitor for morphological evolution. Nature 396, 336-342.

Ruttan, L. A. & M. A. Persinger 1989. Temporal lobe signs and enhanced pleasantness scores for words generated during spontaneous narratives. Perceptual and Motor Skills 69 3 Pt 2: 1101-2.

Ryan, R. (1999), The strong eye of shamanism: a journey into the caves of consciousness. Rochester: Inner Traditions.

Saavedra-Aguilar, J. C., and l S. Gomez-Jeria 1989. Journal of Near-Death Studies, 7: 205-222.

Sabom, M. 1982. Recollections of Death. New York: Harper & Row.

Sabom, M. 1998. Light and death: One doctor's fascinating account of near-death experiences. Grand Rapids, MI: Zondervan.

Sabourin, L. & M. A. Persinger 1987. Specific temporal-lobe signs and enhanced delayed cross-modal matching performance. Perceptual and Motor Skills 64 1: 309-10.

Sackville-West 1943 The eagle and the dove. London: Michael Joseph.

Sadock, Benjamin and Sadock, Virginia 2000. The Comprehensive Textbook of Psychiatry, 7th ed. Lippincott. Williams and Wilkins Press.

Sagan, C. 1979. Broca's Brain. New York: Random House.

Saghir, G. B.,& Robins, E. 1973. Male and female homosexuality. Baltimore, Williams & Wilkins.

Salmela, M. (2002) The problem of affectivity in cognitive theories of emotion. Consciousness & Emotion 3 (forthcoming).

Sancar, A. 1994. Mechanisms of DNA excision repair. Science, 266, 1954-1956.

Sanford, John. 1982. Dreams: God's Forgotten Language. New York: Crossroads.

Santillana & von Dechen, 1969. Hamlet's Mill. Nonpareil Books, Boston.

Sarich, V. 1970. Primate systematics. In Old Word Monkeys. J. R. Napier & P. H. Napier Eds. 175-226. Academic Press, New York.

Savary, L.M., P.H. Berne, and Strephon Kaplan Williams. 1984. Dreams and Spiritual Growth: A Christian Approach to Dreamwork. Mahwah: Paulist Press.

Saver, J.L. & Rabin, J. 1997. The neural substrates of religious experience. Journal of Neuropsychiatry & Clinical Neuroscience, 9 3, 498-510.

Schacter, D. L. 1996. Searching for Memory: The Brain, the Mind, and the Past. New York: Basic Books.

Schaller, G. B. 1963. The Mountain Gorilla. Chicago. University of Chicago Press.

Schechter, E. I. 1984. Hypnotic induction vs. control conditions: Illustrating an approach to the evaluation of replicability in parapsychological data. Journal of the American Society for Psychical Research, 78, 1-27.

Schlemmler, A. 1990. Mysteries of the Mexican Pyramids. Thames & Hudson, London.

Schenk, L., & Bear, D. 1981 Multiple personality and related dissociative phenomenon in patients with temporal lobe epilepsy. American Journal of Psychiatry, 138, 1311-1316.

Schenkel, R. 1966. Play, exploration, and territoriality in the wild lion. In P. A. Jewell & C. Loizos eds.. Play, exploration and territoriality. Academic Press. London.

Schiller, F. C. S. 1994. Riddles of the sphinx: A study in the philosophy of evolution. London: Swan Sonnenschein & Co. Original work published 1891

Schlitz, M., & Braud, W. G. 1997. Distant intentionality and healing: Assessing the evidence. Alternative Therapies, 3 6, 62-73.

Schmahmann, J. (Ed.) (1997) *The Cerebellum and Cognition.* New York: Academic Press.

Schmahmann, J., C. Anderson, N. Newton and R. Ellis (2001) The function of the cerebellum in cognition, affect and consciousness: Empirical support for the embodied mind. *Consciousness & Emotion* 2, 273-309.

Schmidt, L. & Trainor, L. 2001 Frontal brain electrical activity EEG distinguishes valence and intensity of musical emotions. Cognition and Emotion 15:487-500.

Schneider, D. M., and Lauriston Sharp. 1969. The Dream Life of a Primitive People: the Dreams of the Yir Yoront of Australia. Washington, D.C.: American Anthropological Association.

Schock, R. M. 1992. Sphinx, riddle put to rest. Science, 255, 101-103.

Schoonmaker, F. 1979. Denver cardiologist discloses findings after 18 years of near-death research. Anabiosis, 1:1-2.

Schopf, J. W. 1978The evolution of the earliest cells. Scientific American, 1978, 239, 84-100.

Schopf, J. W. 1992. The oldest fossils and what they mean. In J.W. Schopf ed.. Major events in the history of life. New York, Bartlett.

Schopf, J. W. 1999. Cradle of life: The discovery of Earth's earliest fossils. Princeton University Press.

Schopf,J. W. 1993. Science.640.

Schwarcz, et al. 1988 ESR dates for the hominid burial site of Qafzeh. Journal of Human Evolution 17:

Scott, S. K., Young, B. S., Calder, A. J., Hellawell, D. J., Aggleton, J. P., & Johnson, M. 1997. Impaired auditory recognition of fear and anger following bilateral amygdala lesions. Nature, 385, 254-257.

Serafetinides, E. A. 1965 The significance of the temporal lobes and of hemisphere dominance in the production of the LSD-25 symptomology in man. Neuropsychologia, 3, 69-79.

Sergent, J. 1994. Brain-imaging studies of cognitive functions. Trends in Neuroscience, 17, 221-227.

Sethi, P. K., & Raio, S. T. 1976. Gelastic, quiritarian, and cursive epilepsy. Journal of Neurology, Neurosurgery and Psychiatry, 39, 823-828.

Seznec, J. 1981. The Survival of the Pagan Gods: The Mythological Tradition and Its Place in Renaissance Humanism and Art, tr. B. F. Sessions. Princeton: Princeton University Press.

Shafton, Anthony. 2002. Dream-Singers: The African American Way with Dreams. New York: John Wiley & Sons.

Shaji, A.V. & Kulkarni, S.K. 1998. Central nervous system depressant activities of melatonin in rats and mice. Indian Journal of Experimental Biology, 36 3, 257-63.

Shakespeare, William. c. 1564-1616. Julius Caeser. London. Oxford University Press. 1914.

Shaw, M.C. Jedrej and Rosalind, ed. 1992. Dreaming, Religion, and Society in Africa. Leiden: E.J. Brill.

Shear, Jonathan. 2001. Experimental Studies of Meditation and Consciousness. In Religion and Psychology: Mapping the Terrain, edited by W. Parsons. London: Routledge.

Sheils, D. 1978. A cross-cultural study of beliefs in out-of-the-body experiences. Journal of the Society for Psychical Research, 49:697-741.

Shekar, C. (1989), Possession syndrome in India. In C. Ward (Ed.) Altered states of consciousness and mental health, (pp.79-95). Newbury Park, Ca.: Sage.

Sheng, M., & greenberg, M. E., 1990. The regulation and function of c-fos and other immediate early genes in the nervous system. Neuron, 4, 477-485.

Shirer, W. L. 1941. Berlin Diary. New York.

Shirer, W. L. 1960. The Rise and Fall of the Third Reich, Fawcett, New York.

Schwaller de Lubicz, 1988. Sacred Science: The King of Pharonic Theocracy. Inner Traditions International, Vermont.

Sellers, J. B. 1992. The Death of the Gods in Ancient Egypt. Penguin, New York.

Shweder, Richard, and R.A. Levine, 1975. Dream Concepts of Hausa Children: A Critique of the Doctrine of Invariant Sequence. Ethos 3 209-230.

Siddhartha,Gautama. c. 525 BCE. The Dhammapada. Oxford. Clarendon Press. 1881.

Siikala, A. (1978), The rite technique of Siberian shaman. Folklore fellows communication 220. Helsinki: Soumalainen Tiedeskaremia Academia.

Sim, M.K., & Tsoi, W.F. 1992. The effects of centrally acting drugs on the EEG correlates of meditation. Biofeedback & Self Regulation. 17 3, 215-220.

Sitchen, Z. 1980. The stairway to haven. Avon, New York.

Sitchin, Z. 1990 The lost realms. New York. Avon.

Skirda, R. J. & M. A. Persinger 1993. Positive associations among dichotic listening errors, complex partial epileptic-like signs, and paranormal beliefs. Journal of Nervous and Mental Disease 181 11: 663-7.

Slater, E. & Beard, A. W. 1963. ïThe schizophrenic-like psychosis of epilepsy. British Journal of Psychiatry, 109: 95-150.

Slater, E. & Beard, A. 1963 The schizophrenia-like psychoses of epilepsy. I, V. British Journal of Psychiatry 109:95-112, 143-150.

Smart, N. 1969 The religious experience of mankind. New York.

Smirnov, Y. A. 1989 On the evidence for Neandertal burial. Current Anthropology 30: 324.

Smith, A. 1993[1776] An inquiry into the nature and causes of the wealth of nations. Oxford: Oxford University Press.

Smith, Adam. 1776. An Inquiry into the Nature and Causes of the Wealth of Nations. Vol 1. London. Denton & Sons. 1904.

Smith, Carlyle. 1993. REM Sleep and Learning: Some Recent Findings. In The Functions of Dreaming, edited by R. Hoffmann. Albany: State University of New York Press.

Smith, H. W. [1870] 1952.The Christian's Secret of a Happy Life. Old Tappan, N.J.: Revell.

Smyth, C. P. 1990. The Great Pyramid: Its Secrets and Mysteries Revealed. Bell, New York.

Solecki, R. 1971 Shanidar: The first flower people. New York: Knopf.

Solms, Mark. 1997. The Neuropsychology of Dreams: A Clinico-Anatomical Study. Mahway: Lawrence Erlbaum.

Southard, E. E. 1919 Shell-shock and other Neuropsychiatric Problems. Boston.

Spare, Austin O. Anathema of Zos. The Sermon of the Hypocrites. 1927.

Spencer, S. S., et al., 1983 Sexual automatisms in complex partial seizures. Neurology, 33, 527-533.

Sperber, D., Premack, D. & Premack, A., eds. 1995 Causal cognition. Oxford: Clarendon Press.

Spilka, B. & McIntosh D. N. 1995. Attribution theory and religious experience. In Handbook of religious experience, pp. 421-445. R. W. Hood, Jr. ed.. Religious Education Press, Birmingham, Alabama.

Spilka, B., Brown, G. & Cassidy, S. 1992. The structure of religious mystical experience. International Journal for the Psychology of Religion. 2:241-257.

Spilka, B. & D. McIntosh, eds. (1997), The psychology of religion: Theoretical approaches. Boulder, CO: Westview Press.

Spilka, B., P. Shaver, and L. Kirkpatrick. (1997), A general attribution theory for the psychology of religion. In B. Spilka & D. McIntosh (Eds.), The psychology of religion (pp.). Boulder, CO.: Westview Press.

Spitz, R.A., & Wolf, K.M. (1946) Anaclitic depression: An inquiry into the genesis of psychiatric conditions in early childhood. *P.A. Study of the Child, II*. New York: International University Press.

Spratling, W. P. 1904. Epilepsy and Its Treatment. Philadelphia: W. B. Saunders.

St-Pierre, L. S., M. A. Persinger, et al. 1998. Experimental induction of intermale aggressive behavior in limbic epileptic rats by weak, complex magnetic fields: implications for geomagnetic activity and the modern habitat? International Journal.

Stace, W. T. 1960. Mysticism and philosophy. Philadelphia: Lippincott.

Stack, S., & Wasserman, I., 1992. ïThe Effect of Religion on Suicideî. Journal for the Scientific Study of Religion, 31, 457-466Proceedings of the 36th Annual Parapsychological Association Convention, 105-125.

Stark, R. (1997), A taxonomy of religious experience. In B. Spilka & D. McIntosh (Eds.), The psychology of religion: Theoretical approaches (pp.). Boulder, CO: Westview Press.

Steklis, H. D., & Kling, A. 1985. Neurobiology of affiliative behavior in nonhuman primates. In M. Reite & T. Fields Eds.. The Psychobiology of attachment and separation, pp. 93-134. Orlando, FL: Academic Press.

Stephen, Michelle. 1995. A'Aisa's Gifts: A Study of Magic and the Self. Berkeley: University of California Press.

Stephen, Michelle. 1979. Dreams of Change: The Innovative Role of Altered States of Consciousness in Traditional Melanesian Religion. Oceania 50 1:3-22.

Stern, D. 1985. The interpersonal world of the infant. New York: Basic Books.

Stern, E. & Silbersweig, D. 1998 Neural mechanisms underlying hallucinations in schizophrenia. In M. Lenzenweger & R. Dworkin eds., Origins and development of schizophrenia. Washington, DC: American Psychological Association.

Stevens, A. 1982. Archetype: A Natural History of the Self. London: Routledge & Kegan Paul.

Stevens, A. 1993. The Two Million-Year-Old Self. College Station: Texas A&M University Press.

Stevenson, I. 1970. Telepathic impressions: A review and report of thirty-five new cases. Charlottesville: University of Virginia Press.

Stewart, Ian and Cohen, Jack. 1997. Figments of Reality: The Evolution of the Curious Mind. United Kingdom: Cambridge Press.

Stewart, L. S. & M. A. Persinger 2000. Pretraining exposure to physiologically patterned electromagnetic stimulation attenuates fear-conditioned analgesia. International Journal of Neuroscience 100 1-4: 91-8.

Stone, M. 1997 Healing the Mind. New York, W.W. Norton.

Strachan, T., & Read, A. 1996. Human molecular genetics. Wiley, NY.

Strassman, R.J. 2001. DMT: The Spirit Molecule. Park Street Press, Rochester.

Strauss, E., Risser, A., & Jones, M. W. 1982. Fear responses in patients with epilepsy. Archives of Neurology, 39, 626-630.

Storm, L., & Ertel, S. 2001. Does psi exist? Comments on Milton and Wiseman's 1999 meta-analysis of ganzfeld research. Psychological Bulletin, 127, 424-433.

Storm, L., & Thalbourne, M. in press. Paranormal effects using sighted and vision-impaired participants in a quasi-ganzfeld task. Australian Journal of Parapsychology.

Stuss, D.T., & Benson, D.F. 1986. The Frontal Lobes. New York: Raven.

Suddendorf, T. 1999 The rise of the metamind. In M. Corballis & S. Lea eds., The descent of mind. New York: Oxford University Press.

Sudsuang, R., Chentanez, V., & Veluvan, K. 1991. Effects of Buddhist meditation on serum cortisol and total protein levels, blood pressure, pulse rate, lung volume and reaction time. Physiology of Behavior, 50, 543-548.

Suess, L. A. & M. A. Persinger 2001. Geophysical variables and behavior: XCVI. Experiences attributed to Christ and Mary at Marmora, Ontario, Canada may have been consequences of environmental electromagnetic stimulation.

Sundkuler, Bengt G.M. 1961. Bantu Prophets in South Africa. London: Oxford University Press.

Sutin, Lawrence. 1995. The Shifting Realities of Philip K. Dick: Selected Literary and Philosophical Writings. New York, Vintage.

Sutula, T., Cascino, G., Cavazos, J., Parada, I. & Ramirez, L.1988. Hippocampal synaptic reorganization in partial complex epilepsy: evidence of mossy fiber sprouting in epileptic human temporal lobe. Annals of Neurolo

Swaab, D.F, & Fliers, E. 1985. A sexually dimorphic nucleus in the human brain Science, 228, 1112-1114

Swaab, D.F. & Hoffman M.A. 1988. Sexual differentiation of the human hypothalamus: Ontogeny of the sexually dimorphic nucleus of the preoptic area. Developmental Brain Research, 44, 314-318.

Swaab, D.F., Hoffman, M.A. 1990. An enlarged suprachiasmatic nucleus in homosexual men. Brain Research, 537,141-148.

Szpakowska, Kasia. 2001. Through the Looking Glass: Dreams in Ancient Egypt. In Dreams: A Reader on the Religious, Cultural, and Psychological Dimensions of Dreaming, edited by K. Bulkeley. New York: Palgrave.

Swanson, G. (1973), The search for a guardian spirit: The process of empowerment in simpler societies. Ethnology, 12, 359-78.

Targ, E., Schlitz, M., & Irwin, H. J. 2000. Psi-related experiences. In E. Cardena, S. J. Lynn & S. Krippner Eds., Varieties of anomalous experience: Examining the scientific evidence pp. 219-252. Washington, DC: American Psychological Association.

Tart, C. T. 1969. Altered States of Consciousness: A Book of Readings. USA: John Wiley.

Tart, C. T. 1978. A psychophysiological study of out-of-the-body experiences in a selected subject. Journal of the Society for Psychical Research, 62:3-27.

Tart, C. T. Ed.. 1997. Body mind spirit: Exploring the parapsychology of spirituality. Charlottesville, VA: Hampton Road Publishing Company.

Tart, C. T. 2000. States of Consciousness. USA: Backinprint.com.

Tautz, D. 1998. Debatable homologies. Nature, 395, 17-19.

Taylor, D. C. 1972 Mental state and temporal lobe epilepsy. Epilepsia,13, 727-765.

Taylor, D. C. 1975 Factors influencing the occurrence of schizophrenia-like psychosiswith temporal lobe epilepsy. Psychological Medicine, 5, 429-254.

Taylor, Jeremy. 1983. Dream Work. Mahwah: Paulist Press.

Taylor, Jeremy. 1992. Where People Fly and Water Runs Uphill. New York: Warner Books.

Teasdale, J.D. & Barnard, P.J. 1993. Affect, Cognition and Change: Re-modelling Depressive Thought. Hillsdale. Lawrence Erlbaum Associates, Publishers.

Teasdale, J.D., Howard, R.J., Cox, S.J., Ha, Y., Brammer, M.J., Williams, S.C.R. & Checkley, S.A. 1999. Functional MRI study of the cognitive generation of affect. American Journal of Psychiatry, 156, 209-215.

Teasdale, J.D., Segal, Z. & Williams, J.M.G. 1995. How does cognitive therapy prevent depressive relapse and why should attentional control mindfulness training help? Behaviour. Research & Therapy, 33, 25-33.

Tedlock, Barbara. 1987. Dreaming: Anthropological and Psychological Interpretations. New York: Cambridge University Press.

Tedlock, Barbara. 2001. The New Anthropology of Dreaming. In Dreams: A Reader in the Religious, Cultural, and Psychological Dimensions of Dreaming, edited by K. Bulkeley. New York: Palgra

Teilhard de Chardin, Pierre. 1959. The Phenomenon of Man. Trans. B. Wall. New York: Harper & Row.

Teitelbaum, P. 1961.Disturbances in feeding and drinking behavior after hypothalamic lesions.In M.R. Jones Ed., Nebraska Symposium on Motivation, Lincoln: University of Nebraska Press.

Teitelbaum, P., & Epstein, A.N. 1962.The lateral hypothalamic syndrome. Psychological Review, 69, 74-90.

Tellegen, A., Horn, J. M., & Legrand, R. G. 1969. Psychonomic Science, 14, 104,

Tellegen, A., et al. 1988. Journal of Personal and Social Psychology 54: 1031-39.

Terzian, H., & Ore, G. D. 1955. Syndrome of Kluver and Bucy in man by bilateral removal of temporal lobes. Neurology, 5, 373-3

The Power of Dreams. 1994. The Discovery Channel.

The Rig Veda. 1981. Translated by W. D. O'Flaherty. London: Penguin Books.

The Seventh Seal. 1957. Written and directed by Ingmar Bergman. Presented by Svensk Filmindustri. New York. Criterion Collection.

The Thirteen Principal Upanishads. 1931. Translated by R. E. Hume. Dehli: Oxford University Press.

Thelen, E., and Smith, L. (1994). *A Dynamic Systems Approach to the Development of Cognition and Action*. Cambridge, Massachusetts: MIT Bradford.

Theresa, Saint of Avila 1930 Interior castle. London: Thomas Baker.

Thigpen, C. & Cleckley, H. 1957 The Three Faces of Eve. New York, McGraw-Hill.

Thomas a Kempis. [c. 1450] 1989. Imitation of Christ. Chicago: Moody.

Thomas, A.G., Vornov, J.J., Olkowski, J.L., Merion, A.T., & Slusher, B.S. 2000. N-Acetylated alpha-linked acidic dipeptidase converts N-acetylaspartylglutamate from a neuroprotectant to a neurotoxin. Journal of Pharmacology and Experimental Therapies,

Thomas, L. & Cooper, R. 1978 Measurement and incidence of mystical experience. Journal for the Scientific Study of Religion 17:433-437.

Thomas-Keprta, K. L., et al., 2000 Geochim. Cosmochim. Acta
64, 4049-4081.

Thomkins, P. 1987. Mysteries of the Mexican Pyramids. Thames & Hudson.

Thompson, J. E. 1993. The Rise and Fall of Maya Civilization. Pimlico, London.

Tiller, S. G. & M. A. Persinger 1994. Elevated incidence of a sensed presence and sexual arousal during partial sensory deprivation and sensitivity to hypnosis: implications for hemisphericity and gender differences. Perceptual and Motor Skills 79 3 P

Tiller, S. G. & M. A. Persinger 2002. Geophysical variables and behavior: XCVII. Increased proportions of the left-sided sense of presence induced experimentally by right hemispheric application of specific frequency-modulated complex magnetic fields.

Tillich, Paul. 1952. The Courage to Be. Yale University Press.

Tinbergen, N. 1951 The study of instinct. London: Oxford University Press.

Toffelmeir, Gertrude, and K. Luomala. 1936. Dreams and Dream Interpretation of the Diegueno Indians of Southern California. The Psychoanalytic Quarterly 5:195-225.

Tolstoy, L. [1869] 1952. Second epilogue, War and Peace. Trans. L. and A. Maude. Vol. 51, Great Books of the Western World. Chicago: Encyclopedia Britannica.

Tonkinson, Robert. 1970. Aboriginal Dream-Spirit Beliefs in a Contact Situation: Jigalong, Western Australia. In Australian Aboriginal Anthropology, edited by R. M. Berndt. Sidney: University of Western Australia Press.

Tooley, G.A., Armstrong, S.M., Norman, T.R., & Sali, A. 2000. Acute increases in night-time plasma melatonin levels following a period of meditation. Biological Psychology, 53 1, 69-78.

Tow, P.M., & Whitty, C.W.M. 1953.Personality changes after operations of the cingulate gyrus in man.Journal of Neurology, Neurosurgery and Psychiatry, 16, 186-193.

Townsend, J. (1997), Shamanism. In S. Glazier (Ed.), Anthropology of religion: A handbook of method and theory (pp.429-469). Westport, Conn: Greenwood.

Trainor, L. & Trehub, S. 1992 The development of referential meaning in music. Music Perception 9:455-470.

Trimingham, Spencer. 1959. Islam in West Africa. Oxford: Clarendon Press.

Tripp, C. A. 1987. The homosexual matrix. New York, New American Library.

Trompf, G.W. 1990. Melanesian Religion. Cambridge: Cambridge University Press.

Trotsky, L. (1964) *The Age of Permanent Revolution* New York: Dell.

Tupler, R., et al., 2001 Expressing the human genome. Nature 409, 832 - 833.

Turner, V. 1969 The ritual process. New York: Aldine.

Turner, Victor. 1974. Dramas, fields and metaphors. Cornell UP.

Turon, C. 1997. American Association for the Advancement of Science.

Uhl, R. G., Kuhar, B. R., & Snyder, S. H. 1978. Enkephalin containing pathways: Amygdaloid efferents in the stria terminalis. Brain Research, 149, 223-228.

Ullman, C. 1982. Cognitive and Emotional Antecedents of Religious Conversion. New York: Sheed & Ward.

Ullman, M., & Krippner, S. 1989. Dream Telepathy. McFarland, New Jersey.

Unamuno, M. de (1972) *The Tragic Sense of Life*. Princeton: Princeton University Press.

Uno, H., Tarara, R., Else, J., & Sapolsky R. M. 1989. Hippocampal damage associated with prolonged and fatal stress in primates. Journal of Neuroscience, 9, 1705-1711.

Ursin, H., & Kaada,B. R. 1960. Functional localization within the amygdaloid complex in the cat. Electroencephalography and Clinical Neurophysiology, 12, 1-20.

Utts, J. 1996. An assessment of the evidence for psychic functioning. Journal of Scientific Exploration, 10 1, 3-30.

Valle, J. & R. Prince. (1989), Religious experiences as self-healing mechanisms. In C. Ward (Ed.), Altered states of consciousness and mental health: A cross cultural perspective (pp.149-66). Newbury Park: Sage.

Van Bockstaele, E.J. & Aston-Jones, G. 1995. Integration in the ventral medulla and coordination of sympathetic, pain and arousal functions. Clinical and Experimental Hypertension, 17 1-2, 153-65.

Van Den Aardweg, G.J.M. 1980. Parents of homosexuals—not guilty? American Journal Psychotherapy 38,181-189.

Van Dusen, W. 1999. Beauty, wonder, and the mystical mind. West Chester, PA: Chrysalis Books.

Van Dusen, W. 2001. The design of existence: Emanation from source to creation. West Chester, PA: Chrysalis Books.

Van Praag, H. & De Haan, S. 1980. Depression vulnerability and 5-Hydroxytryptophan prophylaxis. Psychiatry Research, 3, 75-83.

Varela, F., Thompson, E., & Rosch, E. (1991/1993) *The Embodied Mind* Cambridge: The MIT Press.

Velikovsky, I. 1950 Worlds in collision. Dell, NY

Venkatesh, B., et al. 1999 Late changes in splicesomal introns define clades in vertebrate evolution. Proceedings of the National Academy of Sciences, 96, 10267-10271.

Venter, C. et al., 2001. The sequence of the human genome. Science, 2001, 1304-1351.

Verhoeven, D. 1994. De levensbeschouwing van studenten aan de KULeuven, een sociaal wetenschappelijke studie. Socologisch onderzoeksinstituut. The meaning system of students at the Catholic University Leuven, a social scientific study.

Vitebsky, P. (2001), Shamanism. Norman: University of Oklahoma Press.

Vochteloo, J. D., & Koolhaas, J. M. 1987. Medial amygdala lesions in male rats reduce aggressive behavior. Physiology and Behavior, 41, 99-102.

Von Grunebaum, G.E., and Roger Callois, eds. 1966. The Dream and Human Societies. Berkeley: University of California Press.

Wade, M., Johnson, N.A., Jones, R., Siguel, V., & McNaughton, M. 1997. Genetic variation segregating in natural populations of Tribolium castaneum affecting traits observed in hybrids with T. fremani. Genetics, 147, 1235-1247.

Wahass, S. & Kent, G. 1997 A comparison of public attitudes in Britain and Saudia Arabia towards auditory hallucinations. International Journal of Social Psychiatry 43:175-183.

Walde, Christine. 1999. Dream Interpretation in a Prosperous Age? Artemidorus, the Greek Interpreter of Dreams. In Dream Cultures: Explorations in the Comparative History of Dreaming, edited by G. G. Stroumsa. New York: Oxford University Press.

Waldron, J. L. 1998. The life impact of transcendent experiences with a pronounced quality of noesis. Journal of Transpersonal Psychology, 30, 103-134.

Waldrop, M. M. 1992. Complexity: The Emerging Science at the Edge of Chaos. New York: Simon & Schuster.

Walker, S. 1972 Ceremonial spirit possession in Africa and Afro-America. Leiden: Brill.

Wallace, Anthony F.C. 1958. Dreams and Wishes of the Soul: A Type of Psychoanalytic Theory among the Seventeenth Century Iroquois. American Anthropologist 60:234-248.

Wallace, R.K. 1970. Physiological effects of transcendental meditation. Science, 167, 1251-1254.

Wallin, N., Merker, B. & S. Brown. Eds. (2000), The origins of music. Cambridge (MA): MIT Press.

Walton, K.G., Pugh, N.D., Gelderloos, P., & Macrae, P. 1995. Stress reduction and preventing hypertension, preliminary support for a psychoneuroendocrine mechanism. Journal of Alternative and Complementary Medicine, 1 3, 263-283.

Walsh, R. (1990), The spirit of shamanism. Los Angeles: Tarcher.

Walton, K., & D. Levitsky. (1994), A neuroendocrine mechanism for the reduction of drug use and addictions by Transcendental Meditation. Alcoholism Treatment Quarterly, 11(1/2), 89-117.

Wang, L. J. 2000. Gain-assisted superluminal light propagation. Nature 406, 277 - 279.

Ward, J.S.M. 1925. The Hung Society.Bakersville Press, London.

Ward, K. 2002. God: A Guide for the Perplexed. Oxford: Oneworld.

Warner, R. 1977 Witchcraft and soul loss. Hospital and Community Psychiatry 28:686-690.

Wasman, M., Flynn, J.P 1962 Directed attack elicited from the hypothalamus. Archives of Neurology, 6, 220-227.

Watanabee, J. & Smuts, B. 1999 Explaining ritual without explaining it away. American Anthropologist 101:98-112.

Waterhouse BD, Moises HC, Woodward DJ. Phasic activation of the locus coeruleus enhances responses of primary sensory cortical neurons to peripheral receptive field stimulation. Brain Research 1998, 790 1-2,33-44.

Watson, J. D., Gilman, M., Witkowksi, J., & Zoller, M. 1992. Recombinant DNA. Scientific American Books, NY

Watt, D. (2000) The centrencephalon and thalamocortical integration: Neglected contributions of periaqueductal gray. Consciousness & Emotion 1, 91-114.

Watt, D. (1998) Affect and the "hard problem": neurodevelopmental and corticolimbic network issues. Consciousness Research Abstracts: Toward a Science of Consciousness, Tucson 1998, 91-92.

Watts, F. & Williams, M. 1988. The Psychology of Religious Knowing. Cambridge: Cambridge University Press.

Watts, A. W. 1963. Psychotherapy east and west. New York: Mentor/New American Library.

Watts, F. 1999. Cognitive neuroscience and religious consciousness. In R.J. Russell, N. Murphy, T. Meyering & M. Arbib Eds. Neuroscience and the Person. Vatican City State, Vatican Observatory & Berkeley, California, Centre for Theology and Natural Sc

Watts, F. 2002. Theology and Psychology. Aldershot, Ashgate.

Wayman, Alex. 1967. Significance of Dreams in India and Tibet. History of Religions 7:1-12.

Weber, M. 1946 The Protestant sects and the spirit of capitalism. In From Max Weber: Essays in sociology, trans. and ed. C. Wright Mills & H. Gerth. New York: Oxford University Press.

Weil, A. A. 1956. Ictal depression and anxiety in temporal lobe disorders. American Journal of Psychiatry, 113, 149-157.

Weinberg, Steven. 1993. Dreams of a Final Theory. Vintage.

Weingarten, S. M., Cherlow, D. G., & Holmgren, E. 1977 The relationship of hallucinations to depth structures of the temporal lobe. Acta Neurochirugica, 24, 199-216.

Weingarten, S.M., Charlow, D.G. & Holmgren, E. 1977. The relationship of hallucinations to the depth of structures of the temporal lobe. Acta Neurochirurgica, 24, 199-216.

Weingartner, H., Gold, P., & Ballenger, J.C., et al. 1981. Effects of vasopressin on human memory functions. Science, 211 4482, 601-603.

Weiss, P. A. (1968) The living system: Determinism stratified. In A. Koestler & J.R. Smythies (Eds.), Beyond Reductionism — New Perspectives in the Life Sciences. The Alpbach Symposium (pp. 3-55). London: Hutchinson.

Wellman, H. 1990 The child's theory of mind. Cambridge, MA: MIT Press.

Wesley, John. c. 1703-1791. A Heart Strangely Warmed: John Wesley's Sermons.

Westwood, J. 1987. The Atlas of Mysterious Places. Guild Publications, London.

Wheeler, M., Stuss, D. & Tulving, E. 1997 Toward a theory of episodic memory: The frontal lobes and autonoietic consciousness. Psychological Bulletin 121:331-354.

White, R. (1959) Motivation reconsidered. Psychological Review 65, 297-333.

White, R. A. 1993. Working classification of EHE's. Exceptional Human Experience: Background Papers: I, 11, 149-150.

White, R. A. 1997. Dissociation, narrative, and exceptional human experience. In S. Krippner & S. Powers Eds., Broken images, broken selves: Dissociative narratives in clinical practice pp. 88-121. Washington, DC: Brunner-Mazel.

Whitehead, A.N. 1926. Religion in the Making. New York. Macmillan.

Whitehead, H. 1988[1921] The village gods of South India. Madras: Asia Education Services.

Wilber, Ken. 2000. Integral Psychology. Boston: Shambhala.

Williams, D. 1956 The structure of emotions reflected in epileptic experiences. Brain, 79, 29-67.

Williams, J.M.G., Watts, F., Macleod, C., & Mathews, A. 1997. Cognitive Psychology and Emotional Disorders. Second Edition. Chichester: John Wiley & Sons.

Wilson, D.S. 2002 Darwin's cathedral. Chicago: University of Chicago Press.

Wilson, Edward O. 1998. Consilience: The Unity of Knowledge. Little Brown, UK.

Wilson, Edward O. 2000 The Study of Human Nature. On Human Nature. Ed. Leslie Stevenson. New York: Oxford University Press.

Wilson, Edward O. 1998. Consilience: The Unity of Knowledge. New York: Alfred A. Knopf.

Wilson, J. A. 1951 The culture of ancient Egypt. Chicago, U. Chicago Press.

Wimmer, H. & Perner, J. 1983 Beliefs about beliefs. Cognition 13:103-128.

Winkelman, Michael. 1995. Psychointegrator Plants: Their Roles in Human Culture, Consciousness and Health, Yearbook of Cross-cultural Medicine and Psychotherapy 1995: p. 20.

Winkelman, M. (1986a), Magico-religious practitioner types and socioeconomic analysis. Behavior Science Research, 20(1-4), 17-46.

Winkelman, M. (1986b), Trance states: A theoretical model and cross-cultural analysis. Ethos, 14, 76-105.

Winkelman, M. (1990), Shaman and other "magico-religious healers": A cross-cultural study of their origins, nature and social transformation. Ethos, 18(3), 308-352.

Winkelman, M. (1992), Shamans, priests and witches. A cross-cultural study of magico-religious practitioners. Anthropological Research Papers #44. Tempe: Arizona State University.

Winkelman, M. (1996), Psychointegrator plants: Their roles in human culture and health. In M. Winkelman & W. Andritzky (Eds.), Yearbook of cross-cultural medicine and psychotherapy Volume 6 (pp.9-53). Berlin: Verlag und Vertrieb.

Winkelman, M. (1997), Altered states of consciousness and religious behavior. In S. Glazier (Ed.), Anthropology of religion: A handbook of method and theory (pp.393-428). Westport, Conn: Greenwood.

Winkelman, M. (1999), Altered states of consciousness. In D. Levinson, J. Ponzetti & P. Jorgensen Encyclopedia of human emotions, (pp.32-38). New York: Macmillan.

Winkelman, M. (2000), Shamanism The neural ecology of consciousness and healing. Westport (CT): Bergin and Garvey.

Winkelman, M. (2002a), Shamanism and cognitive evolution. Cambridge Archaeological Journal, 12(1), 71-101.

Winkelman, M. (2002b), Shamanism as neurotheology and evolutionary psychology. American Behavioral Scientist, 45(12),1875-1887.

Winkelman, M. & D. White (1987), A cross-cultural study of magico-religious practitioners and trance states: data base. In D. Levinson and R. Wagner (Eds.), Human relations area files research series in quantitative cross-cultural data: Vol. 3D (pp.). New Haven: HRAF Press.

Winkelman, M. & C. Winkelman. (1991), Shamanistic healers and their therapies. In W. Andritzky (Ed.), Yearbook of cross-cultural medicine and psychotherapy 1990 (pp.163-182),. Berlin: Verlag und Vertrieb.

Winn, T., B. Crowe & J. Moreno. (1989), Shamanism and music therapy. Music Therapy Perspectives, 7, 61-71.

Witkowski, J. A. 1988. The discovery of split genes. Trends in Biochemical Science.

Woese, C. R., et al., Proc.Natl. Acad. Sci. 87, 4576-4579 1990.

Wolf, Fred Alan. 1991. Parallel Universes: The Search for Other Worlds. Paladin, UK.

Wolf, J. 2000. Taking the Quantum Leap: The New Physics for Nonscientists.

Wolman, B. B. Ed.. 1977. Handbook of parapsychology. New York: Van Nostrand Reinhold.

Woods, M. 1913 Was the Apostle Paul an epileptic? New York: Cosmopolitan Press.

Woolley, C. L. 1965. Ur of the Chaldees. Norton, NY.

Worthing, M. W. 1996. God, Creation, and Contemporary Physics. Minneapolis: Fortress.

Worthington, E., Kurusu, T., McCullough, M. & Sandage, S. 1996 Empirical research on religion and psychotherapeutic processes of outcomes. Psychological Bulletin 19:448-487.

Wright, R. 1991. Time Among the Maya. Futura Publications, London.

Yadid, G., Zangen, A., Herzberg, U., Nakash, R., & Sagen, J. 2000. Alterations in endogenous brain beta-endorphin release by adrenal medullary transplants in the spinal cord. Neuropsychopharmacology, 23 6,709-716.

Yap, P. 1960 The possession syndrome. Journal of Mental Science 106:114-137.

Young, A. W., Aggleton, J. P., & Hellawell, D. J., 1995. Face processing impairments after amygdalotomy. Brain, 118, 15-24.

Young, Serinity. 1999. Dreaming in the Lotus: Buddhist Dream Narrative, Imagery, and Practice Boston: Wisdom Publications.

Young, Serinity. 2001. Buddhist Dream Experience: The Role of Interpretation, Ritual, and Gender. In Dreams: A Reader on the Religious, Cultural, and Psychological Dimensions of Dreaming, edited by K. Bulkeley. New York: Palgrave.

Zachar, P. (2000) Child development and the regulation of affect and cognition in consciousness: A view from object relations theory. In R. Ellis and N. Newton (Eds.), *The Caldron of Consciousness: Motivation, Affect, and Self-organization.* Amsterdam: John Benjamins, 205-222.

Zaleski, C. 1987. Otherworld Journeys: Accounts of Near-Death Experience in Medieval and Modern Times. New York: Oxford University Press.

Ziegler, D.R., Cass, W.A., & Herman, J.P. 1999. Excitatory influence of the locus coeruleus in hypothalamic-pituitary-adrenocortical axis responses to stress. Journal of Neuroendocrinology, 11 5, 361-369.

Zilboorg, G. 1943. Fear of Death. Psychanalytic Quarterly, 12:465- 467.

Zilman, A. L. 1981. Women as shapers of the human adaptation: in Woman the Gatherer. Edited by F. Dalhberg. New York: Yale U. Press.

Zisook, S., Byrd, D., Kuck, J. & Jeste, D. 1995 Command hallucinations in outpatients with schizophrenia. Journal of Clinical Psychiatry 56:462-465.

Zoe 7 Marti, Joseph. 2001. Into the Void: Psychedelics, Hallucinogens, Brain Technology Devices & The Expansion of Consciousness. USA: Zon Worldwide Media.

Zusne, L., & Jones, W. H. 1989. Anomalistic psychology: A study of magical thinking 2nd ed.. Hillsdale, NJ: Erlbaum.

The Transmitter to God
The Limbic System, The Soul and Spirituality
ISBN# 0-9700733-3-13
University Press, California

Astrobiology, The Origin of Life
and the Death of Darwinism

The Origin of Life:
The Earth is an island, swirling in an
ocean of space, and life has been washing
to shore, since the creation.
The age of the universe is unknown...and
the ancestry of life may extend backwards in
time interminably into the long ago...
Cosmic collisions are commonplace, not only between meteors and
planets, but entire galaxies, and life has been repeatedly tossed into the
abyss... only to land on other planets. The genetic seeds of life swarm
throughout the cosmos, and these genetic "seeds," these living
creatures, fell to Earth, encased in stellar debris which pounded the
planet for 700 millions years after the creation. And these "seeds"
contained the DNA-instructions for the metamorphosis of all life,
including woman and man. DNA acts to purposefully modify the
environment, which acts on gene selection, so as to fullfill specific
genetic goals: the dispersal and activation of silent DNA and the
replication of life forms
that long ago lived on other planets.

AMERICA ATTACKED
by Sara Jess, Gabriel Beck
A Comprehensive Retelling of the Events of
September 11, 2001,
How and Why the Attack Was Planned and Carried out,
and the Role of
Osama bin Laden and al-Qeada
in this Murderous Assault on the
United States of America

**Hitler's Diaries
-The Book-
The Mind & God
of Adolf Hitler
ISBN: 0970073399
University Press**

**Hitler's Diaries
The Rise & Fall of Adolf Hitler
-The Movie-
Starring Adolf Hitler
ISBN: 0971644535
100 Minutes, Color
& Black & White
Brain-Mind.com
Productions**

AMERICA ATTACKED
by Sara Jess, Gabriel Beck
A Comprehensive Retelling of the Events of
September 11, 2001,
How and Why the Attack Was Planned and Carried out,
and the Role of
Osama bin Laden and al-Qeada
in this Murderous Assault on the
United States of America

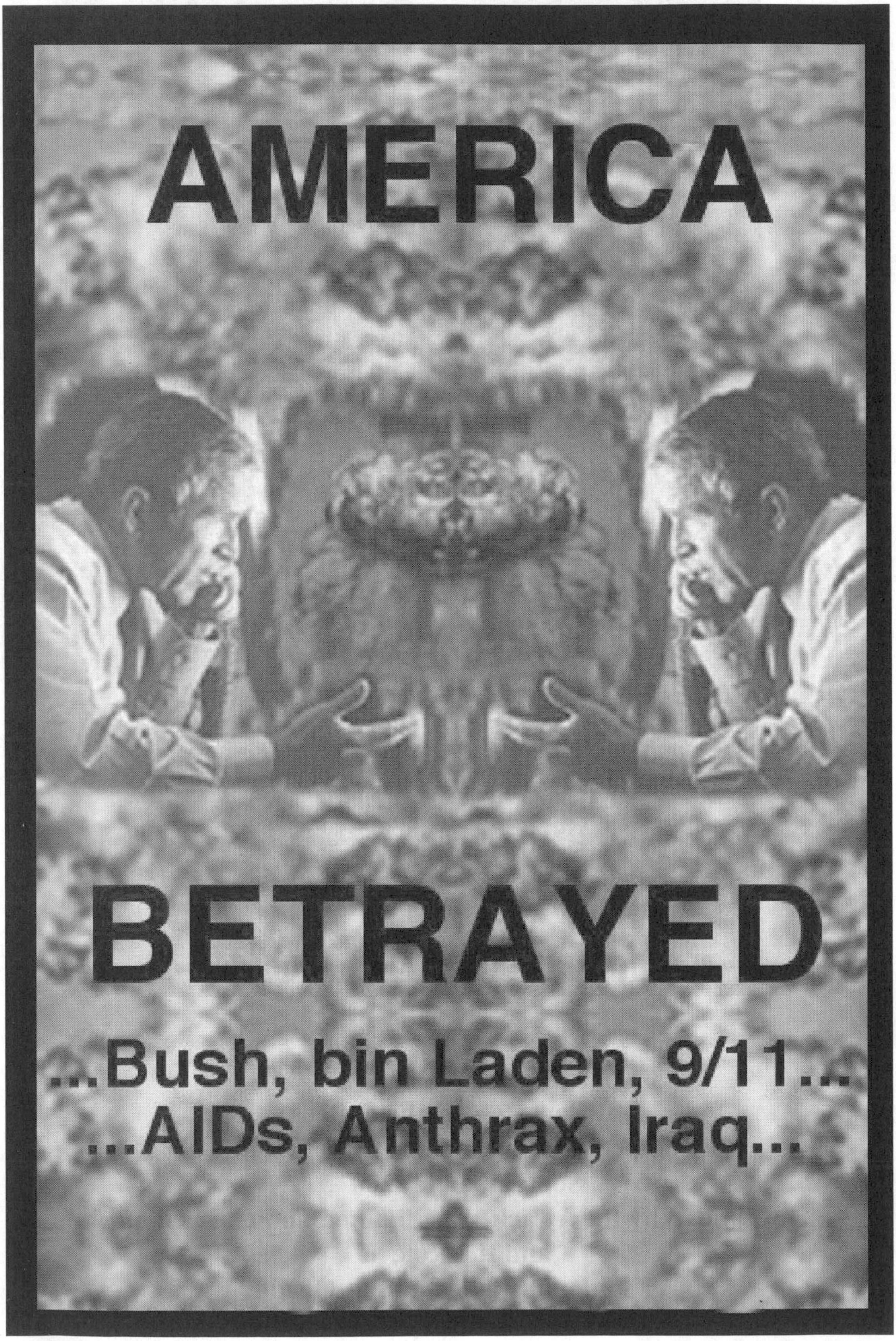
AMERICA
BETRAYED
...Bush, bin Laden, 9/11...
...AIDs, Anthrax, Iraq...

Hitler's Diaries
-The Book-
The Mind & God
of Adolf Hitler
ISBN: 0970073399
University Press

Hitler's Diaries
The Rise & Fall of Adolf Hitler
-The Movie-
Starring Adolf Hitler
ISBN: 0971644535
100 Minutes, Color
& Black & White
Brain-Mind.com
Productions